BRITISH QUALIFICATIONS
31st EDITION

BRITISH
QUALIFICATIONS
31st EDITION

A complete guide to educational,
technical, professional and
academic qualifications
in Britain

CONFEDERATION OF

TOURISM • HOTEL • CATERING
MANAGEMENT

**KOGAN
PAGE**

First published in 1966
This (thirty-first) edition 2001

Kogan Page Limited
120 Pentonville Road
London N1 9JN

Typeset by Saxon Graphics Ltd, Derby

Printed and bound in Great Britain by Biddles Ltd, Guildford and King's Lynn

British Library Cataloguing in Publication Data

A CIP record for this book is available from the British Library.

ISBN 0 7494 3485 6 HB
ISBN 0 7494 3486 4 PB

Foreword

The thirty-first edition of *British Qualifications* has been considerably revised and updated to take account of the many changes in degree, diploma and certificate courses, and also of legislation affecting the structure of higher and further education as a whole.

The editor and compilers are most grateful to the academic registrars and the secretaries of the many bodies they have contacted for information and advice. Without their cooperation, the revision and updating of *British Qualifications* would not have been possible.

Dr Bernard Hephrun
Honourary President

EUROPEAN UNIVERSITY OF IRELAND (EUI)
THE UNIVERSITY OF THE NEW MILLENNIUM
OFFERS POSTGRADUATE & POST-EXPERIENCE
PROGRAMMES AT AFFORDABLE COST
TO PROFESSIONALS & EXECUTIVES

European University's professional development programmes are well-received by the working adults, as its tutorials are delivered and supervised by experts who have direct experience in Industry. EUI is considered to be one of the best in the International market and has the growing alumni of top professionals.

EUI is formed by reputed academics as an independent private university to conduct non-traditional professional degree programmes. EUI believes that the continuing education for mature persons is important and it has designed a special study programme to facilitate those interested in obtaining a professionally-relevant qualification in their respective field of employment or experience.

Unlike other traditional universities, the entry qualification is broadened to accommodate mature candidates with prior learning and experience. In addition to its 'off-campus' distance learning programme, the university also provides realtime lectures and faculty link via its affiliated centres in 8 overseas locations and hopes to expand world-wide by the year 2000.

EUI encourages candidates to undertake a study plan relevant to their current employment. EUI's programmes are uniquely designed to accommodate candidates from various fields at an affordable cost. Most importantly, exemptions are given for prior learning and experience.

EUI offers professional degree programmes leading to PG Diploma, Bachelor, Masters (including an Executive/work based MBA), DBA, PhD at an affordable cost compared to most other competitors. EUI is proud to be the first university to introduce study programme in other International languages including Chinese.

The university provides a fast, convenient, efficient and flexible platform for your growth in this highly competitive and demanding world. EUI is modelled along the well-received American concepts of professional development. The programmes are flexible and designed to meet the demands placed on today's busy professionals to succeed through the new millennium. The programmes are especially geared to meet your individual needs, progressing in line with your development, working on it when it suits you best and deriving all the satisfaction from it, while attaining your aspirations towards gaining a professional degree. **The assessment is based on a) Assignments b) Locally held workshop c) A work based project/dissertation.**

Apply by CV or obtain a form from EUI's web site and forward it to EUI REGISTRY, DOMINIC COURT, 41 LOWER DOMINIC STREET, DUBLIN 1, REPUBLIC OF IRELAND. TEL: + 35 31 8733199 FAX: + 35 31 8733612 EMAIL: EUI.SAV@BTINTERNET.COM www.btinternet.com/~european.university/wwweui.html

London School of Accountancy & Management - LSAM offers Executive MBA (12 months)

The business school has modified its courses to meet the needs and challenges of the new Millennium, the courses offered are modern and dynamic, which includes an Executive MBA.

Offers Professional Qualifications leading to an Advanced Diploma, Post-graduate Diploma and MBA at competitive fees. The MBA is designed to accommodate busy executives via the matured entry route. The tuition is provided by well reputed professionals who have hands on experience in the Industry. LSAM offers Full & Part-time courses and the lectures are specially designed to accommodate working adults in the evenings & weekends. Students can enroll throughout the year.

LSAM, 492 Harrow Road, London W9 3QA. Tel: 44 (0)181 968 6969 Fax: 44 (0)181 960 3026

Contents

How to Use this Book

The reader may find these notes helpful when using the book.

Part 1 is a short introduction to the educational institutions mentioned in later Parts. It describes the organisation of secondary, further and higher education in England and Wales, Scotland and Northern Ireland with a brief description of various types of institution, their place in the system as a whole and the types of qualification for which they provide courses of instruction.

Part 2 covers those examinations for which the secondary schools (and colleges of further education) enter their pupils. As they are almost entirely non-vocational in character, these examinations are not usually mentioned in Part 5. England and Wales, Scotland and Northern Ireland are dealt with separately as each has its own examination structure.

Part 3 is intended as an introduction to the qualifications, usually technical or commercial in nature, which fall under the general heading of further education. These qualifications are usually gained after courses of study at technical college or through correspondence courses. Further information about the qualifications in this Part will be found in Part 5, where they are described under the relevant trade or profession.

Part 4 deals with qualifying courses at Universities. Universities also validate degree courses held at colleges of further and higher education. These institutions and their degrees are listed under the validating university. Degrees, diplomas and certificates are arranged under individual institutions. Those qualifications which are of a vocational or professional nature are also described in Part 5.

Part 5 has an explanation of the various types of professional body and their membership. It also describes the qualifications in each individual trade or profession, arranged in a standard order as follows:

> Membership of Professional Institutions and Associations
> University Qualifications
> National Certificates and Diplomas
> NVQs
> SVQs
> GNVQs
> Useful Addresses

Wherever possible this pattern has been followed, but in a few cases, such as those of Law and Medicine, the nature of the professional structure has dictated a different presentation.

Part 6 describes various accrediting bodies involved in the accreditation of colleges in the independent sector of further and higher education.

Part 7 is a list of study associations and learned societies which are not in the main qualifying bodies and are usually not included in Part 5.

Index of Abbreviations and Designatory Letters

AAB	Associate of the Association of Book-keepers
AACB	Associate of the Association of Certified Book-keepers
AACP	Associate of the Association of Computer Professionals
AACPP	Associate Member of the College of Pharmacy Practice
AAIA	Associate of the Association of International Accountants
AAMS	Associate Member of the Association of Medical Secretaries, Practice Administrators and Receptionists
AASI	Associate of the Ambulance Service Institute
ABDO	Associate of the British Dispensing Opticians
ABEng	Associate Member of the Association of Building Engineers
ABHA	Associate of the British Hypnotherapy Association
ABIAT	Associate Member of the British Institute of Architectural Technologists
ABIPP	Associate of the British Institute of Professional Photography
ABSSG	Associate of the British Society of Scientific Glassblowers
ACA	Associate of the Institute of Chartered Accountants in England and Wales
ACA	Associate of the Institute of Chartered Accountants in Ireland
ACCA	Associate of the Association of Chartered Certified Accountants
ACEA	Associate of the Association of Cost and Executive Accountants
ACertCM	The Archbishop of Canterbury's Certificate in Church Music
ACIArb	Associate of the Chartered Institute of Arbitrators
ACIB	Associate of the Chartered Institute of Bankers
ACIBS	Associate of the Chartered Institute of Bankers in Scotland
ACIH	Associate of the Chartered Institute of Housing
ACII	Associate of the Chartered Insurance Institute
ACILA	Associate of the Chartered Institute of Loss Adjusters
ACIOB	Associate of the Chartered Institute of Building
ACIS	Associate of the Institute of Chartered Secretaries and Administrators
ACP	Associate of the College of Preceptors
ACPM	Associate of the Confederation of Professional Management
ACYW	Associate of the Community and Youth Work Association
ADCM	Archbishop of Canterbury's Diploma in Church Music
AdDipEd	Advanced Diploma in Education
ADI	Approved Driving Instructor
AECI	Association Member of the Institute of Employment Consultants
AFA	Associate of the Institute of Financial Accountants
AFCI	Associate of the Faculty of Commerce and Industry Ltd
AffIManf	Affiliate of the Institute of Manufacturing
AffIMS	Affiliate of the Institute of Management Specialists
AffIP	Affiliate of the Institute of Plumbing
AffIProfBTM	Affiliate of Professional Business & Technical Management
AFIMA	Associate Fellow of the Institute of Mathematics and its Applications
AFISLO Licence	Aerodrome Flight Information Service Of ficer's Licence
AFRCSEd	Associate Fellow of Royal College of Surgeons of Edinburgh
AGCL	Associate Member of the Guild of Cleaners and Launderers
AGI	Associate of the Greek Institute
AGSM	Associate of the Guildhall School of Music and Drama
AHCIMA	Associate of the Hotel and Catering International Management Association
AHFS	Associate of the Council of Health Fitness and Sports Therapists
AHRIM	Association of the Institute of Health Record Information and Management
AIAgrE	Associate of the Institution of Agricultural Engineers
A IAT	Associate of the Institute of Asphalt Technology
AIBCM	Associate of the Institute of British Carriage and Automobile Manufacturers
AIChor	Associate of the Benesh Institute of Choreology
AICHT	Associate of the International Council of Holistic Therapists
AICS	Associate of the Institution of Chartered Shipbrokers

AIDTA	Associate of the International Dance Teachers' Association
AIEM	Associate of the Institute of Executives and Managers
AIExpE	Associate of the Institute of Explosive Engineers
AIFA	Associate of the Institute of Field Archaeologists
AIFireE	Associate of the Institution of Fire Engineers
AIGD	Associate of the Institute of Grocery Distribution
AIHort	Associate Member of the Institute of Horticulture
AIIMR	Associate of the Institute of Investment Management and Research
AIIRSM	Association of the Institute of Risk and Safety Management
AIL	Associate of the Institute of Linguistics
AILAM	Associate of the Institute of Leisure and Amenity Management
AIMBM	Associate of Institute of Maintenance and Building Management
AIMgt	Associate of the Institute of Management
AIMM	Associate of the Institute of Massage and Movement
AInstAM	Associate of the Institute of Administrative Management
AInstBA	Associate of the Institute of Business Administration
AInstBCA	Associate of the Institute of Burial and Cremation Administration
AInstBM	Associate of the Institute of Builders Merchants
AInstCM	Associate of the Institute of Commercial Management
AInstPkg	Associate of the Institute of Packaging
AInstPM	Associate of the Institute of Professional Managers and Administrators
AInstSMM	Associate of the Institute of Sales and Marketing Management
AInstTA	Associate of the Institute of Transport Administration
AInstTT	Associate Member of the Institute of Travel and Tourism
AIOC	Associate of the Institute of Carpenters
AIOFMS	Associate of the Institute of Financial and Management Studies
AIP	Associate of the Institute of Plumbing
AIS	Accredited Imaging Scientist (Royal Photographic Society)
AISOB	Associate of the Incorporated Society of Organ Builders
AISTD	Associate of the Imperial Society of Teachers of Dancing
AISTDDip	Associate Diploma of the Imperial Society of Teachers of Dancing
AITSA	Associate of the Institute of Trading Standards Administration
AIWSc	Associate Member of the Institute of Wood Science
ALA	Associate of the Library Association
ALCM	Associate of the London College of Music
ALI	Associate of the Landscape Institute
ALS	Associate of the Linnean Society of London
AMA	Associate of the Museums Association
AMABE	Associate of the Association of Business Executives
AMASI	Associate Member of the Architects and Surveyors Institute
AMBCS	Associate Member of the British Computer Society
AMBII	Associate Member of the British Institute of Innkeeping
AMIA	Affiliated Member of the Association of International Accountants
AMIAgrE	Associate Member of Institution of Agricultural Engineers
AMIAP	Associate Member of the Institution of Analysts and Programmers
AMIAT	Associate of the Institute of Asphalt Technology
AMIBC	Associate Member of the Institute of Building Control
AMIBCM	Associate Member of the Institute of British Carriage and Automobile Manufacturers
AMInstAEA	Associate Member of the Institute of Automotive Engineer Assessors
AMIBF	Associate Member of the Institute of British Foundrymen
AMICE	Associate Member of the Institution of Civil Engineers
AMIChemE	Associate Member of the Institution of Chemical Engineers
AMIEE	Associate Member of the Institution of Electrical Engineers
AMIED	Associate Member of the Institution of Engineering Designers
AMIEx	Associate Member of the Institute of Export
AMIHIE	Associate Member of the Institute of Highway Incorporated Engineers
AMIHT	Associate Member of the Institution of Highways and Transportation
AMIIExE	Associate Member of the Institution of Incorporated Executive Engineers
AMIM	Associate Member of the Institute of Materials

AMIManf	Member of the Institution of Manufacturing
AMIMechE	Associate Member of the Institution of Mechanical Engineers
AMIMechIE	Associate Member of the Institution of Mechanical Incorporated Engineers
AMIMinE	Associate of the Institute of Mining Engineers
AMIMM	Associate Member of the Institution of Mining and Metallurgy
AMIMS	Associate Member of the Institute of Management Specialists
AMINI	Associate Member of the Nautical Institute
AMInstB	Associate Member of the Institution of British Engineers
AMInstE	Associate Member of the Institute of Energy
AMInstR	Associate Member of the Institute of Refrigeration
AMInstTA	Associate Member of the Institute of Transport Administration
AMIPlantE	Associate Member of the Institution of Plant Engineers
AMIPR	Associate Member of the Institute of Public Relations
AMIPRE	Associate Member of the Incorporated Practitioners in Radio and Electronics
AMIQ	Associate Member of the Institute of Quarrying
AMIQA	Associate Member of the Institute of Quality Assurance
AMIRTE	Associate Member of the Institute of Road Transport Engineers
AMISM	Associate Member of the Institute for Supervision and Management
AMIStrutE	Associate Member of the Institution of Structural Engineers
AMITD	Associate Member of the Institute of Training and Development
AMPA	Associate Member of the Master Photographers Association
AMProfBTM	Associate Member of Professional Business and Technical Management
AMRSH	Associate Member of the Royal Society of Health
AMS (Aff)	Affiliate, Association of Medical Secretaries, Practice Administrators and Receptionists
AMS	Associate of the Institute of Management Services
AMSE	Associate Member of the Society of Engineers (Incorporated)
AMusLCM	Associate in Music of the London College of Music
AMusTCL	Associate in Music of Trinity College of Music, London
AMWES	Associate Member of the Women's Engineering Society
ANAEA	Associate of the National Association of Estate Agents
ANCA	Advanced National Certificate in Agriculture
APMI	Associate of the Pensions Management Institute
APMP	Association for the Project Management Professional
ARAD	Associate of the Royal Academy of Dancing
ARAM	Associate of the Royal Academy of Music
ARB	Architects Registration Board
ARCM	Associate of Royal College of Music
ARCO	Associate of the Royal College of Organists
ARCS	Associateship of the Royal College of Science
ARELS-FELCO	Association for Recognised English Language Teaching Establishments in Britain
ARIBA	Associate of the Royal Institute of British Architects
ARICS	Associate of the Royal Institution of Chartered Surveyors
ARIPHH	Associate of the Royal Institute of Public Health and Hygiene
ARPS	Associate of the Royal Photographic Society
ARSC	Associateship of the Royal Society of Chemistry
ARSCM	Associate Member of the Royal School of Church Music
ASCA	Associate of the Institute of Company Accountants
ASDC	Associate of the Society of Dyers and Colourists
ASE	Associate of the Society of Engineering
ASIS	Accredited Senior Imaging Scientist (Royal Photographic Society)
ASLC	Advanced Secretarial Language Certificate
ASMA	Associate of the Society of Sales Management Administrators Ltd
ASNNA	Associate of the Society of Nursery Nursing Administrators
AssCI	Associate of the Institute of Commerce
AssociateIEEE	Associate of the Institution of Electrical and Electronics Engineers Incorporated
AssocIMechIE	Associate of the Institution of Mechanical Incorporated Engineers
AMInstAEA	Associate of the Institute of Automotive Engineer Assessors

AssocIPD	Associate of the Institute of Personnel & Development
AssocIPHE	Associate of the Institution of Public Health Engineers
AssocMlnstWM	Associate Member of the Institute of Wastes Management
ASTA	Associate of the Swimming Teachers' Association
ASVA	Associate of the Incorporated Society of Valuers and Auctioneers
ATC	Art Teacher's Certificate
ATC Licence	Air Traffic Controller's Licence
ATCL	Associate Diploma in Speech and Drama, Trinity College, London
ATCLTESOL	Associate Diploma in the Teaching of English to Speakers of Other Languages, Trinity College, London
ATD	Art Teacher's Diploma
ATI	Associate of the Textile Industry
ATII	Associate of the Chartered Institute of Taxation
ATPL	Airline Transport Pilot's Licence
ATSC	Associate in the Technology of Surface Coatings
ATT	Member of the Association of Taxation Technicians
ATTA	Association of Therapy Teachers Associate
ATTF	Association of Therapy Teachers Fellow
ATTM	Association of Therapy Teachers Member
AWeldI	Associate of the Welding Institute
BA	Bachelor of Arts
BA(Econ)	Bachelor of Arts in Economics & Social Studies
BA(Ed)	Bachelor of Arts (Education)
BA(Lan)	Bachelor of Languages
BA(Law)	Bachelor of Arts in Law
BA(Music)	Bachelor of Music
BAC	British Accreditation Council for Independent Further and Higher Education
BAcc	Bachelor of Accountancy
BAgr	Bachelor of Agriculture
BAO	Bachelor of Obstetrics
BArch	Bachelor of Architecture
BChD	Bachelor of Dental Surgery
BChir	Bachelor of Surgery
BCL	Bachelor of Civil Law
BCom	Bachelor of Commerce
BCombStuds	Bachelor of Combined Studies
BCommunications	Bachelor of Communications
BCS	Bachelor of Combined Studies
BD	Bachelor of Divinity
BDS	Bachelor of Dental Surgery
BEd	Bachelor of Education
BEng and Man	Bachelor of Mechanical Engineering, Manufacture and Management
BEng	Bachelor of Engineering
BER	Board for Engineers' Registration
BHSAI	British Horse Society's Assistant Instructor's Certificate
BHSI	British Horse Society's Instructor's Certificate
BHSII	British Horse Society's Intermediate Instructor's Certificate
BHSSM	British Horse Society's Stable Manager's Certificate
BLD	Bachelor of Landscape Design
BLE	Bachelor of Land Economy
BLib	Bachelor of Librarianship
BLing	Bachelor of Linguistics
BLitt	Bachelor of Letters
BLS	Bachelor of Library Studies
BM	Bachelor of Medicine
BM, BCh	Conjoint degree of Bachelor of Medicine, Bachelor of Surgery
BM, BS	Conjoint degree of Bachelor of Medicine, Bachelor of Surgery
BMedBiol	Bachelor of Medical Biology
BMedSci	Bachelor of Medical Sciences

BMedSci(Speech)	Bachelor of Medical Sciences (Speech)
BMet	Bachelor of Metallurgy
BMSc	Bachelor of Medical Sciences
BMus	Bachelor of Music
BN Nursing	Bachelor of Nursing, Nursing Studies
BN	Bachelor of Nursing
BPharm	Bachelor of Pharmacy
BPhil (Ed)	Bachelor of Philosophy (Education)
BPhil	Bachelor of Philosophy
BPL	Bachelor of Planning
BFA	Bachelor of Fine Arts
BSc (Architecture)	Bachelor of Science (Architecture)
BSc (DentSci)	Bachelor of Science in Dental Science
BSc	Bachelor of Science
BSc(Econ)	Bachelor of Science in Economics
BSc(MedSci)	Bachelor of Science (Medical Science)
BSc(Social Science)	Bachelor of Science (Social Science)
BSc(Town & Regional Planning)	Bachelor of Science (Town & Regional Planning)
BScEng	Bachelor of Science in Engineering
BScFor	Bachelor of Science in Forestry
BScTech	Bachelor of Technical Science
BSocSc	Bachelor of Social Science
BScAgr	Bachelor of Science in Agriculture
BSSc	Bachelor of Social Science
BSSG	Member of the British Society of Scientific Glassblowers
BTEC HC	Business and Technology Education Council Higher Certificate
BTEC HD	Business and Technology Education Council Higher Diploma
BTEC HNC	Business and Technology Education Council Higher National Certificate
BTEC HND	Business and Technology Education Council Higher National Diploma
BTEC	Business and Technology Education Council
BTech	Bachelor of Technology
BVSc	Bachelor of Veterinary Science
C&G	City and Guilds
CA	Member of the Institute of Chartered Accountants of Scotland
CABE	Companion of the Association of Business Executives
CAS	Certification of Accountancy Studies
CASS	Certificate of Applied Social Studies
CAT	Certificate for Accounting Technicians
CBA	Companion of the British (Theatrical) Arts
CBAE	Companion of the British Academy of Experts
CBIM	Companion of the British Institute of Management
CBiol	Chartered Biologist
CBSSG	Craft Member of the British Society of Scientific Glassblowers
CCETSW	Central Council for Education and Training in Social Work
CChem	Chartered Chemist
CCol	Chartered Colourist
CDipAF	Certified Diploma in Accounting and Finance
CEng	Chartered Engineer
CertBibKnowl	Certificate of Bible Knowledge
CertDesRCA	Certificate of Designer of the Royal College of Art
CertEd	Certificate in Education
CertHSAP	Certificate in Health Services Administration Practice
CertHSM	Certificate in Health Services Management
CertOccHyg	Certificate in Operational Competence in Comprehensive Occupational Hygiene
CertTEL	Certificate in the Teaching of European Languages
CertTESOL	Certificate of Teaching of English to Speakers of Other Languages
CertTEYL	Certificate of Teaching of English to Young Learners
CertYCW	Certificate in Youth and Community Work

CETHV	Certificate of Education in Training as Health Visitor
CFS	Certificate in Financial Services
ChB	Bachelor of Surgery
ChM	Master of Surgery
CHP	Certificate in Hypnosis and Psychology
CHRIM	Certified Member of the Institute of Health Record Information and Management
CIAgrE	Companion of the Institution of Agricultural Engineers
CIEx	Companion of the Institute of Export
CIFE	Conference for Independent Further Education
CIMediE	Companion of the Institution of Mechanical Engineers
CIMgt	Companion of the Institute of Management
CISOB	Counsellor of the Incorporated Society of Organ Builders
CL(ABDO)	Diploma in Contact Lens Fitting of the Association of Dispensing Opticians
CMA	Certificate in Management Accountancy
CMathFIMA	Fellow of the Institute of Mathematics and its Applications
CMBHI	Craft Member of the British Horological Institute
CMIWSc	Certified Member of the Institute of Wood Science
CmpnIAP	Companion of the Institution of Analysts and Programmers
CMS	Certificate in Management Studies
CNAA	Council for National Academic Awards
COES	Certificate of Educational Studies
Companion IEE	Companion of the Institution of Electrical Engineers
Companion IGasE	Companion of the Institution of Gas Engineers
CompIManf	Companion of the Institute Manufacturing
CompIMS	Companion of the Institute of Management Specialists
CompIP	Companion of the Institute of Plumbing
Corporate IRRV	Corporate Member of the Institute of Revenues, Rating and Valuation
CPA	Chartered Patent Agency
CPC	Certificate of Professional Competence, the Institute of Transport Administration
CPE	Common Professional Exam
CPEA	Certificate of Practice in Estate Agency
CPFA	Member of Chartered Institute of Public Finance and Accountancy
CPhys	Chartered Physicist of the Institute of Physics
CPIM	Certificate in Production and Inventory Management
CPL	Commercial Pilot's Licence
CPM	Certified Professional Manager (Society of Business Practitioners)
CPR	Chartered Professional Review
CProfBTM	Companion of Professional Business & Technical Management
CPS	Certificate in Pastoral Studies and Applied Theology
CPsychol	Chartered Psychologist, British Psychological Society
CPT	Continuing Professional Training
CPVE	Certificate of Pre-Vocational Training
CRNCM	Companionship of the Royal Northern College of Music
CSE	Certificate of Secondary Education
CSMGSM	Certificate in Stage Management (Guildhall School of Music and Drama)
CStat	Chartered Statistician
CSYS	Certificate of Sixth Year Studies
CTextATI	Associate of the Textile Institute
CTextFTI	Fellow of the Textile Institute
CVT	Certified Vehicle Technologist
DA	Diploma in Anaesthetics
DAES	Diploma in Advanced Educational Studies
DAvMed	Diploma in Aviation Medicine
DBO	Diploma of the British Orthoptic Society
DCC	Diploma of Chelsea College
DCDH	Diploma in Child Dental Health
DCG	Diploma in Careers Guidance
DCH	Diploma in Child Health

DChD	Diploma of Dental Surgery
DChM	Diploma in Chiropodial Medicine, Institute of Chiropodist and Podiatrists
DCHT	Diploma in Community Health in Tropical Countries
DCL	Doctor of Civil Law
DCLF	Diploma in Contact Lens Fitting
DCLP	Diploma in Contact Lens Practise
DCR(R)or(T)	Diploma of the College of Radiographers
DD	Doctor of Divinity
DDH(Birm)	Diploma in Dental Health, University of Birmingham
DDOrthRCPSGlas	Diploma in Dental Orthopaedics of the Royal College of Physicians and Surgeons of Glasgow
DDPHRCS(Eng)	Diploma in Dental Public Health, Royal College of Surgeons of England
DDS	Doctor of Dental Surgery
DDSc	Doctor of Dental Science
DEng	Doctor of Engineering
DES	Department of Education and Science (now the Department for Education)
DGA	Diamond Member of the Gemmological Association and Gem Testing Laboratory of Great Britain
DGDPRCS	Diploma in General Dental Practice, Royal College of Surgeons of England
DGM	Diploma in Geriatric Medicine
DHE	Diploma in Horticulture, Royal Botanic Garden, Edinburgh
DHMSA	Diploma in the History of Medicine, Society of Apothecaries of London
DHP	Diploma in Hypnosis and Psychotherapy
DIA	Diploma of Industrial Administration
DIC	Diploma of Membership of Imperial College of Science and Technology, University of London
DIH	Diploma in Industrial Health
Dip CD	Diploma in Community Development
DipAD	Diploma in Art and Design
DipAE	Diploma in Adult Education
DipAgrComm	Diploma in Agricultural Communication
DipArb	Diploma in Arbitration
DipArb	Diploma in Arboriculture
DipArch	Diploma in Architecture
DipASE(CofP)	Graduate Level Specialist Diploma in Advanced Study in Education, College of Preceptors
DipAT	Diploma in Accounting Technology
DipBA	Diploma in Business Administration
DipBldgCons	Diploma in Building Conservation
DipCAM	Diploma in the Communication Advertising and Marketing Education Foundation
DipCHM	Diploma in Choir Training, Royal College of Organists
DipClinPath	Diploma in Clinical Pathology
DipCOT	Diploma of the College of Occupational Therapists
DipCT	Diploma in Corporate Treasury Management
DipEd	Diploma in Education
DipEF	Diploma in Executive Finance
DipEH	Diploma in Environmental Health
DipEM	Diploma in Environmental Management
DipEMA	Diploma in Executive and Management Accountancy
DipEngLit	Diploma in English Literature
DipFD	Diploma in Funeral Directing, National Association of Funeral Directors
DipFS	Financial Studies Diploma
DipGAI	Diploma of the Guild of Architectural Ironmongers
DipGSM	Diploma of the Guildhall School of Music and Drama
DipHE	Diploma of Higher Education
DipISW	Diploma of the Institute of Social Welfare
DipLE	Diploma in Land Economy
DipM	Postgraduate Diploma in Marketing, Chartered Institute of Marketing
DipMetEng	Diploma in Meteorological Engineering

DipOccHyg	Diploma of Professional Competence in Comprehensive Occupational Hygiene
DipPharmMed	Diploma in Pharmaceutical Medicine
DipPhil	Diploma in Philosophy
DipProjMan	Diploma in Project Management
DipPropInv	Diploma in Property Investment
DipRAM	Diploma of Royal Academy of Music
DipRCM	Diploma in the Royal College of Music
DipRMS	Diploma in Royal Microscopical Society
DipSc	Diploma in Science
DipSM	Diploma in Safety Management
DipSurv	Diploma in Surveying
DipTCL	Diploma of the Trinity College of Music, London
DipTESOL	Diploma in Teaching of English to Speakers of Other Languages
DipTHP	Diploma in Therapeutic Hypnosis and Psychotherapy
DipTM	Diploma in Training Management, Institute of Personnel and Development
DipTransIoL	Diploma in Translation, Institute of Linguistics
DipUniv	Diploma of the University
DipVen	Diploma in Venereology, Society of Apothecaries of London
DipWCF	Diploma of the Worshipful Company of Farriers
DIS	Diploma in Industrial Studies
Dlit(t)	Doctor of Letters or Literature
DLO	Diploma of Laryngology and Otology
DLORCSEng	Diploma in Laryngology and Otology, Royal College of Surgeons of England
DLP	Diploma in Legal Practice
DM	Doctor of Medicine
DMedRehab	Diploma in Medical Rehabilitation
DMet	Doctor of Metallurgy
DMJ(Clin) or DMJ(Path)	Diploma in Medical Jurisprudence (Clinical or Pathological), Society of Apothecaries of London
DMRD	Diploma in Medical Radio-Diagnosis
DMRT	Diploma in Radiotherapy
DMS	Diploma in Management Studies
DMU	Diploma in Medical Ultrasound
DMus	Doctor of Music
DMusCantuar	The Archbishop of Canterbury's Doctorate in Music
DO	Diploma in Ophthalmology
DO	Diploma in Osteopathy
DOpt	Diploma in Ophthalmic Optics
DOrth RCSEdin	Diploma in Orthodontics, Royal College of Surgeons of Edinburgh
DOrth	Diploma in Orthoptics
DOrthRCSEng	Diplomate in Orthodontics, Royal College of Surgeons of England
DP	Diploma in Psychotherapy
DPA	Diploma in Public Administration
DpBact	Diploma in Bacteriology
DPD(Dund)	Diploma in Public Dentistry, University of Dundee
DPH	Diploma in Public Health
DPhil	Diploma in Philosophy
DPHRCSEng	Diploma in Dental Public Health, Royal College of Surgeons of England
DPM	Diploma in Psychological Medicine
DPS	Diploma in Professional Studies
DPSE	Diploma in Pastoral Studies and Applied Theology
Dr(RCA)	Doctor of the Royal College of Art
DrAc	Doctor of Acupuncture
DRCOG	Diploma of the Royal College of Obstetricians and Gynaecologists
DRDRCSEd	Diploma in Restorative Dentistry, Royal College of Surgeons of Edinburgh
DRE	Diploma in Remedial Electrolysis, Institute of Electrolysis
DRI	Diploma in Radionuclide Imaging
DRSAMD	Diploma in the Royal Scottish Academy of Music and Drama
DSc	Doctor of Science

DSc(Econ)	Doctor of Science (Economics) or in Economics
DSc(Eng)	Doctor of Science (Engineering)
DSc(Social)	Doctor of Science in the Social Sciences
DScEcon	Doctor in the Faculty of Economics and Social Studies
DSCH(Oxon)	Diploma of Surgical Chiropody (Oxon), Oxford School of Chiropody and Paediatric Medicine
DScTech	Doctor of Technical Science
DSocSc	Doctor of Social Science
DSSc	Doctor of Social Science
DSTA	Diploma Member of the Swimming Teachers' Association
DTCD	Diploma in Tuberculosis and Chest Diseases
DTCH	Diploma in Tropical Medicine and Hygiene
DTech	Doctor of Technology
DTI	Department of Trade and Industry
DTM&H	Diploma in Tropical Medicine and Hygiene
DTp	Department of Transport
DUniv	Doctor of the University
DVetMed	Doctor of Veterinary Medicine
DVM	Doctor of Veterinary Medicine
DVM&S	Doctor of Veterinary Medicine and Surgery
DVS	Doctor of Veterinary Surgery
DVSc	Doctor of Veterinary Science
ECG	Executive Group Committees (of the Board for Engineers Registration)
EHO	Environmental Health Of ficer
EMFEC	East Midland Further Education Council
EN	Enrolled Nurse
EN(G)	Enrolled Nurse(General)
EN(M)	Enrolled Nurse (Mental)
EN(MH)	Enrolled Nurse (Mental Handicap)
ENB	English National Board
EngC	Engineering Council
EngTech	Engineering Technician
EurBiol	European Biologist
FABE	Fellow of the Association of Business Executives
FACB	Fellow of the Association of Certified Bookkeepers
FACP	Fellow of the Association of Computer Professionals
FAE	Fellow of the Academy of Experts
FAIA	Fellow of the Association of International Accountants
FAMS	Fellow of the Association of Medical Secretaries, Practice Administrators and Receptionists
FASI	Fellow of the Ambulance Service Institute
FASI	Fellow of the Architects and Surveyors Institute
FASP	Fellow of the Association of Sales Personnel
FBA	Fellow of the British Academy
FBA	Fellow of the British Arts
FBCS	Fellow of the British Computer Society
FBDO	Fellow of the Association of British Dispensing Opticians
FBDO (Hons)	Fellow of the Association of British Dispensing Opticians with Honours Diploma
FBDO (Hons) CL	Fellow of the Association of British Dispensing Opticians with Honours Diploma and Diploma in Contact Lens Fitting
FBEI	Fellow of the Institution of Body Engineers
FBEng	Fellow of the Association of Building Engineers
FBHA	Fellow of the British Hypnotherapy Association
FBHI	Fellow of the British Horological Institute
FBHS	Fellow of the British Horse Society
FBID	Fellow of the British Institute of Interior Design
FBIE	Fellow of the British Institute of Embalmers
FBIPP	Fellow of the British Institute of Professional Photography
FBIS	Fellow of the British Interplanetary Society

FBPsS	Fellow of the British Psychological Society
FCA	Fellow of the Institute of Chartered Accountants in England and Wales
FCAM	Fellow of the Communication Advertising and Marketing Education Foundation
FCB	Fellow of the Communicators in Business Ltd
FCBSI	Fellow of the Chartered Building Societies Institute
FCCA	Fellow of the Association of Chartered Certified Accountants
FCEA	Fellow of the Association of Cost and Executive Accountants
FCGI	Fellowship, City & Guilds
FChS	Fellow of the Society of Chiropodists and Podiatrists
FCI	Fellow of the Institute of Commerce
FCIArb	Fellow of the Chartered Institute of Arbitrators
FCIB	Fellow of the Chartered Institute of Bankers
FCIBS	Fellow of the Chartered Institute of Bankers in Scotland
FCIBSE	Fellow of the Chartered Institute of Building Services Engineers
FCIH	Fellow of the Chartered Institute of Housing
FCII	Fellow of the Chartered Insurance Institute
FCIJ	Fellow of the Chartered Institute of Journalists
FCILA	Fellow of the Chartered Institute of Loss Adjusters
FCIM	Fellow of the Chartered Institute of Marketing
FCIOB	Fellow of the Chartered Institute of Building
FCIPS	Fellow of the Chartered Institute of Purchasing and Supply
FCIS	Fellow of the Institute of Chartered Secretaries and Administrators
FCIT	Fellow of the Chartered Institute of Transport
FCLS	First Certificate for Legal Secretaries
FCMA	Fellow of the Institute of Cost and Management Accountants
FCOphth	Fellow of the College of Ophthalmology
FCOptom	Fellow of the College of Optometrists
FCPM	Fellow of the Confederation of Professional Management
FCPWA	Fellow of the Faculty of Community, Personal, and Welfare Accounting
FCSD	Fellow of the Chartered Society of Designers
FCSP	Fellow of the Chartered Society of Physiotherapy
FCT	Fellow of the Association of Corporate Treasurers
FCTHCM	Fellow of the Confederation of Tourism, Hotel and Catering Management
FCYW	Fellow of the Community and Youth Work Association
FDSRCPSGlas	Fellow in Dental Surgery of the Royal College of Surgeons of Glasgow
FDSRCSEd	Fellow in Dental Surgery of the Royal College of Physicians and Surgeons of Edinburgh
FDSRCSEng	Fellow in Dental Surgery of the Royal College of Physicians and Surgeons of England
FECI	Fellow of the Institute of Employment Consultants
FEIS	Fellow of the Educational Institute of Scotland
FFA	Fellow of the Faculties of Actuaries
FFA	Fellow of the Institute of Financial Accountants
FFARCSEng	Fellow of the Faculty of Anaesthetists of the Royal College of Surgeons in England
FFARCSIrel	Fellow of the Faculty of Anaesthetists of the Royal College of Surgeons in Ireland
FFAS	Fellow of the Faculty of Architects and Surveyors (Architects)
FFCA	Fellow of the Association of Financial Controllers and Administrators
FFCI	Fellow of the Faculty of Commerce and Industry Ltd
FFCS	Fellow of the Faculty of Secretaries
FFHom	Fellow of the Faculty of Homoeopathy
FFPHM	Fellow of the Faculty of Public Health Medicine, Royal College of Physicians of London and Edinburgh and Royal College of Physicians and Surgeons of Glasgow.
FFPHMIrel	Fellow of the Faculty of Public Health Medicine, Royal College of Physicians of Ireland
FFRRCSIrel	Fellow of the Faculty of Radiologists, Royal College of Surgeons in Ireland
FFS	Fellow of the Faculty of Architects and Surveyors (Surveyors)

FGA	Fellow of the Gemmological Association
FGCL	Fellow of the Guild of Cleaners and Launderers
FGI	Fellow of the Greek Institute
FGSM	Fellow of the Guildhall School of Music and Drama
FHCIMA	Fellow of the Hotel and Catering International Management Association
FHFS	Fellow of the Council of Health, Fitness and Sports Therapists
FHG	Fellow of the Institute of Heraldic and Genealogical Studies
FHRIM	Fellow of the Institute of Health Record Information and Management
FHSM	Fellow of the Institute of Health Services Management
FIA	Fellow of the Institute of Acturies
FIAB	Fellow of the International Association of Book-keepers
FIAEA	Fellow of the Institute of Automotive Engineer Assessors
FIAgrE	Fellow of the Institution of Agricultural Engineers
FIAP	Fellow of the Institution of Analysts and Programmers
FIAT	Fellow of the Institute of Asphalt Technology
FIBA	Fellow of the Institution of Business Agents
FIBC	Fellow of the Institute of Building Control
FIBCM	Fellow of the Institute of British Carriage and Automobile Manufacturers
FIBCO	Fellow of the Institute of Building Control Of ficers
FIBF	Fellow of the Institution of British Foundrymen
FIBiol	Fellow of the Institute of Biology
FIBMS	Fellow of the Institute of Medical Laboratory Sciences
FICE	Fellow of the Institution of Civil Engineers
FIChemE	Fellow of the Institution of Chemical Engineers
FIChor	Fellow of the Benesh Institute of Choreology
FICHT	Fellow of the International Council of Holistic Therapies
FICM	Fellow of the Institute of Credit Management
FICorr	Fellow of the Institute of Corrosion
FICS	Fellow of the Institute of Chartered Shipbrokers
FICW	Fellow of the Institute of Clerks of Works of Great Britain Incorporated
FIDTA	Fellow of the International Dance Teachers' Association
FIED	Fellow of the Institution of Engineering Designers
FIEE	Fellow of the Institution of Electrical Engineers
FIEM	Fellow of the Institute of Executives and Managers
FIEx	Fellow of the Institute of Export
FIExpE	Fellow of the Institute of Explosives Engineers
FIFireE	Fellow of the Institution of Fire Engineers
FIFM	Fellow of the Institute of Fisheries Management
FIFST	Fellow of the Institute of Food Science and Technology
FIGasE	Fellow of the Institute of Gas Engineers
FIGD	Fellow of the Institute of Grocery Distribution
FIGeol	Fellow of the Institute of Geologists
FIHEc	Fellow of the Institute of Home Economics Ltd
FIHIE	Fellow of the Institute of Highways Incorporated Engineers
FIHort	Fellow of the Institute of Horticulture
FIHT	Fellow of the Institution of Highways and Transportation
FIIMR	Fellow of the Institute of Investment Management and Research
FIInfSc	Fellow of the Institute of Information Scientists
FIIRSM	Fellow of the International Institute of Risk and Safety Management
FIISE	Fellow of the International Institute of Social Economics
FIL	Fellow of the Institute of Linguistics
FILAM	Fellow of the Institute of Leisure and Amenity Management
FIM	Fellow of the Institute of Materials
FIMA	Fellow of the Institute of Mathematics and its Applications
FIManf	Fellow of the Institute of Manufacturing
FIMarE	Fellow of the Institute of Marine Engineers
FlMatM	Fellow of the Institute of Materials Management
FIMBM	Fellow of the Institute of Maintenance and Building Management
FIMechE	Fellow of the Institute of Mechanical Engineers
FIMechIE	Fellow of the Institute of Mechanical Incorporated Engineers

FIMF	Fellow of the Institute of Metal Finishing
FIMgt	Fellow of the Institute of Management
FIMgt	Fellow of the British Institute of Management
FIMI	Fellow of the Institute of the Motor Industry
FIMM	Fellow of the Institute of Massage and Movement
FIMM	Fellow of the Institute of Mining and Metallurgy
FIMS	Fellow of the Institute of Management Specialists
FIMunE	Fellow of the Institution of Municipal Engineers
FInstAEA	Fellow of the Institute of Automotive Engineer Assessors
FInstAM	Fellow of the Institute of Administrative Management
FInstBA	Fellow of the Institute of Business Administration
FInstBCA	Fellow of the Institute of Burial and Cremation Administration
FInstBM	Fellow of the Institute of Builders Merchants
FInstBRM	Fellow of the Institute of Baths and Recreation Management
FInstCh	Fellow of the Institute of Chiropodists
FInstCM	Fellow of the Institute of Commercial Management
FInstD	Fellow of the Institute of Directors
FInstE	Fellow of the Institute of Energy
FInstLEx	Fellow of the Institute of Legal Executives
FInstMC	Fellow of the Institute of Measurement and Control
FInstNDT	Fellow of the British Institute of Non-Destructive Testing
FInstP	Fellow of the Institute of Physics
FInstPet	Fellow of the Institute of Petroleum
FInstPkg	Fellow of the Institute of Packaging
FInstPM	Fellow of the Institute of Professional Managers and Administrators
FInstPS	Fellow of the Institute of Purchasing and Supply
FInstR	Fellow of the Institute of Refrigeration
FInstSMM	Fellow of the Institute of Sales and Marketing Management
FInstTA	Fellow of the Institute of Transport Administration
FInstTT	Fellow of the Institute of Travel and Tourism
FInstWM	Fellow of the Institute of Wastes Management
FInstWM	Fellowship of the Institute of Wastes Management
FIntMC	Fellow of International Management Centre
FIOC	Fellow of the Institute of Carpenters
FIOM	Fellow of the Institute of Operation Management
FIOP	Fellow of the Institute of Plumbing
FIOP	Fellow of the Institute of Printing
FIOSH	Fellow of the Institution of Occupational Safety and Health
FIPA	Fellow of the Institute of Practitioners in Advertising
FIPD	Fellow of the Institute of Personnel Development
FIPI	Fellow of the Institute of Professional Investigators
FIPlantE	Fellow of the Institution of Plant Engineers
FIPR	Fellow of the Institute of Public Relations
FIQ	Fellow of the Institute of Quarrying
IQA	Fellow of the Institute of Quality Assurance
FIR	Fellow of the Institute of Population Registration
FIRSE	Fellow of the Institute of Railway Signal Engineers
FIRTE	Fellow of the Institute of Road Transport Engineers
FIS	Fellow of the Institute of Statisticians
FISM	Fellow of the Institute of Supervisory Management
FISOB	Fellow of the Incorporated Society of Organ Builders
FISTC	Fellow of the Institute of Scientific and Technical Communicators
FISTD	Fellow of the Imperial Society of Teachers of Dancing
FIStrucE	Fellow of the Institution of Structural Engineers
FISW	Fellow of the Institute of Social Welfare
FITD	Fellow of the Institute of Training and Development
FITSA	Fellow of the Institute of Trading Standards Administration
FLA	Fellow of the Library Association
FLCM	Fellow of the London College of Music
FLCSP(Phys)	Fellow of the London and Counties Society of Physiologists

FLI	Fellow of the Landscape Institute
FLS	Fellow of the Linnean Society
FMA	Fellow of the Museums Association
FMAAT	Fellow Member of the Association of Accounting Technicians
FMPA	Fellow of the Master Photographers Association
FMR	Fellow of the Association of Health Care Information and Medical Records Of ficers
FMS	Fellow of the Institute of Management Services
FN	Fellow of the Nautical Society
FNAEA	Fellow of the National Association of Estate Agents
FNAEAHonoured	Honoured Fellow of the National Association of Estate Agents
FNCP	Fellow of the National Council of Psychotherapists
FNIMH	Fellow of the National Institute of Medical Herbalists
FPMI	Fellow of the Pensions Management Institute
FProfBTM	Fellow of Professional Business and Technical Management
FRAeS	Fellow of the Royal Aeronautical Society
FRAS	Fellow of the Royal Astronomical Society
FRCA	Fellow of the Royal College of Anaesthetists
FRCGP	Fellow of the Royal College of General Practitioners
FRCM	Fellow of the Royal College of Music
FRCO	Fellow of the Royal College of Organists
FRCO(CHM)	Fellow of the Royal College of Organists (Choir-training Diploma)
FRCOG	Fellow of the Royal College of Obstetricians and Gynaecologists
FRCP	Fellow of the Royal College of Physicians of London
FRCPath	Fellow of the Royal College of Pathologists
FRCPEdin	Fellow of the Royal College of Physicians of Edinburgh
FRCPsych	Fellow of the Royal College of Psychiatrists
FRCR	Fellow of the Royal College of Radiologists
FRCS(Irel)	Fellow of the Royal College of Surgeons in Ireland
FRCSEd (C/TH)	Fellow of the Royal College of Surgeons of Edinburgh, specialising in Cardiothoracic Surgery
FRCSEd (Orth)	Fellow of the Royal College of Surgeons of Edinburgh, specialising in Orthopaedic Surgery
FRCSEd (SN)	Fellow of the Royal College of Surgeons of Edinburgh, specialising in Surgical Neurology
FRCSEd	Fellow of the Royal College of Surgeons of Edinburgh
FRCSEng	Fellow of the Royal College of Surgeons of England
FRCSGlasg	Fellow of the Royal College of Physicians and Surgeons of Glasgow
FRCSEng(Oto)	Fellow of the Royal College of Surgeons in England, with Otolaryngology
FRCVS	Fellow of the Royal College of Veterinary Surgeons
FRHS	Fellow of the Royal Horticulture Society
FRIBA	Fellow of the Royal Institute of British Architects
FRICS	Fellow of the Royal Institution of Chartered Surveyors
FRIN	Fellow of the Royal Institution of Navigation
FRINA	Fellow of the Royal Institution of Naval Architects
FRIPHH	Fellow of the Royal Institution of Public Health and Hygiene
FRNCM	Fellow of the Royal Northern College of Music
FRPharmS	Fellow of the Royal Pharmaceutical Society of Great Britain
FRPS	Fellow of the Royal Photographic Society
FRS	Fellow of the Royal Society
FRSC	Fellow of the Royal Society of Chemistry
FRSCM	Fellow of the Royal School of Church Music
FRSH	Fellow of the Royal Society of Health
FRTPI	Fellow of the Royal Town Planning Institute
FSAPP	Fellow of the Society of Advanced Psychotherapy Practitioners
FSBP	Fellow of the Society of Business Practitioners
FSBT	Fellow of the Society of Teachers in Business Education
FSCA	Fellow of the Society of Company Accountants
FSDC	Fellow of the Society of Dyers and Colourists
FSE	Fellow of the Society of Engineers (Inc)

FSElec	Fellow of the Society of Electroscience
FSG	Fellow of the Society of Genealogists
FSG(Hon)	Honorary Fellow of the Society of Genealogists
FSGT	Fellow of the Society of Glass Technology
FSIAD	Fellow of the Society of Industrial Artists and Designers
FSMA	Fellow of the Society of Sales Management Administrators Ltd
FSNNA	Fellow of the Society of Nursery Nursing Administrators
FSS	Fellow of the Royal Statistical Society
FSSCh	Fellow of the School of Surgical Chiropody
FSSF	Fellow of the Society of Shoe Fitters
FSTA	Fellow of the Swimming Teachers' Association
FSVA	Fellow of the Incorporated Society of Valuers and Auctioneers
FTCL	Fellow of the Trinity College of Music
FTI	Fellow of the Textile Institute
FTII	Fellow of the Chartered Institute of Taxation
FTSC	Fellow in the Technology of Surface Coatings
FWeldI	Fellow of the Welding Institute
FYDA	Associate Fellowship of the Youth Development Association
GASI	Graduate Member of the Ambulance Service Institute
GBSM	Graduate of the Birmingham School of Music
GCE	General Certificate of Education
GCGI	Graduateship, City & Guilds
GCSE	General Certificate of Secondary Education
GIBCM	Graduate of the Institute of British Carriage and Automobile Manufacturers
GIBiol	Graduate of the Institute of Biology
GIEM	Graduate of the Institute of Executives and Managers
GIMA	Graduate Member of the Institute of Mathematics and its Applications
GIMI	Graduate of the Institute of the Motor Industry
GInstP	Graduate of the Institute of Physics
GIntMC	Graduate of the International Management Centre
GIS	Graduate Imaging Scientist (Royal Photographic Society)
GLCM	Graduate Diploma of the London College of Music
GMusRNCM	Graduate in Music of the Royal Northern College of Music
GNSM	Graduate of the Northern School of Music
GradBHI	Graduate of the British Horological Institute
GradlAP	Graduate of the Institution of Analysts and Programmers
GradIElecIE	Graduate of the Institution of Electrical and Electronics Incorporated Engineers
GradIISec	Graduate of the Institute of Industrial Security
GradIManf	Graduate of the Institute Manufacturing
GradIMF	Graduate of the Institute of Metal Finishing
GradIMS	Graduate of the Institute of Management Specialists
GradInstNDT	Graduate of the British Institute of Non-Destructive Testing
GradInstPS	Graduate of the Institute of Purchasing and Supply
GradIOP	Graduate of the Institute of Printing
GradIPD	Graduate of the Institute of Personnel and Development
GradIS	Graduate of the Institute of Statisticians
GradISCA	Graduate of the Institute of Chartered Secretaries and Administrators
GradMechE	Graduate of the Institution Mechanical Engineers
GradMInstWM	Graduate Member of the Institute of Wastes Management
GradRNCM	Graduate of the Roya] Northern College of Music
GradRSC	Graduate of the Royal Society of Chemistry
GradStat	Graduate Statistician
GraduateIEIE	Graduate of the Institution of Electrical and Electronics Incorporated Engineers
GradWeldI	Graduate of the Welding Institute
GRC	General Readers Certificate
GRIC	Graduate Membership of the Royal Institute of Chemistry
GRSC	Graduate of the Royal Society of Chemistry
GRSM	Graduate Diploma of the Royal Manchester School of Music

GRSM(Hons)	Graduate of the Royal Schools of Music
GSMA	Graduate of the Society of Sales Management Administrators Ltd
GSNNA	Graduate of the Society Nursery Nursing Administrators
HC	Higher Certificate
HD	Higher Diploma
HDCR (R) or (T)	Higher Award in Radiodiagnosis or Radiotherapy, College of Radiographers
HNC	Higher National Certificate
HND	Higher National Diploma
HonASTA	Honorary Associate of the Swimming Teachers' Association
HonDrRCA	Honorary Doctorate of the Royal College of Art
HonFBID	Honorary Fellow of the British Institute of Interior Design
HonFBIPP	Honorary Fellow of the British Institute of Professional Photography
HonFCP'	Charter Fellow of the College of Preceptors
HonFEIS	Honorary Fellow of the Educational Institute of Scotland
HonFHCIMA	Honorary Fellow of the Hotel, Catering and Institutional Management Association
HonFIEE	Honorary Fellow of the Institution of Electrical Engineers
HonFIExpE	Honorary Fellow of the Institute of Explosives Engineers
HonFIGasE	Honorary Fellow of the Institution of Gas Engineers
HonFIMarE	Honorary Fellow of the Institute of Marine Engineers
HonFIMechE	Honorary Fellow of the Institution of Mechanical Engineers
HonFIMM	Honorary Fellow of the Institution of Mining and Metallurgy
HonFInstE	Honorary Fellow of the Institute of Energy
HonFInstMC	Honorary Fellow of the Institute of Measurement and Control
HonFInstNDT	Honorary Fellow of the British Institute of Non-Destructive Testing
HonFIQA	Honorary Fellow of the Institute of Quality Assurance
HonFIRSE	Honorary Fellow of the Institution of Railway Signal Engineers
HonFIRTE	Honorary Fellow of the Institute of Road Transport Engineers
HonFPRI	Honorary Fellow of the Plastics and Rubber Institute
HonFRINA	Honorary Fellow of the Royal Institution of Naval Architects
HonFRPS	Honorary Fellow of the Royal Photographic Society
HonFSE	I Honorary Fellow of the Society of Engineers (Inc)
HonFSGT	Honorary Fellow of the Society of Glass Technology
HonFWeldI	Honorary Fellow of the Welding Institute
HonGSM	Honorary Member of the Guildhall School of Music and Drama
HonI]tI E	Honorary Member of the Institute of Road Transport Engineers
HonMIFM	Honorary Member of the Institute of Fisheries Management
HonMInstNDT	Honorary Member of the British Institute of Non-Destructive Testing
HonMRIN	Honorary Member of the Royal Institute of Navigation
HonMWES	Honorary Member of the Women's Engineering Society
HonRAM	Honorary Member of the Royal Academy of Music
HonRCM	Honorary Member of the Royal College of Music
HonRNCM	Honorary Member of the Royal Northern College of Music
HonRSCM	Honorary Member of the Royal School of Church Music
HSC	Higher School Certificate
HSE	Health & Safety Executive
HTC	Higher Technical Certificate
IAC	Investment Advice Certificate
ICSF	Intermediate Certificate of the Society of Floristry
IEng	Incorporated Engineer
IMIBC	Incorporated Member of the Institute of Building Control
IncMWeldI	Incorporated Member of the Welding Institute
IPFA	Member of the Chartered Institute of Public Finance and Accountancy
IPR	Incorporated Professional Review
JP	Justice of the Peace
LABAC	Licentiate Member of the Association of Business and Administrative Computing
LAE	Licentiate Automotive Engineer
LAEx	Legal Accounts Executive
LAMDA	London Academy of Music and Dramatic Art

LAMRTPI	Legal Associate Member of the Royal Town Planning Institute
LASI	Licentiate of the Architects and Surveyors Institute
LASI	Licentiate of the Ambulance Service Institute
LBEI	Licentiate of the Institution of Body Engineers
LBIPP	Licentiate of the British Institute of Professional Photography
LCCI	London Chamber of Commerce and Industry
LCEA	Licentiate of the Association of Cost and Executive Accountants
LCFI	Licentiate of CFI International (Clothing and Footwear Institute)
LCGI	Licentiate, City & Guild
LCIBSE	Licentiate of the Chartered Institution of Building Services Engineers
LCP	Licentiate of the College of Preceptors
LCSP(Assoc)	Associate of the London and Counties Society of Physiologists
LCSP(BTh)	Diploma in Body Massage and Physical Culture, London and Counties Society of Physiologists
LCSP(BTh)	Diploma in Health and Beauty Therapy, London and Counties Society of Physiologists
LCSP(Phys)	Diploma in Swedish Massage, London and Counties Society of Physiologists
LDS	Licentiate in Dental Surgery
LDSRCPSGlas	Licentiate in Dental Surgery of the Royal College of Physicians and Surgeons of Glasgow
LDSRCSEd	Licentiate in Dental Surgery of the Royal College of Surgeons of Edinburgh
LDSRCSEng	Licentiate in Dental Surgery of the Royal College of Surgeons of England
LFA	Licentiate of the Institute of Financial Accountants
LFCI	Licentiate of the Faculty of Commerce and Industry
LFCS	Licentiate of the Faculty of Secretaries
LFS	Licentiate of the Faculty of Architects and Surveyors (Surveyors)
LGCL	Licentiate of the Guild of Cleaners and Launderers
LGSM	Licentiate of the Guildhall School of Music and Drama
LHCIMA	Licentiate of the Hotel and Catering International Management Association
LHG	Licentiate of the Institute of Heraldic and Genealogical Studies
LicIPD	Licentiate of the Institute of Personnel & Development
LicIQA	Licentiate of the Institute of Quality Assurance
LICW	Licentiate of the Institute of Clerks of Works of Great Britain Incorporated
LIDPM	Licentiate of the Institute of Data Processing Management
LIEM	Licentiate of the Institute of Executives and Managers
LIIST	Licentiate of the International Institute of Sports Therapy
LILAM	Licentiate of the Institute of Leisure and Amenity Management
LIM	Licentiate of the Institute of Materials
LIMA	Licentiate of the Institute of Mathematics and its Applications
LIMF	Licentiate of the Institute of Metal Finishing
LInstBCA	Licentiate of the Institute of Burial and Cremation Administration
LInstBM	Licentiate of the Institute of Builders Merchants
LIOC	Licentiate of the Institute of Carpenters
LIR	Licentiate of the Institute of Population Registration
LISTD	Licentiate of the Imperial Society of Teachers of Dancing
LISTD(Dip)	Licentiate Diploma of the Imperial Society of Teachers of Dancing
LittD	Doctor of Letters
LLB	Bachelor of Law
LLCM	Licentiate of the London College of Music and Media
LLCM	Performers Diploma of Licentiateship in Speech, Drama and Public Speaking
LLCM(TD)	Licentiate of the London College of Music (Teachers' Diploma)
LLD	Doctor of Law
LLM	Master of Law
LMIFM	Licentiate Member of the Institute of Fisheries Management
LMPA	Licentiate Member of the Master Photographers Association
LMRTRI	Legal Member of the Royal Town Planning Institute
LMSSALond	Licentiate in Medicine, Surgery and Obstetrics & Gynaecology of the Society of Apothecaries of London
LMusLCM	Licentiate in Music of the London College of Music

LMusTCL	Licentiate in Music, Trinity College of Music, London
LNCP	Licentiate Member of the National Council of Psychotherapists
LRAD	Licentiate of the Royal Academy of Dancing
LRAM	Licentiate of the Royal Academy of Music
LRCPEdin	Conjoint Diplomas Licentiate of the Royal College of Physicians of Edinburgh
LRCPSGlasg	Conjoint Diplomas Licentiate of the Royal College of Physicians and Surgeons of Glasgow
LRCSEdin	Conjoint Diplomas Licentiate of the Royal College of Surgeons of Edinburgh
LRCSEng	Licentiate of the Royal College of Surgeons in England
LRPS	Licentiate of the Royal Photographic Society
LRSC	Licentiate of the Royal Society of Chemistry
LRSM	Licentiate Diploma of the Royal Schools of Music
LSBP	Licentiate of the Society of Business Practitioners
LSCP(Assoc)	Associate of the London and Counties Society of Physiologists
LTCL	Licentiate of Trinity College of Music, London
LTh	Licentiate in Theology
LTI	Licentiate of the Textile Industry
MA	Master of Arts
MA(Architectural)	Master of Arts (Architectural Studies)
MA(Econ)	Master of Arts in Economic and Social Studies
MA(Ed)	Master of Arts in Education
MA(LD)	Master of Arts (Landscape Design)
MA(MUS)	Master of Arts (Music)
MA(RCA)	Master of Arts, Royal College of Art
MA(SocSci)	Master of Arts, (Social Science)
MA(Theo])	Master of Arts in Theology
MAAT	Member of the Association of Accounting Technicians
MABAC	Member of the Association of Business and Administrative Computing
MAcc	Master of Accountancy
MACP	Member of the Association of Computer Professionals
MAE	Member of the Academy of Experts
MAgr	Master of Agriculture
MAgrSc	Master of Agricultural Science
MAnimSc	Master of Animal Science
MAO	Master of Obstetrics
MAppSci	Master of Applied Science
MArAd	Master of Archive Administration
MArb	Master of Arboriculture
MArch	Master of Architecture
MArt/RCA	Master of Arts, Royal Co]lege of Art
MasFCI	Master of the Facu]ty of Commerce and Industry
MASI	Member of the Architects and Surveyors Institute
MB, BCh	Conjoint Degree of Bache]or of Medicine, Bachelor of Surgery
MB, BChir	Conjoint Degree of Bachelor of Medicine, Bachelor of Surgery
MB, BS	Conjoint Degree of Bachelor of Medicine, Bachelor of Surgery
MB,ChB	Conjoint Degree of Bachelor of Medicine, Bachelor of Surgery
MBA	Master of Business Administration
MBAE	Member of the British Association of Electrolysis
MBChA	Member of the British Chiropody Association
MBCO	Member of the British College of Ophthalmic Opticians
MBCS	Member of the British Computer Society
MBHA	Member of the British Hypnotherapy Association
MBHI	Member of the British Horological Institute
MBIAT	Member of the British Institute of Architectural Technicians
MBID	Member of the British Institute of Interior Design
MBIE	Member of the British Institute of Embalmers
MBII	Member of the British Institute of Innkeeping
MBSc	Master in Business Science
MBSSG	Master of the British Society of Scientific Glassblowers

MCB	Mastership in Clinical Biochemistry
MCCDRCS(Eng)	Member of the Royal College of Surgeons of England, Clinical Community Dentistry
MCD	Master of Civic Design
MCDH	Master of Community Dental Health
MCGPIrel	Member of the Irish College of General Practitioners
MCh	Master of Surgery
MChD	Master of Dental Surgery
MChemA	Master of Chemical Analysis
MChir	Master of Surgery
MChOrth	Master of Orthopaedic Surgery
MChS	Member of the Society of Chiropodists and Podiatrists
MCIBS	Member of the Chartered Institute of Bankers in Scotland
MCIBSE	Member of the Chartered Institution of Building Services Engineers
MCIH	Corporate Member of the Chartered Institute of Housing
MCIJ	Member of the Chartered Institute of Journalists
MCIM	Member of the Chartered Institute of Marketing
MCIOB	Member of the Chartered Institute of Building
MCIPS	Member of the Chartered Institute of Purchasing and Supply
MCIT	Member of the Chartered Institute of Transport
MCIWEM	Member of the Chartered Institution of Water and Environmental Management
MCom	Master of Commerce
MCommH	Master of Community Health
MCOptom	Member of the College of Optometrists
MCPM	Member of the Confederation of Professional Management
MCPP	Member of the College of Pharmacy Practice
MCPP	Practitioner Member of the College of Pharmacy Practice
MCSD	Member of the Chartered Society of Designers
MCSP	Member of the Chartered Society of Physiotherapy
MCT	Member of the Association of Corporate Treasurers
MCYW	Member of the Community and Youth Work Association
MD	Doctor of Medicine
MDCR	Management Diploma of the College of Radiographers
MDent	Master of Dental Science
MDes	Master of Design
MDes(RCA)	Master of Design, Royal College of Art
MDORCPSGlas	Membership of Dental Orthopaedics, Royal College of Physicians and Surgeons of Glasgow
MDS	Master of Dental Surgery
MDSc	Master of Dental Science
MECI	Member of the Institute of Employment Consultants
MEd	Master of Education
MEd(EdPsych)	Master of Education (Educational Psychology)
MEdStud	Master of Educational Studies
MEng	Master of Engineering
MFA	Master of Fine Art
MFC	Mastership in Food Control
MFCM	Member of the Faculty of Community Medicine
MFDO	Member of the Faculty of Dispensing Opticians
MFHom	Member of the Faculty of Homeopathy
MFPHM	Member of the Faculty of Public Health Medicine, Royal College of Physicians of London and Edinburgh and Royal College of Physicians and Surgeons of Glasgow
MFPHMIrel	Member of the Faculty of Public Health Medicine, Royal College of Physicians of Ireland
MFTCom	Member of the Faculty of Teachers in Commerce
MGDSRCSEd	Membership in General Dental Surgery, Royal College of Surgeons of Edinburgh
MGDSRCSEng	Membership in General Dental Surgery, Royal College of Surgeons of England

MHCIMA	Member of the Hotel and Catering International Management Association
MHort(RHS)	Master of Horticulture, Royal Horticultural Society
MHSM	Member of the Institute of Health Services Management
MIAB	Member of the International Association of Book-keepers
MIAEA	Member of the Institute of Automotive Engineer Assessors
MlAgrE	Member of the Institution of Agricultural Engineers
MIAP	Member of the Institution of Analysts and Programmers
MIAT	Member of the Institute Asphalt Technology
MIBC	Member of the Institute of Building Control
MIBCM	Member of the Institute British Carriage and Automobile Manufacturers
MIBCO	Member of the Institution of Building Control Of ficers
MIBF	Member of the Institute of British Foundrymen
MlBiol	Member of the Institute of Biology
MICE	Member of the Institute of Civil Engineers
MlChemE	Member of the Institution of Chemical Engineers
MICHT	Member of the International Council for Holistic Therapies
MICM	Member of the Institute of Credit Management
MlCorr	Member of the Institute of Corrosion
MICS	Member of the Institute of Chartered Shipbrokers
MICW	Member of the Institute of Clerks of Works of Great Britain Incorporated
M IDTA	Member of the International Dance Teachers' Association
MIED	Member of the Institution of Engineering Designers
MIEE	Member of the Institution of Electrical Engineers
M1EM	Member of the Institute of Executives and Managers
MIEx	Member of the Institute of Export
MlEx(Grad)	Graduate Member of the Institute of Export
MIExpE	Member of the Institute of Explosives Engineers
MIFA	Member of the Institute of Field Archaeologists
MIFF	Member of the Institute of Freight Forwarders
MIFireE	Member of the Institution of Fire Engineers
MIFM	Registered Member of the Institute of Fisheries Management
MIFST	Member of the Institute of Food Science and Technology
MlGasE	Member of the Institution of Gas Engineers
MIGD	Member of the Institute of Grocery Distribution
MIHEc	Member of the Institute of Home Economics
MIHIE	Member of the Institute of HighwayIncorporated Engineers
MIHort	Member of the Institute of Horticulture
MIHT	Member of the Institution of Highways and Transportation
MIIA	Member of the Institute of Internal Auditors
MIIExE	Member of the Institution of Incorporated Executive Engineers
MIIM	Member of the Institute of Industrial Managers
MlInfSc	Member of the Institute of Information Scientists
MIIRSM	Member of the International Institute of Risk and Safety Management
M I ISE	Member of the International Institute of Social Economics
MIL	Member of the Institute of Linguistics
MILAM	Member of the Institute of Leisure and Amenity Management
MIM	Professional Member of the Institute of Materials
MIManf	Member of the Institute of Manufacturing
MlMarE	Member of the Institute of Marine Engineers
MIMatM	Member of the Institute of Materials Management
M IM BM	Member of the Institute of Maintenance and Building Management
MIMC	Member of the Institute of Management Consultancy
MlMechE	Member of the Institution of Mechanical Engineers
MIMechIE	Member of the Institution of Mechanical Incorporated Engineers
MIMF	Member of the Institute of Metal Finishing
MlMgt	Member of the Institute of Management
MIMI	Member of the Institute of the Motor Industry
MlMinE	Member of the Institution of Mining Engineers
MIMM	Member of the Institute of Massage and Movement
MIMM	Member of the Institution of Mining and Metallurgy

MIMS	Member of the Institute of Management Specialists
MINI	Member of the Nautical Institute
MNIMH	Member of the National Institute of Medical Herbalists
MInstAEA	Member of the Institute of Automotive Engineer Assessors
MInstAM	Member of the Institute of Administrative Management
MInstBA	Member of the Institute of Business Administration
MInstBCA	Member of the Institute of Burial and Cremation Administration
MInstBE	Member of the Institution of British Engineers
MInstBM	Member of the Institute of Builders Merchants
MInstCF	Master Fitter of the National Institute of Carpet and Floorlayers
MInstCh	Member of the Institute of Chiropodists & Podiatrists
MInstCM	Member of the Institute of Commercial Management
MInstD	Member of the Institute of Directors
MInstE	Member of the Institute of Energy
MInstLEx	Member of the Institute of Legal Executives
MInstMC	Member of the Institute of Measurement and Control
MInstNDT	Member of the British Institute of Non-Destructive Testing
MInstP	Member of the Institute of Physics
MInstPet	Member of the Institute of Petroleum
MInstPkg	Member of the Institute of Packaging
MInstPM	Full Member of the Institute of Professional Managers and Administrators
MInstPS	Corporate Member of the Institute of Purchasing and Supply
MInstPSA	Member of the Institute of Public Service Administrators
MInstR	Member of the Institute of Refrigeration
MInstSMM	Member of the Institute of Sales and Marketing Management
MInstTA	Member of the Institute of Transport Administration
MInstTT	Full Member of the Institute of Travel and Tourism
MInstWM	Member of the Institute of Wastes Management
MIOC	Member of the Institute of Carpenters
MIOFMS	Member of the Institute of Financial and Management Studies
MIOM	Member of the Institute of Operations Management
MIOP	Member of the Institute of Printing
MIOSH	Member of the Institution of Occupational Safety and Health
MIP	Member of the Institute of Plumbing
MIPA	Member of the Institute of Practitioners in Advertising
MIPD	Member of the Institute of Personnel and Development
MIPI	Member of the Institute of Professional Investigators
MIPlantE	Member of the Institution of Plant Engineers
MIPRE	Member of the Incorporated Practitioners in Radio & Electronics
MIQ	Member of the Institute of Quarrying
MIQA	Member of the Institute of Quality Assurance
MIR	Member of the Institute of Population Registration
MIRRV	Member of the Institute of Revenue, Rating and Valuation
MIRSE	Member of the Institution of Railway Signal Engineers
MIRTE	Member of the Institute of Road Transport Engineering
MISM	Member of the Institute of Supervisory Management
MISOB	Member of the Incorporated Society of Organ Builders
MISTC	Member of the Institute of Scientific and Technical Communications
MIStrucE	Member of the Institution of Structural Engineers
MISW	Member of the Institute of Social Welfare
MITAI	Member of the Institute of Traffic Accident Investigators
MITSA	Member of the Institute of Trading Standards Administration
MIWPC	Member of the Institute of Water Pollution Control
MJur	Master of Jurisprudence
MLD	Master of Landscape Design
MLing	Master of Languages
MLitt	Master of Letters
MLS	Master of Library Science
MMA	Master of Management and Administration
MMedSci	Master of Medical Science

MMet	Master of Metallurgy
MMS	Member of the Institute of Management Services
MMSc	Master of Medical Sciences
MMus	Master of Music
MMus,RCM	Degree of Master of Music, Royal College of Music
MMusArt	Master of Musical Arts
MN	Master of Nursing
MNAEA	Member of the National Association of Estate Agents
MNCP	Full Member of the National Council of Psychotherapists
MNRHP	Full Member of the National Register of Hypnotherapists and Psychotherapists
MNTB	Merchant Navy Training Board
MObstG	Master of Obstetrics and Gynaecology
MOrthRCSEng	Membership in Orthodontics, Royal College of Surgeons of England
MPA	Master of Public Administration
MPH	Master of Public Health
MPharm	Master of Pharmacy
MPhil	Master of Philosophy
MPhil(Eng.)	Master of Philosophy in Engineering
MPhys	Master of Physics
MPPS	Master of Public Policy Studies
MPRI	Member of the Plastics and Rubber Institute
MProfBTM	Member of the Professional Business and Technical Management
MPS	Member of the Pharmaceutical Society of Northern Ireland
MPsychMed	Master of Psychological Medicine
MPsychol	Master of Psychology
MQB	Mining Qualifications Board
MRad MRad (D)	Master of Radiology (Radiodiagnosis) or (Radiotherapy)
MRAeS	Member of the Royal Aeronautical Society
MRCGP	Member of the Royal College of General Practitioners
MRCOG	Member of the Royal College of Obstetricians and Gynaecologists
MRCP	Member of the Royal College of Physicians of London
MRCP(UK)	Member of the Royal College of Physicians of the United Kingdom
MRCPath	Member of the Royal College of Pathologists
MRCPEdin	Member of the Royal College of Physicians of Edinburgh (superceded by MRCP(UK)
MRCPGlasg	Member of the Royal Co]]ege of Physicians of Glasgow (superceded by MRCP(UK)
MRCPIrel	Member of the Royal College of Physicians of Ireland
MRCPsych	Member of the Royal College of Psychiatrists
MRCSEng	Member of the Royal College of Surgeons of England
MRCVS	Member of the Royal Co]lege of Veterinary Surgeons
MRDRCS	Membership in Restorative Dentistry, Royal College of Surgeons of England
MREHIS	Member of the Royal Environmental Health Institute of Scotland
MRIN	Member of the Royal Institute of Navigation
MRINA	Member of the Royal Institution of Naval Architects
MRIPHH	Member of the Royal Institute of Public Health and Hygiene
MRPharmS	Member of the Pharmaceutical Society of Great Britain
MRSC	Member of the Roya] Society of Chemistry
MRSH	Member of the Roya] Society of Hea]th
MRSS	Member of the Royal Statistical Society
MRTPI	Member of the Royal Town Planning Institute
MS	Master of Surgery
MSAPP	Member of the Society of Advanced Psychotherapy Practitioners
MSBP	Member of the Society of Business Practitioners
MSc	Master of Science
MSc(Econ)	Master of Science in Economics
MSc(Ed)	Master of Science in Education
MSc(Eng)	Master of Science in Engineering
MSc(Mgt)	Master of Science in Management

MScD	Master of Dental Science
MScEcon	Master in Faculty of Economic and Social Studies
MScTech	Master of Technical Science
MSE	Member of Society of Engineers
MSFA	Advanced Financial Planning Certificate
MSIAD	Member of the Society of Industrial Artists and Designers
MSocSc	Master of Social Science
MSSc	Master of Social Science
MSSc	Master of Surgical Science
MSSCh	Member of the School of Surgical Chiropody
MSSF	Member of the Society of Shoe Fitters
MSt	Master of Studies
MSTA	Member of the Swimming Teachers' Association
MSTI	Certificate of Insurance Work
MSW	Master in Social Work
MTD	Master of Transport Design
MTech	Master of Technology
MTh	Master of Theology
MTheol	Master of Theology
MTP	Master of Town and Country Planning
MTPI	Master of Town Planning
MTropMed	Master of Tropical Medicine
MUniv	Master of University, (Honorary)
MusB	Bachelor of Music
MusD	Doctor of Music
MusM	Master of Music
MusM(Comp)	Master of Music (Composition)
MusMPerf	Master of Music (Performance)
MVM	Master of Veterinary Medicine
MVSc	Master of Veterinary Science
MWeldl	Member of the Welding Institute
MWES	Member of the Women's Engineering Society
MYD	Member of the Youth Development Association
NCA	National Certificate in Agriculture
NCC	National Computing Centre
NCVQ	National Council for Vocational Qualifications
ND	Diploma in Naturopathy
NDD	National Diploma in Design
NDF	National Diploma in Forestry
NDH	National Diploma in Horticulture
NDSF	National Diploma of the Society of Floristry
NDT	National Diploma in the Science and Practice of Turfculture and Sports Ground Management
NEBS	National Examining Board for Supervision & Management
NNEB	National Nursery Examination Board
NRHP	National Register of Hypnotherapists and Psychotherapists
NVQ	National Vocational Qualifications
NWRAC	North Western Regional Advisory Council for Further Education
ODLQC	Open & Distance Learning Quality Council, formerly CACC, Council for Accreditation of Correspondence Colleges
ONC	Ordinary National Certificate
OND	Ordinary National Diploma
PESD	Private and Executive Secretary's Diploma, London Chamber of Commerce and Industry
PGCE	Postgraduate Certificate in Education
PGDip(RCM)	Postgraduate Diploma of the Royal College of Music
PGDipLCM	Postgraduate Diploma of the London College of Music
PhD	Doctor of Philosophy
PhD(RCA)	Doctor of Philosophy (Royal College of Art)
PIFA	Practitioner of the Institute of Field Archaeologists

I'PI.	Private Pilot's Licence
PPRNCM	Professional Performance of the Royal Northern College of Music
PSC	Private Secretary's Certificate, London Chamber of Commerce and Industry
QC	Queen's Counsel
QIS	Qualified Imaging Scientist
QPA	Qualification in Pensions Administration
RA	Royal Academician
RAD	Royal Academy of Dancing
RADA	Royal Academy of Dramatic Art
RANA	Royal Animal Nursing Auxiliary
RBS	Royal Ballet School
RCM	Royal College of Midwives
RCN	Royal College of Nursing
Ret'dA Bl D	Retired Associate of the British Institute of Interior Design
Ret'dFBID	Retired Fellow of the British Institute of Interior Design
Ret'dMBID	Retired Member of the British Institute of Interior Design
RGN	Registered General Nurse
RHV	Registered Health Visitor
RJDip	Diploma for Retail Jewellers
RJGemDip	National Association of Goldsmiths Gemstone Diploma
RM	Registered Midwife
RMN	Registered Mental Nurse
RNMH	Registered Nurse for the Mentally Handicapped
RP	Registered Plumber
RSA	Royal Society of Arts
RSBEI	Registered Student of the Institution of Body Engineers
RSCN	Registered Sick Children's Nurse
ScD	Doctor of Science
SCE	Scottish Certificate of Education
SCLS	Second Certificate for Legal Secretaries
SCOTVEC	Scottish Vocational Education Council
SCPL	Senior Commercial Pilot's Licence
SenAWeldI	Senior Associate of the Welding Institute
SEng,FInstSMM	Qualified Sales Engineer of the Institute of Sales and Marketing Management
SenMWeldl	Senior Member of the Welding Institute
SFInstE	Senior Fellow of the Institute of Energy
SHNC	Scottish Higher National Certificate
SHND	Scottish Higher National Diploma
SlEDip	Securities Industry Examination Diploma
SlnstPet	Student of the Institute of Petroleum
SLC	Secretarial Language Certificate
SLD	Secretarial Language Diploma
SNC	Scottish National Certificate
SND	Scottish National Diploma
SNNEB	Scottish Nursery Nurses Examination Board
SRD	State Registered Dietitian
SRN	State Registered Nurse
SSC	Secretarial Studies Certificate, London Chamber of Commerce and Industry
StudentlEE	Student of the Institution of Electrical Engineers
Student]MechE	Student of the Institution of Mechanical Engineers
StudlAP	Student of the institution of Analysts and Programmers
Stud]Manf	Student Member of the Institute of Manufacturing
StudIMS	Student of the Institute of Management Specialists
Stud ProfBTM	Student Professional Business and Technical Management
StudSE	Student of the Society of Engineers
StudSElec	Student of the Society of Electroscience
StudWeld I	Student of the Welding Institute
TC	Technician Certificate
TCA	Technician in Costing and Accounting

TCert	Teacher's Certificate
TD	Technician Diploma
TDCR	Teacher's Diploma of the College of Radiographers
TechMInstWM	Technician Member of the Institute of Wastes Management
TechRMS	Technological Qualification in Microscopy, Royal Microscopical Society
TechWeldI	Technician of the Welding Institute
TMBA	Teacher Member of the British Arts
TnIMBM	Technicians of the Institute of Maintenance and Building Management
UCAS	Universities and Colleges Admissions Service
UKCC	United Kingdom Central Council
VetMB	Bachelor of Veterinary Medicine
WJEC	Welsh Joint Education Committee
WMAC	West Midlands Advisory Council for Further Education
WSA	West of Scotland Agricultural College
YHAFHE	Yorkshire and Humberside Association for Further and Higher Education

Part 1

Teaching Establishments

The statutory responsibility for the provision of education in the United Kingdom is shared by the Department for Education and Employment, the Welsh Education Office and the local education authorities of England and Wales, the Scottish Education Department and the education authorities of Scotland, and the Department of Education for Northern Ireland and the education authorities of Northern Ireland. In the United Kingdom education is divided into three stages: Primary education (up to the age of about 11, or 12 in Scotland); Secondary education (from the age of 11 until the pupil leaves school); and Further education (all education and training provided after full-time schooling ends).

This chapter briefly describes secondary schools, further and higher education establishments, and universities.

SECONDARY SCHOOLS

England and Wales

Most secondary schools have been established and are run by local education authorities (LEAs) – outside the Greater London area the councils of non-Metropolitan counties, and the councils of districts in Metropolitan counties. But an increasing number of schools are grant-maintained. This means they are independent of LEA control.

Some schools are provided by the Church of England, the Roman Catholic Church and other Churches or voluntary bodies with the assistance of central government grant and are maintained wholly by local education authorities. These are called 'voluntary controlled', 'voluntary aided' or 'special agreement' schools.

Pupils transfer from primary to secondary schools at about the age of 11 and must stay at school until the age of 16. Children registered at schools in England and Wales are deemed for this purpose to reach the age of 16 on one of two fixed dates in the year, known as the school leaving dates. For those with 16th birthdays between 1 September and 31 January (inclusive) the school leaving date is the end of the Easter term; and for those with 16th birthdays between 1 February and 31 August (inclusive) it is the Friday before the last Monday in May. Pupils intending to go on to take some form of higher education usually stay at school until they are 18, but a growing number of pupils with other objectives remain at school beyond the minimum age in order to improve their qualifications and skills. The system of examinations underwent reform in 1988. The examinations taken mainly at age 16 – the General Certificate of Education Ordinary level (GCE O level) and the Certificate of Secondary Education (CSE) – were replaced by a new single system of examinations called the General Certificate of Secondary Education (GCSE).

The examinations taken mainly at age 18 – the General Certificate of Education Advanced level (GCE A level) – continued, and additional examinations called Advanced Supplementary (AS) levels were introduced alongside them. AS levels were examined for the first time in Summer 1989. This structure was changed in September 2000. The new A level specification has a six-unit structure: the first three units making up the AS and the final three the A2. All six units combined make a whole A level. The first AS levels will be examined in Summer 2000; the first A2 levels in Summer 2002.

At present the main types of school are:

SELECTIVE SCHOOLS

Grammar schools admit pupils on a basis of selection according to ability and provide academic courses up to GCSE and AS/A2 levels. Advanced level examinations are taken by pupils in the senior classes, called the 'sixth form'.

Secondary modern schools provide a wide range of courses, many of them non-academic but also for GCSE qualifications, at least to school-leaving age and beyond for pupils who choose to stay on after the age of 16.

NON-SELECTIVE SCHOOLS

These schools, which are now in the majority, admit children without reference to their ability or aptitude. A variety of school organisations has been adopted, among which the main ones are:

1. **'All-through' comprehensive schools** with an age range of 11–18. This is the most common arrangement.
2. **11–16 comprehensive schools linking with sixth form colleges** or tertiary colleges for pupils over 16. (Tertiary colleges – unlike sixth form colleges – are operated under further education regulations.)
3.. **Middle schools** with lower age limits of 8, 9 or 10 and upper age limits of 12, 13 or 14 linking with comprehensive or occasionally selective upper schools. Middle schools with an age range of 10–13 or 10–14 are deemed secondary. Those with an age range of 9–13 may be deemed either primary or secondary. Those with an age range of 8–12 are deemed primary.

INDEPENDENT SCHOOLS

In addition to the schools maintained by local education authorities and the non-maintained schools for pupils with special needs, there are the independent schools which draw their income from fees, private funds and endowments. They vary considerably in size, standards and academic organisation. Besides those traditionally known as the 'public schools' there are many other establishments, some of them offering specialised provision, eg for minority religious groups, the musically gifted, and so on.

All independent schools have to be registered with the Department for Education and Employment and are subject to inspection by OFSTED. The arrangement under which registered schools could apply to the Department to be 'recognised as efficient', if they met certain standards relating to premises, accommodation, staffing etc, was discontinued in 1978 and the term no longer has any validity. Schools must, however, meet certain minimum standards if they are to continue registered.

Scotland

There are four categories of schools in Scotland – **'public schools'**, equivalent to maintained schools in England and Wales, managed by education authorities; **'grant-aided schools'** conducted by managers other than education authorities, which receive grants directly from the Secretary of State; **'self-governing'** schools which have opted out of local authority control and are funded directly by the Secretary of State, and **'independent schools'** which do not receive any direct assistance from public funds. (A number of pupils following a course of secondary education may receive income-related assistance with the cost of tuition fees at certain independent schools.)

Transfer from primary to secondary education usually takes place in Scotland between the ages of 11 and 12½, ie a year later on average than in England and Wales.

The first two years of secondary education are regarded as an exploratory period during which the progress of each pupil is carefully observed and pupils are given a wide variety of subjects so that they can find out where their particular aptitude, abilities and interests lie. At the end of the second year pupils make their course choices for the third and fourth years. While there is scope for some specialisation at this stage, all pupils continue to follow a broad and balanced curriculum consisting of subjects from eight modes. A typical programme would combine SCE Standard Grades in some modes with SCE Short Courses, National Certificate Modules, or school programmes in others. Standard Grade examinations (generally considered equivalent to GCSE level) are normally taken at the end of the fourth year, at age 15–16. During the fifth and sixth years pupils may combine SCE Higher Grades and the Certificate of Sixth Year Studies (CSYS), with further SCE Short Courses and NC modules. Higher Grade serves as the entry qualification to higher education. The universities, whose first Honours degree courses last four years as against three in most English and Welsh universities, have traditionally been left the task of specialisation. The specialised work of the English upper sixth form often corresponds to that of the first year university courses in Scotland.

In the mid-1980s a major reform of the curriculum and assessment arrangements in the third and fourth years of secondary education in Scotland was introduced by the government. The new system brought in new ways of teaching and assessing traditional subjects and introduced a number of new multi-disciplinary courses together with a range of short courses and a new examination known as the Standard Grade of the SCE. The Ordinary Grade of the SCE, the forerunner of Standard Grade, was phased out gradually between 1986 and 1993. In addition, revised courses and examinations for Higher Grade and the Certificate of Sixth Year Studies were prepared to ensure a smooth progression from Standard Grade.

The Higher Still Development Programme was implemented in 1999–2000 and reformed the structure of upper secondary (16+) education in Scotland. It introduced a unified curriculum and assessment system bringing existing qualifications together into a single framework at five levels. The Scottish Qualifications Authority administers the new Higher Still awards.

Northern Ireland

Secondary education, as in England and Wales, normally begins when pupils reach the age of 11. For most pupils, secondary education takes place either in a **grammar school** or in a **secondary (intermediate) school**, although some schools offer a comprehensive type of secondary education. Education in secondary (intermediate) schools (corresponding to secondary modern schools in England and Wales) and comprehensive schools is free and the cost of education in grammar schools is substantially offset by assistance from public funds in respect of each non-fee-paying pupil. Northern Ireland has a selective system of secondary education where, with the exception of the Craigavon area, pupils leaving primary schools transfer to either grammar or secondary schools. Selection to grammar schools is largely based on results achieved in the Transfer Procedure tests taken in the final year of primary education. The tests are based on the Key Stage 2 programmes of study in English, mathematics and science. The test results are used by grammar schools to help them decide which pupils to admit. Parents who wish their children to be educated at secondary non-grammar schools need not enter them for the tests. In the Craigavon area secondary schools operate on a non-selective basis and pupils, transferring to those schools, need not take the Transfer Procedure tests. Grant-aided schools, owned and managed by an Education and Library Board, are known as controlled schools; others not so owned and managed are known as voluntary schools. Voluntary grammar schools are managed by Boards of Governors, the majority of which now have representatives of the public interest on their boards; other voluntary schools, known as maintained schools, are managed by Boards of Governors, some of whom are nominated by the Education and Library Boards. All voluntary schools receive assistance from public funds.

Secondary (Intermediate) Schools: As the minimum leaving age is 16, all children have at least five years of secondary education. During the first three years, all pupils must follow the statutory curriculum containing subjects of both a practical and general nature; in the fourth and fifth years they have the opportunity of preparing for General Certificate of Secondary Education (GCSE) or other examinations, or of participating in the outward-looking courses which the schools have devised for those who do not wish to take external examinations.

Secondary Grammar Schools: These schools provide seven-year courses leading to the General Certificate of Secondary Education and GCE AS/A2 examinations and to qualifications necessary for entry to universities, other higher educational institutions and the professions. Tuition fees are payable in all grammar schools, but for those pupils considered suitable for the academic curriculum which the schools provide, the costs of tuition are met from public funds.

FURTHER AND HIGHER EDUCATION ESTABLISHMENTS

Higher Education can broadly be defined as any course of study leading to a qualification above level 3, that is GCE AS/A2 level and equivalents.

A wide range of higher education courses are available for both full-time and part-time students in the UK. These courses can lead to diplomas, first degrees, teaching qualifications and post-graduate degrees. Some courses are designed for students interested in seeking knowledge for its own sake, others for those interested in applying knowledge to the solution of problems. Some courses lead to a professional qualification, others fill gaps in knowledge.

Higher education courses can be studied at universities and colleges of higher education. Some further education colleges also offer higher education courses, generally of a vocational nature.

Further Education is full-time education suitable to the requirements of persons over compulsory school age and under age 19, except where it is provided in a school; and education, other than higher education, provided to those over 19. It provides a wide range of academic and vocational courses for 16–18 year olds and for adults; for instance GCSEs, AS/A2 levels, GNVQs and NVQs. Further Education is flexible and can respond to a variety of needs; students can study full-time or part-time, daytime or evening.

England and Wales

There is a wide range of further and higher education establishments, including colleges with various titles. There are also a number of independent specialist establishments, like secretarial and correspondence colleges (see below).

There are 30 ex-polytechnics (granted University status in 1992) which historically have had close links with business and industry. Their students include many people already in employment attending on a part-time basis (including block release), as well as full-time and 'sandwich course' students. Their courses include those for first and second degrees, certain graduate equivalent qualifications and the examinations of the principal professional associations. They also provide courses leading to important qualifications below degree level, eg the Higher National Diploma, the Edexcel BTEC Certificate, and the Diploma of Higher Education.

On 1 April 1993, further education and sixth form colleges left local authority control and became independent corporations in a new sector of publicly funded further education (FE). The sector also includes a small number of designated colleges.

The new FE sector contains 456 institutions ranging in size from a few hundred to over 20,000 students; and in type from general FE to specialist (eg agriculture) colleges. FE colleges have diverse titles, including college of technology, college of arts and technology and regional college. Institutions in the sector are funded by a national funding council (the Further Education Funding Council or FEFC). The FEFC is not only a funding body, it also has a statutory duty to secure sufficient provision for full-time education for 16–18 yr olds who want such education and to ensure adequate provision of vocational, academic, access and basic skill courses for adults and part-timers. Most colleges of further education specialise in providing courses which lead to qualifications below degree level, such as A levels and BTEC qualifications. Some offer degree courses.

Students aged 16–18 who have ordinarily been resident in the UK for three years, and European Community nationals, normally have the right to attend a full-time course without paying tuition fees. Colleges are free to determine fee levels for other students. The FEFC's funding methodology makes explicit allowance for colleges to remit fees for students in receipt of certain types of benefit.

Scotland

In Scotland, most courses of higher education at or near degree level and beyond are provided by the 13 universities and the 10 other higher education institutions. These institutions offer a range of vocationally orientated courses ranging from science, engineering and computing to health care, art and design, music and drama, and teacher training as well as the more traditional 'academic' courses. All the universities and higher institutions are funded by the Scottish Higher Education Funding Council.

The exception is the Scottish Agricultural College at Cleeve Gardens, Oakbank Road, Perth PH1 1HF, which continues to be funded by the Scottish Office Agriculture and Fisheries Department.

Northern Ireland

Responsibility for the provision of further education in Northern Ireland rests with the 5 Education and Library Boards. There are 17 institutions of further education (or further education colleges as they are more commonly called) and these offer a wide range of vocational and non-vocational courses for both full-time and part-time students. In addition, further education colleges are Recognised Training Organisations (RTOs) for the purpose of the Jobskills Programme run by the Training and Employment Agency. In Northern Ireland, university education is provided by The Queen's University of Belfast (QUB) and the University of Ulster (UU) and the Regional Office of the Open University (OU). Together they cater for 36,000 students (full and part-time). The Queen's University provides a full spread of undergraduate and postgraduate degrees over its nine faculties, which are as follows:

Arts; Economics and Social Sciences; Science; Law; Medicine (including Dentistry); Engineering; Agriculture and Food Science; Theology and Education.

The University of Ulster has seven faculties and the Ulster Business School:

Art and Design, Business and Management, Engineering, Humanities, Informatics, Science, Social and Health Sciences and Education.

These were based on four campuses at Belfast, Coleraine, Jordanstown and Londonderry. It offers both primary and postgraduate degrees, courses leading to HNDs and professional qualifications. Many of the courses in both universities are designed to suit the needs of industry, commerce and the professions. Agricultural, Horticulture and Food colleges in Northern Ireland are administered through the Department of Agriculture, as in Scotland.

THE UNIVERSITIES

The universities are independent self-governing bodies. Although largely financed by the Government through the Higher Education Funding Council for England (HEFCE), they do not come under the jurisdiction or control of any Government Department. They derive their rights and privileges from Royal Charter or Act of Parliament and any amendment of their charters or statutes is made by the Crown acting through the Privy Council on the application of the universities themselves. The universities alone decide what degrees they award and the conditions on which they be awarded; they alone decide what students to admit and what staff to appoint. The universities may be regarded as falling into nine main types:

(a)   The two old English universities of Oxford and Cambridge.
(b)   The Scottish universities.
(c)   The Universities of London and Wales
(d)   The 'modern' or 'civic' universities
(e)   The new universities.
(f)   The ten new technological universities
(g)   The Open University.
(h)   The former polytechnics granted university status by the Further and Higher Education Act 1992.
(i)   The privately financed University of Buckingham.

OXFORD AND CAMBRIDGE

The most distinctive feature of these universities is the college system. The colleges are completely autonomous so far as their property, finances and internal affairs are concerned, but the university awards degrees and determines the conditions on which they are awarded. Students become members of the university by becoming members of their colleges; their studies are largely guided by the senior members (generally called 'fellows') of their own colleges.

OXFORD

Colleges for men and women: Balliol College; Brasenose College; Christ Church; Corpus Christi College; Exeter College; Hertford College; Jesus College; Keble College; Lady Margaret Hall; Lincoln College; Magdalen College; Merton College; New College; Oriel College; Pembroke College; The Queen's College; St Anne's College; St Catherine's College; St Edmund Hall; St Hugh's College; St John's College; St Peter's College; Trinity College; University College; Wadham College; Worcester College.

Colleges for women: St Hilda's College; Somerville College.

Postgraduate Colleges and Societies: All Souls College; Green College (a medical graduate college); Linacre College and St Cross College (established 1962 and 1965 as societies for graduates reading for advanced degrees or diplomas of the University in all subjects); Nuffield College; St Anthony's College; Wolfson College (established 1966, with a special concern for studies in the natural sciences).

Permanent Private Halls: Campion Hall (For men. Established 1896 for members of the Society of Jesus only and granted present status in 1918). Greyfriars (For men. Established 1910 and granted present status 1957. Receives undergraduates for tuition in any school, giving priority of acceptance to student members of all branches of the Franciscan Order). Mansfield College (For men and women. Founded 1886 to provide a 'Free Church faculty in theology in Oxford' and a college for the training of non-conformist ministers, mainly of the Congregational Church; granted present status 1955. Receives undergraduates for tuition and graduates for tuition or research in any subject). Regent's Park College (For men and women. Founded 1810 as the 'Baptist Academical Institute in Stepney', established in Oxford between 1927 and 1940; granted present status 1957. Admits theological students and others wishing to read for the BA degree or higher degrees). St Benet's Hall (For men. Established 1897 for members of the English Benedictine Abbey of Ampleforth, Yorkshire only and granted present status 1918).

CAMBRIDGE

Colleges for men and women: Christ's College; Churchill College; Clare College; Corpus Christi College; Downing College; Emmanuel College; Fitzwilliam College; Girton College; Gonville and Caius College; Homerton College; Jesus College; King's College; Magdalene College;Pembroke College; Peterhouse; Queens' College; Robinson College; St Catharine's College; St John's College; Selwyn College; Sidney Sussex College; Trinity College; Trinity Hall.

Colleges for women: Lucy Cavendish Collegiate Society (mature students only); New Hall; Newnham College.

Graduate Institutions: Clare Hall; Darwin College; St Edmund's House; Hughes Hall; Wolfson College.

THE FOUR OLDER SCOTTISH UNIVERSITIES

St Andrews (founded 1411); Glasgow (founded 1451); Aberdeen (founded 1495); Edinburgh (founded 1583).

The tradition of the Scottish universities does not reflect the residential character of the Oxford and Cambridge colleges.

THE UNIVERSITY OF LONDON

The University of London was constituted by Royal Charter in 1836 as a body empowered to examine and confer degrees on students of approved institutions. Until 1900 its work was restricted to these functions but in exercising them it influenced and co-ordinated the activities of the various other colleges of university rank founded from time to time in London (such as Bedford College for Women, 1849). From 1858, London University degrees, except in Medicine, were made available for students other than those in certain recognised institutions. The **external degrees** of the University, which were then instituted, still provide both in the United Kingdom and overseas an academic award of high standing for part-time students and others who are not enrolled in a university. London was the first British university to admit women to its degrees (in 1878). The University is now a teaching body as well as an examining body, and has also become a federation in which are incorporated medical schools associated with hospitals, non-medical colleges (called Schools of the University, eg University College and King's College), together with a number of postgraduate and other institutions. Some other higher education establishments in London are also affiliated to the University and in others ('institutions with recognised teachers') certain members of staff are recognised as teachers of the University.

Non-medical Schools: Birkbeck College (primarily for evening and part-time students); Goldsmith's College; Imperial College of Science and Technology; Institute of Education; King's College; London School of Economics and Political Science; Queen Mary and Westfield College; Royal Holloway and Bedford New College; Royal Veterinary College; School of Oriental and African Studies; School of Pharmacy; University College; Wye College (University Department of Agriculture and Horticulture), Wye, Ashford, Kent.

Theological Schools: Heythrop College, 11–13 Cavendish Square, London W1M 0AN; King's College, Theological Department, Strand, London WC2R 2LS.

Undergraduate Medical and Dental Schools: Charing Cross and Westminster Medical School; London Hospital Medical College; Royal Free Hospital School of Medicine; St Bartholomew's Hospital Medical College; St George's Hospital Medical School; St Mary's Hospital Medical School; United Medical Schools of Guy's and St Thomas's Hospitals; School of Medicine, UCL.

Postgraduate Medical Schools: The British Postgraduate Medical Federation (33 Millman Street, London WC1N 3EJ) was incorporated by Royal Charter, and admitted as a School of the

University, in 1947. Its purposes include the provision of organised and correlated facilities for graduate teaching and research for British and overseas qualified medical and dental practitioners. It consists of the following: Institute of Basic Medical Sciences, Royal College of Surgeons of England, Lincoln's Inn Fields, London WC2A 3PN; Institute of Cancer Research, Royal Cancer Hospital, Fulham Road, London SW3 6JB; Cardiothoracic Institute, Brompton Hospital, London SW3 6HP, 2 Beaumont Street, London W1N 1RB; London Chest Hospital, Bonner Road, London E2 9JX; Institute of Child Health, 30 Guildford Street, London WC1N 1EH; Institute of Dental Surgery, Eastman Dental Hospital, Gray's Inn Road, London WC1X 8LD; Institute of Neurology, National Hospital for Nervous Diseases, Queen Square, London WC1N 3BG; Institute of Ophthalmology, Judd Street, London WC1H 9QS; Institute of Psychiatry, De Crespigny Park, Denmark Hill, London SE5 8AF.

London School of Hygiene and Tropical Medicine (Keppel Street, London WC1E 7HT): The School, which offers instruction for higher degrees and diplomas, represents the union of the former London School for Tropical Medicine with the University teaching departments for the Diploma in Public Health; it is recognised by the University in the faculties of science and medicine and is financed chiefly by the University, but also through research grants and contracts.

Royal Postgraduate Medical School (Hammersmith Hospital, Ducane Road, London W12 0HS): A School of the University, recognised in the faculty of Medicine and providing facilities for research and courses for higher degrees and diplomas.

University Institutes specialising in a particular field of study, usually postgraduate: British Institute in Paris; Courtauld Institute of Art; Institute of Advanced Legal Studies; Institute of Archaeology; Institute of Classical Studies; Institute of Commonwealth Studies; Institute of Germanic Studies; Institute of Historical Research; Institute of Latin-American Studies; School of Slavonic and East European Studies; Institute of United States Studies; Warburg Institute.

Institutions with recognised teachers: These are public educational establishments at which the University has recognised certain teachers giving courses for students reading for degrees or diplomas of the University as internal students. This is the only connection between these establishments and the University.

Jews' College, 11 Montagu Place, London W1H 2BA; London Graduate School of Business Studies, Sussex Place, Regent's Park, London NW1 4SA; Royal Academy of Music, Marylebone Road, London NW1 5HT; Royal College of Music, Prince Consort Road, South Kensington, London SW7 2BS; Trinity College of Music, Mandeville Place, London W1M 6AQ.

THE UNIVERSITY OF WALES

The University of Wales consists of constituent university colleges, and a medical school; University College of Wales, Aberystwyth; University of Wales, Bangor; University of Wales College of Cardiff; University College of Swansea; St David's University College, Lampeter; University of Wales College of Medicine.

THE UNIVERSITY OF DURHAM

The University was founded in 1832 and consists of 14 colleges and societies. All teaching takes place in Departments.

NORTHERN IRELAND

Both QUB and UU are funded largely by the Department of Education for Northern Ireland, on the advice of the Northern Ireland Higher Education Council and the Higher Education Funding Council for England (HEFCE). The OU is funded centrally by the HEFCE.

THE 'MODERN' OR 'CIVIC' UNIVERSITIES

(with the date of foundation)

Victoria University of Manchester, 1880; **University of Birmingham**, 1900; **University of Liverpool**, 1903; **University of Leeds**, 1904; **University of Sheffield**, 1905; **University of Bristol**, 1909; **University of Reading**, 1926; **University of Nottingham**, 1948; **University of Southampton**, 1952; **University of Hull**, 1954; **University of Exeter**, 1955; **University of Leicester**, 1957; **University of Newcastle upon Tyne**, 1851; **University of Dundee**, 1967.

The civic universities mostly originated in the university colleges set up in large towns and cities in the latter half of the nineteenth century and the early years of the twentieth. Until they became universities in their own right, the colleges offered courses leading to the external degrees of London University.

THE NEW UNIVERSITIES

(with date of foundation)
University of Sussex, 1961; **University of Essex**, 1961; **University of Keele**, 1962; **University of York**, 1963; **University of East Anglia**, 1964; University of Kent at Canterbury, 1964; **University of Lancaster**, 1964; **University of Warwick**, 1965; **University of Stirling**, 1967; **University of Ulster**, 1984.

The new universities were established to meet the need for more university places. Their most distinctive features are that they were empowered from the beginning to award their own degrees and that they tried to design courses which break down the conventional departmental structure and enable undergraduates to study different subject areas with equal intensity.

THE TECHNOLOGICAL UNIVERSITIES

Aston University, Birmingham B4 7ET; **University of Bath**, Bath BA2 7AY; **University of Bradford**, West Yorkshire BD7 1DP; **Brunel University**, Uxbridge, Middlesex; **City University**, St John Street, London EC1; **Heriot-Watt University**, Edinburgh EH1 1HX; **Loughborough University**, Leicestershire LE11 3TU; **University of Salford**, Salford M5 4WT; **University of Strathclyde**, Glasgow G1; **University of Surrey**, Guildford GU2 5XH.

The ten new universities received their status as a result of the Robbins report on Higher Education (1963). The University of Strathclyde and Heriot-Watt University were formerly Scottish Central Institutions; the others were Colleges of Advanced Technology (CATs).

THE OPEN UNIVERSITY

The **Open University**, Walton Hall, Milton Keynes, Buckinghamshire is a non-residential distance teaching university.

It received its Royal Charter in 1969. There are no formal entry requirements for admission to undergraduate courses which are based on the credit system and are designed for students 'precluded from achieving their aims through an existing institution of higher education'. Teaching is undertaken by means of a combination of printed material, face-to-face tuition, short residential schools, radio, television, audio and video tapes, computers and home experiment kits. The University also offers continuing education courses including in-service training for teachers, updating courses for managers, scientists and technologists and short courses of community education. Instruction began in 1971.

THE UNIVERSITY OF BUCKINGHAM

The University was founded as the University College at Buckingham, a privately financed institution which admitted its first students in February 1976. It received its Royal Charter early in 1983 and was constituted by the name and style of 'The University of Buckingham'. The University continues to be privately financed and to offer two-year courses, each year consisting of four terms of ten weeks, mainly in the fields of law, accountancy, sciences and economics, which now lead to the degree of Bachelor; it is also enabled to award higher degrees.

THE POST-1992 UNIVERSITIES

The Further and Higher Education Act 1992 led to the dissolution of the Council for National Academic Awards (CNAA) and the granting of university status to the polytechnics. This means that the polytechnics received the full range of degree-awarding powers rather than having their course and degrees validated by the CNAA. As a response to their new status many of the polytechnics have also changed their titles. The 39 institutions which have been affected are listed below (new names are followed by former names in parentheses): **Anglia Polytechnic University** (Anglia Polytechnic); **Bournemouth University** (Bournemouth Polytechnic); **University of Brighton** (Brighton Polytechnic); **University of Central England in Birmingham** (Birmingham

Polytechnic); **University of Central Lancashire** (Lancashire Polytechnic); **London Guildhall University** (City of London Polytechnic); **Coventry University** (Coventry Polytechnic); **De Montfort University, Leicester** (Leicester Polytechnic); **University of East London** (Polytechnic of East London); **University of Glamorgan** (Polytechnic of Wales); **Glasgow Caledonian University** (Glasgow Polytechnic/Queen's College, Glasgow); **University of Greenwich** (Thames Polytechnic); **University of Hertfordshire** (Hatfield Polytechnic); **University of Huddersfield** (Huddersfield Polytechnic); **University of Humberside** (Humberside Polytechnic); **Kingston University** (Kingston Polytechnic); **Leeds Metropolitan University** (Leeds Polytechnic); **Liverpool John Moores** University (Liverpool Polytechnic); **Manchester Metropolitan University** (Manchester Polytechnic); **Middlesex University** (Middlesex Polytechnic); **Napier University** (Napier Polytechnic of Edinburgh); **University of North London** (Polytechnic of North London); **University of Northumbria at Newcastle** (Newcastle Polytechnic); **Nottingham Trent University** (Nottingham Polytechnic); **Oxford Brookes University** (Oxford Polytechnic); **University of Paisley** (Paisley College of Technology); **University of Plymouth** (Plymouth Polytechnic South West); **University of Portsmouth** (Portsmouth Polytechnic); **The Robert Gordon University** (Robert Gordon Institute of Technology); **Sheffield Hallam University** (Sheffield City Polytechnic); **South Bank University** (South Bank Polytechnic); **Staffordshire University** (Staffordshire Polytechnic); **University of Sunderland** (Sunderland Polytechnic); **University of Teesside** (Teesside Polytechnic); **Thames Valley University** (Polytechnic of West London); **University of the West of England at Bristol** (Bristol Polytechnic); **University of Westminster** (Polytechnic of Central London); **University of Wolverhampton** (Wolverhampton Polytechnic).

The **University of Derby**, formerly Derbyshire College of Higher Education, and the **University of Luton**, formerly Luton College of Higher Education, are the two colleges of higher education to achieve university status under the FHE Act 1992. Dundee Institute of Technology became **University of Abertay**.

Part 2

Secondary School Examinations

NATIONAL EXAMINATIONS IN ENGLAND AND WALES

GENERAL CERTIFICATE OF SECONDARY EDUCATION (GCSE)

The General Certificate of Secondary Education (GCSE) was introduced in September 1986 with the first examinations in Summer 1988. It replaced the former GCE O level and CSE examinations and is normally taken by pupils around the age of 16. The great majority of maintained schools in England and Wales, together with independent schools, prepare candidates for the GCSE.

The GCSE is the principal means of assessing the National Curriculum at Key Stage 4, the two years leading up to GCSE examinations. The National Curriculum came into effect for the core subjects English, mathematics and science from September 1992 for first examinations in Summer 1994.

The revised National Curriculum which now includes Physical Education, Design & Technology, IT and a Modern Foreign Language as core subjects has been implemented at Key Stage 4 since September 1996. New GCSE syllabuses in all core subjects have been designed to meet the revised National Curriculum requirements and has been offered in schools since September 1996.

For GCSE, the examination boards in England and Wales are arranged into five Examining Groups; four in England and one in Wales. There is a similar board in Northern Ireland. These were originally formed from confederations of the (university-based) GCE Boards and the (Local Education Authority consortia-based) CSE Boards. Each group awards GCSE certificates but the single system is designed to uphold uniform standards in the value of grades and of what is studied in each subject. The City & Guilds and the Royal Society of Arts Examination Board offer GCSEs in Technology and related subjects.

Main features of the GCSE

Each Examining Group designs its own syllabuses but they are required to conform to criteria laid down by the School Curriculum and Assessment Authority (SCAA), which set out the rules and principles for all courses and all examinations in all subjects. The award of a grade is intended to indicate that a candidate has met the level of knowledge or skill laid down by the criteria.

The new approach to assessment is one of the main features which distinguish the GCSE from the old GCE O level and CSE examinations, by placing emphasis on positive achievement. Candidates have the chance to demonstrate what they know and can do, rather than being marked down for inadequacies.

A further feature of GCSE assessment methods is coursework. Credit is given for assignments set and marked by the teacher, with some external moderation, and the marks awarded form a contribution towards the final grade achieved. The proportion of credit obtained from coursework is subject to limits laid down by SCAA.

Grading

The Government accepted Sir Ron Dearing's recommendation that the GCSE should continue to be graded on the system of letters A to G. An additional starred A award has been available since 1994 to reward outstanding pupil achievement.

In accordance with the emphasis on positive achievement, there are 'differentiated' examination papers. Each scheme of GCSE assessment involves a series of tiered papers targeted at different ranges of ability within the A* to G grading scale.

GCSE (Short Courses) have been designed to be completed in about half the curriculum time of a full GCSE. GCSE (Short Courses) are offered in the following subjects: Art, Design & Technology, Geography, History, IT, Music, Modern Foreign Languages, Physical Education and Religious Education.

GCE ADVANCED LEVEL

GCE A level papers are normally taken after two years' study in the sixth form. The A level system was restructured with effect from September 2000. A new Advanced Subsidiary or AS qualification, comprised of three units, forms the first half of a full A level and is normally taken after one year of sixth form study. A further three units, taken at the end of the second year, constitute the A2. All six units together make a whole A level. Students now have the choice of end-of-course or modular assessment. These reforms aim to give students a broader education at 16+, with the new system allowing them to study several different subjects at AS level before specialising in 3–4 subjects in their second year.

Grading

There are five grades at A level: A, B, C, D and E. The former grade O, equivalent to a GCE O level pass, is no longer relevant with the introduction of the GCSE and the N grade, denoting narrow failure, has also been discontinued. All candidates below grade E are marked as U (unclassified) which replaced grade F and is not certificated.

Special (S) papers are set from the same syllabus as the basic A level papers but with questions designed to test the intellectual grasp of the abler sixth former. Candidates who receive a pass grade in their basic A level papers are eligible to have their work on S papers taken into account. They may be given a supplementary grading of 'Distinction', 'Merit' or 'Ungraded' based on their performance on S papers. Candidates may not normally take more than two subjects at any one sitting.

PRE-VOCATIONAL COURSES

GNVQs are new qualifications which provide an alternative route into further study or employment. They are designed to enable students to develop knowledge and skills relevant to a broad range of occupations. GNVQs form part of the Post-16 Qualifications Framework alongside job-specific NVQs, and general education such as GCSEs/GCE A levels. >From September 2000, Advanced level GNVQs were replaced by the new Vocational A levels. Like ordinary A levels, these normally take two years of full-time study. Intermediate level GNVQs are broadly equivalent to four or five GCSEs at grades A*-C, and normally take one year full-time. Foundation level GNVQs are broadly equivalent to four GCSEs at grades D-G, and also take one year of full-time study.

Many schools and colleges are offering GNVQs and Vocational A levels in all or some of the following subjects at all three levels: Art & Design; Business; Construction & the Built Environment; Engineering; Health & Social Care; Hospitality & Catering; Information Technology; Leisure & Tourism; Manufacturing and Science. Intermediate and Advanced GNVQs are available in Media: Communication and Production, Retail and Distributive Services and Management Studies (Advanced only).

NATIONAL EXAMINATIONS IN SCOTLAND

SCOTTISH CERTIFICATE OF EDUCATION

Examinations leading to the award of the Scottish Certificate of Education (SCE) are available at Standard Grade and also at Higher Grade. Standard Grade is the Scottish counterpart of GCSE and is taken at age 15–16. **Higher Grade** represents one further year of study and is taken at age 16–17 when taken in the fifth year, or 17–18 if taken in the sixth year. In addition, there is the **Certificate of Sixth Year Studies (CSYS)** which may be taken by pupils who are in the sixth year of secondary schooling (17–18) and who already possesses a pass on the **Higher Grade** in the subject concerned. Examinations for the SCE and the CSYS are conducted by the **Scottish Qualifications Authority**. Information regarding present and past secondary school examinations in Scotland may be obtained from the Chief Executive, Scottish Qualifications Authority, Hanover House, 24 Douglas Street, Glasgow G2 7NQ.

In August 1999, reforms to post-16 qualifications were implemented. The Standard Grade, Higher Grade, CSYS and SVQs fall under a new framework called National Qualifications, administered by the SQA. Each National Qualification, with the exception of the Standard Grade, is built on units, courses and group awards.

Standard Grade examinations are taken, normally, at the end of the fourth year of secondary schooling; Higher Grade examinations may be taken at the end of the fifth or sixth year. (These arrangements reflect the fact that transfer to secondary schooling in Scotland takes place normally at the age of 11+.) Standard and Higher Grade examinations are scheduled for May/June each year and most can be taken by Further Education and External candidates as well as by school pupils. Standard Grade awards are made in terms of a seven-point numerical award scale 1–7 where 1 is the highest award. The attainment levels for awards 1–6 are specified by Grade Related Criteria (GRC), details of which may be obtained from the SQA. Award 7 indicates completion of an approved course, albeit without satisfaction of the GRC for award point 6. The Standard Grade award scale generally covers the attainment span of the whole age group at 15+ with an award at point 3 regarded as equivalent to a band C award at (the now discontinued) Ordinary Grade prior to 1986 (see below). In so far as, in a given subject entry, the requirements have been met, an aggregate award for the subject will be made and this will be supported on the Certificate by a profile consisting of a grade for each defined element of the subject concerned. New courses and assessment procedures for Standard Grade have been introduced in a range of subjects. Presentation of school pupils for Standard and Higher Grade examinations is normally based on a broad curriculum and it is common for university candidates in Scotland to possess four or five passes on the Higher Grade. While this breadth of the curriculum, together with the shorter period of secondary schooling in Scotland as compared with England, may present difficulties with regard to the precise comparison of SCE and GCE/GCSE awards in terms of subject content attainment, the respective Certificates nevertheless relate to approximately the same ability range of candidates. Formerly, an SCE Ordinary Grade pass was accordingly recognised as equivalent, subject for subject, to a GCE Ordinary level pass, and their successors, Standard Grade and GCSE awards, are generally regarded as equivalent. The Higher Grade is generally recognised throughout the United Kingdom as performing the same task as the GCE A level. The equivalence of particular Higher Grade pass groupings to GCE A level is determined in accordance with commonly accepted formulae, details of which may be obtained by educational and professional bodies and employers from the Scottish Qualifications Authority.

CERTIFICATE OF SIXTH YEAR STUDIES

In 1968 there was introduced in Scottish schools an examination for sixth year pupils (age 17+) leading to the award of Certificate of Sixth Year Studies. A candidate may be presented for the CSYS provided that in each subject of presentation a pass on the Higher Grade (or equivalent qualification) is already held. The CSYS and SCE Higher grades are currently being phased out and are unlikely to be available after 2001. After this time they will be replaced by National Qualifications. Contact SQA for more details.

NATIONAL EXAMINATIONS IN NORTHERN IRELAND

NORTHERN IRELAND COUNCIL FOR THE CURRICULUM, EXAMINATIONS AND ASSESSMENT

29 Clarendon Road, Belfast BT1 3BG. Tel 028 9026 1200 Fax 028 9026 1234
E-mail: info@ccea.org.uk. Web: www.ccea.org.uk
The Northern Ireland Council for the Curriculum, Examinations and Assessment (NICCEA) conducts GCE AS/A2, GCSE exams and the Transfer Procedure in Northern Ireland. As successor to the Northern Ireland Schools Examinations and Assessment Council and the Northern Ireland Curriculum Council, the Council is responsible for ensuring equivalence of standards with other examining bodies in the United Kingdom. NICCEA has been responsible for advising upon and implementing the Pupil Assessment Arrangements for Northern Ireland.

14

Part 3

Further Education Examinations

INTRODUCTION

Definition of Terms

In discussing qualifications, a number of terms are commonly used as synonyms; this usage may obscure important differences of meaning, causing confusion and misunderstanding. In some contexts, it may be important to make these differences explicit in order to guard against exaggerating or diminishing the quality of accomplishment, which is essential in the concept of qualification. It is especially important to clarify the meaning of *examination, course* and *qualification*.

Examination: an examination is a formal test or assessment, which may focus on one or more of the following: knowledge, understanding, skill or competence. The examination may be set as a written test, an oral test, an aural and oral test (eg foreign language test) or a practical test. Until recently, most forms of assessment in FE were based on a model of examinations dominated by the psychometric model, designed to discriminate between individuals – normative referencing – and took the form of written tests. There was considerable variation in different kinds of written examinations, ranging through essays, question and answer and 'multiple response'. More recently, largely as a result of the introduction of National Vocational Qualifications (NVQs), the purpose and format of many FE examinations has been reappraised, and criterion-referenced examinations which focus on achievement (and in the case of NVQs, competence) are increasingly more common. Many forms of assessment are now an integral part of the learning process with a formative as well as a summative function rather than a separate terminal, summative function. While examinations were historically linked to a *course* as a terminal assessment, it is important to appreciate that this is by no means always the case; the National Council for Vocational Qualifications (NCVQ), for example, stipulates that any fully accredited NVQ may be taken without restriction in terms of course requirements or mode of attendance.

Course: a course implies an ordered sequence of teaching or learning over a period of time. A course is governed by regulations or requirements, frequently imposed by an examining body and, in many cases, the institution providing the course. An important distinguishing feature between different courses is the length of the course. The time may vary from a few days to several years. Some courses offer a terminal award on the basis of course completion, and these courses are set for a given period of time. Other 'set period' courses may prescribe examinations; these may be by continuous assessment, terminal testing or a combination of both. In other courses, the programme of study may be accomplished at a faster or slower rate; such courses normally enjoin continuous assessment or a terminal examination, or both. Many courses require attendance at an institution, while distance-learning, correspondence courses, and various forms of flexible learning courses are usually free of these requirements, although some of these courses may require occasional attendance for residential components or face-to-face tutoring. A successful examination result usually confers a qualification or an award.

Qualification: a qualification is normally a certificated endorsement, from a recognised awarding body, that a level or quality of accomplishment has been achieved by an individual. Qualifications are usually conferred on successful completion of an examination, although not all examinations necessarily offer qualifications. An examination may offer an award which is a part-qualification, or offer no distinction other than passing that examination. Thus, in NVQs, a candidate may acquire a unit of competence which is a part-qualification building towards a full statement of competence, an NVQ. A first year student on a HND course may be required to pass all first year examinations in order to be permitted to continue into the second year; in a sense that student is 'qualified' to continue the course but no qualification is awarded. Some award-bearing examinations may be fully recognised and certificated qualifications in themselves (eg a BTEC HNC) but only part-qualifications for a profession (eg Chartered Engineer).

Apparent anomalies do exist. Some professional bodies and trade associations award qualifications which are recognised within the profession or association but which are not obtained by examination. They are usually awarded on the basis of experience, and payment of a fee, and denote membership or acceptance. When the body also offers an examination route to the same qualification, successful examinees are usually known as 'graduate members'.

Finally, we may notice that a number of terms have such insignificant differences in nuances of meaning that they may be used as synonyms. Thus test and examination may be interchanged, a test normally being less formal or a small examination. An assessment is essentially an estimate of worth and it may be as equally rigorous as any test or examination. Programme and course have virtually the same meaning. As noted above, all qualifications are awards, most awards are qualifications.

ENGLAND AND WALES

I. TECHNICAL QUALIFICATIONS

Technical examinations in England and Wales are designed to cater for four broad overlapping categories of candidates: technologists, technicians, craftsmen and operatives. The awards made to technologists are of degree level.

The Pattern of Courses

The pattern of courses at present operated by the main awarding bodies, City and Guilds of London Institute, the Regional Examining Bodies, and the Business & Technology Education Council (see below) is as follows:

For 16-year-old school-leavers, subject to attainment: (Note: BTEC and City & Guilds programmes can be run in schools – students do not have to be school-leavers) (a) a part-time day course for operatives such as NVQ; or (b) a part-time craft course (C1); or (c) the first year of a part-time day technician course; or (d) a one-year part-time general course, after which they will go on either to the second year of a technical course (T2), or to a BTEC National Certificate or Diploma programme; or (e) in subjects where there is no preliminary general course they may either enter a craft course with a view to later promotion if they are suitable, or study for GCSE in order to qualify for entry into a BTEC National Certificate or Diploma course; or (f) if they have appropriate qualifications, such as four GCE/GCSE passes to a BTEC National Certificate or Diploma course; or (g) entry to a BTEC First Certificate/Diploma programme, which can lead to entry to a BTEC National course.

The 18-year-old school-leaver with the necessary GCE AS/A2 level passes will normally aim at professional qualifications and will take a course leading to a degree, a BTEC Higher National Certificate (part-time) or Diploma (full-time or sandwich), or some other advanced award.

The national pattern of qualifications is changing. Most courses which in the past would have lead to Ordinary National Certificates and Diplomas, the more technical courses offered by the City and Guilds of London Institute and the Higher National Certificates and Diplomas have almost entirely been succeeded by, at the lower level, BTEC National Certificates and Diplomas. These are being replaced by National Vocational Qualifications (NVQs) and General NVQs (GNVQs).

Technologists, Technicians, Craftsmen and Operatives

Technologists: usually fully qualified professional engineers or applied scientists. Their work of design, planning and management depends upon the support of technicians and involves at lower levels craftsmen and operatives.

Technicians: carry out a wide range of responsible jobs between those of technologists on the one hand and operatives on the other, involving mathematical, scientific and technical knowledge. Able students may make their way through BTEC National or Higher National (or equivalent) such as NVQs to professional qualifications; after taking the BTEC Higher National Certificate course, for example, candidates may need a further course of study to satisfy the educational requirements of a professional association. Able 16-year-olds enter either two- or three-year courses leading to BTEC qualifications. Following the BTEC National Certificate or Diploma two years' extra study is required to obtain a BTEC Higher National Certificate or National Diploma.

Craftsmen: skilled workers who normally have been craft apprentices. 16-year-old school-leavers enter a one-year craft course (C1) at the end of which most will go on to the second year of a three-year craftsmanship course (C2–3) ending in an examination for the old Intermediate or new Craft Certificates of the City and Guilds. At the end of a further two years, examinations can be taken for the City and Guilds Advanced Craft Certificate. Craftsmen with the right aptitude may be able to enter BTEC National programmes.

Operatives: principally workers, possessing degrees of skill and knowledge of a narrower and often lower kind than those required by craftsmen, who carry out specific operations involving machinery or plant. Courses, which vary considerably in length, and do not always lead to external examinations, are provided to supplement the training given in industry.

Courses for Professional Qualifications

Most students in further education who go on to become members of professional institutions in science and technology obtain partial or total exemption from the institutions' examinations by means of degrees, BTEC Higher National or National qualifications, or their equivalents, associateships or other exempting qualifications. However, some professional qualifications are obtained on completion of specific courses of direct preparation. For most of the professions students are required to take extra subjects (called 'certificates of supplementary study') and also to obtain responsible experience in industry. Courses are conducted for various professional examinations at many institutions.

College Certificates and Diplomas

A few colleges and polytechnics offer their own certificate or diploma-level courses. These courses are not validated by a recognised validating body such as BTEC. Courses are listed in the relevant sections of Part 5.

National Certificates and Diplomas

Ordinary National Certificates and Diplomas have been replaced by the qualifications offered by the Edexcel Foundation and, in Scotland, by the awards of the Scottish Qualifications Authority (SQA). BTEC qualifications apply in England, Wales and Northern Ireland and are awarded at three levels: First, National, and Higher National.

A number of modules relating to the subject are studied to gain each qualification and the ability of each student is measured using a combination of examinations, continuous assessment and project work.

At each of the levels a student may obtain a Certificate or a Diploma. A Diploma requires study of more modules than a Certificate. Certificates are generally awarded to part-time students.

Edexcel also offers and awards National Vocational Qualifications (NVQs) and General National Vocational Qualifications (GNVQs). The system is slightly different in Scotland, where SQA is responsible for developing, administering and assessing National Certificate modules and for continuing the system of Advanced Courses at Higher National Certificate (HNC), Higher National Diploma (HND) and Professional Development Award levels. The Council also accredits and awards Scottish Vocational Qualifications (SVQs), awards which meet the specific requirements laid down by Industry Lead Bodies. These exist at five levels, with Level 1 indicating competence in mainly routine occupational activities and Level 5 indicating a higher level of professional competence. From August 1992, a range of general SVQs were introduced, initially at Levels 1, 2 and 3. These qualifications offer a broad basis for entry to employment or progression to further education and training, including Higher Education.

There are three main categories of awards: the National Certificate (NC), the Higher National Certificate (HNC), the Higher National Diploma (HND). The National Certificate is available to anyone who has reached 16 years of age and possession of it enables the student to study for the Higher awards. The National Certificate is gained after study of the requisite number of modules. There are no end examinations: ability is measured solely by continuous assessment.

The details of the HNC and HND awards are the same as for BTEC HNC and HND qualifications, except that a wider range of courses is available at HNC than HND level.

The National awards of both BTEC are approximately A level standard and the Higher National awards approach degree standard.

II. BUSINESS AND MANAGEMENT EXAMINATIONS

Postgraduate Courses

A number of courses for graduates or persons with equivalent qualifications are offered in further education establishments. They include short specialist courses in Management and Business Studies and secretarial courses for graduates.

Business Schools

A Master of Business Administration (MBA) is an internationally recognised postgraduate qualification intended to prepare individuals for middle to senior level general managerial positions. Most programmes contain as their core a number of subjects considered essential for understanding the operations of any enterprise. These are: accounting and finance, operations management, business policy, economics, human resource management, marketing, information systems and strategic planning.

Unlike any other Master's programme, the MBA is not only postgraduate, it is also strongly post-experience. A minimum of three years (often more) work experience at an appropriate level of responsibility is generally expected of applicants. The requirement for first degree (or equivalent) is sometimes waived for those holding an impressive track record of over five years at managerial level. Approximately one third of MBA students have engineering or information technology backgrounds. Most undertake the qualification to facilitate change from technical or specialist positions to more generalist ones.

The MBA was conceived originally in the USA at the beginning of the century. Introduced in the Uk in the late 1960s it did not grow in popularity until the late 1980s. The popularity of this degree in the UK can be seen in the rapid expansion in the number of providers; 26 in 1985 and 110 in 1997. There are now over 8000 graduates each year and the number continues to rise. Welcome though this expansion may be it calls for vigilance in maintaining quality and standards. To this end, the Association of MBAs (AMBA) operates a system of accreditation.

The accreditation process, which includes visits to schools by an assessment panel, measures individual MBA programmes against specific accreditation criteria. Of the 110 UK schools now in operation, only 33 offer an Association of MBAs accredited MBA programme. There are also a number of practical implications. The AMBA Business School Loan Scheme, and membership of the Association, is only available to students enrolled on accredited MBA programmes.

AMBA is funded by subscriptions from its invididual MBA members and it is therefore able to offer impartial advice. It also organises MBA Fairs and produces annually the *AMBA-Financial Times Guide to Business Schools*, which is essential reading for intending students. This provides details of almost every UK provider, together with those of all the leading continental European and North American Schools.

Further information, including a list of accredited MBA programmes, can be obtained from the Association of MBAs, 15 Duncan Terrace, London N1 8BZ. Tel: 020 7837 3375 Fax: 020 7278 3634 Internet: www.mba.org.uk

*Ashridge Management College, Berkhamsted, Hertfordshire HP4 1NS; Tel 01442 843491 Fax 01442 842382. ***Aston Business School,** Aston Triangle, Birmingham B4 7ET; Tel 0121–359 3011 Fax 0121–359 2721. **Bangor Institute for Financial Management,** MBA Office, University of Wales, Bangor, Gwynedd LL57 2DG; Tel 01248 351151 ext 2162 Fax 01248 364760. ***University of Bath, School of Management,** Claverton Down, Bath BA2 7AY; Tel 01225 826152 (FT) 01225 826211 (PT) Fax 01225 826473. **The Birmingham Business School,** The Graduate Centre, 46 Edgbaston Park Road, Edgbaston, Birmingham B15 2RU; Tel 0121–414 6693 Fax 0121–414 3553. **University of Central England in Birmingham Business School,** Perry Barr, Birmingham B42 2SU; Tel 0121–331 5530 Fax 0121–331 6543. ***University of Bradford Management Centre,** Emm Lane, Bradford BD9 4JL; Tel 01274 733466 Fax 01274 546866. **University of Brighton Business School,** Mithras House, Lewes Road, Brighton, East Sussex BN2 4AT; Tel 01273 642197 Fax 01273 642153. ***Bristol Business School,** Coldharbour Lane, Frenchay, Bristol BS16 1QY; Tel 0117 9656261 ext 2665 Fax 0117 9583758. **School for Advanced Urban Studies,** University of Bristol, Rodney Lodge, Grange Road, Bristol BS8 4EA; Tel 0117 9741117 Fax 0117 9737308. **University of Bristol Graduate School of International Business, 10 Woodland Road, Clifton, Bristol BS8 1UQ, Tel 0117 973 7683 Fax 0117 973 7687. University of Cambridge: The Judge Institute of Management Studies,** Fitzwilliam House, 32 Trumpington Street, Cambridge CB2 1QY; Tel 01223 337051 Fax 01223 324009. **Canterbury Business School,** University of Kent, Canterbury, Kent CT2 7PD; Tel 01227 764000

Fax 01227 761187. Aberconway Building, Colum Drive, Cardiff CF1 3EU; Tel 029 2087 4000 Fax 029 2087 4198. **City of London Polytechnic,** 84 Moorgate, London EC2M 6SQ; Tel 020 7320 1451 Fax 020 7320 1439. *****City University Business School,** Frobisher Crescent, Barbican Centre, London EC2Y 8HB; Tel 020 7477 8606/7/8 Fax 020 7477 8880. *****Cranfield School of Management,** Cranfield, Bedford MK43 0AL; Tel 01234 751122/752725 Fax 01234 751806. *Durham University Business School, **Mill Hill Lane, Durham DH1 3LB; Tel 0191–374 2233 Fax 0191–374 3748.** *EAP European School of Management, **12 Merton Street, Oxford OX1 4JH; Tel 01865 724545 Fax 01865 251960.** *University of Edinburgh, **50 George Square, Edinburgh EH8 9JY; Tel 0131–339 8855.** *Glasgow Business School, **University of Glasgow, 57 Southpart Avenue, Glasgow G12 8QQ; Tel 0141–339 8855 Fax 0141–330 4808.** University of Greenwich Business School, **Riverside House, Beresford Street, Woolwich, London SE18 6BU; Tel 020 8316 9000 Fax 020 8316 9005.** *Henley Management College, **Greenlands, Henley on Thames, Oxfordshire RG9 3AU; Tel 01491 571454 Fax 01491 410184.** University of Huddersfield, Department of Management, Queensgate, Huddersfield, West Yorkshire HD1 3DH; Tel 01484 422288 ext 2026 Fax 01484 516151. **School of Management, University of Hull,** Cottingham Road, Hull HU6 7RX; Tel 01482 466319 Fax 01482 466319. **Humberside Business School,** Cottingham Road, Hull HU6 7RT; Tel 01482 440550 Fax 01482 471345. *****Imperial College, The Management School,** 53 Prince's Gate, London SW7 2PG; Tel 020 7589 5111 Fax 020 7584 1836. Keele University, School of Management and Ecomomics, Keele, Staffordshire ST5 5BG; Tel 01782 621111 Fax 01782 613847. *****Kingston University Business School,** Kingston Hill, Kingston upon Thames, Surrey KT2 7LB; Tel 020 8547 2000 ext 5568 Fax 020 8547 7026. *****University of Lancaster,** Department of Marketing, School of Management and Organisational Sciences, Gillow House, Lancaster LA1 4YX; Tel 01524 65201. **Lancashire Business School,** University of Central Lancashire, Preston PR1 2TQ; Tel 01772 3719 Fax 01772 562623. *****Leicester Business School,** De Montfort University, PO Box 143, Leicester LE1 9BH; Tel 0116 2577203 Fax 0116 2517548. **Leicester University Management Centre,** Leicester LE1 7RH; Tel 0116 2523952 Fax 0116 2523949. **Liverpool Business School,** 98 Mount Pleasant Buildings, Liverpool L3 5UZ; Tel 0151–207 3581 Fax 0151–707 0423. *****London Business School,** Sussex Place, Regents Park, London NW1 4SA; Tel 020 7262 5050 ext 572 Fax 020 7724 7875. *****London Management Centre,** University of Westminster, 35 Marylebone Road, London NW1 5LS; Tel 020 7911 5000. *****Loughborough University Business School,** Ashby Road, Loughborough, Leicestershire LE11 3TU; Tel 01509 263171 Fax 01509 233313. *****Manchester Business School,** Booth Street West, Manchester M15 6PB; Tel 0161–275 6333 Fax 0161–273 7732. **Manchester Metropolitan University,** Faculty of Management and Business, Aytoun Street, Manchester M1 3GH; Tel 0161–247 3953 Fax 0161–247 6304. **Manchester School of Management,** UMIST, PO Box 88, Manchester M60 1QD; Tel 0161–200 3500 Fax 0161–200 3505. *****Middlesex University Business School,** The Burroughs, London NW4 4BT; Tel 020 8368 1299 Fax 020 8368 1539. **Napier Business School,** Department of Management Studies, Redwood House, 16 Spylan Road, Edinburgh SH10 5BR; Tel 0131–455 3371 Fax 0131–346 8553. **Nene College, Faculty of Management and Business,** Park Campus, Moulton Park, Northampton NN2 7AL; Tel 01604 715000 Fax 01604 7210636. **Newcastle Business School,** Northumberland Building, Newcastle upon Tyne NE1 8ST; Tel 0191–235 8942 Fax 0191–235 8560. *****University of Newcastle upon Tyne,** Department of Industrial Management, 13 Windsor Terrace, Newcastle upon Tyne NE1 7RU; Tel 0191–222 6188 Fax 0191–222 8131. **Nottingham Business School,** The Nottingham Trent University, Chaucer Street, Nottingham NG1 4BU; Tel 0115 9418418 ext 4204 Fax0115 9486512. **School of Management and Finance,** Nottingham University, Nottingham NG7 2RD; Tel0115 9484848 ext 3868 Fax 0115 9500664. **Open Business School,** The Open University, Milton Keynes MK7 6AD; Tel 01908 654705. **Oxford Brookes University, School of Business,** Wheatley, Oxford OX9 1HX; Tel 01865 755920 Fax 01865 755830. **Plymouth Business School,** Drake Circus, Plymouth, Devon PL4 38AA; Tel 01752 232856 Fax 01752 232853. **University of Portsmouth, Portsmouth Business School,** Locksway Road, Milton, Southsea, Hampshire PO4 8JF; Tel 01705 844039 Fax 01705 844059. **Roffey Park Management College,** Forest Road, Horsham, West Sussex RH12 4TD; Tel 01293 851644 Fax 01293 851565. **University of Salford, The Management School,** Salford M5 4WT; Tel 0161–745 5000 Fax 0161–745 5022. *****Sheffield Business School,** Sheffield Hallam University, The Old Hall, Totley Hall Lane, Sheffield S17 4AB; Tel 0114 2720911 Fax 0114 2620894. *****Sheffield University Management School,** PO Box 598, Crookesmoor Building, Conduit Road, Sheffield S10 1FL; Tel 0114 2768555 Fax 0114 2739826. **South Bank University,** Manor House, 56 Clapham Common Northside, London SW4 9RZ; Tel 020 7228 2015 Fax 020 7924 3725. **Southampton University**

Management School, Enterprise Road, Chilworth, Southampton SO1 7NS; Tel 01703 233331 Fax 01703 768608. ***Strathclyde Graduate Business School,** 130 Rotten Row, Glasgow G4 0GE; Tel 0141–553 6000 Fax 0141–552 2501. **Sunderland Business School,** 1–4 Thornhill Park, Sunderland SR2 7JZ; Tel 0191–515 2330 Fax 0191–515 2308. **Surrey European Management School,** University of Surrey, Guildford, Surrey GU2 5XH; Tel 01483 509347 Fax 01483 440807. **Templeton College, The Oxford Centre for Management Studies,** Oxford OX1 5NY; Tel 01865 735422 Fax 01865 736374. **Ulster Business School,** Shore Road, Whiteabbey, County Antrim, Northern Ireland BT37 0QB; Tel 028 9036 5131 ext 310 Fax 028 9036 5117. **University College of Wales,** Aberystwyth, Llandadinam Building, Penglais Campus, Aberystwyth, Dyfed SY23 3DB; Tel 01970 622523 Fax 01970 622524. ***Warwick Business School,** University of Warwick, Coventry CV3 7AL; Tel 024 9052 4306 Fax 024 9052 3719.

The Association of Business Schools

344/354 Gray's Inn Road, London WC1X 8BP. Tel 020 7837 1899 Fax 020 7837 8189. E-mail: abs@the-abs.org.uk

ABS was created in 1992 by the merger of the Council of University Management Schools and the Association for Management and Business Education. It has all of the UK's leading business schools as members with current membership standing at 100.

The main aim of ABS is to advance the education of the public in business and management in particular through the promotion of business and management education, training and development so as to improve the quality and effectiveness of the practice of management in the United Kingdom.

ABS is able to provide general information about the wide range of courses and programmes provided by the UK's business schools.

The Association has also established a subsidiary body called the Management Verification Consortium (MVC) which is an approved awarding body for National and Scottish Vocational Qualifications (N/SVQs) in Management at levels 3, 4 and 5. Around 40 major university business schools spread throughout the United Kingdom are awarding N/SVQs within the Consortium.

Further information about MVC can be obtained from the MVC National Administrator, Mr James Hyde, Management Verification Consortium Ltd, Management House, Cottingham Road, Corby, Northants NN17 1TT.

External Degrees

University of London degrees and diplomas are available to External Students who study privately in their own time.

There are undergraduate programmes in: Accounting and Finance, Banking and Finance, Computer and Information Systems, Divinity, Economics, Economics (Geography), Economics and Management, Economics (Politics and International Relations), Economics (Sociology), Education, English, French, Geography, German, Information Systems and Management, Italian, Jewish History, Joint Modern Languages, Laws, Management, Management with Law, Mathematics, Statistics and Computing, Music, Philosophy, Spanish and Latin American Studies.

There are postgraduate programmes in: Agricultural Development, Agricultural Economics, Applied Environmental Economics, Clinical Dentistry (Prosthodontics), Community Dental Practice, Computing, Dental Diagnostic, Radiology, Dental Public Health, Dental Radiology, Development Finance, Distance Education, Drugs and Alcohol: Policy and Intervention, Economic Principles, English Commercial Law, Environmental Assessment, Environment and Development, Environmental Management, Epidemiology: Principles and Practice, Financial Economics, Financial Management, Financial Policy, Food Industry Management and Marketing, Geography, Health Systems Management, Infectious Diseases, Laws, Livestock Health and Production, Managing Rural Change, Materials, Science and Engineering, MBA in International Management, Occupational Psychology, Organisational behaviour, Public Policy and Management, Sustainable Agriculture and Rural Development. University of London Externa Programme, Room 1, Senate House, Malet Street, London WC1E 7HU, UK.

Tel: 020 7862 8361/8360. Fax: 020 7636 5841. E-mail: enquiries@eisa.lon.ac.uk Website: www.lon.ac.uk/external.

III. ACCREDITING BODIES

Industry Lead Bodies and National Training Organisations

Their key responsibilities are the development of industry-defined standards of occupational competence for a framework of National Vocational Qualifications (NVQs).

All new NVQs developed by industry need approval by the Industry Lead Body before they can be submitted to the National Council for Vocational Qualifications (NCVQ) for final accreditation. Funding for the development of standards and NVQs is provided in part by government. TEED and its predecessors have contributed up to 50 per cent of development costs and provided project managers from The Occupational Standards Branch. The remaining 50 per cent of costs have been provided by the industry, usually in the form of staff time, accommodation for meetings and workshops, overheads, and so on.

The Qualifications & Curriculum Authority

29 Bolton Street, London W17 7PD Tel 020 7509 5555 Fax 020 7509 6666 E-mail: info@qca.org.uk

The QCA is responsible for developing a comprehensive and comprehensible national framework for vocational qualifications in England, Wales and Northern Ireland. National Vocational Qualifications (NVQs), General National Qualifications (GNVQs) and core skills are accredited by the QCA and are components of the framework. Candidates for these are assessed through awarding body organisations, who bestow the qualifications where candidates meet the required standards.

QCA, in partnership with the awarding bodies, is responsible for quality assurance of the system and also for coordinating the marketing of NVQs.

NVQs are based on standards set by employers and employees in each industry and so are practical and relevant to work. The NVQ framework has 5 levels, from routine work at Level 1 to senior management at Level 5. There are no barriers to access, such as age limits or entry requirements – NVQs are open to anyone who can show they can reach the required standard. In 1995 there were over 750 NVQs available, from Construction to Management, Floristry to Marketing.

General National Vocational Qualifications are a vocational alternative to academic qualifications. Each of the 11 GNVQs available concentrates on a broad area of work and can be achieved at Foundation and Intermediate. In September 2000, Advanced level GNVQs were replaced by the new Vocational A levels. GNVQs are the only qualifications to have core skills as a mandatory component.

QCA is also responsible for the National Record of Achievement – a nationally recognised format for recording a person's achievements in education, training and employment and planning for the future – and for the National Database, the most comprehensive and up-to-date information source for vocational qualifications available.

IV. VALIDATING AND EXAMINING BODIES

Council for National Academic Awards (CNAA)

The Council was founded by Royal Charter in 1964 and dissolved 30 September 1992. It had powers to award degrees and other academic distinctions to students who completed approved courses in educational institutions other than universities or who carried out research work under the supervision of an educational or research institution other than a university. The CNAA was the largest single degree awarding body in the UK and about one third of all students, prior to 1992/3, who studied for a degree in this country attended CNAA-approved courses. The Council made the following awards:

FIRST AWARDS

BA, BEd, BEng, LLB, BSc: with 1st Class, 2nd Class (Divisions 1 and 2), 3rd Class Honours or Pass; or unclassified with or without Distinction.

MEng: awarded to students who successfully complete a course of study which is longer and more demanding than the BEng first degree course in Engineering.

GMus (Graduate Diploma in Music): awarded to those students who complete three years' approved full-time study (or equivalent) in Music and who demonstrate competence in musical performance.

DipHE (Diploma of Higher Education): were equivalent in standard and often similar in content to that of the first two years of an Honours degree course.

Certificates of Higher Education: were equivalent to the first year of an Hounours degree course.

HIGHER AWARDS

MA, MBA, MEd, MSc: for successful completion of an approved postgraduate course of study of 48 weeks' duration (or the part-time equivalent).

MPhil, PhD: for successful completion of approved programmes of supervised research.

DSc, DLitt or DTech: for original and important contributions to knowledge and/or its applications.

Postgraduate Diploma: awarded for the successful completion of an approved postgraduate course of study of 25 weeks' duration (or the part-time equivalent).

Postgraduate Certificate: awarded for the successful completion of postgraduate/post-experience courses of 15 weeks' duration (or the part-time equivalent).

Postgraduate Certificate in Education (PGCE): awarded on completion of a one year full-time course; candidates must be British graduates or hold another recognised qualification.

Diploma in Professional Studies: available in the fields of education and nursing, health visiting, midwifery and sports coaching. Students normally hold an initial professional qualification. A minimum of two years' experience is normally expected.

Second Bachelor's Degree: Bachelor in Town Planning (BTP).

Edexcel Foundation

Stewart House, 32 Russell Square, London WC1B 5DN. Tel: 020 7393 4500. Fax: 020 7393 4501. E-mail: enquiries@edexcel.org.uk

Edexcel's BTEC qualifications provide a range of widely accessible, high quality education programmes of study related to employment. It does this by approving nationally recognised qualifications and Certificates of Achievement that equip students both for employment and for further study. Edexcel is working with the National Council for Vocational Qualifications (NCVQ) to help develop the national framework for vocational qualifications through National Vocational Qualifications (NVQs) and General National Vocational Qualifications (GNVQs). Through its approved centres up and down the country, Edexcel promotes the best practice in work related education. It collaborates closely with industry, government and others to ensure that Edexcel programmes serve the interests of individuals, employers and the nation as a whole.

RANGE OF PROGRAMMES AND PROGRAMME PROVISION

The Edexcel Foundation was formed by the merger of BTEC and London Examinations. Edexcel courses and qualifications will continue to be known as BTEC and London Examinations and are nationally and internationally accredited and recognised. Edexcel is now able to provide a national qualification framework which begins as part of the national curriculum in schools and progresses through GCSE, AS/A2 Level, Vocational A levels, NVQ (levels 1 to 5), GNVQ (Foundation and Intermediate) to Development (Continuing Education) units and courses for adults. In addition, the BTEC Award framework provides opportunities for supporting life long learning and achievement by recognising the achievements of individuals and providing flexible reskilling or retraining. Students successfully completing individual subjects of short study programmes receive a Certificate of Achievement. BTEC qualifications are available in a wide range of subjects following main occupational systems, design, distribution, engineering, environmental conservation, horticulture, hotel & catering, information technology, land based industries, leisure services, management, public administration, retail services, science and travel and tourism.

Programmes leading to BTEC qualifications are run in schools, colleges, universities, companies and training centres throughout England, Wales and Northern Ireland. They can be studied through very different modes including full time, day release, evening study, block release, sandwich and, where appropriate, open and distance learning. The detailed content of some national and higher programmes may vary from centre to centre to reflect local and regional needs.

All BTEC First, National and Higher qualifications have a title approved by the Foundation and courses submitted for validation must be chosen from the list of approved programme titles. However, many of the programmes listed in this edition of British Qualifications are shown under their particular emphasis or specialism.

BTEC GNVQs are currently available in Art & Design, Business, Health & Social Care, Leisure &

Tourism, Manufacturing, Construction, the Built Environment, Hospitality & Catering, Science, Engineering, Information Technology, Media: Communication & Production, Retail & Distribution Service, Land & Environment, Performing Arts & Entertainment Industries. BTEC NVQs are available in a range of occupational areas and can be awarded at up to five different levels – starting with level 1 (routine and straightforward) tasks through to level 5 (complex managerial and professional activities).

ACCESS TO QUALIFICATIONS AND LENGTHS OF PROGRAMMES

Set out below are the standard entry qualifications and normal length of programmes. Students should approach the centre where they are intending to study for further information. For a list of approved centres, contact the Edexcel Customer Response Centre (contact details above).

BTEC First Certificate/Diploma: students must be at least 16. No formal exam passes are required. Length of programmes – Certificate, one year part-time; Diploma, one year full-time or two years part-time.

BTEC Intermediate GNVQ: students must be at least 16. No formal exam passes are required. Intermediate GNVQs normally take one year of full-time study, or longer if part-time.

BTEC National Certificate/Diploma: students must be at least 16 and centres may ask for a BTEC First qualification, four GCE O levels/CSE grade 1 passes, GCSE grades A, B or C or an alternative suitable qualification, or experience.

Length of programme – Certificate, two years part-time; Diploma two years full-time, three years part-time or sandwich study.

Vocational A level: students must be at least 16. There are no formal entry requirements. Vocational A levels normally take two years of full-time study, or longer if part time.

BTEC Higher National Certificate/Diploma: students should normally be at least 18 and hold an appropriate BTEC National qualification, or equivalent, or a minimum of 2 suitable GCE A level passes and supporting GCSE passes. These will depend on the individual programme and, where a student enters on the basis of A levels he/she may have to undertake additional bridging studies or a conversion course.

Length of programme – Certificate, two years part-time; Diploma, two years full-time, three years part-time or sandwich study.

BTEC Professional Development Modules & Courses: These programmes and units are designed for people with work experience. Entry qualifications and length of programme vary according to the individual programme of study. Students may be admitted to certain of these studies on the basis of suitable experience and proven ability instead of formal qualifications.

THE BTEC AWARD FRAMEWORK

The BTEC Award Framework allows for the development of qualifications unique to a specific organisation. Each organisation will need to design its own qualification with its own specific aims. These aims should clearly indicate the purpose, coherence, target group and likely progression routes of prospective candidcates.

Consultations with intended users of the qualification help to structure the programme, ensuring it is clearly defined.

V. EXAMINING BODIES

City & Guilds

1 Giltspur Street, London EC1A 9DD
Tel 020 7294 2468
Fax 020 7294 2400
WWW: ww.city-and-guilds.co.uk

City & Guilds is the UK's leading vocational assessment and awarding body. The City & Guilds 'Group' comprises City & Guilds, City & Guilds International, Pitman Qualifications, NEBS Management and City & Guilds Training & Consultancy. Through City & Guilds International, the organisation offers qualifications in over 85 countries world wide, promoting both City & Guilds and Pitman Qualifications awards.

City & Guilds specialises in developing qualifications and assessments suitable for work-related and leisure occupations and for general education. It awards nationally recognised certificates in over 500 subjects, many of which are National Vocational Qualifications (NVQs). Its progressive structure of awards spans seven levels, from basic skills to the highest level of professional achievement. Working closely with lead bodies, employers and training organisations, City & Guilds has developed a range of services to meet their needs.

City & Guilds is an independent body. The regulations and syllabuses for its schemes are drawn up by specialist committees, whose members come from industry, education and government departments.

Qualifications are available across all areas of industry and commerce and include agriculture, horticulture & animal care; business & commercial services; computing & information technology; construction & construction services; creative arts; education, training & development; electrical & electronic engineering; hairdressing & beauty services; health & social care; hospitality & catering; leisure & tourism; media & communication; process industries; production & mechanical engineering; retailing, warehousing & sales; science & technology; sport & recreation; textiles, clothing & leather goods; vehicle & transport engineering.

City & Guilds schemes are designed to provide a combination of practical experience and theoretical knowledge. Courses leading to City & Guilds qualifications are run in approved centres, which include schools, colleges of further education, training organisations, companies and adult education institutes. It is possible to study full-time, part-time, as part of a training scheme, in the evenings, or, where appropriate, through distance learning. There are currently over 7,500 centres offering City & Guilds qualifications, although centres do not offer every award. The pattern and duration of courses vary. City & Guilds does not stipulate minimum course lengths and this will vary according to type of qualification and the way in which individual centres operate.

NVQs

National Vocational Qualifications (NVQs) are based on national standards developed by lead bodies. These standards define the skills or competences needed by people working in particular occupations. City & Guilds, as an awarding body, works with lead bodies to develop qualifications based on these standards, which meet the requirements of industry and are approved as NVQs. These are available at levels 1-5.

City & Guilds offers the largest number of NVQs of any awarding body and they are available in most occupational areas. Up to 30 September 1995, over half of all NVQs issued were awarded by the City & Guilds Group (Annual Review 1994-5).

SVQs

City & Guilds offers a range of Scottish Vocational Qualifications – the Scottish equivalent of NVQs. Areas available include administration; agriculture & horticulture; care; catering & hospitality; customer service; electronic engineering; hairdressing; health; information technology; motor vehicles; road haulage; training & development.

GNVQs

General National Vocational Qualifications (GNVQs) are programmes developed primarily for young people aged 16-19 and are available at three levels – foundation, intermediate and advanced. They are the vocational alternative to GCSEs and A levels and are currently available in 13 occupational areas.

City & Guilds offers GNVQs in Art & Design; Business; Health & Social Care; Land and Environment; Leisure & Tourism; Hospitality & Catering; Science; Manufacturing; Construction & the Built Environment; Retail & Distributive Services; Engineering; Information Technology; Media Communication & Production; Performing Arts.

City & Guilds Progression Awards

These awards are designed to bridge the gap between GNVQs and NVQs, as well as being nationally recognised qualifications in their own right. Initially, Progression Awards will be available in Bakery, Food and Beverage, Furniture, Information Technology and Sport & Leisure.

Assessment

City & Guilds schemes are assessed in a variety of ways. For NVQs and other vocational qualifications the most commonly used method is workplace observation. Candidates are assessed on their ability to perform everyday activities in their place of work or in a realistic working environment. The assessment is carried out by appropriate supervisors/managers who have experience of the work they are required to assess and are skilled in the assessment process. Workplace observation may also be supplemented by any of the assessment methods outlined below.

GNVQs, general education and other schemes are assessed by written papers; multiple choice questions; assignments; oral questioning; projects, or any combination of these.

Senior Awards

City & Guilds senior awards recognise significant achievements by an individual at senior level and offer a progressive employment-based route to professional qualifications. The senior awards are the Licentiateship (LCGI), for combined achievement in education training and employment; Graduateship (GCGI) for project and work-based competence at master's degree level; Membership (MCGI), and Fellowship (FCGI) for the highest level of professional achievement.

Information

For general information about City & Guilds, contact: Customer Services Enquiries Unit, at the above address or telephone 020 7294 2800/1/2/4/5.

The London Chamber of Commerce and Industry Examinations Board (LCCIEB)

Athens House, 112 Station Road, Sidcup, Kent DA15 7BJ
Tel 020 8302 0261

Certificates and Group Diplomas: exams are conducted at four Levels, First, Second, Third and Fourth for candidates of any age. A certificate is awarded to candidates who pass any one of our single subjects. Diplomas are awarded to candidates who pass in certain groups of subjects.

Fourth Level subjects: Meetings; Business Administration; Audio Transcription; Shorthand Transcription; English/French Commercial Correspondence; English/German Commercial Correspondence; English/Spanish Commercial Correspondence; French/English Commercial Correspondence; German/English Commercial Correspondence; Spanish/English Commercial Correspondence.

Third Level: Single subject exams are offered in: Accounting; Advanced Business Calculations; Advertising; Audio Transcription; Auditing; Business Administration; Business and Industrial Administration; Business Information Systems; Business Practice; Business Statistics; Commerce and Finance; Commercial Law; Cost Accounting; Customer Service; Economics; English for Business; English for Commerce; European Community; Information Processing; Management Accounting; Manuscript Transcription; Marketing; Office Organisation and Secretarial Procedures; Principles of Management; Public Relations; Purchasing; Selling and Sales Management; Shorthand; Typewriting; English/French Commercial Correspondence; English/German Commercial Correspondence; English/Spanish Commercial Correspondence; French/English Commercial Correspondence; German/English Commercial Correspondence; Spanish/English Commercial Correspondence.

Second and First Level: LCCIEB offers a broad range of subjects at Second and First Levels which lead up to the subjects listed at Third Level.

Executive Diploma in Business Accounting (EDBA) at Fourth Level: candidates are required to pass Financial Accounting, Cost Accounting and Quantitative Methods, Organisations and their Environment, and the Legal Environment within a period of 24 months.

Group Diplomas: may be awarded for passes in the following subjects which must be passed at the Third Level:

Accounting: a pass in Accounting, plus passes in 2 option subjects.

Advertising: passes in Advertising and Marketing, plus a pass in 1 option subject.

Auditing: passes in Auditing and Accounting plus a pass in 1 option subject.

Business and Industrial Administration: passes in Business and Industrial Administration and Business Information Systems, plus a pass in 1 option subject.

Cost Accounting: a pass in Cost Accounting plus passes in 2 option subjects.

Data Processing: a pass in Information Processing and Business Information Systems, plus a pass in 1 option subject.

Economics: a pass in Economics, plus passes in 2 option subjects.

Management Accounting: a pass in Management Accounting plus passes in 2 option subjects.

Marketing: a pass in Marketing, plus passes in 2 option subjects.

Principles of Management: passes in Principles of Management and Business and Industrial Administration plus 1 option subject.

Public Relations: passes in Public Relations and Marketing plus a pass in 1 option subject.

Selling and Sales Management: passes in Selling and Sales Management and Marketing, plus a pass in 1 option subject.

A Third Level Business Studies Diploma is awarded to candidates who pass 3 qualifying subjects over a period of 12months.

Pool of Option Subjects: Accounting; Advanced Business Calculations; Advertising; Auditing; Business Information Systems; Business & Industrial Administration; Business Statistics; Commerce & Finance; Commercial Law; Cost Accounting; Customer Service; Economics; English for Business; English for Commerce; European Community; Information Processing; Management Accounting; Marketing; Principles of Management; Public Relations; Purchasing; Selling & Sales Management.

Foreign Languages for Industry and Commerce (FLIC) and Spoken English for Industry and Commerce (SEFIC): the LCCIEB offers a system of graduated oral exams which are available at any time on any suitable premises. The system recognises 5 standards of achievement. The languages regularly examined are English, French, German, Italian and Spanish. Exams in other languages are available.

Foreign Languages at Work (FLAW): course certificate awarded at registered centres. Courses are designed and assessed by teachers and monitored by LCCIEB, which certifies the outcomes.

Secretarial and Business Administration Examinations **(also available as single subjects)**

Executive Secretary's Diploma (ESD): candidates must pass in English for Business; Meetings; Transcription (Shorthand and/or Audio); Business Administration; Management Appreciation.

Private Secretary's Diploma (PSD) at Fourth Level: candidates must pass in English for Business; Business Administration; Business Practice; Shorthand and/or Audio Transcription and/or Text Production.

Diploma in Business Administration (DBA3) at Third Level: candidates must pass in Business Administration, Business Practice and either Practical Computing or Information Processing.

Diploma in Secretarial Administration (DSA) at Second Level: candidates must pass in English for Business; Business Administration (Shorthand and/or Audio and/or Transcription and/or Text Production. Diploma in Business Administration (DBA2) at Second Level: candidates must pass in Business Administration, Business Practice and either Practical Computing or Word Processing.

Diploma in Administration at First Level: candidates must pass in Business Administration, English for Business and one of a range of IT and secretarial skills options.

Euroqualifications

A suite of awards for bilingual secretaries / administrators (see Linguistics, Languages and Translation in Part 5).

Diploma in European Business Administration (DEBA): available in French, German and Spanish. Candidates must accumulate, over a 5 yr period, passes in (a) Commercial Correspondence or English for Business; (b) FLIC / SEFIC, Advanced Level; (c) European Community Institutions and, either (d) Shorthand / Audio Transcription / Word Processing / Computer Applications, or (e) Management Appreciation.

European Executive Assistant Certificate (FEAC): available in French, German and Spanish. Candidates must accumulate over a 5 yr period, passes in (a) Commercial Correspondence or English for Business; (b) Shorthand/Audio Transcription/Word Processing/Computer Applications; (c) FLIC/SEFIC, Intermediate Level; (d) European Community Institutions.

Commercial Language Assistant Certificate (CLAC): available in French, German and Spanish. Candidates must accumulate, over a 5 yr period, passes in (a) Commercial Correspondence or English for Business; (b) Shorthand/Audio Transcription/Word Processing/Computer Applications; (c) FLIC/SEFIC, Threshold Level.

Vocational Access Certificate: a pre-vocational qualification beneath NVQ. Level 1 covering a choice from Hairdressing, Catering, Administration, Construction, Retailing, Care, Horticulture and Motor Vehicle Maintenance.

Wordpower and Number power: pre-vocational qualifications beneath NVQ Level 1 in literacy and numeracy.

National Vocational Qualifications (NVQs): LLCIEB offers a wide range of NVQs, Modern Apprenticeships and National Traineeships in mainstream business subjects. These include: Accounting; Administration; Customer Service; Distribution & Warehousing; IT; Key Skills; Management; Owner Management; Quick Service; Retail; Selling; Training & Development (including Assessors and Verifiers).

Joint Examination Board

30a Dyer Street, Cirencester, Gloucestershire CL7 2PP Tel 01285 641747 Fax 01285 650449.
E-mail: jeb@jeb.co.uk

The Joint Examining Board offers Teacher and Trainer certificates and diplomas in the following subjects; Educational Management; Information Technology Skills; Information Technology Advanced; Word Processing; Administration; Office Procedures.

Those who follow one of the above courses and successfully complete their assessments are eligible for a JEB Certificate, while those who combine one of these subject courses with the Principles of Teaching and Training course can achieve a JEB Diploma.

Candidates who already hold a teaching qualification recognised by JEB (BEd, CertEd, Training and Development Award level 3 or 4) are given exemption from the Principles of Teaching and Training course and, by sending a copy of their teaching certificate to the Board, are eligible for a JEB Diploma.

Entry requirements: 5 GCSEs (exemption may be applied for by mature students) and a minimum age of 20. For the Educational Management course a minimum of 2yrs teaching or training experience is also required.

A JEB qualification can lead to employment as a tutor or trainer in a College of Further Education, a training centre or the training department of other commercial organisations. Those with the Educational Management Diploma may advance into the Management Team of their educational organisation.

Methods of study: taught course in a JEB registered centre or distance learning programme in each of the specialist teaching subject areas. Taught courses run in JEB centres in the UK attract schedule 2a FEFC funding. Centres should apply to the Board for registration forms and further information. Those wanting to follow a distance learning course should write or phone the Board for full details of the course in which they are interested and an application form.

JEB has been accredited by NCVQ to offer NVQ awards in Training and Development and which include the D units for Assessors and Verifiers. JEB also offers a Dual T&D NVQ/JEB Administration Teacher and Trainer Certificate or Diploma Award for candidates who match their evidence to the Administration Standards.

AWARDING BODY CONSORTIUM

CENTRA	Duxbury Park, Duxbury Hall Road, Chorley, Lancashire, PR7 4AT
	Tel: 01257 241 428 Fax: 01257 260 357 E-mail: Central123@aol.com
EMFEC	Robins Wood House, Robins Wood Road, Aspley, Nottingham, NG8 3NH
	Tel: 0115 929 3291 Fax: 0115 929 0329 E-mail: enquiries@emfec.co.uk
	www.emfec.co.uk
SRCT	Building 33, University of Reading, London Road, Reading, Berkshire, RG1 5AQ
	Tel: 0118931 6320 Fax: 0118 931 6324 E-mail: srcet@clara.net
SWAFET	Bishops Hull House, Bishops Hull, Taunton, Somerset, TA1 5RA
	Tel: 01823 335491 Fax: 01823 323388

The Awarding Body Consortium (ABC) came into being in October 1998. It comprises four leading examination and assessment organisations: CENTRA, EMFEC, SRCT and SWAFET. These four organisations have a history of providing support and accreditation services in their own right.

The ABC is recognised by the government as an awarding body whose qualifications meet the criteria developed through the Qualifications and Curriculum Authority and are acceptable to the Further Education Funding Council as eligible for funding support.

These organisations aim to ensure that all existing registered centres and those centres wishing to offer ABC schemes have local support to enable them to meet the growing needs of students and trainees attending further education, schools and training organisations.

WELSH JOINT EDUCATION COMMITTEE

245 Western Avenue, Cardiff CF5 2YX Tel 029 2026 5000

The Welsh Joint Education Committee is recognised by the Department of Education and Employment as an examining board offering the following major qualifications: General Certificate of Secondary Education (GCSE); Certificate of Educational Achievement (CoEA); Advanced (A)/Advanced Supplementary (AS) Levels; General National Vocational Qualifications (GNVQs); and National Vocational Qualifications (NVQs). The latter 2 exams are offered in partnership with City & Guilds. In addition the WJEC offers exams in certain craft courses.

OXFORD, CAMBRIDGE & RSA EXAMINATIONS (OCR)

Westwood Way, Coventry CV4 8HS Tel 027 7647 0033 Fax 024 7646 8080

OCR is one of the leading providers of vocational, work-based qualifications in the UK, and is proud to have gained one of the most respected names in education.

OCR offers a range of more than 500 qualifications which include NVQs, GNVQs, single subject exams and a wide range of RSA own brand schemes. The schemes are available at any of OCR's 8,000 registered centres throughout the country.

Qualifications

Subject Examinations:

Stage I: Audio-Transcription; Book-Keeping; Communication in Business; Computer Literacy & Information Technology (CLAIT); English Language; Numeracy; Practical Bookkeeping; Shorthand-Transcription; Text Processing; Typewriting; Word Processing; French Text Processing; German Text Processing; Spanish Text Processing; Word Processing (Audio).

Stage II: Accounting; Audio-Transcription; Business Administration; Communication in Business; Databases; Desktop Publishing; English Language; French Text Processing; German Text Processing; Integrated Business Technology; Legal Text Processing; Medical Audio-Transcription; Medical Word Processing; Numeracy; Practical Book-keeping; Shorthand-Transcription; Spanish Text Processing; Spreadsheets; Text Processing; Typewriting; Word Processing.

Stage III: Accounting; Administration Practice; Audio-Transcription; Business Administration; English Language; Shorthand Transcription; Text Processing; Typewriting; Word Processing.

Languages: French for Catering; Certificate in Business Language Competence (Basic), (Survival), (Threshold), (Operational) and (Advanced) in French, German, Spanish, Italian, and Japanese (Basic only); English for Speakers of Other Languages.

Initial Awards: Designed primarily for 14-16 year olds as a complementary provision to their National Curriculum studies. They provide a foundation for and introduction to GNVQs, NVQs and other vocational programmes. The following range of Initial Award qualifications is available from RSA: Agricultural Studies; Care; Computer Graphics; Environmental Studies; Food Technology; Media Studies; Office Studies; Performing Arts; Retailing; Sports & Recreation; Textiles; Travel & Tourism; Vehicle Studies.

Other Schemes: CLAIT File Management DOS; Computer Keyboard Skills Text; Copy Typing Speed Test; GCSEs (RSA offers GCSEs in Information Technology, Design & Technology; Information Studies; Business Studies); Medical Shorthand Speed Test; National Skills Profile; Initial Text Processing; Communicative English Skills; Spelltest; Certificates of Professional Competence in Road Haulage/Passenger Transport.

National Vocational Qualifications (NVQs)

An increasing number of NVQs, levels 1-5 are offered by RSA in such areas as Accounting, Administration, Arts & Entertainment, Customer Service, Distribution, Information & Library Services, Information Technology, International Trade & Services, Key Skills, Management, Marketing, Purchasing, Retailing, Road Haulage & Distribution, Sales, Sport & Recreation.

General National Vocational Qualifications (GNVQs)

GNVQs are broad-based vocational qualifications designed to allow students flexible progression routes moving onto higher level GNVQs, higher education or further training for employment. GNVQs are available at three levels: Foundation, Intermediate and Advanced.

OCR offers the following GNVQ qualifications nationwide: Art & Design; Business; Land and Environment; Engineering; Health & Social Care; Hospitality & Catering; Information

Technology; Leisure & Tourism; Manufacturing; Media; Communication & Production; Performaing Arts; Retail & Distributive Services; Science.

Teacher, Trainer and Assessment Qualifications

Teacher/Trainer Qualifications: Certificate in Counselling Skills in the Development of Learning; Certificate in Counselling Skills and Learning Support; Teacher and Trainer Certificate and Diplomas (Information Technology); Basic Certificate in the Teaching of Exercise to Music; Certificate and Diploma in Teaching Foreign Languages to Adults; Certificate and Diploma for Teachers of Learners with Specific Learning Difficulties; Certificate for Literacy and Numeracy Support Assistants.

Other Verified Schemes: Small Business Certificate; Vocational Certificate (Information Technology); Diploma in Information Technology; Advanced Diploma in Information Technology; Certificate for Part-Time Youth Workers; Advanced Diploma in the Organisation of Community Groups; Certificate and Diploma in Administrative and Secretarial Procedures; Higher Diploma in Administrative Procedures.

SCOTLAND
The Scottish Qualifications Authority

Hanover House, 24 Douglas Street, Glasgow G2 7NQ

The Scottish Qualifications Authority is Scotland's national body for qualifications. The advanced vocational courses comprise Higher National Certificate (HNC), Higher National Diploma (HNDs) and Professional Development Awards. The Scottish Qualification Authority's qualifications are available in a wide range of occupational areas, including: Tending animals, plants and land; Extracting and providing natural resources; Constructing; Engineering; Manufacturing; Transporting; Providing goods and services; Providing health, social care and protective services; Providing business services; Communicating and entertaining; Developing knowledge and skills.

Courses leading to HNC/HND awards are offered in further education colleges and central institutions throughout Scotland and are open to students of all ages who have appropriate National Certificate Modules, have Scottish Certificate of Education at Ordinary, Standard or Higher Grades (or GCSE/GCE equivalents) or be judged by the college to meet alternative criteria for admission.

HNCs and HNDs are all made up from a number of Higher National Units, each of which is separately recorded on the Record of Education and Training (a cumulative computer-based record of all successfully completed qualifications). A Higher National Certificate requires 12 unit credits and a Higher National Diploma 30 credits. A full-time student would normally complete an HNC over one year and an HND over two years. Although students follow an agreed programme to achieve an HNC or HND, they may take additional units to cater for their special interests.

These new Higher National Units are competence-based: the candidate's work is measured against outcomes and performance criteria specified in advance. The competences will incorporate the standards of the industry lead body, where these are available. The outcomes and performance criteria apply to all students but colleges can tailor their detailed teaching and assessment schemes to respond flexibly to local as well as national needs and employment patterns.

The Scottish Qualifications Authority maintains a comprehensive system of quality assurance which ensures that national standards are maintained. Many professional and technical institutes and professional bodies recognise the Scottish Qualifications Authority qualifications for entry to, or exemption from, professional exams. It is advisable to contact the body or institute to check on membership requirements before you decide on your course of study.

Candidates with vocational qualifications who wish to enter a degree course should apply to the university, central institution or college offering the course. In some cases HNC and HND courses link directly to degree courses. Applicants with vocational qualification awards are normally considered on an individual basis; the university, central institution or college will give you details of the way in which your application will be considered.

To complement the Scottish Qualifications Authority's advanced provision, Scottish Vocational Qualifications (SVQs) have been developed in consultation with employers to meet the needs of particular occupations. There are now job-specific SVQs covering virtually all occupations in Scotland. They are especially suitable for employees undertaking on-the-job training, although some may be offered at a college or training centre, or in partnership. SVQs are equivalent to the National Vocational Qualifications (NVQs) available elsewhere in the UK.

NORTHERN IRELAND

I. TECHNICAL AND COMMERCIAL EXAMINATIONS

Northern Ireland students enter for examinations organised by the Business & Technology Education Council (BTEC) for the award of their Certificates and Diplomas. Students will also continue to enter for the examinations of such bodies as the C&G and OCR, and the numerous professional bodies.

31

Part 4

Awards Made by Universities and Designated Institutions

ADMISSION TO DEGREE COURSES

UNIVERSITY COURSES

Universities usually have a general requirement for admission to a degree course; special requirements may be in force for particular courses. Requirements are usually expressed in terms of subjects passed at GCE A level and the Higher Grade of the SCE. The Universities have a clearing-house to handle applications for university courses, the Universities and Colleges Admissions Service (UCAS), PO Box 67, Cheltenham, Gloucestershire GL50 3SA. UCAS has now replaced UCCA and PCAS, and covers all of the institutions formerly in those schemes, and began operations for the first time for Autumn 1994 entry. All intending students who live in the United Kingdom may obtain information on application procedures from their schools or colleges, which should have the application forms and the UCAS Handbook, or directly from UCAS. The scheme covers all universities and all medical schools. The Committee of Vice-Chancellors and Principals (Tavistock Square, London WC1) publishes annually University Entrance: The Official Guide, which gives details of entry qualifications.

THE OPEN UNIVERSITY

For admission to first degree courses, no formal educational qualifications are necessary. However, students who have successfully completed one or more years of full-time study at the higher education level (or its equivalent in part-time study) may be eligible for exemption from some credit requirements of the BA degree.

BUSINESS SCHOOLS

The degrees awarded by the various University Business Schools are postgraduate and therefore normally require an honours degree as part of their entrance qualification.

AWARDS

The awards made by the universities may be separated into the following categories: First Degrees; Higher Degrees; Honorary Degrees; First Diplomas and Certificates; Higher Diplomas and Certificates.

First Degrees

NOMENCLATURE

Various names are given to the first degrees at British universities. At most universities the first degree in Arts is the BA (Bachelor of Arts) degree and the first degree in Science is the BSc (Bachelor of Science) degree. But at the universities of Oxford and Cambridge and at several new universities the BA is the first degree gained by students in both Arts and Science; the BSc is unknown at Cambridge, but is a higher degree at Oxford. In Scotland the first arts degree at 3 of the 4 old universities is that of MA. There are numerous variations on the Bachelor theme, eg BSc (Econ) (Bachelor of Science in Economics), BCom (Bachelor of Commerce), BSocSc (Bachelor of

Social Sciences), BEng (Bachelor of Engineering), BTech (Bachelor of Technology). The first award in medicine is the joint degrees of MB, ChB (Bachelor of Medicine, Bachelor of Surgery), the designatory letters of which vary from university to university.

STRUCTURE OF COURSES

First degree courses vary considerably in structure, not only between one university and another but also between faculties in one university. The degree examination is usually in 2 sections, Part I coming after 1 or 2 years of the course and Part II 'finals' at the end of the course. The first degree system at some Scottish universities differs substantially from that in English and Welsh universities (see below).

HONOURS OR SPECIAL DEGREES AND PASS OR ORDINARY OR GENERAL DEGREES

Each university decides the form and content of its own degree examinations. These vary from university to university and so, too, do the names given to the various sorts of degree awarded. For example, a 'Special' degree at many universities is a Special Honours qualification awarded on satisfactory completion of a Special Honours course, involving specialised study in a single subject. At Cambridge, a 'Special' is an Ordinary degree, of much lower level, for non-Honours candidates, taken in several subjects.

The first degree structure in all British universities is based on the Honours degree. Most graduates who go on to higher academic qualifications, and those entering, for example, the higher grades in the Civil Service or research would normally have an Honours degree of good class. Successful candidates in Honours degree examinations are placed in different classes, according to their performance, first class being the highest. The other classes given vary from university to university, but the classification most often used is: Class I; Class II (Division I); Class II (Division 2); Class III.

The main categories of Honours degrees are as follows:

Special Honours degrees are one-subject courses (although subsidiary relevant subjects are normally studied as well).

Joint Honours, Combined Honours or Double Honours courses cover 2 or more main subjects to the same level.

General Honours degrees are normally taken in at least 2 main subjects and often 3.

At many universities, a performance in an honours course that does not warrant the award of third class honours will earn a **Pass** degree. Apart from the honours course, there are courses that lead to **Ordinary** (sometimes called **Pass** or **General**) degrees. The candidate is usually examined in several subjects. The results are usually not classed, but at some universities ordinary degrees are awarded with distinction or with honours.

Broadly speaking, it is possible to enter a course for a pass or ordinary degree, or a more difficult course for honours. This is not a uniform distinction: (1) Some courses are regarded from the start as honours or special courses or as pass or ordinary or general courses and the students following them are regarded at all times as honours or pass students.

(2) In other courses, even where students are registered for honours they begin with studies common to both honours and pass courses and are regarded as only potential honours students until they can be set on distinctively honours or pass courses after examinations at the end of the first or second year of the course. Students may sometimes be able to transfer from an honours course to a pass course or vice versa; some pass courses are provided only to cater for students, who, during the course, do not reach the standard of honours and are relegated to an easier course. Most students start and finish in honours courses; the number of direct entry pass degree courses has decreased and few are now established.

NUMBER OF SUBJECTS STUDIED

Excluding medicine and dentistry, the broad subject areas are Arts (or Humanities), Social Science, Pure Science and Applied Science. Most students study one main subject selected from one of these areas. It is possible to distinguish many types of degree course according to the number of subjects studied; these types are a variation on 3 main categories:

(1) Honours course in 1 to 3 subjects or without examinable subsidiary subjects.

(2) Pass or ordinary courses in 1 to 3 subjects with or without examinable subsidiary subjects.
(3) Common studies for pass and honours in 1 to 3 subjects with or without examinable subsidiary subjects.
Students following 1-subject courses do not usually study only that 1 subject; courses in 1 main subject usually include related fields and most 1- and 2-subject courses include the formal study of 1 or more subsidiary or ancillary subjects, which may be and normally are examined in the Part I examination.

LENGTH OF DEGREE COURSE

First degree courses may be preceded by a preliminary year, from which students with the appropriate entry qualifications may be exempted. At the University of Keele the preliminary Foundation year is compulsory for all students and is an integral part of all first degree courses, which last four years. At most universities honours and pass courses in arts, social science, pure and applied science last 3 or 4 years, but courses in architecture, dentistry and veterinary medicine usually last 5 years and complete qualifying courses in medicine up to 6 years. Courses in fine arts and pharmacy may last 4 years; 4-year courses exist mainly in double honours schools, especially when they involve foreign languages and a period of study abroad, and in the technological universities, where some courses include a period of integrated industrial training (sandwich courses).

THE SCOTTISH FIRST DEGREE

The distinctive feature of first degrees at some Scottish universities is the Ordinary MA course, which has no counterpart in England and Wales, and the Ordinary BSc course, both of which last 3 years. The function of the Ordinary MA is to provide a broad, general education. Scottish undergraduates are required to show during their first 2 years of study, over a range of subjects, that they are fit to go onto an honours degree course, which takes 4 years to complete.
Because of the different Scottish school tradition and a lower entry age the level of work in the first year of Scottish first degree courses is, generally, less advanced in those subjects which are taught in school than in first-year courses in England, Wales and Northern Ireland. The wider spread of subjects and the rather less specialised character of many of the courses mean that the level of the Scottish 4-year honours courses reaches a standard about the same as that of the English and Welsh 3-year honours degree course.

AEGROTAT DEGREES

Candidates who have followed a course for a degree but have been prevented from taking the examinations by illness may be awarded a degree certificate indicating that they were likely to have obtained the degree had they taken the examinations.

Higher Degrees

Some Bachelors' degrees: (BPhil, BLitt, etc)
Masters' degrees: (MA, MSc, etc)
Doctor of Philosophy: (PhD or DPhil)
Higher doctorates: (DLitt, DSc, etc)
At Oxford and Cambridge the degree of MA is conferred on any BA of the University without any further course of study or examination after a specified number of years and on payment of a fee. Candidates for a Master's degree at other universities (and at some for the degrees of BPhil, BLitt and BD, which are of equivalent standing) are normally required to have a first degree, although it need not have been obtained in the same university. Masters' degrees are taken after 1 or 2 years' full-time study. The PhD requires at least 2 or, more usually, 3 years' full-time study.
In some universities and faculties students may be selected for a PhD course after an initial year's study or research common to both a PhD and a Master's degree. Candidates for a Master's degree are required either to prepare a thesis for presentation to examiners, who may afterwards question them on it orally, or to take written examination papers; they may be required to do both. All PhD students present a thesis; some may be required to take an examination paper as well. A major development in recent years has been the introduction of MPhil, MSc and similar degrees, awarded at the end of a 1- or 2-year course in a special topic on the results of a written examination and also, in some cases, a thesis. Higher doctorates are designated on a faculty basis, eg DLitt

(Doctor of Letters) and DSc (Doctor of Science). Candidates are usually required to have at least a Master's degree of the awarding university. Senior doctorates are conferred on more mature and established workers, usually on the basis of published contributions to knowledge.

Honorary Degrees

Most universities confer honorary degrees on persons of distinction in academic and public life and on others who have rendered service to the university or to the local community. Normally the degrees so awarded are not less than Masters' degrees.

First Diplomas and Certificates

Courses for first diplomas and certificates are relatively simple in structure; they usually reach a level lower than that required for the award of a degree. There is usually a carefully defined course in a specialised or vocational subject, lasting 1 or 2 years, followed by all candidates. Most courses are full-time.

Higher Diplomas and Certificates

Higher diplomas (eg in public health, social administration, medicine and technology) are awarded either on a full-time or, less often, on a part-time basis according to the subject and the university. Candidates must usually be graduates or hold equivalent qualifications. Diplomas are awarded after formal courses of instruction and success in written examinations. A certificate or diploma in education is awarded to graduates training to become teachers after 1 year's full-time study and teaching practice.

UNIVERSITY OF ABERDEEN

Student Recruitment and Admissions Services, King's College, Aberdeen AB24 3FX Tel: 01224 272090/91 Fax: 01224 272031 e-mail: sras@abdn.ac.uk Website: www.abdn.ac.uk/sras

Undergraduate Admissions: Tel: 01224 273504; Fax: 01224 272031; e-mail: admoff@admin.abdn.ac.uk

Postgraduate Admissions: Tel: 01224 273506; Fax: 01224 272041; e-mail: ptgoff@admin.abdn.ac.uk

First Degrees

ARTS & SOCIAL SCIENCES

BD; BD Hons: *3-4 yrs FT/5-6 yrs PT* Divinity

BLE: *3 yrs* Land Economy (Planning); Land Economy (Rural Surveying); Land Economy (Urban Surveying) *3 yrs FT* Land Economy (May be awarded with Distinction or Commendation to those who have displayed exceptional merit or merit respectively)

BLE Hons: *4 yrs* Land Economy (Planning); Land Economy (Rural Surveying and Planning); Land Economy (Rural Surveying); Land Economy (Urban Surveying and Planning); Land Economy (Urban Surveying)

BSc: *3 yrs FT* Marine Resource Management (May be awarded with Distinction or Commendation to those who have displayed exceptional merit)

BSc Hons: *4 yrs FT* Marine Resource Management

BTh: *3 yrs FT/5 yrs PT* Theology; Theology with French or Gaelic or German or Spanish

LLB: *3 yrs* Instruction Based on Scots Law (May be awarded with Distinction or Commendation)

LLB Hons: *4 yrs* Instruction Based on Scots Law

LTh: *3 yrs FT* Theology

MEDICINE

BSc Health Science Hons: *4 yrs FT/5 yrs PT* Health Science (Specialising in Health Care, Nutrition or Sociology)

BSc Med Sci: *1 yr* (One yr intercalated. Course admission normally after completing Phase II of the MB, ChB curriculum. By taught course and individual study and research leading to the submission of a thesis. Classified 1, 2 (i), 2 (ii), 3, or Pass)

MB; ChB: *5 yrs* (Honours and Commendation may be awarded to those candidates who are specially recommended by the examiners)

SCIENCE & ENGINEERING

BEng Hons: *4 yrs* Engineering; Engineering (Civil & Environmental); Engineering (Civil & Structural); Engineering (Civil with European Studies); Engineering (Civil with Management); Engineering (Civil); Engineering (Electrical & Electronic); Engineering (Electrical and Electronic with Control); Engineering (Electrical and Electronic with European Studies); Engineering (Electrical and Electronic with Management); Engineering (Electronic with Communications); Engineering (Electronics & Software Engineering); Engineering (Electronics and Computer Engineering); Engineering (Integrated Engineering with European Studies); Engineering (Integrated); Engineering (Mechanical and Electrical); Engineering (Mechanical with Computer Aided Engineering); Engineering (Mechanical with Control); Engineering (Mechanical with European Studies); Engineering (Mechanical with Management); Engineering (Mechanical with Materials); Engineering (Mechanical)

BSc Agr/BSc Agr Hons: *3-4 yrs* Agriculture; Animal Science; Crop Science

BSc Eng: *3-4 yrs* Engineering with Foundation Studies; Engineering (Civil); Engineering (Electrical); Engineering (Electronic); Engineering (Mechanical)

BSc/BSc Hons: *3-4 yrs/5yrs with industrial placement* Agriculture-Business Management; Animal Care; Animal Ecology; Animal Health & Welfare; Animal Science; Applied Biology for the Land Based Industries; Biochemistry (With Industrial Placement); Biochemistry (Immunology) (With Industrial Placement); Biochemistry-Microbiology (With Industrial Placement); Biology; Biology (Environmental Science); Biotechnology (Applied Molecular Biology); Chemistry with Accountancy or Biomedical Sciences or Environmental Analytical Chemistry or Study in France or Study in Germany or Management Studies or New Materials Technology or Physics; Chemistry; Computing Science with French or Spanish (With Industrial Placement); Computing Science (With Industrial Placement); Computing Science (Artificial Intelligence) (With Industrial Placement); Computing Science (Business Computing) (With Industrial Placement); Computing Science-Management Studies or Mathematics or Psychology or Statistics; Conservation Biology; Countryside & Environmental Management; Crop & Soil Sciences; Ecology; Environmental Geography; Environmental Microbiology; Environmental Science; Environmental Science (Ecology); Environmental Science (Physical Science); Equine Science; Food Production, Quality & Utilization; Forest Sciences; Genetics (With Industrial Placement); Genetics (Immunology) (With Industrial Placement); Geography; Geography-Geoscience; Geology-Petroleum Geology; Geoscience; Human Geography; Human Life Sciences; Immunobiology; Marine Biology; Mathematics; Mathematics with French or German or Spanish or Gaelic; Mathematics-Physics or Statistics or Zoology; Microbiology (With Industrial Placement); Molecular Biology (With Industrial Placement); Molecular Biology (Biochemistry-Genetics); Molecular Microbiology (With Industrial Placement); Neuroscience; Organic Agriculture; Parasitology; Pharmacology; Physical Geography; Physics; Physics with Chemistry or Gaelic or Geology or German or Philosophy or Spanish or French; Physiology; Plant & Soil Science; Plant Science; Plant Sciences (Cell and Molecular); Psychology with French or Gaelic or German; Psychology; Psychology-Statistics; Renewable Resources; Soil Science; Sport & Exercise Science; Sports Studies (Sport and Society); Statistics; Statistics with Economic Science; Tropical Environmental Science; Zoology *4 yrs FT Biomedical Sciences:* Biomedical Sciences (Molecular Biology); Biomedical Sciences (Pharmacology); Biomedical Sciences (Physiology)

THE ENVIRONMENT

BScFor/BScFor Hons: *3-4 yrs FT* Aboriculture & Amenity Forestry; Forest Management

Higher Degrees

DOCTORATES

DLitt: (For Aberdeen graduates of at least seven yrs' standing, or for staff of at least four yrs' standing, in respect of published work making a substantial contribution to human learning)

DMus: Music (For Aberdeen graduates of at least seven yrs' standing or for staff of at least four yrs' standing, in respect of published work making a substantial contribution to the art of music)

DSc: (For Aberdeen graduates of at least seven yrs' standing or for members of staff of at least four yrs' standing, in respect of published work in pure or applied science)

LLD: Law (For Aberdeen graduates of least seven yrs' standing or for members of staff of at least four yrs' standing, in respect of written work contributing substantially to the study of law)

MD; ChM: Medicine (Aberdeen medical graduates of at least two yrs' standing or for qualified practitioners who have held an approved hospital, research or teaching appointment in the vicinity of Aberdeen or Inverness for at least two yrs prior to submission of thesis)
PhD: *36 mths FT/60 mths PT By thesis:*

MASTER'S DEGREES OR EQUIVALENT

LLM: *1 yr FT/3 yrs PT Taught courses available in:* Commercial Law; Environmental Law & Management; Environmental Law & Science; Environmental Law; European Law; General LLM; International & European Law; International Law; Property Law *12 mths FT/24 mths PT By Research*
MA: *3 yrs FT/6 yrs PT* Combined Studies; European Languages & Twentieth Century Culture; Scottish Archaeology; Scottish Culture & Traditions; Women's Studies
MA Hons (Single, Joint, Combined or General): *4 yrs FT/8 yrs PT* Accountancy; Accountancy with French or German; Accountancy-Anthropology or Economic Science or Entrepreneurship or Finance or French or Geography or German or Legal Studies or Management Studies or Philosophy or Political Economy or Social Research or Sociology or Statistics or Divinity; Anthropology; Anthropology-Celtic or Celtic Civilisation or Cultural History or Divinity or Economic History or Economic Science or English or Geography or German or Hispanic Studies or Legal Studies or Entrepreneurship or Finance or French or History or International Relations or Management Studies or Philosophy or Political Economy or Politics or Religious Studies or Sociology or Psychology; Celtic with Languages & Linguistics or Music Studies; Celtic Civilisation; Celtic Civilisation-English or Geography or Hispanic Studies or History or History of Art or Philosophy or Social Research or Sociology or German; Celtic Studies; Celtic-Cultural History or Divinity or Economic Science or English or French or Geography or German or Hispanic Studies or History or History of Art or Management Studies or Mathematics or Political Economy or Religious Studies or Social Research or Sociology; Computing (Also available with Industrial Placement); Computing-Entrepreneurship or Mathematics or Statistics or or Finance; Countryside & Environmental Management; Cultural History with Film Studies or History of Religions or Music Studies or Women's Studies or Sociology; Cultural History; Cultural History-Divinity or English or French or Geography or German or Hispanic Studies or History or History of Art or International Relations or Philosophy or Politics or Sociology; Divinity with Film Studies or Music Studies or Women's Studies or Language & Linguistics; Divinity; Divinity-English or French or Finance or German or Hispanic Studies or History or History of Art or International Relations or Politics or Social Research or Sociology; Economic History-Economic Science or Finance or Geography or International Relations or Management Studies or Political Economy or Politics or Social Research or Sociology; Economic Science with Women's Studies; Economic Science; Economic Science-English or Finance or French or Entrepreneurship or Geography or German or Hispanic Studies or History or International Relations or Management Studies or Mathematics or Philosophy or Politics or Social Research or Sociology or Statistics; English; English with Film Studies or Music Studies or Women's Studies or Language & Linguistics; English-Entrepreneurship or Finance or French or German or Hispanic Studies or History or History of Art or International Relations or Management Studies or Philosophy or Political Economy or Religious Studies or Social Research or Sociology; English-Scottish Literature; Entrepreneurship; Entrepreneurship-Finance or French or Geography or Hispanic Studies or History or Mathematics or Political Economy or Social Research or Sociology or Statistics; Environmental Geography; European Languages with Education; European Management Studies; European Studies; Finance with Women's Studies; Finance-French or Geography or German or Hispanic Studies or History or International Relations or Legal Studies or Management Studies or Philosophy or Political Economy or Politics or Social Research or Sociology or Statistics; French with Film Studies or Music Studies or Women's Studies or Lanuage & Linguistics; French Studies; French-Geography or German or Hispanic Studies or History or History of Art or International Relations or Management Studies or Mathematics or Philosophy or Political Economy or Politics or Religious Studies or Social Research or Sociology; Gaelic Studies; Geography; Geography-German or History or Hispanic Studies or International Relations or Management Studies or Political Economy or Social Research or Sociology; German with Film Studies or Music Studies or Women's Studies or Language & Linguistics; German Studies; German-Hispanic Studies or History or History of Art or International Relations or

Management Studies or Mathematics or Philosophy or Political Economy or Politics or Religious Studies or Social Research or Sociology; Hispanic Studies with Film Studies or Music Studies or Women's Studies; Hispanic Studies (Latin America); Hispanic Studies (Spain); Hispanic Studies-History or History of Art or International Relations or Management Studies or Mathematics or Philosophy or Political Economy or Politics or Religious Studies or Social Research or Sociology; Historical Studies; History with Film Studies or Music Studies or Women's Studies or Language & Linguistics; History; History of Art with Film Studies or Music Studies or Women's Studies or Language & Linguistics; History of Art; History of Art-Philosophy or Religious Studies; History-History of Art or International Relations or Management Studies or Mathematics or Philosophy or Political Economy or Politics or Religious Studies or Social Research or Sociology; Human Geography; International Relations-Legal Studies or Management Studies or Philosophy or Political Economy or Religious Studies or Sociology; Languages-Literature of Scotland; Legal Studies-Philosophy or Politics or Social Research or Sociology; Management Studies; Management Studies-Mathematics or Political Economy or Politics or Social Research or Sociology or Statistics; Mathematics with Gaelic; Mathematics; Mathematics-Philosophy or Political Economy or Physics or Statistics; Mental Philosophy; Natural Philosophy; Philosophy with Film Studies or Music Studies or Women's Studies; Philosophy-Management Studies or Politics or Psychology or Religious Studies or Social Research or Sociology or Physics or Political Economy; Physical Geography; Political Economy; Political Economy with Women's Studies; Political Economy-Politics or Sociology or Statistics; Politics-International Relations; Politics-Religious Studies or Social Research or Sociology; Psychology with French or German or Gaelic; Psychology; Psychology-Social Research or Sociology or Statistics; Religious Studies with Film Studies or Music Studies or Women's Studies or Language & Linguistics; Religious Studies-Sociology; Rural Development; Scottish Studies; Sociology with Cultural History or Women's Studies; Sociology; Sports & Leisure Management; Statistics; Statistics (Economic Science)

MBA: *30-60 mths PT* Business Administration (Open to graduates (or those with equivalent professional qualifications) with a minimum of three yrs' relevant work experience); Business Administration (Educational Management) (Open to graduates (or those with equivalent professional qualifications) with a minimum of three yrs' relevant work experience)

MCh Orth: *12 mths FT/24 mths PT* Master of Surgery in Orthopaedics

MChem: *5 yrs* Chemistry; Chemistry with Placement in France; Chemistry with Placement in Germany; Environmental Analytical Chemistry; New Materials Technology

MEng: *5 yrs* Civil & Environmental Engineering; Civil & Environmental Engineering with European Studies; Civil & Structural Engineering; Civil & Structural Engineering with European Studies; Civil Engineering; Civil Engineering-Diploma in Management; Electrical & Electronic Engineering; Electrical & Electronic Engineering with European Studies; Electrical & Electronic Engineering with Diploma in Management; Electrical & Electronic Engineering with Control; Electronic Engineering with Communications; Electronic & Computer Engineering; Engineering; Engineering with Safety-Reliability Engineering; Mechanical & Electrical Engineering; Mechanical Engineering; Mechanical Engineering with European Studies; Mechanical Engineering with Materials; Mechanical Engineering with Control; Mechanical Engineering-Diploma in Management; Offshore Engineering

MLE: *12 mths FT/24 mths PT By Research: Taught courses available in:* Land Economy (Awarded after taught course or after research); Property Investment & Development; Rural Surveying; Urban Surveying

MLitt: *12 mths FT/24 mths PT By Research: Taught courses available in:* Applied European Studies; Irish & Scottish Studies; Philosophy; Philosophy & Technology; Scottish Philosophy; Strategic Studies

MMed Sci: *12 mths FT/24 mths PT* (The degree is awarded by exam and/or thesis and/or dissertation)

MPhil: *24 mths FT/42 mths PT* (By thesis)

MRad: *24 mths PT* Radiology (Taught course)

MSc: *12 mths FT/24 mths PT* Agricultural Development; Agricultural Economics; Animal Nutrition; Animal Production; Arboriculture; Biomedical Engineering; Clinical Pharmacology; Ecology; Environmental Analytical Chemistry; Environmental Microbiology; Environmental Remote Sensing; Environmental Science; Ergonomics; European Forestry; European Rural Development; Forest Management; Health Service & Public Health Research; Human Nutrition &

Metabolism; Information Technology & Intelligent Systems; Information Technology (Medical Physics); Intelligent Systems & Applications; International Nutrition; Marine & Fisheries Science; Medical Imaging; Medical Molecular Genetics; Medical Physics; New Materials; Nursing/Midwifery; Occupational Health; Occupational Hygiene; Participatory Forest Management; Petroleum Geology; Pig Production; Reproductive Biology; Rural & Regional Resources Planning; Rural Environmental Management; Safety Engineering, Reliability & Risk Management; Seed Science & Technology; Soil Science; Sports Nutrition; Sustainable Development *36 mths PT only* Project Management (evening and weekend classes. Also available by distance learning); Technology & Management in the Oil & Gas Industry (evening and weekend classes) *36-60 mths PT only* Scottish MSc in Primary Care

MSc (Econ): *12 mths FT/24 mths PT* Business Management; Finance & Investment Management; Health Service Management & Policy *36 mths PT only* Human Resources (evening and weekend classes)

MSc (Entr): *12 mths FT/24 mths PT Taught courses available in:* Entrepreneurship

MTh: *12 mths FT/24 mths PT Taught courses available in:* Biblical Languages; General MTh; Reformation Studies

Honorary Degrees

DD; LLD; DLitt; DSc; DMus

Diplomas

DipLE: *1 yr FT* Land Economy (Rural Surveying); Land Economy (Urban Surveying)

Diploma: *9 mths FT/21 mths PT* Agricultural Development; Agricultural Economics; Animal Nutrition; Animal Production; Applied European Studies; Arboriculture; Biomedical Engineering; Business & Management; Business Administration (Minimum 24 mths PT – evening and weekend classes); Business Administration (Educational Management) (Minimum 24 mths PT – evening and weekend classes); Clinical Pharmacology; Ecology; Entrepreneurship; Environmental Analytical Chemistry; Environmental Microbiology; Environmental Remote Sensing; Environmental Science; Finance & Investment Management; Forest Management; Health Service & Public Health Research; Health Services Management & Policy; Human Nutrition; Information Technology & Intelligent Systems; Information Technology (Medical Physics); Intelligent Systems & Applications; Irish & Scottish Studies; Marine & Fisheries Science; Medical Imaging; Medical Physics; Nursing/Midwifery; Pig Production; Project Management (24 mths PT evening and weekend classes. Also available by distance learning); Reproductive Biology; Rural & Regional Resources Planning; Scottish MSc in Primary Care (PT only is available over minimum of 24 mths); Seed Science & Technology; Soil Science; Strategic Studies; Technology & Management in the Oil & Gas Industry (24 mths PT evening and weekend classes)

DLP: *1 yr FT* Legal Practice (For law graduates intending to enter the Law Society of Scotland or the Faculty of Advocates)

DPS: *12 mths FT/18 mths PT* (For postgraduates who have attended at least three yrs' full-time study in Divinity; one academical yr full-time or not less than 18 mths part-time, or a combination of a period of full- and part-time study of not less than 15 mths)

PgDipMin: *12 mths FT/18 mths PT* Ministry; Pastoral Studies & Pastoral Theology (For postgraduates who have attended at least three yrs' full-time study in Divinity; one academical yr full-time or not less than 18 mths part-time, or a combination of a period of full- and part-time study of not less than 15 mths)

Certificates

Certificate: *12 mths PT* Project Management (Evening and weekend classes only); Technology & Management in the Oil & Gas Industry (Evening and weekend classes only) *4 mths FT* Health Services & Public Health Research; Human Nutrition; Nursing/Midwifery; Occupational Health; Practice of Forestry; Rural Development Forestry *Min 12 mths PT* Business & Management (Evening and weekend classes only); Business Administration; Scottish MSc in Primary Care *Min 6 wks/max 3 yrs PT* Underwater Medicine *Min 8 mths PT/max 36 mths PT* Higher Education; Medical/Health Care Education

UNIVERSITY OF ABERTAY DUNDEE

Information and Recruitment Office, Bell Street, Dundee DD1 1HG Tel: 01382 308080 Fax: 01382 308081 e-mail: iro@abertay.ac.uk Website: www.abertay.ac.uk

* Subject to validation.

First Degrees

BA Hons: *2 yrs* Business Administration *2 yrs FT/4 yrs PT* Nursing Studies (post-registration) *4 yrs FT* Accountancy-Finance; Accounting; Business Studies; Business Studies with Marketing Management or Management Science or Financial Services or Information Technology or French or German or Spanish or Human Resource Management or Communications Management; Computer Arts; Computer Arts with Japanese or Marketing; Economics with European Study; Economics; European Business Law; European Business Management with Languages; European Economy & Society; Financial Services; Health & Behavioural Science; Hospitality Management; Information Management; Information Technology; Law (Including the Diploma in Conveyancing and Executry Law); Management with Marketing Management or Information Technology or French or German or Spanish or Human Resource Management or Accounting; Management with Marketing Management; Management with Financial Services; Marketing with Retail Management or Languages; Marketing; Social & Cultural Studies; Social Science; Taxation and Revenue Law; Tourism

BSc Hons: *2 yrs PT* Advanced Nursing Practice (post-registration) *4 mths FT/24 mths PT* Computing (Applications Development) *4 yrs FT/5 yrs S* Applied Chemistry; Applied Chemistry with Pharmaceutical Chemistry; Applied Chemistry with Environmental Chemistry; Behavioural Science; Bioinformatics; Biological Sciences*; Biotechnology; Business Computing; Civil Engineering; Computer Games Technology with Japanese or Marketing; Computer Games Technology; Computing; Computing (Games Development); Electronics; Environmental Biotechnology; Environmental Science-Technology*; Food & Consumer Sciences; Food Product Design; Food, Nutrition and Health; Forensic Psychobiology; Health and Behavioural Science; Health and Sport Science; Health and Sport Studies; Information Management; Internet and Communication Technologies; Mechatronics; Medical Biotechnology; Microbial Biotechnology; Nursing (post-registration); Nursing (pre-registration); Psychology; Psychology with Biology; Psychology with Computing; Quantity Surveying; Sociology; Sport Coaching & Development

Higher Degrees

MBA: *1 yr FT/24 mths PT/1 yr FT/3 yrs PT* European MBA *1 yr FT/3 yrs PT* Master of Business Administration; MBA (Marketing)
MPhil: *2 yrs FT/4 yrs PT*
MSc: *1 yr FT/2 yrs PT* Electrical Power Engineering-Management
MSc/PGDip: *1 yr FT/2 yrs PT* Bioinformatics; Biotechnology; Counselling Studies; Environmental Management; Health & Counselling; Health Studies; Human Resource Management; Information Technology; International Marketing with Languages; Local Economic Development; Mechatronics; Mechatronics with Project Management; Multicultural Counselling; Software Engineering; Software Engineering (Games and Virtual Environments); Wastewater & Environmental Management
PhD: *3 yrs FT/6 yrs PT*

Diplomas

DipHE: *2 yrs FT* Accounting; Biological Sciences; Chemistry; Civil Engineering Studies; Computing; Construction Studies; Engineering; Environmental Studies; Internet Systems; Surveying *FT/PT* Forensic Psychiatry
Diploma: *1 yr* Management Studies

Certificates

Certificate: *1 yr* Management

ADAMS UNIVERSITY COLLEGE

Lancaster LA1 3JD Tel: 01524 384444 Fax: 01524 384567
Ambleside LA22 9BB Tel: 015394 30211 Fax: 015394 30305
Carlisle CA2 7HY Tel: 01228 814859 Fax: 01228 814803

First Degrees

BEng/BEng Hons: *3 yrs FT/4 yrs S* Agricultural Engineering
BSc/BSc Hons: *3 yrs FT/4 yrs S* Agri-Food Marketing with Business Studies; Agricultural Engineering with Marketing & Management; Agriculture with Animal Science; Agriculture with Agricultural Marketing or Crop Management or Land & Farm Management; Agriculture; Animal Health; International Agri-Food Production & Marketing; Rural Enterprise & Land Management; Rural Environment Protection

Higher Degrees

MSc: *1 yr FT* Natural Resources & Extension *18 mths FT* Crop Protection & Crop Biotechnology

Research Degrees

MPhil/PhD: All land-based subject areas (validated by the Open University)

ANGLIA POLYTECHNIC UNIVERSITY

Cambridge Campus, East Road, Cambridge, Cambridgeshire CB1 1PT Tel: 01223 363271 Fax: 01245 495419 e-mail: info@anglia.ac.uk Website: www.anglia.ac.uk

Chelmsford Campus, Victoria Road South, Chelmsford, Essex CM1 1LL Tel: 01245 493131 Fax: 01245 495419 e-mail: info@anglia.ac.uk Website: www.anglia.ac.uk

Danbury Park Conference Centre, Main Road, Danbury, Chelmsford, Essex CM3 4AT Tel: 01245 222141 Fax: 01245 495419 e-mail: info@anglia.ac.uk Website: www.anglia.ac.uk

(** Taught at Cambridge Campus; *** taught at Chelmsford Campus; **** taught at Danbury Park Conference Centre). All Brentwood courses are now at Chelmsford
Language options can be 3 or 4 yrs.
† Subject to validation.

First Degrees

BA: *3 yrs FT* Business (Entry with HND/accreditation HNC/DHE)
BA Hons: *3 yrs FT* 20th Century European History & Politics**; Accounting***; Art History**; Art History-Studio Art**; Arts Administration-Art History**; Business**; Business Administration***; Business Administration (Corporate Administration)***; Business Administration (Financial Services)***; Business Administration (Human Resource Management)***; Business Administration (Leisure Management)***; Business Administration (Marketing Management)***; Business Administration – Accounting; Business Economics**; Business Law; Business Studies (Leisure Management)***; Communication Studies**; English**; English Language for International Business**; English Language Studies-French or German or Italian or Spanish**; English Language Studies-Intercultural Studies**; European Business**; European Philosophy & Literature**; European Social Policy**; French-German or Italian or Spanish**; French-Intercultural Studies**; French for International Business**; Geography**; German-Intercultural Studies**; German-Italian or Spanish**; German for International Business**; Graphic Design**; Health, Welfare and Social Policy**; History**; Human Geography**; Illustration**; International Management (General)**; Italian-Intercultural Studies**; Italian-Spanish**; Italian for International Business**; Leisure and Tourism***; Lens & Digital Media**; Music**; Philosophy**; Philosophy & Psychology (Self & Mind)**; Printmaking**; Secondary French with QTS***; Sociology**; Spanish-Intercultural Studies**; Spanish for International Business**; Voluntary Sector Management*** *4 yrs FT* Business Studies***; European Business-French Programme**; European Business-German Programme**; European Business-Spanish Programme**; French**; German**; Italian**; Languages & Intercultural Studies; Spanish**

BA/BSc Hons Combined: *3 yrs FT* 20th Century European History & Politics-Social Policy or Law or Sociology or Geography or Politics or Women's Studies or Languages or Printmaking or Music or Lens & Digital Media or Philosophy or Heritage; Animal Behaviour**-Imaging Science or Biomedical Science or Microbiology or Biology or Natural History or Chemistry or Ecology & Conservation or Cell & Molecular Biology or Mathematics or Geography or Environmental Biology or Psychology or Languages; Art-Law or Printmaking or Sociology or Geography or Politics or Women's Studies or Communication Studies or English Language Studies or English or Languages or 20th Century European History & Politics or History or History (Family & Community History) or Philosophy or European Philosophy & Literature or Drama or Film Studies or Graphic Design or Music or Lens & Digital Media; Art History**-Law or Business or Sociology or Geography or Politics or Communication Studies or English or Languages or English Language Studies or Women's Studies or 20th Century European History & Politics or History or History (Family & Community History) or European Philosophy & Literature or Heritage or Philosophy or Printmaking or Graphic Design or Music or Drama or Lens & Digital Media or Film Studies; Audiotechnology**-Imaging Science or Mathematics or Chemistry or Computer Science or Real Time Computer Systems or Ecology & Conservation or Biology or Environmental Biology or Cell & Molecular Biology or Microbiology or Natural History or Biomedical Science or Electronics or Internet Technology or Geography or Business or Communication Studies or Languages or Music; Biology**-Forensic Science or Opthalmic Dispensing or Imaging Science or Chemistry or Natural History or Biomedical Science or Psychology or Environmental Biology or Mathematics or Computer Science or Electronics or Geography or Ecology & Conservation or Languages; Biomedical Science**-Forensic Science or Imaging Science or Opthalmic Dispensing or Microbiology or Psychology or Environmental Biology or Natural History or Chemistry or Mathematics or Computer Science or Electronics or Ecology & Conservation or Geography or Languages; Business**-Opthalmic Dispensing or Psychology or Ecology & Conservation or Internet Technology or Chemistry or Mathematics or Computer Science or Electronics or Sociology or Health, Welfare & Social Policy or Intercultural Studies or Geography or Politics or Women's Studies or English Language Studies or English or Languages or 20th Century European History & Politics or History or History (Family & Community History) or European Philosophy & Literature or Heritage or Philosophy or Printmaking or Music or Drama or Lens & Digital Media or Graphic Design or Communication Studies or Law; Business Studies***-Information Systems or Multimedia or Product Design or Construction Management or Leisure; Cell & Molecular Biology**-Forensic Science or Opthalmic Dispensing or Imaging Science or Biomedical Science or Natural History or Psychology or Chemistry or Mathematics or Statistics/Statistical Modelling or Computer Science or Electronics or Ecology & Conservation or Geography or Languages or Imaging Science or Psychology; Chemistry**-Forensic Science or Opthalmic Dispensing or Natural History or Ecology & Conservation or Electronics or Computer Science or Mathematics or Environmental Biology or Microbiology or Geography or Languages; Combined Sciences**; Communication Studies**-Natural History or Ecology & Conservation or Computer Science or Internet Technology or Real Time Computer Systems or Economics or Health, Welfare & Social Policy or Law or Sociology or Geography or Politics or Women's Studies or English Language Studies or English or Languages or History or History (Family & Community History) or 20th Century European History & Politics or European Philosophy & Literature or Heritage or Philosophy or Printmaking or Music or Lens & Digital Media or Graphic Design; Computer Science**-Forensic Science or Opthalmic Dispensing or Languages or Electronics or Imaging Science or Psychology or Natural History or Ecology & Conservation or Internet Technology or Mathematics or Environmental Biology or Microbiology or Heritage; Criminology**-Forensic Science or Psychology or Sociology or Health, Welfare & Social Policy or Law; Drama-Economics or Music or Lens & Digital Media or Social Policy or Law or Sociology or Geography or Politics or Women's Studies or English Language Studies or English or Languages or History or History (Family & Community History) or Philosophy or 20th Century European History & Politics or European Philosophy & Literature or Printmaking or Graphic Design; Ecology & Conservation**-Opthalmic Dispensing or Imaging Science or Psychology or Mathematics or Natural History or Electronics or Real Time Computer Systems or Geography or Languages or Heritage; Economics**-Mathematics or Sociology or Health, Welfare & Social Policy or Geography or Politics or Women's Studies or English Language Studies or English or Languages or 20th Century European History & Politics or History or History (Family & Community History) or Heritage or

Graphic Design or Music or Law; Education Studies (non QTS)***-English or Art or Science; Electronics**-Imaging Science or Psychology or Real Time Computer Systems or Internet Technology or Mathematics or Geography; English**-Law or Mathematics or Health, Welfare & Social Policy or Geography or Sociology or Politics or Women's Studies or English Language Studies or Languages or 20th Century European History & Politics or Printmaking or Graphic Design or Music or Philosophy or Lens & Digital Media or 20th Century European History & Politics or History or History (Family & Community History) or European Philosophy & Literature or Heritage; English Language Studies**-Health, Welfare & Social Policy or Law or Geography & Countryside Planning or Sociology or Geography or Politics or Women's Studies or 20th Century European History & Politics or History or History (Family & Community History) or European Philosophy & Literature or Heritage or Music or Philosophy; Environmental Biology**-Imaging Science or Natural History or Opthalmic Dispensing or Psychology or Mathematics or Statistics/Statistical Modelling or Forensic Science or Geography or Languages; Environmental Planning***-Law; European Philosophy & Literature**-Psychology or Mathematics or Law or Health, Welfare & Social Policy or Sociology or Languages or 20th Century European History & Politics or Geography or Politics or Women's Studies or History or History (Family & Community History) or Heritage or Printmaking or Music or Lens & Digital Media or Graphic Design; Film Studies-Law or Business or Lens & Digital Media or Geography & Countryside Planning or Sociology or Geography or Women's Studies or Communication Studies or English Language Studies or English or Languages or History or History (Family & Community History) or Philosophy or 20th Century European History & Politics or European Philosophy & Literature or Printmaking or Graphic Design or Music or Drama; Forensic Science**-Psychology or Law or Natural History or Microbiology; Geography & Countryside Planning**-Psychology or Lens & Digital Media or Printmaking or Natural History or European Philosophy & Literature or Art or Graphic Design or Music or Drama or Ecology & Conservation or Mathematics or Statistics/Statistical Modelling or Economics or Law or Business or Sociology or Politics or Women's Studies or Communication Studies or English or Languages or History or History (Family & Community History) or Art History or Philosophy or Heritage; Geography**-Imaging Science or Psychology or Mathematics or Planning or Microbiology or Health, Welfare & Social Policy or Law or Sociology or Politics or Languages or History or History (Family & Community History) or Heritage or Philosophy or Printmaking or Music or Lens & Digital Media or Graphic Design; Graphic Design**-Imaging Science or Natural History or Internet Technology or Law or Mathematics or Statistics/Statistical Modelling or Real Time Computer Systems or Sociology or 20th Century European History & Politics or History or History (Family & Community History) or Philosophy or Heritage or Music; Health, Welfare & Social Policy**-Psychology or Mathematics or Sociology or Women's Studies or Languages or History (Family & Community History) or Politics or Law or History or Heritage; Heritage-Law or Sociology or Politics or Women's Studies or Languages or Philosophy or Printmaking or Music or Lens & Digital Media; Hispanic Cultural Studies-Economics or Social Policy or Law or Business or Sociology or Geography or Politics or Women's Studies or Communication Studies or English Language Studies or English or Languages or History (Family & Community History) or Art History or Philosophy or Heritage or 20th Century European History & Politics or European Philosophy & Literature or Art or Graphic Design or Music or Drama or Film Studies or Printmaking or Lens & Digital Media; History (Family & Community History)-Law or Sociology or Politics or Women's Studies or Languages or Philosophy or Printmaking or Music or Lens & Digital Media; History**-Mathematics or Law or Sociology or Languages or Politics or Women's Studies or Languages or Philosophy or Music or Lens & Digital Media or Printmaking; Housing***-Law; Imaging Science**-Opthalmic Dispensing or Psychology or Natural History or Mathematics or Internet Technology or Real Time Computer Systems or Printmaking or Lens & Digital Media; Information Systems***-Multimedia or Product Design; Internet Technology**-Mathematics or Lens & Digital Media; Languages (French, German, Italian, Spanish)-Opthalmic Dispensing or Natural History or Psychology or Mathematics or Law or Health, Welfare & Social Policy or Sociology or Geography or Politics or Women's Studies or 20th Century European History & Politics or History or History (Family & Community) or Heritage or Philosophy or Printmaking or Music or Lens & Digital Media or Graphic Design; Law**-Psychology or Sociology or Mathematics or Politics or Women's Studies or Philosophy or Printmaking or Music or Lens & Digital Media or Surveying or Product Design; Lens & Digital Media**-Mathematics or

Statistics/Statistical Modelling or Real Time Computer Systems or Sociology or Philosophy or Music; Mathematics**-Opthalmic Dispensing or Statistics/Statistical Modelling or Microbiology or Psychology or Natural History or Real Time Computer Systems or Sociology or Politics or Languages or Printmaking or Music; Microbiology-Opthalmic Dispensing or Natural History or Psychology or Languages; Multimedia-Product Design; Music**-Psychology or Sociology or Philosophy or Printmaking; Natural History**-Psychology; Opthalmic Dispensing**-Psychology; Philosophy**-Social Policy or Sociology or Politics or Women's Studies or Languages or Printmaking; Politics**-Sociology or Women's Studies or Languages; Printmaking**-Real Time Computer Systems or Sociology; Property Management***-Law; Psychology**-Sociology or Women's Studies or Languages; Real Time Computer Systems**-Psychology; Sociology**-Women's Studies or Languages; Statistical Modelling**; Statistics**

BEd Hons: *3 yrs FT* Art (Secondary)*** (With QTS); Primary Education; Primary Education with QTS***; Science (Secondary)*** (With QTS)

BEng: *3 yrs FT* Construction Engineering***; Energy Management***; Engineering Systems; Product Design***

BEng Hons: *2 yrs FT* Telecommunications Engineering*** *3 yrs FT* Control Engineering***; Electronic Engineering***

BOptom: *3 yrs FT* Optometry**

BSc: *2 yrs PT* Health Studies (Radiography)**

BSc Hons: *1 yr FT/6 yrs PT* Community Practice*** *18 mths* Midwifery *3 yrs FT* Advanced Technology***; Architectural Design Technology***; Architecture***; Artificial Intelligence**; Audio & Music Technology**; Biological Sciences**; Biomedical Science**; Building Conservation & Heritage***; Building Economics & Design***; Building Surveying***; Business Facilities Management***; Business Information Systems***; Cell & Molecular Biology**; Chemistry**; Chemistry in Society**; Communications Network***; Communications Technology***; Computer Aided Product Design***; Computer Science**; Computer Software Development***; Conservation & Heritage Studies***; Conservation of Landscape & Buildings***; Construction Management***; Construction Management***-Business; Construction Management***-Information Technology; Earth Sciences**; Electronic Product Design***; Electronics***; Energy & Environmental Conservation***; Engineering Management***; Environmental Assessment & Policy**; Environmental Biology**; Environmental Monitoring & Protection***; Environmental Planning***; Environmental Planning***-Geography or Architecture; Environmental Science**; Environmental Toxicology**; Estate Agency Management***; Estate Management***; European Construction Management***; Forensic Science**; Geochemistry**; Geography**; Geography & Countryside Planning**; Health & Social Studies**/***; Health Technology Management***; Housing***; Information Systems***; Internet Technology**; Leisure, Tourism & the Environment***; Medical Technologies Development***; Medicinal Chemistry**; Microbiology**; Midwifery***; Multimedia Computing***; Multimedia Systems***; Nursing***; Nursing (Adult, Mental Health, Learning Disabilities)***; Nursing***-Social Work (Learning Disabilities); Optical Management**; Physical Geography**; Planning and Development Surveying***; Pre-Registration Midwifery***; Property Management***; Psychology**; Quantity Surveying***; Risk Management***; Social Work**; Software Engineering***; Surveying***; Surveying***-Information Technology or Business

LLB Hons: *3 yrs FT* Law***

Higher Degrees

LLM: *FT* International & European Business Law; International Sports Law***; Legal Practice***

MA/MBA/MSc: *FT/PT* Analytical Chemistry**; Applied Linguistics**; Arts Administration**; Biomedical Science**; Business; Business Management**; Computer Science**; Conservation of Buildings***; Corporate Administration***; Education*; Engineering Management***; English Studies*; Environmental & Water Engineering***; Environmental Analysis**; European Business**; European Business Law**; European Language & Intercultural Studies**; Geography, Health & the Environment**; Graphic Arts; Health & Social Work***; Historical Studies**; Housing; Human Resource Management*; International Business**; International Business Economics**; International Sports Law***; Jewish-Christian Relations**; Legal Practice***; Leisure, Tourism & the Environment***; Management***; Medical Imaging**; Medical Imaging Ultrasound**; Modern Philosophy;** Music**; Music Therapy**; Negotiated Master of Arts**;

Negotiated Master of Science**; Pastoral Theology**; Philosophy**; Radiography**; Social Policy**; Sociology & Politics**; Software Engineering***; Victorian Studies**; Women's Studies**
MPhil/PhD: *FT/PT* (By research in various departments)

Diplomas

Diploma in Higher Education: *1 yr FT* Common Professional Examination*** *2 yrs FT* Environmental Monitoring & Protection***; Nursing (Adult, Mental Health, Learning Disabilities, Child)***; University Modular Scheme** *3 yrs FT* Registered Nurse*** *3 yrs PT* Community Care***
Diploma in Management: *1 yr FT*
Diploma in Nursing (Professional Studies): *1 yr FT*
Diploma in Professional Studies in Education: *1 yr FT* Computer Education***
Diploma in Social Work: *2 yrs FT* **/***
Graduate Diploma in Building Management: *1 yr FT*
HND: *2 yrs FT* Architectural Design Technology***; Building Economics-Design***; Building Management***; Business Information Technology***; Business Studies***; Civil Engineering***; Computer Aided Product Design***; Computing**/***; Energy & Environment Studies***; Estate Agency Management***; Leisure & Tourism***; Multimedia Computing*** *2 yrs FT/3 yrs PT* Audio and Music Technology**; Electronics**
Postgraduate Diploma: *9 mths FT* European Management *FT* Environmental Planning***

Certificates

Certificate in Higher Education: *1 yr FT* Cambridge Interfaculty Scheme**
HNC: *2 yrs PT* Electronics*
PGCE: *1 yr FT* General Primary Education***; Primary Education***; Secondary Education (Art & Design)***; Secondary Education (English)***; Secondary Education (Mathematics)***; Secondary Education (Modern Languages)***; Secondary Education (Music)***; Secondary Education (Science)***

Other Courses

Access Courses (International): *1 yr FT* Art & Design**; Humanities**; Languages**; Music**
Courses: *1 yr FT* Brunei Nurses Adaptation Course; Legal Practice Course (Law Society)***
Foundation Course: Access; Engineering/Computing/Science** *1 yr FT* Life Sciences**; Opthalmics (Radiography)

Degrees validated by Anglia Polytechnic University offered at:

City College, Norwich

Ipswich Road, Norwich NR2 2LJ Tel: 01603 773311 Fax: 01603 773301 e-mail: information@ccn.ac.uk
† Subject to validation.

First Degrees

BA Hons: *1 yr FT top-up* Accounting & Finance (Post HNC/HND top-up degree); Business Administration (Post HNC/HND top-up degree); Hospitality & Tourism Management (Post HNC/HND top-up degree); Human Resource Management (Post HNC/HND top-up degree); Marketing (Post HNC/HND top-up degree); Travel & Tourism Management (Post HNC/HND top-up degree) *3 yrs FT* Accounting-Finance; Business Administration; Human Resource Management; Marketing *Combined Arts: Major/minor combinations:* English; History; Psychology; Sociology *4 yrs S* Hospitality-Tourism Management *PT* Accounting & Finance; Business Administration; Combined Arts/Science; Early Childhood Studies†; Human Resource Management; Marketing; Post Compulsory Education

BSc Hons: *1 yr FT top-up* Business Information Systems *3 yrs FT* Combined Sciences; Environmental Biology; Environmental Health; Human Life Sciences; Psychology *4 yrs S* Environmental Health (Integrated) *PT* Business Information Systems; Environmental Biology; Environmental Health; Health Studies; Human Life Sciences; Nursing Practice; Nursing Studies; Social Studies; Social Studies with Counselling Studies *PT (with flexible attendance)* Nursing Studies/Practice

Higher Degrees

MSc: *PT* Education and Training; Educational Management; Human Resource Management

Diplomas

CCETSW Diploma: *2 yrs FT/PT* Social Work
Diploma in Management Studies: *24 mths PT*
Diploma of Higher Education: *2 yrs PT* Counselling Studies
Higher Diploma: *4 mths FT/24 mths PT* Administrative Procedures
HND: *2 yrs FT* Business; Business & Finance; Business & Marketing; Business & Personnel; Business Information Technology; Computer Aided Engineering; Computing; Early Childhood Studies; Electrical/Electronic Engineering; Hospitality Management or Hospitality Management (Licensed Retail); Leisure Management†; Leisure Management (Events)†; Leisure Management (Sport & Recreation)†; Manufacturing Engineering; Media; Multimedia; Software Engineering; Telecommunications Engineering; Tourism Management; Travel & Tourism Management

Certificates

Access Courses: *1 yr FT/PT* Art & Design; Arts, Humanities & Social Sciences; Engineering; Natural Sciences
Foundation Course: *1 yr FT* Environmental Biology; Environmental Health; Human Life Sciences
HNC: *2 yrs PT* Building Studies; Business & Finance; Business Information Technology; Civil Engineering; Computing; Early Childhood Studies; Electrical Engineering or Electronic Engineering; Housing Studies; Manufacturing-Mechanical Engineering; Media; Motor Vehicle Management & Technology†; Multimedia†; Social Care; Software Engineering; Tourism Management; Travel & Tourism Management
PGCE: *FT/PT* Post-16

Professional Qualifications

Professional Qualifications: *1 yr FT/2 yrs PT/4 mths FT/24 mths PT* **CACA:** Foundation, Certificate and Professional Stages; **CIOB:** Corporate Membership Part 1; **CIH:** Advanced Wardens Certificate; **ENB:** Enrolled Conversion Course; Teaching and Assessment in the Clinical Area

Colchester Institute

Sheepen Road, Colchester, Essex CO3 3LL Tel: 01206 518000 Fax: 01206 763041 e-mail: mark2@colch-inst.ac.uk Website: www.colch-inst.ac.uk

(All Music combinations in conjunction with the University of Essex)

First Degrees

BA: *FT/PT* Combined Studies
BA Hons: *3 yrs* Business Studies with Hospitality Management or Leisure Facility Management or Marketing or Personnel Management or Tourism
BA/BA Hons: *3 yrs FT* Art & Design; Business Administration with Business Systems or Hospitality Management or Leisure Facility Management or Marketing or Personnel Management or Tourism; Communications & Media Studies-English or History or Sociology; English-History or Sociology; History-Sociology; Hospitality Studies with Marketing or Personnel Management or International Operations or Tourism or Leisure Management or Facilities Management or Conference Management Business Systems or Culinary Arts; Leisure Studies with Exercise & Health or Sports Development or Leisure Facilities Management or Tourism *4 yrs (includes 1 yr*

industrial placement) Business Studies with Business Systems or Hospitality Management or Leisure Facility Management or Marketing or Personnel Management or Tourism
BSc Hons: *2 yrs FT* Health & Social Care; Occupational Therapy *3 yrs FT* Ecology & Environmental Biology; Environmental Monitoring & Protection (plus two summer work placements); Marine & Freshwater Biology *4 yrs* Ecology; Music *4 yrs PT* Occupational Therapy

Higher Degrees

MA: *1 yr FT/2 yrs PT* Music *PT* Health & the Arts
MPhil: *18 mths minimum FT/30 mths PT* Music

Diplomas

Diploma: *PT* Therapeutic Counselling (Humanistic Person-Centred)
HND: *2 yrs FT* Art & Design; Business Studies; Environmental Monitoring & Protection (plus two summer work placements); Health & Social Care; Hospitality Management; Leisure Studies *PT* Business; Electronic/Manufacturing Systems; Electronics

Norwich School of Art & Design

St George's Street, Norwich, Norfolk NR3 1BB Tel: 01603 610561 Fax: 01603 615728
e-mail: info@nsad.ac.uk Website: www.nsad.ac.uk

Higher Degrees

MA: *1 yr FT/2 yrs PT* Fine Art

ASTON UNIVERSITY

Aston Triangle, Birmingham B4 7ET Tel: 0121 359 3611 Fax: 0121 333 6350
e-mail: registry@aston.ac.uk Website: www.aston.ac.uk

† Subject to validation.

First Degrees

BEng Hons: *3 yrs FT/4 yrs S* Civil Engineering-Environmental Engineering; Internet Systems *3 yrs-4 yrs (optional yr spent in industry)* Chemical Engineering; Civil Engineering; Communications Engineering; Computer Science-Electronic Engineering; Electrical & Electronic Engineering; ElectroMechanical Engineering; Electronic Engineering with Management Studies; Mechanical Engineering
BSc Combined Hons: *3 yrs FT/4 yrs S* Biology (Language study courses third yr spent abroad); Business Administration; Chemistry; Computer Science; Engineering Management; Engineering Product Design; Environmental Science & Technology; European Studies; French; Geographical Information Systems; German; Health & Safety Management; Human Psychology; Mathematics; Politics; Public Policy & Management; Sociology; Telecommunications
BSc Hons: *3 yrs* Optometry *3 yrs-4 yrs (optional yr spent in industry)* Applied & Human Biology; Applied Chemistry; Chemistry; Computing Science; Engineering Product Design†; Human Psychology; Information Technology for Business; Logistics; Pharmaceutical Sciences; Transport Management *3-4 yrs* Industrial Product Design; Information Mathematics; Product Design-Management; Sustainable Product Design *4 yrs S (3rd yr spend abroad)* European Studies with French or German; French (Option of subsidiary German); French-German or Politics; German (Option of subsidiary French); International Business with French or German; Logistics with French or German; Modern Languages with Translation Studies *4 yrs S (3rd yr spent in industry)* Accounting for Management; Business Computing & IT; Human Resource Management; International Business-Economics; Managerial & Administrative Studies; Marketing

Higher Degrees

DSc: (Apply to Registry for details)
MBA: *1 yr FT* (By taught courses, exam and project)

MPhil: (Awarded after at least one yr FT research)
MSc: *1 yr FT* (By taught courses, exam and project)
PhD: (Awarded after two yrs' minimum research)

DEGREES BY RESEARCH

MSc (by research): Business Management (60 hrs of assessed work in Research Methods); German & Jewish Studies†; Innovation (Coursework plus submission of thesis)

DIPLOMA AND MASTER'S DEGREES BY DISTANCE LEARNING

Diploma/MBA: *2-5 yrs PT*
Diploma/MSc: TESOL/TESP ((Teaching English as a Second Language/Teaching English for Specific Purposes) Diploma: 1-3 yrs. MSc: 1-5 yrs)

MASTER'S DEGREES BY INSTRUCTION

MBA: *1 yr FT/2-5 yrs PT* Business Administration
MChem: *4 yrs FT* Applied Chemistry; Chemical Product Technology
MEng: *4 yrs FT* Computing Science with European Studies; Electronic Systems Engineering; Electronic Systems Engineering with Management Studies *4-5 yrs* Civil Engineering with Environmental Engineering *4-5 yrs S (optional yr spent abroad/industry)* Chemical Engineering with European Studies; Civil Engineering with European Studies; ElectroMechanical Engineering with European Studies†; Mechanical Engineering with European Studies *Optional yr abroad spent in industry* Chemical Engineering; Chemical Engineering & Applied Chemistry; Civil Engineering; ElectroMechanical Engineering; Mechanical Engineering
MPharm: *4 yrs FT* Pharmacy
MSc: *1 yr FT* Business & IT; Business Studies; Comparative European Politics & Cultures; Evidence Based Pharmacotherapy; Financial Management & Control; Information Technology; International Business; Marketing Management; Operational Research & Management Studies; Pattern Analysis Neural Networks; Personnel Management & Business Administration; Public Services Management; TESOL/TESP; Work Psychology & Business *1 yr FT/2-5 yrs PT* Contemporary French Studies; Financial Management & Control; German Cultural Studies; Logistics; Marketing Management; Public Services Management; Risk Management & Safety Technology; Sociolinguistics; Telecommunications Technology; Translation in a European Context† *2-5 yrs PT* Hospital or Community Clinical Pharmacy; Hospital or Community Pharmacy Practice; Occupational Health & Safety; Passenger Transport Management

Honorary Degrees

DSc; MSc

Diplomas

Postgraduate Diploma: *6 mths FT* TESOL/TESP *FT* Business & IT; Business Studies; Financial Management & Control; International Business; Marketing Management; Personnel Management & Business Administration; Telecommunications Technology *FT/PT* Business Administration; Business Administration (Public Service Management); Contemporary French Studies; German Cultural Studies; Marketing Management; Public Service Management; Risk Management & Safety Technology; Sociolinguistics; Translation in a European Context *PT* Health & Safety; Hospital or Community Clinical Pharmacy

Certificates

Certificate: *FT only* Teaching English as a Foreign Language *PT* Evidence Based Pharmacotherapy; Psychiatric Pharmacy

BARNSLEY COLLEGE

Barnsley College, Programme Enquiries, PO Box 266, Church Street, Barnsley S70 2YW
Tel: 01226 216171/216172 Fax: 01226 216166 e-mail: programme.enquiries@barnsley.ac.uk
Website: www.barnsley.ac.uk

* Subject to validation.

First Degrees

BA Combined Hons: *3 yrs FT* Design Pathway; Fine Art Pathway; Graphic Design Pathway; Journalism Pathway; Media Pathway; Performing Arts Pathway; Social Science Pathway; Sport, Recreation & Tourism Pathway

BA Hons: *3 yrs FT* Band Studies; Business & Management Studies; Combined Studies (Humanities) (Two from History, English, Geography and Politics); Creative Music Technology; Health Studies; Popular Music Studies *4 yrs FT* Extended Degree Humanities; Extended Degree Popular Music

BSc Hons: *3 yrs FT* Multi-Media Technologies

Diplomas

DipHE: *2 yrs* Business & Management with Information Technology*; Health Studies; Humanities
HND: Business; Care Practice; Computing; Early Childhood Studies; Electrical/Electronic Engineering; Graphic Design; Hospitality Management; Leisure Management; Leisure Management (Sport & Recreation); Mechanical Engineering; Media Journalism; Multimedia; Performing Arts (Creative Music Technology); Public Services; Travel & Tourism Management

Certificates

Cert HE: Health Care Management

Pre-degree

Foundation yr: *3-4 yrs* For Overseas Students

UNIVERSITY OF BATH

Claverton Down, Bath BA2 7AY Tel: 01225 826826 Fax: 01225 826366 Website: www.bath.ac.uk

First Degrees

BA Hons: *4 yrs FT (includes yr spent abroad)* German & Politics; Modern Languages & European Studies (German and French or Italian or Russian)

BEng: *3 yrs FT/S* Sports Engineering *4 yrs S* Civil Engineering

BEng/MEng Hons: *4-5 yrs S/4 yrs* Electrical & Electronic Engineering (With option 'for the European Market'); Electrical Engineering & Applied Electronics (With option 'for the European Market'); Electronic & Communication Engineering (With option 'for the European Market'); Networks & Information Engineering (With option 'for the European Market')

BSc: *3 yrs FT/S* Sports Technology

BSc Hons: *4 yrs S/4 yrs/*3 yrs FT* Applied Biology; Applied Physics; Biochemistry; Biology; Business Administration; Chemistry; Chemistry with Certificate in Education; Chemistry with Management; Chemistry with Study Abroad; Computer Information Systems; Computer Science; Computer Software Theory; Economics; Economics & Politics; Economics-International Development; General Architectural Studies; International Management & International Management & French or German or Spanish; Mathematical Sciences; Mathematics; Mathematics & Computing; Mathematics & Statistics; Molecular & Cellular Biology; Natural Sciences; Pharmacology; Physics with Computing; Physics; Physics with Communications Technology; Politics with Economics; Psychology; Social Policy & Administration; Social Work & Applied Social Studies; Sociology with Human Resource Management; Sociology; Sport & Exercise Science; Statistics

Higher Degrees

DSc

EdD: Education

MA: Contemporary European Political Culture; Interpreting & Translating

MA (Ed): Educational Management; Educational Technology

MArch: *1 yr FT/3 yrs FT* Architectural Design

MBA: Business Administration

MBioc: *4 yrs FT/S*

MChemistry Hons: *4 yrs FT/S*

MD/MS: (By research and submission of thesis)

MEng: *4 yrs FT* Automotive Engineering (Available with French or German); Biochemical Engineering (Available with a European Language); Chemical Engineering (Available with a European Language); Environmental Chemical Engineering (Available with a European Language); Innovation & Engineering Design (Available with French or German); Management-Manufacturing Systems Engineering (Available with French or German); Mechanical Engineering (Available with French or German) *4 yrs FT/5 yrs S* Aerospace Engineering (Available with French or German) *4 yrs FT/S* Sports Engineering *4 yrs S/5 yrs S* Civil and Architectural Engineering

MMathematics Hons: *4 yrs FT/S*

MPharm: *4 yrs FT/S*

MPhil/PhD: (By research in all schools of the University)

MPhys Hons: *4 yrs FT*

MSc: Aerospace Engineering; Applied Social Psychology; Automotive Engineering; Business & Community; Clinical Pharmacy; Computer Science; Conservation of Historic Buildings; Construction Management (DL); Crop Protection; Development Studies; Dynamics & Control; Electrical Power Systems; Environmental Science, Policy and Planning; European Social Policy Analysis; Facade Engineering; Fiscal Studies; Fluid Power Systems; Geometric Modelling & Design; Health Care Evaluation; Health Psychology; Industrial Systems; Knowledge Transfer; Management; Manufacturing Modelling; Multimedia Technology; Nonlinear Mathematics; Numerical Analysis; Policy & Planning; Purchasing & Supply; Responsibility & Business Practice; Social Research

Honorary Degrees

(Any degree of the University)

Diplomas

Postgraduate Diploma: Development Studies; Environmental Science, Policy & Planning; Fiscal Studies; Language Studies (Interpreting & Translating)

Certificates

Postgraduate Certificate in Education: *1 yr FT* (For prospective secondary school teachers)

BATH SPA UNIVERSITY COLLEGE

Newton Park, Bath, Avon BA2 9BN Tel: 01225 873875 Fax: 01225 875444
Website: www.bathspa.ac.uk

First Degrees

BA Hons: *3 yrs FT* Ceramics; Creative Arts; Creative Music Technology; English; Fine Art; Graphic Design; History; Modern English Studies; Music; Study of Religions; Three-dimensional Design

BA/BSc Hons (modular): *3 yrs FT* Education *3 yrs FT. Major/Minor/Joint combinations of* Creative Studies in English; Cultural Studies; Dance; Design & Technology; English Studies; Environmental Biology; Geography; Health Studies; History; International Education; Irish Studies; Media Communication; Music; Psychology; Remote Sensing & Geographic Information Systems; Sociology; Study of Religions

BSc Hons: *3 yrs FT* Business Studies; Environment, Science & Culture; Environmental Biology; Environmental Science; Food Management; Food Nutrition & Consumer Protection; Geography; Global Futures; Remote Sensing & Geographic Information Systems; Social Sciences; Sociology; Tourism Management

Higher Degrees

DOCTORATES
MPhil/PhD: (By research in a range of disciplines)

MASTER'S DEGREES OR EQUIVALENT
MA: *FT/PT* Contemporary Music & Culture; Contemporary Religions; Creative Writing; Irish Studies; Visual Culture; Visual Culture (Fine Art) *PT* Interactive Multimedia; Literary & Historical Studies; Local & Regional History; Music; Professional Studies (Education)
MEd: *PT*
MSc: *FT/PT* Health Promotion; Healthcare Management; Healthcare Practice; Healthcare Promotion

Diplomas

DipHE: *Modular programme combinations of* Art; Business Studies; Creative Studies in English; Cultural Studies; Dance; Design & Technology; Education; English Studies; Environmental Biology; Geography; Global Futures; Health Studies; History; Information Technology; International Education; Irish Studies; Media Communication; Music; Psychology; Remote Sensing & Digital Terrain Modelling; Sociology; Study of Religions; Textile Design Studies
PGDip: *FT/PT* Contemporary Music & Culture; Contemporary Religions; Creative Writing; Health Promotion; Healthcare Management; Healthcare Promotion; Irish Studies; Professional Studies (Education); Visual Culture; Visual Culture (Fine Art) *PT* Local & Regional History

Certificates

Certificate: *PT* Advanced Professional Study in Education (CAPSE); Further & Adult Education
PGCert: *4 mths FT/24 mths PT* Primary (English Specialism) *FT* Middle Years (Design & Technology); Middle Years (Information & Communications Technology); Middle Years (Music); Middle Years (Science); Primary (Early Years); Primary (Information and Communications Technology); Primary (Maths Specialism); Primary (Science Specialism); Primary Years (Later Years); Secondary (Art); Secondary (Design & Technology); Secondary (English); Secondary (Geography & IT); Secondary (History); Secondary (Information Technology); Secondary (Information and Communications Technology); Secondary (Music); Secondary (Religious Education); Secondary (Science)

THE QUEEN'S UNIVERSITY OF BELFAST

Belfast BT7 1NN Tel: 028 90245133

BA Hons: Most students are admitted to Level 1 of an 18 module programme. Progress towards the degree is measured by modules completed rather than by number of yrs of study. A full-time student will normally complete a BA degree in six semesters, three yrs. A part-time student may take as long as is required to accumulate 18 modules, and students may move between full-time and part-time modes of study from one semester to the next. Full-time students progress at the rate of three modules per semester with module assessment completed by the end of each semester. Students normally take six modules at Level 1, across a minimum of three and a maximum of six subjects. Twelve of the 18 modules must be above Level 1 and six of these must be at Level 3. Students taking up Byzantine Studies, Celtic, Greek and Latin *ab initio* may be required to intercalate a yr for intensive language study on completion of requisite Level 1 modules.

First Degrees

BA Hons: *3 yrs* American Studies; Ancient History with Archaeology or Business Economics or Byzantine Studies or Celtic or Classical Studies or Cultural & Media Studies or Development Studies or Drama or Economic & Social History or English or European Area Studies or European Literature in Translation or French or Geography or Modern History or Music or Philosophy or Policy Studies or Politics or Scholastic Philosophy or Social Anthropology or Sociology or Spanish or Women's Studies; Ancient History; Ancient History-Archaeology or Byzantine Studies or Celtic or English or Greek or History & Philosophy of Science or Modern History or Social Anthropology; Archaeology with Ancient History or Business Economics or Byzantine Studies or Celtic or Classical Studies or Cultural & Media Studies or Development Studies or Drama or Economic & Social History or English or European Area Studies or European Literature in Translation or French or Geography or Modern History or Music or Philosophy or Politics or Scholastic Philosophy or Social Anthropology or Sociology or Spanish or Women's Studies; Archaeology; Byzantine Studies with Ancient History or Spanish or Women's Studies or Business Economics or Celtic or Classical Studies or Cultural & Media Studies or Development Studies or Drama or Economic & Social History or English or European Area Studies or European Literature in Translation or French or Geography or Modern History or Music or Philosophy or Policy Studies or Politics or Scholastic Philosophy or Social Anthropology or Sociology; Byzantine Studies; Celtic; Celtic with Ancient History or Archaeology or Business Economics or Byzantine Studies or Classical Studies or Cultural & Media Studies or Development Studies or Drama or Economic & Social History or European Area Studies or European Literature in Translation or French or Geography or Modern History or Music or Philosophy or Policy Studies or Politics or Scholastic Philosophy or Sociology or Spanish or Women's Studies; Classical Studies with Ancient History or Archaeology or Business Economics or Byzantine Studies or Celtic or Cultural & Media Studies or Development Studies or Drama or Economic & Social History or English or European Area Studies or European Literature in Translation or French or Geography or Modern History or Music or Philosophy or Policy Studies or Politics or Scholastic Philosophy or Social Anthropology or Sociology or Spanish or Women's Studies; Classical Studies; Classics; Drama (Major or Joint Honours); Economic & Social History with Ancient History or Archaeology or Business Economics or Byzantine Studies or Celtic or Classical Studies or Cultural & Media Studies or Development Studies or Drama or English or European Area Studies or European Literature in Translation or French or Geography or Modern History or Music or Philosophy or Policy Studies or Politics or Scholastic Philosophy or Social Anthropology or Sociology or Spanish or Women's Studies; Economic & Social History; Economics-European Area Studies or Politics; English with Ancient History or Archaeology or Business Economics or Byzantine Studies or Celtic or Classical Studies or Cultural & Media Studies or Development Studies or Drama or Economic & Social History or European Area Studies or European Literature in Translation or French or Geography or Modern History or Music or Philosophy or Policy Studies or Politics or Scholastic Philosophy or Social Anthropology or Sociology or Spanish or Women's Studies; English; English-History & Philosophy of Science or Scholastic Philosophy or Theology; Ethnomusicology; Ethnomusicology with Ancient History or Archaeology or Business Economics or Byzantine Studies or Celtic or Classical Studies or Cultural & Media Studies or Development Studies or Drama or Economic & Social History or English or European Area Studies or European Literature in Translation or French or Geography or Modern History or Music or Philosophy or Policy Studies or Politics or Scholastic Philosophy or Social Anthropology or Sociology or Spanish or Women's Studies; Ethnomusicology-Music or Politics or Social Anthropology; European Area Studies; European Area Studies with Ancient History or Archaeology or Business Economics or Byzantine Studies or Celtic or Classical Studies or Cultural & Media Studies or Development Studies or Drama or Economic & Social History or English or European Literature in Translation or French or Geography or Modern History or Music or Philosophy or Politics or Policy Studies or Scholastic Philosophy or Social Anthropology or Sociology or Spanish or Women's Studies; Film Studies (Joint Honours); French with Ancient History or Archaeology or Business Economics or Byzantine Studies or Celtic or Classical Studies or Cultural & Media Studies or Development Studies or Drama or Economic & Social History or English or European Area Studies or English Literature in Translation or Geography or Modern History or Politics or Music or Philosophy or Policy Studies or Scholastic Philosophy or Social Anthropology or Sociology or Spanish or Women's

Studies; Geography or Drama or Scholastic Philosophy; Geography with Ancient History or Archaeology or Business Economics or Byzantine Studies or Celtic or Classical Studies or Cultural & Media Studies or Development Studies or Economic & Social History or English or European Area Studies or European Literature in Translation or French or Modern History or Music or Philosophy or Policy Studies or Politics or Social Anthropology or Sociology or Spanish or Women's Studies; Geography-Social Anthropology; German with Ancient History or Archaeology or Business Economics or Byzantine Studies or Celtic or Classical Studies or Cultural & Media Studies or Development Studies or Drama or Economic & Social History or English or European Area Studies or European Literature in Translation or French or Geography or Modern History or Music or Philosophy or Policy Studies or Politics or Scholastic Philosophy or Social Anthropology or Sociology or Spanish or Women's Studies; Human Geography with Ancient History or Archaeology or Business Economics or Byzantine Studies or Celtic or Classical Studies or Cultural & Media Studies or Development Studies or Drama or Economic & Social History or English or European Area Studies or European Literature in Translation or French or Geography or Modern History or Music or Philosophy or Policy Studies or Politics or Scholastic Philosophy or Social Anthropology or Sociology or Spanish or Women's Studies; Human Geography or English or European Area Studies or European Literature in Translation or French or Geography or Music or Philosophy or Policy Studies or Politics or Scholastic Philosophy or Social Anthropology or Sociology or Spanish or Women's Studies; Modern History with Ancient History or Archaeology or Business Economics or Byzantine Studies or Celtic or Classical Studies or Cultural & Media Studies or Development Studies or Drama or Economic & Social History; Modern History; Music with Ancient History or Archaeology or Business Economics or Byzantine Studies or Celtic or Classical Studies or Cultural & Media Studies or Development Studies or Drama or Economic & Social History or English or European Area Studies or European Literature in Translation or French or Geography or Modern History or Philosophy or Policy Studies or Politics or Scholastic Philosophy or Social Anthropology or Sociology or Spanish or Women's Studies; Music; Music Technology; Philosophy with Ancient History or Archaeology or Business Economics or Byzantine Studies or Celtic or Classical Studies or Cultural & Media Studies or Development Studies or Drama or Economic & Social History or English or European Area Studies or European Literature in Translation or French or Geography or Modern History or Music or Policy Studies or Politics or Scholastic Philosophy or Social Anthropology or Sociology or Spanish or Women's Studies; Philosophy; Policy Studies; Politics or Drama; Politics with Ancient History or Archaeology or Business Economics or Byzantine Studies or Celtic or Classical Studies or Cultural & Media Studies or Development Studies or Economic & Social History or English or European Area Studies or European Literature in Translation or French or Geography or Modern History or Music or Philosophy or Policy Studies or Social Anthropology or Scholastic Philosophy or Sociology or Spanish or Women's Studies; Scholastic Philosophy with Ancient History or Archaeology or Business Economics or Byzantine Studies or Celtic or Classical Studies or Cultural & Media Studies or Development Studies or Drama or Economic & Social History or English or European Area Studies or European Literature in Translation or French or Geography or Modern History or Music or Philosophy or Policy Studies or Politics or Social Anthropology or Sociology or Spanish or Women's Studies; Scholastic Philosophy; Social Anthropology with Ancient History or Archaeology or Business Economics or Byzantine Studies or Celtic or Classical Studies or Cultural & Media Studies or Development Studies or Drama or Economic & Social History or English or European Area Studies or European Literature in Translation or French or Geography or Modern History or Music or Philosophy or Policy Studies or Politics or Scholastic Philosophy or Sociology or Spanish or Women's Studies; Social Anthropology; Sociology; Sociology-Byzantine Studies or Economic & Social History or English or Greek or History & Philosophy of Science or Human Geography or Latin or Modern History or Philosophy or Politics or Psychology or Scholastic Philosophy or Social Anthropology or Social Policy or Women's Studies; Spanish with Ancient History or Archaeology or Business Economics or Byzantine Studies or Celtic or Classical Studies or Cultural & Media Studies or Development Studies or Drama or Economic & Social History or English or European Area Studies or European Literature in Translation or French or Geography or Modern History or Music or Philosophy or Policy Studies or Politics or Scholastic Philosophy or Social Anthropology or Sociology or Women's Studies; Theology-English or History & Philosophy of Science or Scholastic Philosophy or European Area Studies; Women's Studies with Ancient History or Archaeology or Business Economics or Byzantine Studies or

Celtic or Classical Studies or Cultural & Media Studies or Development Studies or Drama or Economic & Social History or English or European Literature in Translation or French or Geography or Modern History or Music or Philosophy or Policy Studies or Politics or Sociology or Spanish; Women's Studies; Women's Studies-Economic & Social History or English or Politics or Social Anthropology or Social Policy or Sociology *3-4 yrs* Ancient History-Archaeology or Byzantine Studies or Celtic or Classical Studies or Economic & Social History or English or Greek or History & Philosophy of Science or Latin or Modern History or Philosophy or Politics or Scholastic Philosophy or Social Anthropology or Spanish; Byzantine Studies-Ancient History or Archaeology or Celtic or Economic & Social History or English or History & Philosophy of Science or Latin or Philosophy or Politics or Psychology or Scholastic Philosophy or Social Anthropology or Social Policy or Sociology or Spanish; Celtic-Ancient History or Archaeology or Byzantine Studies or Classical Studies or English or French or German or Greek or Latin or Music or Philosophy or Politics or Scholastic Philosophy or Social Anthropology or Spanish; Classical Studies-Ancient History or Celtic or English or German or History & Philosophy of Science or Philosophy or Politics or Scholastic Philosophy or Social Anthropology; Economic & Social History-Ancient History or Byzantine Studies or Economics or Greek or History & Philosophy of Science or Human Geography or Latin or Modern History or Philosophy or Politics or Psychology or Scholastic Philosophy or Social Anthropology or Social Policy or Sociology or Spanish or Women's Studies; Economics-Economic & Social History or English or European Area Studies or French or German or Modern History or Politics or Scholastic Philosophy; English-Ancient History or Archaeology or Byzantine Studies or Celtic or Classical Studies or Economics or French or German or Greek or Latin or Modern History or Music or Philosophy or Politics or Psychology or Scholastic Philosophy or Social Anthropology or Social Policy or Sociology or Spanish or Theology or Women's Studies; Greek-Ancient History or Archaeology or Celtic or Economic & Social History or English or French or German or History & Philosophy of Science or Philosophy or Politics or Psychology or Scholastic Philosophy or Social Anthropology or Social Policy or Sociology or Spanish; History & Philosophy of Science-Ancient History or Archaeology or Byzantine Studies or Classical Studies or Economic & Social History or Greek or Latin or Philosophy or Politics or Psychology or Scholastic Philosophy or Social Anthropology or Social Policy or Sociology or Theology; Human Geography-Economic & Social History or Politics or Social Policy or Sociology; Latin-Ancient History or Byzantine Studies or Celtic or Economic & Social History or English or French or German or History & Philosophy of Science or Philosophy or Politics or Psychology or Scholastic Philosophy or Social Anthropology or Social Policy or Sociology or Spanish; Modern History-Ancient History or Archaeology or Economic & Social History or Economics or English or French or Politics or Social Anthropology or Social Policy or Sociology; Music-Celtic or Computer Science or English or Ethnomusicology or French or German or Philosophy or Politics or Psychology or Scholastic Philosophy or Social Anthropology or Spanish; Philosophy-Ancient History or Byzantine Studies or Celtic or Classical Studies or Computer Science or Economic & Social History or English or French or German or Greek or History & Philosophy of Science or Latin or Music or Politics or Psychology or Scholastic Philosophy or Social Anthropology or Social Policy or Sociology or Spanish or Sociology; Politics-Ancient History or Byzantine Studies or Celtic or Classical Studies or Economic & Social History or Economics or English or Ethnomusicology or European Area Studies or French or German or Greek or History & Philosophy of Science or Human Geography or Latin or Modern History or Music or Philosophy or Psychology or Scholastic Philosophy or Social Anthropology or Social Policy or Spanish or Women's Studies; Psychology-Byzantine Studies or Economic & Social History or English or Greek or History & Philosophy of Science or Latin or Music or Philosophy or Politics or Scholastic Philosophy or Social Anthropology or Social Policy or Sociology or Spanish; Scholastic Philosophy-Ancient History or Byzantine Studies or Celtic or Classical Studies or Economic & Social History or Economics or English or French or German or Greek or History & Philosophy of Science or Latin or Music or Philosophy or Politics or Psychology or Social Anthropology or Social Policy or Theology; Social Anthropology-Ancient History or Archaeology or Byzantine Studies or Celtic or Classical Studies or Economic & Social History or English or Ethnomusicology or French or Geography or German or Greek or History & Philosophy of Science or Latin or Modern History or Music or Philosophy or Politics or Psychology or Scholastic Philosophy or Social Philosophy or Social Policy or Spanish or Sociology or Women's Studies; Social Policy-Byzantine Studies or Economic & Social History or English or Greek or History &

Philosophy of Science or Human Geography or Latin or Modern History or Philosophy or Politics or Psychology or Scholastic Philosophy or Social Anthropology or Sociology or Women's Studies *4 yrs* European Studies; French; French-Celtic or Economics or English or German or Greek or Latin or Modern History or Music or Philosophy or Politics or Scholastic Philosophy or Social Anthropology or Spanish; German; German-Celtic or Classical Studies or Economics or English or French or Greek or Latin or Music or Philosophy or Politics or Scholastic Philosophy or Social Anthropology or Spanish; Spanish; Spanish-Ancient History or Byzantine Studies or Celtic or Economic & Social History or English or French or German or Greek or Latin or Music or Philosophy or Politics or Scholastic Philosophy or Social Anthropology

BAgr Pass/Hons: *3 yrs* Agricultural Science *4 yrs* Agriculture
BD Hons: *3 yrs FT* Divinity
BDS: Dentistry
BEng Hons: *3 yrs* Aeronautical Engineering; Architectural Engineering; Chemical with Food Engineering; Chemical Engineering; Civil Engineering; Electrical & Electronic Engineering; Manufacturing Engineering; Mechanical Engineering with Food Engineering; Mechanical Engineering *4 yrs S* Computer Science; Electronic & Software Engineering
BSc: Business Information Technology
BSc Hons: *3 yrs* Accounting; Agricultural Economics-Management; Anatomy; Animal Science; Applied Mathematics-Physics; Archaeology & Palaeoecology; Archaeology – Palaeoecology & Geography; Architecture; Biochemistry; Biological Sciences; Biomedical Science; Business & Information Systems Technology; Chemistry; Chemistry with Extended Studies in Europe; Chemistry-Computer Science or Mathematics or Physics or Statistics or Operational Research; Computational Mathematics; Economics; Environmental Biology; Environmental Planning; Food Science; Food Technology; Genetics; Geography with Extended Studies in Europe or Studies in Europe; Geography & Geology; Geology; Management with Business Economics or Economics or French or Spanish; Management; Management & Information Systems; Marine Biology; Mathematics with Extended Studies in Europe; Mathematics (Applied); Mathematics (Pure); Microbiology; Molecular Biology; Physics; Physics with Astrophysics; Physiology; Plant Science; Psychology; Theoretical Physics; Zoology *4 yrs* Accounting with French or German or Spanish; Economics with French or German *4 yrs S* Agricultural Technology; Finance; Finance with French or German or Spanish
BSc/BEng Hons: *4 yrs S* Computer Science
BTh: *3 yrs FT* Theology
LLB Hons: *3 yrs* Law with Politics; Law *4 yrs* Common & Civil Law with French or Italian or Spanish *4 yrs S* Accounting & Law

Higher Degrees

BArch/MArch/MSc: Architecture
Dip/MSc: Clinical Pharmacy; Community Pharmacy; Computational Science; Computer Science & Applications; Engineering Computation; Environmental Engineering; Finance; Food Safety Management; Medieval Archaeology of the British Isles; Opto-Electronics & Optical Information Processing; Polymer Engineering; Rural Development; Town & Country Planning
LLM: Computers & Law; Human Rights Law
MA: Celtic; Comparative Ethnic Conflict; English Language Teaching; European Literature & Culture; German Studies; Germany in Europe; Hispanic Studies; Irish History; Irish Migration Studies; Irish Politics; Irish Writing; Medieval Studies; Modern Literary Studies; Music; Performance Studies; Political Theory & Social Criticism; Psychoanalytic Studies; Renaissance Music; Renaissance Studies; Twentieth Century Music
MA/Dip: Ancient History; Archaeology; Byzantine Studies; Classics; English Language Study; Ethnomusicology; French; Health Care Ethics & Law; Irish Studies; Music Technology; Philosophy; Scholastic Philosophy; Social Anthropology
MB: Medicine
MBA: Business Administration
MEd/MScEd/EdD/PGCE: Education
MEng: *4 yrs* Aeronautical Engineering; Chemical with Food Engineering; Chemical Engineering; Civil Engineering; Electrical & Electronic Engineering; Environmental & Civil Engineering; Mechanical & Manufacturing Engineering *4 yrs FT/5 yrs S* Computer Science

MMedSc: Education for the Health Care Professions; Laboratory Science
MPharm: *4 yrs* Pharmacy
MSc: Advanced Social Work; Developmental & Educational Psychology; Electronics; Environmental Chemistry; European Management & Policy; Manufacturing Systems Engineering; Materials Science; Midwifery; Nursing; Occupational Psychology; Psychotherapy (Psychoanalytic); Science Communication; Telecommunications
MSc (Ed): Computer Based Learning
MSc/Dip/Cert: Agriculture & Food Science
MSc/Diploma: Applied Environmental Sciences
MSci: *4 yrs* Applied Mathematics & Physics; Applied Physics; Chemistry; Mathematics; Physics with Materials Science or Astrophysics; Physics; Theoretical Physics*5 yrs* Physics with Extended Studies in Europe
MSSc: European Integration; Lifelong Learning; Organisation & Management
MSSc/Dip: Criminal Justice Management; Criminology & Criminal Justice
MSSc/LLM: Human Rights & Criminal Justice
MSW: Social Work
MTh: Theology
PhD: Clinical Psychology

Diplomas

Diploma: Applied Psychotherapy; Applied Social Learning Theory in Child Care; Education (Diploma in Advanced Study); Information Engineering; Laws; Mental Health

Certificates

Certificate: Childcare; Criminal Justice; Education (Certificate in Professional Development); Professional Legal Studies; Psychotherapeutic Studies; Veterinary Pharmacy

UNIVERSITY OF BIRMINGHAM

Edgbaston, Birmingham B15 2TT Tel: 0121 414 3344 Fax: 0121 414 7926
e-mail: admissions@bham.ac.uk Website: www.bham.ac.uk

First Degrees

ARTS & SOCIAL SCIENCES
BA Joint Hons: *3-4 yrs FT* African Studies; American & Canadian Studies; Archaeology & Ancient History; Artificial Intelligence; Business Studies; Classical Literature & Civilisation; Computer Studies; Dance; Drama; East Mediterranean History; Economic & Social History; English; French Studies; Geography; German Studies; Hispanic Studies; History; History of Art; Italian Studies; Latin; Mathematics; Media, Culture & Society; Modern Greek; Music; Philosophy; Political Science (If combined with a language (French, German, Modern Greek, Hispanic Studies or Italian), BA in European Studies is awarded); Portuguese; Russian; Social Policy; Theology *5-9 yrs PT* Integrated Studies
BA Single Hons: *3 yrs FT* African Studies with Anthropology; African Studies; Ancient History; Archaeology; Archaeology & Ancient History; Classical Literature & Civilisation; Classics; Classics & Classical Archaeology; Dance & Theatre Arts; Drama & Theatre Arts; East Mediterranean History; Economic & Social History; English; Geography; History & Social Science; History, Ancient & Medieval; History, Medieval & Modern; International Studies with Economics; International Studies with Russian or Modern Greek; International Studies with Political Science; Media, Culture & Society; Medieval Studies; Music; Philosophy; Political Science; Social Policy; Sociology; Theology *4 yrs* International Studies with French or German or Spanish *4 yrs FT* American and Canadian Studies; French Studies; German Studies; Hispanic Studies; Italian Studies; Modern Greek Studies; Russian
BA/BSc: *3 yrs Joint Honours:* Economic & Social History; Economics; Geography; Philosophy; Planning; Political Science; Social Policy; Sociology; Urban and Regional Planning
BCom Hons: *3 yrs* Commerce (Business Administration)

BCom Hons with Language: *4 yrs* Commerce with French or German or Italian or Spanish or Japanese or Portuguese
BMus Hons: *3 yrs* Music
BSc: *4 yrs* Economics with French or German or Italian or Portuguese or Spanish or Japanese
BSc Hons: *3 yrs* Accounting-Finance; Economics; Economics-Modern Economic History; Mathematical Economics and Statistics; Money, Banking & Finance; Public & Social Policy Management; Public Policy, Government & Management *4 yrs* German; Accounting & Finance with French
BSc Single Hons: *4 yrs* Money, Banking & Finance with French or German or Italian or Spanish or Portuguese
LLB Hons: *3 yrs* Law; Law & Business Studies *4 yrs* Law with French or German

MEDICINE & DENTISTRY
BDS: *5 yrs* Dental Surgery
BMedSci: *3 yrs* Biochemical Studies; Biomedical Materials Science; Cell & Molecular Biology; Cell & Molecular Pathology; Neuroscience; Pharmacology; Physiology
BNurs: *4 yrs* Nursing
BSc: *3 yrs* Physiotherapy
MBChB: *5 yrs* Medicine

SCIENCE & TECHNOLOGY
BEng & BCom Double Hons: *4 yrs* Business Management-Engineering; Mechanical Engineering-Business Management
BEng/MEng Hons: *3-4 yrs* Biomedical Engineering; Mechanical Engineering-Business Studies with Foundation Yr; Chemical Engineering with Biochemical Engineering or Environmental Management or Management or Minerals Engineering or Foundation Yr; Chemical Engineering; Chemical Engineering (International Study); Civil Engineering; Civil Engineering with Computational Mechanics or Environmental Management or Management or Foundation Yr; Communication Systems Engineering with Management; Communication Systems Engineering; Computer & Communication Systems Engineering with Management; Computer & Communication Systems Engineering; Computer Science/Software Engineering; Computer Systems Engineering with Management; Computer Systems Engineering; Electronic & Electrical Engineering with Foundation Yr or Management; Electronic & Electrical Engineering; Electronic & Software Engineering; Electronic Engineering; Engineering with Foundation Yr; Interactive Systems with Management; Interactive Systems; Manufacturing Engineering with Foundation Yr; Manufacturing Engineering; Manufacturing Engineering-Business Studies with Foundation Yr; Material Science-Sports; Materials Science & Technology/Materials Engineering/Metallurgy; Mechanical & Materials Engineering; Mechanical Engineering with Foundation Yr; Mechanical Engineering; Metallurgy/Materials Engineering (Or Metallurgy/Materials with Foundation Yr)
BPhil: *3-4 yrs PT* Continuation Studies
BSc: *3 yrs* Natural Science *4 yrs* Natural Sciences (With 1 yr in Continental Europe)
BSc Joint Hons: *3 yrs* Artificial Intelligence & Computer Science; Geology with Biology; Geology & Geography; Geology-Archaeology; Mathematics-Artificial Intelligence or Computer Science or Psychology *4 yrs* Artificial Intelligence (With study in Continental Europe)-Computer Science (With study in Continental Europe)
BSc Single Hons: *3 yrs* Biochemistry with Biotechnology or Molecular Cell Biology; Biochemistry; Bioinformatics; Biological Sciences (Animal Biology, Biotechnology, Environmental Biology, Genetics, Microbiology, Plant Biology); Computer Science; Computer Science with Business Studies; Environmental Management; Environmental Science; Geography; Medical Biochemistry; Physics; Psychology; Sport & Exercise Science *4 yrs* Biological Sciences with Study in Continental Europe; Computer Science with Study in Continental Europe; Computer Science with Business Studies and study in Continental Europe
BSc/MSci: *3-4 yrs* Chemistry; Chemistry with Bio-Organic Chemistry or Environmental Chemistry or Analytical Science or Business Studies or French or Study in Continental Europe; Environmental Geoscience; Geology; Mathematical Sciences; Mathematics with Study in Continental Europe; Physics with Study in Continental Europe; Physics; Physics-Astrophysics or Electronics or Theoretical Physics or Geophysics or Materials Science or Study in Europe or Space

Research with Study in Continental Europe; Physics; Astrophysics with Biomedical Physics or Electronics or Theoretical Physics or Business Studies; Resource & Applied Geology; Theoretical Physics & Applied Mathematics; Theoretical Physics-Applied Mathematics

Higher Degrees

BD: *2 yrs* Divinity

BPhil: Counselling *1 yr FT/2-4 yrs PT* (By coursework and dissertation. For suitably qualified teachers and others in related professions) *DL* (By coursework and dissertation. For suitably qualified teachers and others in related professions)

EMBA: *1-2 yrs* Business Administration (Jointly with Group de Co, Montpellier, France, and University of Valencia, Spain)

LLM: *1 yr FT* Commercial Law; Comparative, European & Public Law

LLM/MJur: *1 yr FT/6 yrs PT* Law

MA: Russian & East European Studies *1 yr FT* Community Mental Health *1 yr FT/2 yrs PT* Black Theology; English for Special Purposes (ESP); Greek Archaeology; History; History & Communications; Moral Theory; Pastoral Studies; Philosophical Theology; Philosophy; Philosophy of Mind; Playwriting Studies; Religion & Culture; Russian Language & Literature; Shakespeare Studies; Theological Studies; Translation Studies *By a prescribed course of exam and dissertation:* African & Caribbean Literature in English; African Studies; Archaeology; Asian Studies (Contemporary Asia); Asian Studies (Contemporary Japan & Asia); Biblical Studies; Byzantine Studies; Chaucer Studies; Classics; Cultural Studies; Dance Theatre Studies; Egyptology; English Linguistics; English Literature: Meaning & the Production, Transmission & Editing of Texts; English Local History; European Studies – General Pathway; European Studies – Pathways Programme; Practical Archaeology *1 yr FT/2 yrs S* Applied Linguistics; Special Applications of Linguistics; TEFL / TESL; Translation Studies (Linguistics) *2 yrs PT* Counselling *PT* Heritage Management; Social Research

MA/Dip: Applied Linguistics; Applied Social Learning Theory & Counselling; Health & Hospital Management; Health Economics & Health Policy *1 yr* Contemporary Pacific Asia; Democracy & Democratisation; European Integration; European Political Economy; European Studies; Globalisation & Governance; Modern Chinese Politics; Peacekeeping; Political Science; Research Methods *1 yr FT/2 yrs PT* Industrial Archaeology; Industrial Heritage; Islamic Studies

MA/Dip/Cert: Social Policy

MA/Dip/DipSW: Social Work

MBA: *1-2 yrs* Business Administration or Business Administration (Strategic Procurement Management) or Executive Modules; International Banking & Finance; Public Service; Strategic Procurement Management *PT* Executive MBA; Executive MBA (Singapore); International Banking & Finance (Thailand)

MEd: *1 yr FT/2-5 yrs PT* Education

MEng: *3-4 yrs* Mathematical Engineering

MLitt: *2 yrs FT/PT* Ancient History; Ancient Near Eastern Studies; Archaeology; Drama & Theatre Arts; Egyptology; English; Environmental Archaeology; Forensic Archaeology & Heritage Management; French Studies; German Studies; Human Osteology & Palaeopathology; Italian Studies; Music; Philosophy; Russian Language & Literature *4 yrs FT/8 yrs PT* Hispanic Studies

MMus: *1 yr FT/2 yrs PT* Composition

MNatSc: *4 yrs* Chemistry

MPH/DPH: *1 yr FT/2 yrs PT* Public Health

MPhil: Biochemistry; Biological Sciences; Botanic Diversity: Classification, Conservation & Management; Chemistry; Cognitive Science; Computer Science; Earth Sciences; Geography; Mathematics & Statistics; Molecular & Cellular Biology; Physics & Space Research; Physics / Astronomy; Plant Breeding & Crop Improvement; Psychology; Sport & Exercise Science; The Science & Engineering of Materials *1 yr FT* Clinical Immunology; Molecular Immunology; Oncology *1 yr FT/2 yrs PT* African Studies; American Film & Literature; Ancient History & Archaeology; Ancient Near Eastern Studies; Archaeological Practice; Biblical Text Criticism; Byzantine Studies; Byzantine, Ottoman & Modern Greek Studies; Choreography; Classics; Contemporary German Studies; Contextual Theology; Cultural Studies; Drama; Egyptology; English Linguistics; English Literature; French; Geography; German Studies; Greek Archaeology; Hispanic Studies; History; History; History & Communications; History of Art; History, Film &

Television; Holocaust Studies; Islamic Studies; Italian; Medieval History; Modern & Contemporary World History; Modern German Studies; Music; Musical Composition; Ottoman Studies; Ottoman Studies; Philosophy; Russian; Russian & East European Studies; Sport & Exercise Sciences; Theology; US Foreign Policy *4 mths FT/24 mths PT By a prescribed course of exam and dissertation:* Contemporary German Studies

MSc: Accounting & Finance; Advanced Computer Science; Anaesthesia & Intensive Care; Anatomy; Applied Climatology & Meteorology; Applied Genetics; Applied Geophysics; Applied Geophysics; Applied Psychology; Applied Radiation Physics with Medical Physics; Applied Radiation Physics; Biomedical Science & Biomedical Ethics; Business Research; Cancer Studies; Cardiovascular Medicine; Clinical Chemistry; Clinical Neuroscience; Clinical Oncology; Clinical Psychology; Cognitive Science; Conservation & Utilisation of Plant Genetic Resources; Criminology/Criminological Psychology; Educational Psychology; Environmental Health; Environmental Health Aspects of Food; Fetal Medicine; General Practice; General Practice; Geriatric Medicine; Haematology; Health Care Ethics; Hydrogeology; Immunology; Infection; Medical & Radiation Physics; Medicine; Mental Disability Studies; Midwifery; Nursing; Obstetrics & Gynaecology; Occupational Health; Paediatrics & Child Health; Pathology; Pharmacology; Physiology; Physiotherapy; Psychiatry; Public & Environmental Health Sciences; Public Health & Epidemiology; Rheumatology; Science of Occupational Health, Safety & the Environment; Surgery; The Physics & Technology of Nuclear Reactors; Toxicology *1 yr FT* Educational Psychology

MSc (Eng): *1 yr* Advanced Mechanical Engineering; Biochemical Engineering; Communications Engineering; Construction Management; Electronic & Information Technology; Engineering Project Management (Manufacturing); Foundation Engineering; Highway Management & Engineering; Integrated Management Systems; Integrated Manufacturing Systems; Integrated Quality Management; International Highway Engineering; Manufacturing Engineering & Management; Operational Research; Power Electronics & Drives; Water Resources Technology & Management; Water Services Technology; Work Design & Ergonomics

MSc/Dip/Cert: Local Governance *1-2 yrs* Public Service Management

MSc/Diploma: Computer Science; Urbanism; Water Resources Technology; World Space Economy

DOCTORATES

ClinPsyD: *3 yrs FT* Clinical Psychology

DEng; DSc: (In respect of substantial contribution to learning)

DLitt; DD: (In respect of substantial contribution to learning. Confined to Birmingham graduates)

DMus: Music (In respect of substantial contribution to learning. Confined to Birmingham graduates)

LLD: Law (In respect of substantial contribution to learning. Confined to Birmingham graduates)

PhD: *3 yrs FT/6 yrs PT* (For all courses)

HIGHER MEDICAL & DENTAL DEGREES

MD: (By thesis or very exceptionally published work. Award restricted to Birmingham graduates, University staff, University honorary staff)

Honorary Degrees

DLitt; DD; LLD; MD; DDS; DMus; DSc; DEng
MA; MEd; MMus; MEng; MSocSc

Diplomas

Diploma: 20th Century Political Thought & Theory; Advice Work; African Studies; Applied Genetics; Business Administration; Cognitive Science; Communications Engineering; Community Mental Health; Computer Applications in Archaeological Ceramic Analysis; Computer Applications in Landscape Archaeology; Computer Science; Conservation & Utilisation of Plant Genetic Resources; Construction Management; Criminological Psychology; Cultural Studies; Curatorial Archaeology; Development Administration; Development Finance; Economic Development & Policy; Electronics & Information Technology; Engineering Project Management

(Manufacturing); English as A Second/Foreign Language (Also available: TEFL/TESL Distance Learning (Cert/Dip/MA)); Environmental Health; European Studies; European Studies – General Pathway; European Studies – Pathways programme; Health Care Policy & Management; Health Sciences (Scheme A: Multidisciplinary; Scheme B: Nursing); Heritage Management; Highway Management & Engineering; Housing Policy & Practice; Industrial Heritage; Integrated Management Systems; Integrated Manufacturing Systems; Integrated Quality Management; International Social Policy; International Studies; International Studies (Contemporary Pacific Asia); International Studies (Diplomacy); International Studies (European Integration); International Studies (European Political Economy); International Studies (International Economic Management); International Studies (International Political Economy); International Studies (Peacekeeping); International Studies (Security); Legal Studies/CPE; Leisure & Tourism Policy & Practice; Local Government & Development; Managing Quality in Health Care; Manufacturing Engineering & Management; Money & Banking; Operational Research; Pastoral Studies; Philosophical Studies; Physiotherapy; Political Science; Poverty Reduction & Development Management; Power Electronics & Drives; Practical Archaeology; Primary Health Care Policy & Management; Probation Services Management; Psychiatry; Psychology; Public Economic Management; Public Services Management; Rehabilitation Studies; Research & Social Policy; Rural Development; Shakespeare Studies; Social Learning Theory & Practice; Social Policy; Social Research; Social Research & Reflective Professional Practice; Social Sciences; Social Services Management; Social Work & DipSW; Social Work Studies; Special Applications of Linguistics; Tourism Policy & Management; Toxicological Studies; Urban & Regional Studies; Urbanism; Working with Offenders; World Space Economy *1 yr PT* Public Health

Certificates

Certificate: Field Archaeology; Practical Theology; Rehabilitation Studies; Skills Training for Working with Substance Misusers

Degrees validated by University of Birmingham offered at:

Birmingham College of Food, Tourism and Creative Studies

Summer Row, Birmingham B3 1JB Tel: 0121 604 1040 Fax: 0121 200 1376
e-mail: l.ingold@bcftcs.ac.uk Website: www.bcftcs.ac.uk

First Degrees

BA/BA Hons: *3-4 yrs FT/S* Adventure Tourism; Food & Retail Management; Hospitality & Food Management; Hospitality & Leisure Management; Hospitality & Tourism Management; Hospitality Business Management; Leisure Management; Licensed Retail Management; Professional Studies in Child Care; Tourism Business Management
BSc Hons: *3 yrs FT* Tourism Management
BSc/BSc Hons: *3 yrs FT* Food & Consumer Management

Higher Degrees

MA: *1-2 yrs* Adventure Tourism Management; Hospitality Management; Tourism Business Administration
MSc: *1-2 yrs* Hospitality Management

Diplomas

BTEC HND: *2 yrs FT/3 yrs S* Adventure Tourism Management; Business; Business & Marketing; Business & Personnel; Business (Salon Management); Early Childhood Studies; Food & Consumer Management (Home Economics); Food & Retail Management; Hospitality (Subject to validation) with Modern Languages (Subject to validation); Hospitality & Food Management; Hospitality & Leisure Management; Hospitality & Tourism Management; Hospitality Business Management; Leisure & Recreation Management; Licensed Retail Management; Professional Culinary Arts; Tourism with Modern Languages; Tourism Business Management

Postgraduate Diplomas

PGDip: *1 yr FT/2 yrs PT* Adventure Tourism Management; Hospitality Management; Tourism Business Administration

The University of Birmingham, Westhill

Weoley Park Road, Selly Oak, Birmingham B29 6LL Tel: 0121 472 7245 Fax: 0121 415 5399 e-mail: m.miles@westhill.ac.uk Website: www.westhill.ac.uk

First Degrees

BA (QTS): *4 yrs FT* Islamic Studies; Mathematics
BA Hons: *3 yrs FT* Applied Islamic Studies; Applied Theological Studies; Applied Theological Studies (Mission) *PT* Combined Studies
BA Hons Humanities: *3 yrs FT* Humanities (Modular interdisciplinary degree – contact Westhill for details of options)
BA/BSc: *4-6 yrs PT* Combined Studies
BPhil: *2 yrs PT* Counselling; Inter-Professional Health & Community Studies *3 yrs FT* Community, Youth & Play Studies

Higher Degrees

MA: *1 yr FT/2 yrs PT* Applied Theological Studies (Christian or Islamic) *2 yrs min* Modular Interdisciplinary Degree *2 yrs PT* Applied Community Studies; English Studies
MEd: *2 yrs PT* Primary Education

Diplomas

DipHE: *2 yrs FT* Community, Youth & Play Studies
Diploma: *2 yrs PT* Counselling
Diploma/Certificate: *1 yr FT* Church Management; Pastoral Studies; Religious Education (Church Education); Women's Leadership

Certificates

PGCert: *1 yr FT* Early Years; Primary General; Secondary Religious Education

BLACKBURN COLLEGE

Feilden Street, Blackburn, Lancashire BB2 1LH Tel: 01524 55144 Fax: 01524 682700
* Subject to validation (may not run in 2001).

First Degrees

BA: *(HND Top-up):* Business Management
BA Hons: Accounting & Finance (Validated by the University of Glamorgan); English (Language & Literary Studies); Graphic Design *1 yr* Business Administration (HND top-up. Validated by the University of Huddersfield) *2 yrs* Business Studies (HND top-up. Validated by the University of Huddersfield); Leisure Management *3 yrs* Criminology; Leisure Management
BEng: *1 yr* Electronics (HND top-up. Validated by Lancaster University); Engineering (HND top-up. Validated by Lancaster University) *3 yrs* Electronics
BSc: *1 yr* Computing (HND top-up. Validated by Lancaster University) *3 yrs* Computing
LLB Hons: *2 yrs* LLB Top-up (Validated by the University of Glamorgan) *3 yrs* Law: multimode (Validated by the University of Glamorgan)

Diplomas

HC: Social Science
HND: Beauty Therapy; Building Studies; Business; Business with E commerce; Business & Finance; Business & Marketing; Business & Personnel; Care Practice; Computing (with BIT and

Software Engineering Options) (Progression to relevant degree at Lancaster University); Creative Media Production; Criminology; Engineering (Progression to relevant degree at Lancaster University); European Legal Studies; Legal Studies (Validated by the University of Glamorgan); Leisure Studies; Managing Health and Care Services; Popular Music; Public Administration; Sports Studies; Telecommunications (Progression to relevant degree at Lancaster University); Textile Design; Travel & Tourism

BOURNEMOUTH UNIVERSITY

Talbot Campus, Fern Barrow, Poole, Dorset BH12 5BB Tel: 01202 595114 Fax: 01202 595287
e-mail: celder@bournemouth.ac.uk Website: www.bournemouth.ac.uk

First Degrees

BA Hons: *1 yr FT* International Business Administration (Top-Up); International Hospitality & Tourism Management (Top-Up) *2 yrs PT* International Business Administration (Top-Up) *3 yrs FT* Advertising & Marketing Communications; Communication; Computer Visualisation & Animation; Accounting-Finance; Health & Community Development; Accounting-Law; Multi-media Journalism; New Media Production; Scriptwriting for Film & Television; Television Production *4 yrs S* Business Decision Information Systems; Business Information Systems Management; Business Studies with French or Languages or German; Business Studies; Computer Aided Product Design; Financial Services-European Studies; Financial Services; Interior Design; International Culinary Arts Management; International Hospitality Management; International Marketing Management; International Retail Management; Law & Finance; Leisure Marketing; Licensed Retail Management; Product Design; Public Relations; Retail Management; Taxation & Law; Tourism Studies *4-5 yrs PT* Accounting; Business Studies *5-8 yrs PT* Advertising & Marketing Communications; Communication; Health & Community Development; Leisure Marketing; Public Relations; Tourism Studies
BEng: *3 yrs FT* Medical Electronics Design
BEng Hons: *3 yrs FT* Computer Communications; Electronic Systems Design; Applied Computing-Electronics; Medical Electronic Design; Microelectronics & Computing; Multi-media Communications *4 yrs (extended)* Computer Communications; Electronic Systems Design; Applied Computing-Electronics; Medical Electronic Design; Microelectronics & Computing *4 yrs S* Applied Computing-Electronics; Computer Communications; Electronic Systems Design; Medical Electronic Design; Microelectronics & Computing; Multi-media Communications *5 yrs S (extended)* Computer Communications; Electronic Systems Design; Applied Computing-Electronics; Medical Electronic Design; Microelectronics & Computing; Multi-media Communications
BSc Hons: *1 yr FT* Business Information Systems (Top-Up) *1-4 yrs PT* Nursing Studies-Primary Health Care; Specialist Community Practice; Specialist Practice *18 mths* Interprofessional Health & Community Care *2 yrs PT* Computing (Top-Up) *2-4 yrs PT* Midwifery Practice *3 yrs FT* Applied Geography; Applied Psychology & Computing; Archaeology; Clinical Nursing; Environmental Protection; Health Science; Heritage Conservation; Midwifery *4 yrs (extended)* Applied Geography; Archaeology; Business Communication Systems; Environmental Protection; Heritage Conservation *4 yrs PT* Nursing Studies-Primary Health Care *4 yrs S* Business Communication Systems; Business Decision Management; Business Information Systems Management; Business Information Technology; Computer Aided Product Design; Computing; Design Engineering; Food Production, Development & Retailing; Hospitality Business Development; Land-based Enterprise; Landscape & Geographical Sciences; Multi-media Communications; Product Design; Software Engineering Management *5 yrs S (extended)* Applied Psychology-Design; Landscape & Geographical Sciences *5-8 yrs PT* Archaeology; Environmental Protection; Health Science; Heritage Conservation; Landscape & Geographical Sciences; Nursing Practice/ENB
LLB Hons: *4 yrs S* Business Law; Taxation & Law *4-5 yrs PT* Business Law; Taxation & Law

Higher Degrees

LLM: *1 yr FT* Intellectual Property Management; Law; Law & Media Practice; Legal Practice Course *2 yrs PT* Intellectual Property Management; Law; Law & Media Practice

LPC: *1 yr FT* Legal Practice
MA: Health Practice Management; Professional Development (Post-Compulsory Education) *1 yr FT* Computer Animation; Corporate Communication; Digital Entertainment Systems; Digital Special Effects; European Tourism Management; Financial Services; Human Resource Management; Information Systems Management; Intellectual Property Management; International Business Administration; International Business Finance; International Commercial Law; Law; Law & Finance; Law & Media Practice; Marketing Communication; Multi-media Journalism; Music Design for the Moving Image; Radio Production; Sound Design for the Moving Image; Taxation; Tourism & Hospitality Management *15 mths FT* Television & Video Production *18 mths FT* Digital Entertainment Systems; Digital Special Effects *2 yrs PT* Clinical Leadership; Financial Services; Intellectual Property Management; International Business Finance; International Commercial Law; Interprofessional Health & Community Care; Law; Law & Finance; Law & Media Practice; Services Marketing; Taxation *3 yrs PT* Human Resource Management (Professional); Master of Business Administration *5 yrs PT* Design Technology; Interior Design; Sustainable Design
MBA: *3 yrs PT* Business Administration
MEng: Electronic Systems Design; Microelectronics-Computing; Multimedia Communications *4 yrs FT* Design Management; Design Visualisation; Electronic Systems Design; Engineering Business Development; Medical Electronics Design; Microelectronics & Computing; Multimedia Communications
MSc: *1 yr FT* Accounting Management/Affiliate ACCA Membership; Archaeological Resource Management; Archaeological Science (Post-Excavation); Architectural Materials Conservation; Coastal Zone Management; Computer Animation; Corporate Governance/Grad ICSA; Digital Entertainment Systems; Digital Special Effects; Electronic Systems Design; Environmental Quality; Finance; Finance & Law; Forensic Archaeology; International Maritime Management; Microelectronics-Computing; Multimedia Communications; Museums & Collections Management; Osteoarchaeology; Software Engineering; Tourism with Environmental Management; Tourism with Hospitality Education; Tourism Management with Planning; Tourism Management with Marketing; Tourism Management; VLSI Design *1 yr PT* Environmental Quality *1-4 yrs PT* Electronic Systems Design; Microelectronics and Computing; Multimedia Communications; VLSI Design *2 yrs FT* Clinical Nursing *2 yrs PT* Archaeological Materials Conservation; Archaeological Resource Management; Archaeological Science (Post-excavation); Architectural Materials Conservation; Building Conservation; Corporate Governance/Grad ICSA; Forensic Archaeology; Information Systems Management; Museums & Collections Management; Safety Management; Services Marketing; Timber Building Conservation *2-3 yrs PT* Managing Business Information Technology; Tourism & Travel Management *3 yrs PT* Project Management *3-5 yrs PT* Advanced Computing *5 yrs PT* Design Technology; Engineering Project Design; Engineering Project Management; Sustainable Design

DOCTORATES
DBA: Business Administration

Diplomas

Advanced Diploma: Clinical Nursing; Midwifery
CCETSW Diploma: *2 yrs FT* Social Work
Diploma in Higher Education: *18 mths FT* Health & Social Services Management *2 yrs FT* Applied Social Studies
Diploma in Professional Studies: *2-4 yrs PT* Midwifery *5 yrs PT* Clinical Practice
Diploma in Professional Studies in Nursing: *2 yrs FT* Nursing *3 yrs FT* Midwifery with Professional Registration; Nursing with Professional Registration with Child Health or Mental Health or Learning Disabilities *4 yrs PT* Nursing *5 yrs PT* Nursing
HND: *2 yrs FT* Business; Business (Leisure Management); Business Information Technology; Computer Aided Design; Design & Production for Digital Media; Environmental Conservation; Fashion-Textiles; Geography and Coastal Conservation; Land-Based Enterprise; Landscape and Countryside Management; Landscape Conservation; Practical Archaeology; Tourism & Leisure Management; Video Production *3 yrs FT* International Food and Hospitality Management *3 yrs PT* Computer Aided Design; Computing; Engineering (Electronics); Engineering (Mechanical & Production)

Postgraduate Diploma: *1 yr FT* Tourism Management; Tourism Management-Marketing; Tourism Management-Planning; Tourism-Environmental Management; Tourism-Hospitality Education; Tourism-Hospitality Management *1 yr PT* Financial Services; Safety Management *18 mths FT* European Enterprise Management *2 yrs PT* Advanced Technology Management; Archaeological Resource Management; Archaeological Science (Post-excavation); Counselling-Psychotherapy; Electronic Systems Design; Health & Social Services Management; Human Resource Management; International Business Administration; Managing Business Information Technology; Microelectronics-Computing; Multimedia Communications; VLSI Design *28 wks PT* Higher French Studies *3 yrs PT* Advanced Computing; Design Technology; Engineering Product Design; Engineering Project Management; Interior Design; Sustainable Design *7 mths FT* Television & Video Production *9 mths FT* Archaeological Resource Management; Architectural Materials Conservation; Computer Animation; Corporate Communication; Corporate Finance; Corporate Finance & Control; Digital Entertainment Systems; Digital Special Effects; Environmental Quality; European Tourism Management; Financial Services; Forensic Archaeology; Human Resource Management; Information Systems Management; International Business Administration; International Retail Management; Law; Marketing Communication; Music Design for Film and television; Osteoarchaeology; Project Management; Project Management; Software Engineering; Sound Design for Film and Television

Certificates

HNC: *1 yr FT* Computer Aided Design *2 yrs FT* Computing; Design & Production for Digital Media; Design-Ecology & Conservation (Stone & Wood); Heritage Management; Landscape Conservation *2 yrs PT* Business; Computer Aided Design; Computing; Engineering (Electronics); Engineering (Mechanical & Production); Fashion & Textiles; Video Production
Postgraduate Certificate: *1 yr FT* Tourism Management; Tourism Management-Marketing; Tourism Management-Planning; Tourism-Environmental Management; Tourism-Hospitality Education; Tourism-Hospitality Management

Other Courses

Foundation Course: *1 yr FT* Computing & Electronics Foundation (Level 0); Conservation Sciences Foundation (Level 0); Design Engineering Foundation (Level 0)

POSTGRADUATE CERTIFICATES
Postgraduate Certificate: *12 wks PT* Conservation Sciences

Professional Courses

Professional Courses: ACCA; ATII; ATT; CIM

UNIVERSITY OF BRADFORD

Bradford BD7 1DP Tel: 01274 232323 Fax: 01274 305340 e-mail: See end of entry.
Website: www.brad.ac.uk/e-mail: ug-admissions@bradford.ac.uk

or† Subject to validation.

First Degrees

BA Hons: *3 yrs FT* Applied Criminal Justice Studies with Diploma in Social Work; Applied Social Sciences; Applied Social Sciences – Gender Studies & Social Policy; Applied Social Sciences – Social & Welfare Studies; Applied Social Sciences – Social Policy & Administration; Applied Social Sciences – Sociology/Social Psychology; Business Studies & Law; Conflict Resolution; Development & Peace Studies; European Area Studies; European Studies with Management; European Studies & Law; History with French or German or Russian or Spanish; History & Law; History & Philosophy; History (Modern European); Interdisciplinary Human Studies – English; Interdisciplinary Human Studies – Philosophy; Interdisciplinary Human Studies – Psychology; Interdisciplinary Human Studies – Sociology; International Relations & Security Studies; Peace Studies; Peace Studies-Spanish; Politics; Politics with Law; Politics with French or German or

Spanish; Politics & History; Politics & Law *3-5 yrs PT* Social Studies *4 yrs S* Business Studies & Law; European Studies; French; German-French; French-Spanish; German; German-Spanish; International Management with French; Modern Languages; Spanish *5 yrs PT* Local & Regional Studies

BEng Hons: *3 yrs FT* Automotive Electronics; Chemical Engineering; Civil Engineering; Computer-Aided Structural Engineering; Computing & Performance Engineering; Cybernetics with Transportation Systems; Electrical & Electronic Engineering; Electronic, Telecommunications & Computer Engineering; Electronics; Industrial Engineering; Manufacturing Systems with Management or Mechanical Engineering; Materials Technology & Management; Mechanical & Automotive Engineering; Mechanical & Automotive Engineering Systems; Mechanical Engineering; Mechanical Engineering with Management; Mechanical Engineering Systems; Medical Engineering; Medical Systems Engineering; Petroleum Products Engineering; Software Engineering *4 yrs FT/5 yrs S Including integrated Foundation Yr:* Civil Engineering; Cybernetics with Transportation Systems; Electrical & Electronic Engineering; Industrial Engineering; Mechanical Engineering Systems; Medical Systems Engineering; Petroleum Products Engineering *4 yrs S* Automotive Electronics; Chemical Engineering; Civil Engineering; Computer-Aided Structural Engineering; Computing & Performance Engineering; Cybernetics with Transportation Systems; Electrical & Electronic Engineering; Electronic, Telecommunications & Computer Engineering; Electronics; Industrial Engineering; Manufacturing Systems with Management or Mechanical Engineering; Materials Technology & Management; Mechanical & Automotive Engineering Systems; Mechanical & Automotive Engineering; Mechanical Engineering; Mechanical Engineering with Management; Mechanical Engineering Systems; Medical Engineering; Medical Systems Engineering; Petroleum Products Engineering; Software Engineering

BEng/MEng Hons: *4 yrs* Chemical Engineering; Civil Engineering; Computer-Aided Structural Engineering; Electrical & Electronic Engineering; Electronic, Telecommunications & Computer Engineering; Manufacturing Engineering; Manufacturing Systems with Mechanical Engineering or Management; Mechanical & Automotive Engineering; Mechanical Engineering; Mechanical Engineering with Management; Medical Engineering; Petroleum Products Engineering; Software Engineering *5 yrs S* Chemical Engineering; Civil Engineering; Computer-Aided Structural Engineering; Manufacturing Systems with Mechanical Engineering or Management; Mechanical & Automotive Engineering; Mechanical Engineering; Mechanical Engineering with Management; Medical Engineering; Petroleum Products Engineering

BSc Hons: *3 yrs FT* Biomedical Sciences – Cellular Pathology; Biomedical Sciences – Medical Biochemistry; Biomedical Sciences – Medical Microbiology; Biomedical Sciences – Pharmacology; Computer Animation & Special Effects; Diagnostic Radiography; Economics; Economics-History or Politics or Sociology/Social Psychology; Electronic Imaging & Media Communications; Interactive Systems & Video Games Design; Internet Product Design; Media Technology & Production; Midwifery; Nursing (Provisional); Optometry; Pharmaceutical Management; Physiotherapy *3 yrs FT/4 yrs S* Accounting & Finance; Applied Ecology & Conservation; Archaeological Sciences; Archaeology; Bioarchaeology; Business Computing; Business Computing; Business-Management Studies; Chemical Processing; Chemistry with Pharmaceutical & Forensic Science; Chemistry; Civil Engineering; Computer Science; Computing with Mathematics; Computing & Information Systems; Cybernetics & Virtual Worlds; E-commerce Technologies; Environmental Management & Sustainability; Environmental Management & Sustainability; Environmental Management & Technology; Environmental Pollution Management; Environmental Science; Geography & Environmental Science; Health & Safety Management; Integrated Industrial Design; Internet Computing; Internet Computing; Internet Law & Society; Manufacturing Management & Technology; Marketing; Materials, Design & Production; Medical Cybernetics; Medical Electronics; Medical Technololgy in Sport; Multimedia Computing; Personnel in Technology; Physical & Environmental Geography; Technology Management; Virtual Design & Innovation *4 yrs FT Including integrated Foundation Yr:* Electronic Imaging & Media Communications *4 yrs FT/5 yrs S Including integrated Foundation Yr:* Archaeological Sciences (via Science Foundation Yr); Biomedical Sciences (via Science Foundation Yr); Chemical Processing; Chemistry (via Science Foundation Yr); Civil Engineering; Cybernetics; Environmental Science (via Science Foundation Yr)

Higher Degrees

DBA: *4 yrs PT* Business Administration
DPharm: Pharmacy
MA: *1 yr FT* European Languages & Cultural Studies; Finance, Accounting & Management; International Business & Management; International Development Studies; Interpreting & Translating; Interpreting & Translating with International Business; Marketing; Media, Communication & Cultural Studies; Old World Archaeology *1 yr FT/2 yrs PT* Baltic Studies; Community Care; Conflict Resolution; East European Studies; European Integration; European Integration & Law; European/Latin American Relations; Gender & Women's Studies; International Politics & Security Studies; Modern European History; Peace Studies; Social & Welfare Studies; Social Work & Social Care *2 yrs PT* Educational & Vocational Guidance of Adults; European Adult & Continuing Education
MBA: Business Administration
MChem: *4 yrs FT* Chemistry; Chemistry with Pharmaceutical & Forensic Science
MPharm: *4 yrs FT* Pharmacy
MPharm Hons: *5 yrs S* Pharmacy (Leads to simultaneous qualification as a Registered Pharmacist)
MPhil: *1 yr FT/2 yrs PT* (By research in all postgraduate Departments & Schools)
MRes: *2-3 yrs PT* Research Methods (In all postgraduate Departments & Schools); Research Methods (in Graduate School of Social Sciences & Humanities)
MSc: Engineering Quality Improvement; Maintenance & Safety Management (In collaboration with Hogeschool Zeeland, Vlissingen, Netherlands) *1 yr FT* Agricultural Development & Rural Finance; Archaeological Prospection; Business Strategy & Environmental Management; Communications & Real Time Electronic Systems; Development & Project Planning; Engineering Science (Chemical Engineering); Environmental Monitoring & Management; Forensic Anthropology; Human Osteology & Palaeopathology; Human Resource Development & Management; Integrated Quality, Safety & Environmental Management; Local Sustainable Development; Macro-Economic Policy & Planning in Developing Countries; Maintenance & Safety Management; Pharmaceutical Services & Medicines Control; Pollution Monitoring & Control; Project Planning & Management; Project Planning, Appraisal & Financing; Projects & Management Development; Radio Frequency & Microwave Engineering; Radio Frequency Communications Engineering; Real Time Electronic Systems; Real Time Power Electronics & Control Systems; Scientific Methods in Archaeology; Software Engineering; Sustainable Livelihoods for Local Development *1 yr FT/2 yrs PT* Biomedical Sciences; Clinical Pharmacy (Hospital or Community); Ethnicity & Identity; Manufacturing Systems Engineering & Management *1 yr FT/3 yrs PT* Computing; Optometry *18 mths FT* Manufacturing Management; Reliability, Safety & Maintenance Management *3 yrs PT* Advanced Midwifery Practice; Advanced Nursing Practice; Health & Social Services Management; Health Care Practice; Medical Imaging
PhD: *3 yrs FT* Electrical Engineering (Total Technology) *3 yrs FT/5 yrs PT* (By research in all postgraduate Departments and Schools)

Honorary Degrees

DEng; DTech; DSc; DLitt; DUniv
LLD; LLM; MEng; MTech; MSc; MA; MEd; MPharm

Diplomas

Diploma: *9 mths FT* Manufacturing Systems Engineering
Postgraduate Diploma: *16 mths PT* Nuclear Medicine *2 yrs PT* Advanced Midwifery Practice; Advanced Nursing Practice; Educational & Vocational Guidance of Adults; European Adult & Continuing Education; Health & Social Services Management; Health Care Practice; Medical Imaging; Research Methods *9 mths FT* Archaeological Prospection; Biomedical Sciences; Business Strategy & Environmental Management; Communications & Real-Time Electronic Systems; Environmental Monitoring & Management; European Languages & Cultural Studies; Forensic Anthropology; Human Osteology & Palaeopathology; Interpreting & Translating with International Business; Interpreting & Translating; Local Sustainable Development; Media, Communication & Cultural Studies; Old World Archaeology; Pollution Monitoring & Control; Radio Frequency & Microwave Engineering; Radio Frequency Communications Engineering;

Real-time Electronic Systems; Real-time Power Electronics & Control Systems; Scientific Methods in Archaeology *9 mths FT/2 yrs PT* Baltic Studies; Clinical Pharmacy (Hospital or Community); Computing; Conflict Resolution; East European Studies; Ethnicity & Identity; European Integration; European Integration & Law; European/Latin American Relations; Gender & Women's Studies; International Politics & Security Studies; Manufacturing Systems Engineering & Management; Modern European History; Peace Studies

Certificates

PGCE-HE: *PT* Education
Postgraduate Certificate: *1 yr PT* Adult Neurology; Computerised Tomography; Health Care Evaluation; Magnetic Resonance Imaging; Managing Health Services; Multiprofessional Palliative Care; Radiographic Image Interpretation; Respiratory Care; Vascular Imaging & Interventional Radiology *12 wk FT* Human Resource Development & Management; Project Planning, Appraisal & Financing; Projects & Management Development; Sustainable Livelihoods for Local Development

Degrees validated by University of Bradford offered at:

Bradford & Ilkley Community College

Great Horton Road, Bradford, West Yorkshire BD7 1AY Tel: 01274 753189 Fax: 01274 753173
e-mail: schoolsliasison@bilk.ac.uk

† Subject to validation.

First Degrees

BA Hons: *1 yr FT* Communication Design; Communication Design (Level 3 only) *1 yr FT/2-5 yrs PT* Photography (Level 3 only); Social and Community Care (Level 3 only, includes professional qualification) *3 yrs FT* Human Resource Management; Law & European Business; Psychology-Management; Public Sector Management; Women's Studies & Community Studies; Youth & Community Development *3 yrs FT/2-5 yrs PT* Combined Studies (Humanities); Combined Studies (Psychology & Humanities); Combined Studies (Psychology & Sociology); Combined Studies (Psychology & South Asian Studies); Combined Studies (Sociology & Humanities); Combined Studies (Sociology & South Asian Studies); Combined Studies (Sociology); Community Studies; Consumer, Health & Community Studies; Counselling and Psychology in Community Contexts; Design, Crafts & Manufacture; Early Childhood Studies; Education & the Community; European Textile Design; Financial Services; Leisure, Recreation & Community; Management & Organisations; Marketing & Law; Office Systems Management; Organization Studies; Primary Education with QTS; Social & Community Care (Care Management); Social and Community Care (Social Work); South Asian Communities Studies *3 yrs FT/5-8 yrs PT* Applied Social Policy and Community Studies; Art & Design (multidisciplinary choose two from: Electronic Media, Illustration, Painting, Photography, Printmaking, Textiles); Business Administration (Accounting); Business Administration (European Studies); Business Administration (Law); Business Administration (Marketing); Combined Studies; Consumer, Health & Community Studies (Health Studies) *PT* Community Health; Community Health (Level 3 only)
BA Hons with QTS: *3 yrs FT/2-5 yrs PT* Education (Primary, Creative Arts – Art, Music & Drama & Core Subjects); Education (Primary, Humanities – History, Geography & Religious Studies & Core Subjects); Education (Primary, Mathematics); Education (Primary, Science)
BSc Hons: *1 yr* Information Technology Systems (Level 3 only) *3 yrs* Science (Secondary) with Qualified Teacher Status *3 yrs FT* Beauty Therapy with Management; Cosmetic Sciences; Ophthalmic Dispensing with Management
LLB Hons: *3 yrs FT* Law

Higher Degrees

MA: Drawing; Managing Organisational Change *1 yr FT/2 yrs PT* Printmaking; The Politics of Visual Representation *2 yrs PT* Counselling in the Community; Managing Change in Community
MEd: *2-3 yrs PT* Education

Diplomas

DipHE: *2 yrs FT* Social Work *2 yrs FT/3 yrs PT* Care Management; Care Management; Ophthalmic Dispensing with Management; South Asian Communities Studies; Youth & Community Development
Diploma: *1 yr FT* Foundation Studies in Art and Design *1 yr PT* Administrative Management; Management Studies; Marketing
Diploma in Professional Studies: Nursing
HND: *2 yrs FT* Applied Science (Biology, Chemistry, Physics); Beauty Therapy; Beauty Therapy (Media); Building Studies; Business; Business & Finance; Business & Marketing; Business & Personnel; Business Information Technology; Design (Communications); Design (Photography); Hotel, Catering & Institutional Management; Leisure Studies; Public Services; Travel & Tourism Management *2 yrs FT/3 yrs PT* Early Childhood Studies; Electrical/Electronic Engineering; Engineering *2 yrs FT/PT* Metallurgy & Materials (Metals Technology) *PT* Plant Technology & Instrumentaion & Control

Certificates

Advanced Certificate: *1 yr PT* Continuing Education Certificate; Marketing *PT* Business Administration; Computer Studies
Certificate: *PT* Administrative Skills; English (Test for Overseas Students); Management; Marketing; Operational Sales and Marketing; Teaching English as a Second Language to Adults
Certificate of Higher Education: *1 yr FT/PT* Combined Studies; South Asian Communities Studies
HNC: Business, Business and Finance *2 yrs* Building Studies *2 yrs PT* Beauty Therapy; Building Studies (Bridging Course); Business Information Technology; Civil Engineering; Design; Early Childhood Studies; Electrical and Electronic Engineering; Electronic Engineering; Handwoven Textile Design; Mechanical & Production Engineering; Plant Technology; Science (Chemistry); Science (Textile Coloration); Software Engineering; Textiles & Management *3 yrs FT/6-8 yrs PT* Engineering (Instrumentation & Control); Plant Technology *PT* Instrumentation and Control
NVQ4: *3 yrs FT/6-8 yrs PT* Personnel; Training and Development *PT* Accounting; School Administration

UNIVERSITY OF BRIGHTON

Lewes Road, Brighton BN2 4AT Tel: 01273 600900 Fax: 01273 642825

* Subject to validation.

First Degrees

BA Hons: *1-5 yrs PT* Religious Education Studies
BA/BA Hons: *18 mths FT* Business Administration (As top-up) *2-4 yrs FT* Health Studies *3 yrs FT* Editorial Photography; Leisure & Sport Studies *3 yrs FT/4 yrs S* Accountancy with Law; Accounting; Finance; Business Studies with Law; Hospitality Management; International Finance-Capital Market Studies; Language Studies with Business; Language Studies with Linguistics; Leisure & Sport Management; Tourism Management *3 yrs FT/4-6 yrs PT* Digital Music; Geography; Information Management; Media-Computing *3 yrs FT/6-8 yrs PT* Social Science; Three-Dimensional Design for Production *4 yrs S* Business Studies with Marketing; Business Studies with Finance; Business Studies; Computing & Information Systems; Fashion Design with Business Studies; Fashion Textiles Design with Business Studies; International Business; International Hospitality Management; International Retail Marketing; International Tourism Management; International Travel Management; Retail Marketing *FT* Architecture; Business Education with Information Technology; Editorial Photography; Food Retail Management; Graphic Design; Illustration; Information & Media Studies; Interior Architecture; Physical Education; Primary Education (Early or Later Years); Social Policy & Administration; Three-Dimensional Crafts; Three-Dimensional Design for Production *FT/PT* Business Studies; Critical Fine Art Practice; Cultural & Historical Studies; Dance-Visual Art; Fine Art (Painting, Print Making or Sculpture); History of Decorative Arts & Crafts; History of Design; Humanities; Information & Library Studies; Music-Visual Art; Professional Education Studies; Social Work Studies; Theatre-Visual Art; Travel Management; Visual Culture

BA/QTS: *2 yrs FT* Business Education; Design & Technology Education; Modern Languages; Secondary Mathematics Education; Secondary Science Education *4 yrs FT* Design and Technology Education; Primary Education; Upper Primary / Lower Secondary Education (Maths, Science, D & T, English, Modern Foreign Languages, Geography, Information Technology); Upper Primary / Lower Secondary Education (PE)

BEng/BEng Hons: *3 yrs FT/4 yrs S* Automotive Engine Design; Civil Engineering; Civil Engineering Design & Practice; Electrical / Electrical & Electronic / Electronic & Computer Engineering; Electronic & Broadcast Engineering; Electronics with Communications; Engineering; Environmental Engineering; Manufacturing Systems Engineering *3 yrs FT/4 yrs S/PT* Energy and Environmental Sustainability; Sports Technology *3 yrs FT/4-8 yrs PT* Mechanical & Aeronautical Design Engineering *4 yrs S* Mechanical & Aeronautical Design Engineering *3 yrs FT/4-8 yrs PT* Mechanical & Environmental Engineering *4 yrs S* Mechanical & Environmental Engineering *3 yrs FT/4-8 yrs PT* Mechanical Engineering *4 yrs S* Mechanical Engineering

BSc Hons: *1 yr FT* Biological Sciences (Forestry / Horse Studies / Wine Studies) *4 yrs S* Urban Conservation & Environmental Management *3 yrs FT/4-8 yrs PT* Urban Conservation & Environmental Management

BSc Hons/ENB Higher Award: *1 yr FT* Community Health Nursing (Mental Health Nursing) *1 yr FT/2 yrs PT* Community Health Nursing (General Practice Nursing); Community Health Nursing (Children's Nursing); Community Health Nursing (Learning Disabilities Nursing); Community Health Nursing (Nursing in the Home / District Nursing) *1 yr FT/2-5 yrs PT* Professional Practice *1 yr FT/variable PT* Community Health Nursing (Public Health Nursing / Health Visiting) *FT* Community Health Nursing (School Nursing)*PT* Community Health Nursing (Specialist Practitioner Programme) *Up to 5 yrs PT max* Professional Practice (Midwifery); Professional Practice (Midwifery) *Variable PT* Professional Practice (Gerontology)

BSc/BSc Hons: *18 mths FT* Professional Studies in Cognitive Behavioural Psychotherapy (Neurosis / Psychosis) *2 yrs PT* Dietetic Studies; Medical Laboratory Scientific Studies; Occupational Therapy Studies; Physiotherapy Studies *2-3 yrs PT* Professional Practice in Adult Nursing *2-4 yrs PT* Nursing Studies (For registered nurses) *3 yrs FT* Midwifery (Diploma plus top-up for degree – leading to Midwife registration); Physiotherapy; Podiatry; Product Design; Sports & Exercise Science *3 yrs FT/4 yrs S* Computer Studies; Computing & Statistics; Mathematics; Mathematics for Computing; Mathematics for Management; Mathematics-Statistics; Statistics for Management *3 yrs FT/4 yrs S/6 yrs PT* Architectural Technology; Biogeography; Building Studies; Design & Technology; Sports Technology *3 yrs FT/4 yrs S/PT* Computing-Operational Research; Energy Studies-Mathematics; Geography-Geology; Human Ecology; Mathematics-Operational Research; Computing-Media *3 yrs FT/4-8 yrs PT/4 yrs S* Biological Sciences; Biomedical Sciences; Construction Management; Environmental Sciences; Project Management for Construction *4 yrs FT* European Nursing *4 yrs PT* Occupational Therapy *4 yrs S* Computer Science; Product Design *4 yrs S/6 yrs PT* Software Engineering *FT* Chemistry-Energy Studies or Physics; Computing-Mathematics; Exercise Science; Informatique *PT* Building Surveying; Geography; Nursing; Pharmaceutical & Chemical Sciences; Podiatric Studies

Higher Degrees

MA: *1 yr FT* Design by Independent Project; History of Design (European Design History) *1 yr FT/2 yrs PT* Community Health & Social Practice; Cultural & Critical Theory; Health Promotion-Education; Histories & Cultures; History of Decorative Arts & Design; History of Design (Design, Industry and the Marketplace); History of Design (Material Culture: Artefacts and Meanings); Media Assisted Language Teaching & Learning; Mental Health; Public Service Partnership; Public Service Partnership (Community Development); Public Service Partnership (Community Safety); Public Service Partnership (Health); Public Service Partnership (Housing); Public Service Partnership (Social Services); Sequential Design / Illustration; Sport & Leisure Cultures *1 yr FT/2-6 yrs PT* Communication Studies; Information Management *1 yr PT* Counselling Studies *2 yrs PT* Criminal Justice Policy-Management; Fine Art; Fine Art Printmaking; French Language & Media; Health Studies; Housing Policy; Housing Policy & Education; Housing Policy-Management; Learning in Organisations; Marketing; Nursing Studies & Management; Tourism Management *2-4 yrs PT* Information Studies *2-5 yrs PT* Nursing Studies; Nursing Studies-Education; Social & Public Policy *2-5 yrs* Community Care *FT/PT* Community Care *FT* Architecture; Health Promotion (Europe) & Education; Health Studies & Education; Health Studies & Management; Interior

Design; Nursing Studies & Education; Social & Public Policy & Education; Social & Public Policy & Management *FT/PT* Architectural Management; TEFL *PT* Change Management; Community Care & Education; Community Care & Management; Education; Textile Design for Fashion *Variable FT/PT* Sequential Design/Illustration
MBA: Business Administration; European Business; Technology Management
MEng: *3-4 yrs FT/4-5 yrs S (Undergraduate level):* Architectural Structures *PT (Undergraduate level):* Architectural Structures *4 yrs FT/5 yrs S* Civil Engineering; Electrical & Computer Engineering; Electrical & Electronic Engineering; Electronic & Broadcast Engineering; Electronic Engineering; Engineering; Engineering Systems Simulation & Control; Environmental Engineering; Manufacturing Systems Engineering; Mechanical & Aeronautical Design Engineering; Mechanical & Environmental Engineering; Mechanical Engineering *FT/PT* Architectural Studies
MPharm: *4 yrs FT* Pharmacy
MPharm Hons: *4 yrs FT (Undergraduate level):* Pharmacy
MSc: Construction Management; Geoframeworks for Engineering; Information Systems Development; Object Oriented Software Technology; Physiotherapy & Management; Podiatry & Management *1 yr FT/2 yrs PT* International Capital Markets *1 yr FT/6 yrs PT* Computer Technology in Manufacture; Public and Environmental Health *1 yr FT/Up to 6 yrs PT* Community Public Health; Environmental Health; Public Health Medicine *1 yr FT/variable PT* Civil Engineering *1-5 yrs* Financial Management and Strategy *12 mths FT/PT variable* Product Innovation and Development *18 mths DL* Community Pharmaceutical Health Care *2 yrs FT* Health through Occupation *2 yrs PT* Biomedical Sciences; Biomedical Sciences-Management; Clinical Studies; Occupational Therapy; Occupational Therapy-Education; Occupational Therapy-Management *2-5 yrs PT* Diabetes Care; Physiotherapy-Education; Podiatry-Education *4 yrs max* Manipulative Physiotherapy *Variable FT/PT* Manipulative Physiotherapy *DL* Industrial Pharmaceutical Studies *FT* Information Systems *FT/PT* Digital Electronics; Facilities Management; Project Management for Construction *PT* Clinical Pharmacy/Clinical Life Sciences; Environmental Assessment; Physiotherapy; Podiatry; Public Services Organisation; Software Engineering; Technology Management

Diplomas

DipHE: *2 yrs + 1 trm FT/4 yrs PT* Accountancy Studies
Diploma: *1 yr FT/2 yrs PT* Architectural Design; TEFL *1 yr PT* Secondary Education *2 yrs PT* Religious Education; Youth & Community *2-3 yrs FT* Professional Practice in Medical Nursing *2-3 yrs PT* Professional Practice in Special and Intensive Care of the Newborn; Professional Practice in Surgical Nursing *3 yrs FT* Midwifery; Nursing (Adult)*(Professional registration entry):* Nursing (Child); Nursing (Learning Disabilities); Nursing (Mental Health) *3 yrs PT* Professional Practice; Professional Practice (Sexual Health); Professional Practice in Palliative Care *5 mths* Mental Health Studies *PT* Applied Professional Studies; Management Studies; Modern Languages; Primary Education
HND: *2 yrs FT* Business & Marketing; Business & Personnel; Computing (Information Systems or Real Time Systems or Software Engineering); Design; Design (2D & 3D Design & Communication); Engineering (Mechanical/Manufacture/Electronic); Forestry; Hotel, Catering & Institutional Management; Multimedia; Music Production; Sport & Exercise Sciences; Travel & Tourism *2 yrs FT/PT* Wine Studies *3 yrs FT* Horse Studies *FT* Applied Biology; Art & Design (Fine Art/Crafts); Building Services Engineering; Business & Finance; Public Services Organisation; Social Care
PGDip: Printmaking & Professional Practice *1 yr FT/2 yrs PT* Education *2 yrs PT* Law (with CPE) *3 yrs PT* Diabetes *PT* Health and Social Services Management
Postgraduate Diploma: *1 yr FT* Art/Fine Art *1 yr PT* Mathematics Teaching *2 yrs FT* Occupational Therapy *2 yrs PT* Counselling; History of Art & Design

Certificates

CertHE: *1 yr FT/2 yrs PT* Computer Programming; Systems Analysis & Design *2 yrs PT/2 yrs OL* Registered Nurse (General Nursing/Mental Health/Learning Disabilities) *3 yrs PT* Applied Professional Studies
Certificate: *1 yr FT* Management *2 yrs PT* Post-compulsory Education *FT* Teaching English as a Foreign Language *PT* Institute of Management; Languages for Professional Purposes *Up to 7 yrs PT* Art

HNC: *2 yrs PT* Building Studies; Engineering; Engineering (Electronic); Engineering (Electronics for Power or Broadcasting); Hotel Catering & Institutional Management; Multimedia; Music Production; Sport & Exercise Sciences; Travel & Tourism

PGCE: *1 yr FT* Art & Design (Secondary); Business Education (Secondary); Dance; Design & Technology (Secondary); Early Primary Years; Information and Communication Technology; Later Primary Years; PE (Secondary); Secondary Mathematics; Secondary Religious Education

PGCert: Applied Therapeutics; Social Services Management *1 yr PT* Clinical Education; Health and Social Care Education *1-3 yrs* Community Based Rehabilitation; Community Public Health; Developments in Community Health & Social Policy; Evaluating Community Health & Social Practice; Managing Community Health & Social Practice; Policy & Politics of Community Health & Social Practice; Public Service Management *1-3 yrs PT* Education Management

UNIVERSITY OF BRISTOL

Senate House, Tyndall Avenue, Bristol BS8 1TH Tel: 0117 928 9000 Fax: 0117 925 1424

† Subject to validation.

First Degrees

MEDICINE, DENTISTRY & VETERINARY SCIENCE

BDS: *5 yrs FT* Dentistry (6 yrs with pre-dental yr for those with non-science A levels)

BVSc: *5 yrs* Veterinary Science *6 yrs* Medicine (BSc: 4 yrs Veterinary Nursing and Practice Administration)

MBChB: *6 yrs* Medicine (MBChB: 5 yrs Medicine (6 yrs with pre-medical yr for those with non-science A levels))

SCIENCE & TECHNOLOGY

BEng: *3 yrs* Avionic Systems; Civil Engineering; Electrical & Electronic Engineering; Electronic & Communications Engineering; Electronic Engineering; Mechanical Engineering

BSc: *3 yrs* Anatomical Science; Biochemistry with Molecular Biology & Biotechnology; Biochemistry; Biochemistry with Medical Biochemistry; Biology; Biology-Geography; Botany; Cellular & Molecular Pathology; Chemical Physics; Chemistry; Computer Science with Mathematics; Computer Science; Environmental Geoscience; Equine Science; Geography; Geology; Geology-Biology; Mathematics with Statistics; Mathematics; Mathematics-Physics; Microbiology; Neuroscience; Pathology and Microbiology; Pharmacology; Physics; Physics with Astrophysics; Physics-Philosophy; Physiology; Psychology; Psychology-Zoology; Vetinary Pathogenesis; Zoology *4 yrs* Study in Industry; Anatomical Science; Biochemistry with Study in Industry; Chemistry (With a preliminary yr of study); Chemistry-Law; Geology (With a preliminary yr of study); Mathematics with Study in Continental Europe; Mathematics-Physics with Study in Continental Europe; Pharmacology with Study in Industry; Physics (With a preliminary yr of study); Physics & Philosophy with Study in Continental Europe; Physics with Study in Continental Europe

SOCIAL SCIENCES

BA: *3 or 6 yrs* Theological Studies (Taught by Trinity College, Stoke Hill, Bristol BS9 1JP) *3 yrs Joint Schools:* Archaeology-Geology; Drama-English; English-Latin or Philosophy; Greek-Philosophy; Philosophy and Mathematics; Theology-Politics or Sociology *Single Schools:* Ancient History; Archaeology; Classical Studies; Classical Studies with Study in Continental Europe; Classics; Classics with Study in Continental Europe; Drama; Economic & Social History; English; History; History of Art; Music; Philosophy; Theology and Religious Studies *4 yrs* French; French-Latin; German; Hispanic Studies; History with German; History of Art and a Modern Language; Italian; Modern Language-Drama; Music and French or German or Italian; Philosophy and a Modern Language; Politics and a Modern Language; Russian; Spanish *Modern Languages:* French (Two from French, German, Spanish, Italian, Russian, Portuguese); German (Two from French, German, Spanish, Italian, Russian, Portuguese); Italian (Two from French, German, Spanish, Italian, Russian, Portuguese); Russian (Two from French, German, Spanish, Italian, Russian, Portuguese); Spanish (Two from French, German, Spanish, Italian, Russian, Portuguese)

BA Hons: *3 yrs FT* Business Administration with Tourism
BSc Social Sciences: *3 yrs* Accounting with Economics and a Language; Accounting & Finance; Deaf Studies; Early Childhood Studies; Economics; Economics & Accounting; Economics-Econometrics; Economics-Economic History; Economics-Economic History or Mathematics or Politics or Sociology; Economics-Finance; Economics-Mathematics; Economics-Philosophy or Politics or Psychology; Economics-Politics or Sociology; Geography; Politics; Politics-Sociology; Psychology; Social Policy & Planning; Social Policy and Politics or Sociology; Social Work and Social Welfare; Sociology; Sociology and Philosophy; Sociology with Study in Continental Europe *4 yrs* Economics & Study in Continental Europe; Accounting; Economics and Econometrics; with Study in Continental Europe; Economics with Study in Continental Europe
LLB: *3 yrs* Law *4 yrs* Law-French; Law-German

Higher Degrees
DOCTORATES
DEng: Engineering (In respect of research and published work)
DLitt: Literature (In respect of research and published work)
DMus: Music (For Bristol graduates of at least eight yrs' standing or MMus holders of at least four yrs' standing, by composition)
DSc: Science (In respect of research and published work)
EdD: *3 yrs min* Education (By advanced study and dissertation)
LLD: Law (In respect of research and published work)
PhD: *3 yrs FT/6 yrs PT* (By research and dissertation)

MASTER'S DEGREES OR EQUIVALENT
LLM: *1 yr min* Commercial Law; European Legal Studies; International Law; Legal Studies; Public Law
MA: *1 yr FT* Analytical Aesthetics; Composition of Music for Film, Television & Theatre; Film and Television Production; Russian Studies; Slavonic Studies *12 mths FT/24 mths PT* Advanced Musical Studies; Ancient History-Historiography; Ancient Philosophy; Buddhist Studies; Classical Heritage; Classics; Contemporary History; Contemporary Theologies; Building Archaeology-History; Landscape Archaeology; Maritime Archaeology & History; Medieval Studies; Mediterranean Archaeology; Modern & Contemporary Poetry; Modern Spanish Theatre; Myth; Performing Arts in France; Philosophy; Philosophy and History of Science; Philosophy and Law; Post 1945 German Novel; Religion & Gender; Romanticism; Shakespeare & English Literature: Text, Influence & Creativity; Television Studies; Twentieth Century Italian Culture: Voices of Conformity and Dissent; Twentieth-Century German Drama *2 yrs FT* Legal Studies (By advanced study for non-law graduates) *2 yrs PT* Local History; Translation
MCD: *12 mths FT/2 yrs PT* Oral Implantology; Oral Medicine; Oral Pathology; Oral Surgery; Periodontology
MEd: *1 yr FT/2-5 yrs PT* Education (By advanced study and dissertation)
MEng: *4 yrs* Aeronautical Engineering; Aeronautical Engineering with Study in Continental Europe; Avionic Systems; Civil Engineering; Civil Engineering with Study in Continental Europe; Communications & Multimedia Engineering; Computational & Experimental Mathematics; Computer Science; Computer Science with Study in Continental Europe; Computer Systems Engineering; Computer Systems Engineering with Study in Continental Europe; Electrical & Electrical Engineering with Study in Continental Europe; Electrical & Electronic Engineering; Electronic & Communications Engineering; Engineering Design; Engineering Mathematics; Mathematics for Intelligent Systems; Mechanical Engineering; Mechanical Engineering with Study in Continental Europe
MLitt: *2 yrs FT/4 yrs PT* Literature (Research leading to a dissertation with opportunity to upgrade to PhD)
MMus/PhD: *2 yrs FT/4 yrs PT* Music (By research and musical composition)
MPhil: *1 yr FT/2 yrs PT* Art & Social Sciences (By research)
MSc: *1 yr FT/2 yrs PT* Engineering *1 yr FT/3 yrs PT* Meat Science & Technology; Surface & Colloid Science & Technology *1 yr FT/3-5 yrs PT modular* Aerospace Design, Manufacture & Management *12 mths FT* Advanced Computing; Advanced Mechanical Engineering; Advanced Neuro & Molecular Pharmacology; Clinical Optometry; Computer Science; Crop Protection; Economics;

Industrial & Environmental Modelling; Molecular Neuroscience; Ophthalmology; Oral and Maxillofacial Surgery; Oral Surgery; Palaeobiology; Prosthetic Dentistry; Psychology of Health and Disease; Public Policy-Economics; Quantitative Development in Economics; Research Methods in Psychology *12 mths FT/2 yrs PT/5 yrs modular* Communications Systems & Signal Processing; Communications Systems and Signal Processing; Computer Science; Counselling; Counselling at Work; Counselling in Primary Care/Health Settings; Deaf Studies; Development, Administration & Planning; Economics & Econometrics; Economics & Finance; Ethnic Relations; European History; Exercise & Health Science; Gender and International Relations; Information & Library Management; International Policy; International Relations; Orthodontics; Paedodontics; Physics of Advanced Electronic Materials; Policy Research; Policy Studies; Prosthetic Dentistry; Restorative Dentistry; Society & Space; Sociology; Transfusion and Transplantation Sciences; Women's Studies *2 yrs FT* Paediatric Dentistry; Restorative Dentistry *2 yrs PT* Counselling: Supervision & Training; Ecology & Management of the Natural Environment; Engineering Management; Environmental Assessment; Environmental Statement Production; Management Development & Social Responsibility; Management Development & Training *2 yrs PT (home students)/2 yrs FT (overseas students)* Diagnostic Imaging *2-3 yrs PT* Palliative Medicine *3 yrs PT* Family Therapy & Systematic Practice *36 mths FT* Orthodontics *Up to 5 yrs PT modular* Management for Professionals
MSci: *4 yrs* Chemical Physics; Chemistry; Chemistry with Industrial Experience; Chemistry with Study in Continental Europe; Geography; Geography; Geology with Statistics; Mathematics; Mathematics; Mathematics with Study in Continental Europe; Mathematics-Physics; Physics; Physics with Astrophysics; Physics with Study in Continental Europe
MSW: *2 yrs FT* Social Work

MEDICAL
ChM: Medicine (For medical graduates of at least four yrs' standing, by research, or published work, and clinical exam)
DDS: Dentistry (For dental graduates of at least two yrs' standing in respect of research or other contributions to learning)
MD: Medicine (For medical graduates of at least two yrs' standing in respect of research or other contributions to learning)
MSc: *1 yr FT* Neuroscience; Transfusion & Transplantation Sciences
MSc (by research): Aerospace Engineering; Anaesthesia; Anatomy; Biochemistry; Biological Sciences; Cardiac Surgery; Chemistry; Child Health; Civil Engineering; Clinical Radiology; Clinical Veterinary Science; Computer Science; Earth Sciences; Electrical & Electronic Engineering; Engineering Management; Engineering Mathematics; Ethics in Medicine; Experimental Psychology; Geographical Sciences; Interface Analysis; Mathematics; Mechanical Engineering; Medical Physics-Engineering; Medicine; Obstetrics & Gynaecology; Opthalmology; Oral & Dental Science; Palliative Medicine; Pathology and Microbiology; Pharmacology; Physics; Physiology; Primary Care; Psychiatry; Social Medicine; Surgery
PhD: (By Research)

Diplomas
DipHE: *2 yrs FT* Deaf Studies
Diploma: *1 yr FT* Composition of Music for Film, Television & Theatre; Drama; English Legal Studies; Film & Television; Psychology of Health and Disease; Social Sciences in Economics *1 yr FT followed by 1 yr PT* Housing Studies *1 yr FT/2 yrs PT* Arts; Dental Studies; Development, Administration & Planning; Education, Advanced Studies in; Ethnic Relations; Gender & International Relations; International Business; International Business; International Relations; Medical Studies; Philosophy; Science; Social Policy & Social Planning; Sociology; Theology or Religious Studies; Women's Studies *1 yr FT/2-5 yrs PT* Education (By coursework. Graduate School of Education); Policy Research; Social Sciences in Deaf Studies *1 yr FT/25 mths PT* Social Sciences (postgraduate) *1 yr FT/3 yrs PT* Meat Science & Technology; Surface & Colloid Science & Technology *1 yr PT* Business Support; Intellectual Property Law & Practice (For qualified lawyers); Management Studies; Managing Development; Post-Qualifying Studies in Social Work *18 mths-5 yrs modular* Management for Professionals *2 trms FT/2 yrs PT* Engineering *2 yr modular/1 yr continuous* Clinical Optometry *2 yrs FT* Science; Social Work *2 yrs FT/4 yrs PT* Theological

Studies (Trinity College, Bristol) *2 yrs PT* Adult & Continuing Education; Adult Guidance & Counselling Skills; Architectural Conservation; Counselling; Counselling at Work; Counselling in Primary Health Care Settings; Ecology & Management of the Natural Environment; Hearing Therapy; Language Studies; Local History; Management Development & Training; Music Therapy; Occupational Health Nursing; Translation *3-5 yrs PT* Postgraduate Dental Studies *4 yrs PT* Open Studies

Certificates

Certificate: Education (Graduate School of Education) *1 yr FT* Applied Social Studies; Deaf Studies; Opthalmic Nursing *1 yr FT/equivalent PT* Higher Education; Theological Studies *1 yr PT* Engineering (postgraduate); Legal Studies; Management Studies; Public Service Interpreting & Translating; Science (postgraduate) *2 yrs FT* Social Work *3 yrs PT* Biological Science

Open Studies Certificate: *2 yrs PT* American Studies; Arts; Counselling Skills; Ecology & Management of the Environment; Exercise & Health Studies; Languages for Business; Medically & Related Subjects; Nursing Home & Retirement Home Management; Science; Sign Language Interpreting; Social Sciences; Translation *Department for Continuing Education:* European Studies

BRUNEL UNIVERSITY

Uxbridge, Middlesex UN8 3PH Tel: 01895 274000 Fax: 01895 232806
e-mail: bob.westaway@brunel.ac.uk Website: www.brunel.ac.uk/home.html

First Degrees

BA: *3 yrs FT* American Studies or Law; American Studies with Drama or English or History or Human Geography or Music or Film/TV Studies; American Studies-Drama or English or Film & Television Studies or History or Music or Film & Television Studies or Drama or Sociology; American Studies-English or History or Music or Psychology or Social Anthropology; American Studies or Drama or English or History; Film & Television Studies or Social Anthropology or Sociology; American Studies or Drama or English or Film & Television Studies or Human Geography or Music; History; Applied Social Studies; Ballet and Contemporary Dance; Drama; Education Studies with Sports Sciences; Education Studies; English; English or Social Policy; Politics; Film & Television Studies; Film & Television Studies with American Studies or Drama or English or History; History; Humanities; Industrial Design and Technology; Music with American Studies or Drama or English or Film/TV Studies or History; Music or Film/TV Studies or History; Music-American Studies or English or Drama or English or Film & Television Studies or Geology or Human Geography or History or Music or Politics or Law; Social Anthropology or Sociology; American Studies; Social Welfare Studies; Social Work; Youth & Community

BA with QTS: *3 yrs FT* Primary *4 yrs FT* Geography; Secondary & Physical Education with English or Information Technology or Religious Studies

BA/BSc: *3 yrs FT* Geography

BEng/MEng: *3-4 yrs FT/4-5 yrs S* Computer Systems Engineering; Electronic & Electrical Engineering; Electronic & Electrical Engineering (Communication Systems); Electronic & Microelectronic Engineering; Engineering Science & Technology; Information Technology-Industrial Systems; Integrated Engineering; Integrated Engineering (Computer Aided Engineering); Integrated Engineering (Mechatronics); Internet Engineering; Manufacturing Engineering with French or German or Management & Business; Manufacturing Engineering; Mechanical Engineering; Mechanical Engineering with Aeronautics or Automotive Design or Building Services or Electronic Systems; Mechanical Engineering and Design; Special Engineering Programme with Economics and Management; Special Engineering Programme

BSc: *3 yrs* Health Information Science; Product Design; Psychology-Sociology or Social Anthropology; Sociology; Sociology & Communications; Sports Sciences; Statistics and Mathematics *3 yrs FT/4 yrs S* Applied Biochemistry; Applied Biology; Biochemistry; Biology; Business Administration; Business Economics; Business Mathematics with French or German; Cell & Molecular Biology; Communication and Media Studies; Community Health (Community Children's Nursing); Community Health (Community Mental Health Nursing); Community Health (Community Psychiatric Nursing); Community Health (District Nursing); Community

Health (General Practice Nursing); Community Health (Health Visiting); Community Health (Occupational Health Nursing); Community Health (School Nursing); Community Practice Teacher; Computer Science with Mathematics; Computer Science; Computing for Mechanical Engineering; E-commerce; Earth Sciences; Economics or Law; Economics-Business Finance or Management; Engineering with Management; Engineering Science & Technology (Manufacturing); Engineering Science & Technology (Mechatronics); Environmental Geosciences; Ethio-legal Issues in Health Care; Financial Mathematics; Foundations of Engineering; Foundations of Science; Health Promotion; Health Services Administration; Health Studies; Human Geography; Industrial Design; Industrial Design Engineering; Information Systems; Management-Business; Mathematics with Management Studies or French; Mathematics with Computer Science or Engineering or German; Mathematics; Mathematics & Statistics with Management; Medical Biochemistry; Medical Biology; Medical Genetics; Multimedia Technology & Design; Occupational Therapy; Physiotherapy; Politics; Politics-Economics or History or Sociology; Psychology; Social Anthropology; Social Anthropology-Communication or Sociology; Sports Sciences-Business or Computer Studies or Leisure Management *3-4 yrs* Geography; Physical Education

LLB: *3-4 yrs* Business and Finance Law; Law with French or German; Law

UG Associate Study Programme: American Studies-History; Biology; Business Studies; Design; Economics; Education; English; Film & Television Studies; Geography & Earth Sciences; Government; Health Studies; Human Sciences; Law; Management Studies; Manufacturing Engineering Systems; Mathematics; Mechanical Engineering; Music; Social Work; Sports Sciences

Higher Degrees

PG Associate Study Programme: Computer Science; Design; Education; Electrical Engineering; Health Studies; Manufacturing & Engineering Systems; Materials Engineering; Mathematics & Statistics; Mechanical Engineering; Sports Science

DOCTORATES

DSc/DLitt/DTech: (Awarded for distinguished original work, to Brunel graduates or members of staff as appropriate to candidate's field of study)

EdD: Education

EngD: Environmental Technology Research

PhD: *3 yrs FT/4 yrs PT* (Awarded by thesis to graduates (or equivalent) for approved postgraduate research)

MASTER'S DEGREES

LLM: *1 yr FT/2 yrs PT* Child Law & Policy; Commercial Law; Criminal Justice; Law & Politics of the European Union

MA: *1 yr FT/2 yrs PT* Applied Social Studies; Child Law and Policy; Communications & Technology; Community Practice Teacher; Criminal Justice; Design, Strategy & Innovation; Education; Education (Educational Management); Education (Guidance & Counselling Skills); Education (Information Technology in Education); Education (Primary Education); Education (Religious Education); Education (Secondary Education); Education (Severe Learning Difficulties); Education (Special Educational Needs); European Policy Studies; European Politics; Guidance and Counselling Skills; Health Service Policy and Management; Psychoanalytic Studies; Public and Social Administration; Public Services Management; Youth & Community Studies

MBA: Business Administration; Business Administration (Design Management); Business Administration (Strategic Accounting & Finance)

MSc: *1 yr FT/2 yrs PT* Advanced Manufacturing Systems; Applied Psychology; Building Services Engineering; Building Services Engineering Management; Business Finance; Cognition & Consciousness; Community Health (Specialist Practitioner) with Modelling; Computational Mathematics; Counselling in Healthcare & Rehabilitation; Data Communications Systems; Decision Modelling & Information Systems; Design Strategy & Innovation; Distributed Computing Systems Engineering; Distributed Information Systems; Engineering Management; Environmental Change; Environmental Management; Environmental Pollution Science; Environmental Science with Occupational Health with Legislation & Management; Environmental Science; Finance and Investment; Financial Economics; Health Promotion; Health

Service Policy & Management; Human Resources & Employment Relations; Information Management; Information Systems; Integrated Industrial Design; Intelligent Systems; International Money, Finance and Investment; Joining Technology; Management of Innovation & Organisational Change; Management Studies; Medical Anthropology; Medical Genetics with Immunology; Microelectronics Systems Design; Multi-agent Distributed Computing; Neurorehabilitation; Occupational Health & Safety Management; Occupational Therapy; Packaging Technology; Physical Education; Social Anthropology of Children; Sport Coaching; Sport Sciences

Diplomas

Diploma: Dance; European Business Administration; Private & Executive Secretary Diploma
DPSE: Educational Management; Guidance & Counselling Skills; Information Technology in Education; Primary Education; Religious Education; Secondary Education; Severe Learning Difficulties; Special Educational Needs

Certificates

Certificate: Bilingual Secretarial Course; Business Administration; CIPFA Professional; Dance; European Executive Assistant Certificate; ICSA Municipal Administration Parts 1-4
HNC: Computer Studies
PGCE: Biology; Chemistry; Design & Technology; English; Geography; Information Technology; Mathematics; Modern Foreign Languages (French); Modern Foreign Languages (German); Physical Education; Physics; Primary; Religious Education; Science; Secondary *Distance Learning* Chemistry; Physics

UNIVERSITY OF BUCKINGHAM

Buckingham, Buckinghamshire MK18 1EG Tel: 01280 814080 Fax: 01280 822245
Website: www.buckingham.ac.uk

Most degree courses are of two yrs' duration. The Buckingham academic yr consists of four ten-wk terms, beginning in January and July.

First Degrees

BA Hons: History of Art-Heritage Management *2 yrs* Communication Studies-International Business; English Language Studies with Literature; English Language Studies (EFL) for TEFL; English Language Studies (EFL) for Translating or French or Spanish or History or History of Art; English Literature with English Language Studies (EFL); English Literature or Economics or French or Spanish or History of Art; History with English Literature; History; History and English Literature or French or Spanish or History; History of Art with English Literature; History of Art & Heritage Management or French or Spanish or History; Politics with Economics or Law; Politics & Economics; Politics, Economics & Law
BSc (Econ) Hons: *2 yrs* Accounting & Financial Management; Accounting-Economics; Business Economics; Economics
BSc Hons: *2 yrs* Accounting with French or Spanish with Information Systems or International Tourism; Business Studies; Business Studies or Law or Politics; Economics with French or Spanish; Economics, Business & Law; Financial Services; Information Systems with Accounting or Business Studies or Operations Management or French or Spanish or Economics; Information Systems; Marketing with French or Spanish; Psychology with Business Studies or Information Systems or English Language Studies (EFL) or English Literature or French or Spanish or Socio-Legal Studies *3 yrs* International Hotel Management-Business Studies *4 yrs PT* Business Studies
LLB Hons: *2 yrs* Economics or French or Spanish or Management Studies; Law with Business Finance; Law & Politics *2 yrs FT/4 yrs PT* Law

Higher Degrees

LLM: *9 mths FT* International & Commercial Law
MA: *1 yr FT* Biography; Biography; British Studies; Heritage Tourism Management; International Relations; TESOL; Victorian Literature *2 yrs PT* Education Law *9 mths FT* Decorative Arts &

Historic Interiors
MBA: *1 yr FT* The Buckingham MBA
MSc: *1 yr FT* Business Economics; Computing; Economics & Law; Electronic Commerce; International Hotel Management; International Tourism Management; Service Management *2 yrs PT* Service Management; Transformation Management *2-4 yrs PT* Electronic Commerce

Honorary Degrees
DLitt; DSc; DUniv; LLD; MA

Research Degrees
DPhil; LLM; MA; MPhil; MSc

BUCKINGHAMSHIRE CHILTERNS UNIVERSITY COLLEGE

Queen Alexandra Road, High Wycombe, Buckinghamshire HP11 2JZ Tel: 01494 522141
Fax: 01494 524392 e-mail: marketing@bcuc.ac.uk Website: www.bcuc.ac.uk

First Degrees

BA Hons: *3 yrs* Advertising Management; Airline Management; Airport Management; Applied Furniture Studies; Business Studies (and/with Economics; European Studies; Finance; French; German; Human Resource Management; Italian, Law; Leisure Management; Marketing; Spanish; Sports Studies; Tourism; Psychology); Business, Economics & Finance; Ceramics with Glass; Contemporary Furniture Design; Designed Metalwork & Jewellery; Drama Production-Creative Writing; E-Commerce Business; English Studies (and/with Film Studies; Media Studies; Psychology; Sociology) with Drama Production (and/with Film Studies; Media Studies; Psychology; Sociology); English Studies with Film or Media or Philosophy or Sociology or Social Work Studies or Visual Art; English Studies and Drama Production; English Studies (and/with Film Studies; Media Studies; Psychology; Sociology; Creative Writing)-Visual Arts (and/with Film Studies; Media Studies; Psychology; Sociology; Creative Writing); Entertainment Industry Management with Video Production; Entertainment Industry Management; European Business Studies; European Business Studies with French or German or Italian or Spanish; Film (and/with Drama Production; Creative Writing) with Media & Video Production (and/with Drama Production; Creative Writing); Film (and/with Video Production; Visual Arts) with Drama Production (and/with Video Production; Visual Arts); Film & Visual Arts (and/with Sociology; Psychology; Media Studies); Film and Drama Production; Film and English Studies; Film (and/with Creative Writing; Drama Production; Media; Psychology; Visual Arts; Sociology)-English Studies (and/with Creative Writing; Drama Production; Media; Psychology; Visual Arts; Sociology); Fine Art; Furniture Design & Craftsmanship; Furniture Restoration & Craftsmanship; Furniture Studies; Global Tourism; Graphic Design & Advertising; Health & Fitness Management; Hospitality Management; Hospitality Management with French or German or Italian or Marketing or Spanish or Sports Studies or Tourism; Human Resource Management; Human Resource Management (and/with Economics; European Studies; French; German; Italian; Law; Spanish; Finance; Leisure Management; Marketing; Tourism; Psychology); Interior Design; International Business & Marketing Logistics; International Business Studies with French or German or Italian or Spanish; International Business Studies; International Foundation Course; International Marketing; International Marketing with French or German or Italian or Spanish; Jewellery; Landscape Design; Leisure Management; Leisure Management (and/with Football Studies; Golf Studies; Rugby Studies; Sport Studies; Tennis Studies; Marketing; French; Italian; Hospitality Management); LLB; Marketing; Marketing & Operations; Marketing-Operations with Economics or European Studies or Finance or French or German or Human Resource Management or Italian or Law or Leisure Management or Marketing or Spanish or Tourism or Sports Studies; Media with Sociology or Video Production or Visual Arts; Media & Film with Video Production; Media Studies (and/with Creative Writing; Drama Production; English Studies; Video Production); Media Studies & English Studies; Media Studies and Drama

Production; Music Industry Management; Music Industry Management (and/with Live Production; Marketing; Pop Music); Nursing; Outdoor Adventure Recreation; Performance Management; Product Design & Manufacture; Retail Management; Retail Management with Economics or European Studies or Finance or French or German or Human Resources Management or Italian or Law or Leisure Management or Marketing or Spanish or Tourism or Sports Studies; Small Business Management; Sports Industry Management; Sports Industry Management-Cricket or Football or Golf or Rugby or Tennis; Sports Tourism Management; Textile Design & Surface Decoration; Theatre & Music Performance Management; Three Dimensional Multi-Disciplinary Design; Tour Operations Management; Tourist Destination Management; Travel & Tourism Management; Travel & Tourism Management with French or German or Italian or Leisure Management or Marketing or Sports Studies or Spanish; Visitor Attractions Management; Visual Arts-Creative Writing or Drama Production

BEng: *3 yrs* Mechanical Engineering Design

BSc: Adventure Tourism; Building Processes; Business Information Technology; Community Health Care Nursing; Computer Aided Design; Computer Aided Design with Management or Marketing; Computer Aided Design & Manufacture; Computer Engineering; Computing; Computing-Psychology; Creative Multimedia with Video Production or Sociology or Philosophy; Criminology with Social Policy; Criminology; Cultural Tourism; Design Technology; Forest Product Technology; Furnishing & Interior Decoration; Furniture; Health Studies; Innovative Design; Internet Technology; Manufacturing Technology with Management; Multimedia Technology; Nursing; Product Design; Psychology; Psychology and Criminology/Sociology; Psychology-Criminology or Media or Sociology or Welfare Studies or Sociology & Visual Arts; Responsible Tourism; Social Welfare Studies; Social Work Studies with Counselling or European Welfare System or International Welfare System or Social Care or Social Policy; Sociology with Social Policy; Sociology or Media or Law or Film Studies or Criminal Law; Sociology-Criminology or Psychology or Social Policy; Sports Psychology; Tourism

Higher Degrees

MASTER'S DEGREES

MA: *FT/PT* Criticism and Culture; European Human Resource Management; Furniture Design & Technology; Illustration; Interior Design; International Marketing; Music Management; Strategic Leisure Management *PT* Furniture Design and Craftmanship

MBA: *PT* Business Administration

MSc: *2 yrs PT* Business Information Technology; Evolutionary Psychology; Forest Products Technology; Heritage Management and Interpretation; Music Management; Nursing; Policy and Participation; Product Design; Tourism Development and Management; Tourist Development-Management

Diplomas

BTEC Diploma: Foundation Art and Design

DipHE: *3 yrs FT* Complementary Health Studies; Nursing

Diploma: Chartered Institute of Building; Chartered Institute of Marketing; Clinical Nursing/Critical Care Nursing/Nurse Practitioner Studies; Enrolled Nurse & Registered Nurse Conversion; Institute of Personnel & Development; Nursing (Project 2000); Social Work

HND: *Direct Entry to Yr 3:* BA Animal Industry Management; BA Business Studies; BA Equine Industry Management *2 yrs FT* Business Information Technology; Business Studies; Business Studies with Finance or French or German or Human Resource Management or Italian or Marketing or Russian or Spanish or Law or Leisure Management or Tourism or Sports Studies; Combined Awards; Computing; Design (Furniture); Film & Media Studies; Furniture Studies; Graphic Design; Health & Fitness Management; Hospitality Management; Legal Studies; Leisure Management; Music Industry Management; Social Care; Sports Industry Management; Textile Design; Travel and Tourism Management

UNIVERSITY OF CAMBRIDGE

Cambridge, Cambridgeshire CB2 1TN Tel: 01223 337733 Website: www.cam.ac.uk/

ARTS & SCIENCES

BA Hons: Candidates for Honours degrees must reach the prescribed standard in any two or three of the Tripos exams, although in some cases one exam is sufficient. In most subjects there are two Tripos (or final) exams, Part I coming at the end of a one- or two-yr course of study and Part II after one to two yrs more of specialised study. The two parts may be taken in different subjects and both parts are classed.

BA Ord: Intended for those who fail a Tripos exam or Tripos qualifying exam and so become ineligible for the BA Hons. Courses and requirements are specified for students individually by the Applications Committee.

BEd: For students at Homerton College only who read for the Education Tripos during the latter part of the course. The BEd is a recognised qualification for teaching.

BTh (Bachelor of Theology for Ministry): Candidates must pass a qualifying exam, first and second exams, and an exam in pastoral studies.

BMus: Candidates who have obtained Honours in any part of the Music Tripos may take the exam for the degree of MusB in their third or later yrs. It is usually taken as a fourth yr course by those who have already completed the Cambridge BA.

MEng: Awarded to students who complete a four-yr course and obtain either Honours in Part II of Chem Eng Tripos or Part II of Manufacturing Eng Tripos or Part IIb of the Engineering Tripos or Part II of the Electrical & Information Sciences Tripos.

MSCI (Master of Natural Sciences): Awarded to students who complete a four-yr course and obtain Honours in Part 3 of the Natural Sciences Tripos.

MA: Cambridge BAs may be admitted MA without exam not less than six yrs from the end of their first term of residence if two yrs have elapsed since admitted BA.

MEDICINE

MB; BChir: The two degrees are qualifications for provisional registration under the Medical Act 1983, comprising three yrs of pre-clinical medical study and two yrs and one term of clinical study. Candidates must pass or gain exemptions from all Second MB exams (except Population Sciences), and so normally read the Medical & Veterinary Sciences Tripos) They must also obtain Honours from Cambridge, or be in possession of an appropriate degree from another university. Having completed the course in the Cambridge Clinical School, students will take the final MB exam for the degrees of MB, Chir. There is provision for students who have obtained the BA degree and fulfilled the appropriate requirements of the second MB exam to go to the medical school of another university for their clinical training. Such students sit the Final MB, which lasts six yrs.

VETERINARY MEDICINE

VetMB: Students usually spend the first three yrs reading for the Medical & Veterinary Sciences Tripos or Natural Sciences Tripos. After taking BA, students begin a three-yr course at the Department of Clinical Veterinary Medicine. The VetMB degree is awarded after passing the Final Veterinary Exam, which is in three parts.See 'Cambridge University Guide to Courses 1998-99', Cambridge University Press, revised annually. 'Undergraduate Prospectus 1999-2000' available from Intercollegiate Applications Office, Kellet Lodge, Tennis Court Road, Cambridge (gratis). 'Graduate Studies Prospectus, 1998-99' available from the Board of Graduate Studies, Mill Lane, Cambridge (gratis).

First Degrees

ARTS & SCIENCE

BA Hons: *3 yrs* Anglo-Saxon, Norse & Celtic; Archaeology & Anthropology; Architecture; Chemical Engineering; Classics; Computer Science; Economics; Education; Education Studies; Engineering; English; Geography; History; History of Art; Land Economy; Law; Linguistics; Mathematics; Medicinal and Veterinary Sciences; Modern & Medieval Languages; Music; Natural Sciences; Oriental Studies; Philosophy; Social & Political Sciences; Theology & Religious Studies; Veterinary Medicine

BEd: *4 yrs FT*

Higher Degrees

LLM: *1 yr* Law
MBA: (The Judge Institute of Management Studies offers a choice of courses of combined study and work experience leading to the MBA degree)
MEd: *2 yrs PT*
MLitt: *2 yrs* (Supervised research)
MPhil: *1 yr* American Literature; Anglo-Saxon, Norse & Celtic; Archaeological Science; Archaeology; Biological Anthropology; Biological Science; Chemistry; Classics; Computer Speech & Language Processing; Conservation of Natural Science Materials; Criminology; Development Studies; Economic & Social History; Economics; Economics & Development; Education; Engineering; English & Applied Linguistics; English Studies; Environment & Development; Environmental Design & Architecture; Epidemiology; Ethnomusicology; European Literature; European Studies; Geographical Information Systems & Remote Sensing; Historical Studies; History & Philosophy of Architecture; History & Philosophy of Science & Medicine; International Relations; Land Economy; Latin-American Studies; Linguistics; Management Studies; Medical Sciences; Medieval & Renaissance Literature; Medieval History; Microelectronic Engineering & Semiconductor Physics; Musical Composition; Musicology; Oriental Studies; Philosophy; Physics; Polar Studies; Political Thought & Intellectual History; Quaternary Science; Social and Developmental Psychology; Social Anthropology; Sociology & Politics of Modern Society; Statistical Science; Theology; Veterinary Science
MSc: *2 yrs* (Supervised research)
MSt: *2 yrs PT* Applied Criminology & Management (Prison Studies); Applied Criminology & Police Studies; English Local History; Interdisciplinary Design for the Built Environment; Manufacturing Leaders' Programme; Modernism: English Literature, 1890-1939; Primary & Community Care
PhD: *3 yrs* (Supervised research available in all Faculties and Departments)

Diplomas

Diploma: Economics; International Law; Legal Studies *1 yr FT* Computer Science; Management Studies; Public Health; Theology *2 yrs FT* Architecture *FT* Conservation of Easel Paintings (Hamilton Kerr Institute)

Certificates

Certificate: Advanced Study in Mathematics (Mathematical Tripos, Part III) *FT* Conservation of Easel Paintings (Hamilton Kerr Institute)
Postgraduate Certificate: Anglo-Saxon, Norse & Celtic; Archaeology; Chemical Engineering; Engineering; English; History; History of Art; Legal Studies; Natural Science; Theology & Religious Studies *1 yr FT* Education (Teacher-training course)

UNIVERSITY OF CENTRAL ENGLAND IN BIRMINGHAM

Perry Barr, Birmingham B42 2SU Tel: 0121 331 5000

† Subject to validation.

First Degrees

BA Hons: *3 yrs FT* 3-D Design: Design in Business; Accountancy; Accountancy & Finance; Adminstration with Accountancy or Business Information Systems or Finance or Human Resource Management or Marketing or French or Spanish or German; Ceramics with Glass Design; Entrepreneurship; Fashion Design with Product Development; Fashion Design with Retail Management; Furniture Design; Industrial Design; Interior Design; International Business Management with Languages; International Business Management; Jewellery & Silversmithing; Management Design & Communication; Marketing with French or German or Spanish; Marketing; Media & Communication; Performance Design & Communication; Textile Design (Embroidery); Textile Design (Constructed Textiles); Textile Design (Printed Textiles); Textile Design (Retail Management); Theatre Design; Visual Communication: Graphic Design; Visual

Communication: Illustration; Visual Communication: Photography; Visual Communication: Time-Based Media *3 yrs FT/4-5 yrs PT* Criminal Justice & Policing *3 yrs FT/5 yrs PT* Business Information & Systems; English Language & Literature/English; Information & Library Studies; Information Technology; Multimedia Communication & Culture Multimedia *3 yrs FT/6 yrs PT* History of Art & Design *3 yrs FT/Flexible PT* Art & Design (By Negotiated Study) *3 yrs/DL* Insurance Management *PT* Social & Policy Studies

BA/BA Hons: Marketing with French or German or Spanish; Marketing *3 yrs* Entrepreneurship†; Finance; International Business Management with Languages; International Business Management *3 yrs FT/5 yrs PT* Architecture; Environmental Planning & Geography; Garden Design; Geography & Environmental Management; Housing; Landscape Architecture; Town & Country Planning *3 yrs FT/6 yrs PT* Fine Art *4 yrs* Business Studies *4 yrs FT* Primary Education with QTS *5 yrs PT* Business Economics

BEd: *2 yrs FT* Music (Secondary)

BEng: *3 yrs FT/5 yrs PT* Automotive Engineering; Communications & Network Engineering; Electronic Engineering; Electronic Systems; Management of Manufacturing Systems; Mechanical Engineering; Mechanical Engineering Systems

BMus Hons: *4 yrs FT* Classical Music; Jazz†; Raga Sangeet

BSc Hons: Computer Aided Design; Computer Networks for Business; Computing & Electronics; Multimedia Technology; Television Technology & Production *3 yrs* Management *3 yrs FT/5 yrs PT* Business Information Technology; Computing; Electronic Commerce; Engineering Product Design; Information Systems; Software Design & Networks; Software Engineering

BSc/BSc Hons: Clinical Nursing Studies; Community Health Nursing; Diagnostic Radiography; Health Policy & Management; Health Promotion; Health Studies; Mental Health Studies; Midwifery; Nursing; Nursing Studies; Palliative Care; Social Work; Social Work Studies; Speech & Language Therapy; Therapeutic Radiography; Women's Health Studies *3 yrs FT/5 yrs PT* Architectural Technology; Building Surveying; Construction Management-Economics; Estate Management; Quantity Surveying

LLB Hons: *3 yrs FT* Politics with Contemporary Governance or Criminal Justice or Law or Psychology *3 yrs FT/4-5 yrs PT* Law with Politics or Psychology or Sociology *3 yrs FT/4-6 yrs PT* Sociology with Psychology or Law or Politics or Economics

Higher Degrees

LLM: *1 yr* European Legal Studies

MA: Advanced Practice Midwifery & Advanced Midwifery; Advanced Practice Nursing & Advanced Nursing; Art & Education; Careers Guidance; Counselling & Psychotherapy; Design Management; Drama in Education; Education; Educational & Professional Development; Equal Opportunities; Fashion; Fine Art (Practice); Fine Art (Theory & Practice); Health & Social Care; Health Promotion; History of Art & Design; Industrial Design: Ceramics & Glass Product Design; Industrial Design: Furniture Design; Industrial Design: Space; Interior Design & Information Technology; Jewellery, Silversmithing & Related Products; Manager and Human Resource Development; Marketing; Media & Communication; Media Production; Music; Primary Care Management; Radiography; Scenography; Surface Design; Textiles; Visual Communication: Animation; Visual Communication: Design for Communication; Visual Communication: Illustration; Visual Communication: Multimedia Design; Visual Communication: Photography; Visual Communication: Video *1 yr* Immigration Policy Law & Practice *1 yr FT/2 yrs or more PT* Literary Studies *1 yr FT/2 yrs PT* Architecture: Conservation & Renewal; Architecture: Design & Theory; Architecture: Urban Design; Design in Business; Housing; Housing Studies; Landscape Architecture; Town Planning; Town Planning Studies *1 yr PT* Legal Practice; Legal Studies; Public Policy in the Information Society; Research Methodology *2 yrs PT* Law of the Built Environment *3 yrs PT* Information & Business *Distance Learning/PT* English Linguistics; Insurance Management

MA/MSc: *1 yr FT/3 yrs PT* Information & Library Management

MA/PgD: *1 yr FT/2 yrs PT* Criminal Justice Policy & Practice

MPhil: *FT/PT* Architecture; Computing; Education; English; Housing Planning; Information & Library Management; Landscape Architecture; Music; Property & Construction

MSc: Advanced Practice (Midwifery); Advanced Practice (Nursing); Automotive Engineering; Business-Management or Finance or Marketing; Computing; Electronic Information; Electronic Services Management; Knowledge Organisation & Management; Manager & Organisation

Development; Mechanical Engineering; Networked Information Management *1 yr FT/2 yrs PT* Construction Project Management; Facilities Management; Property Business & Management; Real Estate & Management

MSc/PGDip/PGCert: *1 yr FT/2 yrs PT* Customer Focused Logistics; Electronic Commerce; Environmental Pollution Control; Environmental Risk Management; Innovation Management; Logistics; Manufacturing Engineering; Polymer Engineering; Software Technology; Supply Chain Management

PhD: *FT/PT* Computing; Education; English; Information & Library Management; Music

Diplomas

BTEC HND: *2 yrs* Business-Management

DipHE: Art & Design (By Negotiated Study); Ceramics with Glass Design; Fashion Design; Fine Art; Furniture Design; Health Studies; History of Art & Design; Industrial Design; Interior Design; Jewellery & Silversmithing; Management Studies; Nursing; Rehabilitation Studies (Visual Impairment); Social Work; Textiles Design; Theatre Design; Visual Communication

DPS: Continuing Education & Development; Drama in Education; Education; Midwifery; Music; Nursing; Primary Care Management; Primary Education

HND: Art & Design (By Negotiated Study (At Franchise College)); Art & Design (Exhibition and Heritage Display) (At Franchise College); Ceramics & Glass (At Franchise College); Clothing Studies (At Franchise College); Computing & Information Studies; Design (Visual Communication) (At Franchise College); Fashion & Textiles (At Franchise College); Gemmology; Horology; Jewellery & Silversmithing; Legal Studies *2 yrs FT* Building Studies; Computer Aided Design; Electronic Engineering; Horticulture; Land Administration; Multimedia & Networks Technology

ND: 3-D Design; Design (Fashion); Design for Media; Precious Metals & Gemstones

Postgraduate Diploma: Advanced Practice (Midwifery) & Advanced Midwifery; Advanced Practice (Nursing) & Advanced Nursing; Art & Design Technology Diploma in Professional Studies in Education; Art & Education; Automotive Engineering; Broadcast Journalism; Careers Guidance; Counselling and Psychotherapy; Design Management; Drama in Education; Education; Education & Professional Development; Equal Opportunities; Fine Art (Practice); Fine Art (Theory & Practice); Health & Social Care (Medical Imaging & Radiation Practice); Health Promotion; History of Art & Design; Housing; Industrial Design; Industrial Logistics; International Broadcast Journalism; Jewellery, Silversmithing & Related Products; Landscape Architecture; Marketing; Mechanical Engineering; Media & Communication; Media Production; Medical Ultrasound; Music; Nursing; Primary Care Management; Professional Administration; Radiography; Scenography; Textiles, Fashion and Surface Design; Town Planning; Visual Communication *1 yr* European Legal Studies; Immigration Policy Law & Practice *1 yr FT/2 yrs PT* Legal Practice/Legal Practice Course; Legal Studies/Common Professional Examination *1 yr PT* Public Policy in the Information Society; Research Methodology

Certificates

BTEC HNC: *2 yrs PT* Computer Aided Design; Engineering (Electronics); Manufacturing Engineering; Mechanical Engineering; Multimedia & Networks Technology

CertHE: Art & Design (By Negotiated Study); Ceramics with Glass Design; Fashion Design/Textile Design; Fine Art; Furniture Design; History of Art & Design; Industrial Design; Interior Design; Jewellery & Silversmithing; Management Design & Communication; Marketing; Media & Communication; Performance Design & Communication; Primary Care Management - Professional Development; Theatre Design; Visual Communication

Certificate: Community Practice Teaching; Professional Studies in Housing; Professional Studies in Planning

CPS: Careers Guidance; Continuing Education & Development; Drama in Education; Education; Primary Care Management

HNC: Building Studies; Housing Studies; Land Administration; Legal Studies

Postgraduate Certificate: Art & Design; Art-Education; Automotive Engineering; Broadcast Journalism; Careers Guidance; Design Management; Drama in Education; Education; Education & Professional Development; Equal Opportunities; Fine Art; Health & Social Care; History of Art and Design; Industrial Design: Product Design; Interior Design & Information Technology;

International Broadcast Journalism; Jewellery, Silversmithing and Related Products; Mechanical Engineering; Media & Communication; Media Production; Medical Ultrasound; Primary Care Management; Professional Studies in Art Education†; Radiography – Appendicular Reporting; Radiography – Barium Enema; Scenography; Textiles, Fashion & Surface Design; Visual Communication

Postgraduate Certificate in Education (PGCE): Art and Design Education; Primary Education; Secondary (Drama); Secondary (Music)

UNIVERSITY OF CENTRAL LANCASHIRE

Preston, Lancashire PR1 2HE Tel: 01772 201201 Fax: 01772 892935
e-mail: c.enquiries@uclan.ac.uk Website: www.uclan.ac.uk

† Subject to validation.
* With optional foundation yr.

First Degrees

BA Hons: *3 yrs FT* Law and Business or Criminology or English or Politics or Psychology or Sociology; Accounting; Accounting & Financial Studies; Accounting and Business or Business Information Systems or Economics or International Business or Law or Management or Marketing; Advertising; American Studies; American Studies and Film & Media Studies or History; Animation; Asia Pacific Studies; Audio Visual Media Studies and Design Studies or Fashion Promotion Studies or Journalism or Media Technology or Photography or Visual Culture; Business and Accounting or Business Information Systems or Economics or Law or Marketing; Business Enterprise; Business Information Systems and Accounting or Business or Management or Statistics; Business Information Technology; Ceramics, Glass & Plastic (Tableware); Contemporary Music; Contemporary Performing Arts; Criminology & Criminal Justice; Criminology and Ethics or Philosophy or Social Policy or Sociology; Deaf Studies; Deaf Studies and Education or Law or Linguistics or Psychology or Race & Ethnic Studies; Design Studies; Design Studies and Audio Visual Media Studies or Fashion Promotion or Media Technology or Photography or Public Relations; E-Business; Economics and Accounting or Business or Geography or International Business or Law or Marketing or Politics; Education and English or History or Sociology; English & American Literature; English & Theatre studies; English and Education or History or Law; English for International Business; English Language & Literature; English Language Studies; English Literary Studies; Entrepreneurship; Entrepreneurship-Design Studies or Fashion Promotion Studies or Management or Marketing; European & International Studies; European Studies and Film & Media Studies or Sociology; Fashion Promotion Studies and Audio Visual Media Studies or Design Studies or Journalism or Marketing; Film & Media and American Studies or Visual Culture; Film & Media Studies; Film and History; Financial Services; Fine Art; Forensic Science and Criminology; Furniture; Garden Design; Geography; Graphic Design; Health Studies; Health Studies and Education or Psychology or Social Policy or Sociology; Heritage Management; History; History and American Studies or Education Studies or English or Film & Media or Law or Politics or Race & Ethnic Studies or Sociology; Hospitality Studies; Human Resource Management; Illustration; Industrial Design; Interior Design; International Business and Accounting or Economics or Marketing; International Business Studies; Jewellery (mixed media); Journalism; Journalism and English; Languages for International Business (With placements); Leisure Studies; Linguistics and Deaf Studies or French; Management; Management and Business Information Systems or Entrepreneurship† or Marketing or Public Relations or Information Systems; Marketing; Marketing and Business or International Business or Management or Organisation Studies or Public Relations or Tourism & Leisure; Marketing Global; Media Technology and Audio Visual Media Studies; Modern World History; Moving Image; Organisation Studies; Philosophy and Business or English or Health Studies or Politics or Sociology; Photography; Photography and Audio Visual Media Studies or Design Studies or Journalism or Media Technology or Visual Culture; Politics & Government; Politics and History or Philosophy or Social Policy; Psychology and Criminology; Public Relations; Public Relations and Management or Marketing; Pure and Applied Philosophy or Social Policy or Sociology or History; Race & Ethnic Studies and Criminology or Education or Health Studies; Retail

Management; Retail Management and Fashion or Logistics or Marketing; Screenwriting; Social & Cultural History; Social Policy & Administration; Social Work & Community Studies; Social Work & Welfare Studies; Sociology; Sociology and Criminology or History or Law or Politics or Social Policy; Sports Management; Surface Pattern with Crafts; Tourism & Leisure and Business or Management; Tourism Studies; Visual Culture; Visual Culture and Film & Media *4 yrs S* Business Studies; Fashion; Fashion Promotion; Hospitality Management; International Hospitality Management; International Tourism Management; Languages with Tourism; Midwifery; Modern Languages

BA/BSc Hons Combined: Performance Technology *3 yrs FT* Accounting; American Studies; Applied Ethics; Applied Physics; Astronomy; Audio Visual Media Studies; Biochemistry; Business; Business French; Business German; Business Information Systems; Business Spanish; Career Management; Chinese; Computing; Counselling; Criminology; Deaf Studies; Design Studies; Development Studies; Drama; Economics; Ecotourism; Education; Employee Relations; English; English for International Business; Entrepreneurship; Environmental Management; European Studies; Fashion Promotion Studies; Film & Media; Forensic Science; French; Geography; German; Health Sciences for Complementary Medicine; Health Studies; History; International Business; Italian; Japanese; Journalism; Law; Linguistics; Management; Marketing; Mathematical Sciences; Mathematics; Media Sociology; Media Technology; Microbiology; Nursing Studies; Nutrition; Organisation Studies; Philosophy; Photography; Physiology/Pharmacology; Politics; Psychology; Public Relations; Race & Ethnic Studies; Social Policy; Sociology; Spanish; Statistics; Teaching English as a Foreign Language; Tourism & Leisure; Visual Culture *4 yrs S* Computing; French; Music; Music & the Creative Arts; Performance Technology

BEng/BEng Hons: *3 yrs FT* Fire Engineering *4 yrs S* Building Services Engineering; Design & Manufacture; Electronic Engineering; Mechanical Engineering; Mechatronics

BSc Hons: Commercial Management & Quantity Surveying *3 yrs FT* Accounting & Statistics; Applied Physics; Applied Psychology; Architectural Design Management; Astronomy; Astrophysics; Biochemistry; Biochemistry and Business or Forensic Science or French or German or Microbiology or Physiology/Pharmacology; Biological Sciences; Biomedical Science; Building Surveying; Business Administration (Yr 3 entry); Business Computing; Computer Aided Engineering; Computing; Computing and Accounting or Business or Mathematics or Media Technology or Psychology; Conservation and Land Management; Construction Project Management; Development Studies and Economics or Environmental Management or Geography or Race & Ethnic Studies or Tourism & Leisure; Ecotourism; Ecotourism-Development Studies or Environmental Management or French or Geography or Marketing; Electronics; Environmental Engineering; Environmental Management; Environmental Management and Development Studies or Ecotourism or Geography or Law or Politics; Environmental Science; Facilities Management; Fire Safety; Fire Safety Engineering; Fire Safety Management; Food & Nutrition; Forensic Psychology; Forensic Science; Forensic Science and Biochemistry or Criminology or Journalism or Law; Forestry & Woodland Management; Geography; Geography and American Studies or Development Studies or Ecotourism or Environmental Management or Sociology; Health Sciences for Complementary Medicine; Herbal Medicine; Homeopathic Medicine; Information System Design; Mathematical Sciences; Mathematics; Mathematics and Education or Business Information Systems or Computing or Psychology or Statistics or Computation; Media Technology; Media Technology and AVMS or Computing or Journalism; Microbiology; Microbiology and Business or Environmental Management or French or German; Motor Sport; Multi Media System Design; Neuroscience; Nursing Studies; Physics; Physics & Astronomy; Physics and Computing or French or German or Management or Marketing or Mathematics or Media Technology; Physiology-Pharmacology; Physiology/Pharmacology and Biochemistry or Business or French or Health Studies or Microbiology or Psychology; Product Design; Psychology; Psychology and Business or Criminology or Education Studies or Forensic Science or Health Studies or Law or Physiology/Pharmacology or Statistics; Social & Community Forestry; Software Engineering; Sport Psychology; Sports Equipment Design; Sports Science; Statistics; Statistics and Business Information Systems or Economics or Law or Marketing or Psychology; Utilities Management *4 yrs S* Building Surveying; Community Specialist Practitioner; Software Engineering

LLB/LLB Hons: *3 yrs FT* Law *4 yrs S* Law-French or German

Higher Degrees

LLM: Employment Law; Environmental Law
MA: Bioethics; Criminology; Cultural History; Design; Education; English Language Studies; Fine Art; Health Promotion; Health Service Management; Health Studies; History and Theory of Art; Human Resource Management; International Business; International Law & Business; International Marketing; Interprofessional Issues in Health and Welfare; Learning Disabilities; Literary Studies; Literature and the History of Ideas; Social Enquiry; Social Work & Welfare Studies; Substance Misuse; Teaching English for International Business; Tourism, Leisure & Service Management
MBA: Business Administration
MPhys Hons: *4 yrs FT* Applied Physics; Astrophysics; Physics/Astronomy
MSc: Building Heritage & Conservation; Business Administration (Information Technology); Clinical and Health Sciences; Clinical Health Studies; Construction Law; Digital Signal and Image Processing; Environmental Analytical Chemistry; Environmental Toxicology; Food Safety Management; Health Informatics; Health Informatics for Research; Multimedia Computing; PC Interfacing & Software Applications; Psychology Programme; Psychosexual Therapy; Sexual Medicine; Statistical Applications of IT; Waste Management

Diplomas

DipHE: *2 yrs FT* Combined Honours; Law; Management Studies; Nursing (pre-registration alternative route); Nursing (pre-registration); Post-Registration Midwifery
Graduate Diploma: Statistics
HND: Adventure Tourism; Amenity Horticulture (Landscape Design and Management) (Newton Rigg Campus); Animal Science (Newton Rigg Campus); Applied Biology; Building Studies; Business Studies (Newton Rigg Campus); Computing (Business Computing); Computing (Information Systems Applications) (Newton Rigg Campus); Computing (Information Systems Design); Computing (Software Engineering); Countryside Management (Newton Rigg Campus); Engineering (Computer Aided Engineering); Engineering (Mechanical and Production); Farm Management; Forestry; Game and Wildlife Management (Newton Rigg Campus); Hill Farm Management (Newton Rigg Campus); Mechanisation (Agriculture and Forestry); Sports Studies (Outdoor Recreation) (Newton Rigg Campus); Visitor Attraction Management (Newton Rigg Campus); Wildlife Identification (Newton Rigg Campus)
Year 0: Art & Design; Combined Honours; Electronic Engineering; Mechanical Engineering; Science; Social Work & Welfare Studies; Technology for Women

Certificates

Postgraduate Certificate: Advanced Professional Studies; Applied Languages; Child Protection; Counselling Studies; Education; Evidence Based Practice for Lactation Management; Evidence Based Practice in Critical Care in Pregnancy and Childbearing; Evidence Based Practice in Supportive Care for the High Risk Neonate; Family Placement; Forensic Sexology; General Practice; Health Research Methods; History Research; Integrative Therapy in Mental Health Practice; IT for HE; Learning Disabilities; Management; Managing Community Health Councils; Practice Development; Primary Health Care Informatics; Race and Ethnic Studies; Research Methods Psychology; Risk Assessment, Risk Taking and Risk Management in Professional Practice; Specialist Issues in Substance Misuse; Teaching & Learning in Higher Education; Working with Serious and Challenging Mental Health Problems

Other Courses

Professional Courses: *1 yr FT* Common Professional Examination in Law *2 yrs FT* DipSW (Social Work)

Postgraduate Diplomas

Postgraduate Diploma: *1 yr FT* Approved Practice in Teaching Programme; Broadcast Journalism; BSL; Counselling Studies; General Practice; Legal Practice; Multi Professional – Cancer Care; Newspaper Journalism; On-line Journalism; Pain Management; Professional Development; Psychological Studies *2 yrs FT* Social Work

CHELTENHAM & GLOUCESTER COLLEGE OF HIGHER EDUCATION

PO Box 220, The Park, Cheltenham, Gloucestershire GL50 2QF Tel: 01242 532828
Fax: 01242 543444 e-mail: deumark@chelt.ac.uk Website: www.chelt.ac.uk

BA/BA Hons or BSc/BSc Hons: Major/minor/joint combinations: most are three yrs full-time/six yrs part-time, some combinations are four yrs sandwich.
Diplomas: All BA/BSc in the modular scheme (defined or combined) can be studied to diploma level, two yrs full-time, or the Certificate of Higher Education level at one yr full-time. Some of the subject areas are offered as Higher National Diplomas (HNC/HNDs).

First Degrees

BA Hons: *3 yrs FT* Advertising (Professional Media); Design for Interactive Media (Professional Media); Fine Art (Painting, Printmaking, Sculpture); Graphic Design (Professional Media); Landscape Architecture; Photography (Professional Media); Professional Media; Rural Planning; Video (Professional Media) *6 yrs PT* Humanities; Local Policy; Theology
BA/BA Hons or BSc/BSc Hons: *3 yrs FT/6 yrs PT/4 yrs S* Accounting & Financial Management; American Studies; Business Computer Systems; Business Information Technology; Business Management; Combined Arts (Available as minor field only); Community Development; Community Studies; Computing; English Studies; Environmental Management; Environmental Policy; Environmental Science; Exercise & Health Sciences; Film Studies; Financial Services Management; Garden Design; Geography; Geology; Heritage Management; History; Hospitality Management (Catering); Hospitality Management (Hotel); Human Geography; Human Resource Management; International Business Management; International Marketing Management; Landscape Design; Landscape Management; Leisure Management; Local Policy; Marketing Management; Media Communications; Modern Languages (French) (Available as minor field only); Multimedia; Natural Resource Management; Performance Arts; Physical Geography; Politics & Society; Psychology; Religious Studies; Rural Planning; Sociological Studies; Sport & Exercise Sciences; Sport Science; Sports Development; Sports Education; Studies in Modern Writing; Theology; Tourism Management; Urban Design; Visual Arts; Visual Culture; Water Resource Management; Women's Studies
BEd Hons: *2 yrs FT* Primary Education (3-8 Nursery/Keystage 1); Primary Education (7-11 Keystage 2/PE); Primary Education (7-11 Keystage 2/RE); Primary Education (Early Primary 5-11) *3 yrs FT* Primary Education (3-8 Nursery/Keystage 1); Primary Education (7-11 Key Stage 2/RE & PE); Primary Education (Early Primary 5-11)
BSc Hons: Computing; Multimedia; Multimedia Marketing; Sport & Exercise Sciences *1 yr FT/2 yrs PT* Community Studies *2 yrs FT/4 yrs PT* Water Resource Management

Higher Degrees

MA: *1 yr FT/2 yrs or more PT* Biblical Studies; Christian Education; Church School Education; Environmental Policy & Management; Fine Art; Landscape Architecture; Literature Since 1950; Management; Management of Human Resources; Professional Development; Public Services Management; Religion & Society; Religious Education; Special Education Needs; Sports Development; Strategic Marketing; Teaching & Learning; The Arts in Society
MBA: *1 yr FT/2 yrs PT* Business Administration; Financial Services; Information Systems; Management of Operations; Marketing
MEd: *1 yr FT/5 yrs PT* Education
MPhil: *18 mths FT/3 yrs PT (by research)* Agriculture & the Environment; Applied Social Studies; Biblical Studies; Business & Management Studies; Church History; Computing; Countryside Planning; Curriculum Studies; Design; English Studies; Environmental Management; Environmental Science; Film; Financial Services; Fine Art; Geography; Geosciences; Health & Social Care; History; Human Resources Management; Information Technology; Leisure Management Studies; Marketing & Service Culture; Media; Multimedia; Organisational Behaviour; Professional Development; Psychology; Religious Education; Religious Studies; Rural Development; Rural Leisure – Rural Welfare; Social Policy; Sociology; Sports Studies; The Management of Behaviour; Theology; Theory of Art; Women's Studies

MSc: *1 yr FT/2 yrs PT* Commercial Computing; Environmental Policy & Management; Health & Social Care (with Advanced Award in Social Work); Multimedia

DOCTORATES
PhD: *3-4 yrs FT/5-6 yrs PT (by research)* (Available in above areas)

Diplomas

DipHE: *2 yrs FT/4 yrs PT* Business & Finance
DipSW: *FT* Social Work
PGDip: *8 mths FT/18 mths or more PT* Biblical Studies; Business Administration; Christian Education; Church School Education; Commercial Computing; Environmental Policy & Management; Financial Services; Fine Art; Health & Social Care (with Advanced Award in Social Work); Information Systems; Landscape Architecture; Landscape Architecture Conversion Course; Literature Since 1950; Management; Management of Human Resources; Management of Operations; Marketing; Multimedia; Professional Development; Public Services Management; Religion & Society; Religious Education; Special Educational Needs; Sports Development; Strategic Marketing; Teaching & Learning; The Arts in Society

Certificates

Cert HE: *1 yr FT* (All BA/BSc in the modular scheme (defined or combined) can be studied to Certificate level)
PGCE: *1 yr FT* Primary; Secondary
PGCert: *15 wks FT/PT variable* Biblical Studies; Business Administration; Christian Education; Church School Education; Commercial Computing; Environmental Policy & Management; Financial Services; Fine Art; Health & Social Care (with Advanced Award in Social Work); Information Systems; Landscape Architecture; Literature Since 1950; Management; Management of Human Resources; Management of Human Resources; Management of Operations; Marketing; Multimedia; Professional Development; Public Services Management; Religion & Society; Religious Education; Special Educational Needs; Sports Development; Strategic Marketing; Teaching & Learning; The Arts in Society

Professional Qualifications

The College also offers a wide range of professional qualifications.

CITY UNIVERSITY

Undergraduate Admissions Office, Northampton Square, London EC1V 0HB Tel: 020 7477 8000 Fax: 020 7477 8995 e-mail: ugadmissions@city.ac.uk Website: www.city.ac.uk

* Subject to approval.

First Degrees

BA: *3 yrs FT/4 yrs S* Journalism with Economics or Psychology or Sociology or Contemporary History
BEng: *3 yrs FT* Biomedical Engineering with Applied Physics; Civil Engineering with Architecture; Engineering & Energy Management *3 yrs FT/4 yrs S* Aeronautical Engineering; Air Transport Engineering; Civil Engineering; Civil Engineering with Surveying; Computer Systems Engineering; Electrical & Electronic Engineering; Mechanical Engineering; Media Communication Systems *4 yrs S* Business Computing Systems; Computing; Computing (Distributed Information Systems & Communications); Software Engineering
BEng/BSc: *3-4 yrs* Biomedical Engineering and Applied Physics; Civil Engineering; Civil Engineering with Surveying; Computer Systems Engineering; Electrical and Electronic Engineering
BMus; BSc: *3 yrs FT* Music
BSc: *3 yrs* Radiography (Therapeutic) *3 yrs FT* Adult Nursing (with RN); Child Nursing (with RN); Midwifery; Optometry; Radiography (Diagnostic) *3 yrs FT/4 yrs S* Actuarial Science; Actuarial Science (with study abroad); Banking & International Finance; Business Studies with

Psychology; Economics or Sociology; Economics; Economics with Accountancy or Sociology or Psychology; Integrated BSc and ATPL in Air Transport Operations; Investment & Financial Risk Management; Management & Systems; Mathematical Science; Mathematical Science with Computer Science or Finance or Economics or Statistics; Psychology; Psychology with Economics or Sociology; Real Estate Finance and Investment; Risk Analysis and Insurance; Social Sciences; Sociology with Economics or Psychology or Media Studies with Media Studies; Sociology; Sociology *4 yrs FT* Speech and Language Therapy

BSc; MEB: *4 yrs FT/4 yrs S* Banking & International Finance; Business Studies; Investment & Financial Risk Management; Investment and Risk Analysis; Management & Systems; Real Estate Finance and Investment

LLB Hons: *2 yrs FT* Law

Higher Degrees

LLM: *1 yr FT* Environmental Law *1 yr FT/2 yrs PT* Criminal Litigation

MA: *1 yr FT* Broadcast Journalism; Electronic Publishing; International Journalism; Newspaper Journalism; Periodical Journalism *1 yr FT/2 yrs PT* Arts Criticism; Arts Criticism & Management; Arts Management; Communications Policy Studies; Composition (Electroacoustic); Composition (Instrumental & Vocal); Ethnomusicology; International Communications & Development; Museum & Gallery Management; Music Performance Studies; Musicology; Musicology (Women & Gender with Performance); Organisations & Social Change *12 mths PT* Cultural Management

MBA: *1 yr FT/2 yrs PT* Finance; Flexible Master's Programme; Human Resources and Management; International Business; Management of Technology; Marketing *2 yrs PT* Evening MBA Programme

MEng: *4 yrs FT* Engineering & Energy Management *4 yrs FT/5 yrs S* Aeronautical Engineering; Air Transport Engineering; Civil Engineering; Civil Engineering with Surveying; Electrical & Electronic Engineering; Mechanical Engineering

MHM: *2 yrs PT* Health Management

MMath: *4 yrs FT/5 yrs S* Mathematical Science; Mathematical Science or Computer Science with Finance & Economics or Statistics

MPhil: *2 yrs FT/3 yrs PT* Midwifery; Nursing *2 yrs PT* Health Management

MSc: *1 yr FT* Banking & International Finance; Electronic Publishing; Finance, Economics & Econometrics; Object-Oriented Software Systems *1 yr FT/2 yrs PT* Advanced Social Research Methods; Business Systems Analysis & Design; Contemporary Health & Social Policy; Corporate Property Strategy; Counselling Psychology; Disability Management in Work & Rehabilitation; Economic Evaluation in Health Care; Economic Regulation & Competition; Exercise & Health Behaviour; Information Engineering; Insurance & Risk Management; Investment Management; Mathematical Trading & Finance; Media Research & Analysis; Medical Informatics; Music Information Technology; Nursing; Organisational Psychology; Property Investment; Property Valuation and Law; Psychological Counselling; Quality Management, Statistical Methods & Reliability; Research Methods allied to Health Studies *1 yr FT/2-3 yrs PT* Internal Auditing & Management; Shipping, Trade & Finance *1 yr FT/2-4 yrs PT* Healthcare Technologies *1 yr FT/2-5 yrs PT* Midwifery *1 yr FT/3 yrs PT* Analysis & Design of Structures for Hazards; Civil Engineering Structures; Geotechnical Engineering; Information Science; Information Systems and Technology *1-4 yrs PT* Air Transport Management *10 mths FT* Finance *12-18 mths FT* Voluntary Sector Management *14 mths* Trade, Transport & Finance *15 mths PT* Energy Technology and Economics *2 yrs PT* Continuing Education & Training; Pharmaceutical Information Management *2-3 yrs PT* Medical Ultrasound; Nuclear Medicine Technology; Radiography *2-4 yrs PT* Human Communication *3 mths FT/1 yr PT* Actuarial Management; Actuarial Science *3 yrs FT* Speech and Language Therapy *Modular* Health Psychology; Psychology and Health *Up to 5 yrs PT* Modular Programme in Engineering *Up to 7 yrs PT* Clinical Optometry

PhD: *3 yrs FT/5 yrs PT* Midwifery; Nursing

PhD; MPhil: (By thesis after a period of research)

DOCTORATES

DSc: (Awarded for published work. Available only to staff and graduates of the University) *FT/PT* Clinical Psychology; Counselling Psychology

Diplomas

Post-MSc Diploma: *18 mths PT* Counselling Psychology Practice
Postgraduate Diploma: Cultural Management; Energy Technology and Economics *1 yr FT* Actuarial Management; Broadcast Journalism; Electronic Publishing; International Journalism; Newspaper Journalism; Periodical Journalism *1 yr FT/2 yrs PT* Actuarial Science; Business Systems Analysis & Design; Counselling Psychology; Disability Management in Work & Rehabilitation; Economic Regulation & Competition; Exercise & Health Behaviour; Information Engineering; Law (CPE); Medical Informatics; Nursing; Psychological Counselling; Quality Management Statistical Methods & Reliability *1 yr FT/2-3 yrs PT* Analysis & Design of Structures for Hazards; Civil Engineering Structures; Geotechnical Engineering; Music Information Technology *1 yr FT/2-5 yrs PT* Midwifery *1 yr PT* Problem-Centred Interventions for People with a Serious Mental Illness (Thorn Initiative) *12-18 mths* Flexible Master's Programme *16 mths PT* Voluntary Sector Management *18 mths PT* Medical Ultrasound; Nuclear Medicine Technology; Radiography *2 yrs FT* Speech and Language Therapy *2 yrs PT* Continuing Education & Training; Educational Guidance *9 mths FT/2 yrs PT* Internal Auditing & Management *Modular* Health Psychology; Psychology and Health *Up to 4 yrs PT* Modular Programme in Engineering

Certificates

Postgraduate Certificate: *1 yr* The Legal Practice Course *1 yr FT/2 yrs PT* The Bar Vocational Course *1 yr PT* Foundations of Psychological Counselling; Medical Ultrasound; Nuclear Medicine Technology; Radiography *6 mths DL* Disability Management at Work *Up to 3 yrs PT* Modular Programme in Engineering; Modular Programme in Engineering

Degrees validated by City University offered at:

Ashridge

Berkhamsted, Hertfordshire HP4 1NS Tel: 01442 841000 Fax: 01442 841036
e-mail: info@ashridge.org.uk. Website: www.ashridge.org.uk

Higher Degrees

Executive Modular MBA: *1 yr FT/2 yrs PT* Business Administration (City)
MSc: *2 yrs PT* Organization Consulting (Middlesex)

Diplomas

Diploma in General Management: *Flexible over 1, 2 or 3 yrs* General Management (City)

Guildhall School of Music & Drama

Silk Street, Barbican, London EC2Y 8DT Tel: 020 7628 2571 Fax: 020 7256 9438
Website: www.gsmd.ac.uk
* Subject to validation.

First Degrees

BA Hons: *3 yrs FT* Acting; Stage Management & Technical Theatre

Higher Degrees

MMus: *1 yr FT* Composition; Music Performance

Gyosei International College in the UK

London Road, Reading, Berks RGI 5AQ Tel: 01189 209 418 Fax: 01189 931 0137
e-mail: gelderd@gyosei.ac.uk Website: www.gyosei.ac.uk

First Degrees
BA: Business Studies; Culture with Business Studies; Language with Business Studies

Higher Degrees
MA: Business Studies

Inns of Court School of Law
4 Gray's Inn Place, Gray's Inn, London WCIR 5DX Tel: 020 7404 5787 Fax: 020 7831 4188
e-mail: bvc@icsl.ac.uk Website: www.icsl.ac.uk

Courses
BVC: *1 yr FT/2 yrs PT* Bar Vocational Course and Postgraduate Diploma; Bar Vocational Training and Diploma in Professional Legal Skills
LLM: *1 yr FT/2 yrs PT* Criminal Litigation (e-mail: llm@icsl.ac.uk)
LPC: *1 yr FT* Legal Practice Course and Postgraduate Diploma in Legal Skills (e-mail: lpc@icsl.ac.uk)

Laban Centre London
Laurie Grove, New Cross, London SE14 6NH Tel: 020 8692 4070 Fax: 020 8694 8749
e-mail: info@laban.co.uk Website: www.laban.co.uk

First Degrees
BA Hons: *3 yrs FT* Dance Theatre

Higher Degrees
MA: *1 yr FT/2 yrs PT* Dance Studies; Scenography for Dance *2 yrs FT/3-4 yrs PT* Dance Movement Therapy
MPhil: *FT/PT* (By research)

DOCTORATES
PhD: *FT/PT* (By research)

Diplomas
Diploma: *2 yrs FT* Dance Movement Therapy *3/4 yrs PT* Dance Movement Therapy
Postgraduate Diploma: *1 yr FT* Graduate Performance *15 wks PT* Visual Design for Dance
Professional Diploma: *1 yr FT/2 yrs PT* Community Dance Studies; Dance Studies
Specialist Diploma: *1 yr PT* Notating; Teaching Studies
Undergraduate Diploma: *3 yrs FT* Dance Theatre

School of Psychotherapy & Counselling at Regent's College
Regent's College, Inner Circle, Regent's Park, London NW1 4NS Tel: 020 7487 7406
Fax: 020 7487 7446 e-mail: spc@regents.ac.uk Website: www.regents.ac.uk/colleges/spc

Higher Degrees
MA/PGDip: *2-4 yrs PT* Psychotherapy & Counselling

DOCTORATES
MPhil/PhD: (By research)

The Centre for Nordoff-Robbins Music Therapy

2 Lissenden Gardens, London NW5 1PP Tel: 020 7267 4496 Fax: 020 7267 4369
e-mail: admin@nordoff-robbins.org.uk Website: www.nordoff-robbins.org.uk

Higher Degrees

Diploma in Nordoff-Robbins Music Therapy: *18 mths*
Master of Music Therapy: *2 yrs*

CORDWAINERS COLLEGE

182 Mare Street, London E8 3RE Tel: 020 8985 0273 Fax: 020 8985 9340
e-mail: enquiries@cordwainers.ac.uk Website: www.cordwainers.ac.uk

First Degrees

BA Hons: Design, Marketing & Product Development (Footwear/Accessories) (validated by City University)

Higher Degrees

MA (RCA): Menswear/Womenswear (Footwear/Accessories) (with the RCA)
MPhil (RCA): Menswear/Womenswear (Footwear/Accessories) (with the RCA)

Diplomas

BTEC HND: *2 yrs FT* Design & Technology (Footwear/Accessories); Design (Footwear/Accessories); Footwear Technology; Saddlery Technology

COVENTRY UNIVERSITY

Priory Street, Coventry CV1 5FB Tel: 024 7688 7688 Fax: 024 7688 8638
e-mail: coro24@coventry.ac.uk Website: www.coventry.ac.uk
* Subject to approval.

First Degrees

BA Hons: *1 yr FT* English and French or German or Italian or Russian or Spanish; French and German or Russian or Spanish or Italian; German-Italian or Spanish or Russian; Italian and German or Russian or Spanish or French; Professional and Social Studies; Spanish and German or Russian or Italian or French *3 yrs FT* Art and Craft Studies; Business Administration; Business and Accounting or Economics or Finance or Human Resource Management or Marketing or Planning or Supply Chain Management or The Global Economy or Tourism; Business Economics; Business Enterprise; Business-Accounting or Finance or Human Resource Management or Supply Chain Management or The Global Economy or Marketing or Planning or Economics or Tourism; Communication Authoring & Design; Communication, Culture and Media; Consumer Product Design; Dance and Professional Practice; Economics; Economics-Law or Human Resource Management or Planning or Supply Chain Management or Tourism; European Studies; European Studies with English or French or German or Italian or Russian or Spanish; Financial Economics; Fine Art; Geography and Computing or Economics or French or German or Planning or Politics or Sports Science; Graphic Design; Human Resource Management-Finance or Supply Chain Management or The Global Economy or Planning or Tourism; International Economics; International Relations and Politics; Law and History or International Studies or Social Policy or Politics; Leisure Management; Marketing Management; Music & Professional Practice; Music Composition and Professional Practice; People Management; Physical Theatre & Professional Practice; Planning and The Global Economy or Tourism; Politics and Social Policy; Politics-History or International Relations or Psychology or Spanish or Russian or Italian or German or Geography or French; Psychology and Sociology; Psychology and Sociology; Retailing Management; Social Policy and International Relations; Social Welfare; Social Work; Sociology; Sociology & Social

Policy; Sociology and History or International Relations or Politics or Social Policy; Supply Chain Management and Finance or The Global Economy or Planning or Tourism; Marketing and Economics or Finance or Human Resource Management or Planning or Supply Chain Management; The Global Economy; Theatre and Professional Practice; Tourism and Marketing or The Global Economy; Transport Design Futures; Women's Studies and Human Resource Management or Law or Politics or Social Policy or Sociology or Sociology; Women's Studies-Human Resource Management or Law or Politics or Social Policy or Finance or Planning or Supply Chain Management or The Global Economy or Tourism *3 yrs FT/4 yrs S* Business and Property Management; Business Computing; Business Information Technology; Business Information Technology with Accounting or Human Resource Management or International Business or Marketing or Supply Chain Management or Tourism or E-Commerce*; Geography; Information Technology and Law; Multimedia Computing; Performing Arts Technology; Property Management and Law; Sport Management; Tourism Management; Urban and Regional Planning *4 yrs FT* Economics-French or German; English -German or French or Italian or Russian or Spanish (Mandatory yr abroad); European Studies with French or German or Italian or Russian or Spanish (Mandatory yr abroad); French-German or Italian or Russian or Spanish (Mandatory yr abroad); Geography with European Studies; German-Italian or Spanish or Russian (Mandatory yr abroad); History-French or German or Italian or Russian or Spanish (Mandatory yr abroad); Italian-Russian (Mandatory yr abroad); Modern Languages (with QTS) (French/German/Italian/Russian/Spanish. Mandatory yr abroad); Spanish-Italian or Russian (Mandatory yr abroad) *4 yrs FT/5 yrs S* Business Information Technology with Foundation Yr *4 yrs S* Business Information Technology; Business Studies; Equine Studies; Leisure Management (with study in Europe)

BA/BSc Hons: *3 yrs FT/4 yrs S* Geography and Economics or French or German or Planning or Politics or Sports Science*4 yrs FT* Business and Information Technology (International Foundation Yr)

BEng Hons: *3 yrs FT/4 yrs S* Aerospace Systems Engineering; Aerospace Technology; Automotive Engineering; Automotive Engineering Design; Automotive Manufacturing; Automotive Technology; Autotronics; Avionic Systems Engineering; Civil & Environmental Engineering; Civil & Structural Engineering; Civil Engineering; Civil Engineering and Management; Civil Engineering Construction; Civil Engineering Design; Computers, Networking & Communications Technology; Electronic Engineering; Electronics Technology; Manufacturing with Management; Manufacturing Systems and Technology; Mechanical Engineering; Mechanical Technology; Polymer Science & Technology; Telecommunication Systems *4 yrs FT* Civil Engineering with European Studies; Civil Engineering Construction with European Studies; Civil Engineering Design with European Studies *4 yrs FT/5 yrs S* Aerospace Systems Engineering (Foundation)

BEng/BSc Hons: Applied Science and Engineering (Foundation Programme); Geography (Foundation Programme) *1 yr FT* European Engineering Studies; Industrial Product Design (Foundation); Industrial Product Design (Foundation) *3 yrs FT/4 yrs S* Computer and Control Systems *4 yrs FT/5 yrs S* Electronic Engineering (Foundation); Engineering (Foundation)

BSc Hons: *1 yr FT* European Business and Technology *1 yr FT/2 yrs PT* Health Sciences; Mental Health Studies; Nursing Studies *3 yrs FT* Civil Engineering; Health Sciences; Occupational Therapy; Physiotherapy; Psychology; Sport Science with Human Resource Management; Third World Development Studies *3 yrs FT/4 yrs S* Applied Ecology; Applied Statistics; Architectural Design Technology; Biochemistry; Biological Sciences-Computing or Economics or Study in Europe or Business or Marketing; Biomedical Sciences; Building Surveying; Business Decision Methods; Computer Science; Computer Systems; Computing; Computing-Economics; Construction Management; Countryside Change & Management; Design and Technology; Development and Health in Disaster Management; Emergency Risk Management; Engineering (Business & Technology); Environmental Biology; Environmental Monitoring and Assessment; Environmental Science; Geographical Information Systems; Geography; Geography and Computing; Intelligent Computing; International Disaster Engineering-Management; Manufacturing Engineering; Mathematical Sciences; Mathematics; Mathematics and Biological Sciences or Economics or French or Geography or German or Statistics; Mathematics and Computing; Network Computing; Performing Arts Technology; Pharmaceutical Sciences; Software Engineering; Sport Science with Health Sciences; Sports Science or Accounting or

Finance; Sports Science-Mathematical Studies; Statistics and Biological Sciences or Computing or Economics or French or Geography or German or Mathematics *3-4 yrs FT/4 yrs S* Applied Chemistry with Biochemistry or Management Studies or Polymer Science; Chemistry and Biological Sciences or Computing or Geography or Mathematics or Statistics *4 yrs FT* Biochemistry (with study in Europe); Biological Sciences with Study in Europe; Business and Technology with French or German or Spanish; Construction Management with European Studies; Dietetics; Pharmaceutical Sciences (with Study in Europe) *4 yrs FT/5 yrs S* Business Decision Methods; Mathematical Sciences (Foundation Yr); Mechanical Engineering (Foundation) *4 yrs S* Equine & Human Sport Sciences

BSc Hons/MSci: *3-4 yrs FT/4 yrs S* Biological Sciences; Environmental Chemistry; Pharmaceutical Chemistry

Foundation Course: *1 yr FT* Aerospace Systems Engineering *4 yrs FT/5 yrs S* Aerospace Systems Engineering

LLB Hons: *2 yrs FT* Law: Senior Status *3 yrs FT* Business Law; Criminal Justice; Law with English; Law *4 yrs FT* European Law with French or German or Italian or Russian or Spanish (Mandatory yr abroad)

Higher Degrees

MASTER'S DEGREES OR EQUIVALENT

LLM: Human Rights & Criminal Justice

MA: Applied Communication; Automotive Design; Automotive Design Research; Community Care; Design & Digital Media; Diplomacy, Law & Global Change; Disability & Social Justice; European Studies; Fine Art; Human Resource Management; Local Economic Development; Management; Marketing; Peace & Reconciliation Studies; Third World Studies; Town Planning *By Research:* History, International Relations & Politics

MBA: Business Law; Engineering Management; Executive Master of Business Administration; Manufacturing Management; Master of Business Administration (European Business); Master of Business Administration (Finance); Master of Business Administration (Information Technology); Master of Business Administration (International Business); Master of Business Administration (Marketing); Master of Business Administration (Sports Management)

MChem/MSci/BSc: *3-4 yrs FT/4 yrs S* Applied Chemistry

MDes/BA Hons: *3-4 yrs FT* Consumer Product Design; Transport Design

MDes/BSc Hons: *3-4 yrs FT/4-5 yrs S* Industrial Product Design

MEng Hons: *5 yrs S* Automotive Engineering Design

MMath: *4 yrs FT* Mathematics

MSc: Acupuncture; Advanced Information Systems; Applied Software Engineering; Automotive & Automotive Component Manufacture; Automotive Engineering; Competitive Manufacturing; Computing; Control Engineering; E-Commerce; Engineering and Manufacturing Management; Engineering Business Management; Engineering Design; European Construction; Health Psychology; Health Studies; Informatics and Control; Information & Communication Technology for Engineers; Information Technology for Management; Local & Regional Economic Development; Manipulative Therapy; Mathematical Modelling & Computer Simulation; Nursing; Occupational Therapy; Operational Telecommunications; Physiotherapy; Rural Change; Software Development; Software Engineering *4 yrs FT* Environmental Monitoring & Assessment

MSc (by research): Analytical Chemistry; Applied Mathematics; Biomedical Science; Biotechnology; Control Theory & Applications; Disaster Management; Engineering; Environmental Science; Exercise & Health; Geographical Information Systems; Geomorphology; Information Systems; Manufacturing Management; Pharmaceutical Sciences; Plant Improvement for Environmental Stress; Plastics Technology; Polymers; Quaternary Science; Rubber Technology; Software Engineering; Sonochemistry

MSc/PGDip/PGCert: Environmental Management; Integrated Catchment Management

MSci: *4 yrs* Environmental Monitoring and Assessment

MSG/MBA: MaŒtrise des Sciences de Gestion

Diplomas

BTEC Diploma: *1 yr FT* Art & Design (Foundation)

DipHE: *18 mths FT* Midwifery Studies *2 yrs FT* Polymer Science and Technology
DipHE/BSc: *3 yrs FT* Midwifery Studies; Nursing
HNC/HND: *2 yrs FT* Business Information Technology; Computing *2 yrs FT/3 yrs S* Building; Civil Engineering
HND: *2 yrs FT* Applied Chemistry; Business Enterprise; Pharmaceutical Chemistry; Theatre Practice *2 yrs FT/3 yrs S* Colour Aided Design (CAD) *3 yrs S* Horse Studies (Management and Technology)
HND/BA Hons (2+2): *4 yrs FT* Business Information Technology
HND/BEng Hons (2+2): *3 yrs FT/4 yrs S* Aerospace Technology; Electronics Technology *4 yrs FT/5 yrs S* Automotive Technology with Management; Manufacturing; Mechanical Engineering
HND/BSc Hons (2 + 2): *2-4 yrs FT* Biological Sciences; Sport Science; Sport Science and Business Management *4 yrs FT* Applied Chemistry; Computing; Pharmaceutical Chemistry
PGDip: Manufacturing Management; Marketing; Personnel Management; Professional Development in Management
UKCC Professional Register: *18 mths* Midwifery Studies (Part 10) *3 yrs FT* Midwifery Studies (Part 10); Nursing Studies (Part 12, Adult Nursing); Nursing Studies (Part 13, Mental Health Nursing); Nursing Studies (Part 15, Child Branch)

Certificates

PGCert: Business Administration; Management; Manufacturing Management; Partnership Working with the Community; Personnel Management

Degrees validated by Coventry University offered at:

Newman College of Higher Education

Genners Lane, Bartley Green, Birmingham B32 3NT Tel: 0121 476 1181 Fax: 0121 476 1196
e-mail: registry@newman.ac.uk Website:www.newman.ac.uk

First Degrees

BA Hons: *3-4 yrs PT* Early Years Education Studies (Work-based); Management of Professional Development (Work-based)
BA Hons (QTS): *4 yrs* KS2/3 English; MFL 11-18 yrs; Primary; Secondary English 11-16 yrs, 11-18 yrs, 14-19 yrs
BA/BSc: *3 yrs Joint Honours:* (Variety of subjects)
BEd Hons: *3 yrs* Primary; Secondary English 11-16 yrs
BEd Hons KS2/3: *3 yrs* English; ICT, Science
BSc Hons (QTS): *4 yrs* Primary
BSc Hons (QTS) KS2/3: *4 yrs* ICT, Science

Higher Degrees

MA/MA(Ed): *PT* English (Genre Studies) (Postgraduate Certificates & Diplomas are also offered in these fields of study); Historical Studies (Postgraduate Certificates & Diplomas are also offered in these fields of study); Theology & Culture (Postgraduate Certificates & Diplomas are also offered in these fields of study)
MEd/MA (Ed) (Primary): *PT* (Specialised Masters Degree routes in various fields of study)

POSTGRADUATE CERTIFICATES
Postgraduate Certificate in Education: *1 yr* Primary (KS2); Secondary RE 11-18 yrs

Research Degrees
MPhil/PhD

CRANFIELD UNIVERSITY

Cranfield, Bedfordshire MK43 0AL Tel: 01234 750111 Fax: 01234 750875

First Degrees

BEng: *3 yrs* Aero-Mechanical Engineering; Agricultural Engineering; Civil Engineering; Command & Control, Communications & Information Systems (CIS); Computer Systems Engineering; Electrical Engineering; Electrical Engineering with Management; Electronic Systems Engineering; Mechanical Engineering; Mechanical Engineering with Management; Software Engineering

BSc: *3 yrs* Applied Science; Business Information Systems; Diagnostic Radiography; Information Systems Management; Management & Logistics; Therapeutic Radiography

BSc Hons: *4 yrs* Agricultural Engineering; Business Management & the Environment; Environment Management; Physical Geography

Higher Degrees

DSc: (For graduates of some standing who are directly connected with the University)

EngD: *3-4 yrs FT* Engineering (By coursework, exam, project and thesis after research in an approved topic)

MA: *1 yr FT/2 yrs PT* (By written exams, continuous assessment and oral exam if required)

MBA: *1 yr FT/2 yrs PT* Business Administration (By coursework and exam. Previous management experience is essential, minimum of three yrs)

MDA: *1 yr FT/2 yrs PT* Defence Administration (By coursework and exam. Previous defence management experience important)

MEng: *4 yrs* Aeromechanical Systems Engineering; Agricultural Engineering; Civil Engineering; Mechanical Engineering

MPhil: *2 yrs FT* (By thesis after research)

MRes: *1 yr FT* Innovative Manufacturing (By coursework and thesis)

MSc: (All taught MScs are assessed by coursework, exam and thesis, possibly plus group project) *1 yr FT/2 yrs PT* Advanced Materials Manufacturing; Aeronautics; Aerospace Dynamics; Aerospace Vehicle Design; Air Transport; Applied Energy; Applied Psychology; Applied Science & Technology; Astronautics & Space Engineering; Automotive Product Engineering; Business Systems; Computer Applications; Defence Sensor Systems and Data Fusion; Design of Rotating Machines; Digital Battlespace; Digital Signal & Image Processing; Disaster Management; Engineering Design & Development; Environmental Diagnostics; Fresh Produce Management; Geographical Information Management; Human Factors and Safety Assessment in Aeronautics; Management Information Systems; Manufacturing Technology & Production Management; Marketing for the Food, Drink & Related Industries; Mathematical Modelling; Medical Diagnostics; Military Technology; Motorsport Engineering and Management; Natural Resources Management; Offshore and Ocean Technology; Process Systems Engineering; Project Management; Quality Management; Radiographic Studies; Scientific & Applications Software; Security Management; Software Techniques for Computer Aided Engineering; Systems Engineering for Defence; Thermal Power; Transportation Management; Water Management; Water Pollution Control Technology; Water Science; Welding Process Automation

PhD: *3 yrs FT* (Depending on qualifications, by thesis after research in an approved topic)

Honorary Degrees

Any degree may be awarded.

DE MONTFORT UNIVERSITY

DE MONTFORT UNIVERSITY

The Gateway, Leicester LE1 9BH

Tel: 0116 255 1551

Fax: 0116 255 0307

Website: www.dmu.ac.uk

Hammerwood Gate, Kents Hill, Milton Keynes MK7 6HP Tel: 01908 695511

Lansdowne Road, Bedford MK40 2BZ Tel: 01234 351966

Caythorpe Court, Caythorpe, Grantham, Lincolnshire NG32 3EP Tel: 01400 272521

General Contacts: Applied Sciences – Annette Crisp, Tel: 0116 257 4103; Art & Design – Kate Bancham, Tel: 0116 250 6161; Business & Law – Nick O'Mahoney, Tel: 0116 250 6292; Computing & Engineering – Faculty of Admissions Unit, Tel: 0116 257 7451; Education & Sports Science – Moira Harrison, Tel: 0116 2551 1551 ext 3300; Health & Community Studies – Anne Hockick, Tel: 0116 255 1551; Humanities & Social Science – Steph Wyatt, Tel: 0116 250 6326
* Also with a QTS route.
** Distance Learning.
S Sandwich Yr.

First Degrees

BA: *5 yrs PT* Architecture
BA/BA Hons: *1 yr FT/2 yrs PT* Applied Social & Community Studies (Applicants must have completed a Diploma in Social Work or Youth & Community Development) *3 yrs FT* Applied Social Studies (Incorporating the Diploma in Social Work); Architecture; Business Administration; Business Studies; Finance; Fine Art; Health Studies; Human Resource Management; Land Management; Law; Law; Marketing Communications; Marketing Research; Politics-Psychology or Sociology; Property and Business *3 yrs FT/4 yrs S* Accounting-Finance (Vocational and non-vocational); Law; Marketing; Public Administration-Managerial Studies *3 yrs FT/5 yrs PT* Adventure Recreation; Youth & Community Development *3 yrs FT/5-8 yrs PT* Accounting (Vocational and non-vocational); Art History; Business; Ceramics & Glass; Conservation & Restoration; Contemporary Decorative Crafts; Contour Fashion; Decorative Artefacts (Multimedia Textiles); Fashion Design; Fashion Studies; Finance; Fine Art; Footwear Design; Furniture Design; History of Architecture & Design; History of Art & Design; Illustration; Interior Design; Law; Marketing; Metalsmithing & Jewellery; Multimedia Design; Museum & Material Culture Studies; Product Design; Property; Surface Decoration; The Management of Design & Innovation; Valuation & Auctioning: Fine Art & Chattels *3 yrs FT/6 yrs PT* Arts Management; Economics; English; Graphics; History; Politics *3-4 yrs FT/6 yrs PT* Dance; Education Studies; French Studies; German Studies; Hispanic Studies *4 yrs PT* Health Studies *4 yrs S* Accounting & Finance (Voluntary work experience yr); Business Studies (Compulsory work experience yr); European Business Studies (Voluntary work experience yr); Human Resource Management (Voluntary work experience yr); Marketing (Voluntary work experience yr); Marketing Communications (Voluntary work experience yr); Marketing Research (Voluntary work experience yr) *6 yrs PT* American Studies; International Relations; Media Studies; Music Technology; Performing Arts; Photography & Video; Theatre
BA/BA Hons; BSc/BSc Hons: Management Science *Combined Studies:* Chemistry; Computing; English for Specific Purposes; Human Resource Management; Management Science; Psychology
BA/BSc Hons: *3 yrs FT/5 yrs PT* Environment & Development; Environmental Studies/Ecology; Geography of Development; Human Geography; Leisure (and Recreational) Studies; Sociology; Sports Studies *4 yrs S* Business Information Systems
BEd Hons: *4 yrs FT* Education (Primary); Physical Education
BEng Hons/Meng: *3 yrs FT/4 yrs S* Mechanical Engineering
BEng/BEng Hons: *4 yrs S* Mechanical Engineering
BEng/BEng Hons/MEng: *3 yrs FT/4 yrs S* Electronic Engineering
BSc Hons: *3 yrs FT* Land Management; Nursing with Registration; Rural Land Management *3 yrs FT/4 yrs S* Broadcast Technology; Computer & Information Systems; Media Technology *4 yrs FT* Computing; Ecological Science; Midwifery (Pre-Registration) *4 yrs S* Computer Science; Computer Systems; Management Science; Multimedia Computing; Pharmaceutical & Cosmetic Sciences; Software Engineering *45 wks FT* Community Health Nursing *90 wks PT* Community Health Nursing *78 wks* Midwifery (Pre-Registration)
BSc/BSc Hons: *2 yrs FT* Outdoor Recreation Management *2 yrs FT/4 yrs S* Recreation Management *3 yrs FT* Agriculture: Crop Production & Protection; Animal Science (Behavioural Studies); Applied Biology; Chemistry; Chemistry Options; Crop Production & Protection; Environmental Studies/Ecology; Equine Science; Equine Sports Science; Fabric Design & Production; Forestry;

Human Communication (Speech Therapy & Language); Landscape Ecology; Psychology; Psychology, Human; Textile & Clothing Production Management; Textile & Clothing Retail Marketing *3 yrs FT/4 yrs S* Architectural Design Technology & Production; Architectural Design Technology and Production; Biology; Biomedical Science with Chemistry; Biomedical Science with Business Studies; Biomedical Science; Building Surveying; Chemistry; Chemistry with Business Studies; Electronics; Industrial Design (Engineering); Management Science; Management Science-Economics; Water & Environmental Management *4 yrs PT (BSc)/further yr for Hons* Textiles (Manufacturing) *4 yrs S* Analytical Chemistry; Applied Chemistry; Chemistry; Chemistry with Business Studies; Computing; Environmental Chemistry; Information Technology; Land Management; Pharmaceutical & Cosmetic Science; Pharmaceutical Chemistry; Psychology & Sociology; Technology; Technology Management *5 yrs S* Biomedical Science with Business *6 yrs PT* Planning & Development

LLB/LLB Hons: *3 yrs FT/4 yrs PT* Law *4 yrs FT* Law with French or German

Higher Degrees

DAdmin: *2-3 yrs PT* Administration

DBA: Business Administration

DFin: Finance

LLM/MA/PGDip: *15 mths* Business Law

LLM/PGDip: Advanced Legal Practice *15 mths FT* Countryside & Agricultural Law; Environmental Law; Food Law

MA: *1 yr FT* Architectural Conservation; Dance; Economics; European Cultural Planning; Film & Fiction; Fine Art; History-Theory & Criticism of Architecture; Learning & Teaching; Management, Law & Humanities of Sport; Management Science and Economics; Marketing Administration; Performance Studies; Personnel & Development; Photography; Practice/ Research & Advancement in South Asian Design & Architecture (PRASADA); Shakespeare Today; Sports History & Culture; Theatre; TV Scriptwriting; War in History *Supported DL* Human Resource Management *14/24 mths PT* Human Resource Management *2 yrs FT* Conservation of Historic Objects *2 yrs PT* Architectural Conservation; Architectural Practice *26 mths PT* Social & Community Studies (Netherlands)

MA/MEd/MSc: (Awarded by independent study)

MA/MSc/PGDip: *3 yrs PT* Design & Manufacture

MA/PGCert/PGDip: Educational Studies

MA/PGDip: Sport & Leisure Management *1 yr FT/2 yrs PT* Applied Health Studies; Architectural Practice; Art & Design Education; Critical Histories of the Visual Image; Photography; Research/ Management/ Community Health *1 yr PT* Dyslexia Studies *2 yrs min* Therapy, Transpersonal Child Adolescent & Family *2 yrs PT* Community Education; Midwifery; Nursing; Transpersonal Counselling-Psychotherapy (London) *DL* Health & Community Development

MBA: *1 yr FT/2 yrs PT* (AMBA accredited)

MChem: *4 yrs FT/5 yrs S* Chemistry

MPharm: *4 yrs FT* Pharmacy

MPhil/PhD: (Available in most disciplines) *2 yrs min* Fine Art Practice

MRes/PGDip: *1 yr FT* Master of Research

MSc: *1 yr FT* Accounting-Finance; Biotechnology; Conservation Science; Energy and Sustainable Development; Environmental Technology; Strategic Marketing *2 yrs PT* Housing

MSc/IGDS: *3 yrs PT* Industrial Data Modelling

MSc/PGDip: *1 yr FT* Computing; Development & Application of Information Systems; Digital Sound & Image Processing; Information Technology *1 yr FT/2 yrs PT* Information Systems Management *2 yrs PT* Property Development *48 wks FT* Mechatronics

MSc/PGDip/PGCert: Biomedical Science; Clinical Pharmacy *3 yrs FT* Environment Quality Management

Diplomas

BTEC HNC/D: *2 yrs PT* Business-Finance; Clothing & Textiles

BTEC HND: *2 yrs FT* Agriculture: Crop Production & Protection; Animal Science (Behavioural Studies); Applied Biology; Chemistry; Clothing; Computing; Engineering; Equine Science; Fashion; Footwear Fashion-Technology; Forestry; Golf & Lesiure Management; Graphic Design;

Horse Studies; Horticulture (Flower & Ornamental Crop Technology); Land Administration; Landscape Ecology; Management Science; Outdoor Recreational Management; Pharmaceutical Chemistry; Public Administration; Textiles *2 yrs FT/4 yrs PT* Performing Arts

BTEC HND/BA/BA Hons: Public Administration; Public Policy & Management

BTEC HND/BA/BSC Hons: Information Systems

BTEC HND/BSc Hons: Computing; Computing Science

BTEC HND/BSc/BSc Hons: Engineering

Chartered Institute of Housing Professionals Dip: *2 yrs FT* Housing

DipHE: Management Studies (With NVQ Levels 4 and 5 options) *1 yr FT/2 yrs PT* Art & Design; Art & Design (Foundation); Conservation & Restoration *18 mths* Nursing for Enrolled Nurses *2 yrs FT* Health Studies *2 yrs FT/3 yrs PT* Midwifery Studies; Nursing with Registration; Social Work; Youth & Community Development *2 yrs FT/3-4 yrs PT* 3-Dimensional Design Crafts; Fashion & Textiles; Graphic Design; Photography & Video; Product Design; Theatre Crafts *2 yrs PT* Management Studies *3 yrs FT* Midwifery (Pre-Registration)

DipHE/BA/BA Hons: *4 yrs FT* Nursing Studies *4 yrs PT* Midwifery Studies

DipHE/BSc Hons: *40 wks* Health Care Practice

GNVQ Advanced: *2 yrs FT/3-4 yrs PT* Art & Design

Graduate Diploma: *2 yrs FT* Architecture *3 yrs PT* Architecture

Postgraduate Diploma: *1 yr FT* Journalism; Law; Legal Practice *1 yr FT/2 yrs PT* Architectural Practice *1 yr PT* Health & Social Services Management; Law Company Secretaryship

Royal Society of Health Diploma: Environmental Protection

University Diploma: *2 yrs PT* Personnel Management

Certificates

CertHE: *1 yr FT* English Language & Culture for International Students

Certificate: Languages for Business *1 yr FT* Textiles (Students can continue to the 2nd yr of the HND); Women's Access to Information Technology *1 yr PT* Management Studies

IPD Professional Qualification: *3 yrs PT* Personnel & Development (Milton Keynes)

PGCE: *1 yr FT* Art & Design Education; Primary Education; Secondary Education *1 yr PT* Commercial Management; Managing Health Services

PGCE/CertED: *2 yrs PT* Post-Compulsory Education

Post-experience Certificate: *1 yr PT* Advanced Management

University Certificate: *1 yr PT* Housing

Professional Qualifications

ACCA: *4 yrs PT* Accountancy (At Leicester and Milton Keynes)

Chartered Institute of Purchasing & Supply profess

CIM: *2 yrs PT* Marketing (At Leicester and Milton Keynes)

CIMA: *4 yrs PT* Accountancy (At Leicester and Milton Keynes)

Degrees validated by De Montfort University offered at:

De Montfort University Bedford

Lansdowne Road, Bedford MK40 2BZ Tel: 01234 351966 Fax: 01234 793277

First Degrees

BA Hons/BSc Hons: *3 yrs FT Nine pathway options:* Business Studies; Dance & Drama; English & Cultural Studies; Environmental Studies; European Studies; History; Human Geography; Leisure & Recreation Studies; Sociology; Sports Studies

BEd Hons: *4 yrs FT* Primary Education; Secondary Physical Education

Higher Degrees

MA: *1 yr FT/2 yrs PT* Educational Studies; Learning & Teaching; Leisure Management; Literary Studies; Performance Studies; War in History; Women & Representation

MPhil/PhD: *12-48 mths FT/24-60 mths PT* Dance; Education; Environmental Studies; European Studies; History; Leisure & Recreation; Literature; Physical Education; Sociology; Sports
MSc: Chiropractic; Sport & Exercise Science

Diplomas

HND: *2 yrs FT* Performing Arts; Science (Sports Studies)
Postgraduate Diploma: Learning & Teaching; Leisure Management

Certificates

Postgraduate Certificate: Distance Learning; Learning & Teaching; Sport/Leisure Facility Management *1 yr FT* Education (Primary); Education (Secondary)

Professional Qualifications

ACCA: *4 yrs PT* Accountancy

UNIVERSITY OF DERBY

Kedleston Road Campus, Kedleston Road, Derby DE22 1GB Tel: 01332 622222
Fax: 01332 294861

Mickleover Campus, Western Road, Mickleover, Derby 3 5 Tel: 01332 622275

Green Lane Campus, Green Lane, Derby DE1 1RX Tel: 01332 622282

Britannia Buildings, Mackworth Road, Derby Tel: 01332 622222

High Peak College, Harpur Hill, Buxton SK17 9J2 Tel: 01298 71100

First Degrees

BA Hons: *3 yrs FT* Accounting; American Studies; Applied Arts; Applied Community and Youth Studies; Applied Social Work; Art Therapies; Business Administration; Business Studies; Community Health Nursing; Early Childhood Studies; Enterprise Management; European Studies; Fashion Studies; Film & Television Studies; Financial Economics; Health Care; History; Hospitality Management; Human Resource Management; Illustration; Industrial Economics; Law with European Studies; Law with Modern Language; Law; Literature; Management; Management Accounting; Marketing; Modern Languages; Performing & Media Arts; Photography & Time-based Media; Popular Music; Social & Cultural Studies; Social, Cultural & Religious Studies; Sociology; Visual Cultures *3 yrs FT/4 yrs S* Accounting; Textile Design *3 yrs PT* Advanced Professional Studies for Nurses, Midwives & Health Visitors; Applied Community & Youth Studies; Applied Social Work *3-4 yrs FT* Applied Arts; Fine Art; Graphic Design; Marketing; Textile Design; Tourism; Visual Communications *4 yrs S* Fashion Studies; International Business
BA/BSc: (Modular Degree Scheme)
BEd Hons: *3 yrs FT* Primary Education
BEng Hons: Mechanical & Manufacturing Engineering
BSc Hons: Mechanical & Manufacturing Engineering *3 yrs FT* Applicable Mathematics-Computing; Applied Environmental Earth Science; Architectural Conservation; Architectural Technology & Innovation; Artificial Intelligence; Biological Imaging; Biology; Biology & Chemistry; Biology & Chemistry; Biology & Geology; Biology-Environmental Studies; Biology-Geography; Biology-Heritage Conservation; Business Decision Analysis; Chemistry with Environmental Management & Monitoring; Chemistry & Geography; Chemistry & Geology; Chemistry-Environmental Studies; Chemistry-Heritage Conservation; Combined Sciences; Communication Technology-Electronic Systems; Computer Studies with Visualisation; Computer Studies with Artificial Intelligence; Computer Studies; Conservation of Countryside Management; Construction Management; Creative Computing; Development Studies; Diagnostic Radiography; Digital Entertainment; Digital Media; Environment & Biology; Environmental Chemistry; Environmental Monitoring; Environmental Studies & Chemistry; Environmental Studies & Geography; Environmental Studies & Geology; Geography & Geology; Health Services Management; Healthcare Information Management; Information Systems; Live Performance Systems & Sound Engineering; Mathematical Studies with Language; Mathematical Studies;

Mathematics with Statistics & Computing; Music Technology-Audio Systems Design; Occupational Therapy; Operational Research; Product Design; Psychology; Technology Management; Virtual Product Design; Visualisation *3 yrs FT/3 yrs PT* Electrical & Electronic Engineering; Electronics Product Design; Human Sciences *3 yrs FT/4 yrs PT* Construction Management; Development Studies *3 yrs FT/4 yrs S/6 yrs PT* Innovation & Marketing; Product Design; Psychology; Technology Management, Innovation & Business Psychology; Therapeutic Radiography *3 yrs FT/5 yrs PT* Information Systems with Artificial Intelligence; Music Technology & Audio System Design *3-4 yrs FT* Applicable Mathematics & Computing; Applied Environmental Earth Science; Architectural Technology & Innovation; Biological Imaging *3-4.5 yrs PT* Occupational Therapy *4 yrs S* Business Decision Analysis; Computer Studies; Computer Studies with Artificial Intelligence; Computer Studies with Visualisation; Information Systems; Mathematics Studies; Mathematics, Statistics & Computing

Higher Degrees

MA: *1 yr FT/2 yrs PT* Aesthetics & Politics; Counselling; Critical History & Theory of Photography; Culture, Place & Identity; Film & Television Studies; Graphic Design; Performance Sportswear Design; Photographic Studies; Textile Design *1 yr FT/3 yrs PT* Human Resource Management; Marketing Management; Tourism Management *1 yr PT* Religious Pluralism *2 yrs PT* Health Promotion, Risk & Safety *3 yrs PT* Management in Education; Pastoral Studies
MBA: *1 yr FT/3 yrs PT* Business Administration
MEd: *1 yr FT* Counselling; Professional Development in Education
MPhil/PhD: (By research. Available in all departments)
MSc: *1 yr FT* Clinical Supervision; Design, Innovation & Strategic Marketing *1 yr FT/3 yrs PT* Applicable Mathematics; Change & Innovation for Nurses, Midwives & Health Visitors; Clinical Pharmacy; Community Pharmacy; Community Pharmacy; Computing; Environmental Pollution Control; Financial Management; General Practice Management; Health Care; Manufacturing Management; Research Methods; Strategic Management *2-3 yrs PT* Health Services Management; Nursing Studies *3 yrs PT* Medical Ultrasound; Social & Administrative Pharmacy

Diplomas

Diploma: Construction Management
Diploma in Higher Education: *1 yr FT* Education
Diploma in Social Work: *2 yrs FT* Applied Youth & Community Work
Postgraduate Diploma: *1 yr FT* European Business; Law; Management Studies; Mediation Studies *1 yr PT* Counselling Studies; Environmental Management; Operations Management; Professional Studies in Nursing

Certificates

Postgraduate Certificate: Medical Ultrasound (Postgraduate only) *1 yr FT* Education *1 yr PT* Environmental Management; Research Methods in Science

Other Courses

CAMS Foundation Course: *1 yr*
Foundation Course: *1 yr FT* Accountancy; Art

DONCASTER COLLEGE

Waterdale, Doncaster DN1 3EX Tel: 01302 553610 Fax: 01302 553766 e-mail: he@don.ac.uk

* Subject to approval.
† HND conversion.

First Degrees

BA Hons: Advertising; Applied Social Sciences; Business Administration; Business Studies; Combined Studies; Criminological Studies; Cultural Studies; Culture & Communication; Economics & Legal Studies; English Literature & Language; Humanities; International Business;

Personnel or Marketing; Business or Leisure Management or Hospitality Management or Finance; Screenwriting Studies; Socio-legal Studies; Urban & Environmental Studies
BEng: Mining & Electrical Engineering; Mining & Mechanical Engineering; Quarry & Road Surface Engineering
BSc: Business Computing *1 yr* Integrated Business Technology; Integrated Technology; Integrated Technology (Hons)

Diplomas

Diploma: *2 yrs PT* Special Education Needs
HND: Building Services Engineering; Business Information Technology; Business Studies; Business-Finance or Marketing or Leisure or Hospitality or Personnel; Comparative Music Studies; Computer Studies/Software Engineering; Design (Advertising); Electronic Engineering & Computing Technology; Fashion; Fine Art; Graphic Design & Multimedia; Illustration; Legal Studies; Music Technology; Performing Arts (Theatre); Sports Science

DONCASTER COLLEGE
Dearne Valley Business School

Tel: 01302 553666 Fax: 01302 553644
e-mail: joanne.layhe@don.ac.uk Website: www.don.ac.uk/dvbs

First Degrees

BA Hons: *1 yr* Business & Management; Business & Managerial Accounting; Business & Marketing; Business & Personnel; Business Administration; Business Studies *2 yrs S (includes industrial placement):* Business & Management; Business & Managerial Accounting; Business & Marketing; Business & Personnel; Business Administration; Business Studies; International Business *3 yrs S (includes industrial placement):* Business & Management; Business Administration; Business Studies with French; Business Studies with German *4 yrs S (includes industrial placement):* Business & Managerial Accounting; Business & Marketing; Business & Personnel; Business Studies; International Business

Diplomas

HND: Business; Business & Finance; Business & Leisure; Business & Management; Business & Marketing; Business & Personnel

UNIVERSITY OF DUNDEE

Dundee DD1 4HN Tel: 01382 344000 Fax: 01382 345500 Telex: 9312110826 DU G
e-mail: srs@dundee.ac.uk Website: www.dundee.ac.uk

MA: The first and second yr courses are common to both MA and MA Honours students. The first yr course comprises three subjects. In the second yr, students normally take three subjects, at least one of which is continued in the third yr.
MA Hons: In the last two yrs students take either a Single or Joint Honours course, selection for which is made at the end of the second yr of the MA. Direct entry to a three yr Honours degree is also available.
Law and Accountancy: For the LLB, BAcc and BFin all students are admitted initially for the third yr degree but may apply for Honours on satisfactory completion of their second yr.
LLB and LLB Hons: Honours degree may be Single Honours in Law or Joint Honours in Law and an Arts & Social Science subject or Joint Honours in Law and Accountancy or Law with French or German or Spanish. For students reading for the LLB who have already been awarded a degree approved for this purpose, the periods of study may be reduced to two and three yrs respectively for the LLB and LLB Honours degrees.
BSc (Science): Students must take seven courses. In the first yr three different subjects are studied, and the courses taken in subsequent yrs may be either a continuation of subjects already studied or courses in different subjects. One or two subjects may be selected from those available in other

Faculties. The decision between BSc and BSc Hons is made at the end of the second yr and is based on performance in the first two yrs. Direct entry to a three yr Honours degree is also available. Named non-Honours degrees may be obtained in Applied Computing; Applied Computing and Mathematics; Chemistry; Mathematics; Physics; Science.

BEng: The final decision between BEng and BEng Honours need not be made until the third yr. The courses in all three yrs are the same as for Honours. Accelerated three yr BEng Honours degree is also available.

MEng: An extra yr of study for an enhanced Engineering first degree.

MSc: Awarded after a course of special study and exam or by research. A thesis is required in either case. For honours graduates the minimum period of study is four academic terms.

MSci: In Physics requires an extra yr beyond the BSC Honours degree for an enhanced first degree.

MPhil: Awarded in the Faculty of Arts & Social Sciences to graduates with First or Second Class Honours; the degree may be awarded either by thesis or exam (with or without dissertation).

First Degrees

ARCHITECTURE & PLANNING
BSc Hons: *4 yrs FT* Environmental Management; Town & Regional Planning (Fully accredited by RTPI)
BSc/BArch: *5 yrs FT* Architecture (Students must complete one yr's professional practice between BSc and BArch degrees. Gives exemption from RIBA Parts I and II)

FINE ART & DESIGN
BA Hons Fine Art: *4 yrs FT* Drawing & Painting; Printmaking; Sculpture; Time-Based Art
BDes Hons Design: *4 yrs FT* Animation & Electronic Media; Ceramics; Constructed Textiles; Graphic Design; Illustration & Printmaking; Interior & Environmental Design; Jewellery & Metalwork; Printed Textiles

LAW & ACCOUNTANCY
BAcc/BAcc Hons: *3-4 yrs FT* Business Finance; Accountancy; Accountancy; Accountancy with Management and Information Systems
BFin/BFin Hons: *3-4 yrs FT* Finance
LLB/LLB Hons: *3-4 yrs FT* Accountancy & English Law; English Law with French or German or Spanish; Law; Scots Law *4 yrs FT* Law and Contemporary European Studies or History or Philosophy or Politics

MEDICINE & DENTISTRY
BDS: *5-6 yrs* Dentistry (Honours or Commendation may be awarded if the candidate's record throughout the dental course is of sufficient merit. (It is also possible for dental students to intercalate an additional yr during their course to study for the Hons BMSc degree))
BMSc: *1 yr* Medicine (Between phases 2 & 3 of the MB, ChB; and the 2nd & 3rd yr of the BDS, students may study 1 or more of the basic sciences in depth for 1 yr to gain an Honours BMSc degree, thereafter resuming their studies for standard MB, ChB or BDS degrees)
BSc MedSci: *3 yrs* Medicine (A BSc in Medical Science may be awarded to MB, ChB or BDS students on the basis of passes obtained on these courses)
MB; ChB: *5-6 yrs* Medicine (Honours or Commendation may be awarded if the candidate's record throughout the medical course is of sufficient merit)

SCIENCE & ENGINEERING
BEng Hons: *3-4 yrs* Civil Engineering; Civil Engineering & Management; Electronic & Electrical Engineering; Electronic Engineering & Microcomputer Systems; Electronic Engineering & Physics; Electronic Engineering with Management; Mechanical Engineering; Semiconductor Engineering
BSc: *3 yrs* Applied Computing; Applied Computing-Mathematics; Chemistry; Mathematics; Physics

BSc Hons: *3-4 yrs* Accountancy-Applied Computing or Chemistry or Mathematics; Anatomical & Physiological Sciences; Anatomical Sciences; Applied Computing; Applied Mathematics; Applied Physics; Biochemistry or Pharmacology; Biochemistry-Chemistry or Physiological Sciences; Biological Chemistry; Biology; Business Economics, Marketing & Operational Research; Chemistry or Economics or Environmental Science or Mathematics or Pharmacology or Physics or Physiological Sciences with Marketing; Chemistry and Business Economics; Applied Computing or Digital Microelectronics or Economics or Financial Economics; Chemistry or Mathematics or Physics or Psychology; Computing & Cognitive Science; Economics; Economics with Statistics; Environmental Science; Financial Economics; Financial Economics with Statistics; Geography; Mathematics; Mathematics with Statistics; Mathematics and Digital Microelectronics or Economics or Financial Economics or Numerical Analysis or Physics or Psychology; Medicinal Chemistry; Microbiology; Molecular Biology; Molecular Genetics; Pharmacology; Pharmacology & Physiological Sciences; Physics; Physics with French or German or Spanish; Physics and Digital Microelectronics or Environmental Science or Philosophy or Psychology; Physiological Sciences; Psychology; Psychology with Statistics; Zoology

Higher Degrees

DOCTORATES
PhD: Doctor of Philosophy (Awarded to graduates of any university after at least nine terms of full-time study and research)

HIGHER MEDICAL & DENTAL DEGREES
DDSc: Doctor of Dental Science (By thesis or published work submitted at least five yrs after first dental qualification. Must be Dundee graduates or St Andrews graduates having matriculated before 1 August 1967)
M MAS: *1 yr FT* Master of Minimal Access Surgery (Aims to train surgeons in endoscopic surgery)
MChOrth: *1 yr FT* Master of Orthopaedic Surgery (Applicants must have a degree in medicine plus at least two yrs' post-registration experience in orthopaedic surgery)
MD: Doctor of Medicine (By thesis on a medical topic at least five yrs after MB, ChB. Must be Dundee graduates or St Andrews graduates having matriculated before 1 August 1967)
MDSc: *3 trms FT/equiv PT Master of Dental Science in one of:* Oral Medicine & Pathology; Oral Surgery; Primary Dental Care
MFM: *4 trms FT/equiv PT* Master of Forensic Medicine (Intended primarily for overseas doctors wishing to obtain information in forensic medicine. This is carried out mainly by means of medical-legal care work attachments)
MM: *4 yrs* Master of Midwifery
MMedEd: Master of Medical Education (Fifteen mths by distance learning following completion of the University's diploma in Medical Education. By dissertation after special study and research on an approved topic)
MMSc: Master of Medical Science (By dissertation and oral exam after study or research in an approved topic; candidates must be medical, dental or medical science graduates)
MN: *2-7 yrs DL Master of Nursing:* Nursing (Aims to provide updated clinical practice by DL for traditionally trained registered nurses and midwives)
MPC: *2-7 yrs DL* Master of Palliative Care (To enhance multi-professional collaboration in palliative care)
MPH: Master of Public Health (By exam and dissertation after study and research in an approved Public Health topic; candidates must be medical, dental or medical science graduates)
MSSc: Master of Surgical Science (By dissertation and oral exam after study or research in an approved topic; candidates must be medical, dental or medical science graduates)

MASTER'S DEGREES OR EQUIVALENT
LLM: *4 trms FT/equiv PT or DL Master of Laws:* Energy Law & Policy; Environmental Law & Policy; European Energy & Natural Resources Law & Policy; International & Comparative Water Law & Policy; International Business Transactions; Mineral Law & Policy; Petroleum Law & Policy; Petroleum Taxation & Finance; Resources Law & Policy

MA: *3 yrs* American Studies; Contemporary European Studies; Economics; English; Environmental Science; Geography; History; Mathematics; Philosophy; Politics; Psychology; Scottish Historical Studies

MA Hons: *3-4 yrs Joint Honours:* American Studies with French or German or Spanish; American Studies-Business Economics with Marketing or English or Environmental Science or Financial Economics or Geography or History or Philosophy or Politics or Psychology or Economics; Business Economics with Marketing with French or German or Spanish; Business Economics with Marketing-Contemporary European Studies or Environmental Science or Geography or History or Mathematics or Philosophy or Politics or Psychology; Economics with French or German or Spanish; Economics-Contemporary European Studies or English or Environmental Science or Financial Economics or Geography or History or Philosophy or Politics or Psychology; Economics-Environmental Science or Geography or History or Mathematics or Philosophy or Politics or Psychology or Planning; English with French or German or Spanish; English-Geography or History or Mathematics or Philosophy or Politics or Psychology; Environmental Science-Financial Economics or Geography or History or Mathematics or Politics; Financial Economics with French or German or Spanish; Financial Economics-Geography or History or Mathematics or Philosophy or Politics or Psychology; Geography with French or German or Spanish; Geography-History or Philosophy or Politics or Psychology or Planning; History with French or German or Spanish; History-Philosophy or Politics or Psychology; Mathematics-Philosophy or Psychology; Philosophy with French or German or Spanish; Philosophy-Politics or Psychology; Politics with French or German or Spanish; Politics-Psychology; Psychology with French or German or Spanish *Single Honours:* American Studies; Business Economics with Marketing; Contemporary European Studies (Includes at least one of French, German or Spanish); Economics; English; Financial Economics; Geography; History; Philosophy; Politics; Psychology; Scottish Historical Studies; Social Work

MBA: *1 yr FT/2 yrs PT Master of Business Administration in:* Mineral Resources Management; Oil & Gas Management; Water Resources Management

MDes: *1 yr FT* Master of Design (For graduate designers to engage in advanced-level work within a multidisciplinary context)

MEd: *1 yr FT/2-5 yrs PT* Education

MEd Hons: *2 yrs FT/2-6 yrs PT* Master of Education (Open to those with a recognised teaching qualification and at least three yrs' relevant experience. The MEd may be awarded with or without Honours. Exam is by continuous assessment, written exam and a dissertation)

MEng Hons: *4-5 yrs FT* Civil Engineering; Electronic & Electrical Engineering; Electronic Engineering & Microcomputer Systems; Electronic Engineering & Physics; Electronic Engineering with Management; Engineering with French or German or Spanish; Semiconductor Engineering

MFA: *1 yr FT* Master of Fine Art (For graduates specialising in Public Art or Painting, Printmaking, Sculpture or other Fine Art discipline)

MPhil: *4 trms FT/equiv PT Mater of Philosophy in one of:* Applied Population Analysis; Child Protection Studies; Cognitive Science; Community Care Studies; Computing, Text & Cognition; Contemporary European Studies; Continental Philosophy; Continental Philosophy & the Arts; Development & Environment; Economics; Education Research; English Literature; Financial Economics; History (Inter-university course); Logic, Text & Information Technology; Philosophy of Cognitive Science; Politics and Policies in Contemporary Europe; Religion & Metaphysics

MRes: *1 yr FT/3 yrs PT* Civil Engineering

MSc: *4 trms FT/equiv PT Master of Science in:* Applied Computing; Biological Nuclear Magnetic Resonance; Concrete Technology & Construction; Concrete Technology, Construction & Management; Construction & Management; Educational Psychology; Electrical Power Engineering & Management; Electronic Circuit Design & Manufacture; Electronic Imaging; Energy Studies (in one of Energy Economics; Energy & the Environment; Energy Finance; Energy Policy; Energy Utility Management; European Energy); Environmental Health; European Urban Conservation; International Oil & Gas Management; Oil & Gas Economics; Orthopaedic & Rehabilitation Technology; Radiation Physics & Medical Imaging; Remote Sensing, Image Processing & Applications; Water Studies *DL Master of Science in:* Primary Care

MSci Hons: *4-5 yrs* Physics

MSW: *6 trms* Master of Social Work

Honorary Degrees
LLD; DSc; DLitt; MDSc; MMSc; MSc; MA; MPH; MSSc

Diplomas

Dip ASSC: *1 yr PG* Computing, Text & Cognition; Economics; Financial Economics; Logic, Text & Information Technology; Political Science; Politics and Policies in Contemporary Europe

DipEng: *1 yr PG* Concrete Technology & Construction; Concrete Technology, Construction & Management; Electrical & Electronic Engineering; Electrical Power Engineering & Management; Electronic Circuit Design & Manufacture

Diploma: *1 yr FT* Child Protection Studies; Cognitive & Behavioural Psychotherapy (Provides students with key theories and associated practice skills for care and treatment of those with mental health problems. Intended for professionally qualified personnel from health or social services); Environmental Studies (By coursework and dissertation for graduates. Separate Diplomas are awarded in Computer-Aided Architectural Design and European Urban Conservation) *1 yr FT/2-3 yrs PT* Teaching in Higher Education (Intended particularly for teachers in further/higher education involved in staff training/staff development programmes) *1 yr PG* Electronic Imaging (Project-based, supported by specialist master classes and intensive technical instruction); Environmental Health (Similar course content to MSc in Environmental Health); Legal Practice (Course open to LLB graduates of Scottish universities. Completion of this course is a compulsory requirement for admission as a solicitor in Scotland); Public Health (Similar course content to Master of Public Health (MPH)) *1-3 yrs PG PT* Advanced Educational Studies (Intended for practising teachers with at least three yrs' experience) *1-4 yrs FT and DL* Medical Education (Designed for health care professionals who are unable to leave their workplace in order to acquire a range of techniques for improving the practice of medical education in their own working environment) *2 yrs PT* German (Intended for teachers of modern languages not already qualified in German); Spanish (Intended for teachers of modern languages not already qualified in Spanish) *2-5 yrs DL* Orthopaedic & Rehabilitation Technology (For health care professionals) *3 yrs FT* Higher Education in Nursing or Midwifery (Option of upgrading to Bachelor's degree in Nursing or Midwifery by distance learning) *5 trms FT or PT or DL* Community Care Studies (Course for practising social workers) *6 trms* Social Work (Equips students with the knowledge, values and practical skills required of a qualified social worker. Persons holding this diploma are eligible for the Diploma awarded by CCETSW) *9 mths FT* Accountancy & Business Finance (Similar in concise content to MAcc) *DL* Advanced Nursing Studies (Intended for nurses, midwives and health visitors); Applied Computing; Palliative Care (Intended for health care professionals involved in the palliative care of cancer patients)

DipSc: *1 yr* Remote Sensing, Image Processing & Applications

Energy Law: *1 yr FT* Energy & Environment; Energy Economics; Energy Finance; Energy Law & Policy; Energy Policy; Energy Studies; Energy Utility Management; European Energy; European Energy & Natural Resources Law & Policy; Gas Management; International Oil & Gas Management; Oil & Gas Economics; Water Law

Certificates

Certificate: *1 trm* Industrial Health (Course for graduates in medicine and surgery of at least two yrs' standing, or similarly qualified persons); International & Comparative Water Law & Policy; Water Studies *1 trm FT* Medical Education (For those involved in the supervision of postgraduate trainees in general practice, hospital specialities, etc) *1 trm FT or PT or DL* Community Care Studies (For practising social workers) *1 trm PT* Educational Studies (Modules in social context of education; education past and present; the idea of education; teaching & learning) *1 trm* Child Protection Studies (Certificate Course and Advanced Certificate for practising social workers) *DL* Child Protection Studies (Certificate Course and Advanced Certificate for practising social workers) *1 yr PT* Teaching in Higher Education (For HE staff to evaluate their own teaching practice) *15 wks PT* Teaching Modern Languages to Adults (For graduates with a high level of competence in a modern language)

UNIVERSITY OF DURHAM

Old Shire Hall, Old Elvet, Durham DH1 3HP Tel: 0191 374 4685 Fax: 0191 374 7250
e-mail: admissions@durham.ac.uk Website: www.dur.ac.uk

First Degrees

BA Combined Hons: *3 yrs* Combined Studies in Social Sciences *3 yrs FT* Combined Studies in Arts; Natural Sciences

BA Hons: *3 yrs FT* Ancient History; Anthropology; Archaeology; Business Economics; Business Finance; Childhood & Society; Classical Studies; Classics I; Classics II; Community & Youth Work Studies; East Asian Area Studies; Economics; English Language & Linguistics; English Literature; European Studies with French or German or Spanish; Geography; Geography (European Studies); Health & Human Sciences; History; Human Sciences; Japanese with Second Language or Geography or History or Linguistics or Philosophy or Politics; Japanese with a Second East Asian Language; Japanese Studies; Latin; Law with Economics or Politics or Sociology; Mathematics; Medieval Studies; Music; Philosophy; Politics & History of the Middle East with Arabic or Persian or Turkish; Politics with Law; Psychology; Russian with Central and East European Area Studies; Russian; Sociology; Sociology and Social Policy; Sociology with Law; Sport in the Community; Sport-Health; Exercise; Theology; Theology (European Studies); Urban Studies *4 yrs FT* Arabic with Anthropology or Economics or Geography or European Languages or Mid Eastern & Islamic Studies or Politics or Sociology & Social Policy; Arabic with Persian or Turkish; Chinese; Chinese with Second Language or Geography or History or Japanese or Linguistics or Philosophy or Politics; Chinese with Second Asian Language; Chinese & Management Studies; Economics with French; History with French or German; Islamic Studies with Arabic; Japanese & Management Studies; Mathematics (European Studies); Modern Languages (French, German, Russian, Spanish, Italian); Politics (European Studies)

BA Joint Hons: *3 yrs* Classics-Theology; Economics with Mathematics; Economics-History or Law or Politics or Sociology *3 yrs FT* Ancient History-Archaeology; Ancient, Medieval and Modern History; Anthropology-Psychology or Sociology; Archaeology-Anthropology or History; Archaeology-History; Classical Studies; Classics-Theology; East Asian Area and Management Studies; English Literature-Classical Studies or Latin or Linguistics or Music or Philosophy; History-Russian/English; Islamic Studies and Arabic; Latin-Music; Law with Politics or Sociology; Mathematics-Economics; Modern Languages-Linguistics or Music; Music-Theology; Philosophy-Politics or Psychology or Theology; Politics-History or Sociology; Psychology-Sociology; Russian-Politics; Sociology-History or Social Policy; Politics-Sociology

BAEd: *3 yrs FT* Education for Primary School Teachers (4-12 yrs)

LLB Hons: *3 yrs FT* Law *4 yrs FT* European Legal Studies

SCIENCE

BSc (Ed): *2 yrs FT* Primary Teaching (Science)

BSc Hons: *3 yrs FT* Applied Physics; Applied Psychology; Archaeology; Artificial Intelligence; Biology; Biomedical Sciences; Cell Biology; Chemistry; Chemistry (Industrial); Chemistry (International); Childhood and the Arts; Computer Science; Earth Sciences; Ecology; Environmental Development; Environmental Geoscience; Environmental Management; Environmental Technology; Geography; Geography (European Studies); Geography-Environment & Development; Geography-Environmental Management; Geology; Geology & Geophysics; Geophysics; Health & Human Sciences; Information Systems Management; Mathematics; Molecular Biology & Biochemistry; Natural Sciences; Physics; Physics & Astronomy; Plant Sciences; Psychology; Software Engineering; Zoology *4 yrs FT* Computer Science (European Studies); Mathematics (European Studies)

BSc Joint Hons: *3 yrs FT* Computer Science-Mathematics; Mathematics-Physics

Higher Degrees

HIGHER MEDICAL & DENTAL DEGREES

MBBS: Medicine (Joint with Newcastle)

MN: *1 yr FT* 17th Century Studies

MASTER'S DEGREES OR EQUIVALENT

MA: *1 yr FT* Ancient Philosophy; Anthropology; Applied Linguistics; Applied Linguistics with ELT or ELT & Materials Development or ELT, CALL & Educational Technology or ESOL or ESP or French or German or Spanish or Arabic or Japanese Language Teaching or Translation; Arabic & English Translation; Area and Business Studies: Central and Eastern Europe; Classics; Classics & Theology; Contemporary Sociology: Studies in Social, Political & Cultural Order; Counselling; Criminal Justice; East Asian Art & Archaeology; East Asian Research; English Literary Studies; European Political & Economic Integration; Geographic Information for Development; International & European Legal Studies (Taught course); International Boundaries; International Relations; International Relations, Middle East with East Asia or Europe; International Studies; Islamic Studies; Languages Acquisition; Linguistics; Managerial Economics; Medieval History; Modern History; Modern Middle Eastern History; Museum & Artefact Studies; Musicology; Philosophy; Social Anthropology (modern societies); Women's Studies (The Middle East) *1 yr FT/5 yrs PT* Community Studies; Education; Health & Community Care *2 yrs FT* Applied Social Studies; Islamic Studies with a Middle Eastern Language; Middle Eastern Studies with a Middle Eastern Language *2 yrs PT* 17th Century Studies; Archaeological Survey; Archaeology (including Conservation of Historic Objects, Environmental Archaeology, History & Philosophy of Archaeology, Medieval Archaeology, Numismatic Studies, Post Medieval Archaeology, Pre-Historic Archaeology, & Roman Archaeology); Classical Historiography; Composition; Electroacoustic Studies; Entrepreneurship; Environmental Management Practice; Ethnomusicology; Middle East Politics; Middle Eastern Studies; Modern East Asian Studies; Modern European Languages & Culture; Music; Theological Research; Theology; Urban & Regional Change In Europe *2-5 yrs PT* Social Work Studies; Sociology & Social Policy; Sociology of Industrial Society

MBA: *1 yr FT/2 yrs PT/4 yrs PT (DL)* Business Administration *1 yr FT/3 yrs PT* Water Resource Management

MEd: *2 yrs FT* Education (By research thesis) *1 yr FT & 1 yr PT* Education (By research thesis) *3 yrs PT* Education (By research thesis)

MEng Hons: *4 yrs FT* Civil Engineering; Electrical Engineering; Electronic Engineering; Engineering (Overseas Studies); Information Systems Engineering; Manufacturing Engineering; Mechanical Engineering; Unified Engineering

MJur: *1 yr FT/2 yrs PT* Law (By thesis)

MLitt: *2 yrs FT/3 yrs PT* Literature (By research thesis) *1 yr FT & 1 yr PT* Literature (By research thesis)

MMath Hons: *4 yrs FT* Mathematics

MMus: *2 yrs FT/3 yrs PT* Music (By research thesis or one yr taught course full-time plus one yr composition or thesis) *1 yr FT & 1 yr PT* Music (By research thesis or one yr taught course full-time plus one yr composition or thesis)

MPhil: *2 yrs FT* Philosophy (By research thesis) *1 yr FT & 1 yr PT* Philosophy (By research thesis) *3 yrs PT* Philosophy (By research thesis)

MSc: *1 yr FT/2 yrs PT* Applied Archaeological Science; Biological Anthropology; Corporate & International Finance; Elementary Particle Theory; Engineering Geology; Geo-Environmental Engineering; Geographical Information for Development; Geomorphology & Environmental Change; Geophysics; Mathematical Sciences; Spatial Information Technology *2 yrs PT* Environmental Management Practice *4 trms FT/equiv PT* Energy & the Environment; Energy Economics; Energy Finance; Energy Policy; Energy Utility Management; European Management; International Oil and Gas Management; Oil and Gas Economics; Water Studies (Legal Aspects)

MSci Hons: *4 yrs FT* Applied Physics; Chemistry; Geological Sciences; Geophysical Sciences; Mathematics (European Studies); Mathematics-Physics; Physics; Physics-Astronomy; Theoretical Physics

MTheol: *1 yr* Theology (By thesis or by taught course (joint programme of study with the University of Tubingen))

Diplomas

Advanced Diploma: *1 yr FT/2 yrs PT* Entrepreneurship Training & Small Business Development *1 yr PT* Business Counselling; Business Diagnostics & Advising; Enterprise Management; Management of Human Services *15 mths* Moving on with Learning Disabilities *21 mths FT/3 yrs max* Business Administration

Dip ASSC: *1 yr PG* Cognitive Science-Information Technology
Diploma: *1 yr FT* Adult & Community Education; Advanced Arabic; Advanced Japanese; Anthropology; Arabic; Archaeology & Local History; Chinese; Employment Relations; Environmental Management Practice; Japanese; Legal Studies; Philosophy; Psychology
Diploma in Higher Education: *1 yr FT* Community & Youth Work Studies
Diploma in Social Work: Social Work
DipSc: *1 yr* Applied Computing
Postgraduate Diploma: Geographical Information for Development; Spatial Information Technology; Urban & Regional Change in Europe; Youth Work Studies *1 yr FT/2 yrs PT* Philosophy; Theological Research *1 yr FT/Up to 5 yrs PT* Counselling; Education; Health & Community Care; Social Work Studies; Sociology; Sociology & Social Policy; Sociology of Industrial Society *1 yr PT* Environmental Management Practice

Certificates

Advanced Certificate: *1 yr FT* Management Studies; Research & Resource Development; Research for Health Care Professionals *1 yr PT* Business Counselling; Entrepreneurship Training & Small Business Development; Management & Development of Human Resources *2 yrs PT* Further Professional Studies; Lifelong Learning & Professional Development
Certificate: *1 yr FT* Legal Studies *1 yr PT* Counselling Skills; Residential Work with Adolescents; Supervisory Studies *2 yrs PT* Basic Russian; Humanities; Social Sciences *5 mths FT* Certificate of English & Academic Study; Certificate of Intermediate Communication Skills in English
Certificate of Continuing Education: *Up to 5 yrs PT max* Arts; Science; Social Science
Certificate of Higher Education: *Up to 5 yrs PT max* Arts; Community & Youth Work Studies; Science; Social Science
PGCE: Education
Postgraduate Certificate: *1 yr FT* Engineering Geology; Geoenvironmental Engineering; Geographical Information for Development; Urban & Regional Change in Europe *1 yr FT/5 yrs PT* Counselling *6 mths FT* Spatial Information Technology

Degrees validated by University of Durham offered at:

Darlington College of Technology

Cleveland Avenue, Darlington, County Durham DL3 7BB Tel: 01325 503050 Fax: 01325 503000
e-mail: pcoleman@darlington.ac.uk Website: www.darlington.ac.uk

Diplomas

DipHE: *2 yrs PT* Nursing

National Training Centre for Scientific Support to Crime Investigation

Harperley Hall, Crook, County Durham DL15 8DS Tel: 01388 762191 Fax: 01388 742509 e-mail: admin@ntcssci.demon.co.uk Website: www.forensic-training.police.uk

Diplomas

Diploma: Crime Scene Examination (Mixed mode of study including eleven wks full-time plus two yrs' work experience and submission of projects/essays/dissertation); Fingerprint Examination (A diploma in Fingerprint Examination is currently being planned. It is anticipated that it will broadly mirror the above format and should be available from September 2000)

Other Courses

Scottish National Vocational Qualifications: Fingerprint Operations (Level 2); Investigating Scenes of Incident (Level 3); Providing Fingerprint Services (Level 4)

New College Durham

Framwellgate Moor Centre, Durham, County Durham DH1 5ES Tel: 0191 375 4000
Fax: 0191 375 4222 e-mail: Admissions@newdur.ac.uk Website: www.newdur.ac.uk

First Degrees

BA Hons: *3 yrs FT* Management with Business and Administration
BSc Hons: *3-4 yrs FT* Podiatry

Diplomas

Diploma: *2 yrs FT* Social Work
HND: *2 yrs FT* Business & Management; Business & Marketing; Business – Accounting/Financial Management; Business – Administrative Management; Business – Arts & Media Management; Business – Business Administration; Business – Business Information Technology; Business – Communications & Media Management; Business – European Business Management; Business – European Travel & Tourism Management; Business – Graphic Design Management; Business – Heritage Management; Business – Hospitality Management; Business – Human Resource Management; Business – International Business Administration; Business – International Business Administration; Business – International Tourism Management; Business – Leisure & Recreation Management; Business – Media Management; Business – Music Industry Management; Business – Performing Arts Management; Business – Sports & Recreation Management; Business – Tourism Management; Business – Training Management; Business – Travel Industry Management; Business – Visitor Attraction Management; Business – Website Management; Business-Finance; Computing; Multi-Media; Sports Science

Royal Academy of Dancing

Faculty of Education, 36 Battersea Square, London SW11 3RA Tel: 020 7233 0091
Fax: 020 7924 3129 e-mail: smcleod@rad.org.uk Website: www.rad.org.uk

First Degrees

BA Hons: *3 yrs FT* The Art & Teaching of Ballet
BPhil Hons: *16-28 mths modular DL* Ballet & Contextual Studies

St John's College

3 South Bailey, Durham, County Durham DH1 3RJ Tel: 0191 374 3500 Fax: 0191 374 3573
Website: St Johns College via www.dur.ac.uk

First Degrees

BA: *3 yrs FT* Theology & Ministry

Diplomas

Diploma: *2 yrs FT* Theology-Ministry

Certificates

Certificate: *1 yr FT/2 yrs PT* Theology-Ministry

Ushaw College

Durham, County Durham DH7 9RH Tel: 0191 373 1367 Fax: 0191 373 7009
e-mail: p.f.fisher@durham.ac.uk Website: www.dur.ac.uk/ushaw

* Subject to approval.

First Degrees

BA: *3 yrs FT* Theology & Ministry (Jointly with St John's and the Wesley Study Centre)

Higher Degrees

MA: *FT/PT* Theology & Ministry (Jointly with St John's and the Wesley Study Centre)

Diplomas

Diploma: *FT/PT* Theology & Ministry (Jointly with St John's and the Wesley Study Centre)

Certificates

Certificate: *FT/PT* Theology & Ministry (Jointly with St John's and the Wesley Study Centre)

POSTGRADUATE CERTIFICATES
Postgraduate Certificate: *FT/PT* Theology & Ministry (Jointly with St John's and the Wesley Study Centre)

Postgraduate Diplomas

Postgraduate Diploma: *FT/PT* Theology & Ministry (Jointly with St John's and the Wesley Study Centre)

UNIVERSITY OF EAST ANGLIA

Norwich NR4 7TJ Tel: 01603 592216 Fax: 01603 458596
e-mail: j.d.beard@uea.ac.uk Website: www.uea.ac.uk

* Denotes one yr in Europe or the USA.

First Degrees

ARTS
BA Hons: *3-4 yrs School of Development Studies:* Development Studies; Development Studies with a Language; Development Studies with Overseas Study; Development Studies & Natural Resources; Development Studies (Economics, Politics & Social Policy)*School of Economic & Social Studies:* Business Economics; Business Finance & Economics; Economic & Social History & Politics; Economics; Economics & a Modern European Language; Economics & Economic & Social History; Economics with Accountancy; History & Politics; Philosophy; Philosophy & Politics; Philosophy, Politics & Economics; Politics; Politics & Economics; Politics & Sociology; Politics with a Modern European Language; Sociology *School of English & American Studies:* American & English History; American & English Literature; American History with American Politics; American Studies; Drama; English & American Literature; English Literature; English Literature & Drama; English Literature & Philosophy; English Studies; Film & American Studies; Film & English Studies *School of History:* Economic & Social History; English & American History; English History; English History with Landscape Archaeology; European History with Danish or Norwegian or Swedish Language or French Language or German Language or Double Honours Language; History; History & History of Medicine; History with Politics; Modern History *School of Language, Linguists & Translation Studies:* Art History & European Literature; Contemporary European Studies; English & Comparative Literature; English & Comparative Literature; French Studies; French/German Languages (Interpreting & Translating); German Studies; Language with Management & Business Studies; Linguistics with Language; Media Studies with Language; Modern Languages *School of Management:* Accountancy; Accountancy with a European Language; Accountancy with Law; Accounting Information Systems; Business Finance & Economics; Business Management *School of Music:* Music *School of World Art Studies & Museology:* Anthropology, Archaeology & Art History; Art History; Art History & European Literature; History & History of Art *4 yrs School of History:* History with History of Art *School of Social Work:* Psychosocial Studies; Psychosocial Studies with Management
BEd Hons: *School of Education & Professional Development:* Members of the Caring Professions; Overseas Teachers; Serving Teachers
BPhil: *2 yrs FT* Philosophy (By instruction, exam and dissertation) *2 yrs PT* Teaching

LAW
LLB Hons: *3 yrs* Accountancy with Law; English History with Law Minor; French Law & Language; German Law & Language; Law

SCIENCE
BPhil: *2 yrs FT* Mathematical Logic (By instruction, exam and dissertation) *2 yrs PT* Teaching (for Serving Teachers)
BSc: *5 yrs PT* Nursing & Midwifery
BSc Hons: *3 yrs School of Biological Sciences:* Biochemistry; Biochemistry with Biology; Biological & Medicinal Chemistry; Biomedicine; Cell Biology; Ecology; Ecology with Biology; Microbiology; Molecular Biology & Genetics; Plant Biology *School of Chemical Sciences:* Biochemistry; Biological & Medicinal Chemistry; Chemical Physics; Chemistry; Chemistry & Mathematics; Chemistry with Analytical Sciences; Chemistry with Business Studies; Environmental Chemistry; Natural Science *School of Development Studies:* Development Studies & Natural Resources *School of Environmental Sciences:* Ecology; Environmental Chemistry; Environmental Earth Sciences; Environmental Sciences; Geophysical Sciences; Meteorology & Oceanography *School of Information Systems:* Computing for Computer Graphics *4 yrs School of Biological Sciences:* Biochemistry; Biological Sciences; Ecology *School of Chemical Sciences:* Chemical Physics; Chemistry *School of Environmental Sciences:* Environmental Sciences; Geophysical Science *School of Information Systems:* Applied Computing; Business Information Systems; Computer Systems Engineering; Computing for Decision Support Systems; Computing Science; Computing Science & Mathematics; Computing Science & Systems; Electronic Design & Technology; Electronic Engineering; Electronic Systems Engineering; Electronics; Electronics with Business Studies *School of Mathematics:* Applied Mathematics; Biomathematics; Chemistry with Mathematics; Computing Science with Mathematics; Geophysical Sciences; Mathematics; Mathematics with Computing or Management or Economics or Philosophy or Statistics or Environmental Science or Yr in Continental Europe or in Canada; Pure Mathematics *5 yrs PT School of Nursing & Midwifery:* Nursing & Midwifery; Nursing & Midwifery Practice (+ENB Award) *School of Occupational Therapy & Physiotherapy:* Occupational Therapy; Physiotherapy

Higher Degrees

LLM: *1 yr* Family Law & Family Policy; International Commercial & Business Law
MA: American Studies; Applied Linguistics; Applied Research in Education; Art History; Arts of Africa, Oceania & the Americas; Comparative Literature; Comparative Studies in World Art; Creative Writing; Culture & Communication; Curriculum Studies; Development Economics; Development Studies; Economic & Social History; Economics; Education; English History; European Art; European History; European Literature; Film Archiving; Film Studies; Gender Analysis in Development; Human Resource Strategy; Industrial Development; International Child Welfare; International Relations; Linguistics; Literary Translation; Modern Literature; Philosophy; Restoration & Eighteenth Century Literature; Rural Development; Teaching English as a Foreign Language; Theatre Directing; Women & Writing *2 yrs* Social Work (Includes fieldwork)
MBA: *2 yrs PT* Business Administration
MEd: *1 yr* Education (Advanced study, research and thesis)
MEng: *3 yrs* Electronic Engineering; Electronic Engineering (with a yr in USA)
MMus: *1 yr* Conducting (By advanced coursework or performance); English Church Music (By advanced coursework or performance); Music Performance Studies (By advanced coursework or performance); Musicology (By advanced coursework or performance)
MPhil: *2 yrs* Philosophy (By advanced study, research and thesis)
MSc: *1 yr* Agricultural Economics; Agriculture, Environment & Development; Atmospheric Sciences; Biocolloid Chemistry; Biology; Biotechnology; Chemical Physics; Chemical Spectroscopy; Climate Change (Modular programme); Co-ordination Chemistry; Computing Science; Electronics; Environmental Impact Assessment; Environmental Sciences; Heterocyclic Chemistry; Hydrogeology; Land Use Planning; Modelling in Applied Mathematics; Molecular Plant Pathology; Physical Chemistry; Physical Organic Chemistry; Physics; Plant Breeding for Agricultural Development; Pure Mathematics; Resource Assessment for Development Planning; Science Education; Spectroscopic & Physical Methods of Chemical Analysis; Synthetic Organic Chemistry *2 yrs* Accountancy & Finance *2 yrs PT* Health Sciences
MSW: *1 yr FT* Social Work (By advanced coursework and dissertation)
PhD: *3 yrs* (By advanced study, research and thesis)

Honorary Degrees

DCL; LittD; ScD; MusD; MA; MSc

Diplomas

ClinPsyD: *3 yrs FT/2-5 yrs PT* Clinical Psychology
DipHE: *3 yrs FT* Nursing *78 wks FT* Midwifery
Diploma: *1 yr FT* Community Psychiatric Nursing/Community Learning Disability Nursing
LLD; LittD; ScD: *FT/PT* (Awarded for published work by graduates of some yrs' standing. Research degrees can be taken in all the Schools listed above, and also in the Centre for East Anglian Studies & the Centre for Applied Research in Education)

Degrees validated by University of East Anglia offered at:

Lowestoft College

St Peter's Street, Lowestoft, Suffolk NR32 2NB Tel: 01502 583521 Fax: 01502 500031
 e-mail: infocentre@lowestoft.ac.uk

First Degrees

BSc/BSc Hons: Natural Sciences

Otley College

Otley, Ipswich, Suffolk IP6 9EY Tel: 01473 785543 Fax: 01473 785353
e-mail: mail@otleycollege.ac.uk Website: www.otley.ac.uk

† Subject to validation.

First Degrees

BSc Hons: Animal Science & Conservation (in partnership with Suffolk College); Animal Science & Welfare (in partnership with Suffolk College); Food Production (in partnership with Suffolk College); Landscape & Garden Design (in partnership with Suffolk College) *30 mths DL* Conservation Management; Landscape Design & Conservation

Higher Degrees

MA: *30 mths DL* Education for Biodiversity†; Education for Biodiversity†
MSc (by research): Conservation Management

Diplomas

DipHE: Animal Science & Welfare (in partnership with Suffolk College); Conservation & Biodiversity; Landscape & Garden Design (in partnership with Suffolk College); Landscape Design & Conservation *30 mths DL* Animal Science & Conservation (in partnership with Suffolk College); Food Production (in partnership with Suffolk College)
Diploma in Management Studies: *30 mths DL*
Postgraduate Advanced Diploma: *30 mths DL* Conservation Management†

Certificates

Advanced Certificate: *30 mths DL* Biological Surveying
Certificate in Management Studies: *30 mths DL*
Certificate of Education: *30 mths DL*
HNC: *PT/weekends* Agricultural Production & Management; Arboriculture & Woodland Management; Biological Identification; Commercial Floristry & Interior Design; Commercial Horticulture; Food Production & Marketing; Habitat Management; Landscape & Garden Design; Nature Conservation; Organic Production; Sustainable Environments

Suffolk College

Ipswich, Suffolk IP4 1LT Tel: 01473 255885 Fax: 01473 230054
e-mail: info@suffolk.ac.uk Website: www.suffolk.ac.uk

First Degrees

BA/BSc Hons: *Joint, Minor:* History; Literary Studies; Management; Social Policy *Major, Joint, Minor:* Applied Biology; Behavioural Studies; Human Biology; Information Technology *Minor only:* Accounting; Economics; European Business; Garden Design; Hospitality Management; Human Resource Management; Law; Leisure Studies; Marketing; Small Enterprise Management; Tourism Studies *Single:* Animal Science & Conservation (Level 2, Semester 2); Animal Science & Welfare (Level 2, Semester 2); Business Information Technology; Foundation Science; Individual Studies; Performing Arts (Level 3 only); Software Engineering; Software Engineering; Sports Science; Technology Management (Level 3 only) *Single, Major, Joint:* Model Design (Level 2 & 3 only); Spatial Design (Level 1 & 3 only) *Single, Major, Joint, Minor:* Animal Science & Conservation; Animal Science & Welfare; Business Management; Business Management (Level 3); Early Childhood Studies; Environmental Studies; Fine & Applied Arts; Food Production; Graphic Design & Illustration (Level 1 & 3 only); Landscape & Garden Design; Media Studies
BSc Hons: Diagnostic Radiography; Nursing (Adult); Oncology & Radiotherapy Technology

Diplomas

DipHE: Animal Science & Conservation; Animal Science & Welfare; Applied & Human Biology; Early Childhood Studies; Fine & Applied Arts; Food Production; Heritage Studies; Landscape & Garden Design; Midwifery; Nursing; Nursing (Care of the Child); Nursing (Mental Health); Social Work & Nursing (Learning Disabilities) *PT only* Independent Studies
DipHE/DipSW: Social Work
HND/HNC: 3D Design; Business; Business Information Technology; Electrical & Electronic; Graphic Design & Illustration; Hospitality & Leisure Management; Hospitality Management; Manufacturing Engineering; Performing Arts; Performing Arts (Production Design); Software Engineering; Spatial Design; Technology Management; Travel and Tourism Management

Certificates

HNC: Business; Civil Engineering; Computing

UNIVERSITY OF EAST LONDON

Barking Campus, Longbridge Road, Dagenham, Essex RM8 2AS Tel: 020 8223 3000
Fax: 020 8223 2900 e-mail: publicity@uel.ac.uk Website: www.uel.ac.uk

Stratford Campus, Romford Road, London E15 4LZ Tel: 020 8223 3000 Fax: 020 8223 2900
e-mail: publicity@uel.ac.uk Website: www.uel.ac.uk

Docklands Campus, 4-6 University Way, London E16 2RD Tel: 020 8223 3000 Fax: 020 8223 2900
e-mail: publicity@uel.ac.uk Website: www.uel.ac.uk

First Degrees

BA/BA Hons: *1 yr FT* International Social Work; Social Work Studies *3 yrs FT* Accounting with Economics or Finance or Information Systems or Law or Mathematics; Anthropology; Applied Language Studies; Art, Design & Film History; Communication Studies; Criminology & Criminal Justice; Cultural Studies; Design; Development Economics; Economics; Education & Community Studies; European Economics; European Studies with French or German or Italian or Spanish; Fashion Design; Fine Art; Gender & Women's Studies; Graphic Fine Art; Health Promotion; Health Services Management; Health Studies; History; International Business/Business Administration; Literature; Media Studies; Political Economy; Politics; Psychosocial Studies; Social Sciences; Sociology; Textile Design & Surface Decoration; Visual Theories *4 yrs FT* European Studies with French or German or Italian or Spanish; Psychosocial Studies with Professional Studies *4 yrs S* Business Studies with French or German; Business Studies; Business Studies (Business Finance); Business Studies (Human Resource Management); Fashion: Design & Marketing

BA/BSc: *3 yrs FT/4 yrs S* Combined Degree (Triple Subject)

BEng/BEng Hons: *3 yrs FT/4 yrs S* Civil Engineering; Electrical & Electronic Engineering; Electrical & Electronic Engineering (Communications); Electrical & Electronic Engineering (Control); Electrical & Electronic Engineering (Robotics); Integrated Engineering; Manufacturing Engineering Technology; Manufacturing Systems Engineering *4 yrs FT/5 yrs S* Engineering with European & International Options; Extended Engineering

BSc/BSc Hons: *3 yrs FT* Electronic Engineering *3-4 yrs FT/4 yrs S* Animal Biology & Conservation; Applied Biology; Applied Economics; Archaeological Sciences; Architecture; Biochemistry; Biomedical Sciences; Biotechnology; Business Economics; Business Information Systems; Civil Engineering; Combined Studies Technology; Computer-Aided Engineering; Computing & Electronics; Distributed Information Systems; Environmental Biology; Environmental Plant Sciences; Environmental Sciences; Finance, Money & Banking; Fitness & Health; Geographical & Land Information Management; Geographical Information Systems; Geography; Green Technology; Human Biology; Human Physiology; Immunology; Infectious Diseases; Information Systems; Medical Biochemistry; Medical Biotechnology; Microbiology; New Technology Education; New Technology & Multimedia; New Technology, Media & Communications; Pharmacology; Physiotherapy; Product Design; Professional Nature Conservation; Property & Planning Informatics; Psychology; Social Policy Research; Social Policy Research (Health); Social Research; Social Research with Professional Studies; Software Engineering; Spatial Business Informatics; Sports Development; Surveying & Mapping Sciences; Wildlife Conservation *4 yrs FT/5 yrs S* Extended Science & Computing

LLB Hons: *3 yrs FT* Law

Higher Degrees

DBA: Business Adminstration

DClinPsy: Clinical Psychology

EdPsyD/MSc: Educational Psychology

LLM: Law

MA: Architecture (History & Theory); Architecture (Sustainability); Architecture (Teacher Training); Art in Architecture; Child Protection; Cultural Studies; Fine Art Studies: Studio Based Research; Guidance; Independent Study; Learning & Teaching in Higher Education; Legal Studies (Crime & Society); Political Activism & Social Movements; Primary Education Practice; Professional Practice in Education; Psychoanalytic Studies; Public & Community Service; Refugee Studies; Social Work, Advanced; Society & Technology & Science; Strategic Accounting; Visual Theories; Voluntary Sector Studies

MBA: Business Administration

MEng: Civil Engineering

MSc: Advanced Environmental & Energy Studies; Architecture; Architecture: Computing & Design; Business & Management; Business Information Systems; Careers: Development & Management; Careers: Education & Guidance; City Infrastructure Management; Civil Engineering; Distributed Information Systems; Engineering (Modular); Environmental Sciences; Financial Management; Health Promotion; Human Resource Management; Independent Study; International Marketing Management; Logistics; Marketing Management; Occupational Therapy; Occupational Therapy (Paediatrics); Pharmacology; Physiotherapy; Physiotherapy Practice (Orthopaedics or Neurology); Pipeline Technology & Management; Psychology: Counselling, Educational, Occupational & Organisational; Toxicology; Toxicology with Management 6S00146TDOCTORATES

Doctorates: Clinical Psychology; Educational Psychology; Fine Art; Occupational & Organisational Psychology; Surveying

Diplomas

Postgraduate Diploma: Adult Guidance; Architecture; Art in Architecture; Careers Education & Guidance; Civil Engineering; Cultural Studies; Legal Studies; Management Studies; Pharmacology; Professional Practice in Education; Psychoanalytic Observation Studies; Public & Community Service; Social Work; Systemic Therapy; Therapeutic Counselling (Integrative); Voluntary Sector Studies

Certificates

Certificate: *1 yr FT* Child Protection; Design Foundation Course; Education (Primary) (Postgraduate certificate); Fundamentals of Accountancy; Human Resource Management; Management

Professional Qualifications

Professional Qualifications: Chartered Association of Certified Accountants (Levels 1, 2 & 3); Land Surveying: Royal Institution of Chartered Surveyors (Final Exam); Local Government Management Board Diploma in Careers Guidance; Social Work Diploma

THE UNIVERSITY OF EDINBURGH

Old College South Bridge, Edinburgh EH8 9YL Tel: 0131 650 1000 Fax: 0131 650 2147
Telex: 727442 UNIVED G Website: www.ed.ac.uk

First Degrees

ARTS & SOCIAL SCIENCES
BA: *3 yrs Divinity:* Divinity; Religious Studies
BCom Ord: *3 yrs Social Sciences:*
BD Hons: *3-4 yrs Divinity:* (Course may be taken either as a first or second degree)
BD Ord: *3-4 yrs Divinity:* (Course may be taken either as a first or second degree)
BMus Hons: *4 yrs Music:* Music; Music Technology
BMus Ord: *3 yrs Music:* Music; Music Technology
BSc (Nursing) General: *4 yrs* Nursing
BSc (Nursing) Hons: *4 yrs 3 mths Social Sciences:* Nursing (Courses leading to these awards and to qualification as a Registered General or Mental Nurse)
BSc (SocSci) General: *3 yrs Social Sciences:* (Eight courses are required in total from not less than four different subjects, of which one must be taken to third yr and at least one other to second yr level)
BSc Social Work (General): *4 yrs* Social Work (Successful completion of these degrees leads to the professional qualification of DipSW, which is awarded by CCETSW)
BSc Social Work (Hons): *4 yrs* Social Work (Successful Completion of these degrees leads to the professional qualification of DipSW, which is awarded by CCETSW)
LLB Hons: *4 yrs Social Sciences:* Law-Accounting or Business Studies or French or German (Other combinations with Arts or Social Science subjects)
LLB Ord: *3 yrs* Law

MEDICINE
BSc (MedSci) Hons: (Open to students undertaking MB ChB course; awarded after at least two yrs of MB ChB studies and one yr's study in Hons School)
MB; ChB: *5-6 yrs*

SCIENCE & TECHNOLOGY
BEng: *3-4 yrs* Chemical Engineering; Civil & Environmental Engineering; Civil Engineering; Civil Engineering-Construction Management; Computer Science; Computer Science & Electronics; Computer Science-Management Science; Electrical & Mechanical Engineering; Electronics or Electrical Engineering; Electronics-Physics; Engineering; Mechanical Engineering; Mechanical Engineering with Management Techniques or Bioengineering; Physics or Electrical Engineering (Communications) or Electrical Engineering (Environmental & Resource Studies) or Electrical Engineering (Microelectronics); Software Engineering; Structural Engineering with Architecture
BSc Hons: *4 yrs* Agricultural Economics; Agricultural Science; Agricultural Science (Animal Science); Agricultural Science (Crop & Soil Science); Agricultural Science with Environmental Science; Agriculture; Agriculture, Forestry & Rural Economy; Anatomical Sciences or Software Engineering; Anatomy; Artificial Intelligence-Computer Science or Mathematics or Psychology; Astrophysics; Biochemistry; Biological Sciences; Chemical Physics with Industrial Experience; Chemical Physics; Chemistry with a yr in Europe; Chemistry with Industrial Experience; Chemistry; Computational Physics; Computer Science; Computer Science-Management Science

or Mathematics or Physics; Development Biology; Ecological Science; Ecological Science with Environmental Science; Environmental Archaeology; Environmental Chemistry; Environmental Chemistry with Industrial Experience; Environmental Chemistry with a yr in Europe; Environmental Geoscience; Forestry; Genetics; Geography; Geology; Geology & Physical Geography; Geophysics; Immunology; Mathematical Physics; Mathematics; Mathematics-Business Studies or Physics or Statistics; Medical Microbiology; Microbiology; Molecular Biology; Neuroscience; Pharmacology; Physics with Meteorology or Music; Physics; Physiology; Plant Science-Vivology; Psychology; Zoology
BSc Ord: *3 yrs*

VETERINARY MEDICINE
BSc (VetSc) Hons: Veterinary Science (Open to students undertaking the BVM&S course; awarded after at least two yrs of BVM&S studies and one yr's study in Hons School)
BVM&S: *5 yrs* Veterinary Medicine (May be awarded with Distinction for special merit in professional exams over the whole course)

Higher Degrees
DOCTORATES
DClinPsych: *36 mths FT* Psychiatry
DD: (Awarded in respect of published work)
DLitt: Literature (Awarded in respect of published work)
DMus: Music (Awarded in respect of published work (musicologists) and published/unpublished work (composers))
DPsychol: Psychology (Not less than two yrs after graduation; by thesis and oral exam)
DSc: (Awarded in respect of published work)
LLD: Law (Awarded in respect of published work)
PhD: *36 mths FT/60 mths PT* (By thesis after research and in musical composition)

HIGHER MEDICAL DEGREES
DDS: (Not less than two yrs after graduation; by thesis and oral exam)
MD: (Not less than two yrs after graduation; by thesis and oral exam)

HIGHER VETERINARY DEGREES
DVM&S: Veterinary Medicine & Surgery (Not less than two yrs after graduation; by thesis and oral exam)

MASTER'S DEGREES OR EQUIVALENT
LLM: *1 yr FT/2 yrs PT* Law (By written exam and dissertation)
MA: *4 yrs Divinity:* Divinity; Religious Studies *Social Sciences:* Accounting-Economics or Business Studies or Law; Archaeology; Archaeology-Geography or Social Anthropology; Architectural Design; Architectural History; Architectural Studies; Business Studies; Business Studies-Accounting or Economics or French or German or Spanish or Mathematics or Statistics or Geography or Law or Economic History; Economic & Social History; Economic & Social History-Politics; Economic & Social History with Environmental Studies; Economic History; Economic History-Business Studies; Economics; Economics with Environmental Studies; Economics-Accounting or Law or Social Policy or Politics or Social & Economic History or Sociology or Chinese or Mathematics or Statistics; Geography; Geography with Environmental Studies or Gender Studies; Geography-Archaeology or Economic & Social History or Economics or Social Anthropology or Social Policy or Sociology or Politics; International Business; International Business with a Language; Linguistics-Psychology or Business Studies or Social Anthropology or Social History or Social Policy or Sociology; Politics with Environmental Studies or Gender Studies; Politics; Politics-Economic & Social History; Psychology; Psychology-Business Studies or Linguistics; Social & Architectural History; Social Anthropology; Social Anthropology with Development or Environmental Studies or Gender Studies or South Asian Studies; Social Anthropology-Linguistics or Social History or Social Policy or Sociology; Social Policy with Environmental Studies or Gender Studies; Social Policy; Social Policy-Economics or Social & Economic History or Sociology or Law or Politics; Sociology; Sociology with Environmental

Studies or Gender Studies or Scottish Society or South Asian Studies; Sociology-Politics or Psychology or Social Anthropology *5 yrs Arts:* Fine Art

MA General: *3 yrs*

MA Hons: *4 yrs Arts:* American Studies; Ancient Civilisations of the Mediterranean & Middle East; Ancient History; Ancient History-Classical Archaeology or Greek or Latin; Arabic; Arabic-Business Studies or Economics or French or History of Art or Linguistics or Persian or Politics or Social Anthropology or Spanish; Archaeology-Scottish Ethnology; Celtic; Celtic & Archaeology-German or Linguistics or Scandinavian Studies or Scottish Historical Studies; Celtic-English; Chinese; Classical Archaeology-Greek or Latin; Classical Studies; Classics; Classics-Medieval History; English Language; English Language-English Literature or German or History or Linguistics or Scandinavian Studies; English Literature; English Literature & Classics or French or German or History or Scottish Literature or Russian Literature; European Union Studies-Modern European Languages (two of Danish, French, German, Italian, Spanish, Swedish); French; French-Arabic or Business Studies or European History or History of Art or Latin or Linguistics or Philosophy or Politics; German; German-Business Studies or European History or History of Art or Latin or Linguistics or Philosophy or Politics; Greek; Greek-Arabic or Linguistics; History; History of Art; History of Art-Chinese Studies or English Literature or History of Music; History-History of Art or Scottish Historical Studies or Sociology; Italian; Italian-English Literature or European History or Greek or History or Art or Latin or Linguistics or Business Studies; Japanese; Japanese-Linguistics; Latin Studies; Latin-Scottish Historical Studies; Linguistics; Linguistics-Artificial Intelligence or Scottish Ethnology or Social Anthropology; Mathematics; Mental Philosophy; Modern European Languages*; Modern History-Politics; Persian-Politics or Social Anthropology; Philosophy-English Language or Economics or English Literature or German or Greek or Linguistics or Mathematics or Politics or Psychology or Systematic Theology; Russian Studies-European History or Linguistics or Business Studies; Sanskrit; Scandinavian Studies (Danish, Norwegian, Swedish); Scottish Ethnology; Scottish Ethnology-English Language or Celtic or English Literature or Scandinavian Studies or Scottish Historical Studies or Scottish Literature; Scottish Historical Studies; Scottish Literature; Scottish Literature-Scottish Historical Studies; Spanish

MBA: *1 yr FT/30 mths PT* Business Administration (By exam and dissertation)

MChem: *5 yrs* Chemistry; Chemistry with a yr in Europe; Chemistry with Industrial Experience; Environmental Chemistry; Environmental Chemistry with a yr in Europe; Environmental Chemistry with Industrial experience

MChemPhys: *5 yrs* Chemical Physics; Chemical Physics with Industrial Experience

MEng: *5 yrs* Chemical & Process Systems Engineering; Chemical Engineering with European Studies; Chemical Engineering; Civil and Environmental Engineering; Civil Engineering; Civil Engineering-Construction Management; Electrical and Mechanical Engineering; Electronics; Electronics-Electrical Engineering; Mechanical Engineering; Mechanical Engineering with Management Techniques; Structural Engineering with Architecture

MLitt: *24 mths FT/36 mths PT* Literature (By thesis and/or exam)

MMus: *1 yr FT/3 yrs max PT* Music (Candidates examined as composers, or theorists, by exam and submission)

MPhil: *24 mths FT/48 mths PT* (By thesis or exam and thesis and in musical composition)

MPhysics: *5 yrs* Astrophysics; Computational Physics; Mathematical Physics; Physics

MSc: *1 yr FT/3 yrs PT Arts:* Applied Linguistics; Art & Ritual; Celtic Studies; Chinese Literature in the Modern Age; Classical Archaeology; Classics; Comparative & General Literature; English Literature; Enlightenment Studies; European Film Studies; French Medieval & Renaissance Studies; French Studies; German Studies; Hispanic Studies; History; History of Art; Linguistic Theory in Relation to English & its History; Medieval Europe: Language & Text; Modern European & World Literatures; Philosophy; Practice & Theory of Translation; Scandinavian Studies; Scottish History; Speech & Language Processing; Studies in Islamic Art *Law:* Criminology & Criminal Justice *Medicine:* Clinical Imaging; Community Dental Health; Environmental Health; Epidemiology; Forensic Medicine; Health Promotion & Health Education; Neonatology; Neuroscience; Orthodontics; Public Health; Reproductive Biology; Reproductive Health *Science:* Animal Breeding; Animal Science for Development; Applied Animal Behaviour & Animal Welfare; Biodiversity & Taxonomy of Plants; Cognitive Science & Natural Language; Computer Science; Crop Technology; Ecological & Resource Management; Ecological Economics; Education in Forestry & Natural Resources; Environmental Chemistry; Environmental Protection & Management; Extension for Rural Development; Forest Science; Human Ecology; Information Technology: Knowledge-based Systems; Mathematical Education; Mathematics of Nonlinear Models; Physics & Technology of Amorphous Materials; Process Systems Engineering; Remote Sensing & Image Processing Technology; Research in the Natural Environment; Resource Management; Seed Technology; Technology in Rural Development *Social Science:* Advanced Work Studies in Criminal Justice; Cancer Nursing; Childhood Studies; Education; European & Integration Politics; Finance & Investment; Gender & Society; Geographical Information Systems; Logistics & Supply Chain Management; Nationalism Studies; Nursing & Education; Nursing & Health Studies; Nursing (Child Health); Operational Research & Management Science; Policy Studies; Science & Technology Studies; Scotland, Society & Politics; Social & Political Theory; Social Anthropology; Social Research; Sociological Research Methods *Veterinary Medicine:* International Animal Health; Sustainable Rural Development in the Tropics; Sustainable Wildlife Management & Health; Tropical Animal Production & Health; Tropical Veterinary Medicine *12 mths FT/24 mths PT Divinity:* Christianity in the Non-Western World; History & Theology of Christian Doctrine; Ministry; Theology & Ethics of Communication; Theology, Culture & Development

MSc (by research): *12 mths FT/24 mths PT* Veterinary Medicine
MSW: *22 mths FT* Social Work (By exam and dissertation)
MTh: *12 mths FT/24 mths PT* Christianity in the Non-Western World; History & Theology of Christian Doctrine; Ministry; Theology & Ethics of Communication; Theology, Culture & Development

Diplomas

Diploma: *1 yr FT Faculty of Science & Engineering:* Information Technology: Knowledge-Based Systems; Remote Sensing & Image Processing Technology *1 yr FT/2 yrs PT Faculty of Arts:* Speech & Language Processing *Faculty of Medicine:* Clinical Imaging *Faculty of Science & Engineering:* Cognitive Science & Natural Language; Extension for Rural Development; Physics & Technology of Materials; Resource Management; Seed Technology *12 mths FT/24 mths PT Faculty of Divinity:* Christianity in the Non-Western World; History & Theology of Christian Doctrine; Ministry; Theology & Ethics of Communication; Theology, Culture & Development *12 mths FT/30 mths PT Faculty of Social Sciences:* Business Administration *2 yrs PT Faculty of Medicine:* Psychiatry *21 mths FT/3 yrs max Faculty of Social Sciences:* Architecture *21 mths PT Faculty of Medicine:* Orthodontics *Faculty of Social Sciences:* Social & Public Policy *24 mths PT Faculty of Medicine:* Forensic Medicine *9 mths FT Faculty of Arts:* Enlightenment Studies; European Film Studies; French Studies; German Studies; Hispanic Studies; History (Historical research; 9 mths FT/18 mths PT by coursework); Modern European & World Literatures; Russian Studies; Scandinavian Studies *Faculty of Law:* Advanced Legal Studies; Legal Practice (Essential pre-requisite for entry to the legal profession in Scotland) *Faculty of Medicine:* Neonatology; Neuroscience; Reproductive Biology *Faculty of Science & Engineering:* Biodiversity & Taxonomy of Plants; Computer Science; Ecological Economics; Ecology & Resource Management; Environmental Protection & Management; Forest Science; Geographical Information Systems; Geography; Reproductive Biology; Technology in Rural Development *Faculty of Social Sciences:* Design and Digital Media; Finance & Investment; Gender & Society; International & European Politics; Logistics & Supply Chain Management; Nationalism Studies; Nursing; Operational Research & Management Science; Policy Studies; Science & Technology Studies; Scotland, Society & Politics; Social & Political Theory; Social Research; Social Work: Advanced Social Work Studies in Criminal Justice; Sociological Research Methods *Faculty of Veterinary Medicine:* International Animal Health; Sustainable Rural Development in the Tropics; Sustainable Wildlife Management & Health; Tropical Animal Production & Health; Tropical Veterinary Medicine *9 mths FT min/21 mths PT Faculty of Arts:* Applied Linguistics *9 mths FT/18 mths PT Faculty of Science & Engineering:* Process Systems Engineering *9 mths FT/2 yrs max Faculty of Arts:* Celtic Studies; Classical Archaeology; Classics; History of Art; History of Art: Studies in Islamic Art; Practice & Theory of Translation *9 mths FT/2 yrs PT Faculty of Science & Engineering:* Animal Breeding; Animal Science for Development; Applied Animal Behaviour & Animal Welfare; Crop Technology; Education in Forestry & Natural Resources; Environmental Chemistry; Human Ecology; Mathematical Education; Mathematics of Nonlinear Models; Physics *9 mths FT/21 mths PT Faculty of Arts:* Chinese Literature in the Modern Age *Faculty of Social Sciences:*

African Studies; Education; Nursing & Education; Nursing & Health Studies; Social Anthropology *9 mths FT/21 mths PT min Faculty of Medicine:* Community Dental Health; Community Health; Environmental Health; Epidemiology; Health Promotion & Health Education *9 mths FT/21-33 mths max PT Faculty of Music:* Music

Certificates

Advanced Certificate: English Studies (Foreign students six mths full-time; for candidates with two yrs' English studies at overseas universities) *10 wks* English Language Teaching; Teaching English for Specific Purposes (For candidates with a minimum of three yrs ELT experience)
Certificate: *1 yr FT/2 yrs PT* Pastoral Studies
Certificates: *1 yr Faculty of Divinity:* Theology *1-2 yrs Faculty of Divinity:* Pastoral Studies
Higher Advanced Certificate: English Studies (Foreign students nine mths full-time; for candidates with two yrs' English studies at overseas universities)

Other Courses

Licentiate: *3 yrs* Theology *Faculty of Divinity:* Theology

UNIVERSITY OF ESSEX

Wivenhoe Park, Colchester, Essex CO4 3SQ Tel: 01206 873333

First Degrees

BA Hons: Accounting; Accounting & Economics; Accounting & Finance; Accounting & Management; American (United States) Studies (4 yr degree); American History; British & European History; Contemporary History; Democratic Politics; Drama-Literature; Economics; Economics (European Exchange); Economics-Politics; English Language-English Literature or History of Art; English Language-Modern Languages or Mathematics or Literature or Linguistics; English-United States Literature or Latin American Literature; European and Russian Studies; European Culture; European Culture and Society; European Law & Sociology; European Politics; European Society; Film Studies-History of Art or Literature; Financial Economics; History with Modern Languages; History; History of Art with Modern Languages; History of Art; History of Modern Art; History-Economics; History-Literature or Modern Languages or Criminology or Sociology or Economics or History of Art; Humanities; International Economics; Language Studies; Language, Communication & IT; Latin American Studies; Linguistics; Linguistics and Literature; Literature-History of Art or Sociology or Modern Languages; Literature-Sociology or Modern Languages; Modern History; Modern History and International Relations; Modern Languages; Modern Languages and English Language; Modern Languages and Linguistics; European Studies-Modern Languages or Economics or Politics or History or Law; Modern Languages-Linguistics or English Language or TEFL or Philosophy; Philosophy with Modern Languages; Philosophy; Philosophy in the Modern World; Philosophy-Politics or Sociology or Literature or History of Art or History or Modern Languages or Law; Political & Social Thought; Politics with Modern Languages; Politics; Politics, Philosophy & Economics; Modern History-Politics; Politics-Sociology or Literature or Modern Languages or International Relations; Psycholinguistics; Psychology; Social & Cultural History; Sociolinguistics; Sociology; Sociology and Criminology; Sociology and Global Change; Sociology and Public Policy; Sociology, Culture & Media; Sociology, Identity & Biography; Teaching English as a Foreign Language; TEFL-Modern Languages; United States & Latin American Literature
BEng Hons: Audio Engineering; Computer Engineering; Computers & Networks; Computers and Telecommunications; Electronic Engineering; Information Systems Engineering; Internet Engineering; Telecommunication Engineering
BSc Hons: Biochemistry; Biochemistry and Molecular Medicine (4 yr sandwich degree); Biochemistry-Molecular Medicine; Biological Sciences; Business Management; Cell & Molecular Biology; Computer Science; Computer Science (Artificial Intelligence); Computer Science (Robotics & Intelligent Machines); Computer Science (Software Engineering); Computing & Management; Data Management and Analysis; Ecology & Environmental Biology; Economics; Computing-Economics; Electronics and Computers; Financial Economics; Information

Management Systems; International Economics; Internet Computing; Management Economics; Marine & Freshwater Biology; Mathematics with Accounting or Economics or Computing or Finance or Statistics or Operational Research or Modern Languages; Mathematics; Mathematics, Operational Research & Economics; Mathematics-Accounting; Psychology; Sports & Exercise Science; Sports Science & Biology; Statistics & Economics

LLB: English & European Laws; English & French Law; Law; Law-Philosophy

Higher Degrees

Cert/Dip/MA/Doc Prog: Sociology

Dip/DocProg: Financial Studies

Dip/MA: Contemporary Practice of Shakespearian Theatre; Contemporary Theatre Practice; Development Studies; Gender, Culture & Society; Local & Regional History; Social Science Data Analysis; Sociology of Culture; Sociology of Development; Theatre – Shakespeare Text, Theory & Practice; Theatre – Writing; Women's History

Dip/MA/Doc Prog: Applied Linguistics; Comparative History; Computational Linguistics; Continental Philosophy; Descriptive & Applied Linguistics; Descriptive Linguistics; English Language & Linguistics; English Language Teaching; Ethics, Politics & Public Policy; European Social History; Gender History; History of Nationalism & Ethnicity; History of Race, Class & Gender; Language Acquisition; Language Testing & Programme Evaluation; Linguistics; Modern European Philosophy; Phonetics & Speech; Phonology; Psycholinguistics & Neurolinguistics; Sociolinguistics; Syntax

Dip/MEnv: Environmental, Science and Society

Dip/MSc: Accounting & Finance; Accounting & Financial Economics; Economics & Econometrics; Financial & Business Economics; Financial Economics & Econometrics; International Economics; Management Economics

Dip/MSc/Doc Prog: Accounting & Financial Economics; Economics; Financial Studies; Mathematics; Mathematics of Finance; Operational Research with Computer Science; Statistics with Computer Science or Data Analysis; Statistics & Operational Research

LLM: European Business Law; European Community Law; International Human Rights Law; International Trade Law; Law in Transition in the 'New' Europe; Public Law

LLM/MPhil/PhD: Law

MA: Aesthetics & the Visual Arts; Applications of Psychoanalysis in Health Care; Art & Film Studies; Contemporary Practice of Shakespearean Theatre; Criminology; Cultural & Social History; European Art from the Renaissance to Impressionism; European Integration; Film Studies; Gallery Studies; History & Theory of Architecture and Design; International Peacekeeping; Jungian & Post-Jungian Studies; Latin American Art & Architecture; Latin American Government & Politics; Modern Art & Theory; Nation, Citizenship & Identity; Native American Studies; Organisational Analysis & Change; Postcolonial Studies; Pre-Columbian & Native American Art; Psychoanalysis of Groups & Organisations; Psychoanalysis, Psychosis & Health Care; Social & Cultural History; Social & Economic Development; Sociological Research; Sociology; Sociology & Health Studies; Sociology & Panel Data Analysis; Sociology & Psychodynamics of Mental Health; Sociology/Government of Japan; Strategic Change; Study of Contemporary Japan; Study of the Pacific Rim & Japan; Theology & Society; Theory & Practice of Human Rights; Women's History

MA/Doc Prog: Applied Social & Economic Research; British Government & Politics; Comparative Democratisation; European Politics; European Social History; Gender History; Gender Studies; History of Nationalism & Ethnicity; History of Race, Class & Gender; Ideology & Discourse Analysis; International Relations; Language Testing & Programme Evaluation; Latin American Government & Politics; Management Studies; Modern European Philosophy; Philosophy & Psychoanalysis; Political Behaviour; Political Economy; Political Theory; Politics; Post-Communist Politics; Psychoanalysis in Social & Cultural Studies; Psychoanalytic Studies; Quantitative Political Science; Researching British History; Russian Politics; United States Government & Politics

MA/MPhil/PhD: American Studies; Art History & Theory; Government; History; Language & Linguistics; Linguistics; Literature; Local History; Philosophy; Psychoanalytic Studies; Theatre Studies

MEng Hons: Electronic & Computer Systems Engineering; Electronic & Telecommunication Systems Engineering; Electronic Systems Engineering; Information Systems and Networks

MPhil/PhD: Applied Social & Economic Research; Environmental Sciences; Finance; Law; Sociology; Sports Science; Theatre Studies; Theoretical Physics

MSc: Advanced Nursing Practice; Applied Economics & Data Analysis; Cognitive Neurolinguistics; Cognitive Neuropsychology; Computer & Information Networks; Computer Games Engineering; Computer Science (Artificial Intelligence & Agents); Computer Science (Cognitive Science & Natural Language Processing); Computer Science (Distributed Information Management Systems); Computer Science (Robotics & Intelligent Machines); Computer Science (Software Engineering); Computer Studies; Counselling Studies; Developmental Neuropsychology; E-Commerce Technology; E-Commerce Technology (E-Business Solutions); E-Commerce Technology (Information Science); E-Commerce Technology (Networks); Finance; Foundations of Psychoanalytic Psychotherapy; Health Psychology; Health Psychology; Health Service Management & Research; Human & Equine Sports Science; International Management; Physics of Laser Communication; Primary Health Care Management & Commissioning; Software Engineering Methods; Speech & Language Processing; Sports Science (Fitness & Health); Supervisory & Reflective Practice; Telecommunication & Information Systems

MSc/Dip/Cert: Mathematics

MSc/Doc Prog: Computer Science; Psychology

MSc/MPhil/PhD: Accounting; Accounting & Finance; Accounting & Financial Management; Applied Physics; Biochemistry; Biological Chemistry; Biological Sciences; Biological Sciences: Immunology; Biology; Cell & Molecular Biology; Cognitive Science; Computer Science; Economics; Electronic Systems Engineering; Environmental Biology; Environmental Sciences; Health Studies; Mathematics; Microbiology; Neuropsychology; Nursing Studies; Physics; Psychology; Social Policy Studies; Sports Science; Statistics; Theoretical Physics

MSc/MRes: Biotechnology

PhD: Chemistry; Legal Theory

Diplomas

Diploma: Communication Systems; Development Economics; Linguistic Studies; Teaching English as a Foreign Language

Certificates

Certificate: Art History and Theory; English for Language Teaching; Gallery Studies; Linguistic Studies; Literature; Mathematics; Philosophical Studies; Political Science; Proficiency in English for Academic Purposes; Sociology; Teaching English as a Foreign Language; Teaching English for Special Purposes

Degrees validated by University of Essex offered at:

Writtle College

Chelmsford, Essex CM1 3RR Tel: 01245 424200 Fax: 01245 420456
e-mail: postmaster@writtle.ac.uk Website: www.writtle.ac.uk

First Degrees

BEng Hons: Agricultural Engineering

BSc Hons: Agricultural Engineering; Agricultural Engineering with Business Management; Agricultural Mechanisation; Agriculture; Agriculture with Business Management; Agriculture with Science; Agriculture & the Environment; Animal Science; Applied Plant Science; Business Management; Conservation & Environment; Countryside Management; Environmental Assessment; Environmental Studies; Equine Science; Equine Studies with Business Management; Equine Studies; Garden Design, Restoration & Management; Horticultural Crop Production; Horticulture with Business Management; Horticulture; International Horticulture; Landscape & Amenity Management; Landscape & Garden Design; Leisure with Heritage Management; Leisure with Sports Management; Leisure with Rural Leisure and Tourism Management; Leisure

Management; Marketing & Supply Chain Management; Rural Environmental Management; Rural Resource Management; Sports Turf Science and Management

Higher Degrees

MEng Hons: Agricultural Engineering
MSc: Equine Management; Equine Science; Horticulture; International Horticulture; Landscape & Amenity Management; Post-Harvest Technology

Diplomas

Diploma: Management Studies
HND: Agricultural Engineering; Agriculture with pathways in Livestock, Mechanisation, Crops and Business Management; Business; Equine Studies; Floristry with Interior Design; Garden Design; Garden Design and Conservation; Horticulture (Commercial Crop Production); Horticulture (Landscape & Amenity Management); Horticulture (Landscape Conservation); Horticulture (Nursery); Horticulture (Retailing); Horticulture (Sports Turf & Golf Course Management); Leisure Management; Rural Resource Management; Science (Applied Biology for Animal Care) *1 yr FT* Science (Applied Biology for Equine Management)

UNIVERSITY OF EXETER

Northcote House, The Queen's Drive, Exeter EX4 4QJ Tel: 01392 263263 Fax: 01392 263108
e-mail: ADMISSION@exeter.ac.uk.

BA Hons: Modular course as a combination of two subjects taken as major/minor routes.

First Degrees

BA Combined Hons: *3 yrs* Ancient History-Archaeology; History-Ancient History; History-Archaeology; History-Politics *4 yrs* English or Fine Art or Greek & Roman Studies; French-Fine Art; German-Mathematics; Greek & Roman Studies-Italian or Theology; History-Archaeology with European Study; History-Modern Languages: French or German or Italian or Russian or Spanish; Italian-Fine Art; Mathematics-French; Music and Modern Languages: French or German or Italian or Russian or Spanish; Philosophy and Political Economy or Political Economy with European Study or Sociology or Sociology with European Study or Politics or Politics with European Study or History or History with European Study; Politics and French or German or Spanish or Russian or Italian; Sociology and French or German or Italian or Spanish or Russian
BA Law: *1 yr FT* Law (For Exeter Graduates who have read Law with Chemistry or Law & Society)
BA Modern Languages: *4 yrs* Arabic; English and French or Italian or Russian or Spanish; French; French-Arabic; German; German-Italian or Russian or Spanish; Italian; Spanish; Spanish-Arabic
BA Single Hons: English with NAS or Film Studies *3 yrs FT* Ancient History; Arabic & Middle East Studies; Arabic Studies; Archaeology; Classics; Drama; English (Truro College); Geography; Greek & Roman Studies; History; Islamic Studies; Latin; Middle East Studies with Arabic; Music; Theological Studies *4 yrs* Arabic & Islamic Studies; Archaeology with European Study; English with European Study; Geography with European Study; History with European Study; Psychology with European Study
BA Single/Combined Hons in Social Studies: *3 yrs Single Honours:* Accounting & Financial Studies; Business & Accounting Studies; Business & Management Studies; Business Economics; Economic & Political Development; Economics; Economics & Geography; Economics & Politics; Economics & Statistics; History & Society; History, Economy and Culture; Law & Society; Managerial Statistics with Economics; Mathematics with Accountancy; Mathematics; Politics; Politics & Society; Psychology; Sociology *4 yrs Single Honours:* Accounting & Financial Studies with European Study; Business & Accounting Studies with European Study; Business & Management Studies with European Study; Business Economics with European Study; Economics with European Study; Economics & Geography with European Study; Economics & Political Development with European Study; Economics & Politics with European Study with European Study; Economics & Statistics; History, Economy and Culture with European Study; Managerial Statistics with European Study; Politics with European Study; Sociology with European Study

BEng: *3 yrs* Civil Engineering; Electronic Engineering; Engineering and Management; Mechanical Engineering (i.e. available in addition to existing 3/4 yr programmes)
BEng Hons: *3 yrs Cambourne Campus:* Engineering; Mine & Quarry Engineering; Minerals Engineering; Minerals Surveying & Resource Management; Mining Engineering *4 yrs Cambourne Campus:* European Study; Minerals Surveying & Resource Management
BMus: *3 yrs* Jazz (Truro College); Music (Students reading for the BA Single Honours in Music may be permitted to transfer to a one-yr course leading to BMus, after satisfactorily completing the first two yrs of their BA course)
BSc Combined Hons: *3 yrs* Biology-Geography; Chemistry-Law; Computer Science with Mathematics; Engineering and Business Studies; Mathematics with Computer Science; Mathematics-Physics or Theoretical Physics
BSc Hons: *3 yrs* Applied Geology (Cambourne Campus); Biological & Medicinal Chemistry; Biological Sciences; Chemistry; Chemistry with NAS; Cognitive Science; Computer Science; Engineering; Engineering Geology & Geotechnics (Cambourne Campus); Environmental Science & Technology (Cambourne Campus); Exercise & Sports Science; Geography; Mathematical Statistics & Operational Research; Mathematics; Physics; Physics with Australian Study; Physics with Professional Experience; Physics with Medical Applications; Psychology; Pure & Applied Mathematics; Surveying and Environmental Management; Surveying and Environmental Management (Cambourne Campus); Theoretical Physics *Single:* Physics with Quantum & Laser Technology *4 yrs* Computer Science with European Study; Mathematics with European Study
BSc Hons Combined Studies: *3 yrs* Archaeology-Chemistry
LLB: *2 yrs FT* LLB (Available for graduates from other HE institutions with at least second class honours)
LLB Hons: *3 yrs* Law *4 yrs* Law (European); Law with European Study

Higher Degrees

LLM: *1 yr FT* European Legal Studies; International & Comparative Public Law; International Business Legal Studies
MA: *1 yr FT* Applied Population Research; Finance & Investment; Reproductive Health Programme Management *1 yr FT/2 yrs PT* Ancient Drama & Society; Applied Drama; Arab Gulf Studies; Complementary Health Studies; Contemporary European Culture (Language, Literature & Society); Cornish Studies; Criticism & Theory; Economics of the European Union; English Cathedral Music; Ethics, Religion & Society; European Film Studies; European History; European Studies; Experimental Archaeology; History; History & Literature of Witchcraft; History of Cinema & Popular Culture; Homeric Studies; International Relations; Islamic Studies; Italian; Landscape Archaeology; Leadership; Lexicography; Literary Manuscript Studies (French); Literary Translation; Local & Regional History; Maritime History; Medicine, Occupation and Health in Historical Perspective; Medieval Studies; Mediterranean Studies; Middle East Politics; Middle East Politics (Jerusalem Studies); Middle East Studies; Military Archaeology; Musicology; Naval History; Politics (Pan-European Politics); Politics (Political Theory); Public Administration & Public Policy; Renaissance Studies; Roman Myth & History; Russian; Spanish; Staging Shakespeare; Theatre Practice; Theology; War & Society; Wetland Archaeology & Environments *2 yrs FT* Social Work Studies *2 yrs PT* Continuing Professional Development
MBA: *1 yr FT/2 yrs PT* Banking-Finance; Financial Management; General; Human Resource Management; International Business; Marketing
MChem Single Hons: *4 yrs* Chemistry; Chemistry with European Study or Industrial Experience
MEd: *1 yr* Educational Psychology
MEd/PG Dip/PG Cert: *1 yr* Drama & the Creative Arts in Education; Music & the Creative Arts in Education; Special Educational Needs; Teaching English as a Foreign Language; Visual Art & the Creative Arts in Education *PT modular* Adult Continuing Education; Arts in Education; Design & Technology; Information Technology; Language & Literacy in Education; Leadership & Management in Education; Mathematics Education; Primary Education/Early Years Education; Professional & Management Development in LEAs; Professional Studies; Secondary/Tertiary Education; Special Educational Needs
MEng Hons: *4 yrs* Civil Engineering; Electronic Engineering; Engineering; Engineering & Management; Mechanical Engineering

MMath Single Hons: *4 yrs* Mathematics
MMus: *1 yr FT/2 yrs PT* Musical Composition
MPhys Hons: *4 yrs* Physics; Physics with Medical Physics; Physics with European Study; Physics with North American Study; Theoretical Physics; Theoretical Physics with European Study; Theoretical Physics with North American Study or Australian Study *Single:* Physics with Quantum Science & Technology
MSc: *1 yr* Bio-informatics; Biological Research Methods; Computer Science (Autonomous Systems); Economic Psychology; Engineering & Management; Finance & Management; Finance-Marketing; Financial Economics; Financial Management; Industrial Rocks & Minerals; International Management; Mathematics; Medical Physics; Minerals Engineering; Mining Engineering; Mining Geology; Psychological Research Methods *1 yr FT/2 yrs PT* Economics; Economics & Econometrics; Wetland Archaeology & Environment *2 yrs PT* Health Care (Professional Education) *3 yrs PT* Logistics Engineering *PT modular* Health Care

RESEARCH DEGREES
DLitt; DSc; LLD; DMus; DD: (Open to Exeter graduates of at least seven yrs' standing, in respect of published work)
MPhil: *2-3 yrs FT/3-5 yrs PT* (In areas in which staff have research interests) *3 yrs PT* Advanced Social Work/Probation Studies (Open to social workers and probation officers with at least two yrs' experience)
PhD: *3-4 yrs FT/4-7 yrs PT* (In all areas in which staff have research interests)

TAUGHT DOCTORATES
DClinPsych: *3 yrs FT* Clinical & Community Psychology
EdD: Educational Psychology; Mathematics Education; Professional Studies; TEFL

Diplomas

Diploma: *1 yr FT* Economics; Economics & Econometrics; Legal Practice; Mining/Minerals Engineering; Science Studies for Overseas Students in Chemistry or Psychology (Includes tuition in English); Social Work (Open to Social Administration graduates or allied subjects); Theology (Course for ordinands and other non-theologian graduates) *1 yr FT/2 yrs PT* Complementary Health Studies; Health Care; Wetland Archaeology & Environments *2 yrs PT* Continuing Professional Development; Diabetes Care; Mineral Technology; Primary Health Care Management *3 yrs PT* General Practice *36 wks FT* Law (For non-law graduates who wish to qualify as solicitors) *9 mths FT* English & Management; English Law for International Students; Lexicography *PT* Leadership; Respiratory Care
HND: *2 yrs Truro College:* Applied Biology; Computing; Early Childhood Studies; Legal Studies; Outdoor Education; Practical Archaeology; Sports Management & Injury

Certificates

Certificate: Advanced Professional Studies in Education; Complementary Health Studies; Continuing Professional Development; Counselling; Education (Further Education); Health Care; Management Development
PGCE: *1 yr* Education (Secondary & Primary)
Testamur or Diploma: *1 yr* Engineering Studies (Overseas Students); English Language Studies (Overseas Students); Psychology (Overseas Students)
Testamurs of Proficiency: French (Open to Exeter students); German (Open to Exeter students)

Degrees validated by University of Exeter offered at:

St Loye's School of Health Studies

Millbrook House, Millbrook Lane, Topsham Road, Exeter EX2 6ES Tel: 01392 219774 Fax: 01392 435357 e-mail: stloyes@exeter.ac.uk Website: www.ex.ac.uk/Affiliate/stloyes/schhom.htm

First Degrees
BSc Hons: *3 yrs FT* Occupational Therapy

Higher Degrees
MSc: *2 yrs PT* Advanced Course for Occupational Therapists (By distance learning); Health Care (For nurses, midwives and health visitors)

The College of St Mark & St John
Derriford Road, Plymouth, Devon PL6 8BH Tel: 01752 636827 Fax: 01752 761120
e-mail: admissions@marjon.ac.uk Website: www.marjon.ac.uk

First Degrees
BA Hons: *3 yrs* Art & Design; Community Studies; Development Studies; Education Studies; English (Literary Studies); English Language Studies; Geography; History; Human Communication Studies (Speech & Language Therapy); Information Technology; Leisure & Tourism Studies; Media Studies; Public Relations; Sociology; Sport Science & Coaching; Sports & Recreation Studies; Theology; Theology & Philosophy; Youth Studies (Only available with Community Studies)
BEd Hons: *4 yrs FT Primary:* Design & Technology; English; English; Geography; History; Mathematics; Physical Education; Religious Studies; Science *Secondary:* Design & Technology; Mathematics; Physical Education
BEd Ord: *2 yrs FT Secondary:* Design & Technology; Mathematics with Information Technology

Higher Degrees
BPhil (Ed)/MEd: *1 yr FT* English Language Teaching; Teacher Training English Language Training; Teaching English for Specific Purposes *PT* Community & Informal Education; Design & Technology; Education Management; English; Geography; Health Education & Health Promotion; History; Information Technology; Management in Education & Allied Professions; Mathematics Education; Physical Education; Professional Development; School Effectiveness & Improvement; Science Education; Special Educational Needs; TESOL
MA: *FT/PT* Anglo-American Literary Relations; Applied Theology; Tourism & Social Responsibility *PT* Church School/Religious Education
MPhil/PhD: (In collaboration with the University of Exeter)

Diplomas
INSET: Advanced Professional Studies; School Effectiveness; School Improvement; School Leadership; Subject Leadership
PGDip: *1 yr FT* Community & Youth Work

Certificates
INSET: Advanced Professional Studies
PGCE: *1 yr FT* Secondary: Art or Design & Technology or English or Geography with IT or Information Technology or Mathematics or Modern Foreign Languages or Physical Education or Religious Education or Science

Truro College
Tel: 01872 264251 Fax: 01872 222360 e-mail: rosemary@trurocollege.ac.uk
Courses at Truro College are also validated by the University of Plymouth.

First Degrees
BA/BA Hons: *3 yrs* English
BMus/BMus Hons: *3 yrs* Jazz

Diplomas

HND: Applied Biology; Applied Psychology; Community Studies (Development & Youth Work); Computing; Early Childhood Studies; Industrial & Applied Geology; Legal Studies; Media Production: Moving Image; Outdoor Education; Performing Arts; Photography & Digital Imaging; Practical Archaeology; Sound Engineering & Multimedia Integration; Sports Science & Injury Management

Certificates

University Certificate: Modern Languages

FALMOUTH COLLEGE OF ARTS

Woodlane, Falmouth, Cornwall TR11 4RH Tel: 01326 211077 Fax: 01326 212261
e-mail: admissions@falmouth.ac.uk Website: www.falmouth.ac.uk

† Subject to validation.

First Degrees

BA Hons: *3 yrs FT* 3D Design; American Studies†; Broadcasting Studies; English with Media Studies; Film Studies; Fine Art; Graphic Design; History of Modern Art & Design; Illustration; Journalism Studies; Photographic Communication; Spatial Design: Interior & Landscape; Studio Ceramics; Textile Design *5 yrs PT* Fine Art

Higher Degrees

MA: *1 yr FT/2 yrs PT* Contemporary Visual Arts
MA/PGDip: *1 yr FT/2 yrs PT* Interactive Design† *1-2 yrs FT/2-3 yrs PT* History of Modern Art & Design
MPhil/PhD: *Variable FT/Variable PT* Research

Postgraduate Diplomas

PGDip: *1 yr FT* Broadcast Journalism; Broadcast Television; Creative Advertising; Creative Enterprise; Photography: Critical Practice; Professional Writing

UNIVERSITY OF GLAMORGAN

Treforest, Pontypridd, Mid Glamorgan CF37 1DL Tel: 01443 480480 Fax: 01443 480558
e-mail: prospectus@glam.ac.uk Website: www.glam.ac.uk

† Subject to validation.

First Degrees

BA: *1 yr* Animation (Top-Up); Business Administration (Top-Up)
BA Hons: *3 yrs FT* Art Practice; Business Accounting; Business Administration; Combined Studies; Communication Studies; Community and Public Art; Criminal Justice; Criminology; Economics and Politics; Economics and Public Policy; English Studies; English Studies with Media Studies or Philosophy or Psychology or Sociology or Theatre & Media Drama; English Studies and History or Media Studies or Philosophy or Sociology or Theatre & Media Drama; Environment & Social Values; Environmental Sustainability; Graphic Design; History; History and Sociology; Humanities; Joint Honours; Leisure & Recreation Management; Leisure & Tourism Management; Leisure Management with a Language; Major/Minor Honours; Media Practice; Media Studies with English Studies or Psychology or Sociology or Theatre & Media Drama; Media Studies and Cultural Studies or Psychology or Sociology or Theatre & Media Drama or Visual Arts; Product Design; Purchasing & Supply Chain Management; Sociology; Sociology with Criminal Justice or Criminology or Psychology; Textile Design & Garment Manufacture; Theatre & Media Drama; Urban Studies & Human Geography; Visual Arts with Art History; Visual Arts, Theatre & Media-Theatre & Media Drama; Wales *4 yrs S* Accounting & Finance; American

Business Studies; Business Information Management; Business Studies; Enterprise & Small Business; European & International Business Administration; Financial Risk Management; Government with American Business or American Studies or European & International Business or Leisure & Tourism; Government & Politics; Government and Economics or History or Law or Philosophy; Human Resource Management; International Accounting; International Studies; Language and Discourse with Accounting & Finance; Law or Business Studies or Criminal Justice or English Studies or Psychology or Sociology; Law and Business Studies; Marketing; Marketing with Languages; Media & Communication; Politics & Public Policy; Public Management and Statistics; Public Policy and Statistics; Purchasing & Supply Chain Management; Retail Estate Management; Retail Management

BEng/BEng Hons: *3 yrs FT/4 yrs S* Digital Communications; Electronic Engineering; Mechanical & Manufacturing Systems Engineering *4 yrs S* Mechanical Engineering *3 yrs FT* Mechanical Engineering *3 yrs FT/4 yrs S* Mechatronic Engineering; Minerals Resource Development; Product Design *4 yrs S* Civil Engineering; Electrical & Electronic Engineering

BSc: Midwifery; Nursing (Adult; Child; Mental Handicap; Mental Health) *2 yrs PT* Health Promotion *+2-5 yrs PT* Professional Practice in Nursing, Midwifery & Health visiting

BSc Hons: *3 yrs FT/4 yrs S* Architectural Engineering; Architectural Technology; Building Pathology; Environmental & Occupational Health & Safety Management+; Environmental Management+; Environmental Services+; Financial Information Technology; Microbiology; Sports Science with Environmental Pollution Science or Physical Geography; Sports Science; Sports Science and Physical Geography *4 yrs S* Chiropractic

BSc/BSc Hons: *1 yr* Mechanical and Manufacturing Engineering (Top-Up) *3 yrs FT* Applied Earth Sciences; Applied Food Science; Applied Microbiology; Biology; Biology with Chemistry or Environmental Pollution Science or Geology or Minerals Surveying Science; Biology and Environmental Science or Minerals Surveying Science; Chemistry; Chemistry with Biology or Environmental Pollution Science; Chemistry and Biology or Environmental Pollution Science; Civil Engineering; Combined Studies; Environmental Pollution Science; Environmental Pollution Science with Biology or Chemistry or Geology or Physical Geography or Sports Science; Environmental Pollution Science and Geological Science or Sports Science; Forensic Science; Forensic Science with Biology or Criminal Justice; Geography; Geoscience; Joint Honours; Major/Minor; Media Technology (Honours and unclassified route); Media Technology and Media Studies; Microbiology; Minerals Surveying with Environmental Pollution Science or Geology; Minerals Surveying & Resource Development; Multimedia Studies; Multimedia Technology; Nursing (Adult); Nursing (Child); Nursing (Mental Handicap); Nursing (Mental Health); Physical Geography with Astronomy or Environmental Pollution Science or Geological Science or Sports Science; Physical Geography; Physical Geography and Environmental Pollution Science; Physical Geography and Geological Science; Planning & Development Surveying; Psychology with Anthropology; Psychology or Criminal Justice or Criminology or Philosophy or Sociology or Statistics; Psychology and Sociology or Theatre & Media Drama or Visual Arts; Sports Equipment Design *3 yrs FT/4 yrs S* Applied Sciences; Architectural & Building Conservation; Architectural Technology; Astronomy with Geological Science or Physical Geography; Astronomy and Physical Geography; Biotechnology; Building Control Surveying; Building Surveying; Building Technology and Management; Computer Studies; Computing and Geographical Information Systems; Computing Mathematics; Construction Buying; Construction Health & Safety; Construction Management; Construction Planning; Design & Technology; Electrical & Electronic Engineering; Electronics; Electronics with European Business Studies; Electronics-IT Studies; Energy & Environmental Technology; Environmental Biology; Environmental Management; Environmental Services; Financial Information Technology; Geographical Information Systems and Human Geography; Geological Science with Astronomy or Physical Geography or Environmental Pollution Science or Geography or Minerals Surveying Science; Geological Science and Astronomy or Minerals Surveying Science; Information Systems and Accounting; Information Technology with European Business Studies; Interior Design; Mathematics; Mathematics and Accounting & Finance; Multimedia Computing; Multimedia Technology; Natural History; Product Design; Property Valuation Management; Science and Science Fiction; Security Design; Software Engineering; Statistics with Psychology; Statistics and Business Studies; Technical Marketing; Technology & Business Studies; Urban Change & Regeneration *4 yrs S* Applied Sports Science; Computer Studies with Foreign Language & Business; Computing with

Business; Computing-Business; Estate Management Surveying; Information Systems; Information Technology; Information Technology with European Business Studies; Mechanical Engineering; Mechatronic Engineering; Media Technology; Quantity Surveying; Software Engineering; Sports Psychology
LLB Hons: *3 yrs FT* Law

Higher Degrees

MA: Arts & Humanities Research; Combined Studies; Educational Development; Media Production; Professional Development; Writing
MBA: *FT/PT* Business Administration
MChem: *4 yrs FT* Chemistry
MEng: Civil Engineering *5 yrs S* Computer Systems Engineering; Electrical & Electronic Engineering; Electromechanical Systems; Mechanical Engineering
MMath: Mathematics
MPhil: *2 yrs FT* Philosophy
MSc: Advanced Information Systems; Applied Psychology; Built Environment; Civil Engineering; Combined Studies; Communicating Science; Computer Crime & Information Security; Computer Studies; Construction Management; Design Management; Education Management; Electronic & Information Technology; Electronic Product Design; Electronic Product Manufacture; Electronic Technology Management; Engineering Management; Engineering Management; Engineering Project Management; Environmental Conservation Management; Environmental Construction Management; Environmental Waste Management; Facilities Management; Family Health Studies; Geographical Information Systems; Health Care Management; Human Resources Management; Multimedia; Paediatrics; Property Management; Public Health; Public Management; Quality & Environmental Management; Real Estate Appraisal; Reproductive & Sexual Health; Safety, Health & Environmental Management; Science Exercise; Scriptwriting; Security and Computer Science; Social Science Research; Society, Culture & Literature; Technology for Teaching & Learning; Total Quality *1 yr* Financial Management *2 yrs PT* Clinical Practice for Nurses, midwives & Health Visitors; Organisational Leadership & Change
PhD: *3 yrs FT*

Diplomas

DipHE: Health Care; Nursing
Diploma: Midwifery (80 wk course for registered Nurses)
HND: Analytical & Forensic Science; Animal Science; Architectural & Building Conservation; Building Studies; Business Administration; Business Information Technology; Chemistry; Civil Engineering; Coastal Zone & Marine Environment Studies; Computer-Aided Engineering; Computing; Computing (Information Systems); Computing (Network Administration); Construction Management; Electrical & Electronic Engineering; Energy Resources Engineering; Engineering Design; Graphic Design & Print Technology; Graphic Design & Production; Graphic Design (Photography); Holistic and Beauty Therapies; Hospitality Management; Information Systems; Information Technology; Land Administration; Landscape Science; Legal Studies; Leisure Boat Design; Manufacturing & Business Studies; Marine Wildlife Conservation; Mechanical & Manufacturing Engineering; Mechatronic Engineering; Media Technology; Minerals Surveying & Resource Management; Multimedia; Network Administration; Quantity Surveying; Retail Science; Science; Software Engineering; Sports Science (Health & Exercise); Sports Science (Human Movement); Textile Design & Garment Manufacture; Turf Management
Postgraduate Diploma: *1 yr FT* Combined Studies; Media Production *1 yr FT/2 yrs PT* Careers Guidance; Electrical Product Engineering; Human Resource Management; Law *1 yr FT/6 yrs PT* Management; Quality & Environmental Management *2 yrs PT* Applied Psychology; Education Management; Engineering Management; Health Care Management; Higher Educational Development *3 yrs PT* Professional Development in Education

Certificates

PGCert: Applied Psychology; Education Management; Educational Development; Engineering Management; Health Care Management; Human Resource Management; Media Production; Operational Management

Professional Qualifications

Professional Qualifications: Accountancy; Bar Examination; Common Professional Examination; General Management Studies; Legal Practice; Nursing; Purchasing & Supply

UNIVERSITY OF GLASGOW

1 The Square, Glasgow G12 8QQ Tel: 0141 330 3219 Fax: 0141 330 4045
e-mail: sras@gla.ac.uk Website: www.gla.ac.uk

* In association with Glasgow School of Art.
*** In association with the Scottish Agricultural College, Auchincruive.
†† With work placement.

First Degrees

BA: *3 yrs FT* Creative and Cultural Studies; Environmental Studies; Health and Social Studies; Liberal Arts; Scottish Studies *4 yrs FT* Design; Fine Art
BAcc Ord/Hons: *3-4 yrs* Accountancy with Finance or International Accounting or Language; Accountancy; Accountancy-Economics
BArch Ord/Hons: *3-4 yrs* Architecture
BD General: *3 yrs* Divinity
BD Hons: *4 yrs* Divinity
BD Ministry: *3-4 yrs* Ministry
BDes (Hons): *4 yrs* Product Design
BEd (Music) Hons: *4 yrs* Music
BEd (Primary Education) Hons: *4 yrs* Primary Education
BEng: Product Design Engineering
BEng Hons/Ord in Engineering; MEng: *4-5 yrs* Advanced Marine Design (MEng); Aeronautical Engineering; Aeronautical Engineering; Avionics (Aeronautical or Electronical); Civil Engineering; Civil Engineering with Architecture; Electrical Power Engineering; Electronic & Software Engineering; Electronics with Music; Electronics & Electrical Engineering; Electronics & Electrical Engineering (European); Mechanical Design Engineering; Mechanical Engineering; Mechanical Engineering with Aeronautics; Mechanical Engineering (European Curriculum); Microcomputer Systems Engineering; Naval Architecture & Ocean Engineering; Naval Architecture & Ocean Engineering with European Studies; Physics-Electronic Engineering; Product Design Engineering
BIBA: *3-4 yrs* International Business Administration
BMus Ord/Hons: *3-4 yrs* Music
BN: *4 yrs* Nursing (Now available as an honours or general degree)
BSc Des: *3-4 yrs Combined subjects:* Applied Mathematics-Statistics or Physics or Computing Science or Astronomy; Archaeology-Geography or Computing Science; Astronomy-Mathematics or Physics; Biomolecular Sciences; Chemistry-Mathematics or Biology; Computing Science-Geography or Mathematics or Physics or Physiology (Neuroinformatics) or Statistics; Human Biology; Infection Biology; Mathematical Sciences; Mathematics-Physics or Statistics *Single subjects:* Anatomy; Animal Biology; Applied Mathematics; Aquatic Bioscience; Archaeological Studies; Biochemistry; Biomedical Sciences; Biotechnology; Chemical Physics; Chemistry; Chemistry with Medicinal Chemistry; Computing Science; Earth Science; Electronic & Software Engineering; Environmental Biogeochemistry; Environmental Chemistry; Environmental Chemistry & Geography; Genetics; Geography, Geography, Chemistry and the Environment; Mathematics; Medical Biochemistry; Microbiology; Molecular & Cellular Biology; Neuroscience; Parasitology; Pharmacology; Physics; Physiology, Physiology, Sports Science-Nutrition; Physiology-Sports Science; Plant Science; Software Engineering; Sports Science; Statistics; Topographic Science; Virology; Zoology
BSc General & Hons: Applied Plant & Animal Science
BSc Hons: *3-4 yrs Combined subjects:* Applied Mathematics or Astronomy or Computing Science or Physics or Statistics; Philosophy or Management Studies; Archaeology-Computing Science or Geography; Computing Science-Economics or Geography or Management Studies or Mathematics or Physics or Physiology or Psychology or Statistics; Astronomy-Mathematics or

Physics or Philosophy; Mathematics or Physics or Statistics; Management Studies-Physiology; Psychology-Statistics; Economics or Management Studies; Statistics-Management Studies or Mathematics or Economics *Single subjects:* Anatomy; Applied Mathematics; Aquatic Bioscience; Archaeology; Biochemistry; Biomedical Sciences; Biotechnology; Chemical Physics; Chemistry; Chemistry with Medicinal Chemistry; Computing Science; Earth Science; Electronic and Software Engineering; Environmental Biogeochemistry; Environmental Chemistry; Environmental Chemistry and Geography; Genetics; Geography; Immunology; Mathematical Sciences; Mathematics; Medicinal Biochemistry; Microbiology; Molecular and Cellular Biology; Neuroscience; Parasitology; Pharmacology; Physics; Physiology; Physiology and Sports Science; Physiology, Sports Science and Nutrition; Plant Science; Psychology; Software Engineering; Sports Medicine; Statistics; Topographical Science; Virology; Zoology

BTechEd: *4 yrs* Technological Education
BTechnol General & Hons: *3-4 yrs* Agriculture; Countryside Management; Food Technology; Leisure & Recreation Management
BTechS: *4 yrs* Technology Studies; Technology Studies in Technology and Management
BTheol Ord/Hons: *4 yrs* Theology
BVMS: *5 yrs* Veterinary Medicine (May be awarded with Honours or Commendation)
LLB Ord/Hons: *3-4 yrs* Law; Law & French Language; Law & French Legal Studies; Law & German Language; Law & German Legal Studies; Law & Spanish Language; Law & Spanish Legal Studies

Higher Degrees

DOCTORATES
DClinPsy: *3 yrs FT* Clinical Psychology (Two yrs part-time for qualified Clinical Psychologists)
DDS: Dental Surgery (By thesis, open only to Glasgow graduates)
DEng: Engineering (Awarded to graduates of at least seven yrs' standing on published work; non-Glasgow graduates or staff members must do five yrs' research)
DLitt: (Awarded on published work, open only to graduates of seven yrs' standing or officers of four yrs' standing, of any of the Scottish universities)
DMus: Music (Awarded on published work, either composition or musicology (open only to Glasgow graduates of seven yrs' standing, or officers of four yrs' standing)
DSc: Engineering (Awarded to graduates of at least seven yrs' standing on published work; non-Glasgow graduates or staff members must do five yrs' research); Science (Awarded to graduates of at least seven yrs' standing on published work:); Science (Awarded to graduates of at least seven yrs' standing on published work; non-Glasgow graduates or staff members must do five yrs' research)
DVM: Veterinary Medicine (By thesis, open only to Glasgow graduates)
DVS: Veterinary Surgery (By thesis, open only to Glasgow graduates)
LLD: Law (Open to Glasgow graduates of seven yrs' standing, who must submit a published work)
MD: Medicine (By thesis, open only to Glasgow graduates)
PhD: (By thesis and exam (which may not be required))
PhD by Published Work: (Awarded to graduates or members of staff of at least seven yrs' standing on the basis of published work)
Scottish Doctoral Programme: *3 yrs FT* Economics; Educational Studies

MASTER'S DEGREES OR EQUIVALENT
LLM: *1 yr FT* Commercial Law; Criminal Justice; European Legal Studies; International Law; International Law; Legal History; Legal History
MA & MA (Soc/Sci): *3-4 yrs* General Humanities
MA/MA Hons & MA/MA (Soc/Sci) Hons: *3-4 yrs* Accountancy; Anthropology; Applied Social Sciences; Archaeology; Architectural History; Business Economics; Business History; Celtic; Celtic Civilisation; Central and East European Studies; Civil Law; Classical Civilisation; Computing Science; Economic & Social History; Economics; English Language; English Literature; Film & Television Studies; Geography; Hispanic Studies; Hispanic Studies (Spanish and Portuguese); History; History of Art; Islamic Studies; Management Studies; Mathematics; Music; Philosophy; Physics; Politics; Psychology; Scottish History; Scottish Literature; Slavonic & East European

Studies; Slavonic Civilisation; Slavonic Languages and Literatures (Czech, Polish and Russian); Social Policy; Sociology; Statistics; Theatre Studies; Theology & Religious Studies *4 yrs* Greek; Latin *5 yrs* French; German; Italian

MAcc: *1 yr FT/2 yrs PT* International Accounting & Financial Management

MArch: *1 yr FT/2 yrs PT* Architecture

MB, ChB; BDS: *5 yrs* Medicine (May be awarded with Honours or Commendation)

MBA: *1 yr FT/2 yrs PT* Business Administration (By exam and dissertation)

MBA (International): *12 mths FT* Business Administration *2 yrs PT* Business Administration

MCC: *2 yrs PT* Community Care

MEd: *1 yr FT/2 yrs PT* Education (Awarded after exam to graduates who have taken a third yr part-time course, consisting of a first (or Diploma in Education) stage and a second (or Honours) stage); Psychology; Religious Education

MEDes: *5 yrs* Product Design (Candidates spend a minimum of two yrs in a European design school)

MEng/MEng Fast-Track: Product Design Engineering

MLitt: *1 yr FT/2.5 yrs PT* Creative Writing (Other Arts & Humanities subjects available)

MM: *1 yr FT/2 yrs PT* Midwifery

MMus: *1 yr FT/2 yrs PT* Music (By research. Available in Faculty of Arts)

MN: *1 yr FT/2 yrs PT* Nursing (Part-time day release)

MPH: *1 yr FT/2-3 yrs PT* Public Health

MPhil: *1 yr FT/2 yrs PT* (By research or by coursework & dissertation. Available in Faculty of Arts) *1-2 yrs FT/2-3 yrs PT* Advanced 2D/3D Motion Graphics & Virtual Prototyping; Aerial Photography-Geophysical Survey; American Studies; Archaeological Studies; Archaeology (Celtic, Medieval, Mediterranean); Art & Design in Organisational Contexts; Art, Design & Architecture in Education; Classics; Contemporary Economic History; Contemporary French Language; Czech; Decorative Arts (Christie's); Development Studies; Digital Management & Preservation; Dramaturgy; Economic Development; Economic Planning & Policy Analysis; Educational Research; Educational Studies; German Intercultural Studies; German Thought (Modern); Higher Still Related Language Arts, Drama & Media; History; History & Computing; History & Computing (with an emphasis on the history of medicine); History (with an emphasis on the history of medicine); History of Art; Housing Studies; International Finance; Literature, Theology and the Arts; Medieval Celtic Studies; Medieval English Studies; Medieval Scottish Studies; Medieval Studies; Monetary Economics & Finance; Philosophy; Polish; Political Philosophy; Psychology; Renaissance Studies; Romanticism and Modernity; Rural Tourism Management; Russian; Russian & East European Studies; Scottish Literature; Scottish Politics; Scottish Studies; Screen Studies; Slavonic & East European Studies; Slavonic Languages; Slavonic Languages & Literatures; Social History; Social Science Research; Socialist Theories & Movements; Sociology; Theatre Research; Urban Policy *30 mths DL* Medical Law

MRes: *1-2 yrs FT/2-3 yrs PT* Bioinformatics; Biomedical & Life Sciences; Ecological Methods

MSc: *1- 2 yrs FT/2-3 yrs PT* Adult & Continuing Education; Advanced Engineering Mechanics; Advanced Information Systems; Applied Poultry Science; Archaeological Science; Bioinformatics; Clothing Physiology; Desalination Technology; Electronics & Electrical Engineering; Environmental Analytical Chemistry; Geotechnical Engineering; Information Technology; Local Economic Development; Science & Science Education; Sports Medicine; Statistics; Structural Engineering; System Level Integration; Travel Medicine; Water Resources Engineering Management

MSc Economics: *1 yr FT* Economics (Component of the Scottish Doctoral Programme in Economics)

MSc Medical Science: *1-2 yrs FT/2-3 yrs PT* Anatomical Sciences; Clinical Nutrition; Clinical Pharmacology; Clinical Physics; Dental Primary Care; Endodontics; Fixed & Removable Prosthodontics; Forensic Medicine; Human Nutrition; Medical Genetics; Ophthalmology; Oral Surgery; Orthodontics; Palliative Care; Prosthodontics; Surgery

MSci: *3-4 yrs Combined subjects:* Statistics; Applied Mathematics and Astronomy or Physics or Physics; Astronomy-Mathematics or Statistics; Mathematics-Physics or Philosophy; Physics and Electronic Engineering or Music; Physics-Music; Physics-Philosophy *Single subjects:* Anatomy; Applied Mathematics; Aquatic Bioscience; Biochemistry; Biomedical Sciences; Biotechnology; Chemical Physics; Chemistry; Chemistry with Medicinal Chemistry; Genetics; Mathematics;

Medical Biochemistry; Microbiology; Molecular and Cellular Biology; Neuroscience; Parasitology; Pharmacology; Physics; Physiology; Physiology and Sports Science; Plant Science; Statistics; Virology; Zoology
MSW: *1 yr FT* Social Work (For candidates who have passed the Diploma in Social Work)
MTh: *1 yr FT/2-4 yrs PT* Literature, Theology & the Arts; Theology (By research or coursework and dissertation)

Honorary Degrees
MA; MSc; DLitt; DD; LLD; DMus; DSc; DEng; DVMS

Diplomas
Diploma: Cancer Nursing; Palliative Care; Palliative Care Nursing *1 yr DL* Travel Medicine *1 yr FT* Decorative Arts; Legal Practice (With the University of Strathclyde) *1 yr PT* Community Care; Emergency Trauma Nursing Care *3 yrs PT* Housing Studies
Postgraduate Diploma: *1 yr* Adult & Continuing Education; Aerial Photography with Geophysical Survey in Archaeology; Aerospace Engineering; Applied Poultry Science; Archaeological Science; Archaeological Studies; Archaeology (Celtic, Medieval, Mediterranean); Cancer Nursing; Clinical Nutrition; Community Care; Contemporary Economic History; Deocorative Arts (Christie's); Desalination Technology; Educational Management & Leadership; Electronics & Electrical Engineering; Emergency Trauma Nursing Care; English Language; Environmental Analytical Chemistry; Forensic Medicine; Geotechnical Engineering; History; History & Computing; Housing Studies; Human Nutrition; Information Technology; Legal Practice (With the University of Strathclyde); Local Economic Development; Mathematics; Mechanical Engineering; Medieval Celtic Studies; Medieval English Studies; Medieval Scottish Studies; Naval Architecture & Ocean Engineering; Palliative Care; Palliative Nursing Care; Rural Tourism Management; Russian and East European Studies; Social History; Social Science Research; Socialist Theories & Movements; Sociological Studies; Sociology; Statistics; Structural Engineering; Travel Medicine; Water Resources Engineering Management *1-2 yrs* Adult Education *2 yrs* Social Work *2 yrs FT/3 yrs PT* Architecture

Certificates
Advanced Certificate: *16 mths PT* Residential Childcare
Certificate: *1 yr FT* English Language; Housing Studies; Medieval English Studies; PGCE (Primary); PGCE (Secondary) *1 yr PT* Educational Management & Leadership

Degrees validated by University of Glasgow offered at:

Glasgow School of Art
167 Renfrew Street, Glasgow G3 6RQ Tel: 0141 353 4500 Fax: 0141 353 4746
e-mail: info@gsa.ac.uk Website: www.gsa.ac.uk

First Degrees
BA Hons Design: *4 yrs FT Options available:* Ceramics; Interior Design; Silversmithing & Jewellery; Textiles; Visual Communications
BA Hons Fine Art: *4 yrs FT Options available:* Environmental Art; Painting; Photography; Printmaking; Sculpture
BArch: *3 yrs FT/4 yrs PT* Architectural Studies
BArch Hons: *4 yrs FT* Architectural Studies
BDes (Hons): *4 yrs FT* Product Design
BEng Hons: *4 yrs FT* Product Design Engineering (Course delivered jointly with Mechanical Engineering at the University of Glasgow)

Higher Degrees

Diploma: *1-2 yrs FT/3 yrs PT* Architecture (Master of European Design)
MArch: *1 yr FT/2 yrs PT* Architectural Studies (By taught course or research)
MEDes: *5 yrs FT* Product Design
MEng Hons: *5 yrs FT* Product Design Engineering (Course delivered jointly with Mechanical Engineering at the University of Glasgow)
MFA: *2 yrs FT* Fine Art
MPhil: *1 yr FT/2 yrs PT* Art & Design in Organisational Contexts *2 yrs FT* 2D/3D Advanced Motion Graphics & Virtual Prototyping *PT modular* Art, Design & Architecture in Education (In collaboration with University of Glasgow Department of Educational Studies)
PhD: *3 yrs FT/4 yrs PT* Architectural Studies

GLASGOW CALEDONIAN UNIVERSITY

Cowcaddens Road, Glasgow G4 0BA Tel: 0141 331 3000 Fax: 0141 331 3005
e-mail: rhu@gcal.ac.uk Website: www.gcal.ac.uk

First Degrees

BA: *PT* Anomalies of Binocular Vision & Orthoptics; Post Qualifying Social Work; Principles of Contact Lens Practice
BA Hons: *4 yrs FT* European Business Studies; Tourism Management
BA/BA Hons: *3-4 yrs FT* Accountancy; Business; Business & Information Management; Business & Languages; Business Economics; Business Studies; Communication & Mass Media; Consumer & Management Studies; Consumer & Management Studies – Home Economics Route; Consumer & Trading Standards; Fashion with Management; Financial Services; Food Product Design with Management; Hospitality Management; International Travel with Information Systems; Joint Accountancy; Law with Administrative Studies; Leisure Management; Marketing & Communication; Nursing Studies (RN); Retail Management; Risk Management; Social Work; Public Administration & Management *PT* Public Administration & Management *3-4 yrs FT/PT* Social Sciences *6 mths top up* Integrated Product Design
BEng Hons: *3-5 yrs* Business & Manufacturing Systems Engineering *4 yrs FT/5 yrs S* Electrical Power Engineering; Electronic Engineering; Manufacturing Systems Engineering; Mechanical Electronic Systems Engineering *PT* Building Services Engineering; Engineering with options
BEng/BEng Hons: *3/4/5 yrs* Engineering for the Environment *PT* Engineering for the Environment
BSc: *1 yr FT top-up* Applied Graphics Technology with Multimedia; Medical Illustration; Music Technology with Electronics *2-3 yrs* Telecommunications Engineering *3 yrs FT* Civil Engineering; Computer Aided Engineering; Electronic Engineering; Medical Technology; Science; Science with Language & Management Options; Building Services Engineering *PT* Building Services Engineering; Family Planning Programme; Health Studies; Specialist Nursing Practice
BSc Hons: *4 yrs FT* Environmental Civil Engineering; Human Nutrition & Dietetics; Physiotherapy; Radiography
BSc/BSc Hons: *2 yrs top-up FT* Architectural Technology; Information Management Systems; Interior Design *3-4 yrs FT* Applied Biosciences; Biomedical Sciences; Building Surveying; Computational Mathematics; Environment; Environmental Toxicology; Financial Mathematics; Human Nutrition & Food Science; Occupational Therapy; Optometry; Podiatry; Property Management & Development/Property Studies; Psychology; Chemistry with Information Technology & Instrumentation *PT* Chemistry with Information Technology & Instrumentation *3-4 yrs FT/PT* Construction Management; Instrumentation with Applied Physics *3-5 yrs* Computer Studies *3.5-4 yrs* Applied Statistics; Management Science; Mathematics for Business Analysis *4 yrs FT* Building Control; Leisure Management; Quantity Surveying *6 mths top up* Food Technology; Information Technology Studies; Multimedia Technology *PT* Fire Risk Engineering

Higher Degrees

MBA: *1 yr FT* Master of Business Administration
MSc: *1 yr FT* Financial Management; Rehabilitation Science
PgC/PgD/MSc: *1 yr FT* Biomedical Sciences; Computing: European Option; Health Studies

(Nursing); Hospitality Management; Leisure Management; Physiotherapy; Tourism Management *1 yr FT/PT* Advanced Engineering Technology; Construction Management; Engineering for the Environment; Environmental Technology; Fire Risk Engineering; Forensic Psychology (Legal & Criminological); Waste Management

PgC/PgD/MSc/Doctorate: *1 yr FT/PT* Learning Contract Framework

PgD/LLM: *1 yr FT* European & International Trade Law

PgD/MSc: *1 yr FT* Applied Social Sciences; Business Information Systems; Development Management; Entrepreneurial Studies; Fashion Marketing; Informatics: Object Technology; Informatics: Software Development for Multimedia Systems; Information & Administrative Management; Information Management Systems; Maintenance Management; Marketing; Operations Management; Risk & Financial Services; Social Work *1 yr FT/PT* Bulk Solids Handling Technology; Computer Studies; Corporate Administration; Industrial Mathematics; Information & Administration Management; Instrumental Analytical Chemistry; Instrumentation; Logistics; Maintenance Management

Diplomas

Diploma: *1 yr FT* Health & Safety Management

HND: Computer Aided Engineering; Electronic Engineering

PgD: *1 yr FT* Dietetics; Journalism Studies

PgD/PgC: *1 yr FT* Human Resource Management *PT* Management Studies; Media Education

University Diploma: Computer Engineering

Certificates

Certificate: *PT* Counselling Skills

Professional Courses

Professional Courses: *PT* Associateship of the Chartered Institute of Bankers in Scotland; Associateship of the Chartered Institute of Management of Accountants; Association of Chartered Certified Accountants; Chartered Institute of Public Finance & Accounting; Member of Chartered Institute of Bankers in Scotland

UNIVERSITY OF GREENWICH

Wellington Street, Woolwich, London SE18 6PF Tel: 020 8331 8590 Fax: 020 8331 8145
e-mail: courseinfo@greenwich.ac.uk Website: www.gre.ac.uk

First Degrees

BA Hons: French or German or Italian or Spanish; Archaeology; Business, Science & Society; Business or French or German or Italian or Spanish; Economics-Business or Economics or French or German; Education or History or Italian or Philosophy or Politics or Psychology or Sociology or Spanish or Statistics or Theology; Education, Science & Society; English with Business or French or German or Italian or Law or Spanish or Theology; English-French or German or Spanish or Theology or Italian; French or German or Spanish or Italian; Business; History with Business or French or German or Italian or Law or Spanish or Theology; History, Science & Society or French; History-Business or Economics or English or German or Italian or Philosophy or Sociology or Spanish or Statistics or Theology; Landscape Architecture with French or German or Spanish; Law; Law with Education or Italian or Psychology; Law, Science & Society; Law-Business or English or Italian or Life Science or Politics or Psychology or Statistics or Theology; Legal Studies; Life Science-French or German or Italian or Spanish; Philosophy with Business or French or German or Italian or Spanish or Theology; Philosophy, Science & Society; Philosophy-Business or Economics or English or French or German or Italian or Sociology or Spanish or Statistics; Politics, Science & Society; Politics-Business or Economics or English or French or German or Italian or Philosophy or Sociology or Spanish or Statistics or Theology; Politics; Business or French or German or Italian or Law or Spanish or Theology; Psychology with French or German or Italian or Spanish; Psychology-French or German or Italian or Spanish; Social Care with French or German or Italian or Spanish; Sociology; Sociology-Business or French or German or Italian or Spanish; Statistics with Business; Theology, Science & Society; Theology-Business or Economics or French or German or Italian or Sociology or Spanish

BA/BA Hons: Accounting & Finance; Architecture; Arts Management; Arts Management with a Language; Business Administration with a Language; Business Administration; Business Studies or History or Law or Philosophy or Politics or Theology; Business Studies with Information Technology Education or a Language; Business: Central & Eastern Europe; Cultural Geography; Design & Technology Education or a Language; Economics with Psychology or Sociology or European Economics or Economic Development or Banking or Law; Economics; Engineering & Business Management; English; Finance & Financial Information Systems; Financial Services; Garden Design; Geography; Heritage Management with a Language; Heritage Management; History; Humanities; Humanities, Science & Society; International Business with a Language; International Business; International Marketing with a Language; International Marketing; Landscape Architecture; Marketing with a Language; Marketing; Marketing Communications; Marketing Communications with a Language; Media & Communication; Media & Society; Operations Management with a Language; Operations Management; Personnel Management with a Language; Personnel Management; Philosophy; Politics; Primary Teaching Studies (English) with QTS; Primary Teaching Studies (Mathematics) with QTS; Primary Teaching Studies (Science) with QTS; Primary/Secondary Teaching Studies (Design & Technology); Sociology; Sociology with Economics or Law or Psychology; Sociology & Economics; Theological Studies; Tourism Management with a Language; Tourism Management

BEng/BEng Hons: Civil Engineering; Civil Engineering with a European Language or Project Management or Water & Environmental Management; Computer Systems with Software Engineering; Electrical & Electronic Engineering; Electrical Engineering; Electronic Engineering; Engineering & Business Management; Engineering Design & Technology; Mechanical Engineering; Motor Vehicle Engineering with Management

BSc Hons: Complementary Therapies; Complementary Therapies – Aromatherapy; Complementary Therapies – Stress Management; Economics-Statistics; Engineering with Business or Law; Engineering-Law or Business or French or German or Italian or Spanish; Environmental Earth Science; European Study; Environmental Science-Business or Economics or Engineering or French or German or Health or History or Italian or Philosophy or Politics or Spanish or Theology; Environmental Sciences with Business; Health with Economics or Education or French or German or Italian or Law or Spanish; Health, Science & Society; Health-Education or French or German or Italian or Law or Life Science or Spanish; Life & Environmental Sciences or History or Philosophy; Life Science-Business or Economics or Education or Sociology or Statistics or Theology; Medical Biochemistry; Pharmaceutical Sciences; Pharmaceutical Sciences with French or German or Spanish; Philosophy with Law; Psychology with Sociology; Science, Society & French; Science, Society & German; Science, Society & Italian; Science, Society & Spanish; Sociology, Science & Society; Sports Science with Professional Tennis Coaching; Statistics with Italian or Law; Statistics, Science & Society or Italian or Spanish; Statistics-French or German

BSc/BSc Hons: Analytical Chemistry; Analytical Chemistry with European Study; Biochemistry with European Study; Biochemistry; Biological Science; Biological Science with French or Law or German or Spanish or European Study; Biological Science (Biotechnology); Biological Science (Ecology); Biological Science (Physiology); Biological Science-Law; Biomedical Sciences; Building Engineering; Building Surveying; Building Surveying with Conservation Studies or Environmental Studies or Information Technology or Project Management; Chemistry with Business Management or French or German or Spanish or European Study or Law; Chemistry; Chemistry-Business Management or Law; Civil Engineering; Computer Networking; Computing; Computing Science; Design & Construction Management; Design & Construction Management with Information Technology or Urban Environmental Studies; Design Studies; Engineering (Electrical & Electronic); Engineering (Mechanical); Engineering Geology; Environmental Biology; Environmental Biology with European Study; Environmental Chemistry with European Study; Environmental Chemistry; Environmental Conservation; Environmental Control; Environmental Geology; Environmental Health; Environmental Sciences with Law; Environmental Sciences; Estate Management; Estate Management with Conservation Studies or Information Technology or Urban Environmental Studies; Exercise Physiology & Nutrition; Facilities Management; Fitness Science; Geographical Information Systems-Remote Sensing; Geography; Geology; Health with Learning Disabilities or Management or Physiology or Psychology or Sociology or Statistics; Health or Physiology; Health-Learning Disabilities or Management or Psychology or Sociology or Statistics; Horticulture; Housing Studies; Human Nutrition with European Study; Human

Nutrition; Information Systems; Information Systems with Business Management; Landscape Management; Leisure Property Development; Management & Industrial Science; Management Science; Mathematical Studies; Mathematics with Computing; Mathematics for Finance & Accountancy; Mathematics, Statistics & Computing; Medicinal Chemistry; Medicinal Chemistry with European Study; Midwifery (Pre-Registration); Multimedia Technology; Natural Resource Management; Nursing (Adult); Nursing (Child); Nursing (Mental Health); Pharmaceutical Sciences with European Study or Law; Pharmaceutical Sciences; Property Management; Property Valuation; Psychology with Statistics; Psychology; Public Health; Quantity Surveying; Quantity Surveying with Information Technology; Remote Sensing; Science; Science & Society; Science & Technology; Science Education; Sports Science; Statistics with Accounting & Finance or Business Management or Social Science or Computing; Statistics

LLB Hons: Law with Education or French or German or Health or Italian or Psychology or Sociology or Spanish or Statistics; Law

Higher Degrees

MA: Architecture; Arts Management; Crime, Deviance & Punishment; Cultural Tourism Management; Education; Employment Strategy; European Public Policy; Gener & Ethnic Studies; Heritage Management; Landscape Architecture; Landscape Studies; Literature & Criticism; Management of Language Learning; Museum Management; Political Studies; Urban Design

MBA: Business Administration

MChem: Applied Chemistry; Applied Chemistry with European Study

MEng: European Civil Engineering; Mechanical Engineering

MSc: Accounting & Finance; Applied Statistics; Biomedical Sciences; Building Engineering; Building Rehabilitation; Chemical Analysis; Civil Engineering; Coastal and Estuarine Management; Computing & Information Systems; Construction Information Technology; Construction Management & Economics; Contaminated Land Remediation; Distributed Computing Systems; Engineering; Environmental Assessment; Environmental Research; Environmental Science; Facilities Management; Finance & Financial Information Systems; Financial Management; Geographical Information Systems; Geology; Geomaterials; Grain Storage Management; Human Resources Development; Information Systems Engineering; International Banking & Finance; Landscape Management; Management Science; Mechanical & Manufacturing Engineering; Natural Resource Management; Occupational Hygiene; Occupational Safety & Health; Open (Land & Construction Management); Open (Science); Petroleum Geology; Petroleum Geology; Pharmaceutical Science; Post Harvest Horticulture; Real Estate Dev & Inv't (Eur); Real Estate Development & Investment; Real Estate Development & Investment (Europe); Research (Earth Science); Research (Environmental Science); Scientific & Engineering Software Technology; Sociology of Health & Welfare; Sustainable Agriculture; Therapeutic Counselling; Tourism, Conservation & Sustainable Development

Diplomas

BTEC HND: Animal Management; Applied Biology; Applied Photography; Biomedical Science; Building Studies; Business Studies; Civil Engineering Studies; Computer Aided Manufacture; Computing; Computing & Information Systems; Design (Communication); Electrical & Electronic Engineering; Electronic Engineering; Equine Management; Graphic Design; Horticulture (Commercial); Hospitality Management; Landscape Management (Land Use); Leisure Management; Mechanical Engineering; Motor Vehicle Engineering Management; Multimedia; Pharmaceutical Sciences; Professional Writing; Public Services; Science (Chemistry); Science (Health Studies); Sports Science; Tourism Management

Postgraduate Diploma: Environmental Assessment; European Studies; Gender & Ethnic Studies; Grain Storage Management; Literature & Criticism; Management Science; Political Studies; Post Harvest Horticulture; Sociology of Health & Welfare

Certificates

PGCE: Further Education; Primary Education; Secondary Education

HALTON COLLEGE
Kingsway, Widnes, Cheshire WA8 7QQ Tel: 0151 423 1391
* Offered as part of 2+2 degrees with Liverpool University as well as HND.

Higher Degrees
HND: Behavioural Sciences; Biomolecular Sciences*; Biological Sciences; Chemical Sciences*; Sports Sciences

HERIOT-WATT UNIVERSITY
Riccarton, Edinburgh EH14 4AS Tel: 0131 451 3376 Fax: 0131 451 3630
e-mail: admissions@hw.ac.uk Website: www.hw.ac.uk/

First Degrees
BA Hons: *4 yrs* Combined Studies
BEng Hons: *4 yrs* Chemical Engineering; Civil & Environmental Engineering; Civil Engineering; Computing & Electronics; Electrical & Electronic Engineering; Engineering; Environmental Services Engineering; Information Systems Engineering; Mechanical Engineering with Computer Aided Engineering; Mechanical Engineering with Energy Resource Engineering; Offshore Engineering (Civil or Mechanical, Electrical, Chemical); Offshore Engineering-Electrical & Electronic Engineering or Chemical & Processing Engineering or Civil Engineering or Mechanical Engineering; Software Engineering with Architectural Design; Structural Engineering; Structural Engineering
BSc Hons: *4 yrs* Actuarial Mathematics & Statistics; Applied Marine Biology; Biochemistry; Biological Sciences; Biology with Sport & Exercise Science; Brewing & Distilling; Building Economics & Quantity Surveying; Building Services & Quantity Surveying; Building Services Construction Management; Building Surveying; Chemistry with Colour Science; Chemistry with Biochemistry or Computer Science or Environmental Economics or European Language or Pharmaceutical Chemistry or Polymers & Electronical Materials or Management or a yr in N. America; Chemistry; Combined Studies; Computational Physics; Computer Science; Computer Science-Human Computer Interaction or Information Systems or Artificial Intelligence or Software Engineering or Multimedia Studies; Construction Management; Engineering Physics; Environmental Management & Technology; Estate Management; Financial Mathematics; Food Science, Technology & Management; General Physics; Information Technology; Integrated Product Design; International Management; Engineering-Management; Mathematics; Mathematics with Applied Mechanics or Computer Science or Economics or Education or European Language or Finance or Physics or Statistics; Microbiology; Optoelectronics & Laser Engineering; Physics or Education or Environmental Science with Laser Science; Physics; Sports & Exercise Science; Sports & Exercise Science with Psychology or Management; Statistics; Statistics-Economics; Sustainability and Environmental Management
BSc Ord: *3 yrs* General Mathematics

Higher Degrees
DOCTORATES
DEng; DLitt; DSc: *12 mths PT* (Awarded on published work)
PhD: *2 yrs FT/4 yrs PT* (By research) *24 mths FT 36 mths PT* (By research) *48 mths PT*

MASTER'S DEGREES
MA Hons: *4 yrs* Accountancy with European Language; Applied Languages & Translating; Business-Economics; Economics; Economics-Accountancy or Finance; International Business-Finance or Languages; Languages (Interpreting & Translating); Management; Management with Business Law or Human Resource Management or Marketing or Operations Management; Management-Economics or Finance
MArch: *15 mths FT* Architecture
MBA: *12 mths FT/24 mths PT* Business Administration (Up to seven yrs by distance learning)

MChem/MPhys: *4 yrs* Applied Physics with Microelectronics Manufacturing; Chemistry or Management or yr in N. America; Chemistry with Biochemistry or Computer Science or Environmental Economics or a European Language or Industrial Experience or Pharmaceutical Experience or Polymers & Electronic Materials; Chemistry with Colour Science; Computational Physics; Engineering Physics; Optoelectronics & Laser Engineering; Physics with Education or Environmental Science or Laser Science; Physics

MDes: *15 mths FT* Design & Applied Arts; Textile Design with Computer Applications; Visual Communication

MEng: *12 mths FT* Petroleum Engineering *5 yrs* Chemical Engineering with Environmental Management or Energy Resource Engineering or Brewing and Distilling Technology or Food Processing Technology or Pharmaceutical Chemistry or Semiconductor Processing Technology; Civil & Environmental Engineering; Civil Engineering; Electrical & Electronic Engineering; Mechanical Engineering; Structural Engineering *Minor only:* Structural Engineering with Architectural Design *5 yrs FT* Chemical Engineering; Electronics with Microelectronics; Environmental Services Engineering; Manufacturing Engineering; Offshore Engineering with Electrical & Electronic Engineering or Chemical Engineering or Civil Engineering or Mechanical Engineering

MFA: *2 yrs FT* Painting; Printmaking; Sculpture; Tapestry

MLA: *21 mths FT/48 mths PT* Landscape Architecture

MPhil: *12 mths FT/24 mths PT* (By research. Available in every department)

MSc: Petroleum Engineering (By distance learning only); Property Asset Management (By distance learning only) *12 mths FT/24 mths FT* Marine Resource Development and Protection; Materials Engineering; Acturial Science; Arabic-English Translation and Interpreting; Brewing & Distilling; Building & Services Engineering (Also available by distance learning); Building Services Engineering Management (Also available by distance learning); Clothing Management; Colour Science; Construction Management (Building Management) (Also available by distance learning); Construction Management (Contracting Management) (Also available by distance learning); Construction Management (Corporate Strategy) (Also available by distance learning); Construction Management (Project Management) (Also available by distance learning); Digital Systems Engineering; Distributed & Multimedia Information Systems; Drives and Power Engineering; Environmental Pollution Control Management; Equal Opportunities; Facilities Management (Also available by distance learning); Asset Management (Also available by distance learning); Financial Mathematics; Geotechnical Engineering; International Accounting; Financial Studies; International Banking; Landscape Studies; Logistics & Supply Chain Management; Marine Resource Management; Mathematics of Non-linear Models; Optoelectronic & Laser Devices; Personnel Management; IT; Reliability Engineering; Safety Engineering; Reservoir Evaluation Management; Science & Technology of Water Purification; Structural Engineering; Subsea Engineering; System Level Integration; Technical Textiles; Translation; Translation and Conference Interpreting; Water Resource Engineering Management *15 mths FT* Architectural Conservation; Urban Design *2 yrs FT* Town and County Planning; Housing *2 yrs FT/3 yrs PT* Housing; Information Technology *5 yrs PT (Modular) Distance Learning* Malting & Brewing *PT* Occupational Psychology (Evening Course)

MURP: *21 mths FT* Urban and Regional Planning

POSTGRADUATE DIPLOMAS

Postgraduate Diploma: Property Asset Management (By distance learning only) *15 mths FT* Architectural Conservation; Urban Design *9 mths FT/18 mths FT* Architecture; Brewing & Distilling; Information Technology; International Accounting; Financial Studies; International Banking; Landscape Studies; Actuarial Science; Arabic-English Translation and Interpreting; Building Services Engineering (Also available by distance learning); Building Services Engineering Management (Also available by distance learning); Clothing Management; Colour Science; Construction Management (Building Maintenance) (Also available by distance learning); Construction Management (Contracting Management) (Also available by distance learning); Construction Management (Corporate Strategy) (Also available by distance learning); Construction Management (Project Management) (Also available by distance learning); Design (Design & Applied Arts; Visual Communication); Digital Systems Engineering; Distributed and Multimedia Information Systems; Drives and Power Engineering; Environmental Pollution

Control Management; Equal Opportunities; Facilities Management (Also available by distance learning); Asset Maintenance (Also available by distance learning); Financial Mathematics; Geotechnical Engineering; Logistics & Supply Chain Management; Marine Resource Development and Protection; Marine Resource Management; Marketing (Textiles/Fashion/Technical Textiles); Materials Engineering; Mathematics of Non-linear Models; Optoelectronic & Laser Devices; Painting; Personnel Management; IT; Petroleum Engineering (By distance learning); Printmaking; Reliability Engineering; Safety Management; Reservoir Evaluation Management; Science & Technology of Water Purification; Sculpture; Structural Engineering; Subsea Engineering; Tapestry; Technical Textiles; Translation; Conference Interpreting; Water Resource Engineering Management *2 yrs* Town and Country Planning *2 yrs FT/3 yrs PT* Housing

Degrees validated by Heriot-Watt University offered at:

Edinburgh College of Art

Lauriston Place, Edinburgh EH3 9DF Tel: 0131 221 6000 Fax: 0131 221 6001
e-mail: registration@eca.ac.uk Website: www.eca.ac.uk

First Degrees

BA Hons: *4 yrs FT* Design & Applied Arts; Painting; Printmaking; Sculpture; Tapestry; Visual Communication
BA/BA Hons: *3-4 yrs FT Combined Studies:* Environmental Studies
BArch Hons: *4 yrs FT and 1 yr S* Architecture

Higher Degrees

MA Hons: *4 yrs FT and 1 yr S* Landscape Architecture; Town Planning
MArch: *1 yr FT/2 yrs PT* Architecture
MDes: *4 trms FT* Design & Applied Arts; Visual Communication
MFA: *2 yrs FT* Painting, Sculpture, Printmaking or Tapestry
MLA: *2 yrs FT* Landscape Architecture
MPhil: (Apply to College for details)
MSc: *1 yr FT/3 yrs PT* Architectural Conservation; Equal Opportunities; Landscape Studies; Urban & Environmental Development; Urban Design
MURP: *2 yrs FT* Urban & Regional Planning
PhD: (Apply to College for details)

Diplomas

Postgraduate Diploma: *1 yr FT* Architectural Conservation; Architecture; Landscape Architecture; Landscape Studies; Painting; Printmaking, Tapestry, Sculpture, Design & Applied Arts; Urban & Environmental Development; Urban Design; Visual Communication *2 yrs FT/3 yrs PT* Housing; Town & Country Planning

Scottish Borders Campus

Netherdale, Galashiels, Selkirkshire TD1 3HF Tel: 01896 892237 Fax: 01896 758965
e-mail: j.dilger@hw.ac.uk Website: www.hw.ac.uk/sbc/

First Degrees

BA Hons: *4 yrs FT* Business Management; Textile Design
BSc Hons: *4 yrs FT* Biomedical Materials; Clothing Design and Manufacture; Computing for Industry; Fashion Design for Industry; Textile Product Development and Design; Textiles & Fashion Design Management; Textiles International Management, Manufacture and Marketing; Textiles Technology and Manufacture

Higher Degrees

MChem/BSc: Colour Chemistry
MDes/Diploma: Textile Design with Computer Applications
MSc/Diploma: Clothing Management; Colour Science; Personnel Management with Information Technology; Technical Textiles (Joint course with the University of Leeds)

Diplomas

HND: Business Studies; Computing (Software Development)

Certificates

HNC: Computing

UNIVERSITY OF HERTFORDSHIRE

College Lane, Hatfield, Hertfordshire AL10 9AB Tel: 01707 284000 Fax: 01707 284738
e-mail: g.ward@herts.ac.uk

* In conjunction with North Herts College; ** Herts Regional College; *** West Herts College; **** Oaklands College.

First Degrees

BA Hons Humanities: *3 yrs FT* Educational Studies; History; Linguistics; Literature; Philosophy *Minor only:* Computing; Drama; Educational Studies; Environmental Studies; French; German; Humanities; Psychological Studies; Religious Studies; Sociological Studies; Spanish

BA/BA Hons: *3 yrs FT* European Studies; Hospitality Management; Image Making & Design; Linguistics; Literature; Media Production Management; Performing Arts; Philosophy; Political Economy; Social Policy; Social Work *3 yrs FT/4 yrs S/5 yrs PT* Accounting; Business Economics; Business Information Systems; Economics; Economics with Finance; International Economics; Marketing; Tourism Management *3 yrs FT/5 yrs PT* Applied & Media Arts; Economics; Fine Art; History; Humanities; Model Design; Politics; Product Design; Social Policy; Social Sciences; Sociology; Two-Dimensional Design *4 yrs S* International Business Studies *4 yrs S/5 yrs PT* Asia Pacific Business; Business Studies

BA/BSc: *3 yrs FT/4 yrs S/5 yrs PT* Business Joint Honours

BEd Hons: *4 yrs FT* Primary Education

BEng (Extended): Engineering (Preliminary 1 yr FT at *, ***, ****)

BEng/BEng Hons: *3 yrs FT/4 yrs S* Aerospace Engineering; Aerospace Systems Engineering; Automotive Engineering; Civil Engineering; Electrical & Electronic Engineering; Electrical Engineering; Electronics Manufacture *3 yrs FT/4 yrs S/PT* Civil Engineering; Communications Systems; Computer Aided Engineering; Digital Systems; Electronic Engineering; Manufacturing Systems Engineering; Mechanical Engineering; Product Engineering

BSc (Extended): *1 yr FT (then 3 yrs FT/4 yrs S/5 yrs PT)* Combined Modular Scheme (Information Sciences) (In conjunction with *; **; ***; ****); Combined Modular Scheme (Science) (In conjunction with *; **; ***; ****); Science (In conjunction with *; **; ***; ****)

BSc Hons: *3 yrs FT/4-5 yrs PT Combined Awards Modular Scheme:* Astronomy / Astrophysics; Business; Chemistry; Computing; Economics; Electronic Music; Electronics; Environmental Studies; European Studies; French; Geology; German; Human Biology; Law; Linguistics Science; Management Science; Manufacturing Systems; Mathematics; Philosophy; Physics; Psychology; Spanish; Statistics

BSc/BSc Hons: *3 yrs FT* Cognitive Science; Electronic Music; Environmental Geology (combined); Environmental Sciences (Combined); European Studies (Combined) with RM; Midwifery; Multimedia Technology; Music Technology with Paramedic Award; Paramedic Science; Physiotherapy; Psychology; Radiography; Software Systems for the Arts and the Media; Sports Science; Sports Therapy *3 yrs FT/4 yrs FT* Nursing with RN; Nursing with Social Work Studies *3 yrs FT/4 yrs S* Pharmaceutical Science *3 yrs FT/4 yrs S/5 yrs PT* Accounting & Management Information Systems; Analytical Chemistry; Applied Biology; Applied Physics; Astronomy; Astrophysics; Biochemistry; Biotechnology; Business Decision Sciences; Business Joint Honours;

Business Statistics; Chemistry with Scientific Computing; Chemistry; Conservation & Recreation Management; Ecosystem Management; Engineering Geology; Engineering Management; Environmental Biology; Environmental Chemistry; Environmental Management with Business; Environmental Pollution Science; Environmental Studies; Geography; Geography and Geology; Human Physiology; Management Sciences; Mathematics; Mathematics for Business Analysis; Medicinal Chemistry; Microbiology; Molecular Biology; Pharmacology; Physics; Astrophysics; Scientific Computing *4 yrs FT* Mathematics with QTS (With a Yr in Europe or North America); Mathematics with QTS *4 yrs PT* Facilitating Parent Infant Relationships *4 yrs S* Graphic Media Studies *4 yrs S/5 yrs PT* Computer Science; Computing & Networks; Information Systems; Intelligent Systems; Software Engineering

LLB Hons: *2 yrs FT* Law *3 yrs FT* Criminal Justice; Law; LLB with Business

Higher Degrees

LLM: *FT/PT* Business Law; Gender and the Law; International Law; Law; Legal Practice; Medical Law

MA: *FT/PT* Applied Social Studies; the Diploma in Social Work; Art Therapy; Counselling; Crime and Community Safety; Dance Movement Therapy; Dramatherapy; Economics; Education Law and Policy; English Language Teaching and Applied Linguistics; English Language Teaching to Adults (DELTA); Environmental Law and Policy; Health Law; Historical Studies; Human Resource Management & Industrial Studies; Humanities; International Business; Law; Law, Government and Policy; Linguistics & Child Language; Literature; Management; Management Studies; Media Management – Film & Television; Philosophy; Policy Studies; Politics; Social Policy; Social Sciences; Social Work and Welfare: Research & Practice; Sociology; Sociology of Health & Illness

MBA/PgD/PgC: *FT/PT* Business Administration (Executive or International or Standard)

MChem: *4 yrs FT/5 yrs S* Chemistry

MEd: *2 yrs PT (CPD)* Education

MEng: *4 yrs FT/5 yrs S* Engineering

MPhys: *4 yrs FT* Applied Physics; Astrophysics; Physics

MSc: Advanced Manufacturing Technology; Advanced Practice; Analytical Chemistry; Applied Biology; Applied Developmental Research; Astrophysics; Automobile Engineering, Design, Manufacture & Management; Automotive Engineering; Biochemistry; Biotechnology; Chemistry; Clinical Studies; Communications Systems; Composition; Computer Science; Conservation & Recreation Management; Data Communications and Networks; Decision Sciences; Digital Systems; Ecology and Agricultural Biology; Electronic Music; Electronics; Emergency Planning and Disaster Management; Environmental Change & Monitoring; Environmental Chemistry; Environmental Geology; Environmental Management for Business; Environmental Management of Rural Areas; Environmental Studies; Health Research & Evaluation; Human Physiology; Information Systems; Integrated River Basin; International Automotive Engineering; Manufacturing Management; Manufacturing Systems Engineering; Medical Imaging Science (Ultrasound, Magnetic Resonance Imaging, Radio Nuclear Medicine); Medical Systems; Medicinal Chemistry; Microbiology; Molecular Biology; Neuromusculoskeletal Physiotherapy; Numerical Software; Occupational Psychology; Oncological Science; Operational Research; Optimisation; Optoelectronics; Organisational Psychology; Pharmaceutical Sciences; Pharmacological & Clinical Sciences; Pharmacology; Pharmacology & Toxicology; Pharmacovigilance; Physics; Physiotherapy; Pre-hospital Emergency Care and Planning; Quality Engineering; Research Methods in Psychology; Sports Therapy; Toxicology

PhD; MPhil; MRes; MA; MEd; MSc: (Available by research)

Diplomas

DipHE: *2 yrs FT* Social Work

Diploma: Advancing Practice; Analytical Chemistry; Applied Biology; Art Therapy; Astrophysics; Automotive Engineering Design, Manufacture and Management; Biochemistry; Biotechnology; Chemistry; Clinical Studies; Conservation & Recreation Management; Counselling; Crime and Community Safety; Dance Movement Therapy; Data Communications and Networks; Decision Sciences; Dramatherapy; Ecology and Agricultural Biology; Economics; Education of the Hearing Impaired; Electronic Music; Emergency Planning and Disaster Management; Environmental

Change and Monitoring; Environmental Chemistry; Environmental Geology; Environmental Management for Business; Environmental Studies; Forensic Odontology; Health Research and Evaluation; Human Physiology; Human Resource Management & Industrial Relations; Information Systems; Integrated River Basin Management; International Automotive Engineering; International Business; Legal Practice (Law Society); Management; Management Studies (In conjunction with *; **; ***; ****); Media Management – Film & Television; Medical Imaging Science (Ultrasound, Magnetic Resonance Imaging, Nuclear Medicine); Medicinal Chemistry; Microbiology; Molecular Biology; Neuromusculoskeletal Physiotherapy; Numerical Software; Occupational Psychology; Oncological Science; Operational Research; Optimisation; Organisational Psychology; Pharmaceutical Sciences; Pharmacological & Clinical Sciences; Pharmacology; Pharmacology & Toxicology; Pharmacorigilance; Physics; Policy Studies; Politics; Pre-hospital Emergency Care and Planning; Social Policy; Social Sciences; Social Work and Welfare: Research and Practice; Sociology; Sociology of Health and Illness; Sports Therapy; Toxicology

Certificates

CATS: (Postgraduate qualification by Credit Accumulation and Transfer)
Certificate: *PT* Mammographic Practice and Applications/Mammographic Studies; Medical Imaging Science; Post Compulsory Education & Training; Radiographic Reporting (Appendicular and Axial Skeleton); Supervision of Counselling and Therapy; Supervision of Midwives plus ENB-R68
PGCE: *1 yr FT* Primary; Secondary (Mathematics/ Modern Languages/Science/Art/English/Geography)

Degrees validated by University of Hertfordshire offered at:

West Herts College

Hempstead Road, Watford, Hertfordshire WD1 3EZ Tel: 01923 812565 Fax: 01923 812556
e-mail: admis.cas@westherts.ac.uk Website: www.westherts.ac.uk

First Degrees

BA/BA Hons: *3 yrs FT* Advertising-Marketing Communications; Business Administration; Business Administration (Hospitality Management); Humanities; Imagemaking & Design; Media Production Management; Media Production Management – Media Research; Media Production Management – Moving Image
BSc Hons: *1 yr FT* Engineering Foundation; Science Foundation *4 yrs S* Graphic Media Studies

Diplomas

Diploma: *1 yr FT* Advertising; Ceramics; Copywriting & Art Direction; Digital Media Production; Digital Pre Press Design and Technology; Illustration; Innovative Package Design Development; International Public Relations; Journalism, Radio & Advertising; Printmaking; Publishing

THE UNIVERSITY OF HUDDERSFIELD

Queensgate, Huddersfield HD1 3DH Tel: 01484 422288 Fax: 01484 516151

First Degrees

BA: *1 yr FT* Business Information Technology
BA Hons: *1 yr FT* Business Administration; European Business *3 yrs FT* Accountancy with Information Systems; Accountancy & Finance; Architecture /Architecture (International); Business Administration; Business Management; Business Studies; Business Studies with Environmental Management; Communications & Cultures; Community Education; Creative Imaging; Creative Textile Crafts; Economics; English with Creative Writing; English Studies;

History-English or Media; Fashion with Manufacture, Marketing & Promotion; Financial Management & Economics; Fine Art (Drawing & Painting); Geography with Environmental Sustainability or Tourism & Leisure Studies or Transport Studies; Geography; History with Media or Sociology; History; History with Heritage; Humanities; Industrial Design; Installation Art & Events; Interior Design; Law & Accountancy; Management & Accountancy; Media; Moving Image Design; Multimedia Design; Music with English or Theatre Studies or a Modern Language; Music Technology; Politics with Contemporary History or Media Studies or Sociology; Politics; Product Design; Surface Pattern; Textile Design; Theatre Studies; Theatre Studies & Media; Theatre Studies with Music; Transport Design; Virtual Reality Design *4 yrs FT* International Business with Modern Languages *4 yrs S* Artificial Intelligence or Computing Science or French; Business Computing or German or Human Computer Interaction or Multimedia or Operational Research or Psychology or Software Development or Statistics; Business Studies; Business Studies with Environmental Management; Computing & Business Analysis; Computing in Business; Creative Imaging; Economics; Economics-Marketing; Fashion with Manufacture, Marketing & Promotion; Financial Management and Economics; Fine Art (Drawing & Painting); Hospitality Management with a Modern Language; Hospitality Management with Tourism & Leisure; Hospitality Operations Management; Industrial Design; Installation Art & Events; Interactive Multimedia; Interior Design; International Business with Modern Languages; International Hospitality Management with a Modern Language or Innovation; Marketing; Marketing; Marketing, Retailing & Distribution; Moving Image Design; Multimedia with French or German or Human Computer Interaction or Business Computing or Software Development or Statistics; Multimedia Design; Multimedia-E-Commerce; Music with Modern Language; Music Technology; Product Design; Product Innovation, Design and Development; Surface Pattern; Textile Design; Transport Design; Virtual Reality Design
BA/BA Hons: *3 yrs FT/4 yrs S* Hospitality with Licensed House Management
BEd/BEd Hons: *2 yrs FT* Business Studies; Design & Technology; Information Technology; Mathematics; Music; Science
BEng Hons: *4 yrs S* Automotive Design; Automotive Engineering; Computer Aided Engineering; Computer Control Systems; Electro-Mechanical Engineering; Electronic & Communication Engineering; Electronic & Control Engineering; Electronic & Electrical Engineering; Electronic Engineering; Electronic Engineering & Computer Systems; Engineering with Technology Management; Engineering Design: Mechanical; Engineering with Technology Management; Environmental Engineering; Mechanical & Automotive Design; Mechanical Engineering; Precision Engineering
BMus Hons: *3 yrs FT* Music
BSc: *1 yr FT* Computing *3 yrs FT/4 yrs S* Applied Sciences
BSc Hons: *3 yrs FT* Applied Social Studies; Architectural Computer Aided Technology; Behavioural Sciences; Building Conservation; Environmental Science; Geography with Human Biology; Geography/Geography (Applied); Health with Community Studies; Health and Environment; Health-Sports Studies; Midwifery; Physiotherapy; Podiatry; Psychology; Social Work; Sociology *3 yrs FT/4 yrs S* Automotive Technology; Biochemistry; Biology (Molecular & Cellular); Chemistry; Chemistry with Analytical Chemistry or Biochemistry or Business or Chemical Engineering or Environmental Science or Food Science or Medicinal Chemistry; Computer Aided Design; Computing Science; Earth Sciences; Electronic Design; Environment and Human Health; Environmental Science; European Logistics Management with Environmental Sciences; Geography; Human Biology; Mathematical Sciences; Mathematics-Computing; Microbial Sciences; Multimedia Design; Multimedia Technology; Music Technology & Audio Systems; Pharmaceutical Science; Product Design; Technology with Business Management; Textile Design; Virtual Reality Design; Virtual Reality Systems *4 yrs S* Catering Management-Food Sciences or Nutrition; Computing and Management Sciences; Environmental Analysis; Environmental Protection; Food & Nutrition; Food Supply Chain Management; Food, Nutrition & Health; Logistics & Supply Chain Management; Manufacturing & Operations Management; Software Development; Software Development with Artificial Intelligence or Business or Business Computing or French or German or Human Computer Interaction or Management or Mathematics or Multimedia or Operational Research or Statistics; Transport & Logistics Management
BSc/BSc Hons: *1 yr FT* Food Services Management; Logistics
LLB/LLB Hons: *3 yrs FT* Business Law; European Legal Studies; Law

Higher Degrees

MA: *1 yr FT* Health Care Law; Innovation with Entrepreneurial Studies; Interactive Multimedia Production; International Business; International Hospitality Management; Marketing and Management for Designers; Music
MBA: *1 yr FT* Business Administration
MChem: *4 yrs FT* Chemistry
MDes: *1 yr FT* Innovation with Entrepreneurial Studies
MEng: *5 yrs S* Automotive Design; Automotive Engineering; Computer Aided Engineering; Computer Control Systems; Electro-Mechanical Engineering; Electronic & Communication Engineering; Electronic & Control Engineering; Electronic & Electrical Engineering; Electronic Engineering; Electronic Engineering & Computer Systems; Engineering Design: Mechanical; Environmental Engineering; Mechanical & Automotive Design; Mechanical Engineering; Precision Engineering; Software Engineering
MSc: *1 yr FT* Analytical Chemistry; Applied Behavioural Sciences; Computer Integrated Manufacturing & its Management; Designing Worldwide Interactive Systems; Electronic & Computer Based Systems Design; Engineering Control Systems & Metrology; Engineering Design and its Management; Environmental Sustainability; Geography; Health and Social Care; Health Professional Education; Information Systems; Innovation with Entrepreneurial Studies; Interactive Multimedia Production; Marketing; Nutrition & Food Management; Scientific Computing; Social Research & Evaluation; Software Development; Surface and Groundwater Resources; Sustainable Architecture; Textile Technology for Textile Designers

Diplomas

BTEC HND: *2 yrs FT* Automotive Engineering; Business & Management; Chemistry; Electronic & Electrical Engineering; Industrial Measurement & Control; Mechanical & Manufacturing Engineering; Mechanical Engineering *3 yrs S* Business Information Technology; Chemistry; Computing; Hospitality Management; Multimedia; Software Engineering
DipHE: *2 yrs FT* Product Design; Textile Design
Postgraduate Diploma: *1 yr FT* Careers Guidance; Law (CPE) *2 yrs FT* Architecture

Certificates

PGCE: *1 yr FT* Design Technology (Key Stage 2/3) *1-2 yrs FT* Business Studies (Secondary); Design Technology (Secondary); Information Technology (Secondary); Mathematics (Secondary); Music (Secondary); Science (Secondary)
PGCE (Post-Compulsory): *1 yr FT*
PSCE: *1 yr FT* PSCE (Post Compulsory Education and Training)

Other Courses

Foundation Course: *1 yr FT* Architectural Foundation Programme; Automotive Design; Automotive Engineering; Computer Aided Engineering; Electronic & Communication Engineering; Electronic & Electrical Engineering; Electronic Engineering; Electronic Engineering & Computer Systems; Engineering Foundation (General); Environmental Engineering; Mechanical & Automotive Design; Mechanical Engineering; Science Foundation

Professional Courses

Professional Courses: ACCA Professional Course in Accountancy; Legal Practice Course

UNIVERSITY OF HULL

Cottingham Road, Hull HU6 7RX Tel: 01482 465328 Fax: 01482 442290
e-mail: admissions@admin.hull.ac.uk Website: www.hull.ac.uk

* Subject to approval.
† HND conversion.

First Degrees

BA Hons: *3-4 yrs FT* American Studies; British Politics and Legislative Studies; Business and Management; Business Management and Information Technology; Business Studies; Combined Languages; Creative Music Technology with Business Management; Creative Music Technology; Criminology; Dance; Drama; Dutch Studies; Economic & Social History; English; English – Primary Education (With QTS); English and Cultural Studies; European International Studies; European Politics and Legislative Studies; European Studies; Fine Art; French; Geography; German; History; Information & Communication Technology – Primary Education (With QTS); International Relations with International Political Economy; Italian; Leisure & Tourism Management; Leisure and Tourism Management; Management; Management (International); Music; Philosophy; Politics; Politics & International Relations; Politics with Management; Politics, Philosophy & Economics; Scandinavian Studies; Social Anthropology; Social Policy; Social Policy & Criminology; Social Work & Social Policy; Sociology; Sociology & Social Anthropology with Development Studies or Dutch Studies or Danish* or Hiapanic Studies*; Sociology & Social Anthropology; South East Asian Studies; South East Asian Studies & Language with Politics; South-East Asian Studies or Development Studies; South-East Asian Studies & Language with Politics or Development Studies; Spanish; Theatre Studies; Theatre Studies; Theology; Transnational Integrated European Studies (TIES)*PT* Arts & Humanities; French; German; Historical Studies; Philosophy; Social & Behavioural Studies; Social Policy & Administration

BA Joint Hons: *3-4 yrs FT* Business and Management; Business Management and IT; Drama-English or French or German or Italian or Music or Theology or Scandinavian Studies; Dutch Studies or French or German; Business Studies or Italian or Spanish or Scandinavian Studies; Dutch Studies-French or German or Gender Studies or South-East Asian Studies or Spanish; Economic & Social History-Sociology & Anthropology or History*; Economics-Geography or Mathematics or Statistics; English-French or German or History or Italian or Music or Philosophy or Scandinavian Studies or Spanish or Theology or Cultural Studies or Gender Studies; French-German or History or Italian or Music or Philosophy or Politics or Scandinavian Studies or Spanish or Gender Studies; Gender Studies and American Studies or Dutch Studies or English or French or German or Italian or Philosophy or Scandinavian Studies or Social & Economic History* or Social Policy or Sociology & Anthropology or Spanish; Gender Studies-American Studies or Drama or English or History; Geography-Sociology & Anthropology; German-Italian or Scandinavian Studies or Spanish; History-Italian or Politics or Scandinavian Studies; Italian-Spanish or Scandinavian Studies; Management and Sociological Studies or Management Science or Physical Education or Sports Science; Philosophy-Politics or Sociology & Anthropology or Spanish or Theology; Politics-Social Policy or Sociology & Anthropology; Scandinavian Studies and Drama or History or Italian or Spanish; Social Anthropology and South-East Asian Studies; Social Anthropology and South-East Asian Studies (with Language); Social Policy-Sociology & Anthropology; Sociology & Social Anthropology; Sociology and Theology

BMus: *3 yrs* Music

BSc (Econ) Hons: *3 yrs* Economics; Economics & Accounting; Economics & Business Economics; Economics & Economic History; International & Financial Economics

LLB: *3-4 yrs FT* Law with German Law & Language; Law with French Law & Language; Law with Philosophy; Law-Politics; Law *5 yrs PT* Law

SCIENCE

BEng: *3-4 yrs FT* Computer Aided Engineering; Computer Systems Engineering; Electronic Engineering; Information & Computer Control Technology; Integrated Engineering; Mechanical & Manufacturing Engineering; Mechanical & Materials Engineering; Mechanical Design Engineering; Mechanical Engineering; Mobile Telecommunications Technology

BSc Hons: *3-4 yrs FT* Accounting; Accounting (International); Applied Physics; Aquatic Biology; Biological Studies – Primary Education (With QTS); Biology with Education; Biology; Biomedical Sciences; Chemistry with Analytical Chemistry & Toxicology or 21st Century Materials or Environmental Toxicology or French or German or Forensic Science & Toxicology or Drug Design & Toxicology or Education; Chemistry; Coastal Management; Coastal Marine Biology; Computer Science with Information Engineering; Computer Science; Environmental Biology; Environmental Science; Geography; Internet Computing; Internet Computing with Industrial Experience or

Business Management; Marine Biology; Mathematical Modelling-Computer Graphics; Mathematics or Finance; Mathematics with German or French or Spanish; Mathematics – Primary Education (With QTS); Midwifery; Molecular Biology & Biotechnology; Nursing Sciences; Nursing Studies; Philosophy; Physical Geography; Physics; Physics with Medical Technology or Lasers & Photonics; Psychology with Counselling or Occupational Psychology or Sports Science* or Anthropology or Philosophy or Sociology; Psychology; Pure Mathematics; Software Engineering; Software Engineering with Industrial Experience or Study Abroad; Sports & Exercise Science; Sports and Exercise Science *PT* Chemistry; Community Nursing (Children's Nursing); Community Nursing (General Practice Nursing); Community Nursing (Learning Disabilities); Community Nursing (Mental Health Nursing); Community Nursing (Nursing in the Home); Community Nursing (Occupational Health Nursing); Community Nursing (Public Health Nursing); Community Nursing (School Nursing)

BSc Joint Hons: *3 yrs* Computer Graphics and Mathematical Modelling; Geography-Environmental Biology; Internet Computing with Industrial Experience; Internet Computing-Business Management or Business Management with Industrial Experience or Management Science; Mathematics and Economics or Philosophy or Statistics with Biology; Physical Education & Sports Science or Mathematics or Scandinavian Studies or Technology or Management

Higher Degrees

DOCTORATES
ClinPsyD: *3 yrs FT* Clinical Psychology
DBA: *PT*
EdD: *PT*

MASTER'S DEGREES OR EQUIVALENT
LLM: *1 yr FT/2 yrs PT Taught courses available in:* European Public Law; International Business Law; International Law *2 yrs By Research:* Law
MA: *1 yr FT* Democratisation, Nationalism & Ethnicity in Asia; Education; Fine Art; Maritime History; Modern European Cultures & Societies; South East Asian Studies (ESRC-recognised programme) *1 yr FT/2 yrs PT* Applied Ethics; Applied Language & New Technologies; Contemporary Literature & Film; Criminology; Developing Area Studies; English & Cultural Studies: Identities; European Integration & Co-operation (ESRC-recognised programme); Gender & Development; Gender Studies; Global Political Economy (ESRC-recognised programme); International Law & Politics (ESRC-recognised programme); International Politics (ESRC-recognised programme); Legislative Studies (ESRC-recognised programme); Management Systems; Maritime Security; Medieval Vernacular Languages & Literatures; Modern European Cultures & Societies; Performance Theory & Practice; Security Studies (ESRC-recognised programme); Social Work; The Politics & Culture of the Northern Renaissance; Theatre & Contemporary Practice (Scarborough Campus); Theological Understanding of Contemporary Society; Theology; Women & Literature in English *2 yrs PT* Painting (Scarborough Campus); Religious Education (Available at Scarborough Campus on weekends) *FT/PT By Research:* Historical Research; History; Philosophy; Philosophy of the Mind; Theology
MBA: *1 yr FT* E-Business; Education; Engineering Management; Financial Management; General Management; Information Management; Strategic Marketing; Travel & Tourism *2 yrs PT* Executive *FT* School Leadership *PT* Health & Social Care Management; Health Services Management; Public Sector Management (Health & Social Care)
MChem: *4 yrs FT* Forensic Science & Toxicology or Industrial Experience; Chemistry with 21st Century Materials or Analytical Chemistry & Toxicology or Environmental Toxicology or French or German or Drug Design & Toxicology; Chemistry
MD: *FT/PT* Public Health & Primary Care
MEd: *1 yr FT/2 yrs PT* Education *DL* Information & Communication Technology (For TESOL) *PT* Special Educational Needs
MEng: *4 yrs FT* Electronic Communications Engineering; Electronic Control & Robot Engineering; Electronic Design & Manufacture; Electronic Engineering; Environmental Electronics; Integrated Engineering; Mechanical Engineering; Microelectronic Systems Engineering; Mobile Telecommunications Engineering; Optoelectronic Systems Engineering

MMath: *4 yrs FT* Mathematics; Mathematics with Finance

MMus: *1 yr* Music: Analysis, Composition, Musicology or Performance *1 yr FT/2 yrs PT* Music

MPhil: *FT/PT By research on topics in:* Accounting; American Studies; Computer Science; Dance; Drama; Economic & Social History; Economics; Education; Engineering; English; Fine Art; Fisheries; Gender Studies; Geography; Health Studies; Law; Mathematics; Medical Physics; Music; Nursing; Philosophy; Politics; Psychology; Social Policy & Criminology; Sociology & Social Anthropology; South-East Asian Studies; Theatre; Theology

MPhys: *4 yrs FT* Applied Physics; Physics with Medical Technology or Lasers & Photonics; Physics

MPhysGeog: *4 yrs FT* Physical Geography

MSc: *1 yr FT Taught courses available in:* Advanced Materials, Processes & Manufacturing; Applied Social Research (Sociology & Social Anthropology); Aquaculture Planning & Management; Chemistry; Computer Graphics & Virtual Environments; Environmental Policy & Management; Fish Marketing; Fisheries Policy & Planning; Fisheries Science; Food Standards Science; Industrial Psychology; Inland Fisheries Management; Internet Computing (Scarborough Campus); Management of Fisheries Technology; Mathematics; Radiosystems Engineering; Strategic Financial Management *1 yr FT/2 yrs PT Taught courses available in:* Advanced Nursing Practice; Biotechnology & Molecular Biology; Counselling/Counselling Studies; Environmental Policy & Management; Estuarine & Coastal Sciences Management; Gender Research; Health Promoting Practice; Human Ageing: Policy & Practice; Learning Disabilities Nursing *2 yrs FT/3 yrs PT Taught courses available in:* Health Professional Studies *2 yrs PT Taught courses available in:* Palliative Care *Flexible Taught courses available in:* Global Biodiversity: Monitoring & Conservation *FT/PT By research on topics in:* Applied Mathematics; Applied Physics; Applied Social Research; Biological Sciences; Business Studies; Chemistry; Clinical Psychology; Computer Science; Engineering; Fisheries; Industrial Psychology; Mathematics; Medical Physics; Medicine; Nursing; Obstetrics & Gynaecology; Philosophy; Physics; Psychology; Pure Mathematics

MSc (Econ): *1 yr FT/2 yrs PT* Public Policy

PhD: *FT/PT By Research:* Accounting; American Studies; Biological Sciences; Chemistry; Drama; Economic & Social History; Economics; Education; Engineering; English; Fisheries; Geography; Health Studies; History; Law; Mathematics; Music; Nursing; Philosophy; Physics; Politics; Psychology; South-East Asian Studies; Theology

PsyD: *3 yrs FT* Clinical Psychology; Psychology

Diplomas

Postgraduate Diploma: *1 yr FT* Counselling; Mathematics (Advanced with PGCE); Mathematics (Foundation); South-East Asian Studies (Foundation); Statistics (Foundation) *1- 2 yrs PT* Special Educational Needs (Dip/Adv) *2 yrs* Social Work *2 yrs PT* Painting (Scarborough Campus) *20 mths PT* Advanced Nursing Practice; Environmental Policy & Management; Estuarine & Coastal Sciences and Management; Global Biodiversity: Monitoring & Conservation; Health & Social Care Management; Health Professional Studies; Health Promoting Practice; Learning Disabilities Nursing; Maritime Security; Public Sector Management (Health & Social Care); Theological Understanding of Contemporary Society; Theology; Women & Literature in English *3 yrs FT* Nursing Studies *8 mths FT* Psychology (Foundation) *9 mths FT* Advanced Materials, Processes & Manufacturing; Applied Ethics; Applied Language & New Technologies; Applied Social Research; Applied Social Research (Sociology & Anthropology); Aquaculture Planning & Management; Biotechnology & Molecular Biology; Chemistry; Computer Graphics & Virtual Environments; Contemporary Literature & Film; Criminology; Democratisation, Nationalism & Ethnicity in Asia; Developing Area Studies; Engineering Management; English: 'Identities' (Scarborough Campus); Environmental Policy & Management; European Integration & Co-operation; European Public Law; Fish Marketing; Fisheries; Fisheries Policy & Planning; Fisheries Science; Food Standards Science; Gender & Development; Gender Research; Gender Studies; Global Political Economy; Health Professional Studies; Health Services Management; Inland Fisheries Management; International Business Law; International Law; International Law & Politics; International Politics; Internet Computing (Scarborough Campus); Legislative Studies; Management of Fisheries Technology; Management Systems; Maritime History; Medieval Vernacular Languages & Literatures; Modern European Cultures & Societies; Music: Analysis, Composition, Musicology or Performance; Palliative Care; Performance Theory & Practice; Politics & Culture of the Northern

Renaissance; Public Policy; Radio Systems Engineering; Security Studies; Theatre & Contemporary Practice (Scarborough Campus) *FT* Psychology (Foundation)
Undergraduate Diploma: Community Health Studies; Community Health Studies (District Nursing); Community Health Studies (Practice Nursing); Women & Health

Certificates

Postgraduate Certificate: *1 yr FT* Education (Hull and Scarborough Campuses) *1-2 yrs PT* Special Educational Needs (Advanced) *2 yrs PT* Early Years Education (Advanced); Mentoring (Advanced) *5 mths FT* Global Biodiversity: Monitoring & Conservation; Medieval Vernacular Languages & Literatures *PT* Education (College Management); Education (Mathematics Conversion Course); Education (Primary); Education (Secondary); Management; Public Sector Management (Health & Social Care)
Undergraduate Certificate: *2 yrs PT* Archaeology; Art History; British Maritime History; Business Studies; Counselling; Country House Studies; Drama & Theatre Studies; English; Gender Studies & Social Science; Health Services Management; Philosophy and Society; Regional & Local History; Regional Environmental Studies; Regional Maritime Studies; Theology

Degrees validated by University of Hull offered at:

Bishop Grosseteste College

Lincoln LN1 3DY Tel: 01522 527347 Registry direct line: 01522 569404 Fax: 01522 530243
e-mail: registry@bgc.ac.uk Website: www.bgc.ac.uk

* Subject to approval.

First Degrees

BA Hons: *3 yrs FT* Arts in the Community (Drama) *PT study is available* Arts in the Community (Drama); English Literature *3 yrs FT* English Literature; Heritage Studies *PT study is available* Heritage Studies
BA Hons with QTS: *3 yrs FT*
BA/BSc Hons with QTS: *4 yrs FT*

Higher Degrees

MA: *PT* (Taught)
MBA: *PT* Church Management (By research)

Diplomas

Modular Diploma: *PT* Professional Studies (Primary or Special Educational Needs)

Certificates

Modular Certificate: *PT* Professional Studies (Primary)
Postgraduate Certificate: *1 yr FT* Education (Primary) (Modular PGCE commencing Sept 2000*)

KEELE UNIVERSITY

Staffordshire ST5 5BG Tel: 01782 584005 Fax: 01782 632343
e-mail: aaa20@keele.ac.uk Website: www.keele.ac.uk

BA/BSc/LLB Hons: During the three yrs students follow a modular degree pattern, normally choosing two principal subjects and one subsidiary course (studied for one yr). Most students are also able to take one or two supplementary modules from any subject area. Students taking principal courses in the sciences must take a subsidiary course in the Humanities or Social Sciences, and vice versa. Students taking two science subjects or Mathematics and a science subject at principal level have the option to specialise in one in their final yr. Dual honours courses are available in combinations between the principal subjects listed.

MSci: The MSci and the BSc course are common for the first two principal yrs. The final two yrs of the MSci include several integrate topics from the two principal subjects. In the third yr there is a project and research training module. In the fourth yr there is a major project with related dissertation.

BA/BSc Hons: Candidates may be admitted to three-yr courses, for which they will read two subjects at honours level and one at subsidiary level. At least one subject at either subsidiary or principal level must be chosen from the Humanities and Social Sciences combined and at least one at either subsidiary or principal level from the Sciences. Students taking two science subjects or Mathematics and a science subject at principal level have the option to specialise in one in their final yr.

First Degrees

BA/BSc Hons: *3 yrs Dual Honours:* American Studies; Applied Environmental Science; Applied Social Studies; Astrophysics; Biochemistry; Biological & Medicinal Chemistry; Biology; Business Administration; Business Administration (marketing); Chemistry; Computer Science; Criminology; Double Language Option; Economics; Educational Studies; English; English & American Literature; Environmental Management; Environmental Politics & Policy; European Studies; Finance; French; Geography; Geography (Human); Geography (Physical); Geology; German; History; Human Resource Management; International History; International Politics; Law; Management Science; Mathematics; Medicine; Midwifery; Music; Music Technology; Neuroscience; Nursing; Philosophy; Physics; Politics; Psychology; Russian History and Culture; Sociology; Software Engineering; Statistics *Single Honours:* Biomedical Sciences; Cognitive Science; Economic & Financial Management; International Relations; Philosophy, Politics & Economics (PPE); Physiotherapy Studies; Political Economy

Higher Degrees

DOCTORATES

DLitt and DSc: (Awarded for published contributions to knowledge, chiefly to Keele graduates of some standing)

PhD: (At least two yrs full-time to four yrs part-time, following one yr's study for the Master's degree)

MASTER'S DEGREES

MA/MSc/Dip: *1 yr FT/2 yrs PT* American Literature & Culture; Architectural History; Biomedical Engineering; Cellular Engineering; Child Care Law & Practice; Child Law; Clinical Pharmacy; Community Care (Learning Disability); Community Pharmacy; Computing in Earth Sciences; Contemporary History; Counselling; Criminology; Digital Music Technology; Diplomatic Studies; Economics; Education Improvement & Effectiveness; Education Management; Environmental Economics & Policy; Environmental Law & Policy; Environmental Politics; Ethics of Cancer & Palliative Care; Ethics of Social Welfare; European Industrial Relations & Human Resource Management; European Studies; General Legal Studies & Research; General Psychiatry; Gerontology; Global Security; Health Economics Research; Health Population & Nutrition in Developing Countries; Human Resource Management & Industrial Relations; Human Resources in Health; Information Technology: Business Information Systems; Information Technology: Geographical Information Systems; International Relations; Local History; Machine Perception & Neurocomputing; Medical Ethics; Medical Science; Modern Music; Molecular Parasitology & Vector Biology; Music Psychology; Neuromusculoskeletal Health Care; Political Parties & Elections; Politics of Sustainable Development; Primary Medical Care; Social Movements & Revolutions; Social Work; US History & Politics; Visual Arts in Contemporary Culture

MBA: Business Administration (By exam); Health Executive

MChem: *4 yrs* (With Industrial Placement)

MD; MPhil; MS: (By research)

MGeoscience: *4 yrs*

MLifesciences: *4 yrs*

MLitt: *1 yr FT/2 yrs PT* Victorian Studies

MPhys: *4 yrs*

MSci: *4 yrs* Astrophysics; Biochemistry; Biology; Chemistry; Computer Science; Geology; Mathematics; Physics

Diplomas

Diploma: *12 mths PT* Legal Studies *18 mths PT* Health Services Management *24 mths PT* Advanced Therapeutics

Certificates

Postgraduate Certificate: *1 yr PT* Business Administration (Education); Counselling; Counselling Supervision; Education Management; Industrial Relations; Information Technology; Teaching & Learning in Higher Education; Teaching English as a Foreign Language; Therapeutics & Prescribing

Postgraduate Certificate in Education: *1 yr FT* Further Education; Secondary *2 yrs* Science (For graduates in Science or Modern Languages or Social Sciences including Geography. The Certificate may also be taken concurrently with PhD work in Mathematics and Sciences) *2 yrs FT* Information Technology; Maths *2 yrs PT* Further Education

UNIVERSITY OF KENT AT CANTERBURY

Canterbury, Kent CT2 7NZ Tel: 01227 764000 Fax: 01227 827077 Website: www.ukc.ac.uk

Humanities and Social Sciences: All degrees marked with * can be combined as a Joint Honours degree with the following subjects: Classical and Archaeological Studies; Comparative Literary Studies; Computing; Drama; English & American literature; European Studies; French; German; History; History & Theory of Art; Italian; Philosophy; Spanish; Theology.

BA, BSc, LLB Hons: A Pass degree may be awarded, Single, Multi-disciplinary or Joint Honours.
Science, Technology & Medical Studies: † Offered with a yr abroad (four-yr course). †† Offered as a sandwich course (four-yr course). ††† Offered as a four-yr course with a yr's foundation.
MA, MSc: ** By research and thesis.

First Degrees

HUMANITIES & SOCIAL SCIENCES

BA/BSc/LLB Hons: *3-4 yrs Humanities:* American Studies (Art & Film, History or Literature); Classical & Archaeological Studies; Comparative Literary Studies; Computing & the Humanities; Drama & Theatre Studies; English & American Literature; English Culture & Language Studies; English, American & Postcolonial Literature; European Studies (French, German, History, Italian, Spanish or Combined Languages and Sociology, Social Policy or Economics); Film Studies; French; German; History; History & Heritage Studies; History & Theory of Art; History-Law or Politics or Social Anthropology; Italian; Modern Language Studies; Philosophy; Spanish; Theology & Religious Studies; Visual & Performed Arts *Social Sciences:* Accounting & Finance; Accounting & Finance with Computing or French Business Studies or German; Accounting & Finance with Computing; Anthropology; Applied Psychology with Clinical Psychology; Applied Psychology; Applied Social Psychology; Applied Social with Clinical Psychology; British & American Policy Studies; British and French Accounting & Finance; Business Administration or German or Italian or Spanish or Computing; Business Administration-French or Computer Science or Economics; Business Studies; Business-Economics; Computing & the Social Sciences; Conservation Biodiversity-Environmental Management; Economics or Computing; Economics with a Language or Econometrics or Philosophy; English & American Literature-Sociology; English-French Law or German Law or Italian Law or Spanish Law; Environmental Social Science or Spanish; European Economics with French or German; European Economics; European Legal Studies; European Management Science with French or German or Italian or Spanish; European Management Science with Computing with French or German or Italian or Spanish; European Management Science-Business Administration with French or German or Italian or a yr in Finland; European Politics; European Social Psychology; European Studies; European Studies (Economics, Social Policy, Sociology); Industrial Relations & Human Resource Management (Accounting, Economics, Law, Politics & Government, Social Policy, Social Psychology or Sociology); International Relations with French or Italian or German; Law; Law & History; Law & Welfare; Law with a Language (French or German); Law-Philosophy or Economics or Politics & Government or Social Anthropology or Sociology; Management Science; Management Science-Business Administration; Management Science-Computing; Management Science; Economics-

Accounting & Finance or Business Administration or Computing or Mathematics or Politics & Government or Social Anthropology or Social Policy or Sociology; Philosophy-Law or Politics or Social Anthropology or Social Policy & Administration or Sociology; Politics & Government with a yr in Finland or French or German or Italian; Politics & Government; Politics & International Relations with a yr in Finland; Psychology; Psychology with Clinical Psychology; Public Management or Law or Philosophy; Social Policy; Social Anthropology with French or German or Italian or Spanish or a yr in Finland; Social Anthropology; Social Policy; Social Policy with Computing; Social Policy & Public Management; Social Psychology with Computing; Social Psychology; Social with Clinical Psychology; Sociology; Sociology with Italian; Sociology & Social Anthropology with a yr in Finland; Urban Studies (Sociology & Social Policy)

SCIENCE TECHNOLOGY & MEDICAL STUDIES
BA/BEng/BSc Hons: 3 yrs; MPhys: 4 yrs: Actuarial Science; Biochemistry; Biochemistry with Biotechnology or Cell & Molecular Biology or Medical Biosciences or Neurosciences; Biological Chemistry; Biological Sciences; Biology; Business Mathematics; Chemistry with Management Science; Chemistry; Communication Systems Engineering; Communications Engineering; Computer Science; Computer Science & Business Administration; Computer Science with Management Science; Computer Systems Engineering; Electronic Engineering; Electronic Engineering with Medical Electronics; Electronic Systems Engineering; European Computer Science; European Mathematics or Computer Science or Philosophy; Management Science-Mathematics; Mathematics; Mathematics & Statistics; Microbiology; Microbiology with Biotechnology or Medical Biosciences; Physics; Physics (Europhysics); Physics-Chemistry; Psychology with Computing; Social Policy; Theoretical Physics *3-4 yrs* Physics with Astrophysics or Management Science or Management Science (Europhysics) or Space Science & Systems or Space Science & Systems (Europhysics) *Social Sciences:* Financial Mathematics; Molecular & Cellular Biology; Pharmaceutical Chemistry

Higher Degrees
DOCTORATES
DD; LLD; DLitt; DSc: (Awarded on published work to Kent staff or graduates of some yrs' standing)
PhD: *3 yrs FT/4 yrs PT* (By research and thesis or doctoral programme – see MPhil list below for subjects)

MASTER'S DEGREES
LLM: *1 yr FT/2 yrs PT* Criminal Justice; Environmental Law & Conservation; Environmental Law and Policy; European Law; Feminist Legal Studies; International Commercial Law; Law; Medical Law; Socio-Legal Studies
MA: *1 yr FT/2 yrs PT* American Studies; Applied Language Studies: Combined Studies or Computing or Vocational Techniques for Career Linguists; Applied Linguistics; Applied Theology; Cartoons & Caricature; Classical Archaeology; Classical Image & Narrative; Classical Studies; Communication & Image Studies; Comparative Literary Studies; Development Economics; Drama; English; English: American Literary Cultures and Europe; English: Modern Literature & Culture; English: Theory & Culture of Modernism; Environmental Anthropology; Environmental Social Science; European & Comparative Literary Studies; European Economic Integration; European Politics and Democracy Studies; European Studies; Film & Art Theory; Film Studies; French; French & Comparative Literary Studies; German; Health Studies; History; History & Cultural Studies of Science; History & Theory of Art; Image Studies; International Conflict Analysis; International Relations; International Relations & European Studies; Italian; Management; Management of Community Care; Medieval & Tudor Studies; Nationalism, Ethnicity & Race; Performance Space and IT Modelling; Philosophy; Political Sociology; Politics & Government; Postcolonial Studies; Propaganda, Persuasion & History; Psychotherapy; Psychotherapy Studies; Social Anthropology; Social Anthropology & Computing; Social Policy; Sociology & Social Research; Spanish; Spanish & Comparative Literary Studies; Study of Mysticism & Religious Experience; Theology & Religious Studies; Urban Studies; Women's Studies

MBA: *1 yr FT/2 yrs PT* Business Administration; Business Administration (Public Sector)
MClinSci: *PT* Psychotherapy (By coursework and dissertation)
MEBA: *1 yr FT/2 yrs PT* European Business Administration
MPhil: *2 yrs FT/3 yrs PT* Accounting; American Studies; Applied Language Studies: Computing; Applied Linguistics; Applied Mathematics; Biochemistry; Biodiversity Management; Cartoons & Caricature; Chemistry; Classical Studies; Communications & Image Studies; Comparative Literary Studies; Computer Science; Drama; Economics; Electronic Engineering; English; Environment Law & Conservation; Environmental Anthropology; Environmental Social Science; European Studies; Film Studies; Forensic Psychology; French; German; Health Psychology; History; History & Cultural Studies of Science; History & Theory of Art; Industrial Relations; International Conflict Analysis; International Relations; Italian; Law; Law-Philosophy; Learning Disability; Management; Management Science; Medicine and Health Sciences; Medieval and Tudor Studies; Mental Health; Microbiology; Operational Research; Personal Social Services; Philosophy; Physics; Politics & Government; Postcolonial Studies; Psychology; Pure Mathematics; Social Anthropology; Social Policy; Social Psychology; Social Work; Sociology; Spanish; Statistics; Theology & Religious Studies; Urban Studies; Women's Studies
MPhysics: *4 yrs FT* Europhysics with a yr in the USA; Physics; Physics with Astrophysics or Space Science & Systems; Physics; Theoretical Physics
MRes: *1 yr FT/2 yrs PT* Biotechnology
MSc: *1 yr FT/2 yrs PT* Actuarial Science; Analysis and Intervention in Learning Disabilities; Applied Mathematics; Biochemistry; Biodiversity Management; Biotechnology; Chemistry; Cognitive Neuroscience; Communication Systems Engineering; Computer Science; Computer Science (Conversion); Conservation Biology; Electronic Engineering; Environmental Anthropology; Environmental Law & Conservation; Environmental Social Science; Ethnobotany; Forensic Psychology; Group Processes & Intergroup Relations; Health Psychology with Computing; Management Science; Management Science; Medical Signal & Image Processing; Microbiology; Operational Research; Paraclinical Sciences; Physics; Pure Mathematics; Social and Applied Psychology; Statistics; Tourism & Conservation

Honorary Degrees
DCL; DD; DSc; DLitt; MSc; MA; LLM; LLD

Diplomas

Diploma: *PT* Addiction Counselling; Archaeological Studies; Christian Theology & Ministry; Comparative Literary Studies; Counselling; English Literature; History, French & Theory of Art; Italian; Kentish History
Postgraduate Diploma: *1 yr FT/2 yrs PT* Chemistry; Criminal Justice; Environmental Anthropology; Environmental Law & Policy; Management Studies & Business English; Medical Law; Medical Signal & Image Processing; Political Sociology; Psychotherapy Studies; Social Anthropology; Social Anthropology & Computing; Sociology & Social Research
University Diploma: Accounting; Biochemistry; Chemistry; Classical Studies; Comparative Literary Studies; Computer Science; Drama; Economics; Economics & Social Statistics; Electronic Engineering; English & American Literature; English Studies; European Legal Studies; European Management Sciences; Film Studies; French; German; History; History & Theory of Art; History of Sciences; Industrial Relations; Italian; Law; Mathematics; Microbiology; Philosophy; Physics; Physics with Astrophysics; Politics & International Relations; Social Anthropology; Social Policy & Administration; Sociology

Certificates

Certificate: Archaeological Studies; Christian Theology; Comparative Literary Studies; Counselling Studies; English Literature; History of Art; Law & Society; Modern History; Philosophy; Social Sciences; Theory & Practice of Local History

Degrees validated by University of Kent at Canterbury offered at:

Canterbury Christ Church University College

Canterbury, Kent CT1 1QU Tel: 01227 767700 Fax: 01227 470442
e-mail: Admissions@cant.ac.uk.

First Degrees

BA Hons: Ceramics; English; Fine Art (Painting); Fine Art (Printmaking); History; Informal and Community Education; International Business Administration; Music; Radio, Film & Television Studies; Religious Studies; Social Science; Theology *Joint Combined Honours:* Fine Art (Sculpture)
BA Hons with QTS: *3-4 yrs FT* Primary Education
BSc Hons: Business Information Management; Computing; Diagnostic Radiography; Environmental Biology; Environmental Science; Geography; Health Science; Hospitality Services Management; Nursing; Occupational Therapy; Physical and Health Science; Science; Sport Science

Diplomas

Diploma of Higher Education: Business Information Management; Nursing Studies; Social Work
HND: Computing; Hospitality Management; Management Studies; Multimedia Computing; Software Development

Kent Institute of Art & Design

Oakwood Park, Maidstone, Kent ME16 8AG Tel: 01622 757286 Fax: 01622 621100
e-mail: UK/EU: kiadmarketing@kiad.ac.uk e-mail: Overseas: dnorman@kiad.ac.uk
Website: www.kiad.ac.uk

First Degrees

BA Hons: *3 yrs FT* Architecture (RIBA Part 1); Ceramics; Editorial & Advertising Photography; Fashion Design; Fashion Product Development; Fashion Promotions; Fine Art (Graphic Fine Art); Fine Art (Painting); Fine Art (Sculpture); Interior Architecture; Interior Design; Model Making; Product Design; Silversmithing, Goldsmithing & Jewellery Design; Visual Communication (Graphic Design); Visual Communication (Illustration); Visual Communication (Photomedia); Visual Communication (Video with Film) *4 yrs* European Fashion *5 yrs PT* Fine Art
BArch: *2 yrs FT* Architecture (RIBA Part 2)

Higher Degrees

MASTER'S DEGREES OR EQUIVALENT
MA: *1 yr FT/2 yrs PT* Architecture; Art & Architecture; Art Criticism & Theory; Ceramics; Contemporary Photo Imaging; Fashion Design and Promotions; Fashion Product Development; Fashion Theory; Fine Art; Fine Art: International Practice; Graphic Fine Arts; Interior Architecture; Interior Design; Jewellery Design; Painting; Photography; Product Design; Sculpture; Silversmithing, Goldsmithing & Jewellery; Three-Dimensional Design; Visual Communication: New Media Practices

Diplomas

PGDip: *2 semesters FT/3 semesters FT* Architecture; Art & Architecture; Art Criticism & Theory; Ceramics; Contemporary Photo Imaging; Design for Industry Research; Digital Art & Design Research; Fashion Design & Promotions; Fashion Product Development; Fashion Theory; Fine Art; Fine Art: International Practice; Foundry; Graphic Fine Arts; History of Architecture & Design; Interior Architecture; Interior Design; Jewellery Design; Painting; Photography; Product Design; Public Art Research; Sculpture; Silversmithing, Goldsmithing & Jewellery Design; Three Dimensional Design; Visual Communication: New Media Practices

KINGSTON UNIVERSITY

Student Recruitment, Kingston University, River House, 53-57 High Street, Kingston upon Thames, Surrey KT1 1LQ Tel: 020 8547 8276 Fax: 020 8547 8237 e-mail: J.Richardson@kingston.ac.uk Website: www.kingston.ac.uk

Admission Enquiries: Student Enquiry & Applicant Services, Kingston University, Cooper House, 40-46 Surbiton Road, Kingston upon Thames, Surrey KT1 2HX Tel: 020 8547 7053 Fax: 020 8547 7080 e-mail: int.recruit@kingston.ac.uk Website: www.kingston.ac.uk

First Degrees

BA: *1 yr FT top-up* Business Administration *3 or 4 yrs FT* French; French with History of Art, Architecture & Design or Applied Biology or Chemistry or Applied Economics or Applied English Language & Linguistics or English Literature or Environmental Studies or Film Studies or German or History or History of Ideas or Human Geography or Mathematics or Politics or Psychology or Spanish or Women's Studies; German with Art, Architecture & Design History or Applied Economics or Applied English Language & Linguistics or Film Studies or French or History or Politics or English Literature or Psychology or Women's Studies; Spanish with Applied Economics or Applied English Language & Linguistics or Art, Architecture & Design History or English Literature or Environmental Studies or Film Studies or French or History or Politics or Psychology or Women's Studies *3 yrs FT* Accounting & Finance; Architecture; Art, Architecture & Design History; Art, Architecture & Design History with History or Film Studies or Sociology or Women's Studies or History of Ideas or English Literature or English Language (Applied) & Linguistics; Business with Law; Business Economics; Business Management; Development Studies; Economics; Economics (Applied) with History of Ideas or English Language or History or Politics or Sociology or Women's Studies or Environmental Studies or Geology or Mathematics or Statistics; English Language (Applied) & Linguistics; English Language (Applied) & Linguistics with Sociology or Art, Architecture & Design History or History of Ideas or English Literature or Politics or Applied Economics or Film Studies; English Literature; English Literature with History of Art, Architecture & Design or Applied English Language or History of Ideas or Women's Studies or History or Politics or Sociology or Film Studies; European Studies; Fashion; Film Studies; Financial Economics; Fine Art; Graphic Design; History; History with Economics (Applied) or English Literature or Environmental Studies or Film Studies or Art, Architecture & Design History or History of Ideas or Politics or Psychology or Sociology or Human Geography; History of Ideas with English Language (Applied) & Linguistics or Economics (Applied) or English Literature or Film Studies or History or Politics or Psychology or Sociology or Women's Studies or Art, Architecture & Design History; Illustration; Interior Design; International Studies; Landscape Architecture; Politics; Politics with Economics (Applied) or English Language (Applied) or English Literature or History or History of Ideas or Psychology or Sociology or Women's Studies or Environmental Studies; Product & Furniture Design; Property Planning & Development; Psychology with History or History of Ideas or Politics or Sociology or Women's Studies; Social Welfare Studies; Sociology with English Language (Applied) & Linguistics or Economics (Applied) or English Literature or History of Art, Architecture & Design or History or History of Ideas or Politics or Psychology or Women's Studies or Film Studies or Human Geography; Sociology; Women's Studies with History of Art, Architecture & Design or Economics (Applied) or English Literature or History of Ideas or Politics or Psychology or Sociology or Film Studies or Human Geography *3 yrs FT/3-9 yrs PT* Community Care Management; Criminal Justice Studies; Family & Childcare Studies *4 yrs FT* Applied European Languages; Art, Architecture & Design History with French or German or Spanish; Economics (Applied) with French or German or Spanish; English Language (Applied) & Linguistics with French or German or Spanish; English Literature with French or German or Spanish; History with French or German or Spanish; History of Ideas with French; Politics with French or German or Spanish; Psychology with French or German or Spanish; Sociology with Spanish; Women's Studies with French or German or Spanish *4 yrs S* Business with French or German or Spanish; Business Studies

BA (Post Qualification): *3 yrs PT* Professional Studies in Education

BA (QTS): *3 yrs FT* Primary Teaching (English & Drama 3-8/7-11); Primary Teaching (History & Geography 3-8/7-11); Primary Teaching (Maths and IT 3-8/7-11); Primary Teaching (Music 3-8/7-11); Primary Teaching (Science 3-8/7-11)

BA/BSc: *3 yrs FT* Human Geography-Computing or Geology or Statistics or History or Politics or Sociology or Women's Studies or Economics or Internet Computing *3 yrs FT/4 yrs (extended)* Geography *4 yrs FT* Biology (Applied)-French; Geography-French; Human Geography-French

BEng: *3 yrs FT/4 yrs S* Aerospace Engineering; Automotive Systems Engineering Studies; Automotive Systems Engineering Technology; Biochemical Engineering Studies; Biochemical Engineering Technology; Civil Engineering; Civil Engineering Technology; Construction Management; Manufacturing Systems Engineering Studies; Manufacturing Systems Engineering Technology; Mechanical Engineering; Mechanical Engineering Studies; Mechanical Engineering Technology; Motorcycle Engineering Studies; Motorcycle Engineering Technology

BEng/MEng: *3 yrs FT/4 yrs S/4 yrs FT/5 yrs S* Aerospace Engineering; Automotive Engineering; Biochemical Engineering Technology; Civil Engineering; Manufacturing Systems Engineering; Mechanical Engineering; Motorcycle Engineering Studies

BMus: *3 yrs FT* Music; Music Technology

BSc: *3 yrs FT* Communication Systems; Computing-Statistics; Diagnostic Radiography; Environmental Geology; Geographical Information Systems; Geography-Computing or Geology or Mathematics or Statistics or Applied Biology or Economics or Internet Computing; Geology; Geology with Geography or Computing or Applied Biology or Business Management or Economics or Internet Computing; Geology (Applied); Geology (Applied) with Business Management; Health Systems Technology; Internet Computing; Investigative Analysis; Mathematical Sciences; Mathematics-Computing or Statistics; Media Technology; Natural History; Nutrition; Physiotherapy; Sports Science; Statistics with Business Management; Statistics-Internet Computing; Therapeutic Radiography *3 yrs FT/4 yrs (extended)* Biochemistry; Biology (Applied); Biomedical Science; Earth & Planetary Sciences; Earth Science *3 yrs FT/4 yrs (extended)/ 4 yrs FT* Chemistry; Chemistry (Applied) *3 yrs FT/4 yrs (extended)/ 4 yrs FT/4 yrs S* Environmental Science; Environmental Studies *3 yrs FT/4 yrs (extended)/ 4 yrs S* Applied Chemistry; Chemistry; Geology (Applied) with Business Management *3 yrs FT/4 yrs (extended)/4 yrs S/5 yrs S (extended)* Pharmaceutical Science *3 yrs FT/4 yrs S* Chemistry with Business Management; Geographical Information Systems with Business Management or Computing; Mathematics with Business Management; Medicinal Chemistry; Statistics with Business Management *3 yrs FT/6 yrs PT* Earth & Planetary Science; Earth Science *4 yrs (extended)* Science Extended Degrees *4 yrs (extended)/5 yrs (extended)* Science Joint Honours Courses *4 yrs S* Building Surveying; Business Information Technology; Computer Information Systems Design; Computer Science; Construction Economics; Property Planning & Development; Property Studies; Quantity Surveying; Software Engineering; Urban Estate Management

BSc with Foundation Year: Earth & Planetary Science; Environmental Geology; Geographical Information Systems with Business Management; Geographical Information Systems; Geology (Applied); Mathematical Sciences; Mathematics with Business Management; Medicinal Chemistry; Nutrition; Sports Science; Statistics with Business Management

BSc/DipHE: *18 mths FT* Midwifery (Pre-Registered) *2 yrs & 3 mths FT/3 yrs FT* Nursing (Reg) Adult; Nursing (Reg) Child; Nursing (Reg) Learning Disabilities; Nursing (Reg) Mental Health

LLB: *3 yrs FT* Law with French Studies or German Studies or Spanish Studies; Law *4 yrs FT* Law with European Studies; Law with French Law or German Law; Law with Business†

Higher Degrees

LLM/MA: *1-2 yrs PT* Legal Studies

MA: *1 yr FT* Accounting & Finance; Business Management *1 yr FT/2 yrs PT* Architecture – Professional Practice; Architecture, Design & Theory; Art & Design; Composing for Film & TV; Education (Professional Studies); Music *1 yr FT/PT* Marketing *1 yr PT* Employment Relations & Law; Managing Human Resources; Marketing Direct; Strategic Financial Management *2 yrs PT* Local History *3 yrs PT* Social Work – Child Protection; Social Work – Community Care Management; Social Work – Criminal Justice Studies; Social Work – Education & Training; Social Work – Therapeutic Methods *48 wks FT* Film & Television Design

MA/PGDip: *1 yr FT/2 yrs PT* Personnel Management *2 yrs PT* Arbitration & Dispute Resolution Practice

MArch: *3 yrs PT* Architecture

MBA: *2 yrs OL/PT* Master of Business Administration

MChem: *4 yrs FT* Chemistry with Industrial Experience; Chemistry

MEng: *4 yrs FT/5 yrs S* Aerospace Engineering; Aerospace Engineering-Astronautics; Mechanical Engineering
MEnvSci: *4 yrs FT/S* Environmental Science
MGeog: *4 yrs FT* Geography
MGeol: *4 yrs FT/5 yrs (extended)* Applied Geology; Environmental Geology; Geology
MPharmSci: *4 yrs FT/extended* Pharmaceutical Science
MSc: *1 yr FT* Business Information Technology; Environmental Geochemistry & Analysis; Environmental Mineralogy; Minerals, Development & Sustainability *1 yr FT/2 yrs PT* Advanced Manufacturing Systems; Business Economics; Business Economics & Forecasting; Data Communications; Immobilia (European Real Estate Studies); Information Systems; Information Technology *2 yrs PT* Environmental Geochemistry & Analysis; Environmental Mineralogy; Minerals, Development & Sustainability *30 mths PT* Professional Practice (Surveying)
MSc/PGDip: *1 yr FT/2 yrs PT* Management in Construction (with pathways)
MSc/PGDip/PGCert: *1 yr FT/2 yrs PT* Analytical Chemistry; Biomedical Science; Environmental & Earth Resources Management; Pharmaceutical Analysis *1 yr FT/5 yrs PT* Radiography *2 yrs PT* Clinical Data Management; Nutrition Support *4 mths FT/12 mths FT* Medical Biochemistry

Diplomas

Diploma: *2 yrs/Open Learning Programme/PT* Management Studies
HND: *2 yrs FT* Business & Finance; Civil Engineering Studies; Engineering; Geographical Information Systems; Graphic Design; Pharmaceutical Science *3 yrs PT* Computer Applications
PGDip: *1 yr FT* Landscape Architecture; Law *1 yr PT* Education (Professional Studies) *2 yrs FT* Architecture

Certificates

HNC: *PT* Business and Finance
PGCE: *1 yr FT* Primary; Secondary
PGCert: *1 yr PT* Architecture – Professional Practice *6 mths PT* Education (Professional Studies)

Pre-degree

Foundation yr: Art & Design; Civil Engineering; Manufacturing Systems Engineering; Mechanical Engineering

LANCASTER UNIVERSITY

University House, Lancaster LA1 4YW Tel: 01524 65201 Fax: 01524 846243 (undergraduate) / 01524 592065 (postgraduate)
e-mail: ugadmissions / pgadmissions@lancaster.ac.uk Website: www.lancs.ac.uk

Lancaster LA1 3JD Tel: 01524 384444 Fax: 01524 384567

Ambleside LA22 9BB Tel: 015394 30211 Fax: 015394 30305

Carlisle CA2 7HY Tel: 01228 814859 Fax: 01228 814803

BA/BSc Hons with QTS: Subjects of specialisation: English; History; Mathematical Music; Sciences; Physical Education; Design & Technology.
BSc with QTS: Subjects of specialisation: Business Education; Design & Technology; Mathematics; Science.
* Also available with study in USA / Canada.
† Subject to validation.

First Degrees

BA Combined Hons: *3 yrs FT* Educational Studies-Applied Social Science

ARTS & SOCIAL STUDIES
BA Combined Hons: *3 yrs FT* Accounting & Finance-Computer Science; Accounting-Economics; Advertising & the Economics of Competitive Strategy; Advertising, Economics & Marketing; American Studies-Art History or Organisation Studies or Women's Studies; Art History-English;

Art-Art History; Computer Science-Mathematics or Music; Criminology-Educational Studies or Sociology or Women's Studies; Economics-Geography or International Relations or Mathematics or Politics; English Language/Linguistics or Teaching English as a Foreign Language-History or History of Science or International Relations or Music or Philosophy or Politics or Religious Studies; English-History or Music or Philosophy or Religious Studies; Finance & Computer Science; Linguistics or Philosophy or Psychology; Organisation Studies-Psychology or Sociology; Peace Studies-International Relations; Philosophy-Politics or Politics & Economics or Religious Studies; Politics-Religious Thought or Sociology; Religious Studies-Sociology; Theatre Studies-English; Women's Studies with Applied Social Sciences or English or Philosophy or Religious Studies or Sociology *4 yrs FT* English Language; French Studies and Accounting & Finance or Economics or English or Geography or German Studies or History or Italian Studies or Linguistics or Marketing or Mathematics or Music or Philosophy or Politics or Psychology or Spanish Studies or Teaching English as a Foreign Language or Theatre Studies or Spanish Studies or Teaching English as a Foreign Language or English Language; German Studies and Accounting & Finance or Economics or English or Geography or History or Italian Studies or Linguistics or Marketing or Mathematics or Music or Philosophy or Politics or Psychology; Italian Studies and Accounting & Finance or Economics or English or Geography or History or Linguistics or Marketing or Mathematics or Music or Philosophy or Psychology or Spanish Studies; Spanish Studies and Accounting & Finance or Economics or English or Geography or History or Linguistics or Marketing or Mathematics or Music or Philosophy or Politics or Psychology or Theatre Studies

BA Hons: *3 yrs FT* Accounting & Finance; Advertising & Marketing; American Studies; Anthropology of Religion; Applied Social Science; Art: History & Culture; Art: Practice & Theory; Creative Arts; Criminology; Culture, Media & Communication; Economics; Educational Studies; English Language; English Language & Literature; English Literature; Entrepreneurship; History; Human Geography; International Relations & Strategic Studies; Language in Society; Linguistics; Mathematics; Medieval & Renaissance Studies; Music; Musicology; Organisation Studies; Organisation Studies & Human Resource Management; Organisation Studies with Industrial Relations; Philosophy; Politics; Politics with International Relations; Psychology; Religious Studies; Social History; Social Work; Sociology; Theatre Studies; Women's Studies *4 yrs FT* European Studies; French Studies; German Studies

BBA Hons: *4 yrs FT* European Management (Management with French Studies or German Studies or Spanish Studies) *4 yrs S* Management

BMus Hons: *3 yrs FT* Music

LLB Hons: *3 yrs FT* Law *4 yrs FT* European Legal Studies

SCIENCE & TECHNOLOGY

BA Combined Hons: *3 yrs FT* Mathematics-Philosophy or Statistics

BEng Hons; MEng: Communications Engineering; Computer Systems Engineering; Electronic Engineering; Engineering; Mechanical Engineering; Mechatronics

BSc Combined Hons: *3 yrs FT* Accounting & Finance-Computer Science or Mathematics; Biochemistry with Biomedicine or Genetics or Microbiology; Biochemistry-Animal Physiology; Biological Sciences-Medical Statistics or Biomedicine; Computer Science-Linguistics or Mathematics or Music for Multimedia Systems or Software Engineering; Economics-Finance or Mathematics or Operational Research; Mathematics-Educational Studies or Operational Research *4 yrs S* Computing-European Languages or French Studies or German Studies or Italian Studies or Spanish Studies

BSc Hons: *3 yrs FT* Biochemistry; Biological Sciences; Business Computing-Information Systems; Business Studies; Combined Science; Computer Science; Ecology; Environmental Chemistry; Environmental Management; Environmental Mathematics; Environmental Science; Finance; Geography; Geophysical Sciences; International Business (Economics); Management Science; Marketing; Mathematics; Mathematics with Statistics; Operations Management; Physical Geography; Physics with Computational Physics or Cosmology or Theoretical Physics; Physics; Physics Studies; Pollution Science; Psychology; Statistics *4 yrs S* Marketing Management

Higher Degrees

DOCTORATES
DSc; DLitt: (Awarded on published work to Lancaster staff and graduates of some standing)
PhD: *3 yrs min* (Available in all departmental subject areas)

MASTER'S DEGREES
MA/MBA/MMus/MRes/MSc/LLM: *12 mths FT/24 mths PT* 19th Century Literary Research; Advanced Mobile & Personal Radio Communication; Art: Studio Practice; Arts and Humanities Consultancy; Asian Religions; Biomedical Sciences; Business Administration; Conflict Resolution; Contemporary Literary Studies; Contemporary Sociology; Contemporary Theatre Practice; Creative Writing; Cultural Studies; Defence and Security Analysis; Design and Evaluation for Advanced Interactive Environments; Digital Signal Processing Applications in Communications Systems; Diplomacy; Distributed Interactive Systems; Economy & Society; Education; English Literary Research; Environment Culture and Society; European & International Legal Studies; European Environmental Policy & Regulation; Feminist Cultural Theory & Practice; Historical Research; History of Ideas; History of Science; International Law & International Relations; International Relations and Strategic Studies; Lake District Studies; Language Studies; Law in History; Law, Culture & Society; Mechatronics; Medieval Studies; Modern Language Research; Modern Social History; Multimedia Broadcasting Engineering; Organisational Analysis & Behaviour; Peace Studies; Philosophy; Physics; Psychological Research Methods; Religion, Culture and Society; Religious Studies; Ruskin Studies; Shakespeare & Cultural Theory; Society, Science & Nature; Tourism & Leisure; Values & the Environment; Visual Culture; Women & Religion; Women's Studies; Women's Studies-Education or English or Language or Social History or Sociology *12-18 mths PT* Engineering Project Management *21 mths FT* Applied Social Studies *24-36 mths PT* Executive MBA*FT* Accounting-Finance; Contemporary Theatre Practice; Diplomacy; Environmental & Ecological Sciences; Environmental Statistics & Systems; Finance; Information Management; International Business; Linguistics for English Language Teaching; Management; Management and Organisational Learning; Management Science; Medical Statistics; Music; Operational Research; Polymer Science & Technology; Quantitative Finance; Science of the Environment *PT* Defence Communications Engineering; Health Research; Human Resource Development; Information Technology & Learning; International Management; Management Learning; Manufacturing Management; Marketing Management
MChem Hons: *4 yrs FT* Environmental Chemistry
MPhys Hons: *4 yrs FT* Physics; Physics with Computational Physics or Cosmology or Theoretical Physics
MSci: *4 yrs FT* Mathematics; Mathematics with Statistics; Statistics; Theoretical Physics with Mathematics

Honorary Degrees

LLD; DLitt; DSc; DMus; MA; MSc

Diplomas

DipSW: Social Work
Postgraduate Diploma: *12 mths FT* Physics; Polymer Science and Technology; Religious Studies *18 mths PT* Business Administration; Health Research *2 yrs FT* Social Work *2 yrs PT* Computer-aided Design & Manufacture; Defence Communications Engineering; Health Research; Information Technology & Learning; Lake District Studies; Local History *9 mths FT* Accounting-Finance; Business Analysis; Economics; Environmental and Ecological Sciences; Environmental Statistics and Systems; Finance *9-12 mths* Accounting & Finance; Adult Basic Education; Advanced Mobile & Personal Communication; Applied Social Studies; Business Administration; Business Analysis; Chemistry; Defence Communications Engineering; DSP Applications in Communications Systems; Economics; Educational Studies; English; Environmental & Ecological Sciences; Environmental Statistics & Systems; Finance; Health Research; Historical Studies; Human Resource Development; International Relations; Management Sciences (Operational Research); Mathematics; Mechatronics; Multimedia Broadcast Engineering; Physics; Polymer Science & Technology; Religious Studies *FT* Management Sciences (Operational Research) *FT/PT*

Advanced Mobile and Personal Radio Communications; DSP Applications in Communications Systems; Educational Studies; Historical Studies; International Relations; Mechatronics; Multimedia Broadcasting Engineering

Certificates

Certificate of Advanced Studies: *10 wks* Communicative Teaching of English; Development & Management of English Language Education; English for Specific Purposes
Postgraduate Certificate: *PT* Advanced Studies in Educational Research

Degrees validated by Lancaster University offered at:

Blackpool and The Fylde College

The Higher Education Admissions Office, Ashfield Road, Bispham, Blackpool FY2 0HB
Tel: 01253 352352 ext 4346 Fax: 01253 356127
e-mail: visitors@blackpool.ac.uk Website: www.blackpool.ac.uk

First Degrees

BA: *1 yr FT top-up* Business Administration; Food Manufacturing Management; Hotel & Catering Management
BA Hons: *2 yrs top-up FT* Applied Counselling (for people in organisations); Hotel and Catering Management; Quality Management *3 yrs FT* English Language, Literature and Writing; Graphic Design; Hospitality Management; Leisure Enterprises Management; Photography; Scientific and Natural History Illustration; Technical and Information Illustration; Wildlife Photography *4 yrs FT* Hospitality Management with Tourism; Hospitality Management (International Hotel Management)
BEng: *1 yr FT top-up* Mechanical & Production Engineering; Mechatronics
BSc: *1 yr FT top-up* Computing
BSc Hons: *2 yrs top-up FT* Computing; E-Commerce

Edge Hill College of Higher Education

St Helen's Road, Ormskirk, Lancashire L39 4QP Tel: 01695 575171 Fax: 01695 579997
e-mail: enquiries@edgehill.ac.uk Website: www.edgehill.ac.uk

First Degrees

BA/BSc Hons: *3 yrs Joint Honours:* Biology; Critical Criminology; Disability & Community Studies; Drama; Early Childhood Studies; Education Studies; English; Film Studies; Geography; History; Information Systems; Mathematics; Media & Communication; Modern European Studies; Sociology; Sports Studies; Women's Studies; Writing *Single Honours:* Applied Social Sciences; Business and Management Studies; Business Information Systems; Conservation Biology; Earth & Environmental Studies; English; English Language; English Literature; Field Biology & Habitat Management; Geography; History; Human Geography; Journalism; Leisure Management; Marketing Information Systems; Media & Communication; Modern European Studies; New Media; Organisation & Management Studies; Physical Geography; Physical Geography & Geology; Psychology; Science Journalism; Social Work Studies; Sociology; Sports Science; Sports Studies *3 yrs FT Modular major subjects:* Applied Social Sciences; Critical Criminology; Disability & Community Studies; Drama; English; English Language; English Literature; Geography; History; Human Geography; Information Systems; Media & Communications; Modern European Studies; Physical Geography; Sports Science; Sports Studies; Women's Studies
BA/BSc Hons with QTS: *2 yrs FT* Secondary *3 yrs FT* Key Stage 2/3; Primary (Nursery, Lower); Primary (Upper); Secondary
BEng Hons: Chemical Engineering

Higher Degrees

MASTER'S DEGREES OR EQUIVALENT

MA: *1 yr FT/2 yrs PT* European Union Studies; Management Development; Sport & Leisure in Europe *2 yrs & 1 trm PT* Crime, Deviance & Social Policy; Criminology, Rights & Justice; Human Rights & Equal Opportunities; Voicing Women; Writing Studies *2 yrs PT* Education Management; Educational Studies; English Language Studies; History

Diplomas

PGDip/PGCert/MA Programme: *Flexible* Early Years Education; Education Management; Educational Studies; Mathematics Education; Mentoring; Primary Education; Special Educational Needs *Modular* Early Years Education; ICT; Induction & Mentoring; Leadership & Management; Literacy & Numeracy; Management of Pupil Behaviour; School Effectiveness; Special Educational Needs

Certificates

PGCE: *1 yr FT* Primary Teaching (Lower/Upper Primary); Secondary

UNIVERSITY OF LEEDS

Leeds LS2 9JT Tel: 0113 233 4022/3 Fax: 0113 233 4056
Website: www.leeds.ac.uk

† Subject to validation.
* Possibility of study abroad under the Socrates arrangements.

First Degrees

ARTS & SCIENCE

BA Hons: *3-4 yrs FT* Accounting & Finance; Arabic & Islamic Studies; Arabic Studies; Arabic-Classical Literature or English or French or German or Greek Civilization or Italian or Linguistics or Management Studies or Politics or Portuugese or Roman Civilization or Russian or Russian Civilization or Spanish or Theology & Religious Studies or Chinese or Japanese; Asia Pacific Studies-Economics or French or Management Studies or Politics or Russian Civilization; Broadcast Journalism; Broadcasting; Business Economics; Childhood Studies; Chinese Studies (Modern); Chinese-Economics or English or French or Geography or German or History or Italian or Japanese or Linguistics or Management Studies or Politics or Portuguese or Russian or Sociology or Spanish or Russian Civilization; Classical Civilization; Classical Literature-English or History or Theology & Religious Studies or French or Italian or Russian or Russian Civilization or Spanish; Classics; Communications; Computing-Linguistics or Philosophy or Russian Civilization; Cultural Theory & Analysis; Development Studies or Social Policy or Sociology or History; Economic & Social History-Geography or Politics; Economics with Transport Studies; Economics or French or German or Italian or Japanese or Management Studies or Spanish or History with North American Studies or Politics with North American Studies or Russian or Russian Civilization or Social Policy; Economics and Economic & Social History or Geography or History or Philosophy or Politics or Sociology; Education; Education and French† or Geography† or German† or Mathematics† or Music† or Spanish†; English; English Literature-Theatre Studies or Theology & Religious Studies; English-Greek Civilization or History or History of Art or Latin or Linguistics or Music or Philosophy or Roman Civilization or Social Policy or Sociology or French or German or Italian or Portuguese or Russian or Russian Civilization or Spanish; Environmental Management; European Studies; European Union Studies; European Union Studies-Law; Fashion; Fine Art; French or Politics; French or Greek Civilization; German or History or History of Art or Italian or Latin or Japanese or Linguistics or Management Studies or Mathematics or Music or Philosophy or Portuguese or Roman Civilization or Russian or Russian Civilization or Spanish or Theology & Religious Studies with Transport Planning; Geography; Geography; Geography-History or Management Studies or Mathematics or Politics or Sociology or Social Policy or Italian or Russian or Russian Civilization or Spanish; German or Spanish; German-History or History of Art or Italian or Japanese or Linguistics or Music or Management

Studies or Philosophy or Russian or Russian Civilization or Theology & Religious Studies; Graphic Design; Greek; Greek Civilization with Greek; Greek Civilization-History or Theology & Religious Studies or Russian Civilization; History; History & Philosophy of Science; History of Art; History of Art-Music or Philosophy or Sociology or Theology & Religious Studies or Italian or Spanish; Human Resource Management; Ibero-American Studies; International History & Politics; International Studies; Italian; Italian-Japanese or Latin or Linguistics or Management Studies or Music or Philosophy or Politics or Portuguese or Roman Civilization or Russian or Russian Civilization or Spanish or Theology & Religious Studies; Japanese; Japanese-Linguistics or Management Studies or Russian or Russian Civilization; Jewish Civilization; Latin; Latin with Ancient History; Latin-Theology & Religious Studies or Russian or Russian Civilization or Spanish; Law-Accounting; Linguistics; Linguistics-Russian or Russian Civilization or Spanish; Local & Regional History; Management with Transport Studies; Management Studies; Management Studies-Philosophy or Psychology or Portuguese or Russian or Russian Civilization or Spanish; Management-Accounting with Arabic or Chinese or Economics or French or Geography or German or Italian or Japanese or Philosophy or Portuguese or Psychology or Russian Social Policy or Spanish or Sociology; Material Culture, Architecture and Museum Studies; Mathematics-Philosophy or Russian or Russian Civilization; Modern Chinese Studies; Music; Music and Electronic Engineering; Music-Philosophy or Theology & Religious Studies; Philosophy or Sociology; Philosophy; History & Philosophy of Science-History of Art or Theology & Religious Studies or Italian or Russian Civilization; Philosophy-Politics or Social Policy or Sociology or Theology & Religious Studies or Russian or Russian Civilization; Political Studies; Politics & Parliamentary Studies; Politics & Parliamentary Studies or Russian Civilization or Portuguese; Russian or Social Policy or Sociology; Politics or Theology & Religious Studies; Russian or Russian Civilization or Spanish or Russian Civilization; Portuguese-Russian or Spanish; Psychology-Sociology; Roman Civilization with Latin; Roman Civilization or Spanish; Russian or Russian Civilization; Russian Studies; Russian-Sociology or Theology & Religious Studies or Spanish; Social Policy & Administration; Social Policy-History; History of Art or History & Philosophy of Science or Latin or Music or Philosophy or Roman Civilization or Sociology or Theology & Religious Studies or Italian or Portuguese or Russian or Russian Civilization or Spanish or Sociology; Social Policy-Theology & Religious Studies; Sociology or Theology & Religious Studies; Sociology or Spanish; Russian Civilization-Sociology; Theology & Religious Studies; Spanish; Textile & Surface Pattern Design; Textile Design; Textile Management; Theology & Pastoral Studies; Theology & Religious Studies *5-6 yrs PT* Childhood Studies; Classical Civilization; Combined Arts; Combined Business Studies; Combined Social Studies; Continuing Studies; Economic & Social History-Local & Regional History; English; European Studies; Geography; Geography and Local & Regional History; History of Art; History-Local & Regional History; Local & Regional History and Sociology; Music; Philosophy; Politics; Social Policy; Social Policy & Sociology; Sociology; Theology & Religious Studies

BEng Hons/Ord: *3-4 yrs FT* Chemical and Mineral Engineering (STEPS programme available)

BEng Hons/Ord; MEng: *3-4 yrs/4-5 yrs (STEPS)* Architectural Engineering (STEPS programme available); Ceramics Science & Engineering (STEPS programme available); Chemical Engineering (STEPS programme available); Civil & Structural Engineering (STEPS programme available); Communications IT Engineering (STEPS programme available); Electronic & Communications Engineering (STEPS programme available); Electronic & Computer Engineering (STEPS programme available); Electronic & Electrical Engineering (STEPS programme available); Electronic Engineering (STEPS programme available); Energy Engineering (STEPS programme available); Environmental Chemical Engineering (STEPS programme available); Environmental Energy Engineering (STEPS programme available); Fire Engineering (STEPS programme available); Management (STEPS programme available); Mechanical & Manufacturing Engineering (STEPS programme available); Materials Science and Engineering (STEPS programme available); Mathematical Engineering (STEPS programme available); Mechanical Engineering (STEPS programme available); Mechanical with Medical Engineering (STEPS programme available); Mechatronics (STEPS programme available); Metallurgy (STEPS programme available); Mineral Engineering (STEPS programme available); Mineral Industry Environmental Engineering (STFPS programme available); Mining Engineering (STEPS programme available); Safety Engineering

BMus: *4 yrs FT* Music

BSc Hons: *3-4 yrs FT* Accounting-Computing or Information Systems; Anatomical Sciences; Anatomy and Physiology; Animal Nutrition & Physiology; Animal Science; Applied Biology; Applied Biology-Chemistry or Management Studies; Applied Zoology; Artificial Intelligence-Mathematics or Philosophy or Physics; Astronomy-Mathematics; Atmospheric Science; Biochemistry; Biochemistry with Cell Biology or Medical Biochemistry or Molecular Biology or Plant Biochemistry; Biochemistry-Chemistry or Food Science or Genetics or Microbiology or Pharmacology or Physiology or Zoology; Biology; Biology of Plants; Biotechnology; Business and Financial Economics; Chemical Process Technology (STEPS programme available); Chemistry; Chemistry with Analytical Chemistry; Cognitive Science; Colour & Polymer Chemistry; Colour Chemistry; Computer Science; Computing or Philosophy; Computing; French or German Management Studies; Ecology; Economics-Mathematics or Statistics; Engineering Technology; Environmental Biogeoscience; Environmental Chemistry; Environmental Geology; Environmental Science; Environmental Science: Energy Option (STEPS programme available); Fire Safety and Management (STEPS programme available); Fire Science; Food Production Processing & Marketing; Food Science; Food Science (European); Fuel & Combustion Science (STEPS programme available); Genetics; Genetics-Microbiology; Geography; Geography-Geology or Management Studies or Mathematics or Statistics; Geological Sciences; Geophysical Sciences; History & Philosophy of Science-Biology or Food Science or Mathematics or Statistics or Physiology; Human Genetics; Industrial Minerals Technology; Information Systems; Interdisciplinary Science; Management Studies-Information Systems or Statistics; Management Studies-Mathematics or Pharmacology; Mathematical Engineering; Mathematical Studies; Mathematics with Finance; Mathematics or German or History & Philosophy of Science or Music or Philosophy; Mathematics and French or Physics or Statistics; Medical Microbiology; Medical Sciences; Medicinal Chemistry; Microbiology; Microbiology with Immunology; Microbiology-Food Science; Microbiology-Zoology; Molecular Science and Technology or Economics; Music-Computer Science or Mathematics or Physics or Statistics; Neuroscience; Neuroscience-Psychology; Pharmacology; Pharmacology-Physiology or Computer Science or French or German or History & Philosophy of Science or Management Studies or Pharmacology; Philosophy-Chemistry or Mathematics or Physics; Physics; Physics with Astrophysics or Electronics & Instrumentation or Foundation Studies; Physics and French or German or History & Philosophy of Science or Music or Philosophy; Physiology; Psychology; Psychology and History & Philosophy of Science or Music or Philosophy; Safety Management; Sports Science & Physiology; Sports Science (Outdoor Activities); Sports Science and Performance Textiles; Statistics and French or German; Textile Manufacturing (STEPS programme available); Textile Studies (STEPS programme available); Zoology *6 yrs PT* Applied Biology; Applied Psychology; Applied Zoology; Biology; Biology of Plants; Ecology; Geography; Zoology

HEALTHCARE STUDIES
BHSc Hons: *18 mths FT* Midwifery (Post-registration) *2-5 yrs PT* Audiology Studies; Cardiological Science Studies; Healthcare Studies; Midwifery; Nursing (Adult); Nursing Practice; Nursing Studies *3 yrs FT* Midwifery; Radiography (Diagnostic); Radiography (Therapeutic)

LAW
LLB Hons: *3 yrs FT* Law *4 yrs FT* Law-French or Chinese or Japanese; Management Studies†

MEDICINE & DENTISTRY
BChD: *5 yrs FT* Dentistry (May be awarded with Honours. A range of BSc Honours programmes may be intercalated into the dental course)

Higher Degrees
DOCTORATES
DClinPsych: *3 yrs FT* Clinical Psychology
DDSc: *3 yrs FT/4 yrs PT*
EdD: *3 yrs FT/4 yrs PT* Education (Attendance at courses, research and thesis)
PhD: *3 yrs FT/4 yrs PT* (Advanced study, research and thesis)

MASTER'S DEGREES BY INSTRUCTION

LLM: *2 yrs* Law (For graduates, by research and thesis)

MA: Linguistics and English Teaching *1 yr FT* Accounting & Finance; Advertising & Marketing with European Studies; American Literature & Culture; Arabic Studies; Arabic Studies (Middle Eastern Folklore); Bibliography, Publishing & Textual Studies; Communication Studies; Credit Management; English-Arabic-English Interpreting; English-Arabic-English Translating; European Studies in the Logic & the History & Philosophy of Science; Health Management, Planning & Policy; Hospital Management; International Studies; Management Planning & Policy; Middle East Studies; Mongolian Studies; Sculpture Studies; Teaching Arabic as a Foreign Language *1 yr FT/2 yrs PT* Anglo-German Cultural Relations; Applied Translation Studies; Asia Pacific Studies; Biblical Theology; British Government; British History; Business Ethics and Corporate Government; Business Law; Contemporary Ibero-American Studies; Country House Studies; Criminal Justice Studies; Cultural Studies; Development Studies; Disability Studies; Economics; English Language Teaching or Language; Linguistics; European Environmental Policy; European Legal Studies; European Security Studies; European Studies; European Union and Public Policy; European Union Law & Policy; European Union Politics; Feminism & the Visual Arts; Film Music Studies; Francophone Studies; Gender & Work; Geographical Information Systems; Health Care Ethics; Health Services' Studies; History & Philosophy of Science; Human Geography; Human Resource Management; Icelandic Studies; Industrial Policy & Performance; Islamic Studies; Italian Studies; Linguistics; Local & Regional History; Medieval English Literature; Medieval History; Medieval Studies; Medieval Theology; Military History; Modern English Language; Modern History; Modern Jewish Studies; Modern Theology; Philosophy; Phonetics; Political Sociology; Popular Musicology; Post-Communist Studies; Quality Assurance in Health & Social Care; Religion & Locality; Religion, Politics & Society in the 20th Century; Religious Studies & Development Studies; Science & Religion; Sculpture Studies; Siberian Studies; Social & Public Policy; Social History of Art; Social Research; Sociology; Strategic Decision Making; Studio Practice; Theology & Development Studies; Theology & Religious Studies; Transport Economics *10 mths FT/22 mths PT* Democratic Studies *11 mths FT/22 mths PT* Politics of International Resources & Development *11 mths FT/23 mths PT* Africa: Human & Sustainable Development; International Political Economy; International Politics *12 mths FT/24 mths PT* Studio Practice *2 yrs PT* Asia Pacific Studies (Internet); Asia Pacific Studies (Singapore); Healthcare Chaplaincy; Independent Practice (Nursing); Modern English Language *2-3 yrs PT* Environmental Economics; Public Health Management *3 yrs PT* Management & Leadership in Health & Social Care *9 mths FT* Classical Civilisation; Greek; Greek Civilisation; Latin; Roman Civilisation; Theatre Studies *9 mths FT/18 mths PT* American Literature & Culture; English Language & World Englishes; English Literature; Icelandic Studies; Literature from Commonwealth Countries; Shakespeare: Contexts & Receptions; Victorian Literature *9 mths FT/21 mths PT* Modern French Studies *9-12 mths FT/24 mths PT* Italian Studies; Linguistics; Linguistics & English Language Teaching; Linguistics & Language Corpora; Phonetics *PT & DL* Independent Practice (Nursing)

MB; ChB: *5 yrs FT* Medicine (May be awarded with Honours)

MBA; MBA Finance: *1 yr FT* Business Administration; Marketing; Transport Management *2-3 yrs PT* Business Administration (Executive Programme) (For British Managers); Health & Social Services Executive Programme; International Business; Marketing-Transport Management

MChem Hons: *4 yrs* Chemistry; Chemistry with Analytical Chemistry; Medicinal Chemistry; Molecular Science & Technology

MDent Sci: *2-3 yrs FT* Community Dentistry; Dental Radiology; Oral Biology & Oral Biochemistry; Oral Medicine; Oral Pathology; Oral Surgery; Paediatric Dentistry; Restorative Dentistry *3 yrs FT* Orthodontics

MEd: *1 yr FT/2 yrs PT* Curriculum Studies; Education; Educational Administration & Management; Information Technology & Multimedia & Education; Learning Systems Design; Mathematical Education; Modern Languages Education; Post Compulsory Education & Training; Primary Education; Religious Education; Science Education; Secondary Management & Curriculum; Special Educational Needs; TESOL; TESOL for Young Learners *2 yrs PT* Clinical Pharmacy Teaching; English Education Language & Literature; Modern Languages Education *6 mths PT* Work Related Learning

MEng: *3-4 yrs* Analysis and Business in Communication IT *4-5 yrs* Automotive Engineering (STEPS programme available); Civil & Environmental Engineering (STEPS programme available);

Civil & Structural Engineering (Europe) with Construction Management (STEPS programme available); Civil Engineering (STEPS programme available)

MGeog: *4 yrs FT* Geography

MGeol: *4 yrs* Environmental Geology (North America); Geological Sciences (North America)

MGeophys: *4 yrs* Geophysical Sciences (North America)

MMath & MMath (European) Hons: *4 yrs* Mathematics

MMed Sci: *1 yr FT/2 yrs PT* Cellular Pathology; Chemical Pathology; Oncology *3 yrs PT* Anaesthesia; Child Health; Clinical Psychiatry; Community Child Health *30 mths PT* Primary Health Care

MMus: *1 yr FT/2 yrs PT* Composition; Critical Musicology; Historical Musicology; Music Technology; Opera Studies; Performance

MPH: *1 yr FT* Public Health (International Division) *1 yr FT/2 yrs PT* Public Health

MPhys Hons: *4 yrs* Molecular Science & Technology; Physics; Physics with Astrophysics or Electronics & Instrumentation or Foundation Studies; Theoretical Physics

MPsychotherapy: *3 yrs PT* Psychotherapy

MSc: *1 yr FT/2 yrs PT* Biodiversity & Conservation; Catchment Dynamics & Management; Ceramics Processing; Child Forensic Studies: Psychology & Law; Combustion & Energy; Communications Studies; Computational Fluid Dynamics; Crop Protection & Biotechnology; Distributed Multi-Media Systems; Dyeing & Finishing; Engineering Geology; Engineering Materials; Environmental Pollution Control; Exploration & Environmental Geophysics; Fire & Explosion; Food Science; Geochemistry; Geographical Information Systems; Geographical Information Systems for Catchment Management; Human Genetics; Information Systems; Integrated Design of Chemical Plant; International Marketing Management; Medical Engineering and Biomechanics; Medical Physics; Mineral Resource & Environmental Geostatistics; Polymer & Surface Coatings Science & Technology; Technical Textiles; Textile Engineering; Textile Management; Textiles *3 yrs PT* Colour Application Technology; Family Therapy; Pharmaceutical Technology & Quality Assurance; Psychoanalytic Observational Studies; Public Health Management

MSc (Eng): *1 yr FT* Automotive Engineering; International Construction Management & Engineering; Mechanical Engineering; Physical Metallurgy; Public Health Engineering; Radio Communications & High Frequency Engineering; Strengthening & Maintenance of Civil Engineering Structures; Surface Engineering; Transport Planning & Engineering; Tribology in Machine Design; Tropical Public Health Engineering *1 yr FT/2-5 yrs PT* Environmental Engineering & Project Management *12 mths FT* Waste Management *24-60 mths PT* Waste Management

MASTER'S DEGREES BY RESEARCH

ChM; MD: *2 yrs PT* (By research and thesis)

MA; MDS; MEd; MRes; MSc; MSc (Eng): *1 calendar yr FT/2 calendar yrs PT* (By thesis in selected disciplines)

MPhil: *2 yrs FT/3 yrs PT* (Study and research, by thesis)

Honorary Degrees

LittD; LLD; DMus; DD; DSc; DEng; MA; MD; MSc

Diplomas

Advanced Diploma in Education: *1 yr FT/2 yrs PT* Education of Children with Severe Learning Difficulties; Education of Deaf Children

DipHE: *2-5 yrs PT* Healthcare Studies; Nursing Practice *3 yrs FT* Nursing

Diploma: Business Ethics & Corpora; Child Forensic Studies: Psychology & Law; Child Health; Clinical Laboratory Sciences; Criminal Justice Studies; Dental Preventative & Community Studies; History & Philosophy of Science *12 mths FT* Business Administration; Business Administration (Finance); Business Administration (Transport Management) *18 mths PT* Health Care Ethics

Graduate Diploma: Energy Engineering; Mineral Engineering; Mineral Industry Environmental Engineering; Mining Engineering

Graduate Diploma in Education: *1 yr FT* TESOL

Postgraduate Diploma: *12 mths FT* Catchment Dynamics & Management; Chemical Engineering;

European Legal Studies; European Legal Studies; Surface Engineering and Tribology *12 mths FT/24 mths PT* Theology & Religious Studies *12 mths PT* Disability Studies *13 mths FT* Medical Ultrasound *2 yrs* Pharmaceutical Technology & Quality Assurance *20 mths PT* Quality Assurance/Health and Social Care *24 mths PT* Clinical Psychiatry; Family Therapy; Midwifery; Oncology; Pharmaceutical Technology & Quality Assurance; Psychological Observational Studies; Social & Public Policy; Sociology *9 mths FT* Classical Civilisation; Dyeing (Awarded to students with BSc in Colour Chemistry who are of sufficiently high standard in the Honours schemes); Dyeing & Finishing; English-Arabic Translation/Interpreting; Health Management Planning and Policy; Hospital Management; Linguistics & Phonetics; Medical Physics; Technical Textiles; Textile Engineering; Textile Management; Textiles *9 mths FT/18 mths PT* Icelandic Studies; Transport Economics *9 mths FT/21 mths PT* Development Studies; History and Philosophy of Science; Italian Studies; Music; Politics of International Resources & Development *9 mths FT/22 mths PT* Catchment Dynamics & Management Studies; Environmental & Physical Sciences for Business & Service Planning; Environmental & Physical Sciences for Catchment Management; Geographical Information Systems; Geographical Information Systems; Human Geography; Social & Economic Sciences for Business & Service Planning; Social & Economic Sciences for Catchment Management

Certificates

Certificate: Criminal Justice Studies; Learning Difficulties; Management & Public Health in Developing Health Systems; Pharmaceutical Technology & Quality Assurance; Professional Development of Teacher Mentors *2 yrs FT* Engineering Technology *2 yrs PT* Archaeology and Local & Regional History; Child Welfare Studies; Criminology

Degrees validated by University of Leeds offered at:

Askham Bryan College

Askham Bryan, York YO23 3FR Tel: 01904 772277 Fax: 01904 772288

† Subject to validation.

First Degrees

BA Hons: *1 yr FT* Business Management (Post-HND)
BSc Hons: Food Production, Processing & Marketing *1 yr FT* Land Management & Technology (Post-HND)

Higher Degrees

MASTER'S DEGREES OR EQUIVALENT
MSc: *1 yr FT* Modern Approaches to Plant Health

Bretton Hall

Bretton Hall, West Bretton, Wakefield, West Yorkshire WF4 4LG Tel: 01924 830261 Fax: 01924 832016 e-mail: dbrooke@bretton.ac.uk Website: www.bretton.ac.uk

† Subject to validation.

First Degrees

BA Hons: *3 yrs FT* Music; Applied Social Studies; Child & Family Studies; Dance; English; English & Drama; English & Social Studies; Fashion; Fine Art & Arts Education; Fine Art: Ceramics; Fine Art: Painting & Printmaking; Fine Art: Sculpture; Graphic Design; Music & Arts Management; Performance Management; Popular Music Studies; Textile Design; Theatre & Arts Education; Theatre Studies; Theatre: Acting or Design & Technology
BA Hons with QTS: *2 yrs* Secondary Technology *4 yrs FT* Education (Early Years 3-8): Art, English, Environmental Science; Education (Primary 7-11): Art, English, Environmental Science, Music

Higher Degrees
MASTER'S DEGREES OR EQUIVALENT
MA: *FT/PT* Arts Education; Contemporary Performing Arts; Counselling; Creative Writing; Culture & Society; Design; Fine Art
MEd: *2 yrs PT* Education (Modular)

Diplomas
Diploma: *2 yrs FT/4 yrs PT* Social Work
Postgraduate Diploma: *FT/PT* Arts Education; Contemporary Performing Arts; Counselling; Creative Writing; Culture & Society; Design; Fine Art

Certificates
Certificate: Counselling
PGCE: *1 yr FT* Education (Primary): Music, Environmental Studies; Education (Secondary): Art, Design & Technology, Drama, English

Research Degrees
MA (Res); MPhil; PhD: *FT/PT*

College of the Resurrection
Mirfield, West Yorkshire WF14 0BW Tel: 01924 490441 Fax: 01924 492738
e-mail: registrar@mirfield.org.uk Website: www.mirfield.org.uk

First Degrees
BA Hons: *3 yrs FT* Theology & Pastoral Studies

Diplomas
DipHE: *2 yrs FT* Theology & Pastoral Studies

Leeds College of Art & Design
Jacob Kramer Building, Blenheim Walk, Leeds LS2 9AQ Tel: 0113 202 8000 Fax: 0113 202 8001
e-mail: helen.sanders@leeds-art.ac.uk Website: www.leeds-art.ac.uk

First Degrees
BA Hons: *3 yrs FT* Fashion/Clothing; Interior Design; Printed Textiles & Surface Pattern Design; Visual Communications *PT* Fine Art

Diplomas
HND: *2 yrs* Multimedia; Photography/Digital Imaging

Certificates
HECert: Art & Design

Leeds College of Music
3 Quarry Hill, Leeds LS2 7PD Tel: 0113 222 3400 Fax: 0113 243 8798
e-mail: enquiries@lcm.ac.uk Website: www.lcm.ac.uk

First Degrees
BA Hons: *3 yrs FT* Jazz Studies
BMus Hons: *2 yrs FT* Jazz with Contemporary Music
BPA Hons: *3 yrs FT* Performing Arts (Music)

Higher Degrees

MMus: *1 yr FT* Music *1 yr FT/2 yrs PT* Jazz Studies (Validated by the University of Leeds)

Diplomas

DipHE: *2 yrs FT* Jazz with Contemporary Music
Graduate Diploma: *3 yrs FT* Music
HND: *2 yrs FT* Commercial Music Production and Management; Music Production
Postgraduate Diploma: *1 yr FT/2 yrs PT* Jazz Studies (Validated by the University of Leeds)

Certificates

Postgraduate Certificate: *1 yr FT/2 yrs PT* Music

Leeds, Trinity & All Saints

Brownberrie Lane, Horsforth, Leeds LS18 5 HD Tel: 0113 283 7221 Fax: 0113 283 7200
e-mail: e.brier@tasc.as.uk Website: www.tasc.ac.uk

† Subject to validation.

First Degrees

BA Hons: *3 yrs FT* Digital Media & Culture; English with History or Theology; History; Management; Management with History or Media or Psychology or Sociology or Sport, Health & Leisure or Theology; Marketing; Marketing with Psychology or Sociology or Communication & Cultural Studies or Sport, Health & Leisure or History or Theology; Media with Cultural & Communication Studies or English or History or Psychology or Sociology or Sport, Health & Leisure or Theology; Psychology with Sociology; Psychology; Theology *4 yrs FT* English with French or Spanish; Management with French or Spanish; Marketing with French or Spanish; Media with French or Spanish; Primary Education (5-8 or 7-11) with English or History or Physical Education or Theology or Mathematics or Science
BSc Hons: *3 yrs FT* Sport, Health, Exercise & Nutrition

Higher Degrees

MASTER'S DEGREES OR EQUIVALENT
MA: *1 yr FT* Bi-Media; Print Journalism; Radio Journalism *1 yr FT/2 yrs PT* Cultural Analysis *1 yr FT/4 yrs PT* Victorian Studies *2-5 yrs PT* Public Communication
MEd: *2-5 yrs PT* School Development
PhD; MPhil: *2-6 yrs FT/PT* (By research)

Diplomas

Advanced Diploma: Primary Education
Diploma: *1 yr* Communications, Ethics & Media
Postgraduate Diploma: *1 yr* Bi-Media; Print Journalism; Public Communication; Radio Journalism

Certificates

Certificate: *1 yr PT* Media Education
PGCE: *1 yr FT* Secondary Education

Northern School of Contemporary Dance

98 Chapeltown Road, Leeds LS7 4BH Tel: 0113 219 3000 Fax: 0113 219 3030
e-mail: ann.miller@nscd.ac.uk Website: www.nscd.ac.uk

First Degrees

BPA: *3 yrs FT* Dance

Diplomas
DipHE: *2 yrs FT* Dance

Pre-degree
Foundation Course: *1 yr FT* Dance

The College of Ripon & York St John
Lord Mayor's Walk, York YO31 7EX Tel: 01904 656771 Fax: 01904 712512
e-mail: I.waghorn@ucrysj.ac.uk Website: www.ucrysj.ac.uk

First Degrees
BA/BSc Combined Hons: *3 yrs FT/5-8 yrs PT* Art; English Literature; Design & Technology; Management Studies; English Literature and American Studies; History; Language Studies (Linguistics); Women's Studies; Geographical Studies-Community Studies; Physical Education; Community Studies; Geographical Studies; Language Studies (English); Psychology; History-American Studies; Geographical Studies; *FT* Language Studies (English)-Community Studies; Physical Education-Community Studies
BA/BSc Hons: *3 yrs FT/5-8 yrs PT* American Studies (History or Literature); Art & Design; Contemporary Culture and Media; Counselling Studies; Dance: Performance & Communication Arts; Drama: Performance & Communication Arts; English Literature; History; Leisure & Tourism Management; Management Studies; Music: Performance & Communication Arts; Psychology; Sports & Exercise Science; Sports Studies & Physical Education; Theatre, Film & Television Studies; Theology & Religious Studies
BA/BSc Hons with QTS: *4 yrs FT* English Studies (Nursery, Lower or Upper Primary); Information Technology (Upper Primary); Mathematics (Nursery, Lower or Upper Primary); Music (Nursery, Lower or Upper Primary); Theology & Religious Studies (Nursery, Lower or Upper Primary)
BA/BSc Integrated QTS: *4 yrs FT* Design & Technology; Environmental Science
BHSc Hons: *3 yrs FT/4 yrs PT* Occupational Therapy (With professional registration); Physiotherapy (With professional registration)

Higher Degrees
MA: *2 yrs PT* Counselling; Educational Studies; Historical Studies; Leading Innovation & Change; Literature Studies; Management & Organisational Development; Theology & Religious Studies

Diplomas
Graduate Diploma: *2 yrs PT* Counselling; Historical Studies; Literature Studies
Postgraduate Diploma: *2 yrs PT* Dramatherapy; Historical Studies; Leading Innovation and Change; Literature Studies; Theology & Religious Studies

Certificates
Certificate: *1 yr PT* Advanced Educational Studies; Christian Studies; Church School Studies; Counselling; Evangelism Studies *2 yrs PT* Counselling Supervision
Postgraduate Certificate in Education: *1 yr FT* Primary (Nursery, Lower Primary, Upper Primary); Secondary (RE, Music, Design & Technology)

LEEDS METROPOLITAN UNIVERSITY
Admissions Information, Leeds Metropolitan University, City Campus, Leeds LS1 3HE
Tel: 0113 283 2600 Fax: 0113 283 3114 e-mail: b.hughes@lmu.ac.uk Website: www.lmu.ac.uk/
† Subject to validation.

First Degrees
BA Hons: *1-5 yrs PT* Service Sector Management *1 yr FT* Service Sector Management *1 yr FT/2 yrs PT* Applied Social Work; Leisure & Sport Management *2 yrs FT/4 yrs FT* Early Childhood

Education; Secondary Design Technology; Secondary Physical Education *2 yrs PT* Licensed Retail Management; Managing in Health & Social Care Organisations *3 yrs FT* Leisure & Sport Studies; Physical Education; Sport & Recreation Development *3 yrs FT/4 yrs PT* Law with Information Technology *3 yrs FT/4 yrs S/1 yr bridging course* Business Studies; Economics & Public Policy; Economics for Business; Public Relations *3 yrs FT/4 yrs S/4 yrs PT* Accounting-Finance *3 yrs FT/4 yrs S/4-6 yrs PT* Business Information Management; Information & Communication Management *3 yrs FT/4 yrs S/6 yrs PT* Retailing *3 yrs FT/4-6 yrs PT* Graphic Arts & Design *3 yrs FT/5 yrs PT* Community & Youth Studies; Playwork *3 yrs FT/5-6 yrs PT* Childhood Studies; Education Studies; Human Geography; Politics; Social Policy & Administration; Sociology *3 yrs FT/6 yrs PT* Architecture; Art & Design; English; English-History; Fine Art; History & Politics; Humanities; Humanities & Social Studies; Interior Design; Media & Popular Culture; Social Studies; Three-Dimensional Design *3 yrs FT/Variable PT* Garden Art & Design; Landscape Architecture; Urban & Regional Planning *3-4 yrs PT* Business Management *4 yrs FT* Primary Education *4 yrs FT/5-8 PT* Professional Language Studies *4 yrs S/6 yrs PT* Events Management; Hospitality Business Management; International Hospitality Business Management; International Tourism Management *5-6 yrs PT* Housing *Variable FT/PT* Professional Education; Professional Training & Development

BEng Hons: *2 yrs FT/3 yrs S/4 yrs PT* Electronic & Electrical Systems Engineering; Manufacturing Systems Engineering

BSc Hons: Health Care Sciences; Health Sciences; Occupational Health & Safety *1 yr FT* Civil Engineering (Commercial Management) *1 yr FT/2 yrs PT* Community Health Care Nursing; Food Systems & Quality Assurance *1 yr FT/2 yrs S/2 yrs PT* Business Information Technology *12-18 mths FT/3 yrs PT/OL* Project Management *2 yrs PT* Midwifery Studies; Nursing Studies; Primary Health Care Nursing *3 yrs FT* Applied Psychology; Clinical Language Sciences (Speech Therapy); Counselling & Therapeutic Studies; Nursing (Adult Health); Nursing (Mental Health); Physical Activity, Exercise & Health; Physiotherapy; Sport & Exercise Science *3 yrs FT/4 yrs S* Business Computing; Human Nutrition *3 yrs FT/4 yrs S/4 yrs PT* Accounting & Information Systems; Creative Music & Sound Technology; Electronics, Media & Communications; Music Technology ; Mutimedia Technology; Technology & Management *3 yrs FT/4 yrs S/4-6 yrs PT* Business Information Systems; Information Systems *3 yrs FT/4 yrs S/5 yrs PT* Civil Engineering; Computing; Construction Management *3 yrs FT/4 yrs S/5-6 yrs PT* Building Surveying; Project Management (Construction); Quantity Surveying *3 yrs FT/4 yrs S/6 yrs PT* Environmental Health *3 yrs FT/5 yrs PT* Architectural Technology; Biosciences & Health; Health & Environment; Health Studies; Human Biology *3 yrs FT/5-6 yrs PT* Social Sciences (Generic Award); Social Sciences (Joint Award) *4 yrs PT* Fire Safety *4 yrs PT/OL* Building Control Engineering *4 yrs S* Dietetics *4 yrs S/6 yrs PT* Licensed Retail Management *5 yrs PT* Therapeutic Counselling *5-6 yrs PT* Facilities Management

LLB/LLB Hons: *3 yrs FT/4 yrs PT* Law

Higher Degrees

LLM: *FT/PT* Law

MA: Employment Studies and Human Resource Management *DL* Town & Country Planning *FT* European Public Relations *FT followed by PT* Film Production (Fiction); Screenwriting (Fiction) *FT/PT* 3D Design; Applied Social Work; Art & Design; Business Consultancy; Business Studies; Cultural Studies; English: 20th Century Literature; Fine Art; Graphic Arts & Design; International Business; Landscape Architecture; Language Teaching; Local Economic Development; Personnel Management; Professional Education; Professional Housing Studies; Professional Training & Development; Psychoanalytic Studies; Social & Cultural History; Sport & Recreation Development; Sport, Leisure & Society; Town & Regional Planning; Urban Environmental Design; Urban Regeneration; Violence, Abuse & Gender Relations *PT* Architecture; Childhood Studies; Company Direction; Corporate Direction; Finance & Accounting; Foresight & Future Studies; Information & Library Management; Marketing Practice; Physical Education; Policy Studies; Psychotherapy; Therapeutic Counselling

MBA: *PT* Education Leadership

MBA/Executive MBA: *FT/PT* Communication Management; Construction Management; General Management; Public Sector Management

MSc: *DL* Information Management *FT/PT* Accounting; Accounting Information Systems; Advanced Professional Practice – Dietetics; Advanced Professional Practice – Midwifery; Advanced Professional Practice – Nursing; Advanced Professional Practice – Physiotherapy;

Advanced Professional Practice – Speech & Language Therapy; Computer Communications & Networks; Creative Technology; Finance; Health Education & Health Promotion; Hospitality Management; Information Management; Information Studies; Information Systems; International Environmental Health; Nutrition & Dietetics; Physical Activity, Exercise & Health; Project Management; Service Sector Enterprise; Software Development; Sport & Exercise Science; Sports & Exercise Injury Management; Systems Engineering *Open Learning Programme/PT* Facilities Management; Professional Computing *PT* Professional Computing; Construction Law & Arbitration; Educational Leadership; Management & Organisation Development; Management (by Action Research) *PT or by open learning* Professional Computing

Diplomas

Advanced Professional Diploma: Applied Creativity; Consulting in the Community; Leadership & Management; Management of a Professional Services Firm; Strategic Management; Working with Diversity in Professional Helping Relationships
Certified Diploma: Accounting & Finance
DipHE: *FT* International Business Studies *FT/PT* Occupational Health & Safety; Playwork; Rehabilitation Studies in Visual Impairment; Social Work; Youth & Community Work *PT* Housing; Professional Health Care Studies; Therapeutic Counselling
DipHE/BSc Hons: *1 yr PT* Psychosocial Interventions
Graduate Diploma: *FT/PT* Architecture; Landscape Architecture
HND: *3 yrs FT* Events Management
PGDip/MA: *FT/PT/DL* Environmental Sustainability
Postgraduate Diploma: *FT/PT* Dietetics; Law; Legal Practice; Personnel Management; Social Work *PT* Management & Leadership *PT or by open learning* Professional Architectural Studies
Professional Diploma: Diabetes Care

Certificates

Cert HE: Film & Video Production; Visual Studies *1 yr FT* English with Professional Studies; International Foundation Studies *2 yrs PT* Counselling Skills
Cert HE/Dip HE/ Adv Dip: Irish Studies
Cert/Dip: Managing & Developing Sport
Certificate: Mental Health Studies; Personal & Professional Skills; Teaching English as a Foreign Language; United Kingdom Planning Law & Practice; Visual & Creative Studies
HNC/HND: Applied Biology; Biosciences & Health; Building Services Engineering; Building Studies; Business; Business & Public Relations; Business Computing; Business Information Technology; Civil Engineering; Computing; Electrical & Electronic Engineering; Electronics, Media & Communications; Leisure & Sport Management; Multimedia Technology; Musical Instrument Technology; Photography; Technology & Management; Telecommunications; Three Dimensional Design (Crafts); Tourism Management *3 yrs S* Hospitality Business Management *4 yrs PT* Hospitality Business Management
PGCE: *1 yr* Primary; Secondary (Physical Education)
PGCert/PGDip: Management & Leadership
Postgraduate Certificate: *FT/PT* Language Teaching; Public Service Management; Research Methodology *Open Learning Programme/PT* Professional Architectural Studies
Professional Certificate: Professional Development for Deaf People
Vocational Certificate: Workplace Learning

Other Courses

Courses: Assessment of Vocational Education; CELTA; Certificate in Business Information Technology; Certificate in Personal & Professional Skills; Certificate/Diploma in Computing Studies; Continuing Education Diploma in Building Services Engineering; CTESOL; Dementia Care; Diploma in Community Based Health Promotion; Diploma in Planning Studies; Educational Development; Engineering Foundation Courses; Epilepsy Care; General Management; Health-related Exercise & Fitness; Landscape Architecture Conversion Course; Language Teaching; Management Development in Local Government; Managed Care; Management Development; Managing in the Community; Managing Raising Achievement; Mentoring; Moderation &

Assessment; Neurological Care; Organisation and Planning of Events; Personal & Organisational Development; Personal & Professional Development; Personal & Professional Skills Development (Education, Events, Hospitality, Retailing & Tourism Professions); Project Management; Public Relations (Public Sector); Quality in Service Operations; Quality Systems Management in Higher Education; Real Estate Studies; Research Awards Supervision; Research Practice; School Library Studies; Service Systems Management; Small Business Development in the Service Sector; Stroke Care; Supervision; Supervisory Skills; Teaching & Learning in Higher Education; Teaching; Learning & Assessment; Training & Development; Urological Care; Women into Management; Work Experience & Professional Skills

Professional Courses

Professional Courses: ACCA; Certificate in Management; Certificate in UK Planning Law & Practice; CIMA; Diploma in Management Studies; Diploma in Practice Research & ENB 870; Diploma in Social Work; EdD (Professional Doctorate in Education); Engineering Council Part 2 Examination (Civil/Structural Engineering); INSET & Professional Development for Teachers; Institute of Acoustics Diploma in Acoustics & Noise Control; Institute of Administrative Management Certificate/Diploma/Advanced Diploma; Institute of Direct Marketing Diploma; Institute of Directors Diploma in Company Direction; Institute of Legal Executives Part 2; Institute of Public Relations Diploma; Investment Management Certificate; Teaching & Assessing in Clinical Practice ENB 997/998

UNIVERSITY OF LEICESTER

Admissions & Student Recruitment, Academic Office, University Road, Leicester LE1 7RH
Tel: 0116 252 5281/0116 252 2298 (higher degrees) Fax: 0116 252 2447 Telex: 347250 LEICUN G
e-mail: admissions@le.ac.uk or higherdegrees@le.ac.uk Website: www.le.ac.uk

BA Combined Honours: Students take three subjects – normally two for three yrs, and one for two yrs.
* Possible as a four-yr degree with the third yr spent studying abroad.
** May be taken for two yrs by students taking Psychology for three yrs.

First Degrees

BSc Hons: *3 yrs FT Faculty of Medicine:* Medical Biochemistry; Medical Genetics

ARTS & LAW
BA Combined Hons: *3 yrs FT/4-8 yrs PT 1 or 2 yr subjects:* American Studies; Computer Science; German ab initio; History of Science; Italian ab initio; Spanish ab initio *1 yr subjects:* Introductory Latin ab initio *2 or 3 yr subjects:* Ancient History; Archaeology; Economic & Social History; Economics; English; French; Geography; German; History; History of Art; Italian; Politics; Psychology; Pure Mathematics; Sociology; Spanish
BA Single/Joint Hons: *3 yrs* American Studies; Ancient History-Archaeology; Archaeology; Economics and Law; English; Geography; Geography (Social Sciences); History; History and Archaeology or Politics; History of Art; Mathematics; Modern Language Studies *4 yrs* European Studies; French; French-German or Italian or Politics or Spanish; Geography and Archaeology or Economical Social History; German-Italian or Spanish; History and Archaeology or Politics; Italian and Spanish; Modern Languages and the Visual Arts *5 yrs PT* Humanities/World Humanities
LLB Hons: *3 yrs* Law *4 yrs S* Language; Law with French

SCIENCE & MEDICINE
BEng Single Hons: *1 yr FT* Engineering (Foundation) *3 yrs FT/4 yrs S* Engineering (Electrical & Electronic); Engineering (Electronic & Software); Engineering (General); Engineering (Mechanical) *4 yrs FT* Electrical & Electronic Engineering with a Yr in the USA; Electrical & Electronic Engineering with a Yr in Industry; Electrical & Electronic Engineering with a Yr in Industry in Europe; Electronic & Software Engineering with a Yr in the USA; Electronic & Software Engineering with a Yr in Industry; General Engineering with a Yr in the USA; General Engineering with a Yr in Industry; Mechanical Engineering with a Yr in Industry; Mechanical

Engineering with a Yr in Industry in Europe; Mechanical Engineering with a Yr in the USA
BSc Hons: *1 yr FT Faculty of Medicine:* (Additional to medical course. One or more subjects may be taken for one yr normally following the first two yrs of the medical degree course)
BSc Single/Joint Hons: *1 yr FT* Sciences (Foundation) *3 yrs FT* Applied and Environmental Geology; Archaeology; Biological Chemistry; Biological Chemistry with a Yr in Industry; Biological Chemistry (USA); Biological Sciences; Biological Sciences (Biochemistry); Biological Sciences (Environmental Biology); Biological Sciences (Genetics); Biological Sciences (Microbiology); Biological Sciences (Physiology); Biological Sciences (Plant Science); Biological Sciences (Zoology); Chemistry; Chemistry with a Yr in Industry; Chemistry with Business Management; Chemistry (Europe); Computational Mathematics; Computer Science; Computer Science in Europe; Economics; Geography; Geography and Archaeology; Geography and Geology; Geology; Geophysics (Geological); Mathematics with Astronomy; Mathematics; Mathematics with a Yr in Europe; Mathematics (Europe option) with Astronomy (Europe option); Mathematics (USA); Mathematics and Computer Science (Yr in Europe option); Medical Biochemistry; Medical Genetics; Physics; Physics with Astrophysics or Medical Physics or Space Science & Technology; Psychology or Sociology; Psychology with Neuroscience; Sociology

SOCIAL SCIENCES
BA Single/Joint Hons: *3 yrs FT* Business Economics; Contemporary History; Economic & Social History; Economics; Economics and Law; Politics; Politics and Economic & Social History; Sociology
BSc Single/Joint Hons: *3 yrs FT* Business Economics; Communications and Society; Sociology

Higher Degrees
DOCTORATES
DClinPsych: *3 yrs FT* (2-5 yrs PT by thesis)
DLitt; DSc; LLD: (Awarded to Leicester graduates and members of staff on presentation of published work)
EdD: *2-3 yrs FT/3-5 yrs PT*
MD: (Awarded to Leicester graduates, members of staff or others in the Leicestershire area on submission of thesis)
PhD: *3 yrs FT/6 yrs PT* (By research)

MASTER'S DEGREES
LLM: *Faculty of Law:* Criminal Law & Justice; European & International Trade Law; European Higher Legal Studies; European Union Law (Employment/Commercial); Human Rights & Civil Liberties; Law & Employment Relations; Legal Studies; Welfare Law
MA: *Faculty of Arts:* Archaeology & Heritage; Archaeology & Heritage; Archaeology (Post Excavation Skills); English Literature & Literary Research; English Literature-Literary Research; English Local History: Societies, Cultures & Nation; Humanities; Landscape Studies; Modern Literature Theory & Practice; Museum Studies; Pluralism & Cultural Identity; Victorian Studies *Faculty of Law:* Civil Liberties & Human Rights; Criminal Law & Justice; Legal Studies *Faculty of Social Sciences:* Child Welfare Studies; Co-operative Management & Organisational Development; Diplomatic Studies; European Politics; European Urbanisation; International Economic History; International Relations & World Order; Law & Employment Relations; Mass Communications; Policing & Social Conflict; Public Order; Public Order; Social & Cultural Theory; Social Policy; Social Work; Sociology of Sport; Urban History *School of Education:* Applied Linguistics/TESOL; Primary Education; Professional Studies in Education
MA; MSc; MEd; MBA; LLM; MPhil: *1 yr FT/2 yrs PT/DL*
MB/ChB: *5 yrs* Medicine (Honours awarded in cases of exceptional overall merit) *4 yrs (Biological Sciences graduates only)* Medicine (Honours awarded in cases of exceptional overall merit)
MBA: *FT/DL Faculty of Social Sciences:* Business Administration *FT/PT/DL School of Education:* Education Management
MChem: *4 yrs* Biological Chemistry; Biological Chemistry with a Yr in Industry; Biological Chemistry with a Yr in Industry; Biological Chemistry (USA); Chemistry; Chemistry with a Yr in Industry; Chemistry with Business Management; Chemistry with a Yr in Industry; Chemistry with Business Management; Chemistry (Europe); Chemistry (USA)

MEng: *4 yrs* Electrical & Electronic Engineering; Electrical & Electronic Engineering with a Yr in the USA; Electrical & Electronic Engineering with a Yr in the USA; Electronic & Software Engineering; Electronic & Software Engineering with a Yr in the USA; Electronic & Software Engineering with a Yr in the USA; General Engineering; General Engineering with a Yr in the USA; General Engineering with a Yr in the USA; Mechanical Engineering; Mechanical Engineering with a Yr in the USA; Mechanical Engineering with a Yr in the USA *5 yrs* Electrical & Electronic Engineering with Industry; Electrical & Electronic Engineering with Industry in Europe; Electronic & Software Engineering with Industry; General Engineering with Industry; Mechanical Engineering with Industry; Mechanical Engineering with Industry in Europe
MGeol: *4 yrs FT* Applied and Environmental Geology; Geology; Geophysics (Geological)
MMath: *4 yrs* Computational Mathematics; Mathematics; Mathematics with Astronomy; Mathematics (USA)
MPhysics: *4 yrs FT* Physics; Physics with Astrophysics or Space Science & Technology
MSc: *Faculty of Medicine and Biological Sciences:* Assessment & Treatment of Sex Offenders; Clinical Sciences; Forensic & Legal Psychology; Forensic Psychology; Medical Statistics; Molecular Ecology; Molecular Genetics; Molecular Pathology & Toxicology; Occupational Psychology; Pain Management; Psychology at Work *Faculty of Science:* Advanced Electrical & Electronic Engineering; Advanced Mechanical Engineering; Applied Criminology; Earth Observation Science; Embedded Systems & Control; Geographical Information Systems; Information and Communications Engineering; Mineral Exploration; Museum Studies; Natural Resource Management *Faculty of Social Sciences:* Business Analysis & Finance; Clinical Criminology; Crime & Criminal Justice; Criminal Justice; Economics; European Economic Studies; Finance; Financial Economics; International Development & Finance; Marketing; Policing & Crime Prevention; Policing & Professional Development; Policing & Public Order Studies; Political Research; Risk Management; Security & Crime Risk Management; Security & Organisational Risk Management; Security Management; Social Research; Sociology of Sport; Training; Training & Human Resource Management; Training & Performance Management

Honorary Degrees
DLitt; DSc; LLD; DMus; MA; MSc; MMus; LLM

Diplomas
Diploma: *DL* Law & Employment Relations *FT* Applied Linguistics/TESOL; Earth Observation Science; Economics; European Politics; Forensic Psychology; Geographical Information Systems; Landscape Studies; Law & Employment Relations; Medical Statistics; Mineral Exploration; Molecular Ecology; Museum Studies; Natural Resource Management; Security Management & Information Technology; Systems Engineering *FT/PT* Archaeology (Post-Excavation Skills); Civil Liberties & Human Rights; Comparative Policing & Social Conflict; Criminal Law & Justice; Criminology; Diplomatic Studies; Employment Law; European & International Trade Law; European Management; Legal Studies; Museum Studies; Professional Studies in Education; Public Order; Public Order Research & Information Management; Sociology of Sport; Sociology of Sport & Sports Management; Welfare Law *PT* Child Protection Studies; Psychodynamic Counselling

Certificates
Certificate: *1 yr* Education (PGCE) *2 yrs PT Adult Education Department:* Alcohol and Drug Counselling; Archaeology; Architectural History; Behavioural Studies; Counselling; Ecology and Environmental Management; Fine Art; Local History; Modern Biology; Modern Social History; Music; Psychodynamic Studies (Diploma); Psychodynamic Supervision (Cert); Psychology; Sculpture *20 wks PT* Learning by Degrees *8 wks FT* Child Protection Social Work *FT/PT* Professional Studies in Education

UNIVERSITY OF LINCOLNSHIRE & HUMBERSIDE
Brayford Pool, Lincoln LN6 7TS Tel: 01522 882000 Fax: 01522 882088 e-mail: marketing@lincoln.ac.uk Website: www.lincoln.ac.uk

First Degrees

TBA Single Hons: Accountancy; Animation; Applied Social Science; Architecture; Business; Child & Youth Studies; Communications; Criminology; Economics; English; Environmental Management; Environmental Studies; European Business; Fine Art; Graphic Design; Graphic & Digital Art; History; Human Resource Management; Illustration; Interactive Design; Interior Design; International Relations; Journalism; Law; Management; Marketing; Media Production; Museum & Exhibition Design; Phonic Art; Politics; Social Anthropology; Social Policy; Social Work; Tourism; TV & Film Design

BA Joint Hons: Accountancy-Advertising or Animation or Applied Social Science or Architectural Technology or Business or Computing or Electronic Business & Commerce or Engineering or European Studies or Fine Art or Graphic Design or Human Resource Management or Illustration or Information Technology or Interactive Design or Interior Design or Marketing or Media Technology or Modern Languages or Museum & Exhibition Design or Public Relations or TV & Film Design; Advertising-Accountancy or Animation or Applied Social Science or Architectural Technology or Business or Communications or Computing or Criminology or Economics or Electronic Business & Commerce or Engineering or English or Environmental Biology or Environmental Management or Environmental Studies or European Studies or Finance or Fine Art or Food Studies or Forensic Science or Graphic Design or Health Studies or History or Human Resource Management or Illustration or Information Systems or Information Technology or Interactive Design or Interior Design or International Relations or Law or Management or Marketing or Media Production or Media Technology or Modern Languages or Museum & Exhibition Design or Politics or Psychology or Public Relations or Social Anthropology or Social Policy or Tourism or TV & Film Design; Animation-Accountancy or Advertising or Applied Social Science or Architectural Technology or Business or Computing or Electronic Business & Commerce or Engineering or European Studies or Fine Art or Graphic Design or Graphic & Digital Art or Human Resource Management or Illustration or Information Technology or Interactive Design or Interior Design or Marketing or Media Technology or Modern Languages or Museum & Exhibition Design or Public Relations or TV & Film Design; Applied Social Science-Accountancy or Advertising or Animation or Architectural Technology or Business or Computing or Electronic Business & Commerce or Engineering or European Studies or Fine Art or Graphic Design or Human Resource Management or Illustration or Information Technology or Interactive Design or Interior Design or Marketing or Media Technology or Modern Languages or Museum & Exhibition Design or Public Relations or Social Work or TV & Film Design; Architecture-Architectural Technology or Graphic Design or Interior Design or Museum & Exhibition Design; Business-Accountancy or Advertising or Animation or Applied Social Science or Architectural Technology or Computing or Electronic Business & Commerce or Engineering or European Studies or Fine Art or Graphic Design or Human Resource Management or Illustration or Information Technology or Interactive Design or Interior Design or Marketing or Media Technology or Modern Languages or Museum & Exhibition Design or Public Relations or TV & Film Design; Communications-Advertising or Applied Biology or Criminology or Economics or Electronic Commerce or English or Environmental Biology or Environmental Management or Environmental Studies or European Studies or Finance or Food Studies or Forensic Science or Health Studies or History or Information Systems or International Relations or Journalism or Law or Management or Marketing or Media Production or Politics or Psychology or Public Relations or Social Anthropology or Social Policy or Tourism; Criminology-Advertising or Communications or Economics or Electronic Commerce or English or Environmental Biology or Environmental Management or Environmental Studies or European Studies or Finance or Food Studies or Forensic Science or Health Studies or History or Information Systems or International Relations or Journalism or Law or Management or Marketing or Media Production or Politics or Psychology or Public Relations or Social Anthropology or Social Policy or Tourism; Economics-Advertising or Communications or Criminology or Electronic Commerce or English or Environmental Biology or Environmental Management or Environmental Studies or European Studies or Finance or Food Studies or Forensic Science or Health Studies or History or Information Systems or International Relations or Journalism or Law or Management or Marketing or Media Production or Politics or Psychology or Public Relations or Social Anthropology or Social Policy or Tourism; English-Advertising or Communications or Criminology or Economics or Environmental Biology or Environmental Management or Environmental Studies or European Studies or Finance or Food Studies or Forensic Science or Health Studies or History or Information Systems or International

Relations or Journalism or Law or Management or Marketing or Media Production or Politics or Psychology or Public Relations or Social Anthropology or Social Policy or Tourism; Environmental Management-Advertising or Communications or Criminology or Economics or English or Environmental Biology or Environmental Studies or European Studies or Finance or Food Studies or Forensic Science or Health Studies or History or Information Systems or International Relations or Journalism or Law or Management or Marketing or Media Production or Politics or Psychology or Public Relations or Social Anthropology or Social Policy or Tourism; Environmental Studies or European Studies or Finance or Food Studies or Forensic Science or Health Studies or History or Information Systems or International Relations or Journalism or Law or Management or Marketing or Media Production or Politics or Psychology or Public Relations or Social Anthropology or Social Policy or Tourism; Environmental Studies- Advertising or Communications or Criminology or Economics or English or Environmental Biology or Environmental Management or European Studies or Finance or Food Studies or Forensic Science or Health Studies or History or Information Systems or International Relations or Journalism or Law or Management or Marketing or Media Production or Politics or Psychology or Public Relations or Social Anthropology or Social Policy or Tourism; European Studies-Accountancy or Advertising or Animation or Applied Social Science or Architectural Technology or Business or Communications or Computing or Criminology or Economics or Electronic Business & Commerce or Electronic Commerce or Engineering or English or Environmental Biology or Environmental Management or Environmental Studies or Finance or Fine Art or Graphic Design or History or Human Resource Management or Illustration or Information Systems or Information Technology or Interactive Design or Interior Design or International Relations or Journalism or Law or Management or Marketing or Media Production or Media Technology or Modern Languages or Museum & Exhibition Design or Politics or Public Relations or Social Anthropology or Social Policy or Tourism or TV & Film Design; Finance-Advertising or Communications or Criminology or Economics or Electronic Commerce or English or Environmental Biology or Environmental Management or Environmental Studies or European Studies or Food Studies or Forensic Science or Health Studies or History or Information Systems or International Relations or Journalism or Law or Management or Marketing or Media Production or Politics or Psychology or Public Relations or Social Anthropology or Social Policy or Tourism; Fine Art-Accountancy or Advertising or Animation or Applied Social Science or Architectural Technology or Business or Computing or Electronic Business & Commerce or Engineering or European Studies or Graphic Design or Graphic & Digital Art or Human Resource Management or Illustration or Information Technology or Interactive Design or Interior Design or Marketing or Media Technology or Modern Languages or Museum & Exhibition Design or Public Relations or TV & Film Design; Graphic Design-Accountancy or Advertising or Animation or Applied Social Science or Architecture or Architectural Technology or Business or Computing or Electronic Business & Commerce or Engineering or European Studies or Fine Art or Graphic & Digital Art or Human Resource Management or Illustration or Information Technology or Interactive Design or Interior Design or Marketing or Media Technology or Modern Languages or Museum & Exhibition Design or Public Relations or TV & Film Design; Graphic & Digital Art-Animation or Fine Art or Graphic Design or Illustration or Interactive Design or Interior Design or Museum & Exhibition Design or Phonic Art or TV & Film Design; History-Advertising or Communications or Criminology or Economics or English or Environmental Biology or Environmental Management or Environmental Studies or Finance or Food Studies or Forensic Science or Health Studies or Information Systems or International Relations or Journalism or Law or Management or Marketing or Media Production or Politics or Psychology or Public Relations or Social Anthropology or Social Policy or Tourism; Human Resource Management-Accountancy or Advertising or Animation or Applied Social Science or Architectural Technology or Business or Computing or Electronic Business & Commerce or Engineering or European Studies or Fine Art or Graphic Design or Illustration or Information Technology or Interactive Design or Interior Design or Marketing or Media Technology or Modern Languages or Museum & Exhibition Design or Public Relations or TV & Film Design; Illustration-Accountancy or Advertising or Animation or Applied Social Science or Architectural Technology or Business or Computing or Electronic Business & Commerce or Engineering or European Studies or Fine Art or Graphic Design or Graphic & Digital Art or Human Resource Management or Information Technology or Interactive Design or Interior Design or Marketing or Media Technology or Modern Languages or Museum & Exhibition Design or Public Relations or TV & Film Design; Interactive Design-Accountancy or Advertising or Animation or Applied Social Science or Architectural Technology or Business or Computing or Electronic Business & Commerce or Engineering or European Studies or Fine Art or Graphic Design or Graphic & Digital Art or Human Resource Management or Illustration or Information Technology or Interior Design or Marketing or Media Technology or Modern Languages or Museum & Exhibition Design or Public Relations or TV & Film Design; Interior Design-Accountancy or Advertising or Animation or Applied Social Science or Architecture or Architectural Technology or Business or Computing or Electronic Business & Commerce or Engineering or European Studies or Fine Art or Graphic Design or Graphic & Digital Art or Human Resource Management or Illustration or Information Technology or Interactive Design or Marketing or Media Technology or Modern Languages or Museum & Exhibition Design or Public Relations or TV & Film Design; International Relations-Advertising or Communications or Criminology or Economics or English or Environmental Biology or Environmental Management or Environmental Studies or European Studies or Finance or Food Studies or Forensic Science or Health Studies or History or Information Systems or Journalism or Law or Management or Marketing or Media Production or Politics or Psychology or Public Relations or Social Anthropology or Social Policy or Tourism; Journalism-Advertising or Communications or Criminology or Economics or Electronic Commerce or English or Environmental Biology or Environmental Management or Environmental Studies or European Studies or Finance or Food Studies or Forensic Science or Health Studies or History or Information Systems or International Relations or Management or Marketing or Media Production or Politics or Public Relations or Social Anthropology or Social Policy or Tourism; Law-Advertising or Communications or Criminology or Economics or Electronic Commerce or English or Environmental Biology or Environmental Management or Environmental Studies or European Studies or Finance or Food Studies or Forensic Science or Health Studies or History or Information Systems or International Relations or Management or Marketing or Media Production or Politics or Public Relations or Social Anthropology or Social Policy or Tourism; Management-Advertising or Communications or Criminology or Economics or Electronic Commerce or English or Environmental Biology or Environmental Management or Environmental Studies or European Studies or Finance or Food Studies or Forensic Science or Health Studies or History or Information Systems or International Relations or Journalism or Law or Marketing or Media Production or Politics or Psychology or Public Relations or Social Anthropology or Social Policy or Tourism; Marketing-Accountancy or Advertising or Animation or Applied Social Science or Architectural Technology or Business or Communications or Computing or Criminology or Economics or Electronic Business & Commerce or Electronic Commerce or Engineering or English or Environmental Biology or Environmental Management or Environmental Studies or European Studies or Finance or Fine Art or Food Studies or Forensic Science or Graphic Design or Health Studies or History or Human Resource Management or Illustration or Information Systems or Information Technology or Interactive Design or Interior Design or International Relations or Journalism or Law or Management or Media Production or Media Technology or Modern Languages or Museum & Exhibition Design or Politics or Psychology or Public Relations or Social Anthropology or Social Policy or Tourism or TV & Film Design; Media Production-Advertising or Communications or Criminology or Economics or English or Environmental Biology or Environmental Management or Environmental Studies or European Studies or Finance or Food Studies or Forensic Science or Health Studies or History or Information Systems or International Relations or Journalism or Law or Management or Marketing or Politics or Psychology or Public Relations or Social Anthropology or Social Policy or Tourism; Modern Languages-Accountancy or Advertising or Animation or Applied Social Science or Architectural Technology or Business or Computing or Electronic Business & Commerce or Engineering or European Studies or Fine Art or Graphic Design or Human Resource Management or Illustration or Information Technology or Interactive Design or Interior Design or Marketing or Media Technology or Museum & Exhibition Design or Public Relations or TV & Film Design; Museum & Exhibition Design-Accountancy or Advertising or Animation or Applied Social Science or Architecture or Architectural Technology or Business or Computing or Electronic Business & Commerce or Engineering or European Studies or Fine Art or Graphic Design or Graphic & Digital Art or Human Resource Management or Illustration or Information Technology or Interactive Design or Interior Design or Marketing or Media Technology or Modern Languages or Public Relations or TV & Film Design; Phonic Art-Animation or Fine Art or Graphic Design or Graphic & Digital Art or Illustration or Interactive Design or Interior Design or Museum & Exhibition Design or TV & Film Design; Politics-Advertising or Communications or Criminology or Economics or Electronic Commerce or English or Environmental Biology or Environmental Management or Environmental Studies or European

Studies or Finance or Food Studies or Forensic Science or Health Studies or History or Information Systems or International Relations or Journalism or Law or Management or Marketing or Media Production or Psychology or Public Relations or Social Anthropology or Social Policy or Tourism; Public Relations-Accountancy or Advertising or Animation or Applied Social Science or Business or Communications or Computing or Criminology or Economics or Electronic Business & Commerce or Electronic Commerce or Engineering or English or Environmental Biology or Environmental Management or Environmental Studies or European Studies or Finance or Fine Art or Food Studies or Forensic Science or Graphic Design or Health Studies or History or Human Resource Management or Illustration or Information Systems or Information Technology or Interactive Design or Interior Design or International Relations or Journalism or Law or Management or Marketing or Media Production or Media Technology or Modern Languages or Museum & Exhibition Design or Politics or Psychology or Social Anthropology or Social Policy or Tourism or TV & Film Design; Social Anthropology-Advertising or Communications or Criminology or Economics or English or Environmental Biology or Environmental Management or Environmental Studies or European Studies or Finance or Food Studies or Forensic Science or Health Studies or History or Information Systems or International Relations or Journalism or Law or Management or Marketing or Media Production or Politics or Psychology or Public Relations or Social Policy or Tourism; Social Policy-Advertising or Communications or Criminology or Economics or English or Environmental Biology or Environmental Management or Environmental Studies or European Studies or Finance or Food Studies or Forensic Science or Health Studies or History or Information Systems or International Relations or Journalism or Law or Management or Marketing or Media Production or Politics or Psychology or Public Relations or Social Anthropology or Tourism; Social Work-Applied Social Science; Tourism-Advertising or Communications or Criminology or Economics or English or Environmental Biology or Environmental Management or Environmental Studies or European Studies or Finance or Food Studies or Forensic Science or Health Studies or History or Information Systems or International Relations or Journalism or Law or Management or Marketing or Media Production or Politics or Psychology or Public Relations or Social Anthropology or Social Policy or Tourism; TV & Film Design-Accountancy or Advertising or Animation or Applied Social Science or Architectural Technology or Business or Computing or Electronic Business & Commerce or Engineering or European Studies or Fine Art or Graphic Design or Human Resource Management or Illustration or Information Technology or Interactive Design or Interior Design or Marketing or Media Technology or Modern Languages or Museum & Exhibition Design or Public Relations

BEng Single Hons: Engineering

BEng Joint Hons: Engineering-Accountancy or Advertising or Animation or Applied Social Science or Architectural Technology or Business or Computing or Electronic Business & Commerce or European Studies or Fine Art or Graphic Design or Human Resource Management or Illustration or Information Technology or Interactive Design or Interior Design or Marketing or Media Technology or Modern Languages or Museum & Exhibition Design or Public Relations or TV & Film Design

BSc Single Hons: Applied Biology; Applied Microbiology; Architectural Technology; Biomedical Science; Computing; Electronic Business & Commerce; Environmental Biology; Food Studies; Forensic Science; Health Studies; Human Biology; Information Systems; Media Technology; Neuroscience; Psychology; Physiotherapy

BSc Joint Hons: Applied Microbiology-Biomedical Science or History or Neuroscience; Architectural Technology-Accountancy or Advertising or Animation or Applied Social Science or Architecture or Business or Computing or Electronic Business & Commerce or Engineering or European Studies or Fine Art or Graphic Design or Human Resource Management or Illustration or Information Technology or Interactive Design or Interior Design or Marketing or Media Technology or Modern Languages or Museum & Exhibition Design or TV & Film Design; Biomedical Science-Applied Microbiology or Forensic Science or Neuroscience; Computing-Accountancy or Advertising or Animation or Applied Social Science or Architectural Technology or Business or Electronic Business & Commerce or Engineering or European Studies or Fine Art or Graphic Design or Human Resource Management or Illustration or Information Technology or Interactive Design or Interior Design or Marketing or Media Technology or Modern Languages or Museum & Exhibition Design or Public Relations or TV & Film Design; Electronic Business & Commerce-Accountancy or Advertising or Animation or Applied Social Science or Architectural Technology or Business or Computing or Engineering or European Studies or Fine Art or Graphic Design or Human Resource Management or Illustration or Information Technology or Interactive

Design or Interior Design or Marketing or Media Technology or Modern Languages or Museum & Exhibition Design or Public Relations or TV & Film Design; Electronic Commerce-Communications or Criminology or Economics or English or European Studies or Finance or History or International Relations or Journalism or Law or Management or Marketing or Politics or Psychology or Public Relations or Social Anthropology or Social Policy or Tourism; Environmental Biology-Advertising or Communications or Criminology or Economics or English or Environmental Management or Environmental Studies or European Studies or Finance or Food Studies or Forensic Science or Health Studies or History or Information Systems or International Relations or Journalism or Law or Management or Marketing or Media Production or Politics or Psychology or Public Relations or Social Anthropology or Social Policy or Tourism; Food Studies-Advertising or Communications or Criminology or Economics or English or Environmental Biology or Environmental Management or Environmental Studies or Finance or Forensic Science or Health Studies or History or Information Systems or International Relations or Journalism or Law or Management or Marketing or Media Production or Politics or Psychology or Public Relations or Social Anthropology or Social Policy or Tourism; Forensic-Advertising or Communications or Criminology or Economics or English or Environmental Biology or Environmental Management or Environmental Studies or Finance or Food Studies or Health Studies or History or Information Systems or International Relations or Journalism or Law or Management or Marketing or Media Production or Politics or Psychology or Public Relations or Social Anthropology or Social Policy or Tourism; Health Studies-Advertising or Biomedical Science or Communications or Criminology or Economics or English or Environmental Biology or Environmental Management or Environmental Studies or Finance or Food Studies or Forensic Science or History or Human Biology or Information Systems or International Relations or Journalism or Law or Management or Marketing or Media Production or Politics or Psychology or Public Relations or Social Anthropology or Social Policy or Tourism; Human Biology-Applied Microbiology or Health Studies or Neuroscience or Psychology; Information Systems-Advertising or Communications or Criminology or Economics or English or Environmental Biology or Environmental Management or Environmental Studies or Finance or Food Studies or Forensic Science or Health Studies or History or International Relations or Journalism or Law or Management or Marketing or Media Production or Politics or Psychology or Public Relations or Social Anthropology or Social Policy or Tourism; Information Technology-Accountancy or Advertising or Animation or Applied Social Science or Architectural Technology or Business or Computing or Electronic Business & Commerce or Engineering or European Studies or Fine Art or Graphic Design or Human Resource Management or Illustration or Interactive Design or Interior Design or Marketing or Media Technology or Modern Languages or Museum & Exhibition Design or Public Relations or TV & Film Design; Media Technology-Accountancy or Advertising or Animation or Applied Social Science or Architectural Technology or Business or Computing or Electronic Business & Commerce or Engineering or European Studies or Fine Art or Graphic Design or Human Resource Management or Illustration or Information Technology or Interactive Design or Interior Design or Marketing or Modern Languages or Museum & Exhibition Design or Public Relations or TV & Film Design; Neuroscience-Applied Microbiology or Biomedical Science or Human Biology; Psychology-Advertising or Communications or Criminology or Economics or English or Environmental Biology or Environmental Management or Environmental Studies or Finance or Food Studies or Forensic Science or Health Studies or History or Human Biology or Information Systems or International Relations or Management or Marketing or Media Production or Politics or Public Relations or Social Anthropology or Social Policy or Tourism

Higher Degrees

MA: *1 yr PT* Housing; Marketing *2 yrs PT* Art, Design & Critical Theory; Interdisciplinary Design (Museum Studies/Exhibition Studies) *PT* Learning Contract Scheme (work-based learning)
MA/MSc: Social Work
MArch: *PT* Architecture
MBA: *PT* Environmental Management; Finance; General Management; Human Resource Management; Quality Management; Strategic Management
MSc: *2 yrs PT* Construction Project Management; Engineering (Manufacturing Systems); Human Resource Development; Human Resource Management; Information & Learning Technologies; Information Technology in Business; Social Research *PT* Business Project Management; Facilities Management Strategy; Information Systems in Business; Learning Contract Scheme (work-based learning); Systems Thinking

Diplomas

HND: Business Studies; Business-Information Technology; Computing; Information Technology; Media Technology *2 yrs FT* Business Studies
Postgraduate Diploma: Architectural Practice; Construction Project Management; Housing; Human Resource Development; Human Resource Management; Information & Learning Technologies; Information Technology in Business; Interdisciplinary Design; Management Studies; Marketing

Certificates

HNC: Electrical & Electronic Engineering; Mechanical and Manufacturing Engineering; Programming
Postgraduate Certificate: Architectural Practice; Construction Project Management; Housing; Human Resource Development; Human Resource Management; Information & Learning Technologies; Information Technology in Business; Interdisciplinary Design; Management

Degrees validated by University of Lincolnshire & Humberside offered at:

Beverley College

Gallows Lane, Beverley, North Humberside HU17 7DT Tel: 01482 868362 Fax: 01482 866784 e-mail: general@beverleycollege.ac.uk

Diplomas

HND: *2 yrs FT* Business Studies

Bishop Burton College

Bishop Burton, Beverley, East Yorkshire HU17 8QG Tel: 01964 553000 Fax: 01964 553101 e-mail: enquiries@bishopb-college.ac.uk Website: www.bishopb-college.ac.uk

First Degrees

BA Hons: Garden Design
BSc Hons: *3 yrs FT* Animal Science & Management; Countryside Management; Countryside Management & Environmental Arts; Countryside Management and Agriculture; Countryside Management-Heritage Interpretation; Countryside Management-Ornithology; Equine Science-Management *PT* Work Based Degree (Conservation and Environmental Management, Equine Studies, Ornithology Management, Environmental Arts Management, Heritage Design and Management)
BSc Ord: *1 yr* Management-Equine Science

Diplomas

HND: *2 yrs FT* Agriculture; Animal Care (Zoology, Behavioural Science); Countryside Management; Interior Design; Sport & Adventure Management *3 yrs S* Equine Management

Certificates

HNC: *2 yrs PT* Agriculture (Arable Options); Animal Care; Animals as Therapy; Art & Design (Interior Design); Art & Design (Interior Design) – Period Decoration & Style option; Art & Design (Soft Furnishing); Art & Design (Textiles); Business; Business (& Agribusiness); Countryside Management; Craft (Traditional Upholstery); Event Design & Management; Floristry; Heritage Management; Horse Studies (Technology & Management); Horticulture with Plantsmanship; Horticulture (Garden Design); Safety Health & Environmental Management; Wastes Management
1st yr studied at Hull College, remaining 3 yrs at University of Hull: Motor Vehicle Recycling
In-Service Certificate: *2 yrs PT*
Postgraduate Certificate in Education: *2 yrs PT*

East Yorkshire College

St Mary's Walk, Bridlington, East Yorkshire YO16 5JW Tel: 01262 852000 Fax: 01262 852001 e-mail: postroom@east-yorks-coll.ac.uk Website: www.east-yorks-coll.ac.uk

Diplomas

HND: *2 yrs FT* Business Information Systems; Business Studies; Caring Services and Practice; Design (Furniture Studies); Early Childhood Studies

Grimsby College

Nuns Corner, Grimsby DN34 5BQ Tel: 01472 311222/0800 315002 Fax: 01472 879924
e-mail: infocent@grimsby.ac.uk Website: www.grimsby.ac.uk

† Subject to validation.

First Degrees

BA Hons: *3 yrs* Applied Social Science; Business Studies; History and English or Social Science; History-English or Social Science; Leisure†; Marketing; Tourism Operations

Diplomas

HND: *2 yrs* Broadcast and News Journalism; Business; Computer Aided Draughting & Design; Computing; Fashion Imaging & Promotion; Health and Social Care; Hospitality Management; Media Production; Multi-media; Photography & Digital Imaging; Refrigeration & Air Conditioning; Sport (Coaching, Business & Exercise Science)†; Travel & Tourism Operations Management; TV, Film and Video

Hull College

Queen's Gardens, Hull, North Yorkshire HU1 3DG Tel: 01482 329943 Fax: 01482 598733

First Degrees

BA Hons: *3 yrs PT 1st yr studied at Hull College, remaining 3 yrs at University of Hull:* Business
BSc Hons: *4 yrs FT 1st yr studied at Hull College, remaining 3 yrs at University of Hull:* Applied Physics; Computer Aided Engineering; Computer Systems Engineering; Electronic Engineering; Mechanical Engineering; Physics with Medical Technology

Diplomas

HND: *2 yrs FT* 3D Design; Childhood Studies; Creative Studies (In association with the University of Humberside); Graphics (Packaging); Multimedia; Music Production; Telecommunications (In association with the University of Humberside); Theatre Studies (In association with the University of Humberside); Travel & Tourism Management (In association with the University of Humberside); TV & Theatre Design (In association with the University of Humberside)*PT* Beauty Therapy; Computing (Business Information Technology; Software Engineering); Early Years/Childhood Studies; Leisure (Sports & Recreation); Managing Health & Care Services; Motor Vehicle Management

Certificates

HNC: *Open Learning Programme* Engineering (various) *PT* 3D Design; Beauty Therapy; Building Studies; Business and Finance or Marketing or Personnel or Management or Computing; Business Studies; Computing (Business Information Technology; Software Engineering); Early Years/Childhood Studies; Electrical & Electronic Engineering; Furniture Design & Manufacture; Graphics; Managing Health & Care Services; Mechanical Engineering; Multimedia; Performing Arts; Photography; Science (Applied Biology); Telecommunications; Textiles

North Lindsey College

Kingsway, Scunthorpe, South Humberside DN17 1AJ Tel: 01724 281111

Diplomas

HND: *2 yrs FT* Business Studies; Engineering (Electronics & Communications)

Yorkshire Coast College

Lady Edith's Drive, Scarborough, North Yorkshire YO12 5RN Tel: 01723 372105
e-mail: admissions@ycoastco.ac.uk

Diplomas

HND: *2 yrs FT* Business; Computing; Engineering (Computer Integrated); Fashion/Costume; Graphic Design; Hotel Catering & Institutional Management; Information Systems; Leisure Management; Science (Sports Studies); Social Care; Travel & Tourism Management

UNIVERSITY OF LIVERPOOL

PO Box 147, Liverpool L69 3BX Tel: 0151 794 2000

First Degrees

BA Hons: *3 yrs* Accounting; Accounting & Computer Science; Ancient History & Archaeology; Archaeology; Architecture; Building Management & Technology; Business Economics; Business Economics & Computer Science; Business Studies; Classical Studies; Classics; Combined Honours; Construction Project Management; Economic & Social History; Economics; Economics & Computer Science; Economics & Economic History; Economics & Mathematics; Egyptology; English and Communication Studies or Modern History or Philosophy; English Language & Literature or French or German or Modern History or Philosophy or German Laws; English-Communication Studies; Environment & Planning; Financial Economics; Geography; Geography & Archaeology; History; Irish Studies; Mathematics & Philosophy; Modern History & Politics; Music; Music & Popular Music; Philosophy; Philosophy & Politics; Politics; Politics & Communication Studies; Sociology; Sociology & Social Policy *4 yrs* English-French or German or Hispanic Studies; European Business Studies and French or German or Hispanic Studies; European Film Studies and Modern Languages; French; French and Pure Mathematics; French-German or Hispanic Studies; German; German & Hispanic Studies; Hispanic Studies; History and French or German or Hispanic Studies; Latin American Studies; Modern European Languages; Philosophy and French or German or Hispanic Studies
BEng: *3 yrs* Aerospace Engineering; Civil Engineering; Clinical Engineering & Materials Science; Computer Electronics & Robotics; Electrical Engineering; Electrical Engineering & Electronics; Electronic & Communication Engineering; Electronic & Integrated Circuit Engineering; Computer Science-Electronic Engineering; Integrated Engineering with Industrial Management or Manufacturing Systems; Integrated Engineering; Manufacturing Engineering & Management; Materials Science; Materials Science & Management Studies; Materials, Design & Manufacture; Mechanical Engineering with Management; Mechanical Engineering; Mechanical Systems & Design Engineering; Medical Electronics & Instrumentation; Metallurgy & Materials Science *4 yrs With Foundation Yr:* Aerospace Engineering; Civil Engineering; Electrical & Electronic Engineering; Electrical Engineering and Electronics; Engineering Foundation; Integrated Engineering; Integrated Engineering with Industrial Management; Materials Science; Materials Science with a European Language; Mechanical Engineering *4 yrs (extended)* Aerospace Engineering; Civil & Environmental Engineering; Civil & Structural Engineering; Civil & Maritime Engineering; Electrical Engineering; Electrical Engineering & Electronics; Electronics; Engineering with Management or a European Language; Integrated Engineering; Integrated Engineering with Industrial Management or a European Language; Materials Engineering; Mechanical Engineering with Management; Mechanical Engineering; Mechanical Systems & Design Engineering
BSc Combined Hons: *3 yrs*

BSc Hons: *3 yrs* Anatomy & Human Biology; Archaeology; Astrophysics; Biochemistry; Biological & Medical Sciences; Biological Sciences; Chemical Physics; Chemistry with Pharmacology or Materials Science or Oceanography; Chemistry; Combined Honours; Computer and Multimedia Systems; Computer Information Systems; Computer Science; Diagnostic Radiography; Environmental Biology; Environmental Physical Sciences; Environmental Sciences; Genetics; Geography; Geography & Biology; Geology; Geology & Physical Geography; Geophysics with Business Management; Geophysics (Geology, Physics); Human Evolution; Marine Biology; Mathematical Physics; Mathematical Sciences; Mathematical Statistics; Mathematics with Education or Management or Computer Science or Ocean & Climate Studies or Finance; Mathematics; Mathematics-Statistics; Microbial Biotechnology; Microbiology; Molecular Biology; Occupational Therapy; Oceanography with Chemistry; Orthoptics; Pharmacology; Physics; Physics with Materials Science; Physics with Ocean & Climate Studies; Physics and Computer Science; Physics and Mathematics; Physics for New Technology; Physiology; Physiotherapy; Plant Science; Psychology; Psychology and Health Sciences or Neuroscience; Pure Mathematics; Radiation Physics & Environmental Science; Radiotherapy; Zoology *4 yrs* Applied Biochemistry; Applied Biology; Applied Genetics; Applied Molecular Biology; Chemical Sciences; Chemistry with a European Language or Industrial Chemistry or Industrial Management; Computer Information Systems; Computer Science with a European Language; Geophysics with a European Language; Life Sciences; Life Sciences with a European Language; Mathematical Sciences with a European Language; Modular Science/Engineering; Physics with a European Language; Psychology

LLB Hons: *3 yrs* Law *4 yrs* English & German Laws; English and French Laws with French

MEDICINE
BDS: *5 yrs* Dentistry
BN: *4 yrs* Nursing
BVSc: *5 yrs* Veterinary Science
MB; ChB Hons: *5 yrs* Medicine

Higher Degrees
DENTISTRY DEGREES
MDS: Dentistry (For Liverpool BDS graduates of two yrs' standing or for holders of UK registrable dental qualifications who have passed the primary exam for the FDSRCS or equivalent and who complete not less than three terms of higher study and research. By thesis)
Membership in Orthodontics: *3 yrs FT* (Taken with the MDentSci)

DOCTORATES
DEng: (Awarded to Liverpool graduates of at least seven yrs' standing for distinguished published work in engineering)
DMus: Music (Awarded to Liverpool graduates of at least seven yrs' standing in respect of original work or extended original compositions)
DSc: (Awarded to Liverpool graduates of at least seven yrs' standing for distinguished published contributions to science)
LittD: (Awarded to Liverpool graduates of at least seven yrs' standing for published contributions to learning in the Humanities, Education & Continuing Education)
LLD: (Awarded to Liverpool graduates of at least seven yrs' standing for published contributions to learning)
PhD: *2 yrs FT/4 yrs PT* (For non-graduates under certain conditions, not less than three yrs of full-time or four yrs of part-time research. By thesis and oral exam)

MASTER'S DEGREES OR EQUIVALENT
LLM: *1 yr FT/2 yrs PT* European Law; International Business Law; International Law; Medicine and Health Care
MA: *1 yr FT* Archives and Records Management; English by Directed Research; Historical Research (Humanities); Historical Research (Social Sciences); Irish Studies (By Directed Research); Language Teaching & Learning; Philosophy and Literary Theory; Science Fiction Studies *1 yr FT/2*

yrs PT Archaeology; Atlantic Connections: Slavery, Migrations and Identities; Classics; Egyptology; English Renaissance & Romantic Literature; European Union Law & Policy; European Union Politics; Geographies of Globalisation and Development; German Historical Studies; Hellenistic Studies; International Economic History: Globalisation and Change; Latin American Studies; Metropolitan Planning; Modern Languages (German); Modern Languages (Hispanic Studies); Philosophy; Politics & Media Studies; Popular Music Studies; Population Studies; Regional Science; Sociology and Social Policy; The 'Gypsies' and European Culture; Town and Regional Planning; Twentieth Century History; Victorian Literature; Women and the World: Gender Literature and Spirituality; Women's History *2 yrs FT* Social Work *2 yrs PT* Children, Policy Practice & Law; Contemporary Art; Irish Studies; Local History; Manx Studies

MArch: *1 yr FT/2 yrs PT* Architecture (For graduates or holders of approved qualifications)

MBA: *12 mths FT* Business, Finance and Management; Development & Industrialisation; Entrepreneurship; Environmental Management; Football Industries; Human Resource Management; Marketing; Music Industries; Public Sector Management; Urban Regeneration

MCD: *2 yrs FT* (By exam, dissertation and coursework)

MChem: *4 yrs* Chemical Physics; Chemistry with a European Language or Industrial Chemistry or Pharmacology or Management; Chemistry

MDentSci: *12 mths FT/24 mths PT* (For dental graduates who have passed the primary exam for the FDSRCS or equivalent. By exam and dissertation)

MEd: *1 yr FT/Up to 6 yrs PT* Education (For graduates and non-graduates with professional qualifications and/or relevant experience. By essays and dissertation)

MESci: *4 yrs* Geology; Geology & Geophysics; Geophysics (North America)

MMath: *4 yrs* Mathematical Physics; Mathematics

MMus: *1 yr FT/2 yrs PT* Music (After BA Hons in Music, by exam with composition or essays or performance)

MPA: *1-2 yrs* (For graduates or equivalent; by exam and dissertation)

MPhil: *1 yr FT/2 yrs PT* (Graduates, by higher study or research; non-graduates by thesis, oral exam and written exam if required) (Higher research, after BSc Honours or equivalent, or for appropriately qualified non-Honours graduates, possibly following a prescribed preparatory course)

MPhys: *4 yrs* Astrophysics; Chemical Physics; Mathematical Physics; Physics with a European Language; Physics

MPlan: *4 yrs* Planning

MRes: Physical Analysis of Biological Interactions at Surfaces

MSc: Addictive Behaviours; Animal Reproduction; Applied Parasitology & Medical Entomology; Archaeology; Behavioural & Evolutionary Ecology; Biosystems-Informatics; Chemical Process Research and Development; Chemical Research; Clinical Nursing; Cognitive & Affective Neuroscience; Early Hominid Studies; Environmental Assessment; Ethics of Health Care; Evolutionary Psychology; Forensic Behavioural Science; History of Science & Technology; Human Immunity; Information Systems; Investigative Psychology; Managing Catalytic Technology; Mathematical Sciences; Medical Diagnostic Ultrasound; Medical Engineering; Medical Microbiology; Medical Science; Nursing; Nursing (Palliative Care); Pharmacology; Physiology; Pure Mathematics; Radiometrics: Instrumentation & Modelling; Recent Environmental Change; Restoration Ecology of Terrestrial & Aquatic Environments; Software Engineering; Surface & Interface Science; Surface Science & Catalysis

MSc (Eng): *1-2 yrs FT/2-3 yrs PT* Advanced Engineering Materials; Advanced Manufacturing Systems & Technology; Advanced Manufacturing with Lasers; Civil and Earthquake Engineering; Environmental Civil Engineering; Industrial Materials Engineering; Intelligence Engineering; Maritime Civil Engineering; Materials Engineering with Lasers; Mechanical Systems Engineering; Microelectronic Systems & Telecommunications; Product Design & Management; Structural Engineering

MEDICINE

ChM: (At least four yrs after the date of admission to medical degree at an approved university; by thesis)

DClinPsychol: (Normally for graduates with good Honours degree in psychology; by exam and dissertation)

MChOrth: *12 mths FT* (For medical graduates with approved professional qualifications; by exam and dissertation)

MCommH: (Offered at the Liverpool School of Tropical Medicine, for medical graduates and other suitably qualified candidates after a one-yr course by exam and dissertation)

MD: Medicine (At least two yrs after MB, ChB; by thesis)

MPH: *12 mths FT* (For graduates in medicine of two yrs' standing; also for other graduates and non-graduates with higher study or research experience. By coursework, written and oral exam, and dissertation)

MRad: (For medical graduates of at least five yrs' standing in either radio-diagnosis or radiotherapy; by thesis, after research)

MTropMed: *12 mths FT* (Two yrs after admission to medical degree; by exam and dissertation)

MTropPaed: *12 mths FT* (For graduates in medicine with two yrs' experience in paediatric practice. By written, practical and oral exams and dissertation)

VETERINARY DEGREES

DVSc: (For Liverpool veterinary graduates of not less than seven yr's standing for published contributions to veterinary science)

MSc: (One yr's advanced course in Veterinary Parasitology after relevant first degree; by exam)

MVSc: *2 yrs FT/4 yrs PT* Veterinary Science (By higher study after BVSc or equivalent; by thesis or report and exam. One yr's advanced course in a veterinary speciality after BVSc or equivalent; by exam)

Diplomas

Diploma: *1 yr FT* Advanced Engineering Materials; Materials Engineering with Lasers *1 yr FT/2 yrs PT* Forensic Behavioural Science *1 yr FT/Up to 6 yrs PT* Modular Advanced Professional Studies in Education (Through study of a specified number of research and taught modules passed at appropriate levels. For graduates and non-graduates with professional qualifications and/or relevant experience. By essays) *1 yr PT* Irish Studies; Manx Studies *2 yrs FT* Social Work *2 yrs PT* Environmental Assessment *21 mths FT* Civic Design (Holders of the Diploma in Town & Regional Planning may transfer to the second yr of the full-time course) *9 mths FT* Town & Regional Planning (For graduates or holders of approved professional qualifications; by exam and coursework) *9 mths PT* Environmental Civil Engineering; Maritime Civil Engineering; Structural Engineering *PT* Bovine Reproduction (Six modules spread over at least two yrs plus extramural study; after BVSc or equivalent; by exam and dissertation)

POSTGRADUATE MEDICAL

Diploma: *12 mths PT* Prescribing Science *2 yrs PT* Radiology (DMR(D) or (T)) (For medical graduates with two yrs' postgraduate clinical experience) *3 mths FT* Genito-Urinary Medicine & Venereology; Reproductive Health in Developing Countries; Tropical Community Medicine & Health; Tropical Medicine & Hygiene (DTM & H) (For medical graduates) *3 yrs PT* Medical Science *6 mths FT* Tropical Child Health (DTCH) (For medical graduates with appropriate experience)

Certificates

Certificate: *15 mths FT/variable PT* Radiometrics *6 wks FT/22 wks PT* TEFL/ESP

Postgraduate Certificate: *1 yr FT/5 yrs PT* Radioactive Waste Monitoring and Decommissioning *13 wks FT/2 yrs PT* Software Technology

Degrees validated by University of Liverpool offered at:

Chester College of H.E.

Parkgate Road, Chester CH1 4BJ Tel: 01244 375444 Fax: 01244 392821
e-mail: B.Reg@chester.ac.uk Website: www.chester.ac.uk

First Degrees

BA Hons: *3 yrs FT Combined Studies:* Archaeology; Art History; Arts and Cultural Management; Business Administration; Business Studies; Community Studies; Contemporary Culture; Counselling Skills; Dance; Drama & Theatre Studies; Education Studies; English Literature; Fine Art; French; German; Health Studies; History; Lens-based and Digital Media; Media and Performance; Social Science; Spanish; Theology & Religious Studies *4 yrs PT* Humanities

BA/BSc Hons: *3 yrs FT Specialist degree schemes:* Animal Behaviour; Animal Behaviour & Welfare; Applied Biology; Biomedical Sciences; Business Administration with a Language (French, German or Spanish); Business Administration; Business Information Systems; Business Studies with a Language (French, German or Spanish); Business Studies; Computational Mathematics; Contemporary Culture; Countryside and Environmental Management; Environmental Science; Equine Studies; Food, Nutrition & Health; History and Heritage Management; Lens-based and Digital Media; Literature and Film; Mathematics, Statistics & Computing; Social Science; Tourism and Heritage Management; Tourism Management with a Language (French, German or Spanish); Tourism Management

BA/BSc Single Hons: *3 yrs FT* Art; Biology; Computer Science and Information Systems; Drama and Theatre Studies; English Literature; Geography; History; Physical Education and Sports Science; Psychology; Theology and Religious Studies

BEd: *4 yrs S* Early Years-English or Physical Education or Theology & Religious Studies

BSc Hons: *3 yrs FT Combined Studies:* Applied Statistics; Biology; Business Studies; Computer Sciences; Development Studies; Geography; Health Sciences; History of Science; Mathematics; Physical Education/Sports Science; Psychology *PT Combined Studies:* Professional Practice (Nursing & Midwifery)

BTh: *FT/PT* Theology

Higher Degrees

MA: *1 yr FT/2-6 yrs PT* Counselling Studies; Drama Practice; Fine Art; Health & Community Studies; Higher Education (Teaching); Landscape, Heritage & Society; Literary Studies; Military Studies; Professional Practice Nursing; Religion & Spirituality; Victorian Studies *6 yrs PT/Distance Learning* Adult Education; Theological Reflection; Church School Education

MBA: *3 yrs PT* Work Based & Integrative Studies

MEd: (Range of subjects available)

MPhil/PhD: (A range of subject areas offered)

MSc: *1 yr FT/2-6 yrs PT* Applied Sport & Exercise Psychology; Biotechnology; Environmental Biology; Evidence-based Clinical Nutrition; Exercise & Nutrition Science; Health Promotion and Health Education; Higher Education (Management); Information Systems; Mathematics; Psychology (Cognitive and Behavioural Psychotherapies)

MTh: Applied Theology

Diplomas

Advanced Diploma: *2-4 yrs PT* Applied Theology *Distance Learning* Adult Education with Theological Reflection; Church School Education

Diploma and Intermediate Diploma: Institute of Linguists Languages for International Communication (French, German, Spanish)

Postgraduate Diploma: *1 yr FT/2-6 yrs PT* Applied Sport & Exercise Psychology; Biotechnology; Environmental Biology; Evidence-based Clinical Nutrition; Exercise & Nutrition Science; Fine Art; Health & Community Studies; Health Promotion & Education; Higher Education (Management); Higher Education (Teaching); Information Systems; Landscape, Heritage and Society; Literary Studies; Management Studies; Mathematics; Military Studies; Psychology (Cognitive and Behavioural Psychotherapies); Religion & Spirituality; Victorian Studies; Work Based & Integrative Studies *3 yrs PT* Counselling Studies *Distance Learning* Adult Education; Theological Reflection; Church School Education

Undergraduate Diploma: Applied Biology

Certificates

Advanced Certificate: *1-2 yrs PT* Art

Certificate: Counselling Supervision
Church Colleges Certificate: Church School Studies; Religious Studies
PGCE: *1 yr FT* Art (Secondary); Drama (Secondary); Education (General Primary); Mathematics (Secondary); Modern Foreign Languages (Secondary) (French, German or Spanish); Physical Education (Secondary); Religious Studies (Secondary)
Postgraduate Certificate: *PT modular/Distance Learning* Adult Education; Theological Reflection; Church School Education *Up to 6 yrs PT* Access to the Historic Environment for Disabled People; Applied Theology; Cognitive-behavioural Therapy Supervision; Counselling Studies; Drama Practice; Environmental Biology; Evidence-based Clinical Nutrition; Exercise & Nutrition Science; Fine Art; Health and Community Studies; Health Promotion & Health Education; Higher Education; Information Systems; Landscape, Heritage and Society; Literary Studies; Management Studies; Mathematics; Military Studies; Religion & Spirituality; Victorian Studies; Work Based & Integrative Studies

Liverpool Hope University College

Hope Park, Liverpool L16 9JD Tel: 0151 291 3295 Fax: 0151 291 3048

First Degrees

BA: *3 yrs FT Combined Studies:* American Studies; Art; Business & Community Enterprise; Cities, Communities & Regeneration; Drama & Theatre; English; Environmental Studies; French; Geography; Health; History; Human & Applied Biology; Identity Studies; Information Technology; Mathematics; Music; Psychology; Sociology; Sport, Recreation & PE; Theology & Religious Studies *4 yrs FT Combined Studies:* American Studies; European Studies
BDes: *3 yrs FT* Design
BEd: *4 yrs S* Primary (KS1); Primary (KS2) *Specialisations:* Advanced Study of Early Years; Art; English; Geography; History; Human & Applied Biology; Information Technology; Mathematics; Music; Science; Sport, Recreation & PE; Theology & Religious Studies
BSc: *3 yrs FT Combined subjects:* Environmental Studies; Geography; Health; Health & Physical Recreation; Human & Applied Biology; Information Technology; Mathematics; Psychology; Sport, Recreation & PE

Higher Degrees

MASTER'S DEGREES OR EQUIVALENT
MA/PGCert/PGDip: *2 yrs PT* American Studies; Applied Women's Studies; Contemporary History; Contemporary Urban Renaissance; Criminal Justice; Ecclesiastical History; Ecumenical Theology; Music; Play Therapy; Theology & Religious Studies (Women's Spirituality); Twentieth Century Literary Studies
MEd: *5 yrs PT* Art & Design Education; Curriculum Studies; Education Management; French Studies; Geographical & Environmental Education; Health & Social Studies; Information Technology; Primary Science; Religious & Theological Education
MSc: *1 yr FT/2 yrs PT* Applied Psychology; Applied Social Research; Ecology & Environmental Management; Health Studies; Information Technology; Management; Managing Exercise Science

Diplomas

Advanced Diploma: *Up to 6 yrs PT* Art & Design Technology; Curriculum Studies; Ecumenical Studies; European Studies; Geographical & Environmental Studies; Health & Social Studies; Information Technology; Management Studies; Religious & Theological Studies; Science; Theatre Studies

LIVERPOOL JOHN MOORES UNIVERSITY

Enquiry Management Team, Roscoe Court, 4 Rodney Street, Liverpool L1 2TZ
Tel: 0151 231 5090 Fax: 0151 231 3194
e-mail: recruitment@livjm.ac.uk Website: www.cwis.livjm.ac.uk

BA/BA Hons; BSc/BSc Hons Single, Joint, Combined: The subjects listed are available and may be combined with each other in the first yr. Many of these subjects may be taken as Single Honours

in the second and third yrs. Please consult JMU's Prospectus or the *UCAS Handbook* for current combinations and further details.
* Subject to validation.

First Degrees

BA Hons/BSc Hons with QTS: Primary: *4 yrs FT* English; Mathematics; Science
BA Hons/BSc Hons with QTS: Secondary: *4 yrs FT* Design & Technology; Physical Education
BA Hons/BSc Hons with QTS: Upper Primary & Middle: *4 yrs FT* Design & Technology; Mathematics; Physical Education; Science
BA/BA Hons: *3 yrs FT* Accounting & Finance; Applied Community Studies; Architectural Studies; Art History Studies; Business & Economics; Business & Information; Business Administration; Childhood Studies; Chinese & Pacific Asia Studies; Consumer Studies; Dance; Dance and Drama; Drama; Electronic Business; English & Chinese; Fashion & Textiles Design; Fine Art; Food & Nutrition; French & Chinese; Geography; German & Chinese; Global Economy; Graphic Design; Health; History; Home Economics; Housing Studies; Information & Library Management; International Journalism; Journalism; Leisure & Tourism; Literature and Cultural History; Media & Cultural Studies; Media Professional Studies; Multimedia Arts; Pacific Asia Studies and Economics or Geography or History or Politics; Politics; Sports Development (With Physical Education); Women's Studies; Youth and Community Studies; Youth and Community Work *3 yrs FT/4 yrs S* Business Studies; Nutrition; Public Service Management*3-4 yrs FT* Leisure & Tourism; Urban Planning *4 yrs FT* European Studies with French or German or Spanish; International Business Studies with French or German or Italian or Japanese or Chinese or Spanish; Midwifery; Nursing; Nursing (Mental Health Route); Tourism & Leisure with a Modern Foreign Language
BA/BA Hons Modern Language Studies: *3 yrs FT* Applied Social Studies *4 yrs FT* Applied Languages Europe (French & German); Applied Languages Europe (French & Spanish); French or German combined with another main subject; French-German or Italian or Japanese or Spanish; Teaching English to Speakers of other Languages (TESOL) with French or German or Italian or Japanese or Spanish or English for Speakers of other Languages (ESOL)
BA/BA Hons/BSc/BSc Hons Single, Joint & Combined: *3 yrs FT* American Studies; Applied Community Studies; Applied Psychology; Business (Joint only) *Joint only:* Countryside Management; Criminal Justice; Dance/Drama; Earth Science; Economics; English for Speakers of Other Languages (Joint/Combined) *Joint/Combined:* European Studies; Food & Nutrition; French; German; Health; History; Human Geography; Imaginative Writing; Law; Literature and Cultural History; Media & Cultural Studies; Politics; Product Design; Screen Studies; Sociology; Sports Science; Theatre Studies; Women's Studies
BDes: *3 yrs FT* Product Design & Digital Modelling
BEd with QTS: *2 yrs FT* Design & Technology; Information Technology; Science
BEng/BEng Hons: *3 yrs FT* Environmental Engineering *3 yrs FT/4 yrs S* Civil Engineering; Communications & Computer Engineering; Computer Aided Engineering; Computer Engineering; Electrical & Electronic Engineering; Electronic Systems Engineering; Electronics & Communication Engineering; Electronics & Control Systems Engineering; Integrated Engineering; Manufacturing Systems Engineering; Mechanical & Marine Engineering; Mechanical Engineering
BSc: *3 yrs FT* Civil Engineering *3 yrs FT/4 yrs S* Marine Operations
BSc/BSc Hons: *3 yrs FT* Applied Computer Technology; Applied Electronics; Applied Psychology; Astrophysics; Broadcast Technology; Building Maintenance Management; Coaching Science; Countryside Management; Earth Science; Environmental Electronics; Environmental Science & Policy; Geography; Geology; Human Sciences; Information Services Management; Innovative Design; Medical Technology; Natural Sciences; Nutrition; Outdoor and Environmental Education; Pharmaceutical & Chemical Sciences; Physical Geography; Psychology & Biology; Public Health; Science & Football; Sports Science; Sports Technology; Sustainable Technology; Transport; Urban Estate Management; Wildlife Conservation *3 yrs FT/4 yrs S* Applied Biochemistry; Applied Biochemistry & Applied Microbiology; Applied Biology or Medicinal Chemistry; Applied Chemistry with Environmental Chemistry or Industrial Chemistry; Applied Chemistry; Applied Ecology; Applied Microbiology; Applied Plant Science; Applied Zoology; Biological Anthropology; Biomedical Sciences; Biophysics; Biotechnology; Biotechnology Management; Building Surveying; Business Mathematics; Construction Management; Environmental Science;

Environmental Technology Management; Marine Operations; Maritime & Intermodal Transport; Maritime Business & Management; Maritime Studies; Maritime Technology; Mechatronics; Molecular Biology; Multimedia Systems; Paleobiology & Evolution; Product Design Engineering; Quantity Surveying; Software Engineering; Technology; Technology Management *4 yrs FT* Forensic and Biomolecular Science *4 yrs S* Applied Statistics & Computing; Business Information Systems; Business Mathematics; Computer Studies; Information Systems Management; Mathematics, Statistics & Computing

BTech: *3 yrs FT/4 yrs S* Maritime Engineering; Mechanical & Manufacturing Technology
LLB/LLB Hons: *3 yrs FT* Law

Higher Degrees

LLM/PgD/PgC: *1-2 yrs PT* European Community Law for UK Businesses
MA: *1 yr PT* European Studies; Professional Development Programme *2 yrs PT* Writing
MA/MSc: *2 yrs PT* Human Geography
MA/PgD: *1 yr FT/1-2 yrs PT* Information and Library Management *1 yr FT/2 yrs PT* Multimedia Arts *1-2 yrs PT* Criminal Justice *2 yrs FT* Social Work *2 yrs PT* Art History and Theory; Consciousness & Transpersonal Psychology; Counselling
MA/PgD/PgC: *1 yr PT* Fraud Management *1-2 yrs PT* Education/Educational Studies (Specialist routes in Educational Management; PE, Sport & Dance; Primary Education; Special Education Needs; Education Studies) *2 yrs PT* Journalism; Literature and Cultural History; Marketing
MBA: *1 yr FT* Business Administration
MBA/DBA/CBA: *1 yr PT* Business Administration
MBS: *1 yr FT* Business Studies
MChem: *4 yrs FT* Chemistry
MEng: *4 yrs S* Civil Engineering
MPharm: *4 yrs FT* Pharmacy
MPhil/PhD: Accountancy; American Studies; Art and Design; Astrophysics; Biochemistry; Biology; Built Environment; Business and Management Studies; Chemistry; Civil Engineering; Communication and Media Studies; Computer Science; Drama, Dance and Performing Arts; East and South East Asian Studies; Education; Electrical and Electronic Engineering; English Language, Literature and Competitive Studies; Environmental Studies; French; General Engineering; Geography; German and Related Languages; History; History of Art; Law; Library and Information Management; Linguistics; Mechanical, Aeronautical and Manufacturing Engineering; Medicine: Related Studies; Middle Eastern & African Studies; Nursing; Pharmacy; Philosophy; Physical Education & Sports Studies; Physics; Politics & International Studies; Psychology; Social Policy & Administration; Social Work; Sociology; Spanish; Sports Science; Statistics & Operational Research; Town & Country Planning
MPhys: *4 yrs FT* Astrophysics
MRes: *Various programmes in the following areas:* Built Environment; Computing & Mathematical Sciences; Languages; Sports Science
MSc: *1 yr FT* International Banking, Economics and Finance *1 yr FT/2 yrs PT* Computing and Information Systems; Interactive Multimedia Systems *1 yr FT/2-3 yrs PT* Industrial Biotechnology *2 yrs PT* Medical Parasitology; Pathology *3 yrs Distance Learning:* Construction (Health and Safety) Management
MSc/PgD: *1 yr FT* Industrial Pharmacy; Phytomedicinal Products *1 yr FT/2 yrs PT* Design & Management of Manufacturing Systems; Design and Simulation of Mechanical Systems; Instrumental Chemical Analysis/Pharmaceutical Analysis; Intelligent Control; Maritime Operations; Microelectronics and System Design; Occupational Psychology; Pharmaceutical Primary Care; Planning Studies; Technology Management; Urban Renewal *1-2 yrs PT* Drug Use and Addiction *2 yrs FT/3 yrs PT* Environmental Planning
MSc/PgD/PgC: *1 yr FT/2-3 yrs PT* Design Management; Exercise & Health; Product Design; Sports Physiology; Sports Psychology; Sports Science *2 yrs PT* Clinical Pharmacy; Clinical Research; Health Care Management; Health Care Practice *2-5 yrs PT* Health (Promotion, Research and Policy Change) *3 yrs PT* Holistic Approaches to Healing; Water, Energy and the Environment
MSc/PGDip: *1 yr FT* Commercial Property Management
MSc/PGDip/PGCert: *2-5 yrs Distance Learning:* National and International Masters Scheme in Virology

Diplomas

PgD/CCETSW Practice Teaching Award: *1 yr PT* Merseyside Practice Teaching Programme
PgD/PgCert: *1-2 yrs FT* Research *2 yrs PT* Administrative Studies; Legal Practice *4 yrs PT* Architecture *3 yrs S* Architecture; Architecture & Urban Design *4 yrs PT* Architecture & Urban Design

Certificates

PGC: *1 yr FT* Tourism and Leisure Management Development *2-5 yrs PT* Tourism and Leisure Management Development *1 yr PT* Learning and Teaching in Higher Education; Mental Health and Approved Social Work
PGCE: *1 yr FT* Art & Design; Design Technology; Modern Foreign Languages; Physical Education; Science

Professional Courses

ACCA: *1 yr PT* Association of Chartered Certified Accountants
CIMA: *1 yr PT* Chartered Institute of Management Accountants
CIPFA: *1 yr PT* Chartered Institute of Public Finance & Accountancy
IPD: *1 yr PT*

LONDON GUILDHALL UNIVERSITY

Admissions Office, 133 Whitechapel High Street, London E1 7QA Tel: 020 7320 1616
Fax: 020 7320 3462 e-mail: enqs@lgu.ac.uk Website: www.lgu.ac.uk

London Guildhall University operates an undergraduate Credit Accumulation Scheme (CAS). This allows students great choice and flexibility. For full details, please refer to the University's undergraduate prospectus.
† Subject to validation.

First Degrees

JOINT HONOURS
Joint Degree Subjects: *3 yrs FT/4-7 yrs PT Any two of the following may be combined:* 3D/Spatial Design; Accounting; American Studies; Asia Studies; Banking; Business; Business Economics; Business Information Technology; Communications; Computing; Criminology; Design Studies; Development Studies; Economics; English; European Studies; Financial Services; Fine Art; French; German; Insurance; International Relations; Investment; Law; Marketing; Mathematics; Modern History; Multimedia Systems; Politics; Product Development & Manufacture; Professional Communications; Psychology; Public Policy; Sociology; Spanish; Taxation; Textile Furnishing Design; Transport *4 mths FT/24 mths PT* Art & Design History; English
Minor Subjects: Economics *(Any two subjects plus one joint degree subject):* Accounting; Accounting Systems; American Studies; Arabic; Asia Studies; Banking; Business; Business Information Technology; Communications; Computing; Criminology; Design Studies; English Studies; European Studies; Financial Services; Fine Art; French; German; Insurance; International Relations; Investment; Law; Mandarin Chinese; Marketing; Mathematics; Modern History; Politics; Psychology; Public Policy; Sociology; Spanish; Taxation; Transport

SINGLE HONOURS
BA/BA Hons: *3 yrs FT/4-7 yrs PT* Accounting & Finance; Business Administration; Business Economics; Business Enterprise; Business Studies; Communication & Audio-visual Production; Design Studies; Economics; European Business Studies; Financial Economics; Financial Services; Fine Art; Fine Art Practice; Furniture Design & Technology; Global Economics; Insurance Studies; Interior Design & Technology; Legal & Economic Studies/Licence d'Administration Economique et Sociale; Modern History; Multimedia Systems; Politics; Politics, Philosophy & Economy; Professional Communications & Marketing Communications; Psychology; Silversmithing, Jewellery & Allied Crafts; Sociology; Textile Furnishing Design & Manufacture

BSc/BSc Hons: *3 yrs FT/4-7 yrs PT* Human Factors; Computing; Computing & Information Systems; Criminology; Furniture Design & Technology; Furniture Manufacture & Innovation; Mathematics with Business Applications; Multimedia Systems; Musical Instrument Technology; Psychology; Restoration & Conservation; Social Policy & Management; Transport and Shipping
LLB/LLB Hons: *3 yrs FT/4-7 yrs PT* Business Law; Law

SINGLE HONOURS: DEFERRED
BA/BA Hons: *3 yrs FT/4-7 yrs PT* Accounting Studies; Communications; Economic Studies; English Studies; French; German; International Relations; Legal Studies; Modern History; Politics; Sociology; Spanish
BSc/BSc Hons: *3 yrs FT/4-7 yrs PT* Business Information Technology; Computing & Information Systems; Social Policy & Management

Higher Degrees

LLM: *1 yr FT/variable PT* International & Comparative Business Law
MA: *1 yr FT/variable PT* Applied Art & Visual Culture; Audio-visual Production; British & European Politics & Government; Communications Management; Computer Imaging & Animation; Contemporary French/German Studies; Design Research for Disability; Financial Services Management; Human Resources Strategies; Marketing Management; Modern British Women's History; Politics; Psychoanalysis & Culture; Silversmithing, Jewellery & Allied Crafts
MBA: *2 yrs PT* Business Administration
MSc: *1 yr FT/variable PT* Applied Psychology; Care Policy and Management; Counselling Psychology; Economics; Economics and Financial Forecasting; Financial Markets with Information Systems; Financial Markets & Derivatives; Financial Services Regulation & Compliance; Information Systems Development; International Banking and Finance; International Trade & Transport; IT Consultancy; Multimedia Systems; Occupational Psychology; Social Research Methods; Strategic Management Accounting; Systems Auditing; User Interface Design *FT/PT* Economic & Financial Forecasting; Financial Services Management; International Banking & Finance *PT* Care Policy & Management; Psychoanalysis & Culture

Diplomas

Fellowship Diploma: Gem Diamond Practice; Gemmology; Legal Practice
Foundation Diploma: Foundation Studies for Overseas Students
Postgraduate Diploma: Law
University Diploma: Business Studies with English; Commercial Operation of Shipping; English for Commerce; Management Practice; Psychology

Certificates

University Certificate: Business Studies with English; Commercial Operation of Shipping; English as a Foreign Language; English for Commerce; Human Resource Strategies; Management Practice; Management Studies; Psychology

Professional Courses

Professional Courses: Airline Transport Pilot's Licence; Commercial Pilot's Licence (CPL); Common Professional Exam in Law; Crew Resource Management; Instrument Rating (IR); LCCI Certificate in Teaching English in Business; Multi-Crew Co-Operation Certificate (MCC) *Distance Learning/PT evenings* Institute of Credit Management *Flexible Learning* Chartered Institute of Bankers *FT* Chartered Insurance Institute *PT evenings* Association of Chartered Certified Accountants; Association of Taxation Technicians; Certified Diploma in Accounting & Finance; Chartered Institute of Bankers; Chartered Institute of Management Accountants; Chartered Institute of Marketing; Chartered Institute of Taxation; Chartered Insurance Institute; Communication Studies & Advertising; Institute of Chartered Secretaries & Administrators; Institute of Chartered Shipbrokers; Pensions Management Institute

THE LONDON INSTITUTE
Camberwell College of Arts

Peckham Road, London SE5 8UF Tel: 020 7514 6301 Fax: 020 7514 6310
e-mail: enquiries@camb.linst.ac.uk Website: www.camb.linst.ac.uk

† Subject to validation.

First Degrees

BA Hons: *3 yrs FT* Ceramics; Conservation; Drawing; Illustration†; Painting; Photography†; Sculpture; Silversmithing & Metalwork *3 yrs FT/4 yrs PT* Graphic Design

Higher Degrees

MA: *1 yr FT/2 yrs PT* Book Arts; Conservation; Conservation; Printmaking
MPhil: *FT/PT* (Offered in all areas of the College's work)
PGDip: *30 wks* Conservation; Printmaking

Diplomas
PGDip: *30 wks* Book Arts

THE LONDON INSTITUTE
Central Saint Martins College of Art & Design

Southampton Row, London WC1B 4AP Tel: 020 7514 7000 Fax: 020 7514 7024
e-mail: applications@csm.linst.ac.uk Website: www.csm.linst.ac.uk

† Subject to validation.

First Degrees

BA Hons: *3 yrs FT* Arts & Design; Ceramic Design; Fashion; Graphic Design; Jewellery Design; Product Design; Textile Design; Theatre Design *3-4 yrs S* Fashion *5 yrs PT* Fine Art

Higher Degrees

MA: *1 yr 48 wks FT/2 yrs PT* Design Studies; Fine Art; Scenography *1 yr FT* Design (By project) *2 yrs FT* Industrial Design *4 trms FT/8 trms PT* Textile Design *4 trms FT/9 trms PT* Communication Design *48 wks FT over 5 trms* Fashion
MPhil/PhD: (Available by negotiation with the Dean of Research)

Diplomas

PGDip: *1 yr PT* Design Studies *2.5 trms FT/4 trms PT* Textile Design *2.5 trms FT/5.5 trms PT* Communication Design
Postgraduate Diploma: *2.5 trms FT/5.5 trms PT* Textile Design *3 trms FT/5 trms PT* Communication Design

Certificates

Postgraduate Certificate: *1 yr PT* Stained Glass *16 wks FT/32 wks PT* Photography *6 mths FT* Animation

THE LONDON INSTITUTE
Chelsea College of Art & Design

Manresa Road, London SW3 6LS Tel: 020 7514 7751 Fax: 020 7514 7778
e-mail: enquiries@chelsea.linst.ac.uk Website: www.linst.ac.uk

First Degrees

BA Hons: *2 yrs FT accelerated* Interior & Spatial Design; Textile Design *3 yrs FT* Design & Public Art; Design for Communication; Design: Interior & Spatial Design or Design & Public Art or Textile Design or Design for Communication; Fine Art; Fine Art: Media or Painting or Sculpture; Interior & Spatial Design; Textile Design *4-5 yrs PT* Fine Art: Practice & Theory of Visual Art

Higher Degrees

MA: *1 yr FT* Fine Art (Combined Media, Painting, Sculpture) *1 yr FT/2 yrs PT* Design for the Environment (Textile Design, Interior & Spatial Design, Design & Public Art) *3 yrs PT* Art Theory
MPhil/PhD: *By research on topics in:* Fine Art; History & Theory of 19th & 20th Century Art; History of Non-Western Modern Art & Design; Interior & Spatial Design; Public Art & Design; Saddlery Technology; Textile Design

Diplomas

Postgraduate Diploma: *1 yr FT* Fine Art *2 yrs PT* Art Theory

THE LONDON INSTITUTE
London College of Fashion

20 John Princes Street, London W1M 0BJ Tel: 020 7514 7400 Fax: 020 7514 7484
e-mail: enquiries@lcf.linst.ac.uk Website: www.lcf.linst.ac.uk

† Subject to validation.
* School of Fashion Design & Technology.
** School of Fashion Promotion & Management.

First Degrees

BA Hons: *3 yrs FT* Costume & Make Up for the Performing Arts; Design Technology for the Fashion Industry; Fashion Photography**; Fashion Promotion (Journalism, Broadcast & PR)** *4 yrs* Fashion Management** *4 yrs PT* Fashion Studies*/** *4 yrs S* Product Development for the Fashion Industries*
BSc: *4 yrs S* Cosmetic Science

Higher Degrees

MA: *48 wks FT/96 wks PT* Fashion Studies (Design & Technology; Management & Marketing; Communication & Culture; History & Theory)*/**

Diplomas

Access Courses: *1 yr FT* Fashion (Fashion Business, Fashion Promotion Media, Fashion and Media Make Up)
Advanced GNVQ: *2 yrs FT* Business of Fashion**
BTEC Diploma in Foundation Studies: *1 yr FT* Art & Design (Fashion)*
BTEC Diploma/Certificate in Tailoring: *1 yr FT*
BTEC HND: *2 yrs FT* Beauty Therapy & Health Studies**; Cordwainers Design (Footwear and Accessories)*; Cordwainers Footwear Technology*; Fashion Design & Technology*; Fashion Marketing & Promotion**; Fashion Styling & Photography**; Specialist Make Up**
BTEC ND: *2 yrs FT* Beauty Therapy**; Fashion Design & Technology*; Fashion Styling for Hair & Make Up**
Diploma: *1 yr FT* Fashion Portfolio*/**

Certificates

Cert HE: *1 yr PT* Cosmetic Science**
PGCert: *15 wks* Fashion (Buying & Merchandising; Advanced Pattern Cutting)*/**

THE LONDON INSTITUTE
London College of Printing

Elephant & Castle, London SE1 6SB Tel: 020 7514 6569 Fax: 020 7514 8068
Website: www.lcp.linst.ac.uk

† Subject to validation.
* School of Fashion Design & Technology.
** School of Fashion Promotion & Management.

First Degrees

BA Hons: *3 yrs FT* Book Arts & Crafts; Film & Video; Graphic & Media Design; Journalism; Marketing & Advertising; Media & Cultural Studies; Photography; Print Media Management; Publishing; Retail Design Management; Retail Management; Surface Design; Visual Merchandising Management

Diplomas

HND: *2 yrs FT* Design Bookbinding; Journalism; Marketing & Advertising; Printing & Digital Media; Retail Design**; Retail Management; Sound Design; Surface Design

UNIVERSITY OF LONDON
Birkbeck, University of London

Malet Street, London WC1E 7HX Tel: 020 7631 6000 Fax: 020 7631 6270
e-mail: admissions@bbk.ac.uk Website: www.bbk.ac.uk

MA: All courses except those marked * are offered under a 120 credit scheme allowing students to accumulate credits towards a Master's degree over a period of up to four yrs. Those courses marked * must be completed within two yrs if taken on a part-time basis. The full-time course covers a minimum period of one calendar yr. A wide range of modules is available .

MSc: All MScs undertaken on a part-time basis must be completed within two yrs. Courses are arranged on a course unit system, except those marked *. All MSc programmes in the faculty of the Built Environment have a corresponding Diploma.

MPhil/PhD: Research degrees are awarded in the languages, literatures, history and social sciences of the following countries: Bulgaria, Czech Republic, Slovak Republic, Finland, Poland, Russia/Soviet Union, Former Yugoslavia.

Associateships: RCS – Royal College of Science; RSM – Royal School of Mines; C&G – City & Guilds of London Institute.* Joint course with University College London.** Joint course with Royal College of Art.*** Joint course with College of Petroleum Studies, Oxford.

First Degrees

ARTS
BA Hons: *4 yrs PT* Accounting-Management; Classical Studies/Classics; English; Film and Media; French Studies; French-Humanities; French-Management; Geography; German; German and Spanish; French-German with Spanish; German-Humanities; German-Management; Hispanic Studies-Humanities; History; History & Archaeology; History of Art; Humanities; Humanities and Media; Linguistics & Languages; Management; Modern German Studies; Philosophy; Politics & Society; Politics, Philosophy & History; Spanish and Latin American Studies

ECONOMICS
BSc (Econ) Hons: *4 yrs PT* Financial Economics
BSc Hons: *4 yrs PT* Economic & Social Policy

LAW
LLB Hons: *3-4 yrs PT* Law

SCIENCE

BSc Hons: *4 yrs PT* Analytical Chemistry; Biochemical Sciences; Biological Sciences; Chemistry; Economic and Social Policy; Environmental Conservation; Environmental Geology; Environmental Management; Environmental Science; Geography; Geology; Information Systems & Management; Mathematics-Statistics; Molecular Biology; Physical Sciences; Psychology; Science for Society; Statistics and Economics; Statistics and Management

Higher Degrees

MA: *1 yr FT/2 yrs PT* Applied Linguistics; Archaeology; Bilingualism; Contemporary History and Politics; Cultural & Critical Studies; Digital Art History; English Literary Research; Gender, Society & Culture; German; Hispanic Studies; Historical Research; History of Art; History of Art (By research); History of Film and Visual Media; History of Film and Visual Media (By research); Imperialism and Post-Colonial Societies; London Studies; Medieval Studies; Modern French Studies; Modern German Studies; Modern History; Modern Literatures in English; Philosophy; Renaissance Studies; Spanish and Latin America Studies (Cultural History and Critique); Translation Studies; Victorian Studies *2 yrs PT* Arts Policy and Management; Classical Civilisation; Garden History; History of Early Modern England and France, 1529-1774; Interdisciplinary Study of Religion; Islamic Studies; Lifelong Learning; Medicine, Science & Society: Historical & Philosophical Perspectives; Science, Culture and Environment

MRes: *1 yr FT* Bioinformatics; Humanities & Cultural Studies; Structural Biology; Structure of Materials *1 yr FT/2 yrs PT* Business Strategy, Politics and the Environment; E-Commerce Management and Organizational Behaviour; European Politics; Football and the Media; International Business; Law; Management and Organizational Behaviour; Politics and Government; Public Management; Public Policy and Management; Social and Political Theory *2 yrs PT* Earth Sciences

MSc: *1 yr FT/2 yrs PT* Analytical Chemistry; Chemical Research; Cognitive Neuropsychology; Computing Science; E-Commerce; E-Commerce Management and Organizational Behaviour; Economics; Ergonomics; European Politics; Finance; Gender, Society & Culture; Geographic Information Science; Geographic Information Science (By Distance Learning); Global Politics; International Business; Molecular Modelling & Bioinformatics; Politics & Government; Public Policy & Management; Social & Political Theory *2 yrs PT* Applied Biology: Pests, Parasites and Human Welfare; Applied Statistics & Operational Research; Biomolecular Organisation; Career Management-Counselling; Environmental Management (Protected Area Management); Environmental Science; Family & Systemic Psychotherapy; Life Course Development; Medicine, Science & Society: Historical & Philosophical Perspectives; Microbiology; Occupational Psychology; Organisational Behaviour; Physiology; Psychodynamics of Human Development; Race & Ethnic Relations; Science, Culture and Environment; Structural Biology – using the Internet *3 yrs PT* Group Analysis; Psychodynamic Counselling

MSc (by research): *1 yr FT/2 yrs PT* Business Strategy, Politics and the Environment; E-Commerce Management and Organizational Behaviour; Football and the Media; International Business; Public Management

Diplomas

Advanced Diploma: *1 yr PT* Chemistry
Diploma: *2 yrs PT* IT Applications; Modern German Studies
Postgraduate Diploma: *1 yr PT* Business Strategy, Politics and the Environment; E-Commerce; E-Commerce Management and Organizational Behaviour; E-Science; Earth Sciences; Econometrics; Economics; Finance; Gender, Society & Culture; Geo-information and Policy Analysis; International Business; Law; Life Course Development; Psychodynamic Perspectives; Psychodynamics of Human Development; Race and Ethnic Relations; Science, Culture and Environment

Certificates

Advanced Certificate: *1 yr PT* Biology; Chemistry; Evolutionary Biology; Geology; Physical Geography Updated; Plant Ecology & Environmental Science; Powder Diffraction – using the Internet; Principles of Protein Structure – using the Internet; Protein Crystallography – using the

Internet; Psychology; Spatial Information Science; Techniques in Structural Molecular Biology – using the Internet
Certificate: *1 yr PT* Chemistry; Geology *2 yrs PT* Biochemical Sciences; Biology; Molecular Biology; Systemic Practice with Families & Couples
Certificate of Continuing Education: *1 yr PT* Biochemical Science; Biology; Statistics
Postgraduate Certificate: *1 yr PT* E-Commerce; Econometrics; Economics; Economics-Finance; Finance; Race and Ethnic Relations; Science, Culture and Environment

UNIVERSITY OF LONDON
British Institute in Paris
Department of French Studies, 9-11 rue de Constantine, Paris Cedex 07 75340
Tel: +33 1 44 11 73 83 Fax: +33 1 45 50 31 55 Website: www.bip.lon.ac.uk

First Degrees
BA Hons: *3 yrs* French Studies

Higher Degrees
MA: *1 yr FT* Contemporary French Studies *1 yr FT/2 yrs PT* Translation

UNIVERSITY OF LONDON
Courtauld Institute of Art
North Block, Somerset House Strand, Strand, London WC2R ORN Tel: 020 7848 2649
Fax: 020 7848 2410 e-mail: tanya.barratt@courtauld.ac.uk Website: www.courtauld.ac.uk

First Degrees
BA Hons: *3 yrs* History of Art

Higher Degrees
MA: *1 yr* History and Theory of the Art Museums; History of Architecture; History of Art; History of Dress
MA; MPhil; PhD

Diplomas
Diploma: *1 yr* History of Art *3 yrs* Conservation of Paintings; Conservation of Wall Paintings

UNIVERSITY OF LONDON
Goldsmiths College
University of London, New Cross, London SE14 6NW Tel: 020 7919 7171 Fax: 020 7919 7975
e-mail: admissions@gold.ac.uk Website: www.goldsmiths.ac.uk

First Degrees
ARTS
BA Hons: *3 yrs FT* Anthropology; Drama & Theatre Arts; English; Fine Art (Studio Practice & Contemporary Critical Studies); History; History of Art; Media & Communications; Politics; Politics with Economics; Social & Political Sciences; Social Policy; Social Policy with Politics; Sociology; Sociology & Cultural Studies; Textiles *4 yrs FT* Design; Eco Design; European Languages, Culture & Society; Fine Art (Extension Degree); French Studies; German Studies; Spanish & Latin American Studies; Textiles (Extension Degree) *4-5 yrs PT* History *4-6 yrs PT* Anthropology; English; Politics; Politics with Economics; Social Policy; Social Policy with Politics *4-9 yrs PT* Social, Cultural & Creative Processes *5 yrs PT* European Languages, Culture & Society;

French Studies; German Studies; Politics with Economics; Social Policy; Social Policy with Economics or Politics; Spanish & Latin American Studies

BA Hons with QTS: *3 yrs FT Specialisation available in:* Art; Design & Technology with Computing; English; Humanities; Mathematics with Computing; Science; Nursery *4 yrs FT* Education (Secondary) with Design & Technology

BA Joint Hons: *3 yrs FT* Anthropology-Communication Studies or Sociology; Art History-Fine Art; History-Art History; Communication Studies-Sociology; Communications-Cultural Studies; Economics-Politics & Public Policy; English-History or History of Art or Politics; History-Sociology *4 yrs FT* Art History & Fine Art (Extension Degree); European Languages, Culture & Society; European Studies; Spanish or Spanish; Latin American Studies *4-6 yrs PT* Economics-Politics or Public Policy; English-History or History of Art *5 yrs PT* European Languages, Culture and Society; European Studies; Spanish and Latin American Studies

BMus: *3 yrs FT/PT* Music *4 yrs FT* Music (Extension Degree)

SCIENCE & TECHNOLOGY
BSc Hons: *3 yrs FT* Psychology *3 yrs FT/4-6 yrs PT* Computer Science & Statistics; Computing & Information Systems; Mathematics with Computer Science or Statistics; Mathematics; Statistics, Computer Science & Applicable Mathematics *3 yrs FT/4-6 yrs PT/4 yrs S* Computing, Operational Research & Statistics for Business

BSc Joint Hons: *3 yrs FT* Mathematics and/with Computer Science or Statistics; Statistics, Computer Science & Applicable Mathematics *4 yrs FT (includes yr in industry)* Mathematics and/with Computer Science or Statistics; Statistics-Computer Science or Applicable Mathematics *4 yrs FT (includes yr spend abroad)/ 5 yrs PT* Psychology with a European Language *4-6 yrs PT* Computer Science and/with Mathematics or Statistics; Computer Science- Statistics or Applicable Mathematics

Higher Degrees

MA: *1 yr FT* Feature Film; Image & Communication (Photography or Electronic Graphics); Journalism; Radio; Television Documentary; Television Drama; Television Journalism *1 yr FT/2 yrs PT* Advanced Clinical Practice in Art Psychotherapy; Anthropology & Cultural Process; Applied Anthropology & Community & Youth Work; Applied Linguistics: Sociocultural Approaches; Arts Administration & Cultural Policy; Communication, Culture & Society; Contemporary Approaches to English Studies; Contemporary British Politics; Creative and Life Writing; Cultural History; Cultural Studies; Culture, Globalisation & the City; Culture, Science & Technology; Curating; Design Futures; Directing; English, Local & Regional History; Fine Art; Fine Art Administration & Curatorship; Gender, Anthropology & Development; Gender, Culture & Modernity; German; Hispanic Studies; History of Art; Jewish Education and Community Studies; Media & Communication Studies; Performance; Performance & Culture; Scenography; Social Anthropology; Social Policy & Administration; Social Research; Textiles; Theatre Education; Transnational Communications & the Global Media; Twentieth Century Literature and its Contexts; Visual Anthropology; Writing for Performance *1 yr FT/2-3 yrs PT* Art Psychotherapy; Group Psychotherapy *1 yr FT/2-5 yrs PT* Education (Modular) *2 yrs FT* Social Work (CCETSW Diploma) *2 yrs PT* Psychoanalytic Studies; Psychotherapy & Society

MMus: *1 yr FT/2 yrs PT* Composition; Contemporary Music Studies; Ethnomusicology; Historical Musicology; Musical Theory & Analysis; Performance & Related Studies

MPhil; MRes; MSc; PhD

MRes: *1 yr FT/2 yrs PT* English; History; History of Art; Media & Communications; Visual Arts

MSc: *1 yr FT* Occupational Psychology *1 yr FT/2 yrs PT* Mathematics; Psychological Assessment in Organisations *2 yrs PT* Rational Emotive Behaviour Therapy

PhD; MPhil: *2 yrs FT/3 yrs PT* Anthropology; Art Psychotherapy; Community & Youth Work; Computer Science & Information Systems; Cultural Studies; Design; Drama; Education; English; Fine Art; French; German; History; History of Art; Mathematics; Media & Communications; Music; Psychology; Religious Studies; Social Policy & Politics; Social Work; Sociology; Spanish/Latin American Studies; Statistics; Textiles

Diplomas

DipHE: *2 yrs FT* Community & Youth Work; Community Work (Turning Point)

Diploma: *2 yrs PT* Cognitive Approaches to Counselling & Psychotherapy *Modular* Management, Training & Supervision

Postgraduate Diploma: *1 yr FT* Fine Art *1 yr FT/2 yrs PT* Art History; Textiles *1 yr FT/2-4 yrs PT modular* Teaching & Management of Languages *1 yr PT* Advanced Training in Art Psychotherapy *15 mths accelerated/2 yrs FT/3 yrs PT* Art Psychotherapy *2 yrs FT* Social Work (CCETSW) *2 yrs PT* Counselling *3 yrs PT* Group Psychotherapy *4 trms PT* Youth Social Work

Certificates

Certificate: *1 yr FT* Creative Music Technology; English Language for the Arts & Social Sciences; Fine Art; Mathematics; Music; Textiles *1 yr PT* Humanistic & Psychodynamic Counselling; Intercultural Therapy; Language Teaching to Adults; Language, Literature & Drama; Media & Communications; Media & Cultural Studies; Politics & Political Economy; Teaching Music to Adults *1-2 yrs PT* Caribbean Studies; Design & Technology; Jazz & Popular Music Studies; Psychology; Social Anthropology; Social Studies *2 yrs PT* Art & Design; Creative Music Technology; Music; Music Studies; Music Workshop Skills

PGCE: *1 yr FT* Primary with QTS or General Science or Religious Education; Secondary with QTS with Art or Biology or Chemistry or Design & Technology or Drama or English or French or Geography or German or Mathematics or Music or Physics or Social Science (with either Geography or History or Humanities or RE) or Spanish

UNIVERSITY OF LONDON
Heythrop College

Kensington Square, London W8 5HQ Tel: 020 7795 6600 Fax: 020 7795 4200
e-mail: a.clarkson@heythrop.ac.uk Website: www.heythrop.ac.uk

First Degrees

BA Hons: *3 yrs* Biblical Studies; Philosophy; Philosophy, Religion and Ethics; Philosophy-Theology; Theological Studies; Theology for Ministry
BD: *3 yrs* Theology

Higher Degrees

MA: *1 yr FT/2 yrs PT* Christian Spirituality; Pastoral Liturgy; Pastoral Studies; Philosophy; Psychology of Religion *2 yrs PT* Canon Law; Christianity and Inter-religious Dialogue; Contemporary Theology in the Catholic Tradition; Philosophy & Religion
MTh: *1 yr FT/2 yrs PT* Biblical Studies; Christian Doctrine; Church History; Pastoral Theology; Philosophy of Religion
PhD; MPhil

Diplomas

Postgraduate Diploma: *1 yr FT/2 yrs PT* Christian-Jewish Relations; Pastoral Theology; Theology

UNIVERSITY OF LONDON
Imperial College of Science, Technology & Medicine

South Kensington, London SW7 2AZ Tel: 020 7589 5111 Fax: 020 7594 8004
e-mail: admissions@ic.ac.uk Website: www.ic.ac.uk

First Degrees

SCIENCE, TECHNOLOGY & MEDICINE

BEng & Associateship of C&G: *3 yrs* Computing; Electrical & Electronic Engineering; Information Systems Engineering

BEng & Associateship of the RSM: *3 yrs* Environmental and Mining Engineering; Materials with Management; Materials Science & Engineering *4 yrs* Materials with a Yr Abroad or Management & a Yr Abroad

BSc & Associateship of the RCS: *3 yrs* Animal Science; Biochemistry with Management; Biochemistry; Biology with Parasitology; Biology; Biology with Management or Microbiology; Biotechnology; Chemistry-Management; Ecology; Environmental Biology; Mathematics with Management or Mathematical Computation or Statistics or Applied Mathematics/Mathematical Physics; Mathematics; Mathematics-Computer Science; Mathematics (Pure Mathematics); Mathematics, Optimisation & Statistics; Microbiology; Physics with Theoretical Physics; Physics; Plant Science; Zoology *4 yrs* Biochemistry with a Yr in Industry or Management and a Yr in Industry; Biology (with a Yr in Industry/Research or in Europe); Biology with Management (with a Yr in Industry/Research); Biotechnology with a Yr in Industry; Chemistry with Management or Management with a Yr in Industry; Equine Science; Mathematics with a Yr in Europe; Physics with a Yr in Europe or Studies in Musical Performance

BSc & Associateship of the RSM: *3 yrs* Applied Natural Science with Management (Agricultural Science); Applied Natural Science with Management (Environmental Science); Applied Natural Science with Management (Agricultural Business Management); Applied Natural Science with Management (Equine Business Management); Applied Natural Science with Management (Business Management for the Food Chain); Applied Natural Science with Management (Environmental Management); Applied Natural Science with Management (Applied Environmental Science); Applied Natural Science with Management (Horticultural Science); Geology

MB, BS, BSc: *6 yrs* Medicine

Higher Degrees

MBA: *FT/PT* Management

MEng & Associateship of C&G: *4 yrs* Aeronautical Engineering; Aeronautical Engineering with a Yr in Europe; Chemical Engineering with a Yr Abroad; Chemical Engineering; Civil & Environmental Engineering; Civil & Environmental Engineering with a Yr in Europe; Civil Engineering with a Yr in Europe; Civil Engineering; Computing (Artificial Intelligence); Computing (Computational Management); Computing (European Programme of Study); Computing (Mathematical Foundations); Computing (Software Engineering); Electrical & Electronic Engineering; Electrical & Electronic Engineering with a Yr Abroad or Management; Information Systems Engineering; Mechanical Engineering with a Yr Abroad; Mechanical Engineering

MEng & Associateship of the RSM: *4 yrs* Aerospace Materials; Environmental & Earth Resources Engineering with a Yr Abroad; Environmental & Earth Resources Engineering; Materials Science & Engineering; Mining Engineering; Petroleum Engineering

MPhil/PhD: *2-3 yrs By research on topics in:* Agricultural Economics & Business Management; Agriculture; Biological Sciences; Environment; Horticulture

MSc: *1 yr FT* Advanced Chemical Engineering; Advanced Computing; Advanced Mechanical Engineering; Advanced Methods in Taxonomy & Biodiversity; Analogue & Digital IC Design; Applied Mathematics; Applied Optics; Applied Plant Science; Biochemical Research; Biostatistics-Epidemiology; Cardio-Respiratory Nursing; Cardiology; Chemical Research; Clinical Biochemistry; Clinical Chemistry; Clinical Cytology; Clinical Psychiatry; Cognitive Neuroscience; Communications & Signal Processing; Composite Materials; Computational Fluid Dynamics & Structural Mechanics; Computational Genetics & Bioinformatics; Computing for Industry; Computing Science; Concrete Structures; Control Systems; Corrosion of Engineering Materials; Drug Use: Evidence Based Policy & Intervention; Earthquake Engineering & Structural Dynamics; Engineering Geology; Engineering-Physical Science in Medicine; Environmental Diagnosis; Environmental Engineering; Environmental Management (Applied Environmental Science); Environmental Management (Landscape Ecology and Management); Environmental Management (Rural Environmental Policy); Environmental Technology; Finance; Haematology; Health Management; Histopathology; History of Science, Medicine & Technology; Human Molecular Genetics; Human Reproductive Biology; Hydrology for Environmental Management; Immunology; Industrial Design Engineering**; Infectious Diseases; Medical Ethics; Medical Ultrasound; Mineral Deposit Evaluation; Molecular Biology & Pathology of Viruses; Molecular Genetics with Counselling; Molecular Medicine; Neuroscience; Pest Management; Petroleum Engineering; Petroleum Geoscience; Petroleum Production Management***; Plant Biotechnology; Process Systems Engineering; Pure Mathematics; Quantum Fields & Fundamental Forces; Renal

Medicine; Respiratory Medicine; Science Communication; Social Intervention for Public Health; Soil Mechanics; Soil Mechanics & Engineering Seismology; Soil Mechanics & Environmental Geotechnics; Structural Steel Design; Surgical Science; Sustainable Agriculture and Rural Development (Agrobiodiversity or Agroecology or Production in Tropical Environment); Transport*; Vascular Technology & Medicine *1 yr FT/2-5 yrs PT (mixed-mode)* Agribusiness Management; Agricultural Economics; Applied Environmental Economics; Economics of Rural Change; Food Industry Management & Marketing *2-5 yrs DL* Agribusiness Management; Agricultural Economics; Applied Environmental Economics; Biodiversity Conservation; Economics of Rural Change; Environment & Development; Environmental Management; Food Industry Management & Marketing; Managing Rural Change; Sustainable Agriculture & Rural Development

MSci & Associateship of the RCS: *4 yrs* Biochemistry; Biotechnology; Chemistry with a Yr Abroad or Medicinal Chemistry; Chemistry with Conservation Science; Chemistry; Mathematics with a Yr in Europe; Mathematics; Mathematics & Computer Science; Physics; Physics with a Yr in Europe *4 yrs/5 yrs* Biochemistry (with a Yr in Europe); Biotechnology (with a Yr in Europe) *5 yrs* Biochemistry with a Yr in Industry/Research; Biotechnology with a Yr in Industry/Research; Chemistry with a Yr in Industry or Medicinal Chemistry & a Yr in Industry

MSci & Associateship of the RSM: *4 yrs* Applied Natural Science with Management (Horticultural Science); Applied Natural Science with Management (Applied Environmental Science); Applied Natural Science with Management (Environmental Science); Applied Natural Science with Management (Environmental Management); Applied Natural Science with Management (Business Management for the Food Chain); Applied Natural Science with Management (Agricultural Business Management); Applied Natural Science with Management (Agricultural Science); Applied Natural Science with Management (Equine Business Management); Earth Resources; Environmental Geology; Geological Sciences; Petroleum Geology

Diplomas

Diploma: *1 yr FT* Cardiology; Internal Medicine; Medical Imaging *9 mths FT* Obstetrics & Gynaecology; Paediatric Cardiology; Thoracic Medicine *9 mths PT* Primary Care Therapeutics *FT/PT* Drug & Alcohol Studies

Postgraduate Diploma: *1/2-5 yrs DL* Agribusiness Management (Minimum registration period 2 yrs); Agricultural Economics (Minimum registration period 2 yrs); Applied Environmental Economics (Minimum registration period 2 yrs); Biodiversity Conservation (Minimum registration period 2 yrs); Economics of Rural Change (Minimum registration period 2 yrs); Environment & Development; Environmental Assessment; Environmental Management; Food Industry Management & Marketing (Minimum registration period 2 yrs); Managing Rural Change (Minimum registration period 2 yrs); Sustainable Agriculture & Rural Development *9 mths* Agribusiness Management; Agricultural Economics; Applied Environmental Economics; Economics of Rural Change; Food Industry Management and Marketing

UNIVERSITY OF LONDON
Institute of Education

20 Bedford Way, London WC1H 0AL Tel: 020 7612 6560 Fax: 020 7612 6097
e-mail: j.simson@ioe.ac.uk Website: www.ioe.ac.uk/courses

First Degrees

In-Service BEd Hons: *2 yrs FT/3 yrs PT* (For trained, qualified teachers with at least one yr's teaching experience. Wide range of options available)

Higher Degrees
MASTER'S DEGREES OR EQUIVALENT
MA: *1 yr FT/2-4 yrs PT* Adult & Continuing Education; Assessment and Development of Early Literacy; Child Development; Child Development with Early Childhood Education; Comparative Education; Cultural Studies in Education; Curriculum Studies; Economics of Education;

Education & International Development; Education & International Development: Health Promotion; Education (Early Years); Education (Psychology); Education, Gender & International Development; Educational Management & Administration; Educational Psychology (Professional Training FT); Effective Learning; English Studies in Education; European Education; Evaluation & Assessment; Geography in Education; Health Education & Health Promotion; Higher & Professional Education; History in Education; History of Education; Information & Communications Technology in Education; Learning & Teaching of English & Literacy; Mathematics Education; Media Education; Media Studies; Modern Languages in Education; Music Education; Policy Studies in Education; Post-Compulsory Education; Primary Education; Psychology & Education for Special Needs; Psychology of Education; Religious Education; School Effectiveness & School Improvement; Science Education; Social Justice & Education; Sociology of Education; TESOL; Values in Education (Philosophical Perspectives); Vocational Education & Training; Women and Management in Higher Education *1 yr PT* Institute of Personnel & Development *PT* Art & Design in Education; Learning & Teaching of Reading & Writing; Museums & Galleries in Education
MSc: *1 yr FT/2 yrs PT* Child Development; Child Development with Early Childhood Education; Educational Psychology (Professional Training FT) *1 yr FT/2-4 yrs PT* Psychology & Education for Special Needs; Psychology of Education

RESEARCH DEGREES
EdD: *3 yrs FT/4 yrs PT*
PhD; MPhil: *2 yrs FT/3 yrs PT*

Diplomas

Advanced Diploma: *1 yr FT/2-5 yrs PT* Careers Education & Guidance; Education; Education & Psychology for Special Needs; Education Management; Jewish Education; Pastoral Care & Personal-Social Education; Primary Science Education; Psychology *FT* Primary Health Care Education & Development
Advanced Diploma in Professional Studies: *15 mths FT/variable PT* (This course has a modular structure and students accumulate credits towards the diploma. A wide range of modules is available)

Certificates

Further Education Teacher's Certificate: *2 yrs PT* Education
PGCE (Post-Compulsory): *1 yr FT*
PGCE (Primary & Secondary): *1 yr FT 6 mths FT* Primary Health Care Education & Development

UNIVERSITY OF LONDON
Jews' College

Schaller House, Albert Road, London NW4 2SJ Tel: 020 8203 6427 Fax: 020 8203 6420
e-mail: jewscoll@clus1.ulcc.ac.uk

First Degrees

BA Hons: *3 yrs FT/5 yrs PT* Jewish Studies

Higher Degrees

DOCTORATES
PhD: *3 yrs FT/5 yrs PT*

MASTER'S DEGREES OR EQUIVALENT
MA: *1 yr FT/2 yrs PT* Hebrew / Jewish Studies (Three Modules chosen from Bible & Midrash; Jewish Law & Talmud; Rabbinic Thought; and Philosophy) *1 yr FT/2-4 yrs PT* Education & International Development

Diplomas
Postgraduate Diploma: *1 yr FT/2 yrs PT* Jewish Studies

Certificates
Certificate: *1 yr FT/2 yrs PT* Higher Jewish Studies (Can be used as access course for the BA for students without formal entry requirements)

UNIVERSITY OF LONDON
King's College London
James Clerk Maxwell Building, 57 Waterloo Road, London SE1 8WA Tel: 020 7836 5454
Fax: 020 7836 1799 Website: www.kcl.ac.uk

First Degrees
SCHOOL OF BIOMEDICAL SCIENCE
BSc Hons: *3 yrs* Biomedical Science; Biomolecular Science; Cell Biology; Clinical Sciences; Human Biology; Molecular Biology; Molecular Biophysics; Pharmacology; Physiology; Physiology and Pharmacology; Physiotherapy *3-4 yrs* Pharmacology with Management *4 yrs* Pharmacology with Studies in Europe; Pharmacology with Toxicology

SCHOOL OF DENTISTRY
BDS: *5-6 yrs* Dentistry
Foundation Course: *1 yr* Natural Sciences/Dentistry

SCHOOL OF EDUCATION
BA Hons: *3 yrs* Language & Communication; Modern Foreign Languages with Education
BSc Hons: *3 yrs* Mathematics with Education; Physics with Education

SCHOOL OF HEALTH & LIFE SCIENCES
BSc Hons: *3 yrs* Biochemistry; Biochemistry-Immunology or Microbiology or Pharmacology; Biological Sciences; Environmental Sciences; Environmental Biotechnology or Immunology; Microbiology; Immunology; Medical Biochemistry; Microbiology; Molecular Genetics; Nutrition *4 yrs* Environmental Health; Nutrition & Dietetics

SCHOOL OF HUMANITIES
BA Combined Hons: *3 yrs* Classical Studies with English or Applied Computing; Geography-History or Philosophy; German and Classical Studies or History; Greek with English; Greek-Philosophy; Latin with English; Mathematics-Philosophy; Music with Applied Computing; Philosophy with Greek; Philosophy-Theology; War Studies with Applied Computing or History or Philosophy or Theology; War Studies and Classical Studies or Geography *4 yrs* Afro-Portuguese, Brazilian & Religious Studies; Classical, Byzantine & Modern Greek Studies or English or Management with Applied Computing; French; French-Classical Studies or Portuguese Studies; French-German or Hispanic Studies or Mathematics or Modern Greek or Philosophy or Portuguese; German with Applied Computing or English; German-Hispanic Studies or Modern Greek or Music or Portuguese; Hispanic Studies with Applied Computing or English or Modern Greek or Philosophy; Hispanic Studies and Classical Studies; History-Portuguese; Modern Greek with Applied Computing or English; Modern Greek-Portuguese; Philosophy and Hispanic Studies; Portuguese with Applied Computing or English; War Studies and French or German or Modern Greek or Portuguese
BA Hons: *3 yrs* American Studies; Ancient History; Biblical Studies; Classical Archaeology; Classical Studies; Classics; English Language & Literature; French; Geography; History; Music; Philosophy; Religious Studies; Theology; War Studies *4 yrs* American Studies; European Studies; French; German; Hispanic Studies; Modern Greek Studies; Portuguese & Brazilian Studies; US & Latin American Studies
BSc Hons: *3 yrs* Geography

SCHOOL OF LAW
LLB Hons: *3 yrs* Law *4 yrs* English & French Law; Law with German Law or European Legal Studies

SCHOOL OF MEDICINE
Foundation Course: *1 yr* Natural Sciences / Medicine
MBBS: *5-6 yrs* Medicine

SCHOOL OF NURSING & MIDWIFERY
BSc: *18 mths FT* Midwifery Practice (post-registration) *3 yrs FT* Nursing Studies (pre-registration) *3 yrs FT + 6 mths PT* Midwifery Professional Studies (pre-registration)

SCHOOL OF PHYSICAL SCIENCES & ENGINEERING
BEng Hons: *3 yrs* Computer Systems & Electronics; Computer-Aided Mechanical Engineering; Electronic Engineering; Manufacturing Systems Engineering; Manufacturing Systems Engineering with Management; Mechatronics; Telecommunications Engineering
BSc Eng: *3 yrs* Manufacturing Systems and Management
BSc Hons: *3 yrs* Business Management; Chemistry; Chemistry with Analytical Chemistry or Bioscience or Computer Science or Management or Philosophy of Science; Chemistry-Mathematics or Philosophy; Computer Science; Computer Science with Management; Mathematics; Mathematics with Philosophy of Mathematics or Philosophy; Mathematics-Physics or Computer Science or Computer Science (Management) or Management or Physics with Astrophysics; Physics with Astrophysics or Computer Science or French or Management or Medical Applications or Philosophy of Science; Physics; Physics and Philosophy *4 yrs* Chemistry with a Yr Abroad or a Yr in Industry; Chemistry with Management with a Yr Abroad or a Yr in Industry; Physics with a Yr Abroad

Higher Degrees
INSTITUTE OF PSYCHIATRY
MSc: Child & Adolescent Mental Health; Clinical & Public Health Aspects of Addiction; Cognitive Behavioural Therapy; Couple, Relationship & Sexual Therapy; Family Therapy; Mental Health Social Work; Neuroscience

SCHOOL OF BIOMEDICAL SCIENCE
MSc: Aeromedical Research; Aviation Medicine; Biomedical Sciences Research; Disability Studies; Human & Applied Physiology; Pharmacology
MSci Hons: *4 yrs* Physiotherapy

SCHOOL OF DENTISTRY
MClin Dent: Endodontology; Periodontology; Prosthodontics
MSc: Community Dental Practice; Dental Public Health; Dental Radiology; Endodontics; Experimental Oral Medicine; Implant Dentistry; Orthodontics; Periodontology; Sedation & Special Care Dentistry

SCHOOL OF EDUCATION
EdD: Education
MA: Applied Language Studies in Education; Classics Education; Computers in Education; Education Management; English Education; Health Education & Health Promotion; Mathematics Education; Modern Foreign Language Education; Religious Education; Science Education; Theology & Education; Urban Education; Youth Ministry & Theological Education
MRes: Social Sciences
MSc: Health Education & Health Promotion

SCHOOL OF HEALTH & LIFE SCIENCES
MPharm Hons: *4 yrs* Pharmacy
MSc: Aquatic Resource Management; Biopharmacy; Clinical Gerontology; Community

Pharmacy; Forensic Science; General Biochemistry-Molecular Biology; Gerontology; Immunology; Molecular Life Sciences Research; Nutrition; Pharmaceutical Analysis & Quality Control; Pharmaceutical Technology

SCHOOL OF HUMANITIES
MA: Ancient History; Anthropology & Sociology of Religion; Area Studies (Africa or Latin America); Brazilian Studies; Christian Ethics; Classical Archaeology; Classics; English; English Language Teaching & Applied Linguistics; French Literature & Culture; Geography; Geography: Cities, Culture & Social Change; Geography: Environmental & Development; Geography: Monitoring, Modelling & Management of Environmental Change; German (German Language or Modern German Literature); History of Christianity; Imperial & Commonwealth History; Indian Religions; Islamic Studies; Late Antique & Byzantine Studies; Latin American Studies; Medieval History (European Literary & Historical Studies); Medieval Studies (Western Europe); Mediterranean Studies; Modern Greek Studies; Modern Rhetoric & Society; New Testament Studies; Old Testament Studies; Patristics; Philosophy; Philosophy of Psychology; Philosophy of Religion; Portuguese Studies; Romance Languages & Literatures (Portuguese); Spanish & Latin American Studies; Systematic Religion; Text & Performance Studies; Twentieth Century Studies; War Studies
MMus: Analysis, Composition, Historical Musicology
MSc: Geography; Geography: Monitoring, Modelling & Management of Environmental Change; Philosophy & History of Science; Philosophy of Mental Disorder

SCHOOL OF LAW
LLM: Law
MA: Advanced European Legal Studies; Child Studies; International Peace & Security; Medical Ethics & Law
MSc: Construction Law & Arbitration

SCHOOL OF MEDICINE & DENTISTRY
MSc: Clinical Biochemistry; Dermatology; Diabetes & Endocrinology; Epileptology; General Practice; Health Psychology; Histopathology; Medical Engineering & Physics; Medical Informatics; Medical Ultrasound; Mental Health Studies; Nuclear Medicine; Palliative Care; Rheumatology

SCHOOL OF NURSING & MIDWIFERY
MSc: Advancing Health Care Practice; Advancing Midwifery Practice; Advancing Professional Healthcare Practice; Community Health; Nursing Research

SCHOOL OF PHYSICAL SCIENCES & ENGINEERING
MEng Hons: 4 *yrs* Computer Systems & Electronics; Computer-Aided Mechanical Engineering; Electronic Engineering; Manufacturing Systems Engineering with Management; Mechatronics; Mechatronics & Manufacturing Systems; Telecommunications Engineering 5 *yrs* Computer Systems & Electronics with a Yr in Industry; Electronic Engineering with a Yr in Industry; Telecommunications Engineering with a Yr in Industry
MSc: Advanced Computing; Chemical Research; Communications & Radio Engineering; Computer & Internet Systems; Computer-Aided Mechanical Engineering; Construction Law & Arbitration; Electronics Research; Enterprise Information Systems; Imaging & Digital Image Processing; Information Processing & Neural Networks; International Management; Mathematics (Intercollegiate); Mechanical Engineering Research; Mechatronics
MSci Hons: 4 *yrs* with a Yr in Industry; Chemistry with Analytical Chemistry or Bioscience or Computer Science; Chemistry; Chemistry-Mathematics; Computer Science; Mathematics with Philosophy of Mathematics; Mathematics; Mathematics-Physics; Physics; Physics and Philosophy and a Yr Abroad

Diplomas
SCHOOL OF NURSING & MIDWIFERY
DipHE: *2 yrs* Nursing Studies (pre-registration, graduate entry) *3 yrs* Nursing Studies (pre-registration) *PT* Midwifery Practice (pre-registration)

Certificates
College Certificate: Advanced Musical Studies; Family Therapy; Medical Ultrasound; Vascular Ultrasound
Postgraduate Certificate: Education; Sports Law
Undergraduate Certificate: Rehabilitation Engineering

Other Courses
Courses: Aviation Medicine (Basic or Advanced Course); Restorative Dentistry (Postgraduate clinical course)

UNIVERSITY OF LONDON
London School of Economics & Political Science
Houghton Street, London WC2A 2AE Tel: 020 7955 7124/5 (Undergraduate); 020 7955 7160 (Graduate) Fax: 020 7955 6001 (Undergraduate); 020 7955 6137 (Graduate) e-mail: ug-admissions@lse.ac.uk; graduate-school@lse.ac.uk Website: www.lse.ac.uk
Contacts: First Degrees: Admissions Officer, PO Box 13401, Houghton Street, London WC2A 2AS
Graduate Programmes: Graduate Admissions, PO Box 13420, Houghton Street, London WC2A 2AR

First Degrees
BA Hons: *3 yrs* Anthropology-Law; Geography; History; Philosophy; Social Anthropology
BSc Hons: *3 yrs* Accounting & Finance; Actuarial Science; Business Mathematics & Statistics; Econometrics-Mathematical Economics; Economic History; Economic History with Economics or Population Studies; Economics with Economic History; Economics; Economics and Economic History; Environmental Management & Policy; Environmental Policy with Economics; Geography with Economics; Geography-Population Studies; Government; Government and Economics or History; Industrial Relations & Human Resource Management; International Relations; International Relations and History; Management; Management Sciences; Mathematics & Economics; Philosophy; Philosophy and Economics; Population Studies; Russian Studies; Social Anthropology; Social Policy and Administration; Social Policy with Social Psychology; Social Policy-Sociology or Government or Population Studies; Sociology
LLB Hons: *3 yrs* Law *4 yrs* Law with French Law

Higher Degrees
LLM: *1 yr* Labour Law; Law
MA: Area Studies
MA/MSc: History of International Relations
MSc: *1 session* Accounting & Finance; Analysis, Design & Management of Information Systems; Anthropology & Development; Cities, Space & Society; City Design & Social Science; Comparative Politics; Crime, Deviance & Control; Criminal Justice Policy; Decision Sciences; Demography; Development Management; Development Studies; Econometrics & Mathematical Economics; Economic History; Economics; Economics & Economic History; Economics & Philosophy; Environment & Development; Environmental Assessment & Evaluation; European Political Economy; European Politics & Policy; European Social Policy; European Studies; Finance & Economics; Gender; Gender & Development; Gender & Social Policy; Gender & the Media; Global History; Global Market Economics; Global Media & Communications; Health & Social Services; Health Policy, Planning & Financing; Health, Population & Society; Housing; Human Geography Research; Industrial Relations & Personnel Management; International Accounting & Finance; International Health Policy; International Relations; Law and Accounting; Local Economic Development; Management; Management (Public Sector); Management and

Regulation of Risk; Management of Non-Governmental Organisations; Media & Communications; Media & Communications Regulation; Nationalism & Ethnicity; New Media, Information & Society; Operational Research; Organisational & Social Psychology; Philosophy & History of Science; Philosophy of the Social Sciences; Philosophy, Policy & Social Value; Political Sociology; Political Theory; Politics of the World Economy; Population & Development; Public Administration & Public Policy; Public Financial Policy; Real Estate Economics & Real Estate Finance; Regional & Urban Planning Studies; Regulation; Religion & Contemporary Society; Russian & Post-Soviet Studies; Social Anthropology; Social Policy & Planning; Social Policy & Planning in Developing Countries; Social Psychology; Social Research Methods; Sociology; Statistics; Theory & History of International Relations; Voluntary Sector Organisation

Diplomas

Diploma: *1 yr FT* Accounting & Finance; Econometrics; Economics; Housing; Law; Sociology; World Politics

UNIVERSITY OF LONDON

Queen Mary & Westfield College (incorporating St Bartholomew's and the Royal London School of Medicine & Dentistry)

Mile End Road, London E1 4NS Tel: 020 7882 5511/5533 Fax: 020 7882 5588
e-mail: admissions@qmw.ac.uk Website: www.qmw.ac.uk/

First Degrees

ARTS

BA Hons: *3 yrs* English; English-Drama or History; Geography; Geography-Politics; History; History-Politics; Human Geography; Journalism and Contemporary History; Law-Economics or Politics; Medieval History; Modern & Contemporary History; Politics *4 yrs* French; French with Business Studies; French (European Studies); French and Drama or Economics or German or Geography or Hispanic Studies or History or Linguistics or Linguistics & Computer Science or Mathematics or Politics or Russian; French and Russian (European Studies); French or German or Hispanic Studies or Russian; English-French; Hispanic Studies (European Studies); German with Business Studies; German; German (European Studies); German and Drama or Economics or Geography or Hispanic Studies or Linguistics or Linguistics & Computer Science or Mathematics or Politics or Russian; German and Hispanic Studies (European Studies); German and Russian (European Studies); Hispanic Studies; Hispanic Studies with Business Studies; Hispanic Studies (European Studies); Hispanic Studies and Drama or Economics or Geography or Linguistics or Linguistics & Computing or Mathematics or Politics or Russian; Hispanic Studies and Russian (European Studies); History-German Language; Law-German; Politics-German Language; Russian with Business Studies; Russian; Russian (European Studies); Russian and Drama or Economics or Geography or Linguistics or Linguistics & Computer Science or Mathematics or Politics

ECONOMICS

BSc (Econ) Hons: *3 yrs* Economics; Economics, Finance and Management; Economics-History or Politics; Economics/Statistics-Mathematics; Geography; Geography & Economics

LAW

LLB Hons: *3 yrs* Law *4 yrs* English & European Law; Law with German Language

SCIENCE & TECHNOLOGY

BDS: *5 yrs FT* Dentistry
BEng Hons: *3 yrs* Aerospace Engineering; Avionics; Biomedical Materials Science & Engineering; Computer Engineering; Electrical & Electronic Engineering; Electronic Engineering; Engineering Science; Materials Science & Engineering; Mechanical Engineering; Telecommunications *4 yrs with integrated industrial training* Aerospace Engineering; Mechanical Engineering

BEng/BSc/BSc (Eng) Hons with Foundation: Aeronautical Engineering; Astronomy; Chemistry; Electronic Engineering; Environmental Science; Materials; Mechanical Engineering; Physics
BSc (Eng) Hons: Engineering with Business Studies or Environmental Science or French or German or Spanish; Engineering
BSc Hons: *3 yrs by course units* Applied Mathematics; Astronomy; Astrophysics; Biochemistry; Biochemistry with Microbiology; Biological Chemistry; Biology with Business Studies; Biology; Biology-Chemistry; Chemical Physics; Chemistry; Chemistry with Business Studies or Biochemistry or Physics; Chemistry-Mathematics; Computer Science with Business Studies; Computer Science; Mathematics-Computer Science; Discrete Mathematics; E-Science (Subject to approval); Ecology; Environmental Chemistry; Environmental Geography; Environmental Science; Genetics; Genetics-Microbiology; Geography; Marine & Freshwater Biology; Mathematical Sciences for Business, Industry & Finance; Mathematics with Business Studies; Mathematics; Mathematics and Astrophysics or Business Economics or Computing or Physics or Statistics; Molecular Biology; Pharmaceutical Chemistry; Physical Geography; Physics; Physics with Business Studies or Computing; Physics & the Environment; Physics and Computer Science or Economics or Electronics or Materials Science; Pure Mathematics; Statistics; Theoretical Physics; Zoology *4 yrs* Chemistry-German

Higher Degrees

MA: *1 yr FT/2 yrs PT* Euro Intellectual & Cultural History: Civilisation & Barbarism; European Languages, Literatures & Thought; Film & Communication; German; German Language: Development and Structure; History (Contemporary British History Since 1939); Language, Society & Change in Europe; Literature, Culture & Modernity; Modern German Literature: Writers and Theory; Performance Studies (Will commence 2001); Renaissance Studies: Culture and Conflict in Northern Europe (1492-1660); Russian Language and Culture; Writing & Society (1700-1820)
MPhil/PhD: *FT/PT* Aeronautical Engineering; Anatomy; Astrophysics & Astronomy (Mathematics); Biochemistry; Biological Science; Biomedical Materials; Biomedical Sciences; Chemistry; Civil Engineering; Community Sciences; Computer Science; Dentistry; Drama; Economics; Electronic Engineering; English; Environmental Science; European Studies; French; Geography; German; Haematology, Oncology & Imaging; Hispanic Studies; History; Laws; Linguistics; Materials; Mathematics; Mechanical Engineering; Medicine; Medieval Studies; Molecular Pathology, Infection & Immunity; Pharmacology; Physics (Including Astrophysics/Astronomy); Politics; Preventive Medicine; Russian; Space Engineering; Statistics; Surgery, Clinical Neuroscience & Intensive Care
MSc: *1 yr FT/2 yrs PT* Advanced Methods in Computer Science; Astrophysics; Chemical Research; Cities and Culture; Clinical Drug Development; Clinical Microbiology; Dental Materials Science; Dental Public Health; Dental Technology; E-Commerce Engineering; Econometrics; Economics; Experimental Oral Pathology; Financial Economics; Financial Economics and Econometrics; Gastroenterology; Geography; Gerodontics; Globalization and Development; Health Care Research Methods; Information Technology; Internet Computing; Management of Intellectual Property; Materials Research; Mathematics; Medical Electronics & Physics; Orthodontics; Paediatric Dentistry; Periodontology; Primary Care; Prosthodontics; Public Policy; Radiation Physics; Sports Medicine

SCIENCE & TECHNOLOGY
MBBS: *5 yrs FT* Medicine
MEng Hons: *4 yrs* Aerospace Engineering; Aerospace Systems; Communication Engineering; Computer Engineering; E-Commerce Engineering (Subject to approval); Electronic Engineering; Environmental Materials Engineering; Internet Computing; Materials and Mechanical Engineering; Materials Engineering in Medicine; Mechanical Engineering; Mechanical Engineering Systems; Medical Engineering
MSci Hons: *4 yrs* Astronomy; Astrophysics; Chemistry; Computer Science (Subject to approval); Instrumentation Physics; Mathematics; Mathematics with Astrophysics or Statistics; Mathematics (Europe); Pharmaceutical Chemistry; Physics; Physics with Medical Physics; Physics & Electronics; Theoretical Physics

Diplomas

Postgraduate Diploma: *1 yr FT/2 yrs PT* Astrophysics; Banking Law; Clinical Drug Development; Clinical Microbiology; Commercial Arbitration; Computer Law; Copyright Law; EC External Market Law; EC Internal Market Law; Emerging Market Law; Gastroenterology; Health Care Research Methods; Intellectual Property Licensing Law; International Commercial Arbitration Law; International Tax Law; Medical Electronics & Medical Equipment Management; Occupational Therapy; Patent Law; Primary Care; Radiation Physics; Sports Medicine; Telecommunications Law; Trade Mark Law

Certificates

Certificate: *1 yr FT* Astronomy and Astrophysics (Subject to approval); Economics; Intellectual Property Law; Mathematics, Astronomy & Computing; Primary Health Care Management
LLM: *1 yr FT/2 yrs PT* Law

UNIVERSITY OF LONDON

Royal Holloway

Egham, Surrey TW20 0EX Tel: 01784 443979 Fax: 01784 471381 e-mail: liaison-office@rhbnc.ac.uk
Website: www.rhbnc.ac.uk

First Degrees

ARTS

BA Hons: *3 yrs* Ancient & Medieval History; Ancient History; Classical Studies; Classical Studies-Drama; Classical Studies-English or Drama or Latin; Classics; Drama & Theatre Studies; Drama-Music; Economics with French or German or Italian or Japanese Studies or Management or Mathematics or Music or Political Studies or Social Policy or Sociology or Spanish; English Language & Literature; French-Classical Studies or Drama or German or Greek or History or Italian or Latin or Management or Music or Spanish; Geography; Greek; History with Spanish or Japanese Studies; History; History with yr in Europe; Latin; Mathematics-Music; Media Arts; Modern History & Economic History & Politics; Music with French or German or Italian or Japanese Studies or Management Studies or Mathematics or Political Studies or Social Policy or Spanish; Music-Psychology; Politics; Politics-Economics; Social Policy; Social Policy-Politics; Sociology; Sociology with Management or Management or Mathematics or Politics; Sociology-Economics or Social Policy; Sociology-Politics or Social Policy or Economics or Management *4 yrs* English-French or German or Italian or Spanish; European Studies; French with Economics or German or Italian or Management Studies or Mathematics or Music or Political Studies or Social Policy or Sociology or Spanish; French; French-Classical Studies or Drama or German or Greek or Spanish or History or Italian or Latin or Management Studies or Music; German with Economics or French or Italian or Management or History or Japanese Studies or Mathematics or Music or Political Studies or Social Policy or Sociology or Spanish; German; German-Classical Studies or Greek or Italian or History or Latin or Management or Music or Spanish; German-Classical Studies or Drama or Greek or History or Italian or Spanish or Latin or Management; Music; History with a Yr in Europe; International Theatre (France); Italian with Economics or French or German or Management or Mathematics or Music or Political Studies or Social Policy or Sociology or Spanish; Italian; Italian-Management or Music or Spanish; Spanish-History
BMus Hons: *3 yrs* Music
BSc (Econ) Hons: *3 yrs* Economics; Financial & Business Economics; Political Economy

SCIENCE & TECHNOLOGY

BSc Hons: *3 yrs* Applied Physics; Biochemistry; Biochemistry or Psychology with Physiology; Biochemistry (Biotechnology); Biochemistry for Management; Biology with Management; Biology; Botany (Plant Biology); Cognitive Science or Artificial Intelligence or Computer Architecture & Design or Safety Critical Systems; Computer Science with French or Management;

Computer Science; Computer Science-Mathematics or Physics; Environmental Biology; Environmental Geology; Geography; Geography-Geology or Mathematics; Geology; Geology-Astrophysics or Biology or Computing or Mathematics; Information Systems-Management or Spanish or Economics; Management with French or German or Italian or Japanese Studies or Mathematics or Social Policy or Spanish; Management; Management-Information Systems; Mathematics with Economics & Management or Economics or French or German or Italian or Management or Operational Research or Spanish or Statistics; Mathematics; Mathematics-Management or Music or Physics or Psychology; Medical Biochemistry; Modern History, Economic History & Politics with a Yr in Europe; Molecular Biology & Genetics; Physics; Physics with Astrophysics or Music; Physics for Management; Plant Science; Psychology; Science & the Media (Biological Sciences; Geology; Physics pathways); Theoretical Physics; Zoology with Physiology; Zoology

Higher Degrees

MA: *1 yr FT/2 yrs PT* Ancient History; Classics; Cultural Geography; Documentary by Practice; Drama & Theatre Studies; European Business; European Literary & Cultural Studies; Feature Film Screenwriting; Film & Television; Gender and Sexuality; Geography of Third World Development; German; Greek Theatre Performance; Hellenic Studies; Late Antique & Byzantine Studies; Material Culture; Medieval Studies; Modern History: Power, Culture, Society; Modernism & Modern Writers; Physical Theatre; Postmodernism, Literature & Contemporary Culture; Producing Film & Television; Renaissance & Early Modern Europe; Research (Drama & Theatre); Shakespeare; The Politics of Democracy; Victorian Art & Architecture; Victorian Culture and Media; Women's History: Gender & Society in Britain & Europe, 1500-1988
MBA: *1 yr FT* International Management
MMus: *1 yr FT/2 yrs PT* Advanced Musical Studies (Pathways in: Historical Musicology; Theory & Analysis; Performance; Performance Studies; Composition)
MSc: *1 yr FT/2 yrs PT* Analysis in the Chemical Sciences; Basin Evolution & Dynamics; Business Information Systems; Computer Science by Research; Discrete Mathematics & Computing Applications; Economics; Environmental Analysis & Assessment; Financial & Industrial Economics; Geography of Third World Development; Information Security; Mathematics; Medical Sociology; Nanophysics & Low Temperature Physics; Particle Physics; Physics Research; Political Economy; Public Sector Studies; Quaternary Science; Research in Analytical Chemistry; Safety Critical Systems; Secure Electronic Commerce; Social Work; Tectonics

SCIENCE & TECHNOLOGY
MSci: *4 yrs* Applied Physics; Astrophysics; Environmental Geoscience; Geoscience with a Yr in North America; Geoscience; Mathematics; Physics; Physics with a Yr in Europe; Theoretical Physics

Diplomas

Postgraduate Diploma: *1 yr* Geology; Information Security; Psychology; Social Studies; The Politics of Democracy; Victorian Art & Architecture

UNIVERSITY OF LONDON
Royal Veterinary College

Royal College Street, London NW1 0TU Tel: 020 7468 5000 Fax: 020 7388 2342
Website: www.rvc.ac.uk

First Degrees

BVetMed: *5 yrs FT* Veterinary Medicine

Higher Degrees

MSc: *1 yr* Veterinary Microbiology; Veterinary Pathology; Wild Animal Health

UNIVERSITY OF LONDON
School of Oriental & African Studies

Thornhaugh Street, Russell Square, London WC1H 0XG Tel: 020 7637 2388 Fax: 020 7436 4211
e-mail: study@soas.ac.uk Website: www.soas.ac.uk

First Degrees

BA Hons: *3 yrs* African Studies or Development Studies; African Studies or Economics or Geography; Art & Archaeology or Social Anthropology or History or Linguistics or History of Art/Archaeology (Asia, Africa) or Study of Religions or Music or Politics or South Asian Studies; Ancient Near Eastern Languages; Ancient Near Eastern Studies; Bengali-Development Studies or Economics or Geography or History or History of Art/Archaeology or Law or Management or Music or Politics or Social Anthropology or Study of Religions; Chinese (Modern & Classical); Chinese-Comparative Religion; Geography or Gujarati or Urdu or South Asian Studies or Tamil or Tibetan; Georgian-Development Studies or Economics or Geography or History or History of Art/Archaeology or Law or Linguistics or Management or Music or Persian or Politics or Social Anthropology or Study of Religions; History; History of Art (Asia, Africa, Europe); History of Art/Archaeology (Asia, Africa); Law or Development Studies or Economics or Geography or History or Linguistics or Music or Politics; South Asian Studies; Music Studies; Persian; Politics; Sanskrit-Economics or Geography or History or History of Art/Archaeology or Law or Music or Social Anthropology or Study of Religions; Social Anthropology; South East Asian Studies *3-4 yrs* Dutch-Indonesian; Economics-Hindi or Indonesian or Thai; Geography-Hindi or Indonesian or Thai or Urdu or Management or Persian; Hindi-Development Studies or Economics or Geography or History or History of Art/Archaeology or Law or Indonesian or Thai or Music or Politics or Social Anthropology or Study of Religions or History or Law or Music or Politics or Social Anthropology; History of Art/Archaeology (Asia, Africa)-Hindi or Indonesian or Thai *4 yrs* African Language & Culture; Ancient Near Eastern Languages; Arabic; Arabic-Amharic or Development Studies or Economics or Geography or History or History of Art/Archaeology or Law or Linguistics or Management or Music or Politics or Social Anthropology or Study of Religions; Burmese-Development Studies or Economics or Geography or History or History of Art/Archaeology or Law or Management or Music or Politics or Social Anthropology or Study of Religions; Chinese-Development Studies or Economics or Geography or History or History of Art/Archaeology or Indonesian or Korean or Law or Management or Music or Politics or Social Anthropology or Study of Religions or Thai or Georgian or Hebrew or Turkish or Israeli Studies or Persian or Urdu; Hausa-Arabic or Development Studies or Economics or Geography or History or History of Art/Archaeology or Law or Management or Music or Politics or Social Anthropology or Study of Religions; Hindi; Indonesian; Japanese; Korean; Study of Religions-Swahili or Turkish or Vietnamese or Amharic or Arabic or Burmese or Chinese or Gujarati or Hausa or Hebrew or Japanese or Korean or Vietnamese; Swahili-Development Studies or Economics or Geography or History or Law or Music or Politics or Social Anthropology or Study of Religions; Thai; Thai-Japanese; Turkish
BSc: *3 yrs* Development Economics; Economics
LLB: *3 yrs* Law

Higher Degrees

LLM: *1 yr FT/2 yrs PT* Law
MA: *1 yr FT/2 yrs PT* African Language; African Literature; African Studies; African/Asian History; Ancient Near Eastern Languages; Anthropology of Media; Applied Japanese Linguistics; Arabic; Chinese Studies; Comparative Literature (Africa/Asia); East Asian Literature; Eastern Christianity &/or African Christianity; English-Arabic Applied Linguistics & Translation; Environment & Development; History & Culture of Medicine; History of Art &/or Archaeology; Indian Religions; International and Comparative Legal Studies; International Boundary Studies; International Studies & Diplomacy; Islamic Societies & Cultures; Islamic Studies; Japanese Linguistics; Japanese Religions; Japanese Studies; Korean Studies; Language in Africa with Linguistics; Languages and Literatures of South East Asia; Linguistics; Medical Anthropology; Modern Turkish Studies; Near and Middle Eastern Studies; Oriental & African Religions; Pacific

Asian Studies; Popular World Cinema; Religious, Fine and Decorative Arts of South Asia; Sinology; Social Anthropology; Social Anthropology of Development; South Asian Area Studies; South East Asian Studies; The Chinese Business World; The South East Asian Business World; Turkish; Yiddish Studies
MMus: *1 yr FT/2 yrs PT* Ethnomusicology
MSc: *1 yr FT/2 yrs PT* African Politics; Asian Politics; Central Asian Politics; Development Economics; Development Studies; Development Studies; Development Studies with special reference to Central Asia; Economics with reference to Africa; Economics with reference to Africa; Economics with reference to South Asia; Economics with reference to the Asia Pacific Region; Economics with reference to the Middle East; International Politics; Middle East Politics; Political Economy of Development; Politics of Asia and Africa; State, Society & Development; Theory & Method in the Study of Politics; Tourism, Environment & Development

Diplomas
Foundation Diploma: *1 yr FT* Postgraduate Studies
Postgraduate Diploma: *1 yr FT* Asian Arts; Economics *1 yr FT/2 yrs PT* International Studies & Diplomacy; Language in Africa with Linguistics; The Chinese Business World; The South East Asian Business World

UNIVERSITY OF LONDON
The School of Pharmacy
29-39 Brunswick Square, London WC1N 1AX Tel: 020 7753 5831 Fax: 020 7753 5829
e-mail: registry@cua.ulsop.ac.uk Website: www.ulsop.ac.uk

Higher Degrees
MPharm Hons: *4 yrs* Pharmacy
MSc: *12 mths FT* Clinical Pharmacy; Clinical Pharmacy, International Practice & Policy; International Practice & Policy *24 mths PT* Pharmacy Practice (Modular)

Diplomas
Diploma: *10 mths PT* Medicines in Health Care *12 mths PT* Pharmacy Practice (Modular)

UNIVERSITY OF LONDON
University College (UCL)
Gower Street, London WC1E 6BT Tel: 020 7679 2000 (switchboard); 020 7679 3000 (degree enquiries) Fax: 020 7679 3001
e-mail: degree-info@ucl.ac.uk (degree enquiries) Website: www.ucl.ac.uk

First Degrees
ARTS
BA Hons: *3 yrs FT* Ancient History; Ancient History-Egyptology or Social Anthropology; Ancient World Studies; Anthropology-Geography; Archaeology (Egyptian); Archaeology (General); Archaeology (Medieval)*; Archaeology (Western Asia); Archaeology-History of Art; Classics; Contemporary East European Studies; Economics-Business with East European Studies; English*; Geography; Greek (with Latin); History; History-History of Art; History of Art with Material Studies; History of Art; Latin (with Greek); Linguistics; Philosophy*; Philosophy-Economics or Greek or History of Art*; Politics and East European Studies; Viking Studies* *4 yrs FT* Archaeology, Classics and Classical Art; Bulgarian and East European Studies; Czech (with Slovak) and East European Studies; Dutch; Dutch with Management Studies; Dutch-French or German or History of Art or Italian or Scandinavian Studies or Spanish; East European Studies; English-German; Fine Art*; Finnish and East European Studies; French; French and Scandinavian Studies or German or History of Art or Italian or Philosophy or Spanish or Dutch or an Asian or

African Language; German; German with Management Studies; German-History of Art or Italian or Dutch or French or English or History or Jewish Studies or Scandinavian Studies; Hebrew; Hispanic Studies; History of Art-Spanish or Dutch or French or German or Italian or Philosophy; History with a European Language; Hungarian and East European Studies; Icelandic; Italian; Italian and Jewish Studies; Jewish History; Modern European Studies; Modern Iberian & Latin American Regional Studies; Polish-East European Studies; Romanian-East European Studies; Russian with an East European Language; Russian-an East European Language; Russian-French; Russian-German; Russian-History; Russian Studies; Scandinavian Studies; Scandinavian Studies with Management Studies; Serbian/Croatian-East European Studies; Slovak (with Czech)-East European Studies; Ukrainian and East European Studies

ECONOMICS
BSc (Econ) Hons: *3 yrs* Economics; Economics-Geography or Statistics

LAW
LLB Hons: *3 yrs* Law *4 yrs* Law with Advanced Studies or French Law or German Law or Italian Law or Hispanic Law

MEDICINE
MBBS: Medicine (5 or 6 yrs dependent upon qualification on entry)

SCIENCE & TECHNOLOGY
BEng Hons: *3 yrs* Biochemical Engineering; Chemical Engineering; Civil & Environmental Engineering; Civil Engineering; Electronic & Electrical Engineering; Engineering with Business Finance; Mechanical Engineering; Mechanical Engineering with Bioengineering; Naval Architecture & Marine Engineering; Structural Engineering *4 yrs* Civil Engineering
BSc Hons: *3 yrs* Anatomy & Developmental Biology; Anthropology; Anthropology-Geography; Applied Physics; Archaeology (General); Architecture; Astronomy; Astronomy-Mathematics or Physics; Astrophysics; Biochemistry; Biology; Biotechnology; Cell Biology; Chemical Physics; Chemistry with a European Language or Management Studies or Mathematics; Chemistry; Computer Science; Computer Science with Electronic Engineering or Mathematics; Construction Management; Earth & Space Science; Environmental Geography; Environmental Geophysics; Environmental Geoscience; Exploration Geophysics; Genetics; Geography; Geology; Geophysics; History & Philosophy of Science; History & Philosophy of Physics; History, Philosophy & Social Studies of Science; Human Genetics; Human Sciences; Immunology; Information Management; Mathematics; Mathematics with Economics or a European Language or Management Studies or Theoretical Physics; Mathematics-Physics or Astronomy or Computer Science or Statistical Science; Medicinal Chemistry; Molecular Biology; Neuroscience; Palaeobiology; Pharmacology; Physical Sciences; Physics; Physics with Space Science or Medical Physics; Physiology; Physiology-Pharmacology; Planetary Science; Podiatry; Psychology; Science Communication & Policy; Speech Communication; Statistics; Statistics with a European Language; Statistics & Operational Research with Management Studies; Statistics, Computing, Operational Research & Economics (SCORE); Statistics, Operational Research, Economics & a European Language; Theoretical Physics; Town & Country Planning *4 yrs* Speech Sciences

Higher Degrees
DClinPsy: *3 yrs FT* Clinical Psychology
DEdPsy: *3 yrs FT/6 yrs PT* Educational Psychology
DPsy: *3 yrs FT/6 yrs PT* Child and Adolescent Psychoanalytic Psychotherapy
LLM: *1 yr FT/2 yrs PT* Law
MA: *1 yr FT* Area Studies (Latin America); Records & Archives Management (International); Research Methods for the Humanities *1 yr FT/2 yrs PT* Ancient History; Anthropology of Art & Visual Culture; Archaeology; Central and East European Studies; Classics; Comparative Art & Archaeology; Comparative Literature; Cultural Heritage Studies; Dutch Studies (Modern); Economics; Egyptian Archaeology; Electronic Communication & Publishing; English Language (Modern); English: Issues in Modern Culture; English: Renaissance to Enlightenment; Field & Analytical Techniques in Archaeology; French & Theory of Literature; German; German Studies;

Hebrew-Jewish Studies; Hispanic Studies; History; History & Culture of the Dutch Golden Age; History (Modern); History of Art; Holocaust Studies; Italian Studies; Legal & Political Theory; Library & Information Studies; Linguistics; Material Culture; Medieval Studies; Museum Anthropology; Museum Studies; Nationalism and Identity; Philosophy; Phonetics; Politics, Security and Integration; Public Archaeology; Romance Languages & Literatures (Italian); Romance Languages & Literatures (Spanish); Russian-East European Literature & Culture; Russian Studies; Scandinavian Studies (Medieval & West Norse); Scandinavian Studies (Modern); Social Dynamics of Eastern Europe and Russia *1 yr FT/2-5 yrs PT* Archives & Records Management *2 yrs FT* Fine Art

MArch: *1 yr FT* Architectural Design

MEng Hons: *4 yrs* Biochemical with Chemical Engineering; Biochemical Engineering; Biochemical Engineering with Study Abroad; Chemical Engineering with Biochemical Engineering; Chemical Engineering; Chemical Engineering with Study Abroad; Civil Engineering; Civil with Environmental Engineering; Electronic & Electrical Engineering for Europe; Electronic & Electrical Engineering; Electronic Engineering with Management Studies; Electronic Engineering with Communications Engineering or Medical Electronics; Electronic Engineering with Computer Science or Optoelectronics; Engineering with Business Finance; Mechanical Engineering with Bioengineering; Mechanical Engineering; Naval Architecture-Marine Engineering

MFA: *2 yrs FT* Fine Art

MPhil/PhD: *3 yrs FT/Equivalent PT* Anatomy & Developmental Biology; Anthropology; Archaeology; Architecture; Archive Studies; Astronomy; Bacteriology; Biochemical Engineering; Biochemistry; Biology; Biomedicine; Building; Chemical Engineering; Chemistry; Child Health; Civil Engineering; Classics; Computer Science; Dental Public Health/Dentistry; Development Planning; Dutch; Economics; Egyptology Electronic & Electrical Engineering; English; Environmental Design; Environmental Engineering; Environmental Studies; Epidemiology & Public Health; Fine Art; French; Geography; Geological Sciences; German; Haematology; Hebrew & Jewish Studies; Higher Education Development; Histopathology; History; History of Art; History of Medicine; Human Communication Sciences; Immunology; Instrumentation; Italian; Laryngology & Otology; Law; Library & Information Studies; Linguistics; Mathematics; Mechanical Engineering; Medical Physics; Medicine; Molecular Biology; Molecular Endocrinology; Molecular Pathology; Neurology; Nuclear Medicine; Obstetrics & Gynaecology; Oncology; Ophthalmology; Orthopaedics; Paediatrics; Pathology; Pharmacology; Philosophy; Phonetics; Photogrammetry; Physics; Physiology; Planning; Primary Health Care; Psychiatry; Psychology; Scandinavian Studies; Science & Technology Studies; Sexually Transmitted Diseases; Slavonic and East European Studies; Space & Climate Physics; Spanish & Latin American Studies; Statistical Science; Surgery; Surveying; Town & Country Planning; Urology; Virology

MRes: *1 yr FT* Advanced Instrumentation Systems; Computer Vision, Image Processing, Graphics & Simulation; Telecommunications *2 yrs PT* Library Archive & Information Studies

MSc: *1 yr FT* Biochemical Engineering; Clinical Neuroscience; Computer Science; Conservation; Data Communications Networks & Distributed Systems; Economics; Environmental & Resource Economics; European Medical Physics; Hydrographic Surveying; Information Technology; Marine Engineering; Mechanical Engineering; Micropalaeontology; Modernity, Space & Place; Naval Architecture; Ocean & Subsea Engineering; Public Understanding of Environmental Change; Space Science; Surgical Science; Vision, Imaging & Virtual Environments *1 yr FT/2 yrs PT* Anthropology & Ecology of Development; Archaeology; Audiological Science; Chemical Process Engineering; Chemical Research; Community Paediatrics; Dental Public Health; Educational Psychology; Ergonomics; Forensic Archaeological Science; Health Psychology; History of Science, Medicine & Technology; Human Communication; Human Evolution & Behaviour; Hydrogeology; Medical Anthropology; Microwaves & Optoelectronics; Molecular Pathology; Non-Linear Dynamics & Chaos; Orthopaedics; Principles of Conservation; Psychoanalytic Development Psychology; Public Policy; Radiation Physics: Industrial Applications or Medical Applications; Refrigeration & Air Conditioning; Research Methods in Psychology; Social Anthropology; Spacecraft Technology & Satellite Communications; Statistics: Applied Stochastic Systems; Theoretical Psychoanalytic Studies *1 yr FT/2 yrs PT/3 yrs PT* Geographic Information Science; Remote Sensing; Transport *1 yr FT/2-5 yrs PT* Community Eye Health; Health Informatics; Information Science; Molecular Medicine; Prenatal Genetics & Fetal Medicine; Sexually Transmitted Infections and HIV *1 yr FT/2-5 yrs PT/Modular* Audiological Medicine; Bioprocessing;

Community Disability Studies in Developing Countries; Cosmopolitan Development; Defence Systems Engineering; Development-Planning (including: Building-Urban Design in Development, Cosmopolitan Development, Development Administration-Planning, Development-Planning (profiled learning), Economics of Urbanisation-Managing the City Economy, Environment-Sustainable Development, European Property Development-Planning, International Housing Studies, Social Development Practice, Urban Development Planning); Photogrammetry with Remote Sensing; Renal Science (Modular degree programme leading to MSc in Renal Science); Surveying; Systems Engineering; Telecommunications *15 mths FT/2-5 yrs PT/Modular* Mother & Child Health *2 yrs FT only* Ageing & Mental Health; Conservation for Archaeology & Museums *2 yrs PT* Applied Hypnosis; Clinical Biochemistry; Clinical Paediatrics; Musculo-Skeletal & Osteopathic Medicine; Sociology, Health & Health Care; Urology *2-5 yrs PT/Modular* Technical Audiology *25 mths FT* Speech & Language Pathology & Therapy *3 yrs PT* Psychiatric Theory & Research

MSci Hons: *4 yrs FT* Applied Physics; Astronomy; Astronomy-Mathematics or Physics; Astrophysics; Chemical Physics; Chemistry with a European Language or Management Studies or Mathematics; Chemistry; Computer Science with Electronic Engineering or Mathematics; Computer Science; Earth & Space Science; Environmental Geophysics; Environmental Geoscience; Exploration Geophysics; Geology; Geophysics; Mathematics; Mathematics with Economics or a European Language or Management Studies or Theoretical Physics; Mathematics-Physics or Astronomy or Computer Science or Statistics; Medical Physics; Medicinal Chemistry; Palaeobiology; Physical Sciences; Physics; Physics with Space Science; Planetary Science; Theoretical Physics

Diplomas

Diploma: *1 yr FT* Architecture; Biochemical Engineering; Built Environment; Chemical Engineering; Information Technology; Linguistics; Marine Engineering; Mechanical Engineering; Mother & Child Health; Naval Architecture; Ocean & Subsea Engineering; Paediatric Gastroenterology; Phonetics; Photogrammetry; Records & Archives Management (International); Shipping Law; Space Science; Surveying; Systematic Reviews Methodology; Teaching Biomedical Sciences; Town & Country Planning; Travel Health & Medicine *1 yr FT/2 yrs PT* Antiquarian Bookselling; Archives & Records Management; Bioprocessing; Community Dental Health; Computer Science; Ergonomics; Forensic Psychotherapeutic Studies; Geographic Information Science; Hydrogeology; Information Science; International Law; Library & Information Studies; Microwaves & Optoelectronics; Molecular Pathology; Radiation Physics; Refrigeration & Air Conditioning; Remote Sensing; Sexually Transmitted Infections & HIV; Spacecraft Technology & Satellite Communications; Statistics *1 yr FT/2-5 yrs PT* Molecular Medicine *1 yr PT* Applied Hypnosis; Clinical Hypnosis *11 mths FT/22 mths PT* Urology *13 mths FT* Cognitive Behavioural Psychotherapy *2 yrs PT* Higher Education Research & Development; Technical Audiology *22 mths FT* Speech and Language Pathology and Therapy *6 mths FT* Clinical Neurology; Community Eye Health *9 mths FT* Fine Art

Certificates

Certificate: *1 yr FT* Archives & Records Management *1 yr FT/2-5 yrs PT* Molecular Medicine *1 yr PT* Biotransformation Bioprocessing; Downstream Processing; Fermentation Bioprocessing; Principles of Bioprocessing *12 mths FT* Professional Practice and Management in Architecture (RIBA(3) *3 mths FT* Community Eye Health; Development Planning; Planning for Eye Care; Records & Archives Management (International) *4 mths FT* Air Survey Photography

LOUGHBOROUGH UNIVERSITY

Academic Registry, Loughborough, Leicestershire LE11 3TU Tel: 01509 263171 Fax: 01509 223905 e-mail: prospectus-enquiries@lboro.ac.uk Website: www.info.lboro.ac.uk/home.html

First Degrees

All undergraduate courses are only available as Honours degree courses. Sandwich courses lead to the award of the appropriate degree and a supplementary Diploma in Industrial Studies (DIS) or Diploma in Professional Studies (DPS) is awarded for satisfactory completion of integrated or professional training where appropriate. A range of one-yr foundation studies programmes offers progression to a range of science and engineering degrees to candidates who do not have qualifications in appropriate subjects.* Four-yr and ** five-yr versions of these courses lead to the additional award of DIS; *** four-yr versions of these courses lead to the additional award of DPS; **** only available as a four-yr course leading to the additional award of Certificate of Education.

First Degrees

BA: *3-4 yrs* Drama; Drama with English; English; English & History of Art & Design; English & Physical Education & Sports Science; French & German Studies; French & Politics; French-German or Politics; German & Politics; Industrial Design & Packaging Technology; Industrial Design & Technology; Industrial Design & Technology with Education or Social Sciences; Information & Library Studies-Education or English or French or Geography or German or Spanish; International Business; Library & Information Studies; Modern European Studies; Politics; Politics with Economics or Sociology or Social Psychology or Social Policy or Geography or English or Communication & Media Studies with English; Publishing

BA Hons: Fine Art (Painting); Fine Art (Printmaking); Fine Art (Sculpture); Graphic Communication; History of Art and Design with Studio Practice; Illustration; Textile Design (Multi-Media Textiles); Textile Design (Woven Textiles); Three Dimensional Design (Ceramics); Three Dimensional Design (Furniture); Three Dimensional Design (Silversmithing and Jewellery) *3 yrs Joint Honours:* English-History of Art and Design *3-4 yrs PT/6 yrs PT* Textile Design (Printed Textiles)

BEng: *3-4 yrs* Aeronautical Engineering; Automotive Engineering; Automotive Materials; Chemical Engineering; Chemical Engineering with Environmental Protection; Civil Engineering; Electronic & Computer Systems Engineering; Electronic & Electrical Engineering; Engineering Science & Technology; Manufacturing Engineering & Management; Materials Engineering; Materials with Management; Mathematical Engineering; Mechanical Engineering; Product Design & Manufacture; Systems Engineering

BSc: *3-4 yrs* Accounting & Financial Management; Air Transport Management; Architectural Engineering & Design Management; Banking, Finance & Management; Business Economics & Finance; Business Studies (Peterborough); Chemistry; Chemistry with Materials or Analytical Chemistry or Environmental Science; Chemistry with Forensic Analysis; Chemistry with European Language; Commercial Management & Quantity Surveying; Communication & Media Studies; Computer Science; Computing & Management; Construction Engineering Management; Economics with Accounting or French or German or Geography or Politics or Sociology or Social Policy or Spanish; Economics; Engineering Physics; Ergonomics (Applied Human Sciences); Geography; Geography & Physical Education & Sports Science; Geography with Economics; Human Biology; Industrial Design & Packaging Technology; Industrial Design & Technology with Education; Industrial Design & Technology; Information Management & Business Studies; Information Management and Business Studies; Information Management and Computing; International Business; International Economics; Library & Information Management; Logistics; Management Sciences; Mathematics or PE & Sports Science; Mathematics with Economics or Management; Mathematics & Accounting and Financial Management; Mathematics & Accounting and Financial Management; Mathematics & Computing; Mathematics & Education; Medicinal & Pharmaceutical Chemistry; Physical Education & Sports Science; Physical Education & Sports Science-Chemistry; Physical Education, Sports Science & Recreation Management with Management; Physics with PE & Sports Science; Physics; Physics; Physics & Computing; Physics & Mathematics; Psychology; Psychology with Ergonomics; Publishing with English; Recreation Management; Recreation Management-Geography; Retail Management; Retail Management (Automotive); Social Policy; Social Psychology; Sociology; Sports Technology; Transport Management & Planning

Higher Degrees

MA/MBA/MSc: *1 yr FT/2-8 yrs PT* Advanced Process Engineering; Airport Planning & Management; Analytical Chemistry & Instrumentation; Analytical Science; Art & Education; Automotive Systems Engineering; Automotive Systems Engineering; Back Care Management; Banking-Finance; Building Services Engineering; Business Administration; Computer Integrated Manufacture; Computing; Construction Management; Construction Project Management;

Contemporary European Studies; Criminal Justice Studies; Criminology & Criminal Justice; Design of Mechatronics Products; Design Studies; Design, Arts & Crafts Practice; Digital Communication Systems; Economics-Finance; Education; Electrical Power Generation; Engineering Design; Engineering Design & Manufacture; Engineering Management; Environmental Studies; Ergonomics; European Leisure Studies; Exercise Physiology; Financial Economics; Healthcare Risk Management; Industrial Mathematical Modelling; Information & Library Studies; Information Studies; Information Technology; Innovative Construction; International Banking; International Economics & Finance; Management; Manufacturing Management; Materials Engineering; Mathematical Education; Mechanical & Electrical Project Management; Mechatronics & Optical Engineering; Medicinal Chemistry & Drug Metabolism; Modern & Contemporary Writing; Monetary Economics; Multi-media & Internet Computing; Occupational Health & Safety Management; Packaging Technology; Physical Education; Planning & Management of Urban Services; Policy, Organisation & Change in Professional Care; Polymer Technology; Postgraduate Certificate in Education; Recreation Management; Renewable Energy Systems Technology; Security Management; Sport & Leisure Management; Sports Science; Surface Design & Engineering; Teaching Art & Design in Further & Adult Education; Technology & Management for Rural Development; Technology for Development; Theatre & the Representation of Gender; Urban Engineering; Urban Water Supply; Waste & Environmental Risk Management; Water & Environmental Management; Water & Waste Engineering; Women's Studies

MChem: *4-5 yrs* Chemistry; Chemistry with Materials or Analytical Chemistry

MComp: *4-5 yrs* Computer Science

MEng: *4-5 yrs* Aeronautical Engineering; Automotive Engineering; Automotive Materials; Chemical Engineering; Civil Engineering; Communications Engineering; Computer Network & Internet Engineering; Electronic & Electrical Engineering; Electronics & Software Engineering; Engineering Science & Technology; Engineering Science & Technology; Manufacturing Engineering & Management; Materials with Management Studies; Materials Engineering; Mechanical Engineering; Product Design & Manufacture; Systems Engineering; Transportation Electronics Engineering

MMath: *4-5 yrs* Mathematics

MPhil: (Awarded only for research)

MPhys: *4-5 yrs* Physics

PhD; DLitt; DSc; DTech: (The PhD is awarded after two yrs' minimum study by thesis and oral exam. The higher doctorates may be awarded to university members of some yrs' standing, on submission of original work)

Honorary Degrees

DLitt; DSc; DTech; MA; MSc; MTech

Diplomas

Diploma: Economics & Finance; Analytical Science; Combined Studies; Communication Systems; Computing; Design Studies; Digital Communication Studies; Education; Ergonomics; Hazardous Waste Management; Healthcare Risk Management; Human Factors in Information Technology; Information & Library Studies; Information Studies; Information Technology; Interactive Computing Systems Design; International Banking; Investigatory Management; Management; Materials Engineering; Modern & Contemporary Writing; Occupational Health & Safety Management; Packaging Technology; Polymer Technology; Research for Healthcare Professionals; Security Management; Surface Design & Engineering; Technical Laser Safety; Technical Management; Technology for Development

Certificates

BTEC: *1 yr FT/2 yrs PT* Art & Design Foundation Studies; Art & Design Foundation Studies

Certificate: Analytical Science; Back Care Management; Education; Education (Further Professional Studies); Healthcare Risk Management; Investigatory Management; Management; Occupational Health & Safety Management; Security Management; Technical Laser Safety; Technical Management; Technology for Development

UNIVERSITY OF LUTON

Park Square, Luton LU1 3JU Tel: 01582 734111 Fax: 01582 7486260
e-mail: admissions@luton.ac.ul Website: www.luton.ac.uk.

Please note: All degrees are modular.
* Subject to validation.

First Degrees

BA/BA Hons; BSc/BSc Hons: *3-4 yrs FT* American Studies; Applied Social Research; Applied Social Studies; Architectural Technology; Architecture; Artificial Intelligence; Biomedical Sciences; Building Surveying; Business Decision Management; Business Enterprise; Child and Adolescent Studies; Coaching Studies; Comparative Literature; Computer Aided Design & Manufacturing; Computer Applications; Computer Visualisation and Animation; Computing Interaction Design; Construction and Environmental Management; Contemporary English Language Studies; Creative Writing; Criminology; Drama Studies; Earth Science; English; Exercise Physiology; Facilities Management; Genetics; Geographical Information Systems; Health and Exercise Behaviour; Heritage Studies; History; Humanities; Immunology; Information Systems Networking; Interior Design; International Business and Culture; International Tourism Management; Internet and E-Business; Irish History; Media History; Microbiology; Nutrition; Organisational Behaviour; Physical Geography; Post-colonial Studies; Postmodern Social Studies; Product Engineering; Professional Communication; Public Policy & Management; Retail Management; Robotics; Social Science; Software Engineering; Sport and Fitness Management; Sports Therapy; Women's Health (Midwifery); Writing and Women *3-4 yrs FT modular* Accounting; Advertising-Marketing Communications; Applied Statistics; Biochemistry; Biology; Biotechnology; Black & South Asian Studies; British Studies; Building Surveying; Business Administration; Business Information Technology; Business Studies; Business Systems; Cartography; Communication System Design; Community Management; Comparative Literature; Computer Aided Design Technology; Computer Science; Computer System Engineering; Computing; Construction Management; Contemporary English Language Studies; Contemporary History; Criminology; Design & Build; Design & Manufacturing; Digital System Design; Ecology & Biodiversity; Economics-Policy; Educational Studies; Electronics; Engineering Product Development; English Literature; Environmental Geology; Environmental Management; Environmental Science; Epidemiology; European Language Studies (EFL); French; Geography; Geology; German; Graphic Design; Health Care; Health Science; Health Studies; History; Hospitality Management; Human Biochemistry; Human Biology; Human Geography; Human Resource Management; Information Systems Development; Intercultural Communication; International Marketing; Italian; Languages & Stylistics in English; Law; Leisure Management; Linguistics; LLB; Mapping Science; Marketing; Mathematical Sciences; Mathematics; Media Performance; Media Practice; Media Production; Media Technology; Midwifery; Modern English Studies; Modern History; Nursing; Organisational Behaviour; Pharmacology; Physical Geography; Plant Biology; Politics; Post-colonial Studies; Product Design; Psychology; Quantity Surveying; Retail Management; Robotics; Social Policy; Social Studies; Sociology; Software Engineering; Spanish; Sport & Exercise Science; Sport & Fitness Studies; Sport Tourism; Travel & Tourism; Women's Health; Women's Studies

Higher Degrees

MASTER'S DEGREES OR EQUIVALENT
DBA
Executive MBA
LLM
MA: (Subjects by arrangement with the University); Applied Linguistics; Applied Social Studies; Applied Translation; Digital Art; Education Management (International Summer School); Intercultural Communication; International Tourism, Planning and Environment; Management Studies; Media, Culture & Technology; Modern English Studies; Policy Studies; Research (Humanities); Sport and Leisure Management; Twentieth Century British History

MA/MSc: *FT/PT* Competitiveness; Computing and Information Technology; Design and Build; Ecotoxicology & Pollution Monitoring; Entrepreneurship & Business Management; Environmental Analysis; Exercise Science; Financial Aspects of Decision Management; Human Resources Management; Internet Technologies; Marketing; Marketing Management; Professional Practice (Healthcare); Psychological Approaches to Health; Psychology and Culture; Research & Evaluation for Practitioners in Health & Social Services; Research (Sciences); Scientific Technology; Software Engineering; Subject Leadership in Education; Tourism Management; Waste Management
MBA: Construction Project Management; Facilities Management; Financial Management; International Business; Marketing; Public Policy; Sport and Leisure Management; Technology; Tourism Management
MSc: Computer Applications; Entrepreneurship & Business Management; Health Psychology; Software Engineering *FT/PT* Artificial Intelligence; Business Decision Management

Diplomas

HND: *2 yrs FT* Advertising and Marketing Communications; Architectural Technology; Biology; Building Surveying; Business Decision Management; Business Information Technology; Business Studies; Computer Aided Design; Computing; Construction Management; Electronics; Engineering Product Development; Environmental Science; Geographical Information Systems; Geographical Techniques; Geology (Earth Science, Petroleum Geology); Graphic Design; Health & Social Studies; Health Science; Heritage & Historical Studies; Internet and E-Business; Leisure Management; Media Technology; Performing Arts; Public Administration; Public Services; Quantity Surveying; Robotics; Sport & Fitness Management; Sport Science; Travel & Tourism
HND/HNC: *2 yrs FT* Health with Social Studies; Motor Vehicle Engineering with Management

Professional Courses

Professional Courses: Assessors & Verifiers; English as a Foreign Language; Exercise Science; Institute of Linguists (French/German/Spanish/Italian); Institute of Personnel & Development Professional Qualification Scheme; Operating Department Practice; Nursing; Social Work; Teaching English as a Foreign Language; Training & Development; Youth & Community Studies

UNIVERSITY OF MANCHESTER INSTITUTE OF SCIENCE & TECHNOLOGY

Sackville St M60 1QD Tel: 0161 200 4034 Fax: 0161 200 8765
e-mail: nadine.broome@umist.ac.uk Website: www.umist.ac.uk
* Subject to approval.
** Compulsory subsidiary language: French, German, Japanese or Spanish.

First Degrees

BEng Hons: *3 yrs* Aerospace Engineering; Building Services Engineering; Chemical Engineering; Civil Engineering; Communication & Control Engineering with Industrial Experience; Communication & Control Engineering; Computer Systems Engineering; Computing and Communication Systems Engineering with Industrial Experience; Computing and Communication Systems Engineering; Electrical & Electronic Engineering with Industrial Experience; Electrical & Electronic Engineering; Electronic & Microelectronic Systems Engineering with Industrial Experience; Electronic & Microelectronic Systems Engineering; Electronic Engineering with Industrial Experience; Electronic Engineering; Manufacturing Systems Engineering; Mechanical Engineering; Mechanical Engineering with Design, Materials & Manufacture; Mechatronic Engineering; Mechatronic Engineering with Industrial Engineering; Software Engineering *4 yrs S* Computer Systems Engineering with Industrial Experience; Integrated Engineering; Software Engineering with Industrial Experience
BSc Hons: Biochemistry with Industrial Experience; Biological & Computational Science with Industrial Experience; Biological Science with Industrial Experience; Computation with Industrial Experience; Computing Science with Industrial Experience; Computing Science; Computation-Geography with Industrial Experience; Computation-Geography; Information Systems

Engineering with Industrial Experience; Physics with Industrial Experience; Textile Science & Technology with Industrial Experience *3 yrs* Analytical Chemistry; Artificial Intelligence; Biochemistry with Biotechnology with Industrial Experience; Biochemistry with Medical Biochemistry with Industrial Experience; Biochemistry with Medical Biochemistry; Biochemistry with Molecular Biochemistry with Industrial Experience; Biochemistry (Industrial Experience) with Molecular Biology (Industrial Experience) or Biotechnology (Industrial Experience); Biochemistry; Biological & Computational Science (Bioinformatics); Biological Science; Biomedical Materials Science; Chemical Physics; Chemistry with Polymer Science; Chemistry; Computation; Computer-Aided Chemistry; Construction Management; Environmental Chemistry; Information Systems Engineering; Management; Management (Accounting & Finance); Management (Decision Science); Management (Employment & Organisation); Management (Human Resources); Management (International Business Economics); Management (International Studies); Management (Marketing); Management (Operations Management & Technology); Mathematical Physics; Mathematics; Mathematics with Astrophysics; Mathematics, Statistics & Operational Research; Mathematics-Management; Medicinal Chemistry; Optometry; Paper Science; Paper Science with Industrial Experience; Physics or Theoretical Physics or Environmental Science; Physics with Astrophysics or Computational Physics or Optoelectronics; Textile Design & Design Management; Textile Technology & Management *4 yrs* Management-Chemical Sciences; Clothing Engineering & Management with A Modern Language; Clothing Engineering-Management; Computational Linguistics; Fashion & Textiles Retailing with Industrial Experience; Fashion & Textiles Retailing; French and German Language Studies; French Language Studies; German Language Studies; International Management with American Business Studies; Management & Marketing of Textiles or Industrial Experience; Management & Marketing of Textiles with A Modern Language; Management-Chemical Sciences with Industrial Experience; Management-Information Technology; Materials Science & Engineering; Paper Science with Management; Paper Science with Management & Industrial Experience; Quantity Surveying-Commercial Management; Textile Design & Design Management with A Modern Language; Textile Design & Design Management or Industrial Experience; Textile Science & Technology with Industrial Experience; Textile Science & Technology with Modern Language; Textile Science & Technology with a Modern Language or Industrial Experience; Textile Technology & Management with a Modern Language *4 yrs FT* Fashion & Textiles Retailing with A Modern Language *4 yrs S* German; International Management with French; Maths-Language Studies (German); Maths-Language Studies (French); Paper Science with A Modern Language

Higher Degrees

MChem Hons: *4 yrs FT* Analytical Chemistry; Chemical Physics or industrial placement; Chemistry with French or German or Spanish; Chemistry; Computer-Aided Chemistry; Environmental Chemistry; Medicinal Chemistry

MChem PST Hons: *4 yrs FT* Chemistry-Polymer Science & Technology

MEng Hons: *4 yrs FT* Aerospace Engineering; Biomedical Materials Science with Industrial Experience; Biomedical Materials Science; Chemical Engineering or industrial experience; Chemical Engineering with a Language; Civil & Structural Engineering; Civil Engineering; Civil Engineering with French or German or North American Studies; Civil Engineering (Enhanced Course); Communication & Control Engineering with Industrial Experience; Communication & Control Engineering; Communication Systems Engineering and Computing with Industrial Experience; Computer Systems Engineering; Computing-Communication Systems Engineering; Electrical & Electronic Engineering with French with Industrial Experience; Electrical & Electronic Engineering with Industrial Experience; Electrical & Electronic Engineering with French with Industrial Experience; Electrical & Electronic Engineering; Electrical & Electronic Engineering with French; Electronic & Microelectronic Systems Engineering with Industrial Experience; Electronic and Microelectronic Systems Engineering; Electronic Engineering with Industrial Experience; Electronic Engineering; Management-Environmental Engineering Design; Material Science with Business & Management; Materials Science & Engineering with Industrial Experience; Materials Science & Engineering; Materials Science & Engineering (Industrial Experience) or Material Science & Engineering (Ceramics) (Industrial Experience) or Engineering (Metals) (Industrial Experience) or Engineering (Polymers) (Industrial Experience); Materials

Science & Engineering (Ceramics or Metals or Polymers); Mechanical Engineering with Design, Materials & Manufacture; Mechanical Engineering; Mechanical Engineering, Manufacture & Management; Mechatronic Engineering with Industrial Experience; Mechatronic Engineering; Software Engineering

MLangEng: *4 yrs FT* Computational Linguistics

MMath Hons: *4 yrs FT* Mathematics

MNeuro Hons: *4 yrs FT* Neuroscience-Artificial Intelligence; Neuroscience-Molecular Cell Biology; Neuroscience-Computation

MOptom Hons: *4 yrs FT* Optometry

MPhil: *1-2 yrs by research according to qualifications (or 2-3 yrs PT in some cases):* Biomolecular Sciences; Building Engineering; Chemical Engineering; Chemistry; Civil & Construction Engineering; Computation; Computational Linguistics; Control Systems; Corrosion & Protection; Electrical Engineering & Electronics; Environmental Technology; Instrumentation & Analytical Science; Management; Manufacturing; Materials Science; Mathematics; Mechanical Engineering; Optometry & Neuroscience; Paper Science; Physics; Pollution Research; Process Integration; Structural Engineering; Textiles; Total Technology; Translation and Intercultural Studies

MPhys Hons: *4 yrs FT* Mathematical Physics; Physics (with study in Europe) with Astrophysics (with study in Europe) or Computational Physics; Physics or Environmental Science or Optoelectronics or study in Europe or Theoretical Physics; Physics with Industrial Experience; Physics; Physics with Astrophysics; with study in Europe

MRes: *1 yr* Biological Sciences

MSc: *1 yr* Accounting & Finance; Advanced Control; Advanced Engineering Materials; Advanced Manufacturing Technology & Systems Management; Biomolecular Archaeology; Bioreactor Systems; Biotechnology; Business Economics; Business Information Technology; Cereal Processing Technology; Communication Engineering; Computation; Computational Experimental Stress Analysis; Computer Assisted Language Instruction in French and / or German; Computer Systems Design; Computing Science; Corrosion Science & Engineering; Decision Technologies; Electrical Power Engineering; Electronic Commerce; Electronic Instrumentation Systems; Embedded Systems; Engineering Project Management; Environmental Biotechnology; Environmental Management & Technology; Finance; Geotechnical Engineering; Impact and Explosion Engineering; Information Management; Information Systems Engineering; Instrumentation & Analytical Science; International Business; International Construction Project Management; Investigative Ophthalmology & Vision Sciences; Machine Translation; Management & Implementation of Dev Projects; Managerial Psychology; Marketing; Mechanical Engineering Design; Metallic & Ceramic Materials; Multimedia Technology; Natural Language Processing; Numerical Analysis & Computing; Operations Management; Optometry & Vision Sciences; Organisational Psychology; Paper Science; Particle Accelerator Science & Technology; Personnel Management & Industrial Relations; Pharmaceutical Engineering; Physics of the Atmospheric Environment; Plasma Science & Technology; Polymer Science & Technology; Process Integration; Software Engineering & Information Engineering; Statistical Analysis & Stochastic Systems; Structural Engineering; Textile Design Technology & Design Management; Textile Technology; Thermal Power & Fluids Engineering; Translation studies

MTech Hons: *4 yrs FT* Fibre Processing-Product Design

PhD: *(6 modules + 6 modules in other Joint above L1) (or 2-3 yrs PT in some cases): 3-4 yrs by research* Total Technology*(or 2-3 yrs PT in some cases):* Biomolecular Sciences; Building Engineering; Chemical Engineering; Chemistry; Civil & Construction Engineering; Computation; Computational Linguistics; Control Systems; Corrosion & Protection; Electrical Engineering & Electronics; Environmental Technology; Instrumentation & Analytical Science; Management; Manufacturing; Materials Science; Mathematics; Mechanical Engineering; Optometry & Neuroscience; Paper Science; Physics; Pollution Research; Process Integration; Structural Engineering; Textiles; Translation and Intercultural Studies

MANCHESTER METROPOLITAN UNIVERSITY

All Saints, Manchester M15 6BH Tel: 0161 247 2000 Fax: 0161 247 6390
e-mail: enquiries@mmu.ac.uk Website: www.prospectus.mmu.ac.uk

† Subject to validation.
†† Validated by University of Manchester.

First Degrees

BA Hons: *1 yr DL* Clothing *1 yr FT* Business Administration (additional PT yr for Hons) *1 yr FT/2 yrs PT* Social Work Studies; Youth & Community Work Studies *2 yrs FT/3-4 yrs PT* Secondary Education *2 yrs PT* Practitioner Leadership *2-3 yrs PT* Business Studies *3 trms FT + 2 trms PT/4 trms FT* Business Management with Leisure *3 yrs FT* 3-Dimensional Design; Accounting & Finance; Applied Community Studies; Applied Social Studies; Applied Social Studies (by Independent Study); Architecture; Contemporary Crafts; Criminology-Sociology; Design & Art Direction; Embroidery; Fine Art; History; History of Art & Design; History of Film, Photography and Graphic Media; Human Communication; Illustration with Animation; Interactive Arts; Landscape Architecture; Mathematics; Photography; Politics; Sociology; Television Production; Textiles; Theatre Arts (Acting); Health Studies *3-5 yrs PT* Health Studies *3 yrs FT/4 yrs PT* Early Childhood Studies; Financial Services *3 yrs FT/4 yrs S* Consumer Protection; Financial Services (Conversion) *3 yrs FT/4-6 yrs PT* Contemporary Arts *3 yrs FT/5 yrs PT* Business Economics; Economics; Information and Library Management; International Economic Studies *3 yrs FT/6 yrs PT* Social Science *3 yrs FT/6-9 yrs PT* Combined Honours *3 yrs PT* Graphic Design *3-4 yrs FT/5 yrs PT* Humanities/Social Studies Programme *4 yrs FT* Economics with Spanish (with University of Murcia); Accounting & Finance in Europe; Business in Europe; Economics with French (with University of Bourgogne); Financial Economics with French (with University of Caen); International Studies in Social Science (with University of Caen); Modern Languages; Primary Education *4 yrs FT/4-6 yrs PT* Secondary Education *4 yrs S* Business (with overseas exchange); Fashion Design with Technology; Financial Services; Hospitality Management with Culinary Arts; Hospitality Management with Tourism; International Hospitality Management; Public Policy & Administration; Public Policy & Administration; Retail Marketing *5 yrs PT* International Economics Studies

BA/BA Hons: *1 yr 1 yr FT With additional yr for Hons:* Business Administration; Special Educational Needs *3 yrs FT* History of Film, Photography & Graphic Media *3 yrs FT/4-6 yrs PT* English Studies *3 yrs FT/6 yrs PT* Historical Studies

BA/BSc Hons: *3 yrs FT* Information & Communications

BA/HND: *3 yrs FT* Clothing Design and Technology

BEd: *2 yrs FT* Design & Technology *3 yrs FT* Mathematics

BEd Hons: *3 yrs FT* Mathematics Teaching (11-18)

BEng Hons: *3 yrs FT/4 yrs PT* Mechatronics *3 yrs FT/4 yrs S* Communication & Electronic Engineering; Computer & Electronic Engineering; Electrical & Electronic Engineering; Electronic Engineering with Management; Engineering (Communication & Electronic) or Engineering (Communication & Electronic) with study in Europe; Manufacturing Systems Engineering with Language (with language award available involving extra study yr); Mechanical Engineering; Mechatronics *3 yrs FT/4 yrs S/4 yrs PT* Engineering; Mechanical Engineering-Manufacturing Systems *3 yrs FT/4 yrs S/PTDE 4 yrs* Engineering; Manufacturing Systems & Engineering *4 yrs PT* Mechanical Engineering *4 yrs S* Engineering

BSc Hons: *1-2 yrs FT/2-4 yrs PT* Community Health; Osteopathy within Community Health *2 yrs FT/4 yrs PT* Nursing Studies *3 yrs FT* Biological Sciences; Management-Manufacturing Systems; Speech Pathology & Therapy; Sport, Coaching & Exercise Science *3 yrs FT/4-6 yrs mixed mode/6 yrs PT* Psychology *3 yrs FT/4-6 yrs PT/4 yrs S* Environmental Studies *3 yrs FT/4 yrs S* Consumed Product Sciences; Environmental Health; Food & Nutrition; Food Technology Management *3 yrs FT/5 yrs PT* Biomedical Science; Business Economics; Information Management *3 yrs FT/PT* Dental Technology *3-4 yrs FT/4 yrs S/4-6 yrs PT* Environmental Management; Environmental Science *3-4 yrs FT/4-6 yrs PT* Psychology *3-4 yrs PT* Applied Chemistry *3-4 yrs PT/4 yrs S* Applied Chemistry; Polymer Science & Technology *4 yrs FT* Chemical Science; Economics with French; Economics with French (with University of Bourgogne); Psychology-Speech Pathology *4 yrs S* Business Information Technology; Chemistry (with study in Europe); Clothing Product Development; Dental Technology with study in Industry; Food Technology; Garment Technology & Management†; Hospitality Management; International Fashion Marketing† *4-5 yrs PT/4 yrs S* Computing; Information Systems *6-9 yrs PT* Combined Honours

BSc/BSc Hons: *3 yrs FT* Speech Pathology & Therapy *3-4 yrs FT/4 yrs S* Chemistry *3 yrs FT/4 yrs S/4-6 yrs PT* Environment Management *3 yrs FT/5 yrs PT* Economics *3 yrs FT/6-9 yrs PT* Applicable Mathematics *4 yrs S* Dental Technology with study in Industry; Information Technology; Software Engineering *4-5 yrs PT/4 yrs S* Computing; Information Systems

LLB/LLB Hons: *3 yrs FT/4 yrs PT* Law *4 yrs FT* Law with French

COMBINED HONOURS SCHEME (MANCHESTER)
BSc/BSc Hons: *3 yrs FT* Biological Sciences; Chemistry *Combined Studies: choice of two subjects:* Applicable Mathematics; Biology; Business Economics; Business Mathematics; Chemistry; Computing Science; Economics; Environmental Studies; European Studies; Geography; Information Systems; Languages (French, German, Italian or Spanish); Psychology; Sociology *3 yrs FT/6 yrs PT* Materials Science *3 yrs FT/6-9 yrs PT* Applicable Mathematics; Business Mathematics; Computing Science; Economics; Environmental Studies; Geography; Multimedia Technology; Psychology *3 yrs FT/PT* Biology

HUMANITIES / SOCIAL STUDIES PROGRAMME (MANCHESTER)
BSc Hons: *3-4 yrs FT/5 yrs PT* English Studies; European Studies

Higher Degrees

MA: Education *1 yr FT* European Urban Cultures; Human Resource Management; Public Relations *1 yr FT/2 yrs PT* Art as Environment; Critical Theory; European Literature, Cultures & Society; European Philosophy; History; International Politics; Sociology *1 yr PT* Marketing Management; Retail Management *1-2 yrs PT* Social Work Studies *15 mths PT* Management *3 yrs PT* History of Art & Design; History of the Manchester Region; Teaching by Research *48 mths FT/96 wks PT* Textiles; Industrial Design; Interior Design; Communication Design; Fine Art
MBA: *2.5 yrs PT*
MChem: *3-4 yrs PT/4 yrs FT* Chemistry
MEd: *2 yrs PT*
MEng: *4 yrs FT* Electrical & Electronic Engineering *4 yrs FT/5 yrs S* Manufacturing Systems & Engineering; Mechanical Engineering
MEng Hons: *4 yrs FT/5 yrs S* Engineering
MPhil/PhD: (Available in many disciplines)
MSc: *1 yr FT* Clothing Manufacture; Clothing Marketing & Distribution (Distance Learning); Clothing Product Development; Clothing Science; Food Technology; International Fashion Marketing; Polymer Science & Technology *1 yr FT/2 yrs PT* Sport & Exercise Science *2 yrs PT* Management (by action learning and research) *2-5 yrs PT* Hospitality Management; Tourism Management *3 yrs PT* Business Information Technology
PgC/PgD/MSc: *2.5 yrs PT* Manufacturing Systems Engineering & Management (Integrated Graduate Development Scheme (IGDS))
PgC/PgD/MSc by Research: *1 yr FT* Analytical Chemistry; Applicable Mathematics; Artificial Intelligence / Computing / Information Systems; Environmental Protection & Safety; Information Systems; Mathematical Modelling; Multimedia Systems; Polymer Engineering & Technology; Public Health & Risk Management *1 yr FT/3 yrs PT* Computing; Countryside Management; Design & Manufacture *12 mths FT/30 mths PT* Biomedical Science *2-3 yrs* Behavioural Ecology *2-3 yrs PT* Conservation Biology; Stress Management for Practitioners
PgD/MSc: *1 yr FT/2 yrs PT* Applied Environmental Investigation *1 yr FT/2-5 yrs PT* Hospitality Management; Tourism Management *1 yr FT/3 yrs PT* Information Management *1-3 yrs PT* Sports Injury & Therapy *2 yrs PT* Practitioner Research *2-3 yrs PT* Education Management; Management Studies *2-5 yrs PT* Mathematical Education; Science Education *2.5 yrs FT* Manufacturing Systems Engineering & Management
PgDip/MSc: Business Information Technology
Postgraduate Diploma/MA: *1 yr FT/2 yrs PT* Women's Studies *1 yr FT/3 yrs PT* Information & Library Management *2 yrs & 2 trms PT* Employment Law; Industrial Relations *2 yrs FT/PT* Youth & Community Work *2 yrs PT* Practitioner Development *2-3 yrs PT* Professional Studies in Education *2-5 yrs PT* Art & Design Education; Primary Education; Special Educational Needs *3 yrs PT* Public Relations; Teaching By Research
Postgraduate Diploma/MEd: *1 yr FT/2 yrs PT* Careers Guidance *1-5 yrs PT* Management in SEN *2-5 yrs PT* Management Studies

Diplomas

BTEC Diploma: Foundation Studies in Art & Design
Diploma: Accounting & Finance (certified dip); Counselling; Professional Studies (Counselling); Professional studies (Special educational Needs); Professional Studies in Education (Counselling); Specific Learning Difficulties

Diploma in Professional Studies in Education
Diploma of Higher Education: Islamic-Middle Eastern Studies
PgD: *2 yrs* Geographical Information Systems
Postgraduate Diploma: Careers Guidance; Education Management; Food Manufacturing; Human Resource Management; Marketing Management; Mathematical Education; Retail Management; Textiles; Tourism Management *1-3 yrs PT* Teaching in Specific Learning Difficulties

Certificates

Certificate of Higher Education: Islamic Studies; Teaching Speechreading to Adults (Lipreading)
Certificate of Professional Studies: Careers Education & Guidance; Individual/Special Educational Needs; Mathematical Education; Mentoring; Primary Education; Sports Physiotherapy/ Sports Podiatry
Postgraduate Certificate: Education
Postgraduate Certificate in Education: Design & Technology; Further, Adult & Higher Education Professional Development Programme; Primary; Secondary
University Certificate: Careers Education & Guidance (Certificate In Professional Studies); Dental Technology National Certificate *Specialism within the Education subject area:* Individual/ Special Educational Needs (Severe Learning Difficulties); Management in Special Educational Needs; Mathematical Education; Primary Education; Primary School Teaching; Science Education; Special Educational Needs; Teaching (early years)

Professional Courses

Professional Courses: Hospitality Management; Tourism Management *Accounting & Finance* ACCA Certified Diploma in Accounting & Finance (Levels 1, 2 & 3); Associateship of the Institute of Taxation; Association of Taxation Technicians; Chartered Institute of Management Accountants & Certified Accountants *Careers* Certificate in Professional Studies – Careers Education & Guidance *Law* Common Professional Examination; Legal Practice Course *Marketing* Chartered Institute of Marketing (CIM) Diploma *Social Work* CCETSW Certificate of Qualification in Social Work

(VICTORIA) UNIVERSITY OF MANCHESTER

Oxford Road, Manchester M13 9PL Tel: 0161 275 2000 (ug) 0161 275 2617 (pg)
e-mail: ug.prospectus@man.ac.uk (undergrads only) Website: www.man.ac.uk

† 2+2: The first two yrs lead to the award of a Higher National Diploma.
Degrees are validated by:
* University of Huddersfield
** Universities of Leeds/Manchester/Salford/UMIST
*** Liverpool John Moores University
**** (Victoria) University of Manchester
***** University of London

First Degrees

ARTS & THEOLOGY
BA: *PT modular* Archaeology; Combined Studies; Comparative Religion; Environmental Studies; History; History of Art & Architecture; History of Modern Art; Literary Studies; Middle Eastern Studies; Theology & Religious Studies
BA Hons: *3-4 yrs* American Studies; Ancient History-Archaeology; Archaeology; Geography-Archaeology; Latin-Archaeology; Architecture; Art & Archaeology of the Ancient World; Classical Studies; Classics; Combined Studies; Comparative Religion-Social Anthropology; Cultural Heritage; Drama with English; Drama; Drama-Screen Studies; Economic History & Economics; English & American Studies; English Language; English Language & Literature; English-Linguistics or Philosophy; Environmental Management; Geography; Greek; Greek-Archaeology; History; History of Art & Architecture; History of Modern Art; Latin with French; Latin; Latin-English; Latin-Linguistics; Linguistics; Linguistics-Social Anthropology or Sociology; Medieval Studies; Modern History with Economics; Politics-Modern History; Modern Middle Eastern History; Psychology; History-Sociology; Study of Religion & Theology; Study of Religion &

Theology (Biblical Studies); Study of Religion & Theology (Jewish Studies); Study of Religion & Theology (Religion & Society); Study of Religion & Theology (South Asian Studies – provisional) *3-4 yrs by research* Classics-Ancient History *4 yrs* English & A Modern Language; English & Drama; European Studies (French or German or Italian or Spanish or Russian)-Modern Languages (French or German or Italian or Spanish or Russian); French with Latin; French Studies; French-Linguistics; German Studies; German-Linguistics; Hispanic Studies; History of Art-French or German or Italian; History-French or Italian or Spanish; Italian Studies; Italian-Linguistics or Middle Eastern Languages or Russian; Linguistics-Spanish; Middle Eastern Languages with Modern European Languages or Comparative Religion; Middle Eastern Studies
BA Joint Hons Modern Languages: *4 yrs Combination of 2 subjects:* French; German; Italian; Portuguese (second language only & cannot be combined with Spanish); Russian; Spanish
BArch: *2 yrs FT* (After BA Hons in Architecture or equiv & 1 yr's practical experience)
BPI: *1 yr FT* (Completes the professional requirement)
MusB: *3 yrs FT PT modular credit-based course:* Music

ECONOMICS, SOCIAL STUDIES, LAW, EDUCATION
BA: *PT Faculty of Education:* Education
BA (Accg & Law): *4 yrs Faculty of Law:* Accounting & Law
BA (Econ): *3 yrs* (Any area of study)
BA (Econ) Hons: *3 yrs Specialisation in 1 or 2 of the following areas:* Accounting; Econometrics & Social Statistics; Economic & Social History; Economics; Finance; Government; Social Anthropology; Social Policy; Sociology; Studies Related to Business
BA Hons: *3 yrs* Accounting with Business Information Systems; English-Philosophy; International Business, Finance & Economics; Philosophy; Philosophy-Politics *Faculty of Education:* Language, literacy & Communication; Leisure Management *3 yrs FT Faculty of Law:* Government & Law
BEconSc/BEconSc Hons: *3 yrs FT Faculty of Economics:* Economics *Faculty of Education:*
BSc Hons: *4 yrs Faculty of Education:* Speech & Language Therapy
BSocSc/BSocSc Hons: *3 yrs* Politics; Social Anthropology; Social Policy; Sociology
LLB: *3 yrs/4 yrs* Law
LLB Hons: *3 yrs* Law *4 yrs Faculty of Arts:* English & French Law
MLPM Hons: Landscape Planning & Management
MTCP Hons: *4 yrs FT* Town & Country Planning

MEDICINE, DENTISTRY & NURSING
BNurs: *4 yrs*
BSc: *PT* Management of Psychosis; Nursing Studies
MB/ChB: (may include 1 yr in Europe)

SCIENCE
BEng Hons: *3 yrs* Aerospace Engineering; Civil Engineering; Engineering with Business; Mechanical Engineering; Structural Engineering with Architecture
BSc Hons: *Intercalating Medical/Dental students only:* Basic Dental Science; Experimental Immunology & Oncology; History of Medicine; Medical Biochemistry; Pathology *3 yrs* Anatomical Sciences; Artificial Intelligence; Biochemistry; Biology; Biology-Geology; Biomedical Materials Sciences; Biomedical Sciences; Cell Biology with Patent Law; Chemistry; Computer Engineering; Computer Science with Business & Management; Computer Science; Computing & Information Systems; Engineering Business & Management; Environmental & Resource Geology; Environmental Science; Environmental Studies; Genetics; Geochemistry; Geography; Geography-Geology; Geology; Life Sciences; Materials Science & Engineering; Mathematics; Mathematics with Business & Management or English; Mathematics-English; Medical Biochemistry; Microbiology; Molecular Biology; Neuroscience; Pharmacology; Pharmacology-Physiology; Physiology; Plant Science; Psychology; Psychology-Neuroscience; Software Engineering; Zoology *4 yrs* Anatomical Sciences with a Modern Language; Biochemistry with a Modern Language; Biology with a Modern Language; Cell Biology with a Modern Language; Chemistry with Studies in Europe; Genetics with a Modern Language; Life Sciences with a Modern Language with a Modern Language; Mathematics; Microbiology with a Modern Language; Molecular Biology with a Modern Language; Neuroscience with a Modern Language;

Pharmacology with a Modern Language; Physics (with Study in Europe); Physiology with a Modern Language; Plant Science with a Modern Language; Zoology with a Modern Language *4 yrs S* Anatomical Sciences; Artificial Intelligence with Industrial Experience; Biochemistry with Biotechnology; Biochemistry; Biology; Biomedical Materials Science; Biomedical Sciences; Cell Biology; Chemistry; Computer & Information Systems; Computer Science; Computing Engineering; Genetics; Life Sciences; Medical Biochemistry; Microbiology; Microbiology with Biotechnology; Molecular Biology; Neuroscience; Pharmacology; Pharmacology-Physiology; Physiology; Plant Science; Psychology-Neuroscience; Software Engineering; Zoology

Bsc Hons/MChem: *3-4 yrs* Chemistry with Medicinal Chemistry or Polymer Science or Patent Law

BSc/MChem Hons: *4 yrs* Chemistry; Chemistry with Medicinal Chemistry or Polymer Science; Chemistry (with Industrial Experience or Study in Europe)

BSc/MEng: *4 yrs S* Structural Engineering with Architecture

BSc/MPhys: *4 yrs* Study in Europe (with); Physics (with); Physics; Physics with Astrophysics or Business & Management or Theoretical Physics or Technological Physics

Higher Degrees

LLM: *1 yr FT By exam & dissertation:* Law & Economics (2 trms spent in Ghent & Rotterham universities)

LLM International Business Law: *1 yr FT By exam in 3 papers chosen from:* British Tax Law; Conflict of Laws in Business & Commerce; International Economic Law; International Fiscal Law (+ dissertation); Law of the European Communities; Law of the Export Trade; Law of Trade Competition; Partnership & Company Law

MA: *1 yr FT/2 yrs PT By exam & dissertation:* 17th Century Studies; 18th Century Studies; 19th Century Studies; 20th Century Studies; Ancient World Studies; Anglo-Saxon Studies; Archaeological Textile Studies; Archaeology; Architecture; British Romantic Literature; Building Conservation; Colonial & Post-colonial Literature & Theory; Counselling; Cultural Criticism; Cultural History; Drama; Early Modern History; Economic & Social History; Editing & Transmission of Texts; English; English Language; English Literature; Environmental Impact Assessment & Management; European Languages & Culture (Ancient Greek, French, German, Italian, Latin, Portuguese, Russian, Spanish); European Media Studies; French; General History; Geo-social Analysis; German; Health Care Ethics-Law; Health, Space & Society; History; History of Art; Italian; Jewish Studies; Language and Cultural Theory; Languages & Linguistics; Linguistics; Linguistics (European); Management; Medieval History; Middle Eastern Studies; Modern British History; Modern European History; Novel Writing; Old English & Anglo-Saxon Studies; Philosophy & the Environment; Planning & Landscape; Portuguese; Religion & Society in Early Modern Britain & Europe; Religions & Theology; Russian; Spanish; Urban Design & Regeneration; Urban Planning & Development; Urban Planning Studies; Victorian Literature; Women's Writing; Writing & Transmission of Contemporary Poetry *2 yrs PT By exam & dissertation:* Counselling Studies

MA (AppLing): *1 yr FT/2-3 yrs PT By coursework & dissertation: 1-2 yrs FT By thesis:* Government

MA (Econ): *1-2 yrs FT/PT* Development Finance *By exam & dissertation:* Agricultural & Environmental Economics; Applied Social Research; Crime, Law & Society; Development Administration & Management; Development Economics; Development Finance; Development Studies; Econometrics; Economics; Economics & Management of Rural Development; Economics-Econometrics; Environment & Development; Finance; Government; Health & Community; History & Social Anthropology of Science, Technology & Medicine; Industrial Strategy & Trade Policy; Labour Studies; Management & Information; Political Economy; Poverty, Conflict & Reconstruction; Public Policy & Management; Social Anthropology; Social Policy & Social Development; Social Policy & Welfare; Social Research Methods; Social Research Methods-Statistics; Social Work; Social Work & Social Welfare; Sociology; Visual Anthropology; Women's Studies & Feminist Research

MA (Theol): *1 yr FT/2 yrs PT By exam & dissertation:* Biblical Studies; Social & Pastoral Theology with Health Care Ethics or Feminist Studies; Social & Pastoral Theology

MAppLing: *1 yr FT/2-3 yrs PT By coursework & project work*

MArch: *2 yrs FT*

MBA: (2.5-5 yrs MBA in Entrepreneurship for owner-managed and small/medium-sized enterprises) (2.2.5-5 yrs Executive) (30 mths for Financial Management MBA on distance learning basis/ Public Sector MBA can be taken FT or on an Executive basis)

MBSc: *1 yr FT/2 yrs PT*

MChem & Phys Hons: *4 yrs*

MChem Hons: *4 yrs* Chemistry with Business & Management

MEd: *1 yr FT/2-5 yrs PT By exam & dissertation:* Adult Education, Literacy & Community Based Development; Communications, Education & Technology; Education of Hearing-Impaired Children (International); Educational Leadership & Management; Educational Psychology; Educational Studies; Educational Technology & English Language Teaching; Educational Technology & TESOL; English Language Teaching; European Masters in Physical Education; Hearing Impairment; Microprocessors in Education; TESOL

MEng: *4 yrs FT* Biomedical Materials Science; Materials Science with Business & Management; Materials Science-Engineering; Materials Science-Engineering (Ceramics); Materials Science-Engineering (Metals); Materials, Science & Engineering; Metals *4 yrs S* Biomedical Materials Science with Industrial Experience; Materials Science-Engineering; Materials Science-Engineering (Polymers)

MEng Hons: *4 yrs* Aerospace Engineering (Integrated European Programme); Aerospace Engineering (Enhanced & Extended); Civil Engineering; Civil Engineering (Integrated European Programme); Civil Engineering (Integrated Japanese Programme); Computer Science; Engineering with Business; Mechanical Engineering (Integrated European Programme); Mechanical Engineering (Integrated European Programme) with Systems (Integrated European Programme); Mechanical Engineering; Structural Engineering (Integrated European Programme) with Architecture (Integrated European Programme)

MLang: *1 yr FT/2-3 yrs PT By exam & project work*

MLing: *1 yr FT/2 yrs PT By exam & project work*

MMath Hons: *4 yrs*

MML (Master of Modern Languages): *4 yrs* French (Combination of 2 subjects)-German (Combination of 2 subjects) or Italian (Combination of 2 subjects) or Russian (Combination of 2 subjects)

MPharm: *4 yrs FT* Pharmacy

MPsy: *4 yrs* Psychology with Study in Europe

MSc: Earth Sciences *By exam & thesis:* Applications & Management; Geotechnical Engineering; Urban Geoscience *1 yr FT By exam & dissertation:* Community Organisations for Rural Development; Educational Audiology; Educational Psychology; Educational Research; Human Resource Development; Human Resource Management; Organisational Change & Development *1-2 yrs FT/2-3 yrs PT By exam & dissertation:* Accounting & Finance *1-2 yrs FT/PT By exam & thesis:* Advanced Engineering Materials; Applied Mathematics & Fluid Mechanics; Artificial Intelligence (now a specialisation with MSc Advanced Computer Science); Biomedical & Forensic Studies in Egyptology; Clinical Pharmacy; Computational Molecular Biology (Bioinformatics); Computer Science (Advanced computer science: Formal Methods, High Performance Computing, Software Engineering, Artificial Intelligence, Robotics & Intelligence Systems, Advanced Applications); Earth & Environmental Sciences Research Technologies; Electronic Instrumentation Systems; Environmental Engineering; Environmental Monitoring & Modelling; Experimental Condensed Matter Physics; Experimental Particle Physics; Geography (Environmental Monitoring & Modelling, Physical Geography); Geotechnical Engineering; History of Science, Technology and Medicine; Immunology & Immunogenetics; Industrial Pharmaceutical Sciences; Instrumental Applications of Atomic & Molecular Processes; Laser Photonics & Modern Optics; Maintenance Engineering (IGDS); Mathematical Logic & the Foundations of Computer Science; Metallic & Ceramic Materials; Molecular Parasitology & Vector Biology; Molecular Pharmacology; Neuroscience; Nuclear & Radiation Physics; Pharmaceutical Engineering; Pollution & Environmental Control; Polymer Science & Technology; Radio Astronomy; Research Technologies; Statistics; Technical Change & Industrial Strategy; Theoretical Physics; Theoretical Physics *By thesis:* Aeronautical Engineering; Biochemistry; Biotechnology; Cell Biology; Chemistry; Civil Engineering; Computer Science; Electronic & Electrical Engineering; Materials Science; Mechanical Engineering; Nuclear Engineering; Pharmacology; Pharmacy; Physics (incl Astronomy & Radio-Astronomy); Pollution Research; Psychology; Science & Technology *Faculty of Arts:* Physical Geography (by exam & thesis) *Up to 5 yrs PT By exam & thesis:* Applied Psychology

MTPl: *1-2 yrs FT/2 yrs PT* (By exam & dissertation or planning design)
MusM: *1 yr FT/2 yrs PT*
MusM Perf: *1- 2 yrs FT*

DOCTORATES
DD: (Awarded after distinguished research)
DSc: (Awarded in recognition of published work of high distinction to Manchester grads or others who have been engaged in research under the auspices of the Univ for 6 consecutive terms min)
DSosSc: (Conferred by the Univ in recognition of published work)
EngD: *1-2 yrs FT/PT* Materials Science *4 yrs* Computer Science; Electrical Engineering; Engineering
LittD: (Open only to Manchester Masters or PhDs)
LLD: (Awarded after distinguished research)
PhD: (Awarded to grads (or equiv) who have spent 1 yr min in approved P/grad work incl some research and have followed a course of research of 2 yrs min FT or 4 yrs min PT)

MASTER'S DEGREES OR EQUIVALENT
BAppLing: *1 yr FT/2-3 yrs PT*
BD Hons: *2 yrs*
BLang: *1 yr FT/2-3 yrs PT*
BTP: *FT/PT*

MEDICAL & DENTAL
ChM
ClinPsyD: *3 yrs FT*
DDS
MD
MDSc
MPhil: *1-2 yrs FT* Anaesthesia; Animal Biology; Audiology/Audiolgical Medicine; Biochemistry; Biomolecular Science; Biotechnology; Cell biology; Child Dental Health; Child Health; Clinical Biochemistry; Clinical Psychology; Community Dentistry; Computational Methods in Medical Science; Conservative Dentistry; Dental Specialities (Biomaterials Science); Developmental Biology; Diagnostic Radiology; Environmental Biology; Epidemiology Research; General Practice; Genetics; Geriatric Medicine; Haematology; Health Promotion; Immunology; Injury Research; Medical Art; Medical Biophysics; Medical Genetics; Medical Microbiology; Medicine; Microbiology; Molecular Biology; Neuroscience; Nursing; Obstetrics & Gynaecology; Occupational Health; Occupational Hygiene; Oncology; Ophthalmology; Oral & Maxillo-Facial Surgery; Oral Medicine; Oral Pathology; Orthodontics; Orthopaedic Surgery; Pathological Sciences; Periodontology; Pharmacology; Physiological Sciences/Physiology; Plant Sciences; Prosthetic Dentistry; Psychiatric Social Work; Psychiatry; Public Health; Public Health & Epidemiology; Restorative Dentistry; Rheumatology; Surgery; Toxicology
MSc: *1 yr FT/2-3 yrs PT By exam & dissertation:* Audiological Medicine; Audiological Science; Bacteriology & Virology/Molecular Microbiology; Biological Science; Clinical Biochemistry; Clinical Nursing; Clinical Rheumatology; Dental Specialities; Epidemiology & Biostatistics; Family & Individual Cognitive Behaviour Therapy for Psychoses; Investigative Ophthalmology & Vision Science; Nursing Studies; Pharmacology; Physics & Computing in Medicine & Biology; Psychiatric Social Work; Psychiatry; Psychiatry for Developing Countries; Systemic Family Therapy *2-3 yrs PT By exam & dissertation:* Genetic Counselling; Oncology *PT/DL* Occupational Hygiene (Distance Learning); Occupational Medicine (Distance Learning)
PhD: (Details as for MPhil)

RESEARCH DEGREES
MPhil: *1 yr FT/2 yrs PT* Education (Areas of Study as for MEd); Law (Awarded after presentation of a satisfactory thesis involving discussion of & research in a legal subject)*By thesis:* Aeronautical Engineering; Age & Cognitive Performance; Archaeology; Architecture; Biblical Criticism & Exegesis; Celtic Studies; Civil Engineering; Comparative Literary Studies; Drama; English; French; Geography; German; Greek; History; History of Art; Italian; Latin; Linguistics; Middle

Eastern Studies; Military Studies; Music; Nuclear Engineering; Philosophy; Planning & Landscape; Psychology; Russian; Spanish & Portuguese Studies *1-2 yrs FT By thesis:* Accounting & Finance; Development Administration & Management; Development Studies; Econometrics; Economic Studies; Economics & Econometrics; Health Services Management; Management Education; Social Anthropology; Social Policy; Social Policy & Social Work; Sociology; Visual Anthropology; Women's Studies

MRes: *1 yr FT* Biological Sciences; Informatics; Molecular Engineering; Surface & Interface Science & Engineering

MSc: *By thesis:* Profound Learning Disability and Sensory Impairment *1 yr FT/2 yrs PT By thesis:* Animal Biology; Biochemistry; Biomolecular Science; Biotechnology; Cell Biology; Chemistry; Computer Science; Development Biology; Electrical Engineering; Environmental Biology; Genetics; Geography; Geology; History of Science; Immunology; Mathematics; Mechanical Engineering; Metallurgy; Microbiology; Pharmacy; Physics (incl Astronomy & Radio-Astronomy); Plant Science; Policy Research on Engineering; Psychology; Radiological Protection; Science & Technology; Science & Technology Policy; Statistics; Technology & Medicine

Honorary Degrees
DOCTORATES
DocEdPsy
EdD: *4-6 yrs PT* D Counselling

Diplomas

PGDip: *1 yr FT/2 yrs PT* Anthropology & Development; Applied Social Research; Crime, Law & Society; Development Economics; Development Finance; Development Policy & Management; Development Studies; Economics; Government; Industrial Strategy & Trade Policy; Labour Studies; Management & Information; Public Policy & Management; Social Anthropology; Social Policy & Social Development; Social Policy & Social Work; Social Policy & Welfare; Social Policy & Welfare; Sociology; Women's Studies & Feminist Research

Postgraduate/Post-Experience Diploma: *1 yr* Advanced Studies in Musical Composition; Advanced Studies in Musical Performance (Brass Band Direction or Orchestral Studies or Wind Band Direction or Instrumental Studies or Vocal Studies); Art Gallery & Museum Studies; Drama; Industrial Design & Application; Teaching of English Overseas *1 yr FT* Advanced Studies TESOL; Advanced Study in Audiology; Advanced Study in Training & Development for the Public Sector; Applied Geology (see note ie; Applications & Management, Research Technologies, Urban Geoscience); Applied Mathematics & Fluid Mechanics; Bacteriology; Bioinformatics; Biomedical & Forensic Studies in Egyptology; Chemistry (Polymer Science & Technology); Computer Science (plus Software Engineering, Systems Design); Immunology & Immunogenetics; Legal Studies; Materials Science (Advanced Engineering Materials, Metallic & Ceramic Material); Mathematics (plus Mathematical Logic & the Foundations of Computer Science, Numerical Analysis & Computation); Molecular Parasitology & Vector Biology; Physics (Experimental & Theoretical Physics, Experimental Condensed Matter Physics, Experimental Particle Physics, Radio Astronomy); Pollution & Environmental Control; Psychiatric Social Work; Resources & Hazards; Statistics; Technical Change & Industrial Strategy; Urban Planning *1 yr FT/2 yrs PT* Advanced Study in Communications, Education & Technology; Advanced Study in Education; Advanced Study in Education for Human Resource Studies; Advanced Study in Education of Hearing Impaired Children; Advanced Study in Educational Leadership & Management; Advanced Study in Profound Learning Disability and Sensory Impairment; Advanced Study in Rural & Community Development Education; Biomedical Applications of Physics & Computing Sciences; Biomedical Gerontology; Business Administration; Business Information Systems; Clinical Biochemistry; Computational Methods in Medical Science; Health Promotion; Industrial Pharmaceutical Science; Investigative Ophthalmology & Vision Science; Neuroscience; Occupational Health Sciences; Oncology; Pharmacology; Post-qual Studies in Psychiatric Social work; Primary Health Care; Urban Design & Regeneration *1 yr FT/2-3 yrs PT* Biblical Studies; Social & Pastoral Theology (Also available with Feminism Studies or Healthcare Studies Options); Zoroastrian Studies *2 yrs FT* Social Policy & Social Work *2 yrs PT* Advanced Study in Specific Learning Difficulties (Literacy); Family Therapy; Psychiatry

Certificates

PGCE: *1 yr FT*
TESOL

Degrees validated by (Victoria) University of Manchester offered at:

Warrington Collegiate Institute, Faculty of H.E,

Padgate Campus, Crab Lane, Warrington WA2 0DB Tel: 01925 494494 Fax: 01925 494289 e-mail: registry.he@warr.ac.uk Website: www.ucw.warr.ac.uk

First Degrees

BA Hons: *3 yrs FT/ Up to 7 yrs PT* Combined Studies
BA Joint Hons: *3 yrs FT Equally weighted:* Media (Radio Production) or Media (Multimedia Journalism) or Professional Studies (Education) or Sports Studies or Media (Television Production); Business Management & IT-Leisure (Outdoor Recreation) or Media (Radio Production) or Media (Multimedia Journalism) or Media (Television Production); Business Management & IT-Leisure (Sport) or Media (Television Production) or Media (Radio Production) or Media (Multimedia Journalism) or Sports Studies; Business Management & IT-Leisure (Tourism); Business Management & IT or Leisure (Licensed Entertainment); Media (Commercial Music Production)-Business Management & IT or Leisure (Licensed Entertainment) or Leisure (Outdoor Recreation) or Leisure (Sport) or Leisure (Tourism); Media (Multimedia Journalism)-Business Management & IT or Leisure (Licensed Entertainment) or Leisure (Outdoor Recreation) or Leisure (Sport) or Leisure (Tourism); Media (Radio Production)-Business Management & IT or Leisure (Licensed Entertainment) or Leisure (Outdoor Recreation) or Leisure (Sport) or Leisure (Tourism); Media (Television Production)-Business Management & IT; Performing Arts-Business Management & IT or Leisure (Outdoor Recreation) or Leisure (Sport) or Media (Television Production) or Media (Radio Production) or Media (Multimedia Journalism) or Performing Arts; Professional Studies (Education)-Business Management and IT; Professional Studies (Social Work) or Media (Television Production) or Media (Radio Production) or Media (Multimedia Journalism) or Sports Studies or Media (Commercial Music Production); Leisure (Licensed Entertainment)-Business Management & IT *Major/Minor combinations:* Leisure or Media or Performing Arts or Professional Studies (Education) or Sports Studies; Business Management & IT with Business Management & IT or Media or Performing Arts or Professional Studies (Education) or Sports Studies; Leisure (Licensed Entertainment; Outdoor Recreation; Sport; Tourism) with Business Management & IT (NB Commercial Music Production cannot be studied with Professional Studies (Education) or Sport Studies) or Performing Arts (NB Commercial Music Production cannot be studied with Professional Studies (Education) or Sport Studies) or Professional Studies (Education) (NB Commercial Music Production cannot be studied with Professional Studies (Education) or Sport Studies) or Sport Studies (NB Commercial Music Production cannot be studied with Professional Studies (Education) or Sport Studies); Media (Commercial Music Production; Television Production; Radio Production; Multimedia Journalism) (NB Commercial Music Production cannot be studied with Professional Studies (Education) or Sport Studies) with Business Management & IT or Leisure or Media or Professional Studies (Education) or Sport Studies; Performing Arts with Business Management & IT or Leisure or Media or Performing Arts or Professional Studies (Education) or Sport Studies
BA Single Hons: *3 yrs FT* Leisure Management; Media (Commercial Music Production; Television Production; Radio Production; Multimedia Journalism); Media (Multimedia Web Production); Media and Cultural Studies; Performing Arts; Sport Studies *3 yrs FT/ Up to 7 yrs PT* Business Management & IT; Human Resource Management; Information Systems Management; Marketing Management

Higher Degrees

MA: *1 yr FT* Radio Production; Television Production (Granada TV bursaries available) *1 yr FT/2 yrs PT* Media & Cultural Studies; Music & Screen Culture; Screen Studies

Diplomas

DipHE: *2 yrs FT* Diploma in Social Work with DipHE
Diploma/Certificate: *1-2 yrs PT* Counselling
HND: *2 yrs FT* Engineering; Graphic Design *2 yrs FT/3 yrs PT* Mechatronics

Certificates

Certificate in Education: Further, Adult & Higher Education
HNC: *2 yrs PT* Building Studies; Business; Business Information Technology; Caring Services (Social Care); Computer Studies; Electrical & Electronic Engineering; Engineering; Graphic Design; Leisure Studies; Motor Vehicle Management; Social Care; Software Engineering

MIDDLESEX UNIVERSITY

White Hart Lane, London N17 8 HR Tel: 020 8362 5000 Fax: 020 8362 5649
e-mail: admissions@mdx.ac.uk Website: www.mdx.ac.uk

† Subject to validation.

First Degrees

BA Hons: *1 yr FT/Up to 5 yrs PT* Social Science (DipSW top-up) *2 yrs FT* Design & Technology with QTS; Fashion Product Management; Multimedia Arts; Recording Arts; Social Work (with DipSW) *3 yrs FT* Accounting with Business Economics or Business Information Systems or Business Studies or French or German or Human Resource Management or Law Studies or Management or Marketing or Mathematics or Spanish or Statistics or Race & Culture; American Studies with Business Studies or Criminology or Cultural & Intellectual History or Education Studies or English Literary Studies or Environment & Society or Geography or German or History or Italian or Law Studies or Media & Cultural Studies or Philosophy or Political & International Studies or Psychology or Social Science or Spanish or Third World & Development Studies or Gender & Women's Studies or Writing & Publishing Studies; Applied Philosophy; Business Administration; Business Economics with Accounting or Business Information Systems or Business Studies or French or German or Human Resource Management or Law Studies or Management or Marketing or Spanish or Statistics; Business Studies with Accounting or American Studies or Business Economics or Business Information Systems or Communication & Language Studies or Criminology or Economics or English Language & British Culture or French or Geography or German or Health & Policy Studies or Human Resource Management or Information & Communication Technology or Law Studies or Management or Marketing or Mathematics or Media & Cultural Studies or Psychology or Social Policy or Social Science or Sociology or Spanish or Statistics or Third World & Development Studies or Writing & Publishing Studies; Christian Studies with Communication & Language Studies or Cultural & Intellectual History or English Literary Studies or Media & Cultural Studies or Religious Studies or Pastoral Studies; Communication & Language Studies with Business Information Systems or Business Studies or Computer Communications or Criminology or Education Studies or English Language & British Culture or English Literary Studies or Film Studies or History or Information & Communication Technology or Italian or Law Studies or Marketing or Media & Cultural Studies or Race & Culture or Social Science or Spanish or TEFL or Writing & Publishing Studies; Community Dance; Constructed Textiles; Criminology with American Studies or Business Studies or Communication & Language Studies or Economics or Environment & Society or Geography or Health & Policy Studies or Health Studies or History or Interprofessional Health or Law Studies or Political & International Studies or Psychology or Race & Culture or Religious Studies or Social Policy or Social Science or Sociology or Spanish or Statistics or Third World & Development Studies or Writing & Publishing Studies; Criminology or Political & International Studies; Cultural & Intellectual History with American Studies or Art & Design History or Christian Studies or Communication & Language Studies or English Literary Studies or French or German or History or Italian or Media & Cultural Studies or Philosophy or Race & Culture or Religious Studies or Spanish; Dance with Art & Design History or Business Studies or Education Studies or English Literary Studies or Film Studies or French or German or History or Italian or Marketing or Media & Cultural Studies or Philosophy or Race & Culture or Religious Studies or Sociology or Spanish or Third World Studies; Dance Performance; Dance Studies; Design & Technology with Business Information Systems or Business Studies or Education Studies or Information & Communication Technology or Product Design or Psychology; Drama & Theatre Arts with Business Studies or English Literary Studies or French or German or History or Italian or Media & Cultural Studies or Political & International Studies or Spanish; Drama & Theatre Studies or Business Information Technology; Education Studies with Biological Sciences or Design & Technology or English Literary Studies or French or Geography or German or History or Information & Communication Technology or Mathematics or Psychology or Religious Studies or Spanish; Education Studies; English or TEFL; English Language & British Culture with Art & Design History or Business Information Systems or Business Studies or Communication & Language Studies or English Literary Studies or Film Studies or French or German or Information & Communication Technology or Media & Cultural Studies or Philosophy or Political & International Studies or Portuguese or Psychology or Social Science or Spanish or Turkish; English Literary Studies with Art & Design History or Communication & Language Studies or Cultural & Intellectual History or Education Studies or English Language & British Culture or Film Studies or French or German or History or Information & Communication Technology or Italian or Law Studies or Media & Cultural Studies or Philosophy or Portuguese or Psychology or Religious Studies or Social Science or Spanish or TEFL or Turkish; European Cultural History; Fashion; Film Studies with Art & Design History or Business Studies or Communication & Language Studies or Dance or English Language & British Culture or English Literary Studies or History or Italian or Media & Cultural Studies or Music or Philosophy or Psychology or Sociology or Gender & Women's Studies or Writing & Publishing Studies; Film Studies or Third World & Development Studies; French with Business Studies or Caribbean Studies or Cultural & Intellectual History or Education Studies or English Language & British Culture or English Literary Studies or History or Information & Communication Technology or Italian or Law Studies or Media & Cultural Studies or Political & International Studies or Psychology or Social Science or Spanish or TEFL; Gender & Women's Studies or Communication & Language Studies or English Literary Studies or History or Media & Cultural Studies or Politics & International Studies or Psychology or Religious Studies or Social Policy or Social Science or Sociology or Third World & Development Studies; Gender & Women's Studies; German with Business Studies or Cultural & Intellectual History or Education Studies or English Language & British Culture or English Literary Studies or French or Italian or Law Studies or Media & Cultural Studies or Philosophy or Political & International Studies or Psychology or Social Science or Spanish or TEFL; Historical Studies; History with American Studies or Art & Design History or Business Studies or Communication & Language Studies or Cultural & Intellectual History or Education Studies or English Language & British Culture or English Literary Studies or French or German or Information & Communication Technology or Italian or Law Studies or Media & Cultural Studies or Philosophy or Portuguese or Political & International Studies or Religious Studies or Social Science or Spanish or Turkish or Gender & Women's Studies or Art & Design; History & Theory of Media; Human Resource Management with Accounting or Business Economics or Business Information Systems or Business Studies or French or German or Law Studies or Management or Marketing or Mathematics or Spanish or Statistics; International Studies or Management; Law Studies or Business Studies or Criminology or French or German or History or Human Resource Management or Marketing or Mathematics or Philosophy or Political & International Studies or Psychology or Race & Culture or Social Science or Spanish or Statistics with Accounting or American Studies or Business Economics or Business Information Systems; Management with Accounting or Business Economics or Business Information Systems or Business Studies or French or German or Human Resource Management or Law Studies or Marketing or Spanish or Statistics; Marketing with Accounting or Business Economics or Business Information Systems or Business Studies or French or German or Human Resource Management or Law Studies or Management or Mathematics or Spanish or Statistics or TEFL or Social Science or Spanish or Gender & Women's Studies or Writing & Publishing Studies; Media & Cultural Studies with American Studies or Art & Design History or Business Studies or Communication & Language Studies or Criminology or English Language & British Culture or English Literary Studies or Environment & Society or French or Geography or German or Law Studies or Portuguese or Psychology; Media & Cultural Studies; Modern European Philosophy; Music with Communication & Language Studies or Education Studies or English Literary Studies or Film Studies or French or History or Media & Cultural Studies or Philosophy or Psychology or

Sociology or Spanish; Pastoral Studies with Christian Studies or Philosophy or Psychology or Religious Studies or Social Science; Performing Arts; Philosophy; Philosophy/Applied Philosophy/Modern European Philosophy-American Studies or Art & Design History or Criminology or Cultural & Intellectual History or English Language & British Culture or English Literary Studies or Film Studies or French or German or History or Law Studies or Political & International Studies or Portuguese or Religious Studies or Social Science or Spanish or Gender & Women's Studies or Writing & Publishing Studies; Political & International Studies with Criminology or Economics or English Language & British Culture or French or German or History or Italian or Information & Communication Technology or Law Studies or Media & Cultural Studies or Philosophy or Portuguese or Social Science or Spanish or Third World & Development Studies or Turkish; Political Studies; Primary Education with QTS; Race & Culture with Communication & Language Studies or Criminology or Cultural & Intellectual History or Education Studies or English Language & British Culture or History or Information & Communication Technology or Law Studies or Media & Cultural Studies or Portuguese or Psychology or Religious Studies or Social Policy or Social Science or Third World & Development Studies or Turkish or Gender & Women's Studies or History; Religious Studies or Christian Studies or Criminology or Cultural & Intellectual History or Education Studies or English Literary Studies or Information & Communication Technology or Jewish Studies or Media & Cultural Studies or Pastoral Studies or Philosophy or Political & International Studies or Psychology or Race & Culture or Social Science or Social Policy or Spanish; Religious Studies or Health Studies or Interprofessional Health or Mathematics or Media & Cultural Studies or Philosophy or Politics & International Studies or Race & Culture or Religious Studies or Social Science or Sociology or Spanish or Statistics or Third World & Development Studies or Gender & Women's Studies or Writing & Publishing Studies; Social Policy with American Studies or Business Studies or Criminology or Economics or English Literary Studies or Environment & Society or Geography or Health & Policy Studies; Sociology with Business Studies or Criminology or Economics or English Literary Studies or Environment & Society or Geography or Health Studies or History or Interprofessional Health or Mathematics or Philosophy or Political & International Studies or Psychology or Social Policy or Social Science or Spanish or Gender & Women's Studies or Writing & Publishing Studies; Sonic Arts or Art & Design History or Business Studies or Caribbean Studies or Communication & Language Studies or English Language & British Culture or English Literary Studies or French or German or History or Information & Communication Technology or Italian or Law Studies or Media & Cultural Studies or Politics & International Studies or Portuguese or Psychology or TEFL or Third World & Development Studies or Writing & Publishing Studies; Spanish with American Studies; Teaching English as a Foreign Language with Communication & Language Studies or Education Studies or English Literary Studies or French or German or Italian or Portuguese or Psychology or Spanish or Third World & Development Studies or Turkish; Technical Theatre Arts; Theatre Dance; Third World & Development Studies with American Studies or Business Studies or Caribbean Studies or Communication & Language Studies or Criminology or Economics or English Literary Studies or Environment & Society or Geography or Health & Policy Studies or Health Studies or History or Interprofessional Health or Media & Cultural Studies or Political & International Studies or Portuguese or Psychology or Race & Culture or Religious Studies or Social Policy or Social Science or Sociology or Spanish or Statistics or Turkish or Gender & Women's Studies or Writing & Publishing Studies; Visual Communication Design (Graphic Design); Visual Communication Design (Illustration); Writing; Writing & Publishing Studies with American Studies or Business Studies or Communication & Language Studies or Criminology or English Literary Studies or Film Studies or French or German or Information & Communication Technology or Italian or Media & Cultural Studies or Philosophy or Portuguese or Social Science or Spanish or Third World & Development Studies or Turkish *3 yrs FT/4 yrs S* Accounting & Finance; Finance; Hospitality Management; Interior Design; Management; Marketing; Money, Banking & Finance; Social Policy; Sociology; Third World & Development Studies *3 yrs FT/4 yrs S/6 yrs PT* Jewellery *3 yrs FT/5-7 yrs PT* Drama & Technical Theatre Arts; Fine Art; Music; Music (Jazz); Printed Textiles & Decoration *3 yrs FT/6 yrs PT* Applied Arts with Business Studies or Criminology or English Language & British Culture or English Literary Studies or Film Studies; Art & Design History or History or Italian or Media & Cultural Studies or Philosophy or Psychology or Spanish *4 yrs FT* French; German; Latin American Studies (1 yr spent in Latin America); Spanish; Teaching English as a Foreign Language or Spanish or Third World & Development Studies or Turkish with Communication & Language Studies or Education Studies or English Literary Studies or French or German or Italian or Portuguese or Psychology *4 yrs FT/5 yrs PT* Social Science (with or without Diploma in Social Work) *4 yrs S* Business Studies; Human Resource Management; International Management

BA Hons/DipHE: *2-3 yrs FT* Theology for Ministry

BA/BSc Hons: *3 yrs FT* Economics with American Studies or Business Studies or History or Mathematics or Philosophy or Political & International Studies or Social Policy or Social Science or Sociology or Statistics or Third World & Development Studies or English Literary Studies or Health & Policy Studies or History or Interprofessional Health or Maths or Philosophy or Political & International Studies or Psychology or Religious Studies or Social Policy or Social Science or Sociology or Spanish or Statistics or Third World & Development Studies; Geography with Business Studies or Communication & Language Studies or Criminology or Education Studies *3 yrs FT/4 yrs S* Business Economics; Economics; Geography; Product Design *FT/PT* Post-Registration Nursing; Work Based Learning Studies

BEng Hons: *3 yrs FT/4 yrs S* Computer Systems Engineering

BSc: *3 yrs FT* Reproductive Sexual Health; Primary Health Care with Health Studies or Mental Health & Human Relations or Psychology *4 yrs FT* Veterinary Nursing

BSc Hons: *1 yr FT/2 yrs PT* Occupational Health & Safety *18 mths* Pre-Registration Midwifery (DipHE top-up) *3 yrs FT* Information & Communication Technology; Applied Computing with Business Information Systems or Computer Communications; Applied Computing with Applied Computing; Biological Sciences or Health & Environment or Business Studies or Education Studies or Health & Policy Studies or Health Studies or Information & Communication Technology or Law Studies or Mathematics or Mechanical Engineering or Psychology or Social Policy or Spanish or Statistics or Spanish; Business Information Systems with Accounting or Applied Computing or Business Economics or Business Studies or Communication & Language Studies or Computer Communications or Criminology or Economics or English Language & British Culture or French or Geography or Human Resource Management or Information Technology or Law Studies or Management or Marketing or Mathematics or Statistics; Child Healthcare with Health Studies or Mental Health & Human Relations or Primary Healthcare or Psychology or Reproductive Sexual Health; Computer Communications with Applied Computing or Business Information Systems; Computer Systems; Computing Science; Environmental Science with Applied Computing or Biological Sciences or Business Studies or French or Health & Policy Studies or Herbal Medicine (Phytotherapy) or Information & Communication Technology or Interprofessional Health or Law Studies or Mathematics or Psychology or Social Policy or Social Science or Spanish or Statistics; Health & Policy Studies with Applied Computing or Education Studies or Health Studies or Herbal Medicine (Phytotherapy) or Information & Communication Technology or Political & International Studies or Race & Culture or Social Policy or Social Science or Statistics or Third World & Development Studies or Gender & Women's Studies or Writing & Publishing Studies; Health Sciences; Health Studies or Health & Environment with Biological Sciences or Business Studies or Criminology or Management or Psychology or Social Policy or Sociology or Third World & Development Studies; Housing Studies; Information & Communication Technology with Applied Computing or Business Information Systems or Business Studies or Christian Studies or Computer Communications or Criminology or Economics or Education Studies or English Literary Studies or History or Law Studies or Marketing or Media & Cultural Studies or Psychology or Spanish or Writing & Publishing Studies; Information & Communication Technology; Interprofessional Health with Biological Sciences or Health Studies or Herbal Medicine (Phytotherapy) or Mental Health & Human Relations or Psychology or Social Science or Sociology; Mathematics with Accounting or Business Information Systems or Business Studies or Economics or Education Studies or Human Resource Management or Law Studies or Management or Marketing or Psychology or Statistics; Mathematics in Society; Mental Health & Human Relations with Health Studies or Psychology or Social Science; Multimedia; Physiological Measurement or Geography or Health & Policy Studies or Health Studies or Interprofessional Health or Mathematics or Philosophy or Race & Culture or Religious Studies or Social Science or Sociology or Third World & Development Studies or Gender & Women's Studies; Psychology with American Studies or Business Studies or Communication & Language Studies or Criminology or Economics or Education Studies or English Literary Studies or Environment & Society or Statistics or Spanish;

Psychology or History or Interprofessional Health or Philosophy or Political & International Studies or Psychology or Race & Culture or Religious Studies or Social Policy or Spanish or Statistics or Third World & Development Studies or Gender & Women's Studies or Writing & Publishing Studies; Social Science or American Studies or Business Studies or Communication & Language Studies or Criminology or Economics or English Literary Studies or Health & Policy Studies or Health Studies; Statistics or Health & Environment with Business Economics or Health Studies or Mathematics or Social Policy or Social Science or Accounting or Business Information Systems or Economics or Human Resource Management or Law Studies or Management or Marketing or Psychology *3 yrs FT/4 yrs S* Mathematics for Business *3 yrs FT/4 yrs S/5 yrs PT* Environmental Health; Herbal Medicine (Phytotherapy); Social Science *3 yrs FT/4-5 yrs PT* Business Information Systems *3 yrs FT/5 yrs PT* Environmental Science; Human Biology *3-4 yrs FT/5 yrs PT* Sport & Performance Therapy *4 yrs FT* Nursing with Professional Qualification (RN) *4 yrs PT* European Environmental Engineering Science *5 yrs FT with mandatory placement* Traditional Chinese Medicine *5 yrs PT* Osteopathy
LLB Hons: *3 yrs FT* Law

Higher Degrees

Joint Masters: In-Company Management Programmes
LLM: Employment Law
MA: Aesthetics & Art Theory; Applied Philosophy; Choreography; Choreography with Performing Arts; Comparative Contemporary Literature; Criminology; Design; Design for Interactive Media; Design Leadership; Digital Architecture; Digital Arts; East/West Theatre Studies; Economics; Education Management; Electronic Arts; European Cinema; Fine Art; Human Resource Management; International Finance; International Relations; Lifelong Learning; Local Economic Development; Management Practice; Marketing Management; Modern European Philosophy; Money, Banking & Finance; Music/Music Education; Nationalism, Society and Culture in Modern Europe; Performing Arts; Personal & Organisational Development; Political Economy; Popular Literary Fictions; Psychoanalysis; Social Work (with or without DipSW); Spatial Culture; The Theory & Practice of Translation; Translation; Video; Visual Culture
MA/MFA: Theatre Directing
MA/MSc: Geography-Environmental Management; Sustainable Environmental Management; Sustainable Environmental Management; Sustainable Rural Development
MA/PGDip: Research Methods for Business; Special Educational Needs; Specific Learning Difficulties; Tourism Management with Hospitality; Youth Justice, Probation & Applied Criminology *2 yrs PT* Teaching Visual Culture
MBA: Executive MBA
MProf/DProf: Professional Studies
MSc: Arboriculture & Community Forest Management; Business Information Technology; Financial Management; Integrated Pollution Control; Investment & Finance; Mental Health Interventions; Occupational Health & Safety; Water Pollution Control
MSc/PGDip: Housing; Institutional & Community Care; Interactive Multimedia Systems; Interprofessional Healthcare; Practices & Psychodynamics of Residential Care; Psychology & Health; Social Policy *2 yrs FT* Working with the Seriously Ill, the Dying and the Bereaved
MSc/PGDip/PGCert: Applied Health Research; Research Methods

Diplomas

Advanced Diploma: *1 yr PT* Complementary Therapies; Healthcare Ethics & Law; Healthcare Research
DipHE: *1 yr FT* Women's Health *18 mths FT* Adult Nursing; Child Nursing; Mental Health Nursing; Nursing Common Foundation Programme *2 yrs FT* Community Health Studies; Visual Communications Design: Graphic Design *3 yrs FT* Pre-Registration Midwifery
DipHE/BSc Hons: Child Health Studies
Diploma: Management Studies; Professional Practice (Nursing)
Diploma/Certificate: *2 yrs PT* Statistics
HND: *2 yrs FT* Computing; Environmental Health; Fashion; Graphic Design; Health, Fitness & Complementary Therapies; Hospitality Management; Housing Studies; Journalism; Landscape Design & Construction; Networking & Computer Systems; Professional Horticulture *2 yrs FT/3 yrs*

S Electronic Engineering; Electronic Systems with Business Studies *3 yrs FT* Hotel, Catering & Institutional Management
Postgraduate Diploma: *1 yr FT* Healthcare Ethics; Personnel Management

Certificates

Certificate: *2 yrs PT* Management (Healthcare Services) *2-3 yrs PT* Information Technology
Certificate of Higher Education: *1 yr FT* Nursing Programme (Enrolled Nurse Conversion Programme leading to RN (Adult, Mental Health, Children's Nursing))
Foundation Course: *1 yr FT* Art & Design; Biological & Environmental Science; Computing Science; Mathematics; Product Design
HNC/HND: *1-2 yrs FT/2-4 yrs PT* Health Therapies & Sports Fitness *2-3 yrs PT* Computing
PGCE: *1 yr FT* Primary Education *Secondary:* Art & Design; Design & Technology; Drama; English; Information Technology; Modern Foreign Languages; Music
University Certificate/Diploma/Advanced Diploma: Work Based Learning Studies

Professional Qualifications

Professional Qualifications: Professional Diploma of the Institute of Personnel Development (IPD)

NAPIER UNIVERSITY

219 Colinton Rd, Edinburgh EH14 1DJ Tel: 0131 444 2266 Fax: 0131 455 6333

* Subject to validation.

First Degrees

BA: *3 yrs FT* Business with Entrepreneurship; Business Studies; Business Studies with Entrepreneurship; Business Studies-Psychology; Hotel Services Management; Languages with International Business *3-4 yrs FT* Accounting-Economics; Business Studies with Finance; Business Studies with Human Resource Management; Business Studies with Information Management; Business Studies with Operations Management; Tourism Management with Language *4 yrs FT* Marketing Management with Entrepreneurship; Tourism with Human Resource Management; Tourism Management with Entrepreneurship *4 yrs PT* Business Studies *DL* Banking – Financial Services; Criminal Justice; Criminal Justice (Police Studies) *FT* Modular Combined Programmes *PT* Business Studies; Modular Combined Programmes *S* Business Studies with Operations Management; Business Studies with Information Management
BA Hons: *3/4 yrs FT* Business Studies-Psychology* *4 yrs FT* Accounting-Economics; Accounting-Finance; Accounting-Law; Accounting with Entrepreneurship; Business Studies with Entrepreneurship; Business Studies; Hospitality with Human Resource Management; Hospitality Management with Entrepreneurship; Languages with International Business; Marketing Management with Entrepreneurship; Tourism Management with Entrepreneurship; Tourism with Human Resource Management *4 yrs S* Business with Entrepreneurship
BA/BA Hons: *3 yrs FT/4 yrs S* Business Information Management *3-4 yrs FT* Accounting; Accounting-Information Management; Business-Financial Services; Business Economics; Business Studies with Finance; Business Studies with Human Resource Management; Business Studies with Information Management; Business Studies with Operations Management; Business Studies-Languages; Communication; Export Management-Languages or Marketing or Tourism; Financial Services with Business Economics; Financial Services; Graphic Communication Management; Hospitality Management; Hospitality-Languages or Marketing; Journalism; Languages with International Business; Law; Marketing Management; Photography, Film & Television; Publishing; Tourism Management; Tourism Management with Language *3-4 yrs S* Business Studies with Finance; Business Studies with Human Resource Management; Business Studies with Information Management; Business Studies with Operations Management *3.5-4.5 yrs S* Business Studies *4 yrs FT* Interior Architecture; Marketing-Tourism; Social Science *4 yrs PT* Business Studies
BDes: *4 yrs FT* Interdisciplinary Design
BEng: *1 yr PT* Electronics Manufacture *3 yrs FT* Engineering *3-4 yrs FT* Communications Engineering; Electronics Manufacture; Mechatronics; Multimedia Systems; Polymer Engineering;

Product Design Engineering *FT* Computer Networks and Distributed Computing; Computer Systems

BEng Hons: Communication-Electronic or Computer Engineering*; *3/4 yrs FT* Electronic & Computer Engineering (S)*; *4 yrs FT* Electronic & Communication Engineering (S)* *4.5 yrs FT* Computer Systems*; Computing Networks-Distributed Computing*

BEng/BEng Hons: *3-4 yrs FT* Civil & Transportation Engineering (S); Communications Engineering*; Computing-Electronic Systems; Electronic & Electrical Engineering (S)*; Electronics Manufacture*; Energy & Environmental Engineering (S)*; Engineering with Management*; Manufacturing Systems Engineering*; Mechanical Engineering*; Mechatronics*; Multimedia Systems*; Polymer Engineering*; Product Design Engineering*; Software Engineering *4-6 yrs PT* Electronic & Electrical Engineering*; Software Engineering

BMus: *3/4 yrs FT* Music

BSc: *1yr PT* Multimedia Technology (Direct entrants); Network Computing (Direct entrants); Software Technology (Direct entrant) *1-4 yrs PT* Complementary Therapies (Aromatherapy) (up to 5 yrs depending on no. of modules taken – max 3 per semester)*; Complementary Therapies (Reflexology) (up to 5 yrs depending on no. of modules taken – max 3 per semester)*; Homeopathy (up to 5 yrs; offered as PT or FT)*; Midwifery Studies with Health Studies (max no. yrs – 6 for midwifery, 4 for health studies); Nursing (up to 5 yrs) *15 wks PT* Clinical Supervision *2 yrs FT* Software Technology (Direct entrant) *2-3 yrs PT* Nursing (Specialist Practitioner Qualification) *3 yrs FT* Midwifery (Pre-registration)* *3-4 yrs FT* Animal Biology; Business Information Technology; Civil Engineering; Combined Studies (Built Environment); Computer-Aided Design and Information Technology; Computer Aided Design and Business; Construction and Project Management; Construction Engineering; Electronics and Business; Electronics and Information Technology; Environmental Biology; Environmental Toxicology; Health Sciences (Jointly with the Faculty of Science); Immunology and Toxicology; Industrial Technology and Business; Industrial Technology-Information Technology; Information Analysis; Marine and Freshwater Biology; Mechatronics and Business; Mechatronics-Information Technology; Transportation Engineering; Medical Microbiology *4-6 yrs PT* Medical Microbiology *3-4 yrs PT* Information Analysis *4 yrs FT* Business Information Technology; Health and Life Sciences; Health and Social Sciences; Health Science with Health Promotion; Health Sciences; Health Sciences with Gender Health *4 yrs PT* Health Sciences *4-6 yrs PT* Animal Biology; Environmental Biology; Environmental Toxicology; Immunology and Toxicology; Marine and Freshwater Biology *FT* Human Computer Systems; Sport and Exercise Science* *FT/PT* Multimedia Technology (Direct Entrants); Network Computing (Direct Entrants); Software Technology (Direct Entrant) *PT* Construction and Project Management *Up to 5 yrs PT* Mental Health Practice

BSc Hons: *4 yrs FT* Business Information Technology *4.5 yrs FT* Human Computer Systems* *4 yrs S* Industrial Design

BSc/BSc Hons: *1-2 yrs FT* Multimedia Technology (Direct entrants); Network Computing (Direct entrants) *2-3 yrs PT* Nursing (Specialist Practitioner Qualification) *3-4 yrs FT* Animal Biology; Business Information Technology; Combined Studies (Built Environment); Computer-Aided Design-Business*; Computer-Aided Design-Information Technology*; Construction-Project Management; Construction Engineering*; Electronics-Business*; Electronics-Information Technology*; Environmental Biology; Environmental Toxicology*; Health Sciences (Jointly with the Faculty of Science); Immunology-Toxicology; Industrial Technology-Business*; Industrial Technology-Information Technology*; Information Analysis*; Marine-Freshwater Biology; Mechatronics-Business*; Mechatronics-Information Technology*; Medical Microbiology*; Social & Management Sciences; Transportation Engineering*; Transport Studies with Information Management *3-4 yrs FT/4-6 yrs PT/8 yrs Hons PT* Architectural Technology; Building Control; Building Surveying; Estate Management; Planning & Development Surveying; Quantity Surveying *3-4 yrs PT* Information Analysis* *3-4-5 yrs S* Ecotourism; Mathematics with Technology or Computing or Financial Studies *3-4-5 yrs S/4-6 yrs PT* Applied Microbiology & Biotechnology*; Biological Sciences; Biomedical Sciences; Environmental Biology; Toxicology *4 yrs only FT* Accounting-Applied Statistics; Accounting-Mathematics; Applied Statistics-Business Economics; Applied Statistics-Economics; Applied Statistics-Financial Services; Applied Statistics-Music; Applied Statistics-Psychology; Applied Statistics-Sociology; Economics-Mathematics; Financial Services-Mathematics; Health Sciences (Jointly with the Faculty of Health); Health Sciences with Gender Health; Mathematics-Music; Mathematics-Psychology; Mathematics-Sociology;

Mathematics with Statistics *4-5 yrs* Computing; Information Systems *4 yrs PT* Health Sciences (Jointly with the Faculty of Health) *4-6 yrs PT* Animal Biology; Environmental Biology; Environmental Toxicology; Immunology-Toxicology; Marine-Freshwater Biology; Medical Microbiology* *6-8 yrs PT* Construction-Project Management

Higher Degrees

Diploma/MSc: Accounting- Finance (2 yrs for Diploma, 3 yrs for MSc)
LLM: *1 yr FT* International Law
MA: *1 yr FT* Exhibition Interpretation
MBA: *PT or by open learning*
MMus: *FT/PT* Jazz
MSc: Business Management; Information Systems (9 mths: PGDip, 12 mths: MSc); Object Orientated Software Engineering; Publishing *1 yr FT* Administration & Information Management; Advertising Communication; Biology of Water Resource Management; Biomedical Sciences; Electronic Journalism; Electronic Publishing; Electronics (Communications); Electronics (Computer Engineering); Electronics (Digital Systems); Electronics (Manufacture); European Marketing-Languages; Human Resource Management; Information Technology (Engineering Design); Information Technology (Mechatronics); Information Technology (Multimedia Technology); Information Technology (Software Engineering); International Journalism; Newspaper Journalism; Periodical Journalism; Publishing; Publishing Production; Quality Management*; Social & Education Research; Social & Employment Research; Social & Health Research; Social Research; Software Technology; Transportation Engineering *Information Technology:* Computer-Aided Engineering; Engineering Design; Mechatronics; Multimedia Technology; Software Engineering *1 yr FT/2-3 yrs PT* Applied Statistics *1 yr PT* Business Management *15 wks* Information Technology (Software Engineering) *2 yrs PT* Advertising Communication; Applied Statistics; Biomedical Sciences; Electronic Journalism; Electronic Publishing; Human Resource Management; Information Systems; Information Technology (Engineering Design); Information Technology (Mechatronics); Information Technology (Multimedia Technology); Information Technology (Software Engineering); International Journalism; Materials Technology; Newspaper Journalism; Object Orientated Software Engineering; Periodical Journalism; Property & Construction Management; Publishing Production; Social & Education Research; Social & Employment Research; Social and Health Research; Social Research; Software Technology *2-4 yrs OL* Criminal Justice (District Courts); Criminal Justice (Police Studies) *2-5 yrs OL* Property & Construction Management *3 yrs* Materials Technology *3 yrs PT* Accounting-Finance; Electronics (Communications); Electronics (Computer Engineering); Electronics (Digital Systems); Electronics (Manufacture); Plastics Moulding Technology; Publishing; Quality and Business Excellence*; Quality Management* *45 wks FT* Business Management *48 wks FT* Information Technology (Computer Aided Engineering); Information Technology (Mechatronics); Materials Technology *PT* Information Technology (Software Engineering)
MSc/PGDip: Information Technology (Computer Aided Engineering) (32 wks (PGDip), 48 wks (MSc)); Information Technology (Mechatronics) (32 wks (PGDip), 48 wks (MSc)); Materials Technology (32 wks (PGDip), 48 wks (MSc)) *1 yr FT* Information Technology-Financial Services; Masters in Accounting and Finance *2 yrs PT* Biomedical Science-Drug Design* *2-3 yrs DL* Transportation Engineering* *2-3 yrs PT* Advanced Neonatal Nursing Practice* *3 yrs PT* Publishing *DL* Computer Enhanced Mathematics Education *FT/DL* Facilities Management*; Property Management-Investment* *FT/PT* Corporate Strategy-Finance; Drug Design-Toxicology; Ecotourism; Interactive Technologies for e-Commerce*; Midwifery; Nursing; Tourism Management; Wildlife Biology-Conservation* *PT* Electronics Manufacture; Engineering Information Technology (Computer Aided Engineering); Facilities Management*; Internet Technologies for e-Commerce*; Property Management-Investment*
MSc/PGDip/PGCert: *PT* Accounting and Finance
PgD/MSc: Information Systems (9 mths FT (PgD), 12 mths FT (MSc)); Information Technology (Computer-Aided Engineering) (32 wks FT (PgD), 48 wks FT (MSc))
PgDip/MSc: Local Economic Development (2-3 yrs (PgDip), 2-5 yrs (MSc)); Materials Technology (32 wks FT (PgDip), 48 wks FT (MSc)) *1 yr FT* Property and Construction Management (9 mths (PgDip), 1 yr (MSc))

Diplomas

Advanced Diploma: *1 yr FT* Biomedical Sciences *1 yr PT* Biomedical Sciences *2 yrs OL* Careers Guidance for Clients with Special Needs *2 yrs PT* Plastics Moulding Technology *PT (with flexible attendance)* Counselling

DipHE: *2 yrs FT* Diploma in Higher Education (Built Environment) *2-4 yrs PT* Studies for the Church in the Community

Diploma of Higher Education: *3 yrs FT* Midwifery (18 mths FT for registered nurses); Nursing (Adult; Child; Mental Health; Learning Disabilities) (2 yrs FT for grads)

Distance Learning: Certificate/ Diploma in Marketing

District Court Practice & Procedure: *1 yr OL*

Higher National Diploma: *2 yrs FT* Applied Biological Sciences; Business Administration; Civil Engineering; Computing; Electrical Engineering; Engineering*; Engineering – Electrical & Mechanical* *4 yrs PT* Software Engineering

HND: *FT* Applied Biological Sciences

PGDip: *1 yr PT* Management Studies *2 yrs PT* International Law *PT* Marketing, Chartered Institute of Marketing

Postgraduate Diploma: *1 yr FT* Administrative & Information Management; Advanced Electronic Design; Advertising Communication; Applied Statistics; Biology of Water Resource Management; Biomedical Sciences; Business Management; Careers Guidance; Electronic Journalism; Electronic Publishing; Electronics (Communications); European Marketing- Languages; Exhibition Interpretation; Hospitality; Human Resource Management; Information Technology (Engineering Design); International Journalism; International Law; Newspaper Journalism; Object Orientated Software Engineering; Periodical Journalism; Property & Construction Management; Publishing; Publishing Production; Quality Management*; Social & Education Research; Social & Employment Research; Social & Health Research; Social Research *Information Technology:* Engineering Design; Multimedia Technology (1 yr taught then MSc dissertation 16 wks); Software Engineering *1 yr OL* Criminal Justice (District Courts); Criminal Justice (Police Studies); District Court Practice & Procedure *1 yr PT* Local Economic Development *2 yrs PT* Accounting-Finance; Administrative & Information Management; Applied Statistics; Biomedical Sciences; Business Management; Electronic Journalism; Electronic Publishing; Human Resource Management (plus dissertation); Information Systems; Information Technology (Mechatronics); Information Technology (Engineering Design); Information Technology (Multimedia Technology); Information Technology (Software Engineering); International Journalism; Materials Technology; Newspaper Journalism; Object Orientated Software Engineering; Periodical Journalism; Publishing Production; Quality Management (2 yrs PT academic; 1 yr PT dissertation); Social & Education Research; Social & Employment Research; Social & Health Research; Social Research; Software Technology; Transportation Engineering *2-5 yrs OL* Property & Construction Management *3 yrs PT* Electronics (Communications); Plastics Moulding Technology; Publishing *31 wks FT* Software Technology *32 wks FT* Information Technology (Computer Aided Engineering); Information Technology (Mechatronics); Information Technology (Software Engineering); Materials Technology *9 mths FT* Information Systems

Postgraduate/Post-Experience Diploma: *1 yr FT* Careers Guidance; Chartered Association of Certified Accountants; Chartered Institute of Bankers (Stage 2 Associateship) (Stage 3 Membership); Chartered Institute of Management Accountants; Company Secretarial Practice and Share Registration Practice (ICSA); Exhibition Interpretation *1 yr PT* Chartered Institute of Certified Accountants (ACCA); Chartered Institute of Marketing; District Court Practice & Procedure; Institute of Chartered Secretaries & Administrators; Institute of Quality Assurance (A11: Introduction to Quality Assurance; A12: Principles and Techniques of Quality Management); Management; Marketing (Senior Managers Intensive Diploma course) (Diploma in Direct Marketing) (Scottish Power Marketing Training Scheme) *2 yrs PT* Chartered Institute of Marketing; Institute of Purchasing & Supply

University Diploma: *1 yr FT* Accounting *2 yrs FT* Accounting *4 yrs PT* Accounting

Certificates

CertHE: *2 yrs PT* Working with People in the Church and Community *3 yrs PT* Church Studies *FT* Certificate in Higher Education (Built Environment)

Certificate: *1 yr PT* Institute of Chartered Secretaries & Administrators *2 yrs PT* Accounting
Higher National Certificate: *1 yr FT* Applied Biological Sciences *2 yrs FT* Engineering *2 yrs PT* Civil Engineering; Computing; Engineering; Mechatronics*; Polymer Technology
HNC: *2 yrs PT DL* Contracting Management
PGCert: *1 yr DL* Management Studies *1 yr PT* Management Studies
University Certificate: *1 yr FT* Accounting *2 yrs PT* Accounting

UNIVERSITY OF NEWCASTLE UPON TYNE

Newcastle upon Tyne NE1 7RU Tel: 0191 222 6138/8672 Fax: 0191 222 6139 Telex: 53654 UNINEWG
e-mail: admissions-enquiries@ncl.ac.uk Website: www.ncl.ac.uk

First Degrees

BA Combined Hons: *3 yrs* Economics; Education; English Literature; Understanding Asian Cultures (first yr only) *Choice of 3-5 Subjects:* Philosophical Studies: Cosmos & European Traditions; A Science Subject; Accounting; Ancient History; Archaeology; Architectural History and Theory; Biblical Studies; Chinese; Computing Science; English Linguistic Studies; Film Studies (2nd & 3rd yr only); Fine Art (Drawing); French; Geography; German; Greek; Greek & Roman Culture; Greek (New Testament); Hebrew; Hindu Studies (2nd & 3rd yr only); History; History of Art; Japanese; Korean; Latin; Law; Mathematics & Statistics; Medieval Studies; Music; Politics; Portuguese; Psychology; Religious studies; Sanskrit (1st yr only); Science subject; Social Policy; Social Studies; Spanish & Latin American Studies
BA Hon in Architectural Studies & BArch: *5 yrs (3 to BA & 2 to BArch)*
BA Hons: *3-4 yrs* Spanish-Politics; Town Planning (plus 2 yrs Dip in Town Planning)*Arts:* Ancient History; Ancient History-Archaeology; Archaeology; Business & Economic Studies (under review); Business Management; Business Management with Japanese; Business Management with Korean; Economics-Business Management (with Business Training); Classical Studies; Classics; Economics; Economics with Information Systems; Politics-Economics; English Language; English Language-Literature; English Literature; English Literature & Latin; Environmental Planning & Society; European Business Management; Financial & Business Economics; Fine Art; French; French-Politics or Linguistics; Geography; German; German or Politics; Linguistics; Government & European Union Studies with Latin; Greek; History; Humanities; International Business Management; International Management; Latin with Greek; Latin American Studies; Law with French with Japanese or Chinese or Korean or Marketing & Management; Linguistics; Linguistics; Spanish-Linguistics; Modern Languages with Film Studies; Modern Languages with Linguistics; Modern Languages; Modern Languages-Film Studies or Linguistics; Music; Philosophical Studies: Knowledge and Human Interests; Politics; Politics and Social Policy; Politics-History; Psychology; Religious Studies; Politics-Social Policy; Social Policy-Sociology; Sociology; Spanish; Spanish-Linguistics or Politics *3-4 yrs FT* Mechanical & Automotive Engineering; Mechanical & Design Engineering; Mechanical & Manufacturing Engineering; Mechanical & Materials Engineering; Mechanical Engineering; Mechanical Engineering (Europe); Mechanical Engineering-Mechatronics
BDS: *5 yrs FT* Dentistry
BEng Hons: *3-4 yrs FT* Chemical & Process Engineering; Civil & Environmental Engineering; Civil & Structural Engineering; Civil Engineering; Electrical & Electronic Engineering; Electronic Communications; Electronic Engineering; Marine Engineering; Marine Technology; Mechanical Engineering; Microelectronics & Software Engineering; Naval Architecture; Offshore Engineering; Small Craft Technology
BMus Hons: Music; Popular & Contemporary Music
BSc Biomedical Science Hons: *3 yrs* Pharmacology
BSc Hons: *3 yrs* Biochemistry; Biological Sciences; Biology; Biomedical Sciences; Genetics; Medical Microbiology; Microbiology; Molecular Biology; Physiological Sciences *Some 4 yr courses with foundation yr available:* Human Genetics
BSc Hons (Agricultural & Biological): *3 yrs* Agriculture; Agronomy; Animal Production Science; Animal Science; Countryside Management; Domestic Animal Science; Ecological Resource Management; Entomology & Pest Management; Environmental Biology; Environmental Science & Agricultural Ecology; Farm Business Management; Food Marketing; Food Marketing

Management; Marine Biology; Rural Resource Management; Wildlife Biology; Zoology *3-4 yrs* Applied Biology *4 yrs* Agri-Business Management; Food & Human Nutrition

Bsc Hons (Science): *3 yrs FT* Mathematics-Surveying; Mapping Science *Some 4 yr courses with foundation yr available:* Accounting-Financial Analysis; Astronomy-Astrophysics; Chemical Physics; Chemical Technology for Management; Chemistry with Education with Study in North America; Chemistry; Chemistry (with Industrial Training Yr-4 yrs); Chemistry with European Studies (BSc Hons French, German, Spanish); Chemistry; Chemistry (4 yrs with Industrial Training) with Medicinal Chemistry (4 yrs with Industrial Training); Chemistry with Applied Chemistry; Computer Systems Engineering; Computing Science; Economics-Geography; Geographic Information Science; Geography; Mathematical Sciences (Deferred Choice); Mathematics with Education; Mathematics; Mathematics-Statistics; Physic with Medical Applications; Physics with Medicinal Applications; Physics; Psychology; Software Engineering; Statistics with Education; Statistics; Surveying & Mapping Science; Theoretical Physics *4 yrs Some 4 yr courses with foundation yr available:* Accounting-Law; Mathematics (with industrial training)-Physics (with industrial training); Mathematics (with industrial training)-Psychology (with industrial training) *4 yrs S Some 4 yr courses with foundation yr available:* European Business Management (Includes 1 yr at a European Business School)

BSc Hons Combined Studies: *3 yrs, 4 yrs with Foundation Yr:* Astronomy & Astrophysics; Biological Sciences-Biomedical Sciences; Chemistry; Computer Science & Software Engineering; Geography; Mathematics & Statistics; Physics; Psychology; Surveying & Mapping Science

BSc Hons Ed: *4 yrs* English Management Studies; Applied Communications or Social Policy; Language Sciences-Speech

BSc Joint Hons: *3 yrs, 4 yrs with Foundation Yr:* Statistics; Chemistry-Mathematics or Physics or Psychology or Surveying & Mapping Sciences; Economics-Computing Science or Mathematics or Statistics; Economics-Mathematics or Statistics; Geography-Mathematics or Statistics or Surveying & Mapping Science; Mathematics-Accounting or Statistics or Computing Science; Mathematics-Physics or Psychology or Surveying & Mapping Sciences; Physics-Computing Science or Mathematics; Psychology-Statistics; Statistics-Accounting or Chemistry or Computing Science or Economics or Geography or Psychology

LLB Hons: *3 yrs*

MB; BS

Higher Degrees
DOCTORATES

DBA: *30 mths FT/60 mths PT* Business Administration

DClinPsy: *48 mths PT* Clinical Psychology (By thesis; advanced study & research)

DEdPsy: *4-5 yrs PT*

DLitt; DSc; DEng: (For Newcastle grads or academic staff in respect of work of distinction)

EdD: *24 mths FT/4 yrs PT min.* (by research, advanced courses, exams & either thesis or 2 related dissertations for holders of suitable qualifications)

LLD: (For Newcastle grads in respect of independent original work)

MASTER'S DEGREES

LLM: Philosophical Studies of Knowledge & Human Interest *1 yr FT/2 yrs PT* Environmental Legal Studies; Health Sciences; International Legal Studies; International Trade

MA: *1 yr FT/2 yrs PT By course of instruction:* Advanced Historical Studies; Ancient History; Applied Linguistics & Bilingualism; Applied Policy Research; Applied Theology; Archaeology; Architecture; Child & Adolescent Mental Health; Chinese-English, English-Chinese Conference Interpreting; Chinese-English, English-Chinese Translating; Chinese-English, English-Chinese Translating & Interpreting; Classics; Environment Law & Society; European Union Studies; Film Studies; Greek & Roman Archaeology; Heritage Education & Interpretation; History of Roman Italy; Housing Studies; Human Resource Management; International Business Management; International Cultural Change; International Financial Analysis; International Human Resource Management; International Management; International Political Economy; International Studies; International Studies (Research Training); Landscape Design Studies; Linguistics & English Language; Linguistics for TESOL; Media Technology for Teaching English as a Foreign Language;

Museum Studies; Music Technology; Music, Meaning and Culture; Nationalism and Transnational Development; Planning Studies; Planning Studies (International); Popular Music Studies; Religion & Literature; Shakespeare & Renaissance Culture; Town Planning (Europe); Town Planning (Urban Conservation); Twentieth Century Studies: English & American Literature & Film; Urban Conservation; Urban Design; Women's Studies

Master of Architecture: *18 mths PT*

Master of International Housing Science: *2 yrs FT* (by exam & dissertation)

Master of Landscape Architecture: *12 mths FT/2 yrs FT/24 mths PT By exam & dissertation:* (Special regulations for Master's degrees & doctorates exist for members of Univ Staff)

Master of Town Planning: *12 mths FT/2 yrs FT/24 mths PT* (By exam & dissertation)

MBA: (By exam & dissertation) *1 yr FT/30 mths PT* Strategic Telecommunications Management *33 mths PT* Rolls Royce Consortium

MChem: Chemistry; Medicinal Chemistry (undergraduate degree)

MChem, MMath, MPhys: *4 yrs* Astronomy-Astrophysics; Chemical Physics; Chemistry (with study in North America); Chemistry with Medicinal Chemistry; Chemistry; Mathematics; Mathematics-Statistics; Physics with Medicinal Applications; Physics; Theoretical Physics

MEd: Education (Educational Management) (Hou Dhabi); Education (Guidance and Counselling) (Hong Kong); Education (TESOL) *24 mths PT*

MEd, MPhil: *1 yr FT/2 yrs PT* (By adv course, exam & dissertation for holders of suitable qualifications); (By research & thesis for holders of suitable qualifications)

MEng Hons: *4-5 yrs* Chemical & Process Engineering; Civil & Environmental Engineering; Civil & Structural Engineering; Civil Engineering; Electrical & Electronic Engineering; Electronic Communication; Electronic Engineering; Marine Technology; Marine Technology; Marine Technology; Mechanical & Automotive Engineering; Mechanical & Design Engineering; Mechanical & Manufacturing Engineering; Mechanical Engineering; Mechanical Engineering (Europe); Mechanical Engineering-Materials Engineering or Mechatronics; Microelectronics & Software Engineering; Naval Architecture; Offshore Engineering; Small Craft Technology *Foundation yr also available:* Chemical & Process Engineering; Civil Engineering; Electrical & Electronic Engineering; Mechanical Engineering

MFA: Fine Art *2 yrs FT* Master of Fine Art (Course of adv study & research in; Printmaking; Painting; Sculpture)

MLitt: *1 yr FT/2 yrs PT* (By thesis and guided study)

MMath: (undergraduate degree)

MMus: Composition; Performance

MMus Composition, MMus Performance: *1 yr FT/2 yrs PT* (Course of instruction)

MPhil: *1 yr FT/2 yrs PT* (By Research)*PT By thesis:* Museum Studies

MPhys: Astronomy & Astrophysics; Physics; Theoretical Physics

MRes: *1 yr FT* Marine Technology

MSc: *Agriculture & Biological Sciences:* Advanced Silicon Processing & Manufacturing Technologies IGDs; Automation and Control; Computer aided Design & Management; Engineering Geology; Environmental & Resource Assessment; International Agricultural & Food Marketing; Pest Management; Relativity, Astrophysics and Cosmology; Rural Resource & Countryside Management; Tropical Agricultural & Environmental Science; Tropical Coastal Management; Tropical Soils & Sustainable Land Management *Education:* Educational Psychology; Human Communication Sciences; Language Pathology *Engineering:* Advanced Silicon Processing & Manufacturing Technologies; Applied Process Control; Clean Technology; Communications & Signal Processing; Designing Chemical Solutions; Drug Chemistry; Electrical Power; Electronics; Engineering Hydrology; Engineering Mathematics; Environmental Engineering; Geotechnical Engineering; GIS & Archaeology – Time, Space, People and Place; Groundwater Engineering; Hydroinformatics & Hydraulic Engineering; Hydroinformatics & Management Systems; Irrigation with Marketing; Manufacturing Systems Engineering; Marine Engineering; Marine Technology; Mathematical Techniques & their Applications; Mechanical Properties of Solids; Microelectronics; Offshore Engineering; Pipeline Engineering; Quality Engineering; Structural Engineering; Structural Engineering & Construction Management; Sustainable Management of the Water Environment; Transport & Business Management; Transport Engineering & Operations; Transportation Planning & Policy *Science:* Computing Science *1 yr FT Social Sciences:* Computer-Aided Design & Management *1 yr FT/2 yrs PT Medicine:* Disability & Oral Care; Genetics; Health

Sciences; Industrial Biotechnology; Occupational Hygiene; Orthodontics; Psychiatric & Mental Health Nursing Practice; Rehabilitation Management; Restorative Dentistry *1 yr FT/2 yrs PT by research, thesis & in some cases exam Arts:* GIS & Archaeology: Time, Space, People & Place; Science with English *Engineering:* Environmental Biogeochemistry *Science:* Petroleum Geochemistry

POSTGRADUATE BACHELOR'S DEGREE

BPhil: (10 mths FT (followed by dissertation) or 3 yrs PT incl min of 5 wks FT. By exam & dissertation. Educational Studies)

HIGHER MEDICAL DEGREES

DDS: (In respect of independent original work & oral exam. Dental Science)
MD: (By thesis & oral exam if required)

Diplomas

Advanced Educational Studies (DAES): *9 mths FT* (Advanced Diploma in Education (ADE) 24 Mths PT)
Diploma: Business Administration (Derwentside Industrial Agency)
Educational Studies: *9 mths FT*
Postgraduate Diploma: Advanced Historical Studies; Ancient History; Applied Policy Research; Applied Theology; Archaeology; Business Administration; Classics; Counselling in Health and Social Care Settings; Engineering Mathematics; Greek and Roman Archaeology; Heritage Education & Interpretation; History of Roman Italy; Industrial Biotechnology; Irrigation; Landscape Design; Lifelong Learning; Linguistics and English Language; Linguistics for TESOL; Media Technology for TEFL; Music, Meaning and Culture; Popular Music Studies; Professional Practice and Management; Rehabilitation Engineering; Research Skills & Methods in the Social Sciences; Rural Resource and Countryside Management with English; Science; Shakespeare and Renaissance Culture; Sustainable Management of the Water Environment; Town Planning; Town Planning (Urban Conservation); Twentieth Century Studies: English & American Literature & Film; Urban Conservation; Urban Design; Women's Studies *2 semesters* Advanced General Practice; Agricultural Marketing; Applied Process Control; Chemical & Process Engineering; Chinese-English, English-Chinese Translating; Clean Technology; Composition (Music); Computer-Aided Design & Management; Computing Science; Conscious Sedation in Dentistry; Engineering Hydrology; Environmental & Resource Assessment; Environmental Biogeochemistry; Environmental Engineering; Film Studies; Geotechnical Engineering; Groundwater Engineering; Health Sciences; Housing Studies; Hydroinformatics & Hydraulic Engineering; International Agricultural Food Marketing; International Financial Analysis; Landscape Architecture; Lifelong Learning; Management Studies; Museum Studies; Music Technology; Performance (Music); Pest Management; Petroleum Geochemistry; Planning; Quality Engineering; Religion & Literature; Research Skills & Methods in the Social Sciences; Research Training in Political Philosophy History of Political Thought; Structural Engineering; Structural Engineering & Construction Management; Therapeutics; Town & Country Planning; Transport Engineering & Operations; Transportation Planning & Policy; Tropical Coastal Management; Tropical Soils & Sustainable Land Management; Tropical Agricultural & Environmental Science; Understanding & Treatment of Disturbed Behaviour in Childhood & Adolescence

Certificates

Certificate: Conservation & Planning; Conservation Principles & Techniques; Lifelong Learning; Management (Culture & Heritage); Management Studies; Neurological Rehabilitation; Primary Care Research; Proficiency of Modern Foreign Languages
Postgraduate Certificate: Electrical Power Engineering; Engineering Mathematics; Lifelong Learning; Marine Technology; Medical Education; Quality Engineering; Transport Engineering *3 trms* Environmental Engineering; International Political Science
Postgraduate Certificate in Education: *1 yr FT*
Testamur in English Studies for Norwegians: *1 yr FT*

UNIVERSITY COLLEGE NORTHAMPTON

Park Campus, Broughton Green Road, Northampton NN2 7AL Tel: 01604 735500
Fax: 01604 720636 e-mail: admissions@northampton.ac.uk Website: www.northampton.ac.uk

First Degrees

BA Hons: *1 yr FT (HND Top-up):* Business Administration & Management *1 yr FT/2 yrs PT (DipHE Top-up):* Community Health Care Nursing *3 yrs FT* Accounting & Finance; American Studies; Business Entrepreneurship; Business Information Systems; Criminology; Cultural Studies; Early Childhood Studies; Early Years Education with QTS; Electronic Commerce; English; Fashion; Fine Art; Geography; Graphic Communications; History; Marketing; Music; Performance Studies; Primary Education with QTS (General Primary); Social Work; Sociology *4 yrs S* Business Studies; International Business Studies

BSc Hons: *1 yr FT (HND Top-up):* Equine & Estate Studies *3 yrs FT* Earth Science; Architectural Technology; Behavioural Science; Biology; Computing (Computer Communications); Computing (Computer Systems); Computing (Internet Technology); Computing (Software Engineering); Engineering; Environmental Management; Geography; Human Biology; Leather Technology; Midwifery Studies; Nursing Studies (Adult); Nursing Studies (Child Health); Nursing Studies (Learning Disabilities); Nursing Studies (Mental Health); Occupational Therapy; Podiatry; Product Design; Psychology; Sport Science; Wastes Management; Wastes Management & Pollution Control *3 yrs PT (HND/C entry):* Computing *3.5 yrs PT (Professional registration entry):* Gerontology; Health Science Studies; Nursing

LLB: *3 yrs FT*

COMBINED HONOURS DEGREE PROGRAMME

BA Hons/BSc Hons: *3 yrs FT* Business Ent *3 yrs FT/Flexible PT major/minor/elective subjects:* Accountancy; American Studies; Business; Criminology; Drama; Earth Science; Ecology; Economics; Education; English; Fine Art; French; Geography; History; Human Biological Studies; Industrial Archaeology; Industrial Enterprise; Information Systems; Law; Management Science; Mathematics; Media & Popular Culture; Music; Politics; Psychology; Sociology; Sport Studies *Minor/elective subjects:* Architectural Studies; Chemistry & the Environment; Equine Studies; European Union Studies; Fossils; German; Health Studies; History of Art; Marketing Communications; People in Organisations; Philosophy; Property Management; Social Welfare; Spanish; Third World Development

Higher Degrees

International MBA: *1 yr FT*

MA: *1 yr FT* International Business Analysis *1 yr FT/2 yrs PT* Linguistics & Literature; Modern English Studies; Women's Studies *15 mths PT (PGDip entry):* Human Resource Management *18 mths PT* Marketing Management *2 yrs PT* Medical & Healthcare Ethics; Modern History; Policy Studies; Printmaking; Theatre Studies *Flexible PT* Professional Studies in Education

MBA: *1 yr FT* MBA for Women *1 yr PT* (DMS entry) *3 yrs PT*

Mphil: *1-2 yrs FT/2-4 yrs PT*

@First Para:MSc: *1 yr FT* Leather Technology; Management Studies *1 yr FT/2 yrs PT* Applied Psychology; Environmental Management; Office Systems & Data Communication *Flexible PT* Health Studies; Health Studies: Midwifery; Health Studies: Nursing; Health Studies: Occupational Therapy; Health Studies: Physiotherapy; Health Studies: Podiatry; Podiatry

PhD: *2-4 yrs FT/3-6 yrs PT*

Diplomas

Diploma: *1 yr FT* BTEC Diploma in Foundation Studies in Art & Design *1 yr PT* RSA Diploma for Teachers of Learners with Specific Learning Difficulties

Diploma in Higher Education: Registered Nurse *1 yr PT (HNC entry):* Social Care *2 yrs FT/3-4 yrs PT* Social Work *3 yrs FT* Registered Midwife

HND: *2 yrs FT* Animal Welfare & Management; Architectural Technology; Business; Business & Finance; Business & Marketing; Business & Personnel; Business Information Technology;

Computer Systems; Computing; Construction Management; Countryside Management; Engineering; Equine Studies with Estate Studies; Fashion; Graphic Design; Media (Production & Practice); Product Design; Quantity Surveying

PGDip: *2 yrs PT* Management Studies (DMS); Professional Studies in Education

Certificates

Certificate: *1 yr FT* Foundation Course in Leather Technology *1 yr PT* C&G 457 Craft Certificate; C&G 457 Operatives' Certificate; Health Education; Management Studies; Professional Management (IPD) *2 yrs PT* National Certificate in Leather Technology

Certificate in Education: *2 yrs PT* Post-Compulsory Education

HNC: *2 yrs PT* Business & Finance; Business Information Technology; Caring Service (Care Management); Caring Service (Social Care); Computer Systems; Computing; Electrical Engineering; Electronic Engineering; Graphic Design; Mechanical Engineering

PGCert: *1 yr FT* Education (Primary) *1 yr PT* Management

Other Courses

Courses: *2 yrs PT* Enrolled Nurse Conversion *3-5 yrs PT* Chartered Association of Management Accountants (ACCA) *4 yrs PT* Chartered Institute of Management Accountants (CIMA) *Flexible PT* Assessment & Verification Awards; Framework for Continuing Professional Education; Individually produced training & development programmes & consultancy for businesses; Institute of Personnel & Development Diploma; Institute of Quality Assurance; Leather Induction Course; Nursing, Midwifery & Health Visiting; Return to Teaching

*UNIVERSITY OF NORTH LONDON

166-220 Holloway Road, London N7 8DB Tel: 020 7753 3355 Fax: 020 7753 3272
e-mail: Admissions@unl.ac..uk Website: www.unl.ac.uk

† Subject to validation.

First Degrees

BA (QTS): *2 yrs FT* Mathematics

BA Hons: *3 yrs FT* Accounting & Finance; Architecture; Business & Philosophy; Business Administration; Business Economics-Finance; Business Studies; Business Systems Modelling; Caribbean Studies-Leisure Studies; Creative Writing; Economics-History; Ethics; European Studies-Hospitality Management or International Business; Events Management; Facilities Management; Hospitality Management; Hospitality Management-Caribbean Studies; Human Resource Studies-Women's Studies; International Business; International Hospitality Management; International Leisure & Tourism Management; Leisure & Tourism Management; Marketing-French or Spanish & Latin American Studies; Performing Arts; Philosophy-Economics; Sports Management; Theatre Studies-Arts Management; Tourism Studies *3 yrs FT. 2 subjects from 1 group only Group 1:* Accounting; Arts Management; Business Economics; Economics; Economics; Hospitality Management; Human Resource Studies; International Business; Law in Business; Leisure Studies; Marketing; Retail Management; Sports Management; Tourism Studies *Group 2:* Caribbean Studies; Critical Theory; Education Studies; English; Film Studies; French; German; History; Humanities IT; Irish Studies; Philosophy; Spanish & Latin American Studies; Theatre Studies; Women's Studies *4 yrs FT* European Studies or Philosophy; French-Caribbean Studies or Critical theory or English or History or Education Studies or Film Studies or Humanities IT or Irish Studies or Theatre Studies or Women's Studies or German or Spanish & Latin American Studies or Irish Studies; German-Caribbean Studies or Critical Theory or English or History or Philosophy or Education Studies or Film Studies or Humanities IT or Theatre Studies or Women's Studies or Spanish & Latin American Studies; International Business-French or German or Spanish; International Hospitality Management; Spanish & Latin American Studies-Caribbean Studies or Critical Theory or English or History or Philosophy or Education Studies or Film Studies or Humanities IT or Irish Studies or Theatre Studies or Women's Studies

BA/BSc Hons: *3 yrs FT* Applied Psychology-Education Studies or Human Resource Studies or Philosophy or Women's Studies; Arts Management or Business or Film Studies or Theatre Studies; Biological Sciences-Education Studies; Business Economics-Consumer Studies; Business Systems

Modelling; Business-Applied Psychology; Business-Communications Engineering; Business-Computing or Politics or Polymer Engineering; Caribbean Studies-Information Systems or Law; Chemistry-Business or Education Studies or French or German or Philosophy; Critical Theory & Cultural Studies-Economics; Sociology-Environmental Management; Ecology; Environmental Science; European Studies-Politics or Sociology; Film Studies-Arts Management; French and Humanities Information Technology; Health Studies-Philosophy or Sports Management or Women's Studies or Leisure Studies or Social Research or Sociology; Human Geography; Human Nutrition-Sports Management; Human Resource Studies-Consumer Studies; International Business-Politics; Law-Philosophy or History; Mathematical Sciences-Business or Education Studies; Philosophy-Politics; Economics or Philosophy; Retail Management-Human Geography; Social Research-Caribbean Studies or Education Studies or Irish Studies or Marketing or Philosophy or Women's Studies; Statistics-Business or Education Studies; Tourism Studies-Caribbean Studies or Human Geography; Women's Studies-Law
BEd: *1 yr* International Primary and Secondary
BEd Hons: *3 yrs FT* Education (Primary) and early years
BEng Hons: *3 yrs FT/4 yrs S* Electronic & Communication Engineering; Electronic Engineering; Polymer Engineering
BSc Hons: *3 yrs FT* Applied Psychology; Cultural Studies; Environmental Management; Health Studies; Human Geography; Mass Communication; Politics; Public Administration; Social Work; Social Work; Sociology with Health Studies or Politics or Applied Psychology or Social Research *3 yrs FT/4 yrs S* Applied Statistics; Biochemistry; Biological & Medicinal Chemistry; Biomedical Sciences; Biomolecular Science; Business Information Systems; Business Systems Modelling; Chemistry; Chemistry by Research; Computing; Consumer Behaviour; Consumer Studies; Ecology; Electronic Engineering; Electronic Product Technology; Electronics & Communications Engineering; Food & Consumer Studies; Food Science; Health Promotion; Health Studies & Human Nutrition; Human Biology; Human Life Sciences; Mathematical Sciences; Mathematics; Mathematics-Computing; Microbiology; Microcomputer Systems Technology; Multimedia Computing; Multimedia Technology and Applications; Pharmaceutical Science; Psychobiology; Social Research & Statistics; Sports Science; Sports Science & Human Nutrition *Combination of 2 subjects:* Biochemistry; Biological Sciences; Biomedical Science; Chemistry; Communications Systems; Computer Software Development; Computing; Consumer Studies; Ecology; Electronics Product Technology; Human Nutrition; Information Systems; Information Technology; Mathematical Sciences; Mathematics; Microbiology; Philosophy; Polymers; Statistics *4 yrs FT* Environmental Management; Environmental Science; Food Science; Human Nutrition; Microcomputer Systems Technology; Multimedia Technology & Applications; Social Research; Sports Science *4 yrs S* Computer Science
LLB: *3 yrs FT* Law

Higher Degrees

MA: *1 yr FT* Advanced Architecture & Interior Design; Applied Translation Studies; Arts & Heritage Management; City in History; Comparative European Social Studies; Education; Employment Studies & Human Resource Management; European Business Law; Health & Social Policy; Information & Knowledge Management; International Business; International Business Law; International Public Administration; International Tourism Policy; Leisure & Tourism Studies; Literature, Representation & Modernity; Marketing; Mass Communications; Modern Drama & Theatre Studies; Modern European Studies; Post Colonial Studies; Public Policy & Public Law; Social Work; Sport Management; TEFL; Transport Policy & Management
MBA: *1 yr FT* Hospitality & Tourism Management; Business Administration
MSc: *1 yr FT* Computing; Information Services Management; Polymer Science & Engineering

DOCTORATES
MPhil/PhD: (In various subjects)

Diplomas

DipHE: *1 yr FT* Purchasing & Logistics *2 yrs FT* Sports Science & Fitness Evaluation
HND: *2 yrs FT* Accounting & Business Management; Business Management; Computing; Computing & Mathematical Science; Electronic & Communications Engineering; Hospitality &

Business Management; Human Resource & Business Management; Marketing & Business Management; Polymer Science & Engineering; Sports & Leisure Management; Tourism Management
PGDip: *1 yr FT* Computing; Human Resource Management; Legal Studies; Polymer Science & Engineering; Social Research Methodology *2 yrs FT* Architecture

Certificates

PGCE: English; Mathematics Education; Modern Foreign Languages; Music Education; P.E Education; Primary Education
PGCert: International Business; International Tourism Policy; Marketing

Other Courses

HWC: *2 yrs PT* Business Management; Business-Finance; Electronic and Communications Engineering; Polymer Engineering

UNIVERSITY OF NORTHUMBRIA AT NEWCASTLE

Ellison Building, Ellison Place, Newcastle upon Tyne NE1 8ST Tel: 0191 232 6002
Fax: 0191 227 4017 Website: www.unn.ac.uk

† Subject to validation.

First Degrees

BA Hons: *1 yr FT* Accounting & Finance; Business Administration; Dance (Completion Award); Logistics & Supply Chain Management; Travel & Tourism Administration *1 yr FT/2 yrs PT* Social Welfare & Social Work *3 yrs FT* 3D Design: Furniture & Interiors/Jewellery & Fine Product; Accountancy; Architectural Design & Management; Art History & Fine Art; Art History & Information Studies; British and American Cultures; Business Administration; Childhood Studies & Professional Practice Studies; Community Health Care Studies; Contemporary Photographic Practice; Disability Studies & Childhood Studies; Disability Studies & Professional Practice Studies; Care & Education of Very Young Children (CARED)-Disability Studies/Professional Practice Studies; Drama; Economics; Economics-Sociology; English; English & History; English & Women's Cultures; English-Film Studies or History or Women's Cultures; Financial Services; Fine Art; French; French-German or Spanish or Economics or Politics; Geography; German-Spanish or Economics or Politics; Graphic Design; History; History & Art History; History & Sociology; History of Modern Art, Design & Film; History-Politics; Housing Studies; Information & Management; Information Studies-French or German or Spanish; Media Production; Multimedia Design; Performance; Political Economy; Politics; Politics & Economics; Politics & Sociology; Politics-Media Studies; Social Sciences; Social Work; Spanish-German or Economics or Politics; Sport Studies; Transportation Design *3-4 yrs FT* European Studies *4 yrs FT* European Studies-French or German or Spanish; International Business Administration; International Business Studies *4 yrs S* International Business Studies; Business Studies; Design for Industry; Fashion; Fashion Marketing; History with French; Human Resource Management; Marketing; Travel & Tourism Management
BA Hons with QTS: *2 yrs FT* Mathematics; Modern Languages; Science; Technology; Visual Arts *3 yrs FT* Primary
BA/BSc Hons: *3 yrs FT* Sport & Exercise Science; Sport Development; Sport Management (European)
BEng Hons: *3 yrs FT/4 yrs S* Building Services Engineering; Communication & Electronic Engineering; Computer Aided Engineering; Electrical & Electronic Engineering; Manufacturing Systems Engineering; Materials Engineering; Mechanical Engineering *3-4 yrs S* Architectural Environmental Design *4 yrs S* Electronic Engineering for Europe
BEng/BEng Hons: *3 yrs FT/4 yrs S* Engineering Design Technology *36-42 mths or 12-18 mths for holders of an appropriate HND* Electronic Systems Design Engineering
BSc Hons: *1 yr FT* Nursing Science *3 yrs FT* Architectural & Urban Conservation; Business Information Technology; Criminology-Social Research or Sociology; Environmental Management; Environmental Studies; Geography; Geography-Environmental Management or Sports Studies;

Human Organisations; Information & Communication Management; International Health Studies; Landscape Ecology; Mathematics; Midwifery Studies/Registered Midwife; Nursing Studies; Occupational Therapy; Psychology; Psychology with Computing or Sport Science; Sociology *3 yrs FT/4 yrs S* Applied Biology; Applied Chemistry; Applied Life Sciences; Applied Physics; Biomedical Sciences; Biomedical Sciences & Chemistry; Chemistry with Analytical Chemistry or Biochemistry or Biochemical Sciences or Biomedical Sciences or Chemical Engineering or Environmental Chemistry; Computer & Network Technology; Engineering with Business Studies; Environmental Protection Science; Estate Management; Food Science and Nutrition; Housing Development; Mathematics with Business Administration; Mechanical Engineering; Opto-electronic Engineering; Planning & Development Surveying *4 yrs FT* Human Organisations-Social Research; International Business & Technology; Sociology & Social Research *4 yrs S* Applied Chemistry (Europe); Architectural Technology; Building Design Management; Building Surveying; Business Information Systems; Computing with Cognitive Psychology; Computing for Business; Computing for Industry; Computing Studies; Construction Management; Multimedia Computing; Quantity Surveying
BSc/BSc Hons: *1 yr FT/1.5 yrs PT* Applied Business Computing
LLB Hons: *3 yrs FT* Law*4 yrs FT* Exempting Bar Vocational; Exempting with French Law; LLB Exempting (Solicitors')

Higher Degrees

MA: *1 yr FT/2 yrs PT* Design; Fine Art; Marketing; Tourism Management *1-3 yrs* Information & Library Management *FT/PT* Information & Library Management *16 mths FT* European Business Administration *2 yrs FT* Conservation of Fine Art
MBA: *1 yr FT* Business Administration
MChem: *4 yrs FT* Chemistry
MEng: Building Services Engineering
MMath: *4 yrs FT* Mathematics
MSc: *1 yr FT* Computing; Engineering, Science & Technology; Environmental Monitoring & Control; European Master's in Adapted Physical Activity; Optoelectronic & Communication Systems; Product Manufacture *1 yr FT/2 yrs PT* Social Research; Social Science *1 yr FT/2.5 yrs PT* Project Management (Construction/Property/Energy & Environment)

Diplomas

DipHE: *1 yr FT* Playwork *2 yrs FT* Accounting
DipSW: *2 yrs FT* Social Work
HND: *2 yrs FT* Architectural Technology; Building Services Engineering; Building Surveying; Computing for Business; Computing Studies; Construction Management; Electrical & Electronic Engineering; Estate Management; Mechanical & Production Engineering; Quantity Surveying
Postgraduate Diploma: *1 yr FT* Arts Management; Business Information Technology; Careers Guidance; Design; Housing; Information & Library Management; Marketing; Tourism Management *2 yrs FT* Housing Policy & Management

Certificates

PGCE: *1 yr FT* Primary; Secondary

NOTTINGHAM TRENT UNIVERSITY

Burton Street, Nottingham NG1 4BU Tel: 0115 941 8418 Fax: 0115 848 6503
Website: www.ntu.ac.uk
† Subject to validation.

First Degrees

BA/BA Hons: *3 yrs FT* Fashion Marketing & Communication; Accounting & Finance; Broadcast Journalism; Business Economics; Business Management; Business Studies; Business, Leisure & Sports Education; Communication Studies; Contemporary Arts; Criminology; Decorative Arts; Design for Television; Design Studies; Economics; Economics & Financial Services; English;

European Studies; Fashion & Textiles; Fashion Design; Fine Art; Graphic Design; History; Human Geography; Human Services; Humanities; International Business; International Relations; International Studies; Media & Cultural Studies; Photography; Photography in Europe; Politics; Product Design; Psychology & Educational Development; Social Sciences; Social Work; Textile Design; Theatre Design *4 yrs FT* European Economics with a Language; European Studies; International Relations; International Studies; Modern Languages; Specialist Primary Education (with QTS) *4 yrs S* Accounting & Finance; Business & Financial Services; Business & Quality Management; Business Information Systems; Business Studies; Fashion and Textile Management; Fashion Knitwear Design; Furniture & Product Design; Graphic Communications Management; Interior Architecture & Design; International Business; Product Design

BEng/BEng Hons: *3 yrs FT* Civil and Environmental Engineering; Civil and Structural Engineering; Civil Engineering with Management; Civil Engineering; Electrical & Electronic Engineering; Electronics; Electronics & Computing; Electronics and Communications Engineering; Integrated Engineering; Mechanical Engineering; Surveying for Engineering *4 yrs S* Civil & Environmental Engineering; Civil and Structural Engineering; Civil Engineering with Management; Civil Engineering; Electrical & Electronic Engineering; Electronics; Electronics & Communications Engineering; Electronics & Computing; Integrated Engineering; Mechanical Engineering; Surveying for Engineering

BSc/BSc Hons: *3 yrs FT* Animal Science; Applied Physics; Biochemistry & Microbiology; Biomedical Science; Biomolecular Analysis; Building Surveying; Business and Technology; Chemistry; Chemistry with study in the USA; Civil and Environmental Engineering; Civil Engineering; Combined Studies in Sciences; Computational Physics; Computer Science; Computing (Visualisation); Conservation & Countryside Management; Environmental Biology; Environmental Science; Equine Sports Science; Financial and Project Management in Construction; Food Safety Management; Food Science and Technology; Food Supply Chain Management; Geological Engineering; Health Studies; Information Systems; Integrated Engineering; Mathematical Engineering; Mathematical Physics; Mathematics; Mechanical Engineering; Medicinal Chemistry; Multimedia Production; Multimedia Technology; Physics; Physics with Analytical Science; Physics with Astrophysics; Physics with Biomedical Physics; Physiology-Pharmacology; Planning and Development; Policy Science; Product Design; Applied Human Nutrition-Product Development; Property & Surveying; Property Development; Psychology; Quantity Surveying; Real Estate Management; Safety, Health and Environmental Management; Software Engineering; Sport (Administration & Science); Surveying for Engineering *4 yrs S* Applied Biology; Applied Chemistry; Applied Physics; Applied Science; Architectural Technology; Biochemistry & Microbiology; Biomedical Sciences; Building; Building Surveying; Chemistry in Europe; Civil & Environmental Engineering; Civil Engineering; Computer Science; Computer Studies (Information Management, MultiMedia & Virtual Reality, Software Engineering); Computing (Visualisation); Conservation & Countryside Management; Construction Management; Environmental Biology; Environmental Health; Equine Sports Science; Financial and Project Management in Construction; Food Safety Management; Food Science and Technology; Food Supply Chain Management; Geological Engineering; Information Systems; Integrated Engineering; Mathematical Engineering; Mathematics; Mechanical Engineering; Multimedia Production; Multimedia Technology; Physics in Europe; Physiology and Pharmacology; Planning & Development; Product Design; Applied Human Nutrition-Product Development; Property and Surveying; Property Development; Quantity Surveying; Real Estate Management; Residential Development; Safety, Health and Environmental Engineering; Software Engineering; Surveying for Engineering

LLB: *3 yrs FT/4 yrs S 4 yrs* Europe with French or German

University Foundation Degree: *1 yr FT UFD 2 yrs FT* Advanced Horse Management; Advanced Horse Management and Equitation; Applied Animal Studies; Applied Food Studies; Building Design and Construction; Chemistry; Civil Engineering; Countryside and Environmental Management; Financial and Project Management in Construction; Floristry Design; Garden Design; Physics; Science (Applied Biology)

Higher Degrees

LLM: *1 yr FT* Advanced Litigation; Corporate Law
MA: *1 yr FT* Asia Pacific Studies; Cinema Studies; Counselling; Customer Service Management;

Design Studies; Education; Educational Management; English Language Teaching; English Literary Studies; Environmental Education; European Culture & Society; Fashion & Textiles; Global Politics & Culture; Heritage Studies; International Cultural Studies; Investigative Journalism; Newspaper Journalism (†); Online Journalism; Primary Education; Special Educational Needs; Strategic Human Resource Management; Technology Education; Television Journalism; Theory, Culture & Society; Tourism Quality Management; World Politics; Writing

MBA: *1 yr FT* Entrepreneurship; Legal Practice

MChem Hons: *4 yrs FT* Chemistry (with study in the USA); Chemistry (with a yr in Industry); Chemistry; Chemistry in Europe; Medicinal Chemistry (with a yr in Industry); Medicinal Chemistry

MEng/BEng Hons: *5 yrs S* Computer Science; Integrated Engineering; Mathematical Engineering; Mechanical Engineering

MPhys Hons: *4 yrs FT* Applied Physics

MSc: *1 yr FT* Biomedical Science; Biotechnology; Building Engineering; Computational Methods in Engineering; Construction Engineering Design & Management; Construction Procurement Management; E-Business; Employment Relations; Engineering Multimedia; European Biotechnology; European Construction Management; European Traffic and Transportation Sciences; Geotechnical Engineering Design & Management; Human Resource Development & Consulting; Industrial Computing Systems; Integrated Environmental Control; Integrated Environmental Energy Management; Management; Management & Marketing; Management-Information Systems; Marketing Management; Occupational Health & Safety Management; Public Finance & Management; Quality Engineering; Real Time Computing Applications; Research Methods; Residential Development

Diplomas

PGDip: *1 yr FT* Building Engineering; Cinema Studies; Computational Methods in Engineering; Corporate Law; Counselling; Construction Engineering-Design; Employment Relations; Engineering Multimedia; English Language Teaching; English Literary Studies; European Culture and Society; Fashion & Textiles; Geotechnical Engineering Design and Management; Heritage Studies; Industrial Computing Systems; International Cultural Studies; Investigative Journalism; Law; Management Studies; Newspaper Journalism; Occupational Health & Safety Management; Occupational Health and Safety Enforcement; Online Journalism; Personnel Management; Public Finance & Management; Public Services Management; Pumping Technology; Real Time Computing Applications; Research Methods; Television Journalism; Theatre Arts; Theatre Culture and Society; Training Management; World Politics

Certificates

PGCE: *1 yr FT* Further Education; Further Education & Training; Primary; Secondary

Degrees validated by Nottingham Trent University offered at:

Southampton Institute

East Park Terrace, Southampton SO14 OYN Tel: 023 8319000 Fax: 023 8222259 e-mail: ms@solent.ac.uk Website: www.solent.ac.uk

First Degrees

BA Hons: *3 yrs FT* Accountancy; Advertising; Antiques (History & Collecting); Antiques (History & Collecting) with French or German or Spanish; Architectural Technology (Interiors Pathway Available); Business with French or German or Information Management or Spanish; Business Management; Business-Law; Corporate Communication; Criminology; Documentary Imaging and Photography; Fashion; Fashion with Professional Practice; Film studies; Financial Services; Fine Art; Fine Art with Professional Practice; Fine Arts Valuation; Graphic Design; Graphic Design with Professional Practice; Health & Fitness Management; Human Resource Management; Illustration & Animation; Illustration & Animation with Professional Practice; Interdisciplinary Design Practice; International Business; International Design Studies; Journalism; Journalism-

Politics; Legal Studies; Maritime Leisure Management; Marketing; Marketing Design; Media with Cultural studies; Multimedia Design; Photography; Photography & Digital Imaging; Photojournalism; Political Studies; Product Design with Marketing; Product Design with Marketing with Professional Practice; Real Estate Valuation; Social & Community Studies; Social Science; Sports Studies & Business; Tourism Management *3-6 yrs PT* Architectural Technology; Architectural Technology (Interiors); Business Law; Combined Studies; Fashion; Fine Art; Fine Arts Valuation Studies; Graphic Design; Illustration & Animation; International Design Studies; Legal Studies; Maritime Leisure Management; Multimedia Design; Photography; Product Design with Marketing; Real Estate Valuation; Social Studies *3-6 yrs PT/4 yrs S* Business Studies; European Policy; Mechanical Design; Modern Languages

BEng Hons: *3 yrs FT* Merchant Ship Engineering *3 yrs FT/3-6 yrs PT* Electronic Engineering; Engineering; Business; Maritime Technology; Mechanical Design; Yacht & Powercraft Design *3-6 yrs PT* Electronic Engineering; Engineering with Business

BSc: *3-6 yrs PT* Building; Electronics with Business

BSc Hons: *3 yrs* Business Technology Management; Computer Network Communication; Computer Systems & Networks; Leisure & Sports Technology; Marine Geography; Media Technology; Merchant Ship Operations; Psychology; Software Engineering; Yacht Manufacturing & Surveying *3 yrs PT* Computer Network Management *3-6 yrs PT* Combined Studies *4 yrs S* Business Information Technology

BSc/BSc Hons: *3 yrs FT/3-6 yrs PT* Computer Studies; Construction; International Transport Management; Maritime Environmental Management; Maritime Environmental Science; Maritime Studies; Shipping Operations

LLB Hons: Law

Higher Degrees

LLM: *2 yrs PT*

MA: *1 yr FT* Design; Fine Arts Valuation; Media *FT/PT* Exhibition Studies; Film; Fine Art; Health Education & Health Promotion; Managing Human Resources; Marketing Management; Media; Research (Methodology)

MBA: *1 yr FT/3 yrs PT* Finance; General Management; Human Resource Management; International Transport and Logistics; Marketing

MPhil: *FT/PT*

MSc: *1 yr FT* Integrated Systems Engineering; Marine Engineering *1 yr FT/2-3 yrs PT* Computing (Software Engineering); Exclusive Economic Zone (EEZ) Management *2 yrs PT* Computing (Software Engineering); Industrial Systems Technology; Integrated Systems Management (Condition Monitoring); Marine Engineering *2-3 yrs PT* Computing (Software Engineering)

PhD: *FT/PT*

Diplomas

Diploma: *PT* Accountancy-Finance; Housing; Marketing

DMS: *1 yr PT* Management Studies

PGDip: *2-3 yrs PT* Computing (Software Engineering); Condition Monitoring; European Law; European Law and Practice; Research (Methodology) *FT/PT* Electronic Journalism; Film; Marine Engineering; Marketing Management

Certificates

Certificate: *PT* Management; Marketing; Personnel Practice

UNIVERSITY OF NOTTINGHAM

University Park, Nottingham NG7 2RD Tel: 0115 951 5151
e-mail: undergraduate.enquiries@nottingham.ac.uk Website: www.nottingham.ac.uk

First Degrees

ARTS & SOCIAL SCIENCES

BA Hons: *3-4 yrs* American & Canadian Studies; American Studies; Ancient History; Archaeology; Architectural Studies; Architecture; Art History; Classical Civilisation; Classics; Economic & Social

History; Economics with French or German or Hispanic Studies or Russian; Economics & Econometrics; Economics & European Union Studies; English Studies; French Studies; Geography; German; Hispanic Studies; History; Industrial Economics; Industrial Economics or Insurance; Latin; Law or South East Asian or Chinese Law; Law with French or German or American Law or European Law; Management Studies with French or German or Portuguese or Spanish; Management Studies; Modern European Studies; Modern Language Studies; Music; Philosophy; Politics; Psychology; Russian & East European Area Studies; Russian Studies; Russian Studies for Beginners; Social & Cultural Studies; Social Policy & Administration; Sociology; Theology *Joint Honours:* American Studies with International Study; American Studies or International Study; American Studies-English Studies; American Studies-French or History or Latin American Studies or Philosophy; American Studies-History with International Study; Ancient History-Archaeology or History or Latin; Archaeology-Classical Civilisation or English Language or Geography or History or Latin; Art History with Architectural History; Art History-English Studies or German; Beginner's Portuguese-Russian; Classical Civilisation-English Studies or French or German or Philosophy or Theology; Economics with European Union Studies or Econometrics; Economics-Agricultural Economics; Economics-Philosophy; English Studies-Latin or Philosophy or Theology; French-Beginner's Russian or German or History or Hispanic Studies; German-Hispanic Studies; Beginner's Russian-Beginners Russian; History-Law; Politics-American Studies; Philosophy with International Study; Philosophy-Theology; Psychology-Philosophy; Russian Beginners with Film Studies or Hispanic Studies; Russian-Serbo-Croat
BEd & BCombStuds: *3-4 yrs FT* (For students at constituent Colleges of Education. Hons BEd can also be taken by non grad qualified teachers with at least 3 yrs teaching experience)
BPhil (Ed): *FT/PT* (Second 1st degree for qualified teachers (grads & non grads))
BTh: *3 yrs* (For students in Theological Colls – St John's (Nottingham))
LLB Hons: *3 yrs*
LLB Ord: *3 yrs*

MEDICINE & HEALTH SCIENCES
BM/BS: *5 yrs*
BSc Hons: Physiotherapy
MN: *4 yrs FT* Nursing

SCIENCE & ENGINEERING
BPharm Hons: *3 yrs* Pharmacy
BSc Hons: *3 yrs* Agriculture with European Studies; Agriculture; Animal Science; Animal Science with European Studies; Applied Biology; Applied Biology with European Studies; Biotechnology; Biotechnology with European Studies; Environmental Biology with European Studies; Environmental Biology; Environmental Science; European Union Studies; Food Microbiology with European Studies; Food Microbiology; Food Science; Food Science with European Studies; Horticulture; Horticulture with European Studies; Nutrition with European Studies; Nutrition; Nutritional Biochemistry; Nutritional Biochemistry with European Studies; Plant Science
BSc Joint Hons: *3 yrs* Chemistry-Management Studies; Computer Science; Computer Science-Management Studies; Mathematics-Computer Science or Management Studies with European Studies; Microbiology; Molecular Physics-Chemistry
BSc/BEng Hons/MEng: *3-4 yrs* Biochemistry & Biological Chemistry; Biochemistry & Genetics; Biology; Chemical Engineering; Chemistry; Chemistry of Materials; Chemistry-Molecular Physics with German; Civil Engineering with French; Civil Engineering; Computer Science; Electrical & Electronic Engineering; Electrical & Electronic Engineering with a Modern Language; Electronic Engineering with Mathematics; Electronic Engineering with a Language; Electronic Engineering; Environmental Science; Environmental Engineering; Environmental Engineering; Genetics; Geography or German or Japanese or Russian or Spanish or Italian; Manufacturing Engineering & Management with French; Manufacturing Engineering & Management; Mathematical Physics; Mathematics with Engineering; Mathematics (with statistics); Mechanical Design, Materials & Manufacture with French or German or Spanish; Mechanical Engineering; Microbiology; Mining & Minerals Engineering; Mining Engineering; Neuroscience; Physics; Physics with European Language or Medical Physics; Physiotherapy with French or German; Production & Operations Management or Japanese or Russian or Spanish or Italian; Psychology; Zoology

Higher Degrees

DArch: Architecture
EdD: School Improvement/Teacher Education
LLM/PGDip: International Law
MA: Twentieth Century French & Francophone Literature; American Studies with Canadian Studies; American Studies; Ancient & Medieval Philosophies; Archaeology; Architectural Theory & Design; Architecture & Urban Design; Art History; Business Administration; Classical Studies; Counselling Studies; Critical Theory; DH Lawrence & the Modern Age; English Language in Literary Studies; English Language Teaching; Evaluation Research (Human Services); Film Studies; Greek Archaeology & History; Greek Drama; History of Slavery; Human Relations; Indian Philosophy; International Social Policy; Local & Regional History; Mathematical Education; Medieval Archaeology; Medieval English; Modern History; Modern Social History; Musicology; Nineteenth Century Culture & Society; Philosophy; Philosophy (by research); Politics & Critical Theory; Post-compulsory Education; Psychology in Schools; Recent Trends in German Literature; Roman Archaeology; Roman History; Teaching; Teaching & Training in Continuing Education; TESOL; Theological & Pastoral Studies; Theological & Religious Studies; Twentieth Century French Studies; Urban Educational & Social Policy; Victorian Studies; Viking and Anglo-Saxon Studies: Language, Texts and History *4 yrs FT* Lifelong Education; Medieval History; Modern English Language
MA/MSc: Archaeological Materials
MA/MSc/PGDip: *Faculty of Science:* Information Technology
MA/PgD: Agricultural Economics; Architectural Technology; Comparative Politics; Corporate Strategy & Governance; Economic Development & Analysis; Environmental Planning; International Relations; International Studies: Asia-Pacific Region; Landscape & Culture; Management; Modern Cultural Studies; Modern German Studies; Politics & Social Policy; Social Policy; Social Policy & Administration; Social Policy & Community Care; Social Policy & Health; Social Policy & Sustainable Development; Social Work; Strategic Management (By dissertation); Women & Social Policy *4 yrs FT* Health Economics; Health Services Research
MArch: Architecture (Design); Architecture (Practice)
MBA/PgDip: Business Administration (Criminal Justice); Business Administration (Education); Business Administration (Executive); Business Administration (Financial Studies); Business Administration (Health); Business Administration (International); Business Administration (Local Authorities); Business Administration (Voluntary Sector) *4 yrs FT* Business Administration (Modular); Business Administration (Singapore)
MEd: Education
MMath: *4 yrs FT* Mathematics
MMedSci: *Faculty of Medicine:* Obstetric Ultrasound
MMedSci/PgDip: *Faculty of Medicine:* Clinical Education; Clinical Psychiatry; Primary Health Care
MRes: *Faculty of Medicine:* Clinical Research
MSc: Law & Environmental Science; Occupational Health & Safety *Faculty of Engineering:* Construction Management; Electrical Engineering; Electronic Engineering; Human Factors in Manufacturing Systems; Manufacturing Systems; Operations Management & Manufacturing Systems; Process & Project Engineering *Faculty of Medicine:* Immunology & Allergy; Oncology *Faculty of Science:* Applied Biomolecular Technology; Clinical Pharmacy; Crop Science & Management; Intelligent Systems (Artificial Intelligence); Intelligent Systems (Human-Computer Interaction); Occupational Psychology; Plant Genetic Manipulation *1 yr FT/2-3 yrs PT Faculty of Medicine:* Community Paediatrics *4 yrs FT* Renewable Energy & Architecture; Work & Organisational Psychology *Faculty of Medicine:* Continued Professional Development (Physiotherapy); Health Services Research; Molecular Medical Microbiology *Faculty of Science:* Clinical Pharmacy; Rehabilitation Psychology
MSc/PgD: *Faculty of Engineering:* Engineering Surveying & Geodesy; Environmental Engineering; Navigational Technology; Surface Design & Engineering *Faculty of Medicine:* Advanced Nursing Practice & Advanced Nursing Studies; Health Care Policy & Organisation; Sports Medicine *Faculty of Science:* Applied Biomolecular Microbiology; Environmental Management & Ecotoxicology; Environmental Science; Food Production Management; Geographical Information Systems; Occupational Health Psychology

MSc/PgD/PgC: *Faculty of Medicine:* Public Health *Faculty of Science:* Advanced Food Manufacture *Faculty of Science:* Environmental Management
MSci: *4 yrs FT* Chemistry; Physics

Diplomas

PgD: Economics; Economics & Development Economics; Economics & Econometrics; Economics & International Economics
PgD/PgC: *Faculty of Science:* Clinical Nutrition; Structure-Based Drug Design
PGDip: International Education Professionals; Psychology (By research)*Faculty of Medicine:* Molecular Biology
Postgraduate Diploma: Continuing Professional Development and School Improvement; Philosophy

Certificates

Advanced Certificate: English Language Studies; Politics & International Studies
Certificate: Adult Teaching *1 yr FT* Design & Craft; Mathematics & the Teaching of Mathematics; Theory & Practice of Education (Overseas Teachers) *2 yrs FT* Community & Youth Work; Qualification in Social Work *2 yrs PT* Economic Studies; Industrial Relations *3 yrs PT* Archaeology; Geology; Local History; Theological & Pastoral Studies
Certificate in Education: *2 yrs PT* Education of Adults
PGCE: *1 yr*
PGCert: *Faculty of Medicine:* Clinical Science

THE OPEN UNIVERSITY

Walton Hall, Milton Keynes MK7 6AA Tel: 01908 653231
e-mail: crsc-gen@open.ac.uk Website: www.open.ac.uk

First Degrees

BA/BA Honours; BSc/BSc Honours: 3-4 yrs min PT: Undergraduate courses are offered to students studying in their own homes. No entrance qualifications are needed, but students must be over 18 and resident in the EU or other countries where the University has agreed to register students. Degrees are built up through a credit points system. A credit is awarded on completion of a nine-mth course on the basis of continuous assessment and final exam. Courses are worth either 60 or 30 credit points and are offered at first, second and third level. 360 credit points are needed for the BA or BSc degree. A maximum of 120 credit points may be taken concurrently in each academic yr, which runs from February to October. Recognition, in the form of credit transfer, is also given for study previously completed at a higher education level with other institutions. Students may choose from over 130 courses offered in Arts, Computing, Education, Environmental Education, Law, Languages, Mathematics, Science, Social Sciences and Technology.

Higher Degrees

The University offers three research degrees: BPhil; MPhil; and PhD; all by thesis. These involve 1-2-3 yrs of full-time study respectively, or the equivalent in part-time study. There are also PT taught Master's degrees: MA in Education; Dr of Education; MA in Humanities; MA in Open & Distance Learning; MA/MSc in Social Science; MSc in Science; MSc in Mathematics; MSc in Manufacturing: Management & Technology; MSc in Computing for Commerce & Industry; MSc in Development Management; MSc in Environmental Decision Making; MBA; MBA (Technology

Management). The normal entrance requirement for admission to postgraduate study is a first or upper second class Honours degree of a British university, or equivalent. However, access to the MA in Education, the MBA, the MSc in Computing for Commerce & Industry, the MSc in Development Management, and the MSc in Environmental Decision Making, can also be gained by first studying an Open University diploma in that area, for which no previous qualification is required.

MEng: 480-point honours degree awarded to students who have studied approved undergraduate courses at specific levels and who want the highest professional status, Chartered Engineer.

MMath: 480-point honours degree awarded to students who have specialised in mathematics and have studied approved undergraduate courses at specific levels.

HIGHER DOCTORATES
DSc

Honorary Degrees

DUniv

Diplomas

Undergraduate Diplomas: Awarded to students who have successfully studied specific courses in: Classical Studies; Computing; Environment & Development; Pollution Control; European Humanities; Music; French; German; Spanish; Applied Social Sciences; Design & Innovation; Economics; Gender & Development; Geography; Geography & Environment; Information Technology; Mathematics; Modern Social History Research; Statistics and Systems Practice.

Other Courses

Professional and Personal Development: The University also offers a range of individual courses, some of which can also be studied in the undergraduate programme and many of which form part of other qualifications. Qualifications available now or in the immediate future are: *1 yr min PT*: Certificate of Professional Development in Education; Postgraduate Certificate in Teaching and Learning in Higher Education; Professional Certificate of Management; Certificate in Health & Social Care *18 mths* Postgraduate Certificate in Education *2yrs min PT* Advanced Diploma in Special Needs in Education; Postgraduate Diploma in Manufacturing: Management & Technology; Postgraduate Diploma in Computing for Commerce & Industry; Joint Postgraduate Diploma in Computing & Manufacturing; Diploma in Health & Social Welfare; Diploma in Environmental Decision Making; Postgraduate Diploma in Developmental Management; Diploma of Higher Education (Social Work); Diploma in Psychology (Conversion for Postgraduates)

Degrees validated by The Open University offered at:

NESCOT

Reigate Road, Ewell, Epsom, Surrey KT17 3DS Tel: 020 8394 1731 Fax: 020 8394 3030
e-mail: info@nescot.ac.uk Website: www.nescot.ac.uk

First Degrees

BA: *3 yrs FT* Management & Financial Services; Photography & Imaging *FT/PT* Photography Imaging

BA Hons: *3-4 yrs FT* Business Studies

BSc: *1 yr FT* Computer Studies *2 yrs PT* Business Information Technology (Top-Up) *3 yrs FT* Business Information Technology; Facilities Management *3 yrs PT* Environmental Health; Environmental Management *4 yrs FT* Computer Studies (University of Surrey) *4 yrs PT*

Biomedical Sciences; Clinical Science (BR) *6 yrs PT* Environmental Engineering; Facilities Management *PT* Clinical Science (BR); Computer Studies (University of Surrey)
BSc Hons: *1 yr FT* Business Information Technology *3 yrs FT* Biological Sciences; Biomedical Science *3 yrs PT* Biological Sciences *FT* Applied Animal Science; Biological Sciences; Digital Imaging; Osteopathic Medicine *PT* Digital Imaging
BSc/BSc Hons: *3 yrs FT* Applied Animal Science; Applied Physiology; Computer Studies (with a European Option); Digital Imaging; Environmental Health; Pharmacology *3-4 yrs FT* Applied Biology; Biochemistry; Biomedical Science; Biotechnology; Computer Studies; Facilities Management; Immunology; Microbiology *4 yrs FT* Applied Human Physiology; Osteopathic Medicine

Higher Degrees

Master: *1 yr FT* Biomedical Sciences; Immunology (University of Surrey) *5 yrs PT* Biomedical Sciences *FT* Virology (University of Surrey) *PT* Acoustics; Facilities Management; Immunology (University of Surrey); Tech Audiology (University of London); Virology (University of Surrey)
MSc: *FT/PT* Acoustic & Noise Control; Bioanalytical Science; Biomedical Science; Facilities Management; Immunology; Molecular Pharmacology; Research & Valuation for Professional Practice; Virology
PhD: *FT* Research Biological Sciences

Diplomas

BTEC HND: *1 yr PT* Computing (Evenings); Business Information Technology (Evenings) *2 yrs FT* Animal Science; Applied Biology; Business & Finance; Business Information Technology; Multimedia; Performing Arts; Photomedia *3 yrs S* Computing *FT* Biology-Business Studies; Building Studies; Digital Imaging; Leisure Management
DipHE: *2 yrs FT* Biological Sciences
Diploma: *PT* Acoustics & Noise Control

Certificates

BTEC HC: *1 yr FT* Building Studies *2 yrs PT* Applied Biology; Building Studies; Business Information Technology (Evenings); Business (Evenings); Civil Engineering; Computing (Evenings); Digital Imaging; Environmental Health; Housing Studies; Photography *PT* Building Studies (Single Subject); Facilities Management
BTEC HNC: *FT* Bioinformation & Business *PT* Building Services Engineering

Northern College of Education

Hilton Place, Aberdeen AB24 4FA Tel: 01224 283500 Fax: 01224 283900
Website: www.norcol.ac.uk

First Degrees

BA: *FT* Social Work *PT/DL* Early Childhood Studies; Professional Development
BA/BA Hons: *3-4 yrs FT* Community Education (or workplace-based)
BEd Hons: *4 yrs FT* Music (Secondary Music Education); Primary

Higher Degrees

MA Hons: *5 yrs FT* European Languages with Education
MEd: *PT/DL*
MPhil/PhD: *PT* (By research)
MSc: *PT/DL* Advanced Professional Studies

Diplomas

Postgraduate Diploma: *1 yr FT/18 mths workplace based* Community Education *PT/DL* Counselling; Early Education; Educational Management; Educational Studies; Guidance & Pupil Support; ICT & Learning; Primary Education; Professional Development; Special Educational Needs

Certificates

PGCE: *1 yr FT* Primary Education; Secondary Education
Postgraduate Certificate: *PT/DL* Counselling; Early Education; Education Management; Educational Studies; Environmental Studies; Guidance & Pupil Support; Health Education; ICT & Learning; Pastoral Care; Primary Education P3-P7; Primary Science; Professional Development; Rural Education; Special Educational Needs; Teaching Primary Science

The Central School of Speech & Drama

Embassy Theatre, Eton Avenue, London NW3 3HY Tel: 020 7722 8183 Fax: 020 7722 4132
Website: www.cssd.ac.uk

First Degrees

BA: *3 yrs FT* Acting
BA Hons: *2 yrs* Accelerated Degree Circus *3 yrs FT* Alternative Theatre Forms; Drama & Education; Puppetry; Stage Management; Technical Theatre Arts (Set, Costume, Lighting & Sound Design; Scenic Art, Scenic Construction, Costume Construction & Prop Making); Theatre Crafts; Theatre Practice Design

Higher Degrees

MA: *1 yr FT* Advanced Theatre Practice (Performance, Directing, Writing, Design, Puppet & Object Theatre, Dramaturgy, Arts Management, Music & Sound for Performance, Scenography); Performance Studies *FT/PT* Theatre & Drama Education; Theatre & Drama Education
MA/PGDip: *1 yr FT* Voice Studies

Diplomas

Postgraduate Diploma: *1 yr FT* Drama & Movement Therapy

Certificates

PGCE: *1 yr FT* Drama; Media Education with English
Postgraduate Certificate: *1 yr PT* Teaching & Learning in Higher Education *FT/PT* Theatre & Drama Education

OXFORD BROOKES UNIVERSITY

Headington, Oxford OX3 0BP Tel: 01865 741111

First Degrees

BA Hons: *3 yrs FT* Architecture; Business-Retail Management; English Studies; Fine Art; French Studies; German Studies; History of Art; Modern History; Music; Nursing (Learning Disability); Nursing (Mental Health); Publishing; Town and Country Planning *3-4 yrs* Business-Management *4 yrs* European Business Studies
BA Hons with QTS: *3 yrs FT modular* Teacher Education
BA/BA Hons: *1 yr FT* Accounting & Finance; Business Economics; International Banking & Finance; International Business Management; Marketing Management *3 yrs FT* Business Administration & Management; Fine Art; Health Care Studies; Planning Studies *4 yrs FT modular* Languages for Business
BA/BA Hons; BSc/BSc Hons: *3-4 yrs FT modular Joint subjects (combine two):* Accounting & Finance; Anthropology; Biological Chemistry; Biology; Business Administration & Management; Business Statistics; Cell Biology; Cities & Society; Computer Systems; Computing; Computing Mathematics; Computing Science; Ecology; Economics; Educational Studies; Electronics; English Studies; Environmental Chemistry; Environmental Design-Conservation; Environmental Policy; Environmental Sciences; European Culture & Society; Exercise & Health Science; Fine Art; Food Science & Nutrition; French Studies; Geography; Geology; Geotechnics; German Studies; German Studies; History; History of Art; Hospitality Management Studies; Human Biology; Information Systems; Intelligent Systems; Japanese Studies; Law; Leisure Planning; Mapping & Cartography;

Marketing Management; Mathematics; Multimedia Systems; Music; Physical Geography; Planning Studies; Politics; Psychology; Publishing; Retail Management; Sociology; Software Engineering; Spanish Studies; Statistics; Telecommunications; Tourism; Transport and Travel; Water Resources

BEng/BEng Hons: *3 yrs FT/4 yrs S* Automotive Engineering; Civil Engineering; Electronic Engineering; Engineering Foundation; Mechanical Engineering

BSc Hons: *3 yrs FT* Estate Management

BSc/BSc Hons: *3 yrs FT/4 yrs S* Applied Social Studies; Biology; Biotechnology; Building; Cell & Molecular Biology; Civil Engineering; Computer Aided Product Design; Computer Systems; Computer Technology; Computing; Computing Mathematics; Computing Science; Construction Management; Electronics; Environmental Biology; Environmental Geotechnology; Environmental Sciences; Extended Science; Geological Sciences; Hotel & Restaurant Management; Human Biology; Information Systems; Intelligent Systems; Mathematical Sciences; Media Technology; Midwifery; Nursing (Adult); Nursing (Children); Nutrition & Food Science; Occupational Therapy; Physiotherapy; Public Health Nutrition; Software Engineering; Technology Management

LLB Hons: *3 yrs FT modular* Law

Higher Degrees

MA: *FT/PT* Built Resources Studies; Culture & Society in Modern France/Germany/Europe; Education; Education for International Schools; Electronic Media; Environmentalism & Society; European Studies; Historical Studies; Humanities; Humanities; Humanities & Research Methodology; Social Anthropology of Japan; Urban Design

MBA: *FT/PT/DL* Business Administration

MPhil/PhD: (Available in a range of disciplines)

MSc: *FT/PT* Advanced Health Care Practice; Computing; Development Practices; Distributed Systems; Energy Efficient Building; Environmental Assessment & Management; European Property Development & Planning; Geratology; Health Care Studies; Hotel & Catering Management; Housing; International Hotel & Tourism Management; International Management; International Nutrition & Food Processing; Knowledge-based Systems; Petroleum Geology; Petroleum Reservoir Engineering; Planning Studies; Town Centre Planning; Urban Planning

Diplomas

BTEC HND: Civil Engineering Studies

Diploma: Advanced Studies

Postgraduate Diploma: Anthropology; Architecture; Built Resources Studies; Computing; Culture & Society in Modern France/Germany/Europe; Development Practices; Distributed Systems; Education for Professional Health Care Practice; Educational Studies; Electronic Media; Energy Efficient Building; Environmental Assessment & Management; Family Therapy; Geratology; Historic Conservation; Housing; Housing Education; International Nutrition & Food Processing; Knowledge-based Systems; Management Studies; Personnel Management; Petroleum Geoscience; Planning; Planning; Publishing; Urban Design; Urban Planning

Certificates

Certificate: Community Practice Teacher's Certificate; Computing; Management; Tenant Participation

Postgraduate Certificate: Primary Education; Professional Studies in Education; Secondary Education

UNIVERSITY OF OXFORD

University Offices, Wellington Square, Oxford OX1 2JD Tel: 01865 270001 Fax: 01865 270708
Website: www.oxford.ac.uk

BA: The degree of BA is the first degree in both Arts & Science subjects (except for Chemistry, Molecular & Cellular Biochemistry, Engineering, Metallurgy & Science of Materials, and Fine Art). Candidates must reach an appropriate standard in one of the subjects listed.

BM, BCh: All candidates for the BM, BCh must take an honours degree. This is normally obtained by taking the Honour School of Physiological Sciences after completion of the first BM. The last three yrs are devoted to clinical studies and lead to the Oxford BM, BCh.
† Subject to validation.

First Degrees

BA Hons: *3-4 yrs* Ancient & Modern History; Arabic; Arabic with subsidiary language or Islamic Art & Archaeology or Islamic Studies/History or Modern Middle Eastern Studies; Archaeology & Anthropology; Biological Sciences; Chinese; Classical Archaeology-Ancient History; Classics-English or Modern Languages; Computer Science; Economics & Management; Egyptology; Egyptology & Ancient Near Eastern Studies; English; English-Modern Languages; European & Middle Eastern Languages; Experimental Psychology; Geography; Geology; Hebrew; Human Sciences; Japanese; Jewish Studies; Law; Law with Law Studies in Europe; Mathematics; Mathematics-Computer Science; Mathematics-Philosophy; Modern History; Modern History-Economics; Modern History-Modern Languages or Politics; Modern Languages; Music; Persian with subsidiary language or Islamic Art & Archaeology or Islamic Studies/History; Philosophy, Politics & Economics; Physics; Physics-Philosophy; Physiological Sciences; Physiological Sciences (Medicine); Physiology with Philosophy or Psychology; Psychology with Philosophy; Psychology, Philosophy & Physiology; Sanskrit; Theology; Turkish with subsidiary language or Islamic Art & Archaeology
BFA: *3 yrs* Fine Art

Higher Degrees

BCL: *1 yr FT* Law (By exam, or by exam and dissertation)
BD: Divinity (By written and oral exam and by thesis. Open to Oxford graduates only)
BMus: Music (By exam. Open to Oxford graduates only)
BPhil: *2 yrs By exam and thesis:* Philosophy
DPhil: *3-4 yrs FT* (By thesis)
MBA: *1 yr* Business Administration (By coursework and examination)
MBiochem: *4 yrs* Molecular & Cellular Biochemistry
MChem: *4 yrs* Chemistry
MEng: *4 yrs* Chemical Engineering; Civil Engineering; Electrical Engineering; Engineering & Computing Science; Engineering & Materials; Engineering Science; Engineering, Economics & Management; Information Engineering; Materials, Economics & Management; Mechanical Engineering; Metallurgy & Science of Materials
MESC: *4 yrs* Earth Sciences
MFA: *1 yr FT* Master of Fine Art
MJur: *1 yr* Law (By exam or exam and dissertation)
MLitt: *2 yrs FT* (By thesis)
MMath: *4 yrs* Mathematics
MPhil/BPhil: *2 yrs By exam and thesis:* Byzantine Studies; Celtic Studies; Classical Archaeology; Comparative Social Policy; Development Studies; Eastern Christian Studies; Economic & Social History; Economics; English Studies; European Archaeology; European Literature; European Politics & Society; General Linguistics & Comparative Philology; Greek & Latin Languages & Literature; Greek &/or Roman History; International Relations; Judaism & Christianity in the Graeco-Roman World; Latin American Studies; Historical and Comparative Philology-Linguistics; Material Anthropology-Museum Ethnography; Mathematics for Industry; Modern European History; Music (Interpretation & Performance); Oriental Studies; Philosophical Theology; Politics; Russian & East European Studies; Slavonic Studies; Social Anthropology; Sociology; Theology; World Archaeology
MPhys: *4 yrs* Physics
MSc: *1 yr FT By coursework and examination:* Applied Statistics; Archaeological Science; Biology (Integrative Bio-Science); Comparative Social Policy; Computation; Diagnostic Imaging; Economic and Social History; Economics for Development; Educational Research Methodology; Environmental Change and Management; Epidemiology, Evolution and Control of Infectious Diseases; History of Science: Instruments, Museums, Science, Technology; Human Biology; International Relations Research; Management (Industrial Relations and Human Resource Management); Material Anthropology and Museum Ethnography; Mathematical Modelling;

Mathematics and Foundations of Computer Science; Neuroscience; Politics Research; Public Policy in Latin America; Social Anthropology; Sociology; Theoretical Chemistry *1 yr FT/2 yrs PT By coursework and examination:* Educational Studies (Comparative and International Studies in Education, or Teacher Education and Development) *1-3 yrs By Research:* Thesis *2 yrs FT/4 yrs PT by coursework:* Applied Social Studies *3-4 yrs FT* Law with Accounting or Politics; Law with French or German or Spanish; Law-Accounting or Politics *3-4 yrs PT By coursework and examination:* Evidence-Based Health Care; Forestry and Its Relation to Land Use; Software Engineering

MSt: *1 yr FT* Anthropological Archaeology; Archaeological Science; Byzantine Studies; Celtic Studies; Chinese Studies; Classical Archaeology; Classical Armenian Studies; Classical Hebrew Studies; European Archaeology; European Literature; Forced Migration; General Linguistics & Comparative Philology; Greek &/or Latin Languages & Literature; Greek &/or Roman History; Historical Research; Historical Research (Medieval History); History of Art & Visual Culture; Islamic Art & Archaeology; Jewish Studies in the Graeco-Roman Period; Korean Studies; Legal Research; Historical and Comparative Philology-Linguistics; Modern History; Modern Jewish Studies; Modern Middle Eastern Studies; Music (Musicology); Oriental Studies; Philosophical Theology; Philosophy; Professional Archaeology; Psychodynamic Studies; Research Methods in English; Slavonic Studies; Study of Religion; Syriac Studies; Theology; Women's Studies; World Archaeology; Yiddish Studies *2 yrs PT* English Local History

MTh: *FT/PT* Applied Theology (by coursework and thesis)

Diplomas

Postgraduate Diploma: Applied Statistics; Architectural History; Cognitive Therapy; Educational Studies; Evidence-Based Health Care; Human Biology; Jewish Studies; Mathematical Finance; Material Anthropology; Museum Ethnography; Professional Archaeology; Psychodynamic Practice; Social Anthropology; Software Engineering; Theology

Certificates

PGCE: Education
Postgraduate Certificate: Architectural History; Diplomatic Studies; Evidence-Based Health Care; Object Technology; Psychodynamic Counselling *PT* Software Engineering

Degrees validated by University of Oxford offered at:

Westminster College, Oxford

Oxford OX2 9AT Tel: 01865 247644 Fax: 01865 251847
e-mail: marketing@ox-west.ac.uk Website: www.ox-west.ac.uk

First Degrees

BA Hons: *Validated by the Open University Validation Services:* English Literature with Geography or History or Theology; Geography with History or English Literature or Theology; History with Geography or English Literature or Theology; Theology with History or Geography or English Literature *3 yrs FT Validated by Oxford Brookes University:* Theology
BA with QTS: *3 yrs FT Validated by Oxford Brookes University:* Education
BEd Hons: *4 yrs FT* Primary Education (English or French or Mathematics or Religious Studies or Science in the Environment)
BTh Hons: Theology (or by Distance Learning)

Higher Degrees

MEd: *2-3 yrs PT* Education
MTh: *3 yrs PT* Applied Theology

Certificates

PGCE: *1 yr FT* Secondary *Validated by Oxford Brookes University:* Art & Design; English; French; French/Matrise; Geography; German; Information Technology; Maths; Music; Religious Education; Science

UNIVERSITY OF PAISLEY

Paisley PA1 2BE Tel: 0141 848 3000 Fax: 0141 848 3623 Website: www.paisley.ac.uk

† Subject to validation.

First Degrees

BA: *2 yrs FT* Childhood Studies *3 yrs FT* Property Studies

BA/BA Hons: *1-2 yrs FT* Business Accounting; Business Administration *3-4 yrs FT* European Policy Studies; Media: Theory & Production; Social Sciences with Politics or Social Policy or Technology & Society or Psychology or Sociology or Social Work *3-4 yrs FT/4-5 yrs S* Business & Management; Business Analysis; Business Economics; Business Information Technology or Marketing or European Language with Accounting or Human Resource Management or Multimedia or Management; Financial Services; International Marketing; Marketing; Public Management and Administration; Tourism

BA/BA Hons; BSc/BSc Hons: *PT* Biology; Chemistry

BAcc/BAcc Hons: *3-4 yrs FT/4-5 yrs S* Accounting

BEd/BEd Hons: *4 yrs FT* Primary Education

BEng Hons: *4 yrs S* Civil Engineering with Geology; Civil Engineering with Project Management; Civil Engineering with Architectural Studies; Civil Engineering with Environmental Management; Construction Engineering; Mechanical Engineering

BEng/BEng Hons: *3-4 yrs FT/5 yrs S* Chemical Engineering; Computer Engineering; Electronic & Electrical Engineering

BSc: Health Studies; Midwifery (Advanced Studies); Nursing *1 yr FT* Computer Aided Design *1 yr PT* Applied Computing *3 yrs FT* Computer Networking; Computing Technology; Internet Technologies; Manufacturing Management; Mechatronics; Product Design and Development; Science & Technology *3 yrs FT/4 yrs S* Civil Engineering with Environmental Management or Architectural Studies

BSc Hons: *4 yrs FT/4 yrs S* Biochemistry & Microbiology; Biomedical Sciences; Biotechnology; Environmental Biology; Environmental Chemistry; Environmental Industrial Chemistry; Immunology & Biochemistry; Medicinal Chemistry; Microbiology & Immunology; Science with Management *4 yrs S* Biology with Multimedia; Construction & Environmental Management; Construction Management; Physics with Multimedia *5 yrs S* Industrial Chemistry; Pharmaceutical Industrial Chemistry; Science with European Language

BSc/BSc Hons: *Health Studies/Nursing with Community Specialism:* Community Mental Health Nursing; Community Nursing in the Home; District Nursing; Health Visiting; Public Health Nursing; School Nursing *3-4 yrs* Media Technology; Multimedia Systems *3-4 yrs FT* Psychology or Chemistry; Biology *3-4 yrs FT/4 yrs S* Real Estate Management *3-4 yrs FT/4-5 yrs S* Computing Science with French or German or Spanish; Computing Science; Information Systems; Quality Management-Technology; Software Engineering *3-4 yrs FT/5 yrs S* Applicable Mathematics with Computing; Applied Biochemistry; Biology; Geology-Biology or Chemistry or Mathematical Science or Physics; Business Information Technology; Chemistry; Civil Engineering; Earth Science and Environmental Management; Environmental Management; Environmental Science & Technology; Mathematical Sciences; Microelectronic Science; Physics; Science with Geology or European Language or Management or Multimedia; Water and Environmental Management

Combined Awards: *9 mths FT/2-3 yrs PT* Entrepreneurship and Economic Development; Molecular Basis of Disease and Treatment; Skills for Biotechnology and the Biomedical Sciences

Higher Degrees

Combined Awards: *FT/PT* Entrepreneurship and Economic Development; Molecular Basis of Disease and Treatment

MBA: Master of Business Administration *DL* Management of e-Business

MEd: *PT* Education

MRes: Skills for Biotechnology and the Biomedical Sciences

MSc: *FT* Information Systems Development; Multimedia Communications *FT/PT* Advanced Computer Systems Development; Alcohol & Drug Studies; Industrial Chemistry with Software Development or Web Technology; Information Technology or IT Support or European IT Support or Business or Management or Intelligent Systems or Information Systems Provision;

International Marketing; Microelectronic Science; Quality Engineering; Quality Management; Safety Management with Environmental Management; Urban Property Appraisal; Waste Management with Environmental Management *PT* Advanced Social Work; Careers Guidance; Gerontology; Health Studies
MSci: *5 yrs* Technological Physics

Diplomas

DipHE: Education; Health Studies; Manufacturing Management; Midwifery; Midwifery; Modular Scheme Combined Awards; Product Design and Development; Quality Management & Technology; Science & Technology *3 yrs* Nursing (Adult or Mental Health Nursing) *FT* Nursing (Adult or Mental Health Nursing) *PT* Mechatronics
Postgraduate Diploma: *2-3 yrs PT/9 mths FT* Advanced Computer Systems Development; Alcohol & Drug Studies; Careers Guidance; Electronic Product Design for Manufacture; Engineering Design of Buildings; Engineering Geology; Environmental Management; International Marketing; Microelectronics Science; Quality Engineering; Quality Management; Safety Management with Environmental Management; Urban Property Appraisal; Waste Management Environmental Management; Information Technology with Software Development or Web Technology or IT Support or European IT Support or Business or Management or Intelligent Systems or Information Systems Provision *FT* Multimedia Communications; Industrial Chemistry; Information Systems Development; *PT* Advanced Social Work; Business and Financial Management; Education; Educational Studies; Gerontology; Health Studies

Certificates

Cert HE: Health Studies; Mechatronics; Modular Scheme Combined Awards; Product Design and Development; Science Skills for Business
Combined Awards: *PT* Gerontology; Health Studies
PGCE: *9 mths FT* Primary Education; Secondary Education
Postgraduate Certificate: *FT* Information Systems Development; Multimedia Communications *FT/PT* Advanced Computer Systems Development; Careers Guidance; Entrepreneurship and Economic Development; Information Technology; Skills for Biotechnology and the Biomedical Sciences *PT* Advanced Social Work; Alcohol and Drug Studies; Education

UNIVERSITY OF PLYMOUTH

Drake Circus, Plymouth, Devon PL4 8AA Tel: 01752 232140 Fax: 01752 232141
e-mail: JHopkinson@plymouth.ac.uk Website: www.plym.ac.uk

† Subject to validation.
†† Combined with a Minor.
* Available at Seale Hayne Campus.
** Available at Exmouth Campus.
*** Available at Exeter Campus.

First Degrees

BA Hons: Three Dimensional Design: Furniture & Interior Design; Accounting & Finance; Architectural Studies with MediaLab Arts; Architectural Studies with Heritage Studies; Architectural Technology & the Environment; Architecture; Architecture, Design & Structures; Art History; Business Administration; Business of Perfumery; Business Studies; Combined Arts Scheme; Cultural Practice; Culture, Environment and Landscape; Design & Italian; Design: Graphic Communication; Design: Illustration; Design: Photographic Illustration; Design: Photography; Design: Typography; Early Childhood Studies; Education Studies; English; European Business; European Studies; European Studies-Modern Languages (French, German, Italian, Spanish); Fine Art; Fine Art Contextual Practice; Geography; Geography; Geography and Modern Languages (French, German, Italian, Spanish); Heritage; History; International Business; International Business with Modern Languages (French, German, Italian, Spanish); Marketing; Media Arts; Modern Language Studies; Modern Languages; Personnel Management; Steiner (Waldorf) Education; Theatre and Performance; Three Dimensional Design; Three Dimensional

Design- Designer Maker; Three Dimensional Design- Product Design; Visual Arts

BA Joint Hons: *Major/Minor pathways from:* American Studies; Art History; Cultural Practice; Early Childhood Studies; Education Studies; English; European Languages & Culture; Heritage; History; Media Arts; Music; Theatre & Performance; Visual Arts

BEd/BA Hons: *3-8 yrs* Early Childhood Studies** *5-11 yrs* Art & Design-General Primary; English-General Primary; History-General Primary; Mathematics-General Primary; Music-General Primary; Physical Education-General Primary; Science-General Primary

BEng Hons: Composite Materials Engineering; Extended Engineering (Foundation Yr progressing to BEng award); Marine Technology; Mechanical Engineering

BEng Hons/MEng: Civil & Coastal Engineering; Civil Engineering; Communication Engineering; Computer Engineering; Electrical & Electronic Engineering; Electronic Engineering; Robotics and Automated Systems

BSc: Computing; Mechanical Design & Manufacture

BSc Hons: Agriculture; Agriculture-Countryside Management; Agriculture-Environment; Agriculture-Estate Management; Animal Production; Animal Science (Behaviour and Welfare); Applied Economics; Applied Economics; Applied Statistics; Applied Statistics; Applied Statistics & Management Science; Biological Sciences; Building Surveying & The Environment; Business and the Environment; Business and Tourism; Business Economics; Business Economics; Business Information Management Systems; Cell Biology; Chemistry; Chemistry (Analytical); Chemistry (Applied); Chemistry (Environmental); Civil & Coastal Engineering; Civil Engineering; Civil Engineering & Computer-Aided Design; Community Health Care Nursing; Computer Systems & Networks; Computer Systems Engineering; Computing Informatics; Conservation Ecology; Construction Management & The Environment; Cosmetic Science and Perfumery; Criminal Justice Studies; Crop Science; Cultural Tourism; Decision Analysis and Business; Earth Sciences; Ecology; Ecology; Ecotourism; Electrical & Electronic Systems; Electronic Communication Systems; Environmental Design & Management; Environmental Science; European Economics; Extended Science (Foundation yr leading to BSc award); Fisheries and Aquaculture; Fisheries Science; Food and Hospitality Management; Food Biology; Food Production and Quality; Food Quality with Product Development & Nutrition; Food Quality with Management; Geography; Geography; Geological Sciences; Geology; Geology (Applied); Health & Social Care Management; Hospitality and Tourism Management; Hospitality Management; Human Biology; Human Biosciences; Hydrography; International Hospitality Management; International Relations; International Tourism Management; Internet Technologies and Applications; Land and Environmental Management; Law; Marine Biology; Marine Biology; Marine Biology & Coastal Ecology; Marine Biology and Oceanography; Marine Environmental Science; Marine Navigation; Marine Resources; Marine Sports Technology; Marine Technology; Maritime Business; Maritime Business with Logistics; Maritime Business with Maritime Law; Mathematical Studies; Mathematics; Mathematics; Mathematics-Statistics; MediaLab Arts; Microbial & Cellular Biology; Microbiology; Multimedia Production and Technology; Nautical Studies; Ocean Science; Ocean Science; Plant Sciences; Podiatry; Politics; Politics; Psychology; Psychology; Quantity Surveying & the Environment; Rural Estate Management; Rural Resource Management; Social Policy & Administration; Social Policy & Administration; Social Research; Sociology; Sociology; Sports & Health Science; Sports Management; Surf Science & Technology; Sustainable Engineering; Tourism Management; Underwater Science; Wildlife Conservation *Single Honours:* International Relations *2 yrs HND top-up:* Animal Science (Equine) *3 yrs* Community Work & Social Policy-Administration; Social Work plus Diploma in Social Work *4 yrs* Community Work & Social Policy & Administration (& CPE); Social Work & Social Policy with diploma in Social Work

Joint Hons Major/Minor pathways: European Languages & Culture

LLB Hons: Law

Higher Degrees

DClinPsy: Clinical Psychology

MA: Biography & History; Architectural Conservation; Creative Writing; English; Fine Art; Fine Art Contextual Practice; Heritage; History of Art; Media; Publishing; Three Dimensional Design; European Heritage: Planning and Management; Theatre and Performance

MBA: Business Administration

MBM: Business Management

MChem: Chemistry
MD/MS: Medical Studies
MEd: Adult Education; Early Years; Educational Management; Further Education; Language & Literacy; Primary Education; Primary Mathematics; Special Educational Needs
MGeol: *4 yrs* Geology
MMath: Mathematics
MPhil/PhD: Agriculture & Food; Architecture; Arts & Design; Astronomy; Biological Sciences; Business & Management; Civil & Structural Engineering; Computing; Education; Electronic, Communication & Electrical Engineering; English; Environmental Sciences; Geographical Sciences; Geological Sciences; Health Studies; Humanities & Cultural Interpretation; Land Use & Rural Management; Law; Marine Engineering; Marine Studies; Mathematics & Statistics; Mechanical Engineering; Medicine; Meteorology; Modern Languages; Multimedia; Ocean Sciences; Politics; Primary Health Care; Psychology; Shipping & Transport; Social Policy & Social Work; Sociology; Tourism
MRes: Applied Fish Biology; Applied Marine Science; Aquatic Ecotoxicology; Environmental Analytical Chemistry; Global Change; Sustainable Environmental Management
MSc: Biological Diversity; Coastal and Ocean Policy; Competitive Product Engineering; Digital Futures; E-Commerce; Environmental Monitoring and Management; Global Change; Human Communication Research; Management and Marketing for Rural Business; MBM (Finance); Port Management; Rural Property Management; Sustainable Environmental Management; @First Para:Agricultural Business Management; Applied Marine Science; Behavioural Research Methods; Biomedical Sciences; Cancer Studies; Communications Engineering & Signal Processing; Computational Intelligence; Data Storage Systems; Health Care & Practice; Health Psychology; Hydrography; Integrated Services & Intelligent Networks Engineering; International Logistics; International Shipping; Primary Health Care; Psychological Research Methods; Psychology of Health; Remote Health Care (Polar Option); Rural Development; Rural Tourism; Social Research

Diplomas

Diploma: Professional Studies in International Shipping & Logistics Management; Professional Studies in International Shipping & Logistics Management (Europe)
HND: *2 yrs HND top-up:* Adventure Tourism Management
Postgraduate Diploma: Biological Diversity; Coastal and Ocean Policy; Competitive Product Engineering; Digital Futures; E-Commerce; Environmental Monitoring and Management; European Heritage: Planning and Management; Global Change; Human Communication Research; Management and Marketing for Rural Business; Port Management; Rural Property Management; Sustainable Environmental Management; Theatre and Performance; @First Para:Biography & History; Adult Education; Agricultural Business Management; Applied Marine Science; Architectural Conservation; Behavioural Research Methods; Biomedical Sciences; Cancer Studies; Communications Engineering & Signal Processing; Computational Intelligence; Creative Writing; Data Storage Systems; Early Years Education; Educational Management; English; Fine Art; Fine Art Contextual Practice; Further Education; Health Care & Practice; Heritage; History of Art; Humane Architecture; Hydrography; Integrated Services & Intelligent Networks Engineering; International Logistics; International Shipping; Landscape Design; Language & Literacy; Law; Management Studies; Media; Personnel & Development; Primary Education; Primary Health Care; Primary Mathematics; Psychological Research Methods; Psychology of Health; Publishing; Remote Health Care (Polar Option); Rural Development; Rural Tourism; Social Research; Special Educational Needs; Three Dimensional Design *Distance Learning:* Perfumery

Certificates

Postgraduate Certificate: Management Studies

Degrees validated by University of Plymouth offered at:

Dartington College of Arts

Totnes, Devon TQ9 6EJ Tel: 01803 862224 Fax: 01803 863569
e-mail: registry@dartington.ac.uk Website: www.dartington.ac.uk

First Degrees

BA Hons: *3 yrs FT* Arts Management (Two subject awards with Arts Management) with Music (Two subject awards with Arts Management) or Music (Performance) (Two subject awards with Arts Management) or Music (Composition) (Two subject awards with Arts Management) or Performance Writing (Two subject awards with Arts Management) or Theatre (Two subject awards with Arts Management) or Visual Performance (Two subject awards with Arts Management); Music (Single subject awards with interdisciplinary electives); Music (Two subject awards with Arts Management) with Arts Management (Two subject awards with Arts Management); Music (Composition) (Two subject awards with Arts Management) with Arts Management (Two subject awards with Arts Management); Music (Composition) (Single subject awards with interdisciplinary electives); Music (Performance) (Two subject awards with Arts Management) with Arts Management (Two subject awards with Arts Management); Music (Performance) (Single subject awards with interdisciplinary electives); Performance Writing (Two subject awards with arts management) with Arts Management (Two subject awards with arts management); Performance Writing (Single subject awards with interdisciplinary electives); Theatre (Single subject awards with interdisciplinary electives); Theatre (Two subject awards with Arts Management) with Arts Management (Two subject awards with Arts Management); Visual Performance with Arts Management; Visual Performance (Single subject awards with interdisciplinary electives)

Higher Degrees

MA: *1 yr FT/2 yrs PT* Arts Management (Yr runs September to September); Contemporary Music (Yr runs September to September); Devised Theatre (Yr runs September to September); Performance Writing (Yr runs September to September); Visual Performance (time-based arts practices) (Yr runs September to September)
PGDip: *1 yr FT/2 yrs PT* Arts Management (Yr runs September to September); Contemporary Music (Yr runs September to September); Devised Theatre (Yr runs September to September); Performance Writing (Yr runs September to September); Visual Performance (time-based arts practices) (Yr runs September to September)

UNIVERSITY OF PORTSMOUTH

University House, Winston Churchill Avenue, Portsmouth PO1 2UP Tel: 023 9284 8484
Fax: 023 9284 3082 e-mail: admissions@port.ac.uk Website: www.port.ac.uk

First Degrees

BA Hons: Accountancy Studies; Accounting with Finance or Business Law; Accounting; Accounting-Business Information Systems; Applied Languages; Architecture; Business with Sports Administration; Business Economics with French or German or Italian or Russian or Spanish; Business Economics with Business Law; Business Economics; Business Law with French or German or Italian or Russian or Spanish; Business Studies/Administration; Communication Design; Computer Animation; Economic & Business Policy; Economic & Social History; Economics; Economics and Business Policy; Economics-Geography; English & Comparative Literature; English & Creative Studies; English Language & Literature; English Literature; English Studies (For overseas students); History-English or French or German or Politics or Russian or Spanish; European Business; European Social Work; European Studies; European Studies with English as a Foreign Language or French or German or Italian or Portuguese or Russian or Spanish; Extended Business Degree Scheme; Financial Services; Fine Art; French Studies; Russian-French

Studies or German Studies or Italian Studies or Soviet Studies or Spanish Studies; Business Economics-French or German or Italian or Russian or Spanish; Business Law-French or German or Italian or Russian or Spanish; French-Italian Studies; Geography; German Studies; German-French Studies or Italian Studies or Spanish Studies; Health & Social Care; Hispanic-French Studies; History with French or German or Russian or Spanish; History; History-Sociology; Hospitality Management with Tourism; Hospitality Management; Human Geography; Illustration; Information Technology with French with German or Russian or Spanish; Information Technology-French or German or Russian or Spanish; Interactive Media Management; International Business Studies; International Finance & Trade; International Relations with French or German or Spanish or Russian; International Relations-French or German or Spanish or History or Russian; International Relations-Politics; International Trade with English as a Foreign Language or French or German or Italian or Russian or Spanish; Spanish-Italian Studies or Latin American Studies; Languages and International Trade; Latin American Studies/Latin American Development Studies; Moving Image; Photography; Politics; Politics-Sociology; Restoration & Decorative Studies; Social Policy & Administration; Social Policy-Criminology or Politics; Sociology & Social Policy; Spanish Studies; Three Dimensional Studies; Visual Culture

BEng Hons: Civil Engineering; Civil Engineering with European Studies; Communication Systems Engineering; Communications Engineering; Computer Engineering; Computer Technology; Construction Engineering Management; Electronic and Computer Engineering; Electronic and Electrical Engineering; Electronic Engineering; Electronic Engineering (European Programme); Engineering; Engineering Design-Materials; Engineering Geology & Geotechnics; Extended Engineering degree scheme including Civil Engineering; Mechanical and Manufacturing Engineering; Mechanical Engineering

BSc Hons: Applied Environmental Geoscience; Applied Microbiology; Biochemistry; Biology; Biomedical Science; Biomolecular Science; Biotechnology; Business Information Systems; Business Information Technology; Cell Biology; Computer Science; Computer Science (Integrated); Computer Systems Engineering; Computing; Criminology & Criminal Justice; Decision Analysis & Information Technology; Earth Sciences; Electronics; Entertainment Technology; Environmental Assessment (Construction Industry); Environmental Biology; Environmental Science; European Technology Management; Exercise & Health Science; Extended Biology Degree Scheme; Facilities Management; Geographical Science; Geological Hazards; Geology; Geology-Geographical Science; Information Technology & Society; Internet Technology; Leisure Resource Management; Marine Biology; Marine Environmental Science; Mathematics; Mathematics with Computing; Mathematics with Astronomy; Mathematics for Finance & Management; Computer Aided Product Design; Construction Technology; Mathematics for Financial Markets; Mathematics-Statistics; Mechanical & Manufacturing Engineering; Molecular Biology; Palaeobiology & Evolution; Pharmacology; Product Design & Innovation; Property Development; Psychology; Quantity Surveying; Radiography (Diagnostic & Therapeutic); Real Estate Management; Sociology; Sociology & Criminology; Software Engineering; Sports Development; Sports Science; Technology Management with Languages; Technology Management; Technology Management with Computing

Higher Degrees

MA: Advanced Professional Practice in Education; Advanced Professional Practice in Health Care; Applied Linguistics-Modern Language Teaching; Applied Linguistics-TEFL; Applied Social Studies; Art, Design and Media; Arts Enterprise; Arts Management; Arts Programme Development; Business Law; Church & Community Studies; Curriculum Management; Economics For Business; Education In Service; English Language & Literature; English Literature; European Law; European Law and Policy; European Media; European Social Work; European Studies; Financial & Resource Management; Health Professional Education; Historical Landscape Change; History; Learning & Teaching in Higher Education; Maritime Studies; Marketing; Marketing & Electronic Commerce; Mental Health Studies; Modern Language Studies; Partnership Masters Programme; Sales; Translation Studies

MArch: Architecture

MBA

MEng: Civil Engineering with European Studies; Civil Engineering; Communication Systems Engineering; Computer Engineering; Electronic & Computer Engineering; Electronic & Electrical Engineering; Engineering Management

MMath: Mathematics
MPharm: Pharmacy
MSc: Advanced Manufacturing Technology; Applied Psychology (Learning Disability); Aquaculture Economics; Architecture-Environment; Biomedical Science; Building Conservation; Business Economics; Child Forensic Studies (Psychology & Law); Civil Engineering; Clinical Pharmacy; Coastal & Marine Resource Management; Communication Systems Engineering; Contaminated Land; Control Technology; Criminal Justice Studies; Economic Research & Consultancy; Economy Society and Place; Ecotourism; Education & Training Management; Electronic Engineering; Engineering Design; Environmental Engineering; Environmental Resource Management; Financial Decision Analysis; Fisheries Economics; Fisheries Planning & Development; Geographical Information Systems; Geography of Health; Geohazard Assessment; Ground Investigation & Assessment; Healthcare Information Management; Healthcare Information Systems; Heritage & Museum Studies; Heritage Tourism; Historic Building Conservation; Historical Geography and GIS; Human Resource Development; Human Resource Management; Information Systems; Land Information Management & Mapping; Landscape Dynamics & Management; Local & Regional Economics; Maritime Conservation Studies; Mathematical Sciences; Medical Imaging; Microelectronic Systems Design; Microwave Communications; Microwave Solid State Physics; Mobile Robotics; Molecular Biology; Multi-Media Information Systems; Nursing Studies Partnership Programme; Occupational & Environmental Health & Safety Management; Product Engineering; Professional & Policy Studies; Professional & Policy Studies (Age & Ageing or Crime & Police or Community Health; Professional Practice (in Architecture, Surveying, Civil Engineering); Project Management; Property Development & Investment; Psychological Research Methods; Quality Management; Radiation Therapy; Radionuclide Imaging; Real Estate Studies (SE Asia); Signal Processing; Social Research Methods; Surface Engineering; Systems Engineering; Technology Management

Diplomas

HND: Building Studies; Business; Civil Engineering; Computer Animation; Computer Systems Engineering; Computing; Engineering (Electrical and Electronic); Engineering (Mechanical/Manufacture); Restoration & Decorative Studies; Software Engineering; Tourism Management

QUEEN MARGARET UNIVERSITY COLLEGE

Corstorphine Campus, Clerwood Terrace, Edinburgh EH12 8TS Tel: 0131 317 3000
Fax: 0131 317 3248 e-mail: admissions@mail.qmuc.ac.uk
* Subject to validation.

FIRST DEGREES
BA Hons: *3-4 yrs FT* Acting; Communication Studies; Consumer Affairs (subject to validation); Consumer Studies; Corporate Communication; Drama & Theatre Arts; Hospitality and Tourism Management; Information Management; International Hospitality Management; Media and Cultural Studies; Retail Business; Sociology & Social Policy with Psychology; Stage Management & Theatre Production; Tourism Management
BA Hons/BSc Hons: *3-4 yrs FT* Joint Degrees; Psychology and Sociology-Social Policy
BSc Hons: Health Promotion *3-4 yrs FT* Biological & Health Sciences; Food with Marketing; Food and Nutrition; Health Psychology; Human Nutrition; Occupational Therapy; Podiatry; Psychology with Sociology & Social Policy; Public Health Nutrition; Social Sciences and Health; Speech Pathology and Therapy; Veterinary Nursing* *4 yrs FT* Diagnostic Radiography; Dietetics; Nursing; Physiotherapy; Therapeutic Radiography

UNIVERSITY OF READING

PO Box 217, Reading, Berkshire RG6 6AH Tel: 0118 987 5123 Fax: 0118 931 4404
e-mail: schools.liaison@reading.ac.uk Website: www.reading.ac.uk

First Degrees

BA (Ed) Hons: *4 yrs FT Specialisations:* Art; English; Geography & the Environment; Music

BA Combined Hons: *3 yrs FT* Ancient History-Archaeology or Sociology; Archaeology-History of Art or History; Business Economics-Organisational Studies; Classical Studies-English Literature or History of Art or Medieval Studies or Politics or Sociology; Economics-Sociology; English Literature-Classical Studies or History of Art or Sociology; Greek-English Literature or Philosophy; History with Latin; History-Ancient History or Economics or English Literature or History of Art or Philosophy or Sociology; International Relations-Economics; Modern History-International Relations; Music-English Literature or History of Art; Philosophy-Classical Studies or English Literature or Politics or Sociology; Politics-Economics; Psychology-Linguistics or Philosophy or Sociology; Sociology-International Relations *4 yrs FT* Art-History of Art or Psychology; English Literature-German or Italian; Film & Drama-Italian; French-Economics or German or Italian; German-Economics or French or Italian; History-French or German or Italian; Italian with Latin or Film Studies; Italian-Classical Studies; Latin-French or German or Italian; Linguistics with a Foreign Language; Music-French or German or Italian; Philosophy-French or German or Italian

BA Hons: *3 yrs FT* Accounting & Economics; American Studies; Ancient History; Archaeology; Business Economics; Classical Studies; Classics; Economics; Economics & Econometrics; Film & Drama; History; History of Art & Architecture; International Securities, Investment & Banking; Investment & Finance in Property; Latin (Classical & Medieval); Linguistics; Management & Business Administration; Music; Philosophy; Politics & International Relations; Psychology; Sociology *3 yrs FT/4 yrs PT* Community & Youth Studies *3 yrs FT/5 yrs PT* English Language & Literature *4 trms (post-qualifying)* Community Health Studies (Specialisms in: Community Mental Handicap Nursing; Community Psychiatric Nursing; District Nursing, Health Visiting & Practice Nursing) *4 yrs FT* Art; European Studies; French; German; International Management & Business Administration; Italian; Linguistics & Language Pathology; Typography & Graphic Communication

BEng Hons: *3 yrs FT* Electronic Engineering; Integrated Engineering; Mechanical Engineering *4 yrs FT* Electronic Engineering (Access Course); Integrated Engineering (Access Course); Mechanical Engineering (Access Course)

BSc Hons: *3 yrs FT* Agricultural Botany; Agricultural Botany-Studies in Europe; Agricultural Economics; Agriculture; Animal Science; Applied Mathematics; Biochemistry; Biological Sciences; Botany; Botany-Zoology; Building Construction & Management; Building Surveying; Chemistry; Chemistry (All courses available with a yr in Europe) with Archaeology (All courses available with a yr in Europe) or Computer Science (All courses available with a yr in Europe) or Economics (All courses available with a yr in Europe); Chemistry & Food Science; Computer Science; Computer Science-Cybernetics or Psychology; Construction Management; Construction Management, Engineering & Surveying; Crop Protection; Crop Protection-Studies in Europe; Cybernetics & Control Engineering; Environmental Biology; Environmental Chemistry; Environmental Earth Sciences; Environmental Geochemistry; Environmental Science of the Earth & Atmosphere; Food Marketing Economics; Food Studies; Habitat & Soil Management; Horticulture; Human & Physical Geography; Human Cybernetics; Human Geography; Intelligent Systems; Land Management; Mathematical Studies; Mathematics; Meteorology; Microbiology; Molecular Biology; Pathobiology; Physical Geography; Physics; Physics & Electronics; Physics & Photonics; Physics-Meteorology or Music; Physiology & Biochemistry; Psychology; Pure Mathematics; Quantity Surveying; Regional Science (Geography & Economics); Rural Land Management; Rural Resource Management; Rural Resource Science; Statistics; Zoology *4 yrs FT* Land Management; Physics with French or German or Italian or a Yr in Europe; Physics (Access Course) *4 yrs S* Agricultural Botany-International Studies; Applied Statistics; Biotechnology; Crop Protection-Studies in Europe; Crop Science-International Studies; Food Manufacture, Management & Marketing; Food Technology; Landscape Management; Landscape Management-Studies in Europe; Urban Planning & Development

LLB Hons: *3 yrs FT* Law *4 yrs FT* Law with Legal Studies in Europe; Law with French Law

Higher Degrees

MASTER'S DEGREES OR EQUIVALENT

LLM: *1 yr FT/2 yrs PT* Law

MA: *1 yr* Ancient & Modern Philosophy; Ancient Literature; Ancient Philosophy; Ancient Social & Cultural History; Applied Linguistics; Beckett Studies & Irish Literature in English Since 1890; Body & Representation; British Archaeology; Burial Archaeology; Business Economics; Children's Literature; Classical & Medieval Latin; Classical Tradition; Contemporary English Language & Linguistics; Counselling; Counselling & Vocational Guidance; Cypriot & Agean Archaeology; Education & Society; Educational Administration & Institutional Management; English & Language in Education; Equity & Change in the Public Services; Euro-Mediterranean Studies; European Studies; Field Archaeology; Film & Drama; French Studies; Health & Nursing Studies; History of Agriculture & the English Landscape; Information Technology in Education; International Relations; International Security Studies; International Studies; Italian Studies; Learning Disability Studies; Linguistics; Literature & the Visual Arts, 1840-1940; Medieval Studies; Mediterranean Archaeology; Modern History; Moral, Legal & Political Philosophy; Music Education; Organisation, Planning & Management in Education; Philosophy; Prehistoric Archaeology; Primary Education; Roman Archaeology; Rural Social Development; Social Work; Sociology; Teaching English as a Foreign Language; The English Renaissance, Politics, Patronage & Literature; Therapeutic Child Care *2 yrs Taught courses available in:* Linguistics *2 yrs FT* Language Pathology

MAgrSc: *2 yrs* Agricultural Research, Technology & Extension; Tropical Agricultural Development

MBA: *3-5 yrs PT* Construction & Real Estate; Management

MChem: *4 yrs FT* Chemistry

MEng: *4 yrs FT* Cybernetics & Control Engineering; Electronic Engineering; Integrated Engineering; Mechanical Engineering

MFA: *2 yrs* Fine Art

MMath: *4 yrs FT* Applied Mathematics; Mathematics; Pure Mathematics

MMus: *1 yr* Composition; Music Theory & Analysis; Musicology; Organ Historigraphy; Performance Studies

MPhil: *2 yrs Taught courses available in:* Applied Zoology; Environmental Planning; European Studies; International Relations; International Security Systems; International Studies; Language Pathology; Medieval Studies; Plant Breeding & Crop Improvement *21 mths Taught courses available in:* Land Management

MPhys: *4 yrs FT* Physics

MRes: *1 yr* Earth & Atmospheric Sciences; Urban & Regional Studies *21 mths* Regional Science

MSc: *1 yr* Agricultural Development Economics; Agricultural Education & Training; Agricultural Extension; Agricultural Management; Applied & Modern Optics; Applied Meteorology; Biometry; Business Economics; Chemical Research; Construction Management; Construction Management & Engineering Research; Contaminated Land & Groundwater Investigation & Remediation; Dairy Animal Science; Development Economics & Policy; Economic Development & International Trade; Economics; Economics & Econometrics; Engineering & Information Sciences; Engineering Research; Environmental Sedimentology & Geomorphology Research; Food Biotechnology; Food Economics-Marketing; Food Science; Food Technology; Horticulture; Hydrogeology & Groundwater Quality; Information Systems Engineering; International Banking & Financial Services; International Business & Economic Development; International Business & Economic Integration; International Business & Finance; International Business History; International Securities, Investment & Banking; Land Management; Livestock Economics & Planning; Management of Soil Fertility; Management School Improvement; Mathematical Education; Mathematics & Meteorology; Modelling & Management of Surface Freshwater Systems; Multinational Accounting & Financial Management; Numerical Solution of Differential Equations; Nutrition & Food Science; Parallel & Scientific Computation; Pedology, Soil Survey & Land Evaluation; Petroleum Sedimentary Research; Physics Education; Physics of Materials; Physics Research; Plant Biotechnology; Pure & Applied Plant and Fungal Taxonomy; Quality Assurance; Real Estate; Regional Science; Renewable Energy & the Environment; Research Methods in Psychology; Ruminant Animal & Forage Science; School Management; Science

Education; Soil Spatial Analysis & Land Evaluation; Soils & Environmental Pollution; Tropical Agricultural Development; Urban Land Appraisal; Urban Planning & Development; Vegetation Survey & Assessment; Veterinary Epidemiology; Veterinary Laboratory Management; Weather Climate & Modelling; Wildlife Management & Conservation Control 2 *yrs PT* Corporate Real Estate & Faculties Management; Inclusive Environment; Intelligent Building; Project Management 3 *yrs PT* Town & Country Planning

Diplomas

Advanced Diploma: 2 *yrs* Environmental Planning; Land Management; Town & Country Planning
Postgraduate Diploma: 1 *yr* Agricultural Education & Training; Agricultural Extension; Animal Production; Applied & Agricultural Meteorology; Applied & Modern Optics; Applied Meteorology; Careers Guidance in Higher Education; Counselling; Counselling & Vocational Guidance; Educational Administration & Institutional Management; English & Language in Education; English & Language in Education; Equity & Change in the Public Services; Fine Art; General Sociology; Health & Nursing Studies; Hydrogeology & Groundwater Quality; Information Systems Engineering; Laboratory Techniques & Management in Livestock Development; Law; Learning Disability Studies; Management School Improvement; Meteorology; Music Education; Music Teaching in Private Practice; Numerical Solution of Differential Equations; Organisation, Planning & Management in Education; Primary Education; Pure & Applied Plant and Fungal Taxonomy; Renewable Energy & the Environment; Research Methods in Psychology; Rural Extension & Women; Rural Social Development; Social Work; Soil Science; Therapeutic Child Care; Tropical Agricultural Development; Typography & Graphic Communication; Urban Land Appraisal; Vegetation Survey & Assessment; Vocational Guidance; Weather, Climate & Modelling; Wildlife Management, Conservation & Control

Certificates

Certificate: 3 *mths FT* Teaching English as a Foreign Language
PGCE: 1 *yr* Primary Education: Early Years; Primary Education: Junior; Primary Education: Music (7-12 yrs); Secondary Education

THE ROBERT GORDON UNIVERSITY

Schoolhill, Aberdeen AB10 1FR Tel: 01224 262180 Fax: 01224 262185
e-mail: i.centre@rgu.ac.uk Website: www.rgu.ac.uk

† Subject to validation.

First Degrees

BA Hons: 3-4 *yrs FT* Fine Art 4 *yrs FT* Applied Social Sciences
BA/BA Hons: 3-4 *yrs FT* Accounting & Finance; Business Administration; Communication with Modern Languages; Corporate Communication; Design & Craft; Fine Art (Accelerated route); Government, Policy & Management; Hotel & Hospitality Management; Information & Library Studies; Law & Management; Publishing Studies; Retail Management; Social Work; Tourism & Hospitality Management 4 *yrs FT* Business Studies; European Business Administration with Languages
BEng Hons: 3-4 *yrs FT* Electronic & Communications Engineering 4 *yrs FT* Mechanical & Offshore Engineering; Mechanical Engineering
BEng/BEng Hons: 3-4 *yrs FT* Electronic & Computer Engineering; Electronic & Electrical Engineering
BSc: 3 *yrs FT* Mechanical Engineering
BSc (Eng) Hons: Electronic & Electrical Engineering; Engineering Design; Mechanical Engineering
BSc Hons: 3-4-5 *yrs FT* Occupational Therapy; Pharmaceutical Sciences 4 *yrs FT* Architecture; Architecture with Languages; Design for Industry; Interior Architecture; Nursing; Nutrition & Dietetics with State Registration; Physiotherapy; Radiography
BSc/BSc Hons: Applied Biosciences-Management; Applied Chemistry-Management; Applied

Physics-Management; Biological Sciences; Computer Network Management & Design; Computing; Computing-Information; Environmental Science-Management; Environmental Science-Technology *3-4-5 yrs FT* Applied Biosciences & Chemistry; Applied Chemistry; Applied Physics; Architectural Technology; Biosciences with Biomedical Science; Building Surveying; Business Computing; Computer Science; Construction Management; Design for Digital Media; Innovation Management; Nutrition; Quantity Surveying; Technology & Business

Higher Degrees

HND: *3-4 yrs FT* Hospitality Management
MEng: Electronic & Electrical Engineering; Mechanical Engineering
MPharm Hons: *4 yrs FT* Pharmacy
MPhil: *2 yrs FT*
MSc/PgD: *1 yr FT/2 yrs PT* Design and Management of Manufacturing Systems
PhD: *3 yrs FT*

ROYAL COLLEGE OF ART

Kensington Gore, London SW7 2EU Tel: 020 7590 4444 Fax: 020 7590 4500
e-mail: admissions@rca.ac.uk Website: www.rca.ac.uk

Higher Degrees

MA (RCA): *2 yrs* Design Products; Animation; Architecture & Interiors; Ceramics & Glass; Communication Art & Design; Computer Related Design; Constructed Textiles; Fashion Menswear; Fashion Womenswear; Goldsmithing, Silversmithing, Metalwork & Jewellery; History of Design (Joint course with the V&A); Industrial Design Engineering (Joint course with the ICSTM); Painting; Photography; Printed Textiles; Printmaking; Sculpture; Vehicle Design; Visual Arts Administration (Joint course with the Arts Council of England) *3 yrs* Conservation (Joint course with the V&A and the ICSTM)
MPhil (RCA): *2 yrs FT/3-6 yrs PT* (Research degree awarded after the successful completion of an approved programme of supervised research)
PhD (RCA): (A programme of research, not less than two, nor more than six consecutive yrs' duration, by project or thesis, including an oral exam with an external assessor. Topics may be concerned with any subject currently within the RCA curriculum)

ROYAL SCOTTISH ACADEMY OF MUSIC & DRAMA

100 Renfrew Street, Glasgow G2 3DB Tel: 0141 332 4101
e-mail: registry@rsamd.ac.uk Website: www.rsamd.ac.uk

First Degrees

BA: *3 yrs* Acting; Contemporary Theatre Practice; Musical Studies; Scottish Music; Stage Management Studies
BA Hons: *4 yrs* Contemporary Theatre Practice; Musical Studies
BEd (Music) Hons: *4 yrs* Music
BMus Hons: *4 yrs* Music

Higher Degrees

MDra: *1 yr* Acting; Directing; Producing
MMus: *1 yr* Advanced Opera; Composition; Conducting; Opera; Performance

Diplomas

Postgraduate Diploma: *1 yr* Music

UNIVERSITY OF SALFORD

Salford, Greater Manchester M5 4WT Tel: 0161 295 5000 Fax: 0161 295 5999
Website: www.salford.ac.uk/homepage.html

First Degrees

BA Hons: *3 yrs* Applied Consumer Studies; Arabics/English Translation & Interpreting; Contemporary Military & International History; Design Studies; Digital 3D Design for the Entertainment Industry; English & Cultural Studies; English & History; English Language & Literature; Fashion Design; Fashion Design; Geography; Graphic Design; Graphic Design; Hospitality Management; International Studies; Leisure Management; Media & Performance; Performing Arts; Politics & Contemporary History; Spatial/Interior Design; TV & Radio; Urban Geography; Urban Studies; Visual Arts & Culture *3 yrs FT/5 yrs PT* Sociology; Tourism Management *3-4 yrs* Band Musicianship *4 yrs* Computer Science and a Modern Language; Contemporary European Studies and a Modern Language; English and a Modern Language; European Languages; European Studies and a Modern Language; Linguistics and a Modern Language; Media, Language & Business; Modern Languages with Contemporary European Studies; Modern Languages & Linguistics; Modern Languages-Translation & Interpreting Studies *PT* Hospitality & Tourism Management; Leisure & Tourism Management

BA Hons/DipHE: *2-3 yrs FT* Social Work Studies

BA/BSc: Geography with Languages

BA/HND: *2 yrs* Fashion Design; Graphic Design

BEng: *3 yrs FT/4 yrs S* Construction Engineering

BEng Hons: *3-4 yrs* Civil & Environmental Engineering *4 yrs* Civil & Environmental Engineering with European Studies; Civil Engineering

BEng Hons/MEng: *3-4-5 yrs FT* Aeronautical Engineering; Mechanical Engineering *4 yrs* Civil Engineering; Civil Engineering with European Studies or Transport *4-5 yrs* Mechanical Engineering with European Studies; Unified Engineering

BSc: *3 yrs* Popular Music & Recording *PT* Counselling Studies & Social Policy; Exercise & Health Sciences

BSc Hons: *2 yrs FT 2 + 2 course*/4 yrs FT 2 + 2 course*:* Software, Computer Science & Information Systems *3 yrs* Video & Audio Engineering *3 yrs FT* Acoustics; Applied Computing-Mathematical Modelling; Applied Health Imaging; Audio Technology; Biochemical/Biological Science with Studies in the USA; Building with Facilities Management or Production Management or Project Management; Building; Building Surveying with Industrial Placement; Building Surveying; Business Economics; Business Economics with Gambling Studies; Chemistry; Chemistry with Business Studies or Studies in North America; Complementary Medicine and Health Sciences; Complementary Medicine Practice; Computer Systems-Telecommunications Engineering or Health Sciences; Counselling Studies and Complementary Medicine or Social Policy; Diagnostic Radiography; Economics with Sports Economics; Economics; Environmental Geography; Exercise and Health Sciences; Food Industry Management; Geography; Health Sciences; Health Sciences and Social Policy; Housing Studies; Housing, Health & the Environment; Information Technology with Language Training (French or German); Information Technology; Media Technology; Modelling of Physical & Financial Systems; Music, Acoustics and Recording; Nursing: Registered (Child or Adult); Occupational Therapy; Physiotherapy; Podiatry; Political Economy; Politics and Sociology; Product Design and Development; Property Management and Investment; Quality Management; Quantity Surveying with Industrial Placement; Quantity Surveying; Social Economics; Social Policy; Sociology; Sociology and Cultural Studies; Sports Rehabilitation; Video & Audio Engineering *3 yrs FT/4 yrs S* Combined Sciences *3 yrs FT/5 yrs PT* Food Safety & Quality; Sociology *3-4 yrs FT* Aeronautical Engineering; Applied Computing with Mathematical Modelling; Audio Technology; Biochemical Science; Biological Science; Business Information Systems; Business Operation and Control with Studies in North America; Business Operation and Control; Business Studies; Computer Science; Computer Science-Applied Mathematics with Operational Research and Applied Statistics or Information Systems; Environmental and Resource Science; Environmental Sciences; Environmental Technology and Management; Finance and Accounting; Mathematics with Professional Studies; Mathematics; Physiology with Biochemistry *3-4 yrs FT/4-5 yrs FT* Aerospace Business Systems; Manufacturing Business Systems;

Mechanical Engineering *3-5 yrs* Electronic & Electrical Engineering; Robotic & Electronic Engineering *4 yrs* Electronic & Electrical Engineering; Building Surveying with Industrial Placement; Chemical Science; Chemistry with Foundation Yr; Construction Management; Environmental and Resource Science with Further Studies in Europe or China; European Business Studies; Information Technology with Studies in Japan; Modern Languages and Marketing Studies; Prosthetics and Orthotics; Quantity Surveying with Industrial Placement *4 yrs FT* Environmental & Resource Science with Further Studies in Europe/China *PT* Applied Chemistry with Analytical Chemistry; Building; Business; Child Health; Complementary Medicine and Health Sciences (subject to validation); Counselling Studies-Complementary Medicine or Health Sciences; Environmental Health; Food Industry Management; Health Sciences; Health Sciences-Social Policy; Housing Studies; Nursing Studies; Physiotherapy; Politics & Contemporary History; Practice in Midwifery; Psychotherapeutic Interventions; Sexual Health; Social Policy; Sociology; Software Development; Surveying

Bsc Hons/MChem: *3-4 yrs* Chemistry with Analytical Chemistry; Environmental Chemistry

BSc Hons/MPhys: *3-5 yrs* Physics with Acoustics or Additional Studies in Europe or Computing or Environmental Physics or Medical Physics or Laser Applications or Optoelectronics or Space Technology or Foundation Yr; Physics

BSc Joint Hons: *3-5 yrs* Science

BSc/Mchem Hons: *3-4 yrs FT* Chemistry with Medicinal Chemistry

BSc/MPhys: *3-4 yrs FT/4-5 yrs FT* Physics with a Foreign Language or Photonics

Higher Degrees

MA: *FT* Creative Technology; East European Studies & Polish; Social Work Studies; Television Documentary and Features; Translating; Translating & Interpreting; Translation Studies (English-Arabic) *FT/PT* Applied Linguistics; Contemporary European Studies; East European Studies; English Literature and Modernity; Heritage Studies; Intelligence & International Relations; Music: Compositional Studies; Music: Performance; Politics & Contemporary History *PT* Advanced Language Studies; Advanced Social Work Studies; Child Care and Family Services; Community Care; Contemporary Urban and Criminology Studies; Creative Technology; Cultural Studies; Design Management; EU Welfare and Social Care; Gerontology; Television & Radio Scriptwriting

MA/PGDip: *PT* Cultural Studies; Design Management; Gerontology; Welfare & Social Care

MBA: *PT* Transport

MChem: *4 yrs* Applied Chemistry; Chemistry with Biochemistry or Industrial Experience or Medicinal Chemistry or Additional Studies in Europe

MMath: *4 yrs* Mathematics

MPhil; MRes; MSc; PhD: (By research)

MPhys: *4 yrs* Physics with Studies in North America

MSc: *FT* Advanced Manufacturing; Advanced Robotics; Applied Optics; Business with Information Technology; Computer Science; Corporate Finance; Data Telecommunications & Networks; Electronic Control Engineering; Energy Technology for Sustainable Development; Export Management; Gas Engineering; Gas Engineering & Management; Industrial Control Systems; Intelligent Machinery; International Business; Molecular Parasitology-Vector Biology; Operational Research-Applied Statistics; Virtual Environments *FT/PT* Analytical Chemistry; Applied Optics; Computational Physics; Economic Development; Environmental Protection; Environmental Resources; Export Management; Housing (Policy); Housing (Practice); Human Resource Management; Industrial Design; Information Systems; Information Technology in Property & Construction; Managing Information Technology; Marketing; Nursing; Purchasing & Logistics Management; Quality Management; Transport Engineering & Planning *PT* Advanced Radiography Practice; Construction IT; Corporate Communications Management; Food Safety; Geographical Information Systems; Health Practice; Health Sciences; Management Consultancy; Management Development; Management Studies; Manufacturing Systems Engineering & Management; Medical Ultrasound; Nuclear Medicine Technology; Occupational Safety & Health; Operations Management; Pastoral Care in the Working Environment; Product Realisation; Project Management; Sociology; Sports Rehabilitation; Strategic Leadership (Learning & Development); Sustainable Management of Waste; Technology & Society; Technology Management; Transport & Logistics Management

MSc/PGDip: *PT* Complementary Therapy

MSc/PGDip/PGCert: *PT* Clinical Radiographic Reporting Pathway; Mammography Pathway; Medical Imaging Pathway

Diplomas

DipHE: *2 yrs* Accounting; Social Work

Diploma: Nursing; Nursing (Child, Mental Health, Adult); Professional Studies in Midwifery; Professional Studies in Social Work & Nursing *PT* Psychotherapeutic Interventions; Sexual Health

HND: *2 yrs* Applied Consumer Studies; Audio & Video Systems; Building Studies; Business & Finance; Environmental Health; Fashion Design (Sportswear & Fashion); Food Industry Management; Graphic Design; Leisure Management; Media Performance; Media Production; Physical Theatre & Dance; Professional Sound & Video Technology; Quality Management *2 yrs FT* Chemistry; Electronic & Electrical Engineering; Hospitality & Tourism Management; Hospitality Management; Leisure & Tourism Management; Physical Theatre and Dance; Professional Sound & Video Technology; Quality Management

PGDip: *PT* Applied Optics; Childcare & Family Services; Creative Technology; Enterprise Development Processes; Industrial Design; Nursing; Postural Care in the Working Environment; Product Realisation; Sports Rehabilitation; Sustainable Management of Waste

Postgraduate Diploma: *30 wks Foundation Diploma:* Business Administration; Management-English Language *FT* Applied Optics; Business with Information Technology; Corporate Finance; Data Telecommunications & Networks; Electronic Control Engineering; Energy Technology for Sustainable Development; Enterprise Development Processes; Industrial Control Systems; Intelligent Machinery; International Business; Molecular Parasitology & Vector Biology; Natural Gas Engineering; Television Documentary Features; Translating & Interpreting; Translation English-Arabic; Translation Studies *FT/PT* Advanced Social Work Studies; Analytical Chemistry; Applied Linguistics; Business Administration; Computational Physics; Contemporary European Studies; Economic Development; English; Environmental Protection; Environmental Resources; Export Management; Heritage Studies; Housing (Practice/Policy); Human Resource Management; Intelligence & International Relations; Literature & Modernity; Marketing; Music: Compositional Studies; Music: Performance; Politics & Contemporary History; Purchasing & Logistics Management; Quality Management; Transport Engineering & Planning *PT* Advanced Language Studies; Advanced Radiography; Childcare & Family Services; Clinical Radiographic Reporting; Community Care; Corporate Communications Management; Cultural Studies; Design Management; Employment Studies; EU & Social Care; Food Safety; Geographical Information Systems; Gerontology; Health Practice; Housing Practice; Management Consultancy; Management Development; Management Studies; Managing Information Technology; Manufacturing Systems Engineering & Management; Medical Ultrasound; Nuclear Medicine Technology; Nursing; Occupational Safety & Health; Operations Management; Pastoral Care in the Working Environment; Product Realisation; Project Management; Purchasing & Logistics Management; Social Care; Sociology; Sports Rehabilitation; Sustainable Management of Waste; Technology & Society; Technology Management; Television & Radio Scriptwriting; Transport & Logistics Management

Certificates

Foundation Course: *1 yr FT* Art & Design

HNC: Advanced Manufacturing Technology; Assurance / Leisure Management; Building Services Engineering; Building Studies; Business & Finance; Business Information Technology; Digital Communications; Electronic Maintenance; Environmental Health; Food Industry Management; Food Safety & Quality Assurance; Housing Studies; Science (Chemistry); Software Engineering *1 yr* Hospitality and Tourism Management; Hospitality Management; Housing Studies; Leisure Management; Total Quality Management *4 mths FT/24 mths PT* Applied Consumer Studies *PT* Leisure Management

Postgraduate Certificate: *FT* Geography; Transport & Development *FT/PT* Economic Analysis; Music: Compositional Studies; Music: Performance *PT* Advanced Radiography Practice Studies; Business Administration; Housing Studies; Management; Managing Information Technology; Manufacturing Systems Engineering & Management; Medical Ultrasound; Nursing

University Certificate: *PT* Counselling

Degrees validated by University of Salford offered at:

South Devon College

Newton Road, Torquay TQ2 5BY Tel: 01803 400700 Fax: 01803 400701
e-mail: courses@s-devon.ac.uk Website: www.s-devon.ac.uk

Higher Degrees

MEng: Electronic Engineering

The Oldham College

Rochdale Road, Oldham OL9 6AA Tel: 0161 624 5214 Fax: 0161 785 4234
e-mail: info@oldham.ac.uk Website: www.oldham.ac.uk

* 2+2 courses are of four yrs duration; two yrs in an affiliated college and two yrs in the University.

First Degrees

BEng Hons: *4 yrs FT Specialisation available in:* Computer Aided Engineering; Computers; Electronic & Electrical Engineering; Electronic Communication; Electronic Computer Systems; Management & Electronics; Microelectronic Control Engineering; Robotic & Electronic Engineering

Diplomas

HND: *2 yrs FT* Business Information Technology; Engineering

SHEFFIELD HALLAM UNIVERSITY

City Campus, Pond Street, Sheffield S1 1WB Tel: 0114 225 5555 Fax: 0114 225 4023
e-mail: admissions@shu.ac.uk Website: www.shu.ac.uk

† Subject to validation.

First Degrees

BA Hons: *1 yr FT with HND* Business Studies; Public Policy & Management *1 yr FT/2 yrs PT* Community Health Care Nursing *2 yrs FT HND Entry + 4 yrs S* Business Studies *2 yrs PT* Health Care Practice (options in Nursing, Midwifery & Health Visiting) *3 yrs FT* Applied Social Studies; Business Studies; Combined Studies; Communication Studies; Criminology-History; Law-Criminology; Early Years Education (QTS); English Studies; Environmental Policy; European Urban & Regional Studies; Film & Literature; Film Studies (History and Criticism); Film Studies (Photography); Film Studies (Production); Film Studies (Theory); Financial Services; Fine Art (Time-based Art or Printing & Painting or Sculpture); History; History of Art, Design & Film; English-History; Film-History; Housing & Society; Industrial Design (Innovation or Product Design); Information Design; Media Studies; Metalwork & Jewellery; Nursing Studies; Packaging Design; Primary Education with QTS (English or Geography or History or Mathematics or Science or Technology); Social Policy; Law-Social Policy; Social Work Studies; Sociology; Tourism Management; Urban & Regional Studies; Urban & Regional Geography; Urban Studies *3 yrs FT/4 yrs S* Accounting & Management Control; Financial Information Systems; Information Design; Planning Studies; Public Policy & Management; Tourism and Recreation Management; Tourism Management *3 yrs PT* Education Studies; Special Educational Needs *4 yrs S* Housing Studies; International Business with Languages *4 yrs S/5 yrs PT* Community Development and Regeneration; Social Science-Law; Urban Land Economics *5 yrs PT* Computer Studies *6 yrs PT* Communication Studies; English Studies; English-History; Film Studies (Criticism); Film Studies (History); Film Studies (Photography); Film Studies (Production); Film Studies (Theory); Film-History; Film-Literature; Fine Art (Time Based Art, Painting and Printmaking, Sculpture); History; History of Art, Design and Film; Criminology-History; Media Studies

BA Hons/BSc Hons: *3 yrs FT/4 yrs S* Business Property Management; Business Systems Modelling; Electrical & Electronic Engineering; European Politics & Policy; Food & Consumer Studies; Materials Engineering; Mechanical Engineering; Property Development

BEng Hons: *3 yrs FT/4 yrs S* Computer Engineering; Computer-aided Engineering and Design; Electrical and Electronic Engineering; Electronic Engineering; Materials Engineering; Mechanical and Computer-aided Engineering; Mechanical Engineering

BSc Hons: *1 yr* Electronics & Information Technology; Engineering *1 yr FT* Applied Biological Sciences; Instrumentation & Measurement *2 yrs FT* Design and Technology with Education and QTS; Mathematics with Education and QTS with Education and QTS; Science *2 yrs FT HND Entry + 4 yrs S* Quantity Surveying *3 yrs FT* Architecture & Environmental Design; Diagnostic Radiography; Environmental Conservation; Sport-Exercise Science; Nutrition Health and Lifestyles; Occupational Therapy; Outdoor Leisure Management; Physiotherapy; Psychology; Radiotherapy and Oncology; Recreation Management; Sport & Society; Sport Development and Coaching; Sport Equipment Development; Sport Management; Sport Studies; Sport Technology *3 yrs FT/4 yrs S* Applied Chemistry; Biomedical Sciences; Business Property Management; Engineering Physics; Environmental Land Management; Environmental Science and Technology; Food and Consumer Studies; Food Marketing Management; Food Marketing Management; Hotel & Catering Management; Hotel & Tourism Management; Human Biosciences; Mathematics; Media Science; Pharmaceutical Chemistry; Physics; Property Development *4 yrs S* Applied Statistics; Architectural Technology; Biomedical Chemistry; Biomedical Science; Building Surveying; Business & Technology; Business Information Systems; Business Systems Modelling; Civil Engineering; Computer Network Engineering; Computing & Management Sciences; Computing (Networks & Communications); Computing (Software Engineering); Computing (Visualisation); Construction Management; Engineering; Engineering Design and Innovation; Environmental Management; European Computing; Forensic Engineering; Information Engineering and Technology Management; Management Science; Mathematics; Mathematics & Technology; Sport & Exercise Science; Urban Land Economics

BSc Hons (QTS): *1 yr FT/2 yrs PT* Mathematics with Education and QTS *2 yrs FT* Design and Technology with Education and QTS; Mathematics with Education and QTS; Science with Education and QTS *3 yrs FT* Design & Technology with Education and QTS; Physical Education with QTS; Science with Education and QTS

LLB Hons: *4 yrs FT* Maitrise en Droit

Higher Degrees

MA: *1 yr FT* Broadcast Journalism; Imperialism and Culture *1 yr FT/2 yrs PT* British Cultural Studies; Counselling & Psychotherapy; Cultural Policy & Management; Discourse & Text Analysis; Heritage Management; Housing Policy & Practice; Housing Policy Studies; Media Studies; Property Law; Transport Planning & Management; Writing *1 yr FT/3 yrs PT* Communication Studies; Design Innovation Strategy; Industrial Design; Packaging Design; Women's Studies *1 yr FT/Up to 6 yrs PT* Education; Language & Literacy; Leadership and Special Educational Needs; Professional Development & Training; Special Educational Needs *15 mths FT* International Broadcast Journalism; Screen Arts; Urban & Regional Planning; Urban Design *2 yrs FT/4 yrs PT* Fine Art *2 yrs PT* Design Technology Education; Health Care Practice (Nurse Practitioner); Metalwork and Jewellery; Public Health *2 yrs PT/2 yrs OL* Design *3 semesters FT/2 yrs PT* Design; Information Design *3 yrs PT* Accounting & Education; Advanced Social Care; Advanced Social Work; Banking & Finance; Criminal Justice; European Social Work; Film Studies; Globalisation Theory and Modernity; Policy and Social Studies; Social Science Research Methods *4 yrs PT* TESOL *Distance Learning* Further & Higher Education; Technical Authorship

MA/MSc: *FT/PT* Combined Studies (Options from across the University)

MBA: *1 yr FT/2 yrs PT* Facilities Management *1 yr FT/3 yrs PT* Business Administration; Industrial Management *20 mths PT* Financial Services Sector; Financial Studies; Management for Professionals

MEng: *4 yrs S* Civil Engineering

MPhys: *3 yrs FT/4 yrs S* Engineering Physics

MSc: Business; Information Technology & Management; Marketing Management; Process Management *1 yr FT* Computer Studies; International Business; International Marketing; Property Valuation Management; SAP Information Technology & Management *1 yr FT/2 yrs PT* Advanced

Materials; Analytical Science; Bioinformatics; Biomedical Basis of Disease; Clinical Analytical Science; Computer Based Instrumentation & Measurement; Construction Management; Engineering Physics; Environmental Analytical Science; Environmental Management for Business & Commerce; Environmental Management for Conservation & Recreation; Facilities Management; Genetics and Human Disease; Human Neurology; Immunology; Modern Applicable Mathematics; Networked Information Engineering; Organisation Development & Consultancy; Pathological Sciences; Pharmacology & Biotechnology; Project Management; Property Asset Management; Strategic Information Systems Management; Urban Regeneration *1 yr FT/2-3 yrs PT* Advanced Engineering; Computer and Network Engineering; Electronics & Information Technology; Engineering; Engineering with Management; Environmental Management for Conservation and Recreation; Facilities Management; Human Resource Management; Industrial Management; Information Technology & Management; Leisure & Food Studies; Mechatronics; Occupational Therapy; Physiotherapy; Sport and Exercise Science; Sport Management *1 yr FT/2-3 yrs PT/Distance Learning* Countryside Recreation Management; Food Management; Hospitality & Tourism Management; Hospitality Management; International Hospitality Management; International Tourism Management; Tourism Management *1 yr FT/3 yrs PT* Urban & Regional Management *1 yr FT/Up to 6 yrs PT* Education Management; Further & Higher Education; Mathematics Education; Science Education *2 yrs PT* Managing Change *3 yrs PT* Networked Information Engineering; Novell Enterprise Network Management; Operational Research for Health Management; Property Information Management; Radiotherapy Studies; Surface Design & Engineering; Surveying Professional Practice *Distance Learning* Total Quality Management
MSci: *3 yrs FT/4 yrs S* Chemistry; Physics

Certificates

Certificate: *2 yrs PT* Social & Community Research
PGCE: *1 yr FT* Business Education; Design and Technology; Early Years Education (3-8); English; Information Technology; Mathematics; Modern Languages; Primary (5-11); Religious Education; Science *2 yrs FT* Design & Technology; Mathematics; Modern Languages; Science
PGCert: *1 yr FT* Outdoor Management and Development *Distance Learning* Outdoor Management and Development with Business Studies; Applied Statistics; Applied Statistics; Applied Statistics with Statistical Education; Catering Systems Design and Planning; International Hospitality Management; Paediatric Studies in Occupational Therapy

UNIVERSITY OF SHEFFIELD

Sheffield S10 2TN Tel: 0114 222 2000 e-mail: ug.admissions@sheffield.ac.uk
Website: www.shef.ac.uk/~admit/

First Degrees

BA Hons: *3-4 yrs FT* Accounting & Financial Management; American Studies; Archaeology & Prehistory; Archaeology & Prehistory-Medieval History; Architecture; Biblical Studies-English or German or Linguistics or Music or Philosophy; Business Studies; Business Studies or Economics or Information Management or Mathematics; Accounting & Financial Management-Business Studies; East Asian Studies-Business Studies; Economics or Information Management or Japanese Studies; Korean Studies-Business Studies or Economics; Chinese Studies; Chinese Studies-Business Studies; East Asian Studies; Economics; Economics with Econometrics or Mathematics or Statistics; English Language-English Literature or Medieval Literature or Linguistics or Sociology; English Literature; French Studies; French-Business Studies or Economics or German or Hispanic Studies or History or Linguistics or Music or Philosophy or Politics or Russian; French or Russian or German or Hispanic Studies or History or Music or Philosophy; English-Geography or Japanese Studies; Economics or Mathematics or Philosophy or Politics or Social Policy or Statistics or Sociology; German Studies; German-Business Studies or Economics or Hispanic Studies or History or Linguistics or Music or Philosophy or Politics or Russian; Hispanic Studies-Business Studies or Economics or Politics or Catalan Philology or Hispanic Philology; History; History-Sociology or Philosophy or Russian or Spanish; Human Communication and its Disorders; Japanese Studies; Japanese Studies or Politics or Social History or Sociology;

Geography or Mathematics; Japanese Studies-Korean Studies or Sociology or Politics; Journalism Studies; Korean Studies; Landscape Design with Planning; Law or Spanish with French or German; Law-Criminology; Linguistics-Hispanic Studies or Japanese Studies or Korean Studies or Philosophy or Russian; Management-Mathematics; Modern East European Studies; Modern History with Politics; Modern History-Japanese Studies or Politics; Modern Languages; Philosophy; Philosophy-Hispanic Studies or Psychology; Politics; Psychology-Sociology or Cognitive Science or Philosophy; Russian Studies; Russian-Business Studies or East Asian Studies or Economics or Hispanic Studies or Politics; Social & Political Studies; Social History; Social Policy-Sociology; Sociology; Urban Studies and Planning

BA/BSc Hons: *3-4 yrs FT* Geography; Psychology

BA/LLB: *3 yrs* Law

BEng/MEng: *3-4 yrs FT* Aerospace Engineering; Ceramic Science & Engineering with a Modern Language; Ceramic Science & Engineering; Chemical Engineering with a Modern Language; Chemical Process Engineering with Biotechnology; Chemical Process Engineering; Civil & Environmental Engineering; Civil & Structural Engineering; Civil Engineering; Civil Engineering-Law; Computer Systems Engineering; Control Systems Engineering; Electrical Engineering or a Modern Language with Foundation Yr; Electronic Engineering with Foundation Yr or a Modern Language; Electronic Engineering; Electronic Engineering (Communications); Electronic Engineering (Computing); Electronic Engineering (Solid State Devices); Electronic Engineering (Systems) with a Modern Language; Electronic Engineering (Systems); Electronic, Control & Systems Engineering; Food Technology-Chemical Process Engineering; Glass Science & Engineering with a Modern Language; Glass Science & Engineering; Materials Science & Engineering with Foundation Yr or a Modern Language; Materials Science & Engineering; Mechanical Engineering with a Language; Mechanical Engineering; Mechanical Systems Engineering; Medical Materials Science & Engineering; Medical Systems Engineering; Metal Science & Engineering with a Modern Language; Metal Science & Engineering; Polymer Science & Engineering with a Modern Language; Polymer Science & Engineering; Software Engineering; Software Engineering-Law; Structural Engineering & Architecture

BMed Sci: *4 yrs* Clinical Nursing Practice; Paramedical Studies; Speech Science

BMus: *3-4 yrs FT* Music; Music-Hispanic Studies or Philosophy

BSc Hons: *3 yrs* Anatomy & Cell Biology; Animal & Plant Biology; Archaeological Science; Archaeological Science-Geography or Geology; Artificial Intelligence & Computer Science; Biochemistry; Biochemistry-Genetics or Microbiology or Physiology; Biological Sciences; Biological Sciences-Philosophy; Biomedical Science; Biotechnology-Microbiology; Chemistry-Astronomy or Materials Science or Pure Mathematics or Study in Australia/Europe/Industry/Japan/the USA; Computer Science; Computer Science-French or German or Mathematics or Russian or Hispanic Studies; Ecology; Ecology-Geography; Environmental Geology; Environmental Geoscience; Genetics; Genetics-Microbiology; Information Management; Landscape Design & Archaeology; Materials Science-Physics; Mathematics; Mathematics with Study in Europe; Mathematics-Astronomy or Physics; Medical Biochemistry; Microbiology; Microbiology; Molecular Biology; Molecular Biology; Natural Environmental Science; Natural Environmental Science; Neuroscience; Pharmacology or Philosophy or Mathematics; Physics-Astronomy or Electronics or Medical Physics or Materials Science or Study in Europe; Physiology; Physiology-Pharmacology; Plant Sciences; Probability & Statistics; Zoology; Zoology-Genetics

BSc/MChem Hons: *3-4 yrs* Biological Chemistry; Chemistry; Materials Chemistry

BSc/MPhys: *3-4 yrs* Chemical Physics; Physics; Theoretical Physics

MB/ChB: *5-6 yrs FT* Medicine (ASMC)

Higher Degrees

LLM/PGDip: International, Commercial & European Law

MA: Advanced Japanese Studies; Applied Social Studies; Biblical Studies; Design Brief Management; Early Modern Studies; Economics & Finance; Education & Social Research; Information Technology Management; International Criminology; International Political Economy; Landscape Archaeology; Language & Style in Later Middle English; Librarianship; Library & Information Management; Modern History; Planning Research; Political Communication; Politics; Psychoanalytic Psychotherapy; Psychology for Musicians; Psychology of Music; Public Policy; Research Methods in Political Science; Social & Cultural Geographies; Translation Studies

MA/MSc: Economics

MA/PGCert/PGDip: Health & Social Care Practice Management; Philosophy

MA/PGDip: American History; Applied Linguistics; Applied Research & Quality Evaluation; Archaeology & Prehistory; Arts & Heritage Management; Biotechnological Law & Ethics; Catalan Studies; Contemporary French Studies; Contemporary Poetry; Critical Theory & Modern Languages; Disability Studies; Economics of Money, Banking & Finance; Education for Health & Social Care Practice; English Literature; European Studies; Hispanic Studies; History; Holocaust Studies; International Studies; Japanese Language & Society; Journalism Studies; Korean Studies; Landscape Management; Latin American Studies; Law; Leisure Management; Medieval Studies; Modern & Contemporary Fiction; Modern & Contemporary Writing; Modern English Language & Linguistics; Modern French Literature & Culture; Narrative; Nineteenth Century Studies; Political Economy; Practice Teaching; Russian Literary & Cultural Studies; Slavonic Languages

MArch: Advanced Architectural Studies; Architectural Studies

MArch/PGDip: Landscape

MBA: Finance & Accounting; Management; Marketing Management

MMed Sci: Anatomy & Cell Biology; Basic Science Applied to Anaesthesia in Dentistry; Clinical Communication Studies; Clinical Nursing, Midwifery & Public Health Nursing; Clinical Nursing, Midwifery & Public Health Nursing Practice; Clinical Pathology; Endocrinology; Microbial Pathogenicity; Oral Surgery; Primary & Community Care

MMedSci/PgDip: Human Nutrition; Nephrology; Oral Pathology; Palliative Care; Restorative Dentistry

MMet/PGDip: Advanced Metallurgy

MSc: Computer Aided Environmental Design; Engineering Geology & Geotechnics; Environmental Monitoring & Assessment in Drylands; Geo-Environmental Waste Disposal; Language & Communication Impairment in Children; Language, Speech & Auditory Processing; Osteology, Palaeopathology & Funerary Archaeology; Palaeoanthropology; Process Automation; Psychosocial Interventions; Software, Systems & Information Engineering; Steel Construction; Systems, Information & Control Engineering; Textual Computing

MSc Eng: Data Communications

MSc Eng/PGCert: Advanced Software Engineering

MSc Eng/PGCert/PGDip: Civil & Structural Engineering; Control Systems; Structural Dynamics; Structural Engineering

MSc Eng/PGDip: Concrete Engineering; Economy; Polymer & Polymer Composite Science & Engineering; Process Safety & Loss Prevention; Rail Systems Engineering; Structural Integrity

MSc/PGDip: Archaeomaterials; East Asian Business; Environmental Archaeology & Palaeoeconomy; Health Economics & Management; Health Information Management; Health Services Research & Technology Assessment; Information Management; Information Systems; Medical Physics & Clinical Engineering; Pathological Sciences; Software Systems Technology; Sport & Recreation Management

Diplomas

PGDip: Art Psychotherapy; Business Administration; Business Administration (International Management); Cancer Studies; Planning Studies; Psychiatry, Philosophy & Society; Software Systems & Parallel Processing; Town & Regional Planning

PGDip/PGCert: Integrated Design of Structures

Certificates

PGCert: Childhood Disability; Innovation & Technology Management

UNIVERSITY OF SOUTHAMPTON

Highfield, Southampton SO1 1BJ Tel: 023 8059 5000 Fax: 023 8059 3037

All taught degrees, undergraduate and postgraduate, allow intermediate qualifications to be gained at stages, Certificate or Diploma; Postgraduate Certificate/Diploma.
† Subject to validation.

First Degrees

ARTS & SOCIAL SCIENCES

BA Combined Hons: *3 yrs* Archaeology with Spanish or German or French or Italian; Archaeology-Geography or History or Iberian Studies; Economics-Philosophy; European Cultural Studies; History of Art & Design; History-Sociology; Latin American Studies; Mathematics-Philosophy or Politics or Sociology; Modern History-Politics with Economics or Philosophy or Quantitative Methods; Music-Management or Acoustics or Film or Maths; Philosophy-Mathematics or Sociology or Politics; Portuguese- Spanish; Spanish and Film Studies or History *3-4 yrs* English-Film or French or German or History or Music or Philosophy or Spanish *4 yrs* Contemporary Europe; French-Film Studies or History or Philosophy or German or Jewish History & Culture or Music or Spanish or Portuguese; Fashion Studies-French or German or Spanish or British Studies; French-German or History or Music or Philosophy or Portuguese or Spanish; German-Film Studies; German-Music or Philosophy or Spanish or History; Iberian-Latin American Studies; Jewish History & Culture-French or German or History or Spanish; Politics-French or German; Spanish-History or Film Studies or Portuguese

BA Single Hons: *3 yrs* Archaeology; Contemporary Europe; Contemporary Europe (English); English; European Cultural Studies; Fashion; Fine Art; Geography; History; Music; Philosophy; Popular Music; Textile Art; Textiles/Fashion *3-4 yrs* British Studies; German *4 yrs* French; Spanish (Beginners) & Latin American Studies; Spanish (including Catalan & Portuguese)

BSc (Social Sciences) Combined Hons: Accounting & Finance; Accounting-Economics or French or German or Spanish; Accounting-Management Science; Economics-Management Sciences or Econometrics or Economic History or Finance or French or German or Mathematics or Politics; Economics with Actuarial Studies; History-Sociology; Management Sciences & Accounting; Management Sciences-French or German or Spanish; Management Sciences with French or German or Spanish; Politics & International Relations; Politics-Economic History or Law or Sociology or Social Administration; Politics-Sociology; Psychology with Physiology; Social Policy & Administration; Sociology-Social Policy; Sociology-Social Policy with Social Work Studies

BSc (Social Sciences) Single Hons: *3 yrs* Accounting & Finance; Actuarial Studies; Economics; Management Sciences; Politics; Population Sciences; Psychology; Sociology

LLB: *3 yrs* Law *4 yrs* European Legal Studies

MEDICINE

BM: *5 yrs* Medicine

NURSING

BMid: *4 yrs* Midwifery
BN: *4 yrs* Adult Branch; Child Branch
BNSc: *3 yrs* PT Nursing

PHYSIOTHERAPY & OCCUPATIONAL THERAPY

BSc: *3 yrs* Occupational Therapy; Physiotherapy; Podiatry

SCIENCE & TECHNOLOGY

BEng Hons/MEng: *3-4 yrs* Acoustical Engineering; Aerospace Engineering; Civil Engineering; Computer Engineering; Computer Science & Software Engineering; Electrical Engineering; Electromechanical Engineering; Electronic Engineering; Electronics with Microelectronics or Telecommunications or Optical Electronics or Computer Systems or Computational Intelligence; Electronics; Environmental Engineering; Mechanical Engineering; Ship Science; Software Engineering; Water Management & Engineering

BSc Combined Hons: *3 yrs* Acoustics and/with Music; Biochemistry with Chemistry or Nutrition or Pharmacology or Physiology; Biochemistry -Physiology with Foundation Yr; Biochemistry-Pharmacology or Chemistry; Biology-Maths; Biology with Computer Science or Oceanography or Maths; Chemistry with Biochemistry or Computer Science or Environmental Sciences or Geology or Mathematics or Oceanography or Pharmacology or Physics or Medicinal Chemistry or Management; Computer Science with Artificial Intelligence or Distributed Systems & Networks or Image & Multimedia Systems or Parallel Computing or Systems Integration; Environmental

Geology; Geography with Geology or Oceanography; Geology with Biology or Oceanography or Physical Geography; Marine Environmental Chemistry; Marine Geosciences; Marine Sciences with French; Mathematics-Philosophy; Oceanography with Chemistry or Geology or Marine Biology or Physical Geography or Mathematics or Physics; Physiology with Nutrition or Biochemistry or Pharmacology or Psychology; Physiology & Biochemistry with Nutrition; Psychology with Physiology; Physics with Astronomy or Computer Science or Mathematics or Oceanography or Music or Space Science or Laser Science or Chemistry or Theoretical Physics *3-4 yrs* Mathematics with Astronomy or Actuarial Science or Chemistry or Computer Science or German or Music or Management Sciences or Philosophy or Spanish or Economics or Education or Finance or Geography or Oceanography or Operational Research or Physics or Statistics
BSc Double Hons: *4 yrs* Biochemistry-Chemistry
BSc Hons: *3 yrs* Computer Science; Physiology-Pharmacology or Biochemistry with Nutrition
BSc Single Hons: *3 yrs* Biochemistry; Biology; Chemistry; Environmental Sciences; Geography; Geology; Geophysical Sciences; Industrial Applied Mathematics; Marine Environmental Chemistry; Marine Sciences; Mathematical Studies; Mathematics; Molecular Cell Biology; Nutritional Sciences; Occupational Therapy; Oceanography; Pharmacology; Physics; Physiology; Physiology & Biochemistry; Physiotherapy; Plant Science; Psychology; Zoology *4 yrs* Chemistry (with Industrial Training)

Higher Degrees

DOCTORATES
DClinPsy: Clinical Psychology
DLitt; DSc; DSc (Social Sciences); LLD; DMus: (May be awarded to Southampton graduates six yrs after their first graduation, in respect of published work)
DM/MS: (Open to Southampton medical graduates three yrs after qualification (by thesis or published works) and to other medical graduates by thesis following two yrs' work in the Wessex region)
DMus: (For Southampton graduates of five yrs' minimum standing; by composition or thesis and exam)
PhD: *1 yr* (Open to Southampton and other graduates and to non-graduates on certain conditions and with special approval after successful completion of an MPhil; may be taken part-time)

MASTER'S DEGREES
MA: Aesthetics; Applied Linguistics for Language Teaching; Archaeology & Anthropology of Rock Art; Archaeology of Art & Representation; Archaeology of Human Origins; Archaeology of Rome and its Provinces; Architectural Studies; Ceramic & Lithic Analysis for Archaeologists; Contemporary Philosophy: The Analytic & Continental Traditions; Country House Studies; Criminal Justice; Culture & History of Science; Early Modern European Culture: The Renaissance; Education; Education, Experience and Biography; European Fashion & Textile Design (with study abroad)†; European Fine Art (with study abroad); Film Studies; Fine Art Printmaking; French Language & Culture; Gender Studies; Historical Studies; History of Textiles & Dress (with study abroad)†; Jewish History & Culture; Literature, Culture & Modernity; Literature, History & Culture; Material Culture: Archaeology & Design History; Medieval Culture; Modern and Contemporary Art; Multilingualism; Museum Studies: Culture, Collections and Communications; Musical Composition; Musical Performance; Musicology; Osteoarchaeology; Philosophy of Mind; Sculpture; Textile-Fashion Design; Textile Art; Textile Conservation; United States History
MA (Ed): Computer Based Learning; Geography & Environmental Education; Language in Education; Management & Professional Studies; Mathematics Education; Science & Technology Education
MA/MSc: Maritime Archaeology
MBA: Business Administration (for experienced managers); Business Administration (for recent graduates)
MChem: *4 yrs* Chemistry (with Industrial Training)
MEng with European Studies: *4 yrs* Engineering with Foundation Yr
MEng with Tripartite Diploma: *5 yrs* Electronic Engineering with Tripartite Diploma (From the Universities of Southampton and Karlsruche and the Ecole Superieure d'Ingenieurs et Electronique, Paris. Includes two yrs' study abroad)

MEnv: *4 yrs* Environmental Sciences
MGeog: *4 yrs* Geography
MGeol: *4 yrs* Geology
MMath: *4 yrs* Mathematics
MPhil: *2 yrs* (Open to Southampton and other graduates and to non-graduates on certain conditions and with special approval; may be taken part-time); Research Methodology
MPhys: *4 yrs* Physics
MSc: Accounting-Finance; Accounting-Management Science; Applied Digital Signal Processing; Archaeological Science: Archaeological Computing; Audiology; Automotive Dynamics, Noise & Vibration; Aviation Management; Biochemical Pharmacology; Citizenship, Democracy & Political Theory; Cognitive Therapy For Severe Mental Health Problems; Companion Animal Behaviour Counselling; Comparative Politics & Policy; Computer Based Learning and Training; Corporate Risk and Security Management; Development and Security; Development Economics-Economic Policy Analysis; Economics; Economics-Econometrics; Education for Health Professionals; Educational Psychology; Engineering for Development (Infrastructure, Water Supply & Sanitation); Environmental Coastal Engineering; Equal Opportunities Studies; Finance-Economics; Financial Managerial Controls; Gender in Society; Health Education & Promotion; Health Education/Health Promotion; Health Informatics; Health Psychology; Information Engineering; Information Systems; Instrumentation-Transducers; Integrated Environmental Studies; International Banking & Financial Studies; International Financial Markets; International Relations; International Relations & Security Studies; Management Sciences; Marine Engineering; Maritime Engineering Science; Microelectronics Systems Design; Nursing; Oceanography; Operational Research; Optical Fibre Communications; Politics; Professional Studies; Radio Frequency Communication Systems; Risk Management; Social Statistics; Social Work Studies; Sociology & Social Policy; Sound & Vibration Studies; Statistics with Applications in Medicine; Superconductivity & Cryogenics; Transportation Planning & Engineering
MSc (Ed): Biology Education; Chemistry Education; Environmental Sciences Education; Geography Education; Physics Education

MASTER'S DEGREES BY RESEARCH
MSc (Ed): Chemistry

Honorary Degrees

Any University degrees may be awarded.

Diplomas

AdDipN/DipN: Midwifery

CERTIFICATES
PGCE: Biology; Chemistry; English; French; Geography; German; Mathematics; Modern Languages; Physical Education; Physics; Primary Age Range: Mathematics; English; Science

UNIVERSITY OF SOUTHAMPTON
University of Southampton New College

The Avenue, Southampton SO17 1BG Tel: 023 92597276 Fax: 023 92597271
e-mail: vah@soton.ac.uk

† Subject to validation.

First Degrees

BA: Historical & Political Studies; Humanities; Humanities (English Studies & Historical Studies); Humanities (English Studies); Humanities (Historical Studies)
BSc: Applied Social Sciences; Applied Social Sciences (Anthropology); Applied Social Sciences (Criminology); Applied Social Sciences (Psychological Studies); Health & Well-Being; Human Sciences; Sport Science-Psychological Studies; Sport Studies

Degrees validated by University of Southampton offered at:

Chichester Institute of Higher Education

Bishop Otter Campus, College Lane, Chichester, West Sussex PO19 4PE Tel: 01243 816000
Fax: 01243 816080

† Subject to validation.

First Degrees

BA (Ed) Hons: *2 yrs FT* Education *5 trms PT* In-Service Education
BA Hons: *3 yrs* Counselling; Dance; English; Environmental Science; Geography; Health Studies; History; Mathematics; Media Studies; Music; Protecting Children; Related Arts; Religious (Study of); Sports Studies; Theology; Women's Studies *Some subjects are also available in combinations:* Art *FT/PT* Social Studies; Social Work Studies
BA Hons with QTS: *2 yrs FT* Secondary Mathematics-Education *4 yrs FT* Art & Education; Dance & Education; English & Education; Geography & Education; History & Education; Mathematics & Education; Music & Education; Science & Education; Secondary Education & Mathematics; Secondary Education & Physical Education; Study of Religion & Education
BSc Hons: *3-4 yrs FT* Sports Science *FT/PT* Health Science

Higher Degrees

MA: *FT/PT* English Language Teaching Management *PT* English (Creative Writing); Management (Health & Social Care Services); Mathematics Education; Related Arts; Study of Religions
MA (Ed): *PT* In-Service Education
MPhil/PhD: *FT By research on topics in:* Art; Dance; Education; English; Geography; Health Studies; History; Mathematics; Music; Related Arts; Religious Studies; Social Work; Sports Studies; TESOL
MSc: *FT/PT* Sport and Exercise Science

Diplomas

DipHE: Theology & Ministry
Diploma: *2 yrs PT* Independent Professional Counselling
Diploma in Professional Studies: *2 yrs PT* Child Protection; Counselling; Nursing (Post-Registration); Social Work
Postgraduate Diploma: English (Creative Writing); English Language Teaching Management; Management (Health & Social Care Services); Mathematics Education; Mathematics Education; Related Arts; Study of Religions; Study of Religions

Certificates

PGCE: *1 yr FT* Primary Teaching; Secondary Design Technology; Secondary English; Secondary History; Secondary Mathematics; Secondary Physical Education; Secondary Religious Education *2 yrs FT* Secondary Mathematics (conversion course for non-maths graduates with relevant degree)
Postgraduate Diploma: Sport and Exercise Science

King Alfred's College

Winchester SO22 4NR Tel: 01962 841515 Fax: 01962 842280
Website: www.wkac.ac.uk

† Subject to validation.

First Degrees

BA Hons: *1 yr HND top-up:* Business Administration *3 yrs FT* American Studies; Archaeological Practice; Archaeology; Business Management with Business Communications; Dance Studies; Drama Studies; Drama, Theatre & TV Studies; Education Studies; Education Studies (Early

Childhood); English; Historical Practice; History; Media & Film; Performing Arts; Public Services Management; Theology-Religious Studies; Sports Development; Sports Studies *5-8 yrs PT Combined Studies:* Business Studies; English; History; Religious Studies; Tourism & Heritage Management

BA Hons with QTS: *4 yrs FT* Primary Education *Specialisations:* Art; Design & Technology; Drama with English; English; Geography; History; Mathematics; Physical Education; Religious Studies; Science

BA/BSc Combined Hons: American Studies; Archaeology; Business Studies; Dance Studies; Drama Studies; Education Studies; Education Studies (Early Childhood); English for Academic Purposes; English Studies; Historical Practice; History; Leisure Management; Media & Film; Psychology; Theology-Religious Studies; Social Care Studies; Sports Development; Sports Studies; Tourism & Heritage Management

Post-qualifying Award: Social Work Studies

Higher Degrees

MA: *1 yr FT* Theatre for Development *1 yr FT/2 yrs PT* Contemporary Popular Knowledge; Educational Studies; English (Contemporary Literature); Field Archaeology; Regional & Local History & Archaeology; Religion; Social History; Writing for Children *2 yrs PT* Performing Arts *5 yrs PT* Education: Professional Enquiry

MSc: *1 yr FT/2 yrs PT* Disability Studies

Diplomas

DipHE: *2 yrs FT* American Studies; Archaeological Practice; Archaeology; Business Management with Business Communications; Dance Studies; Drama Studies; Drama, Theatre and TV Studies; Education Studies; Education Studies (Early Studies); English Studies; Historical Practice; History; Media & Film; Public Services Management; Social Care Studies; Sports Development; Sports Studies; Theology & Religious Studies; Tourism & Heritage Management

Diploma of Advanced Educational Studies: *Up to 5 yrs PT* Educational Studies

HND: *2 yrs FT* Archaeological Practice; Historical Practice; Leisure Management; Public Services Management; Social Care Studies; Tourism & Heritage Management

Certificates

Certificate of Advanced Educational Studies: *1 trm* Educational Studies *PT* Educational Studies

PGCE: *1 yr FT* Education

Winchester School of Art

Park Avenue, Winchester SO23 8DL Tel: 023 80596900 Fax: 023 80596901
Website: www.soton.ac.uk/~wsart

† Subject to validation.

First Degrees

BA Hons: *3 yrs FT* Fashion; Fashion Studies and British Studies; Fine Art (Painting; Printmaking; Sculpture); History of Art & Design; History of Art & Design-English; Textile Art; Textile Design *4 yrs FT* History of Art and Design-British Studies; Fashion (with Foundation Yr); Fashion Studies-French or German or Spanish; History of Art and Design-Film; Fine Art (Painting; Printmaking; Sculpture) with Foundation Yr; History of Art & Design and French or German or Spanish or Modern Languages; Textile Art (with Foundation Yr); Textile Design (with Foundation Yr)

Higher Degrees

MA: *1 yr FT* Euro Fashion & Textile Design; European Fine Art (Barcelona/Winchester); Fine Art Printmaking; Museum Studies: Culture, Collections & Communication; Sculpture; Textile and Fashion Design; Textile Art *1 yr FT/2 yrs PT* Architectural Studies; Country House Studies; History of Textiles & Dress; Material Culture: Design History; Modern and Contemporary Art *2 yrs FT* Textile Conservation

SOUTH BANK UNIVERSITY

103, Borough Road, London SE1 0AA Tel: 020 7928 8989 Fax: 020 7815 8155
Website: sbu.ac.uk

† Subject to validation.

First Degrees

BA Hons: *3 yrs FT* Accounting & Finance; Acting; Architecture; Arts Management; English; Housing; Human Geography; International Hospitality Management; International Hotel & Tourism Management; International Tourism Management; Marketing; Politics; Tourism and Hospitality Management; Urban and Environmental Planning *3 yrs FT/4 yrs S* European Studies; European Studies with Languages; Hospitality and Tourism Management *3 yrs FT/4 yrs S/3-5 yrs PT* Business Studies; Business Studies with A Language *3 yrs FT/5 yrs PT* Business Administration *4 yrs S* Business Studies; Hospitality Management; Modern Languages & International Business; Tourism Management

BA/BSc Combined Hons: *3 yrs FT Any two of the following may be combined:* Accounting; Business Information Technology; Computing; Criminology; Economics; Electronic Commerce; English Studies; Forensic Science; French; History; Human Geography; Human Resource Management; Law; Management; Marketing; Media Studies; Music; Politics; Psychology; Social Policy; Sociology; Spanish; Sports Science; Tourism; World Theatre

BEng Hons: *3 yrs FT/4 yrs S* Architectural Engineering; Building Services Engineering; Chemical Engineering; Multimedia Engineering *3 yrs FT/4 yrs S/4 yrs PT* Civil Engineering; Construction Engineering; Electronic & Electrical Engineering; Internet Engineering; Mechanical Engineering *4 yrs PT/5 yrs PT* Mechanical Engineering

BSc Hons: *1 yr FT/2 yrs PT* Computer Aided Engineering *3 yrs FT* Criminology; Electronic Commerce; Media & Society; Nursing Studies & Social Work; Nursing Studies (Child Care or Adult or Mental Health); Psychology; Radiography (Imaging & Radiotherapy); Social Policy; Sociology; Sport & Exercise Science *3 yrs FT/4 yrs S* Applied Biology; Architectural Technology; Biochemistry; Biotechnology; Business Information Technology; Chemical Engineering Design; Choice and Design; Civil and Environmental Engineering; Civil Engineering Design; Electrical & Electronic Engineering; Environmental Engineering; Food; Food Science and Technology; Food Studies; Food, Nutrition and Health; Forensic Science; Human Biology; Industrial Design; Industrial Risk Management; Internet Computing; Microbiology; Nutrition; Occupational Health & Safety; Product Design and the Environment; Special Effects; Sports Product Design *3 yrs FT/4 yrs S/5 yrs PT* Building Surveying; Civil Engineering; Computing Studies; Computing Studies; Construction Management; Estate Management; Food Sciences; Nutrition; Quantity Surveying; Social Sciences *3-4 yrs FT/5 yrs PT* Building Services Engineering; Computer Aided Engineering *4 yrs S* Engineering Product Design

LLB Hons: *3 yrs FT/4 yrs PT* Law

Higher Degrees

MA: Housing Studies *2 yrs FT/3 yrs PT* Town Planning *2 yrs PT* Applied European Studies; European Politics *2-3 yrs PT* Education Studies for Health Care Professionals

MBA: Business Administration (General) *1 yr FT* Business Administration (International Management)

MSc: *1 yr FT* Design & Manufacturing Management; European Public Policy; Health Promotion; Health Service & Hospital Management; Manufacturing Management; Mechatronics Engineering; Quality Engineering Management *1 yr FT/1.5 yrs PT* Environmental & Development Education; European Business & Language; International Business; International Marketing *1 yr FT/2 yrs PT* Advance Information Technology; Business Information Technology; Careers Guidance & Counselling; Charity Accounting and Financial Management; Charity Marketing and Fundraising; Civil Engineering Design/Information Technology/Management; Clinical Imaging; Community Healthcare; Computer Science; Construction Economics & Management; Construction Management; Critical and Social Policy; Development Studies; Energy Engineering; Engineering Product Design; Environmental Acoustics; Environmental Civil Engineering; European Politics; Food Safety & Control; Food Standards; Health Education; Housing Policy; Information Analysis; Information Management in Business; Information Systems Management; Information Technology in Business; Knowledge Management Systems; Legal Studies (CPE);

Property Asset Management; Public Service Management; Race and Ethnicity; Real Time Systems; Social Analysis; Social Identity; Social Research Methods; Town Planning; Urban Civil Engineering *1.5 yrs FT/2.5 yrs PT* Computing & Mathematical Education; Property Law *15 mths FT/2 yrs PT* Facilities Management *2 yrs* Health Services Management *2 yrs PT* Applied Radiography; Changing Social Identities; Community Health Nursing; Computer Systems & Networking; Development Studies; Engineering Information Management; Engineering Services Management; Human Resources; Information Systems Engineering; Interprofessional Health & Welfare Studies; Legal Practice; Occupational Health & Safety; Occupational Hygiene; Property Development (Project Management); Sociology of Health & Illness *2.5 yrs FT* Social Work *2.5-5 yrs PT* Midwifery; Nursing; Social Work *3 yrs FT* Estate Management

Diplomas

HND: *2 yrs FT/3 yrs PT* Applied Biology; Building Services Engineering; Business Information Technology; Business Studies; Chemical Engineering; Civil Engineering; Computer Aided Engineering; Computer Studies; Construction Studies; Electrical & Electronic Engineering; Electronic Commerce

Postgraduate Diploma: European Studies *1 yr FT* Careers Guidance & Counselling; Health Service & Hospital Management; Hospital & Health Services Administration; Professional Studies in Midwifery *1 yr FT/1.5 yrs PT* Facilities Management; Information Analysis *1 yr FT/2 yrs PT* Advanced Information Technology; Applied Radiography; Computer & Mathematics Modelling; Construction Management; Devices, Measurement & Instrumentation; Energy Engineering; Engineering Product Design; Environmental Acoustics; Environmental Monitoring & Assessment; Food Safety & Control; Information Systems Engineering; Midwifery; Nuclear Medicine; Personnel Management; Technology Management *1 yr FT/9 mths FT* Environmental & Development Education; European Business & Language *2 yrs FT* Social Work *2 yrs FT/3 yrs PT* Town Planning *2 yrs PT* Estate Management; Health Services Management; International Business; Legal Practice; Management Studies; Urban (Civil) Engineering *9 mths FT/15 mths PT* International Marketing *FT* Health Education *PT* Charity Finance; Clinical Ultrasound; Community Health Nursing; Nuclear Medicine; Nursing; Nursing: Professional Studies

Certificates

Certificate: *9 mths PT* Applied Advice Work

HNC: *2 yrs PT* Building Studies; Business Information Technology; Business Studies; Civil Engineering Studies; Computing; Electrical & Electronic Engineering; Housing Studies; Software Engineering

PGCE: Early Childhood (3-8)

Postgraduate Certificate: *1 yr FT* European Business Systems *1 yr PT* Applied Advice Work; Clinical Ultrasound; Human Resources; Nuclear Medicine *2 yrs PT* Management *PT* Health Management Studies; Managing Health Services; Personnel Practice

STAFFORDSHIRE UNIVERSITY

College Road, Stoke-on-Trent ST4 2DE Tel: 01782 294960 Fax: 01782 294951

BA Hons/BSc Hons: The modular degree scheme allows the subjects listed to be studied in combination either as joint awards or on a major/minor basis.

† Subject to validation.

First Degrees

BA Extended Engineering: *4 yrs FT/5 yrs S* Product Design Technology

BA Hons: *3 yrs FT/4-8 yrs PT* Accounting & Business; Accounting Information Technology; American Studies; Applied Social Studies; Business & Financial Economics; Business & Quality Management; Business Administration; Business Studies with Operations Management or Tourism; Business Studies; Combined Studies; Cultural Studies; Design; Economics; Enterprise & Entrepreneurship; Environmental Studies; European Economics; Fine Art; Geography; Historical Studies; History of Art & Design; Human Resource Management; Interactive Systems Design;

International Business Communications; International Business Management; International Finance & Business; International Relations; Literary Studies; Marketing; Philosophy; Politics; Product Design Technology; Sociology; Sport & Leisure Management; Sport & Leisure Studies; Sport, Recreation & Tourism *4 yrs S* Accounting; Economic Studies; European Media, Culture & Politics; French with Language Studies; Leisure Economics; Media Studies; Recreation Geography & Environment; Social Science

BA Hons/BSc Hons: Accounting; American Studies; Applied Statistics; Biochemistry; Biology; Business Studies; Ceramic Science; Chemistry; Computing; Cultural Studies; Development Studies; Ecology; Economic Studies; Electronics; Environmental Studies; European Culture; Film Studies; French; Geography; Geology; German; History; History of Art & Design; Information Systems; International Relations; Law; Legal Studies; Literature; Media Studies; Microbiology; Molecular Biology; Physiology; Politics; Psychology; Sociology; Spanish; Women's Studies

BEng Extended Engineering: *3 yrs/4 yrs/5 yrs FT/6 yrs S* Computer Aided Engineering; Electrical Engineering; Electronic Engineering; Engineering Design; Environmental Engineering; Manufacturing Engineering; Business; Mechanical Engineering; Mechatronics; Mechatronics & Computer Engineering; Medical Engineering; Small Vehicle Design

BEng/BEng Hons/MEng: *4-5 yrs S* Computer Aided Engineering; Computer Science; Computer Systems; Distributed Interactive Systems; Electrical Engineering; Electronic Engineering; Engineering Design; Environmental Engineering; Graphics, Imaging & Visualisation; Information Systems; Information Technology Strategy; Intelligent Systems; Manufacturing Engineering with Business; Mathematics for Information Technology; Mechanical Engineering; Mechatronics; Medical Engineering; Microelectronics & Computer Engineering; Multimedia Systems; Small Vehicle Design; Software Engineering

BSc Extended Engineering: *4 yrs FT* Business Communications; Computer & Electronics for Information Technology; Environmental Technology; Environmental Transportation Studies; Food Processing Technology; Health Technology; Industrial Marketing; Manufacturing Management; Media Technology; Music Technology; Occupational Health & Environmental Technology; Product Design Technology; Small Vehicle Design; Transportation Studies/Management/Informatics; Transportation Systems Technology

BSc Extended Science: *4 yrs FT* Applied Biology; Applied Chemistry & Analytical Chemistry; Applied Ecology; Applied Geology; Applied Microbiology; Applied Physics; Biochemistry-Microbiology or Molecular Biology or Physiology; Chemistry; Environmental Biology; Environmental Chemistry; Environmental Geology; Environmental Science; Human Biology; Physics; Physics & Electronics; Pollution Science

BSc/BSc Hons: *3 yrs FT/4-8 yrs PT* Applied & Analytical Chemistry; Applied Biology; Applied Computing; Applied Geology; Applied Physics; Biochemistry & Microbiology; Biochemistry & Physiology; Building Surveying; Business Decision Analysis; Business Information Technology; Ceramic Technology; Chemical Sciences; Chemistry; Computer Science; Computing & Applicable Mathematics; Earth Sciences; Electronic & Applied Physics; Enterprise & Business Computing; Environmental Biology; Environmental Chemistry; Environmental Geology; Environmental Science-Biology or Chemistry; Environmental Transportation Studies; Exercise & Health; Facilities Management; Geography; Health Studies; Health Technology; Information Technology Strategy; Manufacturing Management; Mathematics for Information Technology; Media Technology; Physics; Pollution Science; Product Design Technology; Property with Business Studies or French or Geography or German or Spanish; Property & Construction; Property Development & the Environment; Psychology; Psychology & Criminology; Quantity Surveying; Small Vehicle Design; Software Engineering; Sports & Exercise Sciences; Sports Equipment Technology; Sports Sciences-Information Systems or Physiology; Sports Studies; Technology Management; Transportation Studies/Management Informatics; Valuation Surveying *4 yrs S* Animal Biology; Applied Ecology; Biochemistry & Molecular Biology; Business Communications Technology; Computer Systems; Computing & Electronics for Information Technology; Computing Science; Distributed Interactive Systems; Environmental Technology; Food Processing Technology; Graphics, Imaging & Visualisation; Information Systems; Intelligent Systems; Multimedia Systems; Music Technology; Occupational Health & Environmental Technology; Sports Science-Applied Statistics or Biology or Chemistry or Electronics or Geography or Geology or Physics or Biochemistry or Psychology; Transport Systems Technology

LLB: *3 yrs FT* Law

Higher Degrees

LLM: *12 mths FT/PT variable* Business Law; Commercial Law; Critical Legal Studies; Employment Law; Family Law; International Environment Law; International Law; Law; Public Law

MA: *12 mths FT/PT variable* Ceramic Design; Ceramic Design for Production; Ceramics & Craft Management; Child Care, Policy & Practice; Computing in Design; Critical Regional Geographies; Cultural Representation; Culture & Cultural Representation; Design Management; Design Management & Ceramic Design; Development Studies; Economics; Economics of International Trade & European Integration; Electronic Graphics; Electronic Graphics & Design Management; Fine Art; Glass & Craft Management; Graphic Design Management; Higher & Professional Education; Historical Studies; History of Ceramics; History of European Design & Visual Culture; International Relations; Law & Legal Practice; Legal Practice Management; Modern Continental Philosophy; Multimedia Design; Politics; Product Design & Design Management; Social & Cultural Theory; Sustainable Development; Textual & Critical Studies; Women's Studies

MBA: *12 mths FT/3.5 yrs PT* Management Development Programme

MPhil: *FT/PT* (By research in various departments)

MSc: *12 mths FT/PT variable* Analytical Chemistry; Applied Geology; Computer Aided Engineering; Computing for Business; Computing Science; Computing Science: Artificial Intelligence with Distributed Systems or Graphics & Image Processing or Human-Computer Interaction or Information Technology for Strategic Management or Object Technology or Systems Design; Electronic Engineering; Engineering Design; Engineering Mechanics; European Management Strategy; Global Marketing Strategy; Health Psychology; Health Research; Health Studies; Information Technology; Management; Marketing; Media Technology; Operations; Philosophical & Theoretical Psychology; Power Engineering; Procurement & Logistics; Rotating Machines; Social Research Methods; Social Theory & Research; Software Engineering; South East Asian Management Studies; Sport, Health & Exercise Science; Technology & Organisations; Technology Management; Tourism Marketing

PhD: *FT/PT* (By research in various departments)

Diplomas

DipHE: Accounting; American Studies; Applied Statistics; Biochemistry; Biology; Business Studies; Ceramic Science; Chemistry; Computing; Cultural Studies; Development Studies; Ecology; Economic Studies; Electronics; Environmental Studies *3 yrs/4 yrs* Applied Social Studies; European Culture; Film Studies; French; Geography; Geology; German; History; History of Art & Design; Information Systems; International Relations; Law; Legal Studies; Literature; Media Studies; Microbiology; Molecular Biology; Philosophy; Physics; Physiology; Politics; Psychology; Sociology; Spanish; Women's Studies

Diploma: Advice Work & Law; Social Work (CCETSW)

Certificates

Cert HE: Accounting; American Studies; Applied Statistics; Biochemistry; Biology; Business Studies; Ceramic Science; Chemistry; Computing; Cultural Studies; Development Studies; Ecology; Economic Studies; Environmental Studies; European Culture; Film Studies; French; Geography; Geology; German; History; History of Art & Design; Information Systems; International Relations; Law; Legal Studies; Literature; Media Studies; Microbiology; Molecular Biology; Philosophy; Physics; Physiotherapy; Politics; Psychology; Sociology; Spanish; Women's Studies

UNIVERSITY OF ST ANDREWS

St Andrews, Fife KY16 9AJ Tel: 01334 462150 Fax: 01334 463388
e-mail: admissions@st-andrews.ac.uk Website: www.st-and.ac.uk

First Degrees

ARTS
BD Ord/Hons: *3-4 yrs* Divinity

MA General/Hons: *3-4 yrs* Theological Studies *Groups:* Ancient History-Art History or Biblical Studies or Economics or French or German or Greek or Italian or Latin or Mathematics or Philosophy or Spanish or Integrated Information Technology or Linguistics or English or Classics or Classical Studies; Integrated Information Technology-Ancient History or Art History or Greek or Latin or Management; Arabic-Art History or Economics or English or French or German or Italian or Hebrew or International Relations or Latin or Management or Medieval History or Modern History or Social Anthropology or Spanish or Philosophy or Russian; Management-Arabic or Art History or Classics or Economics or English or French or Geography or German or International Relations or Italian or Middle East Studies or Modern History or Philosophy or Psychology or Spanish or Integrated Information Technology; Art History-Classical Studies or English or French or Geography or German or Hebrew or International Relations or Italian or Mathematics or Medieval History or Modern History or Philosophy or Psychology or Russian or Social Anthropology or Spanish or Biblical Studies or Integrated Information Technology or Ancient History or Arabic or Management or Middle East Studies; Arts and Vocational Information Technology; Biblical Studies-Classical Studies or Economics or English or French or German or Greek or Hebrew or Philosophy or Art History or Ancient History; Classical Studies-English or International Relations or Italian or Medieval History or Modern History or Social Anthropology or Theological Studies or Integrated Information Technology or Middle East Studies or Philosophy or Art History or Biblical Studies or New Testament or Scottish History; Classics-Italian or Management or Integrated Information Technology or Philosophy; Economics-English or French or Geography or German or International Relations or Italian or Management or Mathematics or Medieval History or Modern History or Philosophy or Russian or Social Anthropology or Spanish or Statistics or Ancient History or Arabic or Biblical Studies or Middle Eastern Studies; Statistics-Economics or Mathematics or Philosophy or Economics or Management; English-French or Geography or German or Greek or Hebrew or Italian or Latin or Medieval History or Modern History or Philosophy or Psychology or Russian or Scottish History or Social Anthropology or Spanish or Theological Studies or International Relations or Ancient History or Arabic or Art History or Biblical Studies or Classical Studies or Middle Eastern Studies; French-Geography or German or Hebrew or International Relations or Italian or Latin or Management or Medieval History or Modern History or Philosophy or Psychology or Russian or Social Anthropology or Spanish or Theological Studies or Ancient History or Arabic or Art History or Biblical Studies or Economics or English; Geography-International Relations or Management or Medieval History or Modern History or Psychology or Scottish History or Social Anthropology or Spanish or Theological Studies or Italian or Art History or Economics or English or French or Hebrew; German-International Relations or Italian or Latin or Management or Medieval History or Modern History or New Testament or Philosophy or Psychology or Russian or Spanish or Theological or Biblical Studies or Economics or English or Middle East Studies or French; Greek-Hebrew or Italian or Latin or New Testament or Philosophy or Integrated Information Technology or Ancient History or Biblical Studies or English or Spanish; Hebrew-Mathematics or New Testament or Russian or French or Latin or Arabic or Art History or Biblical Studies or English or Geography or Greek or Middle East Studies; International Relations-Italian or Management or Medieval History or Modern History or Philosophy or Psychology or Russian or Scottish History or Social Anthropology or Spanish or Theological Studies or English or Middle East Studies or Arabic or Art History or Classical Studies or Economics or French or Geography or German; Italian-Latin or Management or Medieval History or Modern History or Philosophy or Russian or Scottish History or Social Anthropology or Spanish or Ancient History or Arabic or Art History or Classical Studies or Classics or Economics or English or Geography or Greek or International Relations or Middles East Studies or Spanish or French or German; Latin-Mathematics or Medieval History or New Testament or Philosophy or Russian or Spanish or Hebrew or Integrated Information Technology or Ancient History or Arabic or English or French or German or Greek or Italian or Middle East Studies; Mathematics-Medieval History or Philosophy or Psychology or Scottish History or Statistics or Art History or Economics or Ancient History or Hebrew or Latin or Theological Studies; Medieval History-Philosophy or Psychology or Russian or Social Anthropology or Spanish or Arabic or Art History or Classical Studies or Economics or English or French or Geography or German or International Relations or Italian or Latin or Mathematics or Middle East Studies; Middle East Studies-Social Anthropology or Modern History or Medieval History or Management or Latin or International Relations or Hebrew or Geography or English or Economics or Art History or Arabic or Classical Studies; Middle East Studies-Spanish or Russian or Italian or German; Modern History-New Testament or Philosophy or Russian or Social Anthropology or Spanish or Theological Studies or Arabic or Art History or Classical Studies or Economics or English or French or Geography or German or International Relations or Italian or Management or Middle East Studies or Psychology; Modern Languages with Economics or International Relations or Management with Linguistics; Modern Languages (double or triple languages); New Testament-Classical Studies or German or Greek or Hebrew or Latin or Modern History or Biblical Studies or Classics or Economics or English or French or German or Greek or International Relations or Italian or Arabic or Classical Studies or Latin or Management or Mathematics or Medieval History or Modern History or Psychology; Philosophy or Russian or Scottish History or Social Anthropology or Spanish or Statistics or Theological Studies or Ancient History or Art History; Psychology or Art History or Economics or English or French or Geography or German or International Relations or Management or Mathematics or Medieval History or Modern History or Philosophy or Social Anthropology or Theological Studies; Russian-Social Anthropology or French or German or Italian or Spanish or Art History or Economics or English or Hebrew or International Relations or Latin or Management or Medieval History or Middle East Studies or Modern History or Philosophy; Social Anthropology or Spanish or Classical Studies or English or Geography or International Relations or Italian or Mathematics or Philosophy; Scottish History or Italian or Scottish History; Social Anthropology-Spanish or Theological Studies or Arabic or Art History or Classical Studies or Economics or English or French or Geography or International Relations or Medieval History or Middle East Studies or Modern History or Philosophy or Psychology or Russian; Spanish-Ancient History or Arabic or Art History or Economics or English or Geography or Greek or International Relations or Latin or Management or Medieval History or Middle East Studies or Modern History or Philosophy or Scottish History or French or Social Anthropology or Theological Studies or French or German or Italian or Russian; Theological Studies-Classical Studies or English or French or Geography or German or International Relations or Mathematics or Modern History or Philosophy or Psychology or Social Anthropology or Spanish *Single subjects:* Ancient History with Linguistics; Ancient History; Ancient History & Archaeology; Applied Economics; Applied Mathematics; Applied Mathematics; Arabic; Arabic and Middle East Studies; Art History; Biblical Studies; Classical Studies with Linguistics; Classical Studies; Classics; Development Studies; Economics with Russian or Spanish or Social Anthropology; Economics; English with Linguistics; English Language & Literature; Financial Economics; French with Linguistics; French; Geography with Social Anthropology or Spanish; Geography; German with Linguistics; German; Greek with Linguistics; Greek; Hebrew; History; International Relations; Italian; Latin; Management; Mathematics; Medieval History; Medieval History & Archaeology; Medieval Studies; Middle East Studies with Arabic; Modern History; Modern Languages; Philosophy; Psychology with French or Geography or Linguistics; Psychology; Pure Mathematics; Russian with Geography or Linguistics; Russian; Scottish History; Scottish Studies; Social Anthropology; Social Anthropology with Geography; Spanish with Geography or Linguistics; Spanish; Statistics

SCIENCE

BSc General/Hons; MSci: *3-4 yrs* Management-Computer Science or Economics or Geography or Geoscience; Physics *Single subjects:* Animal Biology; Applied Economics; Applied Mathematics; Astrophysics; Behavioural and Environmental Biology; Biochemistry; Biology; Biology with French or German; Biomolecular Science; Cell Biology or Pathology or Environmental Biology with Environmental and Behavioural Biology or Environmental and Marine Biology or Environmental and Plant Biology or Physiology; Chemistry with Applied Chemistry or Biological Chemistry or Catalysis or French or German or Industrial Placement or Materials Chemistry or Pharmacology; Chemistry; Chemistry (Advanced) with Industrial Yr; Computer Science; Economics with French or Russian or Spanish; Economics; Environmental Biology; Evolutionary & Environmental Biology; Financial Economics; Geography; Geography with French; Geoscience; Human Biology; Internet Computing; Computer Science; French; German; Linguistics; Management with French; Management; Management Science; Marine & Environmental Biology or Geography; Mathematics with French or German; Neuroscience; Physics; Physics with Management or Photonics or Solid State Sciences; Physiology; Plant & Environmental Biology; Psychology; Psychology with French; Pure Mathematics; Quantitative Ecology; Statistics; Statistics

with French or German; Theoretical Physics *Two Subjects:* Biochemistry-Chemistry; Chemistry-Computationer Science or Management Science or Mathematics or Physics or Biochemistry or Geoscience; Physics-Chemistry or Computer Science or Logic & Philosophy of Science or Mathematics; Computer Science or Logic & Philosophy of Science or Management Science or Mathematics or Physics or Statistics or Management or Chemistry or Geoscience; Statistics-Computer Science or Economics or Geography or Logic & Philosophy of Science or Management Science or Mathematics; Economics-Management Science or Mathematics or Management or Statistics; Electronics-Physics; Environmental Biology-Geography or Geology; Geography or Management Sciences or Mathematics or Statistics or Management or Environmental Biology; Geoscience-Environmental Biology or Computer Science or Chemistry or Management or Management Science; Logic & Philosophy of Science-Mathematics or Physics or Computer Science or Statistics; Management Science-Mathematics or Statistics or Computer Science or Economics or Geography or Geoscience; Mathematics-Physics or Psychology or Statistics or Chemistry or Computer Science or Economics or Geography or Logic & Philosophy of Science or Management Science or Theoretical Physics; Psychology-Mathematics; Theoretical Physics-Mathematics
BSc Ord/Hons in Medical Science: *3-4 yrs* Medical Science (Students to the University of Manchester where they can graduate MB, ChB after three yrs of clinical studies)

Higher Degrees
ARTS/DIVINITY
MLitt: 20th Century German Literature and Society; Advanced Language Studies; Ancient Historical Research; Ancient History; Arabic Literature; Art History; Central & East European Studies; Classics & Ancient History; Creative Writing; Cultural Identity Studies; Divinity; Early Medieval Scotland; Economics; Enlightenment Studies; Environmental History & Policy; European Languages & Linguistics; French Studies; German Studies; Greek; Greek & Latin; Health Care Management; Historical Research; History of Photography; Information Technology in Arts; International Security Studies; Islamic History; Late Roman, Byzantine & Early Medieval Studies; Latin; Management, Economics & International Relations; Maritime Studies; Medieval English; Medieval History; Middle East Politics; Middle East Studies; Modern American History; Modern Historical Studies; Modern Historiography; Modern Poetries in English; Museum & Gallery Studies; People & Nation in the Twentieth Century; Philosophy & Anthropology; Reformation Studies; Research in Classics; Romantic Studies; Russian Studies; Scottish History; Scottish Literature; Scottish Studies; Shakespeare Studies; Social Anthropology; Social Anthropology-Amerindian Studies; Spanish-Latin American Studies; Women, Writing & Gender *2 yrs* Philosophy *4 mths FT/24 mths PT*
MPhil: *2 yrs* 20th Century German Literature & Society; Advanced Language Studies; Ancient Historical Research; Ancient History; Arabic Literature; Art History; Central & East European Studies; Classics & Ancient History; Cultural Identity Studies; Divinity; Early Medieval Scotland; Economics; Environmental History & Policy; European Languages & Linguistics; French Studies; German Studies; Greek; Greek & Latin; Health Care Management; Historical Research; History of Photography; International Security Studies; Islamic History; Late Roman, Byzantine and Early Medieval Studies; Latin; Management, Economics & International Relations; Maritime Studies; Medieval English; Medieval History; Middle East Politics; Middle East Studies; Modern American History; Modern Historical Studies; Museum & Gallery Studies; National Trust for Scotland Studies; Philosophy; Philosophy & Anthropology; Research in Classics; Romantic Studies; Russian Studies; Scottish History; Scottish Literature; Shakespeare Studies; Social Anthropology; Social Anthropology & Amerindian Studies; Spanish & Latin American Studies *4 mths FT/24 mths PT* Reformation Studies
MPhil/PhD: Church History; Divinity; Divinity; New Testament; Old Testament; Practical Theology & Christian Ethics
MSc: *1 yr* Biological and Medicinal Chemistry; Mathematics; Optoelectronic & Laser Devices; Statistics
PhD/DLang: Amerindian Studies; Ancient History; Arabic Studies; Art History; Classics & Ancient History; Economic & Social History; Economics; English; French; Geography; German; Greek; International Relations; Latin; Logic & Metaphysics; Management; Maritime Studies; Medieval History; Modern History; Moral Philosophy; Psychology; Russian; Scottish History; Social Anthropology; Spanish

SCIENCE

MPhil/PhD: Applied Mathematics; Astronomy; Biochemistry; Cell Biology; Chemistry; Computational Science; Developmental Biology; Electronics; Ethology; Experimental Pathology; Geography; Marine Biology; Mathematics; Microbiology; Neurobiology; Physical Education; Physics; Physiology; Plant Biology & Genetics; Psychology; Pure Mathematics; Statistics; Theoretical Physics *Taught courses available in:* Geoscience

MSc: *Taught courses available in:* Biological & Medicinal Chemistry; Mathematics; Optoelectronic & Laser Devices; Statistics

Honorary Degrees

DD; LLD; DSc; DMus; DLitt; MA; MSc

Diplomas

Graduate Diploma: 20th Century German Literature & Society; Advanced Language Studies; Ancient Historical Research; Ancient History; Arabic Literature; Art History; Biological & Medicinal Chemistry; Central & East European Studies; Classics & Ancient History; Creative Writing; Cultural Identity Studies; Divinity; Early Medieval Scotland; Economics; Environmental History & Policy; European Languages & Linguistics; French Studies; German Studies; Greek; Greek & Latin; Health Care Management; Historical Research; History of Photography; International Security Studies; Islamic History; Late Roman, Byzantine and Early Medieval Studies; Latin; Management, Economics & International Relations; Maritime Studies; Mathematics; Medieval English; Medieval History; Middle East Studies; Ministry; Modern American History; Modern Historical Studies; Museum & Gallery Studies; National Trust for Scotland Studies; Optoelectronics & Laser Devices; People & Nation in the Twentieth Century; Philosophy; Philosophy & Anthropology; Reformation Studies; Research in Classics; Russian Studies; Scottish History; Scottish Literature; Scottish Studies; Shakespeare Studies; Social Anthropology; Social Anthropology & Amerindian Studies; Spanish; Statistics; Middle East Politics; Romantic Studies

UNIVERSITY OF STIRLING

Stirling FK9 4LA Tel: 01786 467044 Fax: 01786 466800

First Degrees

BA Hons: *4 yrs* Business & Management; Business Computing; Business Law; Business Law-Business Studies or Sports Studies or Economics or Human Resource Management or Marketing or Politics or Spanish; Business Studies with Sports Studies; Business Studies or Sociology or Spanish/Spanish Language or German/German Language; Business Studies and Business Law or Economics or Education or Education/Computing Science or English Studies or Film & Media Studies or French/French Language or Finance or Japanese Studies or Mathematics or Modern Languages or Politics or Psychology or Social Policy or Marketing; Commonwealth Literature-English Studies or Education/English Studies; Conservation Biology; Conservation Science; Economic & Social Policy; Economics with Sports Studies; Economics or German/German Language; Economics and Business Law or Business Studies or Finance or History or Human Resource Management or Japanese Studies or Marketing or Philosophy or Politics or Psychology or Mathematics or Social Policy or Sociology or Spanish Language or French/French Language or Philosophy/Politics or Business Studies/Computing Science or English Studies or English Studies/Commonwealth Literature or English Studies/Film & Media Studies or English Studies/History or English Studies/Religious Studies or French or French/German or French/Spanish or German or German/Spanish or History or History/Religious Studies or Religious Studies or Politics/History or Spanish; Education and Business Studies or Politics; Education/Business Studies or Philosophy or Sociology or Finance; Computing Science with Commonwealth Studies or Scottish Literature or Scottish Studies; English Studies; English Studies or Education or Education/Commonwealth Literature or Education/Film & Media Studies or Education/History or Education/Religious Studies or Film & Media Studies or French or German or History or Japanese Studies or Philosophy or Politics or Religious Studies or Sociology or

Spanish; English Studies and Business Studies; Entrepreneurship; European Studies; Film & Media Studies or English Studies or English Studies/Education or Entrepreneurship or French or German or History or Japanese Studies or Marketing or Philosophy or Politics or Psychology; Film & Media Studies and Business Studies or Social Policy or Sociology or Spanish or Sports Studies; Film & Media Studies or Marketing or Sports Studies; Entrepreneurship; Finance with Sports Studies; Finance; Finance and Business Studies or Computing Science or Economics or French Language or German Language or Human Resource Management or Japanese Studies or Management Science or Marketing or Mathematics or Spanish Language; Finance Studies; French or Japanese Studies or Marketing or Mathematics or Philosophy or Politics or Psychology or Religious Studies or Sociology or Spanish; French and Business Studies or Economics or Education or Education/German or Education/Spanish or English Studies or Film & Media Studies or German or History or Human Resource Management or Economics or Finance or Marketing; French Language and Business Studies; German or Economics or Education or Education/French or Education/Spanish or English Studies or Film & Media Studies or French or History or Japanese Studies or Marketing or Mathematics or Philosophy or Politics or Religious Studies or Sociology or Spanish; German and Business Studies or Human Resource Management or Marketing or Finance; German Language and Business Studies or Economics; Hispanic Studies; History; History with Scottish Studies or Social Policy or Sociology or Education/Religious Studies or Education or Education/English Studies or English Studies or Film & Media Studies or French or German or Japanese Studies or History or Philosophy or Politics; History and Economics or Religious Studies or Spanish; Human Resource Management with Sports Studies; Human Resource Management or Social Policy or Sociology; Human Resource Management and Business Law or Economics or Finance or French Language or German Language or Japanese Studies or Marketing or Psychology or Spanish Language or Politics; International Management Studies with European Languages and Society or Japanese Language & Society; Japanese Studies; Japanese or German or Social Policy or Sociology or Economics; Mathematics and Business Studies or Finance or French or Social Policy or Sociology; Management Science and Finance with Sports Studies; Marketing or Film & Media Studies or Finance or French/French Language or German/German Language or Human Resource Management or Japanese Studies or Business Studies; Marketing and Business Law or Economics or Entrepreneurship or Modern Languages or Politics or Psychology or Social Policy or Sociology or Spanish/Spanish Language or Finance or French or History or German or Human Resource Management or Marketing or Philosophy or Politics or Sociology or Spanish; Mathematics; Japanese Studies and Business Studies or English Studies or Economics or Film & Media Studies or Marketing; Modern Languages and Business Studies; Money, Banking & Finance; Philosophy; Philosophy and Computing Science or Economics or English Studies or Film & Media Studies or French or German or History or Japanese Studies or Politics or Politics/Economics or Psychology or Religious Studies or Social Policy or Sociology or Spanish or Sports Studies; Politics; Politics & Parliamentary Studies; Politics and Business Law or Business Studies or Economics or English Studies or Film & Media Studies or French or German or History or Human Resource Management or Japanese Studies or Marketing or Philosophy or Philosophy/Economics or Religious Studies or Social Policy or Sociology or Spanish or Sports Studies; PPE (Politics, Philosophy, Economics); Psychology; Psychology and Economics or Film & Media Studies or French or Human Resource Management or Marketing or Philosophy or Social Policy or Sociology or Sports Studies; Public Management and Administration; Religious Studies; Religious Studies or Education or Education/English Studies or Education/History or English Studies or Film & Media Studies or French or German or History or Philosophy or Politics or Social Policy or Sociology or Spanish; Retail Marketing; Scottish History; Scottish Literature; Scottish Literature and English Studies or Spanish; Social Work (including DipSW); Sociology & Social Policy or Social Policy; Sociology and Business Studies or Computing Science or Economics or English Studies or Film & Media Studies or French or German or History or Human Resource Management or Japanese Studies or Management Science or Marketing or Mathematics or Philosophy or Politics or Psychology or Religious Studies or Spanish or Sports Studies; Spanish and Business Law or Business Studies or Education or Education/French or Education/German or English Studies or Film & Media Studies or French or German or History or Japanese Studies or Philosophy or Politics or Religious Studies or Scottish Literature or Sociology; Spanish Language and Business Studies or Economics or Finance or Human Resource Management or Marketing; Sport & Exercise Science; Sports Studies; Sports

Studies and Business Studies or Economics or Entrepreneurship or Film & Media Studies or Finance or Human Resource Management or Marketing or Politics or Psychology or Social Policy or Sociology; Technological Economics; Tourism Management

BA/BAcc/BSc: *3 yrs* Accountancy; Adult Education; Aquatic Science; Biochemistry; Biology; Business Law; Business Studies; Chemistry; Computing Science; Economics; English as a Foreign Language; English Language & Business; English Language Teaching; English Studies; Environmental Science; Film & Media Studies; Finance; French; German; History; Human Resource Management; Japanese Studies; Management Science; Marine Biology; Marketing; Mathematics; Philosophy; Politics; Politics, Philosophy, Economics; Psychology; Religious Studies; Scottish Literature; Social Policy; Sociology; Sociology & Social Policy; Software Engineering; Spanish; Technological Economics

BA/BAcc/BSc General: *3 yrs*

BA/BSc General/Hons with DipEd: *3 yrs 3 mths/4 yrs 3 mths* Politics or History/Politics; Education and Biochemistry or Biology/Chemistry or Business Studies or Business Studies/Computing Science or Chemistry or Computing Science or Computing Science/Mathematics or English Studies or English Studies/Commonwealth Literature or English Studies/History or English Studies/Religious Studies or English/Film & Media Studies or French or French/German or French/Spanish or German or German/Spanish or Mathematics or History or History/Religious Studies or Mathematics & its Applications or Religious Studies or Spanish or Biology

BAcc Hons: *4 yrs* Accountancy; Accountancy-Business Law or Business Studies or Computing Science or Economics or French Language or German Language or Management Science or Marketing or Mathematics or Spanish Language or Sports Studies

BSc Hons: Aquaculture; Biochemistry; Biochemistry-Education; Biology; Biology-Computing Science or Education or Education/Chemistry or Environmental Science or Management Science or Mathematics or Mathematics and its Applications or Psychology; Business Law-Management Science; Business Studies-Computing Science; Chemistry and Biology/Education or Education; Computational Ecology; Computing Science or Mathematics and its Applications or Psychology or Spanish Language; Computing Science and Biology or Business Studies or Economics or Education or Education/Mathematics or Entrepreneurship or Environmental Science or Film & Media Studies or Finance or French Language or German Language or Japanese Studies or Management Science or Marketing or Mathematics; Economics and Computing Science or Environmental Science or Mathematics and its Applications or Biology; Education and Biochemistry or Biology/Chemistry or Chemistry or Computing Science or Computing Science/Mathematics or Environmental Science (Geography) or Mathematics or Mathematics and its Applications; Entrepreneurship and Computing Science; Environmental Analysis; Environmental Biology; Environmental Science; Environmental Science (Geography); Environmental Science (Geography)-Education; Environmental Science and Biology or Computing Science or Economics or Film & Media Studies or Management Science or Mathematics or Mathematics and its Applications or Politics; Film & Media Studies and Computing Science or Environmental Science; Finance-Mathematics and its Applications; French Language and Computing Science or Management Science or Mathematics and its Applications; French-Management Science; Freshwater Science; German Language and Computing Science or Management Science or Mathematics and its Applications; German-Management Science; Japanese Studies and Computing Science or Management Science; Management Science; Management Science with Sports Studies; Management Science and Biology or Business Law or Computing Science or Environmental Science or French/French Language or German/German Language or Japanese Studies or Marketing or Mathematics or Mathematics and its Applications or Psychology or Spanish/Spanish Language; Marine Biology; Marketing and Computing Science or Management Science; Mathematics and Biology or Computing Science or Education or Education/Computing Science or Environmental Science or Management Science or Psychology; Mathematics and its Applications or Spanish Language; Mathematics and its Applications and Biology or Computing Science or Economics or Education or Environmental Science or Finance or French Language or German Language or Management Science; Politics and Environmental Science; Psychology or Mathematics or Management Science or Business Studies; Psychology and Biology or Computing Science; Software Engineering; Spanish Language and Computing Science or Management Science or Mathematics and its Applications; Sports Studies and Management

Science; Sustainable Development Studies *3 yrs* Conservation Biology *3 yrs/4 yrs* Freshwater Science; Sport and Exercise Science

Higher Degrees

DOCTORATES
PhD: *2 3 yrs* (By research)

MASTER'S DEGREES
EdD: *3-4 yrs FT/5-6 yrs PT* Education *3-4 yrs FT/5-6 yrs PT (by research)*
MBA: *1 yr FT* Business Administration; Business Administration (Public Service Management); Business Administration (Retailing)
MEd: *1 yr FT/2-5 yrs PT* Education; Management for Tertiary Education
MPhil: Historical Research; Legal and Political Philosophy; Modern French Literature & Society; Modern Poetry; Publishing Studies; Religion, Culture and Critical Theory; The Gothic Imagination *3-4 yrs PT* Education *4 mths FT/24 mths PT*
MSc: *1 yr FT/2 yrs PT* Advanced Social Work Studies in Criminal Justice; Applied Social Research; Aquaculture; Aquatic Pathobiology; Aquatic Veterinary Studies; Banking & Finance; Community Care; Computer Assisted Language Learning & TESOL; Creative and Cultural Industries; Dementia Studies; Economics; Entrepreneurial Studies; Environmental Management; Housing Studies; Human Resource Development; Human Resources Management; Industrial Relations; Information Systems Management; Information Technology; International Business; Investment Analysis; Lifelong Learning; Marketing; Media Management; Media Research; Palliative Nursing Care; Psychological Research Methods; Psychology & Health; Public Relations; Quality Management; Retail Management; School Leadership and Management; Social Work Management; Social Work Studies; Software Engineering; Software Technology; Strategic Management of Housing; Technology Enhanced Learning; Technology Management; TESOL

Honorary Degrees
DUniv; MA

Diplomas

DipHE: *3 yrs* Midwifery; Nursing
Postgraduate Diploma: *1 yr FT* Advanced Educational Studies; Advanced Social Work Studies in Criminal Justice; Applied Social Research; Aquaculture; Aquatic Pathobiology; Aquatic Veterinary Studies; Banking & Finance; Business Administration; Business Administration (Retailing); Community Care; Creative and Cultural Industries; Dementia Studies; Education; Entrepreneurial Studies; Environmental Management; Historical Research; Housing Studies; Human Resource Development; Human Resource Management; Industrial Relations; Information Systems Management; Information Technology; International Business; Investment Analysis; Legal and Political Philosophy; Management for Tertiary Education; Marketing; Media Management; Media Research; Modern French Literature & Society; Modern Poetry; Palliative Nursing Care; Psychological Research Methods; Public Relations; Publishing Studies; Quality Management; Religion, Culture and Critical Theory; Retail Management; School Leadership and Management; Social Work Management; Social Work Studies; Software Technology; Strategic Management & Housing; Technology Enhanced Learning; Technology Management; TESOL; The Gothic Imagination

Certificates

Certificate: *1 yr FT/2 yrs PT* Advanced Educational Studies; English Language Teaching; Enterprise Skills; Further Education; Healthcare Management; Housing Studies; Professional Development; Religious Studies; Tertiary Education (Further Education) *3 yrs FT Major subjects:* Drug and Alcohol Studies

ST MARTIN'S COLLEGE, LANCASTER, AMBLESIDE AND CARLISLE

Tel: 01524 384444 Fax: 01524 384567 e-mail: admissions@ucsm.ar.uk

Lancaster LA1 3JD Tel: 01524 384444 Fax: 01524 384567

Ambleside LA22 9BB Tel: 015394 30211 Fax: 015394 30305

Carlisle CA1 2AA Tel: 01228 616203 Fax: 01228 616235

First Degrees

BA Hons: *4-6 yrs PT* English & History

BA/BSc Hons: *3 yrs FT* English with Modern Languages & TEFL Local Government Management *Major subjects:* Applied Social Sciences; Art & Design; Business & Management Studies; English; Geography; Health Management; Health Studies; History; Religious Studies; Social Ethics *Modular Studies Joint:* Applied Social Sciences; Art & Design; Business & Management Studies; Creative Writing; Design & Technology; Drama; Drama; Economics; Education Studies; English; English with Modern Languages or TEFL Local Government Management; Geography; Health Management; Health Studies; History; Information Technology; Language Studies; Mathematics; Music; Religious Studies; Science, Technology & Society; Social Ethics; Spanish; Sports History; Sports Studies *PT modular* Art & Design; Drama; English; Geography; Health Management; Health Studies; History; Mathematics; Midwifery Studies; Nursing Studies; Religious Studies; Social Ethics; Sports Studies

BA/BSc Hons with QTS (Primary): *3 yrs FT* Advanced Study of Early Years Education; Drama; English & Literary Education; Geographical and Environmental Education; Numeracy and Mathematics Education; Physical Education; Science Education *4 yrs FT* Art & Design; Biological Studies; Design & Technology; English; Geography; History; Information Technology; Mathematics; Music; Physical Education; Religious Studies

BA/BSc Major Degrees: *3 yrs FT* Applied Psychology; Applied Social Sciences; Art & Design; English; Geography; Health Management; Health Studies; History; Religious Studies

BPhil: *1 yr FT* (For qualified teachers and other professionals)

BSc Hons: *3 yrs FT* Diagnostic Radiography; Environmental Studies; Geography of Leisure & Tourism; Leisure & Recreational Management Studies; Leisure and Recreation/Tourism; Management Studies/Leisure and Recreation; Management Studies/Tourism; Multimedia Production & Applied Imaging; Nursing; Occupational Therapy; Outdoor Studies; Sports Science; Tourism/Leisure and Recreation; Tourism/Management Studies *3-6 yrs PT* Child Health Studies; Community Children's Nursing; Community Mental Health Nursing; Community Nursing in the Home; District Nursing; General Practice Nursing; Health Management; Health Promotion; Health Studies; Health Studies (Nurse Practitioner); Learning Disabilities Nursing; Midwifery Studies; Multimedia Production & Imaging Science; Occupational Health Nursing; Primary Health Care; Public Health Nursing/Health Visiting; Radiography Studies; School Nursing; Specialist Practice in the Community

BSc Hons with QTS (Secondary): *2 yrs FT* Mathematics; Science

Higher Degrees

MASTER'S DEGREES OR EQUIVALENT

MA: *2-5 yrs PT* Church School Education; Developing Teacher Expertise; Educational Management; Health Management; Informal & Community Education; Religious & Moral Education; Science & Maths; Special Educational Needs; Sustainable Environments; Writing Studies

MPhil: *24-36 mths FT/24-60 mths PT* Applied Social Science; Art, Design & Technology; Education; English; Geography; History; Imaging Sciences; Mathematics; Music; Nursing Studies & Primary Health Care; Occupational Therapy; Radiography; Religious Studies; Science & Technology; Social Ethics

MSc: *2-5 yrs PT* Challenges in Child Centred Practice; Clinical Leadership in Nursing; Health & Healing Science; Health Promotion and Public Health; Interprofessional Health Studies; Magnetic Resonance Imaging; Medical Diagnostic Imaging; Medical Ultrasound; Primary Health Care Management

PhD: *36-48 mths FT/36-60 mths PT* Applied Social Science; Art, Design & Technology; Education; English; Geography; History; Imaging Sciences; Mathematics; Music; Nursing Studies & Primary Health Care; Performing Arts; Radiography; Religious Studies; Science & Technology; Social Ethics

Diplomas

DipHE: Community & Youth Studies; Counselling; Midwifery; Working with the Older Person
Diploma in Professional Studies: *2-3 yrs PT* Care & Support of the Older Person with Continuing Care Needs; Child Health Studies; Children's Nursing; Health Management; Health Promotion; Health Studies; Nursing; Primary Health Care

Certificates

CertHE: *1 yr PT* Counselling; Health Management; Health Promotion; Health Studies
PGCE: *1 yr FT* 11-18 yrs (Secondary); Art; English with Drama & Media Studies; Geography; History; Information Technology; Mathematics; Modern Languages (French, German, Spanish); Religious Education & Personal and Social Development; Science (Biology, Chemistry, Physics) *2 yrs FT* Information Technology; Mathematics *FT/PT* Primary
Postgraduate Certificate: *12-18 mths PT* Gynaecological Ultrasound; Medical Image Interpretation; Obstetric & Gynaecological Ultrasound; Obstetric Ultrasound; Youth & Community Work

STOCKPORT COLLEGE OF FURTHER & HIGHER EDUCATION

Wellington Road South, Stockport, Lancashire SK1 3UQ Tel: 0161 958 3100 Fax: 0161 480 6636 e-mail: stockcoll@cs.stockport.ac.uk

† 2+2: The first two yrs lead to the award of a Higher National Diploma.
Degrees are validated by:
* University of Huddersfield
** Universities of Leeds/Salford/UMIST
*** Liverpool John Moores University
**** University validated (to be confirmed)
***** University of London
****** UMIST

First Degrees

BA: *PT* Business Studies*
BA Hons: *3 yrs FT (HND Top-up):* Business Administration* *FT* Design & Visual Arts (Advertising)***; Design & Visual Arts (Cont. Textiles)***; Design & Visual Arts (Graphic Design)***; Design & Visual Arts (Illustration)***; Documentary and Fine Art Photography*** *FT/PT* Professional Studies (Early Childhood Studies, Social Work, Learning Difficulties or Social Care)**** *PT* Professional Studies (Education)*****
BEng Hons: *4 yrs FT* Aeronautical/Manufacturing/Mechanical Engineering**†
BSc Hons: Chemistry******† *4 yrs FT* Biochemistry******†; Biology******†

Diplomas

Diploma: *PT* Nursing***

UNIVERSITY OF STRATHCLYDE

Glasgow G1 1XQ Tel: 0141 552 4400 Fax: 0141 552 0775 e-mail: j.gibson@mis.strath.ac.uk
Website: www.strath.ac.uk

ARTS & SOCIAL SCIENCES
Students are admitted to courses leading to a Pass degree; selection for Hons is made in the light of their performance

BA Pass: Students normally take five subjects in the first yr and two of these in the second and third yrs. Subjects as listed under BA Hons. Subjects include Russian as well as those listed under Honours.

BA Hons: For the four-yr course students may be exempted from the first yr on the basis of three good A level passes.

BA Hons: PT. By conversion or addition to BA Pass degree (Arts & Social Sciences). See BA (FT) for available subjects.

BUSINESS
Students are admitted to leading to a Pass degree; selection for Hons is made in the light of their performance.

BA Pass: Students may be exempted from certain first yr classes, reading the study period for the Pass degree to two yrs on the basis of acceptable passes in appropriate subjects at GCE A level gained at an appropriate standard or an HND relevant to the choice of Principal Subjects and gained at an appropriate standard. Students normally take four subjects in the first yr and two of these during the second and third yrs. Compulsory classes in Computing and Statistics must be included in the curriculum.

SCIENCE & TECHNOLOGY
BSc Hons: Students may be exempted from the first yr on the basis of three good GCE A level passes

BEng: Students may be exempted from the first yr on the basis of three good GCE A level passes.

TECHNOLOGY & BUSINESS STUDIES
Students select a Business Studies Principal subject and a Technology Principal subject* In conjunction with Bell College of Technology, Hamilton.

First Degrees
ARTS & SOCIAL SCIENCES
BA Joint Hons: *4-5 yrs Combination of 2 subjects:* Economics; English; European Studies; French; Geography; Geography & Planning; German; History; Human Resource Management; Italian; Law; Marketing; Mathematics; Politics; Psychology; Russian; Scottish Studies; Sociology; Spanish
BA Single Hons: *4-5 yrs* Economics; English; European Studies; French; Geography; Geography and Planning; German; History; Human Resource Management; Italian; Politics; Psychology; Scottish Studies; Sociology; Spanish; Sustainable Development and Regeneration

BUSINESS, LAW & ECONOMICS
BA Hons: *4-5 yrs* International Business and Modern Languages
BA Joint Hons: *4 yrs Combination of 2 subjects:* Accounting; Business Law; Economics; Finance; Geography; History; Human Resource Management; Law; Management Science; Marketing; Mathematics & Statistics; Modern Languages; Politics; Psychology; Sociology; Tourism
BA Single Hons: *4 yrs* Accounting; Business Law; Finance; Human Resource Management; Management Science; Sustainable Development & Regeneration; Tourism
BA/BA Hons: *3-4 yrs FT* Environmental Planning Studies; Hotel & Hospitality Management; International Tourism
LLB/LLB Hons: *4-5 yrs* European Law; Law (based on Scottish Law); Law and a Modern Language

EDUCATION
BA: *3 yrs Single:* Social Work (including Diploma in Social Work)
BA Hons: *3-4 yrs* Applied Music; Community Arts; Community Education; Education and Business; Outdoor Education in the Community; Sport in the Community
BEd Hons: *4 yrs* Primary Education
BSc/BSc Hons: *3-4 yrs* Speech and Language Pathology; Sport and Exercise Science

SCIENCE & TECHNOLOGY
BEng Dipl Eng Hons: *5 yrs FT Single Honours:* Engineering with Business Management and European Studies; Environmental Engineering; Mechanical Engineering
BEng Hons: *4 yrs Single Honours:* Building Design Engineering; Chemical Engineering; Civil Engineering; Environmental Engineering; Manufacturing Systems Engineering; Mechanical Engineering

BEng Hons; MEng: Accounting; Engineering with Business Management and European Studies *4 yrs* Computing *4-5 yrs* Electronics Manufacture; Building Design Engineering; Chemical Engineering with Process Biotechnology; Chemical Engineering; Civil Engineering with Environmental Management or European Studies; Civil Engineering; Computing-Electronic Systems with Business Studies or European Studies; Electrical & Mechanical Engineering with Business Studies or European Studies; Electronic & Electrical Engineering; Electronic and Electrical Engineering; Environmental Engineering; Manufacturing Engineering & Management; Manufacturing Sciences & Engineering (with a diploma in Management for Engineers); Manufacturing Systems Engineering; Mechanical Engineering with Biomedical Engineering or Control Engineering or Energy Studies or Environmental Engineering or Financial Management or Material Engineering; Mechanical Engineering; Naval Architecture & Small Craft or Offshore Engineering; Product Design

BSc/BSc Hons: *3 yrs* Biological Sciences *4 yrs* Applied Chemistry; Applied Physics; Architectural Studies with European studies; Architectural Studies or Molecular Biology; Biochemistry-Biotechnology or Immunology or Microbiology or Pharmacology; Bioscience with Modelling; Business Information Systems; Chemistry with Teaching Qualification; Chemistry; Computer Science with Law; Computer Science; Construction Engineering & Management; Environmental Health; Facilities Management; Forensic & Analytical Chemistry; Mathematics with Teaching qualification (secondary)

BSc/MSci: *3 yrs* Science Studies *4 yrs* Biological Sciences with Teaching Qualification; Biomolecular and Medicinal Chemistry; Immunology-Pharmacology or Microbiology; Laser Physics & Optoelectronics; Mathematical Biology; Mathematics; Mathematics and Computer Science; Mathematics, Statistics and Accounting; Mathematics, Statistics and Economics; Mathematics, Statistics and Finance; Mathematics, Statistics and Management Science; Mathematics-Physics; Pharmaceutical Sciences; Physics with Teaching Qualification (secondary); Physics; Prosthetics & Orthotics; Software Engineering; Statistics

TECHNOLOGY & BUSINESS STUDIES

BSc/BSc Hons: *3-4 yrs FT* Accounting; Accounting/Economics; Computer Science; Computer Science; Economics; Economics; Electronic Technology; Manufacturing; Manufacturing; Marketing; Marketing

Higher Degrees

LLM: *1 yr FT/2 yrs PT* Commercial Law (joint with Glasgow University); Construction Law; Employment Law; Information Technology & Telecommunications law; International Law

MArch: *1 yr FT/2 yrs PT* Advanced Architectural Design

MBA: *1 yr FT/3 yrs PT/4 yrs open learning*

MBM: Business & Management

MEnv: *1 yr FT/2 yrs PT* Environmental Studies

MLitt: *1 yr FT* Journalism Research; Journalism Studies; Literary Linguistics

MPharm: *4 yrs* Pharmacy

MPhil: (By research and thesis)

MRes: *12 mths FT/24 mths PT*

MSc: Adult Guidance; Advanced Academic Studies; Advanced Professional Studies; Advanced Social Work Studies; Bioengineering; Biotechnology; Business Economics; Business Information Technology Systems; Clinical Pharmacy; Communications Control & Digital Signal Processing; Communications Technology and Policy; Computer Aided Building Design; Computer Aided Engineering Design; Computer Integrated Manufacture; Construction Management; Educational Psychology; Electrical Power Engineering; Energy Systems & the Environment; Environmental Science; Equality & Discrimination; Facilities Design & Planning; Facilities Management; Finance; Food Biotechnology; Food Science & Microbiology; Forensic Science; Human Resource Management; Human Resource Management for the Tourism & Hospitality Industries; Immunopharmacology; Industrialisation, Trade, & Economic Policy; Information & Library Studies; Information Management; Information Strategy; Information Technology; Information Technology Systems; Integrated Building Design; International Hospitality Management; International Marketing; Management in Education; Management of Competitive Manufacturing; Marine Technology; Marketing; Occupational Psychology; Operational Research; Personnel

Management; Pharmaceutical Analysis; Pharmacology; Process Engineering; Prothetics & Orthotics; Research Methods in Psychology; Social Research; Tourism; Tourism in Developing Countries; Urban & Regional Planning; Urban Design; Urban Development *3 yrs FT* Advanced Speech and Language Therapy
MSci: *5 yrs FT* Applied Chemistry; Applied Chemistry; Biomedical and Medicinal Chemistry; Biophysics; Chemistry; Forensic and Analytical Chemistry; Laser Physics and Opto Electronics; Mathematics; Physics; Physics and Mathematical Finance; Physics with Simulation

DOCTORATES
DSc: *3 yrs min*
PhD: *3 yrs FT/4 yrs PT*

Honorary Degrees
MA; MSc; MLitt; LLD; DLitt; DUniv

Diplomas
PGDip: *1 yr* Applied Microbiology; Careers Guidance; Environmental Science *1 yr FT* Pharmaceutical Analysis *1-2 yrs PT* Lower Limb Orthotic Biomechanics (by distance learning); Lower Prosthetics Biomechanics (by distance learning) *1-2 yrs PT/DL* Clinical Gait Analysis *21 mths FT* Process Engineering *24 mths PT* Human Resource Management for the Tourism & Hospitality Industries; Personnel Management *9 mths* Advanced Architectural Design; Bioengineering; Biotechnology; Business & Management; Business & Management; Business Economics; Business Information Technology Systems; Clinical Pharmacy; Communications Control & Digital Signal Processing; Community Education Certificate; Computer Aided Building Design; Computer Aided Building Design; Computer Integrated Manufacture; Computer-Aided Engineering Design; Construction Law; Construction Management; Counselling in Primary Care; Early Education; Educational Computing; Educational Technology; Electrical Power Engineering; Energy Systems & the Environment; Energy Systems and the Environment; English Studies; Equality & Discrimination; Facilities Design & Planning; Facilities Management; Finance; Forensic Science; Historical Studies; Human Resource Management; Immunopharmacology; Industrial Mathematics; Industrialisation, Trade & European Policy; Information & Library Studies; Information Management; Information Management; Information Technology & Telecommunications Law; Information Technology Systems; Integrated Building Design; International Hospitality Management; International Marketing; Journalism Studies; Legal Practice; Literary Linguistics; Literary Linguistics; Management of Competitive Manufacturing; Marine Technology; Marine Technology; Marketing; Operational Research; Pharmacology; Pharmacology; Public Policy; Russian Language; Science & Technology Policy; Social Research; Social Research; Teaching Creative Writing; Tourism; Tourism in Developing Countries; Urban & Regional Planning; Urban Design; Urban Development *PT* Biomechanics (distance learning)

UNIVERSITY OF SUNDERLAND
Edinburgh Building, Chester Road, Sunderland SR1 3SD Tel: 0191 515 3000
e-mail: student-helpline@sunderland.ac.uk Website: www.sunderland.ac.uk

Hylton Centre, North Hylton Road, Sunderland SR5 5DB Tel: 0191 511 6000 Fax:0191 6280
Shiney Row Centre, Success Road, Philadelphia, Houghton-le-Spring DH4 4TL Tel: 0191 511 6000 Fax: 0191 511 6180
Tunstall Centre, Sea View Road, Sunderland SR2 9LH Tel: 0191 511 6000 Fax: 0191 511 6589
Please note: many of the programmes listed as full-time are also available part-time. Contact the University for details.

First Degrees
BA: *2 yrs FT* IT Education *3 yrs FT* Business & Legal Studies; Business Administration; Communication, Cultural and Media Studies; Community & Youth Work; Electronic Media; Electronic Media Design; English Education; English Studies; Film & Media Studies; Fine Art; Geography Education; Glass, Architectural Glass & Ceramics; Health Studies; History; Illustration & Design; Interactive Media; IT Education (Key Stage 2/3); IT Education (Secondary); Journalism

Studies; Media Production (TV & Radio); Model Making; Performance Arts Studies; Photography, Video & Digital Imaging; Politics; Social Science; Social Science (Applied); Social Work; Sociology *FT/PT* Computer Studies

BA/BA Hons: *1 yr FT* Business Administration (top-up programme) *2 yrs FT* Business Administration (shortened); Business Education; Key Stage 2/3 Education; Modern Foreign Languages Education (French, German, Spanish); Music Education; Professional Studies (PT only); Technology Education *3 yrs FT* Arts & Design; Business & Accounting; Early Childhood Studies; Interactive Entertainment Systems; Internet Information Systems *3 yrs FT/4 yrs S* Accounting & Computing; Business Computing; Internet Information Systems; Sports & Exercise Development; Sports Sciences *4 mths FT/24 mths PT 4 yrs FT* Primary Education (3-8 yrs & 7-11 yrs); Technology Education *4 yrs S* Business & Marketing; Business & Human Resource Management; Business & Management Studies; Business Studies; International Business with French or German or Spanish; International Business

BEng: *FT/PT* Engineering

BEng/BEng Hons: *3 yrs FT/4 yrs S (5 yrs with option of MEng)* Computer Systems Engineering; Electrical & Electronic Engineering; Manufacturing Engineering; Mechanical Engineering *4 yrs S (5 yrs with option of MEng)* Automotive Design & Manufacture

BSc: Biomedical Science; Pharmacology; Science Education *FT* Geography

BSc/BSc Hons: *2 yrs FT* Information Technology Education; Mathematics Education; Nursing; Science Education; Technology Education *3 yrs FT* Health Studies; Media Systems; Psychology *3 yrs FT/4 yrs S* Applied Geology; Biological Science; Biomedical Sciences; Broadcasting and Multimedia Technology; Chemical & Pharmaceutical Sciences; Computing; Environmental Sciences; Environmental Studies; Information Technology; Pharmacology; Sport & Exercise Development; Sports Sciences; Tourism Development Studies *4 yrs FT* Technology Education

Joint Honours Scheme: *4 mths FT/24 mths PT* American Studies (please contact the university for details of available subject combinations); Business; Business Law; Comparative Literature; Computing; Ecology; Education & Training; English; Environmental Studies; European Studies; French; Gender Studies; Geography; Geology; German; History; History of Art & Design; Human Resource Management; Independent Programmes; Marketing; Mathematical Sciences; Media Studies; Music; Philosophy; Physiology; Politics; Psychology; Religious Studies; Sociology; Spanish; Studies in Linguistics

LLB: *3 yrs FT* Law with Psychology; Law & Accounting; Law & Business Studies

Higher Degrees

Dip SE: Pharmaceutical Sciences; Professional Studies (Pharmaceutical Sciences)

MA: *1 yr FT* Film and Cultural Studies *all incorporating a PG certificate and DIP:* Art & Design in Context; Conservation of Stained Glass; English Studies; Fine Art; Gender, Culture and Development; Glass; Historical Studies; International Studies; Media Production; Peace, Conflict and Justice; Photography; Policy Studies; Teaching English to Speakers of Other Languages; Women, Culture and Identity *PT only all incorporating a PG certificate and DIP:* Children's Literature; Design & Technology Education; Peace, Conflict & Justice; Policy Studies; Post-16 compulsory; Post-Compulsory Education; Special Education Needs; Teaching & Learning with ICT; Training & Development

MBA: *1 yr FT* Business Administration; Business Studies; Finance Management; Human Resource Management; Information Technology Management; International Management; International Marketing; Management Development Programme; Manufacturing Management; Marketing; Operations Management

MPharm: *4 yrs* Pharmacy

MSc: *1 yr FT all incorporating a PG certificate and DIP:* Advanced Nursing Practice; Applied Ergonomics; Clinical Pharmacy; Competitive Manufacture; Computer-Based Information Systems; Computer-Based Plant & Process Control; Decision Support Systems; Environment, Health & Safety; Environmental Management; Health Sciences; Knowledge Engineering; Management of Information Technology; Materials Engineering; Project Management; Scientific Computing; Software Engineering; Wastes Management; Water & Environmental Engineering *FT/PT* Engineering Management; Health & Safety; Project Engineering *PT only all incorporating a PG certificate and DIP:* Business Economics; Clinical Pharmacy; Health Information Management; Human Resource Management; Knowledge Engineering; Systemic Management

Diplomas

HND: Business Information Technology; Business Information Technology for Returners; Computing; Computing for Returners; Information Design; Information Systems; Information Systems; Information Systems for Returners *1 yr FT* Art Foundation; Business Computing Foundation; International Foundation in Business Computing *2 yrs FT* Business

MBA: *PT only* Management Development Programme (incorporates Certificate in Management Studies, Diploma in Management Studies, and MBA)

PGDip: *2 yrs PT* Environmental EuroPro Diploma *3 yrs PT* Graduate Diploma in Psychology *PT* Postgraduate Education in Pharmaceutical Quality Scheme

Undergraduate Diploma: *1 yr FT* Diploma in Nursing *1 yr PT* Diploma in Palliative Care *2 yrs PT* Diploma in Nursing Theory and Practice *30 wks* Diploma in Care of Person with Diabetes

Certificates

HNC: *2 yrs PT* Information Technology Support (SCOTVEC validated); Science (Pharmaceutical)

PGC: *2 yrs PT* Clinical Pharmacy

PGCE: *1 yr FT* Business Education; Design & Technology Education; English Education; Geography Education; Information Technology Education; Mathematics Education; Modern Foreign Languages Education; Music Education; Primary Education; Science Education

PGCert: *1 yr PT* Management Practice (NVQ 4/5); Pharmaceutical Quality Assurance*150 hrs PT* Certificate in Practice Teaching (Social Work)

Undergraduate Certificates: *1 yr PT* Specialist Classroom Support

Degrees validated by University of Sunderland offered at:

City of Sunderland College

Bede Centre, Durham Road, Sunderland SR3 4AH Tel: 0191 511 6000 Fax: 0191 511 6380
Website: www.citysun.ac.uk

First Degrees

BA Hons: Education; Joint Honours (Humanities) *3 yrs FT/4 yrs S* Business Computing
BSc Hons: Health Studies; Science

Other Courses

Certificate: Certificate of Education

Diploma: Management (NEBS); Management Studies; Primary Healthcare

HND/HNC: Biology (Applied); Building Environmental Science; Building Studies; Business; Business Care; Community & Economic Development; Computing; Economics of Industry/Building Law; Electrical Engineering; Housing Management; Leisure Studies; Maintenance Technician Training Scheme; Management for the Motor Vehicle Industry; Mechanical & Production Engineering; Travel & Tourism Management

Matthew Boulton College of Further & Higher Education

Sherlock Street, Birmingham B5 7DB Tel: 0121 446 4545 Fax: 0121 446 3105
Website: www.matthew-boulton.ac.uk

First Degrees

BSc Hons: *3 yrs FT* Podiatry

THE SURREY INSTITUTE OF ART & DESIGN, UNIVERSITY COLLEGE

Farnham Campus, Falkner Road, Farnham, Surrey GU9 7DS Tel: 01252 892607
Fax: 01252 892624 e-mail: slarge@surrart.ac.uk Website: www.surrart.ac.uk

For further details contact the Registry, Farnham Campus, Falkner Road, Farnham, Surrey GU9 7DS Tel: 01252 8926/09/10/11
 e-mail:registry@surrart.ac.uk

† Subject to validation.

First Degrees

BA Hons: *3 yrs FT* Animation; Arts & Media; Design Management; Fashion; Fashion Journalism; Fashion Promotion & Illustration; Film & Video; Fine Art; Graphic Design; Graphic Design (Visual Communication); Graphic Design: New Media; Interior Design; Journalism; Packaging Design; Photography; Product Design (Sustainable Futures); Textiles: Printed & Woven; Three Dimensional Design (Ceramics or Glass or Jewellery & Metalwork) *5 yrs PT* Fine Art; Photo Digital Illustration

Higher Degrees

MA: *3 semesters FT/5 semesters PT* Jewellery & Metalwork *Named subject with specialisms in:* Animation; Ceramics; Design Management; Fashion; Film & Video; Fine Art; Glass; Graphic Design; Interior Design; Journalism; Media & Cultural Studies; Packaging Design; Photography; Sustainable Design; Textiles

Diplomas

Access Courses: *1 yr PT* Access to Art & Design
EdExcel BTEC National Diploma: *2 yrs FT* Fine Art
National Diploma: *1 yr FT/2 yrs PT* Foundation Studies in Art & Design

UNIVERSITY OF SURREY

Guildford, Surrey GU2 7XH Tel: 01483 300800/259192 Fax: 01483 300803/259389
e-mail: p.elliott@surrey.ac.uk Website: www.surrey.ac.uk

Notes: Environmental Studies may not be combined with Biology, Drama, Heritage Studies, History, Media Arts, Religious Studies, Sport Rehabilitation or Theology.
* Subject to validation.

First Degrees

BEng: *3-4 yrs* Aerospace; Bio-Materials Engineering *4 yrs* Information Systems Engineering (accredited under SARTOR (3rd edition) 1997) with A European Language (accredited under SARTOR (3rd edition) 1997)
BSc: *3 yrs* Nursing Studies (Registered Nurse: Learning Disability Nursing) *3-4 yrs* Management and Tourism; Physics with Finance; Science of Materials

EUROPEAN INSTITUTE OF HEALTH & MEDICAL SCIENCES
BSc Hons: Health Sciences (Registered Midwife: Midwifery); Health Sciences (Registered Nurse: Adult Nursing); Health Sciences (Registered Nurse: Child Nursing); Health Sciences (Registered Nurse: Mental Health Nursing)

SCHOOL OF BIOLOGICAL SCIENCES
BSc: *3-4 yrs* Biochemistry (Pharmacology); Microbiology (Medical)
BSc Hons: *3-4 yrs* Biochemistry; Biochemistry (Medical); Biochemistry (Toxicology); Food Science & Microbiology; Microbiology (Biotechnology); Microbiology (Environmental); Molecular Biology; Molecular Microbiology; Nutrition; Nutrition with an integrated foundation yr; Nutrition & Food Science *4 yrs* Nutrition/Dietetics *4-5 yrs* Biochemistry with an integrated foundation yr; Microbiology with an integrated foundation yr; Nutrition with Foundation Yr

SCHOOL OF ELECTRONIC ENGINEERING, IT & MATHEMATICS
BEng Hons: *3-4 yrs* Electronic Engineering; Information Systems Engineering *4 yrs* Electronic Engineering with a European Language; Information Systems Engineering with a European Language *4-5 yrs* Electronic & Information Systems Engineering with an integrated foundation yr
BSc Hons: Computing & German *3-4 yrs* Computer Modelling & Simulation; Computer Science & Engineering; Computing & Information Technology; Mathematics (5 yrs with a period of professional training) with an integrated foundation yr (5 yrs with a period of professional training); Mathematics; Mathematics & Statistics with a European Language; Mathematics and Computing Science with a European Language; Mathematics and Computing Science or Statistics or a European Language; Mathematics and Statistics

SCHOOL OF ENGINEERING IN THE ENVIRONMENT
BEng Hons: *4-5 yrs* Civil Engineering with an integrated foundation yr
BEng Hons/Meng: *3-4 yrs/4-5 yrs* Civil Engineering; Computing; Chemical Engineering; Engineering for the Environment; Environmental Chemical Engineering *3.5 yrs/4.5 yrs* Environmental Chemical Engineering; Chemical Engineering *4 yrs/5 yrs* Civil Engineering with a European Language *4-5 yrs* Chemical Engineering with an integrated foundation yr

SCHOOL OF HUMAN SCIENCES
BSc Hons: *3-4 yrs* Applied Psychology & Sociology; Business Economics with Computing; Economics; Economics & Sociology; Sociology *4 yrs* Psychology

SCHOOL OF LANGUAGE & INTERNATIONAL STUDIES
BA Hons: *3-4 yrs* Language and Business Culture in Europe *4 yrs S* Combined Languages
BSc Hons: *4 yrs S* Computing & German; French & Economics with International Business; French & European Studies; French & Law; German & Economics with International Business; German & European Studies; German & Law; Linguistic & International Studies (entry by selection in yr 2); Russian & Economics with International Business; Russian & European Studies; Russian & Law
LLB Hons: *3 yrs/4 yrs* Law and European Studies *4 yrs S* Law and French; Law and German; Law and Russian

SCHOOL OF MANAGEMENT FOR THE SERVICE SECTOR
BSc Hons: *3-4 yrs* International Hospitality & Tourism Management *4 yrs* Hotel & Catering Management; Retail Management

SCHOOL OF MECHANICAL & MATERIALS ENGINEERING
BEng Hons: *3-4 yrs* Engineering with Business Management; Mechanical Engineering with Mechatronics *4 yrs* Business Management; Engineering with a European Language; Mechanical Engineering with a European Language; Metallurgy with professional experience *4-5 yrs* Engineering with Business Management and an integrated foundation yr; Materials Science & Engineering with an integrated foundation yr; Mechanical Engineering with an integrated foundation yr
BEng Hons/MEng: *3-4 yrs/4 yrs/4.5 yrs* Materials Science & Engineering with a European Language

SCHOOL OF PERFORMING ARTS
BA Hons: *3-4 yrs* Dance & Culture
BMus Hons: *3-4 yrs* Music; Music & Sound Recording

SCHOOL OF PHYSICAL SCIENCES
BSc Hons: *3-4 yrs* Physics with Nuclear Astrophysics or Computational Modelling or Satellite Technology or Medical Physics *4 yrs* Initial Teacher Training; Chemistry; Chemistry with Management Studies or Initial Teacher Training *4-5 yrs* Chemistry with an integrated foundation yr; Physics with an integrated foundation yr
Bsc Hons/MChem: *3-4 yrs* Chemistry *4 yrs* Computer Aided Chemistry
BSc Hons/MPhys: *3-4 yrs* Physics with Medical Physics; Physics

Higher Degrees

MChem: *4 yrs* Analytical & Environmental Chemistry; Chemistry with Biochemistry; Chemistry with Medicinal Chemistry; Chemistry with Instrumentation and Analysis; Chemistry with Industrial Technology; Chemistry with Industrial Management; Chemistry with Food Science; Chemistry with European Experience

MEng: *4 yrs* Computer Modelling and Simulation *4.5 yrs* Aerospace; Engineering for the Environment; Mechanical and Bio-Medical Engineering; Mechanical and Satellite Engineering; Mechanical Engineering; Mechanical Engineering with A European Language *4-5 yrs* Chemical Engineering

MEng Hons: *4-5 yrs* Computer Science & Engineering; Computing & Information Technology; Electronic Engineering; Electronic Engineering with a European Language; Electronics with Digital Broadcasting; Electronics with Mobile Communication; Radio Frequency Engineering; Satellite Engineering; Systems Engineering; Information Systems Engineering; Telecommunications Systems

MMath: *4 yrs* Mathematics

MPhys: *4 yrs* Physics with Satellite Technology; Physics with Nuclear Astrophysics; Physics with Computational Modelling (including research yr); Physics with Finance

EUROPEAN INSTITUTE OF HEALTH & MEDICAL SCIENCES

MSc: *FT/PT* Chiropractic *PT* Occupational Health; Occupational Hygiene; Occupational Safety

MSc/PgD: *FT/PT* Advanced Clinical Practice; Advanced Clinical Practice (Cancer Nursing); Advanced Clinical Practice (Midwifery) *PT* Health Ergonomics; Health Informatics

MSc/PgD/PgC: *PT/DL* Medical Education

MSc/PGDip: *FT/PT* Advanced Clinical Practice (Palliative Care Nursing)

PGCert/PGDip/MSc: *DL* General Practitioner Training *PT* Nutritional Medicine (joint with School of Biological Sciences)

PGDip: *PT* Occupational Health & Safety; Occupational Health Nursing

SCHOOL OF BIOLOGICAL SCIENCES

MSc: *FT* Block Release; Clinical Biochemistry with Molecular Biology *FT/PT* Toxicology *PT* Pharmaceutical Medicine; Quality Systems in the Clinical Environment (General and Pharmaceutical Medicine)

MSc/PgD: *FT/PT* Medical Microbiology *PT* Applied Toxicology; Clinical Pharmacology; Nutritional Medicine (joint with EIHMS)

SCHOOL OF EDUCATIONAL STUDIES

MSc: *PT* Change Agent Skills & Strategies

MSc/PgD/PgC: *FT/PT* Applied Professional Studies in Education & Training *PT* Counselling & Psychotherapy as a Means to Health; Management Consultancy

PGCert: *FT/PT* Education of Adults; Education of Adults

PGCert/PGDip/MSc: *FT/PT* Applied Professional Studies in Educational Learning; Applied Professional Studies in Lifelong Learning

SCHOOL OF ELECTRONIC ENGINEERING, IT & MATHEMATICS

MSc/PgD: *FT/PT* Digital Broadcasting; Information Systems; Machine Intelligence; Medical Imaging; Microwave Engineering & Wireless Subsystems Designs; Microwaves & Optoelectronics; Mobile & Personal Communications; Mobile & Satellite Communications; Mobile Communications Systems; Multimedia Signal Processing & Communications; Multimedia Technology & Systems; Satellite Communication Engineering; Satellite Engineering; Signal Processing; Signal Processing & Machine Intelligence; Telecommunications; Telematics (Communications & Software) *PT* Electronic Engineering

SCHOOL OF ENGINEERING IN THE ENVIRONMENT

MSc/PgD/PgC: *FT/PT* Bridge Engineering; Structural Engineering; Water & Environmental Engineering

SCHOOL OF HUMAN SCIENCES
MSc/PgD: *FT* Social Research & the Environment; Social Research Methods *FT/PT* Applied Economic Studies; Applied Psychology; Business Economics & Policy; Economics; Energy Economics & Policy; Environmental Psychology; Forensic Psychology; Health Psychology; International Economics & Policy; Occupational & Organisational Psychology; Research Methods & Psychological Assessment; Social Psychology
MSc/PgD/PgC: *PT* Social Research

SCHOOL OF LANGUAGE & INTERNATIONAL STUDIES
MA/PgD: *DL Human Studies:* Linguistics (TESOL) *FT/PT* Russian Language & Society; Translation
MSc/PgD: *DL* English Language Teaching Management
PGCert/PGDip/MA: *FT Human Studies:* European Politics, Business & Law

SCHOOL OF MANAGEMENT FOR THE SERVICE SECTOR
MSc/PgD: *FT* Foundation Yr in Management Studies *FT/PT* Food Management; Health Care Management; Tourism Studies *FT/PT/DL* International Hotel Management; Tourism & Hospitality Education; Tourism Management; Tourism Marketing; Tourism Planning & Development
PGCert/PGDip/MSc: *FT/PT/DL* Leisure, Culture & Tourism Management
PgDip/MSc: *FT/PT* Retail Management

SCHOOL OF MECHANICAL & MATERIALS ENGINEERING
MSc/PgD: *FT/PT* Advanced Manufacturing Management & Technology; Advanced Materials Technology; Biomedical Engineering
MSc/PgD/PgC: *FT/PT* Materials for Engineering Applications

SCHOOL OF PERFORMING ARTS
MA/PgD: *FT/PT* Dance Studies; Physical Theatre (joint with Royal Holloway College)
MA/PGDip: *FT/PT* Performance Practice and Theory
MMus: *FT/PT* Music

SCHOOL OF PHYSICAL SCIENCES
MSc: *FT/PT* Chemical Research
MSc/PgD: *FT* Block Release-Medical Physics *FT/PT* Radiation & Environmental Protection

SURREY EUROPEAN MANAGEMENT SCHOOL
LLM/PGDip: *FT/PT/DL* Law; Law
MBA/PgDip: *FT/PT/DL* Business Administration
MSc/PgD: *FT/PT/DL* Financial Services Management; Human Resource Management; International Business Management; International Management; International Marketing Management; Management; Marketing Management; Operations & Logistics Management
PGCert/PGDip/MSc: *FT/PT/DL* Market Research Management
PgDip/MSc: *FT/PT/DL* Relationship Marketing Management

Degrees validated by University of Surrey offered at:

Farnborough College of Technology

Boundary Road, Farnborough, Hampshire GU14 6SB Tel: 01252 405555 Fax: 01252 407041
e-mail: info@farn-ct.ac.uk

*@First Para:*Notes: Environmental Studies may not be combined with Biology, Drama, Heritage Studies, History, Media Arts, Religious Studies, Sport Rehabilitation or Theology.
* Subject to validation.

First Degrees

BA Hons: *3 yrs FT* Accounting; Business Administration; Leisure Management *3 yrs FT/PT* Accounting; Marketing; Social Science & Social Policy
BEng Hons: *3 yrs FT* Aerospace Engineering
BSc Hons: *3 yrs FT* Aeronautical Engineering; Environmental Protection (Conservation Management); Environmental Protection (Pollution Control); Media Technology; Science and Management of Exercise & Health *3 yrs FT/5 yrs PT* Computing

NESCOT

Reigate Road, Ewell, Epsom, Surrey KT13 3DS Tel: 020 8394 1731 Fax: 020 8394 3030

First Degrees

BSc/BSc Hons: *3 yrs FT* Computer Studies (with a European Option)

Higher Degrees

MSc: *FT/PT* Immunology; Virology

St Mary's, Strawberry Hill

Waldegrave Road, Strawberry Hill, Twickenham TW1 4SX Tel: 020 8240 4000 Fax: 020 8240 4255 e-mail: farrugim@smuc.ac.uk

First Degrees

BA Hons: *3 yrs FT* Drama; English; History; Theology & Religious Studies
BA Hons QTS: *4 yrs FT* Primary Teaching-Biology or Drama or English or Geography or History or Physical Education or Theology & Religious Studies; Secondary Teaching-Physical Education
BA Hons/BSc Hons: *3 yrs FT. 2 subjects from different groups Group 1:* English; Irish Studies *Group 2:* Geography; Heritage Studies; Media Arts; Sport Rehabilitation; Theology & Religious Studies *Group 3:* Biology; Drama; Health and Human Biology; History *Group 4:* Classical Studies; Education Studies; Management Studies; Sociology; Sport Science
BSc Hons: *3 yrs FT* Geography; Sociology; Sport Science

Higher Degrees

MA: *1 yr FT* Heritage Interpretation *PT* Applied Linguistics & English Language Teaching; Catholic Schools Leadership; Education Studies; Linguistics in Education; Religion & Education; Religious History; Theology & Religious Studies
MPhil: (In a range of disciplines)
MSc: *PT* Applied Human Science

DOCTORATES
PhD: (In a range of disciplines)

Diplomas

Diploma: *PT* Applied Human Science; Applied Linguistics & English Language Teaching; Catholic Schools Leadership; Education Studies; Linguistics in Education; Religion & Education; Religious History; Theology & Religious Studies

Certificates

PGCE: *1 yr FT* Primary; Secondary

University of Surrey Roehampton

Senate House, Roehampton Lane, London SW15 5PU Tel: 020 8392 3232 Fax: 020 8392 3478
e-mail: enquiries@roehampton.ac.uk Website: www.roehampton.ac.uk

First Degrees

BA Hons: *3 yrs FT/Up to 7 yrs PT* Art for Community; Art History; Bookbinding; Calligraphy; Childhood & Society; Cultural Studies; Dance Studies; Drama & Theatre Studies; Early Childhood Studies; Education; English as a Foreign Language; English Language & Linguistics; English Literature; Film & TV Studies; History; Humanities; Music; Women's Studies *4 yrs FT* French; Marketing; Modern Languages; Spanish; French-Spanish; Marketing

BA Hons QTS: *4 yrs FT With one of the following Subject Specialisms*

BA/BSc Hons: *3 yrs FT/Up to 7 yrs PT* Art for Community; Art History; Biological Anthropology; Biological Sciences; Biology; Biomedical Sciences; Bookbinding; Business Computing; Business Studies; Calligraphy; Childhood & Society; Psychology-Counselling; Cultural Studies; Dance Studies; Drama & Theatre Studies; Early Childhood Studies; Ecology and Conservation; Education; English as a Foreign Language; English Language & Linguistics; English Literature; Environmental Sciences/Environmental Studies (2nd yr entry); Environmental Studies/Environmental Science; Film & Television Studies; French; Geography; Health & Social Care; Health Studies; History; Human & Social Biology; Human Geography; Human Resource Management; Human Sciences; Humanities; Leisure Management; Marketing; Modern Languages; Music; Natural Resource Studies; Nutrition and Health; Painting and Printmaking; Philosophy; Primary Education; Psychology; Retail Management and Marketing; Science of Sport and Exercise; Social Anthropology; Social Policy & Administration; Social Science of Sport; Sociology; Spanish; Sport & Exercise Studies; Theology & Religious Studies; Women's Studies; Zoology *4 yrs FT* French; Marketing-French; Spanish; Modern Languages; Spanish

BEd Hons: *1 yr FT/2-4 yrs PT* In-service Education

BMus Hons: *3 yrs FT/Up to 7 yrs PT* Music

BSc Hons: *3 yrs FT/Up to 7 yrs PT* Anthropology; Biological Sciences; Biomedical Sciences; Business Computing; Business Studies; Ecology & Conservation; Environmental Studies/Environmental Science; Geography; Health & Social Biology; Health Studies; Human & Social Biology; Human Geography; Human Resource Management; Human Sciences; Leisure Management; Marketing; Natural Resource Studies; Nutrition & Health; Philosophy; Psychology; Psychology & Counselling; Retail Management & Marketing; Science of Sport & Exercise; Social Policy & Administration; Social Science of Sport; Sociology; Sport & Exercise Studies; Zoology

SCHOOL OF ELECTRONIC ENGINEERING, IT & MATHEMATICS
BSc Hons: *3-4 yrs* Mathematics with Business Studies

Higher Degrees

MA/GradDip: *1 yr FT/2-4 yrs PT* Ballet Studies; Biblical & Theological Studies; Children's Literature; Choral Education; Early Childhood Studies; Education Management; Education Studies; English Language and Literacy in Education; Primary and Early Childhood Studies; Shakespeare and Performance *2 yrs PT* Landscape and Culture *PT* Art for Community; Art for the Community; Art, Craft & Design Education; Ballet Studies; Biblical & Theological Studies; Biblical & Theological Studies; Children's Literature; Choral Education; Dance Movement Therapy; Dance Movement Therapy; Drama Therapy; Early Childhood Studies; Education Management; Education Studies; English Language & Literacy in Education; English Literature & Politics 1778-1832; Historical Research; International Service; Literature & Politics 1776-1832; Music Therapy; Play Therapy; Play Therapy; Primary & Early Childhood Studies; Shakespeare and Performance; Sport & Exercise Assessment; Sport Culture & Development; Twentieth Century French Cultural Studies; Twentieth Century French Cultural Studies; Twentieth Century Music; Twentieth Century Music; Women Studies; Women, Gender & Writing

MA/GradDip (Education Studies): *1 yr FT/2-4 yrs PT Combined subjects:* Art, Craft and Design Education; Careers Guidance; Choral Education; Education Studies; Educational Management; English Language & Literacy in Education; Music Education; Primary & Early Childhood Studies; Religious Education; Science, Mathematics and Design Technology Education *2 yrs FT/Up to 4 yrs*

PT or PHD: 3 yrs FT/Up to 6 yrs PT By Research in the following Departments: Early Childhood Studies
MPhil/PhD: *1 yr FT/2 yrs PT* Music *2 yrs FT/Up to 4 yrs PT or PHD: 3 yrs FT/Up to 6 yrs PT By Research in the following Departments:* Art; Art & Play Therapy; Biological Sciences; Dance; Drama & Theatre Studies; Education; English (Literature/Language & Linguistics); Film & TV Studies; Health Studies; History; Life Sciences (various); Modern Languages; Psychology & Counselling; Sociology & Social Policy; Sport Studies; Theology & Religious Studies; Women's Studies
MSc/GradDip: Sociology and Anthropology of Travel and Tourism *1 yr FT/2 yrs PT* Behaviour, Biology & Health; Clinical Neuroscience with Immunology; Clinical Neuroscience; Clinical Nutrition; Clinical Nutrition & Immunology; Counselling Psychology; Diabetes; Ecological Management & Monitoring; Ecology for Sustainable Development; Global Studies; Health Studies; Nutrition; Nutrition, Brain & Behaviour; Psychobiology of Stress & Stress Management; Science-Mathematics; Design & Technology-Education; Sociology and Anthropology of Travel and Tourism; Sport & Exercise Assessment; Sport, Culture & Development *2 yrs PT* Counselling Psychology; Management for Ministry; Psychological Counselling & Psychotherapy; Sport & Exercise Assessment; Strategic Training & Development

Diplomas

Advanced Diploma: *1 yr PT* Changing Women's Lives; Diabetes
Diploma: Fundamentals of Dance Movement Therapy *1 yr PT* Arts Management; Health Research *18 mths PT* Early Childhood Studies; ICT in Primary Education *2 yrs PT* Humanistic Counselling & Psychotherapy; Play Therapy; Psychological Counselling; Supervision in Play Therapy *Up to 4 yrs PT Includes the following Dips:* Counselling in Education; Design & Technology Education; Early Childhood Studies; English & Language Teaching; Mathematics Education; Professional Practice; Science Education; Special Education Needs in Mainstream Schools; Teaching of Music

Certificates

Certificate: *1 yr FT* English for Academic Purposes *1 yr PT* Art & Play in Therapeutic Work with Children; Contemporary Issues in Women's Lives; Drugs: Prevention & Education; Early Childhood Education; ICT in Primary Education; Mental Health & Ethnicity; Psychological Counselling; Sociology (Higher Teaching Certificate) *6 mths PT* Dramatherapy *7 mths PT* Play Therapy
Professional Development Education Programme: *Up to 4 yrs PT Includes the following Cert:* Art Education; Boarding Education-CCP; Boarding Staff (Preparatory Level Certificate); Careers Guidance; Children with Literacy Problems; Children with Literacy Problems (Dyslexia); Classroom Assistant (Foundation); Counselling in Education; Design & Technology Education; Diabetes; Early Childhood Studies; English & Language Teaching; English Teaching – Primary; Information Technology Education; Mathematics Education; Mentoring; Peer Support; Personal, Social & Health Education; Professional Practice; Return to Teaching (Primary or Secondary); Role of SENCO; Science Education; Special Needs Education in Mainstream Schools; Special Teacher Assistant; Studying Women's Lives; Teaching and Learning in Higher Education; Teaching of Music; Women In Society

THE UNIVERSITY OF SUSSEX

Falmer, Brighton BN1 9RH Tel: 01273 606755 Fax: 01273 678335

First Degrees

BEng: *3 yrs* Electronic Engineering and Computer Science; Mechanical Engineering with Business Management
BEng/MEng: *3-4 yrs* Electrical & Electronic Engineering; Mechanical Engineering

ARTS & SOCIAL STUDIES
BA: *3 yrs* Applied Psychology; Artificial Intelligence; Contemporary History; Developmental Psychology; Economic & Social History; Economics; English; English with Development Studies; English Language; Geography; Geography & Environmental Studies with Development Studies; History; History with Development Studies; History of Art; Intellectual History; International

Relations; International Relations with Development Studies; Law with North American Studies; Law; Linguistics; Media Studies; Music; Philosophy; Politics; Politics with Development Studies; Psychology; Social Anthropology; Social Anthropology with Development Studies; Social Policy; Social Psychology; Sociology with Development Studies; Sociology *4 yrs* American Studies (History); American Studies (Literature); American Studies (Social Studies); Economics with French/Maitrise Internationale; French; German; German-Italian or Spanish or Linguistics or Russian; Italian Studies; Politics with North American Studies; Russian & East European Studies; Linguistics; Spanish; Italian *6 yrs PT* Cultural Studies
LLB Hons: *3 yrs/4 yrs* European Commercial Law with a Language; Law

SCIENCE
BA: *3 yrs* Contemporary History with Development Studies; Economics with Development Studies; Economics with Economic and Social History; Economics and Applied Quantitative Methods; Philosophy-Engineering; English-Media Studies; Geography with Development Studies; Geography (with a Language); Geography-Environmental Studies; Economics-International Relations; Music-Media Studies; Philosophy-Economics; Philosophy-International Relations; Philosophy-Politics; Philosophy-Sociology; Economics-Politics; Politics-International Relations; Social Psychology with Sociology; Sociology with Social Psychology *4 yrs* Contemporary History (with a Language); Economic & Social History (with a Language); Economics (with a Language); English (with a Language); English Language (with a Language); European Drama with French with German with Italian; French with Development Studies; French-German; French-Italian; Geography (with a Language); History (with a Language); History of Art (with a Language); Intellectual History (with a Language); International Relations (with a Language); Law (with a Language); Linguistics (with a Language); French-Linguistics; Russian-Linguistics; Media Studies (with a Language); Philosophy (with a Language); Politics (with a Language); French-Russian; Social Anthropology (with a Language); French-Spanish; Russian-Spanish *PT* Landscape Studies
BEng: *3 yrs* Broadcast Engineering; Electromechanical Engineering; Electronic and Communication Engineering with Business Management; Mechatronics; Robotics & Automated Manufacture *4 yrs With Foundation Yr:* Engineering
BEng/MEng: *3-4 yrs* Computer Systems Engineering; Electronic and Communication Engineering
BSc: *3 yrs* Artificial Intelligence with Management Studies; Biochemistry with Management Studies or Neurobiology; Biochemistry; Biology; Biology with Management Studies; Biomolecular Science; Computer Science with Management Studies; Computer Science; Computer Science & Artificial Intelligence; Ecology & Conservation; Environmental Science; Environmental Science with Development Studies or Management Studies; General Engineering; Geography; Geography & Environmental Science; Information Technology Systems; Mathematics & Artificial Intelligence; Mathematics & Computer Science; Mathematics & Economics; Mathematics & Statistics with Computer Science or Economics or Environmental Science or Management Studies; Molecular Genetics in Biotechnology; Multimedia and Digital Systems; Natural Science; Neuroscience; Product Design; Psychology *With Foundation Yr:* Arts, Humanities and Social Sciences *4 yrs* Artificial Intelligence with European Studies; Biochemistry with North American Studies; Biochemistry with European Studies; Biology with North American Studies; Biology with European Studies or North American Studies; Chemistry with English Language Tuition; Chemistry-Law; Computer Science with European Studies; Computing Sciences; Environmental Science with European Studies or North American Studies; Environmental Science (with English Language Tuition); Environmental Science-Law; Human Sciences; Physics-Law; Mathematics (with English Language Tuition); Molecular Genetics with French with German with Spanish; Molecular Sciences; Physical Science; Physics (with English Language Tuition); Psychology with North American Studies *With Foundation Yr:* Biological Science; Mathematics *4 yrs S* Biochemistry with Management Studies; Biochemistry with Neurobiology; Biochemistry; Biomolecular Science; Molecular Genetics in Biotechnology
BSc Hons: *3 yrs* Mathematics & Statistics
BSc/MChem Hons: *3-4 yrs* Chemistry *4 yrs* Chemistry with European Studies or North American Studies
BSc/MMaths: *3-4 yrs* Mathematical Physics; Mathematics with European Studies or North American Studies; Mathematics; Mathematics with Computer Science or Economics or

Environmental Science or Management Studies *4 yrs* Mathematics with European Studies or North American Studies

BSc/MPhys: *3-4 yrs* Physics with Astrophysics or Computational Physics or Electronics & Optoelectronics or Environmental Science or Management Studies or Theoretical Physics; Physics; Theoretical Physics *With Foundation Yr:* Astrophysics *4 yrs* Physics with European Studies or North American Studies; Physics-Maths

Higher Degrees

DLitt; DSc: (Conferred on graduates of some yrs' standing in respect of published work)

LLM: *1 yr FT/2 yrs PT* International Commercial Law; International Criminal Law; Law (Master of Laws)

MA: Children & Young People: Their Personal, Linguistic & Cognitive Development; Education (School Effectiveness); Equality & Social Justice in Organisations; Professional Development; Public Service Management; Special Educational Needs *1 yr FT* Contemporary European Studies; Development Economics; Economics of Education, Health & Social Protection; European Economic Integration; Gender & Development; International Economics *1 yr FT/2 yrs PT* Aesthetics; American History; American Literature & Theory Since 1945; Anthropology of Development & Social Transformation; Anthropology of Europe; Applied Linguistics; Applied Policy Studies; Contemporary History; Contemporary War & Peace Studies; Creative Writing, the Arts & Education; Criminal Justice; Culture, Race, Difference; Digital Media; Early Modern History; Education (Independent Studies); English Literature; Environment, Development & Policy; Global Political Economy; History; History of Art: Europe, Asia & America; Human Geography; Intellectual History & the History of Political Thought; International Education; International Relations; Law, Rhetoric & Power; Life History Research: Oral History & Mass-Observation; Literature & Visual Culture; Literature, Religion & Philosophy; Media Studies; Migration Studies; Modern European Literature; Modern French Thought; Modern German Studies (Berlin & Vienna as Cultural Centres); Modern German Studies (German-Jewish Culture & Politics); Music; Philosophy; Philosophy of Cognitive Science; Psychology; Renaissance Theory & Culture; Rural Development; Russian & East European Studies; Social & Political Thought; Social Welfare Studies; Women's Studies *PT modular* Education; Social Work Studies

MBA: *2 yrs PT* Business Administration (Run jointly with Roffey Park Management College)

MChem: *4 yrs FT* Chemical Physics with European Studies or North American Studies; Chemical Physics *4 yrs FT/S* Chemistry

MChem/BSc: *3-4 yrs* Management Studies; Medicinal Chemistry

MEng: *4 yrs* Automotive Engineering; Robotics, Cybernetics and Process Automation *With Foundation Yr:*

MPhil: *2 yrs FT* Development Studies

MPhys: *4 yrs* Physics

MRes: *1 yr FT* Computer Science & Artificial Intelligence; Psychology

MSc: *1 yr FT* Astronomy; Biochemistry; Biochemistry (Genetic Manipulation & Molecular Biology); Chemistry; Experimental Psychology; Mathematics *1 yr FT/2 yrs PT* Cognitive Psychology; Developmental Psychology; Digital Electronics; Evolutionary & Adaptive Systems; Human Centred Computer Systems; Intelligent Systems; Physics; Plant Biotechnology for Emerging Economies; Science & Technology Policy; Technology & Innovation Management *1 yr PT* Cardiology

MSW: *2 yrs FT* Social Work

Honorary Degrees

DLitt; DSc; LLD; DUniv

Master's degrees may be conferred as Hons degrees

Diplomas

Diploma: Archaeology *2 yrs* Social Work *2 yrs PT* Advocacy & Empowerment; Social & Critical Studies; Theology & Biblical Studies; Women's Studies

Postgraduate Diploma: Arts Management; Contemporary European Studies; Digital Electronics *1 yr FT* Law (or CPE) *1 yr PT* Adult Learning & Life Histories; Cardiology; Continuing Education; Creative Writing & Personal Development *2 trms FT/4 trms PT* Cognitive Psychology;

Developmental Psychology; Evolutionary & Adaptive Systems; Human-Centred Computer Systems; Intelligent Systems; Philosophy of Cognitive Science; Psychology *2 yrs PT* Dramatic Writing; Psychotherapeutic Counselling

Certificates

Certificate: Digital Electronics; Environment, Society & Politics; Field Geology; Modern Drama; Science Studies *1 yr PT* Advocacy & Empowerment; Art History; Arts Management; Creative Writing; Drama; Field Biology; Life History Work; Literature (19th century); Local History; Management Development; Managing Voluntary & Community Organisations; Media Studies; Multimedia: Digital Arts; Multimedia: Screen Design; Music; Practical Archaeology; Renaissance Literature; Teaching Adults with Learning Difficulties & Disabilities; Women's Studies
PGCE: *1 yr FT* Education
Postgraduate Certificate: *1 yr PT* Child Care Decision Making

UNIVERSITY OF TEESSIDE

Middlesbrough TS1 3BA Tel: 01642 218121 Fax: 01642 342067
Website: www.tees.ac.uk

† Subject to approval.

First Degrees

BA Hons: *3 yrs FT* Accounting with Law; Accounting and Finance; Business Management; Cultural Studies; Cultural Studies-English Studies; Design Crafts for the Entertainment Industries; Design Marketing; Direct Marketing; English Studies; English-History; Fine Art; Graphic Design; History; Human Resource Management; Industrial Design; Interior Architecture and Design; International Textiles and Surface Pattern; Leisure Management; Leisure Management (Sport); Leisure Management – Hospitality; Leisure Management – Tourism; Marketing; Marketing and Retail Management; Media Studies; Modern and Contemporary European History; Photography; Public Relations; Social and Cultural History; Social Work Studies; Tourism Management *3 yrs FT/4 yrs S* Computer Animation; Computer Games Design; Creative Visualisation *4 yrs S* Business Studies; International Business Studies
BA/BA Hons: Business Administration – Leisure *2 semesters FT/3 semesters FT/PT HND top-up:* Business Administration; Business Administration – Hospitality
BEng Hons: *3 yrs FT/4 yrs S* Chemical Engineering; Chemical Engineering-Food Technology; Computer Engineering-Microelectronics; Construction Engineering; Design Engineering; Electrical Engineering; Electronic Engineering; Instrumentation and Control Engineering; Mechanical Engineering; Telecommunication and Digital Broadcast Engineering
BSc: *2 yrs FT* BSc Yr 2 Computing (direct entry)
BSc Hons: *3 yrs FT/4 yrs S* Nutrition and Health Sciences*2 semesters FT/3 semesters FT/PT* Nutrition and Health Sciences *3 yrs FT* Applied Science and Forensic Investigation; Business Economics; Consumer Science and Consumer Law; Criminology; Diagnostic Radiography; Economics; Health Sciences; Human Biology with Media Studies; Leisure with Sports Studies; Leisure with Heritage Studies; Leisure; Leisure, Tourism and Heritage; Leisure with Multimedia; Occupational Therapy; Physiotherapy; Psychology; Psychology and Criminology; Psychology-Counselling; Social Sciences; Social Work/Learning Disabilities; Sociology; Sport and Exercise (Applied Sports Science); Sport and Exercise (Coaching Science); Sport and Exercise (Exercise Science); Youth Studies *3 yrs FT/4 yrs S* Biomedical Engineering; Biotechnology; Chemical and Medicinal Science; Chemical Technology; Chemistry; Computer Studies; Computer-Aided Design Engineering; Food Science and Nutrition; Food Technology; General Engineering; Information Society; Interactive Computer Entertainment; Media Production; Media Technology; Microbiology; Multimedia; Sport and Exercise (Sports Studies); Sports Therapy; Virtual Reality; Visualisation; Work Psychology *4 yrs S* Business Computing; Computer Science; Informatics; Information Technology; Software Engineering *78 wks FT* Midwifery
BSc/BSc Hons: *2 semesters FT/3 semesters FT/PT* Business Informatics
LLB: *3 yrs FT* Law

COMBINED HONOURS SCHEME

BA Hons: *3 yrs FT Arts & Humanities:* Cultural Studies with Business Studies or French or German or Heritage Studies† or History or Media Studies† or Multimedia or Politics; English with Business Studies or French or German or Heritage Studies† or History or Law or Media Studies† or Multimedia or Politics; History with Business Studies or Cultural Studies or English or French or German or Heritage Studies† or Law or Media Studies† or Multimedia or Politics *Business, Management and Marketing:* Accounting with Information Technology or Law or Marketing or Multimedia or Sport and Exercise; Business Studies with French or German or Information Technology or Law or Media Studies† or Multimedia; Human Resource Management with Marketing or Multimedia† *Media and Contemporary Communications:* Graphic Design with Media Studies† or Multimedia; Media Studies with Business Studies† or Criminology† or Cultural Studies† or English† or French† or German† or Heritage Studies† or Information Technology† or Media Production† or Media Technology† or Multimedia† or Sociology† or Writing for the Media† *Social Sciences and Law:* Cultural Studies with Media Studies† or Multimedia or History; Law with Business Studies or Criminology or French or German or Heritage Studies† or Information Technology or Media Studies† or Multimedia or Psychology or Social Policy or Sociology

BSc Hons: *3 yrs FT Engineering:* Chemical Systems Engineering with Business Studies or French or German or Information Technology or Law; Electronic Systems Engineering with Business Studies or French or German or Information Technology or Law; Material Systems Engineering with Business Studies or French or German or Information Technology or Law *Forensic Investigation:* Forensic Investigation with Criminology† or Law† or Psychology† *Heritage, Leisure, Sport and Tourism:* Leisure with Criminology or Economics or Heritage Studies† or Media Studies† or Multimedia or Politics or Psychology or Sociology or Sports Studies or Youth Studies† with Business Studies; Sport and Exercise (Applied Sport Science) or Psychology; Sport and Exercise (Coaching Science) with Business Studies or Psychology or Psychology; Sport and Exercise (Exercise Science) with Business Studies or Psychology or Sport and Exercise (Sports Studies) with Psychology *Media and Contemporary Communications:* Media Production with Media Studies† or Media Technology; Media Technology with Media Production or Media Studies†; Multimedia with Media Studies† *Psychology:* Psychology with Business Studies or Information Technology or Law or Multimedia or Sociology or Sport and Exercise *Social Sciences and Law:* Criminology with Law or Media Studies† or Politics or Psychology or Social Policy or Sociology or Sport and Exercise; Economics with Business Studies or Multimedia or Politics; Sociology with Criminology or Information Technology or Media Studies† or Psychology

JOINT HONOURS SCHEME

BA Hons: *3 yrs FT Arts & Humanities:* Cultural Studies and English; English and History
BSc Hons: *3 yrs FT Psychology:* Psychology and Counselling† or Criminology

SINGLE HONOURS

BA Hons: *3 yrs FT Heritage, Leisure, Sport and Tourism:* Heritage and Media†; Leisure Management; Leisure Management (Hospitality); Leisure Management (Sport); Leisure Management (Tourism); Tourism Management† *Media and Contemporary Communications:* Graphic Design; Heritage and Media†; Media Studies

BSc Hons: *3 yrs FT Heritage, Leisure, Sport and Tourism:* Leisure, Tourism and Heritage†; Sport and Exercise (Applied Sport Science); Sport and Exercise (Coaching Science); Sport and Exercise (Exercise Science); Sport and Exercise (Sports Studies) *Media and Contemporary Communications:* Computer Animation; Information Technology; Media Production; Media Technology; Multimedia

Higher Degrees

DClinPsy: *3 yrs* Clinical Psychology
MA: Computer Animation; Creative Multimedia; Human Resource Management
MBA: Master of Business Administration
MSc: Advanced Manufacturing Systems; Analytical Chemistry; Biotechnology; Chemical Engineering; Clean Manufacturing Technology; Computer-Aided Graphical Technology Applications; Computing; Digital Systems Technologies; Enterprise Management; Food

Technology; Forensic Psychology; Graduate Enterprise in Multimedia (GEM); Information Technology; International Management; Learning Technologies; Multimedia Applications; Process Manufacturing Management; Rehabilitation Science (with licence to practice Physiotherapy); Social Research Methods; Sport and Exercise Science; Sustainable Engineering; Virtual Reality

Diplomas

DipHE: Social Work
Diploma: *3 yrs FT* Diploma in Nursing
Foundation yr: *1 yr FT* Social Sciences *Undergraduate Diploma:* Extended Computing; Extended Engineering; Extended Science
HND: Building Studies; Built Environment; Business and Administration; Business and Travel and Tourism; Business Information Technology or Hospitality; Business-Finance or Human Resource Management or Leisure or Marketing; Chemical Engineering; Chemistry; Civil Engineering Studies; Computer and Communications Engineering; Computer Animation; Computer Studies; Computer-Aided Design Engineering; Computer-Aided Product Design; Computing (Information Technology); Computing (Software Development); Computing (Software Development); Construction Studies; Creative Digital Imaging; Electrical & Electronic Engineering; Electrical Engineering; Electronic Engineering; Fabrication and Welding; Instrumentation and Control Engineering; Manufacturing Engineering; Mechanical and Production Engineering; Mechanical Engineering; Mechatronics; Media Technology; Motor Vehicle Management; Motor Vehicle Technical Management; Multimedia; Music Technology; Process Technology; Public Administration; Service Sector Management; Sports Studies; Sustainable Resource Management
Postgraduate Diploma: *2 semesters FT* Human Resource Management

Degrees validated by University of Teesside offered at:

THAMES VALLEY UNIVERSITY

St. Marys Road, Ealing, London W5 5RF Tel: 020 8579 2056 Fax: 020 8231 2056
e-mail: learning.advice@tvu.ac.uk Website: www.tuv.ac.uk/

Slough Campus: Wellington Street, Slough, Berkshire SL1 1YG Tel: 01753 534585
Fax: 01753 574264 Wolfson School of Health Sciences: 32-38 Uxbridge Road, Ealing W5 2BS
Tel: 0181 280 5261 Fax: 0181 280 5137

London College of Music and Media: St Mary's Road, London W5 5RF Tel: 020 8579 5000
Fax: 0181 566 2546

First Degrees

BA: *3 yrs FT* Accountancy-Business Finance; Accounting with Business or Finance or Information Systems or Law; Advertising with Business or Digital Arts or Languages or Marketing or Media Studies or Multimedia Computing or Photography or Radio Broadcasting or Sound & Music Recording; Design for Interactive Media with Advertising or Animation or Digital Arts or Film & Television Studies or Media Studies or Journalism or Photography or Radio Broadcasting; Digital Arts with Advertising or Digital Animation* or Languages or Multimedia Computing or Photography or Radio Broadcasting or Sound & Music Recording or Video Production; E-Business; Entrepreneurship; Human Resource Management with Marketing or Psychology or Business; New Media Journalism with Advertising or Business or Digital Arts or Film & Television Studies or Finance or Languages or Law or Media Studies or Multimedia Computing or Photography or Psychology or Radio Broadcasting or Sound & Music Recording or Video Production; Marketing with Advertising or Business or Languages or Media Studies or Psychology; Marketing*; Media Arts with Advertising or Business or Digital Animation* or Digital Arts or Film & Television Studies* or Journalism or Languages or Marketing or Multimedia Computing or Photography or Radio Broadcasting or Sound & Music Recording or

Video Production; Music Technology; Sport, Health & Fitness Management *3 yrs FT/PT* Law with Business; Psychology with Business or Advertising *3-4 yrs FT/3-4 yrs PT* Business Studies; Accounting; Advertising; Entrepreneurship; Human Resource Management; Information Systems; New Media Journalism; Languages; Law; Marketing; Operations Management*; Hospitality Management; Catering & Food Management; Hotel Management; Human Resource Management; Information Systems; Tourism Management; Leisure Management; Media Studies *Flexible* Accounting-Business Finance (Open Learning)
BA/BA Hons: *3-4 yrs FT/3-4 yrs PT* Leisure Management
BSc: *2-4 yrs PT* Community Practice *2-5 yrs OL* Health Studies; Professional Studies – Nursing (wound care) *2-5 yrs PT* Substance Use & Mis-use Studies; Professional Studies – Midwifery; Mental Health Nursing; Child Health Nursing *2-5 yrs PT/OL* Professional Studies – Nursing; Palliative Care/Cancer Care – Marie Curie *3 yrs FT* Media Technology; Midwifery; Multimedia Computing with Digital Animation* or Digital Arts or Information Systems or Photography or Sound & Music Recording or Video Production or Advertising or Languages or Media Studies; New Media Journalism with Advertising or Business or Digital Arts or Film & Television Studies or Finance or Languages or Law or Media Studies or Multimedia Computing or Photography or Psychology or Radio Broadcasting or Sound & Music Recording or Video Production; Nursing – Pre-registration (Adult); Psychology with Counselling Theory; Web & E-Business Computing *3 yrs FT/PT* Health-Community Psychology *3 yrs FT/PT/OL* Information Systems; Information Systems with Accounting or Business or Multimedia Computing *3 yrs PT* Culinary Arts (Kitchen and Larder); Culinary Arts (Pastry) *3-5 yrs FT/PT* Psychology *3-5 yrs PT/OL* Health Promotion *3-7 yrs PT* Health & Social Care for Older People
LLB: *3 yrs FT/PT* Law

Higher Degrees

BMus: *3 yrs FT* Performance/Composition; Popular Music Performance (Guitar, Bass Guitar, Drums, Vocals)
MA: *1 yr FT* Computer Arts; Media *1 yr FT/2 yrs PT* Film & the Moving Image; Human Resource Management *1 yr FT/36 mths PT* Hospitality Management; Leisure Management; Tourism Management *1 yr OL* Marketing *1 yr PT* Counselling *1-5 yrs PT* Collaborative Leadership *2 yrs PT* Computer Arts; Media *2-3 yrs FT* Information Management *2-3 yrs PT* Management & IT *2-5 yrs OL* Midwifery Practice *2-5 yrs PT* Information Management *3-5 yrs PT* Learning and Teaching in Healthcare *30 mths FT/1 yr PT* Professional Practice *30 mths PT* Food Policy
MBA: *1 yr FT/2 yrs PT* MBA (Graduate programme); MBA (Executive programme)
MMus: *1 yr FT/2 yrs PT* Composing Concert Music; Composing for Film & Television; Composing for New Media; Composing for the Theatre; Performance
MSc: *(8 modules above L1) 1 yr FT/2 yrs PT* Executive Development *1 yr PT* Strategic Accounting & Finance (ACCA Stream); Strategic Accounting & Finance (CIMA Stream) *1-2 yrs FT/PT* Corporate Communications *15 mths FT/27 mths PT* Finance-Administration *2 yrs PT* Multimedia Computing *2-3 yrs FT/2-5 yrs PT* Information Management *2-3 yrs PT* Information Systems *3-5 yrs PT* Advancing Nursing Practice

Diplomas

Advanced Diploma: *2 yrs PT* International Culinary Arts (Kitchen & Larder); International Culinary Arts (Pastry)
BTEC: *2 yrs FT* Hospitality with Tourism (National Diploma)
DipHE: *2 yrs FT* Advertising with Business or Digital Arts or New Media Journalism or Languages or Marketing or Media Studies or Multimedia Computing or Photography or Radio Broadcasting or Sound & Music Recording or Video Production; Design for Interactive Media* with Advertising or Animation or Digital Arts or Film & Television Studies or Media Studies or New Journalism or Photography or Radio Broadcasting; Digital Arts with Advertising or Digital Animation* or Languages or Multimedia Computing or Photography or Radio Broadcasting or Sound & Music Recording or Video Production; Human Resource Management with Business or Marketing or Psychology; Information Systems; New Media Journalism with Advertising or Business or Digital Arts or Film & Television Studies or Finance or Languages or Law or Media

Studies or Multimedia Computing or Photography or Psychology or Radio Broadcasting or Sound & Music Recording or Video Production; Marketing; Marketing with Advertising or Business or Languages or Media Studies or Psychology; Media Arts with Advertising or Business or Digital Animation* or Digital Arts or Film and Television Studies* or New Media Journalism or Languages or Marketing or Multimedia Computing or Photography or Radio Broadcasting or Sound & Music Recording or Video Production; Media Technology; Multimedia Computing with Advertising or Digital Animation* or Digital Arts or Information Systems or Languages or Photography or Sound & Music Recording or Video Production or Media Studies; Music Technology; Performance Composition; Popular Music Performance (Guitar, Bass Guitar, Drums, Vocals); Psychology with Counselling Theory; Sport, Health and Fitness Management* *2 yrs FT/PT* Languages with Law or Marketing or Operations Management*; Business Studies with Accounting or Advertising or Finance or Human Resource Management or Information Systems or Journalism*; Business Studies; Health & Community Psychology; Law with Business; Law; Psychology with Business or Advertising *2 yrs OL* Accounting *2 yrs FT/PT/OL* Information Systems; Business; Multimedia Computing *2-5 yrs OL* Health Studies *2-5 yrs PT* Professional Studies – Nursing (wound care) *2-7 yrs PT/OL* Health & Social Care for Older People *3 yrs FT* Accounting with Business or Finance or Information Systems or Law *3-5 yrs OL* Health Promotion **HND:** *2 yrs FT* Business-Accounting*; Business-Human Resource Management*; Business-Marketing*; Business-Operations Management*; Media Technology *2 yrs FT/PT* Business; Business Information Technology; Computing; Culinary Arts Management *2-3 yrs FT/2-3 yrs PT* Hospitality-Hotel Management; Hospitality-Tourism Management; Hospitality, Catering & Food Management; Leisure Management; Travel & Tourism Management

Certificates

Advanced Certificate: *2 yrs PT* Purchasing & Supply
BTEC: *2 yrs FT* Sports & Health Club Operations *2 yrs PT* Food Science & Technology for the Food Industry (National Certificate)
CertHE: *1 yr FT* Sport, Health & Fitness Management
Certificate: *1 yr PT* Management *2 yrs PT* Purchasing & Supply
6S00146TNVQs
NVQ: *1 yr PT* Certificate in Management Skills (NVQ 3) *1-2 yrs OL* Administration (NVQ 1, 2 & 3) *1-2 yrs PT* Housekeeping (NVQ 1 & 2); Supervisory Management (NVQ 3); Management Standards (NVQ 4); Asian Culinary Arts (NVQ 2 & 3); Customer Service (NVQ 2 & 3); Reception (NVQ 2); Food & Drink Service (NVQ 2 & 3); Food Preparation & Cooking (NVQ 2 & 3); Kitchen & Larder (NVQ 3); Patisserie & Confectionery (NVQ 3); Advanced Diploma in International Culinary Arts (NVQ 4) *1-2 yrs PT/OL* Customer Service (NVQ 2 & 3) *12-18 mths PT* Care (NVQ 3) *2 yrs PT* Operating Department (NVQ 3) *2-3 yrs DL* Business Administration (NVQ 3 & 4); Customer Service (NVQ 3 & 4); Procurement (NVQ 3 & 4) *2-3 yrs PT* Management (NVQ 3, 4 & 5) *6-12 mths PT* Care (NVQ 2) *9 mths DL* Training & Development (NVQ 3, 4 & 5) *PT* National Examination Board in Occupational Safety & Health (NVQ 3)

POSTGRADUATE CERTIFICATES

PGCert: *(4 modules above L1) Combined with 8 in Major 1 yr OL* Advanced Certificate in Marketing (CIM); Certificate in Marketing (CIM) *1 yr PT* Advanced Certificate in Marketing (CIM); Certificate in Marketing (CIM); Certificate in Personnel Practice; Further and Adult Education Teacher's Certificate; Teaching and Learning in Further and Higher Education *1-5 yrs PT* Collaborative Leadership *12 mths PT* Certificate in Counselling (pre-practitioner) *2 yrs PT* Certificate for Accounting Technicians (CAT); Hotel & Catering International Management Association Certificate *3-4 yrs PT* Institute of Credit Management Certificate *9 mths OL* Certificate in Training Practice *Variable FT/PT* Certificate in Personnel & Professional Development

Postgraduate Diplomas

PGDip: *(12 modules in L1) 2 or more thematically related 1 yr FT* Legal Practice *1 yr FT/2 yrs PT* Film & the Moving Image; Law (CPE) *1 yr FT/24 mths PT* Food Policy *1 yr PT/OL* Diploma in Marketing (CIM) *1-5 yrs PT* Collaborative Leadership *12 mths OL* Flexible Learning Delivery *12-18 mths OL/9* *mths FT/24 mths PT* University Diploma in Personnel Management *9 mths FT/18 mths PT* Performance *2 yrs PT* Counselling (BAC course accredited) *2-3 yrs FT/2-5 yrs PT* Information Management; Higher Education in Complementary Medicine *9 mths FT/21 mths PT* Hospitality Management; Leisure Management; Tourism Management *24-27 mths OL* Learning and Development *3-5 yrs PT* Advancing Nursing Practice; Learning and Teaching in Healthcare

Professional Courses

Professional Courses: *1-2 yrs PT/3 yrs OL* Chartered Institute of Purchasing & Supply (CIMA) *1-4 yrs PT* Chartered Institute of Management Accountants programme (CIMA) *2-3 yrs OL* Euro Diploma in Purchasing & Supply Management *3 yrs FT/4 yrs PT/3-4 yrs DL* Association of Chartered Certified Accountants (ACCA)

UNIVERSITY OF ULSTER

University House, Coleraine, Co Londonderry BT52 1SA Tel: 028 70344141 Fax: 028 70324697
† Subject to validation.

First Degrees

FACULTY OF ART, DESIGN & HUMANITIES
BA: *3 yrs FT* Irish Studies
BA Hons: *3 yrs FT* English; International Studies; Irish History & Politics; Irish Studies; Media Studies; Modern & Contemporary History; Peace & Conflict Studies; Philosophy; Theatre Studies*3-4 yrs FT* Combined Studies in Art & Design; Design; Fine & Applied Arts; Modern Studies in the Humanities; Textiles & Fashion Design; Visual Communication *4 yrs FT* Applied Languages; International Business Communication
BA Hons Humanities Combined: *3-4 yrs FT Two Subjects:* English; European Studies; French; Geography; German; History; Irish; Japanese Studies; Media Studies; Philosophy; Spanish; Theatre Studies
BMus Hons: *3 yrs FT* Music
BSc Hons: *3-4 yrs FT/4 mths FT/24 mths PT* Technology & Design

FACULTY OF BUSINESS & MANAGEMENT
BA Hons: *3 yrs FT* Retail Management *3-4 yrs FT* Business Finance & Investment; Business Studies with Computing; Consumer Studies; Economics & Government; Law & Economics *3-4 yrs FT/3-7 yrs PT* Accounting *3-4 yrs/Variable PT* Government & Law; Business Studies (with Specialisms) *4 yrs FT* Economics; International Business Studies; Hospitality Management *4 yrs FT/Variable PT* Hospitality Management; Hotel & Tourism Management *4 yrs/Variable PT* Business Studies Public Policy & Management
BSc Hons: Sport, Exercise & Leisure

FACULTY OF ENGINEERING
BEng Hons: *4 yrs FT* Manufacturing Systems Management; Engineering *4-7 yrs PT* Engineering
BEng/BEng Hons: *3 yrs FT* Mechanical Engineering *4 yrs FT* Electronics & Computing *4 yrs PT* Civil Engineering
BEng/MEng Hons: *4-5 yrs* Electronic Systems
BSc Hons: *3-4 yrs FT* Technology & Design *4 mths FT/24 mths PT 4 yrs FT* Biomedical Engineering; Engineering with Business; Environmental Engineering; Environmental Health; Transportation *4 yrs FT/5 yrs PT* Architectural Technology & Management *4 yrs FT/6 yrs PT* Biomedical Engineering; Surveying; Specialisms *4 yrs FT Variable PT* Building Engineering & Management
BSc/BSc Hons: *3-4 yrs* Building Engineering & Management

FACULTY OF INFORMATICS
BEng/MEng: *4 yrs FT/5 yrs S* Software Engineering
BSc Hons: *4 yrs FT* Interactive Multimedia Design *4 yrs FT/5 yrs S* Computing with Enterprise Studies or Marketing with Linguistics; Computing
BSc/BSc Hons: *4 yrs FT* Computing Science; Mathematics, Statistics & Computing

FACULTY OF SCIENCE
BSc: *3 yrs FT* Environmental Science; Geography
BSc Hons: *3 yrs FT* Optometry *4 yrs FT* Biotechnology; Clinical Science; Radiography *4 yrs FT/S* Applied Biochemical Sciences; Biological Sciences; Biomedical Sciences; Environmental Science; Food Technology Management; Geography; Human Nutrition *Variable PT* Applied Chemical Sciences; Life Sciences

FACULTY OF SOCIAL & HEALTH SCIENCES & EDUCATION
BA/BSc Hons: *3 yrs FT* Combined Studies
BSc: *3-4 yrs FT* Community Youth Work
BSc Hons: *2 yrs FT/3-5 yrs PT* Professional Development *2 yrs FT/5 yrs PT* Combined Social Policy *2 yrs FT/6 yrs PT* Communications Studies *3 yrs FT* Linguistic Science *3 yrs FT/5 yrs PT* Organisational Science; Psychology *3 yrs FT Variable PT* Nursing (Professional Development); Sociology *3-4 yrs FT* Social Administration & Policy; Social Psychology; Social Psychology & Sociology *4 yrs FT* Applied Psychology; Communication, Advertising & Marketing; Housing; Nursing; Occupational Therapy; Physiotherapy; Social Work; Speech & Language Therapy *5 yrs PT* Health Sciences *Variable PT* Professional Development in Nursing with Specialist Options

Higher Degrees
DOCTORATES
DEng: *FT/PT* Engineering
DLitt; DSc: (Open to graduates or members of University staff, six yrs after first degree, or in the case of members of staff who are not graduates of the University, not less than six yrs after taking up appointment; by thesis or in respect of published work)
DMedSc: *FT/PT* Medical Science
DNSc: *FT/PT* Nursing Science / Midwifery Science
DPhil: *3 yrs FT/5 yrs PT* (By research, thesis and oral exam)
DPhil by Published Work: *1 yr* (Open to candidates who have an academic association with the University. Short thesis, published work and oral exam)
EdD: *3 yrs FT/5 yrs PT* Education
PhD: Biological Science *FT/PT* Environmental Science; Informatics; Management

MASTER'S DEGREES
LLM: *1 yr FT/2 yrs PT* European Law & Policy
MA: Tourism Management *2 yrs FT* European Business *FT* Accounting; Peace & Conflict Studies *FT/PT* Administration & Law; Anglo-Irish Literature; Applied Arts; Applied Languages & Business; English Poetry; Fine Art; Hospitality Management; Marketing; Media Studies; Newspaper Journalism; Teaching English to Speakers of other Languages; Textile Design; Tourism Management *PT* American Studies; Business Strategy; History; Human Resource Management; Journalism Studies; Modern French Studies; Newspaper Journalism; Twentieth Century Music
MA/PGDip: Applied Languages & Business; English Poetry; Irish History & Politics
MBA: *1 yr FT/2-3 yrs PT* Business Administration *3 yrs PT* Business Administration with Specialisms
MFA: *2 yrs FT/3-4 yrs PT* Fine Art
MRes: *1 yr FT* Research
MSc: Communications & Public Affairs; Industrial Practice; Technology *1 yr FT* International Business *1 yr FT/2 yrs PT* Computing & Information Systems; European Law & Policy *1 yr FT/PT* Computing & Design *2 yrs PT* Executive Leadership *FT* Communication, Public Relations & Advertising; Energy Technology; Food Biotechnology; Information Systems Management; Social Work *FT/PT* Advanced Nursing / Midwifery; Applied Psychology; Biomedical Sciences; Biotechnology; Coastal Zone Management; Construction & Project Management; Ecotoxicology; Electronics & Signal Processing; Electronics & Software Systems; Environmental Business Administration; Environmental Management; Finance & Investment; Health Promotion; Hotel & Catering Management; Human Nutrition; Manufacturing Management; Medical Science; Renewable Energy; Sport, Exercise & Leisure; Toxicology; Water Resource Management; Women's Studies *PT* Advanced Social Work; Biological Sciences; Education & Contemporary Society; Education Management; Environmental Health Protection & Safety; Expert Teaching; Fire Safety

Engineering; Guidance & Counselling; Industrial Practice; Manufacturing Management; Manufacturing Technology Design & Management; Marketing Studies; Prescribing Science; Professional Development in the Community; Property Development; Social Administration & Policy; Social Research Methods

MSc/PGDip: Biomedical Engineering; Human Nutrition & Dietetics; International Business; Marketing Studies; Physiotherapy; Primary Healthcare & General Practice

Diplomas

DipHE: *FT* Accounting; Combined Studies in Art & Design; Design; Fine & Applied Arts; Hospitality Management; Irish Studies; Social Work; Technology & Design; Textiles & Fashion Design; Visual Communication

Diploma: *2 yrs PT* Combined Social & Behavioural Sciences; Community Development & Education; Counselling

PGDip: Coastal Zone Management; Ecotoxicology; Education for Nurses, Midwives & Health Visitors; Energy Technology; Environmental Business Administration; European Law & Policy; Management Studies; Marketing; Medical Science; Renewable Energy; Water Resource Management

Postgraduate Diploma: *1 yr FT* Applied Languages & Business; Business Administration; Communications, Publications & Advertising; European Business; Toxicology *1 yr FT/PT* Biotechnology; Computing & Design; Environmental Management; Food Biotechnology; Teaching English to Speakers of Other Languages *FT* Accounting; Advanced Accounting; Information Systems Management; Newspaper Journalism; Peace & Conflict Studies; Social Work *FT/PT* Administration & Law; Advanced Nursing/Midwifery; Anglo-Irish Literature; Applied Arts; Biomedical Sciences; Coastal Zone Management; Computing & Information Systems; Construction & Project Management; Ecotoxicology; Electronic and Software Sytstems; Electronics & Signal Processing; Energy Technology; English Poetry; Environmental Business Administration; Fine Arts; Health Promotion; Hospitality Management; Human Nutrition with Specialisms; Management Studies; Marketing; Media Studies; Medical Studies; Rehabilitation Science; Renewable Energy; Sport, Exercise & Leisure; Textile Design; Tourism Management; Women's Studies *PT* American Studies; Biological Sciences; Business Strategy; Cultural Management; Education in Contemporary Society; Education Management; Environmental Health Protection & Safety; Fire Safety Engineering; Further & Higher Education; Guidance & Counselling; History; Housing; Human Resource Management; Industrial Practice; Journalism Studies; Manufacturing Management; Manufacturing Technology Design & Management; Modern French Studies; Prescribing Science; Professional Development in the Community; Property Development; Social Administration & Policy; Social Research Methods; Twentieth Century Music

Certificates

Certificate: *PT* Foundation Studies for Mature Students; Foundation Studies in Music

PGCert: Education (Primary Education); Professional & Management Development for Women

Postgraduate Certificate: *FT* Education *FT/PT* Biomedical Sciences; Construction & Project Management *PT* Business Strategy; Community Nursing; Education in Contemporary Society; Education Management; Environmental Health Management; Expert Teaching; Fire Safety Engineering; Further & Higher Education; Guidance & Counselling; Management; Management Studies; Property Development; Specialist Nursing Practice; Specialist Nursing Practice; Workplace Health & Safety Management

UNIVERSITY OF WALES
Cardiff University

Academic Registry, PO Box 927, Cardiff CF10 3UA Tel: 029 20874404 Fax: 029 20874130 e-mail: admissions@cf.ac.uk Website: www.cardiff.ac.uk

MPhil and PhD research degrees are available in each department; LLM by research is available in the Department of Law. LLM, MA, MBA, MEd, MRes, MSc and MScEcon are taught degrees, normally assessed by examination and dissertation.

All students study modules in their 1st yr, the total value of which will be 120 credit points. Foundation yr for overseas students who wish to study Arts & Social Studies, and candidates with inappropriate qualifications who wish to study Sciences.

† Subject to validation.

† Taken with Business Studies or Computer Studies or Legal Studies.

* With first 2 yrs spent at an associated institution.

** Candidates need not decide until the end of the 1st yr which combinations they wish to take to degree level.

First Degrees

BA Hons: *3 yrs* Ancient & Medieval History; Ancient History; Applied Psychology; Archaeology; Archaeology & Ancient History; Archaeology & Medieval History; Communication; Education; English Language Studies; English Literature; History; History & Welsh History; History of Ideas & Philosophy; Journalism, Film & Broadcasting; Language & Communication; Medieval Studies; Music; Philosophy; Psychology; Religious and Theological Studies; Welsh *4 yrs* French; German; Italian; Spanish

BA Joint Hons: *3 yrs (4 yrs if studying a modern foreign language):* Ancient History-German or Education or English Literature or French or History of Ideas or Italian or History or Philosophy or Cultural Criticism or Religious Studies or Social Philosophy & Applied Ethics or Sociology or Spanish or Welsh or Welsh History; Cultural Criticism-Archaeology or English Literature or History of Ideas or Welsh History or Music or Philosophy or Sociology or Religious Studies or Welsh or Italian or Language Studies or German or French or Ancient History or Spanish; Economics-Education or French or German or History or History of Ideas or Italian or Philosophy or Social Philosophy & Applied Ethics or Spanish or Welsh or Welsh History or History or Social Philosophy & Applied Ethics; English Literature-Welsh History or Welsh or Spanish or Religious Studies or Psychology or Philosophy or Music or Language Studies or Italian or History of Ideas or German or French or Education or Cultural Criticism or Archaeology or Ancient History; German-Ancient History or Archaeology or Computing or Economics or Education or English Literature or French or History or History of Ideas or Italian or Japanese or Language Studies or Cultural Criticism or Music or Politics or Pure Mathematics or Religious Studies or Sociology or Spanish or Welsh or Italian; History of Ideas-Welsh History or Spanish or Sociology or Social Philosophy & Applied Ethics or Religious Studies or Politics or Philosophy or History or German or French or English Literature or Education or Economics or Cultural Criticism or Archaeology or Ancient History or Philosophy; History-Welsh or Spanish or Sociology or Social Philosophy & Applied Ethics or Religious Studies or Music or Italian or History of Ideas or German or French or English Literature or Economics or Archaeology or Ancient History or Economics or Cultural Criticism or Archaeology or Ancient History or Politics; Italian-Welsh or Spanish or Sociology or Religious Studies or Philosophy or Music or Language Studies or Japanese or History of Ideas or History or German or French or English Literature or Education; Japanese-French or German or Italian or Spanish or Welsh or Sociology or Social Philosophy & Applied Ethics or Pure Mathematics or Politics or Philosophy or Music or Language Studies or History of Ideas or History or English Literature or Education or Economics or Cultural Criticism or Archaeology or Ancient History; Japanese-Spanish or Italian or German or French; Journalism, Film & Broadcasting-Sociology or Social Policy; Language Studies-Education or English Literature or French or German or Italian or Philosophy or Portuguese or Spanish or Welsh or Welsh History or Social Philosophy & Applied Ethics or Religious Studies or Pure Mathematics or Psychology or Music or History of Ideas or Economics or Archaeology or Ancient History; Language Studies-Welsh or Spanish or Philosophy or Italian or German or French or English Literature or Education or Cultural Criticism or German; Music-Welsh or Sociology or Social Philosophy & Applied Ethics or Religious Studies or Pure Mathematics or Philosophy or Italian or History or French or English Literature or Education or Cultural Criticism or History or English Literature or Education or Economics or Cultural Criticism or Archaeology or Ancient History or French; Philosophy-Welsh History or Welsh or Sociology or Spanish or Religious Studies or Pure Mathematics or Psychology or Politics or Music or Language Studies or Italian or History of Ideas; Politics-Welsh or Spanish or Social Philosophy & Applied Ethics or Religious Studies or Philosophy or Italian or History of Ideas or German or French or Education; Psychology and Philosophy or English Literature or Education; Pure Mathematics-Welsh or Religious Studies or Philosophy or Music or German or

French or Education; Religious Studies-Welsh History or Spanish or Sociology or Social Philosophy & Ethics or Pure Mathematics or Politics or Music or Philosophy or Italian or History of Ideas or History or German or English Literature or Education or Cultural Criticism or Archaeology or Ancient History or Welsh or History; Social Philosophy & Applied Ethics-Welsh History or Spanish or Sociology or Religious Studies or Politics or Music or History of Ideas or French or English Literature or Education or Economics or Archaeology or Ancient History; Social Policy and Journalism, Film & Broadcasting; Spanish or Sociology or Religious Studies or Politics or Language Studies or Italian or History of Ideas or French or English Literature or Education or Economics or Cultural Criticism or History or Politics; Spanish-Welsh or Sociology or Social Philosophy & Applied Ethics or Religious Studies or Philosophy or Language Studies or Japanese or Italian or History of Ideas or German or French or English Literature or Education or Economics or Cultural Criticism or Ancient History; Welsh History-Cultural Criticism or Welsh or Sociology or Religious Studies or Social Philosophy & Applied Ethics or History of Ideas or Education or Economics or English Literature or Archaeology or Ancient History or Religious Studies; Welsh History or Welsh or Spanish; Sociology or Social Philosophy & Applied Ethics or Philosophy or Music or Journalism, Film & Broadcasting or Italian or History of Ideas or History or German or French or Cultural Criticism or Archaeology or Ancient History or German; Welsh or Sociology or Social Philosophy & Applied Ethics; Archaeology or Spanish or Religious Studies or Welsh History or Italian or History of Ideas or History or French or English Literature or Education or Cultural Criticism or Philosophy or Sociology; Welsh-Welsh History or Spanish or Religious Studies or Pure Mathematics or Politics or Philosophy or Music or Language Studies or Italian or History or German or French or English Literature or Education or Economics or Cultural Criticism or Archaeology or Ancient History

BD Hons: *3 yrs* Theology

BEd Hons: *PT* Vocational Training

BEng: *4 yrs FT* Electrical & Electronic Engineering; Electronics; Manufacturing Engineering; Mechanical Engineering

BEng Hons: *3 yrs* Computer Systems Engineering; Environmental Engineering; Manufacturing Engineering; Medical Engineering *3 yrs FT/4 yrs S* Architectural Engineering; Civil & Environmental Engineering; Civil Engineering; Electrical & Electronic Engineering; Electronic Engineering; Integrated Engineering; Mechanical Engineering

BEng/MEng Hons: *4 yrs FT/5 yrs S* Mechanical Engineering

BMus Hons: *3 yrs* Music

BSc: *5 yrs* City & Regional Planning

BSc (Econ) Hons: *3 yrs* Banking & Finance; Business Economics; Economics; History & Politics; Politics; Social Policy; Sociology *4 yrs* European Union Studies

BSc (Econ) Joint Hons: Accounting-Economics; Criminology or Sociology; Social Policy or Social Policy; Economics-Management Studies or Politics or Sociology or Industrial Relations; Politics-Economics or Modern History or Sociology; Social Policy-Industrial Relations; Social Research Methods and Social Policy or Sociology; Sociology and Criminology; Sociology-Economics or Education or Industrial Relations or Psychology or Social Policy

BSc Hons: *3 yrs* Mathematics, Operational Research & Statistics *3 yrs FT* Accounting; Anatomical Sciences; Archaeological Conservation; Archaeology; Astrophysics; Biochemistry with Medical Biochemistry or Molecular Biology; Business Administration; Business Studies & Japanese; Computer Science; Computer Systems Engineering; Environmental Geoscience; Exploration Geology; Geology; Marine Geography; Mathematics; Mathematics, Operational Research & Statistics; Medical Molecular Biology; Optometry; Pharmacology; Physics with Astronomy or Medical Physics; Physics; Physics & Music; Physiology; Geography (Human)-Planning; Psychology; Theoretical & Computational Physics *3 yrs FT/4 yrs S* Applied Biology; Applied Psychology; Biochemistry; Biology; Biotechnology; Business Studies with Japanese; Chemistry with Bioscience; Chemistry or Industrial Experience; Ecology & Environmental Management; Genetics; Mathematics & its Applications; Microbiology; Neuroscience; Zoology

BSc Joint Hons: *3 yrs* Physics; Chemistry-Computing; Mathematics-Computing; Physics-Physics; Mathematics-Physiology; Psychology; Psychology and Criminology

BSc/BArch: *5 yrs* Architectural Studies

BTh Hons: *3 yrs* Theology

LLB Hons: *3 yrs* Law; Law & Criminology *4 yrs* Law & Politics-Sociology; Law-French or German or Italian or Japanese or Spanish

Higher Degrees

EdD: *FT/PT* Education
LLM: *1 yr FT* Legal Aspects of Marine Affairs *1 yr FT/2 yrs PT* Commercial Law; Criminal Justice; Legal Aspects of Medical Practice *2 yrs PT* Canon Law
MA: *1 yr FT* Applied Linguistics; Critical & Cultural Theory; Cultural Politics; Early Celtic Studies; Education; English Literature; European Journalism; Journalism Studies; Language & Communication Research; Medieval British Studies; Music, Culture & Politics; Musicology; Performance Studies; Postmodernity; Sexual Politics; Teaching & Practice of Creative Writing; Welsh *1 yr FT/2 yrs PT* Analytical Philosophy; Ancient History; Ancient History & Society; Archaeology; Ethic & Social Philosophy; History of Philosophy; History/History of Wales; Literature in European Culture; Philosophy; Religious Studies *1 yr FT/3 yrs PT* Welsh Ethnological Studies *2 yrs FT* Social Work *2-5 yrs PT* Education
MBA: *FT/PT* Business Administration
MChem: *4 yrs* Chemistry
MEng Hons: *4 yrs FT/5 yrs S* Architectural Engineering; Civil & Environmental Engineering; Civil Engineering; Electrical & Electronic Engineering; Electronic Engineering; Environmental Engineering; Integrated Engineering; Manufacturing Engineering; Mechanical Engineering; Medical Engineering
MESci Hons: *4 yrs FT/5 yrs S* Earth Sciences
MMus: *1 yr FT* Music
MPharm Hons: *4 yrs* Pharmacy
MPhys: *1 yr FT/2 yrs PT* Physics with Astronomy *4 yrs FT/5 yrs S* Astrophysics; Engineering Physics
MSc: *1 yr FT* Applied Economics; Artificial Intelligence with Engineering Applications; Computing; Educational Psychology; European Regional Development; Financial Economics; Human Resource Management; International Economics, Banking & Finance; International Transport; Marine Policy; Mineral Resources; Occupational Psychology; Population Development; Reproductive Health & Family Planning Management; Social Science Research Methods; Transport & Planning; Urban Planning *1 yr FT/2 yrs PT* Architecture (Environmental Design of Buildings); Care of Collections; Conservation; Criminology & Criminal Justice; Electronic Engineering; Environmental Design of Buildings; Magnetic & Electrical Engineering with Industrial Applications; Sustainability Planning & Environmental Policy with Information Technology Applications; Systems Engineering; Transport & Planning; Women's Studies *1 yr FT/3 yrs PT* Applied Environmental Geology; Civil Engineering; Computing; Geotechnical Engineering; Structural Engineering; Water Engineering *2 yrs FT* City & Regional Planning *2 yrs FT/3 yrs PT* Housing *2 yrs PT* Advanced Social Work; Clinical Engineering; Orthopaedic Engineering *3 yrs PT* Clinical Pharmacy; Clinical Research; Community Pharmacy; Information Systems Engineering; Methods and Applications of Social Research
MSc (Econ): *1 yr FT/2 yrs PT* The European Policy Process
MSc Econ: *1 yr FT/2 yrs PT* West European Labour Studies
MTh: *1 yr FT/2 yrs PT* Biblical Studies; Christian Doctrine; Christian Social Ethics; Church History; Pastoral Theology

Diplomas

Diploma: *FT* Bar Vocational Course; Biological Research; Business Administration; Criminology & Criminal Justice; Electrical Engineering; Electronic Engineering; European Regional Development; Journalism Studies; Legal Practice; Port & Shipping Administration; Psychology; Public & Media Relations; Town Planning *FT/PT* Computing; Practical Theology *PT* Clinical Pharmacy; Clinical Research; Community Pharmacy; Pharmaceutical Medicine

Certificates

Certificate: *FT/PT* Theology & Religion
Certificate in Education/PGCE: *2 yrs PT* In-Service (Further Education) *9 mths FT* Further Education

UNIVERSITY OF WALES
College of Medicine

Heath Park, Cardiff CF14 4XN Tel: 029 20747747 Fax: 029 20742914
e-mail: turnercb@cardiff.ac.uk Website: www.uwcm.ac.uk

† Subject to validation.

First Degrees

BDS: Dental Surgery
BMedSci: Medical Science (Intercalated)
BN: Nursing
BSc: Cellular and Molecular Pathology (Intercalated); Dentistry; Medical Genetics (Intercalated); Medical Science; Pharmacology (Intercalated); Psychology and Medicine (Intercalated); Public Health (Intercalated)*FT/PT* Community Health Studies *PT* Nursing
BSc Hons: Dental Science (Intercalated); Diagnostic Radiography and Imaging; Radiography and Oncology *FT/PT* Occupational Therapy
MM Hons: *FT* Physiotherapy

Higher Degrees

DChD: (By thesis for Wales dental grads of 4 yrs min standing)
MCh: (As MD)
MD: (By thesis or taught PT/FT research)
MPH: *By exam & dissertation:* Public Health
MPhil: (As PhD)
MSc: *By coursework & dissertation:* Administration for Developing Countries; Anaesthesia & Intensive Care; Child Health; Community Healthcare Nursing; Dermatology; Forensic Dentistry; Genetic Counselling; Health Services Management; Medical Education; Medical Illustration; Medical Toxicology; Nursing; Occupational Therapy; Organising High Quality Staffed Housing; Orthodontics; Pain Management; Palliative Medicine; Physiotherapy; Positive Approach to Challenging Behaviour; Preventative Health Care; Psychiatry; Radiography; Reproduction & Health; Sports Medicine; Sports Physiotherapy; Supported Employment; Therapeutics; Wound Healing and Tissue Repair
MScD: *By coursework & dissertation:* Orthodontics
PhD: (By thesis after FT/PT research)

Diplomas

Diploma: Community Health Studies; Midwifery; Project 2000 (3 yr course prepares the nurse to practise both in hospital & community settings)
PGDip: Anaesthesia & Intensive Care; Biomedical Methods; Community Healthcare Nursing; Dental Studies; Dermatological Sciences; Health Service Management; Medical Education; Medical Illustration; Medical Toxicology; Medical Ultrasound; Organising High Quality Staffed Housing; Pain Management; Palliative Medicine; Positive Approach to Challenging Behaviour; Practical Dermatology; Psychological Medicine; Supported Employment; Therapeutics; Wound Healing & Tissue Repair

Certificates

Certificate: Computed Tomography; Health Services Management; Medical Education; Primary Care Management; Professional Practice in Neurosciences; Respiratory Physiotherapy
School Nurse Certificate: Practice Nurse Training; Primary Health Management

UNIVERSITY OF WALES
North East Wales Institute

Plas Coch, Mold Road, Wrexham LL11 2AW Tel: 01978 290666 Fax: 01978 290008
e-mail: enquiries@newi.ac.uk Website: www.newi.ac.uk

† Subject to validation.

First Degrees

BA/BSc Hons: *1 yr FT* Fine Art *3 yrs FT* Business Law; Business Management; Business, Finance & Accounting; Design (Animation or Architectural Glass or Ceramics or Graphic Design or Illustration or Jewellery/Metalwork); English; English with Media Studies or Sociology or Psychology or Welsh Studies; Environmental Studies; Geography-English or History or Media Studies or Welsh Studies; History; History-Media Studies or Welsh Studies; Human Resource Management; Marketing; Primary Education (with QTS); Social Science; Sociology; Youth and Community

BEng Hons: *3 yrs FT* Aeronautical/Mechanical Avionics; Electrical & Electronic Engineering; Manufacturing; Sound/Broadcast Engineering

BN Hons: Nursing

BSc Hons: *3 yrs FT* Applied Community & Health Studies; Architectural Studies; Business Information Systems; Computer Studies; Estate Management (Conservation & the Environmental or Planning & Development or Residential Property Management or Valuation & Property Surveying); Geography; Multimedia Computing; Nursing Studies; Psychology; Sports Science

Higher Degrees

MA: Animation; English; History

MBA: *PT*

MPhil: *2-3 yrs FT* Biochemistry; Chemistry; Physics

MSc: (By research in a range of disciplines) *1 yr FT/2 yrs PT* Nursing

Diplomas

Diploma in Higher Education: Nursing; Psychology; Youth & Community

HND: *2 yrs* Aeronautical Engineering; Business; Computing; Design Crafts; Electrical & Electronic Engineering; Film & TV; Graphic Design; Illustration; Manufacturing Engineering; Mechanical Engineering; Sound/Broadcast Engineering

PGDip: Advanced Nursing Education

UNIVERSITY OF WALES

University of Wales College, Newport

University Information Centre, PO Box 101, Newport NP18 3YH Tel: 01633 432432 Fax: 01633 432850 e-mail: uic@newport.ac.uk Website: www.newport.ac.uk
† Subject to validation.

First Degrees

BA Hons: *2 yrs FT Secondary:* Media & Visual Culture *3 yrs FT/4-6 yrs PT* Animation; Archaeology; Community Justice; Community Studies; Community Studies (Community Education & Development); Community Studies (Education & Training); Community Studies (Social & Labour Studies); Community Studies (Voluntary Sector & Community Work); Community Studies (Youth & Community Work); Design Futures; Documentary Photography; Education (for serving teachers); Fashion Design; Film & Video; Graphics; Interactive Arts; Multimedia; Philosophical Studies; Photographic Art; S.E.N (for serving teachers)

BA Hons QTS: *3 yrs FT With QTS:* Primary Studies; Secondary Design & Technology

BA/BSc Hons: *3 yrs FT/4-6 yrs PT Major, Joint, Minor:* Humanities, Social & Environmental Sciences (3 subjects in 1st yr)-Archaeology (Pre-history) (3 subjects in 1st yr) or English (3 subjects in 1st yr) or Environmental Studies (3 subjects in 1st yr) or European Studies (3 subjects in 1st yr) or Geography (3 subjects in 1st yr) or History (3 subjects in 1st yr) or Information Technology (3 subjects in 1st yr) or Modern Languages (available as a Minor or Joint Subject only) (3 subjects in 1st yr) or Philosophy & Religious Studies (3 subjects in 1st yr) or Sports Studies (3 subjects in 1st yr)

BEd Hons: *3 yrs FT*

BEng Hons: *3 yrs FT/4-6 yrs PT* Electrical and Instrumentation Systems; Electronic & Instrumentation Systems; Integrated Manufacturing Technology

BSc (Ed): *2 yrs FT Secondary:* Design & Technology; Design & Technology with ICT; Mathematics with ICT; Mathematics with Science
BSc Econ Single Hons: *3 yrs FT/4-6 yrs PT* Social Welfare; Social Welfare & Human Behaviour; Social Welfare & Organisations; Social Welfare-Law
BSc Hons: *3 yrs FT/4-6 yrs PT* Accounting & Finance; Accounting Practice; Accounting-Legal Studies; Business & Enterprise; Business & Modern Languages; Business Administration; Business Information Technology; Business-Legal Studies; Computing; Industrial Information Technology
BSc Ord: *3 yrs FT/4-6 yrs PT* Civil & Construction Engineering
IRRV: *3 yrs PT DL Distance Learning:* (3 yrs for full professional qualification)

Higher Degrees

MA: *1 yr FT* Film; Multimedia-Information Design *1 yr FT/2-5 yrs PT* Autism; Education; Special Educational Needs (with various specialist routes) *2 yrs PT* Celto-Roman Studies; Documentary Photography *2-5 yrs PT* Art Education; Creative Arts in Education; Curriculum Studies; Early Years Education; Education & Training; Education Management; Health Education; Religious Education *2.5-3 yrs PT* Philosophy & Religious Studies *2.5-5 yrs PT* Environmental Management *21 mths* Marketing *3 yrs PT* Counselling *3.5 yrs* Marketing *9 mths* Marketing
MBA: *1 yr FT/3 yrs PT*
MPhil: *1 yr FT/3 yrs PT* CAAI (Interactive Arts); High Voltage Engineering Research; Mechatronics Research; SCARAB (Culture, Archaeology, Religion, Biogeography)
MSc: *1 yr FT/3 yrs PT* Electrical/Electronic Technology Management; Human Resource Management; IT Management; Manufacturing Technology Management
MSc Econ: *PT* Management of Human Services

Diplomas

DipHE: *2 yrs FT* Accounting Practice
Diploma in Foundation Studies: *1 yr FT/2 yrs PT* Art & Design
HND: Accounting & Finance (Access & Foundation Prog – 1 yr (1-2 yrs if needed/ Access)); Business & Legal Studies (Access and Foundation Programme – 1 yr (1-2 yrs if needed, flexible)); Business Administration (Access and Foundation Programme – 1 yr (1-2 yrs if needed, flexible)); Business Information Technology (Access & Foundation Prog – 1 yr (1-2 yrs if needed; flexible)); Civil Engineering (Access & Foundation Prog – 1 yr (1-2 yrs if needed; flexible)); Computing (Access & Foundation Prog – 1 yr (1-2 yrs if needed; flexible)); Electrical/Electronic Engineering (Access & Foundation Prog – 1 yr (1-2 yrs if needed; flexible)); Engineering (Access & Foundation Prog – 1 yr (1-2 yrs if needed; flexible)); European Business Studies (Access and Foundation Programme – 1 yr (1-2 yrs if needed, flexible)); Manufacturing Engineering (Access & Foundation Prog – 1 yr (1-2 yrs if needed; flexible)); Mechanical Engineering (Access & Foundation Prog – 1 yr (1-2 yrs if needed; flexible)); Technology & Disability Studies (franchised to Bridgend College) (Access & Foundation Prog – 1 yr (1-2 yrs if needed; flexible)); Telecommunication Engineering (Access & Foundation Prog – 1 yr (1-2 yrs if needed; flexible))
HND/HNC: *2 yrs* Accounting & Finance (and 1 yr HND); Business & Legal Studies (and 1 yr HND); Business Administration (and 1 yr HND); Business Information Technology (and 1 yr HND); Civil Engineering (and 1 yr HND); Computing (and 1 yr HND); Electrical/Electronic Engineering (and 1 yr HND); Engineering (and 1 yr HND); Manufacturing Engineering (and 1 yr HND); Mechanical Engineering (and 1 yr HND); Mechatronics (and 1 yr HND)
PGDip/Cert/In-Service Diploma: *2 yrs PT* (All PT Masters courses)

Certificates

ACCA: *4 yrs PT*
Certificate in Higher Education: *1-2 yrs* Combined Studies
CIM: *1 yr PT Advanced Certificate:* (or Advanced Diploma)
CIMA: *3 yrs PT*
CMS: *1 yr PT*
HNC: Advanced Manufacturing Technology (Merthyr College Franchise); Industrial Measurement & Control (Merthyr College Franchise)
IPD: *3 yrs PT*

PGCE: *Certificate in Higher Education:* Introduction to Secondary Teaching *1 yr FT* Design & Technology; Education & Training; Primary *2 yrs PT* Education & Training
PGDip/PGCert: *1 yr FT* Mediation (Cert – 9 mths/ Dip – another 9 mths)

UNIVERSITY OF WALES
University of Wales Institute, Cardiff
Central Administration, PO Box 377, Western Avenue, Cardiff CF5 2SG Tel: 029 2041 6070
Fax: 029 2041 6911 e-mail: uwicinfo@uwic.ac.uk Website: www.uwic.ac.uk
† Subject to validation.

First Degrees
BA Hons: *1 yr FT* Business Management *1 yr FT/2 yrs PT* Community Studies (Learning Disabilities / Social Work) *2 yrs FT* Education Welsh (Secondary with QTS); Music (Secondary with QTS) *3 yrs FT* Art & Aesthetics; Business Studies; Ceramics; European Business Management; Fine Art; Graphic Communication; Graphic Communication; Industrial Design; Interior Architecture; Primary Education (with QTS) with Art or English or Design Technology or Science or Geography or History or Mathematics or Music or Physical Education or Religious Education or Welsh; Recreation & Leisure Management *3 yrs FT/4 yrs S* Tourism *4 yrs FT* Drama Education (Secondary with QTS) *4 yrs S/4-8 yrs PT* Hospitality Management; International Hospitality Management *5 yrs PT* Sport & Physical Education; Sport Development
BSc Hons: *3 yrs* Sports Development *3 yrs FT* Business Information Systems; Dental Technology; Environmental Risk Management; Housing Studies; Podiatry; Psychology & Communication; Sport & Exercise Science; Sport & Physical Education; Sports Coaching *3 yrs FT/3-6 yrs PT* Electronics Design *3 yrs FT/4 yrs S* Consumer Science; Environmental Health; Food Studies *3 yrs FT/4 yrs S/4-8 yrs PT* Applied Human Nutrition; Biomedical Sciences *3 yrs FT/4-6 yrs PT/4 yrs S* Catering Management *4 yrs FT* Speech & Language Therapy

Higher Degrees
MA: *1 yr FT/2 yrs PT* Art & Design Education; Fine Art *1 yr FT/3 yrs PT* Coaching Science; Sport & Leisure Studies; Therapeutic and Community Recreation *1 yr FT/3-5 yrs PT* Education *1 yr FT/Up to 3 yrs PT* Leisure & Tourism Management *1-2 yrs FT/2 yrs PT* Ceramics *45 wks FT* Design
MBA: *1 yr FT/Up to 3 yrs PT*
MPH: *2 yrs PT*
MSc: *1 yr FT* Dietetics *1 yr FT/2 yrs PT* Biomedical Sciences; Environmental Risk Management; Health / Learning Disabilities; Interprofessional Studies *1 yr FT/2-3 yrs PT* Sport and Exercise Sciences *1 yr FT/3 yrs max PT* Coaching Science *1 yr FT/Up to 4 yrs PT* Food Science & Technology *2 yrs PT* Quality Assurance and Inspection (Social Welfare) *3-6 yrs* Business Information Systems

Diplomas
Diploma: *PT* Food Hygiene; Professional Development in Housing Studies
HND: *1-2 yrs PT* Building Technology & Management *2 yrs* Environmental Studies; Recreation & Leisure Management *2 yrs FT* Applied Biosciences; Architectural Design & Technology; Biomedical Sciences; Business & Finance; Business Information Technology; Computing; Dental Technology; Electrical & Electronic Engineering; Environmental Studies; Health & Social Care; Product Design & Manufacture; Technology of Food *2 yrs PT* Culinary Arts; Hospitality Management; Licensed Trade Management; Mechanical Engineering; Recreation & Leisure Management *3 yrs PT* Building Technology & Management
ND: *4 yrs PT*

Certificates
Certificate: *1 yr FT/1 yr PT* Management; Management Studies; Supervisory Management *26 wks PT* Financial Planning
HNC: *2 yrs PT* Applied Biosciences; Building Technology Management; Business Information Technology; Business Studies; Computer Studies; Hospitality Management Studies; Housing

Studies; Mechanical Engineering; Recreation & Leisure Management; Technology of Food; Wastes Management *2-3 yrs PT* Science (Dental Technology)

PGCE: *1 yr FT* Art and Design; Design and Technology; English & Drama; Home Economics; Mathematics; Modern Foreign Languages; Music; Physical Education; Primary; Science; Welsh *3 yrs FT* History

Postgraduate Certificate: *1 yr FT* Education (Primary); Education (Secondary)-Art & Design or Design & Technology or Home Economics or History or Mathematics or Modern Foreign Languages or Music or Physical Education or Science or Welsh or English & Drama *2 yrs & 1 trm PT* Post Compulsory Education & Training

Postgraduate Certificate in Further Education: *2 yrs + 1 trm PT*

Other Courses

Access Courses: *1 yr PT* Teacher Education; Technology
Foundation Course: *1 yr FT/2 yrs PT* Art & Design

UNIVERSITY OF WALES
University of Wales, Aberystwyth

Old College, Ceredigion SY23 2AX Tel: 01970 622021 (undergrads) & 01970 622023 (postgrads) Fax: 01970 627410 e-mail: undergraduate-admissions@aber.ac.uk Website: www.aber.ac.uk

† Subject to validation.

First Degrees

BA: *1 yr FT* Welsh History-American Studies or Art History or Drama or Economic & Social History or Education or English or Film & Television Studies or Fine Art or French (4 yrs) or Geography or German (4 yrs) or History or Information & Library Studies or International Politics or Irish (4 yrs) or Mathematics or Politics or Spanish (4 yrs) *3-4 yrs FT* American Studies; Art History-American Studies; Drama-American Studies or Art History or Fine Art or History; Geography-American Studies or Art History or Drama or Economic & Social History or Education or English or Film & Television Studies or Fine Art or French (4 Yrs) or Mathematics or Statistics or Physics; Art History; Art History with Fine Art; Art History-Fine Art; Communication and Learning; Drama; Performance Studies-Drama or English or Film & TV Studies; Economic & Social History; Economic and Social History with Economics or Business Studies; Education-American Studies or Art History or Drama or Fine Art; English; English-American Studies or Art History or Drama or Education or Fine Art; European Languages; Film & Television Studies; Film and Television Studies-American Studies or Education or English or Drama or Fine Art or Art History; Fine Art; Fine Art with Art History; Fine Art (Route A); Fine Art-American Studies; Geography with Economics; Geography with Welsh; Geography; Geography (Major); History; History-American Studies or Art History or Economic & Social History or Education or English or Fine Art or French (4 yrs) or Geography or German (4 yrs); Humanities or Drama; Information & Library Studies-German (4 yrs) or History or French (4 yrs) or American Studies or English or Art History or Fine Art or Film & Television or Education or Geography; International Politics-English or French (4 yrs) or Geography or German (4 yrs); Law with Accounting & Finance or Business Studies or Economics or German (4 yrs) or Information Management or Italian (4 yrs) or Marketing or Mathematics or Politics or Spanish (4 yrs) or Welsh; Law; Mathematics-American Studies or Art History or Drama or Film & Television Studies or Fine Art or French (4 yrs) or Geography or German (4 yrs) or History or Irish (4 yrs) or Physics; Politics-Modern History or English or French (4 yrs) or Geography or German (4 yrs); Modern Welsh Studies *4 yrs French*-American Studies or Art History or Drama or Economic & Social History or Education or English or European Studies or Film & Television Studies or Fine Art; Spanish-American Studies or Art History or Drama or Economic & Social History or Education or English or European Studies or Film & Television Studies or Fine Art or French or German or History or Information & Library Studies or International Politics or Mathematics or Politics; Celtic Studies; French; French with Economics or German or Italian or Spanish or Welsh; German with French or Italian or Spanish or Welsh or International Politics; German-American Studies or Drama or Economic & Social History or Education or English or European Studies or Film & Television Studies or French or Geography

or Education; Irish-American Studies or Art History or Drama or English or Film & Television Studies or Fine Art or French or German or History or Information & Library Studies; Modern Languages with Business Studies; Spanish; Spanish with Economics or French or German or Italian or Welsh or International Politics; Welsh

BEng: *4 yrs S* Interactive Multimedia Engineering

BEng/MEng: *4-5 yrs S* Software Engineering

BSc: *3 yrs* Internet Computing *3-4 yrs FT/S* Agriculture with Animal Science or Business Studies or Computing or Countryside Management or Crop Science or Marketing or Organic Agriculture; Animal Science; Applied Mathematics-Pure Mathematics or Statistics; Biochemistry; Biochemistry-Genetics; Biology; Botany; Computer Science with Accounting and Finance or Artificial Intelligence (4 yrs) or Welsh with Spanish; Computer Science or Italian or German or French or Business Studies; Computer Science; Computer Science-Geography or Mathematics or Physics or Statistics; Countryside Conservation; Countryside Management; Countryside Recreation and Tourism; Earth Planetary & Space Science; Education-Mathematics or Statistics; Environmental Biology; Environmental Earth Science with Education; Environmental Earth Science; Environmental Science; Equine Science; Equine Studies; Financial Mathematics; Genetics; Geography; Geography (Major); Information & Library Studies-An Approved Sci Sub; Life Sciences; Marine & Freshwater Biology; Mathematics with Accounting & Finance; Mathematics; Mathematics with Business Studies or Economics or Education; Microbiology; Microbiology-Zoology; Physics with Atmospheric Physics or Business Studies or Education or French (4 yrs) or German (4 yrs) or Italian (4 yrs) or Spanish (4 yrs) or Planetary and Space Physics; Pure Mathematics-Statistics; Rural Resources Management; Tourism Management; Zoology (major or minor) *4 yrs* Internet Computing

BSc Ord: *3 yrs FT* Mathematics; Physics

BSc/MPhys: *4 yrs* Physics with Atmospheric Physics or Business Studies or Education or French or German or Italian or Planetary & Space Physics or Spanish; Physics

BScEcon: *3-4 yrs FT* Accounting & Finance with Law or Welsh or a European Language; Accounting & Finance; Accounting and Finance with Computer Science or Information Management or Mathematics or Statistics or Welsh; Accounting and Finance-Economics; Business Economics; Business Finance; Business Studies; Business Studies with Computer Science or a Modern Language or Law or Mathematics or Economic & Social History or Information Management or Politics; Economics with Economic & Social History or French or Geography or German or International Politics or Mathematics or Politics or Spanish; Economics; Economics-Marketing; European Politics; Information & Library Studies; Information & Library Studies-International Politics or Politics; Information Management with Economics; Information Management with Law or Marketing; Information Management; Information Management, Accounting & Finance; International Politics with Law or Economics; International Politics; International Politics-International History or Strategic Studies or The Third World or Intelligence Studies or French (4 yrs) or German (4 yrs) or Italian (4 yrs) or Spanish or Economic & Social History or History; International Relations with Accounting & Finance or Computer Science or Economics or Education or French (4 yrs) or German (4 yrs) or Information Management or International Politics or Italian (4 yrs) or Law or Politics or Spanish (4 yrs) or Welsh; Marketing; Political Studies; Political Studies-Political Studies; Law; Politics with Law with Welsh; Politics-Economic and Social History or History; The Americas and International Politics*4 yrs* Economics with Italian

LLB: Business Law; Criminal Law; European Law; Public Law *2 yrs* Law *2-3-4 yrs FT/FT* Law; French; German; Italian; Spanish

Higher Degrees

Cert/Dip/MA: *1 yr FT* Practising Human Geography; Space, Place & Politics

Cert/Dip/MSc: *1 yr FT* Bio-Informatics

Cert/Dip/MScEcon: *1 yr FT* Entrepreneurship (Welsh Medium); Postcolonial Politics (Specialist or Research Training); Security Studies (Specialist or Research Training)

LLM: *1 yr FT* International Business Law *1 yr FT/2-3 yrs PT DL* The Law of International Business and the Environment *1 yr FT/Distance Learning* Environmental Law & Management

MA: *1 yr FT* American Literature Since 1945; Art; Art & Art History; Art History; Early British Studies; Economic & Social History of Wales; Historical Studies; History of Wales; Literary

Studies; Postmodern Fiction; Spanish Poetry of the Nineteenth & Twentieth Centuries; Television Studies; Theatre & the World; Theatre, Film & Television Studies; Writing: Process & Practice *1-2 yrs FT* Irish; Medieval Welsh Literature
MBA: *1 yr FT* Business Administration; Business Administration (Environmental Management)
MEd: *PT* Education
MMath: *4 yrs FT* Mathematics
MPhys: *4 yrs FT* Physics; Physics with Atmospheric Physics or Planetary & Space Physics
MRes: *1 yr FT* Advanced Plant Science; Modern Approaches to Crop Improvement
MSc: *1 yr FT* Biological Electron Microscopy; Computer Science; Environmental Techniques in Earth System Science; Equine Science; Improvement & Renovation of Grassland *1 yr FT/2-3 yrs PT DL* Environmental Impact Assessment; Environmental Rehabilitation *FT* Environmental Management Systems & Auditing *2-3 yrs PT DL* Environmental Management Systems & Auditing
MScEcon: International History and Intelligence Studies *1 yr FT* Accounting & Finance; Archive Administration; International History (Specialist or Research Training); International Politics (Specialist or Research Training); Management; Politics of the European Union (Specialist or Research Training); Security Studies (Specialist or Research Training); Strategic Studies (Specialist or Research Training) *1 yr FT/DL* Information & Library Studies; Records Management *3 yrs PT DL* Health Information Management; Management of Library & Information Services

Diplomas

Diploma: *2 yrs PT DL Taught courses normally assessed by exam:* Environmental Auditing *9 mths FT Taught courses normally assessed by exam:* Accounting & Finance; Archive Administration; Art; Biological Election Microscopy; International Business Law; Records Management *9 mths FT/2 yrs PT DL Taught courses normally assessed by exam:* Environmental Impact Assessment; Environmental Rehabilitation

POSTGRADUATE CERTIFICATES
PGC: *1 yr FT* Education (Teacher Training) (Taught element and practical experience element. Continual assessment) *1 yr PT Taught courses normally assessed by exam:* English/Welsh Translation
PGCert: *1 yr DL* Management of Health & Information Services*6 mths FT* Environmental Management

UNIVERSITY OF WALES
University of Wales, Bangor
Gwynedd LL57 2DG Tel: 01248 351151 Fax: 01248 383268
e-mail: g.brindley@bangor.ac.uk Website: www.bangor.ac.uk/home.html
† Subject to validation.

First Degrees

BA Joint Hons: *3-4 yrs FT Certain combinations of the following:* Accounting; Banking; Criminology; Economics; Education (Welsh medium only); English; European Cultural Studies; French; German; History; Linguistics; Management; Marketing; Mathematics; Modern Languages; Music; Physical Education; Psychology; Religious Studies; Social Policy; Sociology; Sports Science; Tourism; Tourism; Welsh; Welsh History; Welsh Literature & Literature of the Media; Women's Studies
BA Single Hons: *3 yrs FT* Accounting & Finance; Banking & Finance; Biblical Studies; Business & Social Administration or Finance or Marketing or a Modern Language; Business Studies-Economics; Marketing-Computer Studies or a Modern Language; Contemporary Studies (History, Literature, Culture); Criminology & Criminal Justice; Economics; English with Journalism; English with Creative Writing; English with Film Studies; English; English with Theatre Studies; English Language; English Literature with English Language; Environmental Planning & Management; Heritage Management; Heritage, Archaeology & History; History with Archaeology; History; Journalism & Media Studies (Welsh medium only); Languages; Leisure & the Environment; Leisure & Tourism Resource Management; Leisure Management with The English Language; Linguistics; Linguistics; Management with Accounting or Banking & Finance

or Agriculture; Media Studies (Welsh medium only) or Journalism (Welsh medium only); Communication (Welsh medium only); Medieval & Early Modern History; Modern & Contemporary History; Music; Political & Social Sciences; Psychology; Religious Studies; Sociology with Social Policy; Sociology; Sociology & Social Policy (Welsh medium only); Sport, Health & Physical Education; Theatre & Media Studies (Welsh medium only); Tourism with Languages; Tourism & Languages; Welsh with Creative Writing or Journalism; Welsh; Welsh History with Archaeology; Welsh Theatre & Media Studies *4 yrs FT* French with Italian or Spanish or German; French with Psychology; French; French Language & Modern France; German with Italian or Spanish; German with Psychology; German Language & Modern Germany; Languages (French, German, Italian, Spanish) with Tourism; Marketing & a Modern Language; Modern Languages with Marketing or Business Studies; Three Language Honours (Chosen from French, German, Italian, Spanish, EFL) *4 yrs PT* Literature, History & Society; Social Studies *4-10 yrs PT* Social Studies

BD: *3 yrs FT*
BEd Hons: *3 yrs FT* Secondary School Design & Technology *Primary Education with following main subjects:* Art, Craft & Design; Design & Technology; English; Geography; History; Mathematics; Music; Physical Education; Religious Studies; Science; Welsh
BEng: *3 yrs FT* Media Electronics *3-4 yrs FT* Computer Systems Engineering; Electronic Engineering
BMus: *3 yrs FT*
BN: *3 yrs FT* Nursing
BSc Joint Hons: *3 yrs FT Certain combinations of the following:* Biochemistry; Chemistry; Management; Marine Biology; Oceanography; Physical Education; Physical Oceanography; Sports Science; Zoology
BSc Single Hons: *2-5 yrs PT* Health Studies *3 yrs FT* Agriculture with Business Management; Agroforestry; Applied Biology; Applied Marine Biology; Biochemistry; Biology with Molecular Biology; Biology; Biomolecular Sciences; Chemistry; Computer Science; Computer Systems with Business Studies or Psychology; Diagnostic Radiography & Imaging; Ecology; Environmental Biology; Environmental Chemistry; Environmental Conservation; Environmental Science; Forestry; Forestry & Forestry Products; Geological Oceanography; Marine Biology; Marine Chemistry; Mathematics with Computer Systems; Mathematics; Midwifery; Ocean Science; Plant Biology; Psychology; Psychology with Health Psychology; Rural Resource Management; Sports Science; World Agriculture; Zoology with Animal Ecology or Marine Zoology; Zoology *4 yrs FT* Agroforestry; Biology with European Dimension; Chemistry with European Experience; Chemistry with Industrial Experience; Environmental Chemistry with Industrial Experience; Forestry; Forestry & Forestry Products; Rural Resource Management; World Agriculture

Higher Degrees

DClinPsy: *3 yrs FT*
MA: *1 yr FT* Analysis (Music); Archive Administration; Arthurian Literature; Banking & Finance; Business Management; Comparative Criminology & Criminal Justice; Countryside Management; Creative Music Technology & Film, Media and the Arts; Creative Writing; Editorial Musicology; English; Ethnomusicology; Gerontology; Heritage Management; Labour History; Linguistics; Medieval History; Modern History; Music; Music in the Christian Church; Musicology; Performance (Music); Religious Studies; Social & Regional History (Wales); Social Research-Social Policy or Sociology or Criminology or Gerontology; Social Work; Welsh History; Welsh Language, Literature & Media Literature; Welsh Music & Celtic Music; Women's Studies *2 yrs FT* Social Work (To include DipSW)
MBA: *1 1/2 yrs FT or 2 1/2 yrs PT semester distance learning 1 yr FT*
MChem: *4 yrs FT*
MEd: *2 yrs PT*
MEng: *4 yrs FT* Computer Systems Engineering; Electronic Engineering
MMath: *4 yrs FT* Mathematics
MMus: *1 yr FT*
MPhil: *2 yrs FT* (By research in Arts, Education, Health & Science Faculties)
MSc: *1 yr FT* Agroforestry; Applied Mathematics; Applied Oceanography; Applied Sports Sciences; Biocomposites Technology; Computed Tomography & Comparative Imaging;

Diagnostic Radiography; Diagnostic Radiography-Trauma or Fluoroscopic Imaging; Ecology; Electronic Engineering; Environmental Chemistry; Environmental Forestry; Experimental Consumer Psychology; Health Education & Health Promotion; Health Studies; Marine Environmental Protection; Marine Geotechnics; Mathematics; Medical Ultrasound; Modern Chemical Laboratory Practice; Nursing Studies; Physical Oceanography; Pure Mathematics; Rural Resource Management; Shellfish Biology, Fisheries & Culture; Water Resources; World Animal Production
MTh: *1 yr FT*
PhD: *3 yrs FT* (By research in Arts, Education, Health & Science Faculties)

Diplomas

DipHE: *2 yrs FT* Electronic Engineering; Instrumental Methods for Science Laboratories
Diploma in Theology: *3 yrs FT*
HND: *2 yrs FT* Agriculture; Electronics Engineering; Equine Studies; Horticultural Technology
Postgraduate Diploma: *9 mths FT* (Courses also available in all subjects listed under MSc & MA); Archive Administration; Computed Tomography; Forestry

Certificates

PGCE: *2 semesters FT* Art; Biology; Chemistry; Early Childhood (Primary); English; French; Geography; German; History; Junior Stage (Primary); Mathematics; Music; Outdoor Activities; Physics; Technology; Welsh
Postgraduate Certificate: *1 yr FT* Community Development; Computed Tomography & Comparative Imaging; Diagnostic Radiography; Diagnostic Radiography-Trauma or Fluoroscopic Imaging; Gerontology; Health Education & Health Promotion; Management; Medical Ultrasound; Translation (Welsh/English)

UNIVERSITY OF WALES

University of Wales, Lampeter

Ceredigion, Wales SA48 7ED Tel: 01570 422351 Fax: 01570 423423 e-mail: recruit@lampeter.ac.uk
Website: www.lampeter.ac.uk
† Subject to validation.

First Degrees

BA Combined Hons: *3 yrs* (A combination of 3 subjects to meet special interests)
BA Joint Hons: *3 yrs* (Combinations (2 subjects) may be taken except the combination Welsh & Welsh Studies)
BA Single Hons: Anthropology & Religion; Archaeology & Anthropology; Creative Studies; Media Studies; North American Studies *3 yrs* Ancient History & Archaeology; Archaeology & Environment; Business Management; Classical Studies; Classics; Cultural Studies in Geography; English Literature; Environmental Management & Resource Development; Geography; History; Latin; Philosophical Studies; Religion Ethics & Society; Theology; Victorian Studies; Welsh Studies *4 yrs* Philosophy; Welsh
BA Single Hons only: *(May not be taken as joint /combined studies):* Ancient & Medieval History; Ancient History & Archaeology; Archaeology & Environment; Environmental Management & Resource Development; Philosophy; Religion, Ethics & Society
BD Hons: *3 yrs* Divinity

Higher Degrees

MA: Byzantine Studies; Church History *2 yrs PT* Ancient History; Ancient Philosophy & Mythology; Archaeological Research; Celtic Christianity; Death & Immortality; Death Studies; Environmental Anthropology; Feminist Theology; Landscape Archaeology; Religion Politics & International Relations; Social Anthropology; Study of Religions: Religious Experience; The Word & Visual Imagination; Visual Representations in History *3 yrs FT* Cultural Landscape Management

MA/MPhil: *1-2 yrs FT/PT* (Most of the subjects listed under BA Single Hons)
PhD: *2-3 yrs FT* (Most of the subjects listed under BA Single Hons) *3-5 yrs PT* (Most of the subjects listed under BA Single Hons)

Diplomas

Diploma: *2 yrs FT* (Similar to joint hons; 1 subject must be Informatics; at the end of the second yr; students have the option to take a third yr to obtain a BA degree)
Licence in Greek: *1 yr FT/2 yrs PT* (Open to grads of all Univs)
Licence in Latin: *1 yr FT/2 yrs PT* (Open to grads of all Univs)
Licence in Religious Studies (LRS): *1 yr FT/2 yrs PT* (Open to grads of all Univs)
Licence in Theology (LTh): *1 yr FT/2 yrs PT* (Open to grads of all Univs)
PgD/PgC: *9 mths FT* (Available on any taught Masters course)

Certificates

Certificate: Screen Translation

UNIVERSITY OF WALES

University of Wales, Swansea

Singleton Park, Swansea SA2 8PP Tel: 01792 295876
e-mail: b.stratford@swan.ac.uk

† Subject to validation.

First Degrees

ARTS & SOCIAL STUDIES
BA Hons: *3 yrs* American Studies; Ancient & Medieval History; Ancient History; Ancient History with Greek or Latin; Ancient History & Civilisation; Ancient History & Civilisation with Greek or Latin; Classical Civilisation; Classical Civilisation with Greek or Latin; Classics; Economics; English; Geography; Greek & Roman Studies with Greek or Latin; History; Politics; Politics with International Relations; Psychology; Teaching English as a Foreign Language *3-4 yrs* Welsh *4 yrs* American Studies; European History with English or German or Italian or Spanish or Welsh or French; European Politics; French; French; German; German; Italian; Italian; Philosophy; Russian; Spanish; Spanish; Spanish with Catalan
BA Joint Hons: *3 yrs* American Studies-English or History or Philosophy or Anthropology; Ancient History & Civilisation-Anthropology or English or Greek or History or Latin or Medieval Studies or Philosophy or Politics or Language Studies; Ancient History-Economic History or English or History or Language Studies or Medieval Studies or Philosophy or Politics or Welsh; Anthropology-English or History or Medieval Studies or Welsh; Classical Civilisation-Economic History or English or Greek or History or Language Studies or Latin or Medieval Studies or Philosophy; Economics-Geography or History or Welsh; English Language-Greek or Greek & Roman Studies or Classical Civilisation or Latin; English-Geography or Greek or Greek & Roman Studies or History or Latin or Medieval Studies or Philosophy or Politics or Sociology or Welsh or Language Studies or Classical Civilisation or Teaching English as a Foreign Language; Geography-History or Welsh; Greek & Roman Studies or Medieval Studies; Greek-Medieval Studies or Philosophy or Welsh or History or Language Studies; History-Latin or Medieval Studies or Philosophy or Politics or Sociology or Welsh; Latin-Medieval Studies or Welsh; Medieval Studies-Sociology or Welsh; Philosophy-Politics or Welsh; Politics-Welsh; Psychology-Welsh; Sociology-Welsh; Teaching English as a Foreign Language-Welsh *4 yrs* American Studies-French or German or Italian or Russian or Spanish or Welsh or History or Philosophy or English; Egyptology-Ancient History or Anthropology or Classical Civilisation; Ancient History-French or German or Italian or Spanish or Welsh; Anthropology-French or German or Italian or Russian or Spanish or Welsh; Catalan and Spanish with Business Studies; Classical Civilisation-Welsh or Spanish or Italian; Economic History-German or Italian or Russian or French or Spanish or History; Economics-French or Spanish or Russian Studies or Italian or Russian or Welsh or German; English Language-French or German or Italian or Russian or Spanish or Spanish with

Business Studies or German with Business Studies or Italian with Business Studies; English-French or German or Italian or Russian or Spanish or Welsh or Greek or Teaching English as a Foreign Language; European Politics-French or German or Italian or Russian or Spanish or Welsh; French-Geography or German† or Greek or Greek and Roman Studies or History or Italian† or Latin or Medieval Studies or Philosophy or Teaching English as a Foreign Language or Language Studies or Language Studies with Business Studies or Politics or Psychology or Russian† or Sociology or Spanish† or Welsh†; Geography-German or Italian or Russian or Spanish or Welsh; German or Language Studies or History or Italian† or Latin or Philosophy or Politics or Psychology or Russian† or Sociology or Spanish† or Welsh† or Language Studies with Business Studies or Teaching English as a Foreign Language; Greek-Greek; Welsh-History; Italian or Russian or Spanish or Welsh or Russian Studies; Italian-Latin or Medieval Studies or Philosophy or Politics or Psychology or Russian† or Sociology or Spanish† or Welsh† or Language Studies or Language Studies with Business Studies or Teaching English as a Foreign Language; Language Studies-Latin or Russian or Russian with Business Studies or Spanish or Spanish with Business Studies or Teaching English as a Foreign Language or Welsh; Latin-Spanish or Welsh; Medieval Studies-Spanish or Welsh; Philosophy-Spanish or Welsh; Politics-Russian or Spanish or Welsh or Russian Studies; Psychology-Russian or Spanish or Welsh; Russian-Sociology or Spanish† or Welsh† or Teaching English as a Foreign Language; Sociology-Spanish or Welsh; Spanish-Welsh† or Teaching English as a Foreign Language; Ancient History & Civilisation-Welsh
BA Single Hons: *3 yrs*
BSc Econ Joint Hons: *3 yrs* American Studies-Anthropology or Economic History or Geography or Politics or Social History or Sociology; American Studies-Economic History or Anthropology or Geography or Politics or Social History or Sociology; Anthropology-Development Studies or Geography or Philosophy or Politics or Psychology or Social History or Social Policy or Sociology; Development Studies-Economics or Geography or International Relations or Politics or Social Policy or Sociology; Economic History-Economics; Economics-Politics or Psychology or Social Policy; Geography-Social Policy or Sociology; Integrated Honours in Social Sciences; Philosophy-Politics or Psychology or Sociology; Politics or Sociology; Psychology-Sociology; Social History-Social Policy or Sociology; Social Policy-Sociology *4 yrs* Development Studies-Spanish
BSc Econ Single Hons: *3 yrs* Anthropology; Development Studies; Early Childhood Studies; Economic & Social History; Geography; Politics with International Relations; Politics; Social Philosophy; Social Policy; Sociology *4 yrs* Social Studies (with foundation yr)

BUSINESS, LAW & ECONOMICS
BSc Hons: *3 yrs* Actuarial Studies; Applied Econometrics; Business Economics; Business Information Technology; Business Studies; Business, Economics-Law; Economics; Financial Economics; Management Science with Mathematics; Management Science; Operational Research; Statistics *4 yrs* Actuarial Studies (with a yr abroad); American Business Studies; American Management Science; Business Information Technology; Business Studies (with a yr abroad); European Business Studies (France, Germany, Italy or Spain); European Business Studies with a Modern Language; European Management Science (France, Germany, Italy, Spain); European Management Science with a Modern Language; Management Science (with a yr abroad) with Mathematics (with a yr abroad); Management Science (with a yr abroad); Statistics (with a yr abroad)
BSc Joint Hons: *3 yrs* Business Management-Economics; Economics-Statistics; Management Science-Statistics or Mathematics *4 yrs* Management Science and Mathematics with a yr abroad.; Management Science-Statistics (with a yr abroad)
LLB Hons: *3 yrs* Law
LLB Joint Hons: *3 yrs* Law and American Studies or Business Studies or Economics or Politics or Psychology or Welsh *4 yrs* Law-American Studies or French or German or Italian or Russian or Spanish or Welsh

ENGINEERING
BEng Hons: *3 yrs* Biochemical Engineering; Chemical Engineering; Civil Engineering; Civil Engineering (with a yr in Industry); Electronic & Electrical Engineering; Electronics with Communications or Computing Science; Materials Science & Engineering; Mechanical Engineering; Product Design & Manufacture *4 yrs* Biochemical Engineering (with a yr in

industry); Chemical Engineering (with a yr in Europe or in industry); Civil Engineering with French or German or Italian or Spanish; Electronic & Electrical Engineering (with a yr in Europe, N America, Australia or Industry); Electronics (with a yr in Europe, N America, Australia or Industry) with Communications (with a yr in Europe, N America, Australia or Industry) or Computing Science (with a yr in Europe, N America, Australia or Industry); Materials Science & Engineering (with a yr in North America); Mechanical Engineering (wih a yr in Europe or North America)

BSc Econ Single Hons: *4 yrs*
Integrated BEng scheme: *4 yrs For students with inappropriate A-levels:* Biochemical engineering; Chemical Engineering; Civil Engineering; Electronic & Electrical Engineering; Engineering (with deferred choice of specialisation); Materials Science with Engineering; Mechanical Engineering

HEALTHCARE STUDIES
BN Hons: *3 yrs* Nursing

SCIENCE
BSc Hons: *3 yrs* Applied Mathematics; Biochemistry; Biological Sciences (and with deferred choice); Biology; Biomolecular & Biomedical Chemistry; Chemical, Analytical & Forensic Science; Chemistry or Computer Science or Environmental Chemistry or Sports Science; Chemistry; Computer Science; Computer Science with Electronics; Computing Mathematics; Environmental Biology; Genetics; Geography; Marine Biology with Welsh or Sports Science; Mathematics; Mathematics (with a deferred choice of specialisation); Medical Genetics; Medical Sciences & Humanities; Physics or Sports Science; Physics with Laser Physics or Medical Physics or Particle Physics & the Foundations of Cosmology; Psychology; Pure Mathematics; Sports Science; Zoology
4 yrs Biochemistry with Italian; Biochemistry (with a yr in industry); Biological Sciences with French or German or Italian or Spanish; Biomolecular & Biomedical Chemistry (with a yr abroad or a yr in industry); Chemical, Analytical & Forensic Science (with a yr abroad or a yr in industry); Chemistry (with a yr abroad or a yr in industry) with Environmental Chemistry (with a yr abroad or a yr in industry); Chemistry (with a yr abroad or a yr in industry); Chemistry (with a yr abroad or a yr in industry) with Business Management (with a yr abroad or a yr in industry); Chemistry (with a yr abroad or a yr in industry) with Law (with a yr abroad or a yr in industry); Chemistry (with a yr abroad or a yr in industry) with Computer Science (with a yr abroad or a yr in industry); Chemistry (with a yr abroad / a yr in Industry) with Sports Science (with a yr abroad / a yr in Industry); Computer Science with French or German or Italian or Spanish or Russian or Welsh; Geography with European Studies; Mathematics with French or German or Italian or Spanish or Russian or Welsh; Philosophy; Physics (with a yr abroad)
BSc Joint Hons: *3 yrs* Biological Sciences (specialising in two subjects); Biological Sciences-Geography or Psychology; Chemistry-Physics; Civil Engineering with Management; Computer Science-Psychology or Topographic Science or Physics; Economics-Geography or Mathematics or Statistics; Electronics with Management with Entrepreneurship; Geography-Topographic Science; Materials Science & Engineering with Management; Mathematics-Physics or Topographic Science; Mechanical Engineering with Management; Process Engineering with Management; Psychology-Law; Pure Mathematics-Statistics
Integrated Schemes: *4 yrs For students with inappropriate A-levels:* Biological Sciences; Biological Sciences (specialising in two subjects); Chemistry; Computer Science; Mathematics; Physics

Higher Degrees

EMBS Hons: *4 yrs* European Master in Business Sciences
LLM: *1 yr FT/2 yrs PT* Commercial and Maritime Law
MA/MSc Econ: *1 yr FT/2 yrs PT* Ancient History; Applied Criminal Justice & Criminology; Applied Social Studies; Business Economics; Child Welfare & Applied Childhood Studies; Development Management; Development Policy and Practice; Diversity of Contemporary Writing; Education; English; Ethics of Health Care; European Politics; French; German Studies; Health Care Law and Ethics; Health Care Management; Health Planning and Development; Hispanic Studies; History; International Relations: Diplomatic & Foreign Policy Studies; Literary Translation (French or German or Spanish or Welsh); Maitrise; Medical Humanities; Modern French & English Studies; Modern Italian Studies; Modern Welsh Writing in English; Philosophy;

Philosophy of Nursing; Political Theory; Social Development, Planning and Management; Social Research; Social Work & Applied Social Studies; Translation with Language Technology; Welsh; Women's Studies

MBA: *1 yr FT/2 yrs PT* Master of Business Administration

MChem Hons: *4 yrs* Chemistry (with a yr abroad or in industry); Chemistry

MEng Hons: *4 yrs* Chemical and Biochemical Engineering; Civil Engineering; Computing; Electronic & Electrical Engineering; Electronics with Computing Science; Electronics with Communications; Materials Science & Engineering; Mechanical Engineering *5 yrs* Electronic & Electrical Engineering (with a yr in Europe, N America, Australia or Industry); Electronics (with a yr in Europe, N America, Australia or Industry) with Communications (with a yr in Europe, N America, Australia or Industry) or Computing Science (with a yr in Europe, N America, Australia or Industry)

MMath Hons: *4 yrs* Mathematics

MPhys Hons: *4 yrs* Physics

MSc: *1 yr FT/2 yrs PT* Advanced Silicon Processing and Manufacturing Technologies; Biochemical Engineering; Chemical Engineering; Clinical Audit & Effectiveness; Colour Application Technology; Communication Systems; Community Services Management; Computational Modelling & Finite Elements; Computer Science; Electrical Engineering; Environmental Biology; Health Information; Health Promotion; Material Engineering; Mechanical Engineering; Medical Radiation Physics; Midwifery; Molecular Biology; Nursing; Printing and Coating Technology; Research in Health and Social Care; Substance Abuse

Degrees validated by University of Wales offered at:
Swansea Institute of Higher Education

Mount Pleasant, Swansea SA1 6ED Tel: 01792 481000 Fax: 01792 481085
e-mail: rachael.earp@sihe.ac.uk

* Subject to validation.

First Degrees

BA Hons: *3 yrs FT* Accounting; Accounting; Architectural Stained Glass; Art History with Art & Cultural Studies; Business Administration; Business-Finance*; Business Education; Ceramics; Ceramics & Glass; Computer Animation; Computer Animation*; English Studies*; Financial Management; Fine Art; Fine Art & Ceramics; General Illustration; Graphic Design; Human Resource Management*; Leisure Management; Leisure Management with Languages*; Marketing*; Media; Multimedia; Painting & Drawing; Photo Journalism; Photography in the Arts; Photojournalism & Media; Public Services; Sports/Recreation Management; Strategic Economics*; Surface Pattern Design; Tourism Management; Tourism Management with Languages* *3-4 yrs FT* Primary Education *4 yrs FT* European Business with Languages *4 yrs S* Business Studies

BA Joint Hons: *3 yrs FT* English-Theatre Studies or Film & TV Studies or Drama & Media Studies or Social Studies; Art Studies; European Studies & Environmental Conservation; Social Studies-Business Studies or Health Studies or European Studies; Theatre Studies and Film & TV Studies

BEng: *3 yrs FT* Automotive Design; Automotive Electronic Engineering; Automotive Engineering; Computer Systems (Electronics); Computer Systems (Laser Technology); Computer Systems (Multimedia); Electronic Engineering; Engineering Design & Manufacture; Engineering Design & Manufacturing; Manufacturing Systems Engineering; Motorsport Engineering & Design

BEng Hons: *3 yrs FT* Internet Engineering

BSc Hons: *3 yrs FT* 3D Computer Animation*; Building Conservation-Management; Business Information Technology; Civil Engineering-Environmental Management; Computer Networks; Computer Systems Security; Computing & Information Systems; Environmental Conservation; Environmental Management of the Built Environment; Environmental Technology-Management; Interactive Spatial Design; Motorsport Management; Multimedia; Music Technology; Packaging Design & Technology*; Product Design; Project & Construction Management; Software Engineering; Strategic Economics; Supply Chain Management; Transport Management; Web Management

LLB: *3 trms* Law

LLB Hons: *3 yrs FT* Law

Higher Degrees

MA: Fine Art; Glass *2 yrs FT/PT* Photography *2 yrs PT* Management of Human Resources
MBA: *1 yr FT/2 yrs PT* (plus dissertation)
MEd: *2 yrs PT*
MPhil: *1 yr FT/2 yrs PT* (By research)
MSc: *1 yr FT/2 yrs PT* Product Design *2 yrs FT* Leisure & Tourism *3 yrs PT* Transport

Diplomas

Diploma in Foundation Studies: *1 yr FT* Art & Design; Product Design
HND: *2 yrs FT* Architectural Stained Glass; Automotive Engineering; Building Studies; Business; Business & Marketing; Business & Finance; Business & Personnel; Business Information Technology; Ceramics; Civil Engineering Studies; Computer Networks; Computer Systems Security; Computing; Electrical; Electronics; General Illustration; Graphic Design; Instrumentation; Internet Engineering; Leisure Studies (Sport and Outdoor Activities)*; Leisure Studies (Tourism)*; Management of Innovation; Mechanical & Manufacturing Engineering; Mechatronics; Photo Journalism; Photography in the Arts; Surface Pattern Design; Technical Graphics; Transport Management *2 yrs PT* Telematics *3 yrs S* European Business Studies; Leisure Studies
PGDip: *1 yr FT/6 yrs PT* Product Design *2 yrs PT* Human Resource Management

Certificates

PGCE: *1 yr FT* Art; Business

Professional Courses

Professional Courses: *PT* AAT; ACCA; Chartered Institute of Marketing; CIMA; FETC; Institute of Personnel & Development

UNIVERSITY OF WARWICK

Coventry, West Midlands CV4 7AL Tel: 024 76523523 Fax: 024 76524752
e-mail: ugadmissions@admin.warwick.ac.uk Website: www.warwick.ac.uk
BEng: *Note:* It is possible to transfer from these degrees to the 4 yr MEng

First Degrees

BA: Gender and Cultural Studies; Sociology-Gender Studies; History (European and American); History (Modern European); History (Renaissance and Modern); Psychology-Philosophy; Politics, International Studies & Gender *By Research. Taught courses available in:* French Studies; History of Art; QTS Specialisms: Art/Drama/English/Mathematics/Music/Science *1 yr FT/2 yrs PT By Research. Taught courses available in:* Film & Television Studies; Philosophy; Philosophy and Literature; Politics
@First Para:3 yrs Ancient History & Classical Archaeology; Classical Civilisation with Philosophy; Classical Civilisation; English & Latin Literature; English & Spanish-American Literature; English and American Literature; English Literature; English Literature and Creative Writing; English-European Literature; English-Theatre Studies; Film & Literature; History-Politics or Sociology; Law and Business Studies; Philosophy with Classical Civilisation; Philosophy or Computer Science; Philosophy-Politics; Philosophy-Psychology; Politics with International Studies; Politics-Sociology; Sociology; Sociology with Social Policy; Theatre & Performance Studies *4 yrs* Comparative American Studies; English-French; English-German Literature; English-Italian Literature; French with Film Studies or Sociology; French with International Studies; French Studies with German or Italian; French-History; German or Business Studies; German with French; German with French or International Studies or Italian; German Studies; German Studies-Italian; Italian with Film Studies or International Studies or French or German or Theatre Studies; Italian and European Literature; Law-Sociology or Business Studies; Politics with French
BA Hons: *3 yrs* Economics-Economic History *4 yrs* French-German Studies or Italian Studies *6 yrs average, by PT evening or daytime study only*

BA Hons QTS
BA/BSc: Economics-Politics; International Studies *3 yrs* Mathematics; Mathematics-Philosophy
BEng: *3 yrs* Civil Engineering; Electronic and Communication Engineering
BSc: Mathematics and Mathematical Learning; MMathStat; MORSE – Mathematics/Operational Research/Statistics/Economics *3 yrs* Accounting & Finance; Biochemistry; Biological Sciences; Engineering-Business Studies; Chemistry; Chemistry with Management; Chemistry with Medicinal Chemistry; Computational Biology; Computer Science; Computer or Business Studies; Management Sciences; Economics; Industrial Economics; Management Sciences; Mathematics with Computing; Microbiology; Microbiology-Virology; Physics and Business Studies; Physics or Economics or Business Studies; Mathematics *4 yrs* International Business; Physics; Physics with Computing; Psychology; Virology
Bsc/BEng: *3 yrs* Computer Systems Engineering; Electrical Engineering; Electronic Engineering; Engineering (General); Engineering Design & Appropriate Technology; Manufacturing Systems Engineering; Mechanical Engineering
BSc/MMaths: *4 yrs* Mathematics
LLB: *3 yrs* Law *4 yrs* European Law; Law
MBChB: Medicine

Higher Degrees

DClinPsych: *4 yrs* Clinical Psychology
EngD: *4 yrs FT*
LLM: International Economic Law (and Diploma); Law in Development
MA: Art & Design Education; Arts Education & Cultural Studies; Continental Philosophy; Creative and Media Enterprises; Culture, Class & Power: Modern Europe since 1850; Drama Education & Cultural Studies; Eighteenth Century Studies; English & European Renaissance Drama; English Language Studies & Methods; English Language Teaching; English Language Teaching for Specific Purposes; English Language Teaching for Young Learners; European Industrial Relations; History of Race in the Americas; Industrial Relations; Language Programme Evaluation and Testing; Organisation Studies; Performance, Social Work; Space and IT Modelling; Philosophy & Literature; Philosophy & Social Theory; Religious Education; Renaissance Studies *By Research. Taught courses available in:* French Studies; History of Art; Modern French Cultural Studies *1 yr FT/2 yrs PT By Research. Taught courses available in:* Children's Literature Studies; Colonial & Post-colonial Literature in English; Comparative Literary Theory; European Cultural Policy & Administration; Film & Television Studies; Gender, Literature & Modernity; Religious & Social History 1500-1700; Research in Film and Television Studies; Social History of Medicine; Social Policy (or Diploma); Sport, Politics & Society *1 yr FT/2 yrs PT by research, thesis & in some cases exam* Humanities (Comparative Cultural Studies/Caribbean Studies/Classics and Ancient History/German Studies/History of Art/Italian/Renaissance Studies *4 yrs PT* Educational Studies *PT By Research. Taught courses available in:* Local & Regional History
MA/Dip: Continuing Education; English; Researching Lifelong Learning
MA/MSc/Dip: Philosophy & Ethics of Mental Health
MA/PGCert: British Cultural Studies
MA/PGCert/PGDip: Translation Studies
MA/PGDip: Philosophy
MBA: *1 yr FT/3 yrs PT* (PT evening/modular. An MBA by distance learning also available (48-96 mths)) *FT/PT Modular:* Business Administration (and Distance Learning Programmes)
MChem: *4 yrs* Chemistry; Chemistry with Medicinal Chemistry
MD (Doctor of Medicine): *2 yrs FT/3 yrs PT* (By Research)
MEd: *2 yrs PT By course work & dissertation:* Continuing Education
MEng: Computer Science *4 yrs* Electronic and Communication Engineering *4 yrs FT* Civil Engineering; Computer Systems Engineering; Electrical Engineering; Electronic Engineering; Engineering (General); Engineering Design & Appropriate Technology; Manufacturing Systems Engineering; Mechanical Engineering
MMathStat: *4 yrs* Mathematics-Statistics
MMedSci (Master of Medical Science): *1 yr FT/2 yrs PT* (By research)
MPA: Public Administration
MPA (European): *1 yr FT/3 yrs PT*

MPhil: *2 yrs FT/3 yrs PT* (By research)
MPhys: *4 yrs* Mathematics-Physics; Physics
MRes: *1 yr FT* Engineering
MS (Master of Surgery): *1 yr FT/2 yrs PT* (By research)
MSc: Engineering Business Management; @First Para:Information Technology for Manufacture; Management Science & Operational Research; Manufacturing Systems Engineering; Process Business Management (and Post-Experience Diploma); Mathematics Education; Quality & Reliability *1 yr FT/2 yrs PT By Research. Taught courses available in:* Advanced Electronic Engineering; Advanced Engineering; Advanced Mechanical Engineering; Community Child Health; Economics & Finance; Financial Mathematics; Interdisciplinary Mathematics; Manufacturing Engineering by Research; Mathematics; Primary Care Management (Certificate / Diploma); Science Education *PT* Instrumental & Analytical Methods in Biological & Environmental Chemistry
MSc/Dip/Cert: Primary Care Management
MSc/PgD: Economics *1 yr FT/2 yrs PT By Research. Taught courses available in:* Quantitative Development Economics
MSc/PGDip: Ecosystems Analysis & Governance; Health Information Science for Health Services Management; Statistics
MSc/PGDip/PGCert: Community Gynaecology
PhD: *3 yrs FT min/4 yrs PT*
Postgraduate Diploma/MA: Applied Social Studies (also as Certificate); Comparative Labour Studies; Gender & International Development; Interdisciplinary Gender Studies; International Political Economy; International Studies; Modern British Studies; Politics; Race & Ethnic Studies; Social & Political Thought; Sociological Research in Healthcare; Sociology of Education; Training & Human Resource Development

HIGHER DOCTORATES
DLitt; DSc; LLD: (Awarded for significant original work)

Diplomas

CCETSW Diploma: Social Work
Diploma: English Language Teaching & Administration; Law in Development *1 yr FT/2 yrs PT By Research. Taught courses available in:* History of Art
Post-experience Diploma: Engineering Business Management; Health Information Science (also as Post-Experience Certificate)
Postgraduate Diploma: Analytical Biology; British Cultural Studies; Design Systems in Production; High Performance Computers & Computation; Human Resource Management; Legal Studies; Music Education & Cultural Studies; Post-Compulsory Education (Further or Higher Education); Primary Health Care Management; Sociology

Certificates

Certificates: *3 yrs/4 yrs* Primary Diabetes Care
Joint Certificate: British Cultural Studies-English Language Teaching
Open Studies Certificate: Archaeology; Classical Studies (Rome or Greece); Community Development & Leadership; Creative Writing; Earth Science; Ecology and Conservation; English Studies; Historical Studies; Marine Ecology; Marine Studies; Philosophical Studies; Religious Studies; Studies in Complementary Health Care; Studies in Women and Gender; Workers' Education in the UK *4 mths FT/24 mths PT* Employment Studies
PGCE: Post-Graduate Certificate in Education
Post-experience Certificate: Engineering Business Management; English Law
Postgraduate Certificate: Labour Market Analysis; @First Para:Design Systems in Production; Industrial Relations; Instrumental & Analytical Methods in Biological & Environmental Chemistry; Post-Compulsory Education (Further & Higher Education); Primary Diabetes Care; Psychotherapy *1 yr FT/2 yrs PT By Research. Taught courses available in:* Religious Education *3 yrs/4 yrs* Language Teaching; Mentoring for Professional Development; Middle Management in Colleges *4 mths FT/24 mths PT* Drama Education

THE UNIVERSITY OF WESTMINSTER

309 Regent Street, London W1R 8AL Tel: 020 7911 5000 Fax: 020 7911 5192
e-mail: admissions@wmin.ac.uk Website: www.wmin.ac.uk

† Subject to validation.

First Degrees

BA Hons: *1 yr FT* Medical Journalism *3 yrs FT* Architecture; Architecture with special pathways in Interior Design or Urban Design; Business with Property; Tourism-Business; Ceramics; Commercial Music; Contemporary Media Practice; Digital Media; Economics for Business; English Language & Linguistics; English Language-English Literature; English Literary & Cultural Studies-Linguistics; English Literary & Cultural Studies; Fashion; Film and Television; Graphic Information Design; Illustration; Land Economy with Business; Management of Business Information; Media Studies; Photographic & Digital Arts; Professional Language Studies; Russian; Social Science; Tourism & Planning; Town Planning; Urban Design with Town Planning; Urban Development with Business Management *3 yrs FT/4 yrs PT min* Business; Business Studies (services); Human Geography; Mixed Media Art; Modern History; Politics; Sociology *4 yrs FT* European Management; International Business (Europe); International Business (with language); Modern Languages with English Language or Linguistics with English Literary & Cultural Studies *4 yrs PT min* Arabic; Chinese; Photography & Multimedia *4 yrs S* Business Information Management & Finance; Business Studies; Fashion Merchandising Management *4 yrs S/5 yrs PT* Housing Management & Development

BA/BSc Hons: *3 yrs FT* Business Computing

BEng Hons: *3 yrs FT* Digital Communications; Electronic Engineering; Real-Time Computer Systems *3 yrs FT/4 yrs S* Technological Design & Innovation

BSc Hons: *1 yr FT* Biological Sciences Level Zero; Computing Level Zero *3 yrs FT* Applied Ecology; Architecture; Artificial Intelligence; Biochemistry; Biochemistry & Microbiology; Biochemistry-Physiology; Biological Sciences; Biotechnology; Biotechnology in Medicine; Cognitive Science; Computational Mathematics; Digital & Photographic Imaging; Environmental Sciences & Business Management; Health Sciences : Homeopathy; Health Sciences: Chiropractic; Health Sciences: Complementary Therapies; Health Sciences: Herbal Medicine; Health Sciences: Nutritional Therapy; Human Nutrition; Human Physiology; Information Systems Engineering; Internet Computing; Leisure Development & Strategic Management; Mathematical Sciences; Microbiology; Multimedia Computing; Nutrition and Exercise Science; Product Design Engineering; Psychological Sciences; Software Engineering; Sports and Exercise Sciences; Town Planning (1 yr Dip); Traditional Chinese Medicine: Acupuncture; Urban Estate Management *3 yrs FT/4 yrs PT* Applied Biology; Biomedical Sciences; Computer Science *3 yrs FT/4 yrs S* Computer Communications and Networks; Industrial Systems & Business Management; Psychology; Statistics and Operational Research *3 yrs FT/4 yrs S/5 yrs PT* Building Surveying; Construction Management or Building Engineering; Construction with Business; Facilities Management; Quantity Surveying *3 yrs FT/5 yrs PT* Computing; Digital Signal Processing; Electronics; Health Sciences: Therapeutic Bodywork; Media Technology; Mobile Communications; Real-Time Computing *4 yrs PT* Photography & Multimedia *4 yrs S* Business Information Technology; Computer Systems Technology *5 yrs PT* Building Control Surveying

GradDip: *2 yrs PT*

LLB: *1 yr FT/2 yrs PT* Commercial Law *3 yrs FT/4 yrs PT min* Law *4 yrs FT* European Legal Studies; Law with French; Law with Spanish

Higher Degrees

LLM: *1 yr FT/2 yrs PT* International Law; Venture Capital; Women and the Law

MA: *1 yr FT* Individual and Organisational Development; International Business & Management; International Finance (with Ecole Superieure de Commerce, Nice); International Journalism; Photographic Journalism *1 yr FT/2 yrs PT* Audio Production; Communication; Communication Policy and Regulation; Computer Imaging in Architecture; Contemporary Chinese Cultural Studies; Design & Media Arts; Design for Interaction; Development Administration; Digital Media; Dispute Prevention and Resolution; Entrepreneurship; Globalisation, Development & Transition; Human Resource Management; Hypermedia Studies; International Finance; Landscape Studies (Architecture); Legal Practice; Marketing; Marketing Communications; Music

Management; Public Policy & Administration; Technical & Specialised Translation; Tourism Management; Translation and Linguistics; Urban Regeneration *1 yr FT/2 yrs PT/DL* Applied Social & Market Research *1 yr FT/2-5 yrs PT* Photographic Studies *1 yr FT/3 yrs PT* Diplomatic Studies *1 yr PT* Advanced Legal Practice *1-3 yrs PT* Advanced Social Work *2 yrs FT/3 yrs PT* Architecture *2 yrs PT* 20th-Century Historical Studies *2-3 yrs PT* Interprofessional Practice *2-4 yrs PT* Journalism Studies *2-5 yrs PT* Continuing Professional Education (Health and Social Care); Film & Television Studies; Photographic Studies *3 yrs PT* Town Planning

MA/LLM: *1 yr FT/2 yrs PT* Entertainment Law; International Commercial Law
MA/MSc: *1 yr FT/2-5 yrs PT* Business Computing
MA/PGCert/PGDip: *1 yr FT/2 yrs PT* Applied Language Studies; Bilingual Translation; International Relations-Political Theory; Twentieth Century Europe: Perspectives and Interpretations *1-3 yrs PT* Social Housing Law *2 yrs PT* French-Francophone Studies *2-5 yrs PT* Community Development *Flexible PT* Housing Studies; Professional Development in the Built Environment
MA/PGDip: *1 yr FT* Urban Design (Europe) *1 yr FT/2 yrs PT* Urban Design
MBA: *1 yr FT* Diplome D'Etudes Superieures with Ecole Superieure de Commerce, Montpellier; International Construction *1 yr FT/2 yrs PT* Tourism *18-24 mths PT by research* Public Services Management (General) *2 yrs PT* Design Management
MSc: *1 yr FT* Advanced Computer Science; Environment & Business; European Logistics, Transport & Distribution Management; European Property Development & Planning; Information Technology Security; Transport Policy: Planning and Management; Urban Design (Europe); Urban Planning *1 yr FT/2 yrs PT* Applied Microbiology; Biomedical Sciences; Business Information Technology; Business Psychology; Clinical Chemistry; Computer Networks & Communications; Computers in Instrumentation; Digital Imaging; Digital Signal Processing Systems; Haematology; Information Management & Finance; Medical Biotechnology; Medical Microbiology; Medical Molecular Biology; Mobile Personal & Satellite Communications; Quantitative Finance; Urban Design; VLSI Systems Design *1 yr FT/2-3 yrs PT* Transport Planning & Management *1 yr FT/2-4 yrs PT* Information Systems Design (Conversion); Parallel and Distributed Computing *1 yr FT/2-5 yrs PT* Advanced Social Work; Business Computing; Computer Science (Conversion); Database Systems; E-Commerce; Interactive Multimedia; IT Security; Software Engineering (+ Conversion) *2 yrs FT/2-3 yrs PT* Health Sciences: Osteopathic Medicine *2 yrs PT* Health Sciences: Osteopathic Medicine; Evaluation of Clinical Practice; Facilities Management; General Practice & Primary Health; Health Psychology; Public Health (Food and Nutrition); Urban Regeneration *2-3 yrs PT* Cognitive Science and Intelligent Computing *2-5 yrs PT* Complementary Therapy Studies; Complementary Therapy: Acupuncture; Complementary Therapy: Bodywork; Decision Sciences *Distance Learning* Payroll Management *Variable PT* Energy, Economics & the Environment
PGC: *1 yr PT* Fire Safety
PGDip: *1 yr FT/2 yrs PT* Legal Practice *2 yrs PT* Personnel Management

Diplomas

Certified Diploma: *1 yr PT/DL* Accounting & Finance
Foundation Course: *1 yr FT* Built Environment Studies; International Built Environment Studies
GradDip: *1 yr FT/2 yrs PT* Psychology *2 yrs PT* Law
HND: Business Administration; Environmental Law *3 yrs FT/4 yrs S* Financial Studies
MSc: *1 yr FT/2-5 yrs PT* Computer Science (Conversion)
PGDip: Conference Interpreting Techniques *1 yr FT* Broadcast Journalism: Print Journalism; Urban Planning *1 yr FT/2 yrs PT* Legal Practice; Technical & Specialised Translation; Translation & Linguistics *2 yrs FT/3 yrs PT* Architecture *3 yrs PT* Town Planning *9 mths FT/2 yrs PT* Diplomatic Studies *Open Learning Programme* Health & Social Services Management; Training & Development

Certificates

Advanced Certificate: *1 yr PT* Marketing
PGC: For Teachers in Primary Care *6 mths FT/1 yr PT* Marketing
PGCert: Team Management *1 yr FT/2 yrs PT* Technical & Specialised Translation; Translation & Linguistics *1 yr PT* Certificate for Teachers in Primary Care; Housing Studies; Management Development; Professional Practice in Architecture

UNIVERSITY OF THE WEST OF ENGLAND, BRISTOL

Frenchay Campus, Coldharbour Lane, Bristol BS16 1QY Tel: 0117 965 6261 Fax: 0117 344 2810
e-mail: admissions@uwe.ac.uk Website: www.uwe.ac.uk

† Subject to validation.

First Degrees

BA Hons: *3 yrs FT* Business Administration; Business Administration with Tourism; Ceramics; Cultural & Media Studies; Cultural & Media Studies-History; Drama-English or Cultural & Media Studies or History†; Economics; English; English- History; Fashion/Textile Design; Fine Arts (Incorporating: Art & Visual Culture, Fine Art, Fine Art in Context); Geography; Graphic Design; History; Illustration; International Business Economics; Modern Languages-Information Systems; Modern Languages-Business Systems; Planning with Leisure; Planning with Transport; Planning-Development; Politics; Science, Society and the Media; Social Science; Sociology; Time-Based Media; Town & Country Planning; Transport & Environmental Management *3 yrs FT/4 yrs S* Accounting & Finance; Business Decision Analysis; Business Decision Analysis with European or American Study; Business Studies with Combined Science; Equine Business Management; Housing Policy and Management *4 yrs FT* Architecture & Planning; European Languages-Law; International Business Studies with Language or Tourism; Modern Languages-European Studies; Primary (QTS) *4 yrs S* Business Information Systems with European or American Study; Business Information Systems; Business Studies with Tourism; Business Studies; Information Systems Analysis with European or American Study; Information Systems Analysis; Marketing

BEng Hons/MEng: *3 yrs FT/4 yrs S/4 yrs FT/5 yrs S* Aerospace Systems Engineering†; Aerospace Manufacturing Engineering; Digital Systems Engineering; Electrical & Electronic Engineering; Electronic Engineering; Manufacturing Systems Engineering; Mechanical Engineering

BSc Hons: *3 yrs FT* Building Surveying; Built Environmental Studies; Business in Property; Combined Sciences; Geography & Environmental Management; Midwifery; Nursing (Adult/Child/Learn.D/Mental Health); Physiotherapy; Psychology; Psychology-Health Science; Radiography (Diagnostic/Therapeutic); Real Estate & Leisure Management; Real Estate (Valuation & Management); Sports, Exercise & Health Sciences *3 yrs FT/4 yrs S* Agriculture & Conservation†; Agriculture & Land Management†; Animal Science; Applied Chemical Sciences; Building Engineering & Management; Building Surveying; Business in Construction; Computing-Mathematics or Statistics (also available with European Study); Construction Management; Engineering; Environmental Biology; Environmental Chemistry; Environmental Engineering; Environmental Health; Environmental Health Studies; Environmental Quality & Resource Management; Environmental Science; Equine Science; Linguistics (Joint Honours); Mathematical Sciences; Mathematical Sciences with European or American Study; Music Systems Engineering; Quantity Surveying; Statistics with European or American Study; Statistics; Valuation & Estate Management; Veterinary Nursing Science *4 yrs FT* Primary (QTS) *4 yrs S* Applied Biochemistry & Molecular Biology; Applied Biological Sciences; Applied Microbiology; Applied Physiology & Pharmacology; Biomedical Sciences; Computer Science; Computing & Information Systems with European or American Study; Computing & Information Systems; Computing for Real-Time Systems with European or American Study†; Computing for Real-Time Systems; Software Engineering

LLB: *3 yrs FT* Law

Higher Degrees

EdD: *PT only* Education

LLM: *FT/PT* European Law & Comparative Awards; Industrial & Commercial Law; International Law; Socio-Legal Studies *PT only* Advanced Legal Practice

MA/MSc: *FT/PT* Cultural & Media Studies; English; European Planning & Development; History; Marketing *PT only* Changing Frameworks in Health & Welfare; Education; Health Psychology†; Learning & Change in Organisations; Legal Studies; Qualitative Methods in Psychology†; Research Methods in Psychology; Strategic Human Resources Management

MA/MSc/PGDip: *FT* Machine Learning & Adaptive Computing *FT/PT* Advanced Language Studies; Biomedical Science; Cellular Pathology; Ceramics – Making & Archiving; Clinical Chemistry; Digital Media; Ecology & Society (Social Science); Environmental Health; European

Business; European Labour Studies†; Film Studies & European Cinema; Fine Art in Context; Haematology; Human Resource Management; Information Technology; International Business Economics; Landscape Studies; Manufacturing & Management Information Systems; Medical Microbiology; Multidisciplinary Printmaking; Politics; Social & Political Theory; Social Research; Social Sciences; Sociology; TEFL & Linguistics *PT only* Cancer Care; Gender & Health; Group Relations & Society; Health & Social Care Research; Health Promotion; Information Systems; Instrumental Analysis; Nuclear Medicine Technology; Primary Health & Community Care; Sports Medicine & Rehabilitation; Trauma Radiography

MA/MSC/PGDip/PGCert: *Distance Learning* Community Safety & Crime Prevention; Countryside Conservation & Management; Town & Country Planning; Urban & Rural Regeneration *FT/PT* Advanced Manufacturing Systems; Advanced Technologies in Electronics†; Analytical Modelling for Engineering Design; Applied Vision, Graphical Modelling & Virtual Reality†; Built Environment Research; Built Environment Studies; Conservation of Buildings & their Environments; Construction Project Management; Equine Business Management; Facilities Management; Guidance: Vocational/Educational; Housing Studies; Intelligent Engineering Systems†; Local Economic Development; Local Environmental Management & Sustainability†; Statistics & Management Science; Systems Engineering & Project Management; Technology Management; Total Quality Management in Engineering†; Total Technology; Tourism & Sustainability; Town & Country Planning; Urban Design† *PT only* Management; Real Estate; Technology Management Aerospace; Total Technology Aerospace; Trauma Radiography

MBA: *FT* UK Route/European Route

Diplomas

PgDip/PgCert: *FT/PT* Counselling; Creative Sound Production; Education (FAHE); European Law & Comparative Awards; International Law; Town Planning Studies

PGDip: *FT* Bar Vocational; Careers Guidance *FT/PT* Analytical Modelling for Engineering Design; Art Therapy; Industrial & Commercial Law; Law (CPE); Legal Practice (LPC); Socio-Legal Studies *PT only* Education; Professional Skills (Law)

Certificates

PGCE: *FT* Education: Primary/Secondary
PGCert: *Open Learning Programme* Health Education

Degrees validated by University of the West of England, Bristol offered at:

Wesley College

College Park Drive, Henbury Road, Bristol BS10 7QD Tel: 0117 959 1200 Fax: 0117 959 1277 e-mail: admin@wescoll.demon.co.uk Website: www.wescoll.demon.co.uk

First Degrees

BA Hons: Theological Studies; Theology & Ministry

Higher Degrees

MA: Theology & Ministry

Diplomas

Diploma: Theological Studies; Theology & Ministry

Certificates

Certificate: Theological Studies; Theology & Ministry

UNIVERSITY OF WOLVERHAMPTON

Wulfruna Street, Wolverhampton WV1 1SB Tel: 01902 321000 Fax: 01902 322686
e-mail: enquiries@wlv.ac.uk Website: www.wlv.ac.uk

Note: Most of the BA & BSc courses listed can be taken in major/minor/joint combinations within the modular degree scheme.

First Degrees

BA: *3 yrs FT* Languages for Business *4 yrs FT* Human Rights; Latin American Studies; Russian; Spanish *4 yrs S* Accounting & Finance; Business Studies; Computer Science; Computing; Design for Multimedia; European Business Administration; Hospitality & Licensed Retail Management; Interactive Multimedia Communication

BA Hons: *3 yrs FT/4 yrs S* Interior Architectural Design

BA/BA Hons: *3 yrs* Design for Multimedia; Education Studies & English; Journalism & Editorial Design; Languages for Business; Marketing and Sports Studies

BA/BSc: *1 yr* Specialist Practitioner *1 yr FT top-up* Business Enterprise *4 yrs FT* French; Language & Communication; Languages

BA/BSc Hons: Accounting; Accounting; Accounting & Finance; American Studies; Analytical Chemistry; Animation; Applied Theology; Applied Theology; Biochemistry; Biology; Biomedical Science; Biotechnology; Business; Business Information Management; Business Law; Ceramics; Chemistry; Computing; Conductive Education; Construction Studies; Criminal Justice; Dance Studies; Deaf Studies; Design & Technology; Design for Interior Textiles; Design Studies; Drama; Earth Science; Ecology; Economics; Education Studies; Electronic Media; Engineering; English; English as a Foreign Language; Environmental Animal Biology; Environmental Chemistry; Environmental Law; Environmental Management; Environmental Science; European and International Law; European Studies; European Studies; Exercise Science; Film Studies; Fine Art as Social Practice; Food Biology; French; French; Furniture Design; Genetics & Molecular Biology; Geography; German; German; German Studies; Glass; Graphic Communication; Health Sciences; History; Human Biology; Human Geography; Human Physiology; Human Resource Management; Illustration; Industrial Product Design; Interactive Multimedia Communication; International Studies; Interpreting British Sign Language/English; Italian Studies; Journalism & Editorial Design; Latin American Studies; Law; Leisure Management; Linguistics; Manufacturing Studies; Marketing; Materials Technology; Mathematical Sciences; Mechatronics; Media & Cultural Studies; Media & Cultural Studies; Medical Communication Studies; Microbiology; Music; Music – Popular; Painting; Pharmacology; Philosophy; Photography; Plant & Crop Science; Politics; Printmaking; Psychology; Public Art; Public Health; Religious Studies; Russian; Russian Studies; Sculpture; Social Policy; Social Policy; Social Welfare Law; Sociology; Spanish; Spanish; Spanish Studies; Special Needs & Inclusion in Society; Sports Studies; Teaching English for Speakers of Other Languages; Tourism; War Studies; Women's Studies; Woods, Metals & Plastics *1-2 yrs Post HND courses:* Applied Social Studies; Built Environment; Business Administration; Business Economics; Business Enterprise; Business Information Technology; Computer Studies; Health Studies; Health Studies (Health Promotion); Health Studies (Primary Health Care); Marketing; Rehabilitation Studies; Tourism *1-2 yrs by research according to qualifications Post HND courses:* Further, Adult & Higher Education

BEd/BEd Hons/BA/ BA Hons with QTS: *3 yrs FT* Primary; Secondary

BEng Hons: *3 yrs FT* Manufacturing Engineering; Mechatronics

BEng Hons/BSc/BSc Hons: *3 yrs FT* Automotive Systems Engineering; Engineering; Manufacturing Engineering; Mechanical Engineering; Mechatronics

BMidwif: *2 yrs FT* (and English National Board Higher Award) *Up to 5 yrs PT* (and English National Board Higher Award)

BSc: *3 yrs* Complementary Therapies; E-Commerce; Early Childhood Studies; Geography; Health Sciences; Manufacturing Studies; Materials Technology; Occupational Health & Safety; Psychology; Public Health; Sports Studies; Sports Technology *3 yrs FT/4 yrs S* Analytical Chemistry; Applied Environmental Geology; Applied Sciences; Architectural Conservation & Management; Architectural Design & Technology; Biochemistry; Biochemistry with Food Science; Biochemistry with Molecular Biology; Biological Sciences; Biomedical Sciences; Biotechnology; Building Surveying; Built Environment; Chemistry; Chemistry with Polymer Science; Civil

Engineering; Civil Engineering Management; Civil Engineering Surveying (Quantities); Computer Aided Engineering Design; Computer Aided Industrial Design; Computer-Aided Design & Construction; Computer-Aided Product Design; Construction Management; Decision Sciences; Digital Product Modelling; Ecology; Engineering-Languages or Business Law or Business; Environmental Animal Biology; Environmental Chemistry; Environmental Management; Environmental Science; Environmental Technology; Food Biology; Genetics & Molecular Biology; Housing Development & Management; Materials & Quality Engineering; Mathematical Sciences; Medicinal Biochemistry; Microbiology; Off-Road Vehicle Design; Physical Geography; Plant & Crop Science; Property & Asset Management; Public Health; Quantity Surveying; Rehabilitation Studies; Sports Technology; Virtual Reality Design; Virtual Reality Manufacturing *4 yrs S* Business Information Systems; Computer Science; Computer Science (Information Systems); Computer Science (Multimedia Terminology); Computer Science (Software Engineering); Computer Studies; Computing; Mathematical Business Analysis
BSc Hons: *1 yr FT* Specialist Practitioner – Behaviour Therapy Nursing *2 yrs FT/Up to 5 yrs PT* Professional Midwifery Studies; Professional Studies (Nursing) *2-5 yrs PT* Nursing with ENB Higher *3 yrs FT* Midwifery (with Registered Midwife Qualification); Nursing (with Registered Midwife Qualification) *4 yrs S* Computer Studies (post-diploma top-up)
LLB: *3 yrs FT/4-6 yrs PT*

Higher Degrees

LLM: *1 yr FT/PT/DL*
MA: *1 yr FT* English Law; European Business Communication *1 yr FT/2-3 yrs PT* Art & Design; Design & Technology; European Studies; Further Vocational Education & Training; International Business; International Studies; Quality Management *1 yr PT* Human Resource Management *PT* English Studies; History *Variable PT* Child Care
MBA: *1 yr FT/3 yrs PT*
MEd: Special Needs and Inclusion in Society
MMedEd: *PT*
MSc: *1 yr FT* Advanced Clinical Nursing Practice *1 yr FT/2 yrs PT* Biomedical Science; Computer Aided Design & Construction; Computer Aided Engineering Design; Computing; Construction Law; Environmental Management; Food Biology *1 yr FT/2-3 yrs PT* Built Environment; Computer Science; Computer Science; Computer Science (Multimedia Technology); Computer Science (Multimedia Technology); Construction Project Management; Environmental Science; Environmental Technology; Health Studies; Land Reclamation *12 mths FT* Applied Microbiology & Biotechnology; Environmental Science; Environmental Technology; Instrumental Chemical Analysis *18 mths PT* Human Resource Development *2 yrs FT* Applied Sport and Exercise Science *2 yrs FT/PT* Virtual Manufacturing in Construction & Engineering *56 wks FT* Development Training & Education *FT/PT* Health Studies *Variable PT* Counselling Psychology

Diplomas

DipHE: *2 yrs FT/4-5 yrs PT* European Office Administration & Communication *3 yrs FT* Registered Nurse *PT* Registered Nurse
Diploma: *2 yrs PT* Social Work with Diploma in Higher Education *3 yrs FT/PT* Registered Nurse with DipHE *FT/PT* Professional Studies in Education
HND: Applied Biology; Biochemistry; Biomedical Science; Biotechnology & Microbiology; Building Studies; Business & Finance; Chemistry; Civil Engineering Studies; Computer Aided Design in Construction; Computing; Design (Figurative, Sculpture & Modelling or Furniture or Typography); Design Network; Engineering (Computer Aided Design); Engineering (Manufacturing Studies); Engineering (Mechanical Engineering); Environmental Management; Environmental Science; Equine Studies; Graphic Communication; Hospitality; Mechatronics; Photography; Physiology & Pharmacology
LLDip: *1 yr FT/2 yrs PT*
PGDip: *32 wks* Childcare *FT/PT* Art & Design; Community Health; Computer and Engineering Design; Construction Law; Construction Project Management; Education; English Studies; History; Human Resource Development; Human Resource Development; Human Resource Management; Legal Practice Course; Management Studies; Specialist Practitioner

Certificates

Certificate: CCETSW Award in Practice Teaching; Further, Adult & Higher Education; Health Education
HNC: Biochemistry; Chemistry; Food Product Design; Food Science with Business
PGCE: *1 yr FT* Further, Adult & Higher Education; Primary School; Secondary School
PGCert: *FT/PT* Art & Design; Computer Aided Engineering Design; Construction Law; English Studies; History; Human Resource Development; Human Resource Management; Management Studies

UNIVERSITY COLLEGE WORCESTER

Henwick Grove, Worcester WR2 6AJ Tel: 01905 855111 Fax: 01905 855132
e-mail: f.fairhurst@worc.ac.uk Website: www.worc.ac.uk

BA Hons/BSc Hons: Modular scheme qualifying with single or joint honours or major/minor honours or a combined studies degree depending on weighting of subjects.
† Subject to validation; * offered in conjunction with Pershore & Hindlip College (at Pershore); ** with Kidderminster College; *** with Pershore & Hindlip College (at Hindlip); **** with Holme Lacy College; ***** with Evesham College; ****** with Stourbridge College; ******* with Worcester College of Technology.

First Degrees

BA: *1 yr FT* Public Services (Top-up Degree); Social Welfare (Top-up degree, in association with North East Worcestershire College)
BA Hons: *1 yr FT* Early Childhood Studies (Top-up degree); Media (Top-up degree) *3 yrs FT* QTS Primary Education (Early Years 3-8 or Later Years 7-11) *4 yrs FT* QTS Primary Education (Art or Biology or English or PE)
BA Hons/BSc Hons: *3 yrs FT* Art & Design; Biological Science; Business Management; Drama; Education Studies; English & Literary Studies; Environmental Science; Geography; Health Studies; Heritage Studies; History; Information Technology; Media & Cultural Studies; Psychology; Sociology; Sports Studies; Women's Studies
BSc Hons: *1 yr FT* Equine Studies (Top-up Degree) *3 yrs FT* Midwifery (February or September entry) *4 yrs FT* Horticulture *Flexible/PT* Equine Sports Coaching (Top-up Degree, in association with the British Horse Society) *FT/PT* Applied Professional Studies for Registered Nurses, Midwives & Health Visitors

Higher Degrees

MASTER'S DEGREES OR EQUIVALENT
MA: *1 yr FT/2 yrs PT* Contemporary Studies: Sociology; Education; English Renaissance Studies; History; Studies in British Theatre *2 yrs PT* 19th Century Studies
MPhil/PhD: *FT/PT* (By research)
MSc: *1 yr FT/2 yrs PT* Education Management *2 yrs PT* Clinical Practice; Environmental Issues; Gerontology; Health & Care

Diplomas

DipHE: *3 yrs FT* Nursing
Diploma: *1 yr FT* Education *2 yrs PT* Management Studies
HND: *2 yrs FT* Animal Care; Computing & Information Technology; Early Childhood Studies 0-8; Environmental Management; Equine Studies; Food Quality & Manufacture; Health & Social Care; Horticulture (Crop Technology); Horticulture (Management & Design of Gardens); Information Technology Management; Media; Outdoor Recreation Management; Sport & Leisure Studies; Sports Studies; Travel & Tourism

Certificates

Certificate: *18 mths PT* Health Service Management; Management Studies
PGCE: *1 yr FT* Early Years (Primary); Education (Secondary) (Major subject in English, Business

Studies & Economics, Geography, History, Design &Technology/Food & Textiles, Mathematics, Modern Languages, Music, Physical Education, Science: Biology, Chemistry or Physics); Later Years (Primary)

UNIVERSITY OF YORK

Heslington, York YO1 5DD Tel: 01904 430000 Fax: 01904 433433
e-mail: admissions@york.ac.uk Website: www.york.ac.uk

The University awards the Bachelor of Arts degree in the Arts, the Mathematical Sciences, the Social Sciences and Psychology, the Bachelor of Science degree in the Applied and Natural Sciences (including Psychology) and the Mathematical Sciences, the Bachelor of Engineering degree in Engineering, the Master of Physics degree in Physics, and the Master of Engineering degree in Computer Systems and Software Engineering and in Electronic Systems Engineering. All courses are Hons degrees, but candidates who fail to reach this standard may be considered for the ordinary degree award. Degree courses are Single Subject & Combined Subject.

First Degrees

BA Hons: *3-4 yrs* Applied Social Science; Archaeology with Education; Economic History with Education; Economics-Economic History or Econometrics or Finance or History or Philosophy or Politics or Sociology; Economic History-Politics or Sociology; Economics-Politics; Philosophy; Educational Studies; English or Writing and Performance; English with Education or Philosophy; English Language & Linguistics; English-History or History of Art or Linguistics or Philosophy or Politics; French & German (Language & Linguistics); French & Linguistics; German & Linguistics; Hindi & Linguistics; History with Economics or Education or French or Sociology; History; History of Art; History-Archaeology; History-History of Art or Philosophy or Politics; Languages & Linguistics or Chinese; Linguistics with Education or Literature or Philosophy; Midwifery Practice; Modern Languages & Linguistics; Music with Education; Music; Philosophy; Philosophy with Education or English or Linguistics; Philosophy, Politics & Economics or English; Philosophy-Linguistics; Philosophy-Sociology or Linguistics or Economic History; Politics with Education; Politics or English or History; Politics-Sociology or Social Policy; Social Policy; Social Policy-Sociology or Politics; Sociology with Education; Sociology

BA/BSc Hons: *3-4 yrs* Archaeology with Education; Biology; Economic History; Economic History with Education; Economics with Education; Economics-Econometrics with Education; English; History with Education with Education; Linguistics; Management, Information Technology and Language or Physics or Statistics; Mathematics with Economics or Education or Linguistics or Physics or a Yr in Europe or Health Services or Physics (with a yr in Europe); Mathematics-Philosophy or Physics; Music with Education; Philosophy with Education; Physics with Education; Politics with Education; Sociology with Education

BA/BSc/BEng Hons: *3-4 yrs* Computer Science; Computer Science with Business Management; Music Technology

BEng Hons: *3 yrs FT/4 yrs S* Electronic & Communication Engineering; Electronic & Computer Engineering; Electronic Engineering; Electronic Engineering with Business Management or Music Technology Systems

BSc Hons: *3 yrs* Biology with Education; Chemistry; Chemistry, Life Systems & Pharmaceuticals; Chemistry, Management & Industry; Chemistry, Resources & the Environment; Computer Science-Mathematics; Economics; Economics & Finance; Environment, Economics & Ecology; Health Sciences; Physics with Astrophysics or Business Management or Computer Simulation or Education or Philosophy; Physics in the Modern World; Psychology *Divinity:* Health Sciences-Mathematics or Sociology *3 yrs FT/4 yrs S* Biology; Ecology, Conservation & Environment; Genetics; Molecular Cell Biology

BSc/MPhys: *3-4 yrs* Physics (optional yr in Europe); Theoretical Physics (optional yr in Europe)

Higher Degrees

MASTER'S DEGREES
Cert/Dip/MA: Local History; Non-Directive Play Therapy
Cert/Dip/MSc: Safety Critical Systems Engineering; Software Engineering; System Safety Engineering

Cert/MA: Railway Studies
Dip/MA: Historical Research; Medieval Studies; Modern History: The Age of Revolutions; Philosophy
Dip/MSc: Environmental Economics & Environmental Management; Psychosocial Interventions
MA: Aesthetics; Applied Educational Studies: Leadership & Management; Applied Linguistics; Archaeological Heritage Management; Archaeological Research; Archaeology of Buildings; Blake & the Age of Revolution; Community Music; Comparative Politics; Conservation Studies (Historic Buildings & Places); Conservation Studies (Historic Gardens & Landscapes); Culture of Modernism; Early Modern History; Education; Educational Studies; English (by research); English Renaissance Literature; Field Archaeology; Foundations of Twentieth Century Philosophy; Historical Archaeology; Historical Research; History (by dissertation); History & Politics (Popular Movements); History of Art; Housing Studies; Language Variation & Change; Linguistics; Local History; Medieval Archaeology; Medieval English Literatures; Medieval History; Medieval Studies; Modern History (History & Culture); Modern History: The Age of Revolutions; Modern Literature & Culture; Music; Philosophy; Phonetics & Phonology; Political Philosophy; Political Philosophy (The Idea of Toleration); Politics; Post-War Recovery Studies; Primary Education; Public Administration & Public Policy; Public Services Management; Qualitative Research Methods; Representations & Contexts, 1750-1850; Romantic & Sentimental Literature, 1770-1830; Science Education; Social Policy; Sociology of Contemporary Culture; Syntax & Semantics; Teaching English to Young Learners; Women's & Gender History; Women's Studies; Writing and Performance (Drama/Film/Television)
MA/MSc/Dip: Music Technology
MChem Hons: *4 yrs FT/S* Chemistry (with a yr in Europe); Chemistry; Chemistry, Life Systems & Pharmaceuticals (with a yr in Europe); Chemistry, Life Systems & Pharmaceuticals; Chemistry, Management & Industry (with a yr in Europe); Chemistry, Management & Industry; Chemistry, Resources & the Environment (with a yr in Europe); Chemistry, Resources & the Environment
MEng Hons: *4 yrs* Avionics; Computer Science; Computer Systems & Software Engineering; Electronic & Communication Engineering; Electronic Engineering or Media Technology; Electronic Engineering with Music Technology Systems or Business Management; Media Technology; Music Technology Systems; Radio Frequency Engineering
MMath Hons: *4 yrs FT* Computer Science with Mathematics; Computer Science-Mathematics; Mathematics or Physics or Linguistics; Mathematics with Computer Science; Mathematics-Linguistics; Mathematics-Physics
MPhil/DPhil: *2 yrs FT/4 yrs PT* Archaeology; Biology; Chemistry; Communication Studies; Computer Science; Economics & Related Studies; Educational Studies; Eighteenth Century Studies; Electronics; English & Related Literature; Environment; Health Sciences; Health Studies; History; History of Art; History of Art; Language & Linguistic Science; Mathematics; Medieval Studies; Music; Music Technology; Philosophy; Physics; Politics; Psychology; Railway Studies; Social Policy & Social Work; Sociology; Women's Studies
MRes: Bioinformatics; Biomolecular Science; Ecology & Environmental Management
MSc: Administrative Science & Development Problems; Archaeological Information Systems; Chemistry; Computer Science; Econometrics & Economics; Economic & Social Policy Analysis; Economic and Social History; Economics; Economics & Finance; Electromagnetic Compatability; Electronics; Environmental Economics; Environmental Economics and Environmental Management; Finance and Econometrics; Health Economics; Health Sciences; Information Processing; Management; Mathematics; Physics; Project Analysis, Finance & Investment; Public Economics; Radio Frequency Communications; Reading and Language; Women, Development & Administration; Zoo Archaeology
MSW: *2 yrs* Social Work

HIGHER DOCTORATES
DSc; DLitt; DMus

Honorary Degrees
DUniv; MUniv

Diplomas

Cert/Dip/MSc: Software Engineering
Diploma: *1 yr FT/2 yrs PT* Applied Educational Studies; Leading & Managing in the Health Service; Professional Managers Programme

Certificates

PGCE: Education *3-4 yrs Secondary:* English Literature *4 yrs S Secondary:* English Literature

EUROPEAN UNIVERSITY OF IRELAND (EUI)
THE UNIVERSITY OF THE NEW MILLENNIUM
OFFERS
POSTGRADUATE & POST-EXPERIENCE
PROGRAMMES AT AFFORDABLE COST
TO PROFESSIONALS & EXECUTIVES

Dr Bernard Hephrun
Honourary President

EUI is built upon the ethos that learning is a life long process and education has no boundaries or limitations, it seeks recognition from employers and professional bodies rather than state educational authorities, by having closer corporation with the Industry.

European University's professional development programmes are well-received by the working adults, as its tutorials are delivered and supervised by experts who have direct experience in Industry. EUI is considered to be one of the best in the International market and has the growing alumni of top professionals.

Candidates will be awarded credit units based on experiential and prior learning, similar to the Credit Assessment and Transfer Scheme (CATS) and Accreditation for Prior Experiential Learning (APEL) in the UK and Ireland are designed to acknowledge prior learning and thus avoid repetition.

Professional Diplomas & Degrees: Advanced certificate & Diplomas, Bachelor, Masters including an accelerated Executive MBA, DBA and Ph.D.

Highest Doctorate: Professional D.Litt, D.Sc & D.Ed. Candidates for this programme must be outstanding.

Examination & Assessment: based on a) Assignments b) Locally held workshop c) A work based project; Doctorate candidate must submit a thesis and will be subject to an oral defence.

The programmes are especially geared to meet your individual needs, progressing in line with your development, working on it when it suits you best and deriving all the satisfaction from it, while attaining your aspirations towards gaining a professional degree. Candidates holding a recognised professional qualification are entitled to credit transfer, such applicants must enclose a detailed CV and copies of supporting documents.

Apply by CV or obtain a form from EUI's web site and forward it to EUI REGISTRY, DOMINIC COURT, 41 LOWER DOMINIC STREET, DUBLIN 1, REPUBLIC OF IRELAND. TEL: + 35 31 8733199 FAX: + 35 31 8733612 EMAIL: EUI.SAV@BTINTERNET.COM www.btinternet.com/~european.university/wwweui.html

London School of Accountancy & Management (LSAM) offers 12 months Executive MBA.

LSAM is well-reputed for its professional development seminars. It is the first business school to introduce seminar based modules, enabling the learning process interesting and valuable rather than difficult and stressful.

The business school has modified its courses to meet the needs and challenges of the new Millennium, the courses offered are modern and dynamic.

LSAM Offers Professional Qualifications leading to an Advanced Diploma, Post-graduate Diploma and MBA at a competitive rate. The MBA is designed to accommodate busy executives via the matured entry route. Assessment is based on assignments and a work-related project.

LSAM is the first business school to offer a work-based MBA (validated by a university), in co-operation with the employer. The tuition is provided by well reputed professionals who have hands on experience in the Industry. LSAM offers Full & Part-time courses. The lectures are specially designed to accommodate working adults in the evenings, weekends or in a series of block workshop groups.

LSAM has affiliated centres Internationally including France, Germany, Italy, Greece, Poland, Hungary, Check Republic, Malaysia, India, Mauratius, Zimbabwe, Hong Kong & China. Write with your details to the Course Director, London School of Accountancy & Management, 492 Harrow Road, London W9 3QA. Tel: 44 (0)181 968 6969 Fax: 44 (0)181 960 3026

Part 5

Qualifications Listed by Trades and Professions

In this part the qualifications and examinations in each trade or profession are, generally speaking, arranged in the following order:

Membership of Professional Institutions and Associations

University Qualifications

National Certificates and Diplomas

NVQs

SVQs

GNVQs

OCR

Other Vocational Awarding Bodies

Useful Addresses

Note: In the main, only qualifying bodies are included; for a full list of learned societies see Part 7.

PROFESSIONAL ASSOCIATIONS

Professional associations vary greatly in size and function. Many qualify people by examination as practitioners in a particular field. Other associations do not conduct examinations for membership, but accept the evidence provided by degrees, diplomas or the qualifications of other bodies. Some, which may be called study associations or learned societies, open their membership to amateurs as well as specialists. This part of the book is mainly concerned with membership of qualifying professional associations. A 'profession' is that kind of occupation in a special area of activity and offering a distinctive service which is followed by persons who have undertaken advanced training and education. People who wish to become members of professional associations must undertake progressive stages of instruction and practical experience before being examined for membership; in qualifying associations there is more than the simple membership structure often found in non-qualifying associations. Admission to 'corporate' membership, that is to the complete rights and privileges of full membership, marks the fact that the candidate has reached, by examination, the degree of competence required of practitioners. Once a member of a professional association, the candidate accepts certain responsibilities towards clients, colleagues and the general public. The use of designatory letters after a member's name is usually allowed.

THE FUNCTIONS OF PROFESSIONAL ASSOCIATIONS

Qualification

Some associations qualify individuals to act in a certain professional capacity. They also try to safeguard high standards of professional conduct. Few associations have complete control over the profession with which they are concerned. Some professions are regulated by the law and their associations act as the central registration authority. Entry to others is directly controlled by associations which alone award the requisite qualifications. If a profession is required to be registered by the law and is controlled by the representative Council, a practitioner found guilty by his Council of misconduct may be suspended from practice or completely debarred by the removal of his name from the register of qualified practitioners. In other professions the consequences of misdemeanour may not be so serious because the profession does not exercise the same degree of control. The professions registered by Statute, and therefore subject to restrictions on entry and loss of either privileges or the right to practise on erasure are:

Professions	Statutory Committee Controlling Professional Conduct
Architects	Architects Registration Council
Dentists	General Dental Council
Doctors	General Medical Council
Professions supplementary to Medicine: Chiropodists; Dieticians; Medical Laboratory Technicians; Occupational Therapists; Orthoptists; Physiotherapists; Radiographers.	Council for Professions Supplementary to Medicine (separate Board for each)
Midwives	United Kingdom Central Council for Nursing,
Nurses	Midwifery and Health Visiting
Opticians	General Optical Council
Patent Agents	Council of the Chartered Institute of Patent Agents
Pharmacists	Statutory Committee of the Pharmaceutical Society
Solicitors	Statutory Committee of the Law Society
Veterinary Surgeons	Disciplinary Committee of the Royal College of Veterinary Surgeons

Certain other professions are closed. Admission to the Bar is controlled by the Inns of Court, although their powers have never been confirmed by Statute. Merchant Navy Officers and Mine Managers are certificated by the Department of Trade and the Health and Safety Executive respectively. No teacher may take up a permanent post in a maintained school in England or Wales unless his qualifications have been accepted by the Department of Education and Science; misconducting teachers are reprimanded or debarred by the Department and not by the teaching profession. By contrast, there has been movement towards self-government in the teaching profession in Scotland. Although some types of professional occupation are not controlled by statute, employment in them may nevertheless be fairly strictly controlled by convention. If a particular association is well enough confirmed and if its examinations are respected, employers may require applicants for appointment to certain posts either to have or to take its qualifications.

Study

Some associations give their members an opportunity to keep abreast of a particular discipline or to undertake further study in it. Such associations are especially numerous in medicine, science and applied science. Many qualifying associations also provide an information and study service for their members. Some of the more famous learned societies confer added status upon distinguished practitioners by electing them to membership or honorary membership.

Protection of Members' Interests

Some associations exist mainly to look after the interests of the individual practitioner and the group. A small number are directly concerned with negotiations over salary and working conditions.

MEMBERSHIP OF PROFESSIONAL ASSOCIATIONS
Qualifying Associations

The principal function of qualifying associations is to examine and qualify persons who wish to become practitioners in the field with which they are concerned. As already indicated, some regulate professional conduct and many offer opportunities for further study. Membership is divided into grades, usually classified as 'corporate' and 'non-corporate'. Non-corporate members are those not yet admitted to full membership, mainly students; they are divided from corporate membership by barriers of age and levels of responsibility and experience. The principal requirement for admission to membership is the knowledge and ability to pass the association's exams; candidates may be exempted from the association's exams if they have acceptable alternative qualifications.

NON-CORPORATE MEMBERS

Non-corporate members are those who are as yet unqualified or only partly qualified. They are accorded limited rights and privileges, but may not vote at meetings of the corporate body. Most associations have a 'Student' membership grade. Students are those who are preparing for the exams which qualify them for admission to corporate membership. Some associations have 'Licentiate' and 'Graduate' membership grades, which are senior to the Student grade.

Graduates are those who have passed the qualifying exams but lack other requirements, such as age and experience, for admission to corporate membership.

CORPORATE MEMBERS

Corporate members are the fully qualified, constituent members of incorporated associations. They are accorded full rights and privileges and may vote at meetings of the corporate body. Corporate membership is often divided into two grades, a senior grade of 'Members' or 'Fellows' and a general grade of 'Associate Members' or 'Associates'.

HONORARY MEMBERS

Some associations have a special class of Honorary Members or Fellows for distinguished members or outsiders.

EXAMINATIONS AND REQUIREMENTS

Non-corporate members normally become corporate members by exam or exemption, with or without additional requirements. The level of many final professional exams is of degree standard and a number of professional qualifications are accepted by the Burnham Committees on the salaries of teachers in maintained schools and colleges for the graduate addition to salary.

The transition from the general grade of membership to the senior is fairly automatic in some associations (eg on reaching a prescribed age), but in others the higher grade is reached only after the submission of evidence of research or progress in the profession.

Qualifying exams are usually conducted in two or more stages. The first stage leads to an Intermediate or Part I qualification, which is at about the standard of GCE A level, or equivalent BTEC award. The second stage leads to a Final or Part II or Part III qualification, which is at about the standard of a degree.

INSTRUCTION

Students may obtain instruction by any of the following means:

(1)   Correspondence courses.

(3)   Some associations maintain their own schools (eg the Architectural Association School and the Law Society's School of Law).

(4)   Courses of direct preparation in universities or colleges of further education.

ACCOUNTANCY

Membership of Professional Institutions and Associations

ASSOCIATION OF ACCOUNTING TECHNICIANS

AAT
ASSOCIATION
OF ACCOUNTING
TECHNICIANS

154 Clerkenwell Road, London EC1R 5AD
Tel: 020 7837 8600
Fax: 020 7837 6970
e-mail: aatuk@dial.pipex.com
Website: www.aat.co.uk

The AAT represents skilled staff in all areas of accounting and finance. It has more than 30,000 Members and 70,000 Students world-wide, and is sponsored by 4 of the major chartered accountancy bodies in the UK.

MEMBERSHIP:
MAAT: Membership is available to registered Students who may apply if they have demonstrated competence at all 3 Stages of the AAT Education and Training Scheme, and can provide evidence of 1 yrs' experience (or part-time equivalent) in an approved accounting function.
FMAAT: Members may apply to become Fellow Members, 5 yrs after they have been admitted to Membership provided that they can supply evidence of either (a) supervisory or management responsibilities held over a prescribed period, or (b) significant specialisation in a relevant area (eg taxation). MAATs and FMAATs receive a range of services designed to maintain and expand their levels of competence. These include: technical bulletins and courses designed to update, broaden and extend skills gained while qualifying; Branch Network (regionalised groups providing access to technical meetings and other presentations and events); professional support and ethical guidance; and *Accounting Technician*, a monthly magazine.

TRAINING:
Registered Students: Flexible open access for Students to register on the Scheme, although entrants must be numerate and have a good command of English. The Education and Training Scheme is competence-based, using a variety of assessment methods. The Scheme is accredited at National and Scottish Vocational Qualification (NVQ/SVQ) Levels 2, 3 & 4 in Accounting (these three Levels are also known as the Foundation, Intermediate and Technician Stages of the AAT's Education and Training Scheme. Students are fully credited for all units successfully completed and NVQ/SVQ Certificates are awarded for each Stage achieved. Students who complete the AAT Education and Training Scheme are eligible to exemptions, should they wish to progress to the senior professional qualifications of the AAT's Sponsoring Bodies. Further information on entry should be sought from the Institute concerned. Benefits to registered Students include receipt of *Accounting Technician* and access to their local Branch.

ASSOCIATION OF CERTIFIED BOOK-KEEPERS

139 Fonthill Road, 3rd Flr, London N4 3HF Tel: 020 7272 3925 Fax: 020 7281 5723
e-mail: icea@enta.net Website: www.icea.enta.net
MEMBERSHIP:
Fellow (FACB): Applicants must pass the ACB's exam or equiv, be at least 21 and have 5 yrs' experience.
Associate (AACB): Applicants must pass the ACB's exam or equiv and have 3 yrs' experience. The Association provides a single subject exam in: (1) Book-keeping; (2) Advanced Book-keeping and Accounting; (3) Computer Applications in Accounting.
No formal qualifications are necessary to register as a student, but applicants must have good knowledge of English. The ACB qualifications are ideal for employees at the first and second levels of work in accounting, costing and internal auditing. Members can describe themselves as Certified Book-Keeper. The qualifications are based on NCVQ competence and the ACB will seek

NCVQ recognition in due course. Exemptions are considered from the applicants who have passed (a) RSA Stage 3, (b) LCC Higher (c) Pitman Level 2 or similar exam.

EXAMINATIONS:
Certified Diploma in Computerised Book-keeping & Accounting: This is a single subject exam in book-keeping and accountancy of 3 hrs' duration. One hr for theory and practice and 2 hrs for practical assignment to prepare day books/spread sheets, prepare ledgers and to draw final accounts using computerised accounts package.
Certified Diploma in Small Business Administration: This is also a single subject exam of 3 hrs' duration in business administration, with special emphasis for small business.

THE ASSOCIATION OF CHARTERED CERTIFIED ACCOUNTANTS

29 Lincoln's Inn Fields, London WC2A 3EE Tel: 020 7396 5800 Fax: 020 7396 5858
e-mail: recruit@acca.org.uk Website: www.acca.org.uk

MEMBERSHIP:
Fellow (FCCA): Long-term Associate members (5 yrs min) advance to Fellowship automatically.
Associate (ACCA): Candidates must pass ACCA's exams and obtain 3 yrs' approved financial experience which can be obtained in industry, commerce, public service or public practice. The world's largest and fastest growing international professional accountancy body, ACCA provides a market-driven set of qualifications based on the highest professional, intellectual and ethical standards. Established almost 100 yrs ago and now representing over 75,000 members and 155,000 students in more than 140 countries world-wide, it's core values are openness, integrity and professional and ethical discipline. Recognized as a professional body under UK companies and financial services legislation, ACCA's role as a professional accountancy body is to train and regulate practising Chartered Certified Accountants. As such, ACCA is responsible for ensuring its members and students are aware of changes in legislation and accounting standards.

NEW SYLLABUS:
ACCA is in the process of launching a groundbreaking new syllabus – to be first examined in December 2001 – which will transform the way the profession is trained in the future. The launch follows extensive consultation with leading employers, members, students and tuition providers world-wide. The new scheme places greater emphasis on corporate strategy, the design and management of business systems, risk assessment and strategic financial analysis whilst retaining the core technical knowledge that ACCA's research showed to be essential to the role of the modern financial professional.

QUALIFYING:
Students must complete the professional examinations (14 papers) and obtain a minimum of 3 yrs' relevant training. Study can be full-time with training obtained later; or part-time by day/evening class, Open Learning or home study whilst working full-time in relevant employment. Training can be obtained in any country and in any employment sector – industry commerce, public practice or public service.

ENTRY LEVELS:
All graduates from recognized universities can register and those with relevant degrees will be exempted from some examinations; some qualifications will qualify for up to nine exemptions. Those who complete Parts 1and 2 of the new scheme may also be eligible to apply for the award of a BSc (Hons) in Applied Accountancy from Oxford Brookes University.
The Certified Diploma in Accounting and Finance (CDipAF): The Certified Diploma is a postgraduate qualification designed to equip managers with an understanding of how to compile, analyse and communicate financial information. The qualification is recognised for exemption from a number of MBA programmes.

Enrolment on the Diploma Register: To enrol on the Certified Diploma Register candidates must hold one of the following: a recognised degree, HND/C, NVQ Level 4 and/or membership of a non-accounting professional body. Candidates who do not hold the above may be admitted on the basis of experience if they are aged 23 or over and can provide an employer's reference to show their experience is relevant to the Diploma.

ACCA Accounting Technician qualification (CAT): This qualification was launched in August 1997 to enable candidates to qualify in accounts supports roles. As there is no formal academic entry requirement, anyone can enrol, providing they are aged 16 or over. Some qualifications, such as A levels, HNC/Ds, RSA, Pitmans and LCCI qualifications will receive exemptions from some CAT examinations.

Mode of Application: Contact ACCA for a registration pack, or view vacancy information and register on-line on the ACCA website.

Application Deadline: Register by 15 August for December examinations or 31 December for the following June examinations.

THE ASSOCIATION OF CORPORATE TREASURERS

Ocean House, 10/12 Little Trinity Lane, London EC4V 2DJ Tel: 020 7213 9728 Fax: 020 7248 2591 e-mail: enquiries@treasurers.co.uk Website: www.treasurers.org
The Association is the only examining body for the profession of corporate treasury management and offers 3 levels of membership.

MEMBERSHIP:

Fellow (FCT): Applicants must satisfy the requirements for membership and should have a total of 5 yrs' experience of senior responsibility for corporate treasury functions.

Membership Qualification (MCT): Individuals who successfully complete the Membership qualification are eligible to become Members of the Association and use the designatory letters **MCT**.

Associate Membership Qualification (AMCT): Individuals who successfully complete the Associateship qualification are entitled to apply for Associate Membership. Once accepted they are entitled to use the designatory letters **AMCT**.

EXAMINATIONS:

The Associate Membership Qualification comprises 6 subjects: Accountancy Practice and Introductory Economics, Financial Analysis, Corporate Taxation, Business Law, Money Management, Corporate Finance and Funding.

The Membership Qualification comprises 3 subjects: Corporate Financial Management, Advanced Funding and Risk Management, Treasury Management.

Exemptions: Exemptions are available on a subject for subject basis from papers I-IV of the Associate qualification with exemption against all four papers for a chartered accountancy qualification. A fast-track route for CIMA students and recently qualified members offers a shortened paper VI (Corporate Finance and Funding) enabling them to qualify at the AMCT level within 5 mths.

The Cash Management Certificate: This is a 6 mth course which improves understanding between providers and users of cash management services. Successful completion of the 5 day residential school and examination allows the use of the designatory letters **Cert CM**.

ASSOCIATION OF FINANCIAL CONTROLLERS AND ADMINISTRATORS

Tower House, Third Floor, 139, Fonthill Road, London N4 3HF Tel: 020 7272 3925 Fax: 020 7281 5723 e-mail: icea@enta.net Website: www.icea.enta.net

MEMBERSHIP:

AAFC (Associate): Applicants are required to pass the Association's exam or equiv, be at least 20 and have had 4 yrs' experience. This qualification is based on NVQ level 4 competency.

FAFC (Fellow): Applicants must hold senior positions in financial management and must be an Associate. They must have at least 5 yrs' experience and be over 25. The Association has a 3-part exam syllabus consisting of 4 papers in each part. Parts 1, 2, and 3 are of first, second and third yr degree standard of the British Universities. Only registered students are permitted to sit the exam.

Applicants to be registered as students must be 18 and must have 5 GCE or GCSE passes including 2 at A level or equivalent or 3 yrs' experience in accounting, finance or allied work.

THE ASSOCIATION OF INTERNATIONAL ACCOUNTANTS

A·I·A

THE ASSOCIATION
OF INTERNATIONAL
ACCOUNTANTS

South Bank Building, Kingsway, Team Valley, Newcastle-upon-Tyne
NE11 0JS
Tel: 0191 482 4409
Fax: 0191 482 5578
e-mail: aia@aia.org.uk
Website: www.aia.org.uk

The AIA is one of Britain's five recognised Qualifying Bodies for accountants and company auditors.

MEMBERSHIP:
Associate (AAIA): Achieved upon passing the AIA professional exams and attaining 3 yrs approved accountancy experience. There are no restrictions as to where experience can be gained; in industry, commerce, the public sector or public practice.
Fellow (FAIA): Granted to Associate members following 5 continuous yrs of post qualifying accountancy experience.

EXAMINATIONS:
Registration as an AIA student is a prerequisite for entry. Candidates must also be in accountancy employment, or a full time student on an approved course of accountancy or business studies. The exams comprise three levels:
Foundation Level: *Module A:* Financial Accounting 1, Economics, Cost Accounting, *Module B:* Law, Auditing & Taxation, Statistics & Data Processing
Professional 1: *Module C:* Auditing, Company Law, Management Information, *Module D:* Business Management, Financial Accounting II, Management Accounting
Professional II: *Module E:* Financial Accounting III, Financial Management, *Module F:* Professional Practice (Auditing), Taxation & Tax Planning. Local variant papers are available to suit individual national requirements, alternatively, students may opt to follow International Accounting Standards or Islamic Accounting. Members holding the AIA's recognised audit qualification wishing to practice as a registered auditor in the UK, may do so under the control of a recognised supervisory body.

ENTRY REQUIREMENTS:
A minimum of 2 A-levels and 3 GCSEs (to include Mathematics and English), or the equivalent overseas qualification. Mature students (21 and over) may be admitted to the course on assessment of their general education and accountancy experience, which must be a minimum of five yrs.

EXEMPTIONS:
Degree holders or those with a BTEC HND in Business Studies (financial stream) are entitled to exemptions from all or part of the Foundation Level. Specific accountancy related degrees and certain recognised professional qualifications also attract exemptions from Professional Level 1.

THE CHARTERED INSTITUTE OF MANAGEMENT ACCOUNTANTS

63 Portland Place, London W1N 4AB Tel: 020 7637 2311 Fax: 020 7631 5309
e-mail: Student-Services@cimaglobal.comWebsite: www.cimaglobal.com
We provide our students and members with the skills to achieve even their most ambitious goals. We are internationally renowned for delivering flexible, comprehensive training programmes and for continuing to support CIMA graduates throughout their careers. Consequently they go on to achieve their aims – whether they want to become the Directors and CEOs of the future, or become internationally transferable managers.

MEMBERSHIP:

Registered Students: Only registered students may sit the exams. Registration requires a minimum of 5 GCE or GCSE passes (any 2 of which must be at A-Level) including Mathematics and English Language. Alternatively the ATT (NVQ Level 3), BTEC Edexcel NC/ND, or Advanced GNVQ in Business is acceptable. For information on other BTEC Edexcel subjects, please contact the Student Services Centre on Tel: +44 20 7917 9251.

Associate (ACMA): An applicant is required to pass the Institute's exams comprising 4 stages and to demonstrate a minimum of 3 yrs' verified, relevant, practical experience in management accounting, basic accounting and financial management. Experience may be gained in industrial, commercial or service organisations in the private or public sectors, or may be obtained by any combination of appointments across these sectors.

Fellow (FCMA): As per ACMA, but a min of 3 yrs' experience are required in a 'senior and strategic position' in addition to the 3 yrs' experience required for Associateship.

EXAMINATIONS:

The syllabus is made up of 3 levels:

Foundation Level: Financial Accounting Fundamentals (FAFN), Management Accounting Fundamentals (FMAF), Economics for Business (FECB), Business Law (FBLW) and Business Mathematics (FBSM). *Please note: FECB, FBLW and FBSM are 2 hr examinations, all other exams allow 3 hrs.*

Intermediate Level: Finance (IFIN), Business Taxation (IBTX), Financial Accounting – UK Standards (IFNA), or International Standards (IFAI), Financial Reporting – UK Standards (IFRP), or International Standards (IFRI), Management Accounting – Performance Management (IMPM), Management Accounting – Decision Making (IDEC), Systems and Project Management (ISPM) and Organisational Management (IORG).

Please note: Students can elect to sit Financial Accounting and Financial Reporting with either the UK Accounting Standards format or the International Accounting Standards format.

Final Level: Management Accounting Business Strategy (FLBS), Management Accounting Financial Strategy (FLFS), Management Accounting Information Strategy (FLIS) and Management Accounting Case Study (FLCS).

THE CHARTERED INSTITUTE OF PUBLIC FINANCE AND ACCOUNTANCY

CIPFA

3 Robert Street,
London WC2N 6BH
Tel: 020 7543 5600
Fax: 020 7543 5700
Website: www.cipfa.org.uk

CIPFA is the leading professional body for public services, whether in the public or private sectors. Membership is available to those who meet the requirements of the Institute's education and training scheme. Once qualified, members possess a recognised and highly-regarded qualification, designated CPFA.

The CIPFA min entry requirements are 5 GCSE passes, including maths and English Language. 2 of these must be at A level. The equiv qualifications for Scotland, Northern Ireland and the Republic of Ireland are also accepted. Exemptions are granted for relevant degrees and/or work experience.

CIPFA's Education and Training Scheme consists of a Foundation Stage and 3 Professional Stages: P1, P2 and P3. Subjects studied are: Foundation – Financial Accounting, Cost Accounting and Quantitative Analysis, Law and Effective Management Skills; P1 – Accounting Theory & Practice, Management Accounting, Auditing, Information and Financial Management; P2 – Financial Reporting and Accountability, Accounting for Decision Making, Public Policy and Taxation, Business Strategy and Management; P3 – Finance and Management Case Study Examination, Project.

FACULTY OF COMMUNITY, PERSONAL AND WELFARE ACCOUNTING

22 Parkthorn Road, Preston PR2 1RX Tel: 01457 834 943
Contact: R Slinger, Registrar
The Faculty is a radical professional association for Accountants, Administrators, Secretaries and Financial Consultants in fields related to Community Provision and Consumer Finance. Members are designated Community Finance Accountants/Consultants.
The Faculty is currently devising a qualification structure based upon progressive methods of assessment, cases and practical experience. It is unlikely that the style or content apart from Foundation Accountancy or Administration skills will be similar to that of other bodies. The training programme will include the following: Management of Community Provision; Debt Counselling; Consumer Credit; Assurance and Insurance Studies; Corporate Planning; Accountancy; and Workers Rights. The Faculty now has only a sole designation for all full members which is that of **Fellow of the Faculty (FCPWA)**. This is based upon individual assessment of the members' ability and experience in the areas outlined above including 3–5 yrs' practical experience. All other applicants are enrolled as ordinary members with no designation. Former members of the old Faculty of Community Accountancy and Administration may use their previous single designation.

EXAMINATIONS:
Personal Financial Planning: The Faculty recognises the Financial Planning Certificate of the Chartered Insurance Institute and the requisite levels of the Life Insurance Association by exam.
Accountancy: The Faculty recognises AAT, CIPFA and parts of some other bodies' exams.
Corporate Administration: The Faculty recognises Chartered, Corporate and Certified Public Secretary qualifications.
NVQs: These are accepted at various levels but on an individual basis.
Non-UK Assessment Scheme: A cross-referenced assessment procedure is used for overseas applicants. All assessments, both for UK and overseas applicants, are on an Endowed Membership basis.
Certificate in Community Interviewing: For those who survey financial matters (jointly with YDA).

THE INSTITUTE OF CERTIFIED BOOK-KEEPERS

20 Bloomsbury Square, London WC1A 2NA Tel: 020 7681 0101 Fax: 020 7681 0202
e-mail: info@book-keepers.org
The Institute of Certified Book-keepers is the largest book-keeping organisation in the world with in excess of 85,000 members and students in the UK and in more than a dozen countries around the world. The Institute has its own 'Oscar' awards ceremony where it awards a 'Luca' to winners in each of several categories.

MEMBERSHIP:
Student Member: Open to any person studying towards the Institute's qualification.
Associate Member(AICB): A person who has passed the ICB Level II Intermediate examination or its equivalent is eligible to become an Associate Member.
Member (MICB): A person who has passed the ICB Level III Advanced examination or its equivalent is eligible to become a Member. A Member may use the title 'Certified Book-keeper'
Fellow (FICB): A Member who is able to demonstrate a minimum of two yrs' relevant working experience may apply for election to the grade of Fellow. A Fellow may use the title 'Certified Book-keeper'.

QUALIFICATIONS:
The Certificate in Book-keeping: The syllabus is divided into a number of different levels – Foundation, Intermediate, Advanced, Associate and Member. Each level comprises three units. Two units in each level are assessed by Continuous Assessment, with the third assessed by Time Constrained Assessment. On successful completion of each Unit students are awarded a Credit by the National Open College Network. The Certificate is awarded on achievement of all six credits.
Level I (Foundation): An introduction to Finance and Basic Book-Keeping is available from September 2000.
Level II (Intermediate): Preliminary matters and credit control (Business documents, Books of prime entry, Credit control); Book-keeping to final accounts (Ledger accounts, The trial balance,

The preparation of final accounts for sole traders); Cash and Related Terms (Banking procedures, Wages and salaries, Dealing with visits from the Inland Revenue and Customs & Excise).

Level III (Advanced): Completing business accounts in book-keeping (Purpose and use of control accounts, Incomplete records, Stock valuation); Partnership accounts and adjustments to final accounts for Book-keepers (Adjustments, Partnerships); Further final accounts in Book-keeping (Non-profit-making organisations, Limited liability companies, Manufacturing accounts.)

Associate Level: RSA Stage 1 Book-Keeping; IAB Intermediate and Foundation Levels only (Grade A/B only); NVQ Levels 2-4 (specific units).

Member Level: RSA Stage 2 Book-Keeping; IAB Final (Grade A/B only). Other qualifications on application. *OTHER AWARDS* The Certificate in Computerised Book-keeping (CB.Cert.); The Diploma in Computerised Book-keeping (CB.Dip.); The Certificate in Payroll Management (PM.Cert.); The Diploma in Payroll Management (PM.Dip.); The Certificate in Small Business Management (BM.Cert.); The Diploma in Small Business Management (BM.Dip.).

THE INSTITUTE OF CHARTERED ACCOUNTANTS IN ENGLAND AND WALES (ICAEW)

Gloucester House, 399 Silbury Boulevard, Central Milton Keynes MK9 2HL
Tel: 01908 248105 Fax: 01908 691165 e-mail: cparkins@icaew.co.uk

MEMBERSHIP:
Associate Chartered Accountant (ACA): Those who have successfully completed formal training and have passed the Institute's professional exams may apply for admission.
Fellow Chartered Accountant (FCA): Associate members of 10 yrs' standing who satisfy the requirements for continuing professional education are eligible.

TRAINING:
Training is available in public practice and increasingly in industrial/commercial organisations and the public sector. Students train under a formal training contract with an authorised training office. Training contracts are of between 3-5 yrs' duration.

ELIGIBILITY FOR ENTRY:
Potential students must meet the following minimum entry requirements: 1) At least 2 GCE A Levels plus at least 3 GCSEs or equivalent

QUALIFYING:
Currently, in order to qualify as a Chartered Accountant, students need to complete these elements of training: 1) Practical work experience in a training office authorised by the Institute; 2) Professional examinations (Professional Stage, Advanced Stage).

PROFESSIONAL EXAMINATIONS:
From September 2000, the ACA qualification will include a Professional and an Advanced Stage:
Professional Stage: Subjects covered are Accounting, Financial Reporting, Audit and Assurance, Taxation, Business Finance and Business Management.
Advanced Stage: Subjects covered are Business Advice, Advanced Technical Knowledge, Advanced Business Management, Acquisition and Management of Knowledge, Communications. (These subjects will be assessed in an Advanced Case Study and a Test of Advanced Technical Competence.) For further information call the Recruitment and Promotion Section on 01908 248108 or e-mail address: etdsrp@icaew.co.uk. Alternatively view the Institute's website: www.icaew.co.uk/careers

INSTITUTE OF CHARTERED ACCOUNTANTS IN IRELAND

Chartered Accountants House,87-89 Pembroke Road,Dublin 4
Tel: 010 3531 6377200 Fax: 010 3531 6680842
e-mail: ca@icai.ie Website: www.icai.ie

MEMBERSHIP:
Associate (ACA): In order to be eligible for membership, candidates must have completed satisfactorily the requisite period of service under training contract with a recognised training firm, have passed all requisite parts of the Institute Exam up to and including the Final Admitting Exam and also have completed satisfactorily a special practical computer course designed by the Institute as a prerequisite for membership.

For graduates, the normal period of contract is 3 1/2yrs, for Post-Graduates 3 yrs and for non-graduates it is 4 yrs or 5 yrs depending on entry route selected. Non-graduates seeking entry into a training contract must be at least 17 and have obtained the requisite standard in the GCE/GCSE or Leaving Certificate Exams. Details on request.

To fulfil the requirements of the EU Directive, members going into the practice are required to meet certain criteria before being granted an auditing certificate.

EXAMINATIONS:
The Institute's exam: The exam is in 3 parts. The syllabus comprises 2 Professional Exams and a Final Admitting Exam. The core subjects throughout the syllabus comprise Business Law, Financial Accounting, Auditing, Management Accounting, Business Finance, Taxation, Information Technology, Financial Management and Business Information Systems.

The Institute places considerable reliance on FT education for its students and, in addition to the facilities available to non-graduates, Postgraduate (leading to the award of Diplomas/Masters degrees) programmes to meet the needs of business and non-business graduates are also available. PT and block-release study during the student's training contract is carried out under the auspices of the Institute's own Centre of Accounting Studies. Training contracts incorporate periods of paid study leave for this purpose.

THE INSTITUTE OF CHARTERED ACCOUNTANTS OF SCOTLAND

CA House, 21 Haymarket Yards, Edinburgh EH12 5BH Tel: 0131 347 0100
e-mail: student.education@icas.org.uk Website: www.icas.org.uk

MEMBERSHIP:
Member (CA): To qualify a candidate must have completed a 3 yr training contract in a training office authorised by the Institute and have passed the Institute's Test of Competence exam (if applicable), the Test of Professional Skills and the Test of Professional Expertise (compulsory).

CA Student: The entry qualification for CA training is a UK university degree, or equivalent qualification from overseas. The Institute distinguishes 2 categories of degree – fully accredited (degree in accounting which gives exemption from the first-level Test of Competence Course and Exam) and Qualifying (non-relevant degrees). Qualifying graduates take the Institute's Test of Competence Course and Exam during the 1st yr of the training contract but may be given single subject exemptions depending on degree content.

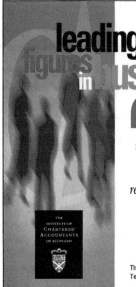
EXAMINATIONS:

Test of Competence: The Syllabus includes Financial Accounting, Principles of Auditing and Reporting, Business Management, Finance, Business Law. Exam is by multiple-choice and narrative questions. (Fully accredited graduates exempt.)

Test of Professional Skills: The syllabus includes Financial Reporting, Assurance and Business Systems, Advanced Finance, Taxation. Exam is by case studies, narrative and computational questions.

Test of Professional Expertise: One multi-discipline case study designed to test candidates' ability to apply their theoretical knowledge and practical skills to problems of the type likely to be encountered by the newly qualified accountant. Additional syllabus material includes Corporate Planning, Corporate Strategies and Management, Business Improvement, Management of Financial Structures, Ethics.

THE INSTITUTE OF COMPANY ACCOUNTANTS

80 Portland Place, London W1N 4DP

(and at 40 Tyndalls Park Road, Clifton, Bristol BS8 1PL Tel 0117 9738261 Fax 0117 9238292)

The Institute traces its origins to the yr 1923. Associateship is gained only through registered studentship, practical experience and the passing of entrance exams. Although the majority of members occupy positions of responsibility in commerce and education the Institute has also a highly successful practising arm. Institute practitioners, who are required first to qualify for a practising certificate, specialise in providing accountancy services to smaller businesses and private individuals.

MEMBERSHIP:

Fellow (FSCA): Associates of at least 3 yrs' standing, who hold positions of suitable responsibility, may apply for election to Fellowship.

Associate (ASCA): On successful completion of the exams, students with at least 3 yrs' approved practical experience may apply for admission to Associateship and use the designation **Incorporated Company Accountant.**

Registered Student: One who is studying for the qualifying exams of the Institute. Applicants must have obtained a degree from an approved university; or GCE/GCSE in 5 subjects, including English and Mathematics and 2 at A level, or the equiv; or by acceptable work experience.

EXAMINATIONS:
The exams are at 4 levels. The 12 papers comprising Levels 1, 2 and 3 may be attempted in any combination and order. At each diet up to 4 papers may be attempted as allowed by the exam timetable. The 4 papers of Level 4 must be attempted at 1 diet after all other papers have been passed. Each paper is of 3 hrs' duration and there are 4 sittings over 2 consecutive days.
Level 1: Financial Accounting 1; Quantitative Techniques; Cost Accounting; Business Law.
Level 2: Economics and the Business Environment; Business Organisation and Management; Information Technology; Taxation 1.
Level 3: Financial Accounting 2; Management Accounting; Company and Partnership Law; General Principles of Auditing and Basic Receivership and Liquidations.
Level 4: Financial Accounting 3; Financial Management or Professional Practice; Internal Auditing; Taxation 2.
Exemptions: Limited exemptions from individual subjects at Levels 1, 2 and 3 may be available in respect of passes at comparable professional exams or through relevant work experience. No exemptions granted at Level 4.

INSTITUTE OF COST AND EXECUTIVE ACCOUNTANTS

Tower House, 139 Fonthill Road, London N4 3HF Tel: 020 7263 5424 Fax: 020 7281 572
e-mail: icea@enta.net Website: www.icea.enta.net

MEMBERSHIP:
Fellow (FCEA): Applicants are required to pass the Institute's exam, be at least 21 and have at least 5 yrs' experience with competence. No one is granted exemption from the Fellowship exam.
Associate (ACEA): Applicants must pass the Institute's exams or equivalent, be at least 20 and have had 4 yrs' appropriate experience and competence as required by NCVQ.
Technician (TCA): The certificate of Technician in Costing and Accounting is issued to those applicants who passed the Associateship Level I and Level II exams and have had appropriate experience for at least 3 yrs and competence as required by NCVQ.

EXAMINATIONS:
CMA: The Institute will issue the Certificate in Management Accountancy to a member, Fellow or Associate, who holds the position of a financial executive, controller or director of a standing organisation approved by the Council, has completed the Institute's training course and is at least 30.
DipEMA: Diploma in Executive and Management Accountancy is restricted to Fellows of the Institute and must pass the Diploma Exam. The Diploma Holder, subject to the standard of achievement being acceptable, will get the opportunity to register with several British Universities to study for MA, MSc, MBA and then PhD in accountancy. Many overseas universities give preference to diploma holders for postgraduate study.
DipEF: Diploma in Executive Finance for non-accountants is designed for executives who are not accountants or do not have any accounting qualifications. This diploma provides non-accountant executives with the background knowledge and awareness of financial terms which will assist them to understand financial information and to communicate effectively with financial personnel.
Registered Students: Only registered students may sit the exam. The applicant must be 18 and have 5 GCE or GCSE passes, including 2 at A level or equiv or 3 yrs' experience in accounting, costing or allied work. The Institute recognises appropriate NCVQ qualifications for admission and for exemption.
The Institute has a 4-part exam syllabus, consisting of 4 papers in each part. The Associateship Levels 1, 2 and 3 are equiv to degree standard whereas Fellowship is equiv to honours degree standard of the British universities. The Institute's qualifications are recognised by the Local Government Management Board for appointments. The Institute issues a ' Practising Certificate' for its practising members, covered by professional indemnity insurance and under the control of the professional and ethical guide for members, registered with the Office of Fair Trading.

THE INSTITUTE OF FINANCIAL ACCOUNTANTS

INSTITUTE OF FINANCIAL ACCOUNTANTS

Burford House,
44 London Road,
Sevenoaks, Kent TN13 1AS
Tel: 01732 458080 Fax: 01732 455848
e-mail: mail@ifa.org.uk
Website: www.ifa.org.uk

The Institute of Financial Accountants, established in 1916, is the largest professional body of its type in the world. It represents members and students in more than eighty countries and provides a qualification and continuous professional development for those who want to become financial accountants. IT sets standards within the profession, both technically and ethically. Financial Accountants are employed in senior positions within industry, commerce and practice. They are professionals who take an active role in financial management.

EXAMINATION STRUCTURE:
Pre-Professional: Financial Accounting 1, Cost Accounting, Business Law & Business Taxation.
Associate Membership: Financial Accounting 2, Management Accounting, Management Information Systems & Principles of Management.
Fellow Membership: Advanced Financial Accounting, Financial Management & Strategic Management.

ENTRY REQUIREMENTS:
The following qualifications will be accepted for admission to the Pre-professional Level: 4 GCSEs including English Language and a quantitative subject plus one A Level or Scottish Higher in an academic subject, NVQ3 in Accounting, GNVQ Advanced, BTEC National Certificate/Diploma, SCOTVEC National Certificate, or IAB Final Examination. Students over 21 with at least 4 yrs relevant experience may be admitted to the pre-professional level.

EXEMPTIONS:
Pre-professional level: HNC Business and Finance with the relevant 'pathway' or Non-relevant degree.
Associate Membership level: HNC 2/HND 2 Business and Finance (Management Accounting and Financial Accounting modules must be taken from the financial 'pathway'), Business degree with Financial and Management Accounting modules, AAT Technician Level, S/NVQ4 in Accounting, CIMA stage 2 or ACCA Papers 1-6.
Fellow Membership level: Accounting Degree, CIMA stage 3 or ACCA Certificate.

MEMBERSHIP:
Associate: A person shall be eligible for admission as an Associate member when he/she has passed either the Associate Level of professional examinations, or received exemption.
Fellow: A person shall be eligible for admission as Fellow when, in addition to five yrs' experience in a senior accountancy capacity, he/she has passed the Fellow Level of the professional examinations, or has received exemptions.

INSTITUTE OF INTERNAL AUDITORS – UK

The Institute of Internal Auditors
UK and Ireland

13 Abbeville Mews, 88 Clapham Park Road, London SW4 7BX
Tel: 020 7498 0101
Fax: 020 7978 2492
e-mail: iia@easynet.co.uk

The Institute of Internal Auditors– UK is the only body whose prime objectives are to represent all internal auditors and to further the profession of internal auditing. Entry to full membership is through professional qualifications achieved through examinations.

EXAMINATIONS:
The syllabus covers every aspect of the discipline of internal auditing proving a broad coverage of management, accounting and finance, with a detailed study of the corporate control process and the means of monitoring that process.

PIIA – the practitioner level which covers: Theory and Principles of Management, Principles and Practices of Accounting, Principles of Control, Information Systems Auditing and Internal Auditing Practices.

MIIA – the professional level which covers: Advanced Management, Financial Management and Business Analysis, Advanced Information Systems Auditing and Advanced Internal Auditing. The

QICA – the specialist qualification in computer auditing. The QICA qualification comprises two levels each with its own examination paper. The first level examination paper is Information Systems Auditing and the second level paper is Specialist Information Systems Auditing.

INTERNATIONAL ASSOCIATION OF BOOK-KEEPERS

IAB

INTERNATIONAL
ASSOCIATION OF
BOOK-KEEPERS

Burford House, 44 London Road, Sevenoaks, Kent TN13 1AS
Tel: 01732 458080
Fax: 01732 455848
e-mail: mail@iab.org.uk
Website: www.iab.org.uk

Contact: Student Registrar (please quote BQ24)

The Association specialises in the promotion of the study and practice of book-keeping and bestows qualifications for employees at the first levels of work in financial accounting. Its aims are: to offer the advantages of a professional association to all book-keepers who meet the requirements for membership; to afford advice and support to members, representation of their interests to external bodies, and guarantees for public confidence; to conduct exams and award qualifications which are recognised as indicators of competence and integrity.

MEMBERSHIP:
Fellowship (FIAB): After successful completion of the exam requirements, or their equiv, and 2 or more yrs' practical book-keeping experience in a senior capacity. Fellows are entitled to use the designation **Registered Book-keeper**.

Membership (MIAB): After successful completion of the Intermediate examination or its equivalent.

EXAMINATIONS:
The Association offers examinations at three levels, *Foundation, Intermediate and Final.* The exams are open access therefore anyone of any experience or qualifications may become a registered student to allow them to study towards the Associations examinations. The exam structure is aimed at giving students a practical knowledge of book-keeping and accounting skills.

The Association also offers a:
Diploma in Computerised Book-keeping, which is an assessment of book-keeping skills using accountancy software; Diploma in Small Business Financial Management, which covers the basic records and requirements of a small business and how that information may be used to control the business; Diploma in Payroll Administration, which covers all aspects of payroll, including the requirements of the Inland Revenue.

EXEMPTIONS:
Foundation: Holders of RSA Stage 1 & 2 Practical Book-keeping, SCOTVEC Financial Record Keeping 1,2 & 3, NVQ 2 in Accounting or equivalent qualifications in Book-keeping or Accounts. Candidates who have attained the age of 19 and have at least three yrs approved book-keeping experience may also be exempt.

Intermediate: Holders of GCSE Accounting (grades A-C), RSA Book-keeping & Accounts Level II, LCCI Book-keeping or Accounts.

Final: Holders of RSA Book-keeping & Accounts Level III, LCCI Book-keeping & Accounts Higher, A Level Accounting (grades A-C) or their equivalent in Book-keeping and Accounts.

University Qualifications

The following universities offer qualifications in Accountancy and related subjects. Full details may be found in Part 4, under the entry for the appropriate university.

FIRST DEGREES AWARDED BY UNIVERSITIES
Aberdeen; Abertay, Dundee; Anglia; Anglia (City College, Norwich); Aston; Belfast; Birmingham; Blackburn; Bournemouth; Bradford; Bradford (Bradford & Ilkley Community College); Brighton; Bristol; Buckingham; Bucks. Coll.; Central England; Central Lancashire; Cheltenham & Gloucester; City; Coventry; De Montfort, Leicester; Derby; Doncaster (Dearne Valley Business School); Dundee; East Anglia; East Anglia (Suffolk College); East London; Edinburgh; Essex; Exeter; Glamorgan; Glasgow; Glasgow Caledonian; Greenwich; Hertfordshire; Huddersfield; Hull; Kent; Kingston; Lancaster; Leeds; Leeds Metropolitan; Lincolnshire; Liverpool; Liverpool John Moores; London (Birkbeck, University of London); London (London School of Economics & Political Science); London Guildhall; Loughborough; Luton; Manchester; Manchester Metropolitan.; Middlesex; Napier; Newcastle; North London; Northampton; Northumbria; Nottingham Trent; Nottingham Trent (Southampton Institute); Oxford Brookes; Paisley; Plymouth; Portsmouth; Reading; Robert Gordon; Sheffield; Sheffield Hallam; South Bank; Southampton; Staffordshire; Stirling; Strathclyde; Sunderland; Surrey (Farnborough College of Technology); Teesside; Thames Valley; Ulster; UMIST; Wales (Cardiff University); Wales (Swansea Institute of Higher Education); Wales (University of Wales College, Newport); Wales (University of Wales, Aberystwyth); Wales (University of Wales, Bangor); Warwick; Westminster; Wolverhampton

HIGHER DEGREES AWARDED BY UNIVERSITIES
Aberdeen; Aston; Birmingham; Bournemouth; Bradford; City; De Montfort, Leicester; Dundee; East Anglia; East London; Essex; Glasgow; Greenwich; Heriot-Watt; Hull; Kent; Kingston; Lancaster; Leeds; Leeds Metropolitan; Liverpool John Moores; London (London School of Economics & Political Science); London Guildhall; Manchester; Napier; Oxford; Reading; Sheffield; Southampton; Ulster; UMIST; Wales (University of Wales, Aberystwyth); Westminster

DIPLOMAS AWARDED BY UNIVERSITIES
Abertay, Dundee; Aston; Bournemouth; Brighton; City; Dundee; Durham (New College Durham); Kent; Lancaster; Leeds Metropolitan; London (London School of Economics & Political Science); Napier; North London; Northumbria; Nottingham Trent (Southampton Institute); Salford; Staffordshire; Thames Valley; Ulster; Wales (University of Wales College, Newport); Wales (University of Wales, Aberystwyth); Westminster

CERTIFICATES AWARDED BY UNIVERSITIES
Bradford (Bradford & Ilkley Community College); East London; Napier; Staffordshire; Wales (University of Wales College, Newport)

OTHER COURSES AWARDED BY UNIVERSITIES
Derby; Manchester Metropolitan.; Northampton

POSTGRADUATE DIPLOMAS AWARDED BY UNIVERSITIES
Heriot-Watt

PROFESSIONAL COURSES AWARDED BY UNIVERSITIES
Huddersfield; Leeds Metropolitan; Liverpool John Moores; London Guildhall; Manchester Metropolitan

PROFESSIONAL QUALIFICATIONS AWARDED BY UNIVERSITIES
De Montfort, Leicester; De Montfort, Leicester (De Montfort University Bedford); Glamorgan

National Certificates and Diplomas

All BTEC National and Higher National programmes in Business and Finance include elements of accountancy in the finance module of the courses.

Scotland
SQA HNC: Accounting; Financial Services
SQA HND: Accounting; Financial Services

NVQs

Level 2: Accounting
Level 3: Accounting; Providing Financial Advice (Excluding Direct Investment)
Level 4: Accounting

SVQs

Level 2: Accounting
Level 3: Accounting
Level 4: Accounting

OCR

OCR offer various awards in Accounting & Book-Keeping. Contact OCR for details.

London Chamber of Commerce and Industry Examinations Board (LCCIEB)

Accounting Levels 3 and 4.

Other Vocational Awarding Bodies

ABC: Book-keeping

ADVERTISING AND PUBLIC RELATIONS

Membership of Professional Institutions and Associations

COMMUNICATION ADVERTISING AND MARKETING EDUCATION FOUNDATION

Abford House, 15 Wilton Road, London SW1V 1NJ Tel: 020 7828 7506 Fax: 020 7976 5140
e-mail: info@camfoundation.com Website: www.camfoundation.com
CAM is the examining body for the principal UK trade and professional associations of the marketing communication industry. The CAM qualifications are industry examined and controlled, developing candidates' careers by giving the essential practical skills and knowledge. Candidates may study through a UK network of colleges providing FT, PT, evening, intensive and distance learning options.

WHAT THE QUALIFICATIONS COVER:
Advanced Diploma in Communication Studies: This is broad-based and can be regarded as an induction for those who work in the marketing communication industry. To achieve the qualification candidates study, and must pass, the following 6 subjects: Marketing; Advertising; Public Relations; Media; Direct Marketing and Sales Promotion; Research and Consumer Behaviour. (An Advanced Certificate is awarded for each subject passed.)
Higher Diploma in Integrated Marketing Communication: This is management orientated for those wishing to develop their career to senior practitioner level. All candidates must pass the Higher Certificate in Management and Strategy and the Higher Certificate in Planning, Implementation and Evaluation. CAM also offers specialist Higher Diploma options in Advertising, Public Relations, Direct Marketing and Sales Promotion.
Entry Requirements:
All candidates applying for **Advanced Diploma** registration must be at least 18 yrs of age and have a minimum of 5 GCSEs including Maths and English at grade C or above, or the equivalent

qualifications. Where English is not the first language, evidence of English language competence to IELTS 6.5 is required. Those with Industry experience but without formal qualifications may apply through discussion with the Registrar. Entrance to the **Higher Diploma** is normally by completion of the Advanced Diploma. Experienced practitioners may gain direct entry if they can prove their experience and competence.

Exemptions:
Applications for exemptions from one or more Advanced Certificate modules are considered on the basis of previous educational qualifications that substantially cover the CAM Syllabi.

Qualifications:
On successful completion of the Advanced Diploma, candidates can apply for Associate membership of the CAM Foundation and use the designation **AmCAM**. On completion of the Higher Diploma candidates can apply for full membership of the CAM Foundation and use the designation **MCAM**. Honorary Fellowships (**FCAM**) are only awarded to those who have made an outstanding contribution to the marketing communication industry.

National Vocational Qualifications (NVQs): (Levels 3 and 4) For Advertising, Direct Marketing and Public Relations were launched at the end of 1994. (Those for Sales Promotion are expected to follow.) To meet the special requirements for awarding NVQs CAM has entered into an agreement with the RSA Examinations Board and formed a new Joint Organisation which has now been accredited.

INSTITUTE OF PRACTITIONERS IN ADVERTISING

44 Belgrave Square, London SW1X 8QS Tel: 020 7235 7020 Fax: 020 7245 9904
e-mail: mark@ipa.co.uk Website: www.ipa.co.uk

MEMBERSHIP:
Fellow (FIPA): Fellows are elected by the Council from among Members of at least 5 yrs' standing and after outstanding service to advertising.

Member (MIPA): Those eligible as Members are generally Directors and Associate Directors of member-agencies. As a rule they should have 5yrs' advertising experience, including 3 yrs as an agency executive or specialist.

Agencies involved in the creating and/or placing of advertising and marketing communications are admitted as Incorporated Practitioners in Advertising. As the Institute is the trade and professional organisation solely for advertising agencies, only people working in member-agencies of the Institute are eligible to apply for personal membership.

THE INSTITUTE OF PUBLIC RELATIONS

The Old Trading House, 15 Northburgh Street, London EC1V 0PR Tel: 020 7253 5151
Fax: 020 7490 0588

MEMBERSHIP:
Members (MIPR): (a) Individuals whose applications are acceptable to the Council provided that they hold the IPR Diploma or have had at least 4 yrs' substantial experience at operating executive level in the practice of and an acceptable academic qualification in public relations. Acceptable academic qualifications are either (i) a CAM Public Relations Diploma, or (ii) FT degree standard course in public relations or other courses where the syllabus has been approved by the Education and Training Committee of the Institute or (iii) such overseas qualifications as shall be specifically approved by the Council; (b) Individuals whose applications are acceptable to the Council provided that they have at least 10 yrs' substantial experience in public relations of which not less than 4 yrs' shall have been in a senior appointment, or who have at least 10 yrs in senior management and at the time of their application hold a senior public relations appointment in a major organisation. Applicants will be required to submit a curriculum vitae with their application giving details of their public relations career and may be required to attend an interview before a Standing Committee of the Institute. Members shall be entitled to exercise full voting rights in the affairs of the Institute and use the letters MIPR after their names. They shall be entitled to a certificate of full membership of the Institute.

Associates (AMIPR): Associate membership shall be open to individuals who have had at least 3 yrs' substantial experience in the practice of public relations and whose applications are acceptable to the Council. Such persons shall be entitled to use the description Associate Member of the

Institute of Public Relations and to use the designatory letters AMIPR after their names. Associates shall be entitled to the same member benefits as full members, to exercise full voting rights if elected before 1 January 1993 in the affairs of the Institute and to a certificate of associate membership.
Affiliates: Affiliate membership shall be open to individuals whose applications are acceptable to the Council and who are working as bona-fide practitioners in public relations or carrying out a specialist role in public relations but do not qualify for any other grade of membership. Affiliates shall be entitled to the same member benefits as full members, but shall not be entitled to put any letters or descriptions after their name or vote at any General Meeting of the Institute.

LONDON SCHOOL OF PUBLIC RELATIONS

David Game House, 69 Notting Hill Gate, London W11 3JS Tel: 020 7221 3399 Fax: 020 7243 1730 e-mail: lsp@easynet.co.uk Website: www.pr-school-london.com
Provides training for those wishing to enter public relations as a career or for those already in PR or an information/communications job who require some formal training. The Diploma issued by the School is a heavyweight introduction for graduates and is backed by leading consultancies. Courses on offer: An Integrated Approach to Public Relations (15 wk evening Diploma). An Advisory Board of Fellows of the Institute of PR act to monitor course standards and the setting of exam papers. The course is also recognised by the National Union of Journalists (NUJ). The School is a recognised training provider by the Public Relations Consultants Association (PRCA).

University Qualifications

The following universities offer qualifications in Advertising and Public Relations and related subjects. Full details may be found in Part 4, under the entry for the appropriate university.

FIRST DEGREES AWARDED BY UNIVERSITIES

Bournemouth; Bucks. Coll.; Central Lancashire; Cheltenham & Gloucester; Doncaster; Exeter (The College of St Mark & St John); Hertfordshire (West Herts College); Lancaster; Leeds Metropolitan; Lincolnshire; Lincolnshire (Lincoln University Campus); London Institute (London College of Fashion); London Institute (London College of Printing); Luton; North London; Nottingham Trent (Southampton Institute); Teesside; Thames Valley; Ulster

HIGHER DEGREES AWARDED BY UNIVERSITIES

Kent; Leeds; Leeds Metropolitan; Leicester; Manchester Metropolitan.; Napier; Stirling; Ulster

DIPLOMAS AWARDED BY UNIVERSITIES

Hertfordshire (West Herts College); Leeds Metropolitan; London Institute (London College of Printing); Luton; Napier; Stirling; Thames Valley; Ulster

CERTIFICATES AWARDED BY UNIVERSITIES

Leeds Metropolitan

POSTGRADUATE DIPLOMAS AWARDED BY UNIVERSITIES

Plymouth (Falmouth College of Arts)

PROFESSIONAL COURSES AWARDED BY UNIVERSITIES

Leeds Metropolitan; London Guildhall

National Certificates and Diplomas

BTEC Higher National Certificates/Diplomas: Advertising (Copywriting and Art Direction)
Scotland
SQA HNC: Advertising and Marketing with Public Relations; Advertising Copywriting
SQA HND: Advertising and Public Relations; Advertising

SVQs

Level 3: Advertising; Public Relations.
Level 4: Advertising; Public Relations.

AGRICULTURE AND HORTICULTURE
Membership of Professional Institutions and Associations

THE INSTITUTE OF HORTICULTURE

14/15 Belgrave Square, London SW1X 8PS Tel: 020 7245 6943 Fax: 020 7245 6943 e-mail: ioh@horticulture.org.uk Website: www.horticulture.demon.co.uk/

MEMBERSHIP:

Membership of the Institute affords recognition of professional status and achievement in horticulture. Membership is available to those working wholly or substantially in horticulture (or in a branch of science or arts directly linked with horticulture) and having the appropriate combination of qualifications and experience. There are membership grades to match the successive stages reached in the career progression of all horticulturists.

Fellowship (FIHort): Attained by nomination and election by those Members who have made an outstanding contribution to horticulture.

Corporate Membership (MIHort): Open to those who have reached a high level either by qualification or achievement in a particular field of experience. The qualifications expected are University Degrees, Botanic Gardens Diplomas, MHort (RHS), HND NVQ Level 4 and ND with suitable experience.

Associate Membership: Open to holders of an ND, C&G Phase III or IV, RHS Diploma (formerly MHort Stage 1) NVQ Level 3 or C&G Phase I or II, but with considerable industry experience.

Affiliate Membership: Granted to those whose main occupation or involvement is in horticulture, but who are not yet deemed eligible to become an Associate or Corporate Member.

Student Membership: Available for those studying for horticultural qualifications.

QUALIFYING EXAMS:

The Institute does not have its own exams, but expects Members to have obtained qualifications in horticulture or highly-related subjects either from a university or a horticultural college. The Institute can provide details of universities and colleges that offer appropriate courses.

University Qualifications

The following universities offer qualifications in Agriculture and Horticulture and related subjects. Full details may be found in Part 4, under the entry for the appropriate university.

FIRST DEGREES AWARDED BY UNIVERSITIES

Aberdeen; Adams; Belfast; Bristol; De Montfort, Leicester; Derby; Edinburgh; Essex (Writtle College); Glasgow; Greenwich; Lincolnshire (Bishop Burton College); Liverpool John Moores; London (Imperial College of Science, Technology & Medicine); London (Wye College); Newcastle; Nottingham; Nottingham Trent; Plymouth; Reading; Wales (University of Wales, Aberystwyth); Wales (University of Wales, Bangor); Wolverhampton; Worcester

HIGHER DEGREES AWARDED BY UNIVERSITIES

Aberdeen; Bath; Belfast; Bournemouth; Bradford; Bristol; Cheltenham & Gloucester; Coventry; East Anglia; Edinburgh; Essex (Writtle College); Greenwich; Hertfordshire; Leeds; London (Birkbeck, University of London); London (Wye College); Loughborough; Manchester Metropolitan.; Middlesex; Newcastle; Nottingham; Plymouth; Reading; UMIST; Wales (University of Wales, Bangor)

DIPLOMAS AWARDED BY UNIVERSITIES

Aberdeen; Central England; Central Lancashire; De Montfort, Leicester; Edinburgh; Greenwich; Hertfordshire; Lincolnshire (Bishop Burton College); London (Wye College); Newcastle; Northampton; Plymouth; Reading; Wales (University of Wales, Bangor); Worcester

CERTIFICATES AWARDED BY UNIVERSITIES

East Anglia (Otley College); Lincolnshire (Bishop Burton College); OU (Northern College of Education)

OTHER COURSES AWARDED BY UNIVERSITIES
Essex (Writtle College)

National Certificates and Diplomas

BTEC National Certificates/Diplomas: Agricultural Merchanting; Agricultural Supply and Marketing; Agriculture; Agriculture (Amenity Landscape Services); Agriculture (Arboriculture); Agriculture (Farm Mechanisation); Agriculture (Game, Wildlife and Habitat Management); Agriculture (Land Use and Recreation); Agriculture (Livestock and Related Crop Production); Agriculture (Livestock Production); Agriculture (Management of Thoroughbred Horses); Agriculture (Mechanised Crop Production); Agriculture (Merchanting); Agriculture (Poultry Options); Agriculture (Production and Management); Amenity Horticulture; Commercial Horticulture; Horticultural Mechanisation; Horticulture; Horticulture (Arboriculture Option); Horticulture (Amenity Option); Horticulture (Amenity Supervision and Leisure); Horticulture (Commercial Crop Production); Horticulture (Garden Centre Sales and Organisation); Horticulture (Garden Centre Studies); Horticulture (Glass House Crop Production); Horticulture (Hardy Fruit Production); Horticulture (Hardy Nursery Stock Production); Horticulture (Landscape Technology); Horticulture (leisure and Horticulture Supervision); Horticulture (Turf Science and Sports Ground Management)
BTEC Higher National Certificates/Diplomas: Agriculture
Northern Ireland
HNDs: Agriculture; Science (Technology of Food).
National Certificates: Agriculture; Amenity Horticulture
Scotland
SQA HND: Agricultural Science; Countryside Recreation & Conservation Management; Horticulture; Horticulture with Plantmanship; Pig Enterprise Management; Poultry Production & Management; Rural Recreation & Tourism; Service Engineering – Agriculture; Horticulture and Construction Plant; Service Engineering – Construction Plant and Agricultural Machinery
SQA HNC: Arboriculture; Agriculture; Amenity Horticulture; Animal Technology; Countryside Recreation & Conservation Management; Horticulture; Pig Production; Poultry Production; Rural Recreation & Tourism; Service Engineering – Agriculture; Horticulture and Construction Plant; Service Engineering – Construction Plant and Agricultural Machinery

NVQs

Level 1: Amenity Horticulture; Commercial Horticulture; General Agriculture.
Level 2: Amenity Horticulture (Arboriculture); Amenity Horticulture (Cemetery and Graveyard Maintenance); Amenity Horticulture (Decorative Horticulture); Amenity Horticulture (Hard Landscape); Amenity Horticulture (Interior Landscaping); Amenity Horticulture (Nursery); Amenity Horticulture (Sports Turf); Environmental Conservation (Landscapes and Ecosystems); Extensive Crop Production; Gamekeeping; Intensive Crop Production; Livestock Markets (Driving Livestock); Livestock Production; Mixed Farming; Poultry Production.
Level 3: Amenity Horticulture (Arboriculture); Amenity Horticulture (Decorative Horticulture); Amenity Horticulture (Hard Landscape); Amenity Horticulture (Sports Turf Maintenance); Extensive Crop Production; Gamekeeping; Intensive Crop Production; Livestock Production; Mixed Farming; Poultry Production.
Level 4: Agriculture (Livestock Management); Agriculture and Commercial Horticulture (Crop Management).

SVQs

Level 1: Amenity Horticulture; Crop & Livestock Production; Intensive Crop Production; Livestock Production; Mechanised Field Crop Production; Mushroom Crop Production.
Level 2: Amenity Horticulture: Arboriculture; Amenity Horticulture: Hard Landscaping; Amenity Horticulture: Nursery – Soft Landscape Maintenance; Commercial Horticulture: Garden Centre Operation; Crop & Livestock Production.
Level 3: Commercial Horticulture: Garden Centre Operation; Constructing & Restoring Landscapes; Crop & Livestock Production; Intensive Crop Production; Livestock Production; Managing Trees & Woodland; Mushroom Crop Production; Nursery Stock Production.
Level 4: Crop Management.

Other Qualifications and Courses

THE ROYAL BOTANIC GARDEN

20A Inverleith Road, Edinburgh EH3 5LR Tel: 0131 248 2825 Fax: 0131 248 2901 Website: www.rbge.org.uk
Contact: Principal, School of Horticulture.
The Higher National Diploma in Horticulture with Plantmanship course consists of HND units in Establishing Plant Collections, Designing Plant Collections, Managing Plant Collections, Plant Classification & Systematics, Plant & Habitat Conservation, Plantmanship. Students who successfully complete the course and who gain the necessary credits may be eligible to enter the third yr of the BSc Horticulture at Strathclyde University and other universities.

AWARDS OF THE ROYAL HORTICULTURAL SOCIETY

RHS Garden, Wisley, Woking, Surrey GU23 6QB Tel: 01483 224234
RHS General Exam in Horticulture: Basic exam for professionals, or for amateur gardeners; 2 written papers on basic understanding of scientific principles and their relationship and application to horticultural skills and practices.
RHS Diploma in Horticulture: Major step up from the RHS General Exam; for professionals and amateur gardeners; period of broad horticultural experience essential ; 4 written papers and, for those who achieve the necessary standard at this stage, a practical and oral exam.
Master of Horticulture (RHS) Award: Premier qualification for horticultural professionals; must have RHS Diploma (or Stage I of MHort (RHS) or NDH Intermediate) plus appropriate professional horticultural experience; 4 written papers: 2 compulsory on principles and applied management in horticulture and 2 candidate's choice in horticultural technology; in addition, for those who achieve the necessary standard, managerial and technical competence assessment including dissertation. Further details, including entry requirements, forms, fees etc, write with sae to Examinations Office, RHS Garden, Wisley, Woking, Surrey GU23 6QB. Tel: 01483 224234 Fax: 01483 212382

Other Vocational Awarding Bodies

Scotland
The pattern of qualifications and teaching establishments in Scotland is similar to that in England and Wales, and Scottish Diplomas and College Certificates in Agricultural subjects correspond with those described above. There are no farm institutes and students at this level would either study PT for the C&G Certificates while working on an approved farm under the Scottish National Apprenticeship scheme or take a course leading to a college certificate. The Scottish Agricultural College operates at 3 centres of study: East of Scotland College of Agriculture (ESA), West Mains Road, Edinburgh EH3 9DF; North of Scotland College of Agriculture (NSA), 581 King Street, Aberdeen AB9 1UD; and West of Scotland Agricultural College (WSA), Auchincruive, Ayr KA6 5HW.

ALTERNATIVE MEDICINE

University Qualifications

The following universities offer qualifications in Alternative Medicine and related subjects. Full details may be found in Part 4, under the entry for the appropriate university.

FIRST DEGREES AWARDED BY UNIVERSITIES

Central Lancashire; Greenwich; Napier; Westminster

HIGHER DEGREES AWARDED BY UNIVERSITIES

Coventry; Liverpool John Moores; Salford; Westminster

DIPLOMAS AWARDED BY UNIVERSITIES
Middlesex

CERTIFICATES AWARDED BY UNIVERSITIES
Warwick

AMBULANCE SERVICE

Membership of Professional Institutions and Associations

AMBULANCE SERVICE INSTITUTE

Registered in Cardiff – Company No: 1290137 Registered Charity No: 298872 Data Protection
Act Registered No: K382661X

2 Appletree Close, Oakley, Near Basingstoke, Hampshire RG23 7HL Fax: 01256 782650 (24 hr)
e-mail: ambservinst.uk@virgin.net Website: www.asi.ac.uk or www.asi-international.com
Official Publication: 'asi INTERNATONAL'®™ No: 2170635
Hon. Secretary & Treasurer: Mr W.R. Jones FASI (Hon)

MEMBERSHIP:
Membership of the Ambulance Service Institute is open to all employees of a NHS Ambulance
Service. There is also a section for Non-NHS personnel such as Voluntary Aid, First Responders,
Non-NHS Ambulance Services, Military Medical and Industrial First Aid/Medical personnel, etc,
who hold a current First Aid certificate or higher qualification issued by a recognised body such
as the British Red Cross Society and/or the St Johns Ambulance and who are being regularly
trained in Ambulance or First Aid duties.
Fellow (FASI): Open to Graduate Members who submit a paper on their research area to the
Board of Management on one or more aspects of Ambulance Service development that may
improve the professional care given to Patients and/or the way in which the service is provided.
Graduate (GASI): Open to Associate Members in order to enable them to further develop and
expand their knowledge of Clinical and/or Management skills for the benefit of Patients and the
general public at large. This grade is also available for Membership by exemption to Ambulance
personnel who can comply with the criteria.
Associate (AASI): Open to Licentiate Members, available in Pre-Hospital Care, Control
Communications & First Line Management. This grade is also available for Membership entry by
exemption to IHCD qualified Ambulance Paramedics who are able to comply with the criteria.
Licentiate (LASI): Open to those who have passed the preliminary exam in Pre-Hospital Care or
Control Communications & First Line Management. This grade is also available for Membership
entry by exemption to IHCD qualified Ambulance Technicians who are able to comply with the
criteria.
Student: Open to both NHS Ambulance Service personnel and Non-NHS Ambulance personnel
who hold a current 'First-Aid at Work', 'First Aid' or other relevant Certificate issued by a
recognised body such as the British Red Cross Society and/or the St Johns Ambulance and who
are being regularly trained in Ambulance and/or First Aid duties.
Affiliate (ASI Affil): Open to individuals, companies or bodies who support the Institutes aims,
objectives and activities without claim to membership by examination or other means.

EXAMINATIONS:
Graduate Grade: The syllabus includes standards of performance & quality control, contractual
procedures – standards-applications and management, major incident planning – all hazards,
human relations, the law & developments in relation to Ambulance Services, budgetary control
within the Ambulance Services, equipment design and evaluation including vehicles, information
technology and communication systems, existing and proposed European and British legislation
applicable to the Ambulance Services of Great Britain.
Associate Grade: 'Pre-Hospital Care' includes papers on anatomy/physiology, advanced
resuscitation, drug administration, neo-natal conditions, emergency childbirth, trauma and
multiple casualty management. 'Control Communications and Management' includes papers on

communication and computer technology, standards of performance, health & safety & welfare at work Act, personnel management, identification of training needs and development, patient complaints evaluation, ORH reports, contractual procedures and contract management.

Licentiate Grade: 'Pre-Hospital Care' includes papers on anatomy/physiology, patient care & examination and diagnosis, resuscitation, emergency childbirth, infectious diseases, trauma management, personal hygiene, use & maintenance of ambulance equipment, road traffic law, advanced driving, health and safety, patient complaints procedures. 'Control Communications & First Line Management' includes papers on communication systems and procedures, control of emergency and priority dispatch cases, non-emergency cases control and journey pre-planning, health & safety, personnel management, training, reports, contract procedures & management and major incidents, patient complaints procedures.

ARBITRATION

Membership of Professional Institutions and Associations

THE CHARTERED INSTITUTE OF ARBITRATORS

International Arbitration Centre, 24 Angel Gate, City Road, London EC1V 2RS Tel: 020 7837 4483 Fax: 020 7837 4185

e-mail: info@arbitrators.org Website: www.arbitrators.org

The Institute exists to promote and facilitate the settlement of disputes by arbitration and alternative dispute resolution.

CORPORATE MEMBERS:

Associates (ACIArb): Associates shall: (a) satisfy the Council that he is in all respects a fit and proper person for admission to the Institute; (b) be engaged in a profession, occupation or calling in which recourse to arbitration is directly or indirectly involved; (c) be not less than 21; (d) possess a general standard of education conforming with the requirements of the Council; and (e) (i) have passed Part I of the exam of the Institute, or (ii) have passed any other exam accepted by the Council as the equivalent, or (iii) have such knowledge and experience of the law and practice of arbitration as the Council may approve.

Members (MCIArb): Members shall be elected by the Council and every candidate for election shall: (a) be an Associate of the Institute and be not less than 25 yrs of age; (b) satisfy the Council that he is in all respects a suitable person for election as a Member; (c) either have passed or been exempted from Part I of the examinations or assessment of the Institute and have passed Part II or any other examination accepted by the Council as the equivalent to Part II. Alternatively the person may be a full member of another association of arbitrators or practitioners of alternative means of dispute resolution which has standards of knowledge of arbitration and alternative dispute resolution law, practice and procedure which are in the opinion of the Council equivalent to those of the Institute for election to membership and satisfy the Council that he has achieved those standards.

Fellows (FCIArb): Fellows shall be elected by the Council and every candidate shall: (a) be a member of the Institute and be not less than 35 yrs of age; (b) satisfy the Council that he is in all respects a suitable person for election as a Fellow; (c) have completed and passed the Institute's personal assessment for Fellowship to the satisfaction of the Council; (d) have passed or been exempted from Part I of the examinations of the Institute and Part II of the examinations of the Institute and have passed or been exempted from Part III of the examinations of the Institute and thereafter have completed and passed the Assessment for Fellowship Programme to the satisfaction of the Council. Upon election to Fellowship by the Council of the Institute, in accordance with (a) and (e) above, the member will be entitled to describe himself as a 'Chartered Arbitrator'.

NON-CORPORATE MEMBERS:

Individual Affiliates/Corporate Affiliates: The Council may elect a person who is not professionally qualified but has an interest in arbitration.

Retired Members: Associates, Members and Fellows, on reaching the age of 60, who are not practising in any occupation directly or indirectly concerned with arbitration, may request to be transferred.

HONORARY MEMBERS:
The Council may elect a person of eminence for services rendered to the Institute and/or arbitration.

University Qualifications

The following universities offer qualifications in Arbitration and related subjects. Full details may be found in Part 4, under the entry for the appropriate university.

HIGHER DEGREES AWARDED BY UNIVERSITIES
Leeds Metropolitan; London (King's College London)

DIPLOMAS AWARDED BY UNIVERSITIES
London (King's College London); London (Queen Mary & Westfield College (incorporating St Bartholomew's and the Royal London School of Medicine & Dentistry))

ARCHAEOLOGY

Membership of Professional Institutions and Associations

THE INSTITUTE OF FIELD ARCHAEOLOGISTS

University of Reading, 2 Earley Gate, PO Box 239, Reading RG6 6AU Tel: 0118 9316446 Fax: 0118 9316448 e-mail: admin@ifa.virgin.net Website: www.archaeologists.net

MEMBERSHIP:
MIFA Member: Open to graduate members with at least 3 yrs' continuous experience who can demonstrate they have satisfactorily exercised responsibility for a substantial archaeological project. Also open to non-graduates or those with non-relevant degrees whose experience and achievements are considered to confer equivalent qualification.
AIFA Associate: Open to graduate members with at least 12 mths' continuous experience who can demonstrate they have satisfactorily exercised delegated or part responsibility for a substantial archaeological project. Also open to non-graduates or those with non-relevant degrees whose experience and achievements are considered to confer equivalent qualification.
PIFA Practitioner: Open to graduate members with at least 6 mths' continuous experience in field archaeology. Also open to non-graduates or those with non-relevant degrees whose experience and achievements are considered to confer equivalent qualification.
Affiliate: Open to those studying archaeology or actively involved in field archaeology who support the Institute's aims and activities.

EXAMINATIONS:
Candidates for all categories of membership must agree to abide by the Institute's Code of Conduct and are examined on the basis of documented evidence of academic qualifications, experience, levels of responsibility held, and demonstrable achievements (eg publications), supported by references from appropriate referees. There is a formal appeals procedure.

University Qualifications

The following universities offer qualifications in Archaeology and related subjects. Full details may be found in Part 4, under the entry for the appropriate university.

FIRST DEGREES AWARDED BY UNIVERSITIES
Belfast; Birmingham; Bournemouth; Bradford; Bristol; Cambridge; De Montfort, Leicester; Derby; Durham; East Anglia; East London; Edinburgh; Exeter; Glasgow; Greenwich; Leicester; Liverpool; Liverpool (Chester College of H.E.); London (Birkbeck, University of London); London (King's College London); London (School of Oriental & African Studies); London (University College

(UCL)); Manchester; Newcastle; Northampton; Nottingham; Oxford; Portsmouth; Reading; Sheffield; Southampton; Southampton (King Alfred's College); St Andrews; Wales (Cardiff University); Wales (University of Wales College, Newport); Wales (University of Wales, Bangor); Wales (University of Wales, Lampeter); Warwick; York

HIGHER DEGREES AWARDED BY UNIVERSITIES
Aberdeen; Belfast; Birmingham; Bournemouth; Bradford; Bristol; Cambridge; De Montfort, Leicester; Durham; Edinburgh; Exeter; Glasgow; Kent; Leicester; Liverpool; London (Birkbeck, University of London); London (King's College London); London (University College (UCL)); Manchester; Newcastle; Nottingham; Oxford; Reading; Sheffield; Southampton; Southampton (King Alfred's College); UMIST; Wales (Cardiff University); Wales (University of Wales, Lampeter); York

DIPLOMAS AWARDED BY UNIVERSITIES
Birmingham; Bournemouth; Bradford; Durham; Edinburgh; Exeter; Exeter (Truro College); Glasgow; Kent; Leicester; Newcastle; Oxford; Southampton (King Alfred's College); Sussex

CERTIFICATES AWARDED BY UNIVERSITIES
Birmingham; Cambridge; Hull; Kent; Leeds; Leicester; Nottingham; Sussex; Warwick

National Certificates and Diplomas
BTEC National Certificates/Diplomas: Practical Archaeology
BTEC Higher National Certificates/Diplomas: Practical Archaeology

Other Vocational Awarding Bodies
ABC: Field Archaeology

ARCHITECTURE
Membership of Professional Institutions and Associations

ARCHITECTS REGISTRATION BOARD
8 Weymouth Street, London W1N 3FB Tel: 020 7580 5861 Fax: 020 7436 5269
e-mail: info@arb.org.uk
The Architects Registration Board is the regulatory body for architects in the United Kingdom. Only those individuals registered with the Architects Registration Board can use the title "architect". In order to be admitted to the Register, it is necessary to have passed recognised exams at a school of architecture in the UK and to have obtained at least two yrs' practical training experience working under the supervision of an architect. Provision also exists for entry onto the Register for those with non-UK qualifications in architecture and practical training experience.

ASSOCIATION OF BUILDING ENGINEERS
Lutyens House, Billing Brook Road, Weston Favell, Northampton NN3 8NW Tel: 01604 404121 Fax: 01604 784220 e-mail: building.engineers @ abe.org.uk Website: www.abe.org.uk
The Association was founded in 1925 under the name of The Incorporated Association of Architects and Surveyors and is the professional body for those specialising in the technology of building.
MEMBERSHIP:
Fellow (FBEng): Must not be less than 32 and must have held a senior appointment in the construction industry for a period of 5 yrs.
Member (MBEng): Graduates holding an accredited classified Hons degree on satisfying the ABE Evaluation of Professional Competence. Exemption from the EPC is granted to corporate members of certain related professional bodies.
Graduate Member (Grad BEng): Must have at least one yr's relevant experience and hold an accredited degree.

Associate Member(ABEng): Must have at least 2 yrs' experience in a professional office and hold a qualification of an academic standard not less than that of a BTEC HNC in construction.

Student: Open to those enrolled on approved courses of study leading to MBEng.

Corporate Members (Fellow and Member): Eligible to register as professional engineer (PEng) with the Society of Professional Engineers and thus entitled to register with the Union Internationale des Ingenieurs Professionnels and use the designation Ingenieur Professionnel Europeen (IngPEur).

BRITISH INSTITUTE OF ARCHITECTURAL TECHNOLOGISTS

397 City Road, London EC1V 1NH Tel: 0800 731 5471 Fax: 020 7837 3194
e-mail: careers@biat.org.uk Website: www.biat.org.uk

MEMBERSHIP:

Member (MBIAT): Open to those applicants who satisfy the Institute that they meet its academic and professional requirements. This grade is only open to those upgrading from Profile or Associate membership. Standard route: to have obtained a degree in Architectural Technology or in a technically-based subject in the Built Environment or an approved HNC/HND in Building Studies including the design options or an alternative BIAT approved higher level qualification. Must then have completed a 2 yr practice qualification logbook under supervision of approved supervisor and have passed a professional interview.

Associate (ABIAT): Open to all applicants who have obtained a qualification as listed in the standard route above.

Profile Membership: Open to applicants with non-standard qualifications or who are self-employed.

Student Membership: Open to all further and higher education students following approved courses and to school students following relevant GCSEs and A levels or GNVQs, who intend to pursue a career in architectural technology.

ROYAL INSTITUTE OF BRITISH ARCHITECTS

(Incorporated 1837)
66 Portland Place, London W1N 4AD Tel: 0906 302 0400 (calls cost 50p per min) Fax: 0207 631 1802
e-mail: bal@inst.riba.net Website: www.architecture.com

MEMBERSHIP:

Non-Corporate Membership – Student: Candidates may enrol as Student members if they are bona fide students of Architecture studying for the RIBA Exam in Architecture or for an exam providing exemption from the RIBA Exam.

Corporate Membership: A person may qualify for election if s/he has passed or received exemption from Parts 1 and 2 of the RIBA Examination in Architecture and the RIBA Exam in Professional Practice, or has obtained a qualification in architecture outside the UK which in the opinion of the admission panel indicates possession of the requisite knowledge and experience of architectural practice. The designation **FRIBA (Fellow)** and **ARIBA (Associate)** are still used but only by those who were members of the Institute before the present charter came into effect in 1971. It is now more common for members of the Institute to use the suffix RIBA, as there is now only 1 class of corporate membership.

Honorary Membership: By election.

Subscriber Membership: Open to anyone with a personal or professional interest in architecture and who is ineligible for corporate or student membership.

EXAMINATIONS:

The RIBA recognises courses at 35 schools of architecture. All students must spend at least 2 yrs in practical training in addition to the academic course before qualifying for RIBA membership. 1 yr of this must be after completing the course, but the other yr is generally taken in the middle of the course. Most schools provide a yr's break after the third academic session. The final yr of the practical training must be spent in an architect's office, but the first practical training period can be spent in other sectors of the building industry such as with contractors, manufacturers, quantity surveyors, engineers, and planners. At least one of the practical training yrs must normally be spent in a UK architectural practice.

Min entry requirements to the RIBA course:

The General Certificate of Education (England, Wales, Northern Ireland): Candidates should have at least 5 GCSE passes and 2 academic A level passes, or 1 subject at A level with 2 AS levels of the GCE. This is a min, and is no guarantee for admission to every school of architecture, many of which will demand higher entrance qualifications and ask for specific A levels. Both the GCE A level subjects should be drawn from the academic field of study. English, Mathematics, Physics and Chemistry are considered to be core subjects. Students with BTEC (or (SCOTVEC) Certificate in Building Studies may be considered if they also have GCSE English Language. Some schools may also require 3 additional subjects to include Mathematics. In Scotland the qualifications are similar, except that at least 3 subjects must be passed at Higher grade and 2 at Ordinary grade. Those without A level art would be expected to prepare a portfolio.

Universities with a recognised course of architecture: Robert Gordon University, Aberdeen; University of Bath; The Queen's University of Belfast; *University of Central England in Birmingham; *University of Brighton; University of Cambridge; University of Wales College of Cardiff; *De Montfort University, Leicester; University of Dundee; Heriot-Watt University, Edinburgh; University of Edinburgh; University of Strathclyde, Glasgow; *Glasgow University and Glasgow School of Art; University of Huddersfield; *University of Humberside; *Leeds Metropolitan University; University of Liverpool; *Liverpool John Moore's University; University College London; University of East London; *University of Greenwich, London; *Kingston University, London; *University of North London; *South Bank University, London; University of Westminster, London; University of Manchester; University of Newcastle upon Tyne; University of Nottingham; Oxford Brookes University, Oxford; University of Plymouth; University of Portsmouth; and the University of Sheffield.* PT courses available.

Other recognised schools of architecture: Canterbury School of Architecture, Kent Institute of Art and Design; Architectural Association, London; School of Architecture and Interior Design, Royal College of Art, London (Part 2 exemption only). The *Description and Regulations* (for the RIBA Exam in Architecture) contains details of the external exam syllabus and may be purchased from the RIBA Education Department. Further information can be found in the careers section of the website.

University Qualifications

The following universities offer qualifications in Architecture and related subjects. Full details may be found in Part 4, under the entry for the appropriate university.

FIRST DEGREES AWARDED BY UNIVERSITIES

Anglia; Bath; Belfast; Brighton; Bristol; Cambridge; Central England; Central Lancashire; Cheltenham & Gloucester; City; Coventry; De Montfort, Leicester; Derby; Dundee; East London; Edinburgh; Glamorgan; Glasgow; Glasgow (Glasgow School of Art); Glasgow Caledonian; Greenwich; Heriot-Watt; Heriot-Watt (Edinburgh College of Art); Huddersfield; Kent (Kent Institute of Art & Design); Kingston; Leeds; Leeds Metropolitan; Lincolnshire; Liverpool; Liverpool John Moores; London (University College (UCL)); Loughborough; Luton; Manchester; Manchester Metropolitan.; Napier; Newcastle; North London; Northampton; Northumbria; Nottingham; Nottingham Trent; Nottingham Trent (Southampton Institute); Oxford Brookes; Paisley; Plymouth; Portsmouth; Robert Gordon; Sheffield; Sheffield Hallam; South Bank; Strathclyde; Ulster; Wales (Cardiff University); Wales (North East Wales Institute); Wales (Swansea Institute of Higher Education); Wales (University of Wales Institute, Cardiff); Westminster; Wolverhampton

HIGHER DEGREES AWARDED BY UNIVERSITIES

Bath; Belfast; Bournemouth; Brighton; Bristol; Cambridge; Central England; Central Lancashire; De Montfort, Leicester; East London; Essex; Glamorgan; Glasgow; Glasgow (Glasgow School of Art); Greenwich; Heriot-Watt; Heriot-Watt (Edinburgh College of Art); Huddersfield; Keele; Kent (Kent Institute of Art & Design); Kingston; Leeds; Leeds Metropolitan; Lincolnshire; Liverpool; Liverpool John Moores; London (London School of Economics & Political Science); London (Royal Holloway); London (University College (UCL)); Manchester; Middlesex; Newcastle; North London; Nottingham; Oxford Brookes; Plymouth; Portsmouth; Royal College of Art; Sheffield; Sheffield Hallam; Southampton; Southampton (Winchester School of Art); Strathclyde; Wales (Cardiff University); Westminster; Wolverhampton

DIPLOMAS AWARDED BY UNIVERSITIES

Anglia; Bournemouth; Brighton; Bristol; Cambridge; Cheltenham & Gloucester; De Montfort; Leicester; East London; Edinburgh; Glamorgan; Glasgow; Heriot-Watt (Edinburgh College of Art); Huddersfield; Kent (Kent Institute of Art & Design); Kingston; Leeds Metropolitan; Lincolnshire; Liverpool; Liverpool John Moores; London (Royal Holloway); London (University College (UCL)); Luton; Newcastle; North London; Northampton; Northumbria; Oxford; Oxford Brookes; Plymouth; Strathclyde; Teesside; Wales (University of Wales Institute, Cardiff); Westminster

CERTIFICATES AWARDED BY UNIVERSITIES

Kingston; Leeds Metropolitan; Leicester; Lincolnshire; London (University College (UCL)); Oxford; Westminster

OTHER COURSES AWARDED BY UNIVERSITIES

Huddersfield; Leeds Metropolitan

POSTGRADUATE DIPLOMAS AWARDED BY UNIVERSITIES

Heriot-Watt

National Certificates and Diplomas

BTEC National Certificates/Diplomas: Design (Architectural Stained Glass)
BTEC Higher National Certificates/Diplomas: Design (Architectural Stained Glass); Design (Interior Architecture)
Scotland
SQA HNC: Architectural Conservation; Architectural Technology
SQA HND: Architectural Conservation; Architectural Technology

ART AND DESIGN

Membership of Professional Institutions and Associations

THE ASSOCIATION OF BRITISH PICTURE RESTORERS

Station Avenue, Kew, Surrey TW9 3QA Tel: 020 8948 5644 Fax: 020 8948 5644
e-mail: apbrlondon@aol.com Website: www.abpr.co.uk

MEMBERSHIP:
Fellowship: Open to practising picture restorers whose work and studio have been examined by the Council of the Association and found to be of a sufficiently high standard.
Associate Membership: Open to practising picture restorers who are in agreement with the aims of the Association. Students of picture restoration may belong as Associate members at a reduced subscription.

EXAMINATIONS:
Before an application is approved the applicant must have at least seven yrs' full-time experience. After approval of the application and when the applicant has sufficient work for consideration, two members of the Council visit the applicants studio to assess both work in progress and finished work. They then report to the Council which comes to a decision on whether or not to admit the applicant as a Fellow of the ABPR. Although the main emphasis will be on assessing their ability, the examiner will also be considering the applicant's attitude, background knowledge, studio and past experience.

THE CHARTERED SOCIETY OF DESIGNERS

32-38 Saffron Hill, London EC1N 8FH Tel: 020 7831 9777 Fax: 020 7831 6277
e-mail: csd@.org.uk

MEMBERSHIP:
Corporate membership of the Society is a recognised professional qualification and entitles members to use the affix
Fellow (FCSD): Granted to members who have had at least 5 yrs' standing and whose work

demonstrates a high degree of competence. Fellowship may also be offered to designers of distinction, or to others appropriately qualified, who are not already Society members and who have had at least 7 yrs' practice or experience.

Member (MCSD): Open to all practising designers, design managers and design educationalists who have had at least 4 yrs' practice or experience and who have the necessary standard of education and professional competence. Evidence of technical skill and creative ability in one or more of the Society's recognised categories of membership must be submitted. Candidates are assessed by interview together with submission of a portfolio of relevant work.

Graduate Membership: On the completion of an accredited degree or BTEC HND course in design, students are eligible for Graduate Membership of the Society without assessment interview. Candidates for Graduate Membership who do not have approved qualifications must submit for an assessment interview. There is no affix.

Student Membership: Open to all students following degree or BTEC HND course in design.

THE ROYAL ACADEMY SCHOOLS

Royal Academy of Arts, Burlington House, Piccadilly, London W1V 0DS
Tel: 020 7300 5650 Fax: 020 7300 8001
The RA Schools award the Royal Academy Schools Postgraduate Diploma. The course lasts for 3 yrs FT in Fine Art, Painting or Sculpture. Candidates for the postgraduate course must have a BA Hons degree or a university degree in Fine Art.

University Qualifications

The following universities offer qualifications in Art and Design and related subjects. Full details may be found in Part 4, under the entry for the appropriate university.

FIRST DEGREES AWARDED BY UNIVERSITIES

Anglia; Anglia (City College, Norwich); Anglia (Colchester Institute); Barnsley; Bath Spa; Blackburn; Bournemouth; Bradford; Bradford (Bradford & Ilkley Community College); Brighton; Bristol; Brunel; Buckingham; Bucks. Coll.; Central England; Central Lancashire; Cheltenham & Gloucester; Coventry; De Montfort, Leicester; Derby; Dundee; Durham; East Anglia (Suffolk College); East London; Edinburgh; Exeter; Exeter (The College of St Mark & St John); Glamorgan; Glasgow; Glasgow (Glasgow School of Art); Glasgow Caledonian; Greenwich; Heriot-Watt (Edinburgh College of Art); Hertfordshire; Hertfordshire (West Herts College); Huddersfield; Hull; Kent; Kent (Canterbury Christ Church University College); Kent (Kent Institute of Art & Design); Kingston; Lancaster; Lancaster (Blackpool and The Fylde College); Leeds; Leeds (Bretton Hall); Leeds (Leeds College of Art & Design); Leeds (The College of Ripon & York St John); Leeds Metropolitan; Lincolnshire; Liverpool (Chester College of H.E.); Liverpool (Liverpool Hope University College); Liverpool John Moores; London (Goldsmiths College); London (School of Oriental & African Studies); London (University College (UCL)); London Guildhall; London Institute (Camberwell College of Arts); London Institute (Central Saint Martins College of Art & Design); London Institute (Chelsea College of Art & Design); London Institute (London College of Printing); Loughborough; Luton; Manchester Metropolitan.; Middlesex; Napier; Newcastle; Northumbria; Nottingham Trent; Nottingham Trent (Southampton Institute); OU (The Central School of Speech & Drama); Oxford; Oxford Brookes; Plymouth; Plymouth (Falmouth College of Arts); Portsmouth; Reading; Robert Gordon; Salford; Southampton; Southampton (Chichester Institute of Higher Education); Southampton (King Alfred's College); Southampton (Winchester School of Art); St Martin; Staffordshire; Strathclyde; Sunderland; Surrey (University of Surrey Roehampton); Surrey Institute; Teesside; Thames Valley; Ulster; Wales (North East Wales Institute); Wales (Swansea Institute of Higher Education); Wales (University of Wales College, Newport); Wales (University of Wales Institute, Cardiff); Wales (University of Wales, Aberystwyth); Wales (University of Wales, Bangor); Westminster; Wolverhampton; Worcester

HIGHER DEGREES AWARDED BY UNIVERSITIES

Anglia; Anglia (Norwich School of Art & Design); Bath; Bath Spa; Bournemouth; Bradford (Bradford & Ilkley Community College); Brighton; Bristol; Brunel; Buckingham; Bucks. Coll.; Central England; Central Lancashire; Cheltenham & Gloucester; City; Coventry; Cranfield; De

Montfort, Leicester; Derby; Dundee; Durham; East Anglia; East London; Edinburgh; Essex; Exeter; Glamorgan; Glasgow; Glasgow (Glasgow School of Art); Heriot-Watt; Heriot-Watt (Edinburgh College of Art); Hull; Keele; Kent; Kent (Kent Institute of Art & Design); Kingston; Lancaster; Leeds; Leeds (Bretton Hall); Leeds Metropolitan; Lincolnshire; Liverpool; Liverpool (Chester College of H.E.); Liverpool (Liverpool Hope University College); Liverpool John Moores; London (Birkbeck, University of London); London (Goldsmiths College); London (Institute of Education); London (Royal Holloway); London (University College (UCL)); London Guildhall; London Institute (Camberwell College of Arts); London Institute (Central Saint Martins College of Art & Design); London Institute (Chelsea College of Art & Design); Loughborough; Luton; Manchester Metropolitan.; Middlesex; Napier; Newcastle; Northumbria; Nottingham Trent; Nottingham Trent (Southampton Institute); Oxford; Plymouth; Plymouth (Falmouth College of Arts); Portsmouth; Reading; Royal College of Art; Salford; Sheffield Hallam; Southampton; Southampton (Chichester Institute of Higher Education); Southampton (Winchester School of Art); St Martin; Staffordshire; Sunderland; Surrey (University of Surrey Roehampton); Surrey Institute; Ulster; Wales (University of Wales College, Newport); Wales (University of Wales Institute, Cardiff); Wales (University of Wales, Aberystwyth); Warwick; Westminster; Wolverhampton; York

DIPLOMAS AWARDED BY UNIVERSITIES

Anglia; Anglia (Colchester Institute); Barnsley; Bath Spa; Bournemouth; Bradford (Bradford & Ilkley Community College); Brighton; Bucks. Coll.; Cambridge; Central England; Central Lancashire; Cheltenham & Gloucester; City (Laban Centre London); Coventry; De Montfort, Leicester; Doncaster; Durham (New College Durham); East Anglia (Suffolk College); East London; Edinburgh; Glamorgan; Glasgow; Greenwich; Heriot-Watt (Edinburgh College of Art); Hertfordshire (West Herts College); Hull; Kent; Kent (Kent Institute of Art & Design); Kingston; Leeds (Bretton Hall); Leeds Metropolitan; Lincolnshire; Lincolnshire (Bishop Burton College); Lincolnshire (Grimsby College); Lincolnshire (Hull College); Lincolnshire (Yorkshire Coast College); Liverpool (Chester College of H.E.); Liverpool (Liverpool Hope University College); London (Goldsmiths College); London (Royal Holloway); London (School of Oriental & African Studies); London (University College (UCL)); London Institute (Camberwell College of Arts); London Institute (Central Saint Martins College of Art & Design); London Institute (Chelsea College of Art & Design); London Institute (London College of Fashion); London Institute (London College of Printing); Loughborough; Luton; Manchester (Warrington Collegiate Institute, Faculty of H.E,); Middlesex; Napier; Newcastle; Northampton; Northumbria; Nottingham Trent; Plymouth; Reading; Salford; Sheffield; Strathclyde; Surrey Institute; Ulster; Wales (North East Wales Institute); Wales (Swansea Institute of Higher Education); Wales (University of Wales College, Newport); Wales (University of Wales, Aberystwyth); Warwick; Wolverhampton

CERTIFICATES AWARDED BY UNIVERSITIES

Anglia; Anglia (City College, Norwich); Bournemouth; Bradford (Bradford & Ilkley Community College); Brighton; Bristol; Cambridge; Central England; Cheltenham & Gloucester; De Montfort, Leicester; East Anglia (Otley College); East London; Essex; Huddersfield; Leeds (Leeds College of Art & Design); Leeds Metropolitan; Leicester; Lincolnshire; Lincolnshire (Bishop Burton College); Lincolnshire (Hull College); Liverpool (Chester College of H.E.); Liverpool John Moores; London (Goldsmiths College); Loughborough; Manchester (Warrington Collegiate Institute, Faculty of H.E,); Manchester Metropolitan.; Middlesex; Northampton; Nottingham; Oxford (Westminster College, Oxford); Salford; Southampton (Chichester Institute of Higher Education); St Martin; Surrey (University of Surrey Roehampton); Wales (University of Wales Institute, Cardiff); Wales (University of Wales, Bangor); Warwick; Wolverhampton

OTHER COURSES AWARDED BY UNIVERSITIES

Derby; Essex (Writtle College); Wales (University of Wales Institute, Cardiff)

POSTGRADUATE DIPLOMAS AWARDED BY UNIVERSITIES

Heriot-Watt

PRE-DEGREE AWARDED BY UNIVERSITIES

Kingston

PROFESSIONAL QUALIFICATIONS AWARDED BY UNIVERSITIES
East London

National Certificates and Diplomas

BTEC National Certificates/Diplomas: Design
BTEC Higher National Certificates/Diplomas: Applied Arts; Design; Design (Advertising); Design (Animation and Electronic Image Making); Design (Display); Design (Electronic Design for Print); Design (Electronic Design for Screen); Design (Electronic Media and Reprography); Design (Electronic Media); Design (Graphic Design); Design (Illustration); Design (Industrial Design); Design (Interior Design); Design (Model Making); Design (Murals); Design (Packaging); Design (Publications); Design (Reprography); Design (Retail); Design (Retail and Exhibition Design); Design (Spatial Design); Design (Technical Illustration); Design (Three Dimensional Studies); Design (Typography); Design (Visual Communication); Design Technology; Electronic Imaging
Scotland
SQA HNC: Arts Administration; Arts Management; Art & Design; Fine Art; Graphic Design; Fashion & Clothing; Fashion with Business Administration; Fashion: Design; Graphic Reproduction; Graphics and Illustration; Interior Design; Performing Arts in the Community; Public Art; Spatial Design (Interior Design)
SQA HND: Art & Design; Arts Management; Fashion & Clothing; Fashion; Design & Production with Retail; Fashion with Business Administration; Graphic Design; Graphics & Illustration; Interior Design; Public Art; Spatial Design (Interior Design).
A range of National Certificate Modules are available within this sector. National Certificate Modules are offered at a variety of centres.

NVQs

Level 2: Exhibition Design; Graphic Design; Interior Design
Level 3: Design
Level 4: Design

SVQs

Level 2: Ceramics Design; Constructed Textile Design; Exhibition Design; Fashion Design; Furniture Design; Graphic Design; Interior Design; Product Design; Surface Pattern Textile Design
Level 3: Design; Delivering Artform Development Programmes
Level 4: Design; Delivering Artform Development Programmes
Level 5: Design

GNVQs

3722 Art and Design

Other Vocational Awarding Bodies

ABC: Art and Craft Studies; Computer Aided Art and Design; Design and Visual Skills; Graphic Design (including Computer Aided Graphic Technology); Graphic Technology; Interior Design and Decorative Techniques; National Diploma in Foundation Studies in Art and Design

ASTRONOMY AND SPACE SCIENCE

Membership of Professional Institutions and Associations

THE BRITISH ASTRONOMICAL ASSOCIATION

Burlington House, Piccadilly, London W1V 9AG
This is an association of amateur observers.

THE BRITISH INTERPLANETARY SOCIETY

27-29 South Lambeth Road, London SW8 1SZ Tel: 020 7735 3160 Fax: 020 7820 1504
e-mail: bis.bis@virgin.net Website: bis-spaceflight.com

MEMBERSHIP:
The Society bases its requirements for its Fellowship grade on recognised professional and scholastic qualifications. Its Membership grade is open to all persons interested in space or astronautics.

Fellows (FBIS): Fellowship is a Corporate Membership grade of the Society and is open to suitably qualified persons. Election to Fellow may be based on one of the following: an outstanding contribution to the work of the Society or to Astronautics or, 5 yrs' continuous membership at the time of application and additionally either; a relevant university degree in Science, Mathematics, Engineering or Medicine plus 5 yrs' relevant scientific, technical or other professional experience; or, at least 10 yrs' relevant scientific, technical or other professional experience.

Members (non-Corporate Grade): No special qualifications are required.

ROYAL ASTRONOMICAL SOCIETY

Burlington House, Piccadilly, London W1V 0NL Tel: 020 7734 4582/3307 Fax: 020 7494 0166 e-mail: info@ras.org.uk Website: www.ras.org.uk/ras

The Society conducts no examinations and Fellowship of the Society (FRAS) implies no kind of professional qualification. New members are proposed by Fellows and elected by Council.

University Qualifications

The following universities offer qualifications in Astronomy and Space Science and related subjects. Full details may be found in Part 4, under the entry for the appropriate university.

FIRST DEGREES AWARDED BY UNIVERSITIES

Belfast; Birmingham; Bristol; Central Lancashire; Coventry; Durham; Edinburgh; Glamorgan; Glasgow; Hertfordshire; Keele; Kent; Kingston; Lancaster; Leeds; Leicester; Liverpool; Liverpool John Moores; London (King's College London); London (Queen Mary & Westfield College (incorporating St Bartholomew's and the Royal London School of Medicine & Dentistry)); London (Royal Holloway); London (University College (UCL)); Manchester; Newcastle; Nottingham Trent; Portsmouth; Salford; Sheffield; Southampton; St Andrews; Sussex; UMIST; Wales (Cardiff University); Wales (University of Wales, Swansea); York

HIGHER DEGREES AWARDED BY UNIVERSITIES

Belfast; Birmingham; Bristol; Central Lancashire; Cranfield; Durham; Glasgow; Hertfordshire; Keele; Kent; Kingston; Lancaster; Leeds; Leicester; Liverpool; Liverpool John Moores; London (Queen Mary & Westfield College (incorporating St Bartholomew's and the Royal London School of Medicine & Dentistry)); London (Royal Holloway); London (University College (UCL)); Manchester; Newcastle; Plymouth; St Andrews; Surrey; Sussex

DIPLOMAS AWARDED BY UNIVERSITIES

Coventry; Hertfordshire; Kent; London (Queen Mary & Westfield College (incorporating St Bartholomew's and the Royal London School of Medicine & Dentistry)); London (University College (UCL))

CERTIFICATES AWARDED BY UNIVERSITIES

London (Queen Mary & Westfield College (incorporating St Bartholomew's and the Royal London School of Medicine & Dentistry))

AUDIOLOGY

HEARING AID COUNCIL

Witan Court, 305 Upper Fourth Street, Central Milton Keynes MK9 1EH Tel: 01908 235700 Fax: 01908 233770

Under the Hearing Aid Council Act 1968, it became an offence to supply a hearing aid commercially to any member of the public unless the individual providing this service was suitably qualified and registered as a dispenser with the Hearing Aid Council. A min period of training under the supervision of a qualified dispenser is necessary as well as passing the Council's exam. The Act does not extend to hearing aids dispensed through the NHS. The Council issues a Code of Practice and in the event of any breach of the rules the Council has the power to take disciplinary proceedings, including the erasure of any name from the register.

University Qualifications

The following universities offer qualifications in Audiology and related subjects. Full details may be found in Part 4, under the entry for the appropriate university.

FIRST DEGREES AWARDED BY UNIVERSITIES
Anglia; Bristol; Central Lancashire; Salford; Wolverhampton

HIGHER DEGREES AWARDED BY UNIVERSITIES
Bristol; London (University College (UCL)); Manchester; Southampton

DIPLOMAS AWARDED BY UNIVERSITIES
Bristol; London (University College (UCL))

CERTIFICATES AWARDED BY UNIVERSITIES
Bristol

SVQs
Level 3: Health Care: Physiological Measurement

AVIATION
Membership of Professional Institutions and Associations

THE GUILD OF AIR PILOTS AND AIR NAVIGATORS
Cobham House, 9 Warwick Court, Gray's Inn, London WC1R 5DJ Tel: 020 7404 4032
Fax: 020 7404 4035 e-mail: gapan@gapan.org Website: www.gapan.org
A Livery Company of the City of London. Application for admission as Upper Freeman or Freeman is welcomed from Pilots or Navigators who meet the criteria given below. Admission is subject to approval by the Court of the Guild.
MEMBERSHIP:
Upper Freemen: Within the preceding 10 yrs shall have engaged in the profession of air pilot or air navigator for a period or periods totalling not less than 5 yrs, and shall be or shall have been the holder of a professional pilot's licence, a flight navigator's licence, a full instructor's rating, or test pilot qualifications. Professional pilots include both civil and military pilots.
Freemen: Hold the qualifications described for Upper Freemen but without having completed the prescribed period of engagement in the profession of air pilot or air navigator (ie from the date of attaining a full commercial rating or obtaining military wings), or hold or have held for not less than 2 yrs a private pilot's licence and have substantial experience as a pilot, or have qualifications and experience as a pilot of airships, balloons, gliders or hang gliders.
Associate: The membership is intended for those pilots or navigators who do not, as yet, meet the above requirements.
Notes: At the discretion of the Court, persons who have contributed or are likely to contribute to the advancement of the profession may be admitted.
The Guild administers charitable trusts to improve air safety and aviation education and works for the improvement of standards and the encouragement of those entering the profession. Each yr it awards several flying scholarships. In conjunction with the Triservice aircrew selection centre at RAF Cranwell, aptitude tests for potential commercial aviators are arranged as required. It also administers the Guild of Air Pilots Benevolent Fund and is responsible for several aviation trophies and awards which are presented annually.
Application forms can be obtained by contacting the Membership Secretary at the above address.

THE GUILD OF AIR TRAFFIC CONTROL OFFICERS

24 The Greenwood, Guildford, Surrey GU1 2ND e-mail: caf@gatco.org Website: www.gatco.org

MEMBERSHIP:

Full Member: Candidates shall be a British Subject, over the age of 18, actually engaged in the Profession and the holder of a current licence or certificate of competency recognised or issued by Her Majesty's Government which enables them to carry out 1 or more of the functions of the Air Traffic Control Service or, by being an Associate Member for at least 3 yrs and, in the opinion of the Executive Council, have merited the status of Full Membership by virtue of their professional conduct and experience.

Associate Member: Candidates shall be over the age of 18, not otherwise qualified for Full Membership and shall have previously held a licence or certificate of competency recognised or issued by Her Majesty's Government which enabled them to carry out 1 or more of the functions of the Air Traffic Control Service or, can prove to the Executive council that they had carried out 1 or more of the functions of the Air Traffic Control Service for which at the time no licence or certificate was required or, be able to satisfy the Executive Council that they are closely allied to and sincerely interested in the profession of Air Traffic Control and that, because of their special qualifications and/or appointment, can contribute to the aims of the Guild.

Student Member: Shall be a British Subject over the age of 18 and be able to prove to the Executive Council or the Membership Secretary that they are engaged in a course of training for the Profession approved by the Executive Council.

Corporate Member: Any company, partnership, association or organisation from any country whose activities concern aviation, and who is able to satisfy the Executive Council of its suitability for membership.

University Qualifications

The following universities offer qualifications in Aviation and related subjects. Full details may be found in Part 4, under the entry for the appropriate university.

FIRST DEGREES AWARDED BY UNIVERSITIES

Bristol; Bucks. Coll.; City; Lincolnshire; London (Queen Mary & Westfield College (incorporating St Bartholomew's and the Royal London School of Medicine & Dentistry)); Loughborough; Salford; York

HIGHER DEGREES AWARDED BY UNIVERSITIES

Bristol; City; Cranfield; Southampton

PROFESSIONAL COURSES AWARDED BY UNIVERSITIES

London Guildhall

NVQs

Level 3 and 4: Controlling Air Terminal Operations
Level 3 and 4: Controlling Aircraft Operations
Level 3: Planning Aircraft Payloads

City & Guilds

7280 Aviation Studies

Statutory Qualifications

CIVIL AVIATION AUTHORITY

Aviation House, Gatwick Airport South, West Sussex RH6 0YR Tel: 01293 573886 Fax: 01293 573827 Website: www.srg.caa.co.uk

The CAA is empowered to grant licences authorising the holder to act as the pilot of an aircraft, an aircraft maintenance engineer, or an air traffic controller. Applicants for any licence must meet the appropriate requirements in respect of age, knowledge, experience and skill, and in most cases medical fitness.

FLIGHT CREW LICENCES

Under the arrangements for the harmonisation of European Flight Crew Licensing requirements between the Member States of the Joint Aviation Authorities, new requirements for both Aeroplane and Helicopter Private and Professional Pilot licensing have now been implemented. The implementation date was 1July 1999 for the Aeroplane requirements and 1January 2000 for the Helicopter requirements. Details of these new requirements may be found in the publications *JAR-FCL1 (Aeroplanes)* and *JAR-FCL2 (Helicopters)* obtainable from: Rapidoc, Willoughby Road, Bracknell, Berkshire RG12 8DW Tel: 01344 861666 Fax: 01344 714440 e-mail: rapidoc@techindex.co.uk. During the current transition period between the old UK National Requirements for Flight Crew Licences and the new European requirements under JAR-FCL, resulting in considerable changes, prospective licence applicants are best advised, for the time being, to seek specific guidance and information either from their local flying training organisation or, in writing, from: Flight Crew Licensing Department, Safety Regulation Group, Civil Aviation Authority, Aviation House, Gatwick Airport South, West Sussex RH6 0YR. Information may also be found by accessing the Flight Crew Licensing website: www.srg.caa.co.uk

AIRCRAFT MAINTENANCE ENGINEER'S LICENCE

Maintenance carried out on civil aircraft is normally carried out by approved organisations or, where permitted, under the supervision of a licensed engineer. All maintenance must be certified as being performed correctly by a licensed engineer or a person authorised by an approved organisation (normally based upon a maintenance licence). To facilitate this, the Civil Aviation Authority issues Aircraft Maintenance Engineer's Licences (AMEL) in various categories to applicants who meet the appropriate experience requirements and who successfully complete the exam(s) for the categories and ratings for which they wish to be licensed. A minimum age of 21 yrs applies. The licences will be issued either in accordance with National or European requirements depending upon the aircraft categories sought.The new European licence, issued under Joint Aviation Requirement (JAR) 66, has been available as a qualification pathway for large aircraft since September 1999 but comes into full effect in June 2001. Licences for smaller aircraft will continue to be issued in accordance with Section L of British Civil Airworthiness Requirements (BCAR) until they too are provided for in JAR-66.

Exams: The examination requirements between JAR-66 and BCAR Section L differ. Before taking the Section L examinations, it is necessary to satisfy the general and specific experience requirements. JAR-66 examinations can be taken at any time but all examinations and the application for JAR-66 licence issue must be completed within a 5 yr period. The examinations for both licence systems are modular and the respective subject matter to be studied is contained in the appropriate requirements.

Guidance Leaflets: A variety of guidance leaflets on the licensing requirements for maintenance engineers is obtainable from: Engineer Licensing Department, Safety Regulation Group, Civil Aviation Authority, Aviation House, Gatwick Airport South, West Sussex RH6 0YR Tel: 01293 573000 Fax: 01293 573779. These documents are also available on the Engineer Licensing website: www.srg.caa.co.uk

AIR TRAFFIC CONTROL LICENCES

Air Traffic Controller's Licence: Persons who provide any type of air traffic control service must, under the conditions of the Air Navigation Order for the time being in force, hold an Air Traffic Controller's Licence authorising them to provide that service at the place in question. The ATC Licence is granted with one or more ratings indicating the type of air traffic control service which the holder is qualified to provide. Subsequently ratings are issued at the initial certification of competence stage where the licence holder wishes to provide the particular type of air traffic control service concerned. Applicants must be at least 20, and must hold the appropriate class current medical certificate. They must also have a thorough knowledge of English and be able to speak without accent or impediment which would interfere with radio-telephone conversation.

Flight Information Service Officer's Licence: Flight Information Service is primarily intended for aerodromes without an air traffic control unit. Similar provisions apply to persons who provide this service – they must hold a Flight Information Service Officer's Licence. Applicants must be at least 18, and hold a Class 3 medical certificate. The FISO Licence is granted to applicants who pass a written exam and a practical RTF test. Exemption from these is given to applicants in certain circumstances, eg holders of an ATC licence who have held a Certificate of Competence in Aerodrome Control within 3 yrs of the application. The FISO Licence must be validated at the place where the holder wishes to provide a service.

Student Air Traffic Controller's Licence: The Student ATC Licence permits the holder to provide an air traffic control service for the purpose of becoming qualified for the grant of a full Air Traffic Controller's Licence. A student may only provide an air traffic control service when the holder is under the supervision of a suitably licensed air traffic controller. Applicants must be at least 18, have passed an appropriate approved rating course and meet the same medical and English Language standards as for the ATC Licence. They must satisfy certain minimum experience requirements and must successfully pass approved courses in ATC subjects for each rating required.

Useful Addresses

Aviation Training Association, Dralda House, Crendon Street, High Wycombe, Buckinghamshire HP13 6LS Tel: 01494 445262 Fax: 01494 439984

BAKERY AND CONFECTIONERY

National Certificates and Diplomas

Scotland
SQA HNC: Bakery Supervisory Management; Baking Technology; Craft Bakery Production
SQA HND: Baking Technology & Bakery Process Management

NVQs

Level 2: Bakery Service; Craft Baking
Level 4: Craft Baking (Technical Operations); Patisserie and Confectionery Specialist

SVQs

Level 2: Craft Baking
Level 3: Craft Baking: Technical Operations

Other Vocational Awarding Bodies

ABC: Cake Decoration; Pastry Cooks and Patissiers; Wired Sugar Flowers

Useful Addresses

Biscuit, Cake, Chocolate and Confectionery Alliance, 37– 41 Bedford Row, London WC1R 4JH Tel: 0171-404 9111 Website: www.bcca.org.uk
Craft Bakery Training Organisation (Scotland), Atholl House, 4 Torpichen Street, Edinburgh EH3 8JQ Tel: 0131-229 1401 Fax: 0131 229 8239 E-mail: master.bakers@samb.co.uk
Incorporated National Association of British and Irish Millers, 21 Arlington Street, London SW1A 1RN Tel: 0171-493 2521 Fax: 0171 493 6785 E-mail: nabim@dial.pipex.com
National Association of Master Bakers, 21 Baldock Street, Ware, Hertfordshire SG12 9DH Tel: 01920 468061 Fax: 01920 461632

BANKING

Membership of Professional Institutions and Associations

THE CHARTERED INSTITUTE OF BANKERS IN SCOTLAND

Drumsheugh House, 386 Drumsheugh Gardens, Edinburgh EH3 7SW Tel: 0131 473 7777
Fax: 0131 473 7788 e-mail: info@ciobs.org.uk Website: www.ciobs.org.uk

MEMBERSHIP:
Fellow (FCIBS): Fellowship is open to Members of at least 10 yrs' standing, currently holding a managerial position in banking and elected by Council for significant contribution to banking and/or the Institute.
Member (MCIBS): Membership is awarded to Associates who have passed the Final exams, which place particular emphasis on management skills and theory.
Associate (ACIBS): Associateship is awarded to Student Members who have gained 9 credits from a selection of the following subjects: Core Introduction to Financial Services, Banking Practice, Banking and the Law, Financial Economics, Business Accounting, Marketing Financial Services, Optional Investment, International Business, Taxation, Business Banking, Management, Mortgage Lending, Call Centre Management, Sales Management, Corporate Finance.

EXAMINATIONS:
Diploma in Financial Services (DipFS): Awarded to students who have passed 6 exams from the following lists: Core Introduction to Financial Services, Optional Legal Environment, Economic Environment, Basic Accounting and Taxation, Introduction to Insurance, Sales and Service, Team Development, Banking Operations, Information Technology, Introduction to Insurance and Telephone Banking, Introduction to Investment, International Services. Entry is open to all employees in the financial services sector. There is a fast track route for those who possess university entry level qualifications and those with a university degree can go directly to the Associateship course.

THE CHARTERED INSTITUTE OF BANKERS

90 Bishopsgate, London EC2N 4DQ
Tel: 01227 762600
Fax: 01227 763788
e-mail: institute@cib.org.uk
Website: www.cib.org.uk

The Chartered Institute of Bankers (incorporating the Institute of Financial Services) merged with The Chartered Building Societies Institute in 1993.

MEMBERSHIP:
Fellow (FCIB): Fellows have been elected to Associateship or hold a comparable qualification. They have 5 yrs' experience in a senior management position and have given service to the Institute and/or banking education above normal work commitments.
Associate (ACIB): Associates are elected from those who have passed the Associateship examinations, have 3 yrs employment in a relevant occupation and have been members of the Institute for 3 yrs.
Ordinary Member: This grade of membership is open to anyone over the age of 18 yrs.
Student Member: Open to those under 18 yrs.

EXAMINATIONS:
Master's in E-Commerce: A pioneering management qualification launched in April 2000. Developed in collaboration with Canterbury Business School, a department of the University of Kent at Canterbury, the programme has been designed to put candidates at the forefront of developing tomorrow's business models.
BSc (Hons) Financial Services and Associateship: Following the Institute's partnership with

UMIST (University of Manchester Institute of Science and Technology) in 1996, the award of the ACIB has been linked to a BSc (Hons) in Financial Services. The programme is designed to be relevant and practical and allows candidates to follow a specialist or generalist route depending on their needs or interests. Direct entry for those holding a degree or the Diploma in Financial Services Management (replacing the Banking Certificate).

Diploma in Financial Services Management (DFSM): A flexible and portable qualification designed to equip candidates with the essential skills and knowledge to help 'fast track' their management careers. The DFSM also acts as the foundation element for the BSc/Associateship.

Diploma and Certificate in the Marketing of Financial Services (DipMFS and CertMFS): Two new higher education qualifications for marketing professionals in the financial services industry offered in partnership with the Chartered Institute of Marketing (CIM). Designed to enable professionals working in the financial services industry to develop a sound understanding of key marketing principles and how they can be applied.

Certificate in Financial Services Practice (CFSP): A qualification that is particularly relevant to, and valued by, those in a customer care or front office role across the whole financial services industry.

Certificate for Financial Advisers (CeFA): A regulatory qualification for financial advisers and intermediaries. CeFA is one of the qualifications you must achieve if you are to 'practise' unsupervised, and it is an alternative to the Financial Planning Certificate (FPC).

Certificate in Mortgage Advice and Practice (CeMAP): CeMAP has been developed in conjunction with the Council of Mortgage Lenders and covers all aspects of the Code of Mortgage Lending Practice. Candidates with CeFA/FPC or equivalent can take a special 'Bridge' paper to complete the qualification.

Professional Investment Certificate (PIC): An advanced qualification, building on existing statutory examinations for financial advisers (CeFA and FPC). It is an alternative to the Advanced Financial Planning Certificate (AFPC).

NVQs: The Institute is involved with a wide range of NVQs directly relevant to the financial sector.

Free-Standing Diplomas: A range of specialist awards based around papers drawn from the BSc/Associateship menu, providing credits towards that qualification, eg Diploma in Mortgage Lending, Diploma in Trust and Estate Practice.

University Qualifications

The following universities offer qualifications in Banking and related subjects. Full details may be found in Part 4, under the entry for the appropriate university.

FIRST DEGREES AWARDED BY UNIVERSITIES

Abertay, Dundee; Anglia (City College, Norwich); Belfast; Birmingham; Bournemouth; Bradford; Bradford (Bradford & Ilkley Community College); Brighton; Bristol; Brunel; Buckingham; Bucks. Coll.; Central England; Central Lancashire; Cheltenham & Gloucester; City; Coventry; De Montfort, Leicester; Doncaster; Dundee; Durham; East Anglia; East London; Essex; Exeter; Glamorgan; Glasgow; Glasgow Caledonian; Greenwich; Heriot-Watt; Hertfordshire; Huddersfield; Hull; Keele; Kent; Lancaster; Lancaster (Blackpool and The Fylde College); Leeds; Leeds Metropolitan; Lincolnshire; Lincolnshire (Lincoln University Campus); Liverpool; London (London School of Economics & Political Science); London (Queen Mary & Westfield College (incorporating St Bartholomew's and the Royal London School of Medicine & Dentistry)); London (Royal Holloway); London (University College (UCL)); London Guildhall; Loughborough; Manchester; Manchester Metropolitan.; Middlesex; Napier; Newcastle; North London; Northumbria; Nottingham Trent (Southampton Institute); OU (NESCOT); Oxford Brookes; Paisley; Portsmouth; Reading; Sheffield; Sheffield Hallam; Southampton; Staffordshire; Stirling; Strathclyde; Surrey; Thames Valley; Ulster; Wales (Cardiff University); Wales (Swansea Institute of Higher Education); Wales (University of Wales, Bangor); Westminster; York

HIGHER DEGREES AWARDED BY UNIVERSITIES

Aberdeen; Bath; Belfast; Birmingham; Bournemouth; Brighton; Bristol; Brunel; Buckingham; Central England; Cheltenham & Gloucester; City; De Montfort, Leicester; Derby; Durham; East Anglia; East London; Edinburgh; Essex; Exeter; Glamorgan; Glasgow; Glasgow Caledonian;

Greenwich; Heriot-Watt; Hull; Lancaster; Leeds Metropolitan; Leicester; Lincolnshire; Liverpool; Liverpool John Moores; London (Birkbeck, University of London); London (Imperial College of Science, Technology & Medicine); London (London School of Economics & Political Science); London (Queen Mary & Westfield College (incorporating St Bartholomew's and the Royal London School of Medicine & Dentistry)); London Guildhall; Loughborough; Luton; Manchester; Middlesex; Napier; Newcastle; Nottingham Trent; Nottingham Trent (Southampton Institute); Reading; Salford; Sheffield; Sheffield Hallam; Southampton; Stirling; Strathclyde; Surrey; Ulster; UMIST; Wales (Cardiff University); Wales (University of Wales, Bangor); Warwick; Westminster; York

DIPLOMAS AWARDED BY UNIVERSITIES
Aberdeen; Anglia (City College, Norwich); Bath; Birmingham; Blackburn; Bournemouth; Bradford; Bradford (Bradford & Ilkley Community College); Brighton; Bucks. Coll.; Cheltenham & Gloucester; De Montfort, Leicester; Doncaster; Doncaster (Dearne Valley Business School); Dundee; Durham (New College Durham); Edinburgh; Kingston; Lancaster; London (Birkbeck, University of London); Loughborough; Manchester; Napier; Newcastle; Northampton; Nottingham Trent (Southampton Institute); Oxford; Paisley; Salford; South Bank; Stirling; Strathclyde; Teesside; Thames Valley; Wales (Swansea Institute of Higher Education); Wales (University of Wales Institute, Cardiff); Wales (University of Wales, Aberystwyth); Westminster; Wolverhampton

CERTIFICATES AWARDED BY UNIVERSITIES
Anglia (City College, Norwich); Cheltenham & Gloucester; Lincolnshire (Hull College); London (Birkbeck, University of London); Northampton; Salford; Wales (University of Wales Institute, Cardiff)

OTHER COURSES AWARDED BY UNIVERSITIES
North London

POSTGRADUATE DIPLOMAS AWARDED BY UNIVERSITIES
Heriot-Watt

PROFESSIONAL COURSES AWARDED BY UNIVERSITIES
London Guildhall

NVQs
Level 2: Banking
Level 3: Banking
Level 4: Banking

SVQs
Level 2: Banking
Level 3: Banking
Level 4: Banking

OCR
OCR offer the following awards:
Banking Levels 2 & 3
Building Society Services Level 2
Providing Financial Advice (Building Societies) Level 3

BEAUTY THERAPY AND BEAUTY CULTURE

Membership of Professional Institutions and Associations

ASSOCIATION OF THERAPY LECTURERS

3rd Floor, Eastleigh House, Upper Market Street, Eastleigh SO51 9FD Tel: 023 8048 8900
Fax: 023 8048 8970 Website: www.fht.org.uk
(Part of the Federation of Holistic Therapists)
This is the largest professional association supporting lecturers in Beauty Therapy, Holistic
Therapies and Health & Fitness subjects. Membership is open to those currently teaching in
Colleges, public or private. Fellowship is open to those with more than 5 yrs' teaching experience.

BRITISH ASSOCIATION OF BEAUTY THERAPY AND COSMETOLOGY LTD

Secretariat, Babtac House, 70 Eastgate Street, Gloucester, Gloucestershire GL1 1QN
Tel: 01452 421114 Fax: 01452 421110

MEMBERSHIP:

Full Member: A person who has gained a recognised qualification in Facial & Body Treatments
(minimum) approved by the Association. Covered by group insurance and entitled to vote.
Student Member: A person undergoing a course of training at an establishment approved by the
Association. Covered by limited group insurance while working under direct supervision of a Full
member. Not entitled to vote.
Specific Skills Member: A person who has gained a recognised qualification approved by the
Association. Covered by group insurance and entitled to vote.
Overseas Member: A person working with the Beauty Profession abroad. Not covered by group
insurance. Not entitled to vote.
Associate Member: A person who has a business or profession related to beauty therapy. Not
covered by group insurance. Not entitled to vote.
Overseas Associate Member: Not covered by group insurance. Not entitled to vote.
Non Practising Member: A person no longer practising beauty therapy. Not entitled to vote.
CIBTAC International is recognised world-wide. CIBTAC is the Awarding Body of BABTAC and
offers an international qualification.

THE BRITISH ASSOCIATION OF ELECTROLYSISTS LTD

(Incorporated 1957)
Secretary, 2a Tudor Way, Hillingdon, Uxbridge, Middlesex UB10 9AB Tel: 01895 239966

MEMBERSHIP:

Full Membership (MBAE): By exam only. Candidates may apply after they have completed the
required Syllabus of Training or if they are qualified electrolysists. All candidates must sit the oral
and practical exams. DRE members, electrolysists who have worked continuously for 5 yrs,
candidates participating in the BAE Epilation course and those who hold C&G Certificates in
Electrical Epilation, a BTEC National Diploma in Beauty Therapy or Confederation of
International Beauty Therapy & Cosmetology Certificate, NVQ Level 3, will all be granted
exemption from the theory paper unless otherwise stated.

THE INSTITUTE OF ELECTROLYSIS

138 Downs Barn Boulevard, Downs Barn, Milton Keynes MK14 7RP Tel: 01908 695297 Fax: 01908
695297 e-mail: institute@electrolysis.co.uk Website: www.electrolysis.co.uk
The Professional organisation for practising Electrolysists and Therapists.

MEMBERSHIP:

There are two categories of membership:
Full- holders who have attained the **Diploma in Remedial Electrolysis (DRE)** and **Associate-**
(AIE). Candidates may apply for entry to the Institute after successfully completing a recognised
course in Epilation. If applying directly after this basic training, and having passed the Institute
entry requirements the candidate becomes an Associate member. Associates then accrue 2 yrs in

practice to qualify for Full membership. Or, an experienced qualified Electrolysist may produce evidence of being in practice for 2 yrs and on passing the full entrance examination would be directly admitted to Full Membership.

EXAMINATIONS:
Consist of a practical, Oral and Sterilisation Paper to qualify for either category of membership. All of these sections, plus a further General Written paper is required for Full membership. Sections may be taken separately and the qualification accumulated.
The Certificate in The Treatment of Dilated Capillaries: This is a new qualification open to Institute members who treat broken capillaries. The high standard of the Practical and Oral examination ensures that referrals from the public are passed on to members practising to a very high standard.
Support
The Institute offers a network system of Mentors and Tutorial support for candidates contemplating or revising for the entry examinations in order to achieve a high rate of success. Workshops and seminars are held regularly to update members of the Institute.

INTERNATIONAL COUNCIL OF HEALTH FITNESS AND SPORTS THERAPISTS
3rd Floor, Eastleigh House, Upper Market Street, Eastleigh SO51 9FD Tel: 023 8048 8900 Fax: 023 8048 8970 Website: www.FHT.ORG.UK
(Part of the Federation of Holistic Therapies)
This professional association supports therapists in the health and fitness industry. Membership is only open to those qualified through awarding bodies such as IIST, S/NVQs and BTEC (Edexcel).

INTERNATIONAL FEDERATION OF HEALTH AND BEAUTY THERAPISTS
3rd Floor, Eastleigh House, Upper Market Street, Eastleigh SO51 9FD Tel: 023 8048 8900 Fax: 023 8048 8970 Website: www.FHT.ORG.UK
(Part of the Federation of Holistic Therapists)
This professional association supports therapists in the Health & Beauty industry. Membership is only open to those qualified through awarding bodies such as VTCT, S/NVQs, BTEC and City & Guilds. Exemptions from these qualification requirements are granted only for those who have other acceptable qualifications and experience.

INTERNATIONAL HEALTH AND BEAUTY COUNCIL
(Listed under Vocational Training Charitable Trust, Beauty Therapy and Beauty Culture Section)

INTERNATIONAL THERAPY EXAMINATION COUNCIL (ITEC)
10/11 Heathfield Terrace,, Chiswick, London W4 4JE Tel: 020 8994 4141 Fax: 020 8994 7880 e-mail: info@itecworld.co.uk

EXAMINATIONS:
The ITEC exams are divided into 4 groups:
Beauty Therapy: Diplomas in Beauty Therapy (Aestheticienne plus Physiatrics), Beauty Specialist . Entry requirements: 5 GCSEs incl English lang or equiv as determined by school/college principal. Min age 16 yrs. Certificates in Beauty Specialist, Facial Make Up, Manicure & Pedicure.
Complementary Therapy: Anatomy, Physiology and Body Massage, Anatomy & Physiology Theory. Diplomas in Aromatherapy, Reflexology, Sports Therapy, Certificates in nutrition and diet (theory only), Sports therapy, Sports Massage, Sports Equipment.
Specialist Subjects: Diplomas in Electrology, Nutrition advisers, Aerobic Teachers, Gym Instructors, Colour Analysis and Image, Fashion, Theatre & Media Make Up, ITEC Honours (open to holder of Aestheticienne, Beauty Specialist and Physiatrics Diplomas.
Certificates: Depilatory Waxing, Stress Management, Aerobic Exercise, Clinical Camouflage.

LONDON COLLEGE OF FASHION
(A Constituent College of the London Institute)
20 John Prince's Street, London W1M 0BJ Tel: 020 7514 7400 Fax: 020 7514 8484

For a list of courses offered please see the London College of Fashion's entry in the Fashion section.

VOCATIONAL AWARDS INTERNATIONAL
(Merged with the Vocational Training Charitable Trust, Health and Beauty Section)

VOCATIONAL TRAINING CHARITABLE TRUST
(Consists of Vocational Awards International, International Institute of Health and Holistic Therapies, International Health and Beauty Council and International Institute of Sports Therapy) 3rd Floor, Eastleigh House, Upper Market Street, Eastleigh, Hampshire SO50 9FD Tel: 02380 684500 Fax: 02380 651493

S/NVQ QUALIFICATIONS:
S/NVQ in Beauty Therapy at Level 2 & 3; S/NVQ in Hairdressing at Level 1, 2 & 3; S/NVQ in Customer Service at Level 2 & 3
Key and core skill units at Levels 1, 2, 3 & 4.

NON-S/NVQ QUALIFICATIONS:
VOCATIONAL TRAINING CHARITABLE TRUST (VTCT)
Foundation Anatomy & Physiology; Diploma in Anatomy & Physiology; Diploma in Nutrition; Emergency First Aid Certificate; Receptionist Diploma; Therapist's First Aid Diploma
INTERNATIONAL HEALTH & BEAUTY COUNCIL (IHBC)
Beauty Consultant Diploma; Beauty Specialist Diploma; Colour Consultancy Diploma; CosmeticMake-Up Certificate; Depilation Certificate; Diploma in Advanced Nail Techniques; Diploma in Electrology; Diploma in Epilation; Ear Piercing Certificate; Face and Body Painting Diploma; Fashion/Photographic Make-Up Diploma; Foundation Certificate in Beauty Therapy; International Beauty Therapist Diploma; International Master's Diploma in Health and Beauty Therapy; International Sugaring Certificate; Make-Up Artiste Diploma; Make-Up Certificate; Make-Up and Manicure Certificate; Manicure Certificate; Manicure and Pedicure Certificate; Mendhi/Henna Skin Decoration Diploma; Nail Art Diploma; Theatrical and Medial Make-Up Diploma; Threading Depilation Certificate; Wax Depilation Certificate
INTERNATIONAL INSTITUTE OF HEALTH & HOLISTIC THERAPIES (IIHHT)
MASSAGE QUALIFICATIONS:
Baby Massage Certificate; Body Massage Certificate; Body Massage Diploma; Indian Head Massage Diploma; Remedial Massage Diploma; Sports Event Massage Certificate; Sports Massage Certificate

HOLISTIC AND COMPLEMENTARY QUALIFICATIONS:
Foundation Certificate in Complementary Therapies; Counselling by a Therapist Certificate; Diploma in Aromatherapy; Advanced Diploma in Aromatherapy; Diploma in Aromatherapy for Carers; Diploma in Holistic Therapies; Diploma in Reflexology; Advanced Diploma in Reflexology; Diploma in Stress Management; Red Vein Treatment Diploma; Remedial Camouflage Diploma

HEALTH AND FITNESS AND ACTIVITY THERAPY QUALIFICATIONS:
Diploma in Special Needs Exercise; Foundation Certificate in Health and Fitness Studies; Diploma in Health and Fitness Studies; Advanced Diploma in Health and Fitness Studies; International Master's Diploma in Health and Fitness Studies; Diploma in Sports Therapy; Advanced Diploma in Sports Therapy; International Master's Diploma in Sports Therapy; Management of Activity Injuries Diploma; Personal Trainer Diploma

University Qualifications

The following universities offer qualifications in Beauty Therapy and Beauty Culture and related subjects. Full details may be found in Part 4, under the entry for the appropriate university.

FIRST DEGREES AWARDED BY UNIVERSITIES
Bradford (Bradford & Ilkley Community College); London Institute (London College of Fashion)

DIPLOMAS AWARDED BY UNIVERSITIES

Birmingham (Birmingham College of Food, Tourism and Creative Studies); Blackburn; Bradford (Bradford & Ilkley Community College); Glamorgan; Lincolnshire (Hull College); London Institute (London College of Fashion); Plymouth

CERTIFICATES AWARDED BY UNIVERSITIES

Bradford (Bradford & Ilkley Community College); Lincolnshire (Hull College); London Institute (London College of Fashion)

National Certificates and Diplomas

BTEC National Certificates/Diplomas: Beauty Therapy
BTEC Higher National Certificates/Diplomas: Beauty Therapy

NVQs

Level 2: Beauty Therapy
Level 3: Beauty Therapy

City & Guilds

3020 Cosmetic Make-up; 3030 Manicure; 3040 Beauty Therapy; 3050 Electrical Epilation.
Scotland
SQA HND: Beauty Therapy
SQA HNC: Beauty

BIOLOGICAL SCIENCES

Membership of Professional Institutions and Associations

INSTITUTE OF BIOLOGY

20-22 Queensberry Place, London SW7 2DZ Tel: 020 7581 8333 Fax: 020 7823 9409
e-mail: info@iob.org Website: www.iob.org
MEMBERSHIP:
Chartered Biologist (CBiol): This designation may be used by Fellows and Members of the Institute.
European Biologist (EuroBiol): This pan-European professional title may be awarded to Fellows and Members of the Institute with appropriate experience.
Fellow (CBiol FIBiol): The senior grade reserved for biologists who have achieved distinction.
Member (CBiol MIBiol): The main grade for professional biologists. The usual entry requirement is a good honours degree in a biological subject followed by at least three yrs' experience in responsible work in biology.
Graduate (GIBiol): The first step towards Chartered Biologist status for biologists who do not yet have sufficient professional experience for the Member grade.
Associate: For those with a third class honours or pass degree or HND/HNC in a biological subject.
Student: For those over 17 yrs of age and studying for a qualification in Bioscience.
Affiliate: For those who share an interest in the advancement of biology who do not fulfil any of the above criteria.

INSTITUTE OF BIOMEDICAL SCIENCE

12 Coldbath Square, London EC1R 5HL Tel: 020 7713 0214 Fax: 020 7436 4946
e-mail: mail@ibms.org Website: www.ibms.org

MEMBERSHIP:
Fellow (FIBMS): Must possess an IBMS accredited MSc or individually approved higher degree or have passed the IBMS Fellowship Exam or Exam by Thesis. Candidates must have been Associates for 2 yrs.
Associate (AIBMS): Must possess an IBMS accredited BSc honours degree or individually approved BSc honours degree. Holders of other qualifications should consult the Institute. Graduate applicants must have at least 1 yr's acceptable experience.
Student Member: Must be on a course directly leading to Associateship, or must have obtained a qualification acceptable for Associateship and be obtaining or intending to obtain the required professional experience.
Affiliate: Must possess a suitable level of educational attainment and further appropriate vocational attainment. Candidates are assessed individually.
Company Member: Suitable organisations and institutions involved in biomedical science can apply.
The Institute recommends an annual achievement of credits for Continuing Professional Development, and it is possible to achieve a CPD Diploma.
(See note on State Registration. To be state registered, medical laboratory scientific officers must by law hold a qualification and have completed a form of training approved by the Medical Laboratory Technicians Board.) The legislation is currently being revised.

THE LINNEAN SOCIETY OF LONDON

Burlington House, Piccadilly, London W1V 0LQ Tel: 020 7434 4479 Fax: 020 7287 9364
e-mail: john@linnean.demon.co.uk
This is a learned society which provides a meeting point for many biological disciplines and publishes scientific journals, symposia volumes and Synopses of the British Fauna. It possesses a large library and the collections of Carl Linnaeus.

MEMBERSHIP:
Fellows (FLS): People of any nationality, 21 or over, who take an active interest in any branch of biological science may be considered for election on the proposal and recommendation of at least 1 Fellow.
Associates (ALS): Restricted to persons aged 18 – 29. Associates may retain Associateship until 30. Eligible to apply for election to Fellowship on reaching 21.
Student Associates: Student Associates must be between 16 and 24 on election and may retain this status until 25. They must be registered as FT or PT students at a university or other IHE.

THE ZOOLOGICAL SOCIETY OF LONDON

Regent's Park, London NW1 4RY Tel: 020 7449 6261 e-mail: marion.hoyland@zsl.org
Membership of the Society does not confer professional status.

MEMBERSHIP:
Ordinary Fellowship: This grade is open to persons of at least 18 who are able to satisfy the Council as to their interest in the purposes and activities of the Society.
Scientific Fellows: Must submit evidence that they are making or have made a contribution to the advancement of Zoology. For example the following are qualifications which may prove acceptable: (i) possession of an approved honours degree in zoology or veterinary science or an equiv qualification, or (ii) possession of a degree or equiv qualification taken partly in zoology with professional position in zoological work (including a post teaching zoological science up to GCE A level standard), or (iii) an original contribution to zoological knowledge of a standard judged adequate by the Council, published in a recognised scientific journal, or (iv) proven practical experience in animal conservation.

University Qualifications

The following universities offer qualifications in Biological Sciences and related subjects. Full details may be found in Part 4, under the entry for the appropriate university.

FIRST DEGREES AWARDED BY UNIVERSITIES
Aberdeen; Abertay, Dundee; Anglia; Anglia (Colchester Institute); Aston; Bath; Belfast;

Birmingham; Bradford; Brighton; Bristol; Brunel; Central Lancashire; City; Coventry; De Montfort, Leicester; Derby; Dundee; Durham; East Anglia; East Anglia (Suffolk College); East London; Edinburgh; Essex; Essex (Writtle College); Exeter; Glamorgan; Glasgow; Glasgow Caledonian; Greenwich; Heriot-Watt; Hertfordshire; Huddersfield; Hull; Keele; Kent; Kingston; Lancaster; Lancaster (Edge Hill College of Higher Education); Leeds; Leeds Metropolitan; Leicester; Liverpool; Liverpool (Chester College of H.E.); Liverpool (Liverpool Hope University College); Liverpool John Moores; London (Birkbeck, University of London); London (Imperial College of Science, Technology & Medicine); London (King's College London); London (Queen Mary & Westfield College (incorporating St Bartholomew's and the Royal London School of Medicine & Dentistry)); London (Royal Holloway); London (University College (UCL)); London (Wye College); Loughborough; Luton; Manchester; Manchester Metropolitan.; Middlesex; Napier; Newcastle; North London; Northampton; Northumbria; Nottingham; Nottingham Trent; OU (NESCOT); Oxford; Oxford Brookes; Paisley; Plymouth; Portsmouth; Reading; Robert Gordon; Salford; Salford (Halton College); Sheffield; Sheffield Hallam; South Bank; Southampton; Southampton (University of Southampton New College); St Andrews; St Martin; Staffordshire; Stirling; Stockport; Strathclyde; Sunderland; Surrey; Surrey (St Mary's, Strawberry Hill); Surrey (University of Surrey Roehampton); Sussex; Teesside; Ulster; UMIST; Wales (Cardiff University); Wales (University of Wales, Aberystwyth); Wales (University of Wales, Bangor); Wales (University of Wales, Swansea); Warwick; Westminster; Wolverhampton; Worcester; York

HIGHER DEGREES AWARDED BY UNIVERSITIES

Aberdeen; Abertay, Dundee; Anglia; Birmingham; Bristol; Brunel; Cambridge; Central Lancashire; Coventry; De Montfort, Leicester; Dundee; Durham; East Anglia; East Anglia (Otley College); Edinburgh; Essex; Exeter; Glasgow; Hertfordshire; Hull; Keele; Kent; Kingston; Leeds; Leeds (Askham Bryan College); Leicester; Liverpool; Liverpool (Chester College of H.E.); Liverpool John Moores; London (Birkbeck, University of London); London (Imperial College of Science, Technology & Medicine); London (King's College London); London (Queen Mary & Westfield College (incorporating St Bartholomew's and the Royal London School of Medicine & Dentistry)); London (University College (UCL)); London (Wye College); Manchester; Manchester Metropolitan.; Napier; Newcastle; Nottingham; Nottingham Trent; OU (NESCOT); Oxford; Paisley; Plymouth; Portsmouth; Reading; Sheffield; Sheffield Hallam; St Andrews; Strathclyde; Surrey; Surrey (NESCOT); Surrey (University of Surrey Roehampton); Teesside; Ulster; UMIST; Wales (University of Wales, Swansea); Warwick; Westminster; Wolverhampton; York

DIPLOMAS AWARDED BY UNIVERSITIES

Aberdeen; Abertay, Dundee; Birmingham; Brighton; Central Lancashire; Coventry; De Montfort, Leicester; East Anglia (Otley College); East Anglia (Suffolk College); Edinburgh; Exeter; Exeter (Truro College); Greenwich; Hertfordshire; Hull; Kent; Leeds; Liverpool; Liverpool (Chester College of H.E.); London (Queen Mary & Westfield College (incorporating St Bartholomew's and the Royal London School of Medicine & Dentistry)); London (University College (UCL)); Luton; Manchester; Napier; Nottingham; OU (NESCOT); Oxford; South Bank; St Andrews; Staffordshire; Strathclyde; Ulster; Wales (College of Medicine); Wales (University of Wales Institute, Cardiff); Wolverhampton

CERTIFICATES AWARDED BY UNIVERSITIES

Bristol; Brunel; Cambridge; East Anglia (Otley College); Leeds Metropolitan; Leicester; Lincolnshire (Hull College); London (Birkbeck, University of London); London (Goldsmiths College); Napier; Southampton; Staffordshire; Sunderland; Sussex; Wales (University of Wales Institute, Cardiff); Wales (University of Wales, Bangor)

National Certificates and Diplomas

BTEC Higher National Certificates/Diplomas: Science (Applied Biology); Science (Biology with Chemistry)

Scotland

SQA HNC: Applied Biological Sciences; Biological Sciences; Biomedical Sciences

SQA HND: Applied Biological Sciences; Biological Sciences; Biomedical Sciences.

A range of National Certificate Modules are available within this sector. National Certificate Modules are offered at a variety of centres.

NVQs

Level 4: Laboratory Operations

SVQs

Level 1: Laboratory Operations
Level 2: Laboratory and associated technical activities
Level 3: Laboratory and associated technical activities
Level 4: Laboratory and associated technical activities

City & Guilds

7550 Science Laboratory Assistants

BREWING

Membership of Professional Institutions and Associations

THE INSTITUTE OF BREWING

33 Clarges Street, London W1Y 8EE Tel: 020 7499 8144 Fax: 020 7499 1156
e-mail: enquiries@iob.org.uk

MEMBERSHIP:
Student Members: Persons engaged in the study of the principles and practices of the brewing, fermentation, distillation and related industries with the object of qualifying for subsequent admission to the category of Associate Member.
Members: Persons who by virtue of their knowledge of the scientific and technical aspects of brewing, fermentation, distillation and related industries are able to further the objects of the Institute.
Associate Members: Have passed the prescribed exam.
Associate Membership Exam: Candidates must be members of the Institute.
Exemptions: Exemption may be granted in respect of BSc Hons in Brewing and Distilling, MSc in Brewing and Distilling and Postgraduate Diploma in Brewing and Distilling (Heriot-Watt University).
Diploma Members: Are Associate Members who have then passed the prescribed exam.

University Qualifications

The following universities offer qualifications in Brewing and related subjects. Full details may be found in Part 4, under the entry for the appropriate university.

FIRST DEGREES AWARDED BY UNIVERSITIES
Heriot-Watt

HIGHER DEGREES AWARDED BY UNIVERSITIES
Heriot-Watt

CERTIFICATES AWARDED BY UNIVERSITIES
Sunderland

BUILDING

Membership of Professional Institutions and Associations

ARCHITECTURE AND SURVEYING INSTITUTE

St Mary House, 15 St Mary Street, Chippenham, Wilts SN15 3WD Tel: 01249 444505
Fax: 01249 443602 e-mail: mail@asi.org.uk Website: www.asi.org.uk

The Institute offers appropriate membership grades to surveyors engaged in all areas of the built environment including private practice, Local and Central Government, Mechanical Engineering Services and technical education. Chartered and Incorporated Engineers are also contained within the various specialist disciplines of Membership. Architects members are required to be registered with the Architects Registration Board.

CORPORATE GRADES:

Fellow (FASI): Open to existing members who have satisfied the requirements for Member level plus additional experience at senior level or those who hold an exempting qualification (min age 35).

Member (MASI): Entry is by honours degree-level examination only. Qualified members are entitled to the designation Corporate Surveyor. Exemption given to relevant qualifications.

NON-CORPORATE GRADES:

Associate Members (AMASI): Primarily reserved for applicants over 30 with a wealth of practical industry-experience but whose technical/educational qualifications do not meet the standard for corporate membership.

Licentiate (LASI): Applicants must hold an approved exempting qualification. Technician: Equates with BTEC/SCOTVEC certificates in Building Studies.

Student: Following an approved FT or PT course of technical education (max age 30).

EXAMINATIONS:

Stage I: Requirements are satisfied by a BTEC HNC in Building Studies or other approved course; exams are no longer held at this stage.

Stage II: Subjects include Technology, Measurement, Law, Contract Documentation, Financial Management, Property Maintenance & Rehabilitation, and Economics of Industry. A BTEC/SCOTVEC HND may give exemption, with candidate being permitted to progress to Corporate Membership by means of experience, a log book and a case study.

Stage III: Subjects similar to Stage II but build on knowledge already gained. This is set at honours degree level and the candidate is then required to demonstrate suitable experience and may attend a professional interview. Direct Member Examination: Open to mature candidates with considerable experience in the industry. A case study-type exam tests ability to handle complex situations such as may be expected throughout a Surveyor's career.

THE CHARTERED INSTITUTE OF BUILDING

Englemere, Kings Ride, Ascot, Berkshire SL5 7TB Tel: 01344 630700 Fax: 01344 630777
e-mail: memenquiry@ciob.org.uk Website: www.ciob.org.uk/

The CIOB is the leading body for professionals in building related disciplines and is committed to the highest possible standards for its members in construction related education.

MEMBERSHIP:

Fellow (FCIOB): Fellowship is the highest class of Institute membership and is awarded only to those members who have reached senior positions in the industry.

Member (MCIOB): A Member must be not less than 23 yrs of age; have passed or be exempt from the CIOB's written examinations; have had a minimum of 3 yrs professional level experience; and have passed the Professional Interview or undertaken the Professional Development Programme (PDP).Mature candidates may be accepted for Corporate membership through the Direct Membership Examination route.

Incorporated (ICIOB): For those who have either a minimum of HND (195 credits) in a construction related area, or who are fully exempt from all the Institute's examinations and preparing for the interview by undertaking either the Professional Development Programme or the Professional Interview.

Associate: An applicant must be not less than 21 yrs of age; have passed or be exempt from Level 1 (minimum HNC) of the Education Framework examinations; and have a minimum of with 2 yrs' experience at higher technician level.

Student: An applicant must be at least 16 yrs of age and have been accepted for, or engaged in, a course of building studies recognised by the Chartered Institute of Building.

EXAMINATIONS:

The content of the CIOB exams assesses candidates' understanding of both technological and managerial aspects of the building process. The new Educational Framework comprises:

Formation Studies: Design & Technology 1; Science for Building Materials; Site Surveying; Business Environment 1; Information and Decision Making; Structures; Assessed Experiential Learning.

Core Studies: Design & Technology 2, Business Environment 2; Legal Studies; Management; Management of Building Production; Building Services; Pre-Contract Studies; Assessed Experiential Learning.

Professional Studies: The candidate must chose four modules from the following areas: Facilities Management, Commercial Management, Project Management, Construction Management, Production Design Management and complete Project Evaluation & Development, Assessed Experiential Learning or Dissertation. Mature candidates with at least 10 yrs of professional level experience have the opportunity of applying for the two part Direct Membership Examination leading to Chartered Builder Status. A detailed breakdown of exam admission regulations and syllabuses available on request. The Professional Interview and the Direct Membership Examination Part A both require the candidate to put forward a report on their professional experience. This report forms the basis for discussions held with an interview panel of senior Members/Fellows to assess the relevance and extent of the person's practical achievements.

INSTITUTE OF ASPHALT TECHNOLOGY

Office 5, Trident House, Clare Road, Stanwell, Middlesex TW19 7QU Tel: 01784 423444
Fax: 01784 423888

MEMBERSHIP:

The Institute provides membership as follows:

Fellow (FIAT): Must be over 40, have been a Member for 5 yrs, and have reached an eminent position in asphalt activities.

Member (MIAT): Must be over 25, be an Associate member and have 5 yrs' experience, or be over 30, have 10 yrs' asphalt experience, and have reached a sufficiently responsible position.

Associate Member (AMIAT): Must have passed relevant exams approved by the Institute.

Associate (AIAT): Must be over 18 and have employment associated with bituminous products.

Student: Must be over 16, with 4 GCSE grades or equivalent, and be training in asphalt technology.

QUALIFICATIONS:

IAT Professional Exam (HNC); Quarry and Roadsurfacing (Degree)

THE INSTITUTE OF BUILDING CONTROL

92-104 East Street, Epsom, Surrey KT17 1EB Tel: 01372 745577 Fax: 01372 748282
e-mail: admin@instobc.demon.co.uk Website: www.demon.co.uk/instobc

MEMBERSHIP:

There are five classes of membership of the Institute:

Fellow (FIBC): This grade is awarded to members who are engaged in a Building Control capacity and have shown outstanding service, either to the Institute or to the Building Control profession.

Member (MIBC): Applicants must be not less than 23 yrs of age and must have successfully completed, or be exempt from, the Institute's Incorporated examination, Parts I and II, and have completed the Assessment of Professional Competence (APC). This grade represents Corporate Membership of the Institute.

Incorporated (IMIBC): Applicants must be not less than 21yrs of age, employed in a Building Control capacity (and/or be pursuing an approved* course of study), and have successfully completed, or be exempt from, the Incorporated examinations, Part I and II.

Associate (AMIBC): Applicants must be not less than 21yrs of age, employed in a Building Control capacity (and/or be pursuing an approved* course of study), and have achieved an HND or HNC pass in a construction related subject, or an equivalent qualification as determined by the Institute's Education & Development Committee. Persons awarded Associate Membership may proceed directly to the Incorporated examination, Part I.

Student: Students joining the Institute and progressing through the membership route will be required to satisfy the criteria and regulations in force at the time of registration. Applicants registering as students of the Institute must be in possession of one of the following academic awards: (a) GCSE or CSE passes in five subjects, including mathematics, a science subject and a subject requiring the use of descriptive English; two GCSE passes at A/S or A Level or two SCE passes in Highers or two SQA passes in Higher Still; (b) an appropriate ONC or OND in a Construction related course; (c) BTEC National Certificate in Building Studies or Civil Engineering; (d) City and Guilds Final or Technical Certificate Parts I and II; (e) a National Vocational Qualification (NVQ) in the Built Environment – Level 3. Additionally students must be not less than 17 yrs of age and must be in approved* employment and/or undertaking an approved* course of study.

Mature Entrants: Mature candidates, ie Associate Members of 35 yrs and above with a minimum of 5 yrs Building Control experience, will be exempt from the Incorporated examination but will be required to produce a Critical Analysis of a Major Task and a Professional Studies module, or complete the Advanced Building Control Surveying and Fire Safety Studies examinations at Incorporated Part II level before proceeding to the Assessment of Professional Competence. Mature candidates who have successfully completed a Critical Analysis of a Major Task and either the Professional Studies Module or the Advanced Building Control Surveying and Fire Studies examinations at Part II can apply to be upgraded to Incorporated Membership.

Exemptions: An exemption list of qualifications accepted by the Institute is available on application from the Institute's headquarters.

Specimen Examination Papers: Specimen past papers may be obtained from the Institute.

PROFESSIONAL EXAMINATIONS:

Following a review of its examination structure and syllabus, the Institute introduced new examinations in June 1995. The scheme comprises an Incorporated examination, Part I and II. Candidates must be registered at the appropriate class of membership and be in possession of the prerequisite qualifications at the time of application. Applicants may register for membership examinations with the Institute at any time of the yr. The Part I and II examinations are held annually each June. The closing date for examination entry is 1 March of the yr in which the examination is to be taken. Late entries will be accepted up to 31 March but the appropriate late entry fee will be levied. The Assessment of Professional Competence (APC) is a separate element and will be held annually.

Notes: (1) Cognate degrees are defined as accredited degrees in Building Control or accredited degrees with a Building Control option or conversion course. (2) Non-cognate degrees are defined as construction related courses, eg building, building surveying, building management, building engineering, construction management, fire engineering, building technology, built environment or other approved derivatives. (3) Guidance notes on the requirements in respect of the Critical Analysis of a Major Task, Professional Studies Module, Career Critique submission, and the path to corporated membership for 'professionals with other appropriate qualifications' are set out in Appendix One. (4) Any candidate who has satisfied fully the requirements of the Construction Industry Council (CIC) and has successfully completed the Assessment Interview conducted by the CIC as the Designated Body for Approved Inspectors will be admitted at Corporate Member level.

THE INSTITUTE OF CARPENTERS

35 Hayworth Road, Sandiacre, Nottingham NG10 5LL Tel: 0115 949 0641 Fax: 0115 949 1664
e-mail: centroff@innotts.co.uk Website: www.central-office.co.uk
Secretary: David Winson

MEMBERSHIP:

Fellow (FIOC): Open to a Member who is 21 or over, who has passed the Institute's own exam, or other qualifications approved by the Institute.

Member (MIOC): Candidates who are *bona fide* craftsmen or women and who have passed the Institute's own Membership exam, or other qualifications approved by the Institute and who are trained as carpenters, joiners, shopfitters, Cabinet Makers, or Wood Machinists. Note: Wood Machinists require a pass in the practical paper of the Institute's Member exam.

Licentiate (LIOC): Candidates who are *bona fide* craftsmen and women who have passed the Practical paper of the Institute's Member Exam, or other qualifications approved by the Institute and who are trained as carpenters, joiners, shopfitters, or Cabinet Makers.

Affiliate: Candidates who are *bona fide* craftsmen and women, who have passed the Institute's Intermediate Exam and are trained or training as carpenters, joiners, shopfitters, or Cabinet Makers.

EXAMINATIONS:

Fellowship: Performance Criteria provides for the requirements of organisation and supervision in the woodworking industry. The exam consists of 2 papers, each of 3 hrs duration: (i) Joiner or Carpentry Practice; (ii) A general paper relating to workshop and site supervision organisation.

Member: Performance Criteria requires a knowledge of carpentry and joinery to an advanced stage (NVQ Level 3). The exam consists of: a 7 hr pre-determined practical task and a 3 hr Associated Vocational Technology (Job Knowledge) paper relating to Joinery/Shopfitting and Carpentry.

Licentiate: The 7 hr practical task as stated above.

Intermediate: Performance Criteria requires a basic knowledge of carpentry and joinery as required for NVQ Level 2. The exam consists of a 4 hr pre-determined practical task and a 1½ hr Associated Vocational Technology (Job Knowledge) paper relating to Joinery and Carpentry.

Pre-Vocational Certificate: For those in secondary school education, or NVQ Level 1/2 wood occupation trainee, the syllabus is designed to be incorporated into the secondary school, college/training centre curriculum and is approved by SCAA3. Certification requires success in each of the following elements: (a) A 1½ hr job knowledge paper; (b) a 3 hr practical task; (c) Course-work assessment.

THE INSTITUTE OF CLERKS OF WORKS OF GREAT BRITAIN INCORPORATED

41 The Mall, London W5 3TJ Tel: 020 8579 2917/8 Fax: 020 8579 0554
e-mail: gensec@icwgb.sagehost.co.uk

MEMBERSHIP:

Fellow (FICW): Any person of 40 who has been a Member for more than 10 yrs and who:(i) has been a practising Clerk of Works for more than 15 yrs and is still practising; or (ii) has been a Lecturer at a recognised educational establishment concerned with subjects connected with the profession of Clerks of Works for more than 15 yrs and is still practising; or (iii) has been engaged partly as a Clerk of Works and partly as a Lecturer for an aggregate of more than 15 yrs and is engaged in either of those professions as at the date of his/her election.

Member (MICW): Any person practising as a Clerk of Works and who: (i) is 23 and who has passed the Final Exam of the Institute comprising Part 1, Part 2 and Professional Practice Exam Part III, and has been recommended by the Examination Board for election as a Member of the Institute; or (ii) is at least 40 and who has passed the Mature Entrants Exam set by the Institute and is practising as a Clerk of Works and has been recommended by the Examination Board for election as a Member of the Institute; or (iii) is 45, a Licentiate at the time of application having held that grade of membership for not less than 5 yrs and can produce evidence of having practised as a Clerk of Works for not less than 8 consecutive yrs immediately preceding application (or 10 yrs not immediately preceding application) and recommended for election as a Member of the Institute; or (iv) is at least 50 and can produce evidence of having practised as a Clerk of Works for not less than 10 consecutive yrs immediately preceding the application (or a total period of 12 yrs not immediately preceding the application) of which not less than 5 yrs must have been in a capacity which at the discretion of the Examination Board shall be deemed to require a level of practical experience and responsibility at least comparable with the technical ability of a person in sub-clauses (i), (ii) and (v) hereof and has been so interviewed by the Examination Board and recommended for election as a Member of the Institute; or (v) is at least 30, is qualified by exam and experience and is lecturing at a recognised education establishment in subjects connected with the profession of Clerk of Works and has done so for a period not less than 2 yrs and has been interviewed by the regional examining board and recommended by the Examination Board for election as a Member of the Institute.

Licentiate (LICW): (i) Any person of 22 who has passed the Part I Final Exam. (ii) Any person of 23 who has passed an exam accepted by the Examination Board as being equiv to the Part I Final Exam and whose application is supported by evidence of not less than 2 yrs' supervisory experience in the construction industry. (iii) Any person of 30 who is practising as a Clerk of Works and can produce evidence of having so practised for at least 3 consecutive yrs immediately preceding the application plus 3 yrs' supervisory experience (or for a total period of 8 yrs not immediately preceding the application). (iv) Any person of 25 being a lecturer at a college or teaching establishment and is teaching subjects considered suitable by the Examination Board as related to the profession of Clerk of Works.

Probationer: (i) Any person of 21 who has passed the Intermediate Exam and in the opinion of the Examining Board possesses adequate experience of a supervisory or practical nature; or (ii) Any person of 22 who has passed an exam accepted by the Examination Board as being equiv to the Intermediate Exam and whose application is supported by evidence of not less than 1 yr's supervisory experience in the construction industry; or (iii) Any person of 30 who is practising as a Clerk of Works and can produce evidence of having so practised for not less than 1 yr preceding the application plus 2 yrs' supervisory experience (or supervisory experience for a period of 5 consecutive yrs not immediately preceding the application); or (iv) Any person of 40 who has been accepted as a candidate for the Mature Entrants Exam, and recommended for election as a Probationer of the Institute.

Student: Any person of 18 following a course of Instruction recognised by the Institute Examination Board as a suitable preparatory course leading to the Institute's Exam.

EXAMINATION:
The Intermediate Exam is common to all candidates and consists of 4 papers: Construction Technology 1, Materials Science 1, Surveying and Levelling/Calculations 1, Site Procedures and Administration 1. Candidates may not take the Final Exam until they have passed or been exempted from the Intermediate. Final Part I consists of 4 papers common to all candidates: Construction Technology 2, Construction Services 1, Contractors' Plant and Equipment 1 and Construction Science 1. Plus papers in Construction Technology 3 (choice of Building, Civil Engineering, Engineering Services 1, Landscaping), Concrete Technology (common to all except Engineering Services) and Engineering Services 2. Final II is common to all candidates and is divided into 2 Groups. Group A consists of papers on Professional Practice and Procedure and Elements of Law and Maintenance and Repair. Group B comprises papers on Measurement and Specification and Materials Inspection and Testing. Final III is a Professional Practice Exam which comprises an oral and practical identification of materials.

Exemptions: Total exemption is granted from the Intermediate and whole or partial exemption from the Final Exam in respect of certain qualifications, including the following: HND, HTD (Building or Civil Engineering) and HNC, HTC (Building or Civil Engineering); OND, TED and ONC, BTEC (Intermediate only); C&G Construction Technician's Certificate; C&G Full Technological Certificate; Certificate of the National Examining Board for Supervisory Studies; NVQ/SVQ Level 3 Site Inspection (New Works).

INSTITUTE OF MAINTENANCE AND BUILDING MANAGEMENT

Keets House, 30 East Street, Farnham, Surrey GU9 7SW Tel: 01252 710994 Fax: 01252 737741 e-mail: imbm@btconnect.com

MEMBERSHIP:
Fellows (FIMBM): They will have been Corporate Members of the Institute for at least five consecutive yrs, have appropriate qualifications and experience and have a proven record of service to the Institute or to the industry at regional, national or international level.

Members (MIMBM): They are persons whom the Executive Council deem to have the appropriate building management or maintenance experience and knowledge. The roles and responsibilities of Members will fall within the following parameters: (a) Managerial responsibility for organisation operation, management function or department concerned with the management maintenance and modification of property and its services; (b) Responsible for/contribute to the formulation of policy for the management maintenance and modification of property and its services; (c)

Responsible for the planning/or execution and/or monitoring of operations concerned with the management maintenance and modification of property and its services; (d) Responsible for the design of products, artefacts, methods and systems used/required for the management, maintenance and modification of property and its services; (e) Responsible for the provision and/or utilisation of management services to enable the management, maintenance and modification of property and its services. (May include financial, contractual, personnel, information, marketing, public relations, research responsibilities); (f) Responsible for the delivery and/or development and/or management of qualifications at advanced management or technical levels relating to the management, maintenance and modification of property and its services. Members should possess an Honours degree level education. A direct entry route to Membership is available via professional report and interview.

Associates (AIMBM): They are persons whom the Executive Council deem to have the appropriate building management or maintenance experience and knowledge. The roles and responsibilities of Associates will fall within the following parameters: (a) Contribute to the management of organisation operation. Responsible/contributory responsibility for management function or department concerned with the management maintenance and modification of property and/or its services; (b) Responsible for/contributory responsibility for the execution and/or monitoring of operations concerned with the management maintenance and modification of property and/or its services; (c) Responsible for/contributory responsibility for the provision and/or utilisation of management services to enable the management maintenance and modification of property and/or its services. (May include financial, contractual, personnel, information, marketing, public relations and research responsibilities); (d) Responsible for the supervision of management, administrative and technical personnel (within level and scope of responsibility) concerned with the management, maintenance and modification of property and/or its services; (e) Responsible for the delivery and/or management of qualifications at trade, technical or supervisory levels relating to the management, maintenance and modification of property and its services. Associates should hold a relevant Degree, HND or an appropriate NVQ at level 4.

Technicians (TIMBM): They are persons whom the National Council deem to have appropriate building management or maintenance experience and knowledge. The roles and responsibilities of Technicians will fall within the following parameters: (a) Responsible for the supervision of personnel involved in administration and/or technical operations relating to the management maintenance and modification of property and/or its services; (b) Contribute to the execution and/or monitoring and/or administration of operations concerned with the management maintenance and modification of property and/or its services; (c) Responsible for the execution and/or monitoring and/or administration of discrete and/or small works relating to the management, maintenance and modification of property and/or its services. Technicians should hold an HNC or an appropriate NVQ at level 3.

Affiliates: They are persons not employed in building or building maintenance organisations but having an interest in building or building maintenance are invited by the Council to join the IMBM.

EXAMINATIONS:

The Institute is the professional body for the establishment of standards of competence and conduct for those employed in Building Maintenance and Estates services in both the private and public sectors.

S/NVQs: The Institute recognises a broad range of construction related qualifications at levels appropriate to the membership grades. The Institute is the Standards Setting Body for Building Maintenance and Estates Services and has developed S/NVQs at levels 3 & 4 which correspond to Technician and Associate grades of membership respectively.

PQS: The Institute has also developed a course based honours degree programme – the Professional Qualification Structure (PQS). The PQS/BSc (Hons) Building Maintenance Management is a part-time programme consisting of three individually examined and certified stages. Completion of part 1and/or 2 enables students to be considered for Associate Membership. Completion of part 3 allows students to be considered for full Membership. The PQS has an entry requirement of HNC, which may be achieved through APL/APEL. Credit transfers are available between the PQS and the Building Maintenance and Estates Service S/NVQS.

Offers of membership (all levels): Applicants should note that qualifications AND industry experience are taken into account when assessing membership applications.

University Qualifications

The following universities offer qualifications in Building and related subjects. Full details may be found in Part 4, under the entry for the appropriate university.

FIRST DEGREES AWARDED BY UNIVERSITIES
Anglia; Brighton; Bristol; Brunel; Bucks. Coll.; Central England; Central Lancashire; Coventry; De Montfort, Leicester; Derby; Edinburgh; Glamorgan; Glasgow Caledonian; Greenwich; Heriot-Watt; Huddersfield; Kingston; Leeds Metropolitan; Liverpool; Liverpool John Moores; London (University College (UCL)); Loughborough; Luton; Napier; Northumbria; Nottingham Trent; Nottingham Trent (Southampton Institute); Oxford Brookes; Paisley; Plymouth; Portsmouth; Reading; Robert Gordon; Salford; Sheffield Hallam; South Bank; Staffordshire; Strathclyde; Teesside; UMIST; Wales (Swansea Institute of Higher Education); Westminster; Wolverhampton

HIGHER DEGREES AWARDED BY UNIVERSITIES
Anglia; Bath; Birmingham; Bournemouth; Brighton; Bristol; Cambridge; Central England; Central Lancashire; Coventry; Dundee; Glamorgan; Glasgow Caledonian; Greenwich; Heriot-Watt; Kingston; Leeds; Leeds Metropolitan; Lincolnshire; London (Imperial College of Science, Technology & Medicine); London (University College (UCL)); Loughborough; Luton; Manchester; Napier; Nottingham; Nottingham Trent; Portsmouth; Reading; Salford; Sheffield; Sheffield Hallam; South Bank; Strathclyde; Ulster; UMIST; Westminster; Wolverhampton

DIPLOMAS AWARDED BY UNIVERSITIES
Abertay, Dundee; Anglia; Birmingham; Blackburn; Bradford (Bradford & Ilkley Community College); Bucks. Coll.; Central England; Central Lancashire; Coventry; Derby; Dundee; Glamorgan; Greenwich; Lincolnshire; Luton; Napier; Northampton; Northumbria; Nottingham Trent; Paisley; Portsmouth; Salford; South Bank; Strathclyde; Teesside; Ulster; Wales (Swansea Institute of Higher Education); Wolverhampton

CERTIFICATES AWARDED BY UNIVERSITIES
Anglia (City College, Norwich); Bradford (Bradford & Ilkley Community College); Brighton; Central England; Leeds Metropolitan; Lincolnshire; Lincolnshire (Hull College); Manchester (Warrington Collegiate Institute, Faculty of H.E,); Salford; South Bank; Ulster

POSTGRADUATE DIPLOMAS AWARDED BY UNIVERSITIES
Heriot-Watt

National Certificates and Diplomas

BTEC National Certificates/Diplomas: Builders' Merchants Studies; Builders' Merchants Studies (Timber); Building Studies; Construction; Construction and Land Use
BTEC Higher National Certificates/Diplomas: Building Studies; Building Studies (Architectural); Building Studies (Quantity Surveying); Building Studies (Surveying)
Scotland
SQA HNC: Building; Building Services Plant Engineering; Building Supervision; Built Environment: Architectural Technology; Built Environment: Building Control; Built Environment: Building Control and Inspection; Built Environment: Fire Safety; Built Environment: General; Built Environment: Quantity Surveying; Construction Management; Construction Practice.
SQA HND: Building Control; Building Inspection and Supervision; Building Maintenance Management; Building Services; Building Services Engineering; Building Services Plant Engineering; Building Supervision; Building Surveying; Built Environment; Built Environment Studies; Built Environment: Architectural Technology; Built Environment: Building Control; Built Environment: Building, Inspection and Supervision; Built Environment: Building Maintenance Management; Built Environment: Fire Safety; Built Environment: General; Built Environment: Quantity Surveying; Construction Management; Construction Surveying.

NVQs

Level 1: Accessing Occupations (Construction); General Construction Operations; Building Craft Occupations; Decorative Occupations (Construction); Floorcovering (Construction); General Construction Operations; Glazing; Insulation Installing; Interior Systems (Construction); Plant Maintenance; Plant Occupations (Construction); Roofing Occupations; Trowel Occupations (Construction); Wood Occupations (Construction)

Level 2: Applied Waterproof Membranes (Construction); Bricklaying (Construction); Chimney Engineering (Construction); Demolition (Construction); Earthmoving Plant Operations (Construction); Facade Maintenance (Construction); Fence Erection; Fitted Interiors (Construction); Floorcovering (Construction); Formworking (Construction); Glazing; Installation of Glass Support Structures; Interior Systems (Construction); Lifting Plant Operations (Construction); Lightning Conductor Engineering (Construction); Mastic Asphalting (Construction); Plant Maintenance; Plant Operations – Bored or Driven Works (Construction); Plastering Solid and Fibrous (Construction); Roof Sheeting and Cladding (Construction); Roof Slating and Tiling (Construction); Scaffolding (Construction); Steelfixing (Construction); Steeplejacking (Construction); Stonemasonry (Construction); Thatching; Thermal Insulation; Tunnelling Operations (Construction); Wall and Floor Tiling (Construction); Wood Occupations (Construction); Wood Preserving – Industrial Pre-Treatment (Construction)

Level 3: Bricklaying (Construction); Building Services Engineering – Buying; Building Services Engineering – Estimating; Building Services Engineering – Site Supervision; Building Site Supervision; Construction Contracting; Construction Plant and Equipment Supervision; Demolition (Construction); Floorcovering; Formworking (Construction); Glazing; Installing Architectural Glazing Systems; Interior Systems (Construction); Lightning Conductor Engineering (Construction); Maintenance Operations (Construction); Mastic Asphalting (Construction); Painting and Decorating (Construction); Plant Maintenance (Construction); Plant Operations (Construction); Plastering Solid and Fibrous (Construction): Roof Sheeting and Cladding; Roof Slating and Tiling; Scaffolding (Construction); Site Inspection; Site Technical Support; Steeplejacking (Construction); Stonemasonry (Construction);Wall and Floor Tiling (Construction); Wood Occupations (Construction)

Level 4: Building Control; Building Services Engineering – Design; Building Services Engineering – Services and Maintenance Management; Building Services Engineering – Site Management; Building Site Management; Construction Contracting; Construction Plant and Equipment Management

Level 5: Construction Project Management

SVQs

Level 1: Construction: Accessing Occupations or Decorative Occupations or Floorcovering Occupation or General Building Operations or General Construction Operations or Glazing or Plant Occupations or Industrial Painting or Trowel Occupation or Fixing Cable Supports or Fixing Cables or Highways Maintenance.

Level 2: Construction: Applied Waterproof Membranes; or Bricklaying or Carpentry & Joinery or Ceiling Fixing or Construction Operations or Facade Maintenance – Cleaning or Floorcovering Occupations or Formworking or General Building Operations or Glazing or Industrial Painting or Painting & Decorating or Plant Maintenance or Plant Operations – Bores/Driven Works or Plant Operations – Earth Moving or Plant Operations – Lifting or Plastering or Roof Sheeting & Cladding or Roof Slating & Tiling or Scaffolding or Shopfitting or Stonemasonry or Wall & Floor Tiling or Wood Machining or Fence Erection or Highways Maintenance.

Level 3: Constructing Contracting; Construction: Bricklaying or Carpentry & Joinery or Ceiling Fixing or Formworking or General Construction Operations or Glazing or Industrial Painting or Mason Paving or Painting & Decorating or Plant Equipment Supervision or Plant Maintenance or Plant Operations or Plastering or Roof Slating & Tiling or Scaffolding or Shopfitting or Stonemasonry or Wall & Floor Tiling or Wood Machining or Highways Maintenance.

Level 4: Construction Contracting; Construction: Plant & Equipment Management; Highways Maintenance.

Level 5: Construction Project Management.

GNVQs

3727 Construction and the Built Environment

Useful Addresses

Builders' Merchants Federation, Parnall House, 5 Parnall Road, Staple Tye, Harlow, Essex CM18 7PP Tel: 01279 439654 Fax: 01279 430127 E-mail: training@bmf.org.co.uk
Construction Industry Training Board, Bircham Newton, Nr Kings Lynn, Norfolk PE13 6RH Tel: 01485 577577 Fax: 01485 577689
Construction Industry Training Board (Northern Ireland), 17 Dundrod Road, Crumlin, Belfast BT29 4SR Tel: 01232 825466 Fax: 01232 825693
Institute of Maintenance and Building Management, Keets House, 30 East Street, Farnham, Surrey GU9 7SW Tel: 01252 710994 Fax: 01252 737741

BUILDING SOCIETIES

NVQs

Level 2: Building Society Services

SVQs

Level 2: Building Society Services

Useful Addresses

Building Societies Association, 3 Savile Row, London W1X 1AF Tel: 0171 437 0655 Fax: 0171 734 6416

BUSINESS STUDIES

Membership of Professional Institutions and Associations

THE INTERNATIONAL FACULTY OF BUSINESS QUALIFICATIONS

Laurom House, The Oaks Business Village, Revenge Road, Lordswood, Kent ME5 8UD
Tel: 01634 869200 Fax: 01634 869149
The International Faculty of Business Qualifications was formed to fulfil two main objectives:
1. To provide business qualifications through coaching, assessment and review.
2. To validate the awards of professional institutes and centres of learning and training which offer qualifications and awards in business subjects.
The Faculty places special emphasis on accreditation of prior learning. Assessment of skills gained through life and work experience is an essential feature of our programmes, providing a route to recognised business qualifications for applicants who may not have had the opportunity to study or train, but who have acquired the necessary skills through experience and proven ability. Assessment of skills and recognition awards already achieved leads to the granting of certificates and diplomas in the appropriate subjects.
The Faculty also assesses the skills of tutors and trainers and can award individual certification to deliver approved courses.
The validation of the awards of professional institutes is carried out through an assessment of entry requirements and procedures which should comply with international standards and practices. The differing business practices in different countries of the world can be accommodated.

MEMBERSHIP GRADES:
Student: Applicants must achieve success in appropriate subjects at a level which, in the opinion of the Council of the Faculty, is satisfactory for the purposes of admission to Student Membership Grade.

Associate (AIFBQ): Applicants for 'Associate' grade must have passed the examinations of the Faculty incorporating all of the subjects included in the syllabus. Exemption on a subject-for-subject basis will be granted, at the discretion of the Board, to applicants who hold degrees and qualifications from universities and / or awarding bodies approved for this purpose by the Faculty, or can demonstrate competence in the practice of specific skills.

Fellow (FIFBQ): Applicants must have passed the examinations of the Faculty as for Associate membership or have been exempted and must have at least five yrs' experience in the practice of skills approved by the Council of the Faculty.

THE BRITISH ASSOCIATION OF COMMUNICATORS IN BUSINESS

42 Borough High Street, London SE1 1XW Tel: 020 7378 7139 Fax: 020 7378 7140
e-mail: bacb@globalnet.co.uk Website: www.bacb.org.uk

MEMBERSHIP GRADES:
Fellow (FCB): Fellows are elected by the Council and must be of the highest standing in the field of internal corporate communication.

Member (MCB): One who has been engaged in internal corporate communications for at least 10 yrs and has demonstrated his or her professional ability and competence to the satisfaction of the Membership Committee. Experience must include having had management responsibilities.

Associate Member: A person who is engaged in corporate communication.

Student: Must be enrolled in a formal course of relevant further education and / or be studying on-the-job training or otherwise for a relevant exam.

THE FACULTY OF COMMERCE AND INDUSTRY

52 Market St, PO Box 99, Wigan, Lancashire WN1 1HX Tel: 01695 622226 Fax: 01695 627199
The Faculty, established in 1982 to provide a bridge between commerce and industry, is international in scope and dimension with members in over thirty countries. Membership is open to all those engaged in management and senior supervisory positions in Commerce and Industry. The Faculty publishes the *International Management Focus,* holds social and business functions, and provides an international forum to bring together those engaged in Commerce and Industry.

ENTRY QUALIFICATIONS:
Fellow (FFCI): Applicants must be over the age of 25 at the time of application, already be an Associate of the Faculty, and have at least five yrs' experience in a management or senior supervisory position considered appropriate by the Council of the Faculty.

Associate (AFCI): Applicants must be over the age of 20 at the time of application, and have passed or been exempted from the entrance examination of the Faculty and have at least two yrs' experience in a management or senior supervisory position considered appropriate by the Council of the Faculty.

Student: Applicants must be over the age of 16 at the time of application, and have passed such examinations as the Council of the Faculty consider appropriate for admission to the Faculty's entrance examination programme.

THE INSTITUTE OF BUSINESS ADMINISTRATION

16 Park Crescent, London W1N 4AH Tel: 020 7612 7028 Fax: 020 7612 7027
e-mail: iba-uk@dial.pipex.com Website: www.ibauk.org
Promotes professional standards of administration and management in small and medium- sized organisations.

MEMBERSHIP:
Fellow (FInstBA): Candidates must be at least 25, be a member or have Associate status in IBA and have at least 5 yrs' relevant work experience at senior level within an organisation.

Member (MInstBA): Candidates must be at least 21, have Associate status in IBA, at least 3 yrs' relevant work experience in an administrative capacity and have completed an approved programme of study.

Associate (AInstBA): Candidates must be at least 19 and have successfully completed an approved programme of study.

Licentiate: Candidates must be registered on to a suitable course relating to a junior level business administration role and be interested in further developing their personal professional studies.

PROGRAMMES OF STUDY:

The IBA syllabus covers a variety of topics important to administrators of small and medium-sized enterprises and includes Operations, Office and Records, Financial, Law, Premises and Staff. A network of centres providing programmes leading to the IBA Diploma in Business Administration is being set up and IBA has a number of DL programmes for those unable to attend a college. ICSA Foundation and Pre-Professional level examination success are recognised as approved programmes of study.

THE INSTITUTE OF CHARTERED SECRETARIES AND ADMINISTRATORS

16 Park Crescent, London W1N 4AH Tel: 020 7580 4741 Fax: 020 7323 1132
e-mail: icsa@dial.pipex.com Website: www.icsa.org.uk/
ICSA is the body which sets the international standards of the profession and through which Chartered Secretaries are qualified and supported. The Institute provides a broad-based programme focusing on business practice, law, accountancy, finance and regulation. Members are employed in a variety of sectors including business, local government, charities and universities, with the core membership employed as Company Secretaries.

MEMBERSHIP:

Associate (ACIS): Successful completion of the exams plus 3 to 6 yrs ' relevant experience is required for this grade of membership.

Fellow (FCIS): Fellows must be at least 25, and have 8 yrs' relevant experience, 3 of which must have been at senior level.

EXAMINATIONS:

The qualifying scheme consists of three programmes – Foundation, Pre-Professional and Professional, encompassing the four core themes of Corporate Finance, Corporate Law, Administration and Management. The Institute operates a policy of open entry onto the Foundation programme and exemptions are available from some qualifying scheme modules for holders of relevant degrees and professional qualifications.

THE INSTITUTE OF COMMERCE

50 Burnhill Road, Beckenham, Kent BR3 3LA Tel: 020 8663 3577 Fax: 020 8663 3212
e-mail: ioc@wadetrade.com
EXAMINATIONS:

Diploma in Business Studies (DBS): Economics, Business Law, Business Organisation, Managing the Finance Function, Introduction to Information Technology & Statistics

Certificate in Management Studies (CMS): Marketing, Business Planning, Business Principles, Organisational Behaviour

Diploma in Management Studies (DMS): Management Practice, Marketing Management, Operations Management, Human Resource Management

Diploma in International Business (DIB): Practice & Procedures in International Business, International Marketing, Business Development in Overseas Markets, Import/Export Agency Management.

University Qualifications

The following universities offer qualifications in Business Studies and related subjects. Full details may be found in Part 4, under the entry for the appropriate university.

FIRST DEGREES AWARDED BY UNIVERSITIES

Abertay, Dundee; Adams; Anglia; Anglia (City College, Norwich); Anglia (Colchester Institute); Aston; Barnsley; Bath; Bath Spa; Birmingham; Blackburn; Bournemouth; Bradford; Bradford (Bradford & Ilkley Community College); Brighton; Bristol; Brunel; Buckingham; Bucks. Coll.; Central England; Central Lancashire; Cheltenham & Gloucester; City; City (Gyosei International

College in the UK); Coventry; De Montfort, Leicester; De Montfort, Leicester (De Montfort University Bedford); Derby; Doncaster; Doncaster (Dearne Valley Business School); Dundee; Durham (New College Durham); East Anglia; East Anglia (Suffolk College); East London; Edinburgh; Essex; Essex (Writtle College); Exeter; Glamorgan; Glasgow; Glasgow Caledonian; Greenwich; Heriot-Watt (Scottish Borders Campus); Hertfordshire; Hertfordshire (West Herts College); Huddersfield; Hull; Keele; Kent; Kent (Canterbury Christ Church University College); Kingston; Lancaster; Lancaster (Blackpool and The Fylde College); Leeds; Leeds (Askham Bryan College); Leeds Metropolitan; Lincolnshire; Lincolnshire (Grimsby College); Lincolnshire (Hull College); Liverpool; Liverpool (Chester College of H.E.); Liverpool (Liverpool Hope University College); Liverpool John Moores; London (Imperial College of Science, Technology & Medicine); London (King's College London); London (Queen Mary & Westfield College (incorporating St Bartholomew's and the Royal London School of Medicine & Dentistry)); London (University College (UCL)); London (Wye College); London Guildhall; Loughborough; Luton; Manchester; Manchester (Warrington Collegiate Institute, Faculty of H.E,); Manchester Metropolitan.; Middlesex; Napier; Newcastle; North London; Northampton; Northumbria; Nottingham Trent; Nottingham Trent (Southampton Institute); OU (NESCOT); Oxford Brookes; Paisley; Plymouth; Portsmouth; Reading; Robert Gordon; Salford; Sheffield; Sheffield Hallam; South Bank; Southampton (King Alfred's College); St Martin; Staffordshire; Stirling; Stockport; Strathclyde; Sunderland; Surrey; Surrey (Farnborough College of Technology); Surrey (University of Surrey Roehampton); Sussex; Teesside; Thames Valley; Ulster; UMIST; Wales (Cardiff University); Wales (North East Wales Institute); Wales (Swansea Institute of Higher Education); Wales (University of Wales College, Newport); Wales (University of Wales Institute, Cardiff); Wales (University of Wales, Aberystwyth); Wales (University of Wales, Bangor); Wales (University of Wales, Swansea); Warwick; Westminster; Wolverhampton; Worcester; York

HIGHER DEGREES AWARDED BY UNIVERSITIES

Aberdeen; Abertay, Dundee; Anglia; Aston; Bath; Belfast; Birmingham; Bournemouth; Bradford; Brighton; Bristol; Brunel; Buckingham; Bucks. Coll.; Central England; Central Lancashire; Cheltenham & Gloucester; City; City (Ashridge); City (Gyosei International College in the UK); Coventry; Cranfield; De Montfort, Leicester; Derby; Dundee; Durham; East Anglia; East London; Edinburgh; Exeter; Glamorgan; Glasgow; Glasgow Caledonian; Greenwich; Heriot-Watt; Hertfordshire; Huddersfield; Hull; Keele; Kent; Kingston; Lancaster; Leeds; Leeds Metropolitan; Leicester; Liverpool; Liverpool John Moores; London (Birkbeck, University of London); London (Royal Holloway); London (School of Oriental & African Studies); London (Wye College); London Guildhall; Loughborough; Luton; Manchester; Middlesex; Napier; Newcastle; North London; Northampton; Northumbria; Nottingham; Nottingham Trent; Oxford; Oxford Brookes; Paisley; Plymouth; Reading; Salford; Sheffield; Sheffield Hallam; South Bank; Southampton; Staffordshire; Stirling; Strathclyde; Sunderland; Surrey; Sussex; Teesside; Thames Valley; Ulster; UMIST; Wales (Cardiff University); Wales (University of Wales, Aberystwyth); Wales (University of Wales, Bangor); Wales (University of Wales, Swansea); Warwick; Westminster; Wolverhampton

DIPLOMAS AWARDED BY UNIVERSITIES

Aberdeen; Anglia; Anglia (City College, Norwich); Anglia (Colchester Institute); Aston; Barnsley; Bath Spa; Birmingham; Birmingham (Birmingham College of Food, Tourism and Creative Studies); Blackburn; Bournemouth; Bradford; Bradford (Bradford & Ilkley Community College); Brighton; Bristol; Brunel; Bucks. Coll.; Central England; Central Lancashire; Cheltenham & Gloucester; Coventry; De Montfort, Leicester; Derby; Doncaster; Doncaster (Dearne Valley Business School); Durham; Durham (New College Durham); East Anglia (Suffolk College); Edinburgh; Glamorgan; Greenwich; Heriot-Watt (Scottish Borders Campus); Hertfordshire; Huddersfield; Kent; Kingston; Lancaster; Leeds; Leeds Metropolitan; Lincolnshire; Lincolnshire (Beverley College); Lincolnshire (East Yorkshire College); Lincolnshire (Grimsby College); Lincolnshire (North Lindsey College); Lincolnshire (Yorkshire Coast College); London (Birkbeck, University of London); London (School of Oriental & African Studies); London (Wye College); London Guildhall; Luton; Manchester; Middlesex; Napier; Newcastle; North London; Northampton; Northumbria; Paisley; Portsmouth; Salford; Sheffield; South Bank; Southampton (King Alfred's College); Staffordshire; Stirling; Strathclyde; Sunderland; Teesside; Thames Valley; Ulster; Wales (Cardiff University); Wales (North East Wales Institute); Wales (Swansea Institute of Higher Education); Wales (University of Wales Institute, Cardiff); Wales (University of Wales, Aberystwyth); Westminster; Wolverhampton

CERTIFICATES AWARDED BY UNIVERSITIES
Aberdeen; Anglia (City College, Norwich); Bournemouth; Bradford (Bradford & Ilkley Community College); Bristol; Brunel; Cheltenham & Gloucester; Coventry; East Anglia (Suffolk College); Huddersfield; Hull; Keele; Leeds Metropolitan; Lincolnshire (Bishop Burton College); Lincolnshire (Hull College); London Guildhall; Manchester (Warrington Collegiate Institute, Faculty of H.E,); North London; Northampton; Salford; Sheffield Hallam; South Bank; Staffordshire; Ulster; Wales (University of Wales College, Newport); Wales (University of Wales Institute, Cardiff)

OTHER COURSES AWARDED BY UNIVERSITIES
Essex (Writtle College); North London; Northampton

PROFESSIONAL COURSES AWARDED BY UNIVERSITIES
London Guildhall

National Certificates and Diplomas

BTEC National Certificates/Diplomas: Business and Finance
BTEC Higher National Certificates/Diplomas: Business
Scotland
HNC: Applied Consumer Studies; Business Development for Footballers; Business Information Technology; Business Information Systems; Business Information Management; Business Administration with Gaidhealtachd Studies; Business Information Technology; Business Information Technology Administration and Travel and Tourism; European Business and Administration; European Business Management; European Studies with Marketing; European Trade and Business
HND: Business Information Management; Business Information Systems; Business Information Technology; Business Studies; Business Technology; Applied Consumer Studies; Business Administration with Gaidhealtachd Studies; Business Administration with Information Technology; Business Information Technology; Business Administration and Travel and Tourism; European Business and Administration; European Business Management; European Studies with Marketing; European Trade and Business. A range of National Certificate Modules are available within this sector.

NVQs

BTEC Continuing Education Modules of Study and Continuing Education Certificate in Business Administration
Level 2: Customer Service; International Trade and Services
Level 3: Business Information; Customer Service; International Trade and Services
Level 4: Business Counselling; Developing Union Organisation; International Trade and Services

GNVQs

3723 Business

OCR

OCR offer various awards in business administration. Contact OCR for details.

Pitman Qualifications

Word Processing; Keyboarding; Practical Data Processing; Understanding Computers; Practical Spreadsheet Processing; Computerised Accounts; Text Production Skills; Text Production Skills (French); Text Production Skills (German); Text Production Skills (Spanish); Disk Management
Certificate: Basic Business Skills Administration NVQ Levels 1,2,3,4; Customer Service NVQ Levels 2 and 3.

Useful Addresses

Institute of Chartered Secretaries and Administrators, 16 Park Crescent, London W1N 4AH Tel: 0171 580 4741 Fax: 0171 323 1132 E-mail: icsa@dial.pipex.com

Small Firms Lead Body, PO Box 393, Northampton NN1 4YG Tel: 01604 234618 Fax: 01604 633546
E-mail: sfedi@compuserve.com

CATERING AND INSTITUTIONAL MANAGEMENT

Membership of Professional Institutions and Associations

BRITISH INSTITUTE OF INNKEEPING

Wessex House, 80 Park Street, Camberley, Surrey GU15 3PT Tel: 01276 684449 Fax: 01276 23045
e-mail: info@bii.org Website: www.bii.org
Founded in 1981, the Institute is the professional body for the licensed retail sector.

MEMBERSHIP:
There are a wide range of grades available allowing membership of the British Institute of
Innkeeping – from those who have just started their careers in licensed retailing to those who have
been in the industry for many yrs. The grade of membership awarded depends on both experience
and qualifications taken and is determined by a points system. Members can benefit from a wide
range of services offering business, personal and financial benefits.

EXAMINATIONS:
National Vocational Qualifications: With a partner, the Institute is an Awarding Body for On-
Licensed Premises Management (Level 4) and On-Licensed Premises Supervision (Level 3). The
parallel Scottish Vocational Qualifications (Levels 3 & 4) are also awarded.
National Licensee's Certificate: Aims to introduce the basics of licensing law and the social
responsibilities of licensees to new entrants to the profession, although it is also relevant to
existing licensees.
National Entertainment Licensee's Certificate: A qualification for the late night sector in licensed
retail. It is aimed at those running establishments which require Public Entertainment Licences
and encompasses basic licensing law and the social responsibilities attached to the running of a
premises with such a licence.
Certificate of Induction: A three-day minimum training course leading to an MCQ and short-
answer question exam consisting of 2 parts (incorporating the National Licensee's Certificate as
Part 2). The qualification is intended to introduce the complexities of running on-licensed
premises and the technical skills required but also outlines the regulatory regime surrounding the
running of a business.
Qualifying Examination: This comprises a 5 part examination, including a practical test (the
National Licensee's Certificate forms Part 2), which covers the technical, operational and
administrative aspects of licensed house management and control. Three papers are 'open book'.
Subjects are studied at a higher level than in the Certificate of Induction. This qualification is used
by many pub owning companies for their employees.
Door Supervisor's National Certificate: A pre-entry, pre-registration qualification for door
supervisors working in licensed premises.
Advanced Qualifications: Aimed at licensees and senior staff in pubs, bars and pub/restaurants
to help them run more profitable businesses, these qualifications in Catering Management,
Practical Trainer Financial Management, Business Development, Customer Service Management,
Leadership & Motivation, Cellar & Beer Quality Management, Spirit Retail and Wine Retail are
available nationwide through Institute Accredited Trainers. The Diploma in Licensed Retailing is
also available and requires 5 Advanced Qualifications as a prerequisite. All Institute qualifications
carry points which count towards initial membership and progression through the Institute's
membership grades.
Professional Barperson's Certificate A qualification for barstaff in all types of licensed premises.
Including work-based training and multiple-choice examinations, the qualification is made up of
clusters of units aimed at different parts of the sector.

CONFEDERATION OF TOURISM, HOTEL AND CATERING MANAGEMENT

118-120 Great Titchfield Street, London W1P 7AJ Tel: 020 7612 0170 Fax: 020 7612 0170
Website: www.cthcm.com

The Confederation of Tourism Hotel and Catering Management was established in 1982 to provide recognised standards of management training appropriate to the needs of the hotel and travel industries, via its syllabi, examinations and awards. Those studying for the examinations of the Confederation are offered a structured learning process, encompassing both the theoretical and practical aspects of the industry, together with a clearly defined path of development through progressive grades of membership. The Confederation offers four externally examined Diploma training programmes, each of which will normally take an academic yr to complete, and four grades of membership each indicating a level of personal development.

TRAINING PROGRAMMES:

Diploma in Hotel Management: Aims to provide students with a broad understanding of the operational aspects of the international hotel industry, and a knowledge of the underlying principles involved.

Syllabus content: Food and beverage operations, food science, hygiene and nutrition, front office operations, facilities and accommodation operations, hospitality costing and control, supervisory management, marketing, tourism, computing, business communication.

Advanced Diploma in Hotel Management: Aims to provide an understanding of the managerial, decision making and leadership aspects of the international hotel industry and to develop independent research and study skills which will be required when working at senior managerial level in the industry.

Syllabus content: Food and beverage management, food and beverage production, facilities and accommodation management, management accounting, human resource management, management research report.

Diploma in Travel Agency Management: Aims to provide students with a broad understanding of the operational aspects of travel agency management and airline ticketing, along with an understanding of the tourism industry.

Syllabus content: Travel geography, the tourism industry, travel agency operations, fares and ticketing levels one and two, computer reservations systems, travel agency law, business computing, sales and marketing, finance for the travel industry.

Advanced Diploma in Tour Operation and Management: Aims to provide an understanding of the managerial, decision making and leadership aspects of the international tour operation industry and to develop the independent research skills which will be required when working as a senior manager in the industry.

Syllabus content: Tour operations, tour management, resort representation, advanced fares calculation, advanced computer reservation systems, brochure and website design.

ADMISSIONS REQUIREMENTS:

The selection of students for admission to the courses at Diploma level is at the discretion of individual educational establishments. No specific educational qualifications are required, although it is desirable for applicants to have completed formal secondary education. For selection on to a course at Advanced Diploma level the applicant must have been successful in, or exempted from, the Diploma level course. Exemptions are granted at the discretion of the Confederation on the basis of previous education and experience.

Examination results and certificates

Each candidate will receive a record of performance in one of four grades for each component of the examination. The grades are Distinction, Credit, Pass and Referral. Qualifications are awarded to those candidates who achieve at least a pass grade in all components of their course.

GRADES OF MEMBERSHIP:

Student Member: This classification is for those who have enrolled on a CTHCM course at a registered CTHCM centre.

Associate Member (AMCTHCM): Awarded to those who have passed or been exempted from the Diploma level examination. Holders of equivalent qualifications acceptable to the Confederation may also be granted associate membership.

Member (MCTHCM): Awarded to those who have passed or been exempted from the Advanced Diploma level examinations, and hold at least two yrs' experience in the industry. Holders of equivalent qualifications acceptable to the Confederation may also be granted membership, as may those who have at least ten yrs relevant experience.

Fellow (FCTHCM): Awarded at the discretion of the Confederation to those who have achieved positions of significant responsibility in the industry, or who have made notable contributions to the work of the Confederation.

GUILD OF INTERNATIONAL PROFESSIONAL TOASTMASTERS

Life President: Ivor Spencer, 12 Little Bornes, Alleyn Park, London SE21 Tel: 020 8670 5585 Fax: 020 8670 0055 e-mail: ivor@ivorspencer.com Website: www.ivorspencer.com

Applicants must be professional toastmasters. They are required to complete a questionnaire, after which they may be invited to an oral exam conducted by the Executive Committee; menu cards must be submitted as evidence that applicants have been engaged as toastmasters.

In general, candidates must be of a calibre to enable them to officiate at major (eg royal and civic) occasions and to manage many types of public and social function.

Successful candidates are placed on a yr's probation, at the end of which there is a final exam consisting of written and oral tests. The Guild also awards its trophy to the Best After Dinner Speaker of the yr. Ivor Spencer created The Guild of International Professional Toastmasters Best After Dinner Speaker Award of the Yr, which has been established for thirty yrs. Its recipients have been former Prime Minister Baroness Thatcher, Lord Tonypandy, Bob Monkhouse, Sir Peter Ustinov and other very eminent speakers. The Award still continues, but the name has been changed to THE IVOR SPENCER BEST AFTER-DINNER SPEAKER AWARD OF THE YR.

HOTEL AND CATERING INTERNATIONAL MANAGEMENT ASSOCIATION

191 Trinity Road, London SW17 7HN Tel: 020 8672 4251 Fax: 020 8682 1707
e-mail: pds@hcima.co.uk Website: hcima.org.uk

Founded in 1971 from the merger between the Hotel and Catering Institute and the Institutional Management Association, the HCIMA is the professional body for managers in all sectors of the 'Hospitality' industry throughout the world.

MEMBERSHIP:

Fellow (FHCIMA): Captains of Industry – Members (MHCIMA) who have been members of the Association for over 10 yrs may apply to become HCIMA fellows.

Member (MHCIMA): Established managers – senior managers who have a considerable background of experience and a moderate amount of structured learning or graduates with appropriate management experience.

Associate (AHCIMA): Managers – experienced supervisors and managers with some structured learning or recent graduates with limited experience.

Intermediate: Aspiring Managers – supervisors with little or no structured learning or those with an appropriate qualification and limited experience.

Student: Students following HCIMA-accredited courses of study, GNVQ Intermediate/ Advanced, NVQ Level 3 and above.

HCIMA PROGRAMMES OF STUDY:

The HCIMA offers two programmes of study. These programmes are intended for hospitality professionals who wish to gain a qualification while continuing with full-time employment. The **HCIMA Professional Certificate** is designed for those working at supervisory level in the hospitality industry, with at least 2 yrs previous experience. The **HCIMA Professional Diploma** is designed for managers who normally hold a position involving section or departmental responsibilities. Courses are available at over 50 colleges in the UK, with the option of studying part-time, by distance learning, or for those with appropriate prior experience, on a 1 yr full-time basis for the Diploma. These programmes have been developed to provide a framework for continuing professional development. That is, experience and knowledge are consolidated to assist in decision-making and optimising job performance. Skills and competencies are recognised in each area of the hospitality industry and subject areas are designed to be accessible to all individuals working in this sector. Further details may be obtained from the HCIMA direct.

INTERNATIONAL INSTITUTE OF HOSPITALITY TOURISM & MANAGEMENT (IIHTM)

Secretary General: Mr R. A. Wright BA (Hons). DMS., MA., MEd.,

Registered Office: 43 Gower Street, London WC1E 6HH Tel: 020 7274 2166 Fax: 020 7274 1226 e-mail: Intloffice@clc-london.ac.uk

The Institute aims to provide a service to all categories of personnel in the Hotel, Catering, Tourism and Food Industries throughout the world. It offers recognised examinations and qualifications in all of these sectors. It maintains high academic standards through its Council, appointed from senior members of industry and education. Standards are also supported by consultation with industry and other examining bodies in the relevant fields. The Institute's courses are offered world-wide on the basis of equal opportunity for all.

The Institute has two areas of work

Membership – offering suitably qualified and experienced personnel the opportunity to obtain recognition for their qualification and experience via corporate membership of the Institute.

Educational qualifications – the Institute offers a variety of educational courses and examinations to be studied at recognised centres throughout the world. These are at different levels: successful completion can lead to awards ranging from **student members to fellowship award of the Institute.**

MEMBERSHIP:

Fellowship (FIIHTM): Awarded to distinguished members of the industry in recognition of their work and contribution to the various industries covered by the Institute.

Membership (MIIHTM): Awarded by the Institute to holders of the Institute's Higher Diploma and who have 2 yrs' experience in the industry. Holders of equivalent qualifications acceptable to the Institute may also be granted Membership. Candidates who have at least 10 yrs' experience in the industry in a relevant craft, supervisory or management position may also be granted Membership.

Associate Membership (AMIIHTM): Associate Membership will be awarded to holders of the Institute's Advanced Diploma. Holders of equivalent qualifications may also be granted Associate Membership.

Student Membership: Students who have completed secondary education and are enrolled on an Institute's Certificate level course at a recognised and registered centre must register as Student Members. On successful completion of their course they will be eligible to proceed to the appropriate category of membership.

EXAMINATIONS:

The Institute will provide course structures, syllabus, schemes of work and subject modules in a variety of areas. These are continuously updated, amended and additions made. Please contact the Institute for up-to-date material in any area that you are interested in. Please note that full course materials will only be sent to recognised centres whose registration is up to date.

The Institute will set and hold examinations at **Certificate**, **Diploma**, **Advanced Diploma** and **Higher Diploma** level at recognised centres throughout the world. These will be at times and intervals to suit the academic yr in each country. The examinations will be externally set, marked and moderated covering all subjects at the various levels. The Institute will also accredit and issue Certificates for approved single subject examinations. This process is in addition to the accreditation of full-time courses.

Current programmes of study are as follows:

1. **Certificate in Hotel, Restaurant and Tourism Management**
2. **Diploma in Hotel, Restaurant and Tourism Management**
3. **Advanced Diploma in Hotel, Restaurant and Tourism Management**
4. **Higher Diploma in Hotel, Restaurant and Tourism Management**
5. **Certificate in Travel & Tourism Management**
6. **Diploma in Travel & Tourism Management**
7. **Advanced Diploma in Travel & Tourism Management**

Syllabi, course structure, sample examination papers and course guidelines are available from the Institute.

University Qualifications

The following universities offer qualifications in Catering and Institutional Management and related subjects. Full details may be found in Part 4, under the entry for the appropriate university.

FIRST DEGREES AWARDED BY UNIVERSITIES

Abertay, Dundee; Anglia (Colchester Institute); Birmingham (Birmingham College of Food, Tourism and Creative Studies); Bournemouth; Brighton; Buckingham; Bucks. Coll.; Central Lancashire; Cheltenham & Gloucester; Derby; Doncaster; East Anglia (Suffolk College); Glasgow Caledonian; Hertfordshire; Huddersfield; Kent (Canterbury Christ Church University College); Lancaster (Blackpool and The Fylde College); Leeds Metropolitan; Luton; Manchester Metropolitan.; Middlesex; Napier; North London; Oxford Brookes; Plymouth; Portsmouth; Queen Margaret; Robert Gordon; Salford; Sheffield Hallam; South Bank; Strathclyde; Surrey; Thames Valley; Ulster; Wales (University of Wales Institute, Cardiff); Wolverhampton

HIGHER DEGREES AWARDED BY UNIVERSITIES

Birmingham (Birmingham College of Food, Tourism and Creative Studies); Bournemouth; Buckingham; Glasgow Caledonian; Huddersfield; Hull; Leeds Metropolitan; Manchester Metropolitan.; Oxford Brookes; Sheffield Hallam; Strathclyde; Surrey; Thames Valley; Ulster;

DIPLOMAS AWARDED BY UNIVERSITIES

Anglia (City College, Norwich); Anglia (Colchester Institute); Barnsley; Birmingham (Birmingham College of Food, Tourism and Creative Studies); Bournemouth; Bradford (Bradford & Ilkley Community College); Brighton; Bucks. Coll.; Durham (New College Durham); East Anglia (Suffolk College); Glamorgan; Greenwich; Huddersfield; Hull; Kent (Canterbury Christ Church University College); Lincolnshire (Grimsby College); Lincolnshire (Yorkshire Coast College); Middlesex; Napier; Salford; Strathclyde; Ulster; Wales (University of Wales Institute, Cardiff);

CERTIFICATES AWARDED BY UNIVERSITIES
Bournemouth; Brighton; Leeds Metropolitan; North London; Salford; Wales (University of Wales Institute, Cardiff)

OTHER COURSES AWARDED BY UNIVERSITIES
Leeds Metropolitan

POSTGRADUATE DIPLOMAS AWARDED BY UNIVERSITIES
Birmingham (Birmingham College of Food, Tourism and Creative Studies); Thames Valley

PROFESSIONAL COURSES AWARDED BY UNIVERSITIES
Manchester Metropolitan

National Certificates and Diplomas

BTEC National Certificates/Diplomas: Food and Environmental Health; Hotel Administration; Hotel, Catering and Institutional Operations; Hotel, Catering and Institutional Operations (Accommodation Operations); Hotel, Catering and Institutional Operations (Catering Operations); Hotel, Catering and Institutional Operations (Food and Drink Service); Hotel, Catering and Institutional Operations (Food Industry); Hotel, Catering and Institutional Operations (Food Preparation); Hotel, Catering and Institutional Operations (Front Office Operations); Hotel, Catering and Institutional Operations (Housekeeping and Catering); Hotel, Catering and Institutional Operations (Housekeeping); Hotel, Catering and Institutional Operations (Vegetarian Catering)

BTEC Higher National Certificates/Diplomas: Food Industry Management; Hotel, Catering & Institutional Management; Hotel, Catering & Institutional Management (Culinary Arts); Hotel, Catering and Institutional Management (Tourism)

NVQs

Level 1: Catering & Hospitality (Food Preparation and Cooking); Catering & Hospitality (Guest Service); Catering & Hospitality (Housekeeping); Catering & Hospitality (Kitchen Portering); Catering & Hospitality (Portering); Catering & Hospitality (Preparing and Serving Food); Catering & Hospitality (Reception); Catering & Hospitality (Serving Food and Drink – Bar); Catering & Hospitality (Serving Food and Drink – Counter / Take Away); Catering & Hospitality (Serving Food and Drink – Table); Catering & Hospitality (Serving Food and Drink – Vending)

Level 2: Catering & Hospitality (Food Preparation and Cooking); Catering & Hospitality (Guest Service); Catering & Hospitality (Housekeeping); Catering & Hospitality (Preparing and Serving Food); Catering & Hospitality (Reception); Catering & Hospitality (Serving Food and Drink – Bar); Catering & Hospitality (Serving Food and Drink – Function); Catering & Hospitality (Serving Food and Drink – Table)

Level 3: Catering & Hospitality (Food Preparation and Cooking – Kitchen and Larder Work); Catering & Hospitality (Food Preparation and Cooking – Patisserie and Confectionery); Catering & Hospitality (Food Preparation and Cooking – Vegetarian); Drink Service Advanced Craft; Drinks Dispense Systems (Installation and Maintenance); Food Service Advanced Craft; Kitchen Supervision; Multi-Skilled Hospitality Supervision; On-Licensed Premises Supervision; Restaurant Supervision

Level 4: Kitchen Management; Kitchen and Larder Specialist; Multi-Skilled Hospitality Management; On-Licensed Premises Management; Restaurant Management

SVQs

Level 1: Catering and Hospitality: Food Preparation & Cooking or Guest Service or Housekeeping or Kitchen Portering or Portering or Preparing & Serving Food or Reception or Serving Food & Drink – Bar or Serving Food & Drink – Take-away or Serving Food & Drink- Table or Serving Food & Drink – Vending.

Level 2: Catering & Hospitality: Food Preparation & Cooking or Guest Service or Housekeeping or Preparing and Serving Food – Quick Service or Reception or Serving Food & Drink – Bar or Serving Food and Drink – Function or Serving Food and Drink – Table.

Level 3: Catering and Hospitality: Food Preparation & Cooking – Kitchen & Larder Work or Food

Preparation & Cooking – Patisserie & Confectionery or Food Preparation & Cooking – Vegetarian or Drink Service Advanced Craft or Food Service Advanced Craft or Front Office Supervision or Kitchen Supervision or Multi-Skilled Hospitality or On Licensed Premises Supervision or Restaurant Supervision.

Level 4: Front Office Management or Kitchen Management or Multi-Skilled Hospitality Management or On Licensed Premises Management or Patisserie and Confectionery Specialist or Restaurant Management.

GNVQs
3728 Hospitality and Catering

Other Vocational Awarding Bodies
ABC: Book-keeping for Hotel and Catering Industry; Food Costing; Food Hygiene; Introductory Catering; Modern Cookery; Purchasing, Costing and Control for the Hotel and Catering Industry; Vegetarian Wholefood Cookery

Useful Addresses
Food and Drink Federation, 6 Catherine Street, London WC2B 5JJ Tel: 020 7836 2460 Fax: 020 7836 0580
Hospitality Training Foundation, International House, High Street, Ealing, London W5 5DB Tel: 020 8579 2400 Fax: 020 8840 6217

CERAMICS

University Qualifications
The following universities offer qualifications in Ceramics and related subjects. Full details may be found in Part 4, under the entry for the appropriate university.

FIRST DEGREES AWARDED BY UNIVERSITIES
Bath Spa; Bristol; Bucks. Coll.; Central England; Central Lancashire; De Montfort, Leicester; Dundee; Glasgow (Glasgow School of Art); Kent (Canterbury Christ Church University College); Kent (Kent Institute of Art & Design); Leeds; Leeds (Bretton Hall); London Institute (Camberwell College of Arts); London Institute (Central Saint Martins College of Art & Design); Loughborough; Manchester; Plymouth (Falmouth College of Arts); Sheffield; Staffordshire; Wales (Swansea Institute of Higher Education); Wales (University of Wales Institute, Cardiff); Westminster; Wolverhampton

HIGHER DEGREES AWARDED BY UNIVERSITIES
Bristol; Central England; Kent (Kent Institute of Art & Design); Leeds; Manchester; Royal College of Art; Staffordshire; Surrey Institute; UMIST; Wales (University of Wales Institute, Cardiff)

DIPLOMAS AWARDED BY UNIVERSITIES
Central England; Hertfordshire (West Herts College); Kent (Kent Institute of Art & Design); Staffordshire; Wales (Swansea Institute of Higher Education)

CERTIFICATES AWARDED BY UNIVERSITIES
Central England; Staffordshire

National Certificates and Diplomas
BTEC National Certificates/Diplomas: Design (Ceramics)
BTEC Higher National Certificates/Diplomas: Design (Ceramics); Design (Glass and Ceramics); Science (Ceramic Technology)

NVQs

Level 2: Ceramics Design; Decorating Ceramic Items (Automotive); Fire Ceramic Items; Forming Ceramic Items (Automotive); Heat Treatment; Retractories; Kiln Operations
Level 3: Heat Treatment

City & Guilds

0680 Industrial Ceramics

Useful Addresses

Association for Ceramic Training and Development, St James House, Webberly Lane, Longton, Stoke on Trent ST3 1RJ Tel: 01782 597016 Fax: 01782 597015

CHEMISTRY

Membership of Professional Institutions and Associations

THE OIL AND COLOUR CHEMISTS' ASSOCIATION

Priory House, 967 Harrow Road, Wembley, Middlesex HA0 2SF Tel: 020 8908 1086
Fax: 020 8908 1219 e-mail: Enquiries@occa.org.uk

MEMBERSHIP:
Fellows (FTSC): Must be not less than 33, have been Ordinary Members for not less than 10 yrs, be engaged in positions of superior responsibility in the coatings industry, *either* have been Associates of the professional grade for at least 8 yrs *or* have not less than 15 yrs' experience in the science or technology of coatings in positions of superior responsibility. They must have made an outstanding contribution to the field or have reached a position of eminence in the industry.
Associates (ATSC): May be appointed from among those who are or are not already Licentiates. The former must have practised the science or technology of surface coatings for at least 3 yrs, have superior skill and maturity in the profession, hold the CGLI Insignia Award *or* submit written evidence of work at an acceptable standard. Such candidates may be required to take an oral exam. Candidates who are not already Licentiates are considered in 2 categories. Those not less than 24 must be Ordinary Members and have been Ordinary Members or Students for 2 yrs, hold the GRSC or GInstP or an exempting degree, have approved experience and may be required to take an oral exam. Candidates not less than 30 must be Ordinary Members and have been Ordinary Members or Students for 2 yrs, have been engaged in relevant practice for at least 7 yrs, have attained positions of considerable standing in the industry and must usually take an oral exam.
Licentiates (LTSC): Must be Ordinary Members and have been Ordinary Members or Students for 1 yr, be at least 22 and satisfy 1 of the several specified requirements. Candidates may be required to take an oral exam and will be required to submit written evidence on a subject directly associated with the science and technology of surface coatings.
Students: Are usually less than 25 and are engaged on relevant courses of training.
Ordinary Members: Are chemists and other scientifically trained persons, or persons technically trained in the oil and colour industries who comply with the standard of competence laid down by the Council.

THE ROYAL SOCIETY OF CHEMISTRY

Burlington House, Piccadilly, London W1V 0BN Tel: 020 7437 8656 Fax: 020 7437 8883
e-mail: education@rsc.org Website: www.rsc.org or www.chemsoc.org

MEMBERSHIP:
Fellow (CChem FRSC): Fellows must have at least 5 yrs' approved experience in a senior position since being admitted as a Member (or since being qualified for admission). Non-members who do

not possess the necessary academic qualification but who have made outstanding contributions to chemistry or the advancement of the profession may be admitted to Fellowship.

Member (CChem, MRSC): Requirements are Graduateship, with at least 4 yrs' subsequent approved experience. Entry normally follows a 2 yr period of structured assessment. Fellows and Members have the additional designation Chartered Chemist (CChem).

Graduate (GRSC): This is a qualification comparable to a good honours degree in chemistry. Candidates must have obtained at least a second-class Hons degree on a course accredited by the Society.

Licentiate (LRSC): This category is for chemists who have the equivalent of a pass degree in chemistry. The requirements are an accredited degree including chemistry as a main subject.

Student Member: This category is for those who are undergoing approved education in preparation for professional membership.

Associate Member: This is a category of membership open to those who share an interest in chemistry and in the advancement of the science or its practitioners through the activities of the Society. No formal qualifications are required and no designatory letters are awarded.

EXAMINATIONS:

Since July 1994, exams for GRSC are no longer available. Admission to that category of membership is via an accredited Hons degree.

Masters in Chemical Analysis (MChemA): For intending public analysts or their deputies. The Society offers specialist qualifications for Qualified Persons in relation to the Pharmaceutical Directive 75/319/EEC, and also in health, safety, environmental auditing, analytical and water chemistry through a registration function.

SOCIETY OF COSMETIC SCIENTISTS

GT House, 24/26 Rothesay Road, Luton, Beds LU1 1QX Tel: 01582 726661 Fax: 01582 405217
e-mail: ifscc.scs@btinternet.com Website: www.scs.org.uk
The object of the Society, formed in 1948, is to promote the status of the cosmetic industry, by means of lectures, symposia, publications and education.

MEMBERSHIP:

Honorary Members: Are elected.

Members: At the date of their election Members must possess the following qualifications: a degree granted by a British university in Chemistry, Chemical Engineering, Pharmacy, Medicine, Biology, Physics or related sciences; or the Diploma in Cosmetic Science awarded by the Society; or an equivalent of such degrees as recognised by Council; (Advice on degree equivalents will be sought from other scientific bodies, eg University of London, Royal Society of Chemists, Pharmaceutical Society of Great Britain); At least 1 yr of experience essentially devoted to some scientific aspect(s) of cosmetics and/or technologically closely related products.

Associates: At the date of their election Associates must possess 1 of the following qualifications: BTEC higher certificate or BTEC higher diploma in an appropriate scientific subject; or a recognised equivalent, together with at least 1 yr of experience essentially devoted to some scientific aspect(s) of cosmetics and/or technologically closely related products, or; an educational standard in 2 scientific subjects of the GCE A level or a recognised equivalent of such qualifications, together with at least 3 yrs' experience essentially devoted to some aspect(s) of cosmetics and/or technologically closely related products, or; an educational standard in 2 scientific subjects of the GCE O level or GCSE together with at least 5 yrs' experience essentially devoted to some scientific aspect(s) of cosmetics and/or technologically closely related products, or; at least 7 yrs' experience in cosmetics and toiletries or closely related products, or; any other qualification which, in the opinion of Council, makes the candidate worthy of Associate Membership.

Students: Are defined as: those pursuing the Society's Diploma or other educational course leading ultimately to Membership or Associate Membership of the Society, or; those who, in the opinion of the Membership Committee, have the required academic qualifications and who are gaining, or actively seeking to gain, approved experience and expecting admission to Membership or Associate Membership of the Society, at the time of their election to Student Membership, Students must have a minimum qualification of 2 scientific subjects of the General Certificate of Secondary Education, Ordinary Level, or a recognised equivalent. Membership of this grade is temporary: it covers only the period that a candidate for membership is under training. All Student Memberships are reviewed at the end of 3 yrs. Re-election is only permitted if the Membership Committee is satisfied of the Student's ultimate intention to become a member; all Bye-Laws concerning Student Membership are subject to the discretion of Council.

EXAMINATION:

Diploma: The Society runs a 1yr PT day-release course – the Certificate Course in Cosmetic Science, in conjunction with the London College of Fashion, leading to the Diploma in Cosmetic Science. Also available by distance learning.

University Qualifications

The following universities offer qualifications in Chemistry and related subjects. Full details may be found in Part 4, under the entry for the appropriate university.

FIRST DEGREES AWARDED BY UNIVERSITIES

Aberdeen; Abertay, Dundee; Anglia; Aston; Bath; Belfast; Birmingham; Bradford; Brighton; Bristol; Brunel; Central Lancashire; Coventry; De Montfort, Leicester; Derby; Dundee; Durham; East Anglia; East London; Edinburgh; Essex; Exeter; Glamorgan; Glasgow; Glasgow Caledonian; Greenwich; Heriot-Watt; Hertfordshire; Huddersfield; Hull; Keele; Kent; Kingston; Lancaster; Leeds; Leicester; Liverpool; Liverpool John Moores; London (Birkbeck, University of London); London (Imperial College of Science, Technology & Medicine); London (King's College London); London (Queen Mary & Westfield College (incorporating St Bartholomew's and the Royal London School of Medicine & Dentistry)); London (Royal Holloway); London (University College (UCL)); Loughborough; Luton; Manchester; Manchester Metropolitan.; Napier; Newcastle; North London; Northampton; Northumbria; Nottingham; Nottingham Trent; OU (NESCOT); Oxford; Oxford Brookes; Paisley; Plymouth; Portsmouth; Reading; Robert Gordon; Salford; Salford (Halton College); Sheffield; Sheffield Hallam; South Bank; Southampton; St Andrews; Staffordshire; Stirling; Stockport; Strathclyde; Sunderland; Surrey; Sussex; Teesside; Ulster; UMIST; Wales (Cardiff University); Wales (University of Wales, Aberystwyth); Wales (University of Wales, Bangor); Wales (University of Wales, Swansea); Warwick; Westminster; Wolverhampton; York

HIGHER DEGREES AWARDED BY UNIVERSITIES

Aberdeen; Anglia; Aston; Belfast; Birmingham; Bradford; Bristol; Cambridge; Central Lancashire; Coventry; De Montfort, Leicester; Durham; East Anglia; Edinburgh; Essex; Exeter; Glamorgan; Glasgow; Glasgow Caledonian; Greenwich; Heriot-Watt; Heriot-Watt (Scottish Borders Campus); Hertfordshire; Huddersfield; Hull; Keele; Kent; Kingston; Lancaster; Leeds; Leicester; Liverpool; Liverpool John Moores; London (Birkbeck, University of London); London (Imperial College of Science, Technology & Medicine); London (King's College London); London (Queen Mary & Westfield College (incorporating St Bartholomew's and the Royal London School of Medicine & Dentistry)); London (Royal Holloway); London (University College (UCL)); Loughborough; Manchester; Manchester Metropolitan.; Newcastle; Northumbria; Oxford; Paisley; Reading; Salford; Sheffield Hallam; Southampton; St Andrews; Staffordshire; Surrey; Sussex; Teesside; UMIST; Wales (North East Wales Institute); Wales (University of Wales, Bangor); Warwick; Westminster; Wolverhampton; York

DIPLOMAS AWARDED BY UNIVERSITIES

Aberdeen; Abertay, Dundee; Coventry; De Montfort, Leicester; Edinburgh; Exeter; Glamorgan; Glasgow; Greenwich; Hertfordshire; Huddersfield; Hull; Kent; Kingston; Lancaster; London (Birkbeck, University of London); Manchester; Newcastle; Paisley; Salford; St Andrews; Staffordshire; Teesside; Wolverhampton

CERTIFICATES AWARDED BY UNIVERSITIES

Bradford (Bradford & Ilkley Community College); Brunel; London (Birkbeck, University of London); London (Goldsmiths College); Salford; Southampton; Staffordshire; Wales (University of Wales, Bangor); Wolverhampton

National Certificates and Diplomas

BTEC Higher National Certificates/Diplomas: Applied Chemistry; Science (Applied Chemistry and Scientific Instrumentation); Science (Chemistry and Computing); Science (Chemistry with Biology); Science (Chemistry)

Scotland

SQA HNC: Applied Chemistry; Applied Chemistry with Business Studies; Chemistry; Chemistry (Colour Materials); Chemistry with Instrumental Analysis.
SQA HND: Applied Chemistry; Applied Chemistry with Business Studies; Applied Chemistry with Environmental Studies; Chemistry; Chemistry with Environmental Studies; Chemistry with Instrumental Analysis.
SQA (Advanced Diploma) in Chemistry Analysis with Environmental Studies

City & Guilds

7550 Science Laboratory Assistants

Useful Addresses

Chemical Industries Association, Kings Buildings, Smith Square, London SW1P 3JJ Tel: 020 7834 3399 Fax: 020 7834 4469

CHIROPODY
Membership of Professional Institutions and Associations

OXFORD SCHOOL OF CHIROPODISTS AND PODIATRY

6 Wesley Lane, Bicester, Oxon OX6 7JU Tel: 01869 248538 Fax: 01869 322667

MEMBERSHIP:
All successful students are eligible to become full members of The Institute of Chiropodists and Podiatrists.

EXAMS/QUALIFICATIONS:
Students have to sit three theory examinations (Preliminary, Intermediate and Final). The Final exam is set and conducted by the Institute of Chiropodists and Podiatrists. Students also have to take a Final Practical Assessment which is also conducted by an Inspector from the Institute of Chiropodists and Podiatrists. All successful students gain the qualification
Diploma in Surgical Chiropody – DSCh(Ox). Exemptions are possible where prior learning is given credit. The training course covers both theoretical and practical aspects of chiropody and takes 18 mths to complete. The theoretical part of the course is completed by distance learning as well as attendance of training days at the school. Students must complete a minimum of 300 hrs' practical training, including not only clinical work but training in other environments.

THE BRITISH CHIROPODY AND PODIATRY ASSOCIATION

New Hall, Bath Road, Maidenhead, Berkshire SL6 4LA Tel: 01628 632440 Fax: 01628 674483

MEMBERSHIP:
Fellow (FSSCh): A fellow has to have been in practice for 5 yrs and completed the Advanced course on Orthotics and Biomechanics. He must also be elected by the appropriate Council of the Association.
Member (MSSCh): Obtained by having completed both the theory and practice of chiropody in accordance with The Open College of Chiropody and Podiatry's curriculum. Any member, MSSCh or FSSCh, automatically becomes a Member of the British Chiropody and Podiatry Association (MBChA).

THE INSTITUTE OF CHIROPODISTS AND PODIATRISTS

27 Wright Street, Southport, Merseyside PR9 0TL Tel: 01704 546141 Fax: 01704 500477
e-mail: secretary@inst-chiropodist.org.uk Website: www.inst-chiropodist.org.uk
Institute Chiropody Course: The theory is conducted by distance learning with the practical element totalling six wks full time at the Institute School in Sheffield. Students have access to a tutor helpline, attend a seminar and pass theoretical examinations before commencing the practical. Successful candidates are eligible for full membership (MInstChP) of the Institute. The Institute of Chiropodists and Podiatrists is the only body offering Chiropody courses that are accredited by the Open and Distance Learning Quality Council.

Applications for **Membership (MInstChP)** are also considered from state registered chiropodists, persons who have been in full time practice for at least 3 yrs and pass a written, practical and oral exam and from graduates of the Institute Chiropody Course.

The **Diploma in Chiropodial Medicine (DChM)** is granted to members who have completed 6 modules on chiropodial subjects, including Physical Therapy and Biomechanics. Each of Modules 1 to 4 has at least 1 seminar (optional) and modules 5 and 6 have 2 weekend seminars with practical studies (compulsory). A recognised First Aid Certificate must be obtained for Module 4. Modules 1 to 4 have written exams and Modules 5 and 6 have practical and written exams.

THE SOCIETY OF CHIROPODISTS AND PODIATRISTS

53 Welbeck Street, London W1M 7HE Tel: 020 7486 3381 Fax: 020 7935 6359
e-mail: enq@scpod.org Website: www.feetforlife.org

MEMBERSHIP:

Member (MChS): To gain membership of the Society, applicants must have completed the Society's 3 yr FT course of training leading to the award of its Diploma in Podiatric Medicine (DPodM) coupled with a first degree in podiatry or podiatric medicine approved by the Society (usually a BSc (Hons) Podiatry) and by the Chiropodists Board of the Council for Professions Supplementary to Medicine; or, in the case of those holding foreign qualifications, they must have successfully applied for, and have received, state registration from the said Chiropodists Board (SRCh).

Fellow (FChS): Awarded solely on the grounds of superior professional ability and experience and is attainable by exam only. Candidates are not eligible to sit the final clinical exam for Fellowship until they have completed a minimum of 4 assessed modules of post-registration study approved by the Society's Fellowship Panel.

Surgery (FPodS): Fellow of the Surgical Faculty of the College of Podiatrists. Members of the Society of Chiropodists and Podiatrists who complete the Society's PG course of training in foot surgery are awarded Fellowship of the Surgical Faculty of the Society's College of Podiatrists when they pass their final practical exam. Fellows of the Surgical Faculty are qualified to undertake more advanced skin and soft tissue surgery than are non-Fellows as well as a range of surgical procedures on the foot involving bone and tendon.

EXAMINATIONS:

Teacher's Certificate of the Society of Chiropodists: This qualification is for State Registered Chiropodists and Members of the Society and consists of 2 written papers and oral tests on the principles of teaching and theory of chiropody. Exemption from the teaching section will be granted to those who hold a C&G Teachers Certificate or other appropriate qualification and who have been employed in a School of Chiropody on a regular basis for at least 1 yr.

Training: All the schools now teach a BSc (Hons) in Podiatry. All the schools are departments of Universities or colleges of higher education. Students should be at least 18 at the start of the course and should have attained 5 GCE or GCSE passes (grades A, B or C) to include English language and preferably 2 science subjects. Normally, 2 of the passes should be at A level (or 4 at Advanced Supplementary level). Students with the Scottish Certificate of Education should have attained 5 standard grade passes (grades 1 to 3) of which 3 should be higher grade passes (grades A to C). Where students have passes in excess of the minimum requirements, the number together with the grades of the passes, may be taken into account in assessing their entry qualifications. Qualifications deemed to be equivalent may be taken into account. NB: These are minimum requirements. Individual institutions may lay down higher entry requirements, and prospective students are advised to make early contact with the listed institutions of their choice. Institutions have their own requirements for mature students, whose qualifications and experience are judged on their merits.

Courses of training are offered at the following:

England

Birmingham School of Chiropody and Podiatric Medicine, Matthew Boulton College; Department of Podiatry, Brighton University; Durham School of Podiatric Medicine; Huddersfield School of Podiatry, University of Huddersfield; London Foot Hospital and School of Podiatric Medicine, University College London; Northampton School of Podiatry, Nene University College; Northern College of Chiropody, University of Salford; Plymouth School of Podiatry, University of Plymouth; Wessex School of Podiatry, LSU College of Higher Education, Southampton

Wales
Cardiff School of Podiatry, Cardiff Institute of Higher Education
Scotland
Edinburgh School of Podiatry, Queen Margaret University College; Glasgow School of Podiatric Medicine, Glasgow Caledonian University
Northern Ireland
Northern Ireland School of Podiatric Medicine, The Queen's University Belfast

CHIROPRACTIC

Membership of Professional Institutions and Associations

BRITISH CHIROPRACTIC ASSOCIATION

Blagrave House, 17 Blagrave Street, Reading, Berkshire RG1 1QB Tel: 0118 950 5950 Fax: 0118 958 8946 e-mail: enquiries@chiropratic-uk.co.uk Website: www.chiropractic-uk.co.uk.

Chiropractors are accepted as members of the Association after qualifying from a FT course of at least 4 yrs at an accredited college of chiropractic. Members are categorised in Full, Semi-Active, Provisional, or Associate gradings and have to abide by the Association's Code of Ethics and Bye Laws.

TRAINING:
The only internationally recognised training in the United Kingdom is carried out at present at the Anglo-European College of Chiropractic, Parkwood Rd, Bournemouth, Dorset BH5 2DF Tel: 01202 436200 and now leads on qualification to a MSc(Hons) Chiropractic in Sciences. Courses commence in September each yr and the current minimum educational requirements for entry are 3 A Level passes which must include biology or zoology and chemistry and 5 GCE/GCSE Level passes which must include English and physics. A prospectus of the course may be obtained from the Anglo-European College of Chiropractic in Bournemouth. In 1997, the University of Glamorgan established an undergraduate 4 yr full time course leading to a BSc in Chiropractic, and a 2 yr MSc course was established at the University of Surrey. The profession is now regulated by statute by the General Chiropractic Council which opened a register in June 1999, to which all practitioners will need to apply for registration by June 2001.

University Qualifications

The following universities offer qualifications in Chiropractic and related subjects. Full details may be found in Part 4, under the entry for the appropriate university.

FIRST DEGREES AWARDED BY UNIVERSITIES

Glamorgan; Westminster

HIGHER DEGREES AWARDED BY UNIVERSITIES

De Montfort, Leicester (De Montfort University Bedford); Surrey

CERTIFICATES AWARDED BY UNIVERSITIES

Loughborough

THE CHURCHES

The Anglican Communion

THE CHURCH IN WALES

The Board of the Ministry of the Church in Wales, 39 Cathedral Road, Cardiff CF11 9XF
Tel: 029 20231638 Fax: 029 20387835 e-mail: ministry@rb.churchinwales.org.uk

The Church in Wales expects candidates for ordination to satisfy the requirements of recognised theological courses.

University graduates usually spend at least 2 yrs at a theological college and, if they are non-theological graduates, are encouraged to study for a university degree or diploma in Theology. Non-graduate candidates must have obtained at least 5 passes at GCSE and normally study for a university diploma in Theology or a degree in Theology if they have obtained the necessary grades at GCE A level. These requirements may be modified in the case of older candidates.

THE CHURCH OF ENGLAND

Ministry Division of The Archbishops' Council, Church House, Great Smith Street, London SW1P 3NZ Tel: 020 7898 1399 Fax: 020 7898 1421 e-mail: mark.sowerby@mindiv.c-of-e.org.uk Website: www.cofe.anglican.org

ORDAINED MINISTRY:

Candidates under 30: Grads in theology spend 2 yrs on a FT course at a theological college and have to fulfil the Bishops' requirements. Non-grads and Grads in subjects other than theology are required to spend 3 yrs on a FT course at a theological college and have to fulfil the Bishops' requirements.

Candidates aged 30-49: (a) Candidates for the ordained ministry (stipendiary and non-stipendiary) are required to do either a 2-yr FT course at a theological college or a 3-yr PT course. (b) Candidates for permanent non-stipendiary ministry are required to do a 3-yr PT course.

Candidates aged 50 and over: As for candidates 30-49 except that the exact nature of training is at the discretion of the Bishop.

QUALIFICATIONS:

Church's Ministry Certificate: Those who have completed to the satisfaction of the Ministry Division Moderators a course of study approved by the Ministry Division are entitled to a Certificate. A booklet *Theological Training* describes the colleges and courses which offer approved training. This may be obtained from the Ministry Division.

OTHER CHURCH OF ENGLAND QUALIFICATIONS:

Church of England Readers' Certificate: This is the normal qualification for Readers who have completed a nationally moderated 3 yr course. Contact: Tel: 0207 898 1419, E-mail: Wendy.Thorpe@mindiv.c-of-e.org.uk WWW: www.readers.cofe.anglican.org

Lambeth Studentship in Theology: A Diploma of equivalent standard to an Hons degree, open to men and women baptised in any denomination. Non-residential, under personal supervision. Holders of a recognised Theology qualification may work for the Diploma by thesis, others take a 2-part exam, some of which is done by prepared essays. Valuable for further study for clergy and others, or as a way of acquiring a first qualification in Theology. Contact: Hon Sec The Revd Canon Martin Kitchen PhD, 3 The College, Durham DH1 3EQ E-mail: martin@3college.sonnet.co.uk

Church Army: A recognised training course for pastoral work and evangelism for men and women at the Church Army's own college in Sheffield. Details from the Candidates' Secretary, Church Army, Independents Road, Blackheath, London SE3 9LG.

THE SCOTTISH EPISCOPAL CHURCH

The Theological Institute, Old Coates House, 32 Manor Place, Edinburgh EH3 7EB Tel: 0131 220 2272 Fax: 0131 220 2294 e-mail: tisec@scotland.anglican.org

Candidates for stipendiary and non-stipendiary ordained and lay ministry are assessed according to the Provincial Curriculum for ministerial training, which is designed to take account of previous and concurrent theological study, as, for example, at a University. Training may be undertaken FT or PT with the Theological Institute.

FT is normally for 3 yrs, in conjunction with a BD at Edinburgh University, or 2 yrs for theological graduates. PT training is for 3 yrs at the Institute's Regional Centres.

There are no formal entry qualifications, but students must be sponsored by Bishops' Selections.

The Free Churches

BAPTIST UNION OF SCOTLAND

Baptist House, 14 Aytoun Road, Glasgow G41 5RT Tel: 0141 423 6169
e-mail: admin@scottishbaptist.org.uk

TRAINING:

There are 2 basic forms of Ministerial Training Scheme: Collegiate and Non-Collegiate.

Collegiate courses are provided at the Scottish Baptist College, 12 Aytoun Road, Pollokshields, Glasgow G41 5RN. Tel: 0141 424 0747.The College course normally lasts 4 yrs leading to the award of the College's degree: BD in Theology & Pastoral Studies. A Diploma of Pastoral Studies is also available after a 1 yr course for students already qualified in academic theology. Non-Collegiate candidates holding a University theological or divinity degree will normally be required to undertake Homiletics, Pastoral Theology, Baptist History and Baptist Principles. Candidates who have obtained the Cambridge CRS will normally be required to undertake a further 2 yrs of General Theological Training including the Diploma of Pastoral Studies. Candidates with a Bible College Diploma will be required to take a further 3 yrs of General Theological Training including the Diploma of Pastoral Studies. In some special circumstances a candidate is allowed to qualify by examinable Correspondence Courses together with Baptist History and Baptist Principles. Details of these Courses are only available through the Superintendent after the applicant has been accepted as a candidate.

All candidates, collegiate or non-collegiate, are required after settlement to do further guided reading and essay work. For the college-trained candidates, this is prescribed by the Principal. For non-collegiate candidates, the work is set through the Superintendent of the Baptist Union of Scotland.

Only after successful completion of this work and general approval by the Ministerial Recognition Committee that proof of ministry has been given is a person's name admitted to the Accredited List of Ministers.

The College also offers a Certificate and Diploma of Higher Learning in Theology after yrs 1 and 2 of the degree course. The College's Degree, Certificate and Diploma are validated by the University of Paisley.

BRISTOL BAPTIST COLLEGE

The Promenade, Clifton Down, Clifton, Bristol BS8 3NJ Tel: 0117 946 7050 Fax: 0117 946 7787 e-mail: admin@bristol-baptist.ac.uk Website: www.bristol-baptist.ac.uk

Candidates for the Baptist Ministry must have reached a satisfactory level of education. It will normally be required that they pursue a course of preparation at one of the affiliated theological colleges.

TRAINING AT A BAPTIST THEOLOGICAL COLLEGE:

The length of training varies between 3 and 4 yrs. The colleges work in association with a university and students normally work for a degree in theology. Candidates for training for Baptist-Ministry must obtain the prior recommendation of the Association to which their local church belongs. The colleges are as follows: Bristol Baptist Coll, The Promenade, Clifton Down, Clifton, Bristol BS8 3NJ; Northern Baptist Coll, Brighton Grove, Rusholme, Manchester M14 5JP; Regent's Park Coll, Oxford OX1 2LB; Spurgeon's Coll, 189 South Norwood Hill, London SE25 6DJ; North Wales Baptist Coll, Ffordd Ffriddeodd, Bangor (Baptist Union of Wales); South Wales Baptist Coll, Cardiff CF2 3UR (Baptist Union of Wales); Baptist Theological Coll of Scotland, Glasgow G41 5RT (Baptist Union of Scotland).

A PRESCRIBED COURSE OF STUDY:

Candidates for the Accredited Ministry of the Baptist Union who have not been trained at a Baptist College are required to attend a residential Selection Conference which is usually held annually. A candidate attending such a conference must first have obtained a minimum of 5 GCSE passes and 1 A level pass together with a public exam in Theology such as the Cambridge Certificate/Diploma in Religious Studies, and have been commended by his/her local Association. A successful applicant is enrolled as a probationer for a period of 2 yrs, and required to fulfil other criteria additional to the above.

THE CHURCH OF SCOTLAND

Church of Scotland Offices, 121 George Street, Edinburgh EH2 4YN Tel: 0131 225 5722 Fax: 0131 220 3113

Director of Vocational Services, Board of Ministry

Qualifications for those under 40: University entrance qualifications appropriate to their age.

Those over 23 normally require 3 Higher Passes in the SCE exams in subjects acceptable to the University. Technical qualifications, eg HNC, may contribute to this. Those over 40 should be of good education and experience.

Length of Course: For those who begin their studies before their 23rd birthday – 6 yrs; for those 23–30 when they start – 5 yrs; for those 31–40 – 4 yrs; for those over 40 – each case considered individually.

Courses: Regular Course – a primary degree course followed by 3 yrs' study for the BD degree at the Faculty of Divinity of a Scottish University. Alternative Course – Study for the BD as a first degree (4 yrs) at a Faculty of Divinity of a Scottish University followed by 1 or 2 yrs' further study (according to age), the nature of which must be approved by the Committee on Education and Training of the Church of Scotland.

Application: Intending candidates should make formal application to the above address. They must have been communicant members of the Church of Scotland for at least 3 yrs, be accepted by the Committee on Vocational Guidance after interview by extended interview process and subsequently be nominated as candidates for the Ministry by their local Presbytery. During the theological course candidates are expected to participate in three supervised placements in parish and non-parish settings. On completion of their academic course, a further 15 mths full time placement is required prior to ordination as a Minister of Word and Sacrament.

METHODIST CHURCH IN IRELAND

Board of Examiners, Secretary: Rev Dr W.B. Fletcher BD, 33a Ardenlee Avenue, Belfast BT6 0AA
Candidates for training must normally have the standard of general education for university entrance. They must be accredited Local Preachers of the Methodist Church. Candidates are examined by written papers in Holy Scripture and Theology and by oral aptitude and personality tests.

After admission to training, candidates normally spend six yrs before Ordination, the first three being in Edgehill Theological College, Belfast. The subjects of the course for a diploma or degree of Queen's University of Belfast include New Testament Greek, Hebrew, the English Bible, Theology, Church History, Pastoral Psychology, Homiletics. Following college three yrs are spent as a probationer Minister working on a circuit under a superintendent Minister. During probation the candidate continues study within a tutorial system and is examined by continuous assessment. Special regulations apply to mature candidates. Regulations are identical for men and women.

THE METHODIST CHURCH

Formation in Ministry Office, (Initial Development of Ministries), 25 Marylebone Road, London NW1 5JR Tel: 020 7486 5502 e-mail: Foundationtraining@methodistchurch.org.uk
Candidates for Diaconal or Presbyteral Ministry in the Methodist Church start their preparation by obtaining the consent of their District Vocations Committee to enter the process of training and personal development called Foundation Training. Foundation Training requires one yr (full time) or 2 yrs (part time) to complete. During or after the process a person may apply to become a candidate for ordained ministry. The process of selection takes six mths (and is usually concurrent with the end period of Foundation Training). To be allowed to enter into training for Presbyteral Ministry following Foundation Training, a candidate must also have been recognised as a trained Local Preacher which involves taking the Methodist Local Preachers' Training Course, Faith & Worship. Accepted candidates receive one or two further yrs of theological training. This training may be in a residential or non-residential training institution and in most cases will lead to a degree or diploma qualification in theology or ministry. Upon completion of training, a candidate will be appointed to serve as a Methodist Minister for 2 yrs on probation before ordination.

The residential colleges are as follows: The Queen's College, Somerset Road, Edgbaston, Birmingham B15 2QY (an ecumenical college affiliated to the University of Birmingham); Wesley House, Jesus Lane, Cambridge (affiliated to the University of Cambridge); Wesley College, Henbury Hill, Westbury on Trym, Bristol BS10 7QD (affiliated to the University of Bristol); Hartley Victoria College, Luther King House, Brighton Grove, Rusholme, Manchester M14 5JP (affiliated to the University of Manchester); Wesley Study Centre, 55 The Avenue, Durham DH1 4EB (affiliated to the University of Durham). Non-residential training is available through locally based courses throughout England, Scotland and Wales.

THE MORAVIAN CHURCH IN GREAT BRITAIN AND IRELAND

Moravian Church House, 5-7 Muswell Hill, London N10 3TJ Tel: 020 8883 3409
Fax: 020 8365 3371
e-mail: moravianchurchhouse@btinternet.com Website: www.moravian.org.uk
Candidates for Moravian Church Service must be members of The Moravian Church and would normally be expected to have completed the Lay Training Course. They should make an initial application to the Provincial Board of the Moravian Church. Their qualifications are examined by the Church Service Advisory Board, which reports on them to the Provincial Board, with whom the final decision rests.
Normally the standard of general education should be that of a university degree or Certificate and the knowledge of special subjects required for the work of the Ministry should be that of a university divinity degree or Certificate together with a thorough acquaintance with the history, principles and methods of the Moravian Church. Candidates who have completed any part of a general or divinity course before applying to enter the Ministry of the Moravian Church are only required to take such further training as each may need. Special study courses may be prepared for mature candidates.
Candidates requiring a full course are trained at a suitable Theological college or university, often an Anglican College, in the light of the Fetter Lane Agreement between the two churches. In addition to this basic training, candidates receive further subsequent guidance for the Ministry during a period of supervised service under the direction of experienced Ministers.
A further class of non-stipendiary Ministers has been established for those who wish to serve on a non-maintained basis. Training varies according to candidates' needs. In all cases applications should be made to the address given above.

THE PRESBYTERIAN CHURCH IN IRELAND

The Director of Ministerial Students, 26 College Green, Belfast BT7 1LN Tel: 028 90316831
Fax: 028 90580040 e-mail: dms@union.org.uk
Qualifications: Under 30 – a non-theological degree; over 30 but under 40 (as reckoned on the 1st October following application) – either a non-theological degree or 2 yrs non-graduating Arts or 4 modules of part-time B.D. study or 6 modules of part-time study in Humanities acceptable to the Board of Studies; over 40 – not normally accepted.
Courses: 3 yrs' theological study at Union Theological College, Belfast, or another university/college recognised by the General Assembly. Subjects include: Old Testament, including Elementary Biblical Hebrew; New Testament, including Elementary Hellenistic Greek; Church History; Systematic Theology; Philosophy of Religion, Christian Ethics and Comparative Religion; Practical Theology. Theological studies are followed by a 2 yr period as a probationer (1 yr if over 35 yrs of age).
Method of Application: Candidates obtain an application form from the Director of Ministerial Students, and return same before 15 December in any yr. Candidates then seek the commendation of their Kirk Session and the nomination of their local Presbytery. Nominated candidates attend a Mini summer School and residential interview in June, preceded by psychological and vocational tests and followed by an Applicants' Course of distance learning and a congregational placement. Suitable candidates are recommended by the Board of Studies to the General Assembly of the following June. Women are eligible on the same basis as men.

THE PRESBYTERIAN CHURCH OF WALES

United Theological College, King Street, Aberystwyth, Ceredigion SY23 2LT Tel: 01970 624574
Fax: 01970 626350 e-mail: esl998@aber.ac.uk
Candidates for the ministry in the Presbyterian Church of Wales are trained at the United Theological College, Aberystwyth (Tel: 01970 624574). The College, which is a member of the Aberystwyth/Lampeter School of Theology of the University of Wales, offers courses leading to the BD, the BTh,(3 yrs full-time), the MPhil, MTh and PhD degrees of the University of Wales. It is open to both ministerial students and to any who wish to qualify for allied professions (teaching, social science, etc). Candidates for the BTh degree should normally have attained at least 2 subjects at GCSE/A Level and candidates for the BD degree should normally have attained at least 2 subjects at GCSE/A Level at Grade C or the equivalent.

Candidates for the ministry in the Presbyterian Church of Wales are required to spend a fourth yr in pastoral training during which instruction is given in Pastoral Work and Counselling, Preaching and Sermon Preparation, the Theory and Practice of Worship, Christian Education, Youth and Children's Work, Mission and Evangelism, Prayer and the Spiritual Life.

THE SALVATION ARMY

UK Headquarters, 101 Queen Victoria Street, London EC4P 4EP Tel: 020 7236 5222
Salvation Army officers engaged in FT service are ordained ministers of religion, and are commissioned following a 2-yr period of residential training at the William Booth Memorial Training College, Denmark Hill, London SE5 8BQ. This course is part of a comprehensive study programme, which includes 1 yr's preparatory study by distance learning means and up to 5 yrs of post-commissioning in-service training, including short residential seminars.
Officers may be appointed to corps (church) work, to social service centres (for which additional professional qualifications are required) or to administrative posts.

QUALIFICATIONS FOR ADMISSION:
Single men and women and married couples over 18 are accepted for training following recommendation by local SA centres and attendance at an assessment conference. Older people can be accepted for training if they will be able to complete 15 yrs or more of service following their commissioning. For those over 40 there is the possibility of an alternative pattern of training involving distance learning, placements and short residential periods. Although academic achievement is taken into account, there are no formal min requirements.
Other courses: The Salvation Army Counselling Service offers training modules. Various training courses relating to SA Christian work, youth work and social service are provided. Correspondence courses are also provided by the Training College in a variety of subjects related to theology and Christian ministry.

THE SCOTTISH CONGREGATIONAL COLLEGE

The Principal, 340 Cathedral Street, Glasgow G1 2BQ Tel: 0141 332 7667
The Scottish Congregational College manages training for Christian ministry mainly in Scottish Congregational Churches. Candidates normally follow an approved course of theological training in a Scottish university or a theological institute with further professional and practical training under the supervision of the college. The college also is involved in the continuing professional development of ministers, lay training and adult education. Information can be obtained from the address above.

THE UNITARIAN AND FREE CHRISTIAN CHURCHES

Essex Hall, 1-6 Essex Street, London WC2R 3HY Tel: 020 7240 2384 Fax: 020 7240 3089
e-mail: ga@unitarian.org.uk Website: www.unitarian.org.uk
Candidates accepted for training for the ministry in the Unitarian and Free Christian Churches take courses of training either at Manchester Academy & Harris College, Oxford, the Unitarian College (Luther King House, Brighton Grove, Rusholme, Manchester) or the Memorial College, Aberystwyth (for Welsh speaking candidates).The course at Manchester Academy and Harris College, Oxford varies from 2 to 4 yrs in the light of candidates' qualifications. All candidates for training are expected to study for an Oxford degree in Theology or Theology & Philosophy or an Oxford Certificate in Theology/Religious Studies.
Qualification through the Unitarian College, Manchester (now an Associate Member of the Partnership for Theological Education) depends on the attainment of the College Certificate. This is awarded upon satisfactory completion of a specified course of training, which normally includes, in addition to courses at the College, courses at the University of Manchester (for a degree in Arts or Theology, for the Certificate in Theology, or the Diploma in Social and Pastoral Theology) and part of the common core curriculum of the Partnership. Training normally takes 3 or 4 yrs, but both the length and nature of the course can be varied according to circumstances.
Candidates for the ministry of the **Non-subscribing Presbyterian Church of Ireland** are expected to take a degree course at a university recognised for the purpose before taking a course of theological training at Manchester Academy & Harris College, Oxford, the Unitarian College, Manchester or a recognised university in Northern Ireland.

UNITED FREE CHURCH OF SCOTLAND

11 Newton Place, Glasgow G3 7PR Tel: 0141 332 3435 Fax: 0141 333 1973
e-mail: ufcos@charis.co.uk Website: ufcos.org.uk
The post-school educational preparation required by the United Free Church of Scotland consists of a course of general education at a university and a postgraduate course in Theology as provided by the Divinity Faculties of the Scottish Universities. The Ministry is open to both men and women. Candidates for the Theological course which lasts for 3 yrs must have the approval of their Presbytery. Those who have previous qualifications or been engaged in other occupations may be allowed to undertake a modified course.

THE UNITED REFORMED CHURCH

86 Tavistock Place, London WC1H 9RT Tel: 020 7916 2020 Fax: 020 7916 2021
e-mail: training@urc.org.uk
Stipendiary Ministry: URC Ministers (both men and women) are usually trained in the Church's theological colleges which are validated by the Church. Most students take a qualification of the university to which their college is attached. This could be a degree in Theology or a diploma. Normally the length of the training course varies between 3 and 4 yrs. Candidates for training must be recommended by their local church and District Council and by the Synod Ministerial Committee of their area. The colleges are as follows: Westminster Coll, Cambridge Tel: 01223 741084 Fax: 01223 300765; The Northern Coll, Brighton Grove, Manchester Tel: 0161 249 6404 Fax: 0161 248 9201 E-mail: lkh@luther-king-house.org.uk; Mansfield Coll, Oxford Tel: 01865 2491; Queen's Coll, Birmingham Tel: 0121 454 1527. In certain cases it is possible to train part-time on an Ecumenical Course. The minimum requirement is a diploma in theology and 800 hrs placement in a church.
Non-Stipendiary: A training programme for a Non-Stipendiary Ministry is open to men and women who are committed members of the URC; PT study usually takes 4 yrs. Candidates must be recommended by their local church, District Council and the Synod Ministerial Committee in their area. A Director of Training guides the student. Most students study PT on a recognised ecumenical course with an additional programme to study reformed history ethics and worship, but some train full-time in college. A Leaving Certificate for a call to the ordained ministry is granted. Training is arranged by the Board of Studies of the Training Committee.
Church Related Community Workers: Church Related Community Workers help lead and strengthen the local church's mission through community development in an area where specialist help is required to meet unusual needs. Candidates must be members of the URC showing capabilities for leadership. CRCWs are trained in Theology and Community Work at the Partnership for Theological Education, Manchester.
Lay Preacher's Certificate: Training for Learning & Serving is the title of the qualifying course for the United Reformed Church Lay Preacher's Certificate. The course takes three yrs. Work is done in local groups and there are five residential weekend courses each yr. Candidates are also expected to undertake some practical work in churches.

WESLEYAN REFORM UNION

Church House, 123 Queen Street, Sheffield S1 2DU Tel: 0114 2721938
The Wesleyan Reform Union has no training college of its own and encourages candidates for its Ministry to enter a Bible College for 2 or 3 yrs. All candidates are, however, under the personal supervision of a Union Tutor who directs a Biblical Studies & Training Department offering fairly extensive courses. Candidates attend Headquarters once a yr for an oral exam in Theology conducted by the Tutor in the presence of the Union Examination Committee; they also take written exams.

The Roman Catholic Church

Candidates for the priesthood in the RC Church attend a residential seminary course of at least 6 yrs. Among subjects studied are Philosophy, Psychology, Dogmatic and Moral Theology, Scripture, Church History, Canon Law, Liturgy, Catechetics, Communications and Pastoral Theology. Each College/Seminary has its own arrangement for the University education of its students (eg Durham, Glasgow etc). Those who do not attend University take a final internal exam. Candidates wishing to serve in the diocesan priesthood train at 1 of the following seminaries: Allen Hall, 28 Beaufort Street, Chelsea, London SW3 5AA; St Cuthbert's Coll, Ushaw, Durham; St John's Seminary, Wonersh, Surrey; Oscott Coll, Sutton Coldfield, West Midlands; Scotus Seminary, 2 Chesters Road, Bearsden, Glasgow.British seminaries abroad are: The English Coll, Valladolid, Spain; The Scots Coll, Salamanca, Spain; The English Coll, Rome; The Scots Coll, Rome. The Beda Coll, Rome, offers a 4 yr course for mature students. Many of these seminaries have links with universities and students may take a university degree as part of their course. A candidate wishing to become a member of a Religious Order, eg Benedictine, Franciscan, Dominican, etc, trains at an institute of the Order. The acquisition of a university degree frequently forms part of the training. Jesuits and others train at Heythrop College, which is now a constituent College of London University, where students enter for the theological and philosophical degrees of the university.

Students wishing to serve in missionary territories train in the institute of a missionary congregation, eg the White Fathers, the Mill Hill Fathers, etc. Most missionary students complete part of their studies at the Missionary Institute, London N20.Blackfriars (64 St Giles, Oxford OX1 3LY Tel: 01865 278400 Fax: 01865 278403): Blackfriars is the House of Studies of the English Dominicans, and is also the Permanent Private Hall of Oxford University. It offers full ordination courses for clerical students, both Dominican and non-Dominican. It also offers courses in theology and philosophy for lay people. Maryvale Institute (Maryvale House, Old Oscott Hill, Kingstanding, Birmingham B44 9AG Tel: 0121 360 8118 Fax: 0121 366 6786): A variety of distance learning courses are available with residential schools. The Institute is an Affiliated Institute of Maynooth University, Associated Institute of the Open University and Associated College of Hull University.

UNIVERSITY QUALIFICATIONS
The following universities offer qualifications in The Churches and related subjects. Full details may be found in Part 4, under the entry for the appropriate university.

FIRST DEGREES AWARDED BY UNIVERSITIES
Aberdeen; Bath Spa; Belfast; Birmingham; Birmingham (The University of Birmingham, Westhill); Bristol; Bristol (Wesley College); Brunel; Cambridge; Cheltenham & Gloucester; Derby; Durham; Durham (St John's College); Durham (Ushaw College); Edinburgh; Exeter; Exeter (The College of St Mark & St John); Glasgow; Greenwich; Hertfordshire; Hull; Kent; Kent (Canterbury Christ Church University College); Lancaster; Leeds; Leeds (College of the Resurrection); Leeds (Leeds, Trinity & All Saints); Leeds (The College of Ripon & York St John); Liverpool (Chester College of H.E.); Liverpool (Liverpool Hope University College); London (Heythrop College); London (Jews' College); London (King's College London); London (School of Oriental & African Studies); London (School of Slavonic & East European Studies); London (University College (UCL)); Manchester; Middlesex; Newcastle; North London; Nottingham; Oxford; Oxford (Westminster College, Oxford); Sheffield; Southampton (Chichester Institute of Higher Education); Southampton (King Alfred's College); St Andrews; St Martin; Stirling; Sunderland; Surrey (St Mary's, Strawberry Hill); Surrey (University of Surrey Roehampton); Wales (Cardiff University); Wales (University of Wales Institute, Cardiff); Wales (University of Wales, Bangor); Wales (University of Wales, Lampeter); Wolverhampton

HIGHER DEGREES AWARDED BY UNIVERSITIES
Aberdeen; Anglia; Bath Spa; Belfast; Birmingham; Birmingham (The University of Birmingham, Westhill); Bristol; Bristol (Wesley College); Cambridge; Cheltenham & Gloucester; Coventry (Newman College of Higher Education); Derby; Dundee; Durham; Durham (Ushaw College); Edinburgh; Essex; Exeter; Exeter (The College of St Mark & St John); Glasgow; Hull; Hull (Bishop Grosseteste College); Kent; Lancaster; Leeds; Leeds (The College of Ripon & York St John); Liverpool (Chester College of H.E.); Liverpool (Liverpool Hope University College); London (Birkbeck, University of London); London (Goldsmiths College); London (Heythrop College); London (Institute of Education); London (Jews' College); London (King's College London); London (London School of Economics & Political Science); London (School of Oriental & African Studies); Manchester; Newcastle; Nottingham; Oxford; Oxford (Westminster College, Oxford);

Salford; Sheffield; Southampton (Chichester Institute of Higher Education); Southampton (King Alfred's College); St Andrews; St Martin; Surrey (St Mary's, Strawberry Hill); Surrey (University of Surrey Roehampton); Wales (Cardiff University); Wales (University of Wales College, Newport); Wales (University of Wales, Bangor); Wales (University of Wales, Lampeter); Warwick

DIPLOMAS AWARDED BY UNIVERSITIES

Aberdeen; Bath Spa; Birmingham; Birmingham (The University of Birmingham, Westhill); Brighton; Bristol; Bristol (Wesley College); Brunel; Cambridge; Cheltenham & Gloucester; Durham; Durham (St John's College); Durham (Ushaw College); Edinburgh; Exeter; Hull; Kent; Lancaster; Leeds; Leeds (College of the Resurrection); Leeds (The College of Ripon & York St' John); Liverpool (Chester College of H.E.); Liverpool (Liverpool Hope University College); London (Heythrop College); London (Jews' College); London (King's College London); Manchester; Newcastle; Oxford; Salford; Southampton (Chichester Institute of Higher Education); Southampton (King Alfred's College); St Andrews; Surrey (St Mary's, Strawberry Hill); Sussex; Wales (Cardiff University)

CERTIFICATES AWARDED BY UNIVERSITIES

Birmingham; Birmingham (The University of Birmingham, Westhill); Brighton; Bristol; Bristol (Wesley College); Brunel; Cambridge; Cheltenham & Gloucester; Durham (St John's College); Durham (Ushaw College); Edinburgh; Exeter (The College of St Mark & St John); Hull; Kent; Leeds (The College of Ripon & York St John); Liverpool (Chester College of H.E.); London (Goldsmiths College); Manchester; Manchester Metropolitan.; Nottingham; Oxford (Westminster College, Oxford); Sheffield Hallam; Southampton (Chichester Institute of Higher Education); Stirling; Wales (Cardiff University); Warwick

OTHER COURSES AWARDED BY UNIVERSITIES

Edinburgh

POSTGRADUATE CERTIFICATES AWARDED BY UNIVERSITIES

Durham (Ushaw College); Warwick

POSTGRADUATE DIPLOMAS AWARDED BY UNIVERSITIES

Durham (Ushaw College)

CINEMA, FILM AND TELEVISION
Membership of Professional Institutions and Associations

LONDON INTERNATIONAL FILM SCHOOL

24 Shelton Street, Covent Garden, London WC2H 9HP Tel: 020 7836 9642/0207 240 0168 Fax: 020 7497 3718 e-mail: film.school@lifs.org.uk Website: www.lifs.org.uk
One of the foremost independent film schools in Europe, accredited by the Broadcasting, Entertainment, Cinematograph and Theatre Union (BECTU).

QUALIFICATIONS:
Diploma Course (2 yrs) in The Art and Technique of Film Making: Courses begin September, January and May to equip students with all the skills associated with film production, including: lighting, sound, editing, scripting, directing, set design and the use of 16mm & 35mm cameras. Students applying should have a university degree, art college diploma, or GCEs or GCSEs with 2 subjects at A level and 5 at O level (or overseas equivalent). Students are interviewed whenever possible and are not normally accepted immediately on finishing secondary education. All applicants are required to submit a 3-min film script illustrated by sketches or photographs. Experience of film making, television and photography will also be taken into account. Address all enquiries to the Administrator.

THE NATIONAL FILM AND TELEVISION SCHOOL

Beaconsfield Studios, Station Road, Beaconsfield, Buckinghamshire HP9 1LG Tel: 01494 671234 Fax: 01494 674042 e-mail: cad@nftsfilm-tv.ac.uk Website: www.nftsfilm-tv.ac.uk

QUALIFICATIONS:
The School offers a 2 yr course providing professional training in 10 specialist areas: cinematography; fiction direction; documentary direction; producing; editing; screen sound; animation direction; screenwriting; screen music and screen design. This course is in the process of being validated as an MA. The School also offers a 1 yr project led Advanced Programme. Both the 2 yr course and the Advanced Programme begin in January each yr. NFTS graduates occupy positions of responsibility in both films and television and equally create projects of their own.
Admission: There are no age limits, but most successful candidates will be between 22 and 28, or often older for the Advanced Programme. They will have submitted work and a summary of any professional experience. Whilst many successful applicants will have a high level of academic training, an undergraduate degree is not a prerequisite to obtaining a place, providing applicants have a relevant professional qualification or can demonstrate equivalent industrial or practical experience. Graduates of the 2 yr Course are eligible to apply for the Advanced Programme alongside people who apply directly from outside.

BRITISH KINEMATOGRAPH SOUND AND TELEVISION SOCIETY (BKSTS)/THE MOVING IMAGE SOCIETY

63-71 Victoria House, Vernon Place, London WC1B 4DA Tel: 020 7242 8400 Fax: 020 7405 3560
MEMBERSHIP:
Fellowships: Are conferred upon those who have contributed outstanding service to the industries. The award of the Fellowship is at the discretion of the Council and differs from all other grades in this respect.
Full Membership (MBKS): Is for those aged at least 25 and/or employed for 5 yrs in the technical areas of film, television, sound or related industries. Members are entitled to use the designatory letters **MBKS**. All applicants must be proposed by a paid-up Full Member.
Associate Membership: Is open to those, over the age of 18, who are engaged or interested in the technical areas of film, sound, television or related industries.
Interim Membership: Is for applicants who have completed their training and/or are beginning a career in the industry. Interim Members may apply for Associate or Corporate Membership when they have gained experience.
Student Membership: Is for anyone over the age of 16 undergoing recognised industrial or HE training relevant to Society's activities.

University Qualifications

The following universities offer qualifications in Cinema, Film and Television and related subjects. Full details may be found in Part 4, under the entry for the appropriate university.

FIRST DEGREES AWARDED BY UNIVERSITIES

Anglia; Belfast; Bournemouth; Bradford; Brunel; Bucks. Coll.; Central England; Central Lancashire; Cheltenham & Gloucester; De Montfort, Leicester; Derby; Doncaster; East Anglia; East London; Essex; Exeter; Glamorgan; Huddersfield; Kent; Kent (Canterbury Christ Church University College); Kent (Kent Institute of Art & Design); Kingston; Lancaster (Edge Hill College of Higher Education); Leeds; Leeds (The College of Ripon & York St John); Lincolnshire; Liverpool; Liverpool (Chester College of H.E.); Liverpool John Moores; London (Birkbeck, University of London); London Institute (London College of Printing); Manchester; Manchester (Warrington Collegiate Institute, Faculty of H.E,); Manchester Metropolitan.; Middlesex; Napier; Newcastle; North London; Northumbria; Nottingham; Nottingham Trent (Southampton Institute); Plymouth (Falmouth College of Arts); Reading; Salford; Sheffield Hallam; Southampton; Southampton (King Alfred's College); Southampton (Winchester School of Art); Staffordshire; Stirling; Sunderland; Surrey (University of Surrey Roehampton); Surrey Institute; Thames Valley; Wales (Cardiff University); Wales (Swansea Institute of Higher Education); Wales (University of Wales College, Newport); Wales (University of Wales, Aberystwyth); Wales (University of Wales, Bangor); Warwick; Wolverhampton

HIGHER DEGREES AWARDED BY UNIVERSITIES

Aberdeen; Birmingham; Bournemouth; Bristol; Central England; Cheltenham & Gloucester; De

Montfort, Leicester; Derby; East Anglia; Edinburgh; Essex; Exeter; Glasgow; Hertfordshire; Kent; Kingston; Leeds Metropolitan; London (Birkbeck, University of London); London (Goldsmiths College); London (Queen Mary & Westfield College (incorporating St Bartholomew's and the Royal London School of Medicine & Dentistry)); London (Royal Holloway); London (School of Oriental & African Studies); London Guildhall; London Institute (Central Saint Martins College of Art & Design); Manchester (Warrington Collegiate Institute, Faculty of H.E,); Middlesex; Newcastle; Nottingham; Nottingham Trent; Nottingham Trent (Southampton Institute); Reading; Royal College of Art; Salford; Sheffield Hallam; Southampton; Surrey Institute; Wales (North East Wales Institute); Wales (University of Wales College, Newport); Wales (University of Wales, Aberystwyth); Warwick; Westminster

DIPLOMAS AWARDED BY UNIVERSITIES
Bournemouth; Bristol; Bucks. Coll.; Central England; De Montfort, Leicester; Edinburgh; Hertfordshire; Hull; Kent; Lincolnshire (Grimsby College); Newcastle; Nottingham Trent (Southampton Institute); Salford; Southampton (King Alfred's College); Staffordshire; Thames Valley; Wales (North East Wales Institute)

CERTIFICATES AWARDED BY UNIVERSITIES
Bournemouth; Leeds Metropolitan; Staffordshire

POSTGRADUATE DIPLOMAS AWARDED BY UNIVERSITIES
Plymouth (Falmouth College of Arts)

National Certificates and Diplomas
BTEC National Certificates/Diplomas: Design (Film and Television)
BTEC Higher National Certificates/Diplomas: Design (Film and Television); Design (Video Production)
Scotland
SQA HNC: Animation Production; Audio Engineering; Broadcasting Analysis and Production; Interactive Multimedia (Design and Production); Media Skills in the Community; Media Analysis and Production; Radio Broadcasting; Sound, Video and Television Techniques; Television and Video Production; Video Production Skills; Visual Information.
SQA HND: Audio Engineering; Interactive Multimedia: Design and Production; Radio and Television Production; Sound, Video and Television Techniques; Television and Radio Production; Television Production; Video Production.

NVQs
Level 2: Set Dressing
Level 3: Animation Assistance; Visual Arts Practice
Level 4: Art Direction; Visual Arts Practice

SVQs
Level 3: Broadcast, Film and Video Make-up/Hair; Broadcast, Film and Video Production; Broadcast, Film and Video Production Research
Level 4: Broadcast, Film and Video Production; Broadcast Journalism

CLEANING, LAUNDRY AND DRY CLEANING

Membership of Professional Institutions and Associations

BRITISH INSTITUTE OF CLEANING SCIENCE
3 Moulton Court, Anglia Way, Moulton Park, Northampton NN3 6JA Tel: 01604 678710
Fax: 01604 645988 e-mail: info@bics.org.uk Website: www.bics.org.uk

The Institute is a body of individuals and companies who support the objective of improving the opportunities for Education, Training & Qualification through the cleaning industry. It offers appropriate qualifications at all levels and successful completion of these will entitle the individual to membership in the appropriate grade. It is possible to join as a student member prior to qualification. The Institute works closely with City & Guilds both in regard to their City & Guilds 764-1 and 764-2 Certificates in Cleaning Science and as a Joint Awarding body for NVQ Interior Building Cleaning Levels 1 & 2.The Institute also offers qualifications for the Cleaning Operators Proficiency Certificate, the Food Premises Cleaning Certificate and the Car Valeting Certificate. The Cleaning Operators Proficiency Certificate and the Food Premises Cleaning Certificate are both approved prior to learning for NVQ qualifications.

THE GUILD OF CLEANERS AND LAUNDERERS

Secretariat, 1 Wellfield Road, Offerton, Stockport, Cheshire SK2 6AS Tel: 0161 483 4655 Fax: 0161 483 4655

MEMBERSHIP:

Fellows (FGCL): Entrance to the College of Fellows is by election.

Associate Membership (AGCL): (a) *By Exam:* the applicant should have satisfied the requirements for Licentiateship as indicated below, and should have a minimum of 5 yrs' managerial or technical experience in the textile care of associated industry, and have been a Guild Member for at least 1 yr. (b) *By Exemption:* applicants should have at least 5 yrs' managerial or practical experience in textile care associated industries. They should also be able to demonstrate to the Guild Examination Board that they hold appropriate equivalent qualifications of the type required for Licentiateship.

Licentiateship (LGCL): Open to any member of the Guild, of any age, who has qualified by exam only in: Advanced Laundry or Advanced Drycleaning Technology; plus 3 practical subjects from Stain Removal, Dry Cleaning Practice, Garment Finishing, Silk Finishing, Leather Cleaning, and has relevant certificates in or experience of management.

Membership: Open to people who are directly employed in the drycleaning and laundry industry and allied trades. The Guild also has **Honorary Members** and **Overseas Members.**

EXAMINATIONS:

National Diploma in Laundry and Cleaning Technology: The Diploma is awarded to students who have obtained Advanced Certificates in Laundry and Dry Cleaning together with certain other practical exams.

CERTIFICATES:

Laundry Management and Technology; Advanced Laundry Technology; Advanced Dry Cleaning Technology; Intermediate Dry Cleaning Technology; Principles of Laundering; Introduction to Dry Cleaning; Business Administration; Customer Relations; Stain Removal; Garment Finishing; Advanced Garment Finishing; Suede and Leather Cleaning; Commercial and Industrial Dry Cleaning. Candidates seeking to qualify at Advanced Laundry or Dry Cleaning Technology level would normally have GCSEs in English, Mathematics and a science subject or an equivalent or higher qualification. Some of the above qualifications are superseded by NVQ/SVQs at levels 1 & 2.

NVQs

Level 1: Cleaning (Building Interiors); Dry Cleaning; Laundering (Finishing); Laundering (Washing)

Level 2: Cleaning (Building Interiors); Cleaning: On Site Care of Carpets and Soft Furnishings; Cleaning: Windows, Glass and Facade Surfaces; Cleaning: Within Food Premises; Dry Cleaning; Laundering

SVQs

Level 1: Cleaning: Building Interiors; Cleaning: Highways and Land

Level 2: Cleaning: Building Interiors; Cleaning: Care of Carpets and Soft Furnishings; Cleaning: Highways and Land; Cleaning: Windows, Glass and Façade Surfaces

COLOUR TECHNOLOGY

BRITISH DECORATORS ASSOCIATION

32 Coton Road, Nuneaton, Warwickshire CV11 5TW Tel: 024 76353776 Fax: 024 76354513
e-mail: bda@primex.co.uk Website: www.british-decorators.co.uk
The Association is a registered trade and employers' organisation, catering exclusively for needs of professional painting and decorating trade employers. The Association conducts no exam, but all membership applications are scrutinised at Branch level to ensure that only *bona fide* firms are admitted. The Council, or any Region or Branch, with the prior consent of the Council, may confer **Life Membership** on any person in recognition of meritorious service to the painting industry. Painting and decorating trade employers wishing to become **Members** of a Branch of the Association must be vetted, and supply references which are checked. **Associate Membership** is available to acceptable companies supplying goods or services to the painting and decorating trade.

University Qualifications

The following universities offer qualifications in Colour Technology and related subjects. Full details may be found in Part 4, under the entry for the appropriate university.

FIRST DEGREES AWARDED BY UNIVERSITIES
Heriot-Watt; Leeds

HIGHER DEGREES AWARDED BY UNIVERSITIES
Bristol; Heriot-Watt; Heriot-Watt (Scottish Borders Campus); Leeds

DIPLOMAS AWARDED BY UNIVERSITIES
Leeds

CERTIFICATES AWARDED BY UNIVERSITIES
Bradford (Bradford & Ilkley Community College)

POSTGRADUATE DIPLOMAS AWARDED BY UNIVERSITIES
Heriot-Watt

City & Guilds

6052 Painting and Decorating Skills; 6091 Basic Painting and Decorating Skills

Useful Addresses

The British Coatings Federation, James House, Bridge Street, Leatherhead, Surrey KT22 7EP Tel: 01372 360660 Fax: 01372 376069

COMMUNICATIONS AND MEDIA

University Qualifications

The following universities offer qualifications in Communications and Media and related subjects. Full details may be found in Part 4, under the entry for the appropriate university.

FIRST DEGREES AWARDED BY UNIVERSITIES
Abertay, Dundee; Anglia; Anglia (Colchester Institute); Barnsley; Bath; Bath Spa; Birmingham; Bournemouth; Bradford; Bradford (Bradford & Ilkley Community College); Brighton; Bristol; Brunel; Buckingham; Bucks. Coll.; Central England; Central Lancashire; Cheltenham & Gloucester; City; Coventry; Cranfield; De Montfort, Leicester; Derby; Doncaster; Dundee; East Anglia; East Anglia (Suffolk College); East London; Exeter (The College of St Mark & St John);

433

Glamorgan; Glasgow (Glasgow School of Art); Glasgow Caledonian; Greenwich; Heriot-Watt; Heriot-Watt (Edinburgh College of Art); Hertfordshire; Hertfordshire (West Herts College); Huddersfield; Hull; Kent; Kent (Canterbury Christ Church University College); Kingston; Lancaster; Lancaster (Edge Hill College of Higher Education); Leeds; Leeds (Leeds College of Art & Design); Leeds (Leeds, Trinity & All Saints); Leeds Metropolitan; Leicester; Lincolnshire; Lincolnshire (Lincoln University Campus); Liverpool; Liverpool (Chester College of H.E.); Liverpool John Moores; London (Birkbeck, University of London); London (Goldsmiths College); London (Royal Holloway); London Guildhall; London Institute (London College of Fashion); London Institute (London College of Printing); Loughborough; Luton; Manchester (Warrington Collegiate Institute, Faculty of H.E,); Manchester Metropolitan.; Middlesex; Napier; North London; Northampton; Northumbria; Nottingham Trent; Nottingham Trent (Southampton Institute); Oxford Brookes; Paisley; Plymouth; Plymouth (Falmouth College of Arts); Portsmouth; Queen Margaret; Robert Gordon; Salford; Sheffield Hallam; South Bank; Southampton (Chichester Institute of Higher Education); Staffordshire; Stirling; Sunderland; Surrey; Surrey (Farnborough College of Technology); Surrey (St Mary's, Strawberry Hill); Sussex; Teesside; Thames Valley; Ulster; UMIST; Wales (Cardiff University); Wales (North East Wales Institute); Wales (Swansea Institute of Higher Education); Wales (University of Wales College, Newport); Wales (University of Wales Institute, Cardiff); Wales (University of Wales, Bangor); Wales (University of Wales, Lampeter); Wales (University of Wales, Swansea); Westminster; Wolverhampton; Worcester; York

HIGHER DEGREES AWARDED BY UNIVERSITIES

Bath; Bath Spa; Bournemouth; Bradford; Brighton; Bristol; Central England; Cheltenham & Gloucester; City; Coventry; East Anglia; Glamorgan; Heriot-Watt; Heriot-Watt (Edinburgh College of Art); Hertfordshire; Hull; Kent; Kent (Kent Institute of Art & Design); Kingston; Leeds; Leeds (Leeds, Trinity & All Saints); Leeds Metropolitan; Leicester; Liverpool John Moores; London (Birkbeck, University of London); London (Goldsmiths College); London (Institute of Education); London (London School of Economics & Political Science); London (Queen Mary & Westfield College (incorporating St Bartholomew's and the Royal London School of Medicine & Dentistry)); London (Royal Holloway); London (University College (UCL)); London Guildhall; London Institute (Central Saint Martins College of Art & Design); Loughborough; Luton; Manchester; Manchester (Warrington Collegiate Institute, Faculty of H.E,); Manchester Metropolitan.; Middlesex; Napier; North London; Nottingham Trent (Southampton Institute); Oxford Brookes; Plymouth; Portsmouth; Sheffield; Sheffield Hallam; Southampton; Staffordshire; Stirling; Strathclyde; Sunderland; Surrey; Surrey Institute; Sussex; Thames Valley; Ulster; UMIST; Wales (University of Wales College, Newport); Westminster; York

DIPLOMAS AWARDED BY UNIVERSITIES

Anglia (City College, Norwich); Barnsley; Blackburn; Bournemouth; Bradford; Bradford (Bradford & Ilkley Community College); Brighton; Bucks. Coll.; Central England; Cheltenham & Gloucester; Durham (New College Durham); Edinburgh; Exeter (Truro College); Glamorgan; Glasgow Caledonian; Greenwich; Heriot-Watt (Edinburgh College of Art); Hertfordshire; Hertfordshire (West Herts College); Huddersfield; Kent (Kent Institute of Art & Design); Lancaster; Leeds (Leeds College of Art & Design); Leeds (Leeds, Trinity & All Saints); Lincolnshire; Lincolnshire (Grimsby College); Lincolnshire (Hull College); London Institute (Central Saint Martins College of Art & Design); Loughborough; Luton; Napier; Northampton; OU (NESCOT); Oxford Brookes; Plymouth; Salford; Southampton (King Alfred's College); Staffordshire; Stirling; Teesside; Thames Valley; Ulster; Wolverhampton; Worcester

CERTIFICATES AWARDED BY UNIVERSITIES

Anglia (City College, Norwich); Brighton; Central England; Cheltenham & Gloucester; Glamorgan; Leeds (Leeds, Trinity & All Saints); Leeds Metropolitan; Lincolnshire (Hull College); London (Goldsmiths College); OU (The Central School of Speech & Drama); Salford; Staffordshire; Sussex

PROFESSIONAL COURSES AWARDED BY UNIVERSITIES

London Guildhall

National Certificates and Diplomas

BTEC National Certificates/Diplomas: Media
BTEC Higher National Certificates/Diplomas: Media
Scotland
SQA HNC: Communication; Communication Administration for the Voluntary Sector; Communication for Business; Communication in Europe; Communication of Technical Information; Gaelic Communication; Media Production; Media Analysis and Production; Media Skills in the Community
SQA HND: Communication; Communication in Europe; Communication of Technical Information

NVQs

Level 2: Digital Imaging
Level 3: Digital Imaging

GNVQs

3733 Media: Communication and Production

City & Guilds

2790 Video and Television Production; 7700 Media Techniques: Television and Video Competencies; 7790 Media Techniques: Journalism and Radio Competencies

COMPUTING AND INFORMATION TECHNOLOGY

Membership of Professional Institutions and Associations

ASSOCIATION OF COMPUTER PROFESSIONALS

204 Barnett Wood Lane, Ashtead, Surrey KT21 2DB Tel: 01372 273442 Fax: 01372 277778
e-mail: acp@btinternet.com Website: www.btinternet.com/acp
The main objectives of the Association of Computer Professionals are to prepare candidates through exams for a successful career in computing and to provide high standards of proficiency throughout the Industry. Several British universities and colleges of higher education accept the Advanced Diploma as an entry qualification to Postgraduate and Master of Science degree courses, subject to interview.

EXAMINATIONS:
Single-subject Certificates in Word Processing, dBase III+, Lotus 1-2-3 and other software packages. Certificate in Computer Programming: Computer Fundamentals, Computer Programming and Operating, and Programming Problem and Project.
Diploma in Computer System Design: Systems Analysis and Design, Software Methodology, Computer Systems for Small Businesses and Coursework.
Advanced Diploma in Computer Studies: The Principles of Information Processing, Systems Analysis and Design, Programming, Computer Management, System Operation and Project.

MEMBERSHIP:
Fellow (FACP): An honorary award made by the Council of the Association.
Member (MACP): Must have passed or been exempted from the Diploma exams or have a minimum of 8 yrs' approved experience in the computer industry.
Associate Member (AACP): Must have passed or been exempted from the Certificate exams or have a minimum of 3 yrs' approved experience.
Student Member: Applicants must be at least 17, attained a satisfactory standard of secondary education and be undergoing appropriate training for the Association's exams. Candidates for these exams must be registered with the Association as student members.

THE BRITISH COMPUTER SOCIETY

1 Sandford Street, Swindon, Wilts SN1 1HJ e-mail: bcshq@bcs.org.uk Website: www.bcs.org.uk
The Society has a range of membership grades designed to accommodate almost everyone with
an active interest in computers and computer systems.

PROFESSIONAL MEMBERSHIP:

Fellow (FBCS): A Chartered Professional grade. For election to fellow applicants should be at least
30 and have been an MBCS for at least 1 yr. A minimum of 8 yrs of practical experience are also
required, 5 of them in a position of substantial responsibility. Fellows of the Society are entitled to
use the post-nominal letters FBCS and the title Chartered Information Systems Practitioner.

Member (MBCS): A Chartered Professional grade. Eligibility is dependent on age (minimum 24
for MBCS), academic qualifications, experience and current level of responsibility. Eligibility to
apply for the professional grade is determined by a simple points system – points are awarded for
academic qualifications, training and relevant work experience. Further information is available
via our website www.bcs.org.uk/joinbcs/member.htm. Routes are also available for those with no
formal academic qualification. Members are entitled to use the post nominal letters **MBCS** and the
title **Chartered Information Systems Practitioner.**

Associate Member (AMBCS): A Professional but non-chartered grade. Eligibility is dependent
upon age (minimum 22), academic qualifications, experience and current level of responsibility.
Requirements for academic qualification and responsibility are lower than that of Member, but the
experience required is similar.

OTHER GRADES:

Companion (CompBCS): The Companion grade is intended to cover senior members of other
Professionals who, although not qualifying as Information Systems Engineers, do have significant
involvement within IT. Eligibility is dependent on age (minimum 30), academic qualifications,
experience and eminence or authority in a particular discipline. Those elected to this grade are
entitled to use the post-nominal letters **CompBCS** and to describe themselves as a Companion of
The British Computer Society.

Graduate: For those who have achieved the necessary academic qualification for one of the
professional grades and are gaining the required training and experience.

Student: Open to those who have embarked in a course of study for an appropriate academic
qualification leading to one of the professional grades of membership.

Affiliate: Affiliate membership is open to anyone with an interest in computing.

INSTITUTIONAL MEMBERSHIP:

Business Affiliate: Open to business and public organisations.

Educational Affiliate: Open to institutions of further and higher education.

Schools Affiliate: Open to schools within the UK.

ENGINEERING COUNCIL QUALIFICATIONS:

The British Computer Society is a Chartered Engineering Institution and professional members
who meet the Engineering Council requirements may apply for the qualifications of Chartered
Engineer (CEng) and Incorporated Engineer (IEng). The criteria for registration are set out in the
Engineering Council policy document *Standards and Routes to Registration (SARTOR)* and, in terms
of training and experience, are similar to those for BCS Professional Membership. However, with
certain limited exceptions, applicants must have an academic qualification, which has been
accredited for CEng or IEng by one of the Engineering Institutions. The qualifications now include
250 computing related degree courses, which are accredited by the BCS.

European Engineer: Members registered as Chartered Engineers may also apply for the
qualification 'European Engineer'. The qualification is awarded by the Federation Europeene
d'Association Nationales d'Ingenieurs (FEANI) and entitles those registered to use the letters Eur
Ing.

For further details about membership requirements and annual subscriptions, please contact
Customer Services on 01793 417424. Abated rates are available for retired members and those in
full time education.

THE BCS PROFESSIONAL EXAMINATION

The BCS Professional examination has a modular structure set in three stages: Certificate, Diploma
and Professional Graduate Diploma, plus a Professional Project at Diploma or Professional
Graduate level. Combined with the right amount of work experience, successful completion of the

Diploma (equivalent to HND level) can provide a route to Associate Member of the BCS and achievement of the Professional Graduate Diploma (equivalent to honours degree level) can provide a route to full Member status.

Certificate: Considered equivalent to the first yr of a HND. It consists of a 2 hr written paper on each of the compulsory modules: Information systems, Software Development, Technology.

Diploma: Examined at an academic level equivalent to a HND. It consists of a 2 hr written paper on the compulsory core module – Professional Issues in Information Systems Practice – PLUS a 2 hr written paper on each of three modules chosen from the following list: Architecture, Computer Networks, Database Systems, Multimedia, Object-Oriented Programming, Project Management, Services Management, Software Development, Systems Analysis, Systems Design, Systems Software.

Professional Graduate Diploma: Examined to the level of a University Honours Degree. It consists of a 3 hr written paper on each of the 4 modules chosen from the following list: Advanced Database Management Systems, Computer Graphics, Computer Services Management, Distributed and Parallel Systems, Knowledge Based Systems, Management Information Systems, Network Information Systems, Programming Paradigms, Safety Critical and Realtime Software, Software Engineering, Systems Design Methods, User Interface Design. Alternatively, candidates can take the the Professional Graduate Diploma by submission of a dissertation on a topic that has been agreed by the BCS. Such candidates may also be required to undergo an oral examination. In addition, candidates undertake a **Professional Project**, at either **Diploma Level** (examined to the level expected of a HND project) or **Professional Graduate Diploma Level** (examined to the level expected of a university honours degree project). The purpose of the Professional Project is to demonstrate an appropriate level of Professional competence in the development of a suitable computer-based system. There are no formal entry requirements for the examination and candidates must determine their own suitability for each module they want to enter. However, candidates will be expected to have general education to GCE 'A' Level equivalent, have ability to communicate in English, and to draw practical experience when answering examination questions. A formal course of instruction is not mandatory but the examination should not be undertaken without adequate preparation. The examiners recommend 140 hrs of study time per module for the Certificate and Diploma, and 200 hrs per module for the Professional Graduate Diploma. These are total hrs and include tuition, self-study, assignments and exercise.

INFORMATION SYSTEMS EXAMINATIONS BOARD (ISEB)

The British Computer Society, 1 Sanford Street, Swindon, Wilts SN1 1HJ Tel: 01793 417417 Fax: 01793 480270 E-mail: iseb@hq.bcs.org.uk WWW:www.bcs.org.uk/iseb/index.html

Business Systems Development

The scheme has been defined to cover the general aspects of business systems development; the topics emphasise the personal and business oriented aspects of analysis and design. The technical areas in the syllabus are intended to test analysts' and/or designers' understanding rather than expert knowledge. Individual modular certificates are available in the following areas: Analysis and Design Techniques, Behaviour and Process Modelling, Business Activity Modelling, Business Organisation, Business Systems Investigation, Data Management Essentials, Data Modelling, Database and Physical Process Design, Function Modelling, Graphical User Interface Design, Information and Communications Technology, Object-Oriented Modelling, RAD and Prototyping Essentials, Requirements Engineering, SSADM Essentials, System Design and Implementation, User Centred System Development.

How is the qualification structured? There are two types of qualification available:

1. Certificates in Business Systems Development.
2. Diplomas in Business Systems Development.

The modular certificates are assessed by 1 hr written examinations, the majority of which are 'open book'. All modules count as a single credit towards achieving a Diploma, unless otherwise specified. Diplomas are available in 5 specialised areas: Systems Analysis and Design, Data Management, SSADM 4+, Business Analysis, Rapid Application Development. To achieve a Diploma, candidates must obtain the appropriate core module(s), any required optional modules and pass an oral examination.

Entry requirements: These qualifications are aimed at practitioners with a basic knowledge of Information Systems and Technology. Although there are no formal examination entry requirements, ISEB recommends that candidates have: General education to GCE 'A' Level or equivalent; At least 6 mths' experience in a business or administration environment; Attended a training course offered by an accredited training provider. Note:- It may be that training suppliers will impose their own course entry criteria.

Project Management for Information Systems
The **Certificate in Project Management for Information Systems** is awarded on the basis of the candidate assessment, a written examination and an oral examination. The **Diploma in Project Management** is awarded upon successful completion of 5 written projects (minimum 3,000 words each) and an oral examination. Candidates must have the requisite number of yrs work experience, which varies depending on whether they want to attempt the Certificate through an accredited training course (normally 2 wk residential) or the direct entry route, or the Diploma through achievement of the Certificate or direct entry route. In addition, holders of the Open University M865 or the APMP qualification can apply for exemption from the written examination. These qualifications are aimed at practitioners with previous experience or training in people management, motivation and control. The syllabus reflects the general and well established techniques of managing highly technical and often complex projects, these techniques may apply to any type of project but are related here to the particular problems experienced within IS developments. The Diploma also focuses on the behavioural competence necessary to effect good project management.

IT Service Management
Foundation Certificate in IT Service Management: Awarded on the basis of a multiple-choice paper with 40 questions, lasting 1 hr. Candidates should have the basic working knowledge of IT and attend an accredited training course, which normally lasts 3 days.

Manager's Certificate in IT Service Management: Awarded upon successful completion of two 3 hr written examination papers based on a case study. This qualification is aimed at experienced IT professionals involved in the implementation and/or management of service management functions. Candidates should have at least 5 yrs' practical experience, have had substantial decision-making responsibility affecting the support or delivery of IT services, and have attended an accredited training course (normally two 1 wk courses). The Foundation Certificate is a prerequisite for entrance to examination leading to the Manager's Certificate. The syllabus for both these qualifications is based on Service Support & Service Delivery booked in the CCTA's IT Infrastructure Library (ITIL) and complies with the terms of the ISO9001 Quality Standard. The 2 papers of the Manager's Certificate correspond accordingly.

Certificate in Business and Management Skills: Awarded on the basis of course assessment through individual and group case studies, and the independent review of a portfolio and video evidence submitted to ISEB at the end of the course. Candidates must attend an accredited training course. This qualification is aimed at IT professionals, particularly those responsible for the delivery and support of key IT services, who are looking to expand their knowledge and understanding of wider business and management issues. The course is based upon wide experience and best practice within the IT industry.

Information Communications Technology: These Diplomas are set in 2 stages. Stage One is in three parts: Part A (Certificate in Business Strategies) and Part C (Certificate in Resource Management) are both compulsory. The candidate's choice for Part B will determine the Diploma awarded. The choices are Certificate in Call Centre Management, Certificate in Network Services Management, Certificate in Telecommunications Management and Certificate in E-Business Management. Certificates are awarded upon successful completion of a 3 hr written examination. Diplomas are awarded on the basis of Stage Two: a project demonstrating assimilation of all the course material. The available course Diplomas are:

Management Diploma in Telecommunication, Management Diploma in E-Business, Management Diploma in Network Services and **Diploma in Call Centre Management**. Candidates must have the requisite level of education and number of yrs work experience. Stage One of the diploma reflects the knowledge required to manage a complex operation using technical and human resources; Stage Two demonstrates the application of all the elements from Stage One.

Foundation Certificate in Software Testing: Awarded on the basis of a multiple-choice paper with 40 questions, lasting 1 hr. Candidates should attend an accredited training course leading to the Certificate, although direct entry route is available. This qualification is for anyone with an IT background and an interest in testing, including software developers, testers, test analysts, test

engineers, test consultants, test managers, project managers and quality managers. It will ensure candidates understand the basics of software testing. There will eventually be 3 levels of Software Testing qualifications; the additions will be a Practitioner Certificate and a Practitioner Diploma.
Certificate in Information Security Management Principles: Awarded on the basis of a multiple-choice paper with 100 questions, lasting 2 hrs. Candidates must have a minimum of 12 mths experience in IT and attend an accredited training course leading to the Certificate. However, if 6 mths of that experience was spent in security control activity (eg. closely related to one or more of the ten sections of BS7799), a direct entry route is available. This qualification is designed to provide the foundation of knowledge necessary for individuals who have security responsibility as part of their role, or who are thinking of moving into a security related function. The syllabus reflects the general and well established techniques of Information Security, incorporating the latest technological principles.
DSDM Certificates: The **DSDM Essentials** qualification is awarded on the basis of a multiple-choice paper with 60 questions, lasting 1 hr. The **DSDM Practitioners Certificate** is awarded by ISEB under the guidance and development of DSDM Consortium. Candidates must submit an application to the DSDM secretariat, including their CV and copies of DSDM Course Attendance Certificates (if applicable). The Practitioners Certificate is awarded in the basis of a project synopsis of 2000 words and an oral examination. Candidates should have at least 2 yrs' practical experience, including 6 mths on RAD projects, and attend a 3 day accredited training course. There is also an experienced route available. The DSDM Consortium also offer the following courses:
DSDM Aware (1 day) and **Managing DSDM Projects** (2 days). Contact them direct for more details: DSDM Secretariat, Kent House, 81 Station Road, Ashford, Kent TN23 1PP Tel: 01233 661003 Fax: 01233 661004 E-mail: secretariat@dsdm.org.uk WWW: www.dsdm.org.uk
European Computer Driving Licence (ECDL): This is a Europe-wide qualification, which enables candidates to demonstrate their competence in computer skills. Testing is carried out at audited test centres, and consists of written and practical tests. ECDL is open to anyone regardless of age, education or experience, and attendance on a training course is not mandatory. The syllabus is designed to cover the key concepts of computing, its practical applications and their use in the workplace and society in general. It is divided into 7 modules, all of which must be passed before the ECDL Certificate is awarded. The modules are Basic Concepts of Information Technology, Using the Computer and Managing Files, Word Processing, Spreadsheets, Databases and Filing Systems, Presentation and Drawing, Information Network Services.

INSTITUTE FOR THE MANAGEMENT OF INFORMATION SYSTEMS

5 Kingfisher House, New Mill Road, Orpington, Kent BR5 3QG Tel: 0700 00 23456
Fax: 0700 00 23023 e-mail: central@imis.org.uk Website: www.imis.org.uk

MEMBERSHIP:
Fellow (FIMIS): An applicant must hold an appropriate senior position, in his/her company and/or profession.
Full Member (MIMIS): Requires a minimum of 8 yrs' appropriate experience (excluding training).
Associate Member (AIMIS): Requires a minimum of 4 yrs' appropriate experience (excluding training) depending on academic background.
Licentiate Member (LIMIS): Awarded to applicants with less than 4 yrs' appropriate experience and with certain approved professional qualifications.
Student Member: Available to those studying for a recognised qualification in IS. 4 syllabus levels.
Practitioner Member: Available to those who are not full time students for the Institute's examinations but spend a substantial amount of their working wk in some aspect of IS.

EXAMINATIONS:
Foundation: No prerequisites to this course. Each module is designed to introduce the student to the basic elements of IS and Management practices.
Diploma: Continues on from the Foundation level although entry is also available to candidates who comply with the 4 GCSE entrance requirements. The general standard equates to Ordinary National Certificate/Diploma.
Higher Diploma: Extends and compliments the Diploma course equating to HNC/Diploma.

Graduate Diploma: Hons degree level standard and recognised by the University of Greenwich, London. This qualification enables graduates to participate as fully qualified professionals in the development of computer based systems.

INSTITUTION OF ANALYSTS AND PROGRAMMERS

Charles House, 36 Culmington Road, Ealing, London W13 9NH Tel: 020 8567 2118
Fax: 020 8567 4379 e-mail: dg@iap.org.uk Website: www.iap.org.uk
The Institution is the leading international organisation for professional Analysts and Programmers. Its membership includes some of the world's most influential computer professionals.

MEMBERSHIP:
There are 4 grades of membership: Fellow(FIAP), Member(MIAP), Associate Member(AMIAP) and Graduate(GradIAP). The student category provides an opportunity for those starting out in the profession to associate themselves with the Institution and to receive some of the benefits of membership. The category of Student carries no designatory letters. Applications for admission to the Institution are evaluated by a system of points, which takes account of the quantity and quality of the applicant's formal training and working experience in what the IAP regards as the essential Core Subjects of Analysis, Programming, and Business. Points may be gained in all of these subjects through formal courses, distance learning, private study and in the workplace.

Student: For admission as a student an applicant should be training for the profession and intend to apply for one of the grades of membership of the Institution as soon as he or she is qualified to do so.

Graduate (GradIAP): For admission as Graduate an applicant will need at least 250 points. All 250 of these points must have been gained from a course of formal study and examination approved by the Institution. This total must include at least 100 points in Analysis and 100 points in Programming.

Associate Member (AMIAP): For admission as Associate Member an applicant will need at least 350 points. This total must include at least 100 points in Analysis or Programming. The balance may be made up with further points gained in the Core Subjects, Additional Subjects or by workplace experience. Typically these requirements can be met by applicants with either a good honours degree (or equivalent) in computer science, or with a minimum of four yrs' work experience.

Member (MIAP): For upgrading to Member an applicant will need at least 650 points. This must include at least 100 points each in Analysis or Programming, with a combined total in these two subjects of at least 400 points, plus at least 50 points in Business. The balance may be made up with further points gained in these Core Subjects or Additional Skills, but at least 150 points out of the total must have been gained in the workplace. Those seeking direct admission as Member will need at least 700 points. Typically these requirements can be met by applicants with a degree (or its equivalent) in computer science and four yrs' relevant workplace experience, or with at least eight yrs' workplace experience.

Fellow (FIAP): Applicants who are considered to have exceeded the requirements for Member by a substantial margin, and who have spent a considerable part of their working time in positions of substantial responsibility, may be considered by the Council of the Institution for admission to the grade of Fellow. Only the most outstanding professionals can meet the standards required for admission to the Institution's most senior grade, and applications are subject to the most vigorous scrutiny.

INTERNATIONAL ASSOCIATION OF BUSINESS COMPUTING

31 High Street, Wootton Bassett, Swindon SN4 7AF Tel: 01793 848152 Fax: 01793 848153
e-mail: admin@iabc.demon.co.uk Website: WWW.IABC.DEMON.CO.UK

AIMS:
The Association is a non-profit making, independent and apolitical body whose aim is to provide vocational qualifications in business computing and information systems, offering equal opportunities to all through open access courses available for anyone considering pursuing an academic or commercial career in computing, or wishing to enhance their present situation with additional qualifications.

EXAMINATIONS:

Courses are assessed by exams which take place twice yearly in June and December. There are 2 levels: Certificate and Diploma. No prior educational qualifications required to enter at certificate level.
Certificate: Comprises Introduction to Computer Systems, Computer Programming, Information Technology, Word Processing.
Diploma: Comprises Systems Analysis, Program Design & Implementation, Computers for Managers, Practical Project.

University Qualifications

The following universities offer qualifications in Computing and Information Technology and related subjects. Full details may be found in Part 4, under the entry for the appropriate university.

FIRST DEGREES AWARDED BY UNIVERSITIES

Aberdeen; Abertay, Dundee; Anglia; Anglia (City College, Norwich); Aston; Bath; Bath Spa; Belfast; Birmingham; Blackburn; Bournemouth; Bradford; Bradford (Bradford & Ilkley Community College); Brighton; Bristol; Brunel; Buckingham; Bucks. Coll.; Cambridge; Central England; Central Lancashire; Cheltenham & Gloucester; City; Coventry; Cranfield; De Montfort, Leicester; Derby; Doncaster; Dundee; Durham; East Anglia; East Anglia (Suffolk College); East London; Edinburgh; Essex; Exeter; Exeter (The College of St Mark & St John); Glamorgan; Glasgow; Glasgow Caledonian; Greenwich; Heriot-Watt; Heriot-Watt (Scottish Borders Campus); Hertfordshire; Huddersfield; Hull; Keele; Kent; Kent (Canterbury Christ Church University College); Kingston; Lancaster; Lancaster (Blackpool and The Fylde College); Lancaster (Edge Hill College of Higher Education); Leeds; Leeds (The College of Ripon & York St John); Leeds Metropolitan; Leicester; Lincolnshire; Lincolnshire (Hull College); Lincolnshire (Lincoln University Campus); Liverpool; Liverpool (Chester College of H.E.); Liverpool (Liverpool Hope University College); Liverpool John Moores; London (Goldsmiths College); London (Imperial College of Science, Technology & Medicine); London (King's College London); London (Queen Mary & Westfield College (incorporating St Bartholomew's and the Royal London School of Medicine & Dentistry)); London (Royal Holloway); London (University College (UCL)); London Guildhall; Loughborough; Luton; Manchester; Manchester (Warrington Collegiate Institute, Faculty of H.E,); Manchester Metropolitan.; Middlesex; Napier; Newcastle; North London; Northampton; Northumbria; Nottingham; Nottingham Trent; Nottingham Trent (Southampton Institute); OU (NESCOT); Oxford; Oxford Brookes; Paisley; Plymouth; Portsmouth; Reading; Robert Gordon; Salford; Salford (The Oldham College); Sheffield; Sheffield Hallam; South Bank; Southampton; St Andrews; St Martin; Staffordshire; Stirling; Strathclyde; Sunderland; Sunderland (City of Sunderland College); Surrey; Surrey (Farnborough College of Technology); Surrey (NESCOT); Surrey (University of Surrey Roehampton); Sussex; Teesside; Thames Valley; Ulster; UMIST; Wales (Cardiff University); Wales (North East Wales Institute); Wales (Swansea Institute of Higher Education); Wales (University of Wales College, Newport); Wales (University of Wales Institute, Cardiff); Wales (University of Wales, Aberystwyth); Wales (University of Wales, Bangor); Wales (University of Wales, Swansea); Warwick; Westminster; Wolverhampton; Worcester; York

HIGHER DEGREES AWARDED BY UNIVERSITIES

Aberdeen; Abertay, Dundee; Anglia; Aston; Bath; Belfast; Birmingham; Bournemouth; Bradford; Brighton; Bristol; Brunel; Buckingham; Bucks. Coll.; Cambridge; Central England; Central Lancashire; Cheltenham & Gloucester; City; Coventry; Cranfield; De Montfort, Leicester; Derby; Dundee; Durham; East Anglia; East London; Edinburgh; Essex; Exeter; Exeter (The College of St Mark & St John); Glamorgan; Glasgow; Glasgow Caledonian; Greenwich; Heriot-Watt; Heriot-Watt (Scottish Borders Campus); Hertfordshire; Huddersfield; Hull; Keele; Kent; Kingston; Lancaster; Leeds; Leeds Metropolitan; Leicester; Lincolnshire; Liverpool; Liverpool (Chester College of H.E.); Liverpool (Liverpool Hope University College); Liverpool John Moores; London (Birkbeck, University of London); London (Goldsmiths College); London (Imperial College of Science, Technology & Medicine); London (King's College London); London (London School of Economics & Political Science); London (Queen Mary & Westfield College (incorporating St Bartholomew's and the Royal London School of Medicine & Dentistry)); London (Royal Holloway); London (University College (UCL)); London Guildhall; Loughborough; Luton; Manchester; Manchester Metropolitan.; Middlesex; Napier; Newcastle; North London;

Northampton; Northumbria; Nottingham; Nottingham Trent; Nottingham Trent (Southampton Institute); Oxford; Oxford Brookes; Paisley; Plymouth; Portsmouth; Reading; Royal College of Art; Salford; Sheffield; Sheffield Hallam; South Bank; Southampton; Staffordshire; Stirling; Strathclyde; Sunderland; Surrey; Sussex; Teesside; Thames Valley; Ulster; UMIST; Wales (Cardiff University); Wales (University of Wales Institute, Cardiff); Wales (University of Wales, Aberystwyth); Wales (University of Wales, Swansea); Warwick; Westminster; Wolverhampton; York

DIPLOMAS AWARDED BY UNIVERSITIES
Aberdeen; Abertay, Dundee; Anglia; Anglia (City College, Norwich); Aston; Barnsley; Bath Spa; Birmingham; Blackburn; Bournemouth; Bradford; Bradford (Bradford & Ilkley Community College); Brighton; Brunel; Bucks. Coll.; Cambridge; Central England; Central Lancashire; Cheltenham & Gloucester; City; Coventry; De Montfort, Leicester; Doncaster; Dundee; Durham; Durham (New College Durham); East Anglia (Suffolk College); Edinburgh; Exeter; Exeter (Truro College); Glamorgan; Glasgow; Glasgow Caledonian; Greenwich; Heriot-Watt (Scottish Borders Campus); Hertfordshire; Huddersfield; Hull; Kent; Kent (Canterbury Christ Church University College); Kingston; Lancaster; Leicester; Lincolnshire; Lincolnshire (East Yorkshire College); Lincolnshire (Grimsby College); Lincolnshire (Hull College); Lincolnshire (Yorkshire Coast College); Liverpool (Chester College of H.E.); Liverpool (Liverpool Hope University College); London (Birkbeck, University of London); London (King's College London); London (University College (UCL)); Loughborough; Luton; Manchester; Manchester Metropolitan

National Certificates and Diplomas
BTEC National Certificates/Diplomas: Computer Studies; Computing, Business and Electronics; Information Technology Applications
BTEC Higher National Certificates/Diplomas: Computer Studies; Computer Studies (Business Data Processing); Computer Studies (Computer Systems Maintenance); Computer Studies (Industrial Data Processing); Computer Studies (Software Engineering); Computing; Information Technology *Scotland*
SQA HNC: Business Information Management; Business Information Systems; Computer Aided Draughting; Computer Aided Draughting and Design; Computer Aided Engineering (Electronics); Computer Aided Engineering (Manufacture); Computer Aided Landscape Technology; Computer Aided Manufacture; Computer Applications; Computer Aided Applications for Business; Computer Applications with Management Skills; Computer Controlled Engineering; Computer Graphic Design and Production; Computer Installation Support Engineering; Computer Networks and Information Management; Computer Support and Maintenance; Computer Technology and Instrumentation; Computing; Computing and Business Administration; Computing and Electronics; Information Systems; Information Technology; Information Technology Applications; Information Technology and Business Administration; Information Technology and Computer Systems; Information Technology Applications; Information Technology Support; Information Technology Systems; Microcomputer Servicing and Support; Microcomputer Support; Microcomputer Systems Support; Microprocessor Engineering Systems with Diagnostics; Multimedia Computing.
SQA HND: Business Information Management; Business Information Systems; Business Information Technology; Computer Aided Draughting and Design; Computer Aided Electronics with Management Studies; Computer Aided Engineering; Computer Aided Engineering (Manufacture with Management Studies); Computer Aided Landscape Technology; Computer Applications Management; Computer Graphic Design and Production; Computer Networks and Information Management; Computer Technology and Instrumentation; Computing; Computing and Business Administration; Computing and Electronics; Computing and Telecommunications; Computing (Foreign Language); Computing: Software; Computing: Software Development; Computing: Support; Information and Media Technology; Information and Office Management; Information Technology and Business Administration; Information Technology Systems; Information Technology with Teaching, Caring and Special Needs; Microcomputer Servicing and Support; Microprocessor Engineering with Diagnostics; Multimedia Computing; Multimedia Development and Production.

NVQs

Level 1: Operating Information Technology; Using Information Technology
Level 2: Information Systems Analysis; Install Information Technology Products; Operating Information Technology; Servicing Software (Support Centre); Software Creation; Support Users of Information Technology; Using Information Technology
Level 3: Implement Information Technology Solution; Information Systems Acquisition; Information Systems Analysis; Information Systems Design and Programming; Servicing Software (Field and Support Centre); Support Users of Information Technology; Use and Support of Information Technology
Level 4: Information Systems Development

SVQs

Level 1: Operating Information Technology; Using Information Technology
Level 2: Information Systems Analysis; Install Information Technology Products; Operating Information Technology; Support Users of Information Technology; Using Information Technology
Level 3: Implement Information Technology Solution; Information Systems Acquisition; Information Systems Analysis; Information Systems Design and Programming; Support Users of Information Technology; Use and Support of Information Technology
Level 4: Information Systems Development

GNVQs

3732 Information Technology

OCR

OCR offers the **Cambridge Certificate in Information Technology (CIT)** and **Computer Literacy & Information Technology (RSA CLAIT)** and various other awards. Contact OCR for further details.

City & Guilds

2230 Microcomputer Technology; 4180 Computer Programming & Information Processing; 4190 Data Processing for Computer Users; 4240 Preliminary Applications Programming Certificate; 4242 Basic Competence in Information Technology; 4250 Applications Programming Certificate; 4351 Computer Aided Draughting & Design using Autocad; 7261 Information Technology; 9351 Introductory Computer Programming.

London Chamber of Commerce and Industry Examinations Board (LCCIEB)

Level 1: Using Information Technology
Level 2: Using Information Technology
Level 3: Use and Support of Information Technology

Other Qualifications

NCC Certificate in Systems Analysis & Design: Awarded on the basis of an exam held in conjunction with the NCC Basic Course in Systems Analysis. The course is usually 6 wks FT (but may be done PT) and is intended to train students in investigation, analysis, design and implementation of business systems that involve a computer system. The exam consists of an assessment of course performance by the Education and Training Institute, a written exam; and an oral exam conducted by external examiners appointed by the Board. Holders of the Certificate should be capable of carrying out basic systems work as a member of a team under supervision.
Modular and Practitioner Certificates in SSADM 4+: The qualifications for SSADM 4+ follow a modular structure. The **Foundation Certificate in SSADM 4+** is achieved by attending a three-day accredited course and gaining a pass in a written examination. Candidates can then take up to 6 modular courses (2 to 3 days each) and examinations, for example: **Advanced Data**

Modelling; Physical Design; and Graphical User Interface Design. Candidates achieving the Foundation Certificate and at least 3 modular Certificates are entitled to take an oral examination which leads to the **Practitioner Certificate in SSADM 4+.**

Certificate in Project Management for Information Systems: Awarded on the basis of an exam following an accredited course. The Certificate is intended for those who have experience in project management, and wish to acquire formal training, and for those who have been working in information systems and are about to take project responsibility. The courses leading to this qualification last 80 hrs, usually in two 5-day modules. The exam consists of assessed course work, a written exam; and an oral exam conducted by two examiners appointed by the Board. Certificate holders should be competent in the basic skills of project management and be capable of taking responsibility for the life-cycle of small to medium-sized projects.

Diploma in Project Management for Information Systems: Awarded on the basis of 5 in-depth projects and an oral examination, the Diploma is intended for those who have considerable experience in project management. The holders are expected to be highly competent in all aspects of project management, and capable of taking full responsibility for medium-sized to large projects.

Foundation Certificate in IT Service Management: Awarded on the basis of an exam following attendance at a 3-day accredited course. It is aimed at those who wish to become familiar with the best practice for IT service management, as defined by the IT Infrastructure Library developed by the CCTA. There are no formal entry requirements, but a basic level of IT literacy is useful.

Business and Management Skills for IT Professionals: Awarded on the basis of a rigorous course assessment this Certificate is intended to give the holder practical guidance on business management skills. The course lasts five days; familiarity with the terminology of the IT Infrastructure library book of the same name, upon which the syllabus is based is an advantage.

Qualifications in Telecommunications Management: Certificate-level qualifications awarded on the basis of a written exam following attendance at courses accredited by the Board. Diploma-level qualifications awarded on the basis of a two-stage process. Stage 1 is completed by achieving the Certificate in Business Strategies, the Certificate in Resource Management, plus one of the certificates from either Telecommunications Technology, Call Centre Management, or Network Services Management. Stage 2 requires a project report and oral examination where considered necessary by the examiners. On completion, candidates will hold one of the following, depending on the technical third Certificate and the subject of the project: Management Diploma in Telecommunications; Diploma in Call Centre Management; or Diploma in Network Services Management.

Foundation Certificate in Software Testing: Awarded on the basis of a written exam following attendance at an accredited 3-day training course. The Certificate is intended for those who wish to be aware of the techniques and terminology of software testing. At a later stage, a Practitioner Certificate (8-day course) and a Diploma will be available.

Certificate in Information Security: Awarded on the basis of attending accredited training (1 wk), and passing a written exam. The objective of the Certificate is to ensure that the holder has a basic understanding of concepts relating to Information Security management, current legislation, national and international standards and current business and technical environments.

Certificate in Data Protection: Awarded on the basis of a 1-wk accredited training course and a written exam. The Certificate indicates familiarity with current UK Data Protection Legislation.

Certificate in IT Infrastructure Management: Awarded on the basis of an exam following attendance at courses approved or accredited by the Board. The syllabus is based on the IT Infrastructure Library developed by the Central Computer and Telecommunications Agency. The exam consists of assessed course work, and a written exam set and marked by the Board's examiners. There are no specific criteria for admission but it is unlikely that anyone with less that 5 yrs' relevant experience will have the appropriate background to benefit from the courses. The training for this exam takes the form of two 1-wk courses.

Address: Information Systems Examinations Board, The British Computer Society, 1 Sanford Street, Swindon SN1 1HJ Tel: 01793 417417 Fax: 01793 417458 E-mail: ISEB@hq.bcs.org.uk

Pitman Qualifications

Word Processing Techniques; Keyboarding; Practical Data Processing; Understanding Computers; Practical Spreadsheet Processing; Computerised Accounts; Text Production Skills; Text Production Skills (French or German or Spanish); Disk Management; Desktop Publishing

Other Vocational Awarding Bodies
ABC: introductory and Further Information Technology

Useful Addresses
Information Technology NTO, 16-18 Berners Street, London W1P 3DD Tel: 020 7580 6677 Fax: 020 7580 5577

CONFERENCE EXECUTIVES

Membership of Professional Institutions and Associations

ASSOCIATION FOR CONFERENCES AND EVENTS – ACE INTERNATIONAL

Riverside House, High Street, Huntingdon, Cambridgeshire PE29 3SG Tel: 01480 457595 Fax: 01480 412863 e-mail: ace@martex.co.uk Website: www.martex.co.uk/ace
Membership of the Association exists in over 30 countries outside Great Britain and it is open to all those concerned with the organisation and administration of conferences, business events, meetings, seminars, symposia, study tours and incentive travel in addition to those who supply services and various facilities for the industry. The Association organises professional training in conference related skills for members and non-members, as well as working with colleges in joint training initiatives. ACE initiated the establishment of occupational standards and the development of a framework of NVQs for the Events Industry. These have now been accredited and will be awarded by the City and Guilds Institute.

COUNSELLING

Membership of Professional Institutions and Associations

BRITISH ASSOCIATION FOR COUNSELLING

1 Regent Place, Rugby, Warwickshire CV21 2PJ Tel: 01788 578328 Fax: 01788 562189 e-mail: bac@bac.co.uk Website: www.counselling.co.uk
MEMBERSHIP:
BAC membership is open to those practising counselling or psychotherapy, using counselling skills within another role or training in counselling. All BAC members are required to work in accordance with the Codes of Ethics and Practice. Membership alone is not a qualification. There are currently 4 codes; for counsellors, for supervision of counsellors, for trainers and counselling skills.
ACCREDITATION:
Accreditation as an individual counsellor will be awarded to individual members who successfully demonstrate that they meet one of the following criteria: (i) 450 hrs of formal counsellor training comprised of 250 hrs of theory and 200 hrs of skills training and at least 450 hrs of supervised counselling practice over a min of 3 yrs; (ii) Completion of a BAC Accredited course plus supervised counselling practice as (i) above; (iii) 10 unit combination of counsellor training (1 unit = 75 hrs) and yrs of supervised practice (1 unit = 150 hrs min per yr); (iv) 10 yrs of supervised counselling practice with a min of 150 practice hrs per yr. In all cases members must have an agreed ongoing arrangement for counselling supervision of 1 1/2 hrs individual or equivalent monthly, have undertaken 40 hrs of personal therapy or an equivalent activity, and give evidence of serious commitment to ongoing personal and professional development. This

could be indicated by regular participation in further training, support study etc. Accreditation is renewed on an annual basis.

United Kingdom Register of Counsellors: There are two forms of registration under this system: Independent for counsellors accredited by BAC and COSCA (Confederation of Scottish Counselling Agencies); Sponsored for counsellors working in counselling organisations that provide a counselling service.

CENTRAL SCHOOL FOR COUNSELLING TRAINING

New Roman House, 10 East Road, London N1 6AD Tel: 020 7253 9944 or 0800 243463 (freephone enq Fax: 020 7253 9945 e-mail: enquiries@csct.ltd.uk Website: www.csct.ltd.uk

CSCT has been running training programmes for over 20 yrs. Courses are offered at a national training centre in London and at colleges throughout the UK. All are approved by the DfEE as vocational qualifications and externally validated by the AQA.

QUALIFICATIONS:

Introductory courses: Introduction to Counselling; Counselling Children & Adolescents; Counselling in the Workplace; Cognitive Counselling; Drugs and Alcohol Counselling; Dealing with Grief and Loss

Level One Certificates: Counselling Theory; Counselling Skills; Specialist Counselling Skills

Level Two Advanced Certificate: Counselling Skills & Theory

Level Three Part-time Diploma: Therapeutic Counselling (psychodynamic/cognitive)

Full-time Diploma: Therapeutic Counselling (psychodynamic/cognitive); Supervision of Counsellors and Therapists

University Qualifications

The following universities offer qualifications in Counselling and related subjects. Full details may be found in Part 4, under the entry for the appropriate university.

FIRST DEGREES AWARDED BY UNIVERSITIES

Anglia (City College, Norwich); Birmingham (The University of Birmingham, Westhill); Bradford (Bradford & Ilkley Community College); Bucks. Coll.; Central Lancashire; Hull; Lancaster (Blackpool and The Fylde College); Leeds (The College of Ripon & York St John); Leeds Metropolitan; Liverpool (Chester College of H.E.); Liverpool John Moores; Salford; Southampton (Chichester Institute of Higher Education); Surrey; Surrey (University of Surrey Roehampton); Teesside

HIGHER DEGREES AWARDED BY UNIVERSITIES

Abertay, Dundee; Birmingham; Bournemouth; Bradford (Bradford & Ilkley Community College); Brighton; Bristol; Brunel; Central England; City; City (School of Psychotherapy & Counselling at Regent's College); De Montfort, Leicester; Derby; Durham; East London; Essex; Greenwich; Hertfordshire; Keele; Lancaster; Leeds (Bretton Hall); Leeds (The College of Ripon & York St John); Leeds Metropolitan; Liverpool (Chester College of H.E.); Liverpool John Moores; London (Birkbeck, University of London); London (Imperial College of Science, Technology & Medicine); London Guildhall; Manchester; Nottingham; Nottingham Trent; Reading; Sheffield Hallam; South Bank; Surrey; Surrey (University of Surrey Roehampton); Thames Valley; Ulster; Wales (University of Wales College, Newport); Wales (University of Wales Institute, Cardiff); Wolverhampton

HONORARY DEGREES AWARDED BY UNIVERSITIES

Manchester

DIPLOMAS AWARDED BY UNIVERSITIES

Anglia (City College, Norwich); Anglia (Colchester Institute); Birmingham; Birmingham (The University of Birmingham, Westhill); Bournemouth; Brighton; Bristol; Central England; City; Derby; Durham; East London; Hertfordshire; Hull; Kent; Leeds (Bretton Hall); Leeds (The College of Ripon & York St John); Leeds Metropolitan; Leicester; Liverpool (Chester College of H.E.); London (Goldsmiths College); London (King's College London); Manchester (Warrington Collegiate Institute, Faculty of H.E.,); Napier; Newcastle; Nottingham Trent; OU (Northern College of Education); Reading; South Bank; Southampton (Chichester Institute of Higher Education); St Martin; Strathclyde; Surrey (University of Surrey Roehampton); Ulster

CERTIFICATES AWARDED BY UNIVERSITIES

Bristol; Central Lancashire; City; Durham; Exeter; Glasgow Caledonian; Hertfordshire; Hull; Keele; Kent; Leeds (Bretton Hall); Leeds (The College of Ripon & York St John); Leeds Metropolitan; Leicester; Liverpool (Chester College of H.E.); London (Goldsmiths College); Manchester; OU (Northern College of Education); Oxford; Salford; South Bank; St Martin; Surrey (University of Surrey Roehampton); Ulster

OTHER COURSES AWARDED BY UNIVERSITIES

Manchester Metropolitan

POSTGRADUATE DIPLOMAS AWARDED BY UNIVERSITIES

Central Lancashire

National Certificates and Diplomas

BTEC Higher National Certificates/Diplomas: Caring Services (Counselling)

Other Vocational Awarding Bodies

ABC: Counselling

CREDIT MANAGEMENT

Membership of Professional Institutions and Associations

THE INSTITUTE OF CREDIT MANAGEMENT

The Water Mill, Station Road, South Luffenham, Oakham, Leicestershire LE15 8NB
Tel: 01780 722900 Fax: 01780 721888 e-mail: info@icm.org.uk

MEMBERSHIP:
Fellow (FICM): There is no direct admittance to Fellowship, so applicants must be current members of the Institute. Applicants for Fellowship must also meet any two of the following three criteria: (a) be able to prove 7 yrs in senior management positions; (b) be able to demonstrate that they have made a notable contribution to the credit profession over a number of yrs; (c) show evidence of active participation in Institute national or branch affairs by having held office over a number of yrs.
Member (MICM): Entry to this grade is open to those who are able to demonstrate a minimum of 5 yrs management level experience in the credit profession or its ancillary services.
Graduate Member (MCIM(Grad)): Entry is by successful completion of the Institute's Certificate and Diploma examinations.
Associate Member (AICM(Cert)): Entry is by successful completion of the Institute's Certificate examinations.
Affiliate: Entry to this grade is open to those who: (i) are at least 21; (ii) have experience in credit management. This is a non-professional grade without designatory letters and without the right to vote on the Institute's affairs at national level.
Student: The Institute has an open entry policy and does not require applicants to satisfy any age or educational criteria before being admitted.

PROFESSIONAL EXAMINATIONS:
Certificate: A candidate for the Certificate examinations must be registered as a student of the Institute. The subjects are: Business Environment; Accounting; Business Law; Introductory Credit Management.
Diploma: A candidate for the Diploma must normally have passed or been exempted from all

Certificate subjects. The subjects are: Advanced Credit Management; Practice Credit Management; Credit Management Law; Legal Proceedings and Insolvency. In both qualifications candidates may take any number of subjects at one sitting.

The Foundation Award in Credit Management: This is a stand-alone qualification that is awarded to students who successfully complete the Certificate subject Introductory Credit Management. Students are only eligible for this award when on registration with the Institute they confirm that, initially at least, it is their intended end-point qualification.

EXEMPTIONS:
Exemption from Certificate subjects may be granted to students holding passes in comparative subjects in schemes of equivalent or higher standard eg ONC or OND Business Studies, a BTEC National Award, NVQs or a SCOTVEC equivalent. Exemptions are granted from Diploma subjects to students who have successfully completed comparable subjects in degree courses, in BTEC Higher National Awards, SCOTVEC equivalents, or in the Final Stages of the exams of recognised professional bodies.

University Qualifications

The following universities offer qualifications in Credit Management and related subjects. Full details may be found in Part 4, under the entry for the appropriate university.

PROFESSIONAL COURSES AWARDED BY UNIVERSITIES
London Guildhall

DANCING

Membership of Professional Institutions and Associations

THE BENESH INSTITUTE OF CHOREOLOGY

36 Battersea Square, London SW11 3RA Tel: 020 7223 0091 Fax: 020 7924 3129
e-mail: beneshinstitute@rad.org.uk Website: www.rad.org.uk / www.benesh.org
The Benesh Institute fosters and co-ordinates developments in Benesh Movement Notation in all its applications, trains Benesh choreologists and clinical notators, conducts exams, maintains a library of movement scores and registers works for copyright protection.

AWARDS:
Proficiency Certificates: Elementary, Intermediate and Advanced levels.
Teachers' Certificates: Elementary, Intermediate and Advanced levels.

MEMBERSHIP:
Fellowship of the Institute is awarded for outstanding work in the furtherance and development of Benesh Movement Notation.
Associateship of the Institute is awarded on the successful completion of study programmes and is recognised by major dance companies as the professional qualification.

THE BRITISH BALLET ORGANIZATION

39 Lonsdale Road, Barnes, London SW13 9JP Tel: 020 8748 1241 Fax: 020 8748 1301 e-mail: info@bbo.org.uk Website: www.bbo.org.uk

MEMBERSHIP:
Membership is by exam. 3 levels of membership include: Student, Executant and Teaching. Teachers from societies validated by the Council for Dance Education and Training may apply for provisional registration.

EXAMINATIONS:
Teaching Qualifications by exam in Ballet, Tap and Jazz, Teacher Training Scheme and Ballet Scholarship Scheme for BBO students. Exams in the British Ballet Organization syllabus from Pre-Primary to Advanced Standards in Ballet, Tap, Jazz and Modern Dance.

IMPERIAL SOCIETY OF TEACHERS OF DANCING

Imperial House, 22/26 Paul Street, London EC2A 4QE Tel: 020 7377 1577 Fax: 020 7247 8979
e-mail: admin@istd.org Website: www.istd.org

MEMBERSHIP:

Fellowship Membership (FISTD): Holders of Licentiate Diploma status may enter for the highest qualification of the Society from the age of 28 and after 8 yrs' teaching experience. Successful candidates may apply to train as an examiner of the faculty.

Licentiate Diploma (LISTD Dip): The Licentiate Diploma is granted on successful completion of the written papers in the History and Development of Western Dance, Anatomy and Physiology.

Licentiate Membership (LISTD): Candidates may enter for the Licentiate exam from the age of 23 and after 5 yrs' teaching experience.

Associate Diploma (AISTD Dip): Candidates aged 21 and upwards may enter for the Associate Diploma exam after 3 yrs' teaching experience. Associate Diploma status permits the teacher to become fully registered.

Associate Membership (AISTD): Students aged 18 and upwards may enter for the Associate exam to gain a teaching qualification and provisional registration.

Student Membership: Can be applied for by candidates who have been successful in the Elementary, Intermediate or Advanced exams in any of the Theatre Faculties. The Associate, Licentiate, Fellowship and Diploma examinations are qualifications which are recognised and approved by the Council for Dance Education and Training.

EXAMINATIONS:

Grade/Class Exams: Can be taken in Classical Ballet (Cecchetti and Imperial Methods), Classical Greek Dance, Modern Theatre Dance (including Tap), National Dance (including Scottish Dancing) and South Asian Dance. There are 8 levels of exam from Pre-Primary to Grade VI, although the content varies from faculty to faculty.

Medal Tests: Can be taken in Ballroom, Latin American, Sequence, Disco, Classical Greek, Jazz, National and Scottish Country and Highland Dancing. The levels ascend from Bronze to Silver, Gold, Gold Star and Supreme Award in up to 4 divisions.

Professional Exams: Can be taken in all Faculties and are linked with Membership of the Society as detailed above.

INTERNATIONAL DANCE TEACHERS' ASSOCIATION LIMITED

International House, 76 Bennett Road, Brighton BN2 5JL Tel: 01273 685652 Fax: 01273 674388
e-mail: info@idta.co.uk Website: www.idta.co.uk

This Association is the result of mergers between various teachers' organisations. The Association conducts professional exams at **Associate (AIDTA), Member (MIDTA)**, and **Fellow (FIDTA)** level in Ballet, Ballroom, Latin, Modern Jazz, Freestyle, Rock and Roll, Sequence, Theatre Craft and Tap Dancing and minor (amateur) exams in the same branches plus Gymnastic Dance, Country and Western and Dance Exercise. The Association is an Awarding Body recognised by the DfEE. It has been successful in developing a National Curriculum programme for Dance in Physical Education, and an NVQ Level 3 in Training and Development contextualised for dance teachers, through the OCR.

THE ROYAL ACADEMY OF DANCING

36 Battersea Square, London SW11 3RA Tel: 020 7223 0091 Fax: 020 7924 3129
e-mail: info@rad.org.uk Website: www.rad.org.uk
A teaching, training and examining body of classical ballet.

MEMBERSHIP:

Student Membership: Optional for students who have passed the Pre-Elementary and Elementary Executant exams and mandatory for sitting the Intermediate exam.

Full Membership: Mandatory on passing the Intermediate Executant exam and the Teaching Certificate exam.

Teaching Membership: Mandatory for teachers who enter candidates for exams or assessments.

REGISTRATION:

A Register of Teachers, who enter children and students for exam, is held by the Academy.

GRADE EXAMINATIONS:
For children from the age of 5, starting at Pre-Primary and Primary, and progressing through 8 grades, Grade 1 to Grade 8 Award for Girls.

MAJOR EXAMINATIONS:
For students who study Classical Ballet, possibly with a view to either performing or teaching. 5 levels Pre-Elementary (optional). Elementary, Pre-Intermediate (optional), Intermediate, Advanced and Solo Seal.

TEACHING EXAMINATIONS:
ARAD Advanced Teaching Dip: The Academy's highest teaching exam requiring a depth of knowledge of the principles of classical ballet and a high standard of teaching. Open to holders of the RAD Teaching Diploma, LRAD's and BA (Hons) degree.
RAD Teaching Dip: Written exams in Anatomy & Technique, History of Ballet, Psychology, Child development & Learning and Music in relation to the teaching of dance, in addition to holding the Teaching Certificate and 5 yrs teaching experience. Teaching diploma, Membership and Registration Services, London.

TEACHING PROGRAMMES & QUALIFICATIONS FROM THE FACULTY OF EDUCATION:
BA (Hons) degree in the Art and Teaching of Ballet: A 3 yr practical teacher training course validated by the University of Durham, combining Performance, Education, Dance History and the contextual disciplines of Music and Labanotation, College of the Royal Academy of Dancing, London.
Dip PDTC (RAD London): A 1 yr teaching course for ex-professional dancers. Professional Dancers Teaching Course, Education and Training Dept., London.
RAD Teaching Certificate: A 3 yr distance learning programme comprising teaching experience, course attendance, assessment and monitoring, and a final exam. Teaching Certificate Programme, Registration Dept., London.
Intensive Teaching Course: A 1 yr intensive course for the mature practising teacher. Includes the Teaching Certificate examination and written papers, and a credit towards the RAD Teaching Certificate programme. College of the Royal Academy of Dancing, London.
Professional Dance Notators Diploma in Benesh Movement Notation: A full time, academy based programme which takes place over one yr, equipping dancers with the necessary skills to become professional Benesh Notators and Reconstructors.
BA(Hons) Benesh Movement Notation: An Academy-based programme centred around company placements, taking place over 24 mths, enabling students to develop skills and experiences learned from the Diploma programme.
BA(Hons) Classical Ballet teaching: A part time distance learning programme taking place over 24 or 36 mths, this provides the highest possible level in practical teaching supported by relevant theoretical studies.
BPhil(Hons) Ballet and Contextual Studies: A part time distance learning programme taking place over 16 or 28 mths, validated by the university of Durham, this combines theoretical study and academic research.

ROYAL BALLET SCHOOL

155 Talgarth Road, London W14 9DE Tel: 020 8748 6335 Fax: 020 8563 0649
e-mail: trbs@aol.com Website: www.royal-ballet-school.org.uk
The Royal Ballet School (RBS) takes senior students from the ages of 16 to 18.It also has a Lower School at White Lodge, Richmond Park, Surrey, where entry is at 11, with occasional places at 12 and 13 yrs, and provides a specialist education in ballet combined with general education. Many of the Lower School pupils graduate to the Upper School, where they are trained with other students who have been successful in the entrance auditions held in London and the regions. General education continues to A Level standard.

University Qualifications

The following universities offer qualifications in Dancing and related subjects. Full details may be found in Part 4, under the entry for the appropriate university.

FIRST DEGREES AWARDED BY UNIVERSITIES

Bath Spa; Birmingham; Brighton; City (Laban Centre London); De Montfort, Leicester; De Montfort, Leicester (De Montfort University Bedford); Durham (Royal Academy of Dancing); Hull; Leeds (The College of Ripon & York St John); Liverpool (Chester College of H.E.); Liverpool John Moores; Middlesex; Northumbria; Southampton (Chichester Institute of Higher Education); Southampton (King Alfred's College); Surrey; Wolverhampton

HIGHER DEGREES AWARDED BY UNIVERSITIES

Birmingham; City (Laban Centre London); De Montfort, Leicester; Hertfordshire; Hull; Middlesex; Southampton (Chichester Institute of Higher Education); Surrey; Surrey (University of Surrey Roehampton)

DIPLOMAS AWARDED BY UNIVERSITIES

Bath Spa; Brunel; City (Laban Centre London); Hertfordshire; Southampton (King Alfred's College); Surrey (University of Surrey Roehampton)

CERTIFICATES AWARDED BY UNIVERSITIES

Brighton; Brunel

PRE-DEGREE AWARDED BY UNIVERSITIES

Leeds (Northern School of Contemporary Dance)

National Certificates and Diplomas

BTEC Higher National Certificates/Diplomas Performing Arts (Community Dance); Performing Arts (Dance)

Other Qualifications and Courses

LABAN CENTRE LONDON

Laurie Grove, London SE14 6NH Tel: 020 8692 4070 Fax: 020 8694 8749 e-mail: info@laban.co.uk Website: www.laban.co.uk
EXAMINATIONS:
(All degree courses are validated by City University, London)
BA(Hons)/Diploma Dance Theatre: 3 yrs FT.
Professional Diploma Dance Studies: 1 yr FT, 2 yrs PT.
Professional Diploma Community Dance Studies: 1 yr FT, 2 yrs PT.
Specialist Diploma Teaching Studies in Contemporary Dance: 1 yr (study blocks).
Specialist Diploma Dance Notating: 40 wks, 2 half days per wk.
Study Yr Abroad: 1 yr FT.
Independent Study Programme: 1 yr FT.
MA Dance Studies: 1 yr FT, 2-3 yrs PT.
MA in Dance Movement Therapy: 2 yrs FT, 3-4 yrs PT.
Postgraduate Diploma Dance Movement Therapy: 2 yrs FT, 3-4 yrs PT.
MA Scenography: 1 yr FT, 2 yrs PT.
Graduate Diploma Performance (Transitions Dance Company): 1 yr FT.
Graduate Diploma Visual Design for Dance: 15 wks, 1 day per wk.
MPhil/Phd Research Degrees: 1-2 yrs FT, 2-7 yrs PT.
For information about our annual Easter School and International Summer School, contact the Short Courses Administrator on the number given above.

MIDDLESEX UNIVERSITY: LONDON COLLEGE OF DANCE

10 Linden Road, Bedford MK40 2DA Tel: 01234 213331 Fax: 01234 217284

COURSES:
BA (Hons) Dance: This 3 yr degree programme is part of the Dance sector of The School of Art, Design and Performing Arts of Middlesex University. A high level of performance skills in classical ballet and modern dance is nurtured in this course, as well as theoretical studies. Integrated studies include dance history, music, drama, choreography, repertoire etc. Modules

include Teaching the Growing Child in Yr 2 and Teaching the Developing Artist in Yr 3. Entry requirements: 2 A Levels and at least 3 GCSE passes in other subjects – these must include English. Dance Standard: Elementary level of Ballet.

LONDON CONTEMPORARY DANCE SCHOOL

Director Veronica Lewis MBE, 17 Duke's Road, London WC1H 9AB Tel: 020 7387 0152 Fax: 020 7383 4851 e-mail: info@theplace.org.uk Website: www.theplace.org.uk

All courses, including the degree courses, are predominantly practical and include a rigorous training in contemporary dance and ballet with music, stage design and costume, choreography and a wide range of other dance and movement studies. Students have the possibility to create their own dances, to work with established choreographers and to perform publicly in the course of their 3 yrs at the School. Entry is by audition.

COURSES:

BA(Hons) Contemporary Dance: 3 yrs FT. Entry requirement: 2 A Levels and 3 O Levels or equivalent. The course is open to professional dancers.
Certificate in Contemporary Dance and Choreography: 1 yr.
MA/Postgraduate Diploma: 1 yr FT. Specialisation Performance/Choreography/Video & Film.
MPhil & PhD: Research degrees.

MIDDLESEX UNIVERSITY DANCE DEPARTMENT

Incorporating London College of Dance, Trent Park, Bramley Road, London N14 4XS
Tel/Fax 0181 362 6148 and London College of Dance, 10 Linden Road, Bedford MK40 2DA
Tel: 01234 213331 Fax: 01234 217284.
Institution grant status – Mandatory.

COURSES:

Courses at Trent Park are:
BA (Hons) Dance Performance: UCAS Code W450 P BA/DANP.
BA (Hons) Performing Arts (Dance): UCAS Code W430 P BA/DPA.
BA (Hons) Dance: UCAS Code W455 Z BA/DAN – based at Bedford Campus, London College of Dance.
BA (Hons) Dance Studies: Combines Dance with another subject, eg Education, Spanish, Psychology, and Media and Cultural Studies.
MA Choreography: Based at both campuses. The Dance Department focuses its work on the synthesis of theory and practice and has established strong links with the dance profession in order to enhance the study of dance as a vital artform.
BA (Hons) Community Dance: UCAS code WW49P/ComDan (subject to validation).
MA Choreography with Performing Arts

DURATION OF COURSES:
All BA (Hons) degrees – 3 yrs.
Both MA degrees – 1 yr FT or 2 yrs PT.

DENTISTRY

Registrable Qualifications

In order to qualify as dental surgeons and to be placed in the Dentists Register, maintained by the General Dental Council, 37 Wimpole Street, London W1M 8DQ Tel 0171 887 3800, in accordance with the provisions of the Dentists Act 1984, students must obtain one of the following qualifications:

A first Degree in Dentistry conferred by a university in the UK.

A diploma as a Licentiate in Dental Surgery conferred by one of the Royal Colleges of Surgeons of England and Edinburgh, the Royal College of Physicians and Surgeons of Glasgow. Certain dental qualifications awarded abroad are recognised by the Council as admitting the holders to the UK register without exam. Inquiries should be made to the Council concerning the eligibility of dentists holding qualifications awarded outside the UK.

DENTAL TECHNICIANS

Dental Technicians are craft workers who make dental appliances. They usually work in a hospital, local authority, dental practice or commercial laboratory making up appliances prescribed by a registered dentist. Many technicians train on the job and attend day-release and evening classes to prepare for the BTEC Diploma in Dental Technology. A 3-yr FT training course is available at a number of dental teaching hospitals in England and Wales in conjunction with technical colleges. Some colleges also have 3 yr FT courses independent of dental teaching hospitals. To be employed in the hospital service the BTEC Diploma course must be followed by an additional 1 yr's experience in an approved hospital laboratory. A voluntary register of Technicians is administered by the Dental Technicians Education and Training Advisory Board, 5 Oxford Court, St James' Road, Brackley, Northamptonshire NN13 7XY, from whom further information is available.

DENTAL NURSES

BRITISH ASSOCIATION OF DENTAL NURSES

11, Pharos Street, Fleetwood, Lancashire FY7 6BG Tel: 01253 778631 Website: www.badn.org.uk

British Association of Dental Nurses, 11 Pharos Street, Fleetwood, Lancashire FY7 6BG
Tel: 01253 778631

Membership of the Association is open to all dental nurses, qualified or unqualified. Dental Nurses work normally with dentists in general practice or in public dental services. Their duties might include booking appointments, keeping records, mixing fillings, helping with dental X-rays and other chairside work. Training in general practice is mainly given by dentists themselves which should be supplemented by PT evening courses, leading to the National Certificate, but there are also FT courses of training at various dental hospitals. Entry requirements depend on the individual institutions.* Usually candidates should be 16 to 18 yrs old. The courses take the form of lectures, tutorials and practical work in various dental departments. A salary is paid during training in dental hospital. Dental hospitals conduct their own Intermediate and Final exams and award **Certificates of Proficiency.** They may also prepare their students for the **National Certificate of the National Examining Board for Dental Nurses**. Training is also available in the Army, Royal Navy and Royal Air Force.

*National Examining Board for Dental Nurses, 110 London Street, Fleetwood, Lancashire FY7 Tel: 01253 778417: In order to qualify for the National Certificate a dental nurse must have completed at least 24 mths' full-time employment at the chairside and passed the National Examination and the qualification will not be awarded until the completion of the stipulated 24 mths. There are no formal educational requirements or age restrictions for entry to the National Certificate exam.

Eligibility for courses of study: There may be requirements for entry to a course of study at a training establishment and it is suggested that this is checked with the individual college or dental hospital.

DENTAL HYGIENISTS

Dental Hygienists are permitted to carry out certain kinds of dental work under the direction of a registered dentist, including cleaning, scaling and polishing teeth and giving instruction on matters relating to oral hygiene. They are employed in hospitals, in the public health services and also by general dental practitioners; dental hygienists may work only under the direction and in accordance with the written prescription of a registered dentist. The direct personal supervision of a registered dentist who is on the premises is required when a dental hygienist administers local infiltration analgesia.

Courses in dental hygiene are provided by the dental hospitals in Belfast, Birmingham, Bristol, Dundee, Cardiff, Liverpool, Newcastle upon Tyne, Manchester, Sheffield, Edinburgh, Glasgow and Leeds, and in London by Guy's Hospital, King's College Hospital, London Hospital (combined course in dental therapy & dental hygiene), and the Eastman Dental Hospital. Entry requirements vary and applications are considered individually on merit; detailed information may be obtained from the hospitals. Applicants should have received a good general education including 5 passes at O level in GCE or GCSE passes with at least 1 science subject (Biology, Chemistry or General Science). Training Schools also require applicants to have trained as a Dental

Nurse. Candidates without previous clinical experience but who possess two A Level passes at grade E or above (or Scottish Higher Grade pass at grade C or above), may also be eligible for entry to the course. The course currently extends over 2 yrs. Dental Hygienists are also trained in the Armed Forces. Dental Hygienists who have completed the course of training and have passed the exam for the **Diploma in Dental Hygiene** are entitled to have their names entered in the **Roll of Dental Hygienists** kept by the **General Dental Council**, 37 Wimpole Street, London W1M 8DQ Tel 0171 887 3800. Only enrolled dental hygienists are permitted to practise and to use the title 'dental hygienist'.

DENTAL THERAPISTS

Dental therapists are employed in hospitals and in the community dental service. They work under the direction of a registered dentist who prescribes the treatment to be given, which includes simple fillings, extraction of deciduous teeth, cleaning, scaling and polishing teeth and administration of preventive substances. They also give instruction in dental health. Dental therapists are not permitted to work in general practice.

Training courses in dental therapy are available in London at St Bartholomew's and the Royal London School of Medicine and Dentistry and the Eastman and also at Cardiff, Liverpool and Sheffield. The course lasts 27 mths and the entry qualifications required are the same as those for a dental hygienist. Dental therapists who have completed the course of training and have passed the exam for the **Diploma of Dental Therapy** as a Dental Therapist are entitled to have their names entered in the **Roll of Dental Therapists** kept by the **General Dental Council**, 37 Wimpole Street, London W1M 8DQ Tel 0171887 3800. Only enrolled dental therapists are permitted to practise and to use the title 'dental therapist'.

University Qualifications

The following universities offer qualifications in Dentistry and related subjects. Full details may be found in Part 4, under the entry for the appropriate university.

FIRST DEGREES AWARDED BY UNIVERSITIES

Belfast; Birmingham; Bristol; Dundee; Leeds; Liverpool; London (King's College London); London (Queen Mary & Westfield College (incorporating St Bartholomew's and the Royal London School of Medicine & Dentistry)); Manchester; Middlesex; Newcastle; Wales (College of Medicine)

HIGHER DEGREES AWARDED BY UNIVERSITIES

Bristol; Edinburgh; Glasgow; Leeds; Liverpool; London (King's College London); London (Queen Mary & Westfield College (incorporating St Bartholomew's and the Royal London School of Medicine & Dentistry)); London (University College (UCL)); Manchester; Newcastle; Sheffield; Wales (College of Medicine)

DIPLOMAS AWARDED BY UNIVERSITIES

Bristol; Edinburgh; Hertfordshire; Leeds; London (King's College London); London (University College (UCL)); Newcastle; Wales (College of Medicine)

CERTIFICATES AWARDED BY UNIVERSITIES

Wales (University of Wales Institute, Cardiff)

OTHER COURSES AWARDED BY UNIVERSITIES

London (King's College London)

National Certificates and Diplomas

BTEC National Certificates/Diplomas: Science (Dental Assisting); Science (Dental Technology)
BTEC Higher National Certificates/Diplomas: Science (Dental Technology)
Scotland
SQA HNC: Dental Technology
SQA HND: Dental Technology

DIETETICS

Membership of Professional Institutions and Associations

THE BRITISH DIETETIC ASSOCIATION

5th Floor, Elizabeth House, 22 Suffolk Street, Queensway, Birmingham B1 1LS Tel: 0121 616 4900 Fax: 0121 616 4901 e-mail: info@bda.uk.com Website: www.bda.uk.com.

MEMBERSHIP:
For registration with the Dieticians Board of the Council for Professions Supplementary to Medicine, a candidate must hold a recognised qualification in Dietetics. To qualify for membership of The British Dietetic Association one must be eligible for state registration.
State Registered Dieticians (SRD): May use the letters SRD.
Affiliate Membership: May be granted to graduates with a qualification in Nutrition who are working in the field of Applied Human Nutrition.
Honorary Associates: Are elected for distinguished contributions to the field of Human Nutrition and Dietetics.

University Qualifications

The following universities offer qualifications in Dietetics and related subjects. Full details may be found in Part 4, under the entry for the appropriate university.

FIRST DEGREES AWARDED BY UNIVERSITIES

Brighton; Coventry; Edinburgh; Glasgow Caledonian; Leeds Metropolitan; London (King's College London); Queen Margaret; Robert Gordon

HIGHER DEGREES AWARDED BY UNIVERSITIES

Leeds Metropolitan; Ulster; Wales (University of Wales Institute, Cardiff)

DIPLOMAS AWARDED BY UNIVERSITIES

Glasgow Caledonian; Leeds Metropolitan; London (King's College London)

DISTRIBUTION

Membership of Professional Institutions and Associations

THE INSTITUTE OF LOGISTICS AND TRANSPORT

Logistics and Transport Centre, Earlstrees Court, Earlstrees Road, Corby, Northants NN17 4XQ Tel: 01536 740100 Fax: 01536 740101 Website: www.iolt.org.uk

MEMBERSHIP GRADES:
Fellows (FCIT, FILT): Fellowship of the Institute is open to those Chartered Members who have at least 7 yrs' experience in a position or positions of high responsibility in the management of logistics or transport. Fellowship is also granted to people who have attained a position of eminence in logistics or transport.
Chartered Member (MCIT, MILT): Candidates for election or transfer to the grade of Chartered Member should hold the Institute's Advanced Diploma or an exempting qualification (usually an approved degree) and have at least 5 yrs' relevant experience in logistics or transport, including at least 2 at a senior level. A postgraduate programme is available to candidates whose qualifications meet only part of the requirements for exemption from the Advanced Diploma. The Professional Route enables experienced logistics or transport professionals, who do not fully meet the academic requirements for Chartered Membership, to demonstrate that they broadly satisfy the Institute's criteria. Alternatives include writing a professional essay, delivering a professional paper, submitting previously published works and/or undergoing a professional interview.

Candidates are required to provide evidence of their experience through a CV and an application form.

Member (MILT): Candidates for election or transfer to the grade of Member should hold an approved qualification at level 3 or 4* in logistics or transport and have management responsibility which involves planning, making decisions, directing and accountability for the use and performance of resources. Candidates with a level 3 qualification should have at least 3 yrs' relevant work experience; candidates with a level 4 qualification should have at least one yr's relevant work experience. Candidates are required to provide evidence that they meet the above criteria, either by a CV or though the application form. Candidates without an appropriate qualification but with management responsibility over an extended period (at least 5 yrs) may submit a portfolio of evidence for consideration under the Accreditation of Prior Experience (APA) process.

Affiliate: Affiliate Membership is open to those who are interested in logistics or transport and who support the aims of the Institute but who may not, for a variety of reasons, qualify for Membership. This grade includes those studying for educational qualifications in logistics or transport.

*Level 3 qualifications include relevant N/SVQs at level 3 and the ILT Certificate qualification. Level 4 qualifications include relevant N/SVQs at level 4, relevant HNC/HNDs and the ILT Diploma.

QUALIFICATIONS:

ILT Introductory Certificate: An introduction to logistics and business management designed for career changes, unemployed people and potential supervisors. It provides a broad overview of the basic logistics functions.

Certificate in Logistics: A choice of a modular, competence based programme for first line managers and supervisors involved in warehousing, transport, inventory planning, operational planning and materials handling, or a modular structure programme providing a sound basis for a transport career in Logistics.

Diploma in Transport: A choice of a modular, competence based programme for middle managers with functional responsibilities in warehousing, transport, inventory or materials management; or the alternative programme demonstrating knowledge and understanding application to transport at the operational management level. Also suitable for graduates entering the profession.

Advanced Diploma in Logistics: A choice of a competence based programme for senior managers covering all aspects of supply-chain strategy and management.

NVQ and SVQ Assessment: All of the qualifications above are linked to N/SVQs and candidates therefore have the opportunity to gain additional qualifications.

MSc in Logistics or Passenger Transport Management: The MSc in Logistics or Passenger Transport Management are masters degrees validated by Aston University, with distance learning materials and support provided by the Institute of Logistics and Transport. This 3-yr programme for professionals addresses strategic issues in passenger transport management or logistics.

European Accreditation: Those achieving the Certificate, Diploma and Advanced Diploma in Logistics options are eligible for accreditation by the European Certification Board for Logistics (ECBL). Studies for all these qualifications can be followed by attending a registered or approved training centre or by distance learning. Students on any of the Institutes's qualification courses need to register as an Affiliate of the Institute.

Refer to Transport section for the ILT's transport management qualifications.

NB: Refer to the section on Transport for further ILT qualifications.

University Qualifications

The following universities offer qualifications in Distribution and related subjects. Full details may be found in Part 4, under the entry for the appropriate university.

FIRST DEGREES AWARDED BY UNIVERSITIES

Aston; Central Lancashire; Coventry; Cranfield; Huddersfield; Loughborough; Northumbria; Plymouth

HIGHER DEGREES AWARDED BY UNIVERSITIES

Aston; Central England; Cranfield; East London; Edinburgh; Exeter; Glasgow Caledonian; Heriot-Watt; Salford

DIPLOMAS AWARDED BY UNIVERSITIES
Edinburgh; Salford

POSTGRADUATE DIPLOMAS AWARDED BY UNIVERSITIES
Heriot-Watt

National Certificates and Diplomas

BTEC National Certificates/Diplomas: Distribution Studies
BTEC Higher National Certificates/Diplomas: Distribution Studies; Distribution Studies (Food Production)

GNVQs

3735 Retail and Distributive Services

OCR

OCR offer the following awards:
Distributive Operations Level 1
Distribution & Warehousing Operations Levels 2, 3 & 4
Retail Operations Levels 2, 3 & 4
Retail Operations (Dairy & Hire) Level 3
Mail Operations Level 2
Hire of Goods & Services Levels 1 & 2 (accreditation to be confirmed)

City & Guilds

Scotland
SQA HNC: Distribution Supervisory Management with Retail.

Useful Addresses

Distributive Occupational Standards Council, Coda Centre, 189 Munster Road, London SW6 6AW, Tel: 020 7386 5599 Fax: 020 7386 9599

DIVING

DIVING CERTIFICATES

Health & Safety Executive, Diving Operations Strategy Team, 3rd Floor, South Wing, Rose Court, 2 Southwark Bridge, London SE1 9HS Tel: 020 7717 6701 Fax: 020 7717 6911
The Health and Safety Executive (HSE) issues diver competence certificates to divers who have been assessed as competent by HSE recognised diver training organisations. A list of recognised diver training organisations can be obtained from HSE.HSE issues certificates for the following competencies: SCUBA, Surface Supplied, Surface Supplied (Top Up) and Closed Bell. Divers who have qualified abroad may be able to dive in the UK waters using their non-UK qualifications without having to obtain a HSE certificate. HSE publishes a list of Approved Qualifications which may also be accessed at www.open.gov.uk/hse/spd/divequal.htm
FIRST AID AT WORK:
As part of diver training and assessment, divers are taught diving physiology and diving medicine. At the same time they must also gain a first aid at work qualification (unless they already have a valid one). While it is not a requirement for every diver to refresh it every three yrs (with the exception of offshore divers, who should), the diving contractor has a responsibility to ensure that there are sufficient divers in a dive team with in-date first aid at work qualifications. Refresher training should be taken during the final three mths before the current certificate expires (at an organisation recognised by HSE).

DRAMATIC AND PERFORMING ARTS
Membership of Professional Institutions and Associations
THE BRITISH (THEATRICAL) ARTS
12 Deveron Way, Rise Park, Romford, Essex RM1 4UL Tel: 01708 756263

MEMBERSHIP:
The Association, which conducts exams in Dramatic Art, Classical, Stage Ballet, Mime, Tap and Modern Dance has the following grades of membership:
Fellow (FBA): This grade is reserved for teacher members of at least 10 yrs' standing who have presented students gaining teacher membership. The Art's examiners and adjudicators are drawn from this group.
Advanced Teacher Member: Teacher Member (TMBA)Member, Non-Teacher Associate Member (AMBA);Companion (CBA);Student Member
Exams are conducted at Elementary, Intermediate and Advanced standards for teachers and performers. There are Bronze, Silver and Gold Medal tests for Preliminary-Advanced and non-professional adult students. Further details on application.

University Qualifications
The following universities offer qualifications in Dramatic and Performing Arts and related subjects. Full details may be found in Part 4, under the entry for the appropriate university.

FIRST DEGREES AWARDED BY UNIVERSITIES
Anglia; Barnsley; Bath Spa; Belfast; Birmingham; Brighton; Bristol; Brunel; Bucks. Coll.; Central England; Central Lancashire; Cheltenham & Gloucester; City (Guildhall School of Music & Drama); City (Laban Centre London); Coventry; De Montfort, Leicester; De Montfort, Leicester (De Montfort University Bedford); Derby; Durham (Royal Academy of Dancing); East Anglia; Essex; Exeter; Glamorgan; Glasgow; Greenwich; Hertfordshire; Huddersfield; Hull; Hull (Bishop Grosseteste College); Kent; Lancaster; Lancaster (Edge Hill College of Higher Education); Leeds; Leeds (Bretton Hall); Leeds (Northern School of Contemporary Dance); Leeds (The College of Ripon & York St John); Liverpool (Chester College of H.E.); Liverpool (Liverpool Hope University College); Liverpool John Moores; London (Goldsmiths College); London (Queen Mary & Westfield College (incorporating St Bartholomew's and the Royal London School of Medicine & Dentistry)); London (Royal Holloway); London Institute (Central Saint Martins College of Art & Design); London Institute (London College of Fashion); Loughborough; Luton; Manchester; Manchester (Warrington Collegiate Institute, Faculty of H.E,); Manchester Metropolitan.; Middlesex; North London; Northampton; Northumbria; Nottingham Trent; OU (The Central School of Speech & Drama); Plymouth; Plymouth (Dartington College of Arts); Queen Margaret; Reading; Royal Scottish AMD; Salford; South Bank; Southampton (Chichester Institute of Higher Education); Southampton (King Alfred's College); St Martin; Sunderland; Surrey (St Mary's, Strawberry Hill); Surrey (University of Surrey Roehampton); Ulster; Wales (Swansea Institute of Higher Education); Wales (University of Wales, Aberystwyth); Wales (University of Wales, Bangor); Warwick; Wolverhampton; Worcester

HIGHER DEGREES AWARDED BY UNIVERSITIES
Belfast; Birmingham; Bristol; Central England; City; City (Laban Centre London); De Montfort, Leicester; De Montfort, Leicester (De Montfort University Bedford); East Anglia; Essex; Exeter; Glasgow; Greenwich; Hertfordshire; Hull; Kent; Lancaster; Leeds; Leeds (Bretton Hall); Liverpool (Chester College of H.E.); London (Goldsmiths College); London (King's College London); London (Queen Mary & Westfield College (incorporating St Bartholomew's and the Royal London School of Medicine & Dentistry)); London (Royal Holloway); London Institute (Central Saint Martins College of Art & Design); Loughborough; Manchester; Middlesex; Newcastle; Northampton; Nottingham; OU (The Central School of Speech & Drama); Plymouth (Dartington College of Arts); Portsmouth; Reading; Royal Scottish AMD; Southampton (Chichester Institute of Higher Education); Southampton (King Alfred's College); St Martin; Surrey; Surrey (University of Surrey Roehampton); Thames Valley; Wales (Cardiff University); Wales (University of Wales College, Newport); Wales (University of Wales, Aberystwyth); Warwick; Worcester

DIPLOMAS AWARDED BY UNIVERSITIES

Barnsley; Bath Spa; Bristol; Brunel; Central England; City (Laban Centre London); Coventry; De Montfort, Leicester; De Montfort, Leicester (De Montfort University Bedford); Doncaster; Durham (New College Durham); East Anglia (Suffolk College); Exeter (Truro College); Hertfordshire; Hull; Kent; Leeds (Bretton Hall); Leeds (Northern School of Contemporary Dance); Leeds (The College of Ripon & York St John); Lincolnshire (Hull College); Liverpool (Liverpool Hope University College); Luton; Manchester; Northumbria; Nottingham Trent; OU (NESCOT); OU (The Central School of Speech & Drama); Salford; Southampton (King Alfred's College); Surrey (St Mary's, Strawberry Hill); Sussex

CERTIFICATES AWARDED BY UNIVERSITIES

Brighton; Brunel; Central England; Hull; Lincolnshire (Hull College); Liverpool (Chester College of H.E.); London (Goldsmiths College); Middlesex; OU (The Central School of Speech & Drama); Sussex; Wales (University of Wales Institute, Cardiff)

POSTGRADUATE CERTIFICATES AWARDED BY UNIVERSITIES

Warwick

POSTGRADUATE DIPLOMAS AWARDED BY UNIVERSITIES

Thames Valley

PRE-DEGREE AWARDED BY UNIVERSITIES

Leeds (Northern School of Contemporary Dance)

Speech and Drama

EXAMINATIONS TAKEN AFTER EXTERNAL STUDY

LONDON COLLEGE OF MUSIC AND MEDIA, Thames Valley University, St Mary's Road, Ealing, London W5 5RF Tel 020 8231 2364 Fax 020 8231 2433
E-mail: lcm.exams@tvu.ac.uk Website: elgar.tvu.ac.uk/lcmexams

Performers' Diploma of Associateship in Speech and Drama, and in Public Speaking (ALCM): The exam is both theoretical and practical. Candidates must be at least 16.

Performers' Diploma of Licentiateship in Speech and Drama and in Public Speaking (LLCM): Candidates must hold the Associateship Diploma before entering for this qualification.

Teacher's Diploma in Speech and Drama (LLCM(TD)): Candidates must be at least 18. This is a qualification for private teaching only. The LLC(TD) is accepted as a qualification for membership of the Society of Teachers of Speech and Drama.

Diploma in Drama in Education (LLCM(Ed)): Candidates must hold an ALCM Diploma in Speech, Drama and Communication.

Verse Speaking: Grades and Diplomas.

Music Theatre: Grades and Diplomas.

Reading: Grades only.

Acting: Grades and Diplomas.

Group Performance: Grades only.

Spoken English in Religion: Grades and Diplomas.

Diploma of Fellowship – Performer in Speech and Drama and in Public Speaking (FLCM): Licentiates of the College (LLCM or LLCM(TD)) may enter for the Fellowship Diploma in the same subject. This is a practical exam with no paperwork.

Performers' Diploma of Associateship in Music (ALCM): The exam is both theoretical and practical. All orchestral instruments and voice.

Performers' Diploma of Licentiateship in Music (LLCM): Candidates must hold ALCM before entering for this qualification.

Teacher's Diploma of Associateship in Music (ALCM(TD)): Candidates must be at least 15.

Teacher's Diploma of Licentiateship in Music (LLCM(TD)): Candidates must be at least 18, and must hold ALCM or ALCM(TD) before entering for this qualification.

Diploma of Fellowship: Performer in Music. Also available by thesis, composition or conducting.

GRADED EXAMINATIONS:
Introductory Examinations: Music, Speech and Drama for beginners.
Grades I-VIII: Practical in Music, Speech and Drama and Oral Communication.
Grades VI-VIII: Written exams in Speech and Drama and Oral Communication. Grade VIII paperwork is a compulsory section of the Grade VIII Speech and Drama Practical Exam.
Grades I-VIII: Written exams in Music. Grade V theory is a prerequisite for Grade VIII practical exam. Certificates are awarded as Pass, Merit and Honours. Introductory exams and 8 Grade exams are offered for all instruments and voice.

TRINITY COLLEGE LONDON 89 Albert Embankment, London SE1 7TP Tel:020 7820 6100
Fax: 020 7820 6161 E-mail: info@trinitycollege.co.uk WWW:www.trinitycollege.co.uk
Performer's Certificate in Speech and Drama: Candidates must present a programme of drama, verse and prose, and a prepared talk which is followed by a viva voce.
Associate Diploma (ATCL) in Speech and Drama: Candidates must present a programme of drama, verse and prose and give an impromptu talk which is followed by a viva voce. There is a 3 hr written paper. Candidates are required to have reached the age of 16 when taking the examination.
Licentiate Diploma (LTCL) in Speech and Drama: Candidates may enter as teachers or performers. In addition to the practical test, candidates must take two 3hr papers. Candidates are required to have reached the age of 18.
Fellowship Diploma (FTCL) in Speech and Drama: The exam involves a Performance exam and the writing of a Dissertation. Candidates must already hold the LTCL Diploma. Graded exams are available in Speech and Drama at all levels from Elementary to Advanced.
Certificate in Effective Communication: A 4 pt practical exam, consisting of a formal presentation, impromptu speaking, reading and a question and answer section. Graded exams are available in Effective Communication at all levels from Introductory to Advanced.
Licentiate Diploma for Teachers of English to Speakers of Other Languages (LTCL): This involves two 2½ hr written papers, a hr demonstration of class teaching and an oral interview.
Certificate in the Teaching of European Languages (CertTEL): A course of initial training in the teaching of the selected language, available at selected institutes conducting courses approved by Trinity College.
Certificate in the Teaching of English to Speakers of Other Languages (CertTESOL): A course of initial training available at institutions conducting courses approved by Trinity College.
Certificate in the Teaching of English to Young Learners (CertTEYL): A course for those who wish to teach English at Primary Level. Available at selected institutions conducting courses approved by Trinity College. Graded exams in spoken English for speakers of other languages are available at all levels, from Elementary to Advanced. There are new professional diplomas in acting, dance and stage management:
National Advanced Certificate in Professional Acting
National Certificate in Professional Dance (Classical Ballet)
National Diploma in Professional Acting
National Diploma in Professional Acting (Musical Theatre)
National Diploma in Professional Dance
National Diploma in Professional Dance (Musical Theatre)
National Diploma in Professional Stage Management and Production Skills
An extensive range of music exams is also available (see Trinity College of Music in the music section).

GUILDHALL SCHOOL OF MUSIC & DRAMA, Silk Street, Barbican, London EC2Y 8DT Tel: 020 7628 2571 Fax: 020 7256 9438 WWW: www.gsmd.ac.uk *FT DRAMA & TECHNICAL THEATRE COURSES:*
BA (Hons) in Acting/Professional Acting Course (AGSM): 3 yrs. Candidates are normally expected to have 2 A Level passes for the BA course or equiv qualifications meeting University General Entrance Requirements. Minimum age on entry: 18.
BA (Hons) in Stage Management and Technical Theatre: 3 yrs. Candidates are expected to have 2 A Level passes or equiv qualifications meeting University General Entrance Requirements.

GUILDHALL EXAMINATIONS SERVICE:
Speech Communications and Drama examinations are available in the following subjects: LGSM Diploma for Teachers of Speech and Drama and Speaking Skills; Performance Diploma in Solo Acting; Performance Certificate in Solo Acting, Verse Speaking and Speaking Skills; Grade Examinations in Speech and Drama, Verse Speaking, Prose Reading, Character Study, Scene Study, Group Performance, Speaking Skills – Individual and Group; Speech Communication Arts Levels 1-6 Core Skills – individual assessment within a group examination of communication arts. An extensive range of music exams is also available.

ROYAL SCOTTISH ACADEMY OF MUSIC AND DRAMA, 100 Renfrew Street, Glasgow G2 3DB Tel: 0141 332 4101 Fax: 0141 332 8901 e-mail: registry@rsamd.ac.uk Website: www.rsamd.ac.uk

DRAMA COURSES:
BA (Acting): 3-yr course designed for those intending to pursue a professional career in acting. Admission is by competitive audition.

BA (Stage Management Studies): 3-yr course designed for those intending to pursue careers at a high level in stage management, production management or design. Admission is by competitive interview.

BA (Contemporary Theatre Practice): 3-yr FT course with extension by selection to a 4th Hons yr offering a practical, creative experience and theoretical understanding of a variety of uses of drama, using devising as its main approach to performance. Admission is by competitive audition. This course is designed for those who wish to make their own theatre work and is therefore not suitable for those wishing to focus solely on acting as a career.

MDra (Acting or Directing or Producing): Full-time over one calendar yr (Jan-Dec) or part-time by accumulation of credits over a maximum of 5 yrs. Certain units can also be taken as short courses not leading to a degree. Entry is open to performers and/or practitioners who have already undertaken a practical course of study in drama or who have relevant professional experience. Admission is by competitive audition/interview. Minimum entry age 21.

WELSH COLLEGE OF MUSIC AND DRAMA, Drama, WCMD, Castle Grounds, Cathays Park, Cardiff CF1 3ER Tel: 029 20342854/ 371440 Fax: 029 20237639 e-mail: info@wcmd.ac.uk Website: www.wcmd.ac.uk

BA (Theatre Studies): A 3-yr course leading to the BA Degree of the University of Wales. The course provides a practical training for actors, designers and stage managers along with some useful background study. The acting and stage management options are fully accredited by the NCDT. The course is designated for mandatory grant aid.

Advanced Diploma Courses: 1-yr post-diploma/post-graduate courses are available in Acting, Design, Stage Management and Arts Management or Directing. The courses provide supplementary professional training for intending theatre professionals. The acting and stage management courses are fully accredited by the NCDT. Grants for these courses are made at the discretion of the student's local authority.

Training for the Stage and for Teaching

There are **stage schools** which take children from about the age of 8 and usually combine drama and dancing with a general education. In many cases ex-pupils of stage schools go on to receive FT training at a drama school. Parents who are considering their children for a dramatic career should bear in mind, however, that stage school is not always the best method of entry into the profession. The completion of ordinary education followed by **drama school** training is usually a better alternative. Advice should be sought from a professional body. A number of colleges of further education in England and Wales run 1 or 2 yr courses in speech and drama, which include general education courses and sometimes A Level courses. These, whilst giving students an opportunity to explore their interests in drama, are not to be regarded as theatre training.

To become a **teacher**, in a maintained school it is necessary to obtain qualified teacher status by taking a recognised teacher training course such as a 3 or 4 yr BEd or a postgraduate Certificate in Education or the Scottish equivalent. Single and/or joint degree courses in drama or theatre are offered at several universities. However, these courses are primarily academic and not a training for an actor. Drama may be offered as a main subject or part of a degree course at some colleges and polytechnics. Some also offer drama as a main subject in their creative or performing arts degrees. These courses include more practical training. Students who wish to take a university

degree including drama/theatre studies, or a recognised course for teachers, must have the educational qualifications necessary for entry to university or colleges of education.

NATIONAL COUNCIL FOR DRAMA TRAINING, 5 Tavistock Place, London WC1H 9SS
Tel: 020 7387 3650 Fax: 020 7387 3650 e-mail: ncdt@lineone.net Website: www.ncdt.co.uk
NCDT consists of representatives from Equity, employers' organisations and drama schools. It exists in order to encourage and maintain the highest possible standards of vocational education and training for the professional actor and stage manager/technician and to provide a forum within which the various sides of the profession can discuss matters of common interest in relation to training. There are two Boards, one for acting courses and one for stage management/technical theatre courses. Industry professionals monitor drama school performances to ensure that the product as well as the process is reviewed.

ROYAL ACADEMY OF DRAMATIC ART, 18 Chenies Street, London WC1E 7PA
Tel: 020 7636 7076 Fax: 020 7323 3865 e-mail: enquiries@rada.ac.uk Website: www.rada.org
Acting Diploma Course: Diploma: 9-term (3 yrs) FT training for the professional theatre. Entry by audition. Age 18+.
Technical Theatre and Stage Management Diploma Course: Diploma: 6-term FT training in all aspects of technical theatre and stage management. Selection by interview. Age 18+.
Specialist Technical Diploma Courses: Diploma: 4-term FT practical training under repertory conditions. Selection by interview. A strong portfolio of work is required. Age 18+. Courses are available in: Scenic Construction, Stage Electrics, Property Making, Scenic Art, Wardrobe.
British Theatre in Foundation Course: Foundation Course: 1 yr FT foundation training in acting skills and an introduction to the technical aspects of the theatre. Entry by recommendation letter from a drama teacher or other relevant educationalist. Ages 17-19.

National Certificates and Diplomas

BTEC National Certificates/Diplomas: Design (Theatre Studies); Performing Arts; Performing Arts (Community Performance); Performing Arts (Music); Performing Arts (Popular Music); Stage Design Construction; Stage Management
BTEC Higher National Certificates/Diplomas: Design (Theatre Studies); Performing Arts; Performing Arts (Applied Music); Performing Arts (Community Dance); Performing Arts (Community Theatre); Performing Arts (Dance); Performing Arts (Drama); Performing Arts (Jazz); Performing Arts (Jazz, Popular and Commercial Music); Performing Arts (Music Composition); Performing Arts (Music); Performing Arts (Popular Music); Performing Arts (Professional Community Arts Practitioner); Performing Arts (Small Scale Theatre); Performing Arts (Stage Management); Performing Arts (Stagecraft); Performing Arts (Theatre and Media Production); Stage Management
Scotland
SQA HNC: Theatre Arts
SQA HND: Theatre Arts

GNVQs

3737 Performing Arts and Entertainment Industries

Other Vocational Awarding Bodies

ABC: Performance Arts

Useful Addresses

Arts and Entertainment Technical Initiative, Lower Ground, 14 Blenheim Terrace, London NW8 0EB Tel: 020 7328 6174

DRIVING INSTRUCTORS

REGISTER OF APPROVED DRIVING INSTRUCTORS

Need for Registration: The Register of Approved Driving Instructors (ADI) and the licensing scheme for trainee instructors are administered under the provisions of the Road Traffic Act 1988 by the Department of Environment, Transport and the Regions (DETR).It is an offence for anyone to give professional instruction (that is instruction paid for by or in respect of the pupil) in driving a motor car unless: (a) his or her name is on the Register of Approved Driving Instructors; or (b) he or she holds a ' trainee's licence to give instruction' issued by the Registrar.

Qualification for Registration: Anyone who wants to be an ADI must: (a) have held a full motor car driving licence for periods amounting in aggregate to at least 4 yrs out of the 6 yrs preceding the date of application. (After passing the driving test, any unexpired portion of a provisional licence counts towards the required 4-yr period.); (b) not have been under a disqualification for driving for any part of the 4 yrs preceding the date of application; (c) be a fit and proper person to have their name entered in the Register (non-motoring offences, as well as motoring offences not resulting in disqualification which are not regarded as spent are taken into account in assessing an applicant's suitability); and (d) pass the Register qualifying exam.

The Qualifying Exam: This consists of a written exam, a driving ability test and an instructional ability test.

Further Information: From the Driving Standards Agency, Stanley House, Talbot Street, Nottingham NG1 5GU Tel: 0115 9012618 Fax: 0115 9012600.

NVQs

Level 3: Driving Instruction

Useful Addresses

Association of National Truck Trainers, Huntingdon House, 87 Market Street, Ashby de la Zouch, Leicestershire LE65 1AH Tel: 01530 417234 Fax: 01530 417236

Joint Industry Council for Lift Truck Operating Standards & VQs, LANTRA, National Agricultural Centre, Kenilworth, CV8 2LG Tel: 01203 696996 Fax: 01203 696732

TRANSFED, Regency House, 43 High Street, Rickmansworth, Hertfordshire WD3 1ET Tel: 01923 896607 Fax: 01923 896881

ECONOMICS

University Qualifications

The following universities offer qualifications in Economics and related subjects. Full details may be found in Part 4, under the entry for the appropriate university.

FIRST DEGREES AWARDED BY UNIVERSITIES

Aberdeen; Abertay, Dundee; Anglia; Aston; Bath; Belfast; Birmingham; Bradford; Bristol; Brunel; Buckingham; Bucks. Coll.; Cambridge; Central England; Central Lancashire; City; Coventry; De Montfort, Leicester; Derby; Doncaster; Dundee; Durham; East Anglia; East Anglia (Suffolk College); East London; Edinburgh; Essex; Exeter; Glamorgan; Glasgow; Glasgow Caledonian; Greenwich; Heriot-Watt; Hertfordshire; Huddersfield; Hull; Keele; Kent; Kingston; Lancaster; Leeds; Leeds Metropolitan; Leicester; Lincolnshire (Lincoln University Campus); Liverpool; Liverpool (Chester College of H.E.); Liverpool John Moores; London (Birkbeck, University of London); London (Goldsmiths College); London (London School of Economics & Political Science); London (Queen Mary & Westfield College (incorporating St Bartholomew's and the Royal London School of Medicine & Dentistry)); London (Royal Holloway); London (School of Oriental & African Studies); London (School of Slavonic & East European Studies); London (University College (UCL)); London Guildhall; Loughborough; Luton; Manchester; Manchester Metropolitan.; Middlesex; Napier; Newcastle; North London; Northampton; Northumbria;

Nottingham; Nottingham Trent; Oxford; Oxford Brookes; Paisley; Plymouth; Portsmouth; Reading; Salford; Sheffield; South Bank; Southampton; St Andrews; St Martin; Staffordshire; Stirling; Strathclyde; Surrey; Sussex; Teesside; Ulster; Wales (Cardiff University); Wales (University of Wales, Aberystwyth); Wales (University of Wales, Bangor); Wales (University of Wales, Swansea); Warwick; Westminster; Wolverhampton; York

HIGHER DEGREES AWARDED BY UNIVERSITIES

Aberdeen; Anglia; Birmingham; Bradford; Bristol; Brunel; Buckingham; Cambridge; City; Coventry; De Montfort, Leicester; Dundee; Durham; East Anglia; Edinburgh; Essex; Exeter; Glasgow; Greenwich; Heriot-Watt; Hertfordshire; Hull; Keele; Kent; Kingston; Lancaster; Leeds; Leicester; Liverpool; Liverpool John Moores; London (Birkbeck, University of London); London (Institute of Education); London (London School of Economics & Political Science); London (Queen Mary & Westfield College (incorporating St Bartholomew's and the Royal London School of Medicine & Dentistry)); London (Royal Holloway); London (School of Oriental & African Studies); London (School of Slavonic & East European Studies); London (University College (UCL)); London (Wye College); London Guildhall; Loughborough; Manchester; Middlesex; Newcastle; Nottingham; Nottingham Trent (Southampton Institute); Oxford; Portsmouth; Reading; Salford; Sheffield; Southampton; St Andrews; Staffordshire; Stirling; Strathclyde; Sunderland; Surrey; Sussex; UMIST; Wales (Cardiff University); Wales (University of Wales, Swansea); Warwick; York

DIPLOMAS AWARDED BY UNIVERSITIES

Aberdeen; Birmingham; Bristol; Cambridge; City; Dundee; Edinburgh; Essex; Exeter; Hertfordshire; Hull; Kent; Lancaster; Leeds; Leicester; London (Birkbeck, University of London); London (London School of Economics & Political Science); London (School of Oriental & African Studies); London (Wye College); Loughborough; Manchester; Nottingham; Salford; St Andrews; Staffordshire; Strathclyde

CERTIFICATES AWARDED BY UNIVERSITIES

London (Birkbeck, University of London); London (Queen Mary & Westfield College (incorporating St Bartholomew's and the Royal London School of Medicine & Dentistry)); Nottingham; Salford; Staffordshire

OCR

OCR offer the following awards:
Stage II: Practical Finance; Principles of Finance; Spreadsheets

EMBALMING

Membership of Professional Institutions and Associations

THE BRITISH INSTITUTE OF EMBALMERS

21c Station Road, Knowle, Solihull, West Midlands B93 0HL Tel: 01564 778991 Fax: 01564 770812 e-mail: international.bie@virgin.net Website: www.bie.org.uk

MEMBERSHIP:
Fellow (FBIE): Fellowship is granted by the National Council of the Institute upon invitation from the Fellows themselves. It is given for exceptional services to the Institute or the science in general.
Member (MBIE): Membership is authorised by the National Council of the Institute, which demands certain qualifications from the applicant. Information may be obtained from the National Office.

NATIONAL EXAMINATIONS BOARD OF EMBALMERS

39 Poplar Grove, Kennington, Oxford OX1 5QN Tel: 01865 735788 Fax: 01865 730941

The Board examines candidates who wish to become qualified members of the British Institute of Embalmers (which is not itself an examining body).

REGISTRATION:
Information packs (available from the above office and the International Office of the British Institute of Embalmers, 21c Station Road, Knowle, Solihull, West Midlands B97 0HL) contain lists of approved schools and tutors. The Board only accepts Candidates from these accredited Tutors, and so it is essential to register with one of these Tutors initially. Candidates are then taught through a Modular Programme, with the Board setting a first (Foundation) Module, which must be passed prior to continuing on the course. After successfully completing the Foundation Module, Candidates need to apply for registration with the British Institute of Embalmers, as a Student Member.

EXAMINATIONS:
The Board sets 'school based' tests at the conclusion of each of the 5 modules, and the marks attained in these tests count towards the Board's final exam. The **final exam:** consists of a theoretical exam and a practical exam; the former must be passed before the latter may be attempted. The theoretical exam contains questions from the whole syllabus covering Anatomy and Physiology, (elementary) Pathology, Bacteriology and Chemistry, and a comprehensive understanding of the theory of Embalming. The practical exam consists of the embalmment of a subject. Applicants for the practical exam must already have performed 30 complete embalmments, 12 of which have been subjected to a post mortem exam.

EMPLOYMENT AND CAREERS SERVICES

Membership of Professional Institutions and Associations

THE INSTITUTE OF CAREERS GUIDANCE
27a Lower High Street, Stourbridge, West Midlands DY8 1TA Tel: 01384 376464 Fax: 01384 440830 e-mail: hq@icg-uk.org Website: www.icg-uk.org

MEMBERSHIP CATEGORIES:
Full Member: Subscribes to Code of Ethics and Standards. Commitment to Continuous Professional Development. DCG Parts 1 & 2/S/NVQ Level 4 in Guidance (or equivalent).
Associate: Subscribes to Code of Ethics and Standards. Commitment to Continuous Professional Development. DCG Part 1/S/NVQ Level 3 in Guidance.
Student: Studying FT for DCG, new Qualification in Careers Guidance (QCG) or PT whilst unemployed.
Affiliate: Subscribes to Code of Ethics and Standards. Interest in Guidance.
Fellow (Qualified): 10 yrs Practice + Full Membership.
Fellow (Academic): Research (recognised by Council).
Fellow (Honorary): Good Works (elected at final Council meeting of the yr).

RECRUITMENT AND EMPLOYMENT CONFEDERATION (FORMERLY THE INSTITUTE OF EMPLOYMENT CONSULTANTS)
3rd Floor, Steward House, 16a Commercial Way, Woking, Surrey GU21 1ET Tel: 01483 766442 Fax: 01483 714979 e-mail: info@rec.uk.com Website: www.rec.uk.com

MEMBERSHIP:
Fellow (FREC): Candidates for Fellowship must be recruitment consultants of at least ten yrs' standing, able to show evidence of the highest standards of professional conduct throughout their career. They must have been members of the REC for 3 yrs and need sponsorship from 2 Fellows of the REC.
Member (MREC): Candidates must show evidence of *one* of the following qualifications: Foundation Vocational Award plus 2 1/2 yrs proven relevant experience *or* Certificate in Recruitment Practice plus 2 yrs proven relevant experience *or* successful completion of 5 REC-

approved training courses plus 3 yrs proven relevant experience. Candidates with 6 yrs relevant experience *or* 5 yrs relevant experience plus a degree are exempt from these conditions.

Associate Members (AREC): Candidates must show evidence of *one* of the following qualifications: Foundation Vocational Award plus 6 mths proven relevant experience *or* Certificate in Recruitment Practice *or* successful completion of 3 REC-approved training courses plus 2 yrs proven relevant experience. Candidates with 4 yrs relevant experience *or* 3 yrs relevant experience plus a degree are exempt from these conditions.

Affiliate Membership: Granted to anyone supporting the purpose and objects of the Institute.

Student Membership: Granted to anyone enrolled on an educational course recognised by the Institute.

EXAMINATIONS:

Foundation Vocational Award in Employment Agency Practice: Run by the REC.

Certificate in Recruitment Practice (Cert RP): Run jointly by the REC and the AQA (Assessment & Qualifications Alliance).

University Qualifications

The following universities offer qualifications in Employment and Careers Services and related subjects. Full details may be found in Part 4, under the entry for the appropriate university.

HIGHER DEGREES AWARDED BY UNIVERSITIES

Central England; Greenwich; London (Birkbeck, University of London); Manchester Metropolitan.; Napier; Nottingham Trent; Paisley; South Bank; Surrey (University of Surrey Roehampton)

DIPLOMAS AWARDED BY UNIVERSITIES

Bristol; Central England; Durham; East London; Glamorgan; Huddersfield; London (Institute of Education); Manchester Metropolitan.; Napier; Northumbria; Nottingham Trent; Paisley; Salford; South Bank; Strathclyde

CERTIFICATES AWARDED BY UNIVERSITIES

Central England; Manchester Metropolitan.; Paisley; Surrey (University of Surrey Roehampton); Ulster; Warwick

PROFESSIONAL COURSES AWARDED BY UNIVERSITIES

Luton; Manchester Metropolitan.

AERONAUTICAL ENGINEERING

Membership of Professional Institutions and Associations

THE ROYAL AERONAUTICAL SOCIETY

4 Hamilton Place, Hyde Park Corner, London W1V 0BQ Tel: 020 7499 3515 Fax: 020 7499 6230
The Society is the one multidisciplinary professional institution dedicated to the entire aerospace industry. As a nominated body of the Engineering Council it is also able to nominate suitably qualified engineers for registration at all 3 sections of the Register.

CORPORATE MEMBERSHIP:

Fellows (FRAeS): Must have the qualifications necessary for Membership, have made outstanding contributions in the profession, attained a position of high responsibility or have had long experience of high quality.

Member (MRAeS): Must be over 25 yrs of age, have passed an approved exam (normally of the level of a UK 1st degree), and have a min of 4 yrs' experience which includes a 2-yr period of training and 2 yrs in a position of responsibility. Alternatively, a person without a degree is eligible to become a Member on reaching the age of 35 if that person can demonstrate adequate additional experience and responsibilities within the aerospace industry.

Companion (CRAeS): Applicants must be the calibre for Fellowship but do not, for one reason or another, meet the requirements for that grade.

Associate Members (AMRAeS): Must be over the age of 23, have passed an approved exam (eg BTEC HNC) and had a minimum of 5 yrs' satisfactory experience of which 2 yrs have been devoted to practical training. A person of at least 30 yrs of age, with 10 yrs of relevant experience may also be eligible for Associate Membership if they can demonstrate adequate additional experience and responsibilities within the aerospace industry. Alternatively, a graduate who has completed the training for full membership may also join at this level.

Associates(ARAeS): Applicants must be over 21 yrs of age, have passed an approved exam and have had a minimum of 3 yrs' satisfactory experience of which 2 yrs have been devoted to practical training.

Graduates (GradAeS): Applicants must be between the ages of 21 and 32. They must have an academic qualification acceptable for Corporate membership.

Students: Applicants must be in full time education and have the objective of becoming engaged in the profession of aeronautics.

Affiliates: This class is open to those ineligible for other classes but who are associated with or have an interest in aeronautics.

University Qualifications

The following universities offer qualifications in Aeronautical Engineering and related subjects. Full details may be found in Part 4, under the entry for the appropriate university.

FIRST DEGREES AWARDED BY UNIVERSITIES
Belfast; Brighton; Bristol; Brunel; City; Coventry; Cranfield; Glasgow; Hertfordshire; Kingston; Liverpool; London (Imperial College of Science, Technology & Medicine); London (Queen Mary & Westfield College (incorporating St Bartholomew's and the Royal London School of Medicine & Dentistry)); Loughborough; Manchester; Salford; Sheffield; Southampton; Surrey (Farnborough College of Technology); UMIST

HIGHER DEGREES AWARDED BY UNIVERSITIES
Bath; Belfast; Brighton; Bristol; City; Cranfield; Kingston; London (Queen Mary & Westfield College (incorporating St Bartholomew's and the Royal London School of Medicine & Dentistry)); Loughborough; Manchester

DIPLOMAS AWARDED BY UNIVERSITIES
Glasgow; Wales (North East Wales Institute)

National Certificates and Diplomas

Scotland
SQA HNC: Aeronautical Engineering (Aircraft Manufacture)
SQA HND: Aeronautical Engineering

NVQs

Level 2: Aircraft Engineering Maintenance
Level 3: Aircraft Engineering Maintenance

City & Guilds

2080 Aeronautical Engineering Craft Studies; 2580 Aeronautical Engineering Technicians; 2590 Aeronautical Engineering Competencies

AGRICULTURAL ENGINEERING
(See also Agriculture and Horticulture)

Membership of Professional Institutions and Associations

BRITISH AGRICULTURAL AND GARDEN MACHINERY ASSOCIATION
14-16 Church Street, Rickmansworth, Hertfordshire WD3 1RQ Tel: 01923 720241 Fax: 01923 896063
e-mail: info@bagma.com Website: www.bagma.com

EXAMINTIONS:
BAGMA Management Diploma: The course is designed to introduce potential and junior managers in agricultural and garden machinery dealerships to the modern management skills needed to operate a successful business.
Part A: *1. Financial Aspects:* Cost Accounting, Management Accounting, Financial Planning and Control; *2. Legal Aspects:* **The Law of Contract, Torts of Importance in Business, Business and Transport Law.**
Part B: *Dealership Management Functions and Services:* **General, Sales and Personnel Management, Marketing and Stock Control.**
After the conclusion of the course candidates will also be required to attend an interview with the Diploma Board and to submit a project on a case study.
BAGMA have also published Occupational Standards for Service Engineering which have recently been accredited by QCA as NVQ Level 2 and 3 for Agricultural and Garden Machinery retail trades. BAGMA have also developed National Traineeships for service and partsales staff and a Modern Apprenticeship for service engineers. Supervisors of the future are likely to have come through the NT/MA route, both of which include N/SVQ qualifications and key skills.

THE INSTITUTION OF AGRICULTURAL ENGINEERS
West End Road, Silsoe, Bedford MK45 4DU Tel: 01525 861096 Fax: 01525 861660
e-mail: secretary@iagre.demon.co.uk Website: www.iagre.demon.co.uk

CORPORATE MEMBERS:
Fellow (FIAgrE); Companion (CIAgrE); Member (MIAgrE).
NON-CORPORATE MEMBERS:
Associate Member (AMIAgrE); Associate (AIgrE); Student.
ENGINEERING COUNCIL REGISTRATION:
Members with appropriate academic qualifications, training and experience are eligible to apply to the Institution for Eng Council registration as Chartered Engineer, Incorporated Engineer and Engineering Technician. Full particulars of requirements for membership are obtainable from the Secretariat.

University Qualifications
The following universities offer qualifications in Agricultural Engineering and related subjects. Full details may be found in Part 4, under the entry for the appropriate university.

FIRST DEGREES AWARDED BY UNIVERSITIES
Aberdeen; Adams; Cranfield; Edinburgh; Essex (Writtle College); London (Wye College); Newcastle; Reading; Wales (University of Wales, Aberystwyth)

HIGHER DEGREES AWARDED BY UNIVERSITIES
Adams; Bath; Birmingham; Bristol; Cranfield; East Anglia; Edinburgh; Essex (Writtle College); Greenwich; London (Wye College); Reading; Wales (University of Wales, Aberystwyth); Wales (University of Wales, Swansea)

DIPLOMAS AWARDED BY UNIVERSITIES
Edinburgh; London (Wye College)

OTHER COURSES AWARDED BY UNIVERSITIES
Essex (Writtle College)

NVQs

Level 2: Service Engineering – Agricultural and Groundcare Machinery
Level 3: Service Engineering – Agricultural and Groundcare Machinery

SVQs

Level 2: Services Engineering Agricultural Machinery; Services Engineering Garden Machinery
Level 3: Services Engineering Agricultural Machinery; Services Engineering Garden Machinery.

City & Guilds

3940 Agricultural Mechanics

AUTOMOBILE ENGINEERING

Membership of Professional Institutions and Associations

THE INSTITUTE OF AUTOMOTIVE ENGINEER ASSESSORS

Stowe House, Netherstowe, Lichfield, Staffs WS13 6TJ Tel: 01543 251346 Fax: 01543 415804 e-mail: secretary@iaea.demon.co.uk

CORPORATE MEMBERSHIP:
Fellow (FInstAEA): A Member who has rendered special services to the Institute may be elected to Fellowship by a resolution passed at a General Meeting of the Institute.
Member (MInstAEA): A Member shall be an Incorporated Member who is not under 30 yrs of age and has satisfied the Council that he has been engaged for at least 5 yrs in assessing work in connection with automobile claims.
Incorporated Member (IMInstAEA): This class of Member shall be a person who is not under 25 yrs of age, has a motor trade apprenticeship or equivalent training, has passed the Institute's written and practical estimating examinations and has satisfied the Council that he has at least 2 yrs assessing experience in connection with automobile claims.

EXAMINATIONS:
Written Exams for Corporate Membership. Candidates must satisfy the examiners in all 4 sections of the Institute's Written Exams. Exemption in respect of training or qualification may be granted by the Institute in exceptional circumstances.

THE INSTITUTE OF THE MOTOR INDUSTRY

Fanshaws, Brickendon, Hertford SG13 8PQ Tel: 01992 511521 Fax: 01992 511548

MEMBERSHIP:
Fellow(FIMI): A person qualified by training and experience to hold a senior management position (relevant NVQ Level 5 or equivalent qualification).
Member (MIMI): A person qualified by training and experience to hold a middle management position (relevant NVQ Level 4 or equivalent qualification).
Associate Member (AMIMI): A person qualified by training or experience to industry vocational level (relevant NVQ Level 3 or equivalent qualification).
Affiliate (AffIMI): A person over the age of 18 who is employed in the industry but not qualified for corporate membership (relevant NVQ Level 2 or equivalent qualification).
Graduate: A person over 21studying for an Institute recognised qualification meeting or contributing to entry criteria for corporate membership.
Student: A person aged 16 to 21 registered as working towards an Institute vocational qualification.

QUALIFICATIONS:
The Institute also awards two vocational engineering qualifications subject to experience as well as academic and skill competence. These are **Certificated Automotive Engineer (CAE)** for

suitably qualified vehicle technicians and **Licentiate Automotive Engineer (LAE):** For master technicians. The Institute certificates the following management qualifications which lead to membership at the levels shown in brackets: Supervisory Studies (AMIMI); Certificate of Management (MIMI); Diploma in Motor Industry Management (FIMI).

The Institute is an Awarding Body for a comprehensive range of NVQs covering vehicle mechanical, body repair and refinishing, sales, customer service, parts, administration, management and Training/ Development.

INSTITUTE OF VEHICLE ENGINEERS (FORMERLY INSTITUTE OF BRITISH CARRIAGE & AUTOMOBILE MANUFACTURERS)

31 Redstone Farm Road, Hall Green, Birmingham, West Midlands B28 9NU Tel: 0121 778 4354 Fax: 0121 702 2615 e-mail: info@ivehe.org Website: www.ivehe.org

Institute of British Carriage and Automobile Manufacturers changed its name to Institute of Vehicle Engineers by special resolution and was incorporated with Companies House on 12th January 2000.

MEMBERSHIP:

Fellowship (FIVehE): Open to persons, min age 40, who have been members (MIVehE) for not less than 5 yrs and who submit a precis describing any significant contribution(s) to the Institute and/or vehicle manufacturing or any branch thereof.

Membership (MIVehE): Open to persons, min age 25, who are registered as CEng or IEng or meet the Institute's academic requirements. Alternatively who have completed non-technical professional training and held a responsible position of direction in a practical, technical, administrative, commercial or any branch of vehicle construction industry for not less than 2 yrs.

Associate Membership (AMIVehE): Open to persons, min age 23, who are registered as EngTech or meet the Institute's academic requirements. Alternatively who have received a good general education and have completed relevant approved courses. They shall have been formally trained, hold or have held a responsible position in practical, technical, commercial, administration or any branch of the vehicle construction industry.

Associate (AIVehE): Open to persons, min age 21, with a basic level of academic achievement, training and experience in vehicle construction or any branch thereof.

Licentiate or Certified Vehicle Technologist (LVT or CVT): Additional qualifications for complying with the Institute's technical requirements.

EXAMINATIONS:

Potential members are expected to be registered with the Engineering Council or hold a BEng degree, HND, ONC or equiv NVQ or have served an appropriate apprenticeship with the relevant NVQ.

University Qualifications

The following universities offer qualifications in Automobile Engineering and related subjects. Full details may be found in Part 4, under the entry for the appropriate university.

FIRST DEGREES AWARDED BY UNIVERSITIES
Bradford; Brighton; Brunel; Central England; Coventry; Greenwich; Hertfordshire; Huddersfield; Kingston; Leeds; Loughborough; Oxford Brookes; Sussex; Wales (Swansea Institute of Higher Education); Wolverhampton

HIGHER DEGREES AWARDED BY UNIVERSITIES
Bath; Central England; Coventry; Cranfield; Hertfordshire; Huddersfield; Leeds; Loughborough; Newcastle; Royal College of Art

DIPLOMAS AWARDED BY UNIVERSITIES
Central England; Coventry; Greenwich; Hertfordshire; Huddersfield; Lincolnshire (Hull College); Luton; Teesside; Wales (Swansea Institute of Higher Education)

CERTIFICATES AWARDED BY UNIVERSITIES
Anglia (City College, Norwich); Central England; Manchester (Warrington Collegiate Institute, Faculty of H.E)

OTHER COURSES AWARDED BY UNIVERSITIES
Huddersfield

National Certificates and Diplomas

BTEC National Certificates/Diplomas: Engineering (Historic Vehicle Restoration); Engineering (Motor Vehicle Studies)
BTEC Higher National Certificates/Diplomas: Engineering (Motor Vehicle Studies)
Scotland
SQA HNC: Automotive Engineering; Automotive Management with Technology
SQA HND: Automotive Engineering and Management

NVQs

Level 2: Automotive Glazing
Level 3: Automotive Glazing

SVQs

Level 1: Maintaining Passenger Carrying Vehicles (Body Trades); Maintaining Passenger Carrying Vehicles (Electrical); Maintaining Passenger Carrying Vehicles (Mechanical); Vehicle Maintenance (Service Replacement).
Level 2: Maintaining Passenger Carrying Vehicles (Body Trades or Electrical or Mechanical); Vehicle Body Fitting; Vehicle Mechanical & Electronic Systems Unit Replacement (Light Vehicle); Vehicle Body Fitting.
Level 3: Maintaining Passenger Carrying Vehicles (Body Trades or Electrical or Mechanical); Vehicle Body Refurbishing or Body Repair; Vehicle Mechanical & Electronic Systems Maintenance & Repair (Light Vehicle or Heavy Vehicle).

City & Guilds

3810 Motor Vehicle Craft Studies; 3820 Vehicle Restoration; 3830 Repair and Servicing of Road Vehicles; 3840 Vehicle Parts Personnel; 3890 Repair & Servicing of Motorcycles; 3900 Motor Vehicle Technicians; 3980 Vehicle Body Competencies; 3991 Motorcycle Repair and Maintenance Skills; 3992 Motor Vehicle Repair and Maintenance; 3993 Cycle Maintenance and Repair Skills; 3995 Motor Cycle Skills

Other Awards

The **National Craft Certificate** is awarded by the National Joint Council for the Motor Vehicle Retail and Repair Industry, 201 Great Portland Street, London W1N 6AB, Tel 0171 307 3408 Fax 0171 580 6376 to motor vehicle mechanics (light and heavy), auto-electricians, vehicle body repairers and motorcycle mechanics. The Council also awards an NJC Certificate in Parts Distribution. Applicants are required to pass appropriate C&G, BTEC or SQA exams and RTITB Services Ltd practical skills tests. This certificate is recognised by the Department of Education in Northern Ireland, Scottish Education Department, Motor Industry Training Council and Transport Training Services Ltd (Northern Ireland). It will also award the NCC to people in possession of NVQs Level 3 in Vehicle Mechanical & Electronic Systems Maintenance and Repair for Light Vehicles, Heavy Vehicles & Motor Cycles, Vehicle Body Repair, Vehicle Refinishing and Vehicle Parts Distribution and Supply. It normally takes 3 yrs to qualify.
WELSH JOINT EDUCATION COMMITTEE: Now offers City and Guilds of London Institute's examinations

MICHELIN TRAINING AND INFORMATION CENTRE

The Edward Hyde Building, 38 Clarendon Road, Watford, Hertfordshire WD1 1SX Tel: 01923 415000 Fax: 01923 415250 Website: www.michelin.co.uk/mtic
Specialist training and advice service. An extensive portfolio of tyre retailers, garages, motorcycle dealers and vehicle fleet operators, as well as the more specialised areas of Earthmover, Agricultural and Industrial tyres. Also the facility for specially-tailored and on-site courses depending on requirements.

Technical Training: Tyre Technology from basics to advanced geometry and vehicle handling. Practical courses in fitting, balancing, wheel alignment and the application of all tyre related equipment.

Sales Training: Retail tyre sales, field sales for the dealer representative and advanced sales techniques.

Telephone Training: Basic and advanced telephone techniques, effective use of the telephone and telephone sales in a retail environment.

Management Training: Supervisory training, human resource management, communication, leadership, motivation and staff appraisal.

Training the Trainer: These courses are designed to enable companies to take advantage of specialist skills and experience available within their own organisation and develop selective personnel to pass on those skills.

Training Facilities: 3 lecture rooms (fully equipped), and 2 video role play studios available for hire.

Useful Addresses

Automotive Management and Development, Regency House, 43 High Street, Rickmansworth, Hertfordshire WD3 1ET Tel: 01923 896607 Fax: 01923 896881

Motor Industry Training Council, 201 Great Portland Street, London W1N 6AB Tel: 020 76373 Fax: 020 7436 5108 Website: www.mitc.co.uk

BUILDING SERVICES ENGINEERING

Membership of Professional Institutions and Associations

THE CHARTERED INSTITUTION OF BUILDING SERVICES ENGINEERS

Delta House, 222 Balham High Road, London SW12 9BS Tel: 020 8675 5211 Fax: 020 8675 5449 e-mail: tchamberlain@cibse.org Website: www.cibse.org

The activities of the Institution embrace the whole field of Building Services Engineering which is concerned with the human, scientific and technical aspects of the design, construction, operation and maintenance of all the engineering elements associated with the built environment other than its structure, as well as similar elements associated with certain industrial processes. Such engineering services include heating, ventilation, air conditioning, refrigeration, lighting, electrical power and utilisation, lifts and passenger conveyors, fire protection, gas utilisation, fuel efficiency and energy conservation. CIBSE is a joint awarding body for an NVQ Level 5 in Construction Project Management and Level 3/4 in Building Services. The Institution is a full nominating and authorising body of the Engineering Council, thus able to register members as CEng (Member), IEng (Associate) and Eng Tech (Licentiate) and authorised to accredit degree courses in building services engineering.

Fellow (FCIBSE): The senior grade of membership. Minimum age at least 35.

Member (MCIBSE): Applicants must be at least 25, have received practical training and obtained appropriate professional experience in Building Services Engineering. To satisfy the academic requirements, applicants must have obtained an approved 3 yr BEng, plus matching section or an approved 4 yr MEng degree.

Associate (ACIBSE): Applicants must be at least 23, have received 2 yrs' appropriate training and have a minimum of 3 yrs' experience. The academic requirements can be satisfied by completing exams at HNC level in an acceptable engineering subject, or equivalent. From September 1999 the academic requirement will be a 3 yr BEng degree in an appropriate subject.

Licentiate (LCIBSE): Applicants must be over 21 and possess an acceptable BTEC National Certificate with certain specified Units in Mathematics. Applicants must also have had appropriate training and experience.

Graduate: Applicants must have obtained acceptable qualifications at degree level. Applicants must also be receiving practical training and experience in Building Services Engineering.

Student: Applicants must be enrolled on a recognised course of study leading to the award of a qualification appropriate to Building Services Engineering.

University Qualifications

The following universities offer qualifications in Building Services Engineering and related subjects. Full details may be found in Part 4, under the entry for the appropriate university.

FIRST DEGREES AWARDED BY UNIVERSITIES
Bristol; Brunel; Central Lancashire; Glamorgan; Glasgow Caledonian; Greenwich; Northumbria; Reading; South Bank; Strathclyde; Ulster; UMIST; Wales (University of Wales College, Newport); Westminster

HIGHER DEGREES AWARDED BY UNIVERSITIES
Brunel; Dundee; Greenwich; Heriot-Watt; Leeds; Loughborough; Northumbria; Nottingham Trent; Sheffield; UMIST

DIPLOMAS AWARDED BY UNIVERSITIES
Brighton; Doncaster; Dundee; Northumbria; Nottingham Trent; South Bank; Wales (University of Wales Institute, Cardiff)

CERTIFICATES AWARDED BY UNIVERSITIES
Leeds Metropolitan; Salford

OTHER COURSES AWARDED BY UNIVERSITIES
Leeds Metropolitan

POSTGRADUATE DIPLOMAS AWARDED BY UNIVERSITIES
Heriot-Watt

National Certificates and Diplomas

BTEC National Certificates/Diplomas: Building Services Engineering; Building Services Engineering (Controls); Building Services Engineering (Electrical Installations); Building Services Engineering (Gas Distribution); Building Services Engineering (Gas Utilisation); Building Services Engineering (HVAC); Building Services Engineering (Plumbing); Building Services Engineering (Refrigeration); Building Services Engineering (Surveying)

BTEC Higher National Certificates/Diplomas: Building Services Engineering; Building Services Engineering (Commercial); Building Services Engineering (Controls); Building Services Engineering (Electrical Installations); Building Services Engineering (Gas Distribution); Building Services Engineering (Gas Utilisation); Building Services Engineering (HVAC); Building Services Engineering (Plumbing); Building Services Engineering (Refrigeration); Building Services Engineering (Surveying)

Scotland

SQA Certificate: Building Services Engineering

SQA HNC: Building Services Plant Engineering

SQA HND: Building Services Engineering; Building Services, Plant Engineering

NVQs

Level 3: Mechanical Engineering Systems (heating and ventilating installation); Mechanical Engineering Systems (heating & ventilating systems rectification)

City & Guilds

6050 Master Plumber's Certificate (Pilot); 7690 Building Services Supervisors/Caretakers

Useful Addresses

Chartered Institute of Building Services Engineers, Delta House, 222 Balham High Road, London SW12 9BS Tel: 020 8675 5211 Fax: 020 8675 5449

Engineering Services Training Trust Ltd (ESSTL), Gear House, Saltmeadows Road, Gateshead NE8 3HA Tel: 0191 490 1155 Fax: 0191 477 5737

Insulation and Environmental Training Trust Ltd (IETTL), Charter House, 450 High Road, Ilford, Essex IG1 1UF Tel: 020 8514 2120 Fax: 020 8478 1256 Website: members.aol.com/ticaacad/index.htm

CHEMICAL ENGINEERING

Membership of Professional Institutions and Associations

THE INSTITUTION OF CHEMICAL ENGINEERS

165-189 Railway Terrace, Rugby, Warwickshire CV21 3HQ Tel: 01788 578214 Fax: 01788 560833 e-mail: memserv@icheme.org.uk Website: www.icheme.org
The Institution of Chemical Engineers (IChemE) is the qualifying and professional body for chemical engineers and has over 25,000 members world-wide.
The IChemE Vision: 'To be at the forefront of chemical engineering as a leading international body, qualifying, serving and representing chemical engineers and promoting the advancement of the discipline.'
World-Wide Representation: Approaching 30% of IChemE's members are based outside the UK. IChemE membership supports chemical engineers in over 80 countries, with the satellite office in Melbourne looking after IChemE's 3,000 Australian members.
MEMBERSHIP:
There are 4 grades of membership which cater for every age, qualification and range of experience. Those in the Corporate grades of Member and Fellow are recognised as Chartered Chemical Engineers.
Fellow (FIChemE): Have met the requirements for the grade of Member and have held an *important* post of responsibility in chemical engineering for a period of time.
Member (MIChemE): Must reach the required standards of academic achievement (usually an accredited honours degree), training and experience and hold a post of responsibility in chemical engineering.
Associate Member (AMIChemE): A grade recognising practising professional chemical engineers who hold a degree level qualification but who do not fully satisfy the requirements for the grade of Member. Individuals who fully satisfy the Engineering Councils' requirements for Incorporated Engineer (IEng) registration may also join at this grade.
Affiliate: The general grade for those who wish to associate themselves with the work of the IChemE but do not, as yet, have the necessary qualifications or experience for the grade of Associate Member. There will be a subset of this grade exclusively for student members who will be able to use the title 'Affiliate Student'.

University Qualifications

The following universities offer qualifications in Chemical Engineering and related subjects. Full details may be found in Part 4, under the entry for the appropriate university.

FIRST DEGREES AWARDED BY UNIVERSITIES

Aston; Belfast; Birmingham; Bradford; Cambridge; Edinburgh; Heriot-Watt; Huddersfield; Lancaster (Edge Hill College of Higher Education); Leeds; London (Imperial College of Science, Technology & Medicine); London (University College (UCL)); Loughborough; Newcastle; Northumbria; Nottingham; Oxford; Paisley; Salford (Halton College); Sheffield; South Bank; Strathclyde; Surrey; Teesside; UMIST; Wales (University of Wales, Swansea)

HIGHER DEGREES AWARDED BY UNIVERSITIES

Aston; Bath; Belfast; Birmingham; Bradford; Heriot-Watt; London (Imperial College of Science, Technology & Medicine); London (University College (UCL)); Loughborough; Newcastle; Teesside; UMIST; Wales (University of Wales, Swansea)

DIPLOMAS AWARDED BY UNIVERSITIES
Leeds; London (University College (UCL)); Newcastle; South Bank; Teesside

CERTIFICATES AWARDED BY UNIVERSITIES
Cambridge

National Certificates and Diplomas

Scotland
SQA HNC: Chemical Engineering

Useful Addresses

Chemical Industries Association, Kings Buildings, Smith Square, London SW1P 3JJ Tel: 020 7834 3399 Fax: 020 7834 4469

The Institution of Chemical Engineers, Davis Building, 165–189 Railway Terrace, Rugby CV21 3HQ Tel: 01788 578214 Fax: 01788 560833

CIVIL ENGINEERING

Membership of Professional Institutions and Associations

THE INSTITUTION OF CIVIL ENGINEERS

1 Great George Street, Westminster, London SW1P 3AA Tel: 020 7665 2106 Fax: 020 7233 0515 e-mail: careers@ice.org.uk Website: www.ice.org.uk

The Institution of Civil Engineers is a UK based international organisation with 80,000 members from Students to Fellows. Its membership is mainly UK based although about 20% is overseas. The ICE is a centre of learning and offers a wide range of activities to enable members continually to update their competence. It assesses and qualifies Civil Engineers to the highest standards throughout the world. There are various grades of membership as described below.

MEMBERSHIP:
Fellows (FICE): This is the highest level of membership and is a mark of the position and expertise that has been acquired. They will normally have a achieved a position of responsibility in the promotion, design, construction. Maintenance and management of important engineering work; hold high educational qualifications and either made some outstanding or notable contribution to the science of engineering or materially advanced the practice of engineering from the academic, research, technical or management standpoint. They will normally have completed a programme of at least 7 days continuing education.

Members (MICE): Should normally hold an approved academic qualification to MEng level, have completed an Approved Training Scheme or a period of experience in lieu, have undertaken a programme of at least 30 days' continuing education, have had responsible experience in one of the many branches of civil engineering, be at least 25 and have passed the relevant Professional Review.

Associate Members (AMICE): Should normally hold an approved academic qualification to at an accredited IEng degree, have completed an Approved Training Scheme or a period of experience in lieu, have undertaken a programme of at least 15 days' continuing education, have had responsible experience in one of the many branches of civil engineering, be at least 23 and have passed the relevant Professional Review .

Technician Members: Must hold an approved academic qualification, have completed an Approved Training Scheme or a period of experience in lieu and have passed the relevant Professional Review.

Graduates: Must hold an approved academic qualification leading to one of the professional qualification classes and must be engaged either in an acceptable form of approved training or practical experience or in suitable postgraduate studies.

Students: Must be at least 16 and be studying for the profession on a course approved by the Institution.

University Qualifications

The following universities offer qualifications in Civil Engineering and related subjects. Full details may be found in Part 4, under the entry for the appropriate university.

FIRST DEGREES AWARDED BY UNIVERSITIES

Aberdeen; Abertay, Dundee; Aston; Bath; Belfast; Birmingham; Bradford; Brighton; Bristol; City; Coventry; Cranfield; Dundee; East London; Edinburgh; Exeter; Glamorgan; Glasgow; Glasgow Caledonian; Greenwich; Heriot-Watt; Hertfordshire; Kingston; Leeds; Leeds Metropolitan; Liverpool; Liverpool John Moores; London (Imperial College of Science, Technology & Medicine); London (University College (UCL)); Loughborough; Manchester; Napier; Newcastle; Nottingham; Nottingham Trent; Oxford; Oxford Brookes; Paisley; Plymouth; Portsmouth; Salford; Sheffield; Sheffield Hallam; South Bank; Southampton; Strathclyde; Surrey; Ulster; UMIST; Wales (Cardiff University); Wales (University of Wales College, Newport); Wales (University of Wales, Swansea); Warwick; Wolverhampton

HIGHER DEGREES AWARDED BY UNIVERSITIES

Aberdeen; Aston; Bath; Belfast; Brighton; Bristol; City; Cranfield; Dundee; Durham; East London; Exeter; Glamorgan; Greenwich; Heriot-Watt; Leeds; Liverpool; Liverpool John Moores; London (Queen Mary & Westfield College (incorporating St Bartholomew's and the Royal London School of Medicine & Dentistry)); London (University College (UCL)); Loughborough; Manchester; Plymouth; Portsmouth; Sheffield; South Bank; Surrey; Wales (Cardiff University)

DIPLOMAS AWARDED BY UNIVERSITIES

Abertay, Dundee; Anglia; City; Coventry; East London; Glamorgan; Greenwich; Kingston; Liverpool; Napier; Oxford Brookes; Portsmouth; South Bank; Teesside; Wales (Swansea Institute of Higher Education); Wolverhampton

CERTIFICATES AWARDED BY UNIVERSITIES

Anglia (City College, Norwich); Bradford (Bradford & Ilkley Community College); East Anglia (Suffolk College); Leeds Metropolitan; Napier; South Bank; Wales (University of Wales College, Newport)

PRE-DEGREE AWARDED BY UNIVERSITIES

Kingston

National Certificates and Diplomas

BTEC National Certificates/Diplomas: Civil Engineering Studies
BTEC Higher National Certificates/Diplomas: Civil Engineering Studies
Scotland
SQA HNC: Civil Engineering.
SQA HND: Civil Engineering.

ENGINEERING DESIGN

Membership of Professional Institutions and Associations

THE INSTITUTION OF ENGINEERING DESIGNERS

Courtleigh, Westbury Leigh, Westbury, Wiltshire BA13 3TA Tel: 01373 822801 Fax: 01373 858085 e-mail: ied@inst-engg-design.demon.co.uk Website: www.ied.org.uk

DIVISIONAL STRUCTURE:
The Institution is organised into three separate sections – Engineering Design Division, Product Design Division and CADD Division. Membership to these divisions is based on the following requirements.

CORPORATE MEMBERSHIP:
Fellows (FIED): By portfolio assessment for persons of outstanding ability in the profession who have at least 10 yrs' experience, of which 6 yrs were devoted to Engineering Design, Product Design or CADD and who hold a qualification of HNC or equivalent, and are not less than 30.
Members (MIED): Must have at least 3 yrs' experience, of which 2 yrs were devoted to Engineering Design, Product Design or CADD and hold a qualification of HNC or equivalent, and are not less than 23.
NON-CORPORATE MEMBERSHIP:
Associates: Must have at least 2 yrs' drawing office experience and hold a qualification not less than ONC equivalent, and are not less than 22.
AFFILIATE MEMBERSHIP:
Graduate & Diplomate Membership: Available for persons with appropriate educational qualifications but without adequate experience/responsibility for admission to an appropriate Corporate or Non-Corporate grade.
Students: Must be actively or prospectively engaged in engineering/product/CAD as apprentices or trainees, be engaged in a suitable course of study, and are not less than 18.
ENGINEERING COUNCIL REGISTRATION:
Corporate Members to the Engineering Division may be nominated for Registration as Chartered Engineers or Incorporated Engineers and Non-Corporate Members as Engineering Technicians, depending on their qualifications, training and experience.

University Qualifications

The following universities offer qualifications in Engineering Design and related subjects. Full details may be found in Part 4, under the entry for the appropriate university.

FIRST DEGREES AWARDED BY UNIVERSITIES

Anglia; Aston; Bath Spa; Bournemouth; Bradford; Brighton; Brunel; Bucks. Coll.; Central England; Central Lancashire; De Montfort, Leicester; Derby; East London; Exeter (The College of St Mark & St John); Glamorgan; Glasgow; Glasgow (Glasgow School of Art); Greenwich; Heriot-Watt; Hertfordshire; Huddersfield; Kent (Kent Institute of Art & Design); Leeds (The College of Ripon & York St John); Lincolnshire; Liverpool; Liverpool John Moores; London (Goldsmiths College); London Institute (Central Saint Martins College of Art & Design); Loughborough; Luton; Manchester Metropolitan.; Middlesex; Napier; Northampton; Northumbria; Nottingham Trent; Nottingham Trent (Southampton Institute); Portsmouth; Robert Gordon; South Bank; Southampton (King Alfred's College); St Martin; Staffordshire; Strathclyde; Sunderland; Surrey (University of Surrey Roehampton); Sussex; Teesside; UMIST; Wales (Swansea Institute of Higher Education); Wales (University of Wales College, Newport); Wales (University of Wales Institute, Cardiff); Wales (University of Wales, Bangor); Wales (University of Wales, Swansea); Warwick; Westminster; Wolverhampton

HIGHER DEGREES AWARDED BY UNIVERSITIES

Aberdeen; Bath; Birmingham; Bournemouth; Bristol; Bucks. Coll.; Central England; Coventry; Cranfield; Exeter; Exeter (The College of St Mark & St John); Glasgow; Glasgow (Glasgow School of Art); Huddersfield; Kent (Kent Institute of Art & Design); Leeds; Liverpool John Moores; London (Birkbeck, University of London); London (Imperial College of Science, Technology & Medicine); London (University College (UCL)); London Institute (Central Saint Martins College of Art & Design); Loughborough; Manchester Metropolitan.; Napier; Nottingham Trent; Portsmouth; Royal College of Art; Salford; Sheffield Hallam; South Bank; Staffordshire; Strathclyde; Surrey (University of Surrey Roehampton); Wales (Swansea Institute of Higher Education); Wolverhampton

DIPLOMAS AWARDED BY UNIVERSITIES

Bath Spa; Bournemouth; Central England; De Montfort, Leicester; Glamorgan; Hertfordshire; Huddersfield; Kent (Kent Institute of Art & Design); London (University College (UCL)); Loughborough; Luton; Manchester; Napier; Northampton; Paisley; Salford; Sheffield; South Bank; Strathclyde; Wales (Swansea Institute of Higher Education); Wales (University of Wales Institute, Cardiff)

CERTIFICATES AWARDED BY UNIVERSITIES

Brunel; Central England; Exeter (The College of St Mark & St John); Liverpool John Moores; London (Goldsmiths College); Manchester Metropolitan.; Middlesex; Sheffield Hallam; Wales (University of Wales College, Newport); Wales (University of Wales Institute, Cardiff); Wolverhampton

OTHER COURSES AWARDED BY UNIVERSITIES

Bournemouth; Huddersfield

National Certificates and Diplomas

BTEC Higher National Certificates/Diplomas: Engineering ((Manufacturing/Design); Engineering (Product Design and Manufacture)
Scotland
SQA HNC: Engineering (Design); Engineering Design and Manufacture

NVQs

Level 3: Civil Engineering Site Supervision; Engineering Construction: Design and Draughting; Engineering Design
Level 4: Civil Engineering Site Management

ELECTRICAL, ELECTRONIC AND MANUFACTURING ENGINEERING

Membership of Professional Institutions and Associations

THE INSTITUTION OF ELECTRICAL ENGINEERS
Savoy Place, London WC2R 0BL Tel: 020 7240 1871 Fax: 020 7497 3609 Website: www.iee.org.uk
CORPORATE MEMBERSHIP:
Honorary Fellows (HonFIEE): Are elected by the Council. There are corporate and non-corporate Honorary Fellows.
Fellows (FIEE): Are members of the profession who have met the requirements for MIEE and have carried superior responsibility for at least 5 yrs.
Members (MIEE): Must have satisfied the educational requirements of an accredited MEng or equivalent and have provided evidence that they are (a) competent to practise as a Chartered Engineer, and (b) committed to professional development throughout their career in engineering. Member and Fellow candidates have to be, disregarding temporary unemployment, engaged in or associated with any branch of engineering.
NON-CORPORATE MEMBERSHIP:
Companion (Companion IEE): Are not normally Engineers by profession but must satisfy the Council that they have rendered important services to electrical/electronic/software/systems/information and manufacturing engineering. They are not eligible for election as Fellows.
Associate Members (AMIEE): Are persons who have a minimum of a Pass degree on an Honours degree course or its equivalent, and are working in an activity relevant to the interests of the Institution as illustrated by IEE's Professional Groups.
Associates: Must be aged at least 21, of good education (at least that necessary for enrolment for tertiary education) and be interested in the advancement of electrical/electronic/software/systems/information and manufacturing engineering and their applications.
Students: Must be studying for the profession and intending to satisfy the requirements for AMIEE. Comprehensive information on the IEE including membership application forms can be found on the internet at www.iee.org.uk/

THE INSTITUTION OF LIGHTING ENGINEERS

Chief Executive: Richard Frost, Lennox House, 9 Lawford Road, Rugby CV21 2DZ Tel: 01788 576492 Fax: 01788 540145 e-mail: ile@ile.co.uk Website: www.ile.co.uk

MEMBERSHIP:

Fellows: Persons who (a) (i) are at least 35, and (ii) have been in the grade of Member for at least 5 yrs, and (iii) have made a substantial contribution towards furthering the objectives of the Institution or (b) have, in the opinion of the Council, such experience and eminence in the profession, that his/her admission as a fellow would conduce to the interests of the Institution.

Members: Persons who are at least 25 and (a) (i) have obtained a degree in an approved engineering/science subject, and (ii) have received at least 2 yrs' training in lighting installations or equipment, and (iii) have 3 yrs' approved experience, or (b) (i) complies with all the requirements of (a) but with an academic qualification in a non-engineering field acceptable to the council, or (c) (i) have obtained a qualification not less than a BTEC HNC in an approved engineering/science subject, and (ii) have at least 2 yrs' training in the industry, and (iii) have 5 yrs' approved experience, or (d) (i) complies with all the requirements of (c) but with an academic qualification in a non-engineering field acceptable to the council, or (e) (i) persons who are at least 30, and (ii) are a Corporate Member of an EC approved professional body authorised to register Chartered Engineers, and (iii) have 3 yrs' approved experience in the industry, or (f) at least 35, and (i) have attained a satisfactory level of general education, and (ii) have received at least 2 yrs' training and satisfy the Council of this by submission of evidence in the form of a written thesis, and (iii) have at least 10 yrs' experience in the lighting industry, and (iv) attend a professional interview, and (v) have been a Non- Corporate Member of the Institution in the grade of Affiliate for a min of 5 yrs. Note: persons elected to the grade of Member by routes (b), (d) or (f) will not be eligible for registration with the Engineering Council as a CEng or IEng.

Associate Members: Persons who are at least 23 and (a) (i) have obtained a qualification not less than BTEC HNC in an approved engineering/science subject, and (ii) have at least 2 yrs' training in the industry, and (iii) have at least 3 yrs' experience in the industry, or (b) (i) complies with all the requirements of (a) but with an academic qualification in a non-engineering field acceptable to the Council, or (c) (i) have obtained a qualification not less than BTEC NC in an approved engineering/science subject, and (ii) have 2 yrs' training in the profession, and (iii) have a minimum of 5 yrs' experience in the industry, or (d) complies with all the requirements of (c) but with an academic qualification in a non- engineering field acceptable to the Council, or (e) persons over 35 who (i) have attained a satisfactory level of general education, and (ii) have a minimum of 15 yrs' experience in the industry and can satisfy the Council of this by submission of a written thesis, and (iii) attend a professional interview, and (iv) have been a Non-Corporate Member of the Institution in the grade of Affiliate for a min of 3 yrs. Note: persons elected to the grade of Associate Member by routes (b), (d) or (e) are not eligible for registration with the Engineering Council as an IEng or an EngTech.

Affiliate: (a) (i) persons of 21 or more, and (ii) have obtained an ILE Final Certificate in Lighting Technology, or (b) (i) be at least 30, and (ii) have a minimum of 10 yrs' experience in the industry and show, by presentation of a thesis, that his/her knowledge of lighting or associated subject is equivalent to that gained in an ILE Final Certificate in Lighting Technology.

Associate: Every candidate for election or transfer to the grade of Associate shall be anyone interested in the objects of the Institution who is over 21.

Student: Every candidate for election to the grade of Student shall be under 26 and satisfy the Council that he/she has obtained a satisfactory standard of general education and is undergoing an approved training in lighting or the design or development of lighting installations or equipment.

University Qualifications

The following universities offer qualifications in Electrical, Electronic and Manufacturing Engineering and related subjects. Full details may be found in Part 4, under the entry for the appropriate university.

FIRST DEGREES AWARDED BY UNIVERSITIES

Aberdeen; Abertay, Dundee; Anglia; Aston; Bath; Belfast; Birmingham; Blackburn; Bournemouth; Bradford; Brighton; Bristol; Brunel; Central England; Central Lancashire; City; Coventry; Cranfield; De Montfort, Leicester; Derby; Dundee; East Anglia; East London; Edinburgh; Essex;

Exeter; Glamorgan; Glasgow; Glasgow Caledonian; Greenwich; Heriot-Watt; Hertfordshire; Huddersfield; Hull; Kent; Kingston; Lancaster; Leeds; Leeds Metropolitan; Leicester; Lincolnshire; Lincolnshire (Hull College); Liverpool; Liverpool John Moores; London (Imperial College of Science, Technology & Medicine); London (King's College London); London (Queen Mary & Westfield College (incorporating St Bartholomew's and the Royal London School of Medicine & Dentistry)); London (University College (UCL)); Loughborough; Luton; Manchester Metropolitan.; Napier; Newcastle; North London; Northumbria; Nottingham; Nottingham Trent; Nottingham Trent (Southampton Institute); Oxford; Oxford Brookes; Paisley; Plymouth; Portsmouth; Reading; Robert Gordon; Salford; Salford (South Devon College); Salford (The Oldham College); Sheffield; Sheffield Hallam; South Bank; Southampton; St Andrews; Staffordshire; Strathclyde; Sunderland; Surrey; Sussex; Teesside; Ulster; UMIST; Wales (Cardiff University); Wales (North East Wales Institute); Wales (Swansea Institute of Higher Education); Wales (University of Wales College, Newport); Wales (University of Wales, Bangor); Wales (University of Wales, Swansea); Warwick; Westminster; Wolverhampton; York

HIGHER DEGREES AWARDED BY UNIVERSITIES
Aberdeen; Abertay, Dundee; Aston; Bath; Belfast; Birmingham; Bournemouth; Bradford; Brighton; Bristol; Brunel; Central England; City; Coventry; Dundee; Durham; East Anglia; Essex; Exeter; Glamorgan; Glasgow; Glasgow Caledonian; Greenwich; Heriot-Watt; Hertfordshire; Huddersfield; Hull; Kent; Leeds; Leeds Metropolitan; Leicester; Liverpool; Liverpool John Moores; London (King's College London); London (Queen Mary & Westfield College (incorporating St Bartholomew's and the Royal London School of Medicine & Dentistry)); London (University College (UCL)); Loughborough; Manchester; Napier; Newcastle; Northumbria; Nottingham; Oxford; Paisley; Plymouth; Portsmouth; Reading; Salford; Sheffield Hallam; South Bank; Southampton; St Andrews; Staffordshire; Strathclyde; Surrey; Sussex; Ulster; UMIST; Wales (Cardiff University); Wales (University of Wales College, Newport); Wales (University of Wales, Bangor); Wales (University of Wales, Swansea); Warwick; York

DIPLOMAS AWARDED BY UNIVERSITIES
Anglia; Anglia (City College, Norwich); Anglia (Colchester Institute); Barnsley; Birmingham; Blackburn; Bournemouth; Bradford; Bradford (Bradford & Ilkley Community College); Brighton; Central England; Central Lancashire; Coventry; Derby; Dundee; East Anglia (Suffolk College); Glamorgan; Glasgow; Glasgow Caledonian; Greenwich; Hertfordshire; Hertfordshire (West Herts College); Huddersfield; Kent; Lancaster; Lincolnshire (Hull College); Lincolnshire (North Lindsey College); London (University College (UCL)); Luton; Middlesex; Napier; Northampton; Northumbria; Nottingham Trent; Paisley; Portsmouth; Salford; South Bank; St Andrews; Staffordshire; Strathclyde; Sussex; Teesside; Ulster; Wales (Cardiff University); Wales (North East Wales Institute); Wales (Swansea Institute of Higher Education); Wales (University of Wales Institute, Cardiff); Wales (University of Wales, Bangor)

CERTIFICATES AWARDED BY UNIVERSITIES
Anglia; Anglia (City College, Norwich); Bournemouth; Bradford (Bradford & Ilkley Community College); Brighton; Central England; Leeds Metropolitan; Lincolnshire; Lincolnshire (Hull College); Manchester (Warrington Collegiate Institute, Faculty of H.E,); Newcastle; North London; Northampton; South Bank; Sussex; Wales (University of Wales College, Newport)

OTHER COURSES AWARDED BY UNIVERSITIES
Bournemouth; Huddersfield; North London

POSTGRADUATE DIPLOMAS AWARDED BY UNIVERSITIES
Heriot-Watt

PRE-DEGREE AWARDED BY UNIVERSITIES
Kingston

National Certificates and Diplomas
BTEC National Certificates/Diplomas: Engineering (Broadcast Audio Engineering); Engineering (Communications); Engineering (Electrical/Electronic); Engineering (Electrical Media Systems)
BTEC Higher National Certificates/Diplomas: Engineering (Audio and Video Systems);

Engineering (Audio and Visual Systems); Engineering (Communications); Engineering (Computer Systems Engineering); Engineering (Electrical Power); Engineering (Electrical/Electronic); Engineering (Electronic Instrumentation and Computer Control); Engineering (Electronics); Engineering (Manufacture)
Scotland
SQA HNC: Electrical Engineering; Electrical Engineering (Oil and Gas Production); Electrical Power Engineering; Electronic and Electrical Engineering; Electronic Communications Engineering; Electronic Engineering & Communication Systems; Electronic Service Engineering; Electronic Systems; Electronic Technology; Electronics; Electronics with Data Communication; Electronics with Music Technology; Engineering (Manufacture); Engineering Manufacture with Quality Assurance
SQA HND: Electrical, Electronic & Mechanical Engineering; Electronic & Electrical Systems; Electronic Engineering; Electronic Engineering with Management; Electronic and Electrical Engineering; Electronic & Electrical Engineering with Management; Electronics with Data Communications; Electronics in Manufacturing; Electronic Systems; Engineering Manufacture with Quality Assurance. SQA Advanced Certificate in Engineering Practice (Electrical & Electronic)

NVQs

Level 1: Cabling & Wiring Loom Manufacture; Electronic Product Assembly; Engineering Assembly; Fabricating & Fixing Electrical Cable Supports; PCB (Printed Circuit Board) Assembly; Process Engineering Maintenance; Surface Mount Technology & Automatic Assembly of PCBs
Level 2: Electrical and Electronics Servicing; Electricity Distribution & Transmission Engineering Support; Engineering Manufacture (Foundation); Installing Electrical Systems Equipment; Maintaining Electricity Generation Systems; Operating Single Electricity Generation Systems; Process Engineering Maintenance
Level 3: Electrical and Electronics Servicing; Electricity Distribution & Transmission Engineering; Installing & Commissioning Electrical Systems & Equipment; Maintaining Electricity Generation Systems; Operating Multiple Electricity Generation Systems; Process Engineering Maintenance
Level 4: Engineering Manufacture

SVQs

Level 1: Cable & Wiring Loom Manufacture; Electronic Product Assembly; Printed Circuit Board Assembly; Installing Fibre Optic Communication Links; Surface Mount Technology & Automatic Assembly of PCBs.
Level 2: Electronic Product Assembly & Rectification: Installing & Maintaining Aerial Equipment & Associated Feeders; Printed Circuit Board Assembly & Repair; Technical Services: Semiconductor Fabrication.
Level 3: Erecting & Maintaining Wood Pole Overhead Lines; Erecting & Maintaining Steel Tower Overhead Lines; Installing & Maintaining Electrical Transmission Substation Plant & Apparatus; Installing & Maintaining Electricity Substation Plant & Apparatus; Technical Services: Semiconductor Fabrication.

City & Guilds

2240 Electronics Servicing; 2320 Electronic and Electrical Engineering; 2360 Electrical Installation; 2380 BS 7671:1992 Requirements for Electrical Installations (IEE Wiring Regulations, 16th ed.); 2720 Telecommunications & Electronic Engineering

Other Awards

THE ELECTRONICS EXAMINATION BOARD

Savoy Hill House, Savoy Hill, London WC2R 0BS Tel: 020 7836 3357 Fax: 020 7497 9006
e-mail: eeb@iie.org.uk
The Board comprises representatives from the British Radio Equipment Manufacturers' Association, the Radio, Electrical and Television Retailers' Association, the Cable

Communications Association, the Association of Manufacturers of Domestic Electrical Appliances, National Homecare Ltd, Granada Home Technology, the Institution of Incorporated Engineers and the Institution of Electrical Engineers. It conducts exams jointly with the C&G.

Electronic Servicing Certificate: This is a 4yr PT (day release) course with an exam at Part I level taken at the end of the first yr, Part II level at the end of the third yr when the Electronic Servicing Certificate is awarded, and the Part III level at the end of the fourth yr. The course separates at the end of the second yr, half-way through Part II, into Television on the one hand, and Control Systems Technology on the other. The course to Part II level is offered by some centres on a FT basis. The C&G arranges the written papers and the Board conducts the practical tests at the end of the first, third and fourth yrs. The Joint Advisory Committee of the 2 bodies advises on syllabuses and exam standards.

Progression Award (6958, Level 2): This course is offered in partnership with City & Guilds and has been designed to show the underpinning knowledge for the related NVQ at Level 2. The course has 2 pathways: Consumer/Commercial Electronics and Domestic Electrical Appliances. City & Guilds arrange the written papers and the Board provides the practical assignments and arranges the moderation of the assignments. City & Guilds and the Board collaborate closely on the standards and syllabus of these courses.

Useful Addresses

National Electrotechnical Training Organisation, 34 Palace Court, London W2 4HY Tel: 020 7313 4846 Fax: 020 7221 7344
The Institution of Electrical Engineers, Savoy Place, London WC2R 0BL Tel: 020 7240 1871 Fax: 020 7240 7735*For Telecommunications*
Telecommunications Vocational Standards Council, Blackfriars House, 399 South Row, Central Milton Keynes MK9 2PG Tel: 01908 240120 Fax: 01908 240201

ENERGY ENGINEERING

Membership of Professional Institutions and Associations

THE INSTITUTE OF ENERGY

18 Devonshire Street, London W1N 2AU Tel: 020 7580 7124 Fax: 020 7580 4420
e-mail: info@instenergy.org.uk Website: www.instenergy.org.uk
The Institute was formerly the Institute of Fuel and is a nominated body of the Engineering Council.

CORPORATE MEMBERSHIP:
Senior Fellows, Fellows and Members may use the description Chartered Energy Engineer and are normally eligible for registration as Chartered Engineers.
Honorary Fellows (HFInstE): Persons of great distinction who have rendered exceptional service to the Institute. Limited to 12 in number.
Fellows (FInstE): Corporate Members aged 33 or over, with 5 yrs' professional experience in energy with superior responsibility, having satisfied or gained exemption from the exam qualification for Corporate Membership and having held the class of Member for 3 yrs.
Members (MInstE): Chartered Engineers aged 25 and over, with a minimum aggregate of 4 yrs' approved training and experience in energy. They must hold: (a) any degree acceptable to the Engineering Council; or (b) Engineering Council Part 2 exam in a relevant combination of subjects. Other qualifications are sometimes accepted but only if judged equivalent in every respect to the above.
Members (MInstE): Corporate Members aged 25 and over, with a minimum aggregate of 4 yrs' approved training and experience in energy. They must hold an acceptable honours degree. Other qualifications are sometimes accepted but only if judged equivalent in every respect to the above.

NON-CORPORATE:
Associate Members are normally eligible for registration as Incorporated Engineers and Licentiate

Members are normally eligible for registration as Engineering Technicians.

Companions: Those not necessarily qualified as engineers but who have rendered important service to energy.

Associate Members (AMInstE): Incorporated engineers aged 23 and over, who have an academic qualification recognised by The Engineering Council, with a minimum of 5 yrs' relevant training and experience.

Associate Members (AMInstE): Non-Engineers aged 23 and over, who have achieved The Institute of Energy's NVQ Level 4 in Energy Management or an equivalent academic level in an energy related subject, with a minimum of 5 yrs' relevant training and experience.

Licentiate Members (LMInstE): Engineering Technicians aged 21 and over, who have an academic qualification recognised by The Engineering Council, with a minimum of 4 yrs' relevant training and experience.

Licentiate Members (LMInstE): Non-Engineers aged 21 and over, who have achieved an academic level in energy related subjects, with a minimum of 4 yrs' relevant training and experience.

Associates: Those over 21, of good education, in a responsible position, actively interested in the promotion of energy and qualified to concur with members in its advancement.

Graduates: Those over 21, possessing the academic qualifications for corporate membership.

Students: Those over 18 engaged in a course of study leading to the academic qualification for corporate membership.

Group Members: Corporate bodies of any legal form concerned as organisations with energy. They nominate up to2 representatives.

EXAMINATIONS:

The Institute does not conduct exams for entry but accepts instead the qualifications listed above. At Incorporated Engineer level, the Institute assesses a

Diploma exam in Energy Technology (late Fuel Technology; formerly known as the Licentiateship Exam). This is set up by various colleges around the UK to an approved syllabus and the results are moderated by the Institute. The Institute also awards a **Diploma in Energy Management** for energy managers. **Training in Energy Management through Open Learning (TEMOL)** and an **S/NVQ in Managing Energy** are also awarded. Contact the Membership and Education Department for information on courses accredited for registration to The Engineering Council, approved for membership and for CPD.

THE INSTITUTE OF PETROLEUM

61 New Cavendish Street, London W1M 8AR Tel: 020 7467 7100 Fax: 020 7255 1472
e-mail: ip@petroleum.co.uk Website: www.petroleum.co.uk

MEMBERSHIP:

Membership of the Institute of Petroleum is open to all individuals, companies and other associations wishing to further its aims, which are 'the advancement of technical knowledge relating to the international oil and gas industry'. It is a non-qualifying body. The Institute will increase the knowledge and understanding of the oil industry by young people so that they see it as providing stimulating and fulfilling opportunities.

Honorary Fellows: Persons of eminence, who may or may not be actively engaged in the petroleum industry. These positions shall normally be for life, but the Council may at its discretion elect a person for the period of their tenure of some particular official position.

Fellows (FInstPet): A Member for not less than 5 yrs who satisfies the Council that he has appropriate professional, technical, scientific or academic qualifications and that he has held, for not less than 5 yrs, a position of responsibility concerned with petroleum.

Members (MInstPet): Shall be not less than 18 and shall satisfy the Council that he is a fit and proper person to belong to the Institute and that he is desirous of furthering its objects.

Student Members (SInstPet): A Student Member shall be not less than 18 and shall satisfy the Council that he is undertaking an FT or S course of study, approved by the Council, and intends to become a Member of the Institute.

Collective Membership: Companies and other associations which are interested in and desirous of assisting in the work of the Institute may be elected Collective Members under the conditions laid down in the Institute's By-laws.

University Qualifications

The following universities offer qualifications in Energy Engineering and related subjects. Full details may be found in Part 4, under the entry for the appropriate university.

FIRST DEGREES AWARDED BY UNIVERSITIES

Anglia; Bradford; Brighton; City; Glamorgan; Heriot-Watt; Leeds; London (Imperial College of Science, Technology & Medicine); Napier; Strathclyde

HIGHER DEGREES AWARDED BY UNIVERSITIES

City; Cranfield; Dundee; Durham; East London; Heriot-Watt; Leeds; London (Imperial College of Science, Technology & Medicine); Oxford Brookes; South Bank; Staffordshire; UMIST

DIPLOMAS AWARDED BY UNIVERSITIES

Aberdeen; Anglia; City; Dundee; Glamorgan; Leeds; South Bank; Ulster

POSTGRADUATE DIPLOMAS AWARDED BY UNIVERSITIES

Heriot-Watt

NVQs

Level 1: Processing Operations: Hydrocarbons
Level 2: Refinery Field Operations; Processing Operations (Extractive Industries); Processing Operations: Hydrocarbons
Level 3: Processing Operations: Hydrocarbons; Refinery Control Room Operations

Useful Addresses

British Nuclear Fuels plc, Risley, Warrington WA3 6AS Tel: 01925 832000 Fax: 01925 822711
Electricity Training Association, 30 Millbank, London SW1P 4RD Tel: 020 7963 5859 Fax: 020 7963 5999
National Energy Action, St Andrews House, 90-92 Pilgrim Street, Newcastle upon Tyne, NE1 6SG Tel: 0191 261 5677 Fax: 0191 261 6496

ENVIRONMENTAL ENGINEERING

(See also Building Services Engineering)

Membership of Professional Institutions and Associations

THE CHARTERED INSTITUTION OF WATER AND ENVIRONMENTAL MANAGEMENT

15 John Street, London WC1N 2EB Tel: 020 7831 3110 Fax: 020 7405 4967
e-mail: admin@ciwem.org.uk Website: www.ciwem.org.uk
CIWEM, founded in 1895, is the leading Professional Body in Water and Environmental Management, in recognition of which the Institution was granted a Royal Charter in 1995.In the Royal Charter granted to CIWEM, Water and Environmental Management is defined as the application of engineering, scientific or management knowledge and expertise to the provision of works and services designed to further the beneficial management, conservation and improvement of the environment. This includes: Environmental management; Resource protection, development, use and conservation; Integrated pollution control; Public health, water and sanitation services; Flood defence and land drainage; and Recreation, amenity and conservation activities.

EXAMINATIONS:
PG Certificate in Water & Environmental Management: Provides the broad understanding of water and environmental management issues needed by those active in all facets of the industry.

PG Diploma in Water & Environmental Management: Provides a high standard knowledge in a series of specially chosen options tailored to industry needs. The courses are all modular and may be taken singly or in combinations. The Certificate will be awarded after successful completion of all 4 compulsory modules and the Diploma after the successful completion of a further 4 optional modules.

SOCIETY OF ENVIRONMENTAL ENGINEERS

Owles Hall, Buntingford, Hertfordshire SG9 9PL Tel: 01763 271209 Fax: 01763 273255 Telex: 01763 273255 e-mail: see@owles.demon.co.uk Website: www.environmental.org.uk

This is a learned society formed in 1959 to cover the whole field of environmental engineering and to provide a forum for the dissemination and discussion of knowledge in that field. The major subjects covered by the Society's current work are the testing of industrial and military equipment, the development and use of packaging materials and methods, safety and comfort in road, rail, sea or air travel and contamination control.

MEMBERSHIP:

Membership is confined to those of professional status whose main responsibilities are environmental research, testing or the manufacture of equipment for such research and testing. The SEE has conditional nominated body status with the Engineering Council and is able to assess the competence of environmental engineering candidates for registration to CEng, IEng and Eng Tech. The requirements for Membership are an honours degree in an engineering subject plus at least 2 yrs' training and experience in Environmental Engineering.

Associate Members are required to have an academic qualification plus at least 3 yrs' training and experience. Those with no qualifications may join the SEE as **Associates**.

Student Membership is also available.

University Qualifications

The following universities offer qualifications in Environmental Engineering and related subjects. Full details may be found in Part 4, under the entry for the appropriate university.

FIRST DEGREES AWARDED BY UNIVERSITIES

Aberdeen; Abertay, Dundee; Anglia; Anglia (City College, Norwich); Anglia (Colchester Institute); Aston; Bath Spa; Belfast; Birmingham; Bournemouth; Bradford; Brighton; Bristol; Central England; Central Lancashire; Cheltenham & Gloucester; Coventry; Cranfield; De Montfort, Leicester; De Montfort, Leicester (De Montfort University Bedford); Derby; Dundee; Durham; East Anglia; East Anglia (Suffolk College); East London; Edinburgh; Essex (Writtle College); Exeter; Glamorgan; Glasgow; Glasgow Caledonian; Greenwich; Heriot-Watt; Heriot-Watt (Edinburgh College of Art); Hertfordshire; Huddersfield; Hull; Keele; Kent; Kent (Canterbury Christ Church University College); Kingston; Lancaster; Leeds; Leeds (The College of Ripon & York St John); Lincolnshire (Lincoln University Campus); Liverpool; Liverpool (Chester College of H.E.); Liverpool (Liverpool Hope University College); Liverpool John Moores; London (Birkbeck, University of London); London (Imperial College of Science, Technology & Medicine); London (King's College London); London (London School of Economics & Political Science); London (Queen Mary & Westfield College (incorporating St Bartholomew's and the Royal London School of Medicine & Dentistry)); London (Royal Holloway); London (University College (UCL)); London (Wye College); Loughborough; Luton; Manchester; Manchester Metropolitan.; Middlesex; Napier; Newcastle; North London; Northampton; Northumbria; Nottingham; Nottingham Trent; Nottingham Trent (Southampton Institute); OU (NESCOT); Oxford Brookes; Paisley; Plymouth; Portsmouth; Reading; Robert Gordon; Salford; Salford (Halton College); Sheffield; Sheffield Hallam; South Bank; Southampton; Southampton (Chichester Institute of Higher Education); St Andrews; St Martin; Staffordshire; Stirling; Strathclyde; Sunderland; Surrey; Surrey (University of Surrey Roehampton); Sussex; Ulster; UMIST; Wales (Cardiff University); Wales (North East Wales Institute); Wales (Swansea Institute of Higher Education); Wales (University of Wales College, Newport); Wales (University of Wales Institute, Cardiff); Wales (University of Wales, Aberystwyth); Wales (University of Wales, Bangor); Wales (University of Wales, Lampeter); Wales (University of Wales, Swansea); Westminster; Wolverhampton; Worcester; York

HIGHER DEGREES AWARDED BY UNIVERSITIES
Aberdeen; Abertay, Dundee; Anglia; Aston; Bath; Belfast; Bournemouth; Bradford; Brighton; Bristol; Brunel; Cambridge; Central England; Central Lancashire; Cheltenham & Gloucester; City; Coventry; Cranfield; De Montfort, Leicester; De Montfort, Leicester (De Montfort University Bedford); Derby; Dundee; Durham; East Anglia; East London; Edinburgh; Essex; Glamorgan; Glasgow Caledonian; Greenwich; Heriot-Watt; Hertfordshire; Huddersfield; Hull; Keele; Kent; Kingston; Lancaster; Leeds; Leicester; Lincolnshire; Liverpool; Liverpool (Chester College of H.E.); Liverpool (Liverpool Hope University College); Liverpool John Moores; London (Birkbeck, University of London); London (Imperial College of Science, Technology & Medicine); London (London School of Economics & Political Science); London (Queen Mary & Westfield College (incorporating St Bartholomew's and the Royal London School of Medicine & Dentistry)); London (Royal Holloway); London (School of Oriental & African Studies); London (University College (UCL)); London (Wye College); Loughborough; Luton; Manchester; Manchester Metropolitan.; Middlesex; Newcastle; Northampton; Northumbria; Nottingham; Oxford Brookes; Paisley; Plymouth; Portsmouth; Reading; Salford; Sheffield; Sheffield Hallam; South Bank; Southampton; Stirling; Strathclyde; Sunderland; Surrey; Surrey (University of Surrey Roehampton); Ulster; UMIST; Wales (University of Wales College, Newport); Wales (University of Wales, Aberystwyth); Wales (University of Wales, Bangor); Wales (University of Wales, Lampeter); Wales (University of Wales, Swansea); Wolverhampton; Worcester; York

DIPLOMAS AWARDED BY UNIVERSITIES
Aberdeen; Abertay, Dundee; Anglia; Anglia (Colchester Institute); Bath; Bath Spa; Bournemouth; Bradford; Bristol; Cheltenham & Gloucester; De Montfort, Leicester; Derby; Dundee; Durham; Edinburgh; Glamorgan; Greenwich; Hertfordshire; Hull; Kent; Lancaster; Leeds; Leeds Metropolitan; Leicester; Liverpool; Liverpool (Chester College of H.E.); Liverpool (Liverpool Hope University College); London (Wye College); Luton; Newcastle; Nottingham; Oxford Brookes; Paisley; Reading; Salford; South Bank; Staffordshire; Stirling; Strathclyde; Sunderland; Ulster; Wales (University of Wales Institute, Cardiff); Wales (University of Wales, Aberystwyth); Westminster; Wolverhampton; Worcester

CERTIFICATES AWARDED BY UNIVERSITIES
Anglia (City College, Norwich); Bournemouth; Bristol; Cheltenham & Gloucester; Derby; Durham; East Anglia (Otley College); Hull; Liverpool (Chester College of H.E.); London (Birkbeck, University of London); Newcastle; OU (Northern College of Education); Staffordshire; Warwick

OTHER COURSES AWARDED BY UNIVERSITIES
Essex (Writtle College); Huddersfield

POSTGRADUATE CERTIFICATES AWARDED BY UNIVERSITIES
Bournemouth

POSTGRADUATE DIPLOMAS AWARDED BY UNIVERSITIES
Heriot-Watt

National Certificates and Diplomas
BTEC Higher National Certificates/Diplomas: Engineering (Environmental Engineering); Water and Environmental Engineering
Scotland
SQA HNC: Applied Ecology; Applied Environmental Science; Environmental Monitoring & Safety; Environmental Sciences; Environmental and Heritage Science; Environmental Biology
SQA HND: Environmental Management; Environmental Protection & Management; Environmental Sciences; Environmental Technology; Applied Ecology; Applied Environmental Science; Environmental and Heritage Evaluation; Environmental Biology

NVQs
Level 2: Environmental Conservation (Landscape & Ecosystems)
Level 3: Environmental Conservation (Landscape & Ecosystems)

SVQs

Level 2: Environmental Conservation (Landscapes & Ecosystems)
Level 3: Environmental Conservation (Landscapes & Ecosystems);
Level 4: Environmental Management

FIRE ENGINEERING

Membership of Professional Institutions and Associations

THE INSTITUTION OF FIRE ENGINEERS

148 New Walk, Leicester LE1 7QB Tel: 0116 255 3654 Fax: 0116 247 123 e-mail: info@ife.org.uk
Website: www.ife.org.uk

CORPORATE MEMBERSHIP:
Fellow (FIFireE): Applicants must normally be at least 30, have passed the Graduate and Membership exams and have been engaged for a sufficient period in an important position in fire engineering. Fellowship may also be conferred on persons of eminent scientific attainment.
Member (MIFireE): Applicants must have completed not less than 4 yrs' continuous FT or PT service and training in fire engineering by 30 June in the yr of passing the Membership exam. Transfer from the Graduate grade follows the passing of the Membership exam.
Associate (AIFireE): Applicants must be regularly engaged in fire engineering having completed not less than 4 yrs continuous FT or PT employment in that profession by the day of the election and be in possession of a degree from a recognised University in appropriate scientific subjects, or be a member, in an appropriate comparable grade, of a recognised Professional Institution, and be properly proposed by 3 corporate members.

NON-CORPORATE MEMBERSHIP:
Graduate: Applicants must pass the Graduateship exam or have been exempted from it; they must be not less than 20 when elected and must have served for 3 yrs FT or PT.
Student: Applicants must be engaged professionally or PT and regularly trained in fire engineering. The Institution may also elect **Honorary Fellows.**

EXAMINATIONS:
The Institution conducts a Preliminary Exam, which qualifies for the award of a **Preliminary Certificate and an intermediate examination (for the award of intermediate certificate) from 1998.**
The Graduateship Exam is linked in the UK with the Statutory Station Officers' Exam, success in which is required for promotion to Station Officer. Candidates must be serving FT or PT and must have completed 3 yrs' service in a capacity approved by the Institution.
The Membership Exam is open to Graduates of the Institution who have been regularly trained in fire engineering and have completed not less than 4 yrs' continuous FT or PT service and training in fire engineering.

University Qualifications

The following universities offer qualifications in Fire Engineering and related subjects. Full details may be found in Part 4, under the entry for the appropriate university.

FIRST DEGREES AWARDED BY UNIVERSITIES

Central Lancashire; Glasgow Caledonian; Leeds; Leeds Metropolitan

HIGHER DEGREES AWARDED BY UNIVERSITIES

Glasgow Caledonian; Leeds; Ulster

DIPLOMAS AWARDED BY UNIVERSITIES

Ulster

CERTIFICATES AWARDED BY UNIVERSITIES
Ulster

SVQs
Level 2: Emergency Fire Services: Fire Fighting
Level 3: Emergency Fire Services: Operations or Supervision & Command

Useful Addresses
Fire Services Awarding Body, Layden House, 76-86 Turnmill Lane, London EC1M 5LG Tel: 020 7296 6600 Fax: 020 7296 6666

GAS ENGINEERING

Membership of Professional Institutions and Associations

THE INSTITUTION OF GAS ENGINEERS
Eur. Ing. Chris Bleach, BSc, CEng, MIGasE, Chief Executive, 21 Portland Place, London WIN 3AF Tel: 020 7636 6603 Fax: 020 7636 6602 Website: www.igaseng.com

HONORARY MEMBERSHIP:
Honorary Fellow (HonFIGasE) : Elected at the Council's invitation.

CORPORATE MEMBERSHIP:
Allows use of 'Chartered Gas Engineer' and registration as Chartered Engineer (CEng).
Fellow (FIGasE): Suitably senior Chartered Engineer Members or non-Members over 30.
Member (MIGasE): Over 25, with MEng degree level qualification (MEng or BEng plus further learning), practical training and / or responsible experience.

NON-CORPORATE MEMBERSHIP:
Companion (Companion IGasE): Elected at the Council's invitation.
Professional Associate: Non engineers, over 25, academically or professionally qualified at degree level and gas industry experience / responsibility.
Associate Member (Graduate Grade): Over 21, holding MEng degree level qualification.
Associate Member (Technician Engineer Grade): Over 23, with engineering degree level qualifications, practical training and / or responsible experience. Allows registration as Incorporated Engineer (IEng).
Associate Member (Technician Grade): Over 21 with National Certificate or NVQ Level 3 or equivalent in engineering, practical training and / or responsible experience. Allows registration as Engineering Technician (EngTech).
Associates: Over 21 with sufficient professional experience to participate.
Industrial Affiliates: Firms or other un-incorporated associates, limited companies, public authorities and institutions, or other bodies corporate in or associated with the gas industry.
Student: Between age 16 and 29 studying for a suitable academic qualification.
Note: Mature Routes to CEng and IEng available for over 35s.

University Qualifications
The following universities offer qualifications in Gas Engineering and related subjects. Full details may be found in Part 4, under the entry for the appropriate university.

HIGHER DEGREES AWARDED BY UNIVERSITIES
Dundee; Salford

DIPLOMAS AWARDED BY UNIVERSITIES
Dundee; Salford

NVQs

Level 2: Mechanical Engineering Services (Gas Services Installation & Maintenance – Domestic).
Level 3: Gas Network Engineering

SVQs

Level 2: Mechanical Engineering Services – Gas Services Installation & Maintenance: Domestic.
Level 3: Mechanical Engineering Services – Gas Services Installation

Useful Addresses

Gas Industry National Training Organisation, The Business Centre, Edward Street, Redditch, Worcestershire B97 6HR Tel: 01527 584848 Fax: 01527 69802

GENERAL ENGINEERING

Membership of Professional Institutions and Associations

BOARD FOR ENGINEERS' REGULATION (BER)

The principal task of the BER is to determine the standards and criteria for the education, training, competence and commitment required for the registration of engineers and technicians. Having set the standards the Institutions accredit relevant courses at universities and colleges, and approve programmes of training and experience. The criteria set out below will take effect in 1999, following a major review. Registration provides a recognised guide to the competence of an engineer and as in other professional fields of medicine, law or accountancy denotes a qualification of national – and international – currency, known and understood by employers. The BER is concerned also with the standards of professional conduct which engineering institutions stipulate for their members and which define a level of high integrity in all aspects of the work of qualified engineers.

The Register and Registration

The Register is designed to maintain an up-to-date and detailed record of qualified engineers. It has 3 sections: chartered engineer, incorporated engineer and engineering technician and registration can be achieved in 2 Stages in each of these sections as follows: Initial Stage – Achieving the required academic qualification; Final Stage – Satisfying the requirements for training and responsible experience (Known as Initial Professional Development (IPD))Registration is undertaken through an engineering institution which is a nominated body of the Engineering Council. An annual registration fee is payable and each registrant can apply for a registration card and a Certificate of Registration for which a charge will be made. The standards required for registration in each of the sections and their 2 Stages are set out below:

Chartered Engineer section

An engineering education exemplified by an accredited MEng degree in engineering or completion of The Engineering Council Examination. A period of approved training at the appropriate level, and a period of responsible engineering experience during which the education and training are applied at the appropriate level. IPD is followed by a Professional Review with interview. The total period of IPD will vary from a minimum of 4 yrs where there is a formally structural approved training programme to a minimum of 6 yrs where training is more informal. Those entered on the Register at the Final Stage , are authorised to use the style or title of Chartered Engineer and the designatory letters – **CEng.**

Incorporated Engineer section

An engineering education to a standard exemplified by an accredited BEng degree. A period of approved training at the appropriate level and a period of responsible engineering experience during which the education and training are applied at the appropriate level. IPD is followed by a Professional Review with Interview. The total period of IPD will vary from a minimum of 4 yrs where there is a formally structural approved training programme to a minimum of 6 yrs where training is more informal. Those entered on the Register at the Final Stage are entitled to use the style or title Incorporated Engineer and the designatory letters **IEng.**

Engineering Technician section

Initial Stage – An engineering education which provides a level of understanding of engineering principles broadly equivalent to that required for an EDEXCEL or SQA-SCOTVEC National Award or Advanced GNVQ. Final Stage – [As above but excluding the Professional Review with interview].Those entered on the Register at the Final Stage are entitled to use the style or title Engineering Technician and the designatory letters **EngTech.** Movement from one section of the Register to another is possible for those seeking progressive career opportunities.

EXAMINATIONS:

The Engineering Council Examination sets the academic standard for initial registration in the chartered engineer section of the Council's Register (although most registrants meet this standard by the award of a degree that is accredited as being at least equivalent in standard to the Examination).The Council conducts its Examination world-wide for those whose circumstances prevent them from pursuing an accredited degree programme, and for those who have non-accredited degrees and wish to undertake further qualification to meet the required standard. Prospective candidates for the Examination must confirm their eligibility for entry by completing Form ECX(Q), available from the address given below.

The Part 1 Examination: The scope and standard of the Part 1 Examination is not less than that of an examination set at a point about 12 mths through a 3-yr FT UK degree course. Candidates must satisfy the examiners in 6 subjects: 4 compulsory subjects and 2 subjects from a list of 4 optional ones. The minimum entry requirement is two GCE A Level passes or an equivalent qualification. Exemption may be gained from Part 1 by those holding relevant qualifications, eg a Higher or Advanced Diploma in an appropriate engineering discipline.

The Part 2 Examination: The Examination is in 3 parts: Part 2(A) consists of 5 subjects chosen from 30 normally available. Candidates are advised to choose subjects appropriate to the particular engineering discipline they wish to pursue. Part 2(B) is a single subject, The Engineer in Society, compulsory for all candidates. Part 2(C) consists of a project. The standard of the Part 2 Examination is that of an accredited honours degree in Engineering as awarded by a UK University. The entry requirement is a pass in Part 1 or an equivalent exempting qualification. Full details of the examination are published in:©Guidance and Rules for Candidates – May 1990 and Subsequent Examinations©Syllabuses – May 1999 and Subsequent Examinations. An order form for these and other publications together with a full information pack on the Examinations may be obtained from: The Engineering Council Examinations Department, 10 Maltravers Street, London WC2R 3ER Tel 0171-240 7891. Fax 0171-379 5586 e-mail, Exams@engc.org.uk

National & Scottish Vocational Qualifications

N/SVQs may be accepted as evidence of learning and competence required for registration. At present, each award is assessed for the contribution it makes by a procedure published by the Council in 'Guidance for Institutions and Awarding Bodies on Occupational Standards, N/SVQ and Registration'.

THE ENGINEERING COUNCIL

10 Maltravers Street, London WC2R 3ER Tel: 020 7240 7891 Website: www.engc.org.uk

The Engineering Council was established by Royal Charter in 1981, augmented by a new Supplemental Charter in January 1996. The mission of the Engineering Council is to enhance the standing and contribution of the UK engineering profession in the national interest and to the benefit of society. A vital aspect of the work of the Engineering Council is to stimulate awareness of the importance of registered engineers and technicians as central figures in the competitiveness of British industry and commerce and therefore essential to the wealth of the nation. Equally important is the task of promoting among young people the idea of the engineering profession as a desirable and interesting career and encouraging them to study relevant subjects. The nominated Institutions of the Engineering Council are as follows: The Institute of Acoustics; The Royal Aeronautical Society; The Institution of Agricultural Engineers; The Chartered Institution of Building Services Engineers; The Institution of Chemical Engineers; The Institution of Civil Engineers; The British Computer Society; The Association of Cost Engineers; The Institution of Electrical Engineers; The Institution of Energy; the Institution of Engineering Designers; The Institution of Fire Engineers; The Institution of British Foundrymen; The Institution of Gas Engineers; The Institute of Healthcare Engineering and Estate Management; The Institute of Highway Incorporated Engineers; The Institution of Incorporated Engineers; The Institution of

Incorporated Executive Engineers; the Institution of Lighting Engineers; The Institution of Marine Engineers; The Institute of Materials; The Institute of Measurement and Control; The Institution of Mechanical Engineers; The Institution of Mining and Metallurgy; The Royal Institution of Naval Architects; The British Institution of Non-Destructive Testing; The Institution of Nuclear Engineers; Institute of Physics Plumbing; The Institute of Quality Assurance; The Institution of Road Transport Engineers; The Institution of Structural Engineers; The Chartered Institute of Water and Environmental Management; The Institution of Water Officers; The Welding Institute.

INSTITUTE OF MEASUREMENT AND CONTROL

87 Gower Street, London WC1E 6AF Tel: 020 7387 4949 Fax: 020 7388 8431
e-mail: records@instmc.org.uk Website: www.instmc.org.uk

CORPORATE MEMBERS:
Honorary Fellow (HonFInstMC): Election is at the discretion of the Council.
Fellow (FInstMC): Must be at least 33, have been Members for at least 3 yrs and have had at least 8 yrs' professional experience, involving superior responsibility for at least 5 yrs.
Member (MInstMC): Must be at least 25 and have been awarded a degree accredited by the Engineering Council; *or* passed The Engineering Council's Exams *;or* equivalent qualifications in science or mathematics. They must also have had at least 4 yrs' FT experience practising measurement and control technology, and a min of 2 yrs' professional training approved by the Council. There is a route for candidates who do not satisfy the academic requirements.

NON-CORPORATE MEMBERS:
Companion: Must be 33 and have acquired national distinction in an executive capacity in the field of measurement and control.
Graduate: Must have obtained the educational qualifications required for Membership.
Licentiate: Must be 23 and have obtained an BTEC or SCOTVEC Higher National Award or equiv. They must have had 5 yrs' relevant experience.
Associate: Must be 21 and have obtained an appropriate qualification such as BTEC or SCOTVEC National Certificate.
Student: Must be at least 16 and no more than 28, and be engaged on a recognised course of study complying with the educational requirements for the class of Graduate, Licentiate or Associate.
Affiliate: Open to anyone interested.
Companion Companies: Organisations with interests in measurement and control.

THE INSTITUTION OF BRITISH ENGINEERS

Clifford Hill Court, Clifford Chambers, Stratford upon Avon, Warwickshire CV37 8AA Tel: 01789 298739 Fax: 01789 294442 e-mail: info@britishengineers.com Website: www.britishengineers.com

MEMBERSHIP:
Vice President: Vice Presidents are normally the chair of the Institution's Active Regional Branch in a particular area/country. These VP's form the IBE International Council.
Fellow (FIBE): Sales and marketing directors of engineering companies and directors in other disciplines are awarded this grade.
Member (MIBE): Sales and marketing managers of engineering companies and managers in other disciplines are awarded this grade.
Associate Member (AMIBE): Persons below the level of manager who are employed in engineering companies are awarded this grade.
Graduate Member (GradIBE): For persons studying for a career in engineering or desirous of entering the engineering profession, but do not have the necessary experience and understanding of engineering to qualify for Associate Membership. Graduate Members will be currently undertaking a level of study or training that is equivalent or similar to NVQ Level 2 or above. On achieving the necessary level of experience and understanding they would normally be required to seek upgrading to AMIBE.
Qualified Sales Engineer (SEng): Persons in FT employment in engineering companies at any level who have the technical qualifications and experience necessary are awarded the designatory letter SEng. The minimum requirements are: (i) a minimum academic standard in engineering eg BTech, HND, HNC or equivalent; (ii) at least 5 yrs' FT training including 2 yrs' practical training; and (iii) proven performance over at least 5 yrs in selling, sales management or marketing within the industry.

Bi-Lingual Engineer (BLEng): The Institution has introduced its BLEng qualification because the Engineering Industries are chronically short of Engineers with foreign language capabilities. BLEng is for persons who can satisfy all the requirements for Associate Membership of the IBE and who are fluent both orally and in writing, with a high technical bias, in at least 2 modern languages, one of which must be English. The designatory letters BLEng precede the membership designatory letters: ie BLEng, AMIBE.

Diploma in Business Engineering: The DBE is a new qualification at bachelor degree level for engineers who are involved in the senior management of engineering companies. It assumes that engineering training to HND, HNC or CGLI Full Technological Certificate or equivalent has been achieved and focuses on the elements of Strategy, Planning, Finance, Marketing and Human Resources that are essential to the ongoing growth and profitability of an engineering enterprise. The designatory letters DBE precede the membership designatory letters: ie DBE, FIBE.

Cetificate of Competence in Engineering Practice: The Institution has introduced its GradIBE qualification to encourage young engineers and will be granted to Graduate Members who attain a qualification at, or equivalent to, NVQ Level 2 standard.

THE INSTITUTION OF INCORPORATED ENGINEERS

Savoy Hill House, Savoy Hill, London WC2R 0BS Tel: 020 7836 3357 Fax: 020 7497 9006
e-mail: info@iie.org.uk Website: www.iie.org.uk
Incorporated Engineers form the mainstream of professional engineering practitioners and act as exponents of today's technology. They provide leadership and control in a managerial role, combined with a practical approach and a detailed understanding of particular technologies.

CORPORATE MEMBERSHIP:

Fellow (FIIE); Member (MIIE): Candidates must satisfy the technical education requirements governing Graduateship (see below) and have suitable industrial training and experience. They meet the criteria for registration with the Engineering Council in the professional engineering section as Incorporated Engineers (IEng).

NON-CORPORATE MEMBERSHIP:

Associate (Associate IIE): Associates of the Institution benefit from the full range of member support available to all members. They are committed to developing their careers in association with IIE, or are working towards achievement of other classes of membership.

Graduate (Graduate IIE): A number of HNCs, HNDs and degrees have been accredited by the Institution; contact the IIE for up-to-date details.

Associate Member (AMIIE); Associate Technician (Associate Technician IIE): Contact the IIE for up-to-date details of qualifications. Associate Members meet the criteria for registration with The Engineering Council as Engineering Technicians (EngTech).

Student (Student IIE): Student members must show that they are following regular courses of further education, as approved by the Council, and that they intend to satisfy the requirements of admission to Graduateship or Associate Membership.

INSTITUTION OF INCORPORATED EXECUTIVE ENGINEERS

Wix Hill House, West Horsley, Surrey KT24 6DZ Tel: 01483 222383 Fax: 01483 211109
e-mail: exec@iiexe.demon.co.uk

MEMBERSHIP:

Member (MIIExE): Applicants must be at least 23 and have engineering education and training which will qualify them for registration by the Engineering Council as Incorporated Engineers. Their employment must entail a high degree of personal responsibility for the technical details of engineering installation work, or the maintenance of engineering plant and equipment, or the technical work associated with planning, design, sales or services, or a high degree of managerial and executive responsibility for technical work in a branch of engineering. (Head Office will be pleased to give guidance.)

Associate Member (AMIIExE): Candidates must be: Engineers who satisfy the Membership Committee: (a) that they are at least 21, and (b) that they have had engineering training of an adequate character and standard; (c) that they possess an engineering educational qualification which will qualify them for registration by the Engineering Council; (d) that the duties of their present business or employment include either:(i) responsibility for the planning and layout of work associated with the installation of engineering services equipment and apparatus and/or control of operative labour employed on the site or sites, the requisitioning of materials and plant applicable thereto, or (ii) responsibility for the general maintenance of engineering plant and equipment, and/or for the control of operative labour, or (iii) responsibility for the inspection or sale of important engineering apparatus, equipment or service, or for technical work, or (iv) responsibility for work of a technical character within a branch of engineering and/or the control of operative labour.

Associate: Account is taken of the level of executive or supervisory responsibility exercised by the applicant in his employment. He/she must be over 30 and desire to use the Institution's educational or social facilities.

Student: The Institution welcomes any candidate who satisfies the Membership Committee that they are following a recognised course of study leading to a technical qualification acceptable to the Membership Committee, and that they are aged 17 to 25.

EXAMINATION:
An exam scheme leading to the award of the Diploma in Engineering Management, following attendance at courses of study, is administered by the Institution. The course is also available by distance learning.

THE SOCIETY OF ENGINEERS (INCORPORATED)
Guinea Wiggs, Nayland, Colchester, Essex CO6 4NF Tel: 01206 263332 Fax: 01206 262624

MEMBERSHIP:
Hon Fellows (Hon FSE): Persons of distinguished position or scientific attainment nominated and elected by the Council.

Fellow (FSE): The highest grade of membership requiring major responsibilities for at least 7 yrs in design, research and management in engineering.

Members (MSE): Must have satisfied all 3 parts of the Society's Graduateship Exams, or the recognised equivalents and have at least 3 yrs in a position of professional responsibility. Corporate Members are recognised by the Society of Professional Engineers as satisfying the requirements for entry to their Register of professional engineers, which entitles applicants to use the designation Professional Engineer (PEng), or (PEng)(UK) for engineers working overseas.

Associate Member (AMSE): Must have passed the Society's Part I and Part II exam or other approved exams and have had at least 5 yrs' experience of engineering, of which 2 yrs should be practical or site experience. (This is a non-corporate grade.)

Engineering Associate (ASE): Must have passed the Society's Part I exams and have at least 5 yrs' experience of engineering, of which 2 yrs should be practical or site experience. (This is a non-corporate grade.)

Associates: Persons qualified in some other science, art or profession allied to engineering and therefore not qualified for any other class of membership of the Society, but whose association with the Society is considered conducive to the general advancement of special techniques or engineering knowledge.

Students (StudSE): Must have a good general education and be studying for the profession.

EXAMINATIONS FOR MEMBERSHIP:
The exams, which are of degree standard, are held under several separate headings for Civil, Electrical, Mechanical, Power and Machines, Telecommunications and Electronics, Works and Chemical Engineers, are arranged in 3 stages, Part I General Engineering, Part II Design and Part III Management.

Exemption is granted to holders of the following British qualifications, as well as many overseas qualifications:

All parts: Corporate Members by exam of Royal Aeronautical Society; Chartered Institution of Building Services; Institution of Chemical Engineers; Institution of Civil Engineers; Institution of Electrical Engineers; Institution of Electronic and Radio Engineers; Institution of Gas Engineers; Institution of Marine Engineers; Institute of Measurement Control; Institution of Mechanical Engineers; Institution of Mining Engineers; Institution of Mining and Metallurgy; Institution of Production Engineers; Institution of Structural Engineers; The Society of Professional Engineers Ltd; and Welding Institute.

Part III: A Diploma in Management awarded after 1 yr FT or 2 yrs PT at a UK college.

Parts III & I: A degree in engineering awarded within the UK, including CNAA degrees; the Diploma of Geometra.

Parts II & I: Relevant HND and HNC, with endorsement, obtained prior to 1968.

Part I: HND and HNC; C&G Overseas HC; C&G Full Technological Certificate in technical subject plus O level English; or C&G Licentiateship; CEI or Engineering Council Parts I and II; Engineering Degree at Overseas University; the Diploma of Geometra or Perito (Italy).

WOMEN'S ENGINEERING SOCIETY

2 Queen Anne's Gate Buildings, Dartmouth Street, London SW1H 9BP Tel: 020 7233 1974 Fax: 020 7233 1973 e-mail: info@wes.org.uk Website: www.wes.org.uk

MEMBERSHIP:

Honorary Membership (HonMWES): Open to men or women distinguished in science or engineering or whom the Society wishes to honour for services rendered to the Society or to causes in which it is interested.

Membership (MWES): Open to women over 25 who have received recognised education and training in the theory and practice of engineering or related sciences and are occupying or have occupied in a professional or administrative capacity positions of responsibility associated with engineering. In cases of exceptional responsibility the education and training requirements may be waived.

Associate Membership (AMWES): Open to women with qualifications similar to those for membership but the required standard of responsibility and seniority is not so high.

Student Membership: Open to women who are engaged upon work of an engineering or scientific character and/or are undergoing a course of education or training with a view to qualifying for election to the class of Associate Members.

Junior Membership: Open to women aged between 16 and 19 who are undergoing FT education with the intention of entering a course of training in engineering or science.

Associateship: Open to men or women aged at least 24 who are of good education and who, by their connection with engineering, the sciences, arts or otherwise, will by their association with the Society assist in the general advancement of its work and its aims and objects.

Group Member: The Council may elect to this class universities, polytechnics, technical colleges and other such organisations where women are under training to become engineers.

Company Member: The Council may elect to this class companies, corporations and other organisations which employ engineers and are interested in supporting the aims of the Women's Engineering Society.

University Qualifications

The following universities offer qualifications in General Engineering and related subjects. Full details may be found in Part 4, under the entry for the appropriate university.

FIRST DEGREES AWARDED BY UNIVERSITIES

Aberdeen; Birmingham; Blackburn; Bradford; Brighton; Bristol; Brunel; Cambridge; Coventry; East London; Edinburgh; Exeter; Glasgow Caledonian; Greenwich; Heriot-Watt; Hertfordshire; Hertfordshire (West Herts College); Huddersfield; Hull; Lancaster; Leeds; Leicester; Lincolnshire; Liverpool; Liverpool John Moores; London (Queen Mary & Westfield College (incorporating St Bartholomew's and the Royal London School of Medicine & Dentistry)); London (University College (UCL)); Loughborough; Manchester; Manchester Metropolitan.; Napier; Northampton; Northumbria; Nottingham; Nottingham Trent; Nottingham Trent (Southampton Institute); Oxford; Oxford Brookes; Plymouth; Portsmouth; Reading; Salford; Sheffield Hallam; South Bank; Southampton; Staffordshire; Strathclyde; Sunderland; Surrey; Sussex; Teesside; Ulster; UMIST; Wales (Cardiff University); Wales (University of Wales College, Newport); Wales (University of Wales, Swansea); Warwick; Wolverhampton

HIGHER DEGREES AWARDED BY UNIVERSITIES

Aberdeen; Anglia; Bath; Birmingham; Brighton; Bristol; Cambridge; Coventry; Cranfield; Dundee; Durham; East London; Exeter; Glasgow; Glasgow Caledonian; Greenwich; Heriot-Watt; Hertfordshire; Huddersfield; Hull; Leeds; Leicester; Liverpool John Moores; London (Imperial College of Science, Technology & Medicine); Loughborough; Manchester; Newcastle;

Northumbria; OU (NESCOT); Plymouth; Sheffield Hallam; South Bank; Southampton; Strathclyde; Sunderland; Ulster; UMIST; Wales (Cardiff University); Warwick

DIPLOMAS AWARDED BY UNIVERSITIES
Abertay, Dundee; Blackburn; Bradford (Bradford & Ilkley Community College); Bristol; De Montfort, Leicester; Kingston; Manchester (Warrington Collegiate Institute, Faculty of H.E,); Napier; Northampton; OU (NESCOT); Plymouth; Salford (The Oldham College); Strathclyde; Teesside

CERTIFICATES AWARDED BY UNIVERSITIES
Anglia (City College, Norwich); Brighton; Cambridge; Exeter; Leeds; Manchester (Warrington Collegiate Institute, Faculty of H.E,); Napier; Newcastle; Wales (University of Wales College, Newport)

National Certificates and Diplomas
BTEC National Certificates/Diplomas: Engineering
BTEC Higher National Certificates/Diplomas: Computer Aided Engineering; Engineering; Engineering and Business Studies
Scotland
SQA HNC: Computer-Aided Engineering (Manufacture); Computer Controlled Engineering; Computer Installation Support Engineering; Engineering; Engineering Multiskilling; Engineering Practice; Integrated Engineering; Mechanical & Computer-Aided Engineering; Multidisciplinary Engineering.
SQA HND: Computer-Aided Engineering (Manufacture with Management Studies); Engineering; Facilities Engineering; Integrated Engineering; Integrated Engineering & Manufacture; Mechanical & Computer-Aided Engineering; Multidisciplinary Engineering.

SVQs
Level 1: Engineering Finishing; Engineering Maintenance
Level 2: Engineering Finishing; Engineering Foundation; Engineering Installation and Commissioning; Engineering Maintenance
Level 3: Engineering Finishing; Engineering Installation and Commissioning; Engineering Maintenance; Engineering Technical Services.

GNVQs
3731 Engineering

City & Guilds
2010 Basic Engineering Competencies; 2140 Engineering Systems Maintenance Competencies; 2200 Engineering Craft Supplementary Studies; 2301 Computer-aided Engineering Competencies; 2920 Engineering Master Certificate; 6053 General Operative Skills – Basic Engineering

Other Vocational Awarding Bodies
ABC: Engineering Studies

Useful Addresses
Occupational Standards Council for Engineering, Broadway House, Tothill Street, London SW1H 9NQ Tel: 020 7233 0935 Fax: 020 7233 0940
Engineering Services Training Trust Ltd, Gear House, Saltmeadows Road, Gateshead, NE8 3AH Tel: 0191 490 1155 Fax: 0191 477 5737
Engineering Training Authority, Vector House, 41 Clarendon Road, Watford WD1 1HS Tel: 01923 238441 Fax: 01923 256086
Engineering Training Council (Northern Ireland), INTERPOINT, 20-24 York Street, Belfast BT15 1AQ Tel: 01232 329878 Fax: 01232 310301

MARINE ENGINEERING

Membership of Professional Institutions and Associations

THE INSTITUTE OF MARINE ENGINEERS

80 Coleman Street, London EC2R 5BJ Tel: 020 7382 2600 Fax: 020 7382 2670
e-mail: mem@imare.org.uk Website: www.imare.org.uk

MEMBERSHIP:

Honorary Fellows (HonFIMarE): Persons of distinguished scientific attainment, or of distinction in Engineering, or of eminence, who have given distinguished service to the Institute.

CORPORATE MEMBERSHIP:

Fellows (FIMarE): Persons who are at least 30 and either: (a) have academic qualifications not lower than the standard accepted by the Institute for accreditation with the Engineering Council for inclusion in the Chartered Engineers' section of the Register; and (b) have a minimum of 2 yrs' training of a nature approved by the Institute or a longer period of experience in lieu of training; and (c) have held for not less than 5 yrs a superior position of professional responsibility in maritime engineering disciplines including marine engineering, naval architecture, offshore/subsea engineering and structural/civil/mechanical/electrical engineering with marine applications.

Members (MIMarE): Persons who are at least 25 and: (a) have academic qualifications not lower than the standard accepted by the Institute for accreditation with the Engineering Council for inclusion in the Chartered Engineers' section of the Register; and (b) have a minimum of 2 yrs' training of a nature approved by the Institute or a longer period of experience in lieu of training; and (c) have not less than 2 yrs' professional experience in maritime engineering disciplines.

NON-CORPORATE MEMBERSHIP:

Associate Members: Persons who are at least 23 and: (a) have academic qualifications not lower than the standard accepted by the Institute for accreditation with the Engineering Council for inclusion in the Incorporated Engineer section of the Register; and (b) have a minimum of 2 yrs' training of a nature approved by the Institute or a longer period of experience in lieu of training; and (c) have not less than 2 yrs' professional experience in maritime engineering disciplines including marine engineering, naval architecture, offshore/subsea engineering and structural/civil/mechanical/electrical engineering with marine applications. Under certain circumstances Associate Members who do not possess the required academic qualification may be elected to Corporate Membership. Such members will not however, be able to register as Chartered Engineers.

Companions: Persons who are at least 30 yrs of age and have attained a standard of education, training, qualification and experience which, although not in the engineering profession, is at least equivalent to that necessary for election to the category of Member. They should also have held a responsible position for at least 2 yrs and have an aggregate of further education, training and responsible experience of not less than 7 yrs.

Graduate Members: Persons who are at least 21 and have academic qualifications not lower than the standard accepted by the Institute for accreditation with the Engineering Council for inclusion in the Chartered Engineers' section of the Register at Stage I and be involved in training of a nature approved by the Institute.

Associates: Persons who are in a position to further the objects and purposes of the Institute, be at least 21 and: (a) have academic qualifications not lower than the standard accepted by the Institute for accreditation with the Engineering Council for inclusion in the Engineering Technician section of the register; and (b) have a minimum of 2 yrs' training of a nature approved by the Institute or a longer period of experience in lieu of training; and (c) have not less than 1 yr's experience in maritime engineering disciplines including naval architecture, offshore/subsea engineering and structural/civil/mechanical/electrical engineering with marine applications.

Consociates: Candidates for election to the class of Consociates shall be persons including students, who, in the opinion of the Institute are likely to have a sufficient interest in, or may contribute to, the activities of the Institute.

Note: That as maritime engineering is multidisciplinary, the Institute accepts individuals with relevant qualifications other than in Marine Engineering, eg Naval Architecture, Offshore/Subsea Engineering, Structural/Civil/Mechanical/Electrical Engineering with Marine applications.

University Qualifications

The following universities offer qualifications in Marine Engineering and related subjects. Full details may be found in Part 4, under the entry for the appropriate university.

FIRST DEGREES AWARDED BY UNIVERSITIES
Aberdeen; Heriot-Watt; Liverpool; Liverpool John Moores; London (University College (UCL)); Newcastle; Nottingham Trent (Southampton Institute); Plymouth; Robert Gordon; Southampton; Strathclyde

HIGHER DEGREES AWARDED BY UNIVERSITIES
Aberdeen; Cranfield; Heriot-Watt; Liverpool; London (University College (UCL)); Newcastle; Nottingham Trent (Southampton Institute); Plymouth; Portsmouth; Southampton; Stirling; Strathclyde

DIPLOMAS AWARDED BY UNIVERSITIES
Aberdeen; Glamorgan; Hull; Liverpool; London (University College (UCL)); Nottingham Trent (Southampton Institute); Plymouth; Stirling; Strathclyde

CERTIFICATES AWARDED BY UNIVERSITIES
Newcastle

POSTGRADUATE DIPLOMAS AWARDED BY UNIVERSITIES
Heriot-Watt

National Certificates and Diplomas

Scotland
SQA HNC: Engineering (Shipbuilding); Marine Engineering
SQA HND: Engineering (Marine); Maritime Studies

NVQs

Level 2: Boat Building; Boat Outfitting; Boat Repairing; Fishing Vessel Engineering
Level 3: Boat Building & Maintenance; Fishing Vessel Engineering
Level 4: fishing Vessel Engineering

SVQs

Level 2: Boat Building; Boat Outfitting; Boat Repair; Fishing Vessel Engineering; Fishing Vessel Operations.
Level 3: Fishing Vessel Engineering; Fishing Vessel Operations: Inshore Area or Unlimited Area.
Level 4: Fishing Vessel Engineering; Fishing Vessel Operations: Limited Area or Unlimited Area.

Other Examinations

(See Navigation and Seamanship)

Useful Addresses

Engineering and Marine Training Authority, Vector House, 41 Clarendon Road, Watford WD1 1HS Tel: 01923 238441 Fax: 01923 256086

MECHANICAL ENGINEERING

Membership of Professional Institutions and Associations

THE INSTITUTION OF MECHANICAL ENGINEERS
1 Birdcage Walk, Westminster, London SW1H 9JJ Tel: 020 7222 7899 Fax: 020 7222 4557

MEMBERSHIP:

Honorary Fellows (HonFIMechE): Persons of distinguished scientific attainment, or of distinction in Engineering, or of eminence who have given distinguished service to the Institution.

Fellows (FIMechE): Established mechanical engineers who, in addition to meeting the requirements for Member hold posts of greater responsibility. Fellows are entitled to register as Chartered Engineers.

Members (MIMechE): Established mechanical engineers who, in addition to the requirements for Associate Member have completed a period of responsible professional practice. Members are entitled to register as Chartered Engineers.

Associate Members (AMIMechE): Persons who have satisfied the practical and professional training requirements, and meet the academic requirements either partially or in full (min honours degree or equiv).

Graduates: Usually persons with a mechanical engineering or other acceptable degree.

Students: Persons following an appropriate engineering course at degree level or a pre-academic yr of practical training. In addition, there are 2 classes for persons who do not aspire to full qualification as Chartered Engineers:

Associates: Persons engaged or interested in mechanical engineering.

Companions: Persons occupying distinguished positions in a related profession or who have rendered important services to mechanical engineering. The academic standard for Membership is an accredited degree in Mechanical, Electro-Mechanical, Manufacturing Systems or similar engineering fields. A list of accredited courses is available on enquiry from the Bury St Edmunds Office of the Institution (Karen Borley, Northgate Avenue, Bury St Edmunds, Suffolk IP32 6BN Tel 01284 763277 Fax 01284 704006)

University Qualifications

The following universities offer qualifications in Mechanical Engineering and related subjects. Full details may be found in Part 4, under the entry for the appropriate university.

FIRST DEGREES AWARDED BY UNIVERSITIES
Aberdeen; Abertay, Dundee; Aston; Belfast; Birmingham; Bradford; Brighton; Bristol; Brunel; Bucks. Coll.; Central England; Central Lancashire; City; Coventry; Cranfield; De Montfort, Leicester; Derby; Dundee; Edinburgh; Exeter; Glamorgan; Glasgow; Glasgow Caledonian; Greenwich; Heriot-Watt; Hertfordshire; Huddersfield; Hull; Kingston; Lancaster; Lancaster (Blackpool and The Fylde College); Leeds; Leicester; Lincolnshire; Lincolnshire (Hull College); Liverpool; Liverpool John Moores; London (Imperial College of Science, Technology & Medicine); London (King's College London); London (Queen Mary & Westfield College (incorporating St Bartholomew's and the Royal London School of Medicine & Dentistry)); London (University College (UCL)); Loughborough; Manchester; Manchester Metropolitan.; Middlesex; Napier; Newcastle; Northumbria; Nottingham; Nottingham Trent; Nottingham Trent (Southampton Institute); Oxford; Oxford Brookes; Paisley; Plymouth; Portsmouth; Reading; Robert Gordon; Salford; Sheffield; Sheffield Hallam; South Bank; Southampton; Staffordshire; Strathclyde; Sunderland; Surrey; Sussex; Teesside; Ulster; UMIST; Wales (Cardiff University); Wales (University of Wales College, Newport); Wales (University of Wales, Swansea); Warwick; Wolverhampton

HIGHER DEGREES AWARDED BY UNIVERSITIES
Aberdeen; Abertay, Dundee; Aston; Bath; Belfast; Birmingham; Brighton; Bristol; Brunel; Central England; City; Cranfield; De Montfort, Leicester; Durham; Exeter; Glamorgan; Glasgow; Greenwich; Heriot-Watt; Huddersfield; Hull; Kingston; Lancaster; Leeds; Leicester; Liverpool; Liverpool John Moores; London (Imperial College of Science, Technology & Medicine); London

(King's College London); London (Queen Mary & Westfield College (incorporating St Bartholomew's and the Royal London School of Medicine & Dentistry)); London (University College (UCL)); Loughborough; Manchester; Napier; Newcastle; Plymouth; Sheffield Hallam; South Bank; Staffordshire; UMIST; Wales (University of Wales College, Newport); Wales (University of Wales, Swansea); Warwick

DIPLOMAS AWARDED BY UNIVERSITIES
Barnsley; Bournemouth; Brighton; Central England; Central Lancashire; Coventry; Glamorgan; Glasgow; Greenwich; Huddersfield; Lancaster; London (University College (UCL)); Manchester; Manchester (Warrington Collegiate Institute, Faculty of H.E,); Napier; Northumbria; Paisley; Portsmouth; Teesside; Wales (North East Wales Institute); Wales (Swansea Institute of Higher Education); Wales (University of Wales Institute, Cardiff); Wolverhampton

CERTIFICATES AWARDED BY UNIVERSITIES
Anglia (City College, Norwich); Bournemouth; Bradford (Bradford & Ilkley Community College); Central England; Lincolnshire; Lincolnshire (Hull College); Napier; Northampton; Paisley; Wales (University of Wales College, Newport); Wales (University of Wales Institute, Cardiff)

OTHER COURSES AWARDED BY UNIVERSITIES
Huddersfield

PRE-DEGREE AWARDED BY UNIVERSITIES
Kingston

National Certificates and Diplomas
BTEC National Certificates/Diplomas: Engineering (Mechanical/Manufacture)
BTEC Higher National Certificates/Diplomas: Engineering (Mechanical Engineering); Engineering (Mechanical/Manufacture); Engineering (Mechatronics)
Scotland
SQA HND: Mechanical Engineering; Mechanical & Computer Aided Engineering; Petroleum and Mechanical Engineering; Mechatronics
SQA HNC: Mechanical Engineering; Mechanical and Production Engineering; Mechanical & Computer Aided Engineering; Mechatronics

SVQs
Level 1: Engineering Assembly; Engineering Machining
Level 2: Engineering Assembly; Engineering Construction: Lifting & Positioning Capital Plant & Steel Structures; Engineering Machining; Machining & Assembly Operations.
Level 3: Engineering Assembly; Engineering Construction (Design); Engineering Construction: Erecting Capital Plant Steel Structures; Fabricating Steel Structures; Engineering Construction: Installing Mechanical Plant; Engineering Construction: Installing Pipework Systems; Engineering Construction: Maintaining Mechanical Systems of Plant & Equipment;

City & Guilds
2550 Mechanical Engineering Technicians; 2050 Mechanical Engineering and Mechanical Engineering Maintenance Craft Studies

MINING ENGINEERING
Membership of Professional Institutions and Associations
INSTITUTE OF EXPLOSIVES ENGINEERS
Centenary Business Centre, Hammond Close, Attleborough Fields, Nuneaton, Warwickshire CV11 6RY Tel: 024 7635 0846 Fax: 024 7635 0831 e-mail: info@iexpe.org Website: www.iexpe.org

CORPORATE AND NON-CORPORATE MEMBERS:

Fellows (FIExpE): Members of the Institute who are over 35 yrs of age, and have had at least 15 yrs' experience in pursuits connected with explosives engineering, and are, to the satisfaction of Council, either: (1) recognised by others, in their own specialist field, as a leading authority by having planned, negotiated, organised and supervised work of a sufficiently complex nature and responsibility; or (2) recognised by scientific and academic bodies as a research leader or technical innovator in their chosen field; or (3) a regular, authoritative contributor to scientific or technical papers on explosives-related sciences, engineering or related topics; or (4) known to have contributed greatly to the improvement in safety practices and standards within the explosives industry.

Honorary Fellows (HonFIExpE): The status of Honorary Fellow may be accorded to someone who is, to the satisfaction of Council, worthy. Honorary Fellows shall be either distinguished persons, who from their position have been or are enabled to render assistance to the Institute, or persons eminent for science and experience in pursuits connected with explosives engineering, whether or not currently engaged in the practice of that profession.

Members (MIExpE): The status of Member of the Institute of Explosives Engineers shall be accorded by the Council to candidates not less than 23 yrs old who shall have: (a) passed or been exempted from the appropriate examinations stipulated by the Council; and (b) either (i) been trained and become qualified for, and shall have held for at least three yrs, a responsible post engaged in explosives engineering or equivalent technical explosives management duties; or (ii) been trained and become qualified as Ammunition Technical Officers or Ammunition Technicians Class I in the Army, or their equivalents in the British or appropriate foreign armed services; and (c) been approved for admission by an Individual Membership Committee comprising 3 members of Council none of whom shall be elected representatives of Company Members; or (d) exceptionally, applicants who do not hold adequate academic and/or professional qualifications which would permit exemption from the Institute examinations, and who are applying for membership without examination, shall be required to demonstrate their competence by submitting a thesis of 5000 words in length on a topic related to explosives technology. This thesis may be supported by appropriate diagrams, graphs and photographs. The candidate shall be interviewed by an examining board appointed for the purpose and this board shall ascertain whether the applicant has knowledge adequate to have completed the thesis by his own original work and shall report its findings to the Membership Committee.

Associates (AIExpE): The status of Associate of the Institute of Explosives Engineers shall be granted by the Council to candidates not less than 23 yrs old who shall have: (a) either (i) been trained and become qualified to hold a responsible post as a skilled operative in such pursuits as explosives development, manufacture or use; or (ii) been trained and become qualified as a serviceman or related civilian whose duties involve the handling and use of military explosives and associated munitions, but whose expertise does not equate to the standards laid down in paragraph 11(b); or (b) reached a responsible position and gained adequate experience, but who have not yet sat or been exempted from the examinations for full membership status; and (c) attended for interview by members of Council, if so required.

Student: The status of Student shall be granted by the Council to candidates of at least 18 yrs of age who are either following a course of study or otherwise learning a trade which requires knowledge of the science and/or practice of explosives technology. Students are not entitled to use any designatory letters after their name.

Company Membership: The status of Company Member may be accorded to any company, firm, or sole trader engaged in the development and/or manufacture of explosives or associated munitions or in the use of explosives in mining, tunnelling, quarrying, demolition, excavation, underwater or offshore work, or other appropriate commercial or government enterprise, as approved by Council. Admission to Company Membership shall be granted provided that suitable applicants are proposed by one Company Member or Council Member, and seconded by another Company Member or Council Member, and approved by the Council. These provisions of Company Membership shall apply to British and appropriate foreign enterprises.

Company Affiliate: Any company, firm or sole trader shall be admissible as a Company Affiliate provided that the applicant satisfies Council that it has an appropriate interest in explosives technology.

THE INSTITUTE OF QUARRYING

7 Regent Street, Nottingham, Nottinghamshire NG1 5BS Tel: 0115 9411315 Fax: 0115 9484035
e-mail: iq@qmj.co.uk Website: www.inst-of-quarrying.org/iq/

CORPORATE MEMBERSHIP:

Fellow (FIQ): Must: (a) be employed in the industry; and (b) be at least 33 yrs of age; and (c) have met the Membership requirements (see below); and (d) have had at least 7 yrs' experience in the industry, including 4 yrs in a position of senior managerial charge.

Member (MIQ): Must: (a) be employed in the industry; and (b) be at least 23 yrs of age; and (c) have passed the Professional Examination of the Institute or possess an exempting qualification; and (d) have completed a period of training and experience in the industry, of which not less than 3 yrs was in a position of responsible charge.

NON-CORPORATE MEMBERSHIP:

Associate: Must: (a) have reached the age of 21, passed the Professional Examination of the Institute; *or* (b) have reached the age of 21, have obtained an approved technical or administrative qualification and have at least 1 yr of experience in the industry; *or* (c) have reached the age of 21 and have completed 3 yrs' experience in the industry.

Note: Mature candidates' rights are available to Associates over the age of 38 yrs who have 10 yrs' experience in the industry, including 5 yrs in a position of managerial charge. The applicant can qualify for the corporate grades of Fellow or Member through the preparation of a thesis or by passing the Quarrying Operations and Safety and Legislation papers of the Institute's Professional Examination.

Student: Must: (a) be at least 16 yrs of age and normally not more than 21 (unless extended at the discretion of the Council); and (b) be engaged in a FT course of study or training relating to the industry.

EXAMINATIONS: The **Professional Exam** is at HNC level. Qualifications in Quarrying at HNC level or above give complete exemption. Qualifications in Engineering at HNC level or above give partial exemption. An Assisted Private Study Scheme for the **Professional Exam** is available at Doncaster College. Special exemptions may be granted to 'mature students' who are over 38 with 10 yrs in the industry.

THE INSTITUTION OF MINING AND METALLURGY

Danum House, South Parade, Doncaster DN1 2DY Tel: 01302 320486 Fax: 01302 380900
e-mail: hq@imm.org.uk Website: www.imm.org.uk

MEMBERSHIP:

Honorary Fellows (HonFIMM): Are elected by the Institution's Council from amongst existing Fellows in recognition of their distinguished attainments and contribution to the advancement of the minerals industry and associated branches of technology.

Companions: Are persons who are not eligible for corporate membership and are elected by the Institution's Council in recognition of their distinguished achievements in, or contribution to, the international minerals industry. They must be at least 30 at the time of their election and must be able to satisfy the Council as to their fitness and propriety for this class of membership.

Fellows (FIMM): Must be at least 30 and have been a Member, or have satisfied the conditions for admission as a Member. They should have had at least 5 yrs' experience in responsible charge of important operations, or as a consultant or holder of an important academic or research post in relevant subjects.

Members (MIMM): Must be at least 25 and, having satisfied the appropriate academic requirements, should also have had at least 2 yrs of practical training followed by a min 2 yrs of responsible work in the minerals industry.

Associate Members (AMIMM): Must be at least 23 and, having satisfied the appropriate academic requirements, should have at least 2 yrs of approved training and be in a position of responsibility at the time of their application.

Technician Members: Must be not less than 21 and, lacking the academic standard for corporate or associate membership, should nevertheless have passed such examinations as the Institution's Council may prescribe from time to time. They must also have undergone such appropriate training and obtained such professional experience, again, as the Council may prescribe.

Affiliates: Must be not less than 24 and, lacking academic qualifications for the previously mentioned classes of membership, must be engaged professionally in the minerals industry.
Graduates: Must be not less than 20 and have satisfied the exam requirements of the Council and be engaged in professional training or work in the minerals industry.
Students: Must be not less than 18 and being educated or trained for the profession of environmental engineering, mining, metallurgy, mineral technology, geology, geotechnical engineering, or petroleum engineering.

University Qualifications

The following universities offer qualifications in Mining Engineering and related subjects. Full details may be found in Part 4, under the entry for the appropriate university.

FIRST DEGREES AWARDED BY UNIVERSITIES
Birmingham; Exeter; Leeds; London (Imperial College of Science, Technology & Medicine); London (University College (UCL)); Nottingham; Oxford Brookes

HIGHER DEGREES AWARDED BY UNIVERSITIES
Dundee; Exeter; Leeds; Leicester

DIPLOMAS AWARDED BY UNIVERSITIES
Exeter; Glamorgan; Leeds; Leicester

National Certificates and Diplomas

BTEC National Certificates/Diplomas: Mining Engineering; Mining Engineering (Coal Preparation); Mining Engineering (Mining and Electrical); Mining Engineering (Mining and Mechanical)
BTEC Higher National Certificates/Diplomas: Mining Engineering; Mining Engineering (Coal Preparation); Mining Engineering (Mining and Electrical); Mining Engineering (Mining and Mechanical)

NVQs

Level 1: Land Drilling; Mobile Plant Operations (Extractive Industries)
Level 2: Land Drilling; Mobile Plant Operations (Extractive Industries); Drilling Operations (Extractive Industries)
Level 3: Shotfiring Operations (Extractive Industries – Quarries)

SVQs

Level 1: Offshore Drilling Operations; Drilling
Level 2: Land Drilling; Offshore Drilling Operations.
Level 3: Offshore Drilling Operations.

Useful Addresses

EPIC, 36-38 London Road, St Albans AL1 1NG Tel: 01727 869008 Fax: 01727 843318

NUCLEAR ENGINEERING

Membership of Professional Institutions and Associations

THE INSTITUTION OF NUCLEAR ENGINEERS
(A Nominated Body of the Engineering Council.)
Allan House, 1 Penerley Road, London SE6 2LQ Tel: 020 8698 1500 Fax: 020 8695 6409 e-mail: inuce@lineone.net Website: www.meek.clara.net/inuce

CORPORATE MEMBERSHIP:

Fellows: Must be nuclear engineers or scientists who satisfy the requirements for Member and who have established a superior professional reputation by holding, normally for at least 5 yrs, an important position of responsibility in the nuclear field. They will normally be over 35. The usual route to Fellowship is by transfer from the class of Member.

Members: Must be engineers and scientists who hold an approved degree or have passed the Engineering Council Exam Parts I and II or have equivalent qualifications; they must have undergone structured training or experience in lieu, have had practical experience over a period amounting to at least 3 yrs, have attained a position of professional responsibility in the nuclear field and be at least 25. Applicants accepted for corporate membership will normally be eligible for registration with the Board for Engineers' Registration as Chartered Engineers.

NON-CORPORATE MEMBERSHIP:

Graduate Member: Candidates should normally be at least 21. The requirements are an approved degree in engineering or natural sciences or pass in EC Exam Parts I and II or equivalent approved qualifications; candidates must also be engaged in professional work or training in the nuclear field.

Note: The Institution does not at present hold Graduate Exams.

Associate Member: Candidates must be 23 or over and have reached a satisfactory standard of technical competence in the nuclear field. The requirements are BTEC, HNC or HND in appropriate subjects at an approved institution or the possession of certain other approved qualifications, together with 5 yrs' engineering experience of which 2 yrs must have been devoted to practical training and 3 yrs must have been in the nuclear field. Applicants accepted for this class of membership will normally be eligible for registration with the Board for Engineers' Registration as Incorporated Engineers.

Associate: This class is open to persons who are not qualified for Corporate Membership but who show a keen interest in nuclear matters and would usually hold a position of some responsibility. They should be at least 30.

Technician Member: The requirements for this class of membership are a minimum of three yrs engineering experience, of which at least two yrs must have been devoted to approved practical training in the nuclear field, and that the applicant has attained the age of 21 yrs. An engineering education to the standard of a BTEC or SCOTVEC National Certificate in an acceptable subject is required; older qualifications eg an Ordinary National Certificate, or a City and Guilds of London Institute (CGLI) Part II Final Technicians Certificate or the CGLI Radiation Safety Practice Stage II Certificate are also acceptable. In future, as NVQs at the appropriate level become available, these too will be acceptable. The requirements for training and experience are: (a) a recognised apprenticeship lasting not less than three yrs in mechanical maintenance or fitting, electrical maintenance or fitting, instrumentation maintenance or fitting, or other relevant discipline. In addition, the candidate must have received training in safety and quality assurance appropriate to work in the nuclear field and have worked in the nuclear industry for at least two yrs *or* (b) a systematic course of training designed to ensure that the candidate has a comprehensive knowledge of the techniques required to work in a specialist field, installing, maintaining, repairing, commissioning, building or operating equipment in the nuclear industry. The candidate should be able to demonstrate a thorough understanding of the standards, quality assurance and safety of the work and to have worked in the industry for not less than 2 yrs. All applicants for technician grade, and for registration with the Engineering Council as EngTech are required to provide a short personal statement about their career to date, outlining what work experience they have received, what work-related training they have attended and what responsibilities they hold. This brief cv should be similar to that for a job application and should not exceed one A4 page. For those who lack the academic qualifications stipulated, there is a mature candidate route to Technician Membership. Further details are available from the Institution. The Institution also elects Radiological, Medical and Student members.

University Qualifications

The following universities offer qualifications in Nuclear Engineering and related subjects. Full details may be found in Part 4, under the entry for the appropriate university.

FIRST DEGREES AWARDED BY UNIVERSITIES
Liverpool

HIGHER DEGREES AWARDED BY UNIVERSITIES
Durham; London (Queen Mary & Westfield College (incorporating St Bartholomew's and the Royal London School of Medicine & Dentistry)); London (University College (UCL)); Manchester; UMIST

DIPLOMAS AWARDED BY UNIVERSITIES
London (Queen Mary & Westfield College (incorporating St Bartholomew's and the Royal London School of Medicine & Dentistry)); London (University College (UCL))

NVQs
Level 2: Nuclear Decommissioning

City & Guilds
7410 Radiation Safety Practice

Useful Addresses
British Nuclear Fuels, Risley, Warrington WA3 6AS Tel: 01925 832000 Fax: 01925 822711

PLANT ENGINEERING

Membership of Professional Institutions and Associations

THE INSTITUTION OF PLANT ENGINEERS

77 Great Peter Street, Westminster, London SW1P 2EZ Tel: 020 7233 2855 Fax: 020 7233 2604 e-mail: mail@iplante.org.uk Website: www.iplante.org.uk

CORPORATE MEMBERSHIP:

Fellow (FIPlantE): Applicants must be 25 or over, have academic qualifications at University MEng degree level in Engineering or equivalent; have had at least 6 yrs' combined training and experience and responsibility in senior plant engineering positions. Alternatively, applicants can be of mature age and submit an acceptable written paper. Both these routes are eligible for consideration for CEng registration. The third route to Fellow is for those over 35 who do not require CEng registration.

Member (MIPlantE): Applicants must be 23 or over, have obtained a pass degree or HNC/HND in an engineering discipline, plus a Matching Section, have had 4 yrs' combined training and experience and 2 yrs in responsible appointments. Alternatively, applicants can be over 35, have had 15 yrs' combined training and experience and 2 yrs in responsible positions, and submit an acceptable written paper. Both these routes are eligible for IEng registration. The third route to Member is for those over 26 who do not require IEng registration.

NON-CORPORATE MEMBERSHIP:

Associate Member (AMIPlantE): Applicants must be 21 or over, have had 4 yrs' combined training and experience and have obtained a BTEC/SCOTVEC NC/ND in an engineering discipline or ONC/D or C&G Part II in EngC approved subjects. This grade is eligible for EngTech registration.

Graduate Member: Applicants must be over 18 and have obtained the BTEC/SCOTVEC NC/ND or HNC/HND or degree in EngC approved subjects and be engaged on an EngC approved system of training and experience.

Student Member: Applicants must be over 16 and be studying an approved course of engineering. The Institution is associated with the EngC and can register certain grades of membership as CEng, IEng or EngTech.

University Qualifications

The following universities offer qualifications in Plant Engineering and related subjects. Full details may be found in Part 4, under the entry for the appropriate university.

HIGHER DEGREES AWARDED BY UNIVERSITIES
Newcastle; Wales (University of Wales, Aberystwyth)

DIPLOMAS AWARDED BY UNIVERSITIES
Bradford (Bradford & Ilkley Community College)

CERTIFICATES AWARDED BY UNIVERSITIES
Bradford (Bradford & Ilkley Community College)

National Certificates and Diplomas

BTEC National Certificates/Diplomas: Engineering (Plant and Process Plant); Engineering (Process/Plant/Instrumentation)
BTEC Higher National Certificates/Diplomas: Engineering (Plant and Process Plant); Engineering (Process/Plant/Instrumentation)
Scotland
SQA HNC: Engineering (Plant); Plant Engineering; Plant Engineering (Oil & Gas Production); Plant Engineering & Services

NVQs

Level 2: Engineering Maintenance for Processing Industries
Level 3: Engineering Maintenance for Processing Industries

City & Guilds

3930 Maintenance and Repair of Construction Plant; 0601 Process Plant Operation; 6520 Auxiliary Plant Operators; 6542 Power Plant Operators

PRODUCTION ENGINEERING

Membership of Professional Institutions and Associations

INSTITUTE OF OPERATIONS MANAGEMENT
The University of Warwick Science Park, Sir William Lyons Road, Coventry CV4 7EZ
Tel: 024 76692266 Fax: 024 76692305 e-mail: iom@iomnet.org.uk Website: www.iomnet.org.uk
MEMBERSHIP:
Fellows (FIOM): Must be over 30 yrs of age, and have at least 8 yrs' experience in the field *or* have passed/been exempt from the exams prescribed by the Institute, and have a minimum of 4 yrs' relevant experience.
Members (MIOM): Must be over 22 yrs of age, and have at least 5 yrs' experience in the field *or* have passed/been exempt from the exams prescribed by the Institute, and have a minimum of 2 yrs' relevant experience.
Associates: Must be 18 or over and either actively engaged or interested in operations management.
Students: Must be 18 or over and pursuing a relevant course of study.
EXAMINATIONS:
Introductory Certificate: This provides an introduction to operations management and is aimed

at those new to the profession, those already working in the field but without formal qualifications, and those employed in associated areas. Units cover Production & Inventory Control Techniques; The Business Environment; Quantitative Methods; and Information Technology. There is an optional Industrial Project endorsement (75 hrs).

Diploma: This course is designed for the practitioner / professional manager working in the field. Modules include: The Business Environment; Manufacturing Planning & Control & Master Planning; Material & Capacity Requirements Planning; Inventory & Logistics Management; Shop Floor Control and Just in Time; and Managing Organisations. An NVQ in Management Level 4 may be awarded for the appropriate elements if a competency based programme is followed (360 hrs).

Advanced Diploma: This is approached through an industrially-based project and is aimed at those who will evaluate and develop present techniques and systems, or who will design and implement tomorrow's technologies.

THE INSTITUTION OF MANUFACTURING ENGINEERS

Rochester House, 66 Little Ealing Lane, London W5 4XX Tel: 020 8579 9411
The Institute of Manufacturing Engineers merged with the Institute of Electrical Engineers in September 1991. All regulations for membership are applicable as for Institution of Electrical Engineers (q.v.).

University Qualifications

The following universities offer qualifications in Production Engineering and related subjects. Full details may be found in Part 4, under the entry for the appropriate university.

FIRST DEGREES AWARDED BY UNIVERSITIES
Lancaster (Blackpool and The Fylde College); Nottingham; Salford

HIGHER DEGREES AWARDED BY UNIVERSITIES
Portsmouth; Sunderland

DIPLOMAS AWARDED BY UNIVERSITIES
Bournemouth; Northumbria

CERTIFICATES AWARDED BY UNIVERSITIES
Bournemouth; Bradford (Bradford & Ilkley Community College

National Certificates and Diplomas

SQA Advanced Certificate: Engineering Practice (Manufacture & Engineering Support)

NVQs

Level 1: Engineering Material Processing; Process Engineering Maintenance
Level 2: Engineering Manufacture (Foundation); Engineering Production; Process Engineering Maintenance
Level 3: Engineering production; Process Engineering Maintenance
Level 4: Engineering Manufacture

SVQs

Level 1: Engineering Material Processing; Process Engineering Maintenance.
Level 2: Engineering Manufacture Foundation; Engineering Material Processing; Process Engineering Maintenance.
Level 3: Engineering Material Processing; Process Engineering Maintenance.

City & Guilds

0670/1 Iron & Steel Production Technology

REFRIGERATION ENGINEERING

Membership of Professional Institutions and Associations

THE INSTITUTE OF REFRIGERATION

Kelvin House, 76 Mill Lane, Carshalton, Surrey SM5 2JR Tel: 020 8647 7033 Fax: 020 8773 0165
e-mail: ior@ior.org.uk Website: www.ior.org.uk

MEMBERSHIP:
Fellow (FInstR): A person who has been engaged for not less than 5 yrs in a position of special responsibility or leadership in refrigeration or an allied field and has obtained a degree or equivalent in a subject approved by the Council; or has been engaged for not less than 10 yrs in a position of responsibility or leadership in refrigeration or an allied field of which not less than 5 yrs has been in a position of special responsibility or leadership and has obtained a National HD or equivalent qualification in a subject approved by the Council; or has been engaged for not less than 15 yrs in a position of responsibility or leadership in refrigeration or an allied field of which not less than 5 yrs has been in a position of special responsibility or leadership.

Member (MInstR): A person who has been engaged for not less than 3 yrs in a position of important responsibility or leadership in refrigeration or an allied field and has obtained a degree or equivalent qualification in a subject approved by the Council; or has been engaged for not less than 5 yrs in a position of important responsibility or leadership in refrigeration or an allied field and has obtained a National HC or equivalent qualification in a subject approved by the Council; or has been engaged for not less than 10 yrs in an important position of responsibility or leadership in refrigeration or an allied field.

Associate Member (AMInstR): A person who has been engaged for not less than 3 yrs in a position of some responsibility in refrigeration or an allied field and has obtained a National Certificate or equivalent qualification in a subject approved by the Council; or has been engaged for not less than 5 yrs in a position of some responsibility in refrigeration or an allied field and has obtained a C&G Craft Certificate or equivalent qualification in a subject approved by the Council; or has been engaged for not less than 7 yrs in a position of some responsibility in refrigeration or an allied field.

Affiliate: A person who is actively involved in the science, art or application of refrigeration or allied fields and who has not yet attained the condition for transfer to another grade of membership.

Student: A person who is receiving instruction at an approved institute of learning in subjects relevant to the science, art or application of refrigeration or allied fields with a view to qualifying for a higher grade of membership in due course.

University Qualifications

The following universities offer qualifications in Refrigeration Engineering and related subjects. Full details may be found in Part 4, under the entry for the appropriate university.

HIGHER DEGREES AWARDED BY UNIVERSITIES
London (University College (UCL)); Southampton

DIPLOMAS AWARDED BY UNIVERSITIES
Lincolnshire (Grimsby College); London (University College (UCL))

NVQs

Level 2: Mechanical Engineering – Small Commercial Refrigeration & Air Conditioning Systems
Level 3: Mechanical Engineering Services – Ammonia Refrigeration Systems; Mechanical Engineering Services – Commercial and Industrial Refrigeration Systems other than Ammonia; Mechanical Engineering Services – Commercial & Industrial Air Conditioning Systems

SVQs

Level 2: Mechanical Engineering Services: Small Commercial Refrigeration & Air Conditioning Systems.

Level 3: Mechanical Engineering Services: Ammonia Refrigeration Systems or Commercial & Industrial Halocarbon Refrigeration Systems.

Useful Addresses

Air Conditioning and Refrigeration Industry Board, Kelvin House, 76 Mill Lane, Carshalton, Surrey SM5 2JR Tel: 020 8647 7033 Fax: 020 8773 0165 E-mail: instor@ibm.net

ROAD, RAIL AND TRANSPORT ENGINEERING

Membership of Professional Institutions and Associations

INSTITUTE OF HIGHWAY INCORPORATED ENGINEERS

20 Queensberry Place, London SW7 2DR Tel: 020 7823 9093
e-mail: secretary@ihie.org.uk Website: www.ihie.org.uk
In 1989 the Highway and Traffic Technicians Association changed its name to IHIE. Previous to 1972 the HTTA had been the Association of Highway Technicians, formed in 1965. IHIE is part of the NVQ awarding bodies for transportation qualifications and civil engineering design. Enquiries to OUVS or Edexcel. The Institute is a nominated and licensed institution with the EC and Fellows and Members may register with the Council as IEng or EngTech, as appropriate.
Fellow (FIHIE): Must satisfy the requirements of the EC for registration as an Incorporated Engineer, have passed a Professional Review, and hold a position of responsibility in highways, transportation or allied fields. The minimum academic qualification until 2002 is an Edexcel HNC in Civil Engineering or equivalent.
Member (MIHIE): Must satisfy the requirements of the EC for registration as an Engineering Technician, have passed the Technician Professional Review, and be employed in highways, transportation or allied fields. The minimum academic qualification is a BTEC NC in Civil Engineering Studies or equivalent.
Associate Member (AMIHE): Must have passed the first stage of the Incorporated Professional Review and satisfy EC academic entry requirements or have at least 10 yrs' experience.
Graduate Members: Must have an HNC, HND or degree; or have passed a Technician Initial Professional Development Assessment.
Student Members: Must be undergoing appropriate training or have undergone such training or be still studying.

THE INSTITUTE OF ROAD TRANSPORT ENGINEERS

22 Greencoat Place, London SW1P 1PR Tel: 020 7630 1111 Fax: 020 7630 6677
e-mail: irte@irte.org Website: www.irte.org
The Institute of Road Transport Engineers (IRTE) is a professional engineering institute on the list of Engineering Council Nominated Bodies. The Institute sets standards to improve engineering, commercial and management skill, knowledge and competence of all whose occupation or vocation is concerned with design, production, operation and maintenance of road vehicles of all types used in the carriage of persons, passengers, goods and equipment. In partnership with government bodies and industry the Institute promotes improvement in design and construction and use of all types of road transport vehicles. To promote continuing professional development the Institute encourages the training of its engineers to acquire theoretical and practical qualifications.

MEMBERSHIP:
Modern Apprentices: The Institute encourages young people in road transport engineering to obtain professional recognition and support early in their careers. To this end an initiative has been launched, in recognition of the training being given, to encourage trainees undertaking a Modern Apprenticeship in Vehicle Maintenance and Repair to join the Institute and obtain the benefit from membership from the onset of their career.
Honorary Fellow: A person who has made a considerable contribution to the sphere of transport.

Fellows, Full Members and Associate Members: Road transport engineers who, in the opinion of the Council, merit admission to membership and satisfy the Institute with respect to the educational and vocational requirement as specified by the Council at the time of application.

Technicians and Associates: Persons who, in the opinion of the Council, merit admission to membership and who satisfy the Institute with respect to the educational and vocational requirements as specified by the Council at the time of application but who have not had such a degree of responsibility or experience as would qualify them for admission as a Corporate Member.

Affiliates: Persons who, in the opinion of the Council, merit admission to Affiliateship by virtue of their occupation within the road transport or related industry.

Students: Persons over 16 but not over 25 who are or will be pursuing such course of study as seen fit by the Council.

THE INSTITUTION OF HIGHWAYS AND TRANSPORTATION

6 Endsleigh Street, London WC1H 0DZ Tel: 020 7387 2525 Fax: 020 7387 2808 e-mail: iht@iht.org Website: www.iht.org.uk

(See also Transport, Road Transport Engineering, Works and Highway Engineering) The Institution is currently an assessment centre for transportation NVQ/SVQ's and offers assessment services for: Highway Maintenance Level 3 & 4, Traffic Management & Systems Engineering Level 4, Transport Planning Level 5, Transport & Technical Support Level 3 and Road Safety Level 3 & 4.The Institution is a Conditionally Nominated Body of the Engineering Council and can offer Professional Review for registration as Incorporated and Chartered Engineers.

MEMBERSHIP:

Fellows (FIHT): Must hold a degree or qualification acceptable to the Institution on a FT Level 4/5 NVQ/SVQ and have held an important position of independent responsibility in connection with highway or transportation engineering for at least 4 yrs *or* have at least 10 yrs' experience in highways and/or transportation, and have held an important senior position of independent responsibility in connection with highways and transportation for 4 yrs minimum.

Members (MIHT): Must hold an approved degree or professional qualification and have at least 2 yrs' relevant work experience *or* be a registered Incorporated Engineer and have at least 8 yrs' relevant work experience *or* hold a recognised professional qualification and have at least 10 yrs' relevant work experience *or* have 80% NVQ/SVQ Level or 50% NVQ/SVQ Level 5.

Associate Member (AMIHT): Must hold an approved degree and be engaged in highway or transportation work *or* have at least 5 yrs' relevant work experience *or* have 40% NVQ/SVQ Level 4 *or* 25% NVQ/SVQ Level 5.

Students: Must be at least 18 and be currently involved in a FT course of studies and/or in service training in highways and transportation.

Note: There is no entrance exam for any grade of membership.

INSTITUTION OF RAILWAY SIGNAL ENGINEERS

3rd Floor, Savoy Hill House, Savoy Hill, London WC2R 0BS Tel: 020 7240 3290 Fax: 020 7240 3281 e-mail: training@irse.u-net.com Website: www.irse.org

MEMBERSHIP:

Fellows (FIRSE): Must be at least 30 and have been Members for at least 3 yrs, with at least 5 yrs' superior responsibility; or be at least 35, engaged in the profession and have an appropriate knowledge of, and eminence in, the science of railway signalling or telecommunications.

Members (MIRSE): Must be not less than 25, have been regularly trained, held a responsible position for at least 2 yrs and have satisfied the requirements of the Exam Regulations; or be not less than 28, have held a responsible position for at least 5 yrs and have the minimum educational qualifications applicable to a Chartered Engineer in an associated engineering discipline or its equivalent; or not be less than 35, have had 10 yrs' experience in a position of responsibility in the profession and be holding a position of senior responsibility.

Associate Members: Must be not less than 23 yrs of age, have been engaged in the profession or an allied profession which has the necessary relevance to railway signalling and/or telecommunications for a period of 2 yrs and have achieved an academic standard to the min level necessary to satisfy the Engineering Council's requirements for registration as Incorporated Engineer; or alternatively have 7 yrs' experience in a position of responsibility in the profession.

Engineering Technicians: Must be not less than 21 yrs of age, have undertaken a period of engineering training at the appropriate level of not less than 2 yrs on a structured approved programme, have at least 2 yrs' responsible engineering experience and have achieved an engineering qualification to the min level necessary to satisfy the Engineering Council's requirements for Engineering Technicians.

Students: Must be aged 16-28, be employed and be receiving regular and practical training in some branch of the profession. The Institution also elects

Honorary Fellows (Hon FIRSE).

IRSE EXAMINATION REQUIREMENTS FOR CORPORATE MEMBERSHIP:
The aim of the IRSE Examination is to establish the professional competence of educationally qualified electrical, electronic and communications engineers in railway signalling and communication engineering. It is intended to test the main concepts of the subject material without bias to any one Railway Practice and it is designed to demonstrate that the student has reached the necessary professional educational standard required by a Signalling or Telecommunications Engineer for Corporate Membership of the Institution. This standard is typified by the exercising of judgement in the preparation, assessment, amendment or application of specifications and procedures, and is applicable to personnel engaged in the following activities:

1. Signalling/Telecommunications principles, practices, rules and regulations for the safe operation of railway traffic.
2. Design and development of Signalling/Telecommunications equipment and systems.
3. Preparation and understanding of the equipment drawings and specifications and/or design.
4. Planning, site installation and testing of Signalling/Telecommunications equipment and systems.
5. Practices related to assembly, wiring and testing of Signalling/Telecommunications equipment and systems.
6. Maintenance and servicing of Signalling/Telecommunications equipment and systems.

In order to meet the examination requirements for corporate membership, candidates must, within a period of 5 yrs, obtain a pass in Module 1, plus 3 of the remaining 6 optional modules. It is possible to obtain exemptions from individual modules where you can demonstrate that you have passed an examination by a recognised body, which has substantially covered the syllabus of a particular IRSE examination module. Due to the specialised nature of the IRSE Examination, the scope for exemption is fairly limited. Claims for exemption must be made within 5 yrs of obtaining the particular qualification for which recognition is being claimed. The reason for this condition is that the exemption is based on information that may not be available where a qualification has been discontinued or changed.

Modules Available:
Module 1. Safety of Railway Signalling and Communications – No exemptions will be given.
Module 2. Signalling the Layout – Please apply, no exemptions currently agreed.
Module 3. Signalling Principles – Please apply, no exemptions currently agreed.
Module 4. Communications Principles – This is the most commonly sought after exemption. Many of the applicants for exemption claim that Telecommunications has been part of their Degree course and that, on this basis, exemption should be granted. Unfortunately it has been clear that the content of the Telecommunications element within a typical university Engineering Degree is, at best, a basic overview. Occasionally, students study a Telecommunications topic for their final yr project, but these tend to be about a research topic narrowly specialising in a particular field and the Council is not convinced that such study justifies module exemption. As a basic guideline, therefore, please do not ask for exemption to this module unless: your university study has been predominantly in Telecommunications; or your university study has included Telecommunications and your present career is railway telecommunications engineering.
Module 5. Signalling & Control Equipment, Applications Engineering – Please apply, no exemptions currently agreed.
Module 6. Communications Equipment, Applications Engineering – Please apply, no exemptions currently agreed.
Module 7. Systems, Management & Engineering – Please apply, no exemptions currently agreed.

University Qualifications

The following universities offer qualifications in Road, Rail and Transport Engineering and related subjects. Full details may be found in Part 4, under the entry for the appropriate university.

FIRST DEGREES AWARDED BY UNIVERSITIES
Napier

HIGHER DEGREES AWARDED BY UNIVERSITIES
Birmingham; Bristol; Cranfield; Leeds; London (Imperial College of Science, Technology & Medicine); Napier; Newcastle; Plymouth; Portsmouth; Salford; Strathclyde; Surrey

DIPLOMAS AWARDED BY UNIVERSITIES
Birmingham; Napier; Newcastle; Plymouth; Salford; Strathclyde

CERTIFICATES AWARDED BY UNIVERSITIES
Newcastle

NVQs

Level 1: Roadbuilding
Level 2: Rail Transport Engineering Maintenance (Communication); Rail Transport Engineering Maintenance (Electrification); Rail Transport Engineering Maintenance (Permanent Way); Rail Transport Engineering Maintenance (Plant); Rail Transport Engineering Maintenance (Signal Fault Finding); Rail Transport Engineering Maintenance (Signals); Rail Transport Engineering Maintenance (Traction and Rolling Stock); Roadbuilding
Level 3: Rail Transport Engineering Maintenance (Communication); Rail Transport Engineering Maintenance (Electrification); Rail Transport Engineering Maintenance (Permanent Way); Rail Transport Engineering Maintenance (Plant); Rail Transport Engineering Maintenance (Signals); Rail Transport Engineering Maintenance (Traction and Rolling Stock)
Level 4: Highways Maintenance

SVQs

Level 1: Highways Maintenance
Level 2: Highways Maintenance; Rail Transport Engineering Maintenance: Communication or Electrification or Permanent Way or Plant or Signal Fault Finding or Signals or Traction & Rolling Stock
Level 3: Highways Maintenance; Rail Transport Engineering Maintenance: Communications or Electrification or Permanent Way or Plant or Signals or Traction & Rolling Stock
Level 4: Highways Maintenance

City & Guilds

6140 Roadwork; 6156 Streetworks Excavation and Reinstatement; 6230 Roadwork Supplementary Certificate

Useful Addresses

Rail Industry Training Council, Africa House, 64-78 Kingsway, London WC2B 6AH Tel: 020 7320 0436 Fax: 020 7320 0193
Transportation Vocational Group, Institute of Logistics and Transport, 80 Portland Place, London W1N 4DP Tel: 020 7467 9400 Fax: 020 7467 9440

SHEET METAL ENGINEERING

SVQs

Level 1: High Pressure Aluminium Die Casting
Level 2: High Pressure Aluminium Die Casting

STRUCTURAL ENGINEERING

Membership of Professional Institutions and Associations

THE INSTITUTION OF STRUCTURAL ENGINEERS

11 Upper Belgrave Street, London SW1X 8BH Tel: 020 7235 4535 Fax: 020 7235 4294
e-mail: mail@istructe.org.uk Website: www.istructe.org.uk

MEMBERSHIP:
The Institution authorises its corporate members to use the designatory initials **FIStructE** or **MIStructE**. Such corporate members may be registered by the Institution with the Engineering Council and thereby become additionally entitled to use the designation **CEng** (Chartered Engineer).

Fellows (FIStructE): Must be over 35, have passed the exam for Membership and subsequently have been engaged in a position of responsibility for at least 5 yrs. Alternatively, there is a direct entry route to Fellowship for individuals over 45, with an appropriate academic qualification, who have achieved a position of eminence in the profession.

Members (MIStructE): Must be at least 25, have an academic qualification equivalent to an accredited degree and have passed the Membership exam with relevant training and practical experience in structural engineering.

Graduates: Persons who have normally obtained an accredited degree in Civil or Structural Engineering or equivalent qualification and intend to study the profession of structural engineering.

Associate Members (AMIStructE): Must be at least 23, have relevant training and practical experience, and must possess appropriate academic qualifications equivalent to a 3 yr degree, and have passed the Institution's exam for Associate-Membership leading to registration as **IEng** (Incorporated Engineer).

Students: Persons not less than 17 who are studying or intend to study the profession of structural engineering.

EXAMINATIONS:
Chartered Membership: Part 3 exam, a 7 hr paper on structural design and practice.
Associate Membership: Associate Membership exam, a 6 hr paper on structural engineering practice.

University Qualifications

The following universities offer qualifications in Structural Engineering and related subjects. Full details may be found in Part 4, under the entry for the appropriate university.

FIRST DEGREES AWARDED BY UNIVERSITIES

Aberdeen; Bradford; Coventry; Edinburgh; Heriot-Watt; Leeds; Liverpool; London (University College (UCL)); Manchester; Newcastle; Nottingham Trent; Nottingham Trent (Southampton Institute); Sheffield; UMIST

HIGHER DEGREES AWARDED BY UNIVERSITIES

Aberdeen; Brighton; Glasgow; Heriot-Watt; Liverpool; London (Imperial College of Science, Technology & Medicine); Newcastle; Plymouth; Sheffield; Surrey; UMIST; Wales (Cardiff University)

DIPLOMAS AWARDED BY UNIVERSITIES

Glasgow; Liverpool; Newcastle

POSTGRADUATE DIPLOMAS AWARDED BY UNIVERSITIES

Heriot-Watt

NVQs

Level 2: Engineering Construction; Engineering Construction – Supporting Engineering Construction Activities; Fabricating Constructional Steelwork
Level 3: Engineering Construction – Fabricating Steel Structures; Fabricating Constructional Steelwork

WATER ENGINEERING

University Qualifications

The following universities offer qualifications in Water Engineering and related subjects. Full details may be found in Part 4, under the entry for the appropriate university.

FIRST DEGREES AWARDED BY UNIVERSITIES

Cheltenham & Gloucester; De Montfort, Leicester; Greenwich; Oxford Brookes; Paisley; Plymouth; Stirling

HIGHER DEGREES AWARDED BY UNIVERSITIES

Abertay, Dundee; Anglia; Birmingham; Cranfield; Dundee; Durham; East Anglia; Glasgow; Heriot-Watt; Huddersfield; Liverpool John Moores; London (Imperial College of Science, Technology & Medicine); London (University College (UCL)); Loughborough; Middlesex; Napier; Newcastle; Plymouth; Southampton; Surrey; Ulster; Wales (Cardiff University); Wales (University of Wales, Bangor)

DIPLOMAS AWARDED BY UNIVERSITIES

Dundee; Glasgow; London (University College (UCL)); Napier; Newcastle; Plymouth; Ulster

CERTIFICATES AWARDED BY UNIVERSITIES

Dundee

POSTGRADUATE DIPLOMAS AWARDED BY UNIVERSITIES

Heriot-Watt

National Certificates and Diplomas

BTEC National Certificates/Diplomas: Engineering (River and Inshore Craft); Water Engineering (Water and Waste Water Operations)
BTEC Higher National Certificates/Diplomas: Water Technology

NVQs

Level 2: Operating Process Plant (Sludge); Operating Process Plant (Waste Water): Operating Process Plant (Water)
Level 3: Water Services Operations – Distribution Control

SVQs

Level 2: Water Services Operations: Distribution Control; Well Services: Mechanical Wireline or Electric Logging or Tubing Operations
Level 3: Water Services: Technical Distribution Operations; Well Service: Electric Logging

City & Guilds

6590 Water Industry

Useful Addresses

Board for Education and Training in the Water Industry, 1 Queen Anne's Gate, London SW1H 9BT Tel: 020 7957 4524 Fax: 020 7957 4557

EXPORT

Membership of Professional Institutions and Associations

INSTITUTE OF EXPORT

Export House, 64 Clifton Street, London EC2A 4HB
Tel: 020 7247 9812
Fax: 020 7377 5343
e-mail: education@export.org.uk
Website: www.export.org.uk

THE INSTITUTE OF
EXPORT

QUALIFICATIONS:
Professional Qualification in Export: The Institute provides a 2 yr PT nationally taught professional qualification in International Trade. It is run in over 50 colleges of F & HE. Part 1, The Advanced Certificate in International Trade has 4 subjects: Operating in the Global Economy, the Business Environment, International Physical Distribution and the Finance of International Trade. Part 2, (2nd Yr), has 4 subjects: International Market Planning, International Logistics and Purchasing, Management of International Trade and Practical Global Trading. Completion of both Part 1 and Part 2 entitles eligibility for graduate membership of the Institute. Candidates for Part 1 must be at least 18, for Part 2 they must be at least 19 and have passed Part 1. Exemptions from individual subjects in the Part 1 exam may be granted for equivalent qualifications. Each case is considered individually.

MEMBERSHIP:
Membership: Open to any individual engaged in international trade. Full Membership is dependent on appropriate educational qualifications, experience and career achievements. All members have to be elected by the Council, and the grades of membership are as follows:
Fellow (FIEx): By application from any person who can demonstrate outstanding achievements and has reached a position of eminence in their career. No one may join the Institute at this grade.
Companions (CIEx): By invitation to any person who has demonstrated outstanding achievements at the highest level.
Members by Experience (MIEx): By application from any person who has the requisite number of yrs' experience in international trade and holds a position of responsibility.
Associate Member (AMIEx): By application from any persons who do not qualify for Full Membership by experience or educational qualifications yet have obtained a sufficient level of achievement to justify their election to this grade.
Graduate Member (MIEx (Grad)): By application from any person who has passed the Institute's professional exams or their equivalents, as agreed by the Institute's Education Committee.
Affiliate: By application from any persons who are seeking to improve their knowledge and understanding of overseas trade and international business administration and management.
Student Member: By application from any person of least 18 yrs of age with 4 O Level qualifications, including English Language, or 4 GCSE passes at grades A, B or C or an acceptable equivalent and 1 A Level pass, or equivalent, or ITAS Level 2 S/NVQ. Candidates aged 21 yrs and over who lack formal academic qualifications but have had 3 yrs' practical experience in overseas trade may be accepted at the Institute's discretion. All students of the Institute are required to pass the professional exams within 4 yrs of the date of their registration unless a special extension is granted. Overseas students must demonstrate competence in English and comparable qualifications.

University Qualifications

The following universities offer qualifications in Export and related subjects. Full details may be found in Part 4, under the entry for the appropriate university.

FIRST DEGREES AWARDED BY UNIVERSITIES
Napier

HIGHER DEGREES AWARDED BY UNIVERSITIES
Salford

DIPLOMAS AWARDED BY UNIVERSITIES
Salford

NVQs

Level 2: International Trade & Services
Level 3: International Trade & Services
Level 4: International Trade & Services

London Chamber of Commerce and Industry Examinations Board (LCCIEB)

International Trade and Services Level 2, 3 and 4.

FASHION

University Qualifications

The following universities offer qualifications in Fashion and related subjects. Full details may be found in Part 4, under the entry for the appropriate university.

FIRST DEGREES AWARDED BY UNIVERSITIES

Brighton; Central England; Central Lancashire; Cordwainers; De Montfort, Leicester; Derby; East London; Glasgow Caledonian; Heriot-Watt (Scottish Borders Campus); Huddersfield; Kent (Kent Institute of Art & Design); Kingston; Leeds; Leeds (Bretton Hall); Leeds (Leeds College of Art & Design); Liverpool John Moores; London Institute (Central Saint Martins College of Art & Design); London Institute (London College of Fashion); Manchester Metropolitan.; Middlesex; Northampton; Northumbria; Nottingham Trent; Nottingham Trent (Southampton Institute); Salford; Southampton; Southampton (Winchester School of Art); Surrey Institute; UMIST; Wales (University of Wales College, Newport); Westminster

HIGHER DEGREES AWARDED BY UNIVERSITIES

Central England; Cordwainers; Heriot-Watt; Heriot-Watt (Scottish Borders Campus); Kent (Kent Institute of Art & Design); London Institute (Central Saint Martins College of Art & Design); London Institute (Chelsea College of Art & Design); London Institute (London College of Fashion); Manchester Metropolitan.; Northampton; Nottingham Trent; Royal College of Art; Southampton (Winchester School of Art); Surrey Institute

DIPLOMAS AWARDED BY UNIVERSITIES

Bournemouth; Central England; Cordwainers; De Montfort, Leicester; Doncaster; Kent (Kent Institute of Art & Design); Lincolnshire (Grimsby College); London Institute (London College of Fashion); Middlesex; Northampton; Nottingham Trent; Salford

CERTIFICATES AWARDED BY UNIVERSITIES

Bournemouth; Central England; London Institute (London College of Fashion); Northampton

OTHER COURSES AWARDED BY UNIVERSITIES

Northampton

POSTGRADUATE DIPLOMAS AWARDED BY UNIVERSITIES

Heriot-Watt

National Certificates and Diplomas

Level 2: Footwear Repair
Level 3: Fashion Design; Handcraft Tailoring
Level 4: Costume Design and Realisation

NVQs

Level 2: Footwear Repair
Level 3 : Fashion Design; Handcraft Tailoring
Level 4 : Costume Design and Realisation

SVQs

Level 2: Design: Constructed Textile Design or Fashion
Level 3: Costume Supervision & Maintenance
Level 4: Costume Design & Realisation

City & Guilds

4600 Clothing and Knitting Craft; 4690 Clothing Machine Mechanics; 4921 Shoe Repair

College Associateships and Diplomas

CORDWAINERS COLLEGE

182 Mare Street, London E8 3RE Tel: 020 8985 0273 Fax: 020 8985 9340
e-mail: enquiries@cordwainers.ac.uk Website: www.cordwainers.ac.uk

HIGHER EDUCATION:
BA (Hons) in Design, Marketing & Product Development (Footwear/Accessories): *3 yrs FT. Entry at 18+ with either Foundation course in Art & Design; or BTEC ND General Art & Design; or BTEC ND in Footwear Technology; or BTEC ND in Design specialising in Fashion/Textiles or Footwear/Accessories; or 2 A Levels plus 5 GCSEs at grade C or better; or extensive relevant industrial/commercial experience, with a portfolio of work.*
BTEC HND in Design (Footwear/Accessories): 2 yrs FT. Entry at 18+ with 1 A Level plus 4 GCSEs at grade C or better; BTEC ND in a relevant subject area; or Foundation course in Art & Design with a portfolio of work supporting academic achievements and / or work experience.
BTEC HND in Footwear Technology: Entry requirements as for HND in Design.
BTEC HND in Saddlery Technology: 2 yrs FT. Entry at 18+ with 1 A level plus 4 GCSEs at grade C or above or Diploma in Saddlery Studies or equivalent / related work experience.

FURTHER EDUCATION:
BTEC ND in Design & Technology (Footwear/Accessories): 2 yrs FT
BTEC GNVQ Advanced in General Art and Design: 2 yrs FT
Diploma in Saddlery Studies: 2 yrs FT. For the courses listed above entry is at 16+ with 4 GCSEs at grade C or better; BTEC First Diploma; or CPVE with appropriate profile and supporting portfolio of work.
BTEC Diploma in Foundation Studies in Art and Design: 1 yr FT. Entry at 17+ with 5 GCSEs at Grade C or better; or one A Level plus 4 GCSEs at Grade C or better; or 2 A Levels plus 3 GCSEs at Grade C or better and a portfolio of work.
BTEC Intermediate in Design: 1 yr FT. Entry at 16+ having completed a compulsory course of secondary education.
Short Courses, PT, FT and Evening Classes: Details are available from the Admissions Officer together with information about planned course developments in Design, Technology and Craft Skills.
Note: In exceptional circumstances the normal academic requirements may be waived for mature applicants or those of outstanding ability or with experience of industry or commerce. Many of the courses are suitable for adult returners and enquiries are welcome

LONDON COLLEGE OF FASHION

(A Constituent College of the London Institute)
20 John Princes Street, London W1M 0BJ Tel: 020 7514 7400 Fax: 020 7514 7484 e-mail: enquiries@lcf.linst.ac.uk Website: www.lcf.linst.ac.uk

SCHOOL OF FASHION DESIGN & TECHNOLOGY:
BA (Hons) Design Technology for the Fashion Industry: 3 yrs FT. Options in Menswear, Womenswear or Accessories.

BA (Hons) Product Development for The Fashion Industry: 4 yr course. Entry requirements: min age of 18, 2 A Levels plus 5 GCSEs or equivalent qualifications or experience.

BA(Hons) Costume and Make Up for the Performing Arts: 3 yrs FT. Entry requirements: min age of 18, 2 A Levels plus 5 GCSEs or equivalent qualifications or experience. Options in Specialist Make Up and Hair, Costume Interpretation, Technical Effects for Costume and Make Up.

HND Fashion Design & Technology: 2 yrs FT. Entry requirements: min age of 18, 4 GCSE passes (Grade C or above) plus 1 A Level or pass at BTEC National Diploma.

ND Fashion Design & Technology: 2 yrs FT. Entry requirements: min age of 16, 4 GCSE passes (Grade C or above).

HND Cordwainers Design (Footwear and Accessories): 2 yrs FT. Entry requirements: min age of 18, 4 GCSE passes (Grade C or above) plus 1 A Level or pass at BTEC National Diploma.

HND Cordwainers Footwear Technology: 2 yrs FT. Entry requirements: min age of 18, 4 GCSE passes (Grade C or above) plus 1 A Level or pass at BTEC National Diploma.

BTEC Diploma Foundation Studies in Art and Design: 1 yr FT. Entry requirements: min age of 18, A Level pass plus 3 GCSEs or equivalent qualifications. Options in Fashion Design and Illustration, Fashion Textiles, Fashion Design and Manufacture, Theatre, Fashion Photography, Styling and Make Up, Accessories.

Certificate in Tailoring: 1 yr FT. Entry requirements: min age of 18.

Diploma in Tailoring: 1 yr FT. Entry requirements: min age of 18.

SCHOOL OF FASHION PROMOTION & MANAGEMENT:

BA (Hons) Fashion Promotion: 3 yrs FT. Entry requirements: 5 GCSE passes (Grade C or above – including English Language) plus 2 A Levels or pass at BTEC National Diploma, Scottish Highers or GNVQ Advanced.

BA (Hons) Fashion Management: 3 yrs FT or 4 yrs PT. Entry requirements: 5 GCSE passes plus 2 A Levels or pass at BTEC National Diploma, Scottish Highers or GNVQ Advanced.

BA (Hons) Fashion Photography: 3 yrs FT. Entry requirements: 5 GCSE passes plus 2 A Levels or pass at BTEC National Diploma, Scottish Highers or GNVQ Advanced.

BSc (Hons) Cosmetic Science: 4 yr SW. Entry requirements: 5 GCSE passes plus 2 A Levels or pass at BTEC National Diploma, Scottish Highers (to include a science).

Certificate in Cosmetic Science: 1 yr PT. Entry requirements: 2 A Level passes or BTEC/OND (both to include chemistry and/or biology).

HND Beauty Therapy and Health Studies: 2 yrs FT. Entry requirements: 4 GCSE passes (Grade C or above – to include, Biology, English Language and Mathematics) plus 1 pass at A Level in an academic subject and study of one other A Level subject or BTEC National Diploma in a science subject or a Registered Nurse's qualification.

HND Specialist Make Up: 2 yrs FT. Entry requirements: min age of 18, 4 GCSE passes (at Grade C or above) plus 1 A Level (preferably in art) or a pass at BTEC National Diploma.

HND Fashion Marketing and Promotion: 2 yrs FT. Entry requirements: min age of 18, 4 GCSE passes (at Grade C or above) plus 1 A Level or a pass at BTEC National Diploma.

HND Fashion Styling and Photography: 2 yrs FT. Entry requirements: 4 GCSE passes plus 1 pass at A Level or equivalent qualification or experience.

ND Design Fashion Styling for Hair and Make Up: 2 yrs FT. Entry requirements: min age of 16, 4 GCSE passes (at Grade C or above), show a portfolio of work in art and design.

ND Beauty Therapy: 2 yrs FT. Entry requirements: min age of 16, 4 GCSE passes (at Grade C or above – preferably including a science subject) or equivalent qualifications.

Advanced GNVQ in Business of Fashion: 2 yrs FT. Entry requirements: 4 GCSE passes (Grade C or above) or equivalent qualification.

Fashion and Media Make Up (First Level/Access): 1 yr FT. Entry requirements: min age of 19, highly motivated and evidence of creative ability and capacity to complete concentrated course.

Fashion Promotion Media (First Level/Access): 1 yr FT. Entry requirements: min age of 19, be able to demonstrate good communication skills and creative flair as well as a broad interest in Fashion, the Visual Arts and the Media.

Fashion Business (First Level/Access): 1 yr FT

CROSS COLLEGE COURSES:

BA Hons Fashion Studies: 4 yrs PT. Entry requirements: min age of 18, 2 A Level passes plus 5 GCSEs (Grade C or above) or equivalent qualifications or experience.

First Diploma Fashion Portfolio: 1 yr FT. Entry requirements: min age of 16, 3 GCSEs (Grade C or above).

MA Fashion Studies: 1 yr FT, 2 yr PT. Entry requirements: good honours degree. Options in Communication and Culture, Design and Technology, Management and Marketing, History and Theory.

PG Certificate in Fashion: Options in Advanced Pattern Cutting and Manufacture, Buying and Merchandising, Fashion and Lifestyle Journalism.

Other Vocational Awarding Bodies

ABC: Aspects of Multicultural Fashion (Production Techniques); Machine Knitting; Pattern Cutting; Sewing and Textiles
CENTRA: Machine Knitting; Pattern Cutting; Sewing and Textiles

Useful Addresses

British Footwear Association, 5 Portland Place, London W1N 3AA Tel: 020 7580 8687 Fax: 020 7580 8696
British Leather Confederation, Leather Trade House, Kings Park Road, Moulton Park, Northampton NN3 6JD Tel: 01604 679999 Fax: 01604 679998
CAPITB Trust, 80 Richardshaw Lane, Pudsey, Leeds LS28 6BN Tel: 0113 239 3355 Fax: 0113 239 4118
Worshipful Company of Saddlers, Saddlers Hall, 40 Gutter Lane, London EC2V 6BR Tel: 020 7726 8661 Fax: 020 7600 7386

FISHERIES MANAGEMENT

Membership of Professional Institutions and Associations

INSTITUTE OF FISHERIES MANAGEMENT

22 Rushworth Avenue, West Bridgford, Nottingham NG2 7LF Tel: 0115 9822317 Fax: 0115 9826150 e-mail: chris@randall.force9.co.uk Website: www.ifm.org.uk
The Institute of Fisheries Management is an international organisation of fisheries professional, lay and student members sharing a common interest in the modern management of recreational and commercial fisheries.

MEMBERSHIP:
Fellows (FIFM): Persons who are qualified as Members and who, in the opinion of the Council, have made a significant contribution to fisheries management in the field of research, development or otherwise, and/or in furthering the interests and objectives of the Institute, may be invited to become Fellows.
Honorary Members (Hon MIFM): Persons who have rendered special services to fisheries management or to the Institute, or who are distinguished in some other sphere.
Registered Members (MIFM): Persons who have been engaged in, or involved with, fisheries management for at least 5 yrs and who: (a) hold the Diploma of the Institute; or (b) hold an appropriate University degree or CNAA degree; or (c) hold such alternative qualifications as the Council may from time to time deem appropriate.
Licentiate Members (LMIFM): Persons who have been engaged in, or involved with, fisheries management for at least 2 yrs and who: (a) hold the diploma or a Certificate of the Institute; or (b) hold an appropriate degree as in (b) above; or (c) hold such alternative qualifications as the Council may from time to time deem appropriate.
Associate Members: Persons employed in fisheries management (whether in a FT or PT capacity and whether in a paid or honorary capacity) not eligible as Members or Licentiate Members.
Subscriber Members: Persons or bodies not qualifying for membership in any other category and appearing to have an interest in fisheries management.
Junior Members: Persons under the age of 25 inclusive who are interested in fisheries

management and who are not in regular employment or in receipt of a salary or wages.

The IFM runs 3 correspondence courses: The **Certificate and Diploma in Fisheries Management and the Certificate in Fish Farming** are accepted qualifications by employers such as the Environment Agency. Details from V.L. Holt at above address. The Certificate Courses can each be completed in one yr. The duration of the Diploma course is two yrs, and it has been credit-rated recently by the Open University Validation Service. Persons gaining the Diploma are now entitled to 60 credit points at Level 1 and 15 credit points at Level 2, which can be used to contribute towards an Open University degree.

University Qualifications

The following universities offer qualifications in Fisheries Management and related subjects. Full details may be found in Part 4, under the entry for the appropriate university.

FIRST DEGREES AWARDED BY UNIVERSITIES
Plymouth; Stirling

HIGHER DEGREES AWARDED BY UNIVERSITIES
Aberdeen; Hull; London (King's College London); Portsmouth; Stirling; Wales (University of Wales, Bangor)

DIPLOMAS AWARDED BY UNIVERSITIES
Aberdeen; Hull; Stirling

National Certificates and Diplomas

BTEC National Certificates/Diplomas: Fishery Studies
BTEC Higher National Certificates/Diplomas: Fishery Studies

NVQs

Level 2: Fish Husbandry (Shellfish); Fish Husbandry (Fin Fish)
Level 3: Fish Husbandry

SVQs

Level 2: Fish Husbandry
Level 3: Fish Husbandry

FLORISTRY

Membership of Professional Institutions and Associations

THE SOCIETY OF FLORISTRY LTD
6 Carroll Avenue, Ferndown, Dorset BH22 8BP Tel: 0870 2410432 Fax: 0870 2410432
Fellowship is only granted to paid up persons holding the National Diploma of the Society of Floristry Limited. Membership is open to all persons engaged in the floral industry.

EXAMINATIONS:

Intermediate Certificate of the Society of Floristry (ICSF): Intermediate exams are held annually and are open to students taking a recognised course of floristry training or the equiv 3 yrs relevant experience in the industry.

National Diploma of the Society of Floristry (NDSF): The National Diploma exam is also held annually. This is the highest award for professional floristry in the UK. Entry qualification is the Intermediate Certificate of the Society of Floristry.

Attending a seminar is a compulsory component for both exams.

University Qualifications

The following universities offer qualifications in Floristry and related subjects. Full details may be found in Part 4, under the entry for the appropriate university.

CERTIFICATES AWARDED BY UNIVERSITIES
East Anglia (Otley College); Lincolnshire (Bishop Burton College)

OTHER COURSES AWARDED BY UNIVERSITIES
Essex (Writtle College)

National Certificates and Diplomas

BTEC National Certificates/Diplomas: Floristry
BTEC Higher National Certificates/Diplomas: Floristry

NVQs

Level 2: Floristry
Level 3: Floristry

SVQs

Level 2: Floristry
Level 3: Floristry

City & Guilds

0190 Floristry

FOOD SCIENCE AND NUTRITION

Membership of Professional Institutions and Associations

INSTITUTE OF FOOD SCIENCE AND TECHNOLOGY (UK)

5 Cambridge Court, 210 Shepherds Bush Road, London W6 7NJ Tel: 020 7603 6316
e-mail: info@ifst.org/membership@ifst.org Website: www.ifst.org

MEMBERSHIP:

Fellow (FIFST): Fellows (not less than 33) have the necessary qualifications for Membership and not less than 7 yrs' appropriate experience in food science or technology in addition to the relevant period of qualifying experience for Membership (see below). They must *either* have made a substantial contribution to food science and technology *or* have reached a position of suitable seniority and authority in the profession.

Member (MIFST): Members *either* have an appropriate degree with first or second class Honours or an equivalent academic or professional qualification together with at least 3 yrs' suitable experience if the qualification is in food science or food technology, or at least 4 yrs' if a major element of Food Science & Technology is included; *or* have an acceptable degree or academic or professional qualification, together with at least 4 to 6 yrs' appropriate experience, depending on the nature and subject of the qualifications.

Licentiate: Must *either* have an appropriate degree or academic or professional qualification; *or* an acceptable academic or professional qualification (minimum level HND)

Student Member: Are in approved FT courses of study in the U.K. or Europe.

Affiliate: Persons, while ineligible for any other grade of membership, qualify for this grade by virtue of their activities relating to food science and technology.

Academic requirements for membership: University, academic or professional qualifications acceptable by the Institute include not only those in Food Science or Food Technology, but also in any other relevant disciplines, eg Chemistry, Microbiology, Biochemistry, Engineering, Chemical Engineering, etc.

EXAMINATIONS:
Higher Certificate in Food Premises Inspection: Issued by IFST, the Higher Certificate meets the requirements of the Department of Health Code of Practice No 9, that Inspections of Food Premises should only be undertaken by officers who are suitably qualified and experienced.

University Qualifications

The following universities offer qualifications in Food Science and Nutrition and related subjects. Full details may be found in Part 4, under the entry for the appropriate university.

FIRST DEGREES AWARDED BY UNIVERSITIES

Abertay, Dundee; Adams; Bath Spa; Belfast; Central Lancashire; East Anglia (Otley College); East Anglia (Suffolk College); Glamorgan; Glasgow; Glasgow Caledonian; Greenwich; Heriot-Watt; Huddersfield; Kingston; Leeds; Leeds (Askham Bryan College); Leeds (Leeds, Trinity & All Saints); Leeds Metropolitan; Lincolnshire (Lincoln University Campus); Liverpool (Chester College of H.E.); Liverpool John Moores; London (King's College London); Luton; Manchester Metropolitan.; Newcastle; North London; Northumbria; Nottingham; Nottingham Trent; Oxford Brookes; Plymouth; Queen Margaret; Reading; Robert Gordon; Salford; Sheffield; Sheffield Hallam; South Bank; Southampton; Staffordshire; Surrey; Surrey (University of Surrey Roehampton); Teesside; Ulster; Wales (University of Wales Institute, Cardiff); Westminster; Wolverhampton

HIGHER DEGREES AWARDED BY UNIVERSITIES

Aberdeen; Belfast; Bristol; Central Lancashire; Cranfield; De Montfort, Leicester; Glasgow; Heriot-Watt; Huddersfield; Kingston; Leeds; Leeds Metropolitan; Liverpool (Chester College of H.E.); London (King's College London); Manchester Metropolitan.; Nottingham; Oxford Brookes; Plymouth; Reading; Sheffield; Sheffield Hallam; South Bank; Strathclyde; Surrey; Surrey (University of Surrey Roehampton); Teesside; Thames Valley; Ulster; Wales (University of Wales Institute, Cardiff); Wolverhampton

DIPLOMAS AWARDED BY UNIVERSITIES

Aberdeen; Birmingham (Birmingham College of Food, Tourism and Creative Studies); Bristol; East Anglia (Otley College); East Anglia (Suffolk College); Glasgow; Lincolnshire (Lincoln University Campus); Liverpool (Chester College of H.E.); London (King's College London); Manchester Metropolitan.; Nottingham; Oxford Brookes; South Bank; Ulster; Wales (University of Wales Institute, Cardiff)

CERTIFICATES AWARDED BY UNIVERSITIES

Aberdeen; East Anglia (Otley College); Liverpool (Chester College of H.E.); Wales (University of Wales Institute, Cardiff)

POSTGRADUATE DIPLOMAS AWARDED BY UNIVERSITIES

Thames Valley;

National Certificates and Diplomas

BTEC National Certificates/Diplomas: Science (Technology of Food)
BTEC Higher National Certificates/Diplomas: Science (Applied Food Studies); Science (Food Development and Production); Science (Food Science); Science (Technology of Food)
Scotland
SQA HNC: Food Production Management; Food Science; Food Microbiology; Food, Health & Consumer Studies
SQA HND: Food Science; Food, Health & Consumer Management.
Advanced Diploma: Food Safety

NVQs

Level 1: Food & Drink Manufacturing Operations; Meat Processing
Level 2: Food & Drink Manufacturing Operations

Level 3: Food & Drink Manufacturing Operations; Meat Processing (Technical Operations)
Level 4: Food & Drink Manufacturing Operations; Meat Processing Management (Technical and Production)

City & Guilds
1230 Flour Milling

Other Vocational Awarding Bodies
ABC: Nutrition

Useful Addresses
British Soft Drinks Association, 20-22 Stukeley Street, London WC2B 5LR Tel: 020 7430 0356 Fax: 020 7831 6014
Food & Drink NTO, 6 Catherine Street, London WC2B 5JJ Tel: 020 7836 2460 Fax: 020 7836 0580
Meat Training Council, PO Box 141, Winterhill House, Snowdon Drive, Milton Keynes MK6 1YY Tel: 01908 231062 Fax: 01908 231063

FORESTRY AND ARBORICULTURE

Membership of Professional Institutions and Associations

THE ARBORICULTURAL ASSOCIATION
Ampfield House, Ampfield, Nr Romsey, Hampshire SO51 9PA Tel: 01794 368717 Fax: 01794 368978
e-mail: treehouse@dial.pipex.com
MEMBERSHIP:
Fellows: Professional arboriculturists with qualifications, experience and proficiency to standards approved by the Association. Applicants for Fellowship must have held personal membership or have been employed by a corporate member for at least 5 yrs.
Associates: Persons professionally concerned with arboriculture and who hold one of the following qualifications: National Diploma in Arboriculture (RFS); National Diploma in Arboriculture (BTEC); Certificate in Arboriculture (RFS); NCH (Arboriculture option); Surrey Certificate in Arboriculture (Merrist Wood); City and Guilds Special Certificate in Tree Surgery for Craftsmen; AA Technician's Certificate in Arboriculture; other qualifications relevant to the above may be considered.
Affiliate: All others with a professional involvement in arboriculture including members of related professions with interests in arboriculture.
Corporate Members: Civic Amenity Societies, Associations, Local Authorities, Companies, Partnerships, Institutions, Public Bodies, Government Departments, and similar bodies having sympathy with the objectives of the Association.
Ordinary Members: All other persons interested in the planting, care and conservation of amenity trees and woods.
Students: Persons engaged in FT/S training or education with a maximum time limit of 3 yrs of membership in this category unless extended at the discretion of the Council.

INSTITUTE OF CHARTERED FORESTERS
7A St Colme Street, Edinburgh EH3 6AA Tel: 0131 225 2705 Fax: 0131 220 6128
e-mail: icf@charteredforesters.org Website: www.charteredforesters.org
MEMBERSHIP:
Fellows: Hold a degree or diploma in forestry or related science and have passed the Institute's Professional Exams, have been engaged in forestry in Britain in a professional capacity for at least 5 yrs and been a member for at least 10 yrs. (Forestry is defined in its broadest context and includes professionals practising in all aspects of tree management, including forest management,

arboriculture, urban forestry and environmental forestry.)

Ordinary Members: Have similar academic qualifications, have passed the Institute's Professional Exams and have been engaged in forestry in a professional capacity for at least 2 yrs.

Associates: Are engaged in forestry and intend to qualify for full membership.

Affiliates: Are not professional foresters but are interested in the objectives of the Institute and include some corporate bodies.

Students: Are enrolled for a course in forestry approved by Council.

EXAMINATIONS:

Entry to Corporate Grades (ie Fellow and Ordinary Membership) is open to Associates who have obtained an approved qualification in forestry, and have passed the Institute's Professional Exams, which consist of theory papers, a project, field work and an oral exam.

THE ROYAL FORESTRY SOCIETY OF ENGLAND, WALES AND NORTHERN IRELAND

102 High Street, Tring, Hertfordshire HP23 4AF Tel: 01442 822028 Fax: 01442 890395
e-mail: rfshq@rfs.org.uk Website: www.rfs.org.uk

QUALIFICATIONS:

Certificate in Arboriculture: The syllabus for the written exam covers Botany, Nursery Work, Planting, Maintenance, Pests, Tree Surgery, Legal Questions and Care and Use of Tools. The award of the Certificate is dependent upon the candidate holding specified arboricultural proficiency tests offered by the National Proficiency Tests Council.

Professional Diploma in Arboriculture: The syllabus covers the same general field as the Certificate, but in greater detail. Candidates should be at least 23 and must have been in arboriculture-related industries for 3 yrs. Both the Certificate and the DipArb(RFS) are taken by private study or at various colleges, often on a day-release basis. They are suitable for those employed in botanical gardens, woodlands, local authority work and tree surgery companies.

University Qualifications

The following universities offer qualifications in Forestry and Arboriculture and related subjects. Full details may be found in Part 4, under the entry for the appropriate university.

FIRST DEGREES AWARDED BY UNIVERSITIES
Aberdeen; Bucks. Coll.; Central Lancashire; De Montfort, Leicester; Edinburgh; Wales (University of Wales, Bangor)

HIGHER DEGREES AWARDED BY UNIVERSITIES
Aberdeen; Bournemouth; Bucks. Coll.; Edinburgh; Wales (University of Wales, Bangor)

DIPLOMAS AWARDED BY UNIVERSITIES
Aberdeen; Brighton; Central Lancashire; De Montfort, Leicester; Edinburgh; Wales (University of Wales, Bangor)

CERTIFICATES AWARDED BY UNIVERSITIES
Aberdeen; East Anglia (Otley College)

National Certificates and Diplomas

BTEC National Certificates/Diplomas: Forestry
BTEC Higher National Certificates/Diplomas: Forestry

NVQs

Level 1: Forestry
Level 2: Amenity Horticulture (Arboriculture); Forestry (Establishment & Maintenance or Harvesting)
Level 3: Amenity Horticulture (Managing Trees & Woodlands); Forestry (Contracting); Forestry (Supervising and Operating)
Level 4: Forestry

SVQs

Level 1: Forestry; Amenity Horticulture
Level 2: Forestry: Establishment & Maintenance or Harvesting or Contracting
Level 3: Forestry: Supervising & Operating; Managing Trees & Woodlands
Level 4: Forestry

City & Guilds

0140 Tree Surgery

Other Vocational Awarding Bodies

ABC: RFS Certificate in Arboriculture

Useful Addresses

Forestry and Arboriculture Safety and Training Council, Forestry Commission, 231 Corstorphine Road, Edinburgh EH12 7AT Tel: 0131 314 6247 Fax: 0131 316 4344

FOUNDRY TECHNOLOGY AND PATTERN MAKING

Membership of Professional Institutions and Associations

THE INSTITUTE OF BRITISH FOUNDRYMEN
Bordesley Hall, The Holloway, Alvechurch, Birmingham B48 7QA Tel: 01527 596100 Fax: 01527 596102 e-mail: info@ibf.org.uk Website: www.ibf.org.uk
Formed 1904, granted first Royal Charter in 1921; Third Supplemental Charter granted in 1994. The Institute is a Nominated Body of the Engineering Council and the granting of the Third Supplemental Charter has aligned its own membership requirements with those required by the Engineering Council. The Charter has also introduced the new grade of Affiliated Member.
MEMBERSHIP:
Fellows (FIBF): Persons wishing to apply for the grade of Fellow have to be 35 yrs of age or over and to have the required academic qualifications. They must also prove that they have obtained a position of eminence within the industry and have held this position for at least 3 yrs.
Members (MIBF): Should be at least 25 yrs of age and have achieved the required academic standard, and have held a position of responsibility within the industry for at least 3 yrs.
Associate Members: Applicants with suitable qualifications may apply to join at this grade of membership at the age of 21 yrs. Associate Members who are registered Incorporate Engineers may use the designatory letters **I Eng AMIBF** after their name.
Associates: Available to anyone not less than 18 yrs of age who can satisfy the General Council that they have a bona fide interest in the cast metals industry.
Affiliate Members: Have to prove they have attained a responsible position within their Company.
Students: This grade is available to anyone under the age of 23 yrs who is studying on a course related to Cast Metals Technology. The Institute is a Nominated Body of the Engineering Council and may nominate its members for Chartered Engineer (CEng), Incorporated Engineer (IEng) and Engineering Technician (EngTech) status. It can also make submission for those suitably qualified members to become a Registered European Engineer (EurIng).Fellows and Members who are registered as Chartered Engineers may call themselves 'Chartered Foundrymen'. Those who are registered as Incorporated Engineers may refer to themselves as 'Incorporated Foundrymen'.

City & Guilds

1700 Foundry Craft Competencies; 2110 Patternmaking Craft Studies

FREIGHT FORWARDING

Membership of Professional Institutions and Associations

THE BRITISH INTERNATIONAL FREIGHT ASSOCIATION (BIFA)
Redfern House, Browells Lane, Feltham, Middlesex TW13 7EP Tel: 020 8844 2266
Fax: 020 8890 5546 e-mail: bifa@btconnect.com Website: www.bifa.org
Incorporates The Institute of Freight Professionals.

MEMBERSHIP:
BIFA membership is corporate, open to forwarding and international freight services companies which satisfy strict entrance criteria. Membership of the IFP is for individuals within any sector of the freight industry. IFP professional qualification centres around a required level of appropriate experience and knowledge, and all relevant learning, whether by traditional or vocational qualification, higher or further education or specialised short courses is accredited according to its level. There are 4 categories of membership to accommodate those in the freight industry throughout their career development.
Affiliate: Caters for those at the beginning of their careers and no special entrance criteria are needed. It also applies to those who interface with the industry and do not seek professional qualification in it.
Associate: Those at this level have already achieved a mid-point in learning and/or experience.
Full Professional Membership: Awarded to those who have a high enough proven level of experience and learning to be considered a professional.
Fellow: Conferred by status, experience and time.

EXAMINATIONS:
Exams may be taken if this is the chosen learning method, but are no longer essential. The Advanced Certificate in International Trade (ACIT) is taken at FE colleges. There are also IFP modules available by correspondence, followed by a comprehensive tender project. These courses may be done in their entirety or as selected modules. Each is a stand-alone subject that is individually accredited. Qualification by NVQs is becoming very popular, the most relevant being International Trade and Services. Any NVQ with appropriate operational or business knowledge is also accredited according to level and direct relevance. Because of the wider scope of knowledge now needed by the forwarder, there can be no single qualification that will cater adequately for all sector needs. The qualifications of the specialist sector institutes such as the Institute of Export, the Institute of Logistics and Transport, the Institute of Chartered Shipbrokers, the United Kingdom Warehousing Association and the like are therefore also accredited as appropriate. Another pathway towards professional qualification is higher education and these courses too are accredited as appropriate.

University Qualifications

The following universities offer qualifications in Freight Forwarding and related subjects. Full details may be found in Part 4, under the entry for the appropriate university.

HIGHER DEGREES AWARDED BY UNIVERSITIES
Plymouth

DIPLOMAS AWARDED BY UNIVERSITIES
London Guildhall; Plymouth

CERTIFICATES AWARDED BY UNIVERSITIES
London Guildhall

NVQs

Level 1: Cargo Operations
Level 2: Cargo Operations

FUNERAL DIRECTING, BURIAL AND CREMATION ADMINISTRATION

Membership of Professional Institutions and Associations

THE INSTITUTE OF BURIAL AND CREMATION ADMINISTRATION
Kelham Hall Newark, Nottinghamshire NG23 5QX Tel: 01636 708311 Fax: 01636 708311

MEMBERSHIP:

Fellows (FInstBCA): Are elected from those Members on whom, in the opinion of the Institute's Council, it would be in the interest of the Institute to confer the status of Fellow. The primary requirement shall be that such person shall have: (a) upon some subject with which the Institute is concerned in its objects, prepared and submitted to the Council or had published a paper or thesis, or prepared and delivered at a general meeting or conference of the Institute or similar organisation an address or lecture, which in the opinion of the Council is of value and interest to the Institute in any of its objects; or (b) performed any service which in the opinion of the Council has been of outstanding importance to the Institute or in connection with matters relating to any of the objects of the Institute.

Members (MInstBCA): Are elected from those who: (a) are holders of the Final Diploma of the Institute; or (b) have held Associate Membership for a period of 5 yrs, and are in FT employment in a senior managerial capacity or hold any other appointment of a senior administrative or supervisory character in a burial or cremation undertaking.

Associate Members (AInstBCA): Are elected from 2 groups of applicants: (a) those who have for at least 2 yrs been employed in a supervisory or administrative appointment in a burial or cremation undertaking or a public service ancillary thereto for the disposal of the dead; and (b) Registered Licentiates or Students of the Institute who have passed 5 modules of the Institute's Diploma course.

Registered Licentiates (LInstBCA): Are elected from those employed FT or PT in the service of a burial or cremation undertaking or a public service ancillary thereto for the disposal of the dead, but are not eligible for any other category of membership.

Students: Must be gainfully employed in a burial or cremation undertaking or a public service ancillary thereto for the disposal of the dead. They may be required to pass an approved exam before enrolling for the Institute's Exams.

EXAMINATIONS:

The Institute administers a Diploma Course which is studied by correspondence and supplemented by attendance at a seminar at Stoke Rochford Hall in Lincolnshire. For further details contact: Gary Marshall, Education and Training Officer, Institute Education Service, 18 Albert Crescent, Keresley, Coventry CV6 2GG, Tel 01203 832260. The Institute also administers a course for the training of cemetary operatives titled the COTS scheme, in partnership with Berkshire College of Agriculture. For further details contact: Tim Morris 107 Parlaunt Road, Langley, Slough SL3 8BE, TEL 0181 5464463 , 0374973712 (mobile).

NATIONAL ASSOCIATION OF FUNERAL DIRECTORS
618 Warwick Road, Solihull, West Midlands B91 1AA Tel: 0121 711 1343 Fax: 0121 711 1351
e-mail: info@nafd.org.uk Website: www.nafd.org.uk/www.funeral-directory.co.uk

MEMBERSHIP:

Full Members (Category A): Are businesses engaged in (but not necessarily exclusively) the practice of Funeral Directing within the United Kingdom, the Isle of Man and the Channel Islands. The nominated representative may be the proprietor or a senior executive. Member firms are required to pass an entrance exam consisting of an inspection of premises and facilities; also an assessment of the knowledge and capability of the senior representative, unless he or she holds the Diploma in Funeral Directing.

Full Members (Category B): Are businesses engaged in (but not necessarily exclusively) supplying goods or services to the funeral profession as set out below:(i) Proprietors or Directors of cemeteries and/or crematoria (not being public authorities) or their nominees; (ii) Manufacturers and suppliers of funeral directors' merchandise and equipment; (iii)

Manufacturers and main distributors of hearses, but not their agents; (iv) Proprietors or directors of embalming services; (v) Persons, firms or companies who hire to Funeral Directors, operate or own a hearse or hearses and a passenger car or cars, if accepted into membership after 3rd May 1978.

Overseas Members: Are funeral directors, ancillary businesses and allied professional associations who operate outside the United Kingdom.

EXAMINATIONS:

Diploma in Funeral Directing (DipFD): The Diploma is awarded only to Registered Students who have passed a written exam based on the Association's own **Manual of Funeral Directing**, and a practical oral exam on funeral arranging and have also been working in a funeral director's business for at least 2 yrs, carried out 25 funeral arrangements and be over the age of 18.

NVQ in Funeral Services: This qualification is for persons employed within the funeral profession. The programme offers assessment in the workplace with minimum disruption to day-to-day activities. For those that do not wish to take a formal examination.

NVQs

Level 2: Funeral Services
Level 3: Funeral Services

FURNISHING AND FURNITURE

Membership of Professional Institutions and Associations

NATIONAL INSTITUTE OF CARPET AND FLOORLAYERS
4d St Mary's Place, The Lace Market, Nottingham, Nottinghamshire NG1 1PH Tel: 0115 958 3077 Fax: 0115 941 2238 e-mail: nicf@cfa.org.uk Website: www.nicf.carpetinfo.uk

MEMBERSHIP:

There are 5 levels of membership in the Institute:

Master Fitter (MInstCF): Obtained by the completion of a written exam and an assessment of past work by a regional assessor.

Approved Fitter: Obtained by the completion of a written exam; business references are also required.

Associate Membership: For those not actively involved with carpet fitting but who have an interest in the profession.

Trainee Membership: For students and apprentices.

Patron Membership: For manufacturers and large retail outlets.

University Qualifications

The following universities offer qualifications in Furnishing and Furniture and related subjects. Full details may be found in Part 4, under the entry for the appropriate university.

FIRST DEGREES AWARDED BY UNIVERSITIES
Bucks. Coll.; Central England; Central Lancashire; De Montfort, Leicester; Kingston; London Guildhall; Loughborough; Nottingham Trent; Wolverhampton

HIGHER DEGREES AWARDED BY UNIVERSITIES
Bucks. Coll.; Central England

DIPLOMAS AWARDED BY UNIVERSITIES
Bucks. Coll.; Central England

CERTIFICATES AWARDED BY UNIVERSITIES
Central England; Lincolnshire (Bishop Burton College); Lincolnshire (Hull College)

National Certificates and Diplomas

BTEC National Certificates/Diplomas: Design (Furniture); Design (Furniture Making and Restoration); Furniture
BTEC Higher National Certificates/Diplomas: Design (Furniture); Design (Furniture Making and Restoration); Furniture
Scotland
SQA HNC: Antique Furniture Restoration; Furniture Construction and Design; Furniture Craftsmanship.
SQA HND: Furniture Construction and Design; Furniture Craftsmanship; Antique Furniture Restoration Business.

NVQs

Level 1: Furniture Production Operations; Producing Hand-Crafted Furniture
Level 2: Assembled Furniture Production; Producing Hand-Crafted Furniture; Upholstered Furniture Production
Level 3: Furniture Production; Producing Hand-Crafted Furniture; Traditional Upholstery

SVQs

Level 1: Producing Hand-Crafted Furniture
Level 2: Producing Hand-Crafted Furniture
Level 3: Producing Hand-Crafted Furniture

City & Guilds

5550 Furniture Craft Subjects and Advanced Studies; 5640 Furniture Crafts; 5790 Furniture Subjects Advanced, Design and Construction

Useful Addresses

British Furniture Manufacturing, 30 Harcourt Street, London W1H 2AA Tel: 020 7724 0851 Fax: 020 706 1924

GEMMOLOGY AND JEWELLERY

Membership of Professional Institutions and Associations

THE GEMMOLOGICAL ASSOCIATION AND GEM TESTING LABORATORY OF GREAT BRITAIN (GAGTL)

27 Greville Street, London EC1N 8TN Tel: 020 7404 3334 Fax: 020 7404 8843
e-mail: gagtl@btinternet.com Website: www.gagtl.ac.uk/gagtl

MEMBERSHIP:
Fellow (FGA): Fellowship is granted to those who are successful in the Diploma Exam in Gemmology and who are approved for membership by the Council of Management.
Member: Ordinary membership is open to all who support the aims and objectives of the organisation and who are approved by the Council of Management.
Diamond Member (DGA): This membership is granted to those who are successful in the Gem Diamond Diploma Exam and who are approved for membership by the Council of Management.

EXAMINATIONS:
The Diploma Exam in Gemmology: Is taken after a correspondence course run by the Association or at classes run by the Association and at FE Colleges. It is necessary to qualify in the Preliminary Exam before taking the Diploma Exam. The Diploma Exam, taken at the end of the course, is theoretical and practical. The syllabus includes Elementary Crystallography, Physical and Optical

Properties of Gems, Occurrence, Identification and Fashioning of Gemstones. Successful students are awarded the Diploma in Gemmology.

The Gem Diamond Exam: May be taken after study of the Correspondence Course run by the Association or at classes run by the Association and at FE Colleges. The Exam is theoretical and practical, and the syllabus includes Physical and Optical Properties of Diamond, Grading of Gem Diamond, Occurrence, Fashioning, Identification, and Appraisal of Diamond. Successful students are awarded the Gem Diamond Diploma. The practical component of this course and exam is offered as a separate certificate qualification.

THE NATIONAL ASSOCIATION OF GOLDSMITHS

78A Luke Street, London EC2A 4PY
Tel: 020 7613 4445
Fax: 020 7613 4450
e-mail: nag@jewellersuk.com
Website: www.progold.net

QUALIFICATIONS:
JET (Jewellery, Education and Training) 1 & 2: Taken after a 2 yr correspondence course run by the Association. There is an exam at the end of the 2nd yr which includes theoretical and practical tests. Candidates successful in the exam are entitled to style themselves **PJDip**. The syllabus covers Jewellery Merchandise and Materials, Gemstones, Hallmarks, Horology, Salesmanship and Business subjects.

The Gemstone Diploma: Taken after a 1 yr correspondence course run by the Association. Candidates successful in the exam are entitled to style themselves **RJGem.Dip**. The exam includes theoretical and practical tests.

The JET Management Course: A 1 yr correspondence course run by the Association. Diploma awarded on marks gained throughout the course. Successful candidates are entitled to style themselves **NAG Management Dip**. Syllabus covers Dealing with Staff, Customer Complaints, Time Management and People Management.

The JET Valuations Diploma Course: A 1 yr correspondence course, with an exam, run by the Association. Successful candidates are entitled to style themselves **PJV**. Syllabus covers Law, Antique & Collectable Jewellery, and Preparing a Schedule. All applicants must hold a recognised gemstone qualification.

University Qualifications

The following universities offer qualifications in Gemmology and Jewellery and related subjects. Full details may be found in Part 4, under the entry for the appropriate university.

FIRST DEGREES AWARDED BY UNIVERSITIES
Bucks. Coll.; Central England; De Montfort, Leicester; Dundee; Glasgow (Glasgow School of Art); Kent (Kent Institute of Art & Design); London Guildhall; London Institute (Central Saint Martins College of Art & Design); Loughborough; Middlesex; Sheffield Hallam

HIGHER DEGREES AWARDED BY UNIVERSITIES
Central England; Kent (Kent Institute of Art & Design); London Guildhall; Royal College of Art; Surrey Institute

DIPLOMAS AWARDED BY UNIVERSITIES
Central England; Kent (Kent Institute of Art & Design); London Guildhall

CERTIFICATES AWARDED BY UNIVERSITIES
Central England

National Certificates and Diplomas

BTEC National Certificates/Diplomas: Design (Jewellery); Design (Silversmithing and Jewellery Design)
BTEC Higher National Certificates/Diplomas: Design (Jewellery); Design (Silversmithing and Jewellery Design)

SVQs
Level 1: Manufacturing Jewellery & Allied Products
Level 2: Manufacturing Jewellery & Allied Products
Level 3: Manufacturing Jewellery & Allied Products

City & Guilds
7660 Silverware; 7670 Jewellery

Useful Addresses
Jewellery and Allied Industries Training Council, 10 Vyse Street, Birmingham B18 6LT Tel: 0121 237 1109 Fax: 0121 237 1113

GENEALOGY

Membership of Professional Institutions and Associations

THE HERALDRY SOCIETY
PO Box 32, Maidenhead, Berks SL6 3FD Tel: 0118 932 0210
The Heraldry Society is a registered charity which aims to encourage interest in its subject through publications, lectures, visits and related activities. It maintains contact with heraldic societies in many parts of the country and abroad. Membership is unlimited. Examinations (also open to non-members) are set at three levels: Elementary and Intermediate, both comprising written examination papers; and Advanced, requiring a dissertation. The Intermediate examination may only be taken after passing the Elementary; but the Advanced may be taken independently. Success at any of the three levels gains an appropriate certificate, while success at all three levels taken in order gains the **Diploma** of the Society. Fellowship (FHS) may be awarded by the Council to distinguished scholars in the field. Honorary Fellowship (Hon FHS) may be conferred upon those who have rendered outstanding service to the Society.

THE INSTITUTE OF HERALDIC AND GENEALOGICAL STUDIES
Northgate, Canterbury, Kent CT1 1BA Tel: 01227 768664 Fax: 01227 765617
e-mail: ihgs@ihgs.ac.uk Website: www.ihgs.ac.uk
A registered charity constituted as an incorporated educational trust to make provision for training, study and research in family history and related disciplines. Full library, archive and research facilities are provided at the above address where a wide range of courses leading to qualification in genealogical research is conducted. PT, correspondence and residential courses.
MEMBERSHIP:
Fellowship (FHG): Is normally awarded to those members and honorary members with broadly based knowledge and extensive experience of heraldry and genealogy whose high degree of expertise is deemed worthy of recognition.
Licentiates (LHG): Have completed a prescribed course of study and research over not less than 4 yrs', are above 25, have passed the exams prescribed by the examining board and have submitted an approved dissertation or thesis. They are expected to have had not less than 5 full yrs' experience in research. Licentiateship is not determined by membership continuity. Those following approved courses elsewhere may apply for admission to exams. A series of graded assessments and certificate exams are offered leading the student from the beginning of study, through **Record Agent** to the higher levels of qualification in **Genealogy**. Courses are suitable for those who wish to study genealogy, heraldry and related subjects auxiliary to history either as a vocation or an academic discipline.
Associates: Are unqualified supporting members with use of library etc.

SOCIETY OF GENEALOGISTS

14 Charterhouse Buildings, Goswell Road, London EC1M 7BA Tel: 020 7251 8799 Fax: 020 7250 1800 e-mail: info@sog.org.uk Website: www.sog.org.uk

The Society (founded 1911) is a registered educational charity, established to encourage and foster the study, science and knowledge of genealogy. This it does chiefly through its library, publications, lectures and courses. It does not hold exams.

MEMBERSHIP:

Honorary Fellows (FSG(Hon)): Any person, Member or not, may be elected to Honorary Fellowship for very distinguished services to genealogy by the existing Fellows. Their number is limited to 10.

Fellows (FSG): Members of not less than 5 yrs' standing may be elected to Fellowship for distinguished services to the Society or to genealogy by the existing Fellows. Their number is limited to 100.

Members: Members are elected by the Executive Committee. The number is unlimited and there are presently over 14,700.

GEOGRAPHY

University Qualifications

The following universities offer qualifications in Geography and related subjects. Full details may be found in Part 4, under the entry for the appropriate university.

FIRST DEGREES AWARDED BY UNIVERSITIES

Aberdeen; Anglia; Aston; Bath Spa; Belfast; Birmingham; Bournemouth; Bradford; Brighton; Bristol; Brunel; Cambridge; Central England; Central Lancashire; Cheltenham & Gloucester; Coventry; Cranfield; De Montfort, Leicester; De Montfort, Leicester (De Montfort University Bedford); Derby; Dundee; Durham; East Anglia; East London; Edinburgh; Exeter; Exeter (The College of St Mark & St John); Glamorgan; Glasgow; Greenwich; Hertfordshire; Huddersfield; Hull; Keele; Kent (Canterbury Christ Church University College); Kingston; Lancaster; Lancaster (Edge Hill College of Higher Education); Leeds; Leeds (The College of Ripon & York St John); Leeds Metropolitan; Leicester; Liverpool; Liverpool (Chester College of H.E.); Liverpool (Liverpool Hope University College); Liverpool John Moores; London (Birkbeck, University of London); London (King's College London); London (London School of Economics & Political Science); London (Queen Mary & Westfield College (incorporating St Bartholomew's and the Royal London School of Medicine & Dentistry)); London (Royal Holloway); London (School of Oriental & African Studies); London (University College (UCL)); Loughborough; Luton; Manchester; Manchester Metropolitan.; Middlesex; Newcastle; North London; Northampton; Northumbria; Nottingham; Nottingham Trent; Oxford; Oxford (Westminster College, Oxford); Oxford Brookes; Plymouth; Portsmouth; Reading; Salford; Sheffield; Sheffield Hallam; South Bank; Southampton; Southampton (Chichester Institute of Higher Education); Southampton (King Alfred's College); St Andrews; St Martin; Staffordshire; Stirling; Strathclyde; Sunderland; Surrey (St Mary's, Strawberry Hill); Surrey (University of Surrey Roehampton); Sussex; Ulster; UMIST; Wales (Cardiff University); Wales (North East Wales Institute); Wales (University of Wales College, Newport); Wales (University of Wales Institute, Cardiff); Wales (University of Wales, Aberystwyth); Wales (University of Wales, Bangor); Wales (University of Wales, Lampeter); Wales (University of Wales, Swansea); Westminster; Wolverhampton; Worcester

HIGHER DEGREES AWARDED BY UNIVERSITIES

Aberdeen; Birmingham; Bristol; Cambridge; Cheltenham & Gloucester; Coventry; Cranfield; Dundee; Durham; Edinburgh; Exeter (The College of St Mark & St John); Glamorgan; Glasgow; Greenwich; Huddersfield; Hull; Keele; Kingston; Lancaster; Leeds; Leicester; Liverpool; Liverpool (Liverpool Hope University College); Liverpool John Moores; London (Birkbeck, University of London); London (Institute of Education); London (King's College London); London (Queen Mary & Westfield College (incorporating St Bartholomew's and the Royal London School of

Medicine & Dentistry)); London (Royal Holloway); London (University College (UCL)); Manchester; Middlesex; Nottingham; Plymouth; Portsmouth; Salford; Sheffield; Southampton (Chichester Institute of Higher Education); St Andrews; St Martin; Staffordshire; Sussex

DIPLOMAS AWARDED BY UNIVERSITIES
Bath Spa; Bournemouth; Durham; Edinburgh; Hull; Kingston; Lancaster; Leeds; Leicester; Liverpool (Liverpool Hope University College); London (King's College London); London (University College (UCL)); Luton; Manchester Metropolitan.; Salford; Staffordshire

CERTIFICATES AWARDED BY UNIVERSITIES
Brunel; Durham; Exeter (The College of St Mark & St John); London (Birkbeck, University of London); London (Goldsmiths College); Oxford (Westminster College, Oxford); Salford; Southampton; St Martin; Staffordshire; Sunderland; Wales (University of Wales, Bangor)

National Certificates and Diplomas

BTEC National Certificates/Diplomas: Geographical Information Systems
BTEC Higher National Certificates/Diplomas: Geographical Information Systems

GEOLOGY

Membership of Professional Institutions and Associations

THE GEOLOGICAL SOCIETY
Burlington House, Piccadilly, London W1V 0JU Tel: 020 7434 9944 Fax: 020 7439 8975
e-mail: enquiries@geolsoc.org.uk Website: www.geolsoc.org.uk/
To be elected to Fellowship, the candidate shall either: (*a*) hold an honours degree in geology or a cognate subject for the time being awarded from a University or Higher Education Establishment in the UK and recognised by the Council, or an equivalent qualification recognised by the Council, and have at least 2 yrs' relevant postgraduate experience; or (*b*) have not less than 6 yrs' relevant experience in geology or a cognate subject. Persons who are not yet qualified for election to Fellowship can apply for Associateship or Undergraduates can apply for Junior Associateship. The Society is recognised by the DTI as the chartering authority for professional geoscientists in the UK and is able to confer the title Chartered Geologist (CGeol) upon Fellows who are appropriately qualified.

University Qualifications

The following universities offer qualifications in Geology and related subjects. Full details may be found in Part 4, under the entry for the appropriate university.

FIRST DEGREES AWARDED BY UNIVERSITIES
Aberdeen; Anglia; Belfast; Birmingham; Brighton; Bristol; Brunel; Cheltenham & Gloucester; Derby; Durham; East Anglia; Edinburgh; Exeter; Glamorgan; Greenwich; Hertfordshire; Keele; Kingston; Lancaster; Lancaster (Edge Hill College of Higher Education); Leeds; Leicester; Liverpool; Liverpool John Moores; London (Birkbeck, University of London); London (Imperial College of Science, Technology & Medicine); London (Royal Holloway); London (University College (UCL)); Luton; Manchester; Nottingham Trent; Oxford; Oxford Brookes; Paisley; Plymouth; Portsmouth; Sheffield; Southampton; St Andrews; Staffordshire; Sunderland; Wales (Cardiff University); Wolverhampton

HIGHER DEGREES AWARDED BY UNIVERSITIES
Aberdeen; Birmingham; Bournemouth; Bristol; Cheltenham & Gloucester; City; Durham; East Anglia; Exeter; Glasgow; Greenwich; Heriot-Watt; Hertfordshire; Keele; Kingston; Lancaster; Leeds; Leicester; Liverpool; London (Imperial College of Science, Technology & Medicine);

London (Royal Holloway); London (University College (UCL)); Manchester; Newcastle; Nottingham; Oxford Brookes; Plymouth; Sheffield; St Andrews; Staffordshire; Ulster; UMIST; Wales (Cardiff University); Wales (University of Wales, Bangor)

DIPLOMAS AWARDED BY UNIVERSITIES
Aberdeen; City; Exeter (Truro College); Glamorgan; Glasgow; Hertfordshire; Leeds; Leicester; London (Royal Holloway); London (University College (UCL)); Manchester; Newcastle; Oxford Brookes; Paisley; Reading; Staffordshire; Ulster

CERTIFICATES AWARDED BY UNIVERSITIES
Durham; London (Birkbeck, University of London); Nottingham; Staffordshire; Sussex

POSTGRADUATE DIPLOMAS AWARDED BY UNIVERSITIES
Heriot-Watt

National Certificates and Diplomas
BTEC National Certificates/Diplomas: Science (Geological Technology)
BTEC Higher National Certificates/Diplomas: Science (Geological Technology); Science (Industrial Geology)

GLASS TECHNOLOGY

Membership of Professional Institutions and Associations

SOCIETY OF GLASS TECHNOLOGY
Don Valley House, Savile St East, Sheffield S4 7UQ Tel: 0114 263 4455 Fax: 0114 263 4411 e-mail: sgt@glass.demon.co.uk Website: www.sgt.org
MEMBERSHIP:
Honorary Fellows (HonFSGT): Are elected in recognition of conspicuous service to the Society or distinguished contributions to knowledge in Glass Technology. The number of Honorary Fellows is limited, at any one time, to 12.
Fellows (FSGT): Are elected, having rendered special service to the Society and having been members for at least 5 yrs. The other requirements for Fellowship are: (i) a degree or other qualifications acceptable to the Society, (ii) having been engaged in the Glass or an allied industry or in a technical institution associated with Glass for a period of at least 7 yrs, (iii) either having made a noteworthy contribution to knowledge in some branch of Glass Technology or attained a position of responsibility in the industry or in a teaching institution coupled with positive and adequate service to the Council through one of the Committees.
Ordinary Member: A person interested in the objects of the Society.

University Qualifications
The following universities offer qualifications in Glass Technology and related subjects. Full details may be found in Part 4, under the entry for the appropriate university.

FIRST DEGREES AWARDED BY UNIVERSITIES
Bucks. Coll.; De Montfort, Leicester; Sheffield; Wales (Swansea Institute of Higher Education); Wolverhampton

HIGHER DEGREES AWARDED BY UNIVERSITIES
Royal College of Art; Staffordshire; Sunderland; Surrey Institute

DIPLOMAS AWARDED BY UNIVERSITIES
Central England; Wales (Swansea Institute of Higher Education)

CERTIFICATES AWARDED BY UNIVERSITIES
Central England

National Certificates and Diplomas

BTEC National Certificates/Diplomas: Design (Architectural Stained Glass); Science (Glass Component Technology)
BTEC Higher National Certificates/Diplomas: Design (Architectural Stained Glass)

NVQs

Level 1: Glass Processing; Scientific Glass Product Fabrication
Level 2: Glass Batch Processing Operations; Glass Forming Operations; Glass Melting Operations; Glass Processing; Production Support Operations – Glass (Cold End Operations); Scientific Glass Product Fabrication
Level 3: Glass Decorating; Glass Manufacturing Processes and Production Operations; Scientific Glass Product Fabrication

SVQs

Level 1: Construction: Glazing
Level 2: Construction: Glazing
Level 3: Construction: Glazing

Useful Addresses

Glass Qualifications Authority, BGMC Building, Northumberland Road, Sheffield S10 2UA Tel: 0114 266 1494 Fax: 0114 266 0738

HAIRDRESSING

Membership of Professional Institutions and Associations

HAIRDRESSING AND BEAUTY INDUSTRY AUTHORITY (HABIA)

Fraser House, Netherhall Road, Doncaster DN1 2PH Tel: 01302 380000 Fax: 01302 380028
e-mail: enquiries@habia.org Website: www.habia.org
HABIA is recognised by the Government as the National Training Organisation for the hairdressing and beauty therapy industries in the UK. Established in 1997, it incorporates the Hairdressing Training Board (HTB), the Beauty Industry Authority (BIA) and HTB Scotland. It is responsible for improving upon the already high , professional standing of the British hairdressing and beauty industries through the development of high quality standards tailored to the present and future needs of employers. The National Occupation Standards for hairdressing and beauty that HABIA develops form the basis for the National Vocational Qualifications (NVQs) and Scottish Vocational Qualifications (SVQs).HABIA develops learning programmes for hairdressing and beauty therapy, ranging from guidance for dyslexic hairdressing students and Modern Apprenticeship frameworks to the latest in management practice for salon owners. It researches and communicates industry training needs and works with awarding bodies to design qualifications for delivery in over 700 hairdressing and beauty schools. HABIA also has partners in Italy, Spain and the USA, and welcomes other countries to participate. Assessment for the following S/NVQ qualifications is only available through approved assessment centres, which are eligible to be HABIA Member Schools.
Level 1: Assesses skills needed to assist salon staff (hairdressing only)
Level 2: Covers basic skills required to be a competent junior hairdresser or beauty therapist
Level 3: Expands on technical skills needed at Level 2 and reflects responsibilities undertaken by senior salon staff
Level 4: Accredits competencies demonstrated in managing a salon.

THE INCORPORATED GUILD OF HAIRDRESSERS, WIGMAKERS AND PERFUMERS

Unit 1E Redbrook Business Park, Wilthorpe Road, Barnsley S75 1JN

National Diploma of Hairdressing Ladies and Men's (formerly known as the **General Certificate in Ladies and Men's Hairdressing**): Awarded by the Guild of Hairdressers. The qualification is open to all hairdressers and to those in training who have completed 85% of any course recognised by the Examination Council or have certification by the Hairdressing Training Board (until certification is in operation those completing a 2 yr NVQ Course may take this exam). It is not confined to Guild Members. Holders of the Certificate are accepted by the Hairdressing Council for admission as registered hairdressers. The Diploma will be awarded to all successful candidates who obtain 60% or more of the maximum marks in each section, those candidates who show a high standard throughout the whole exam and gain more than 70% in each section will receive a 'Credit' or more than 80% in each section will receive an 'Honours' Diploma. The exam includes practical tests.

University Qualifications

The following universities offer qualifications in Hairdressing and related subjects. Full details may be found in Part 4, under the entry for the appropriate university.

DIPLOMAS AWARDED BY UNIVERSITIES

London Institute (London College of Fashion)

NVQs

Level 1: Hairdressing
Level 2: Hairdressing
Level 3: Hairdressing

SVQs

Level 1: Hairdressing
Level 2: Hairdressing
Level 3: Hairdressing

City & Guilds

3013 Wigmaking

Other Vocational Awarding Bodies

ABC: Hairdressing (Science and Design)

Useful Addresses

Hairdressing and Beauty Industry Authority, Second Floor, Fraser House, Netherhall Road, Doncaster DN1 2PH Tel: 01302 380000, Fax: 01302 380028

HEALTH AND HEALTH SERVICES

Membership of Professional Institutions and Associations

BRITISH INSTITUTE OF OCCUPATIONAL HYGIENISTS

Suite 2, Georgian House, Great Northern Road, Derby DE1 1LT Tel: 01332 298087 Fax: 01332 298099

AWARDS:
Modules in specified aspects of Occupational Hygiene

Certificate of Operational Competence in Comprehensive Occupational Hygiene (CertOccHyg)

Diploma of Professional Competence in Comprehensive Occupational Hygiene (DipOccHyg)
Examinations for the Modules are open to candidates who meet stated minimum educational requirements or who attend a course in the subject. Candidates for Certificate and Diploma awards are required to produce evidence of having been engaged in the practice of occupational hygiene at an appropriate level, and over an appropriate range of activity, for a specified time before they can be considered for an award. Exams for these two awards are designed to assess the candidate's ability to practise at the appropriate level and are therefore different from each other in scope. Each exam consists of a written exam and an oral exam. The written exam may be taken before the specified period of time has elapsed, but the award of competency will not be given until the oral exam has also been passed.

CHARTERED INSTITUTE OF ENVIRONMENTAL HEALTH

Chadwick Court, Hatfields, London SE1 8DJ Tel: 020 7928 6006 Fax: 020 7928 0353
e-mail: education@cieh.org.uk Website: www.cieh.org.uk
The Institute is a chartered professional and educational body dedicated to the promotion of environmental health.

MEMBERSHIP:
Corporate membership: Full membership is open only to persons who are qualified for appointment as environmental health officers in England, Wales and Northern Ireland and who have passed an assessment of professional competence.
Graduate membership: For persons who hold a Diploma in Environmental Health, or the Certificate of Registration of the Environmental Health Officers Registration Board.
Affiliate membership: For persons working in the field of Environmental Health.
Associate membership: For graduates working in the field of Environmental Health.
EXAMINATIONS:
The Certificate of Registration of the Environmental Health Officers Registration Board is awarded to persons who successfully complete a degree or MSc course in Environmental Health which is approved by the Institute, and complete a 12 mth period of assessed practical training during the course, or a 1 yr period of assessed work experience at the end of the course and the CIEH professional examinations. The Diploma in Environmental Health is no longer offered. Persons who hold the Certificate of Registration, or the Diploma, are considered to be fully qualified to practice as Environmental Health Officers. The Assessment of Professional Competence (APC) may be taken by fully qualified environmental health officers who have at least 2 yrs' post-qualification experience and who have been graduate members of the Institute for at least a yr. The APC is a test of professional skills, not technical knowledge. The Royal Environmental Health Institute of Scotland (q.v.) administers the qualification of environmental health officers in Scotland.

INSTITUTE OF HEALTH PROMOTION AND EDUCATION

c/o Prof A.S. Blinkhorn, Dept Oral Health & Development, University Dental Hospital, Higher Cambridge Street, Manchester M15 6FH Tel: 0161 275 6610 Fax: 0161 275 6610 Website: www.iphe.org.uk
MEMBERSHIP:
Fellows: Persons with appropriate qualifications who in the opinion of the Council have made a major contribution to the practice or development of Health Education and Health Promotion through their work for the Institute.
Members: Persons employed FT in Health Education and/or Health Promotion who hold a recognised professional qualification or whose experience satisfies the Council that they understand the principles of health education and are competent to undertake its practice; or Associate members of 5 yrs' standing who satisfy the Council that they are competent to undertake the practice of Health Education and Health Promotion.
Associate Members: Persons who hold a professional qualification in an appropriate field and who devote part of their time to Health Education and/or Health Promotion work.
Corporate Members: Organisations or groups engaged in or associated with work in Health

Education and/or Health Promotion.

Other classes of Membership: Honorary Life Member; Student Member; Journal Subscriber.

INSTITUTE OF HEALTH RECORD INFORMATION AND MANAGEMENT (UK)

115 Willoughby Road, Boston, Lincolnshire PE21 9HR Tel: 01205 368870

MEMBERSHIP:

Fellow FHRIM: A distinction awarded by the Association to those Associates who have made a significant contribution within the Health Records field.

Associate AHRIM: Members holding the full professional qualification.

Certified Member CHRIM: First Level professional qualification, for those who have passed the certificate exam, acknowledged by the letters CHRIM

Licentiate: A class of membership open to affiliates after 2 yrs' membership giving the option to take an extended role in the Association at local level.

Students: A class of membership for those wishing to take the Association's professional exams.

Affiliate: Open to those not wishing to study for a professional qualification but wishing to belong to a professional organisation.

EXAMINATIONS:

Certificate Exam: Must be registered students of the Association and have GCSE passes at grades A-C or equivalent in at least 5 subjects.

Exemptions: Registered Students who have passed recognised alternative exams may apply for exemption from the Certificate Exam.

Diploma Award: Must have passed the Certificate Exam or hold an equivalent qualification and have GCSE passes at grades A-C in 5 subjects.

National Clinical Coding Qualification: Designed to encourage the development of accurate disease and therapeutic coding and consistency of quality and practice throughout the UK. Holders of this qualification become Accredited Clinical Coders (ACC).

Certificate of Technical Competence: A work place assessment of competence of the individual (Open to non-members).

Certificate of Technical Competence at Supervisory Level: A work based assessment for supervisors (Open to non-members).

THE INSTITUTE OF HEALTHCARE MANAGEMENT

7-10 Chandos Street, London W1M 9DE Tel: 020 7460 7654 Fax: 020 7460 7655 e-mail: enquiries@ihm.org.uk Website: www.ihm.org.uk

MEMBERSHIP:

Full Membership (MIHM): Open to persons who have 2 yrs' healthcare management experience, or 5 yrs' senior management experience outside of the health sector and a recognised professional or managerial qualification or demonstrable relevant experiential learning.

Associate Membership: Open to persons who do not yet satisfy all the criteria for full membership. Further information on membership benefits and qualifications are available from the Membership and Education Departments at the Institute.

THE ROYAL ENVIRONMENTAL HEALTH INSTITUTE OF SCOTLAND

3 Manor Place, Edinburgh EH3 7DH Tel: 0131 225 6999 Fax: 0131 225 3993 e-mail: rehis@rehis.org.uk Website: www.rehis.org

Member: Membership of the Institute is open to those holding appropriate qualifications. Associate membership is available to others who have an interest in the objectives of the Institute.

Environmental Health Officer (EHO) Training in Scotland: The qualification for appointment as an EHO in Scotland is the Institute's Diploma in Environmental Health. Qualified EHOs from other countries may be accepted by the Institute as equivalent. Candidates for the Diploma must be in possession of a BSc (Hons) in Environmental Health from Edinburgh or Strathclyde Universities. Each University has its own specific entry requirements. In addition candidates must complete an approved course of 48 wks practical training with a local authority. This training, which is monitored by the Institute, can be carried out during the university holiday periods or end-on after completing the Degree.

Diplomas in the Inspection of Red Meat, White Meat and Other Foods: Candidates for these qualifications must complete an approved course of training with Glasgow College of Food Technology in conjunction with Glasgow University Veterinary Department. Each applicant must satisfy the entrance qualifications of the College and the Meat Hygiene Service. In addition each candidate must complete 200 hrs practical training under the supervision of the Meat Hygiene Service. Contact: Tom Bell, Director of Professional Development.

THE ROYAL INSTITUTE OF PUBLIC HEALTH AND HYGIENE

28 Portland Place, London W1N 4DE Tel: 020 7580 2731 Fax: 020 7580 6157
e-mail: info@riphh.org.uk Website: www.riphh.org.uk
The Royal Institute of Public Health & Hygiene is an independent organisation promoting the advancement of public health and hygiene through education and training, information and quality testing. The Royal Institute runs courses and symposia on topical health issues and is the awarding body for recognised qualifications in Food Safety, Nutrition, Salon Hygiene and Anatomical Pathology Technology.

MEMBERSHIP:
The Royal Institute has an international membership representing a cross-section of health professionals and hygiene specialists whose work involves the protection and improvement of the public health.
For full criteria and further information about membership contact the Royal Institute's Membership Department.

QUALIFICATIONS:
The Royal Institute has over 40 yrs' experience as an awarding body, offering a portfolio of qualifications which are directly relevant to the workplace and is acknowledged by the UK Government and the food industry as one of five organisations providing appropriate standards for training in food hygiene and safety. Nearly 70,000 candidates each yr take Royal Institute or Royal Institute accredited qualifications in **Food Hygiene and Safety, HACCP Principles, Nutrition and Health, Salon Hygiene (Hairdressing and Beauty Therapy) and Anatomical Pathology Technology**.
Further information on the Royal Institute's qualifications and registered training centres is available from the Royal Institute's Examinations Department.

THE ROYAL SOCIETY FOR THE PROMOTION OF HEALTH

38A St George's Drive, London SW1V 4BH Tel: 020 7630 0121 Fax: 020 7976 6847
e-mail: rshealth@rshealth.org.uk Website: www.rsph.org.uk
The Royal Society for the Promotion of Health acts to promote the health of the population through the provision of information to the public, professions and government. As an awarding body it offers qualifications in Food Hygiene (including Meat Inspection and HACCP), Health and Safety, Nutrition, Pest Control, Environmental Protection, Health Promotion and Counselling. Members of the Society, from a wide variety of professions and occupations, participate in a growing regional branch network, and the work of policy advisory groups. They benefit from a lively journal, a full conference programme, membership benefits and use of the designation Fellow/Member/Associate Member of the Royal Society for the Promotion of Health (FRSH, MRSH, AMRSH).

University Qualifications

The following universities offer qualifications in Health and Health Services and related subjects. Full details may be found in Part 4, under the entry for the appropriate university.

FIRST DEGREES AWARDED BY UNIVERSITIES

Aberdeen; Abertay, Dundee; Anglia; Anglia (City College, Norwich); Anglia (Colchester Institute); Barnsley; Bath Spa; Birmingham (The University of Birmingham, Westhill); Bournemouth; Bradford (Bradford & Ilkley Community College); Brighton; Bristol; Brunel; Bucks. Coll.; Central England; Central Lancashire; Cheltenham & Gloucester; Coventry; De Montfort, Leicester; Derby; Durham; Durham (New College Durham); East London; Glamorgan; Glasgow; Glasgow Caledonian; Greenwich; Huddersfield; Kent (Canterbury Christ Church University College);

Leeds (Leeds, Trinity & All Saints); Leeds Metropolitan; Lincolnshire (Lincoln University Campus); Liverpool; Liverpool (Chester College of H.E.); Liverpool (Liverpool Hope University College); Liverpool John Moores; London (King's College London); London (University College (UCL)); Luton; Manchester Metropolitan.; Middlesex; Napier; North London; Northampton; Northumbria; Nottingham Trent; OU (NESCOT); Oxford Brookes; Paisley; Plymouth; Portsmouth; Queen Margaret; Reading; Salford; Southampton; Southampton (Chichester Institute of Higher Education); Southampton (University of Southampton New College); St Martin; Staffordshire; Strathclyde; Sunderland; Sunderland (City of Sunderland College); Sunderland (Matthew Boulton College of Further & Higher Education); Surrey (University of Surrey Roehampton); Teesside; Ulster; Wales (College of Medicine); Wales (North East Wales Institute); Wales (Swansea Institute of Higher Education); Wales (University of Wales Institute, Cardiff); Wales (University of Wales, Bangor); Wolverhampton; Worcester; York

HIGHER DEGREES AWARDED BY UNIVERSITIES

Aberdeen; Abertay, Dundee; Anglia; Anglia (Colchester Institute); Bath; Bath Spa; Belfast; Birmingham; Bournemouth; Bradford; Brighton; Bristol; Brunel; Central England; Central Lancashire; Cheltenham & Gloucester; City; Coventry; De Montfort, Leicester; Derby; Dundee; Durham; East Anglia; East London; Edinburgh; Essex; Exeter; Exeter (St Loye's School of Health Studies); Exeter (The College of St Mark & St John); Glamorgan; Glasgow; Glasgow Caledonian; Hertfordshire; Huddersfield; Hull; Keele; Kent; Lancaster; Leeds; Leeds Metropolitan; Liverpool; Liverpool (Chester College of H.E.); Liverpool (Liverpool Hope University College); Liverpool John Moores; London (Imperial College of Science, Technology & Medicine); London (Institute of Education); London (King's College London); London (London School of Economics & Political Science); London (Queen Mary & Westfield College (incorporating St Bartholomew's and the Royal London School of Medicine & Dentistry)); London (University College (UCL)); Loughborough; Luton; Manchester; Manchester Metropolitan.; Middlesex; Napier; Newcastle; Northampton; Nottingham; Nottingham Trent (Southampton Institute); Oxford; Oxford Brookes; Paisley; Plymouth; Portsmouth; Reading; Salford; Sheffield; Sheffield Hallam; South Bank; Southampton; Southampton (Chichester Institute of Higher Education); Southampton (King Alfred's College); St Andrews; St Martin; Staffordshire; Stirling; Sunderland; Surrey; Surrey (University of Surrey Roehampton); Ulster; Wales (College of Medicine); Wales (University of Wales College, Newport); Wales (University of Wales Institute, Cardiff); Wales (University of Wales, Aberystwyth); Wales (University of Wales, Bangor); Wales (University of Wales, Swansea); Warwick; Westminster; Wolverhampton; York

DIPLOMAS AWARDED BY UNIVERSITIES

Aberdeen; Anglia (Colchester Institute); Barnsley; Bath Spa; Belfast; Birmingham; Blackburn; Bournemouth; Bradford; Brighton; Bristol; Bucks. Coll.; Cambridge; Central England; Cheltenham & Gloucester; City; De Montfort, Leicester; Dundee; Durham; Edinburgh; Exeter; Glamorgan; Greenwich; Hertfordshire; Hull; Keele; Lancaster; Leeds; Leeds Metropolitan; Lincolnshire (Grimsby College); Lincolnshire (Hull College); Liverpool (Chester College of H.E.); Liverpool (Liverpool Hope University College); London (Imperial College of Science, Technology & Medicine); London (King's College London); London (Queen Mary & Westfield College (incorporating St Bartholomew's and the Royal London School of Medicine & Dentistry)); London (University College (UCL)); London Institute (London College of Fashion); Loughborough; Luton; Manchester; Middlesex; Napier; Newcastle; Nottingham Trent; Oxford; Oxford Brookes; Paisley; Plymouth; Reading; Salford; South Bank; Southampton (Chichester Institute of Higher Education); St Andrews; St Martin; Sunderland; Surrey (University of Surrey Roehampton); Ulster; Wales (College of Medicine); Wales (University of Wales Institute, Cardiff); Warwick; Westminster; Wolverhampton; Worcester; York

CERTIFICATES AWARDED BY UNIVERSITIES

Aberdeen; Anglia (City College, Norwich); Barnsley; Birmingham; Brighton; Central England; Central Lancashire; Cheltenham & Gloucester; City; De Montfort, Leicester; Dundee; Durham; Exeter; Glamorgan; Hull; Leeds; Lincolnshire (Hull College); Liverpool (Chester College of H.E.); Liverpool John Moores; London (King's College London); London (Queen Mary & Westfield College (incorporating St Bartholomew's and the Royal London School of Medicine & Dentistry));

Loughborough; Northampton; OU (Northern College of Education); Oxford; Paisley; Salford; South Bank; St Martin; Stirling; Surrey (University of Surrey Roehampton); Wales (College of Medicine); Wales (University of Wales, Bangor); Wolverhampton; Worcester

OTHER COURSES AWARDED BY UNIVERSITIES
Leeds Metropolitan; Sunderland (City of Sunderland College)

National Certificates and Diplomas

BTEC National Certificates/Diplomas: Environmental Health Studies; Science (Health Studies)
BTEC Higher National Qualifications are offered in: Environmental Health Studies; Science (Health Studies)
Scotland
SQA HNC: Health & Fitness; Health Care
SQA HND: Health & Fitness

NVQs

Level 2: Blood Donor Support; Health Care – Technical Cardiology; Physiological Measurement (Technical Cardiology)
Level 3: Diagnostic and Therapeutic Support; Dialysis Support; Health Care – Technical Cardiology; Health Care Physiological Measurement – Audiology; Health Care – Physiological Measurement – Neurophysiology; Health Care Physiological Measurement – Respiratory; Physiological Measurement (Audiology); Physiological Measurement (Neurophysiology); Physiological (Respiratory); Physiological Measurement (Technical Cardiology)

GNVQs

3724 Health and Social Care

Other Vocational Awarding Bodies

ABC: Community and Health Care

HOME ECONOMICS

Membership of Professional Institutions and Associations

INSTITUTE OF CONSUMER SCIENCES INCORPORATING HOME ECONOMICS
21 Portland Place, London W1B 1PY Tel: 020 7436 5677 Fax: 020 7436 5677 e-mail: icsc@btclick.com
CORPORATE MEMBERSHIP:
Corporate Membership (MICSc): You have full voting powers and may use the letters MICSc after your name. You are eligible if: (1) you have a minimum of 3 yrs' work experience in the field of consumer sciences, home economics and allied technologies plus a first degree or its equivalent at Ordinary or Honours level in a title recognised for membership by the Institute; (2) you have a minimum of 4 yrs' work experience plus a BTEC Higher National Diploma/Certificate or SQA or their equivalent in a title recognised for membership by the Institute, or degrees/diplomas recognised for corporate membership in other disciplines where the holder is currently employed within the field of home economics and allied technologies including social work; (3) you are in a position of responsibility or have extensive freelance/other experience within consumer sciences allied employment. You may not have a particular consumer science or home economics qualification but may be offered membership at the discretion of the Standards Board or those it delegates.

NON-CORPORATE MEMBERSHIP:
Associate (AICSc): You are a holder of a degree or a HND or their equivalent in the subject discipline or a related accepted discipline. If you are a registered post graduate research student you will probably be eligible for associate membership. AICSc awarded for members with a degree or equivalent working towards membership.
Professional Affiliate: You are ineligible for any other grade of membership but are involved in appropriate activities relating to the subject discipline.
Student: You are a full time student on any course in the UK or overseas which could lead directly to any qualification accepted for Associate Membership.
Corporate Forum: Organisations which educate, or employ consumer scientists, or have a declared interest in the theory and practice of consumer science.

DEGREES:
Courses related to the field of Consumer Sciences and Home Economics are widely available, and include the following: consumer studies; food studies; textiles and clothing; design; development; manufacturing; psychology; marketing and business studies; consumer education and social policy. Degree courses also exist which allow greater specialisation in particular areas such as: food science; food technology; food and nutrition; food marketing management; textiles; textile design; fashion management; clothing design and manufacture; hotel management; catering management; hospitality management; retail management; retail design management and food retail management. There are degree courses in consumer protection/ consumer and trading standards, which can lead to employment as a trading standards officer or to related work in consumer advice. Postgraduate qualifications include: diplomas and higher degrees in such subjects as food technology, textile technology and marketing; professional qualifications for social workers and dieticians; teaching qualifications BEd in Design and Technology or a PGCE (postgraduate certificate in education).

University Qualifications

The following universities offer qualifications in Home Economics and related subjects. Full details may be found in Part 4, under the entry for the appropriate university.

FIRST DEGREES AWARDED BY UNIVERSITIES
Liverpool John Moores

CERTIFICATES AWARDED BY UNIVERSITIES
Wales (University of Wales Institute, Cardiff)

National Certificates and Diplomas

BTEC National Certificates/Diplomas: Home Economics; Home Economics (Food and Consumer Studies)
BTEC Higher National Certificates/Diplomas: Home Economics; Home Economics (Applied Consumer Studies)
Scotland
SQA HNC: Home Economics
SQA HND: Home Economics

City & Guilds
3320 Cookery Certificates; 3330 Preliminary Cookery

Other Vocational Awarding Bodies
Modern Cookery; Vegetarian Wholefood Cookery

HORSES AND HORSE RIDING

Membership of Professional Institutions and Associations

THE BRITISH HORSE SOCIETY

Stoneleigh Deer Park, Stareton, Kenilworth, Warwickshire CV8 2XZ Tel: 01926 707700
Fax: 01926 707800 e-mail: enquiry@bhs.org.uk Website: www.bhs.org.uk
All exams are practical and oral. The Certificates are officially recognised within the UK and internationally.

HORSE KNOWLEDGE AND RIDING EXAMINATIONS:
Minimum age is 16 yrs. Candidates are required to take these exams in progression from Stage I upwards. *Riding* and *Care* sections of the Stages exams may be taken separately.

RIDING INSTRUCTORS:
Fellowship of the British Horse Society (FBHS): Open to Gold BHS members, minimum age 25, open to holders of the BHSI certificate. The exam covers Equitation, Training the Horse, and ability in instructing over a very broad field at an advanced level **(International Level 4)**.
Instructor's Certificate (BHSI): Must be Gold BHS members, min age 22. Candidates must pass the BHS Stable Manager's certificate and the Equitation and Teaching section **(International Level 3)**.
Intermediate Instructor's Certificate (BHSII): Must be Gold members of the BHS, min age 20 yrs. Candidates must pass the Riding and Care sections of Stage 4 and Intermediate Teaching Test to obtain the Intermediate Instructor's certificate. They must also hold a current Health & Safety First Aid at Work Certificate **(International Level 2)**.
Assistant Instructor's Certificate (BHSAI): Must be Gold members of the BHS and have reached the age of 17 yrs 6 mths. Candidates under the age of 18 yrs must hold 4 GCSEs, A, B or C (or equiv), 1 of which must be English. Candidates passing the Stage 2 and Preliminary Teaching Test have been awarded the Preliminary Teacher's Certificate. They must log 500 hrs of teaching experience and also hold a current Health & Safety First Aid at Work Certificate and complete the Stage 3 to gain the BHSAI certificate **(International Level 1)**.

STABLE MANAGERS:
BHS Groom's Certificate: Open to Gold BHS members who must be at least 17 yrs and hold a minimum of the Horse Knowledge & Care sections of Stages 1 & 2. Holders are qualified to look after horses in general use under supervision.
BHS Intermediate Stable Manager (BHS IntSM): Open to Gold BHS members who must be at least 19 and hold a minimum of the Horse Knowledge & Care sections of Stages 1 & 2 and the Groom's Certificate. Holders are qualified to manage a small to medium yard without supervision.
BHS Stable Manager's Certificate (BHS SM): Open to Gold BHS members, candidates must be at least 22 and hold the Intermediate Stable Manager's Certificate. Holders are qualified to run a large yard of horses including those in competition at higher levels.
BA(Hons) Equine Sports Coaching: Offered in conjunction with University College Worcester, this degree incorporates the BHSI and/or FBHS certificates, plus additional modules, to obtain the degree. The aim is to produce high quality coaches who can apply scientific training and coaching techniques to equestrian sport. Please contact BHS for more details.

EQUESTRIAN TOURISM (B.E.T.):
In conjunction with the Trekking and Riding Societies of Scotland and Wales and the Association of Irish Riding Establishments, the BHS offers qualifications for:
Assistant Ride Leader: Must be 17 and hold the BHS Riding and Road Safety Certificate or S/NVQ Riding on the Road unit and a current Health & Safety First Aid at Work Certificate. An assistant ride leader may work FT or PT and is competent to take a ride of up to 2 hrs' duration or assist a ride leader on longer rides.
Ride Leader: Must be 18 and hold the Assistant Ride Leader Certificate and a current Health & Safety First Aid at Work Certificate. A ride leader is someone who is able to take sole charge of first time or more experienced riders and is also capable of taking charge of a centre for a temporary period not exceeding one mth.

Holiday Riding Centre Manager: Must be over 22 and hold the Ride Leader Certificate *or* have operated a BHS, TRSS, WRTA or AIRE Centre for a minimum of 3 yrs. Holders are qualified to operate a riding holiday centre both from the practical and financial aspects. An expert to whom the others, including tourist organisations, can turn to for advice. The Ride Leader and Holiday Riding Centre Manager Certificates are recognised by FITE (Fédération Internationale de Tourisme Equestre).

S/NVQs: The Society is an awarding body for S/NVQs in the horse industry and currently awards the following: Level One: Horse Care; Level Two: Horse Care; Level Three: Horse Care and Management. These awards are available for those working with riding and working horses, and in studs.

University Qualifications

The following universities offer qualifications in Horses and Horse Riding and related subjects. Full details may be found in Part 4, under the entry for the appropriate university.

FIRST DEGREES AWARDED BY UNIVERSITIES
Bristol; Coventry; De Montfort, Leicester; Essex (Writtle College); Liverpool (Chester College of H.E.); London (Wye College); Northampton; Nottingham Trent; Plymouth; Wales (University of Wales, Aberystwyth); Worcester

HIGHER DEGREES AWARDED BY UNIVERSITIES
Bristol; Essex (Writtle College)

DIPLOMAS AWARDED BY UNIVERSITIES
Brighton; Bucks. Coll.; Coventry; De Montfort, Leicester; Greenwich; Lincolnshire (Bishop Burton College); Northampton; Wales (University of Wales, Bangor); Wolverhampton; Worcester

CERTIFICATES AWARDED BY UNIVERSITIES
Lincolnshire (Bishop Burton College)

OTHER COURSES AWARDED BY UNIVERSITIES
Essex (Writtle College)

National Certificates and Diplomas

BTEC National Certificates/Diplomas: Horse Studies; Horse Studies (Farriery); Horseracing Industry Operations
BTEC Higher National Certificates/Diplomas: Horse Studies; Horse Studies (Technology and Management); Saddlery Technology
Scotland
SQA HNC: Horse Management
SQA HND: Horse Management

NVQs

Level 1: Horse Care
Level 2: Horse Care; Racehorse Care
Level 3: Farriery; Horse Care & Management; Racehorse Care & Management

SVQs

Level 1: Horse Care
Level 2: Horse Care
Level 3: Horse Care & Management

Useful Addresses

The Animal Care and Equine Training Organisation, Second Floor, The Burgess Building, The Green, Stafford ST17 4BL Tel: 01785 227399, Fax: 01785 229015, Website: www.horsecareers.co.uk
The British Horse Society, Stoneleigh Deer Park, Kenilworth, Warwickshire CV8 2XZ Tel: 01926 707700, Fax: 01926 707800

HOUSING

Membership of Professional Institutions and Associations

THE CHARTERED INSTITUTE OF HOUSING
Octavia House, Westwood Way, Coventry CV4 8JP Tel: 024 76694433 Fax: 024 76695110

MEMBERSHIP:

Fellow (FCIH): Must have been employed by a housing organisation for at least 8 yrs, have had **Corporate** Membership of the Institute for at least 7 yrs, and have completed at least 3 yrs **Continuing Professional Development (CPD)** to be eligible. All Fellows have to complete an annual CPD programme. Fellowship denotes an individual who is a senior member of the housing profession.

Corporate Member (MCIH): Denotes that an individual is fully professionally qualified in housing. There are 4 routes: a) The Institute's Professional Qualification (PQ) and Test of Professional Practice (TPP); b) Completion of a course recognised by the Institute plus TPP; c) Direct Final Examination and Interview; d) Special routes giving exemption from some of the requirements for those who meet eligibility criteria. All applicants for Corporate membership should have 2 yrs' experience in housing and be currently employed by a housing organisation.

Honorary Member: Honorary members are individuals elected by the Institute's Council. Honorary membership reflects a long standing commitment and contribution to housing and activities of the Institute.

Affiliate (previously Associate): Available to anyone interested in housing matters, committed to improving housing practice and who has suitable practical knowledge, experience and character.

Associate Member (ACIH): A new grade to give recognition to those who have *either* a) completed the CIH PQ or a fully recognised alternative, but not TPP; *or* b) passed the Direct Final but not yet eligible for Corporate membership due to not having completed 2 yrs of non-Corporate membership.

Housing Practitioner (Cert.CIH): Denotes that an individual has a CIH recognised Housing Qualification (full list available on request) and is currently working in housing.

Students: Anyone who is currently undertaking or is eligible to undertake any housing qualification recognised by the Chartered Institute of Housing.

EXAMINATIONS:

Professional Qualifications: There are 2 routes through the Professional Qualification, non-graduate and graduate. Non-graduates complete a 2 yr Stage 1 followed by a 2 yr Stage 2. Graduates complete a 1 yr Stage 1 and the 2 yr Stage 2. Both graduates and non-graduates are required to take a *Test of Professional Practice (TPP)*. The Professional Qualification is offered on a PT basis at various centres throughout the country. DL versions of the courses are available through UNISON.

Certificated Courses: The Chartered Institute of Housing offers a range of certificated courses at various centres throughout the UK. The courses are as follows: National Certificate in Supported Housing, The Advanced Certificate for Wardens, National Certificate in Caretaking and Concierge Services, National Benefits Certificate, the National Certificate in Tenant Participation. The CIH has now established a distance learning centre which offers the following certificate courses: **National Certificate in Support Housing, National Certificate in Tenant Participation, National Certificate in Housing Management and Maintenance, National Certificate in Travellers Site Management, National Certificate in Leasehold Management, National Certificate in Housing Aid and Advice.**

Institute Recognised Courses: The Institute recognises a number of PT and FT courses which are available at various centres throughout the UK. All individuals are also required to complete the Institute's Test of Professional Practice if they are intending to pursue *Corporate Membership*.

National/Scottish Vocational Qualifications (N/SVQ): N/SVQs Level 2, 3 and 4 in Housing and Special Needs Housing are currently on offer at a number of centres throughout the UK.

University Qualifications

The following universities offer qualifications in Housing and related subjects. Full details may be found in Part 4, under the entry for the appropriate university.

FIRST DEGREES AWARDED BY UNIVERSITIES
Anglia; Central England; Greenwich; Leeds Metropolitan; Liverpool John Moores; Middlesex; Northumbria; Nottingham Trent (Southampton Institute); Salford; Sheffield Hallam; South Bank; Ulster; Wales (University of Wales Institute, Cardiff); Westminster; Wolverhampton

HIGHER DEGREES AWARDED BY UNIVERSITIES
Anglia; Brighton; Bristol; Central England; De Montfort, Leicester; Glasgow; Heriot-Watt; Leeds Metropolitan; Lincolnshire; London (London School of Economics & Political Science); London (University College (UCL)); Middlesex; Newcastle; Oxford Brookes; Sheffield Hallam; South Bank; Stirling; Wales (Cardiff University); Westminster; York

DIPLOMAS AWARDED BY UNIVERSITIES
Birmingham; Bristol; Central England; De Montfort, Leicester; Glasgow; Heriot-Watt (Edinburgh College of Art); Leeds Metropolitan; Lincolnshire; London (London School of Economics & Political Science); Middlesex; Newcastle; Northumbria; Nottingham Trent (Southampton Institute); Oxford Brookes; Stirling; Ulster

CERTIFICATES AWARDED BY UNIVERSITIES
Anglia (City College, Norwich); Central England; De Montfort, Leicester; Glasgow; Lincolnshire; Salford; South Bank; Stirling; Wales (University of Wales Institute, Cardiff); Westminster

POSTGRADUATE DIPLOMAS AWARDED BY UNIVERSITIES
Heriot-Watt

National Certificates and Diplomas
BTEC National Certificates/Diplomas: Housing Studies
BTEC Higher National Certificates/Diplomas: Housing Studies
Scotland
SQA HNC: Housing

NVQs
Level 2: Housing; Special Needs Housing
Level 3: Housing; Special Needs Housing
Level 4: Housing; Special Needs Housing

SVQs
Level 2: Housing
Level 3: Housing
Level 4: Housing

HYPNOTHERAPY

Membership of Professional Institutions and Associations

BRITISH HYPNOTHERAPY ASSOCIATION
67 Upper Berkeley Street, London W1H 7DH Tel: 020 7723 4443
Founded in 1958, the British Hypnotherapy Association is the leader in hypnotherapy with a 40 yr record of quality service to the public. The Association is an organisation of practitioners who have had at least 4 yrs of relevant training and who comply with adequate standards of competence and ethics in hypnotherapy. The practitioners are also trained to use hypno-analysis when appropriate. Their methods are based on the findings from the lifelong follow ups of results which they routinely do with all their patients.

MEMBERSHIP:
Fellows (FBHA): May be elected from among members for important contributions to the advancement of psychotherapy or hypnotherapy from the viewpoint of the patients.

Full Members (MBHA): In addition to having completed the required training, have had at least 5 yrs' of experience as practitioners and have shown a satisfactory standard in the membership exam. Previously published work is accepted for the exam if it conforms to all the requirements.

Associates (ABHA): Have completed adequate appropriate training in this work (see below).

EXAMINATION:
Full Membership Exam: In the form of a thesis; the minimum length required is 5000 words.

TRAINING:
Training to the standards required by the BHA is offered only by The Psychotherapy Centre. The minimum educational requirement is a university degree or equivalent. Candidates must be psychotherapy patients themselves with a practitioner recommended for this purpose by the Association before admission to the course, insight into oneself being essential for understanding and helping patients. The course can be taken PT or FT – 4 yrs is the minimum length including the therapy. The aim of the course is to produce practitioners fully competent in the treatment of emotional problems, psychogenic disorders and relationship difficulties.

Note: In recent yrs there has been a rapidly increasing problem of people claiming, especially in hypnotherapy, qualifications or memberships which they don't have. It's advisable for anyone to check with us any claims as to qualifications in hypnotherapy.

INDEXING

Membership of Professional Institutions and Associations

SOCIETY OF INDEXERS

Globe Centre, Penistone Road, Sheffield S6 3AE Tel: 0114 281 3060 Fax: 0114 281 3061
e-mail: admin@socind.demon.co.uk Website: www.socind.demon.co.uk

MEMBERSHIP:
Ordinary Membership: Is open to all individuals and institutions concerned with indexing. To acquire recognition as qualified indexers, individual members may apply for admission to the Society's Register of Indexers. Each applicant's theoretical knowledge and practical technique and experience are scrutinised by assessors; if they are adjudged to conform with standards laid down by the Society, the applicant's admission to the Register is approved, and the member is designated a **Registered Indexer**.

TRAINING:
Society of Indexers 'Training in Indexing': Complete indexing course based on the principle of open learning and consisting of a set of 5 training manuals, tutorial support and tests. Successful completion of 5 formal tests will entitle a member of the Society to the status of Accredited Indexer. The course (but not the tests) may be taken by non-members. Accredited Indexers are encouraged to acquire the status of Registration.

INDUSTRIAL SAFETY

HM INSPECTORATE OF HEALTH AND SAFETY

Information Centre, Broad Lane, Sheffield S3 7HQ Tel: 0114 289 2000 Fax: 0114 289 2333

An inspector's role is to ensure the maintenance and improvement of health and safety standards in the workplace. It is a job which has a positive impact on society and where you are promoting the well being of the working population and the public who could be affected by work activities. HSE inspects a variety of workplaces, from factories, farms and construction sites to fairgrounds, hospitals and universities. You will encounter challenging conditions such as noise, fumes, dust, heat and cold. Inspection involves examining all aspects of the workplace including areas at height, with restricted access and outside. You will also be talking to a range of people and need to show a sensitivity to your audience. Once at a site, you will be applying powers of observation, both sensory and investigative, to identify and discover any deviations from good work practice or the law. Decisions need to be taken to determine what course of action is appropriate should a risk be identified. Although inspectors work on their own and are on the move much of the time, they have full support of their team and the specialist knowledge and expertise of HSE is available for reference and advice.

Training

All trainee inspectors of Health and Safety receive an initial basic training over the first two yrs. During this time your work will be managed to ensure that, through on-the-job training and development provided by experienced colleagues, you gain knowledge of a wide range of industry and types of organisation. Your practical experience gained through site visits, will be underpinned by formal training towards the Post Graduate Diploma in Occupational Health and Safety and the Level 4 NVQ in Health and Safety Regulation and will give you an outstanding opportunity for development.

Recruitment

Our inspectors come from a variety of backgrounds. Normally we expect applicants to have a degree or equivalent qualification. Exceptionally, we will consider applications from those without a degree or equivalent who can demonstrate clearly the intellectual qualities required. In addition, all applicants will need to offer at least two yrs work experience, which could be either paid or voluntary employment. The work of an inspector involves considerable travel, including to remote locations, with equipment and responding to incidents outside normal working hrs. Therefore, you must have a full and valid driving licence which is recognised in the UK before you can apply. Finally, if you are to make the most of the opportunities HSE has to offer, you should be prepared to move both now and in the future. If you would like to know more, ring HSE's PERSONNEL HELPLINE on Tel: 0151-951 3366.

MINING QUALIFICATIONS BOARD (MQB)

Safety Policy Directorate, Rose Court, 2 Southwark Bridge, London SE1 9HS Tel: 020 7717 6301 Fax: 020 7717 6908 e-mail: john.freeman@hse.gov.uk Website: www.open.gov.uk/hse/spdmg.htm The HSE MQB's First and Second Class Certificate of Competency are the certificates of qualification required under the Management and Administration of Safety and Health at Mines Regulations 1993 (MASHAM) for appointment respectively as manager and under-manager in mines of coal, shale and fireclay in the UK. To qualify for the First Class Certificate, applicants must hold an approved degree or HND in Mining Engineering or dual BTEC HND Mining/Electrical or Mining/Mechanical. The same applies to the Second Class Certificate although in this case the HNC is also accepted. Applicants for both certificates must also be able to demonstrate that they have gained appropriate practical experience and are required to pass the HSE/MQB legislation exam. The HSE also awards certificates to Mining Mechanical and Mining Electrical Engineers and Mechanics and Electricians Class I and Class II. Applicants for these certificates must normally possess an approved academic qualification and must have the necessary practical experience. Engineers are also required to pass the MQB's legislation exam. [Note: Under the MASHAM regulations there is also an Electricians Qualification and Mechanic's Qualification for persons trained in work underground who follow approved apprenticeship schemes.] Other certificates granted are

(1) Mines Surveyor: For those with HNC or BTEC HND in Mining Surveying/Minerals Resource Management or have passed the intermediate exam of the RICS in the mining surveying section *and* a pass in the MQB practical examination

(2) Deputy's: Applicants for (1) and (2) must have the necessary practical experience. Award of all qualifications is governed by the Mining Qualifications Board Rules.

THE NATIONAL EXAMINATION BOARD IN OCCUPATIONAL SAFETY AND HEALTH (NEBOSH)

Dominus Way, Meridian Business Park, Leicester LE3 2QW Tel: 0116 263 4700 Fax: 0116 282 4000 e-mail: info@nebosh.org.uk Website: www.nebosh.org.uk

The two-part NEBOSH National Diploma: Covers at least the underpinning knowledge for N/SVQ 3 (NEBOSH Diploma Part 1) and N/SVQ 4 (NEBOSH Diploma Part 2) in Occupational Health and Safety Practice. Part 1 requires approximately 170 hrs' tuition and Part 2 about 190 hrs, both plus significant private study. Component modules are: (i) the management of risk; (ii) legal and organisational factors; (iii) the workplace; (iv) work equipment; and (v) agents. In Part 1 only there is an additional module on communication and training skills. Assessment is by 5 assignments and a final examination for each Part. The Diploma is professional-level qualification allowing, with relevant experience, membership of the Institution of Occupational Safety and Health.

The NEBOSH Specialist Diploma in Environment Management: Designed to equip people who have an appropriate professional-level qualification to undertake responsibilities in relation to the risks of damage to the environment posed by work activities. Assessment comprises one written paper and a workplace-based project (an environmental audit).

The NEBOSH National General Certificate: An examined basic qualification for people who are not safety specialists but who have responsibilities in health and safety at work, such as managers, supervisors and employee representatives. The study duration is 80-100 hrs and there are no formal entry qualifications. Assessment comprises 2 written papers and a practical assessment (a health and safety inspection and report).

The NEBOSH National Certificate in Construction Safety and Health: Available for those working in the construction sector. Assessment is as for the National General Certificate with an additional construction paper. Syllabuses, guides for students and lists of courses leading to NEBOSH qualifications may be obtained on request from the Board's office (www.nebosh.org.uk). Courses leading to most NEBOSH awards are widely available by PT, FT block release, and distance/open learning modes.

Membership of Professional Institutions and Associations

BRITISH SAFETY COUNCIL

70 Chancellors Road, London W6 9RS Tel: 020 8741 1231 Fax: 020 8741 4555
e-mail: mail@britsafe.org Website: www.britishsafetycouncil.org
The British Safety Council is an internationally recognised organisation in the field of health and safety representing more than 12,000 companies covering the whole spectrum of commerce and industry. It conducts 30,000 delegate days of training a yr and offers the following qualifications for those who are, or aspire to being, professional health, safety and environmental practitioners.

QUALIFICATIONS:
Diploma in Safety Management (DipSM): An examined international qualification, covering the key areas of competence in Risk Assessment and Risk Management; Communications (at all levels); Occupational Health (including Workplace Wellness programmes); Total Loss Control Techniques (Case Studies); Developing a Safety Culture; Health and Safety Legislation (including EU-based regulations). The exam comprises 450 multi-choice questions, covering all aspects, and can be taken after successfully completing 5 distinct modules of training, together with 300 hrs additional study. An alternative, extended course of training is designed for overseas students. Exams are conducted throughout the yr at various centres, and Diploma holders can use the designatory letters **DipSM**. The Diploma is presented at the Houses of Parliament or other prestigious London venues. The qualification is recognised by the HSE as appropriate for a competent person. The DipSM provides underpinning knowledge for the mandatory units for the NVQ in Occupational Health and Safety Practice. The Diploma is accepted, with relevant experience, for admission to the International Institute of Risk and Safety Management as a full member, and allows delegates to use the designatory letters **MIIRSM**. Entry may also be granted by attaining NVQ Level 3 or 4 in OHSP No 3044.

Diploma in Environmental Management (DipEM): This is a three-part course covering Regulatory Framework; Environmental Assessments & Audits; Emissions to Air, Water & Land; Waste Management & Minimisation; Environmental Monitoring; Treatment Systems, Introducing ISO 1400 series; Project Management. Holders are eligible for Associate Membership of the Institute of Environmental Management. *Certificate in Safety Management (CSM):* An examined qualification for those who are coming into Occupational Health and Safety for the first time, managers and supervisors with safety responsibilities, and safety representatives. The exam comprises a paper of 200 or more multi-choice questions covering the fundamentals of safety management. The Certificate is accepted by the International Institute of Risk and Safety Management for Associate Members Grade, and entitles the person to the designatory letters **AIIRSM**. The Council is an approved NVQ centre.

Contact for Courses: Mhorag Gilchrist, Training Sales Manager, Tel: 020 8600 5525
Contact for Entry: Fiona Harcombe, Press and PR Manager, Tel: 020 8600 5569

THE INSTITUTION OF OCCUPATIONAL SAFETY AND HEALTH

The Grange, Highfield Drive, Wigston, Leicestershire LE18 1NN Tel: 0116 257 3100 Fax: 0116 257 3101 e-mail: membship@iosh.co.uk

CORPORATE MEMBERSHIP:

Fellows (FIOSH): Corporate Members may be elected to this grade if they have been a Corporate Member for a minimum of 5 yrs and have achieved eminence in the field of safety and health, attained a senior position in their work organisation, or carried out original academic or research work.

Member (MIOSH): Corporate Membership may be gained by a combination of relevant academic qualifications such as an accredited degree or diploma in occupational safety and health and a minimum of 3 yrs' professional experience in the field of occupational safety and health. Corporate Members with general health & safety responsibilities, as opposed to specialising in areas such as ergonomics, may apply to become Registered Safety Practitioners (RSPs).

NON-CORPORATE MEMBERSHIP:

Graduate: This grade is granted to persons who meet the academic but not the experience criteria for Corporate Membership.

Technician Safety Practitioner (TechSP): Technician level is open to personnel assisting more highly qualified OSH professionals, or dealing with routine matters in low risk sectors. A TechSP must hold a recognised qualification such as Level 3 of the VQs for OHS Practice.

Affiliate: This grade is open to any other person with an interest in health and safety.

INTERNATIONAL INSTITUTE OF RISK AND SAFETY MANAGEMENT

70 Chancellors Road, London W6 9RS Tel: 020 8600 5537 Fax: 020 8741 1349
e-mail: enquiries@iirsm.org Website: www.iirsm.org
Professional body for health and safety practitioners. Comprehensive range of membership benefits include: designatory letters, free technical and legal helplines, Health and Safety Manager's Newsletter, Safety Management Magazine, certificate and membership card. A non-profit making charity for the advancement of accident prevention.

NEW SYLLABUS:

Fellow (FIIRSM): Awarded by the Board of Governors to persons who have submitted a successful fellowship petition after 5 yrs of membership.

Member (MIIRSM): Open to holders of the British Safety Council Diploma in Safety Management, NVQ Level 3 in Occupational Health & Safety plus 3 yrs' experience, NVQ Level 4 in Occupational Health & Safety, Parts 1 & 2 of the NEBOSH Diploma or a Post-graduate Diploma in Health & Safety.

Associate (AIIRSM): Open to holders of the British Safety Council Certificate in Safety Management, NEBOSH Certificate or Part 1 of the NEBOSH Diploma.

Affiliate: Open to all individuals who have an interest in Health & Safety.

Student: Open to individuals who are studying for recognised safety qualifications.

University Qualifications

The following universities offer qualifications in Industrial Safety and related subjects. Full details may be found in Part 4, under the entry for the appropriate university.

FIRST DEGREES AWARDED BY UNIVERSITIES

Aston; Bradford; Glamorgan; Leeds; Leeds Metropolitan; Middlesex; South Bank; Wolverhampton

HIGHER DEGREES AWARDED BY UNIVERSITIES
Aberdeen; Aston; Bournemouth; Bradford; Brunel; City; Glamorgan; Greenwich; Liverpool John Moores; Loughborough; Manchester; Middlesex; Newcastle; Nottingham; Nottingham Trent; Paisley; Salford; South Bank; Sunderland; Surrey; Ulster

DIPLOMAS AWARDED BY UNIVERSITIES
Aston; Bournemouth; City; Glasgow Caledonian; Leeds Metropolitan; Loughborough; Manchester; Nottingham Trent; Salford; Ulster

CERTIFICATES AWARDED BY UNIVERSITIES
Dundee; Loughborough

POSTGRADUATE DIPLOMAS AWARDED BY UNIVERSITIES
Heriot-Watt

NVQs
Level 3: Safety Services (Offshore)
Level 3: Occupational Health and Safety Practice; Safety Services (Offshore)
Level 4: Occupational Health and Safety Practice; Occupational Health and Safety Regulation

SVQs
Level 2: Safety Services
Level 3: Safety Services (Offshore)

Other Qualifications
The Centre for Hazard and Risk Management (CHARM) at Loughborough University offers a **University Diploma in Occupational Health and Safety Management.** The Diploma award is based on, and assessed by, the course attendance of 5 separate weekly modules, associated course work, 4 exam papers and a project. The programme is intended for those with major health and safety responsibilities who wish to obtain a postgraduate qualification in this field and is also run at Certificate and MSc level. For more information contact Sandy Edwards, the course administrator, on 01509 222158 or e-mail s.p.edwards@lboro.ac.uk.

Other Vocational Awarding Bodies
ABC: Occupational Health and Safety – Practice and Management

INSPECTION, MEASUREMENT AND CONTROL
University Qualifications
The following universities offer qualifications in Inspection, Measurement and Control and related subjects. Full details may be found in Part 4, under the entry for the appropriate university.

FIRST DEGREES AWARDED BY UNIVERSITIES
Anglia; Liverpool; Sheffield; Sheffield Hallam; Strathclyde; UMIST; Wales (University of Wales College, Newport)

HIGHER DEGREES AWARDED BY UNIVERSITIES
Bath; Coventry; Glasgow Caledonian; Huddersfield; London (Imperial College of Science, Technology & Medicine); London (University College (UCL)); Portsmouth; Salford; Sheffield; UMIST; Westminster; York

DIPLOMAS AWARDED BY UNIVERSITIES
Bradford (Bradford & Ilkley Community College); Huddersfield; Salford; South Bank; Wales (Swansea Institute of Higher Education)

CERTIFICATES AWARDED BY UNIVERSITIES
Bradford (Bradford & Ilkley Community College)

National Certificates and Diplomas

Scotland
SQA HNC: Industrial Measurement and Process Control; Process Control

City & Guilds

2250 Maintenance Craft Studies in Measurement and Control; 2750 Industrial Measurement and Control Technicians

INSURANCE AND ACTUARIAL WORK

Membership of Professional Institutions and Associations

ASSOCIATION OF AVERAGE ADJUSTERS
200 Aldersgate Street, London EC1A 4JJ Tel: 020 7956 0099 Fax: 020 7956 0161

MEMBERSHIP:
Fellows: Must be Average Adjusters who have qualified by passing the Association's exam.

EXAMINATIONS:
The examination consists of 5 theoretical modules requiring written answers, 1 module requiring the candidate to prepare a practical adjustment.

THE CHARTERED INSTITUTE OF LOSS ADJUSTERS

Peninsular House, 36 Monument Street, London EC3R 8JL Tel: 020 7337 9960
e-mail: info@cila.co.uk Website: www.cila.co.uk

MEMBERSHIP:
Fellows (FCILA): Must have been Associates for at least 5 yrs, and have been continuously in practice as loss adjusters whilst they have been Associates and fulfilled CPD requirements.
Associates (ACILA): Members who have passed the exams, are at least 25 and have been in practice for 5 yrs are eligible for election as Associates.
Licentiates: Persons who are elected, having passed the Institute's exams but are not able to meet the age or experience requirements for Associateship.
Ordinary Members: Must be at least 18 and be in practice as adjusters in a firm of loss adjusters.

THE INSTITUTE'S EXAMINATION:
The exam comprises 5 subjects and covers insurance law and claims procedure, report writing and the adjustment of various kinds of losses such as liability, property, burglary and third party claims. It cannot be taken until ordinary members have completed a minimum of 2 yrs in practice.

THE SOCIETY OF CLAIMS TECHNICIANS
Contact details as above.
The society was created in 1999 to provide an examination for anyone working in insurance claims. There are two written exams and an additional requirement to satisfactorily complete an inter-personal skills course. Completion of the exams leads to the award of Associate (ASCT). A further five yrs' experience leads to FSCT.

THE CHARTERED INSURANCE INSTITUTE
20 Aldermanbury, London EC2V 7HY Tel: 020 8989 8464 Fax: 020 8726 0131 e-mail: info@cii.co.uk. Website: www.cii.co.uk
MEMBERSHIP:
Open to anyone employed or engaged in insurance.

QUALIFICATIONS:

Fellowship (FCII): Open to Associates who complete an election programme.

Associateship (ACII): Recognised world-wide as the hallmark of a professional insurance education. The syllabus comprises 10 exam subjects and is ideal for the career professional, entry standards: minimum 2 A levels and 2 GCSE's or BTEC National Certificate or aged 25 and over. Chartered titles – either Chartered Insurer or Chartered Insurance Practitioner – are available to all Fellows and eligible Associates.

Certificate of Insurance Practice (MSTI): Ideal for those who work at a technical level. Comprising of 5 exam subjects, successful candidates are eligible to become members of the Society of Technicians in Insurance and are awarded 4 exemptions towards the Associateship. Entry standards: minimum 4 GCSE's or aged 21 and over. (NVQ Levels 3 and 4)

Insurance Foundation Certificate: Provides a broad knowledge of insurance at a foundation level. There are no entry requirements. (NVQ Level 2)

Advanced Financial Planning Certificate (MSFA): Demonstrates the attainment of a highly qualified level in the financial services field. Entry standards: the Financial Planning Certificate. Successful candidates are eligible to become members of the Society of Financial Advisers and are awarded 3 exemptions towards the Associateship.

Financial Planning Certificate: Designed for new or experienced financial advisers and support staff.

THE FACULTY AND INSTITUTE OF ACTUARIES

E-mail: careers@actuaries.org.uk Website: www.actuaries.org.uk

Faculty of Actuaries, Maclaurin House, 18 Dublin Street, Edinburgh, EH1 3PP
Tel: 0131 240 1300 Fax: 0131 240 1313

Institute of Actuaries, Napier House, 4 Worcester Street, Oxford OX1 2AW Tel: 01865 268228 Fax: 01865 268253Actuaries are experts in assessing the financial impact of tomorrow's uncertain events. They enable financial decisions to be made with more confidence by analysing the past, modelling the future, assessing the risks involved, and communicating what the results mean in financial terms.

MEMBERSHIP:

The high regard in which the actuarial profession is held is earned through a good deal of effort and dedication. To become an actuary you must be a competent mathematician and be able to communicate effectively and clearly. There is a minimum entry requirement of grade B at A Level, SCE higher grade, or equivalent. Overall, your degree discipline is not important, although a mathematical or statistical degree has been the most common entry qualification. Undergraduate degree courses in actuarial science and 1 yr FT postgraduate diploma courses are available and may result in exemption from some of the exams. To qualify as an actuary you must pass the professional examinations. The earlier subjects provide a thorough understanding of the mathematical, statistical and financial techniques required in the later subjects and used in the workplace. The later subjects examine the 4 main areas of actuarial practice: investment, life insurance, general insurance and pensions. The Fellowship exam tests one practice area in greater depth.

QUALIFICATIONS:

Fellow of the Faculty of Actuaries (FFA): Any student of the Faculty who has completed the exams may be admitted as a Fellow.

Fellow of the Institute of Actuaries (FIA): Fellows of the Institute of Actuaries must have attained the age of 23 yrs, have passed all of the professional examinations and have also completed 3 yrs' practical actuarial work.

Associate of the Faculty of Actuaries (AFA): Any student of the Faculty who has completed all but the 400 series (Fellowship) subjects and who have completed a professionalism course.

Associate of the Institute of Actuaries (AIA): As for Associates of the Faculty of Actuaries but also can apply to those students who have passed all of the professional examinations but have not attained the age of 23 yrs of age or have not completed 3 yrs' relevant work experience.

Diploma in Actuarial Techniques: The joint Diploma in Actuarial Techniques is awarded to students of the Faculty and Institute of Actuaries who pass relevant professional examinations.

Certificate in Finance and Investment: The joint Certificate in Finance and Investment is awarded to students of the Faculty and Institute of Actuaries who pass relevant professional examinations.

University Qualifications

The following universities offer qualifications in Insurance and Actuarial Work and related subjects. Full details may be found in Part 4, under the entry for the appropriate university.

FIRST DEGREES AWARDED BY UNIVERSITIES
Anglia; Central England; City; Glasgow Caledonian; Heriot-Watt; Kent; London (London School of Economics & Political Science); London Guildhall; Nottingham; Southampton; Wales (University of Wales, Swansea)

HIGHER DEGREES AWARDED BY UNIVERSITIES
Central England; City; Kent; Leicester; Southampton

DIPLOMAS AWARDED BY UNIVERSITIES
City

POSTGRADUATE DIPLOMAS AWARDED BY UNIVERSITIES
Heriot-Watt

PROFESSIONAL COURSES AWARDED BY UNIVERSITIES
London Guildhall

NVQs
Level 2: Insurance (General); Insurance (Intermediaries); Insurance (Life Offices)
Level 3: Insurance (General); Insurance (Intermediaries); Insurance (Life Offices)
Level 4: Insurance (Intermediaries); Insurance (Life Offices)

SVQs
Level 2: Insurance (General); Insurance (Intermediaries); Insurance (Life offices)
Level 3: Insurance (General); Insurance (Intermediaries); Insurance (Life offices)
Level 4: Insurance (Intermediaries); Insurance (Life offices)

OCR
OCR offer the following awards:
Insurance (General) Levels 2, 3 & 4
Insurance (Intermediaries) Levels 2, 3 & 4
Insurance (Life Offices) Levels 2, 3 & 4
Providing Financial Advice (Insurance) Level 3

Useful Addresses
National Training Organisation for Insurance Related Financial Services, 20 Aldermanbury, London EC2V 7HY, Tel: 020 7417 4404, Fax: 020 7726 0131

JOURNALISM

Membership of Professional Institutions and Associations

THE CHARTERED INSTITUTE OF JOURNALISTS

2 Dock Offices, Surrey Quays Road, London SE16 2XU Tel: 020 7252 1187 Fax: 020 7232 2302
e-mail: cioj@dircon.co.uk

MEMBERSHIP:
Fellow (FCIJ): Elected by the council from members who have given outstanding service.
Member (MCIJ): Must have been engaged in FT journalism for at least 3 yrs or 1 yr if holding recognised diploma or other qualification.

Student: Undergoing preparation for professional membership.
Affiliate: Engaged in the communication industry other than as a journalist, or as an occasional contributor to the media whose major income derives from sources other than journalism.

NATIONAL COUNCIL FOR THE TRAINING OF JOURNALISTS

Latton Bush Centre, Southern Way, Harlow, Essex CM18 7BL
Tel: 01279 430009
e-mail: NCTJTRAINING@aol.com
Website: www.NCTJ.com

JOURNALISM:
The National Council runs the official training scheme for entrants to newspaper journalism. There are 2 ways of entering. One way is for the entrant to persuade a provincial editor to give him or her a 6 mth trial and then permanent employment. During the first 2 yrs, training is given on and off the job. The other way is selection for the 1 yr FT courses of preparation accredited by the National Council followed by permanent employment and during the first 18 mths, training on the job. The educational requirements for these courses are at least 2 GCE A Levels in England, 3 Highers in Scotland, including English, and at least 2 GCSE passes at Grade C or above, and 1 A and 5 GCSE passes, including English, in Northern Ireland. Direct entrants need to have at least 5 GCE O Level or GCSE passes including English Language, but many editors now require at least 1 A Level. After at least 18 mths in the industry, trainees take the National Certificate examination, the recognised professional exam. Panels of newspapermen take part and it includes oral and written exams in practical journalism. The **National Certificate** is awarded to successful candidates. The following colleges offer a 1 yr FT pre-entry course before on-job training for the National Councils National Certificate: Brighton CT Crawley College; Darlington CT; East Surrey College; Gloucestershire College of Arts and Technology; Gwent Tertiary College; Harlow College; Harrow College, Harrow; Sheffield College; Southend College of A & T; Sutton Coldfield College; Warwickshire College.
HND in Journalism Studies: May be taken at Cardonald College, Glasgow. A limited number of graduates attend a 1 yr postgraduate journalism course at Liverpool Comm College; Cardiff University; University of Central Lancashire, Preston; or Strathclyde University/Glasgow Caledonian University (joint); De Montfort University Leicester; Trinity & All Saints College, Leeds; University of Ulster, Belfast, before entry into the industry. Graduate Fast-Track Courses (18 or 20 wks): Cornwall College; Harlow College; Sheffield College; Highbury College, Portsmouth; Lambeth College, Vauxhall Centre; Liverpool Community College. Degree Courses: Bournemouth University; University of Central Lancashire, Preston; University of Sheffield; Staffordshire University. Day Release Courses: City of Liverpool Comm College; Wulfrun College, Wolverhampton. The NCTJ also offers distance learning courses in newspaper and periodical journalism. 6 different NVQs at Level four in Newspaper and Periodical Journalism. NVQs in Customer Service, Business Administration and Training & Development are also available.

PHOTOGRAPHY:
The National Certificate in Photo Journalism of the National Council for the Training of Journalists: This test is taken by trainee press photographers after 2 yrs (18 mths for pre-entry trainees) on job experience on provincial newspapers. The educational qualifications for direct entry to press photography are at least 5 O Levels or GCSESs including English in England and Wales with exceptions for industrial or course experience and 3 O grades including English in Scotland. Training is given on and off the job at special 12 wk block release courses. The council has a 1 yr FT pre-entry course in press photography for which you need 1 A Level and 4 O Levels including English Language, or 2 Highers and 3 O grades including English for Scottish applicants.

University Qualifications

The following universities offer qualifications in Journalism and related subjects. Full details may be found in Part 4, under the entry for the appropriate university.

FIRST DEGREES AWARDED BY UNIVERSITIES

Barnsley; Bournemouth; Central Lancashire; City; Lancaster (Edge Hill College of Higher Education); Leeds; Lincolnshire (Lincoln University Campus); Liverpool John Moores; London (Queen Mary & Westfield College (incorporating St Bartholomew's and the Royal London School of Medicine & Dentistry)); London Institute (London College of Printing); Manchester (Warrington Collegiate Institute, Faculty of H.E.); Napier; Nottingham Trent; Nottingham Trent (Southampton Institute); Plymouth (Falmouth College of Arts); Sheffield; Sunderland; Surrey Institute; Thames Valley; Wales (Cardiff University); Wales (Swansea Institute of Higher Education); Wales (University of Wales, Bangor)

HIGHER DEGREES AWARDED BY UNIVERSITIES

Bournemouth; City; Leeds (Leeds, Trinity & All Saints); Liverpool John Moores; London (Goldsmiths College); Napier; Nottingham Trent; Sheffield; Sheffield Hallam; Strathclyde; Surrey Institute; Ulster; Wales (Cardiff University); Westminster

DIPLOMAS AWARDED BY UNIVERSITIES

Barnsley; Central England; City; De Montfort, Leicester; Glasgow Caledonian; Hertfordshire (West Herts College); Leeds (Leeds, Trinity & All Saints); Lincolnshire (Grimsby College); London Institute (London College of Printing); Middlesex; Napier; Nottingham Trent; Nottingham Trent (Southampton Institute); Strathclyde; Thames Valley; Ulster; Wales (Cardiff University); Westminster

CERTIFICATES AWARDED BY UNIVERSITIES

Central England

POSTGRADUATE DIPLOMAS AWARDED BY UNIVERSITIES

Central Lancashire; Plymouth (Falmouth College of Arts)

National Certificates and Diplomas

BTEC Higher National Certificates/Diplomas: Media (Journalism)
Scotland
SQA HND: Journalism

NVQs

Level 4: Newspaper Journalism (Press Photography); Newspaper Journalism (Production Journalism); Newspaper Journalism (Writing); Periodical Journalism (Subbing); Periodical Journalism (Writing)

SVQs

Level 3: Newspaper Journalism: Graphics Journalism.
Level 4: Newspaper Journalism: Production or Writing; Press Photography; Writing.

OCR

OCR offer the following awards:
Newspaper Journalism (Press Photography) Level 4
Newspaper Journalism (Writing) Level 4
Newspaper Journalism (Production Journalism) Level 4
Periodical Journalism Foundation Units
Periodical Journalism (Writing) Level 4
Periodical Journalism (Subbing) Level 4
Periodical Journalism (Advertisement Production) Levels 2, 3 & 4

City & Guilds

7790 Media Techniques: Journalism and Radio Competencies

Useful Addresses

Periodicals Training Council, Queens House, 55-56 Lincoln's Inn Fields, London WC2A 3LJ Tel: 020 7404 4168 Fax: 020 7404 4167

Newspaper Publishers' Association, 34 Southwark Bridge Road, London SW1 9EU Tel: 020 7928 6928 Fax: 020 7928 2067

Newspaper Society, Bloomsbury House, Bloomsbury Square, 74–77 Great Russell Street, London WC1B 3DA Tel: 020 7636 7014 Fax: 020 7631 5119

LAND AND PROPERTY

Membership of Professional Institutions and Associations

THE COLLEGE OF ESTATE MANAGEMENT

Whiteknights, Reading, Berkshire RG6 6AW Tel: 0118 986 1101 Fax: 0118 975 5344
e-mail: info@cem.ac.uk Website: www.cem.ac.uk

COURSES:

The College offers 2 distance learning courses which meet the academic requirements of the Royal Institution of Chartered Surveyors: the Diploma in Surveying (The College of Estate Management) and the BSc in Estate Management (University of Reading). Other undergraduate level distance learning courses offered by the College meet the academic requirements of the Chartered Institute of Building, the Architects and Surveyors Institute and the Construction Industry Board. At postgraduate level, the College offers the University of Reading's MSc in Real Estate and MBA in Construction and Real Estate. It also offers Postgraduate Diplomas in Arbitration, Building Conservation, Facilities Management, Property Investment and Project Management. Most courses are taught by a combination of written instructional material supplemented by audio and video tapes, with assignments for completion by the student and assessment by tutors. The majority of courses are also supplemented by short face-to-face teaching sessions at regional centres.

THE INSTITUTE OF REVENUES, RATING AND VALUATION

41 Doughty Street, London WC1N 2LF Tel: 020 7831 3505 Fax: 020 7831 2048 e-mail: irrv.org.uk Website: www.irrv.org.uk

The Institute offers professional and technical qualifications for all those whose professional work is concerned with Local Authority revenues and benefits, valuation for rating, property taxation and the appeals procedure. The Institute's qualifications are widely recognised throughout the profession.

CORPORATE MEMBERSHIP:

Corporate (IRRV): Corporate membership is granted by the Institute to those people who have passed the Institute's full professional exams with exemptions available to qualified members of certain other professional associations, including the Royal Institution of Chartered Surveyors and the Chartered Institute of Public Finance and Accountancy.

NON-CORPORATE MEMBERSHIP:

Technician: Available to persons who have passed the Institute's Technician exam or who have been exempted therefrom by possessing appropriate qualifications and practical experience.

Student: Open to those preparing for the Institute's exams.

Affiliate: Open to any person maintaining an interest in the work of the Institute, but cannot be used to imply a professional association with the Institute.

EXAMINATIONS:

The Institute conducts full professional exams at 3 levels. The exams conducted for Scottish candidates take account of differences in Scottish Law. The Institute also conducts Technician exams in revenues and housing benefits.

Exemptions: May be granted from certain parts of the Institute's exams in respect of certain post A Level qualifications, degrees and the exams of other professional associations.

ISVA – THE PROFESSIONAL SOCIETY FOR VALUERS AND AUCTIONEERS

3 Cadogan Gate, London SW1X 0AS Tel: 020 7235 2282 Fax: 020 7235 4390
e-mail: educ.memb@isva.co.uk Website: www.isva.co.uk

MEMBERSHIP:
Fellows (FSVA): Must be at least 30, have passed ISVA's Unit 5 and 6 examinations or equivalent thereto and have satisfied the Professional Assessment requirements. In addition applicants must have been in practice in the profession for at least 10 yrs or for at least 5 yrs as a principal or a manager and have been an Associate of ISVA for at least 2 yrs.
Associate (ASVA): Applicants must be at least 21, have passed ISVA's Unit 5 and 6 examinations or equivalent thereto and have satisfied the Professional Assessment requirements.
Student: Applicants must be at least 16 and should have obtained a standard of general education represented by 5 GCSE passes at Grade A, B or C, including English Language and Mathematics, 3 of which must have been passed at the same time. Intermediate and Advanced GNVQ accepted. For NVQ entry telephone for further information.

EXAMINATIONS:
Exams are held at Units 1–6 in the following divisions: General Practice; Agricultural Practice; Fine Arts and Chattels; Plant and Machinery. There is also a special entry route for non-cognate degree holders and those over the age of 30 with 10 or more yrs' experience in the profession. All students are required to complete the Professional Assessment as well as passing the exams. This is undertaken over a 2 yr period of approved employment and comprises a journal and a pre-qualification assignment.

THE NATIONAL ASSOCIATION OF ESTATE AGENTS

Arbon House, 21Jury Street, Warwick CV34 4EH Tel: 01926 496800 Fax: 01926 400953
Telex: DX18120 WARWICK e-mail: info@naea.co.uk Website: www.naea.co.uk

MEMBERSHIP:
Open to application by practising estate agents. The minimum criteria for the main grades are:
Associate (ANAEA): 21 yrs old and 3 yrs' experience in estate agency. Applicants must also pass an admission test.
Fellow (FNAEA): 25 yrs old, 5 yrs' experience in estate agency and the NAEA Certificate of Practice in Estate Agency, Certificate in Residential Lettings & Management or comparable qualification. Other grades include Affiliate, Special Associate, Student, Honorary and Retired Member. Full details are available from the Head of the Membership Department.

QUALIFICATIONS:
The NAEA Certificate of Practice in Estate Agency: The highest available qualification in estate agency. It is open to both NAEA members and non-members. Successful candidates are entitled to use the designatory letters CPEA.
The NAEA Certificate in Residential Lettings & Management: The highest available qualification in residential lettings and property management. It is open to NAEA members and non-members. Successful candidates are entitled to use the designatory letters CRLM. Preparation courses for examination for both CPEA and CRLM are studied via distance learning. Information pack form NAEA Education & Training Department. The Association regularly organises a series of half and full-day courses throughout the UK on a wide range of professional topics. In addition, the NAEA National Assessment Centre offers N/SVQ at Levels 2 & 3 in Residential Estate Agency and Residential Lettings and Property Management.

PROPERTY CONSULTANTS SOCIETY

107A Tarrant Street, Arundel, West Sussex BN18 9DP Tel: 01903 883787 Fax: 01903 889590
e-mail: david@propco.freeserve.co.uk
The principal objects of the Society are to provide a central organisation for surveyors, architects, valuers, auctioneers, land and estate agents, master builders, and constructional engineers, who practise as consultants in their own branches of the profession and including members of the legal profession specialising in estate matters.

EXAMINATIONS: (not currently being held).
Fellow (FPCS): Minimum age 27.
Associate (APCS): Minimum age 21.Entrance is judged on experience, training etc.

THE ROYAL INSTITUTION OF CHARTERED SURVEYORS

Membership Department, Surveyor Court, Westwood Way, Coventry CV4 8JE Tel: 020 7222 7000
or 024 76694757 e-mail: info@rics.org Website: www.rics.org

MEMBERSHIP:
Fellow (FRICS): A Professional Associate of 5 yrs' standing may apply for transfer to the
Fellowship. He or she will need to demonstrate career advancement as well as increased expertise
and management responsibility. Contact Barbara Rollason for further information.
Professional Associate (ARICS): Member of the RICS having successfully undergone an
extensive period of practical training coupled with degree-level education or an equivalent course
of professional study in order to gain the qualification.
Technical Surveyor (TechRICS): Member of the RICS having successfully undergone an extensive
period of practical training and holding a BTEC/SCOTVEC HNC/HND qualification.
Probationer: Member of the RICS having successfully completed a degree or equivalent course
satisfying the academic requirement of the RICS.
Student: Member of the RICS currently studying for a RICS accredited qualification.

EDUCATION & TRAINING:
The majority of candidates join the Institution as a student whilst studying for, or on completion
of, an approved degree or diploma course. Entrants must have attained the minimum standard of
education for university matriculation. The majority of entrants to the profession qualify by
undertaking a related FT, S, PT or Distance degree/diploma course accredited by the Institution.
Entrants with an A Level (or equivalent) may enrol on a related BTEC/SQA HNC/HND that will
lead to qualification as a Technical Surveyor, or may then afford advanced entry to a relevant
degree course. Graduates from non-surveying backgrounds may embark on FT, PT or distance
taught fast track graduate conversion courses of 1 to 2 yrs' duration. All candidates must also
undergo a minimum period of 2 yrs' Professional Assessment comprising professional training
and practical experience, and a professional interview.
**The Royal Institution of Chartered Surveyors now incorporates the Society of Surveying
Technicians and The Incorporated Society of Valuers and Auctioneers.**

University Qualifications

*The following universities offer qualifications in Land and Property and related subjects. Full details may
be found in Part 4, under the entry for the appropriate university.*

FIRST DEGREES AWARDED BY UNIVERSITIES

Aberdeen; Adams; Anglia; Birmingham; Bristol; Cambridge; Central England; Central Lancashire;
City; Coventry; De Montfort, Leicester; East London; Essex (Writtle College); Glamorgan;
Glasgow Caledonian; Greenwich; Heriot-Watt; Kingston; Leeds (Askham Bryan College);
Liverpool John Moores; Loughborough; Napier; Newcastle; Northampton; Northumbria;
Nottingham Trent; Nottingham Trent (Southampton Institute); Oxford Brookes; Paisley;
Plymouth; Portsmouth; Reading; Sheffield Hallam; South Bank; Staffordshire; Wales (North East
Wales Institute); Wales (University of Wales, Aberystwyth); Wales (University of Wales, Bangor);
Westminster

HIGHER DEGREES AWARDED BY UNIVERSITIES

Aberdeen; Belfast; Bournemouth; Bristol; Cambridge; Central England; Cheltenham & Gloucester;
City; De Montfort, Leicester; Durham; East Anglia; Edinburgh; Glamorgan; Greenwich; Heriot-
Watt; Kingston; Liverpool John Moores; London (London School of Economics & Political
Science); London (Wye College); Napier; Nottingham Trent; Paisley; Plymouth; Portsmouth;
Reading; Sheffield Hallam; South Bank; Sussex; Ulster; Wales (University of Wales, Bangor);
Wolverhampton

DIPLOMAS AWARDED BY UNIVERSITIES
Aberdeen; Anglia; Birmingham; Bournemouth; Central England; De Montfort, Leicester; Durham; Edinburgh; Glamorgan; London (Wye College); Napier; Northumbria; Paisley; Plymouth; Reading; South Bank; Ulster

CERTIFICATES AWARDED BY UNIVERSITIES
Central England; Durham; Ulster

OTHER COURSES AWARDED BY UNIVERSITIES
Essex (Writtle College)

POSTGRADUATE DIPLOMAS AWARDED BY UNIVERSITIES
Heriot-Watt

National Certificates and Diplomas

BTEC National Certificates/Diplomas: Land Administration; Land Administration (Estate Management); Land Administration (Geographical Techniques); Land Administration (Housing); Land Administration (Planning); Land and Countryside Studies; Rural Studies; Rural Studies (Countryside Recreation); Rural Studies (Countryside Management); Rural Studies (Environmental Management); Rural Studies (Leisure Attraction Management); Upland Resource Management; Urban and Countryside Conservation
BTEC Higher National Certificates/Diplomas: Land Administration; Land Administration (Estate Management); Land Administration (Geographical Techniques); Land Administration (Housing); Land Administration (Planning); Land Administration (Valuation and Property Management); Rural Environment Management; Rural Resource Management; Rural Studies; Rural Studies (Recreation Land Management)

NVQs

Level 2: Residential Estate Agency; Residential Property Letting and Management Agency
Level 3: Accommodation Supervision; Residential Estate Agency; Residential Property Letting and Management Agency; Selling Residential Property
Level 4: Accommodation Management; Property Management; Valuation

SVQs

Level 2: Residential Estate Agency: Residential Property Letting and Management Agency
Level 3: Residential Estate Agency: Residential Property Letting and Management Agency

GNVQs

3736 Land and Environment

OCR

OCR offer the following awards:
Residential Estate Agency Levels 2 & 3

THE PLANNING INSPECTORATE

PLANNING INSPECTORS

The Planning Inspectorate, Department of the Environment, Transport and the Regions, Tollgate House, Houlton Street, Bristol BS2 9DJ Tel: 0117 987 8104 Fax: 0117 987 8769 Website: www.planning-inspectorate.gov.uk
Planning Inspectors conduct local inquiries and carry out site inspections in accordance with the statutory functions of the Secretary of State for the Environment, Transport and the Regions and

the National Assembly for Wales. Candidates are selected on the basis of written and oral tests. Successful candidates receive initial training, followed by a period under close supervision. The recruitment grade is Housing and Planning Inspector, above which there are 4 higher grades. Candidates must be corporate members of the Royal Town Planning Institute, the Royal Institute of British Architects, the Institute of Civil Engineers or the Royal Institute of Chartered Surveyors (any relevant sub-division); or be registered architects; or be barristers called to the English or Northern Ireland bars, advocates called to the Scottish bar or solicitors admitted in England, Scotland or Northern Ireland. They must have had either relevant experience of the operation of the Planning or Housing Acts or substantial experience in a senior administrative or managerial post requiring knowledge of judicial or quasi-judicial procedures.

Useful Addresses

Institute of Maintenance and Building Management, Keets House, 30 East Street, Farnham, Surrey GU9 7SW Tel: 01252 710994 Fax: 01252 737741
Residential Estate Agency Training and Education Association, 18 Southernhay West, Exeter EX1 1PR Tel: 01392 423399 Fax: 01392 423373

LANDSCAPE ARCHITECTURE

Membership of Professional Institutions and Associations

THE LANDSCAPE INSTITUTE

6-8 Barnard Mews, London SW11 1QU Tel: 020 7350 5200 Fax: 020 7350 5201
e-mail: mail@l-i.org.uk Website: www.l-i.org.uk or www.1stlandscape.co.uk

CORPORATE MEMBERS:
There are two grades of Corporate Membership of The Landscape Institute. The most senior grade is **Fellow(FLI)** with the other grade being **Member(MLI)**. All corporate members must be educated to at least first degree level in landscape architecture, landscape management or landscape science, have postgraduate professional experience and have passed the Institute's Professional Practice Examination. Corporate members of the Institute are entitled to describe themselves as Chartered Landscape Architects.

NON-CORPORATE MEMBERS:
Associates: Have completed a recognised degree- or postgraduate-level course and are gaining professional experience before taking the Institute's Professional Practice Exam.
Students: Are studying a degree- or postgraduate-level course in landscape architecture at one of the universities with courses accredited by the Institute.

EXAMINATIONS:
The Institute's exam leading to Corporate Membership is the Professional Practice Exam. It consists of a written paper and an oral exam, in which the candidate's competence to act as a practising member of the profession is tested. Candidates must complete at least 2 yrs' relevant experience as an Associate member before taking this exam. Success in the Professional Practice Exam entitles candidates to apply for Corporate Membership.

University Qualifications

The following universities offer qualifications in Landscape Architecture and related subjects. Full details may be found in Part 4, under the entry for the appropriate university.

FIRST DEGREES AWARDED BY UNIVERSITIES

Bucks. Coll.; Central England; Central Lancashire; Cheltenham & Gloucester; De Montfort; Leicester; East Anglia (Otley College); East Anglia (Suffolk College); Essex (Writtle College); Greenwich; Kingston; Leeds Metropolitan; Lincolnshire (Bishop Burton College); Liverpool; Manchester; Manchester Metropolitan.; Northumbria; Nottingham Trent; Reading; Sussex

HIGHER DEGREES AWARDED BY UNIVERSITIES
Bristol; Central England; Cheltenham & Gloucester; Essex (Writtle College); Greenwich; Heriot-Watt; Heriot-Watt (Edinburgh College of Art); Leeds Metropolitan; Leicester; Liverpool (Chester College of H.E.); Manchester; Newcastle; Portsmouth; Sheffield

DIPLOMAS AWARDED BY UNIVERSITIES
Bournemouth; Central England; Central Lancashire; Cheltenham & Gloucester; De Montfort, Leicester; East Anglia (Otley College); East Anglia (Suffolk College); Glamorgan; Greenwich; Heriot-Watt (Edinburgh College of Art); Kingston; Leeds Metropolitan; Leicester; Newcastle; Plymouth

CERTIFICATES AWARDED BY UNIVERSITIES
Bournemouth; Cheltenham & Gloucester; East Anglia (Otley College)

OTHER COURSES AWARDED BY UNIVERSITIES
Essex (Writtle College)

POSTGRADUATE DIPLOMAS AWARDED BY UNIVERSITIES
Heriot-Watt

National Certificates and Diplomas
BTEC National Certificates/Diplomas: Landscape Construction; Landscape Studies
BTEC Higher National Certificates/Diplomas: Landscape Construction; Landscape Studies

SVQs
Level 1: Amenity Horticulture
Level 2: Amenity Horticulture; Amenity Horticulture: Interior Landscaping or Sports Turf
Level 3: Amenity Horticulture; Amenity Horticulture: Sports Turf Maintenance
Level 4: Amenity Horticulture

Useful Addresses
British Landscape ITO, 11a North Queen Street, Keighley, West Yorkshire BD21 3DL Tel: 01535 691179 Fax: 01535 691182

LAW

University Qualifications
The following universities offer qualifications in Law and related subjects. Full details may be found in Part 4, under the entry for the appropriate university.

FIRST DEGREES AWARDED BY UNIVERSITIES
Aberdeen; Abertay, Dundee; Anglia; Belfast; Birmingham; Blackburn; Bournemouth; Bradford; Bradford (Bradford & Ilkley Community College); Brighton; Bristol; Brunel; Buckingham; Bucks. Coll.; Cambridge; Central England; Central Lancashire; City; Coventry; De Montfort, Leicester; Derby; Doncaster; Dundee; Durham; East Anglia; East Anglia (Suffolk College); East London; Edinburgh; Essex; Exeter; Glamorgan; Glasgow; Glasgow Caledonian; Greenwich; Hertfordshire; Huddersfield; Hull; Keele; Kent; Kingston; Lancaster; Lancaster (Edge Hill College of Higher Education); Leeds; Leeds Metropolitan; Leicester; Lincolnshire (Lincoln University Campus); Liverpool; Liverpool John Moores; London (Birkbeck, University of London); London (King's College London); London (London School of Economics & Political Science); London (Queen Mary & Westfield College (incorporating St Bartholomew's and the Royal London School of Medicine & Dentistry)); London (School of Oriental & African Studies); London (University College (UCL)); London Guildhall; Luton; Manchester; Manchester Metropolitan.; Middlesex;

Napier; Newcastle; North London; Northampton; Northumbria; Nottingham; Nottingham Trent; Nottingham Trent (Southampton Institute); Oxford; Oxford Brookes; Plymouth; Portsmouth; Reading; Robert Gordon; Sheffield; Sheffield Hallam; South Bank; Southampton; Southampton (University of Southampton New College); Staffordshire; Stirling; Strathclyde; Sunderland; Surrey; Sussex; Teesside; Thames Valley; Ulster; Wales (Cardiff University); Wales (North East Wales Institute); Wales (Swansea Institute of Higher Education); Wales (University of Wales College, Newport); Wales (University of Wales, Aberystwyth); Wales (University of Wales, Bangor); Wales (University of Wales, Swansea); Warwick; Westminster; Wolverhampton

HIGHER DEGREES AWARDED BY UNIVERSITIES

Aberdeen; Anglia; Belfast; Birmingham; Bournemouth; Bradford; Brighton; Bristol; Brunel; Buckingham; Cambridge; Central England; Central Lancashire; City; Coventry; De Montfort, Leicester; Dundee; Durham; East Anglia; East London; Edinburgh; Essex; Exeter; Glasgow; Glasgow Caledonian; Heriot-Watt; Hertfordshire; Huddersfield; Hull; Keele; Kent; Kingston; Lancaster; Lancaster (Edge Hill College of Higher Education); Leeds; Leeds Metropolitan; Leicester; Liverpool; Liverpool (Liverpool Hope University College); Liverpool John Moores; London (Birkbeck, University of London); London (King's College London); London (London School of Economics & Political Science); London (Queen Mary & Westfield College (incorporating St Bartholomew's and the Royal London School of Medicine & Dentistry)); London (School of Oriental & African Studies); London (University College (UCL)); London Guildhall; Loughborough; Manchester; Manchester Metropolitan.; Middlesex; Napier; Newcastle; North London; Nottingham; Nottingham Trent; Oxford; Plymouth; Portsmouth; Reading; Sheffield; Sheffield Hallam; South Bank; Southampton; Staffordshire; Strathclyde; Surrey; Sussex; Ulster; Wales (Cardiff University); Wales (University of Wales, Aberystwyth); Wales (University of Wales, Bangor); Wales (University of Wales, Swansea); Warwick; Westminster; Wolverhampton

DIPLOMAS AWARDED BY UNIVERSITIES

Aberdeen; Belfast; Birmingham; Blackburn; Bournemouth; Bradford; Brighton; Bristol; Bucks. Coll.; Cambridge; Central England; Central Lancashire; City; De Montfort, Leicester; Derby; Doncaster; Dundee; Durham; East London; Edinburgh; Exeter; Exeter (Truro College); Glamorgan; Glasgow; Hertfordshire; Huddersfield; Hull; Keele; Kent; Kingston; Leeds; Leeds Metropolitan; Leicester; Liverpool John Moores; London (Birkbeck, University of London); London (King's College London); London (London School of Economics & Political Science); London (Queen Mary & Westfield College (incorporating St Bartholomew's and the Royal London School of Medicine & Dentistry)); London (University College (UCL)); London Guildhall; Manchester; Napier; North London; Nottingham Trent; Nottingham Trent (Southampton Institute); Plymouth; Reading; South Bank; Staffordshire; Strathclyde; Sussex; Thames Valley; Ulster; Wales (Cardiff University); Wales (University of Wales, Aberystwyth); Warwick; Westminster; Wolverhampton

CERTIFICATES AWARDED BY UNIVERSITIES

Belfast; Bristol; Cambridge; Central England; City; Dundee; Durham; Kent; Leeds; Leeds Metropolitan; London (King's College London); London (Queen Mary & Westfield College (incorporating St Bartholomew's and the Royal London School of Medicine & Dentistry)); Staffordshire; Sussex; Wolverhampton

OTHER COURSES AWARDED BY UNIVERSITIES

Anglia; Central Lancashire

POSTGRADUATE DIPLOMAS AWARDED BY UNIVERSITIES

Central Lancashire; Thames Valley

PROFESSIONAL COURSES AWARDED BY UNIVERSITIES

Huddersfield

PROFESSIONAL QUALIFICATIONS AWARDED BY UNIVERSITIES

Glamorgan

National Certificates and Diplomas
Scotland
SQA HNC: Legal Services
SQA HND: Legal Services

NVQs
Level 4: Legal Practice

England and Wales
MAGISTRATES:
Justices of the Peace (JPs) are appointed on behalf of the Crown by the Lord Chancellor who is advised by committees established for the purpose in every county, metropolitan district, and some of the larger cities and towns. Although JPs do not need to be legally qualified they must be suitable as to character, integrity and understanding of the work they have to do and it is necessary that their suitability in these respects should be generally recognised in their community. They must be broadly representative of the community, but political views are taken into account only so far as may be necessary to ensure that no Magistrates Bench becomes unduly representative of any one party .New JPs must take a course of basic training. This is designed to help them to understand the nature of their duties, to acquire enough knowledge of the law to follow normal cases and to understand the nature and objects of sentencing. The first stage of training takes place before the JP may sit to adjudicate. It consists of attending court as an observer and of instruction on the JP and his office, practice and procedure in the courts and methods of punishment and treatment. The second stage must be completed within 1yr of appointment. It consists of further instruction and visits to penal establishments. JPs appointed to juvenile court panels receive additional special training for the purpose .

JUDGES:
As the courts are the Queen's Courts, the Crown makes all appointments to the judiciary, acting on the advice of Ministers. Recommendations for the highest appointments (the Lords of Appeal in Ordinary, the Lord Chief Justice, the Master of the Rolls, the President of the Family Division and the Lords Justices who are the judges of the Court of Appeal) are made by the Prime Minister. The Lord Chancellor makes the recommendations for the High Court and Circuit judges, recorders and the metropolitan and other stipendiary magistrates. Appointments are made from among judges or practising lawyers. To qualify for the most senior posts candidates must either be a High Court judge or have had at least 15 yrs' practice as a barrister. High Court or Circuit judges must have been barristers for at least 10 yrs or Recorders for at least 5 yrs; Recorders must have been barristers or solicitors for at least 10 yrs. Most of the higher offices are filled from the ranks of **Queen's Counsel (QC)**: barristers who have been in practice for some yrs and have established a good reputation may apply to the Lord Chancellor for a patent to become Queen's Counsel (known as òÁtaking silk' because a QC wears a silk gown in court). The office of stipendiary magistrate is open only to barristers or solicitors of at least 7 yrs' standing.

OFFICERS OF THE COURT:
Officers of the Court include judicial and administrative staff; the former include Masters and Registrars, the latter secretaries and clerks to the judges and the staff who administer the court service. Details are given in òÁThe English Legal System' (HMSO). Qualifications for the judicial offices vary somewhat, but most appointments are limited to established barristers and solicitors.

THE LEGAL PROFESSION:
The legal profession consists of 2 branches. Each performs distinct duties, although there is a degree of overlap in some aspects of their work.
Solicitors undertake all ordinary legal business for their clients (with whom they are in direct contact). They may also appear on behalf of a client in the magistrates' and county courts and in some circumstances in the Crown Court.
Barristers (known collectively as the òÁBar' and collectively and individually as òÁCounsel') advise on legal problems submitted by solicitors and conduct cases in court; in the High Court advocacy may be practised only by barristers.

CORONERS:
Coroners must be barristers, solicitors or legally qualified medical practitioners of not less than 5 yrs' standing. They are appointed by local authorities.

Scotland

The 2 main **civil** courts in Scotland are the Court of Session (the supreme civil court, subject only to the House of Lords), and the Sheriff Court. The courts exercising **criminal** jurisdiction are the High Court of Justiciary, the Sheriff Court and District Courts. Responsibility for prosecutions in most criminal cases in Scotland rests with the Lord Advocate as Senior Scottish Law Officer acting on behalf of the Crown. The Department which handles criminal matters on behalf of the Lord Advocate is the Crown Office. Prosecutions in the High Court of Justiciary are taken on behalf of the Crown by the Lord Advocate, the Solicitor General (the Second Law Officer) and by the Advocates-Depute. A staff of local prosecutors called **procurators fiscal** carry out prosecutions in the Sheriff Courts and in the district courts. Procurators fiscal are civil servants. They must be either advocates or solicitors, but are usually solicitors. Police report details of an alleged crime to the local fiscal, who has discretion whether to prosecute subject to the direction and control of the Lord Advocate and Crown Office. In Scotland, there are 49 procurators fiscal. There are also depute procurators fiscal in busy areas. The bench of a **district court** may be constituted by a **lay judge** sitting alone or by 2 or more or by a **stipendiary magistrate,** who is a professional lawyer of at least 5 yrs' standing. The District Court has the same summary criminal jurisdiction and powers as a sheriff. Lay judges of the district court are justices of the peace drawn from 3 sources: the justices appointed by the Secretary of State for Scotland on behalf of the Queen; all burgh magistrates and police judges in office on 15 May 1975 were appointed JPs; and district and islands councils are empowered to appoint up to ¼ of their number as 'x officio' justices. For each court, a justices' committee is elected to advise the local authority about administration of the district court, to approve a rota of justices, to supervise training and to ensure effective administration of justice. Further provisions relate to the training of justices and to the requirements that justices who sit on the bench must undergo training appropriate to their experience. Above the district court, the **Sheriff Courts** deal with offences committed within the area over which they have jurisdiction. Each Sheriff Court has jurisdiction within the Sheriffdom in which it is located and at the head of the judiciary of each Sheriffdom (there are 6 Sheriffdoms in all) is the Sheriff Principal. The Sheriffdoms are sub-divided into a total of 49 districts, and there is a total of 107 Sheriffs. In addition to its criminal jurisdiction, the **Sheriff Court** deals with most civil litigation. The supreme criminal court is the **High Court of Justiciary**, which sits in Edinburgh and which sits also on circuit in several major towns and cities. The High Court of Justiciary also sits (in a court of at least 3 judges) as the **Court of Criminal Appeal,** hearing appeals from the High Court as court of first instance, from the Sheriff Court and the district court. There is no further appeal in criminal cases. The supreme civil court is the **Court of Session**, which sits in Edinburgh and may hear cases transferred to it and appealed from Sheriff Courts. (There is a right of appeal from the Court of Session to the House of Lords.) Cases originating in the Court of Session are decided by judges sitting singly whose decisions are subject to review by several judges. The total number of judges is 27, of whom 19, called Lords Ordinary, mainly decide cases in the first instance. 1 Judge is FT Chairman of the Scottish Law Commission. This branch of the court is called the Outer House. The 8 other judges are divided into 2 Divisions forming the Inner House. The First Division is presided over by the Lord President of the Court of Session and the Second Division by the Lord Justice-Clerk. The main business of each Division is to review the decisions of the Lords Ordinary or inferior courts which have been appealed to it.

Children: Lay people, carefully selected and trained, make up children's panels in local areas; from these panel groups of 3 panel members form individual hearings. An official, called the Reporter, decides whether a child should come before a hearing. The hearing's main task is to decide, after the grounds for referral to the hearing have been accepted by the child and his parent, what measures of compulsory care (if any) are most appropriate for the child. If the grounds for referral are not accepted, the case must first go to the Sheriff Court for proof.

Organisation and Administration: The Court of Session regulates its own procedure and that in civil proceedings in the Sheriff Court, while the High Court of Justiciary regulates its own procedure and that in criminal proceedings in the Sheriff Court and district courts. The Court of Session, Criminal Courts Rules Councils and Sheriff Court Rules Council, consisting of judges and legal practitioners, advise the courts about amending the rules. The Secretary of State for Scotland is responsible for organisation and administration of the sheriff courts and, to a lesser extent, the supreme courts. (Administration of district courts is a district and islands council responsibility.)

THE LEGAL PROFESSION:
The profession consists of **Solicitors** and **Advocates.**

Northern Ireland

As in England and Wales, the **superior courts** are the Court of Appeal, the High Court and the Crown Court. The latter is an exclusively criminal court. The Court of Appeal hears appeals in civil cases from the High Court and in criminal cases from the Crown Court and cases stated on a point of law from, *inter alia*, the County Court and the Magistrates' Courts. Appeals lie from the Court of Appeal to the House of Lords. The judges of the Court of Appeal and the High Court are appointed by the Crown on the advice of the Lord Chancellor of Great Britain. The Lord Chief Justice is President of the Court of Appeal, the High Court and the Crown Court. To qualify for appointment to the Court of Appeal a person must be either a High Court judge or a barrister who has practised for not less than 15 yrs at the Northern Ireland Bar; appointment to the High Court requires practice at the same Bar for not less than 10 yrs. The Crown Court is served by judges of the Court of Appeal and the High Court and county court judges.

Inferior Courts: As in England and Wales, the **county courts** are principally civil courts dealing with general claims not exceeding £15,000, but in Northern Ireland they also hear appeals from conviction in the Magistrates' Courts for summary offences. They are served by county court judges who are appointed by the Crown on the advice of the Lord Chancellor from barristers or solicitors who have practised for not less than 10 yrs in Northern Ireland or lawyers who have been deputy judges for not less than 3 yrs.

Magistrates' Courts: Magistrates' Courts deal principally with minor criminal offences (summary offences) and are presided over by Resident Magistrates (stipendiaries), who are persons who have practised in Northern Ireland for at least 7 yrs as barristers or solicitors. Resident Magistrates are appointed by the Crown on the advice of the Lord Chancellor. Juvenile courts consist of a Resident Magistrate and 2 lay members, 1 of whom must be a woman. JPs or lay magistrates are appointed by the Lord Chancellor. Except in certain circumstances, such as an urgent sitting of a remand court, they do not sit as justices.

Coroners: Coroners must be barristers or solicitors of not less than 5 yrs standing practising in Northern Ireland.

THE LEGAL PROFESSION:
The legal profession in Northern Ireland consists of barristers and solicitors belonging to professional bodies organised on similar lines to those in England and Wales.

Qualification as a Barrister at the Bar of England and Wales

Introduction: Barristers of the Bar of England and Wales fall into 2 categories: (1) those qualified to practise at the Bar of England and Wales (this includes practice in employment); (2) those qualified as Barristers who do not have the right to practise in England and Wales. In order to qualify, both categories must (a) join an Inn of Court; (b) complete the academic stage of training; (c) complete the vocational stage of training. Those intending to practise at the Bar of England and Wales must: (i) Attend the 1 yr FT or 2 yr PT Bar Vocational Course (BVC) at one of the validated institutions and successfully complete the assessments (from 1997 this course will be offered by a number of validated institutions), (ii) Serve 1 yr in pupillage. Currently, those wishing to follow the non-practising route must pass the Bar Exam to complete the Vocational Course.

Joining an Inn of Court: It is currently necessary to join 1 of the 4 Inns of Court (Lincoln's Inn, Inner Temple, Middle Temple, Gray's Inn) before embarking on the vocational stage of training. In order to be admitted to an Inn it is generally necessary to hold a 2nd class hons degree or better or, in the case of undergraduates, to be reading for such a degree. Before being called to the Bar, students must complete 12 qualifying sessions or dinners. For further information, contact the Student Officer at the appropriate Inn of Court (Lincoln's Inn, London WC2A 3TL, Inner Temple, London EC4Y 7HL, Middle Temple, London EC4Y 9AT, Gray's Inn, London WC1R 5EU).

The Academic Stage of Training: There are 3 ways in which the academic stage of training may be completed: (1) by obtaining a òÁqualifying law degree' (ie one which satisfies the requirements of the General Council of the Bar), including certain specified subjects known as foundation subjects and being passed at II(ii) honours level or above; (2) by obtaining a degree regarded as being of a comparable standard but not in law, or/and covering all the necessary subjects in English law, and taking a specified 1yr FT or 2 yr PT course (Diploma in Law or Common Professional Exam) at an approved Institution; (3) in exceptional cases, being accepted by an Inn of Court as a non-graduate mature student and following a 1 yr FT or 2 yr PT course in (Diploma in Law or Common Professional Examination) at an approved institution. Further details about completing either the academic, or the vocational stage of training may be obtained from The General Council of the Bar, 2/3 Cursitor Street, London EC4A 1NE.

The Vocational Stage of Training: From September 1997 all students, including those from overseas jurisdictions who would previously have taken the Bar Examination for non-intending practitioners, will be required to attend a Bar Vocational Course (BVC) at one of the validated institutions throughout the country. A list if these institutions is available on request from the Education and Training Department at the General Council of the Bar. The purpose of the course is to ensure that students intending to become a barrister acquire the skills, knowledge of procedure and evidence, attitudes and competence in two optional areas to prepare them, in particular, for the more specialised training in the twelve mths of pupillage which follows so that they are adequately equipped for when they are eventually briefed. The FT Bar Vocational Course runs for one academic yr, the PT course for 2 yrs.

Pupillage: Those intending to practise at the Bar of England and Wales must serve one yr in pupillage in the chambers of a Barrister. In the first six mths of such pupillage students may not take instructions from clients but may do so thereafter. Every practising Barrister's work is different because the Bar is a profession of individuals whose talents and abilities vary. Types of professional practice are: Common Law, Criminal Law, Family Law, Commercial Work, Chancery and European International Practice. Further information is available from the General Council of the Bar, Education and Training Department, 2/3 Cursitor Street, London EC4A 1NE.

Qualification as a Barrister in Northern Ireland

To qualify for practice as a barrister in Northern Ireland a candidate must be admitted to the degree of Barrister-at-Law by the **Honorable Society of the Inn of Court of Northern Ireland,** Royal Courts of Justice, Belfast BT1 3JF, Tel Belfast 01232 235111. Enquiries to Under Treasurer. A candidate must be at least 21, hold a degree conferred by a university of the United Kingdom or the Republic of Ireland or by the Council for National Academic Awards of not lower than 2nd class hons, have attended a course at the Institute of Professional Legal Studies, Queen's University, Belfast, and obtained the Certificate of Professional Legal Studies. Before attending the Institute, candidates must first be admitted as students of the Inn of Court of Northern Ireland.

Qualification as a Solicitor in England and Wales

To practise as a solicitor in England and Wales a person must have been admitted as a solicitor, his or her name having been entered on the Roll of Solicitors, and must hold a practising certificate issued by **The Law Society,** Ipsley Court, Berrington Close, Redditch, Worcestershire B98 0TD Tel 0870 606 2555. Persons will be admitted as solicitors only if they have passed the appropriate exams and have completed a training contract and Professional Skills Course. The Law Society controls the training of solicitors. Most solicitors become members of the Society, but membership is not compulsory. Intending solicitors other than Fellows of the Institute of Legal Executives and Justices' Clerk's Assistants, are required to serve a period of training with a practising solicitor after they have completed the Legal Practice Course.

TRAINING CONTRACT:

A candidate who wishes to start training must enrol as a student with The Law Society and satisfy the Society that they have successfully completed the academic stage of training. The training contract to be served by all intending solicitors, other than Fellows of the Institute of Legal Executives and Justices' Clerk's Assistants is 2 yrs. The law graduate who holds a qualifying law degree must complete the Legal Practice Course at a recognised institution, and then serve under the training contract for 2 yrs. The non-law graduate must first pass the Common Professional Exam (CPE) or the Postgraduate Diploma in Law, having attended either a 1 yr FT or 2 yr PT preparatory course. He or she may then serve under the training contract for 2 yrs after completion of a Legal Practice Course. Fellows of the Institute of Legal Executives and Justices' Clerk's Assistants may obtain up to 8 exemptions from the CPE by virtue of similar subjects passed in their Fellowship exams. After passing or being exempted from the CPE, the Fellow/Justices' Clerk's Assistant may be exempt from serving under a training contract following successful completion of an LPC. A Professional Skills Course must be taken prior to application for admission.

THE COMMON PROFESSIONAL EXAM/ POSTGRADUATE DIPLOMA IN LAW:
Subjects: Obligations 1 & 2, Foundations of Criminal Law, Equity & Law of Trust, Law of the EU, Property Law & Public Land, one other area of legal studies.FT courses for the CPE are offered by the College of Law, the Universities of Anglia Polytechnic, Birmingham, Bournemouth, Central England in Birmingham, Central Lancashire, City, De Montfort, East Anglia, Exeter, Glamorgan, Huddersfield, Keele, Kingston, Leeds Metropolitan, London Guildhall, Manchester Metropolitan, Middlesex, North London, Northumbria at Newcastle, Nottingham Trent, Oxford Brookes, South Bank, Staffordshire, Sussex, Thames Valley, Westminster and Wolverhampton, BPP Law School. PT 2 yr courses are offered by the Universities of Central England in Birmingham, Central Lancashire, City, De Montfort, Glamorgan, Holborn College, Huddersfield, Leeds Metropolitan, London Guildhall, Manchester Metropolitan, North London, Northumbria, Nottingham Trent, South Bank, Staffordshire, Thames Valley, Westminster, West of England, Wolverhampton and Worcester College of Technology. DL courses are offered by the College of Law and the Universities of De Montfort, Manchester Metropolitan, Northumbria at Newcastle, Nottingham Trent, BPP Law School, West of England and Wolsey Hall College in Oxford.

THE LEGAL PRACTICE COURSE:
Compulsory subjects: Litigation & Advocacy, Conveyancing, Business Law & Practice. 3 elective subjects: from a range of Corporate Client or Private Client topics (the range of elective available can differ from institution to institution).Persuasive subjects: Accounts, Professional Conduct and Client Care, European Union Law, Revenue Law. These areas pervade the compulsory and elective subjects of the course. Legal Skills: Practical legal research, writing and drafting, interviewing and advising, advocacy. These skills form an integral part of the compulsory and elective subjects. FT courses for the LPC are offered by: College of Law, Bournemouth, Manchester Metropolitan University, Huddersfield University, Leeds Metropolitan University, Northumbria at Newcastle, Sheffield, Glamorgan, Wales (Cardiff), Bristol, Anglia Polytechnic University, BPP Law School, Exeter, Westminster, De Montfort, Nottingham Trent, Staffordshire, Central England at Birmingham, Wolverhampton, West of England, London Guildhall, Thames Valley and Oxford Institute of Legal Practice. PT, 2 yr courses are available at the Universities of Central England, Central Lancashire, Northumbria at Newcastle, Manchester Metropolitan, Glamorgan, Huddersfield, Leeds Metropolitan, John Moores (Liverpool), South Bank, Staffordshire, North London, Hertfordshire, Westminster, De Montfort, Nottingham Trent, London Guildhall and the College of Law, Wolverhampton, BPP Law School.

THE PROFESSIONAL SKILLS COURSE:
From June 1998 a new model Professional Skills Course will be implemented. The aim of the Professional Skills Course is to build on the foundations laid in the LPC so as to develop a trainee's professional skills. Providers of the course, trainees and their employers are encouraged to regard the course as the first stage of a trainee's lifetime professional development. Building upon the LPC, the course will provide training in three subject areas, viz: Financial and Business Skills; Advocacy and Communication Skills; Ethics and Client Responsibilities. Elective topics will also be chosen which fall within one or more of these three core areas. All trainees will have to complete all sections of the course satisfactorily before being admitted. The course will last for 12 days and must be taken during the training contract. Subject to the Law Society being satisfied that the syllabuses will be properly covered and that appropriate tutors and teaching material will be used, it should be possible for the course to be provided by firms in-house, or by local law societies as well as by approved teaching institutions and commercial organisations.

QUALIFIED LAWYERS FROM OTHER JURISDICTIONS:
UK lawyers together with lawyers form certain foreign jurisdictions and EU lawyers can apply for admission under the Qualified Lawyers Transfer Regulations 1990. The European Community Directive on the mutual recognition of Higher Education Diplomas came into force on 4th January 1991. Under the Directive lawyers from EU jurisdictions may apply for admission following

successful completion of aptitude tests in areas of the Common Law compulsory for students in England and Wales. Lawyers from other common law jurisdictions are required to pass such aptitude tests as well as completing up to 2 yrs' post-admission experience either before their home court or in employment in England and Wales. For information on any of the routes to qualification, contact Information Services at the Law Society. Tel 0870 606 2555, or www.lawsociety.org.uk

Qualification as a Solicitor in Scotland

Solicitors in Scotland have their names inserted in a Roll of Solicitors and are granted annual **Certificates** entitling them to practise by **The Law Society of Scotland,** 26 Drumsheugh Gardens, Edinburgh EH3 7YR, Tel: 0131-226 7411 Fax: 0131-225 2934 E-mail: lawscot@lawscot.org.uk Website: www.lawscot.org.uk. A Certificate is granted to candidates who are at least 21, have completed a term of practical training and passed approved exams. (The Law Society will be happy to provide copies of its careers information leaflets on request.)The academic training in Scotland is largely undertaken by 5 of the Universities.

THE QUALIFYING EXAMINATIONS:
97% of those who qualify as Solicitors in Scotland do so by taking an LLB (Ord or Hons) at a Scottish university (or an Arts degree followed by LLB) followed by the Diploma in Legal Practice, and a period of in-office training. Non-LLB graduates may take the **Professional Exams of the Law Society** *all* intending entrants, graduates and non-graduates, to the profession in Scotland to obtain the Diploma in Legal Practice, after the completion of LLB Degree studies, or the Society's Exams. The Diploma is a University award, obtained after 1 yr of FT study, and provides training in the practical skills required by solicitors. The Diploma Course is followed by a 2 yr training contract in a solicitor's office, during the latter yr of which the trainee may apply to hold a qualified practising Certificate, enabling him or her to appear in Court.
Note on England and Wales: A solicitor admitted in Scotland may immediately apply to sit the Law Society's Exam to qualify for practice in England and Wales.

Qualification as a Solicitor in Northern Ireland

The solicitors' professional body in Northern Ireland is the **Law Society of Northern Ireland**, Law Society House, 98 Victoria Street, Belfast BT1 3JZ, Tel 01232 231614/5. It has overall responsibility for education and admission to the profession. Admission to training is generally dependent upon possession of a law degree from a recognised university. Law graduates must complete a 2 yr apprenticeship, one yr of which is comprised of a professional vocational course, at the Institute of Professional Legal Studies, The Queen's University of Belfast. After the completion of the 2 yr apprenticeship, they may be admitted as solicitors, but they are restricted from practising on their own account until they have served for 3 yrs as the qualified assistant of a practising solicitor. Non-law graduates must complete a 2 yr FT academic course in law at the Law Faculty, followed by the 2 yr apprenticeship, and may then be admitted on the same conditions as indicated above.

Qualification as an Advocate in Scotland

Barristers in Scotland are called Advocates. Scottish Advocates are not only members of the **Faculty of Advocates**, Advocates' Library, Parliament House, Edinburgh EH1 1RF, Tel 0131-226 5071, but also members of the College of Justice and officers of the Court. The procedure for the admission of Intrants is subject in part to the control of the Court and in part to the control of the Faculty; the Court is responsible for most of the formal procedures and the Faculty for the exams and periods of professional training. Prospective Intrants must produce evidence that they hold a degree with Honours, Second Class (Division 2) or above, in Scottish Law at a Scottish University, or a degree in Scottish Law at a Scottish University together with a degree with Honours, Second Class (Division 2) or above, in another subject at a United Kingdom University or an ordinary degree with distinction in Scottish Law at a Scottish University and also submit the names of 2 persons of standing in the community from whom references may be obtained. A notice is posted outside Parliament House for a period of 21 days declaring the candidates intention to present a Petition. At the end of this period the Petition is presented to the Court. After the Petition has been remitted by the Court to the Faculty the candidate is considered to have **Matriculated** as an

Intrant. The Faculty **Exams in Legal Scholarship** are conducted on the standard known as the òÁLLB standard' at the Scottish universities. Subject-for-subject exemptions are granted to Intrants who have passed exams at this standard in the course of a curriculum for a law degree at a Scottish university. Every Intrant must pass or be exempted from exams in 9 compulsory subjects and 2 optional subjects. The compulsory subjects include Roman Law, Jurisprudence, Constitutional and Administrative Law, Scottish Criminal Law, Scottish Private Law, Commercial Law and Business Institutions, Evidence, International Private Law and European Law and Institutions. In addition, during pupillage every Intrant must sit an exam (on a higher standard) in Evidence, Practice and Procedure. A Diploma in Legal Practice from a Scottish University is also required, although in exceptional cases this requirement may be waived.

Professional Training consists of a period of 21 mths' training in a Solicitor's office (in some cases 12 mths), followed by a period of about 9 mths' pupillage to a practising member of the Faculty. During the first 3 or 4 wks of pupillage pupils undertake a Foundation Course. Intrants who have passed all the necessary exams and undergone the necessary professional training may apply to be admitted to membership of the Faculty and are admitted at a public meeting of the Faculty. Once admitted to the Faculty, Intrants are introduced to the Court by the Dean of Faculty, make a Declaration of Allegiance to the Sovereign in open Court and are then admitted by the Court to the public office of Advocate.

Legal Executives

THE INSTITUTE OF LEGAL EXECUTIVES (ILEX)

Kempston Manor, Kempston, Bedford MK42 7AB Tel: 01234 841000 Fax: 01234 840373
e-mail: info@ilex.org.uk Website: www.ilex.org.uk

Legal Executives are usually employed in solicitors' offices as specialists in various aspects of legal work. They carry varying degrees of responsibility, depending on how the office is organised, up to full control of their departments, subject to the ultimate responsibility of the solicitor concerned. The Legal Executive training scheme is now the principal non-graduate route to qualification as a solicitor.

MEMBERSHIP:

Fellowship: Open to Members who are 25 or over and have completed at least 5 yrs in qualifying employment, including 2 consecutive yrs after qualifying as a Member of the Institute.

Members: Those who have passed the Institute's Membership Qualifications.

Students: Those who are registered with the Institute and are preparing for the Membership Qualifications. The minimum enrolment requirement is 4 GCSEs in approved academic subjects, or the equivalent. Mature students over 21 can be exempted the usual enrolment requirement.

EXAMINATIONS:

Part I of the Membership Exam: Covers a broad range of principles of law and legal practice and introduces students to most of the work which goes on in a solicitor's office. Since September 1998, the Part I Exam has been available in both traditional, exam-based and vocational format.

Part II of the Membership Exam: Comprises 3 substantive law papers at degree level and 1 specialist practice option. The papers must be selected to reflect a chosen area of procedural specialisation. Parts I and II would take a PT student around 4 yrs to complete.

Diplomas: Awarded to non-members of the Institute who pass individual Part II exam subjects.

Legal Accounts Exams: Available for those who specialise in the finance work of solicitors' offices.

Vocational Qualifications: In law topics, designed for non-lawyers, are also available through the Institute's subsidiary company, ILEX Paralegal Training. ILEX and EDEXCEL are in partnership as the joint awarding body for NVQs in legal practice.

Legal Experts

THE ACADEMY OF EXPERTS

2 South Square, Gray's Inn, London WC1R 5HP Tel: 020 7637 0333 Fax: 020 7637 1893 e-mail: admin@academy-experts.org Website: www.academy-experts.org

Membership of the Academy is open to all individuals and bodies who can satisfy the Council that they are fit and proper persons. There are different categories of membership.

Fellows (FAE): Must be able to demonstrate an appropriate standard of technical competence in their profession or calling; must have wide knowledge and experience as an Expert; and must possess knowledge of legal procedures and the law of evidence.

Members (MAE): Must be able to demonstrate an appropriate standard of technical competence in their profession or calling as an Expert.

Associates: Are those interested in giving Expert advice and seeking to qualify as Members. Those passing the exams are awarded AMAE.

NON-PRACTISING MEMBERS:
Honorary Fellow (HonFAE): An Honorary member of the Academy is entitled to use the designatory title of an honorary fellow, but is described as an honorary member.

Companion (CAE): Companions shall be individuals of high standing whose experience does not meet the requirements for practising individual membership. Companions will have similar standing to Fellows.

Affiliated Individual Members: Executives of bodies which themselves qualify as an Affiliated Corporate Member.

Affiliated Corporate Members: Any body, incorporated or unincorporated, which is sufficiently connected with, or has an interest in, the use of Experts, enabling (a) any such body to nominate a representative to attend meetings of the Academy; (b) such representatives to be eligible for election to the Council.

Subscribing Members: Lawyers qualified to practise in any jurisdiction.

Qualified Dispute Resolver: Must be able to demonstrate an appropriate standard of knowledge and experience of one or more of the categories of dispute resolver. Currently these are Mediator, Conciliator, Arbitrator and (QDR) Expert Determiner. *Membership prior to July 1995 maintains the designatory letters FBAE & MBAE.

TRAINING:
The Academy provides training at various levels and in various forms and courses are run on a wide variety of practical and intellectual matters, including Ethics & Responsibilities, Report Writing & Presentation of Evidence and Practise & Procedure in the EU. In addition, Mediators' Qualifying Courses as well as Continuation Training and ADR Familiarisation Courses for the Legal Profession and Dispute Resolvers are held.

EXAMINATIONS:
Held twice yrly. Mandatory for upgrade to full status. Shortly to be mandatory for upgrade to fellow.

THE COUNCIL FOR LICENSED CONVEYANCERS

16 Glebe Road, Chelmsford, Essex CM1 1QG Tel: 01245 349599 Fax: 01245 341300
e-mail: clc@theclc.gov.uk

The Council is the Regulatory Body for Licensed Conveyancers. It sets training requirements and carries out examining, licensing, and disciplinary functions. The basic educational requirement for registration as a student is 4 GCSE passes (or equivalent) in English Language and 3 other approved subjects at A, B or C. However, mature students over 25 without qualifications may be accepted with relevant practical experience only. LLB and LPC students will be exempt from the equivalent subjects.

EXAMINATIONS:
The Council's exams are in two parts: Foundation and Finals.

Foundation: Comprises Introduction to Licensed Conveyancing, Conveyancing Practice & Procedure (both assessed assignments), and 2 examinations, Land Law and Law of Contract.

Finals: Comprise 3 subjects, Conveyancing Law & Practice, Landlord & Tenant and Accounts. Tuition for the CLC exams is available on a PT basis at a number of colleges and universities throughout the country, and the correspondence course is available direct from the Council for Licensed Conveyancers.

PRACTICAL TRAINING:
Students are also required to complete 2 yrs' practical experience in conveyancing with either a Licensed Conveyancer or Solicitor who are entitled to practise as sole principals, or within a

conveyancing department of a bank, building society, property developer of local authority. This can be achieved PT or FT whilst studying for the exams.

LICENCE HOLDERS:

After successfully completing the exams and practical training, a student is eligible to apply for a limited licence, that is as an employed conveyancer for a further 3 yrs. Only after this period can a limited licence holder apply for a full licence, that is as a sole principal providing conveyancing services directly to the public, by way of an interview with the Council's Licence and Practice Committee after submitting a Business Plan, CV and Cash Flow Forecast. The decision to issue a full licence rests solely with that Committee. Altough a young profession, its numbers are increasing daily as it is seen as an alternative career to becoming a solicitor for those wishing to pursue conveyancing. Those interested in entering the profession should contact the Council's Director of Education and Licensing, Mrs Enid Watson, for advice and information at the above address.

THE INSTITUTE OF LEGAL CASHIERS AND ADMINISTRATORS

146–148 Eltham Hill, Eltham, London SE9 5DX Tel: 020 8294 2887 Fax: 020 8859 1682
e-mail: info@ilca.org.uk

MEMBERSHIP:

The Institute was formed in 1978 and provides its members with a code of ethics plus various services including an advisory service and a register of vacancies. Membership is divided into 4 categories: **Ordinary, Diploma, Associate and Fellow Members**.

EXAMINATIONS:

The Institute has its own structured exam scheme which was developed in conjunction with the Law Department of the University of the West of England. Because of the varied ages and backgrounds of those joining the Institute there are no formal requirements for taking the exams, however, it is envisaged a typical career path would be:

Diploma: For new entrants to the profession. It is intended to test their immediate working knowledge of the office environment.

Associate: Designed to test career students on a deeper understanding of the many legal and accounting topics they will meet in working life. Members are recommended to have 2 or more yrs' experience before embarking on this. Correspondence courses are available for the Diploma and Associate exams.

Fellowship: The Institute's highest qualification. Allows Associates to follow a specialised course of study on a subject approved by the Institute's Education & Training Committee. The Institute also provides training courses on relevant topical subjects.

Useful Addresses

Law Society, 113 Chancery Lane, London WC2A 1PL Tel: 020 7242 1222

LEISURE AND RECREATION MANAGEMENT

MEMBERSHIP OF PROFESSIONAL INSTITUTIONS AND ASSOCIATIONS

INSTITUTE OF GROUNDSMANSHIP

19-23 Church Street, The Agora, Wolverton, Milton Keynes MK12 5LG Tel: 01908 312511
Fax: 01908 311140 e-mail: iog@iog.org Website: www.iog.org

MEMBERSHIP:

Fellows: Must have 5 yrs' experience in the Industry and hold the NDT in Turfculture.

Full Members: Must be persons over 18 employed in Groundsmanship or a related profession for at least 3 yrs. Others so employed can become **Professional Associate Members**, while anyone under 18 employed or training in Turfculture will be accepted as a **Junior Member**. Full time students are accepted free as **Student Members**. Any Corporation concerned in any trade relating to and concerning the Grounds Management industry is eligible to be a **Corporate Member** of the

Institute. Any club, college or organisation concerned in the promotion of sport or concerned in the promotion of any objects similar to the objects of the Institute is eligible to be an **Affiliate Member** of the Institute.

PROFESSIONAL EXAMINATIONS:

ND in the Science and Practice of Turfculture and Sports Ground Management (NDT): The exam is open to all employed in the profession of groundsmanship who hold the Intermediate Diploma or equivalent. The exam consists of 3 parts, a number of written papers and a series of practical/oral tests and a dissertation. The

Intermediate Diploma (NID): Follows a similar pattern, without the dissertation, and is less demanding.

The National Technical Certificate: Based on Amenity Horticulture NVQ/SVQ Level 2, Sports Turf Maintenance, and qualifies candidates for the Intermediate Diploma examination.

The National Practical Certificate: The initial stage in the training and qualification of groundsmen.

INSTITUTE OF LEISURE AND AMENITY MANAGEMENT

ILAM House, Lower Basildon, Reading, Berkshire RG8 9NE Tel: 01491 874800 Fax: 01491 874801 e-mail: info@ilam.co.uk. Website: www.ilam.co.uk

MEMBERSHIP:

ILAM was formed in 1983 by the amalgamation of 4 existing professional bodies. The Institute has a rapidly expanding membership and members' responsibilities include: leisure and sports centres, arts and entertainment complexes, parks, gardens and playgrounds, museums and tourist attractions, countryside recreation, health and fitness clubs.

Member (MILAM): Those engaged in the leisure industry in a position of responsibility.

Associate (AILAM): Those working in the leisure industry who do not fulfil the full membership requirements of the Institute.

Students: Those engaged on a course or training scheme within the leisure management field.

Corporate Affiliate: Public bodies wishing to join ILAM on an organisational basis.

Commercial Affiliate: Commercial companies wishing to join ILAM on an organisational basis.

QUALIFICATIONS:

The new ILAM Professional Qualification Scheme was launched in August 2000. There are now 5 professional levels to the Scheme, as well as 2 technical qualifications. The professional qualification requires candidates to complete a work-based project of a given length to a standard set by the Institute which is appropriate to the qualification being sought.

Professional Qualifications

ILAM First Award: For those new to the industry or with a junior position in the industry. Completion is by work-based projects.

ILAM Certificate in Leisure Operations: For candidates who have a basic working knowledge and understanding of the leisure industry and who hold junior supervisory positions with leisure organisations. Completion is by work-based projects.

ILAM Certificate in Leisure Management: For candidates who have a reasonable understanding of the Leisure Industry and who hold junior or supervisory management posts with a minimum of 400 hrs relevant work experience. Completion is through a combination of exemptions, examinations and projects.

ILAM Diploma in Leisure Management: For candidates who can successfully demonstrate their managerial ability at a middle management level and who hold at least middle management posts and who aspire to senior management level. Completion is through a combination of exemptions, examinations and projects.

ILAM Advanced Diploma in Leisure Management: For candidates who can successfully demonstrate their managerial ability at a senior level and who hold posts at senior management level. Completion is through a combination of exemptions, examinations and projects. To ensure that leisure managers are kept up to date, ILAM offers a comprehensive programme of Continuing Professional Development courses and seminars. The Institute is also approved to train and assess in TDLB units for Assessors and Verifiers. A range of open/distance learning materials has been produced by the Institute, designed to help with NVQs and the ILAM Certificate of Achievement.

Technical Qualifications
ILAM Certificate in Technical Operations (Operations & Maintenance of Swimming Pool Water Treatment & Plant). Also the **National Aquatic Rescue Standards for Pool Lifeguards** is a new lifesaving course run in association with the Swimming Teachers Association. Both the above courses provide the underpinning knowledge that is required for the S/NVQ Operational Services (Level 2) and the material used is SPRITO approved.

INSTITUTE OF SPORT AND RECREATION MANAGEMENT (ISRM)

Giffard House, 36-38 Sherrard Street, Melton Mowbray, Leicestershire LE13 1XJ
Tel: 01664 565531 Fax: 01664 501155 e-mail: ralphriley@isrm.co.uk Website: www.isrm.co.uk

EXAMINATIONS:

Institute of Sport & Recreation Operations Certificate: A broad based vocational training and accreditation programme which focuses on health and safety, effective customer care and the efficient technical operation of sport and recreation facilities. These courses deliver the underpinning knowledge required for S/NVQ Level 2.

ISRM Supervisory Management Certificate: Provides a national standard of training and accreditation for sport and recreation facility supervisors. These courses deliver the underpinning knowledge required for S/NVQ Level 3.

Institute of Sport & Recreation Management Certificate: A prestigious nationally recognised qualification relating to the management of sports halls, leisure centres, swimming pools and associated facilities. These courses deliver the underpinning knowledge required for S/NVQ Level 4.

ISRM Diploma: A higher level exam for qualified ISRM members designed to provide sport and recreation facility managers with the knowledge and understanding to progress to senior management levels within the sport and recreation industry and/or manage major facilities, and to give recognition to professionals qualified at this level.

University Qualifications

The following universities offer qualifications in Leisure and Recreation Management and related subjects. Full details may be found in Part 4, under the entry for the appropriate university.

FIRST DEGREES AWARDED BY UNIVERSITIES

Anglia; Anglia (Colchester Institute); Barnsley; Bath; Birmingham (Birmingham College of Food, Tourism and Creative Studies); Blackburn; Bournemouth; Bradford (Bradford & Ilkley Community College); Brighton; Bristol; Brunel; Bucks. Coll.; Central Lancashire; Cheltenham & Gloucester; Coventry; De Montfort, Leicester; De Montfort, Leicester (De Montfort University Bedford); Doncaster; Durham; East Anglia (Suffolk College); East London; Essex (Writtle College); Exeter (The College of St Mark & St John); Glamorgan; Glasgow; Glasgow Caledonian; Hertfordshire (West Herts College); Huddersfield; Hull; Kent (Canterbury Christ Church University College); Lancaster (Blackpool and The Fylde College); Lancaster (Edge Hill College of Higher Education); Leeds (Leeds, Trinity & All Saints); Leeds (The College of Ripon & York St John); Leeds Metropolitan; Lincolnshire (Grimsby College); Liverpool John Moores; Loughborough; Luton; Manchester; Manchester (Warrington Collegiate Institute, Faculty of H.E,); Manchester Metropolitan.; North London; Nottingham Trent (Southampton Institute); Portsmouth; Salford; Sheffield Hallam; Southampton (King Alfred's College); St Martin; Staffordshire; Strathclyde; Surrey; Surrey (Farnborough College of Technology); Surrey (University of Surrey Roehampton); Teesside; Thames Valley; Ulster; Wales (Swansea Institute of Higher Education); Wales (University of Wales Institute, Cardiff); Wales (University of Wales, Bangor); Wolverhampton

HIGHER DEGREES AWARDED BY UNIVERSITIES

Aberdeen; Anglia; Bucks. Coll.; Central Lancashire; Cheltenham & Gloucester; De Montfort, Leicester; De Montfort, Leicester (De Montfort University Bedford); Glasgow Caledonian; Lancaster; Lancaster (Edge Hill College of Higher Education); Leeds Metropolitan; Loughborough; Luton; North London; Sheffield; Sheffield Hallam; Surrey; Surrey (University of Surrey Roehampton); Thames Valley; Ulster; Wales (University of Wales Institute, Cardiff)

DIPLOMAS AWARDED BY UNIVERSITIES
Anglia; Anglia (City College, Norwich); Anglia (Colchester Institute); Barnsley; Birmingham (Birmingham College of Food, Tourism and Creative Studies); Blackburn; Bournemouth; Bradford (Bradford & Ilkley Community College); Bucks. Coll.; Central Lancashire; Cheltenham & Gloucester; De Montfort, Leicester; De Montfort, Leicester (De Montfort University Bedford); Doncaster; Durham (New College Durham); East Anglia (Suffolk College); Greenwich; Lincolnshire (Bishop Burton College); Lincolnshire (Hull College); Lincolnshire (Yorkshire Coast College); Luton; OU (NESCOT); Salford; Southampton (King Alfred's College); Teesside; Ulster; Wales (Swansea Institute of Higher Education); Wales (University of Wales Institute, Cardiff); Worcester

CERTIFICATES AWARDED BY UNIVERSITIES
Cheltenham & Gloucester; Leeds Metropolitan; Liverpool John Moores; Manchester (Warrington Collegiate Institute, Faculty of H.E,); Salford; Wales (University of Wales Institute, Cardiff); Wales (University of Wales, Bangor)

OTHER COURSES AWARDED BY UNIVERSITIES
Essex (Writtle College)

POSTGRADUATE DIPLOMAS AWARDED BY UNIVERSITIES
Thames Valley

National Certificates and Diplomas
BTEC National Certificates/Diplomas: Leisure Studies; Leisure Studies (Outdoor Recreation)
BTEC Higher National Certificates/Diplomas: Leisure Management; Leisure Studies; Outdoor Activity and Environmental Management; Recreation and Leisure Management
Scotland
SQA HNC: Countryside Recreation and Conservation Management; Leisure and Recreation Management; Leisure Management; Sport and Exercise Science; Sport and Hospitality; Sports Coaching; Sports Coaching with Sports Development; Sports Coaching Practices and Development; Sports Therapy
SQA HND: Countryside Recreation and Conservation Management; Leisure and Beauty Services; Leisure and Recreation Management; Sport and Exercise Science; Sport and Hospitality Management; Sports Coaching with Sports Development; Sports Therapy

NVQs
Level 1: Sport, Recreation and Allied Occupations
Level 2: Mechanical Ride Operation (Leisure Parks, Piers & Attractions); Sport and Recreation (Sport and Play Installations); Sport, Recreation and Allied Occupations – Activity Leadership; Sport Recreation and Allied Occupations – Coaching, Teaching and Instructing; Sport, Recreation and Allied Occupations – Operational Services; Sport, Recreation and Allied Occupations: Spectator Control
Level 3: Sport, Recreation and Allied Occupations: Operations and Development Sport, Recreation and Allied Occupations: Spectator Control; Sports Administration
Level 4: Spectator Control; Sport and Recreation (Coaching); Sport and Recreation Management (Facilities); Sport and Recreation Management (Sports Development)

SVQs
Level 1: Sport, Recreation and Allied Occupations
Level 2: Horticulture (Greenkeeping – Sports-turf, Sports Ground Maintenance); Sport and Recreation: Sport and Play Installation: Sport, Recreation and Allied Occupations: Activity Leadership or Coaching, Teaching and Instruction or Operational Services; Playwork
Level 3: Maintaining Sports-turf; Sport, Recreation and Allied Occupations: Operations and Development; Playwork; Outdoor Education, Development Training, Recreation: Development Training or Outdoor Education or Recreation

GNVQs

3725 Leisure and Tourism

OCR

OCR offer various teaching & management awards in Leisure, Recreation & Sports. Contact OCR for details.

City & Guilds

4810 Recreation and Leisure Industries

Useful Addresses

National Training Organisation for Sport, Recreation and Allied Occupations, c/o Sheffield College – Norton Centre, Dyche Lane, Sheffield S8 8BR Tel 0114 237 4259 Fax: 0114 237 3927
Sport Play and Recreation Industries National Training Executive (SPRINT), Unit 58, Business Development Centre, Stafford Park 4, Telford TF3 3BA Tel: 020 7388 9999

LIBRARIANSHIP AND INFORMATION WORK

Membership of Professional Institutions and Associations

THE INSTITUTE OF INFORMATION SCIENTISTS

39-41 North Road, London N7 9DP Tel: 020 7619 0624/0625 Fax: 0207619 0627
e-mail: iis@dial.pipex.com Website: www.iis.org.uk

MEMBERSHIP:
Fellowship: May be granted to Members who, after 10 yrs in information work, satisfy the Council that they have attained distinction by virtue of work in a senior position or of original work in the information field or have otherwise given distinguished service to the Institute. The Council may admit to **Honorary Fellowship** anyone of distinction.

Members: Are admitted by Council and should comply with the following conditions: (a) being at least 25 yrs of age; (b) holding at least a degree granted by a British University, or a qualification accepted by Council as equivalent; and (c) either (i) holding a qualification approved by Council and having at least 2 yrs' approved experience in Information Work, at least 1 of which must be subsequent to gaining the approved qualification provided that Council may at its discretion require a greater amount of experience subsequent to his gaining the approved qualification if that qualification is deemed to be equivalent to less than 3 yrs' experience in Information Work, or (ii) having at least 5 yrs' approved experience in Information Work, at least 4 of which must be subsequent to gaining the degree or equivalent.

Affiliates: Are admitted by Council and should comply with the following conditions: (a) being a member of an association or institute or engaged in professional graduate level work whose field of activity is deemed by Council to be relevant to that of the Institute; or (b) having the necessary academic qualifications and being employed in information work but lacking sufficient experience to qualify for admission as a Member or being under 25; or (c) having been or are being employed in information work and attending an undergraduate course in a subject other than Information Science; or (d) having been or are being concerned directly with information work in the course of one's employment or profession or studying information work but not qualifying for any other grade of membership.

THE LIBRARY ASSOCIATION

7 Ridgmount Street, London WC1E 7AE Tel: 020 7255 0500 Fax: 020 7255 0501
e-mail: info@la-hq.org.uk Website: www.la.hq.org.uk

MEMBERSHIP:
Fellow (FLA): Is a fully qualified Chartered Member of The Library Association normally of at

least 5 yrs' standing in the grade of Associate who has been elected by the Council to the Fellowship (the higher category of Chartered Membership) upon acceptance of evidence of continuing professional development and contribution to the profession.

Associate (ALA): Is a fully qualified Chartered Member of The Library Association, who is a graduate and has the necessary practical training and experience required by the Association, and has demonstrated his/her professional competence through submission to the Association of an acceptable application based on his/her professional development since completing his/her academic studies.

QUALIFYING EXAMINATION:
Before commencing the post-course practical training and experience required, candidates for Associateship must first successfully complete an accredited degree or postgraduate qualification (or equiv) in library and information studies.

Courses of Study accredited by the Library Association are available at the following institutions: Robert Gordon's University; University of Wales, Aberystwyth; University of Central England in Birmingham; University of Brighton; University of Bristol; University of Strathclyde; Leeds Metropolitan University; Liverpool John Moores University; University of North London; Thames Valley University; University Coll London; City University; Loughborough University; Manchester Metropolitan University; University of Northumbria at Newcastle; University of Sheffield and Queen Margaret College, Edinburgh.

University Qualifications

The following universities offer qualifications in Librarianship and Information Work and related subjects. Full details may be found in Part 4, under the entry for the appropriate university.

FIRST DEGREES AWARDED BY UNIVERSITIES
Anglia; Bournemouth; Brighton; Central England; Cranfield; De Montfort, Leicester; Durham; Essex; Glamorgan; Glasgow Caledonian; Kent (Canterbury Christ Church University College); Leeds Metropolitan; Liverpool John Moores; London (Birkbeck, University of London); Loughborough; Manchester (Warrington Collegiate Institute, Faculty of H.E,); Manchester Metropolitan.; Napier; Oxford; Robert Gordon; Wales (University of Wales, Aberystwyth); Wolverhampton

HIGHER DEGREES AWARDED BY UNIVERSITIES
Bournemouth; Bristol; Central England; City; De Montfort, Leicester; Glasgow Caledonian; Leeds; Leeds Metropolitan; Lincolnshire; Liverpool; Liverpool John Moores; London (University College (UCL)); Loughborough; Manchester Metropolitan.; Northumbria; Sheffield; South Bank; Southampton; Stirling; Strathclyde; Ulster; UMIST; Wales (University of Wales, Aberystwyth); Wales (University of Wales, Bangor)

DIPLOMAS AWARDED BY UNIVERSITIES
Belfast; Bournemouth; City; Kent (Canterbury Christ Church University College); Lincolnshire; London (University College (UCL)); Loughborough; Napier; Northumbria; South Bank; Stirling; Strathclyde; Ulster; Wales (University of Wales, Aberystwyth); Wales (University of Wales, Bangor)

CERTIFICATES AWARDED BY UNIVERSITIES
Lincolnshire; London (University College (UCL))

National Certificates and Diplomas

Scotland
SQA HNC: Librarianship and Information Sciences
SQA HND: Information Services

NVQs

Level 2: Archive Services; Records Services; Information and Library Service
Level 3: Archive Services; Records Services; Information and Library Service
Level 4: Archive Management; Records Management; Information and Library Service

SVQs

Level 2: Information and Library Services; Archive Services; Records Services
Level 3: Information and Library Services; Records Services
Level 4: Information and Library Services; Archive Services; Records Management

OCR

OCR offer the following awards:
Archive Services Levels 2 & 3
Archive Services Management Level 4
Information & Library Services Levels 2, 3 & 4
Records Services Levels 2 & 3
Records Management Level 4

City & Guilds

7370 Library and Information Assistants Certificate

Useful Addresses

Information & Library Services Lead Body, c/o 7 Ridgmount Street, London WC1E 7AE
Tel: 020 7636 7543 242 2244 E-mail: angela.frampton@la-hq.org.uk

LINGUISTICS, LANGUAGES AND TRANSLATION

Membership of Professional Institutions and Associations

THE GREEK INSTITUTE
(Founded in 1969)
34 Bush Hill Road, London N21 2DS Tel: 020 8360 7968 Fax: 020 8360 7968

QUALIFICATIONS:
Diploma in Greek Translation: 3 papers of 3 hrs each. Paper 1: **General Translation**. To translate 2 passages, 1 from Greek into English and 1 from English into Greek. Each passage to be about 750 words. Papers 2 & 3: **Specialised Translation**. To translate 2 passages in each paper, 1 from Greek into English and 1 from English into Greek. Each passage to be about 750 words. The passages will be of a specialised nature and will relate to *any* of the following areas: Humanities, Social Science, Tourism, Medicine, Science, Law or Business Studies. Dictionaries are allowed. Candidates must satisfy the examiners in all 3 papers in order to pass. The standard of this examination is about the same as a first degree at a British university. Successful candidates may use the designation **DipGrTrans**.
Advanced Certificate: 2 papers of 3 hrs each and an oral test of 20 mins. Paper 1: Translations from and into Greek. Paper 2: Candidates will write essays in Greek on 3 different topics – a) Modern Greek Literature (1 prescribed text); (b) Modern Greek History *or* History of Cyprus (20th Century); and (c) Geography and Tourism (on a specified region of Greece or Cyprus). The standard of this examination is about the same as GCE A Level in Modern Greek.
Examinations: The Greek Institute conducts examinations for a **Preliminary Certificate** (1 paper, 2 hrs, and an oral test of 15 mins at Elementary Level), an **Intermediate Certificate** (1 paper, 2½ hrs and an oral test of 20 mins at GCSE Level), and for the **Advanced Certificate** and the **Diploma in Greek Translation** (see above). The Greek Institute Qualifications are included in the list of Vocational Qualifications approved by the Secretary of State for Education under section 3(1) and Schedule 2(A) to the Further and Higher Education Act 1992.Successful candidates in the **Diploma in Greek Translation** and in the **Advanced Certificate** may be elected **Fellows** and **Associates** and may append after their names the designation **FGI** or **AGI** respectively. Ordinary membership is open to anyone who is interested in Greece, Cyprus or in Modern Greek Studies.

THE INSTITUTE OF LINGUISTS

Saxon House, 48 Southwark Street, London SE1 1UN Tel: 020 7940 3100 Fax: 020 7940 3101 e-mail: info@iol.org.uk Website: www.iol.org.uk

MEMBERSHIP:

Fellow (FIL): Available only to those who have been Members for 3 yrs and have attained a position of higher professional standing.

Member (MIL): The Institute admits applicants to membership on the basis of a degree in languages, or a degree with languages as a major component, an Institute qualifying exam such as the Diploma in Languages for International Communication or the Diploma in Translation. Applicants must have 3 yrs' experience in work requiring linguistic skills; 1 yr must be prior to the date of application. Membership (and Fellowship), if based on a full pass in the Diploma exam, is accepted by a number of Institutions as a degree equivalent.

Associate (AIL): The qualifying exams for this grade of membership are the Intermediate Diploma or equivalent.

Diploma in Translation (DipTransIoL): A post-graduate qualification in professional translation work. Some applicants for membership may be required to take an oral exam. The minimum ages for entry into the 3 classes of membership above are: Fellow 25; Member 21; Associate 18.There are 2 unqualified grades.

University Qualifications

The following universities offer qualifications in Linguistics, Languages and Translation and related subjects. Full details may be found in Part 4, under the entry for the appropriate university.

FIRST DEGREES AWARDED BY UNIVERSITIES

Aberdeen; Abertay, Dundee; Anglia; Anglia (Colchester Institute); Aston; Bath; Bath Spa; Belfast; Birmingham; Birmingham (The University of Birmingham, Westhill); Bournemouth; Bradford; Bradford (Bradford & Ilkley Community College); Brighton; Bristol; Brunel; Buckingham; Bucks. Coll.; Cambridge; Central England; Central Lancashire; Cheltenham & Gloucester; City (Gyosei International College in the UK); Coventry; Coventry (Newman College of Higher Education); De Montfort, Leicester; De Montfort, Leicester (De Montfort University Bedford); Derby; Doncaster; Doncaster (Dearne Valley Business School); Dundee; Durham; East Anglia; East London; Edinburgh; Essex; Exeter; Exeter (The College of St Mark & St John); Glamorgan; Glasgow; Glasgow Caledonian; Greenwich; Heriot-Watt; Hertfordshire; Hertfordshire (West Herts College); Huddersfield; Hull; Keele; Kent; Kent (Canterbury Christ Church University College); Kingston; Lancaster; Lancaster (Blackpool and The Fylde College); Lancaster (Edge Hill College of Higher Education); Leeds; Leeds (Bretton Hall); Leeds (Leeds, Trinity & All Saints); Leeds (The College of Ripon & York St John); Leeds Metropolitan; Leicester; Lincolnshire; Liverpool; Liverpool (Chester College of H.E.); Liverpool (Liverpool Hope University College); Liverpool John Moores; London (Birkbeck, University of London); London (British Institute in Paris); London (Goldsmiths College); London (King's College London); London (London School of Economics & Political Science); London (Queen Mary & Westfield College (incorporating St Bartholomew's and the Royal London School of Medicine & Dentistry)); London (Royal Holloway); London (School of Oriental & African Studies); London (School of Slavonic & East European Studies); London (University College (UCL)); London Guildhall; Loughborough; Luton; Manchester; Manchester Metropolitan.; Middlesex; Napier; Newcastle; North London; Northampton; Northumbria; Nottingham; Nottingham Trent; Nottingham Trent (Southampton Institute); OU (Northern College of Education); Oxford; Oxford Brookes; Paisley; Plymouth; Plymouth (Falmouth College of Arts); Portsmouth; Reading; Robert Gordon; Salford; Sheffield; Sheffield Hallam; South Bank; Southampton; Southampton (Chichester Institute of Higher Education); Southampton (King Alfred's College); Southampton (University of Southampton New College); Southampton (Winchester School of Art); St Andrews; St Martin; Staffordshire; Stirling; Strathclyde; Sunderland; Surrey; Surrey (St Mary's, Strawberry Hill); Surrey (University of Surrey Roehampton); Sussex; Teesside; Thames Valley; Ulster; UMIST; Wales (Cardiff University); Wales (North East Wales Institute); Wales (Swansea Institute of Higher Education); Wales (University of Wales College, Newport); Wales (University of Wales Institute, Cardiff); Wales (University of Wales, Aberystwyth); Wales (University of Wales, Bangor); Wales (University of Wales, Lampeter); Wales (University of Wales, Swansea); Warwick; Westminster; Wolverhampton; York

HIGHER DEGREES AWARDED BY UNIVERSITIES

Aberdeen; Abertay, Dundee; Anglia; Aston; Bath; Bath Spa; Belfast; Birmingham; Birmingham (The University of Birmingham, Westhill); Bradford; Brighton; Bristol; Buckingham; Cambridge; Central England; Central Lancashire; Cheltenham & Gloucester; Coventry; Coventry (Newman College of Higher Education); De Montfort, Leicester (De Montfort University Bedford); Dundee; Durham; East Anglia; Edinburgh; Essex; Exeter; Exeter (The College of St Mark & St John); Glasgow; Greenwich; Heriot-Watt; Hertfordshire; Hull; Keele; Kent; Lancaster; Lancaster (Edge Hill College of Higher Education); Leeds; Leeds Metropolitan; Leicester; Liverpool; Liverpool (Liverpool Hope University College); Liverpool John Moores; London (Birkbeck, University of London); London (British Institute in Paris); London (Goldsmiths College); London (Institute of Education); London (King's College London); London (London School of Economics & Political Science); London (Queen Mary & Westfield College (incorporating St Bartholomew's and the Royal London School of Medicine & Dentistry)); London (Royal Holloway); London (School of Oriental & African Studies); London (School of Slavonic & East European Studies); London (University College (UCL)); London Guildhall; Loughborough; Luton; Manchester; Middlesex; Napier; Newcastle; North London; Northampton; Nottingham; Nottingham Trent; Oxford; Oxford Brookes; Plymouth; Portsmouth; Reading; Salford; Sheffield; South Bank; Southampton; St Andrews; Strathclyde; Sunderland; Surrey; Surrey (St Mary's, Strawberry Hill); Surrey (University of Surrey Roehampton); Sussex; Ulster; UMIST; Wales (Cardiff University); Wales (University of Wales, Aberystwyth); Wales (University of Wales, Bangor); Wales (University of Wales, Lampeter); Wales (University of Wales, Swansea); Warwick; Westminster; Wolverhampton; York

DIPLOMAS AWARDED BY UNIVERSITIES

Aberdeen; Aston; Barnsley; Bath; Bath Spa; Birmingham; Birmingham (Birmingham College of Food, Tourism and Creative Studies); Bournemouth; Bradford; Brighton; Bristol; Bucks. Coll.; Dundee; Durham; Edinburgh; Essex; Exeter; Glasgow; Greenwich; Hull; Kent; Leeds; Leicester; Liverpool; Liverpool (Chester College of H.E.); Liverpool (Liverpool Hope University College); London (Birkbeck, University of London); London (Goldsmiths College); London (King's College London); London (School of Oriental & African Studies); London (University College (UCL)); London Guildhall; Napier; Newcastle; Portsmouth; Salford; South Bank; Southampton (King Alfred's College); St Andrews; Staffordshire; Strathclyde; Surrey (St Mary's, Strawberry Hill); Sussex; Thames Valley; Ulster; Westminster; Wolverhampton

CERTIFICATES AWARDED BY UNIVERSITIES

Anglia; Bradford (Bradford & Ilkley Community College); Brighton; Bristol; Brunel; Cambridge; Central Lancashire; De Montfort, Leicester; Durham; Edinburgh; Essex; Exeter; Exeter (The College of St Mark & St John); Exeter (Truro College); Glasgow; Hull; Leeds Metropolitan; Liverpool (Chester College of H.E.); Liverpool John Moores; London (Goldsmiths College); London (Jews' College); London Guildhall; Middlesex; Newcastle; North London; Oxford (Westminster College, Oxford); Sheffield Hallam; Southampton; Southampton (Chichester Institute of Higher Education); Staffordshire; Wales (University of Wales Institute, Cardiff); Wales (University of Wales, Bangor); Warwick; Westminster; Wolverhampton

OTHER COURSES AWARDED BY UNIVERSITIES

Leeds Metropolitan

POSTGRADUATE CERTIFICATES AWARDED BY UNIVERSITIES

Wales (University of Wales, Aberystwyth); Warwick

POSTGRADUATE DIPLOMAS AWARDED BY UNIVERSITIES

Heriot-Watt

PROFESSIONAL COURSES AWARDED BY UNIVERSITIES

Luton

National Certificates and Diplomas

Scotland
SQA HNC: Languages & the Business Environment; Languages & Management Skills; Languages & Scottish Tourism; Languages & Communications.
SQA HND: Languages & Business for Europe; Languages & the Business Environment; Languages with Communication, Europe: Languages & Management Skills; Languages & Scottish Tourism.

NVQs

Level 5: Interpreting

OCR

OCR offer **Certificates in Business Language Competence (CBLC)** in French, German, Italian, Japanese, Spanish & Russian. **CBLCs** are offered at 5 levels: Basic, Survival, Threshold, Operational and Advanced. OCR also offer **Language Units** in English, Dutch, French, German, Italian, Irish, Japanese, Portuguese, Russian, Spanish & Welsh. **Language Units** are offered at 4 levels. Contact OCR for details.

City & Guilds

3375 Vocational Languages; 3450 French; 3460 German; 3470 Spanish; 3480 Italian

London Chamber of Commerce and Industry Examinations Board (LCCIEB)

Foreign Languages for Industry and Commerce (FLIC); Spoken English for Industry and Commerce (SEFIC); English for Business; English for Commerce; English for the Tourism Industry
Euroqualifications
Commercial Language Assistant Certificate (available in English for non-native English speakers, French, German and Spanish)

Other Vocational Awarding Bodies

ABC: Business Language Certificate; Practical Languages

Useful Addresses

Languages National Training Organisation, 20 Bedfordbury, London WC2N 4LB Tel: 020 7379 5134 Fax: 020 7379 5082P

MANAGEMENT

Membership of Professional Institutions and Associations

ASSOCIATION FOR PROJECT MANAGEMENT

Thornton House, 150 West Wycombe Road, High Wycombe, Buckinghamshire HP12 3AE
Tel: 01494 440090 Fax: 01494 528937 e-mail: secretariat@apm-uk.demon.co.uk

MEMBERSHIP:
Fellow (FAPM): Those who have met the requirements for the class of Member and have carried superior responsibility for over 5 yrs in the field of project management.
Member (MAPM): Those who practise, develop, teach or use the techniques of project management and who can demonstrate that they have the qualifications, experience and competence in project management required by the Association.
Associate: Those not actively involved in project management, or have not gained the level of experience required for full membership.
Student: Those attending a recognised FT or PT Higher Education course. Maximum age for this grade is 30.

COMPANY MEMBERSHIP:
Higher Educational Institutes: Available to universities, technical colleges and other academic bodies to provide an interface with the Association.
Corporate: Available to all companies or organisations who are, wholly or mainly, engaged in project activities from design through manufacturing and procurement to execution, or in providing services to industry and commerce including professional firms.

EXAMINATIONS:
Certificated Project Manager (CPM): The qualification and title – Certificated Project Manager (CPM) – is available to Members and Fellows who pass a test of competence and have experience as a project manager. This involves the successful completion of a 5000 word thesis on a project the member has managed and attendance at an intensive professional interview. The status of Certificated Project Manager is recognised throughout Europe by the National Project Management Organisation affiliated to the International Project Management Association (IPMA).
Association for Project Management Professional (APMP): This professional qualification recognises an individual's baseline knowledge and competent experience in project management. The written examination is in 2 parts: (i) multiple choice; and (ii) particular questions whose answers demonstrate the candidate's competence in project management.

THE ASSOCIATION OF BUSINESS EXECUTIVES
Executive Secretary: John Towers

William House, 14 Worple Road, London SW19 4DD
Tel: 020 8879 1973 Fax: 020 8946 7153
e-mail: info@abeuk.com
Website: www.abeuk.com

The Association of Business Executives was founded in 1973 by a group of industrialists, educationalists and politicians as a non-profit-making organisation. The object of the Association is the promotion and advancement of efficient administration and management in industry, commerce and the public service by the continued development of the study and practice of administration and management. The primary objective of ABE is that students successfully completing its examinations will be more effective managers. Membership is not restricted to UK residents and examinations are conducted in over 80 countries world-wide with over 25,000 students sitting examinations each yr.

MEMBERSHIP:
Associate Membership (AMABE): Open to students who have sat and passed the Diploma exams of the Association.
Member (MABE) & Fellow (FABE): Students and Associate Members may advance to the grade of Member after acquiring 4 yrs of suitable executive experience or 2 yrs for holders of the ABE Advanced Diploma. Entry to Fellowship is open to suitably qualified persons who have made a significant contribution to the promotion of the Association at home and overseas.

BUSINESS ADMINISTRATION

EXAMINATIONS:
Certificate Course: No formal qualifications are required but applicants must demonstrate competence in the English Language by the attainment of 1 of the following: British Council – Intermediate Certificate in English/Upper Advanced Certificate in English; LCCI – English for Business (EFB) 1st & 2nd Level; Pitman/City & Guilds – English for Speakers of Other Languages (ESOL)/English for Business and Communication.
Syllabus: Introduction to Business, Introduction to Quantitative Methods, Introduction to Accounting, Introduction to Business Communication.
Diploma Level: Applicants must have attained 1 of the following entry requirements: ABE Certificate; 2 GCE A Levels plus 4 GCSE passes at Grade A, B or C, 2 of which must be English and Maths. Such overseas qualifications which follow University of London guidelines may be accepted by the Registrar as being equivalent to the above. In addition the ABE also welcomes applications for student membership from intending Diploma candidates who, although not holding a formal qualification, have been in appropriate employment for at least 2 yrs. A reference

letter from employer(s) must accompany all such applications. The decision of the Council as to the suitability of the candidate shall be final.

Syllabus:

Part 1: Economics, Organisational Behaviour, Finance & Accounting 1, Business Communication.

Part 2: The compulsory papers are: Principles of Marketing, Quantitative Methods, Finance & Accounting 2, Human Resource Management. Students must also pass 1 of the following options: Principles of Business Law, System Analysis.

Advanced Diploma in Business Administration: Applicants must have attained 1 of the following qualifications: ABE Diploma; a recognised degree; other recognised qualifications of approved Overseas Institutions Higher Education.

Syllabus: The 3 compulsory papers are: Corporate Strategy, Management Organisation, International Business. Students must also sit 2 of the following options: Strategic Marketing, Corporate Finance, Strategic Human Resource Management, Managing the Information Resource.

BUSINESS INFORMATION SYSTEM

EXAMINATIONS:

Diploma Level: The entry requirements are the same as the Diploma Level in Business Administration (see above).

Syllabus: Part 1: The 3 compulsory papers are: Computer Applications in Business & Finance, Computer Fundamentals, Business Communication. Students must also sit 1 of the following subjects: Management Organisations, or Finance & Accounting. 1. **Part 2:** The 4 compulsory papers are: Networks & Distributed Systems, Principles of Programming, Quantitative Methods, Systems Analysis. Students must also sit 1 of the following subjects: Management 2, Marketing, Finance & Accounting 2.

Advanced Diploma: The entry requirements are the same as the Advanced Diploma Level in Business Administration (see above).

Syllabus: The 4 compulsory papers are: Contemporary Application Development Methods, Internet Systems Development, Managing Systems Change, Relational Database Applications in Business. Students must also sit 1 of the following subjects: Strategic Management, Financial Management.

TRAVEL, TOURISM & HOSPITALITY

EXAMINATIONS:

Certificate: The entry requirements are the same as the Certificate Level in Business Administration (see above).

Syllabus: Introduction to Business Communication, Introduction to Accounting, Introduction to Business, Introduction to Travel, Tourism & Hospitality.

Diploma Level: The entry requirements are the same as the Diploma Level in Business Administration (see above).

Syllabus: Part 1: Economics, Organisational Behaviour, Finance & Accounting 1, Travel, Tourism & Hospitality. **Part 2:** Principles of Marketing, Travel, Tourism & Hospitality Operations Management, Human Resource Management. Plus 2 options from: Finance & Accounting 2, Principles of Business Law, Systems Analysis.

Advanced Diploma: The entry requirements are the same as the Advanced Diploma Level in Business Administration (see above).

Syllabus: 5 subjects to be passed: Corporate Strategy, International Travel, Tourism & Hospitality, Tourism & the Environment. Plus 2 options from: Management Organisation, International Business, Strategic Marketing, Strategic HRM, Managing the Information Resource.

EXEMPTIONS:

Holders of the ABE Diploma exams can obtain exemptions from many professional bodies.

POSTGRADUATE OPPORTUNITIES:

Successful completion of the ABE Advanced Diploma will qualify students for entry into many MBA and other postgraduate programmes in the UK and overseas. Students are, however, advised that most institutions offering postgraduate qualifications will expect entrants to satisfy their other admission criteria, ie to pass the GMAT test and/or TOEFL and to provide evidence of experience in industry or commerce. Many universities will accept holders of the Advanced Diploma who do not have the requisite industrial experience onto the final yr of the bachelor degrees.

BUSINESS MANAGEMENT ASSOCIATION

Mr Peter J. van Berckel, 50 Burnhill Road, Beckenham, Kent BR3 3LA Tel: 020 8663 3577
Fax: 020 8663 3212
Secretary General M.H. Pilley, 11 Bourne Close, Ware, Hertfordshire SG12 0PX Te: 01920
462769The Association aims to provide a professional body of business managers for the
promotion and exchange of management skills, knowledge and business planning techniques.

MEMBERSHIP:
Fellow (FBMA): Candidates must be at least 25 and must have passed the Final Exam of the
Association. Exemption conditions as per Membership Grade apply to this category.
Member (MBMA): Candidates must be at least 21 and must have passed the Final Exam of the
Association. Exemption from the Final Exam is granted to candidates who are Members of
approved professional organisations, or who have passed equivalent exams.
Student Membership: All exams of the Association are restricted to registered students.
Candidates for Student Membership must be at least 16 and must have passes in at least 3 subjects
to GCSE Level or their equivalents, one of which must be English Language. Mature students may
be granted exemption from the educational requirements where evidence can be provided of at
least 4 yrs' experience in employment approved by the Council of the Association.

EXAMINATIONS:
Business Management Association Certificate in Business Studies: (1) Accounting & Finance;
(2) Business Law; (3) Business Administration & Management;(4) Sales & Marketing.
Business Management Association Diploma in Business Studies: The Certificate above is
required plus (1) Public Relations; (2) Business Economics; (3) Personnel & Industrial Relations;
(4) Elements of Banking. Certificates and Diplomas also awarded in International Trade and
Independent Consultancy. Exemption from the qualifying exams may be granted to mature
candidates with senior management experience.

THE INSTITUTE FOR SUPERVISION & MANAGEMENT

Stowe House, Netherstowe, Lichfield, Staffordshire WS13 6TJ Tel: 01543 251346 Fax: 01543 415804
The ISM has over 20,000 corporate members drawn from supervisors and managers in all sections
of the economy. A member may be allocated to one of four grades:
Corporate Membership is allocated to:
Fellowships (FISM): Awarded to those members who have completed a suitable course of study
approved by the Governing Body and have attained a management position involving a higher
degree of responsibility for man-management than that required for Corporate Member.
Member (MISM): Must normally have had five yrs' experience in supervision, although
exceptions are made for those whose appointments involve higher levels of responsibility or
qualifications.
Associate Member (AMISM): Awarded to anyone in a supervisory post who has successfully
completed the Institute's Certificate or a course of similar standard in Management.
Non-corporate membership is allocated to:
Affiliate: Awarded to anyone who has completed the ISM introductory award in Supervision.

TRAINING AND EDUCATION
The ISM currently accredits over 500 centres to run its traditional and competence-based (NVQ)
Courses. Its traditional courses include:
Introductory Award which gives candidates an outline of the work and skills of supervisor. It is
suitable for newly appointed supervisors or those aspiring to this level of management (40-50 hrs).
Certificate in Management is the main award of the Institute which seeks to impart the
knowledge and skills which the first-line manager needs to broaden his/her understanding of
management. The programme is assessed through work-based assignments (including a
mandatory project) and oral presentation (180 hrs, provides the underpinning knowledge for
NVQ Level 4).
Diploma in Management seeks to apply the skills and knowledge acquired on the Certificate
course to middle management requirements (180 hrs, provides the underpinning knowledge for
NVQ Level 5).
S/NVQ Awards: The Institute is also an awarding body for S/NVQ Level 3 and NVQ Levels 4 and
5 in Management, S/NVQ Level 3 in Customer Service, NVQ Level 2 in Customer Service and

NVQ Level 3 in Training and Development.

Award for First Line Managers: For people in post, who want a more detailed course on the principles of management (120 hrs provides the underpinning knowledge for NVQ Level 3).

Consolidation Course in Management: For experienced managers who have had no formal training, but would like to consolidate their acquired knowledge with appropriate theoretical training (108 hrs).

Managing Customer Care Award: A stand alone qualification of 44 hrs. It provides the underpinning knowledge for NVQ Level 3 (customer service).

Certificate in Training Management: A stand alone qualification of 108 hrs. It provides the underpinning knowledge for NVQ Level 3 (training and development).

Quality Assured Awards: Aspire and Insignia: provide accreditation for tailored programmes having management or leadership content.

World Class Awards: a family of awards based on the 4 pillars: occupational competence, managing people, managing processes and developing people.

Learning Together: A flexible, continuing professional development tool for groups and individuals.

INSTITUTE OF ADMINISTRATIVE MANAGEMENT

40 Chatsworth Parade, Petts Wood, Orpington, Kent BR5 1RW Tel: 01689 875555 Fax: 01689 870891
e-mail: enquiries@instam.org Website: www.instAM.org

The Institute of Administrative Management is the only organisation in the UK specialising in the promotion of administrative management in the fields of industry and commerce, from the large multinational to the small, independent firms, central and local governments, the armed forces, public utilities and nationalised industries.

MEMBERSHIP:

Fellow (FInstAM): To qualify for election as a Fellow the applicant must either have been a member of the IAM for at least 5 yrs, be at least 30 yrs old and occupy a senior post or meet other criteria as laid down by the Admissions Committee.

Member (MInstAM): Applicants should be over 28 yrs (exceptionally 26), have at least 5 yrs' administrative management experience and meet the criteria as laid down by the Admissions Committee. Alternatively, the applicant must have passed the Institute's Advanced Diploma exam. Members are entitled to use the letters MInstAM; those who have passed the Advanced Diploma are entitled to use the letters MinstAM (AdvDip).

Associate (AInstAM): Associate Members of the IAM are entitled to use the designatory letters AInstAM if they are 25 or over and have at least 2 yrs' administrative management experience. Alternatively, if they have passed the Diploma exam they can use the letters AinstAM (Dip).

Affiliate: In order to qualify for Affiliate Membership to enter for the Institute's Advanced Diploma exams, an applicant must hold one of the following qualifications or similar level qualification: HNC/D, UK Degree, NEBS Management Diploma, N/SVQ Level 4 in Management or Administration.

Student: In order to qualify for student registration to enter for the Institute's Diploma exams, a minimum of 4 GCE O Level subjects or GCSE subjects are required, one of which must be English, as well as 1 pass at A Level. Approved equivalent qualifications will be accepted. Students who do not meet these criteria can enter for the Certificate only (as will a candidate who has had at least 3 yrs' relevant work experience).

Corporate Partners: Company Membership of the IAM is open to all organisations. Please apply to Institute for further information.

EXAMINATIONS:

Certificate in Administrative Management: This is an open access route to the IAM's qualifications, and consists of 3 modules (which are the first 3 modules of the Diploma).

Diploma in Administrative Management: The Diploma is a 1 yr PT programme. It consists of 6 modules and a Case Study or Work Project Report. The titles of the individual modules are: Business Administration; Systems & Activities; The Individual and the Organisation; Human Resources; Effective Management; Management Information; plus the Case Study or Work Project Report. To obtain the Diploma it is necessary to successfully complete 7 modules. To obtain the Certificate it is necessary to pass the first 3 exams only.

Advanced Diploma in Administrative Management: This is a 2 yr PT programme. The syllabus consists of 4 compulsory modules, 2 optional modules (from a choice of 5) and a Case Study or Work Project Report. The titles of the core modules are: Managing Contemporary Issues; Managing Financial Resources; Managing People and Managing Processes. The optional modules are: Managing Facilities; Managing Marketing; Managing Information – Analysis and Presentation; Managing Training and Development; Managing Information and Technology.

THE INSTITUTE OF COMMERCIAL MANAGEMENT

The Fusee, 20a Bargates, Christchurch, Dorset BH23 1QL Tel: 01202 490555 Fax: 01202 490666 e-mail: instcm@instcm.co.uk Website: www.instcm.co.uk

The Institute is an acknowledged specialist in the design and development of progressive and multifunctional programmes of study for use by universities, business schools, colleges, International Development and government agencies. As a recognised international examining board for those undertaking professional business and management studies, the Institute also examines and certifies candidates to an internationally consistent standard. Working with education providers world-wide, ICM offers examinations and certification in the following areas: Accounting, Banking and Finance; Business and Management Studies; Communication Studies; Computer Studies; Hospitality Management; Information Technology; International Trade; Languages; Legal Studies; Marketing Management; Public Relations; Purchasing and Supply Management; Retail and Distribution Management; Safety Management; Sales Management and Marketing; Security Management; Sports and Leisure Management; Travel and Tourism Management.

Recognition of ICM Awards: Subject to status, students holding ICM Diploma, Advanced Diploma and Graduate Diploma level qualifications are accepted onto undergraduate and postgraduate degree programmes offered by institutions in the EC, Eastern Europe, North America, the Middle East, the Far East, SE Asia, sub-Saharan Africa and Australasia. The Institute's awards are also recognised by the majority of the world's leading professional examining boards for either subject or registration purposes.

ICM Vocational Education Awards: ICM programmes are designed to address a wide variety of personal development and training needs. Unless a candidate undertakes a Single Subject examination, all ICM programmes are multi-subject and candidates are required to undertake formal and externally set and marked examinations in all subjects within any programme.

Certificate Level Programmes: These are introductory and foundation programmes designed for school leavers and adults with few or no formal academic qualifications (3 to 6 mths FT/9 mths PT).

Diploma Level Programmes: Designed for business students and working adults (1 to 2 yrs FT/2 to 3 yrs PT). Most Diploma level programmes offer study equivalent to the first yr of a degree, and relevant ICM Diploma awards are accepted by institutions of HE for degree entry purposes.

Advanced Diploma Programmes: Designed for business students, supervisors, managers and mature working adults with existing business qualifications (1 yr FT/2 yrs PT). Offering learning equivalent to 2 yrs of undergraduate study, most Advanced Diploma programmes are taken as an end in themselves, but can also be used for entry at appropriate level to first degree studies.

Graduate Diploma Programmes: Designed for practising managers and business students, these are 1 yr postgraduate courses (some exemptions depending on experience) which, subject to status and exam grades, qualify the holder for entry onto a wide range of Masters programmes.

INSTITUTE OF DIRECTORS

116 Pall Mall, London SW1Y 5ED Tel: 020 7839 1233 Fax: 020 7930 1949 Website: www.iod.co.uk

The IoD is a chartered institute, whose 50,000 members form a unique and influential global network spanning the whole spectrum of business leadership. The Institute's principal objectives are to advance the interests of its members as company directors, to provide business facilities and services of all kinds for these members, and to help directors enhance their professional competence.

MEMBERSHIP:

Fellow (FInstD): Open to IoD members of 1 yr's standing who are: (a) directors for minimum of 5 yrs, with 10 yrs' business experience, who hold the IoD Diploma in Company Direction or equivalent; or (b) directors for minimum of 10 yrs.

Member (MInstD): Open to: (a) directors of 1 yr's standing, with 5 yrs' business experience who have attended the IoD's foundation course covering the role and responsibilities of directors and the board; or (b) directors of 3 yrs' standing, with 7 yrs' business experience.

Associate Member: Open to directors waiting to qualify for Member grade; partners in professional practice and those with professional qualifications working in industry or commerce; sole proprietors; senior executives.

TRAINING:

The IoD's Director Development department is the premier specialist provider of director training services, with a reputation for delivering relevant, practical learning experiences. It is uniquely concerned with the development needs of company directors whatever their experience, company size or type of business; whether or not they are IoD members. The learning approach draws upon and enhances directors' knowledge, skills and understanding, and focuses on helping them to improve business performance. The unique directors' programme, the **IoD Company Direction Programme** covers the essentials of directing a successful modern company. A certificate of Completion is provided for attending the entire programme; however, those who wish to achieve a recognised qualification can undertake an assessment, successful completion of which leads to the award of the prestigious **IoD Diploma in Company Direction**. The Diploma is also a major step towards becoming a **Chartered Director**, the new professional status launched by the IoD in 1999. Offered at the IoD in London and 6 regional UK centres: Durham, Edinburgh, Leeds/Wakefield, Loughborough, Salford, Stirling, Ulster and Wolverhampton. There is also a concise programme which equips newly-appointed and prospective directors with the knowledge and confidence to fulfil their new appointment effectively. The IoD also provides an extensive range of business and boardroom publications, and runs conferences on topical issues of interest to directors.

INSTITUTE OF EXECUTIVES AND MANAGERS

Abbey Lakes Hall, Orrell, Wigan, Lancashire WN5 8QZ Tel: 01695 622226 Fax: 01695 627199

The Institute was originally founded over 30 yrs ago to provide an organisation international in dimension for executives and managers in all vocations.

MEMBERSHIP:

Fellow (FIEM): Candidates must: (i) already be a Member of the Institute; (ii) be not less than 30 yrs of age; *or* (iii) already be an Associate of the Institute; (iv) be not less than 35 yrs of age.

Member (MIEM): Candidates must: (i) already be a Graduate of the Institute; ii) be not less than 25 yrs of age; (iii) hold the Institute's Diploma in Executive Management.

Graduate (GIEM): Candidates must: (i) be an Associate or Licentiate of the Institute; (ii) be not less than 21 yrs of age; (iii) hold the Institute's Certificate in Executive Management.

Associate (AIEM): Candidates must: (i) be a Licentiate of the Institute; (ii) be not less than 25 yrs of age; (iii) hold such academic qualifications and have such practical experience as the Council of the Institute considers appropriate.

Licentiate (LIEM): Candidates must: (i) be a Student of the Institute; (ii) be not less than 21 yrs of age; (iii) hold such academic qualifications and have such practical experience as the Council of the Institute considers appropriate.

Student: Candidates must not be less than 16 yrs of age and hold such academic qualifications and have such practical experience as the Council of the Institute considers appropriate.

EXAMINATIONS:

Diploma in Executive Management (DEM): A comprehensive distance learning study programme, available direct from the Institute and through certain accredited universities and colleges. Taking the form of modular study packages, audio cassette programmes and video cassette programmes, these programmes cover a wide range of topics including Finance for Non Financial Managers and Marketing, etc. The Diploma is an aggregation of subjects, each individual subject carrying a certain number of credits. To be awarded the Diploma candidates need to have aggregated 6 credits. Individual subjects carry a certificate of completion and an indication of the credits earned towards the Diploma. Candidates for the Diploma Programme must hold the Certificate in Executive Management, or similar qualifications which in view of the Council of the Institute would equate to 3 credits on the Certificate scale.

Certificate in Executive Management (CEM): A comprehensive distance learning study programme, available direct from the Institute and through certain accredited universities and colleges. Taking the form of modular study packages, audio cassette programmes and video cassette programmes, these programmes cover a wide range of topics including Appreciation of Accounting for Non Financial Managers, Personnel Interviewing and Selection, etc. The Certificate is an aggregation of subjects, each individual subject carrying a certain number of credits. To be awarded the Certificate candidates need to have aggregated 3 credits. Individual subjects carry a certificate of completion and an indication of the credits earned towards the Certificate.

BENEFITS:

Designation: All grades of members, except students, may use the designation òÁManagement Executive'. Certificate and Diploma holders need not necessarily be members of the Institute.

Publications: Members receive a regular copy of the Institute's magazine *Management Executive*, a copy of the Institute's òÁBudget Summary' and annually the Institute's diary. All members receive a free subscription to *International Management Focus*.

Group Membership: The Institute has negotiated 'Group Membership Benefits' for car hire, hotels, travel etc.

Social: The Institute offers a full and active social programme.

Employment: The Institute gives every support to all members seeking employment and those wishing to have vacancies filled. Any members seeking employment will be placed, if they wish, on the Institute's employment register, and allowed to advertise in situations wanted free of charge in the Institute's magazine. Any members or their employers wishing to fill vacancies can advertise situations vacant in the Institute's magazine at greatly reduced rates.

INSTITUTE OF MANAGEMENT CONSULTANCY

5th Floor, 32-33 Hatton Garden, London EC1N 8DL Tel: 020 7242 2140 Fax: 020 7831 4597
e-mail: consult@imc.co.uk. Website: www.imc.co.uk

The Institute of Management Consultancy (IMC) is the professional body that sets and maintains high standards of quality, independence, objectivity and integrity for Certified Management Consultants (CMC) in the UK. It also provides the opportunity to advance to the status of Fellow grade Certified Management Consultant (FCMC).

MEMBERSHIP:

Affiliate Membership: Offered to all individuals and organisations who are interested in management consultancy.

Associate Membership (AIMC): An Associate is a management consultant, or a potential management consultant, who has chosen to work towards the CMC qualification and has agreed to abide by the IMC Code of Conduct. The applicant must provide evidence of 1 of the following: at least 1 yr's experience as a management consultant; at least 5 yrs' experience in management or a functional specialism; an MA in management consultancy or an MBA with a management consultancy module or an MBA plus an appropriate short course for management consultancy core skills; current work as a consultant within an IMC Certified Practice. Associates are entitled to use the designation AIMC.

QUALIFICATIONS:

Gaining the Certified Management Consultant (CMC) qualification: A CMC is a management consultant who has demonstrated competence and understanding in a range of consultancy situations against an agreed standard, and has signed up to the IMC Code of Conduct. The assessment process requires the applicant to collect evidence of competence, experience, education and training. It is therefore necessary to have quality experience as a management consultant before applying to become a CMC. Candidates are unlikely to be successful if they have less than 3 yrs' experience. The assessment process includes: submission of a professional record to demonstrate competence against IMC standards; an assignment study which is a detailed description, critique and reflection on a real consultancy project that considers the successes and difficulties encountered; an hr-long interview; CV, application form and 3 references. Qualified members are entitled to use the CMC designatory letters and logo.

Fellow grade Certified Management Consultant (FCMC): This is a management consultant of some seniority who has demonstrated substantial additional experience and continuing professional development beyond that required to become CMC, and continues to abide by the IMC Code of Conduct. This level of membership recognises competence at a strategic level gained over a period of not less than 5 yrs FT after becoming a CMC. Individuals cannot join directly at Fellow level.

INSTITUTE OF MANAGEMENT SERVICES

1 Cecil Court, London Road, Enfield, Middlesex EN2 6DD Tel: 020 8366 1261 Fax: 020 8367 8149
e-mail: ims@imgtserv.co.uk Website: www.imgtserv.co/uk/imgtserv/

MEMBERSHIP:

Corporate Membership: There are 2 levels, Fellow and Member. Entry is based upon a combination of experience and qualifications, although both grades are open to experienced personnel holding positions of responsibility, irrespective of qualifications.

Non-Corporate Membership: There are 2 levels, Affiliate and Associate. Associate grade requires both experience and the Institute's Certificate. Affiliate grade is the equivalent of student, and open to those either already engaged in, or having an interest in, management services.

EXAMINATIONS:

The Certificate is designed to qualify for Associate grade and requires candidates to take 5 vocational based tests. These range across the spectrum of Methods Investigations and Study to Work Measurement and Change Management. The Diploma consists of MCI or NVQ4 core and IMS assignments. In addition, candidates have to submit a project or a log book of their management services work in order to obtain the award. There is a reserved grade of MMS(Dip) for members holding the Diploma and Certificate.

THE INSTITUTE OF MANAGEMENT SPECIALISTS

Head Office, Warwick Corner, 42 Warwick Road, Kenilworth, Warwickshire CV8 1HE
Tel: 01926 855498 Fax: 01926 513100

THE INSTITUTE OF MANAGEMENT SPECIALISTS DIPLOMA:

Companion (CompIMS): Must have held Fellow grade for min 4 yrs.

Fellow (FIMS): Must hold PHd, MBA, university degree or membership of a professional institute, plus an appropriate number of yrs' experience at top level as a professional management specialist or as a specialist involved in modern management and technology linked to one or more of the disciplines which include: commerce, industry, computing, information technology, management services, finance, marketing, engineering, science, administration, manufacturing, training or proven associated disciplines.

Member (MIMS): Must hold degree, DBA, DMS, HND, BTEC, SQA, C&G, NEBSM or similar/equivalent awards, plus appropriate experience in one or more of the disciplines as under Fellow.

Associate (AMIMS): Must hold CMS, HNC, BTEC, SQA, C&G, NEBSM or similar/ equivalent awards, plus appropriate experience in one or more of the disciplines as under Fellow.

THE INSTITUTE OF MANAGEMENT SPECIALISTS CERTIFICATE:

Graduate (GradIMS): Must hold OND/ONC, BTEC, SCOTVEC, C&G, NEBSM or similar/equivalent awards, plus appropriate experience in one or more of the disciplines as under Fellow.

Affiliate (AffIMS): Is designed for those who wish to join IMS and intend to develop a career in management, but who do not yet hold the necessary qualifications or experience for Associate Membership.

Student (StudIMS): Must be at least 18 yrs of age and hold 4/5 O Levels, GCSEs, CFSs. 4 passes are acceptable with appropriate experience. Alternatively acceptable are a Foundation Course, First Yr Certificate or Diploma, or a specialised short course with work or office experience.

EXAMINATIONS:

The Institute's exam structure consists of its Certificate and Diploma of Merit. Success in the exams plus practical experience at an appropriate level of responsibility are requisites for membership. Exemption from these exams is allowed to those who hold appropriate PHd, MBA or university, BTEC, SQA, C&G or equivalent awards. Exemption is also allowed to those who hold membership of professional bodies whose standards of entry to membership are not less than those of the Institute. In all cases applicants must have the necessary experience at an appropriate level of responsibility. The Institute conducts its own flexible open-learning course (Home Study) leading to exams for the Institute's Certificate and Diploma of Merit. Entry standards for the Certificate of Merit Course is open to student members holding 4 O Levels at grades A or B, including English, Mathematics, and a Science subject. Min age 18. The Diploma of

Merit Course is open to members holding the Certificate of Merit of the Institute or similar qualifications acceptable to the Management Educational & Examinations Board of the Institute. Also, in addition to the above, a large range of Distance Learning Courses are available from Head Office.

THE INSTITUTE OF MANAGEMENT

Membership Department, Management House, Cottingham Road, Corby, Northamptonshire NN17 1TT Tel: 01536 204222 Fax: 01536 201651 e-mail: member@inst.mgt.org.uk Website: www.inst.mgt.org.uk

MEMBERSHIP:

Companion (CIMgt): The main qualification is eminent achievement in the practice of management. Admission is by invitation of the Board of Companions and the number of Companions is limited.

Fellow (FIMgt): Managers who meet all of the criteria for the grade of Member and who also have extensive experience in general management posts with a substantial strategic element (scope and duration) at Board level, or at the equivalent of Board level in organisations of significance.

Member (MIMgt): Managers with an appropriate combination of general management experience and who hold a recognised management/academic/professional qualification; or managers with an extended period of general management experience.

Associate (AIMgt): Those with some management experience and who, in addition, are undertaking or who hold a recognised management/academic/professional qualification. It may also be applicable to those who are recognised to be gaining the required general management experience.

Affiliate: Those wishing to be identified with the aims of the Institute or who are primarily operating outside a management role and not yet possessing appropriate qualifications.

Student: FT and PT students (minimum age 16).

QUALIFICATIONS:

The institute offers two distinct types of qualification: a Certificate/Diploma in Management or Vocational Qualification in Management. Most candidates who are already managers, however, undertake a combined programme leading to both. Assessment is via a range of assessment methods on a continuous basis. The institute's philosophy is such that all knowledge should be applied within the workplace and the assessment methodology ensures that candidates are asked to reflect on the knowledge and present how the understanding of knowledge can be applied in the working environment. Contact: Sharon Deathridge, Accreditation Development Manager Tel: 01536 204222

THE INSTITUTE OF PROFESSIONAL MANAGERS AND ADMINISTRATORS

La Dependance, Route de Vinchelez, Jersey JE3 2DA Tel: 01534 485500 Fax: 01534 485500 e-mail: success@cpmtraining.com

MEMBERHSIP:

Membership is international.

Fellow (FInstPM): Open to those holding top managerial or administrative posts in commerce, industry or government, or to those who have made an outstanding contribution to management *in their own countries or internationally* or to those who have been professionally involved in the training of managers.

Member (MInstPM): Open to those holding middle/senior management or administration positions, and to those holding management qualifications recognised by the Institute who have also had adequate practical experience.

Associate Member (AInstPM): Open to those holding junior management, administration or supervisory posts, and to those who have undertaken courses on management or administration recognised by the Institute. Transfer to full membership is possible via an Advanced Certificate Examination.

EXAMINATIONS:

Diploma and Higher Diploma Certificates: A wide range of managerial, business and administrative Training Programmes and examinations are available through the Institute's associate college.

Advanced Certificates: 4 Advanced Certificates are available. Only Members are eligible to sit these examinations: (1) Management, Administration and Human Resources; (2) Business Studies; (3) Financial Bookkeeping and Accounting; (4) Tourism, Hotel and Hospitality Management.

INSTITUTE OF VALUE MANAGEMENT

46 Passmore, Tinkers Bridge, Milton Keynes MK6 3DZ Tel: 0870 9020905 Fax: 0870 9020905
e-mail: ivm@btinternet.com
The Institute aims to establish Value Management as a process for achieving value in every sector of the economy and to provide support in the innovative use of Value Management techniques.

MEMBERSHIP:
Corporate Membership: Open to any company or organisation practising or promoting Value techniques. Each corporate member may nominate up to 10 members of their organisation as representatives to the Institute. A member nominated by a corporate body can hold executive office and has full voting rights.
Ordinary Membership: Open to any professional person who has an interest in and can demonstrate an involvement in, practising Value techniques.
Student Membership: Open to students who have an interest in Value Management and who are registered FT students possessing a valid student card.
Fellow: Awarded to a member as a special honour for outstanding contribution to the field of Value Management.

CERTIFICATION & ROLL OF PRACTITIONERS:
Certificate & Training: The Institute has worked very closely with the Commission of the European Communities to establish a European Training System and Certification Procedure.
Roll of Practitioners: The Institute maintains an authorised list of Value Practitioners who are members of the Institute. Launched in 1998 its European Training and Certification System. This European Commission funded initiative offers, through the IVM's Certification Board, certification in the following categories: **Certifcated Value Analyst(CVA); Professional in Value Management(PVM); Certificated Value Manager(CVM); Trainer in Value Management(TVM)**. The Certification Board also approves basic and advanced courses in Value Management that have been designed by Trainers in Value Management. The Institute provides a list of trainers.

PROFESSIONAL BUSINESS AND TECHNICAL MANAGEMENT

Head Office, Warwick Corner, 42 Warwick Road, Kenilworth, Warwickshire CV8 1HE
Tel: 01926 855498 Fax: 01926 513100

MEMBERSHIP:
Companion (CProfBTM): Must have held Fellow grade for a min of 4 yrs.
Fellow (FProfBTM): Must have held Fellow grade for a min of 4 yrs. Must hold MBA or university degree, HND or membership of a professional institute. Plus an appropriate number of yrs' experience at top level in professional business management, professional technical management or modern technology and systems. Involving fields of activity linked to one or more of the disciplines which include: business, administration, commerce, industry, computing, technology, engineering, information technology, science, marketing, finance, training, accounting or proven associated disciplines.
Full Member (MProfBTM): Must hold DBA, DMS, HNC, OND, BTEC, SQA, C&G, NEBSM or similar/equivalent awards. Plus appropriate experience in one or more of the disciplines as under Fellow.
Associate Member (AMProfBTM): Must hold CMS, HNC, OND, ONC, BTEC, SQA, C&G, NEBSM or similar/equivalent awards. Plus appropriate experience in one or more of the disciplines as under Fellow.
Affiliate (AffProfBTM): Is designed for those who wish to join PBTM and intend to develop a career in Business or Technical Management, but who do not yet hold the necessary qualifications or experience for Associate Membership.
Student Member (StudProfBTM): Must be at least 18 yrs of age and hold 4/5 O Levels, GCSEs,

CFSs. 4 passes are acceptable with appropriate experience. Alternatively acceptable are a Foundation Course, First Yr Certificate or Diploma, or a specialised short course with work or office experience.

EXAMINATIONS:
PBTM's exam structure consists of its own Certificate and Diploma of Merit. Success in the exams plus practical experience at an appropriate level of responsibility are requisites for membership. Exemption from these exams is allowed to those who hold appropriate university, BTEC, SQA, C&G or equivalent awards, also to those who hold membership of a professional body whose standards of entry to membership are not less than those of PBTM. In all cases applicants must have the necessary experience at an appropriate level of responsibility. PBTM conducts its own **Flexible, Open-Learning Courses** (Home Study) leading to exams for the PBTM Certificate and Diploma of Merit. Entry standards for the Certificate of Merit course is open to student members holding 4 O Levels grades A or B, including English, Mathematics and a Science subject. Min age 18. The Diploma of Merit course is open to members holding the Certificate of Merit of PBTM or similar qualifications acceptable to the Management Education & Examinations Board of Professional Business and Technical Management. Also, in addition to the above, a large range of Distance Learning Courses are available from Head Office.

THE SOCIETY OF BUSINESS PRACTITIONERS
Tel: 01270 526339 Fax: 01270 526339 Website: www.mamsasbp.com
Postal address: PO Box 11, Sandbach, Cheshire CW11 3GE

MEMBERSHIP:
Fellow (FSBP): Elected on the basis of a high level of achievement in Business Practice and/or a significantly important contribution to Business Education/Practice.
Certified Professional Manager (CPM): Senior membership open to business practitioners who have the SBP Postgraduate Diploma in Business Administration (or its equiv) and who satisfy other requirements.
Members (MSBP): Elected after obtaining the SBP Advanced Diploma in Business Administration and additional diplomas (or equiv), and having satisfied other requirements.

EXAMINATIONS:
The Society conducts bi-annual exams, internationally, for all its qualifications. Preparatory tuition offered internationally at approved centres. Exam reciprocal exemption agreements are in force with other professional institutes. Exam reciprocal exemptions are in force with other professional institutes and agreed entrance to BBA and MBA degree programmes with selected universities.
Diploma in Business Administration: Entry requirements: min age 18. Must be registered Student and have at least 1 of following: (1) 4 GCSEs passed at grade C, or higher, 1 of which must be English Language, with 2 GCE passes at A Level; (2) BTEC Cert or Dip in Business & Finance; (3) Passed Matric or entrance exams of a recognised university; (4) Passed LCCI Stage I (Intermediate) level exams or RSA exams at Stage III level; (5) An equivalent qualification from a recognised professional institute or educational establishment; (6) Mature students may enter on the basis of general educational qualifications and an acceptable level of business experience.
Diploma in Marketing Management: Same entry requirements as for Diploma in Business Administration.
Advanced Diploma in Business Administration: Entry requirements: Must have SBP Diploma in Business Administration (or equivalent) and meet its entry conditions.
Advanced Diploma in Marketing Management: Same entry requirements as for Advanced Diploma in Business Administration.
Postgraduate Diploma in Business Administration: Entry requirements: Must have SBP Advanced Diploma in Business Administration (or equivalent) and/or a recognised degree in a relevant subject.
Postgraduate Diploma in International Marketing: Same entry requirements as for Postgraduate Diploma in Business Administration.

University Qualifications
The following universities offer qualifications in Management and related subjects. Full details may be found in Part 4, under the entry for the appropriate university.

FIRST DEGREES AWARDED BY UNIVERSITIES

Aberdeen; Abertay, Dundee; Adams; Anglia; Anglia (Colchester Institute); Aston; Barnsley; Bath; Belfast; Birmingham; Birmingham (Birmingham College of Food, Tourism and Creative Studies); Blackburn; Bournemouth; Bradford; Bradford (Bradford & Ilkley Community College); Brighton; Bristol; Brunel; Buckingham; Bucks. Coll.; Central England; Central Lancashire; Cheltenham & Gloucester; City; Coventry; Coventry (Newman College of Higher Education); Cranfield; De Montfort, Leicester; Derby; Doncaster (Dearne Valley Business School); Dundee; Durham; Durham (New College Durham); East Anglia; East Anglia (Suffolk College); Edinburgh; Essex; Essex (Writtle College); Exeter; Glamorgan; Glasgow; Glasgow Caledonian; Greenwich; Heriot-Watt; Hertfordshire; Huddersfield; Hull; Keele; Kent; Kent (Canterbury Christ Church University College); Kingston; Lancaster; Lancaster (Edge Hill College of Higher Education); Leeds; Leeds (Leeds, Trinity & All Saints); Leeds (The College of Ripon & York St John); Leeds Metropolitan; Leicester; Lincolnshire (Bishop Burton College); Lincolnshire (Lincoln University Campus); Liverpool; Liverpool (Chester College of H.E.); Liverpool John Moores; London (Birkbeck, University of London); London (Imperial College of Science, Technology & Medicine); London (King's College London); London (London School of Economics & Political Science); London (Queen Mary & Westfield College (incorporating St Bartholomew's and the Royal London School of Medicine & Dentistry)); London (Royal Holloway); London (School of Oriental & African Studies); London (University College (UCL)); London (Wye College); London Guildhall; London Institute (London College of Fashion); Loughborough; Luton; Manchester; Manchester (Warrington Collegiate Institute, Faculty of H.E,); Manchester Metropolitan.; Middlesex; Napier; Newcastle; North London; Northampton; Northumbria; Nottingham; Nottingham Trent; Nottingham Trent (Southampton Institute); OU (NESCOT); OU (Northern College of Education); Oxford; Oxford Brookes; Paisley; Plymouth; Portsmouth; Queen Margaret; Reading; Robert Gordon; Salford; Sheffield; Sheffield Hallam; South Bank; Southampton; St Andrews; St Martin; Staffordshire; Stirling; Strathclyde; Sunderland; Surrey; Surrey (St Mary's, Strawberry Hill); Sussex; Ulster; UMIST; Wales (Cardiff University); Wales (University of Wales, Aberystwyth); Wales (University of Wales, Bangor); Wales (University of Wales, Lampeter); Wales (University of Wales, Swansea); Warwick; Westminster; Wolverhampton; York

HIGHER DEGREES AWARDED BY UNIVERSITIES

Aberdeen; Abertay, Dundee; Anglia; Anglia (City College, Norwich); Aston; Bath; Birmingham; Birmingham (Birmingham College of Food, Tourism and Creative Studies); Bournemouth; Bradford; Bradford (Bradford & Ilkley Community College); Brighton; Bristol; Brunel; Buckingham; Bucks. Coll.; Cambridge; Central England; Central Lancashire; Cheltenham & Gloucester; City; City (Ashridge); Coventry; Cranfield; De Montfort, Leicester; Derby; Dundee; Durham; East London; Edinburgh; Essex; Exeter; Exeter (The College of St Mark & St John); Glamorgan; Glasgow; Glasgow Caledonian; Greenwich; Heriot-Watt; Hertfordshire; Hull; Kent; Lancaster; Lancaster (Edge Hill College of Higher Education); Leeds; Leeds (The College of Ripon & York St John); Leeds Metropolitan; Leicester; Lincolnshire; Liverpool; Liverpool (Liverpool Hope University College); Liverpool John Moores; London (Birkbeck, University of London); London (Imperial College of Science, Technology & Medicine); London (Institute of Education); London (King's College London); London (London School of Economics & Political Science); London (Royal Holloway); London (University College (UCL)); London (Wye College); London Guildhall; Loughborough; Luton; Manchester; Manchester Metropolitan.; Middlesex; Napier; Newcastle; North London; Northampton; Northumbria; Nottingham; Nottingham Trent; Nottingham Trent (Southampton Institute); OU (NESCOT); Oxford Brookes; Paisley; Plymouth; Portsmouth; Reading; Royal College of Art; Salford; Sheffield; Sheffield Hallam; South Bank; Southampton; Southampton (Chichester Institute of Higher Education); St Andrews; St Martin; Staffordshire; Stirling; Strathclyde; Sunderland; Surrey; Surrey (University of Surrey Roehampton); Sussex; Teesside; Thames Valley; Ulster; UMIST; Wales (University of Wales College, Newport); Wales (University of Wales, Aberystwyth); Wales (University of Wales, Lampeter); Wales (University of Wales, Swansea); Warwick; Westminster; Wolverhampton; York

DIPLOMAS AWARDED BY UNIVERSITIES

Aberdeen; Abertay, Dundee; Anglia; Anglia (City College, Norwich); Aston; Barnsley; Birmingham; Bournemouth; Bradford; Bradford (Bradford & Ilkley Community College); Brighton; Bristol; Brunel; Bucks. Coll.; Cambridge; Central England; Central Lancashire;

Cheltenham & Gloucester; City; City (Ashridge); Coventry; De Montfort, Leicester; Derby; Doncaster (Dearne Valley Business School); Durham; Durham (New College Durham); East London; Edinburgh; Essex (Writtle College); Exeter; Glamorgan; Glasgow Caledonian; Greenwich; Hertfordshire; Huddersfield; Hull; Kent; Kent (Canterbury Christ Church University College); Kingston; Lancaster; Lancaster (Edge Hill College of Higher Education); Leeds; Leeds (Leeds College of Music); Leeds (The College of Ripon & York St John); Leeds Metropolitan; Leicester; Lincolnshire; Liverpool (Chester College of H.E.); Liverpool (Liverpool Hope University College); Liverpool John Moores; London (Birkbeck, University of London); London (Goldsmiths College); London (Wye College); London Guildhall; Loughborough; Luton; Middlesex; Napier; Newcastle; Northampton; Nottingham; Nottingham Trent; Nottingham Trent (Southampton Institute); OU (Northern College of Education); Oxford Brookes; Paisley; Plymouth; Portsmouth; Reading; Salford; Sheffield; South Bank; Southampton (Chichester Institute of Higher Education); Southampton (King Alfred's College); St Martin; Stirling; Strathclyde; Sunderland; Surrey (University of Surrey Roehampton); Ulster; Wales (College of Medicine); Wales (University of Wales, Aberystwyth); Warwick; Wolverhampton; Worcester

CERTIFICATES AWARDED BY UNIVERSITIES
Aberdeen; Abertay, Dundee; Bournemouth; Bradford (Bradford & Ilkley Community College); Brighton; Bristol; Central England; Central Lancashire; Cheltenham & Gloucester; Coventry; De Montfort, Leicester; Derby; Durham; East London; Exeter; Glamorgan; Hull; Keele; Leeds Metropolitan; Lincolnshire; Lincolnshire (Hull College); Liverpool (Chester College of H.E.); London (University College (UCL)); London Guildhall; Loughborough; Napier; Newcastle; North London; Northampton; Nottingham; Nottingham Trent (Southampton Institute); OU (Northern College of Education); Oxford Brookes; Plymouth; Salford; South Bank; St Martin; Stirling; Sunderland; Sussex; Ulster; Wales (University of Wales Institute, Cardiff); Wales (University of Wales, Bangor); Warwick; Westminster; Wolverhampton; Worcester; York

OTHER COURSES AWARDED BY UNIVERSITIES
Leeds Metropolitan; Manchester Metropolitan.; Sunderland (City of Sunderland College)

POSTGRADUATE DIPLOMAS AWARDED BY UNIVERSITIES
Birmingham (Birmingham College of Food, Tourism and Creative Studies); Central Lancashire; Heriot-Watt; Thames Valley

PROFESSIONAL COURSES AWARDED BY UNIVERSITIES
Leeds Metropolitan

PROFESSIONAL QUALIFICATIONS AWARDED BY UNIVERSITIES
Glamorgan

National Certificates and Diplomas
BTEC Higher National Certificates/Diplomas: Production Management; Public Sector Management; Total Quality Management
Scotland
SQA HNC: Administration and Information Management; Administrative Management; Business Development for Footballers; Business Information Management; Human Resources Management; Management; Managing Support Services (Facilities).
SQA Certificate: Management.
SQA HND: Administrative Management; Administration and Information Management.
SQA Diploma: Management; Management Support Services; Management with Manufacturing; Management with Marketing; Management with Operations; Management with Personnel; Management Support Services.

NVQs
Level 3: Management; Owner Management – Business Planning
Level 4: Management; Owner Management – Business Management and Development; Project Management
Level 5: Operational Management; Project Management; Strategic Management

SVQs

Level 1: Administration
Level 2: Administration
Level 3: Administration; Supervisory Management
Level 4: Administration; Management
Level 5: Operational Management

City & Guilds

7630 Animal Management; 7760 Pet Store Management

Diploma in Management Studies (DMS)

The DMS is a post-experience postgraduate diploma award designed to raise a student's understanding of management processes and the management of the environment, and to improve managerial performance. It is a national award designed for students with graduate or equivalent qualifications and with relevant experience. Courses vary in length from 25 wks FT to 2 yrs PT. The course is normally in 2 parts, allowing transfer between colleges. Stage 1 provides an introduction to the functional areas underlying management: behavioural studies, marketing, production and operations management, accounting and finance and quantitative methods. Stage 2 provides a more integrative approach to the practice of management, leading to an organisation-based project. All courses offer skills training, eg in interviewing and negotiating, and work in computing. Although most are courses in general management, with course participants from industry, commerce, the professions and the public sector, there are some specialist courses and a number of courses offer specialist options.

Admission of Students: The DMS is suitable for a variety of candidates with the potential to meet the learning demands of Diploma programmes, including graduates from a variety of disciplines and mature and experienced managers. Entrants would normally be expected to have at least 2 yrs of management experience.

National Examining Board for Supervision and Management

NEBS Management is Specialist Awarding Body for Management Qualifications – committed to developing qualifications to meet the needs of today's managers at all levels across commerce and industry. For over 35 yrs we have been awarding management qualifications to team leaders and managers. NEBS Management programmes are available throughout the UK and Ireland and through an expanding international network. A full range of management qualifications are available from the NEBS Management Introductory Award through the NEB Management Diploma or S/NVQs levels 3 to 5. Awards are linked into City and Guilds at Licentiateship and Graduateship levels. We also have a portfolio of focused awards for managers in small businesses, as well as NVQs in Personnel Management.

Useful Addresses

Management Charter Initiative, Russell Square House, 10–12 Russell Square, London WC1B 5BZ
Tel 020 7872 9000 Fax 020 7872 9099

MANUFACTURING

Membership of Professional Institutions and Associations

THE INSTITUTE OF MANUFACTURING

Head Office, Warwick Corner, 42 Warwick Road, Kenilworth, Warwickshire CV8 1HE
Tel: 01926 855498 Fax: 01926 513100

THE INSTITUTE OF MANUFACTURING DIPLOMA:

Companion (CompIManf): Must have held Fellow grade for a min of 4 yrs.

Fellow (FIManf): Must hold PHd, MBA, university degree or membership of a professional institute. Plus an appropriate number of yrs' experience at top level in professional manufacturing, manufacturing management, or modern and advanced manufacturing technology and systems. Involving fields of activity linked to these disciplines which include: industry, commerce, computing, science, engineering, information technology, production, administration, marketing, finance, training, safety, quality or other fields within the manufacturing industry.

Full Member (MIManf): Must hold degree, DBA, DMS, HND, BTEC, SCOTVEC, C&G, NEBSM or similar/equivalent awards, plus appropriate experience in one or more of the disciplines as under Fellow.

Associate Member (AMIManf): Must hold CMS, HNC, BTEC, SCOTVEC, C&G, NEBSM or similar/equivalent awards, plus appropriate experience in one or more of the disciplines as under Fellow.

Affiliate (AffIManf): Is designed for those who wish to join the Institute and intend to develop a career in manufacturing or manufacturing management, but who do not yet hold the necessary qualifications or experience for Associate Membership.

THE INSTITUTE OF MANUFACTURING CERTIFICATE:

Graduate Member (GradIManf): Must hold OND/ONC, BTEC, SCOTVEC, C&G, NEBSM or similar/equivalent awards, plus appropriate experience in one or more of the disciplines as under Fellow.

Student Member (StudIManf): Must be at least 18 and hold 4/5 O Levels, GCSEs, CFSs. 4 passes are acceptable with appropriate experience. Alternatively acceptable are a Foundation Course, First Yr Certificate or Diploma, or a specialised short course with work or office experience.

EXAMINATIONS:

The Institute's exam structure consists of its Certificate and Diploma of Merit. Success in the exams plus practical experience at an appropriate level of responsibility are requisites of membership. Exemption from these exams is allowed to those who hold PHd, MBA, university degree, BTEC, SCOTVEC, C&G or equivalent awards. Exemption is also granted to those who hold membership of professional bodies whose standards of entry to membership are not lower than those of the Institute. In all cases applicants must have the necessary experience at an appropriate level of responsibility. The Institute conducts its own flexible, open-learning (home study) courses leading to exams for the Institute's Certificate and Diploma of Merit. Entry standards: the Certificate of Merit Course is open to student members holding 4 O Levels Grades A or B, including English, Mathematics and a Science subject. Min age 18.The Diploma of Merit Course is open to members holding the Certificate of Merit of the Institute or similar qualifications acceptable to the Management Education & Examinations Board of the Institute. Also, in addition to the above, a large range of Distance Learning Courses are available from Head Office.

University Qualifications

The following universities offer qualifications in Manufacturing and related subjects. Full details may be found in Part 4, under the entry for the appropriate university.

FIRST DEGREES AWARDED BY UNIVERSITIES

Bradford; Bradford (Bradford & Ilkley Community College); Brunel; Bucks. Coll.; Central England; Central Lancashire; Coventry; Glamorgan; Glasgow Caledonian; Hertfordshire; Huddersfield; Hull; Lincolnshire; Liverpool; Liverpool John Moores; London (King's College London); London Guildhall; Luton; Manchester Metropolitan.; Newcastle; Nottingham; Paisley; Portsmouth; Salford; Staffordshire; Strathclyde; Sunderland; Ulster; UMIST; Wales (North East Wales Institute); Wales (Swansea Institute of Higher Education); Wales (University of Wales College, Newport); Wolverhampton

HIGHER DEGREES AWARDED BY UNIVERSITIES

Bath; Birmingham; Bradford; Brighton; Bristol; Brunel; Coventry; Cranfield; De Montfort, Leicester; Derby; Glamorgan; Hertfordshire; Huddersfield; Kingston; Lancaster; Lincolnshire; Liverpool; Liverpool John Moores; Loughborough; Manchester Metropolitan.; Middlesex;

Northumbria; Nottingham; Portsmouth; Robert Gordon; Salford; South Bank; Strathclyde; Sunderland; Surrey; Teesside; Ulster; UMIST; Wales (University of Wales College, Newport); Warwick

DIPLOMAS AWARDED BY UNIVERSITIES
Birmingham; Bournemouth; Bradford; Coventry; Glamorgan; Greenwich; Lancaster; Paisley; Portsmouth; Salford; Strathclyde; Ulster

CERTIFICATES AWARDED BY UNIVERSITIES
Anglia (City College, Norwich); Coventry; Lincolnshire; Salford

National Certificates and Diplomas

Scotland
SQA HNC: Engineering (Manufacture); Engineering Manufacture with Quality Assurance; Manufacturing Engineering; Manufacturing
SQA HND: Electronics in Manufacturing; Engineering Manufacture with Quality Assurance; Manufacturing; Manufacturing Engineering with Industrial Management; Manufacturing Engineering & Management; Manufacturing Systems Engineering; Manufacturing Technology & Management
SQA Diploma in Management with Manufacturing

NVQs

Level 1: Food & Drink Manufacturing Operations; Food & Drink Manufacturing Operations (Distilling); Furniture Production Operations; Manufacturing Products from Textiles; Manufacturing Sewn Products; Manufacturing Textiles; Mattress Manufacturing; Paper Manufacturing; Performing Manufacturing Operations.
Level 2: Assembled Furniture Production; Assembly, Fabrication, Manufacturing Processes (Signmaking); Carton Manufacture; Fibreboard Manufacture; Food & Drink Manufacturing Operations; Food & Drink Manufacturing Operations (Distilling); Footwear Manufacture; Leather Production; Leathergoods Manufacture; Manufacturing Ceramic Items; Manufacturing Jewellery & Allied Products; Manufacturing Products from Textiles; Manufacturing Sewn Products; Manufacturing Textiles; Meat & Poultry Processing & Manufacturing Operations; Paper Manufacturing; Performing Manufacturing Operations; Process Manufacture (Chemicals); Tube Making; Wire Rope Making
Level 3: Carton Manufacture; Food & Drink Manufacturing Operations; Furniture Production; Manufacturing Textiles; Paper Manufacturing; Process Manufacture (Chemicals); Properties Manufacture; Tube Making

SVQs

Level 1: Food and Drink Manufacturing Operations; Paper Manufacturing; Performing Manufacturing Operations
Level 2: Food and Drink Manufacturing Operations; Paper Manufacturing; Performing Manufacturing Operations; Sign Making
Level 3: Food and Drink Manufacturing Operations; Paper Manufacturing; Sign Making
Level 4: Food and Drink Manufacturing Operations

GNVQs

3726 Manufacturing

City & Guilds

4540 Footwear Manufacturing Operatives; 4560 Leather Manufacturing Operatives; 4570 Leather Manufacturing Craft; 4700 Leather Goods Manufacture; 5630 Stringed Keyboard Instrument Manufacture

MAPMAKING AND TOPOGRAPHY

University Qualifications

The following universities offer qualifications in Mapmaking and Topography and related subjects. Full details may be found in Part 4, under the entry for the appropriate university.

FIRST DEGREES AWARDED BY UNIVERSITIES
East London; Glasgow; Luton; Newcastle; Wales (University of Wales, Swansea)

HIGHER DEGREES AWARDED BY UNIVERSITIES
London (University College (UCL)); Portsmouth

DIPLOMAS AWARDED BY UNIVERSITIES
London (University College (UCL))

National Certificates and Diplomas

BTEC National Certificates/Diplomas: Cartography
BTEC Higher National Certificates/Diplomas: Cartography

MARKETING AND SALES

Membership of Professional Institutions and Associations

THE CHARTERED INSTITUTE OF MARKETING
Moor Hall, Cookham, Maidenhead, Berkshire SL6 9QH Tel: 01628 427500 Fax: 01628 427499

MEMBERSHIP:
All grades are awarded following an assessment during which account is taken of the candidate's academic/vocational qualifications and marketing resource management experience. Applicants for admission to membership grades other than Student, Licentiate or Graduate, must be employed, at the time of their application, within at least 1 of the following areas: Advertising; Conduct of Marketing Education; Conduct of Marketing or Sales Training; Direct Marketing; International Marketing; Market Research; Marketing Consultancy; Marketing Services; Merchandising; Physical Distribution; Product/Brand Management; Public Relations; Sales Promotion; Sales.
Graduate: A person who holds a recognised university degree majoring in marketing, CIM Postgraduate Diploma or equivalent level marketing professional body qualification or less than 3 yrs' experience in marketing and less than 1 yr's experience in marketing resource management.
Licentiate: A person who has a CIM Certificate or CIM Advanced Certificate or HNC/HND Marketing or Business Studies or NVQ Level 2 or 3 in marketing, sales or customer services and less than 1 yr's experience in marketing resource management.
Associate Member (ACIM): A person who holds a recognised university degree in marketing, CIM Postgraduate Diploma or equivalent level marketing professional body exam or NVQ Level 5 in marketing or sales and at least 1 yr's experience in marketing resource management. To comply with Privy Council requirements ACIMs may only hold this grade for a max of 6 yrs. After this period they are required to upgrade to Full Member (MCIM) or revert to their previous grade.
Member (MCIM): A person who holds a recognised university degree in marketing, CIM Postgraduate Diploma or equivalent diploma, or Chartered Professional Body admission exam or NVQ Level 5 in marketing or sales; at least 3 yrs' experience in marketing, including 1 yr's experience in marketing resource management.
Fellow (FCIM): A person who has the academic qualifications required for a Member and a proven record of expertise, experience and success, holding a role such as Chief Exec, Exec Director, Senior Marketing Exec, Prof of Marketing or Senior Academic for at least 5 yrs.

EXAMINATIONS:
The 3-tiered syllabus comprises the **Postgraduate Diploma in Marketing, Advanced Certificate in Marketing** and **Certificate in Marketing**. Available at over 300 study centres world-wide and through DL or intensive study, each qualification is in June and December.
The Postgraduate Diploma in Marketing, the Advanced Certificate and the Certificate in Marketing embraces the marketing concept, and reflects the key knowledge and skills areas required by professional marketing and sales practitioners. The emphasis is on the practical application of marketing theory, problem solving and marketing planning from a fundamental level progressing to a more strategic focus at Diploma Level.
The Postgraduate Diploma in Marketing (DipM) is internationally-recognised and with the relevant experience gives eligibility for full membership of the CIM and Chartered Marketer Status. The Open University validation service have awarded the CIM Diploma 70 Master points. Modules include Integrated Marketing Communications Strategy, International Marketing Strategy and a Strategic Marketing Management Section comprising Planning & Control and Analysis & Decision (case study). Student registration forms, study centre lists and further information regarding exemptions and entry points may be obtained from: *The Education Dept*, Tel: 01628 427120 Fax: 01628 427158 e-mail: education@cim.co.uk.

THE INSTITUTE OF SALES AND MARKETING MANAGEMENT

Romeland House, Romeland Hill, St Albans, Hertfordshire AL3 4ET Tel: 01727 812500
Fax: 01727 812525 e-mail: sales@ismm.co.uk
The Institute of Sales and Marketing Management offers a suite of four professional qualifications in sales and sales management. The qualifications are fully recognised by the Department for Education and Employment and the Qualifications and Curriculum Authority under Schedule 2(a) of the Further and Higher Education Act 1992.The courses include a Foundation Award in Sales and Marketing, a Certificate in Operational Sales and Marketing and two Advanced Certificates, one in Account Management and one in Sales Management. The programme is available through Colleges of Further Education, approved private training centres and in-company training departments, and as a distance learning course through RRC Business Training. Membership of the ISMM is awarded on the basis of achieving these or other recognised qualifications or in recognition of a proven track record in sales and sales management.

MANAGING & MARKETING SALES ASSOCIATION EXAMINATION BOARD

PO Box 11, Sandbach, Cheshire CW11 3GE Tel: 01270 526 339 Fax: 01270 526 339
e-mail: info@mamsasbp.com Website: www.mamsasbp.com
MEMBERSHIP:
Student Member: Registered for 2 yrs to undertake the MAMSA exams.
Graduate Member: Annual membership of holders of MAMSA qualifications (GradMAMSA).
Professional Members & Fellows: Annual Membership.

EXAMINATIONS:
Intermediate Diploma in Selling: Entry requirements: min age 18 yrs.
Standard Diploma in Salesmanship: Entry requirements: as above *or* 5 GCSEs at grade C or above *or* 20 yrs old with 2 yrs' approved employment.
Certificate in Sales Marketing: Entry requirements: as for Salesmanship.
Higher Diploma in Sales Marketing: Entry requirements: as for Salesmanship.
Advanced Diploma in Sales Management: Entry requirements: 5 GCSEs at grade C or above and 1 A Level, including English and a branch of Mathematics *or* BTEC ONC Business award *or* 3 yrs' experience in selling and marketing.
Certificate/Diploma in Marketing Strategy & Management: Entry requirements: as for Sales Management.
Diploma in Business Administration & Practices: Entry requirements: as for Sales Management.
Advanced Diploma in the Practice of Business Management: Entry requirements: as for Sales Management.
Certificate in Quality Services
Diploma in Supervisory Skills
Distance learning courses available for all diplomas and for in-company groups.

THE SOCIETY OF SALES MANAGEMENT ADMINISTRATORS LTD

40 Archdale Road, East Dulwich, London SE22 9HJ Tel: 020 8693 0555 Fax: 020 8693 0555
e-mail: ssma@totalise.co.uk

EXAMINATIONS:

The Society is the only professional body which awards specialist certificates and diplomas in all the four major divisions of selling, namely: Selling & Sales Management, Marketing, Retail Management and International Trade. The examinations are held twice a yr (May and November). The subjects for the Certificate in Selling & Sales Management, Certificate in Marketing, Certificate in Retail Management and Certificate in International Trade are : (i) Business Communications; (ii) Accounting & Finance. The subjects for the Advanced Certificate in Selling & Sales Management, Advanced Certificate in Marketing, Advanced Certificate in Retail Management, and Advanced Certificate in International Trade are: (iii) Selling & Sales Management; (iv) Marketing; (v) Principles of Selling; (vi) Principles of Management; (vii) Retail Management; (viii) International Trade & Payments. The subjects for the Diploma in Selling & Sales Management, Diploma in Marketing, Diploma in Retail Management and Diploma in International Trade are: (ix) Consumer Affairs; (x) Management Information Systems; (xi) Export Practice; (xii) Elements of Export Law. A dissertation on a relevant topic is essential for the Advanced Diploma in Selling & Sales Management, Advanced Diploma in Marketing, Advanced Diploma in Retail Management and Advanced Diploma in International Trade. N/SVQs candidates may apply for exemptions or membership according to age, qualifications and experience.

MEMBERSHIP:

Registered students are eligible to take the Society's professional exams. They must be over 18. Registration expires after 3 yrs, and it is renewable.

Fellow (FSMA): Candidates must have been Associate Members for at least 2 yrs, and been engaged in selling, retailing, marketing and international trade ; or holding a position of responsibility ; or must have been a lecturer in sales and related subjects for at least 2 yrs.

Associates (ASMA): Candidates must have passed the Society's professional exams or been exempted from them, and been engaged in selling, sales management, retailing, marketing, and international trade ; or holding a position of responsibility; or must have been a lecturer in sales and related subjects for at least 2 yrs.

Graduates (GSMA): Candidates must have been recommended by their employers as fit and proper persons to benefit from membership, or must have shown proof of outstanding selling abilities, eg agents of mail order firms.

University Qualifications

The following universities offer qualifications in Marketing and Sales and related subjects. Full details may be found in Part 4, under the entry for the appropriate university.

FIRST DEGREES AWARDED BY UNIVERSITIES

Abertay, Dundee; Adams; Anglia (City College, Norwich); Anglia (Colchester Institute); Aston; Bournemouth; Bradford; Bradford (Bradford & Ilkley Community College); Brighton; Bristol; Buckingham; Bucks. Coll.; Central England; Central Lancashire; Cheltenham & Gloucester; Coventry; De Montfort, Leicester; Derby; Doncaster; Doncaster (Dearne Valley Business School); Dundee; East Anglia (Suffolk College); Glamorgan; Glasgow Caledonian; Greenwich; Hertfordshire; Hertfordshire (West Herts College); Huddersfield; Keele; Kent (Canterbury Christ Church University College); Kent (Kent Institute of Art & Design); Lancaster; Lancáster (Edge Hill College of Higher Education); Leeds (Leeds, Trinity & All Saints); Lincolnshire; Lincolnshire (Grimsby College); Lincolnshire (Lincoln University Campus); London (Wye College); London Guildhall; London Institute (London College of Printing); Luton; Manchester (Warrington Collegiate Institute, Faculty of H.E,); Manchester Metropolitan.; Middlesex; Napier; Newcastle; North London; Northampton; Northumbria; Nottingham Trent (Southampton Institute); Oxford Brookes; Paisley; Plymouth; Queen Margaret; Reading; Sheffield Hallam; South Bank; Staffordshire; Stirling; Strathclyde; Sunderland; Surrey (Farnborough College of Technology); Surrey (University of Surrey Roehampton); Teesside; Thames Valley; Ulster; UMIST; Wales (North East Wales Institute); Wales (Swansea Institute of Higher Education); Wales (University of Wales College, Newport); Wales (University of Wales, Aberystwyth); Wales (University of Wales, Bangor); Wolverhampton

HIGHER DEGREES AWARDED BY UNIVERSITIES

Abertay, Dundee; Aston; Bournemouth; Bradford; Brighton; Bristol; Bucks. Coll.; Central England; Central Lancashire; Cheltenham & Gloucester; City; Coventry; Cranfield; De Montfort, Leicester; Derby; Dundee; East London; Exeter; Glasgow Caledonian; Heriot-Watt; Huddersfield; Hull; Kingston; Lancaster; Leeds; Leeds Metropolitan; Leicester; Lincolnshire; Liverpool; Liverpool John Moores; London (Wye College); London Guildhall; Luton; Manchester Metropolitan.; Middlesex; Newcastle; North London; Northampton; Northumbria; Nottingham Trent; Nottingham Trent (Southampton Institute); Paisley; Portsmouth; Reading; Salford; Sheffield; Sheffield Hallam; South Bank; Staffordshire; Stirling; Strathclyde; Sunderland; Surrey; Thames Valley; Ulster; UMIST; Westminster

DIPLOMAS AWARDED BY UNIVERSITIES

Anglia (City College, Norwich); Aston; Birmingham (Birmingham College of Food, Tourism and Creative Studies); Blackburn; Bournemouth; Bradford (Bradford & Ilkley Community College); Brighton; Bucks. Coll.; Central England; Cheltenham & Gloucester; Coventry; Doncaster; Doncaster (Dearne Valley Business School); Durham (New College Durham); Lincolnshire; London (University College (UCL)); London (Wye College); London Institute (London College of Fashion); London Institute (London College of Printing); Luton; Manchester Metropolitan.; Napier; Newcastle; Northampton; Northumbria; Nottingham Trent (Southampton Institute); Paisley; Salford; South Bank; Stirling; Strathclyde; Teesside; Thames Valley; Ulster; Wales (Swansea Institute of Higher Education); Wales (University of Wales College, Newport)

CERTIFICATES AWARDED BY UNIVERSITIES

Bournemouth; Bradford (Bradford & Ilkley Community College); Central England; Cheltenham & Gloucester; East Anglia (Otley College); Lincolnshire (Hull College); Manchester Metropolitan.; North London; Nottingham Trent (Southampton Institute); Wales (University of Wales College, Newport); Westminster

POSTGRADUATE DIPLOMAS AWARDED BY UNIVERSITIES

Heriot-Watt

PROFESSIONAL COURSES AWARDED BY UNIVERSITIES

Leeds Metropolitan; London Guildhall; Manchester Metropolitan

PROFESSIONAL QUALIFICATIONS AWARDED BY UNIVERSITIES

De Montfort, Leicester

National Certificates and Diplomas

BTEC Higher National Certificates/Diplomas: Business and Marketing
Scotland
SQA HNC: Marketing; Marketing & Communication; Marketing Design
SQA HND: Marketing; Marketing & Communication; Marketing Design

NVQs

Level 2: Selling; Telephone Selling; Vehicle Selling; Visual Merchandising
Level 3: Selling; Vehicle Selling; Visual Merchandising
Level 4: Field Sales Management; Visual Merchandising

SVQs

Level 2: Customer Service; Selling; Telephone Selling
Level 3: Customer Service; Direct Marketing; Sales Supervision; Selling; Selling Residential Property
Level 4: Field Sales Management; Direct Marketing

MARTIAL ARTS

Membership of Professional Institutions and Associations

THE SOCIETY OF MARTIAL ARTS/COLLEGE OF HIGHER EDUCATION OF MARTIAL ARTS

PO Box 34, Manchester M9 8DN Tel: 0161 702 1660 Fax: 0161 702 1660
e-mail: sma@societyofmartialarts.ssnet.co.uk
The Society offers appropriate membership grades to practitioners of martial arts. The College offers graduateship qualifications through distance learning and exams, and arranges postgraduate studies in martial arts for qualified students through universities. Exemptions are granted to those with relevant degree or postgraduate qualifications in sports science or martial arts.

MEMBERSHIP GRADES:
Student Member: This class of membership is open to anyone undergoing an approved FT or PT education in marital arts.
Graduate Member (GradSMA): This class of membership is open to marital artists who have completed the Graduateship exam offered by the Society or an approved degree course qualification with a black belt or equivalent grade in martial arts.
Full Member (MSMA): Open to Graduate Members with relevant experience. Some practitioners with many yrs' experience may be able to join directly as a Full Member, provided they complete a thesis in martial arts research.
Fellow Member (FSMA): In general candidates must have relevant experience. Some candidates with many yrs' experience and who have made an exceptional contribution to the field of martial arts may be elected to this class of membership directly.
Affiliate Member status: This is available to organisations promoting martial arts.

GRADUATESHIP IN MARTIAL ARTS:
Through the College of Higher Education of Martial Arts.
Entry requirements: At least 'C' grades at GCSE in English, Maths and Science. Candidates over 25 may enrol as mature students. All candidates without formal qualifications must attend an interview.
Part 1: Candidates must be competent practitioners of any form of martial arts; exemptions are allowed only to those who are holders of a black belt (1st Dan) or equivalent qualification in martial arts.
Part 2: Students are normally expected to have completed Part 1 before continuing with the programme. The subjects offered for study in Part 2 carry a total of 360 credits (3 yrs).
First year core subjects (total 120 credits): Introduction to Sports Science; Human (Functional) Anatomy; Human Physiology; Introduction to Coaching Science; History of Martial Arts; Philosophy (Metaphysics, Epistemology, Aesthetics and Ethics); Sports Sociology; one optional subject to be chosen by the student from any department at an accredited university.
Second year core subjects (total 120 credits): Exercise Physiology; Biomechanics; Acquisition of Martial Arts Motor Skills; Law and Martial Arts; Research Methods; Statistics; Sports Pedagogy; one optional subject to be chosen by the student from any department at an accredited university.
Third year core subjects (total 120 credits): Pediatric Exercise Science; Assessing and Evaluating Martial Arts Skills; Sports Nutrition; Sports Psychology; Epidemiology of Martial Arts injuries.
Research project (total 40 credits).
Assessment: Subjects studied in yrs 1 to 3 are assessed by either 3 written assignments (25%), or by one review paper (50%). In both cases, a 3 hr unseen paper makes up the balance of the total marks. The research dissertation in usually a written presentation of c.10,000 words followed by a viva voce. The pass mark for all papers is 50%.
Mature students' route to Graduateship in Martial Arts: This route is by 1 yr FT research. Candidates submit a thesis of 30,000 words followed by a viva voce and one publication.

MASTERSHIP IN MARTIAL ARTS:
Students with a degree in Martial Arts can follow our advance research for 1 yr and submit a thesis of 40,000 words followed by a viva voce and one publication.

MASSAGE AND ALLIED THERAPIES
(See also Beauty Therapy and Beauty Culture)

Membership of Professional Institutions and Associations

INTERNATIONAL COUNCIL OF HOLISTIC THERAPISTS
(Part of the Federation of Holistic Therapists)

3rd Floor, Eastleigh House, Upper Market Street, Eastleigh SO51 9FD Tel: 023 8048 8900 Fax: 023 8048 8970 Website: www.fht.org.uk
This professional association supports therapists in Holistic Therapies including Aromatherapy, Reflexology, Indian Head Massage, Body Massage, and many more. Membership is only open to those qualified through awarding bodies such as IIHHT, VTCT, S/NVQs, BTEC and City & Guilds. Exemptions from these qualification requirements are granted only for those who have other acceptable qualifications and experience.

INTERNATIONAL INSTITUTE OF HEALTH AND HOLISTIC THERAPIES
(Listed under Vocational Training Charitable Trust, Beauty Therapy and Beauty Culture Section)

THE LONDON AND COUNTIES SOCIETY OF PHYSIOLOGISTS

330 Lytham Road, Blackpool FY4 1DW Tel: 01253 408443 Fax: 01253 401329
e-mail: admin.lcsp@ic24.net Website: www.lcsp.uk.com

MEMBERSHIP:
Full Membership: Open to those persons who have passed the written and practical sections of the qualifying exam and who have not less than 3 yrs' FT practical experience in the profession. Such membership carries the designating letters LCSP(Phys), LCSP(Chir) or LCSP(BTh) according to whether the member is approved by the Council as a practitioner in physical and manipulative therapy, chiropody or health and beauty therapy.
Associate Membership (LSCP (Assoc)): Open to those persons who have passed the written and practical section of the qualifying exam, and who have less than 3 yrs' FT practical experience in the profession.
Fellowship (FLCSP): Conferred on members who have given distinguished service to the profession or Society.
Honorary Membership: May be conferred by the Council on outside persons who are genuinely associated with the profession and work of the Society.
Student Membership: Open to bona fide registered students of the profession.

EDUCATION AND EXAMINATION:
The Society recognises the Northern Institute of Massage (NIM) as its official training establishment, but may also approve of such other sources of training or apprenticeship submitted by an applicant for membership at the discretion of the Council. Students who have successfully completed the tuition course of the NIM may apply to take their final qualifying exam for the Diploma of the NIM under the auspices of the Society, such exam also qualifying the successful candidate for Membership of the Society. The Exam consists of 2 written papers and a practical exam. Exemptions from the written exam may be granted on a subject-for-subject basis to holders of certain qualifications recognised by the Society, eg qualified nurses, medical auxiliaries, etc. Exemptions from the practical exam can only be granted in special circumstances where the applicant is known to be an established practitioner of the profession, and such applicants for admission will, in every case, be required to attend for interview before the Council of the Society.

THE NORTHERN INSTITUTE OF MASSAGE

14-16 St Mary's Place, Bury, Lancashire BL9 0DZ Tel: 0161 7971800
e-mail: northern@institute1924.freeserve.com.uk Website: www.nim56.co.uk
The College offers PT and home study extension courses in Remedial Massage, Manipulative Therapy and allied subjects. Official training establishment to the London and Counties Society of Physiologists. Training approved by the Institute of Baths Management as providing persons employed in remedial baths with a recognised level of performance. The College is accredited by

the Open and Distance Learning Quality Council, and is a Member of the Association of British Correspondence Colleges. The courses are approved by London Licensing Boroughs.

EXAMINATIONS:
Diploma in Remedial Massage: Leading to LCSP(Phys) qualification.
Higher Grade Diplomas in Advanced Remedial Massage & Manipulative Therapy: Subsequent to satisfactory completion of postgraduate training in Advanced Massage, Electro-therapy and Manipulative Therapy.

University Qualifications

The following universities offer qualifications in Massage and Allied Therapies and related subjects. Full details may be found in Part 4, under the entry for the appropriate university.

FIRST DEGREES AWARDED BY UNIVERSITIES
Greenwich

MATERIALS

Membership of Professional Institutions and Associations

The IMM merged with the ILDM in August 1993 to form the Institute of Logistics (q.v.).

THE INSTITUTE OF MATERIALS

1 Carlton House Terrace, London SW1Y 5DB Tel: 020 74517 300 Fax: 020 7839 4534
e-mail: admin@materials.org.uk Website: www.materials.org.uk
The Institute of Materials was formed on 1 January 1992 following an earlier amalgamation of The Metals Society and The Institute of Metallurgists. The Institute of Metallurgical Technicians was incorporated into the latter in 1984. The Institute also amalgamated with The Plastics and Rubber Institute and the Institute of Ceramics on 1 January 1993.

MEMBERSHIP:
Fellow (FIM): A person with an outstanding reputation in the field of Materials.
Professional Member (MIM): A person with proven technical competence in the field of Materials, innovative by character and capable of developing the science and technology of Materials.
Member: A person who is not a Materials Scientist or Technologist but has a general interest in the profession and who may be expected to be a professional engineer in the field of Metallurgy, Materials, Polymers or Ceramics, or a scientist of a closely allied discipline.
Associate (AMIM): 1. A person with a 1st degree in the science of engineering of materials and who has completed the Institute's Training requirements, or early career development, towards professional member status. **2. Incorporated Engineer:** A person typically with an HNC/HND qualification who understands and can apply existing technology but is not necessarily of an innovative character.
Technician: A person capable of following prescribed routines which are dictated by a professional member or incorporated engineer.
Student: This grade of membership is open to persons pursuing a 1st qualification in the field of Materials.
Affiliate: Those generally interested in Materials but who would not necessarily qualify for the grades previously mentioned. As a nominated body of the Engineering Council, the Institute is also empowered to nominate members in relevant grades to the Engineering Technician, Incorporated Engineer and Chartered Engineering Sections of their Register.

University Qualifications

The following universities offer qualifications in Materials and related subjects. Full details may be found in Part 4, under the entry for the appropriate university.

FIRST DEGREES AWARDED BY UNIVERSITIES
Aberdeen; Birmingham; Bradford; Heriot-Watt; Heriot-Watt (Scottish Borders Campus); Hull; Leeds; Liverpool; London (Imperial College of Science, Technology & Medicine); London (Queen Mary & Westfield College (incorporating St Bartholomew's and the Royal London School of Medicine & Dentistry)); London (University College (UCL)); Loughborough; Manchester; Manchester Metropolitan.; Newcastle; Northumbria; Nottingham; Oxford; Plymouth; Portsmouth; Sheffield; Sheffield Hallam; St Andrews; Strathclyde; Surrey; UMIST; Wales (University of Wales, Swansea); Wolverhampton

HIGHER DEGREES AWARDED BY UNIVERSITIES
Aberdeen; Belfast; Birmingham; Brunel; Cranfield; Heriot-Watt; Hull; Leeds; Liverpool; London (Birkbeck, University of London); London (Imperial College of Science, Technology & Medicine); London (Queen Mary & Westfield College (incorporating St Bartholomew's and the Royal London School of Medicine & Dentistry)); Loughborough; Manchester; Napier; Reading; Sheffield; Sheffield Hallam; Sunderland; UMIST

DIPLOMAS AWARDED BY UNIVERSITIES
Edinburgh; Hull; Liverpool; Loughborough; Manchester; Napier

POSTGRADUATE DIPLOMAS AWARDED BY UNIVERSITIES
Heriot-Watt

National Certificates and Diplomas
BTEC National Certificates/Diplomas: Materials Technology
BTEC Higher National Certificates/Diplomas: Materials Technology; Science (Materials)
Scotland
SQA HNC: Polymer Technology

NVQs
Level 1: Engineering Material Processing; Process Operations (Chemical & Pharmaceutical); Process Operations (Refractories & Building Products)
Level 2: Materials Preparation; Process Operations (Chemical & Pharmaceutical); Process Operations (Man-made Fibre); Process Operations (Refractories & Building Products); Processing Raw Materials; Producing Surface Coatings; Product Coating
Level 3: Materials Preparation; Process Operations (Chemical & Pharmaceutical); Process Operations: Technical Support (Chemical & Pharmaceutical); Product Coating

Useful Addresses
ECC International Ltd, John Keay House, St Austell, Cornwall PL25 4DJ Tel: 01726 74482 Fax: 01726 623019
Refractories Clay Pipes and Allied Training Industry, 156 Broomspring Lane, Sheffield S10 2FE Tel: 0114 275 9345

MATHEMATICS

Membership of Professional Institutions and Associations

THE INSTITUTE OF MATHEMATICS AND ITS APPLICATIONS
Catherine Richards House, 16 Nelson Street, Southend-on-Sea, Essex SS1 1EF Tel: 01702 354020 Fax: 01702 354111 e-mail: Membership@ima.org.uk Website: www.ima.org.uk
MEMBERSHIP:
Fellow (CMath FIMA): Corporate Membership with Chartered Status. Fellows have demonstrated seniority or distinction in professional activities involving mathematics. As a guide,

the minimum period after which an honours mathematics graduate might qualify is 7 yrs' for mathematics in research or 10 yrs' for those using or applying mathematics.

Member (CMath MIMA): Corporate Membership with Chartered Status. Members have an appropriate degree, a minimum period of 4 yrs' postgraduate training and experience and a position of responsibility involving the application of mathematical knowledge or training in mathematics.

Associate Fellow (AFIMA): Corporate Membership. This grade is still in existence but was closed to further admissions in December 1997.

Graduate (GIMA): Grade leading to Chartered Status. Graduates hold an honours degree in mathematics or have obtained an honours degree in a related subject and are participating in training or work experience in which mathematical knowledge of a similar level is attained.

Licentiate: Grade leading to Chartered Status. Licentiates hold an ordinary degree or pass degree or HND in mathematics or a degree where mathematics is only a subsidiary component. A more extensive period of postgraduate training and experience are required to meet chartered status requirements.

Student: Grade leading to Chartered Status. Students are undertaking a course of study which will lead to a qualification that meets Graduate or Licentiate Member requirements.

Companion: Grade for non-professional members. No academic requirements are required for entry into this grade.

THE MATHEMATICAL ASSOCIATION

259 London Road, Leicester LE2 3BE Tel: 0116 270 3877 Fax: 0116 244 8508
Awards of the Association are available to practising teachers.

University Qualifications

The following universities offer qualifications in Mathematics and related subjects. Full details may be found in Part 4, under the entry for the appropriate university.

FIRST DEGREES AWARDED BY UNIVERSITIES

Aberdeen; Anglia; Aston; Bath; Belfast; Birmingham; Birmingham (The University of Birmingham, Westhill); Bradford; Brighton; Bristol; Brunel; Cambridge; Central Lancashire; City; Coventry; Derby; Dundee; Durham; East Anglia; East London; Edinburgh; Essex; Exeter; Exeter (The College of St Mark & St John); Glamorgan; Glasgow; Glasgow Caledonian; Greenwich; Heriot-Watt; Hertfordshire; Huddersfield; Hull; Keele; Kent; Kent (Canterbury Christ Church University College); Kingston; Lancaster; Lancaster (Edge Hill College of Higher Education); Leeds; Leeds (Leeds, Trinity & All Saints); Leeds (The College of Ripon & York St John); Leicester; Liverpool; Liverpool (Chester College of H.E.); Liverpool (Liverpool Hope University College); Liverpool John Moores; London (Birkbeck, University of London); London (Goldsmiths College); London (Imperial College of Science, Technology & Medicine); London (King's College London); London (London School of Economics & Political Science); London (Queen Mary & Westfield College (incorporating St Bartholomew's and the Royal London School of Medicine & Dentistry)); London (Royal Holloway); London (University College (UCL)); London Guildhall; Loughborough; Luton; Manchester; Manchester Metropolitan.; Middlesex; Napier; Newcastle; North London; Northampton; Northumbria; Nottingham; Nottingham Trent; Oxford; Oxford Brookes; Paisley; Plymouth; Portsmouth; Reading; Salford; Sheffield; Sheffield Hallam; Southampton; Southampton (Chichester Institute of Higher Education); Southampton (King Alfred's College); St Andrews; St Martin; Staffordshire; Stirling; Strathclyde; Sunderland; Surrey; Surrey (University of Surrey Roehampton); Sussex; Ulster; UMIST; Wales (Cardiff University); Wales (University of Wales Institute, Cardiff); Wales (University of Wales, Aberystwyth); Wales (University of Wales, Bangor); Wales (University of Wales, Swansea); Warwick; Westminster; Wolverhampton; York

HIGHER DEGREES AWARDED BY UNIVERSITIES

Aberdeen; Bath; Belfast; Birmingham; Bradford; Bristol; Brunel; Cambridge; Central England; City; Coventry; Cranfield; Derby; Dundee; Durham; East Anglia; Edinburgh; Essex; Exeter; Glamorgan; Glasgow; Glasgow Caledonian; Heriot-Watt; Hull; Keele; Kent; Lancaster; Leeds; Leicester; Liverpool; Liverpool (Chester College of H.E.); Liverpool John Moores; London

(Goldsmiths College); London (Imperial College of Science, Technology & Medicine); London (King's College London); London (London School of Economics & Political Science); London (Queen Mary & Westfield College (incorporating St Bartholomew's and the Royal London School of Medicine & Dentistry); London (Royal Holloway); London (University College (UCL)); London Guildhall; Loughborough; Manchester; Manchester Metropolitan.; Middlesex; Newcastle; Northumbria; Nottingham; Nottingham Trent; Oxford; Plymouth; Portsmouth; Reading; Salford; Sheffield Hallam; South Bank; Southampton; Southampton (Chichester Institute of Higher Education); St Andrews; St Martin; Staffordshire; Stirling; Surrey (University of Surrey Roehampton); Sussex; Teesside; Ulster; UMIST; Wales (University of Wales, Bangor); Warwick; York

DIPLOMAS AWARDED BY UNIVERSITIES

Bradford; Edinburgh; Glasgow; Hull; Kent; Lancaster; Lancaster (Edge Hill College of Higher Education); Liverpool (Chester College of H.E.); London (King's College London); Manchester; Newcastle; Nottingham Trent; Plymouth; Reading; Salford; South Bank; St Andrews; Stirling; Strathclyde; Ulster

CERTIFICATES AWARDED BY UNIVERSITIES

Brighton; Brunel; Cambridge; Derby; Essex; Exeter (The College of St Mark & St John); Huddersfield; Leeds Metropolitan; Liverpool (Chester College of H.E.); London (Goldsmiths College); Manchester Metropolitan.; Middlesex; Newcastle; North London; Nottingham; Oxford (Westminster College, Oxford); Sheffield Hallam; Southampton; Southampton (Chichester Institute of Higher Education); St Martin; Wales (University of Wales Institute, Cardiff); Wales (University of Wales, Bangor)

POSTGRADUATE DIPLOMAS AWARDED BY UNIVERSITIES

Heriot-Watt

National Certificates and Diplomas

BTEC National Certificates/Diplomas: Mathematical Studies
BTEC Higher National Certificates/Diplomas: Mathematical Studies; Mathematical Studies (Applied Statistics in Operation Research); Mathematical Studies (Business Decision Analysis); Mathematical Studies (Computer Based Mathematics); Mathematical Studies (Mathematics, Statistics and Computing); Mathematics and Statistics; Mathematics, Statistics and Computing; Mathematics, Statistics and Physics *Scotland*
SQA HNC: Applicable Mathematics with Computing; Mathematics, Statistics & Computing.
SQA HND: Applicable Mathematics with Computing; Mathematics, Statistics & Computing.

City & Guilds

3615 Key Skills; 3750 Numeracy; 3794 Numeracy (Numberpower)

MEDICAL HERBALISM

Membership of Professional Institutions and Associations

THE NATIONAL INSTITUTE OF MEDICAL HERBALISTS

56 Longbrook Street, Exeter, Devon EX4 6AH Tel: 01392 426022 Fax: 01392 498963
e-mail: nimh@ukexeter.freeserve.co.uk Website: www.btinternet.com nimh{
MEMBERSHIP:
Fellow (FNIMH): Fellowship of the Institute may be offered to a member who has rendered conspicuous service to the Institute and who has been in active membership for more than 10 yrs.
Member (MNIMH): Those who have successfully completed the training and passed all exams are eligible to apply for membership of Institute.

TRAINING:
The School of Phytotherapy, Bucksteep Manor, Bodle Street Green, Hailsham, East Sussex, runs a 4 yr tutorial course with intensive theory and practical work. There is also a FT course at the School. Middlesex University, Scottish School of Herbal Medicine, University of Central Lancashire and University of Westminster run a 4 yr BSc (Hons) degree course in Herbal Medicine.

University Qualifications
The following universities offer qualifications in Medical Herbalism and related subjects. Full details may be found in Part 4, under the entry for the appropriate university.

FIRST DEGREES AWARDED BY UNIVERSITIES
Middlesex

MEDICAL SECRETARIES

Membership of Professional Institutions and Associations

ASSOCIATION OF MEDICAL SECRETARIES, PRACTICE MANAGERS, ADMINISTRATORS AND RECEPTIONISTS

Tavistock House North, Tavistock Square, London WC1H 9LN Tel: 020 7387 6005
Fax: 020 7388 2648 e-mail: amspar@atlas.co.uk Website: www.amspar.co.uk
MEMBERSHIP:
Fellow (FAMS): May be conferred in recognition of services to the Association.
Member (MAMS): Open to (1) Holders of the Association's Diploma in Medical Secretarial Studies; (2) Holders of the Diploma or Certificate in Practice Management upon qualifying; and (3) Holders of the Diploma in Health Services Reception, or following 10 yrs' relevant experience in a health care environment.
Associate Member (AAMS): Holders of the Association Certificate in General Practice Reception, Certificate in Medical Terminology or Certificate in Medical Secretarial Studies or qualification by five yrs' relevant experience in the Health Care environment.
Affiliate (AMS (AFF)): Affiliateship is open to any person currently working in the medical field for under 5 yrs.
DIPLOMAS AND CERTIFICATES:
Diploma in Health Services Reception: FT/PT course normally over 12 mths, open to school leavers, mature students or those already in post.
Diploma in Medical Secretarial Studies: FT/PT course for school leavers, mature students or those already working in a health care environment.
Diploma in Practice Management: PT course normally 12-18 mths, suitable for those working within general practice either in a management or administrative role or those with a minimum of 3 yrs' relevant experience. AMSPAR is a registered awarding body approved by the Department for Education and Employment. AMSPAR qualifications are endorsed by the BMA.

MEDICINE
A student who wishes to qualify as a doctor in the UK must first obtain, by exam, a primary qualification which confers a title to registration under the Medical Act. He/she is then entitled to apply for
provisional registration and, after satisfactorily completing 1yr as a resident House Officer in approved hospitals, he or she is eligible to apply for **full registration**. The **General Medical Council,** 178 Gt Portland St, London W1N 6JE Tel 0171-580 7642, e-mail gmc@gmc-uk.org, is

charged with the responsibility under the Medical Act 1983 of keeping a Register of all duly qualified medical practitioners.

Primary Qualifications

Primary qualifications entitling the holder to provisional registration in accordance with Part II of the Medical Act 1983 are as follows:

(i)The degrees of Bachelor of Medicine and Bachelor of Surgery awarded by universities in the UK.

(ii) The conjoint diplomas of Licentiate of the Royal College of Physicians of London and Licentiate of the Royal College of Surgeons of England and Licentiate in Medicine and Surgery of the Worshipful Society of Apothecaries of London (LRCP Lond LRCS Eng LMSSA Lond); and the conjoint diplomas of Licentiate of the Royal College of Physicians of Edinburgh and Licentiate of the Royal College of Surgeons of Edinburgh and Licentiate of the Royal College (formerly Faculty) of Physicians and Surgeons of Glasgow (LRCP Edin, LRCS Edin, LRCPS Glasg) conferred by the United Examining Board.

DIPLOMAS OF THE ROYAL COLLEGE OF PHYSICIANS OF EDINBURGH, THE ROYAL COLLEGE OF SURGEONS OF EDINBURGH AND THE ROYAL COLLEGE OF PHYSICIANS AND SURGEONS OF GLASGOW (LRCPEd, LRCSEd, LRCPSGlasg):

The United Examining Board has replaced the Scottish Triple Qualification Board of Management as the examining body. The Scottish Triple Qualification (LRCPEd, LRCSEd, LRCPSGlasg) is issued by the Royal College of Physicians of Edinburgh, the Royal College of Surgeons of Edinburgh and the Royal College of Physicians and Surgeons of Glasgow acting in co-operation after examination in Scotland by the UEB.

DIPLOMAS OF THE ROYAL COLLEGE OF PHYSICIANS OF LONDON, THE ROYAL COLLEGE OF SURGEONS OF ENGLAND AND THE WORSHIPFUL SOCIETY OF APOTHECARIES:

The UEB has replaced the Examining Board in England as the examining body. An English Triple Qualification, (LRCPLon, LRCSEng, LMSSALon) is issued by the RCP of London. RCS of England and the Society of Apothecaries acting in conjunction after examination in England by the UEB. The Scottish Triple is also gained after examination by the UEB. For particulars of the **United Examining Board's exam**, please write to: The Registrar, United Examining Board, Apothecaries Hall, Blackfriar's Lane, London EC4V 6EJ.

THE COUNCIL FOR PROFESSIONS SUPPLEMENTARY TO MEDICINE

Park House, 184 Kennington Park Road, London SE11 4BU Tel: 020 7582 0866 Fax: 020 7820 9684 Website: www.cpsm.org.uk

This was appointed by Act of Parliament; its function is to co-ordinate and facilitate the work of 12 Statutory Boards for the following professions: Chiropody; Dietetics; Medical Laboratory Sciences; Occupational Therapy; Orthoptics; Physiotherapy; Radiography; Prosthetics & Orthotics; Art, Music and Dramatherapy; Clinical Science; Paramedics; and Speech & Language Therapists. The Boards' principal functions are to promote high standards of professional education, training and professional conduct, and to maintain and publish registers of qualified practitioners. Members of the 12 Professions Supplementary to Medicine must register with their appropriate Board if they wish to be employed in any part of the NHS, NHS Trusts or Local Authority Social Services Departments; it is a requirement to practise in most other parts of the public service. The Boards accept registration students who have successfully gained approved qualifications, listed below:

Chiropody: BSc/BSc (Hons) Podiatry.

Dietetics: The Dieticians Board approves certain courses of training and qualifications which are also approved for membership of the British Dietetic Association. These are 4 yr BSc (Hons) degree courses and 2 yr postgraduate* diploma courses.

Medical Laboratory Sciences: For up-to-date information on registration requirements please contact the MLT Board directly.

Occupational Therapy: BSc/Bsc (Hons) Occupational Therapy and postgraduate* courses.

Orthoptics: BSc/BSc (Hons) Orthoptics.

Physiotherapy: BSc/BSc (Hons) Physiotherapy and postgraduate* courses.

Radiography: BSc/BSc (Hons) Radiography (Diagnostic or Therapeutic) and Oncology.

Prosthetics & Orthotics: BSc/BSc (Hons) Prosthetics & Orthotics.

Arts Therapies: Degree in art/drama/music followed by an approved postgraduate* diploma course.

Clinical Science: *Either* membership of the Registration Council for Scientists in Health Care, *or* contact the CS Board directly.

Paramedics: *Either* possession of the appropriate certification from the Institute of Health Care Development, *or* contact the Paramedics Board directly.

Speech & Language Therapists: *Either* membership of the Royal College of Speech & Language Therapists, *or* contact the SLT Board directly.

Note: *Postgraduate in time, not necessarily in level.

THE ROYAL COLLEGE OF PHYSICIANS AND SURGEONS OF GLASGOW

232–242 St Vincent Street, Glasgow G2 5RJ Tel: 0141 221 6072 Fax: 0141 221 1804

Fellow (FRCSGlasg): Elected from fellows of the Royal College of Surgeons of the UK and Ireland. The Fellowship exam may be taken in Surgery in General, Otolaryngology or Ophthalmology. In each case the exam is in 2 parts, A and B. Part A consists of an MCQ paper covering the basic sciences (Anatomy, Physiology and Pathology) plus an oral exam in Anatomy only. Part A Ophthalmology consists of an MCQ in Anatomy of the eye and orbit, head and neck, ophthalmic physiology and ophthalmic pathology.

Surgery in General: Part B consists of a written paper; oral exam in Principles of Surgery & Surgical Physiology, Operative Surgery and Surgical Pathology; and a clinical exam.

Otolaryngology: Part B consists of a written paper; oral exams in Principles of Surgery & Surgical Physiology, Head & Neck Surgery and Rhinology, Otology & Audiology; and a clinical exam.

Ophthalmology: Part B consists of a written paper; oral exams in Basic Sciences, Ophthalmic Medicine & Surgery, General Medicine / Neurology; and a clinical exam.

DIPLOMA EXAMINATIONS:

Geriatrics: Diploma in Geriatric Medicine (DGM RCPSGlasg): Candidates must hold a medical qualification and have had hospital / general practice experience in the care of the elderly.

Paediatrics: Diploma in Child Health (DCH RCPSGlasg): Candidates must hold a medical qualification and demonstrate 6 mths' full- time experience in the care of children incl. hospital and community exposure.

Membership (MRCP(UK)): See Membership of the Royal College of Physicians above.

THE ROYAL COLLEGE OF PHYSICIANS OF EDINBURGH

9 Queen Street, Edinburgh EH2 1JQ Tel: 0131 225 7324 Fax: 0131 220 3939
e-mail: l.telford@rcpe.ac.uk Website: www.rcpe.ac.uk

HIGHER QUALIFICATIONS:

Fellow (FRCPEdin): Elected from among the Members of the Royal Colleges of Physicians of the UK.

Membership (MRCP(UK)): The MRCP(UK) is designed to select those suitable for higher specialist training in the UK, leading eventually to a **Certificate of Completion of Specialist Training(CCST)** Awarded by the Specialist Training Authority (STA) of the medical Royal Colleges. The Examination may also be taken by those who do not intend to pursue a career in hospital medicine and this is one of the reasons why the Colleges have not followed the example of other countries in only awarding their Fellowship or Membership once specialist status has been obtained. The MRCP(UK) comprises two parts. Examination regulations, examination calendars and application forms can be obtained from the Royal Colleges of Physicians of Edinburgh, Glasgow and London.

Certificate in Transfusion Medicine: The exam is designed primarily for overseas practitioners who wish to work in a hospital blood bank. Portfolios of 3,000 words describing 1 case study managed by the candidate, illustrating clinical and laboratory aspects, must be submitted. Examination regulations, applications and past examination papers can be obtained from The Registrar at the above address.

THE ROYAL COLLEGE OF RADIOLOGISTS

38 Portland Place, London W1N 4JQ Tel: 020 7636 4432 Fax: 020 7323 3100
Candidates for the
Final Fellowship (FRCR): Examination must be registered medical practitioners: (a) for

Radiology: have at least 2 yrs of general clinical experience plus 3 yrs of radiology training; for Oncology: have at least 6 yrs of clinical training including a minimum of 3 yrs in clinical oncology; and (b) hold the First FRCR Examination or an accepted equivalent.

Membership is open to those who: (a) are medically qualified; (b) are duly registered in the country where they practise; (c) have been appointed to a training post in a recognised dept. of Clinical Radiology or Clinical Oncology or (d) hold qualifications in radiology recognised by the Council for this purpose.

THE ROYAL COLLEGE OF SURGEONS OF EDINBURGH

Nicolson Street, Edinburgh EH8 9DW Tel: 0131 527 1600 Fax: 0131 527 6406
Website: www.rcsed.ac.uk

MEMBERSHIP:

Membership (MFRCSEd) Surgery in General: The MCQ component consists of 2 multiple choice question papers. The 1st paper tests the candidates knowledge of Sections 1-9 of the Edinburgh Syllabus and the 2nd paper is an examination of the specialists subjects covered by Sections 10-19 of the Edinburgh Syllabus. The Final Assessment consists of 3 oral exams – 1 in Critical Care, 1 in Principles of Surgery, including Operative Surgery and Applied Anatomy, and 1 in Clinical Surgery and Pathology based on the experience demonstrated in the candidates logbook – and 1 clinical exam.

Membership (MFRCSEd) Ophthalmology:
Part 1: Consists of 2 multiple choice question papers on the basic sciences.
Part 2: Consists of a multiple choice question paper (MCQ 3) and 1 oral exam on applied basic sciences, optics and refraction and 1 Objective Structured Clinical Examination (OSCE) which includes practical refraction.
Part 3: Consists of 1 multiple choice question paper (MCQ 4) and 2 oral exams – in Clinical Opthalmology in Relation to Medicine and Neurology; and Opthalmic Surgery and Pathology – and 2 clinical exams in Clinical Opthalmic Medicine and Surgery; and Clinical Opthalmology in Relation to Medicine and Neurology.

Membership (MFRCSEd) Accident and Emergency: The MCQ component consists of 2 multiple choice question papers. The 1st paper tests the candidates knowledge of sections 1-9 of the Edinburgh Syllabus and the 2nd paper is an examination of the specialists subjects covered by Sections 10-19 of the Edinburgh Syllabus. The Assessment consists of a multiple choice question paper, 2 oral exams – in Surgery; and Medicine – and 3 clinical exams in Surgery; Medicine; and Accident and Emergency Medicine.

THE ROYAL COLLEGE OF SURGEONS OF ENGLAND

35/43 Lincoln's Inn Fields, London WC2A 3PN Tel: 020 7405 3474 Fax: 020 7831 9438
e-mail: exams@rcseng.ac.uk

The postgraduate educational work of the College is conducted in co-operation with the Faculty of Dental Surgery and the Faculty of General Dental Practitioners. A number of changes in the College's exams are in prospect at the time of going to press and the up-to-date position should be checked directly with the College. The principal exams in surgery are the **Membership (MRCSEng), Fellowship (FRCSEng)** and **Fellowship with Otolaryngology (FRCSOtoEng).** The FRCS and FRCSOto finish in Nov 2000. There is a subsidiary diploma in Otolaryngology, namely the **Diploma in Laryngology and Otology (DLORCSEng).** The principal exam in dental surgery is the **MFDS** – the Membership of the Faculty of Dental Surgery. The **Fellowship in Dental Surgery (FDSRCSEng)** finishes in 2002. The Faculty of Dental Surgery also holds exams for the: **Membership in Clinical Community Dentistry (MCCDRCSEng); Diploma in Dental Public Health (DDPHRCSEng);** and the **License in Dental Surgery (LDSRCSEng).** The new intercollegiate speciality examinations are now available:

Membership in Orthodontics (MOrth), Membership in Restorative Dentistry (MRD), Membership in Paediatric Dentristry (MPaedDen) and **Membership in Surgical Dentistry (MSurgDent).** The principal exam in general dental practice is the **Membership in General Dental Practice (MFGDPEng).** There is also a **Diploma in General Dental Practice (DGDPRCSEng).**

THE SOCIETY OF APOTHECARIES OF LONDON

Apothecaries' Hall, Black Friars Lane, London EC4V 6EJ Tel: 020 7236 1189 Fax: 020 7329 3177

MEMBERSHIP:

Licentiate in Medicine, Surgery and Obstetrics & Gynaecology (LMSSA Lond): Granted as part of the United Examining Board after exam to candidates who have completed the full curriculum of medical studies at an approved Medical School.

EXAMINATIONS:

Written, Clinical and Oral covering the principles and practice of Medicine, Surgery, Obstetrics & Gynaecology and Pathology & Bacteriology. Licentiates must complete 12 mths of satisfactory House Officer service in order to apply for Full Registration with the General Medical Council. **Diplomates:** The Society also awards, after exam, Diplomas in Medical Jurisprudence, Genitourinary Medicine, Musculoskeletal Medicine, Sports Medicine, the Medical Care of Catastrophes, Regulatory Toxicology, Clinical Pharmacology and the History and Philosophy of Medicine. A Mastership in Medical Jurisprudence is also awarded by exam.

Membership of Professional Institutions and Associations

BRITISH INSTITUTE OF MUSCULOSKELETAL MEDICINE

34 The Avenue, Watford, Herts WD1 3NS Tel: 01923 220999 Fax: 01923 222099
e-mail: bimm@compuserve.com Website: www.bimm.org.uk

There are currently 350 Members in the Institute, and Membership is open to registered doctors in the UK who have an interest in musculoskeletal medicine and experience in 1 or more of the following branches of medicine: orthopaedics, rheumatology, sports medicine and osteopathy. Courses are run several times a yr and there is a Diploma in Musculoskeletal Medicine from the Society of Apothecaries of London and a MSc course in association with the London College of Osteopathy and University College London. The Institute is affiliated to the International Federation of Manual Medicine (FIMM).

MEMBERSHIP OF THE ROYAL COLLEGE OF PHYSICIANS

Membership (MRCP(UK)): Candidates for the Exam for Membership of the Royal Colleges of Physicians of the UK may enter through the Royal College of Physicians of Edinburgh or the Royal College of Physicians and Surgeons of Glasgow or the Royal College of Physicians of London. Candidates for Part I must have been qualified as medical practitioners for at least 18 mths. Part I consists of a multiple-choice question paper and may be taken in General Medicine or Paediatrics. Candidates may apply for exemption from this if they are holders of specified Fellowships, Memberships or Postgraduate Diplomas, listed in the regulations. Before being admitted to Part II, candidates must have completed a period of training lasting 18 mths after full registration with the General Medical Council (ie 2½ yrs after graduation in medicine). Of this period not less than 12 mths should have been spent in posts involving the admission and hospital care of acutely ill medical patients (18 mths for candidates not fully registered with the General Medical Council). The Part II Exam consists of (a) a written test in 3 sections; (b) an oral test; (c) a clinical test and candidates have the choice of being examined in either General Medicine or Paediatrics. Part II must be completed within 7 yrs of success at Part I.

THE ROYAL COLLEGE OF ANAESTHETISTS

48-49 Russell Square, London WC1B 4JY Tel: 020 7813 1880 Fax: 020 7908 7366
e-mail: exams@rcoa.ac.uk Website: www.rcoa.ac.uk

Fellowship of the Royal College of Anaesthetists (FRCA): The Fellowship examination consists of 2 parts, Primary and Final. Entry to the Primary FRCA examination is conditional upon the candidate having undertaken at least 12 (but ideally 18) mths of approved anaesthetic training in the UK or Republic of Ireland. Entry to the Final FRCA exam requires a minimum of 30 mths of anaesthetic training, including at least 18 mths of approved training in the UK or Republic of Ireland. Exemption from the Primary FRCA exam may be granted to holders of certain overseas qualifications. Further details can be obtained from the College.

THE ROYAL COLLEGE OF GENERAL PRACTITIONERS

14 Princes Gate, Hyde Park, London SW7 1PU Tel: 020 7581 3232 Fax: 020 7225 3047
e-mail: info@rcgp.org.uk Website: www.rcgp.org.uk
The aims of the College are to encourage, foster and maintain the highest possible standards in general medical practice. Entry to membership is by exam; the grade of **Associate** is intended for general practitioners who have not yet gained the necessary experience to take the exam and for those in general practice or other branches of medicine who support the aims of the College, but who do not wish, or are not eligible to become members.
Fellow (FRCGP): There are 2 forms of fellowship for members of the College: Fellowship by nomination is for members who have made a significant contribution either to the science or practice of medicine or to the aims of the College; Fellowship by assessment is open to all members of the College of 5 yrs' continuous standing.
Member (MRCGP): Candidates must be fully registered medical practitioners who have passed the membership exam and completed vocational training.
Exam: The examination consists of 4 modules, 2 written papers, an assessment of consulting skills and an oral examination. The modules may be taken at different times but must be passed within 3 yrs of application to complete the examination.
Eligibility: You must be eligible to be an independent practitioner of general practice or undergoing vocational training with this in view.
Membership by Assessment of Performance: General Practitioners who have been in independent practice in the UK for at least 5 yrs may elect to be assessed on evidence of good quality practice. This has 3 components: a portfolio of evidence that the College's assessment criteria have been met; evidence of consulting skills; and an evaluation following a practice visit.

THE ROYAL COLLEGE OF OBSTETRICIANS AND GYNAECOLOGISTS

27 Sussex Place, Regent's Park, London NW1 4RG Tel: 020 7772 6200 Fax: 020 7723 0575
e-mail: coll.sec@rcog.org.uk Website: www.rcog.org.uk
MEMBERSHIP:
Fellow (FRCOG): Members who have been judged by the Council to have advanced the science and/or practice of Obstetrics and Gynaecology or have attained such a position in the medical profession or in other fields as to merit promotion to Fellowship.
Member (MRCOG): Registered medical practitioners who have passed the Membership exam.
EXAMINATIONS:
Part 1 Membership: 2 multiple-choice question papers covering basic sciences.
Part 2 Membership: 2 essay papers plus 1 multiple-choice question paper in obsterics and gynaecology, and an oral exam. Candidates must obtain a pass mark in the paper section in order to progress to the oral.
Training: Candidates must complete the following periods of post-registration training for the Part 2 exam: (a) **Obstetrics:** 12 mths' recognised appointment; (b) **Gynaecology:** 12 mths' recognised appointment. Candidates whose Part 2 training forms and certificates reach the College after 1 September 2002 will be required to complete 4 yrs in recognised posts in obstetrics and gynaecology.
Diploma (DRCOG): Candidates must have permanent British or Irish registration or be eligible for it and have complied with the following requirement:
Obstetrics/Gynaecology: 6 consecutive mths' residence in a combined appointment recognised by the College for the exam.
The Exam: Covers obstetrics, including family planning, cytology, postnatal care of mother and child and the disabilities which may arise from childbirth and those aspects of gynaecology necessary to the practice of a general practitioner, including cervical cytology. It consists of a multiple-choice question paper and an objective structured clinical exam (**OSCE**).

THE ROYAL COLLEGE OF PATHOLOGISTS

2 Carlton House Terrace, London SW1Y 5AF Tel: 020 7451 6700 Fax: 020 7451 6701
e-mail: info@rcpath.org Website: www.rcpath.org.
Examinations Dept Tel: 020 7451 6757

MEMBERSHIP:
Fellowship: Members of at least 8 yrs' standing may be considered for election to Fellowship.
Membership: Persons must hold an approved medical or science degree or equivalent, or an approved dental or veterinary qualification. Admission may be gained by exam or submission of published works.

EXAMINATIONS:
Training programmes are approved for all pathology specialities and subspecialities. The exact examination arrangements vary for each speciality but they all involve a Part 1 and a Part 2 which include *inter alia* written, practical and oral components. In addition, the College offers a **Diploma in Dermatopathology, Diploma in Forensic Pathology** and a **Diploma in Cytopathology**. Further details may be obtained from the Exams Department at the above address.

THE ROYAL COLLEGE OF PHYSICIANS OF LONDON

11 St Andrews Place, Regent's Park, London NW1 4LE Tel: 020 7935 1174 Fax: 020 7224 2032
e-mail: Linda.Cuthbertson@rcplondon.ac.uk Website: www.rcplondon.ac.uk

MEMBERSHIP:
Fellow (FRCP): Elected from among Members of the Royal College of Physicians of London or Members of the Royal Colleges of Physicians of the UK of at least 4 yrs' standing and distinction, and from among other distinguished persons holding medical qualifications. Provisions exist to elect persons without being members or without holding medical qualifications, but only in exceptional circumstances.
Member (MRCP): Elected from among distinguished persons holding medical qualifications. There is also an honorary category for persons who are not medically qualified.
Membership (MRCP(UK)): See under Examinations below.

EXAMINATIONS:
Membership (MRCP(UK)): Candidates in General Medicine may enter through any of the 3 UK College of Physicians.
Part 1: Consists of a multiple choice question paper.
Part 2: Consists of a written test plus and oral/clinical test. A full copy of the regulations may be obtained from the address above. The College also offers a **Diploma in Geriatric Medicine, Diploma in Medical Rehabilitation** and **Diploma in Tropical Medicine and Hygiene**.

THE ROYAL COLLEGE OF PSYCHIATRISTS

17 Belgrave Square, London SW1X 8PG Tel: 020 7235 2351/5 Fax: 020 7245 1231
e-mail: adean@rcpsych.ac.uk Website: ad/bf/Postgrad/EXT 159

MEMBERSHIP:
Fellow (FRCPsych): Open, by election, to Members of not less than 5 yrs' seniority, on the nomination of 2 Fellows. Particular attention is paid to qualifications and professional standing, to appointments held, and to contributions to research and to the literature and the practice of psychiatry.
Member (MRCPsych): Candidates must be registered with the GMC and have undergone approved training for at least 2 1/2 yrs. They must pass both parts of the MRCPsych exam. The College also has
Honorary Fellows, Inceptors, Corresponding Fellows, New Associates and Affiliates.

University Qualifications

The following universities offer qualifications in Medicine and related subjects. Full details may be found in Part 4, under the entry for the appropriate university.

FIRST DEGREES AWARDED BY UNIVERSITIES
Aberdeen; Anglia; Belfast; Birmingham; Bournemouth; Bradford; Brighton; Bristol; Brunel; Cambridge; Central Lancashire; City; Coventry; Cranfield; De Montfort, Leicester; Derby; Dundee; Durham; East Anglia; East London; Edinburgh; Essex; Exeter; Glasgow; Glasgow Caledonian; Greenwich; Hertfordshire; Huddersfield; Hull; Keele; Kingston; Lancaster; Leeds; Leicester; Liverpool; Liverpool (Chester College of H.E.); Liverpool John Moores; London

(Imperial College of Science, Technology & Medicine); London (King's College London); London (Royal Holloway); London (University College (UCL)); Loughborough; Luton; Manchester; Manchester Metropolitan.; Napier; Newcastle; North London; Northampton; Northumbria; Nottingham; Nottingham Trent; OU (NESCOT); Paisley; Portsmouth; Queen Margaret; Robert Gordon; Salford; Sheffield; Sheffield Hallam; South Bank; Southampton; St Andrews; St Martin; Staffordshire; Strathclyde; Sunderland; Surrey; Surrey (University of Surrey Roehampton); Sussex; Teesside; Ulster; UMIST; Wales (Cardiff University); Wales (College of Medicine); Wales (University of Wales Institute, Cardiff); Wales (University of Wales, Swansea); Warwick; Westminster; Wolverhampton

HIGHER DEGREES AWARDED BY UNIVERSITIES

Aberdeen; Anglia; Belfast; Birmingham; Bournemouth; Bradford; Brighton; Bristol; Brunel; Cambridge; Central Lancashire; City; Coventry; Cranfield; De Montfort, Leicester; Derby; Dundee; Durham; East London; Edinburgh; Exeter; Glamorgan; Glasgow; Glasgow Caledonian; Greenwich; Hertfordshire; Hull; Keele; Kent; Kingston; Lancaster; Leeds; Leicester; Liverpool; Liverpool John Moores; London (Imperial College of Science, Technology & Medicine); London (King's College London); London (Queen Mary & Westfield College (incorporating St Bartholomew's and the Royal London School of Medicine & Dentistry)); London (School of Oriental & African Studies); London (University College (UCL)); Loughborough; Manchester; Manchester Metropolitan.; Napier; Newcastle; Nottingham; Nottingham Trent; OU (NESCOT); Oxford Brookes; Paisley; Plymouth; Portsmouth; Salford; Sheffield; Sheffield Hallam; South Bank; St Andrews; St Martin; Strathclyde; Surrey; Surrey (NESCOT); Surrey (University of Surrey Roehampton); Sussex; Ulster; Wales (College of Medicine); Wales (University of Wales Institute, Cardiff); Wales (University of Wales, Bangor); Wales (University of Wales, Swansea); Westminster; Wolverhampton; Worcester

DIPLOMAS AWARDED BY UNIVERSITIES

Aberdeen; Abertay, Dundee; Birmingham; Bournemouth; Bradford; Brighton; Bristol; Central England; City; Dundee; Edinburgh; Exeter; Glamorgan; Glasgow; Greenwich; Hertfordshire; Leeds; Leicester; Liverpool; London (Imperial College of Science, Technology & Medicine); London (King's College London); London (Queen Mary & Westfield College (incorporating St Bartholomew's and the Royal London School of Medicine & Dentistry)); London (University College (UCL)); Manchester; Napier; Oxford Brookes; Paisley; Plymouth; Salford; Sheffield; South Bank; Strathclyde; Sussex; Ulster; Wales (Cardiff University); Wales (College of Medicine); Wales (University of Wales Institute, Cardiff); Wolverhampton

CERTIFICATES AWARDED BY UNIVERSITIES

Aberdeen; Aston; Brighton; Bristol; Central England; Central Lancashire; City; Derby; Dundee; Hertfordshire; Keele; London (King's College London); London (University College (UCL)); Newcastle; Paisley; Salford; South Bank; Staffordshire; Ulster; Wales (College of Medicine); Wales (University of Wales, Bangor)

OTHER COURSES AWARDED BY UNIVERSITIES

Leeds Metropolitan; London (King's College London)

POSTGRADUATE DIPLOMAS AWARDED BY UNIVERSITIES

Central Lancashire

National Certificates and Diplomas

BTEC Higher National Certificates/Diplomas: Orthotics and Prosthetics

Additional Qualifications Registrable

Medical practitioners who hope to become consultants or specialists need to obtain additional qualifications – a higher degree or a diploma or Member or Fellow (as the case may be) of 1 of the Royal Colleges – or a postgraduate diploma (see below).Additional qualifications registrable in accordance with the Medical Act 1983 are as follows:(i) Higher degrees in Medicine, Surgery and other subjects (usually the degrees of Doctor of Medicine and Master of Surgery) awarded by universities in the UK, the National University of Ireland and the University of Dublin; (ii) Membership of the Irish College of General Practitioners; (iii) Membership and Fellowship of the Royal Colleges listed below: Royal Coll of General Practitioners; Royal Coll of Obstetricians and Gynaecologists; Royal Coll of Pathologists; Royal Coll of Physicians of Edinburgh and London; Royal Coll of Physicians and Surgeons of Glasgow (including the Faculty of Public Health Medicine); the Faculty of Occupational Medicine of the Royal Coll of Physicians in London; Royal Coll of Psychiatrists; Royal Coll of Physicians of Ireland; (iv) Fellowship of the Coll of Ophthalmologists; (v) Fellowship of the Royal Colleges listed below: Royal Coll of Surgeons of Edinburgh; Royal Coll of Surgeons of England; Royal Coll of Radiologists; Royal Coll of Surgeons in Ireland (including the Faculties of Anaesthetists and Radiologists); Royal Coll of Anaesthetists.

HIGHER DEGREES

The higher degrees most commonly awarded after an exam and/or thesis are those of **Doctor of Medicine and Master of Surgery,** the latter being usually the senior degree. (Medical graduates may also take the degrees of **Master of Science and Doctor of Philosophy,** but these are not, save in the cases noted below, registrable as additional qualifications.) Higher degrees are awarded by each of the British licensing universities as follows (there are usually requirements relating to age and/or post-registration experience):

Aberdeen: MD; ChM; Queen's Belfast: MD; MCh; MAO (Master of Obstetrics); Birmingham: MD; Bristol: MD; ChM; Cambridge: MD; MChir; Dundee: MD; ChM; Edinburgh: MD; ChM; Glasgow: MD; Leeds: MD; ChM; Leicester: MD; Liverpool: MD; ChM; Master of Orthopaedic Surgery (MChOrth) (The degree of **Master of Orthopaedic Surgery** is open, after a course lasting at least 1 yr, to medical graduates and to graduates in subjects other than medicine who hold a diploma of Fellowship of 1 of the Royal Colleges of Surgeons or who are surgeon Fellows of the Royal College of Physicians and Surgeons of Glasgow. Candidates are required to submit a thesis and to take an exam.)

London: MD; MS; Manchester: MD; ChM; Newcastle upon Tyne: MD; Nottingham: DM; Oxford: DM; MCh; Sheffield: MD; ChM; Southampton: DM; MS; Wales: MD; MCh; Dublin: MD; MCh; MAO; NU Irel: MD; MCh; MAO.

Other Postgraduate Awards

Universities, the Royal Colleges and other bodies confer degrees and diplomas in specialist areas of Medicine, usually after FT or PT courses of instruction. In most cases candidates must either be registered medical practitioners or have a medical qualification which entitles them to registration on the British Medical Register and have been in practice for a yr or so before taking the exam, which may consist of Primary and Final exams or Part I and II exams. Full details are given in the *Guide to Postgraduate Degrees, Diplomas and Courses in Medicine,* available from IntelliGene, Woodlands, Ford, Midlothian EH37 5RE Scotland, and published in association with the National Advice Centre for Postgraduate Medical Education at The British Council.

ACCIDENT AND EMERGENCY MEDICINE AND SURGERY:
MMed Sc in Surgery of Trauma: University of Birmingham: 1 yr FT.

ANAESTHETICS:
MSc (Med Sci) Anaesthesia: University of Glasgow: 2 yrs FT.
MSc in Anaesthesia and Intensive Care: University of Wales College of Medicine: 2 yrs FT.

AUDIOLOGY:
MSc in Educational Audiology: University of Manchester: 1 yr FT.
MSc in Audiological Medicine: University of London (University College): 1 yr FT.
MSc in Audiological Medicine: University of Manchester: 1 yr FT.
MSc in Audiology: University of Manchester: 1 yr FT at the Department of Audiology and Education of the Deaf.
MSc in Audiology: University of Southampton: 1 yr FT or 6 mths FT plus research project undertaken externally over an equiv period.
Diploma in Audiology: University of Southampton: 6 mths FT.
Diploma in Audiology: University of Manchester: 1 yr FT.
Certificate in Audiology: University of Southampton: 6 mths FT.
MSc in Auditory Sciences: University of London (University College): 1 yr FT.

BACTERIOLOGY:
Diploma in Bacteriology: University of Manchester: 1 yr FT course.
MSc in Bacteriology: University of Manchester: 1 yr FT.
PhD in Bacteriology: University of Manchester: 3 yrs FT.
MMedSc in Bacteriology: Queen's University of Belfast: 1 yr FT/4 yrs PT.
MMedSc in Anatomy & Cell Biology: University of Sheffield: 1 yr.
MMedSc in Ultrastructural Anatomy & Pathology: Queen's University Belfast: 1 yr FT.
MSc in Anatomical Science: University of Glasgow: 2 yrs FT.
MSc in Mineralised Tissue Biology: University of London (University College): 1 yr FT/2 yrs PT.
MSc in Physiology: University of London (University College): 1 yr FT.

BIOCHEMISTRY:
MSc in Clinical Biochemistry: University of Dublin, Trinity College: 3 yrs.
MSc in Clinical Biochemistry: University of Leeds: 1 yr FT.
MSc in Clinical Biochemistry: University of London (Intercollegiate, organised by Charing Cross Hospital): 2 yrs PT.
MSc in Clinical Biochemistry: University of London (Royal Postgraduate Medical School): 2 yrs PT.
MSc in Clinical Biochemistry: University of Newcastle upon Tyne: 1 yr FT.
MSc in Clinical Biochemistry: University of Surrey: 1 yr FT/2 yrs block release.
MSc in Biochemistry: University of London (University College): 1 yr FT.
MSc in Analytical Biochemistry: University of Dundee: 1 yr FT.
MSc in Medical Biochemistry: Brunel University: PT/FT.
MSc in Biomedical Science Research: University of London (King's College): 1 yr FT/2 yrs PT.
Diploma in Bioanalytical Chemistry: University of Dundee: 9-12 mths FT.
MSc in Biosensors: University of Newcastle upon Tyne: 1 yr FT.

CARDIOLOGY:
MSc in Cardiovascular Studies: University of Leeds: 1 yr FT.
MSc (Med Sc) Medical Cardiology: University of Glasgow: 2 yrs FT.
Diploma in Cardiology: University of Leeds: 1 yr FT.
Diploma in Cardiology: University of London (National Heart & Lung Institute): 1 yr FT.
Diploma in Cardiology: University of London (Royal Postgraduate Medical School): 1 yr FT.

CLINICAL CYTOLOGY:
MSc in Clinical Cytotechnology: University of London (St Mary's Hospital Medical School): 1 yr FT or 2 yrs PT.
Diploma in Gynaecological Cytotechnology: University of London (St Mary's Hospital Medical School): 6 mths.
MSc Clinical Cytopathology: University of London Imperial College (St Mary's Hospital Medical School): 1 yr FT/2 yrs PT.
DMRD: University of Edinburgh: 2 yrs FT.
DMRD: University of Liverpool: 2 yrs PT.
DMRD: University of Wales (College of Medicine).
Master of Radiology (MRad): University of Aberdeen: 2 yrs FT.

DERMATOLOGY:
MSc (MedSc) in Dermatology: University of Glasgow: 2 yrs FT.
Diploma in Dermatology: University of London (St John's Institute of Dermatology): 9 mths/1 yr FT.
Diploma in Dermatological Sciences: University of Wales College of Medicine: 1 yr FT.
Diploma in Practical Dermatology: University of Wales College of Medicine: Distance learning.
MSc in Dermatology: University of Wales College of Medicine: 1 yr.
MSc in Clinical Dermatology: University of London (St John's Institute of Dermatology): 1 yr FT.

ENDOCRINOLOGY:
MSc/MMedSc in Endocrinology: University of Sheffield: 1 yr FT.
Diploma in Endocrinology: University of London (Royal Postgraduate Medical School): 1 yr FT.
MMedSc in Clinical and Molecular Endocrinology & Diabetes: University of Birmingham: 1 yr FT.

MSc in Neuroendocrine Cell Biology: University of London (University College & Royal Postgraduate Medical School): 1 yr FT.

MSc in Steroid Endocrinology: University of Leeds: 1 yr FT.

EPIDEMIOLOGY:

Diploma in Epidemiology: Royal College of Physicians: 1 yr FT.

MSc in Communicable Disease Epidemiology: University of Cambridge: 1 yr FT/2 yrs PT.

MSc in Environmental Epidemiology & Policy & Tropical Medicine: University of London (School of Hygiene & Tropical Medicine): 1 yr FT/2 yrs PT.

MSc in Epidemiology: University of London (School of Hygiene & Tropical Medicine): 1 yr FT/2 yrs PT.

MSc in Epidemiology & Health Planning: University of Wales (College of Swansea and College of Medicine): 1 yr FT.

MSc in Infectious Diseases: University of London (Royal Postgraduate Medical School): 1 yr FT.

MPhil in Epidemiology: University of Cambridge.

FAMILY PLANNING:

Certificate in Family Planning: Joint Committee on Contraception.

Certificate in Advanced Family Planning (including insertion of intra-uterine devices): Joint Committee on contraception.

FORENSIC:

MSc in Forensic Science: University of London (King's College): 1 yr FT.

MSc or Diploma in Forensic Science: University of Strathclyde.

Diploma & Certificate in Forensic Medicine: University of Glasgow.

Diploma & MSc in Forensic Behavioural Science: University of Liverpool: 1 yr FT for diploma; 2 yrs PT for MSc.

Diploma in Forensic Psychiatry: University of London (Institute of Psychiatry): 1 yr FT/2 yrs PT.

Diploma in Forensic Toxicology: University of Glasgow: 1 yr.

GENERAL MEDICINE:

Diploma in Internal Medicine: University of London (Royal Postgraduate Medical School): 1 yr FT.

Diploma in Medical Science (DipMedSc) in Internal Medicine: University of Newcastle upon Tyne: 1 yr FT.

Master of Medical Science (MMedSc) in Internal Medicine: University of Newcastle upon Tyne: 1 yr FT.

MSc (MMedSc) in Internal Medicine: University of Glasgow: 2 yrs FT.

GENERAL PRACTICE:

Diploma in Primary Medical Care: University of Keele: 2 yrs PT.

MSc in Primary Medical Care: University of Keele: 1 yr (additional to diploma).

MMedSc in General Practice: University of Birmingham: 2 yrs PT.

MSc General Practice: University of London (United Medical Schools): 2 yrs PT.

GENERAL SURGERY:

MMedSc or PhD: University of Birmingham.

Master of Surgery ChM: University of Bristol.

Master of Surgery MCh: University of Oxford.

MSc in Organ Transplantation: University of London (Royal Free Hospital): 1 yr FT.

GENETICS:

MSc in Medical Genetics: University of Newcastle upon Tyne: 1 yr FT.

MSc (MedSc) Medical Genetics: University of Glasgow. 1 yr FT.

Diploma in Clinical Genetics: University of London (Institute of Child Health): 9 mths FT.

GERIATRIC MEDICINE:

MSc/Diploma in Advanced Clinical Practice (Cancer Nursing/Care of the Elderly): University of Surrey: 2 yrs PT.

MSc (MedSc) in Geriatric Medicine: University of Glasgow: 2 yrs FT.

MSc in Gerontology: University of London (King's College): 2 yrs PT (FT possible).

MSc in Gerontology: University of Liverpool: 2 yrs PT.

MSc Social Gerontology: University of Southampton.

HAEMATOLOGY:
MSc (MedSc) in Haematology: University of London (Royal Postgraduate Medical School): 1 yr FT.
MSc (MedSc) in Haematology: University of Glasgow: 2 yrs FT.

IMMUNOLOGY:
MSc in Immunology: University of Birmingham: 1 yr FT.
MSc in Immunology: University of London (Royal Postgraduate Medical School): 1 yr.
MSc in Clinical Immunology: University of Leeds: 1 yr FT.
MSc in Immunology of Infectious Diseases: University of London (School of Hygiene & Tropical Medicine): 1 yr FT.
MSc in Medical Genetics with Immunology: Brunel University: PT/FT.
MSc in Medical Immunology: University of London (United Medical Schools): 2 yrs FT.
MSc in Medical Immunology: University of London (Imperial College): PT.
MSc in Medical Immunology: University of London (King's College): 2 yrs PT.

MEDICAL DEMOGRAPHY:
MSc in Medical Demography: University of London (London School of Hygiene & Tropical Medicine): 1 yr FT/2 yrs PT.
Diploma in Medical Demography: As above: 1 yr FT.

MEDICAL EDUCATION:
Diploma in Medical Education: University of Dundee: 1-4 yrs' distance learning.
Diploma in Medical Education: University of Wales College of Medicine: 1 yr FT/2 yrs PT.
Master in Medical Education: University of Dundee: 1-4 yrs' distance learning (following Diploma)/9 mths FT.
MSc & MPhil in Medical Education: University of Wales College of Medicine: 1 yr FT/2 yrs PT.

MEDICAL JURISPRUDENCE:
MPhil in Medical Ethics & Law: University of Glasgow: 2 yrs FT.
MA Medical Ethics & Law: University of London (King's College). 1 yr FT/2 yrs PT.
LLM in Legal Aspects of Medical Practice: University of Wales College of Cardiff. 1 yr FT/2 yrs PT.
MTh in Christian Social Ethics: University of Wales College of Cardiff: 1 yr FT/2 yrs PT.

MEDICAL PARASITOLOGY:
MSc in Medical Parasitology: University of London (London School of Hygiene & Tropical Medicine): 1 yr FT.
MSc/MVSc in Applied Parasitology and Medical Entomology: University of Liverpool: 1 yr FT.
MSc in Clinical Parasitology: University of London (Royal Free Hospital School of Medicine, London School of Hygiene & Tropical Medicine): 2 yrs PT.

MEDICAL PHYSICS AND BIOMEDICAL ENGINEERING:
MSc in Information Technology (Medical Physics): University of Aberdeen: 1 yr FT/2 yrs block release.
Diploma in Information Technology (Medical Physics): University of Aberdeen: 9 mths.
MSc in Medical Physics: University of Aberdeen: 1 yr FT.
Diploma in Medical Physics: University of Aberdeen: 9 mths FT.
MSc in Medical Physics: University of Leeds: 2 yrs PT.
MSc in Radiation Physics: University of London (Intercollegiate): 1 yr FT.
MSc in Medical Electronics & Physics: University of London (St Bartholomew's Hospital Medical School): 1 yr FT/2 yrs PT.
Postgraduate Diploma in Biomechanics (by distance learning): University of Strathclyde: 9 mths.
MSc in Biophysics and Medical Physics: University of London (Birkbeck College). 2 yrs PT.
MSc in Ergonomics: University of London (University College): 1 yr FT/2 yrs PT.
MSc in Biomedical Engineering: University of Aberdeen. 1 yr FT/2 yrs block release.
Diploma in Biomedical Engineering: University of Aberdeen: 9 mths.
Diploma in Biomedical Engineering: University of Dundee: 9 mths FT.
MSc in Biomedical Engineering Science: University of Dundee: 1 yr FT.
MSc/Diploma in Biomedical Engineering: University of Surrey: 1 yr FT.

MSc in Biomedical Instrumentation: University of Dundee: 1 yr FT.
MSc in Medical Radiation Physics: Brunel University: PT/FT.
MSc in Physical Sciences in Medicine: University of Dublin: 3 yrs PT.
MSc/Diploma in Radiation & Environmental Protection: University of Surrey: 1 yr FT/2 yrs PT.
MSc in Electronic Engineering (options in Medical Electronics): University of Wales College of Cardiff: 1 yr FT/2 yrs PT.
MSc in Medical Imaging: University of Aberdeen: 1 yr FT/2 yrs block release.
Diploma in Medical Imaging: University of Aberdeen: 9 mths.
Diploma in Orthopaedic Technology: University of Dundee: 9 mths FT.
MSc Engineering & Physical Science in Medicine: University of London (Imperial College): 1 yr FT.
Certificate in Rehabilitation Engineering: University of London (King's College): 1 yr PT.
Diploma in Rehabilitation Engineering: University of London (King's College): 1 yr PT.
MSc/Diploma in Bioengineering: University of Strathclyde: 1 yr FT/2 yrs PT.
MSc in Medical Engineering & Physics: University of London (Intercollegiate organised by King's College): 2 yrs PT.

MEDICAL STATISTICS & DATA MANAGEMENT:
MSc in Applied Stochastic Systems: University of London (University College): 1 yr FT/2 yrs PT.
MSc in Health Informatics: University of Glasgow: 1 yr FT.
MSc in Medical Statistics: University of London (London School of Hygiene and Tropical Medicine): 1 yr FT.
MSc/Diploma in Medical Statistics: University of Newcastle upon Tyne: 1 yr FT.

MICROBIOLOGY:
MSc in Medical Microbiology: University of London (London School of Hygiene & Tropical Medicine): 1 yr FT.
MSc/Diploma in Medical Microbiology: University of Surrey: 2 yrs PT.
MSc/Diploma in General & Medical Microbiology: University of London (University College, School of Hygiene & Tropical Medicine): 1 yr FT.
MSc in Medical Biochemistry: University of Newcastle upon Tyne: 1 yr FT.
MSc/Diploma in Clinical Microbiology: University of London (London Hospital): 2 yrs PT.
MSc in Medical Microbiology (PhD also available): University of Manchester: 15 mths FT/9 mths FT + 6 mths research.

MOLECULAR BIOLOGY:
MSc in Applied Molecular Biology & Biotechnology: University of London (University College): 1 yr FT.
MSc in Applied Molecular Biology of Infectious Diseases: University of London (London School of Hygiene & Tropical Medicine): 1 yr FT.
MSc in Molecular Biology: University of Manchester: 1 yr FT.NEPHROLOGY:
Diploma in Nephrology and Hypertension: University of London (Royal Postgraduate Medical School): 1 yr FT.

NEUROSCIENCE/NEUROLOGY:
MSc in Speech & Language Pathology & Therapy: University of London (Institute of Neurology): 2½ yrs FT.
MSc in Neuroendocrine Cell Biology: University of London (University College & Royal Postgraduate Medical School): 1 yr FT.
MSc in Neurological Science: University of London (University College): 1 yr FT.
MSc in Neuroscience: University of London (Institute of Psychiatry/Ophthalmology). 1 yr FT.
MSc in Human Communication: University of London (Institute of Neurology). 1 yr FT/2 yrs PT.
Diploma in Clinical Neurology: University of London (Institute of Neurology): 6 mths.

NUCLEAR MEDICINE:
MSc in Nuclear Medicine: University of London (London Hospital): 1 yr FT/PT.
MSc Nuclear Medicine: University of London (Institute of Nuclear Medicine): 1 yr FT/PT.
MSc in Nuclear Medicine: University of London (Royal Postgraduate Medical School): 1 yr FT/2 yrs PT.
MSc in Radiation Biology: University of London (Intercollegiate organised by University College): 1 yr FT/2 yrs PT.

NUTRITION:
MSc/Diploma in Human Nutrition & Metabolism: University of Aberdeen: 1 yr FT; Diploma 9 mths FT.
MSc in Nutrition: University of London (King's College): 1 yr FT.
MSc in Human Nutrition: University of London (London School of Hygiene & Tropical Medicine): 1 yr FT.
MMed Sc in Human Nutrition: University of Sheffield: 1 yr FT.
Diploma in Human Nutrition: University of Aberdeen: 9 mths.
Certificate in Nutrition and Child Health: University of London Institute of Child Health.

OBSTETRICS AND GYNAECOLOGY:
Diploma in Obstetrics & Gynaecology (DGO): University of Dublin.
Licentiate in Midwifery (LM): University of Dublin.
Master of Obstetrics & Gynaecology (MObstG): University of Liverpool: 18 mths FT.
MSc/Diploma in Advanced Midwifery Practice: University of Surrey & Royal College of Midwives: 1 yr FT + 1 yr PT.
MSc in Reproductive Biology: University of Edinburgh: 1 yr FT.
MSc in Human Reproductive Biology: University of London (Royal Postgraduate Medical School): 1 yr FT.
MMedSci in Assisted Reproduction Technology: University of Nottingham: 1 yr FT.
Diploma in Obstetrics & Gynaecology: University of London (Royal Postgraduate Medical School; Institute of Gynaecology): 5½ mths FT.

OCCUPATIONAL MEDICINE:
Certificate in Aviation Medicine (Cert A Med): Faculty of Occupational Medicine, Royal College of Physicians – RAF Institute of Aviation Medicine: 4 fortnight courses.
Certificate in Occupational Health: University of Aberdeen & Institute of Occupational Medicine Ltd, Edinburgh: 10 wks FT.
Certificate in Occupational Hygiene: University of Aberdeen & Institute of Occupational Medicine Ltd, Edinburgh: 10 wks FT.
Certificate in Underwater Medicine: University of Aberdeen: 3 yrs (modular).
Diploma in Aviation Medicine (DipAvMed): Faculty of Occupational Medicine, Royal College of Physicians – RAF Institute of Aviation Medicine: 6 mths.
Diploma in Occupational Health (DipOccH): University College Dublin: 2 yrs PT.
Diploma in Occupational Therapy: University of London (London Hospital Medical College): 25 mths FT.
MSc in Ergonomics: University of Aberdeen & Institute of Occupational Medicine Ltd, Edinburgh: 1 yr FT.
MSc in Occupational Health: University of Aberdeen & Institute of Occupational Medicine Ltd: 1 yr FT or 2 yrs PT.
MSc/Advanced Diploma in Occupational Health: University of Surrey: Modular Course.
MSc in Occupational Health Sciences: University of Manchester: 1 yr FT/2 yrs PT.
MSc in Occupational Hygiene: University of Aberdeen & Institute of Occupational Medicine Ltd (Edin): 1 yr FT or 2 yrs PT.
MSc in Occupational Hygiene: University of Newcastle upon Tyne: 1 yr FT.
MSc/Advanced Diploma in Occupational Hygiene: University of Surrey: modular with research and dissertation.
MSc/Advanced Diploma in Occupational Safety: University of Surrey: Modular credit accumulation.
MMedSci in Occupational Medicine: University of Birmingham: 1 yr FT.
MA in Health Services Management: University of Manchester: 9 mths FT.

OPHTHALMOLOGY:
MSc in Ophthalmology: University of Glasgow (Tennent Institute of Ophthalmology): 2 yrs FT.
MSc in Community Eye Health: University of London (Institute of Ophthalmology): 1 yr FT.
Diploma in Community Eye Health: University of London (Institute of Opthalmology): 6 mths.
MSc (by advanced study and research) in Ophthalmology: University of Bristol, Bristol Eye Hospital: 1 academic yr plus a period of research for dissertation.
MSc (Med Sc) Ophthalmology: University of Glasgow: 2 yrs FT.

Certificate in Community Eye Health: University of London (Institute of Ophthalmology): 2 mths.
Certificate in Tropical Ophthalmology: University of London (Institute of Ophthalmology): 2 mths.
ORTHOPAEDICS:
Master of Orthopaedic Surgery (MChOrth): University of Liverpool: 1 yr FT.
MSc in Orthopaedics: University of London (University College): 1 yr FT or 2 yrs PT.
MSc in Orthopaedics: University of London (Institute of Orthopaedics): 1 yr.
OTO-LARYNGOLOGY: (See also Audiology)
MSc (MedSc) in Oto-Laryngology: University of Glasgow: 2 yrs FT.
PAEDIATRICS:
Certificate in Community Paediatrics for GPs: University of Sheffield: 1 yr PT.
Diploma in Child Health: University of Dublin: 6 wks PT.
Diploma in Community Paediatrics: University of Sheffield: 1 yr PT.
Diploma in Community Paediatrics: University of Warwick: 2 yrs PT.
Diploma in Child & Adolescent Psychiatry: University of London (Institute of Child Health/Psychiatry): 1 yr FT.
Master in Clinical Genetics: University of London (Institute of Child Health): 1 yr FT.
Diploma in Clinical Genetics: University of London (Institute of Child Health): 9 mths FT.
Diploma in Community Based Rehabilitation: University of London (Institute of Child Health).
Diploma in Clinical Paediatrics: University of London, Institute of Child Health: 1 yr FT.
Diploma in Tropical Child Health (DTCH): University of Liverpool (Liverpool School of Tropical Medicine & Dept of Child Health): 6 mths FT.
Diploma in Paediatric Surgery: University of London (Institute of Child Health): 1 yr FT.
MSc in Community Paediatrics: University of London (Institute of Child Health).
MSc in Community Paediatrics: University of Newcastle upon Tyne: 2 yrs PT.
MSc in Community Paediatrics: University of Warwick: 1 yr FT/4 yrs PT.
MSc in Mother and Child Health: University of London (Institute of Child Health).
Master in Tropical Paediatrics (MTropPaed): University of Liverpool (Liverpool School of Tropical Medicine & Dept of Child Health): 1 yr FT.
PATHOLOGY:
Diplomas in Clinical & Chemical Pathology (DCP): University of London (Royal Postgraduate Medical School): 1 yr FT.
MSc in Experimental Pathology (Toxicology): University of London (Royal Postgraduate Medical School): 1 yr FT.
MMedSc in Clinical Pathology: University of Sheffield. 1 yr FT.
MMedSc in Pathology: Queens University, Belfast: 2 yrs FT.
MMedSc in Ultrastructural Anatomy & Pathology: Queens University, Belfast: 1 yr FT.
MSc (Med Sc) in Diagnostic Histopathology: University of Glasgow: 2 yrs FT.
MSc in Image Analysis in Histology: University of London Royal Postgraduate Medical School: 1 yr FT.
PHARMACOLOGY/PHARMACY:
MSc in Pharmaceutical Analysis: University of Strathclyde: 1/2 yrs FT.
MSc in Pharmaceutical Services & Medicines Control: University of Bradford: 1 yr FT.
MSc in Pharmaceutical Technology: University of London (King's College): 1 yr FT/2 yrs PT.
MSc in Pharmaceutical & Quality Control: University of London (King's College): 1 yr FT or 2 yrs PT.
MSc in Biopharmacy: University of London (King's College): 1 yr FT/2 yrs PT.
Diploma in Pharmaceutical Analysis: University of Strathclyde: 1 yr FT.
Diploma in Clinical Science: University of Wales (College of Cardiff & Welsh School of Pharmacy): 2 yrs PT.
Diploma in Clinical Pharmacy: University of Wales (College of Cardiff & Welsh School of Pharmacy): 2 yrs PT.
Diploma in Regulatory Affairs: University of Wales (College of Cardiff & Welsh School of Pharmacy): PT.
MSc in Clinical Pharmacy: University of Strathclyde: 1–2 yrs FT or 2 yrs PT.

MSc(MedSc) Clinical Pharmacology: University of Glasgow: 1/2 yrs FT.
MSc in Clinical Pharmacology: University of Aberdeen: 1 yr FT.
MSc in Pharmacology: University of Manchester: 1/2 yrs FT.
MSc in Pharmacology: University of Strathclyde: 1/2 yrs FT.
Postgraduate Diploma in Pharmacology: University of Strathclyde: 1 yr FT.
MSc in Biochemical Pharmacology: University of Southampton: 1 yr FT.
MSc or
Postgraduate Diploma in Clinical Pharmacology: University of Aberdeen: 1 yr FT.
Diploma in Radiopharmaceutical Sciences: University of London (King's College): 2 yrs PT.
MSc in Experimental Drug Research: University of London (King's College): 2 yrs PT.
MSc in Pharmacology: University of London (King's College): 1 yr FT.
Postdoctoral Diploma in Pharmaceutical Sciences: University of London (King's College): 1 yr FT.
Postgraduate Diploma in Clinical Pharmacology: University of Aberdeen: 1 yr FT.PSYCHIATRY:
MMedSc in Clinical Psychiatry: University of Leeds: 3 yrs PT.
MMedSci (Psychotherapy): University of Aberdeen.
MSc in Psychiatry: University of Manchester: 3 yrs PT.
MSc in Psychiatry: University of London (Institute of Psychiatry): 2 yrs PT.
MPhil in Psychiatry: University of Edinburgh: 3 yrs PT.
MPhil in Psychiatry: University of London (Institute of Psychiatry): 3 yrs.
MSc in Clinical Psychotherapy: University of London (St George's Hospital): 3 yrs PT.
Diploma in Psychiatry: University of Edinburgh: 2 yrs PT.
Diploma in Child & Adolescent Psychiatry: University of London (Institute of Child Health/Psychiatry): 1 yr FT.
Diploma in Cognitive & Behavioural Psychotherapy: University of Dundee: 1 yr FT/2 yrs PT.
Diploma in Forensic Psychiatry: University of London (Institute of Psychiatry): 1 yr FT/2 yrs PT.
Diploma in Psychotherapy: University of Liverpool: 2 yrs PT.
Diploma in Psychotherapy: University of Sheffield: 4 yrs PT.
MMedSc in Psychiatry: University of Birmingham: 3 yrs PT.
Board Certification in Psychiatry: University of London (Institute of Psychiatry).
Diploma in Addiction: University of London (Institute of Psychiatry): 1 yr.
Diploma in Clinical Hypnosis: University of Sheffield: 8 mths PT.
Diploma in Family & Marital Therapy: University of London (Institute of Psychiatry): 1 yr.
Diploma in Social Work (Mental Illness): University of London (Institute of Psychiatry): 1 yr.
MSc in Clinical Psychology: University of London (Institute of Psychiatry): 2 yrs.
MSc in Family Therapy: Brunel University: 2 yrs PT.
MSc/Diploma in General Psychiatry: University of Keele: 1/2 yrs PT.
MSc in Mental Health Studies: University of Surrey: 3 yrs.
MSc in Health Psychology: University of London (University College): 2 yrs PT.
MSc in Advanced Mental Health Studies: University of Dundee: 1 yr FT/2 yrs PT.
Master in Psychological Medicine: University of Liverpool: 1 yr's approved research.
Diploma/MSc in Forensic Behavioural Science: University of Liverpool: 1 yr PT (Diploma), 2 yrs PT (MSc).
Diploma in Inter-Cultural Therapy: University College London: 1 yr PT.
Diploma in Art Therapy: University of Sheffield: FT.
MSc in Behavioural Psychotherapy: University College London: 13 mths FT.
MSc/Diploma in Environmental Psychology: University of Surrey: 1 yr FT/2 yrs PT.
MSc/Diploma in Health Psychology: University of Surrey: 1 yr FT/2 yrs PT.
MSc/Diploma/DClinPsych in Clinical Psychology: University of Surrey: 3 yrs FT.

PUBLIC HEALTH MEDICINE: (formerly Community Medicine)
Certificate in Health & the Family in Developing Countries: University of Wales (College of Medicine): 3 mths.
Certificate in Health Care: Practice Nursing: University of Exeter.
Certificate in Health Care: Professions allied to medicine: University of Exeter.
Certificate in Marketing for Health Care & Public Services: University of Leeds (Nuffield Institute for Health Service Studies): 8–9 mths PT.
Certificate/Diploma/MSc in Public Health: University of Aberdeen: 4 mths FT (Certificate); 9 mths FT (Diploma); 1 yr FT (MSc).

Diploma in Advanced Study in Education for Primary Health Care: University of Manchester: 9 mths FT/2 yrs PT.

Diploma in Business Administration (Health, Population & Nutrition in Developing Countries): University of Keele: 9 mths FT.

Diploma in Community Dental Health: University of Edinburgh: 9 mths FT/21 mths PT.

Diploma in Community Eye Health: University of London (Institute of Ophthalmology): 6 mths.

Diploma in Community Health: University of Edinburgh: 9 mths FT/21 mths PT.

Diploma in Environmental Health: University of Edinburgh: 9 mths FT/21 mths PT.

Diploma in Health Management, Planning & Policy: University of Leeds (Nuffield Institute of Health Service Studies): 1 yr FT.

Diploma in Health Medicine: University of Cambridge: 1 yr FT.

Diploma in Health Promotion & Health Education: University of Edinburgh: 9 mths FT/21 mths PT.

Diploma in Health Sciences: University of Edinburgh: 9 mths FT/21 mths PT.

Diploma in Hospital Management: University of Leeds (Nuffield Institute of Health Service Studies): 1 yr FT.

Diploma in Management (for Doctors): University of Keele: 18 mths PT.

Diploma/MSc in Health Education & Health Promotion: University of Leeds (Nuffield Institute of Health Service Studies).

Diploma/MSc in Hospital or Primary Health Care Management for Developing Countries: University of Birmingham: 9 mths FT (Diploma); 1 yr FT (MSc).

MA in Health Services Studies: University of Leeds (Nuffield Institute of Health Service Studies): 1 yr FT/2 yrs PT.

MA in Hospital Management: University of Leeds (Nuffield Institute of Health Service Studies): 1 yr FT.

MA in Quality Assurance in Health & Social Care: University of Leeds (Nuffield Institute of Health Service Studies): 20 mths.

Master in Community Health (MCommH): University of Liverpool (School of Tropical Medicine): 1 yr FT.

Master in Health Management: City University, London: 2 yrs PT.

MBA (Health & Social Services option): University of Leeds (Nuffield Institute of Health Service Studies): 24-36 mths.

MBA (Health Executive Programme): University of Keele: 2 yrs PT.

MBA (Health, Population & Nutrition in Developing Countries): University of Keele: 1 yr FT.

MMedSci in Primary & Community Care: University of Sheffield: 1 yr FT.

MPH: University College Dublin: 1 yr FT/2 yrs PT.

MPH: University of Dundee: 1 yr FT.

MPH: University of Glasgow: 1 yr FT/2 yrs PT.

MPH: University of Leeds: 1 yr FT.

MPH: University of Liverpool: 1 yr FT.

MPH: University of Wales (College of Medicine): 1 yr FT.

MPH for Warm Climate Countries: University of Leeds (Nuffield Institute of Health Service Studies): 1 yr FT.

MSc in Communicable Disease Epidemiology: University of London (School of Hygiene & Tropical Medicine): 1 yr FT/2 yrs PT.

MSc in Community Dental Health: University of Edinburgh: 1 yr FT/2 yrs PT.

MSc in Community Health: University of Dublin (Trinity College): 1 yr FT.

MSc in Community Health: University of Edinburgh: 1 yr FT/2 yrs PT.

MSc in Community Health in Developing Countries: University of London (School of Hygiene & Tropical Medicine): 1 yr FT.

MSc in Community Medicine: University of Manchester: 2 yrs PT.

MSc in Environmental Health: University of Dundee: 1 yr FT.

MSc in Environmental Health: University of Edinburgh: 1 yr FT/2 yrs PT.

MSc in Environmental Health (Water Quality Management): University of Surrey: 6½ mths FT.

MSc in Epidemiology & Health Planning: University of Wales (College of Swansea/Medicine): 1 yr FT.

MSc in Health Care: University of Exeter.

MSc in Health Care: Professional Education: University of Exeter.

MSc in Health Informatics: University of Glasgow: 1 yr.

MSc in Health Planning & Financing: University of London (LSE & School of Hygiene & Tropical Medicine): 1 yr FT/2 yrs PT.

MSc in Health Promotion: University of London (School of Hygiene & Tropical Medicine): 1 yr FT/2 yrs PT.

MSc in Health Promotion & Health Education: University of Edinburgh: 1 yr FT/2 yrs PT.

MSc in Health Sciences: University of Edinburgh: 1 yr FT/2 yrs PT.

MSc in Health Sciences: University of London (St George's Hospital): 2 yrs PT.

MSc in Health Services Management: University of London (School of Hygiene & Tropical Medicine): 1 yr FT/2 yrs PT.

MSc in Preventative Health Care for Developing Countries: University of Wales (College of Medicine): 1 yr FT.

MSc in Public Health in Developing Countries: University of London (School of Hygiene & Tropical Medicine): 1 yr FT.

MSc in Public Health Medicine: University of London (School of Hygiene & Tropical Medicine): 1 yr FT/2 yrs PT.

MSc in Public Health Medicine: University of Newcastle upon Tyne: 2 yrs PT.

MSc in Sociology as Applied to Medicine: University of London (Royal Holloway & Bedford New College): 1 yr FT.

MSc/Postgraduate Diploma in Environmental Management & Health: University of Surrey.

Postgraduate Diploma in Quality Assurance in Health & Social Care: University of Leeds (Nuffield Institute of Health Service Studies): 15 mths.

Postgraduate Diploma/MA in Health Management, Planning & Policy: University of Leeds (Nuffield Institute of Health Service Studies): 1 yr FT.

Postgraduate Diploma/MA in Hospital Management: University of Leeds (Nuffield Institute of Health Service Studies): 1 yr FT.

Postgraduate Diploma/MSc in Health Service Management: South Bank University: 3 trms (Diploma); 4 trms (MSc).

MSc(Econ)/Diploma: University of Wales: 1 yr FT.

RADIOTHERAPEUTICS AND CLINICAL ONCOLOGY:

Diploma/MSc in Clinical Oncology: University of Edinburgh: 2 yrs FT.

Diploma in Clinical Oncology: University of London (Institute of Cancer Research): 9 mths.

MSc in Cancer Sciences: University of London (University College): 2 yrs PT.

MSc (MedSc) in Oncology: University of Glasgow: 2 yrs PT.

MSc in Clinical Cytopathology: University of London (St Mary's Hospital): 1 yr FT or 2 yrs PT.

REHABILITATION:

Certificate in Rehabilitation Engineering: University of London (King's College): 1 yr PT.

Diploma in Rehabilitation Engineering: University of London (King's College): 1 yr PT.

Diploma in Rehabilitation Technology: University of Dundee: 9 mths FT.RHEUMATOLOGY:

MMedSc in Rheumatology: University of Birmingham: 1 yr FT.SOCIOLOGY OF MEDICINE:

MSc Sociology as applied to Medicine: University of London (Royal Holloway and Bedford New College): 1 yr FT.

SPORTS MEDICINE:

Diploma in Sports Medicine: University of London (London Hospital): 24 wks FT.

Diploma in Sports Medicine: University of Dublin (Trinity College): 1 yr FT.

MMedSc in Sport & Exercise Science: University of Sheffield: 1 yr FT.

Certificate & Diploma in Sports Physiotherapy: Association of Chartered Phsyiotherapists in Sports Medicine, Crewe and Alsager College of Higher Education: 6 mths (Certificate), 2 yrs PT (Diploma).

MPhil in Sports Medicine: University of London British Postgraduate Medical Foundation.

MSc in Sports Medicine: University of Nottingham: 2 yrs PT.

MSc in the Science of Sports Coaching: University of Sheffield: 1 yr FT.

SURGERY: (See General Surgery)

THORACIC MEDICINE:

Diploma in Thoracic Medicine: University of London (National Heart & Lung Institute): 1 yr FT.

Diploma in Tuberculosis and Chest Diseases: University of Wales (College of Medicine): 6 mths FT.

MSc in Thoracic Medicine: University of London (National Heart & Lung Institute): 1-2 yrs FT.

TOXICOLOGY:

MSc in Applied Toxicology: University of Surrey: 3- 7 yrs.

Master in Applied Toxicology: University of Portsmouth.

MSc in Toxicology: University of Surrey: 1 yr FT or 2 yrs PT.

MSc/Diploma in Toxicology: University of Birmingham: 1 yr.

MSc/Postgraduate Diploma in Toxicology: University of Surrey: 1 yr FT/2 yrs PT.

Diploma in Toxicology: University of Dublin (Trinity College): 2 yrs PT.

TROPICAL MEDICINE AND HYGIENE:

Diploma in Tropical Medicine and Hygiene (DTM&H): Royal College of Physicians (London School of Hygiene & Tropical Medicine): 3 mths FT. A DTM&H is also awarded by the University of Liverpool (3 mths FT).

Diploma in Tropical Child Health (DTCH): University of Liverpool (Liverpool School of Tropical Medicine): 6 mth FT.

Master of Tropical Medicine (MTropMed): University of Liverpool (Liverpool School of Tropical Medicine): 1 yr FT.

Master in Community Health (MCommH): University of Liverpool (Liverpool School of Tropical Medicine): 1 yr FT.

Master in Tropical Paediatrics: University of Liverpool (Liverpool School of Tropical Medicine): 1 yr FT.

MSc in Infection & Health in the Tropics: University of London (School of Hygiene & Tropical Medicine): 1 yr FT.

MSc in Medical Entomology: University of London School of Hygiene and Tropical Medicine: 12 mths FT.

UROLOGY:

Diploma in Urology: University of London (Institute of Urology & Nephrology): 1 yr FT.

VASCULAR MEDICINE:

MSc Vascular Medicine and Technology: University of London (St Mary's Hospital): 1 yr FT/2 yrs PT.

VENEREOLOGY:

Diploma in Venereology: University of Liverpool: 3 mth FT.

VIROLOGY:

MSc in Virology: University of London (London School of Hygiene & Tropical Medicine): 1 yr FT.

MSc in Medical Virology: Univesity of London Royal Free Hospital School of Medicine and London School of Hygiene and Tropical Medicine: 2 yrs PT (day release).

MSc in Medical Virology: University of Manchester: 1 yr FT.

Summary of Registrable Additional Qualifications granted by Licensing Bodies in the United Kingdom and Ireland

Licensing Body	Qualifications	Designatory Letters
University of Aberdeen	Doctor of Medicine,	
	Master of Surgery	MD, ChMAberd
Queen's University, Belfast	Doctor of Medicine,	
	Master of Surgery	MD, MchBelf
	Master of Obstetrics	MAOBelf
University of Birmingham	Doctor of Medicine	MDBirm
University of Bristol	Doctor of Medicine	MDBrist
	Master of Surgery	ChMBrist
University of Cambridge	Doctor of Medicine,	
	Master of Surgery	MD, MchirCamb
University of Dundee	Doctor of Medicine,	
	Master of Surgery	MD, ChMDund

University of Edinburgh	Doctor of Medicine,	
	Master of Surgery	MD, ChMEdin
University of Glasgow	Doctor of Medicine	MDGlasg
University of Leeds	Doctor of Medicine,	
	Master of Surgery	MD, ChMLeeds
University of Leicester	Doctor of Medicine	MDLeics
University of Liverpool	Doctor of Medicine,	
	Master of Surgery	MD, ChMLpool
	Master of Orthopaedic Surgery	
		MchOrthLpool
University of London	Doctor of Medicine,	
	Master of Surgery	MD, MSLond
University of Manchester	Doctor of Medicine,	
	Master of Surgery	MD, ChMManc
University of Newcastle upon Tyne	Doctor of Medicine	MDNcle
University of Nottingham	Doctor of Medicine	DMNottm
University of Oxford	Doctor of Medicine,	
	Master of Surgery	DM, MchOxfd
University of Sheffield	Doctor of Medicine,	
	Master of Surgery	MD, ChMSheff
University of Southampton	Doctor of Medicine,	
	Master of Surgery	DM, MSSoton
University of Wales	Doctor in Medicine,	
	Master in Surgery	MD, MchWales
University of Dublin	Doctor in Medicine,	
	Master in Surgery	MD, MchDubl
	Master in Obstetric Science	MAODubl
National University of Ireland	Doctor of Medicine,	
	Master of Surgery	MD, MChNUIrel
	Master of Obstetrics	MAONUIrel

Anaesthetics:

Royal College of Anaesthetists	Fellow	FRCA
Faculty of Anaesthetists,		
Royal College of Surgeons in Ireland	Fellow	FFARCSIrel

Public Health Medicine:

Faculty of Public Health Medicine,		
Royal College of Physicians of London		
and Edinburgh and Royal College of		
Physicians and Surgeons of Glasgow	Member, Fellow	MFPHM, FFPHM
Royal College of Physicians of Ireland	Member, Fellow	MFPHMIrel,
		FFPHMIrel

General Practice:

Royal College of General Practitioners	Member, Fellow	MRCGP, FRCGP
Irish College of General Practitioners	Member	MCGPIrel

Medicine:

Royal College of Physicians of London	Member, Fellow	MRCPLond,
		FRCPLond, MRCP(UK)
Royal College of Physicians of		
Edinburgh	Member, Fellow	MRCPEdin,
FRCPEdin, MRCP(UK)		
Royal College of Physicians and		
Surgeons of Glasgow	Member, Fellow	MRCP RCPSGlasg,
		FRCP RCPSGlasg,
		MRCP(UK)

Royal College of Physicians of Ireland

Obstetrics and Gynaecology:

Royal College of Obstetricians and Gynaecologists	Member, Fellow	MRCOG, FRCOG

Occupational medicine:

Faculty of Occupational Medicine, Royal Colleges of Physicians of London	Member, Fellow	MFOM, FFOM

Pathology:

Royal College of Pathologists	Member, Fellow	MRCPath, FRCPath

Psychiatry:

Royal College of Psychiatrists	Member, Fellow	MRCPsych, FRCPsych

Ophthalmology:

College of Ophthalmologists	Fellow	FCOphth

Radiology:

Royal College of Radiologists (England)	Fellow	FRCR
Faculty of Radiologists, Royal College of Surgeons in Ireland	Fellow	FFRRCSIrel

Surgery:

Royal College of Surgeons of Edinburgh	Fellow	FRCSEdin
Royal College of Surgeons of England	Fellow	FRCSEng
Royal College of Physicians and Surgeons of Glasgow	Fellow	FRCS RCPSGlasg FRCPSGlasg
Royal College of Surgeons in Ireland	Fellow	FRCSIrel

Summary of Registrable Qualifications granted by Licensing Bodies in the United Kingdom and Ireland

Licensing Body	Qualifications	Designatory Letters
University of Aberdeen	Bachelor of Medicine, Bachelor of Surgery	MBChBAberd
Queen's University, Belfast	Bachelor of Medicine, Bachelor of Surgery	MBBChBelf
University of Birmingham	Bachelor of Medicine, Bachelor of Surgery	MBChBBirm
University of Bristol	Bachelor of Medicine, Bachelor of Surgery	MBChBBrist
University of Cambridge	Bachelor of Medicine, Bachelor of Surgery	MBBChirCamb
University of Dundee	Bachelor of Medicine, Bachelor of Surgery	MBChBDund
University of Edinburgh	Bachelor of Medicine, Bachelor of Surgery	MBChBEdin
University of Glasgow	Bachelor of Medicine, Bachelor of Surgery	MBChBGlasg
University of Leeds	Bachelor of Medicine, Bachelor of Surgery	MBChBLeeds
University of Leicester	Bachelor of Medicine, Bachelor of Surgery	MBChBLeic

University of Liverpool	Bachelor of Medicine, Bachelor of Surgery	MBChBLpool
University of London	Bachelor of Medicine, Bachelor of Surgery	MBBSLond
University of Manchester	Bachelor of Medicine, Bachelor of Surgery	MBChBManc
University of Newcastle upon Tyne	Bachelor of Medicine, Bachelor of Surgery	MBBSNcle
University of Nottingham	Bachelor of Medicine, Bachelor of Surgery	BMBSNottm
University of Oxford	Bachelor of Medicine, Bachelor of Surgery	BMBChOxfd
University of Sheffield	Bachelor of Medicine, Bachelor of Surgery	MBChBSheff
University of Southampton	Bachelor of Medicine	BMSoton
University of Wales	Bachelor in Medicine, Bachelor of Surgery	MBBChWales
Royal College of Physicians of London	Licentiate	LRCPLond
Royal College of Surgeons of England	Licentiate	LRCSEng
Royal College of Physicians of Edinburgh	Licentiate	LRCPEdin
Royal College of Surgeons of Edinburgh	Licentiate	LRCSEdin
Royal College of Physicians and Surgeons of Glasgow	Licentiate	LRCPSGlasg
Society of Apothecaries of London	Licentiate in Medicine and Surgery	LMSSALond

METALLURGY

Membership of Professional Institutions and Associations

INSTITUTE OF CORROSION

4 Leck House, Lake Street, Leighton Buzzard, Bedfordshire LU7 8TQ Tel: 01525 851771
Fax: 01525 376690 e-mail: admin@icorr.demon.co.uk Website: www.icorr.org

MEMBERSHIP:
Fellows (FICorr): Candidates must be 35 or over and have an established reputation as a corrosion scientist or corrosion technologist. They should have made a notable contribution to the understanding or practice of corrosion prevention and control and/or have rendered special services to the Institute.

Professional Members (MICorr): Candidates must be 25 or over and be able to demonstrate knowledge and experience in the field of corrosion science and technology. Normally an academic qualification at degree standard or equivalent is needed although occasionally this requirement may be waived.

Technican (TechICorr): Candidates must be 25 or over, have some academic knowledge (eg passed the Institutes Fundamentals of Corrosion Course*) and be actively and practically involved in the practice of corrosion science and corrosion technology.

Ordinary Members: Ordinary members must indicate that they have an interest in the practice of corrosion science and corrosion technology.

Student Members: Students must be 18 or over and be studying corrosion science or corrosion technology or related subjects. Students must apply for transfer to other grades of membership within 6 mths of ceasing to be a student or within 6 yrs of first becoming a Student Member.

Note: *Details of current courses available from the Institute.

THE INSTITUTE OF METAL FINISHING

Exeter House, 48 Holloway Head, Birmingham B1 1NQ Tel: 0121 622 7387 Fax: 0121 666 6316

MEMBERSHIP:

Fellow (FIMF): Must usually be at least 35, have an established and mature reputation in the field of Metal Finishing and have made a marked contribution to the science or practice of Metal Finishing.

Member (MIMF): Must be experienced in Metal Finishing *or* that, being holders of an appropriate postgraduate qualification they have 1 yr's approved experience *or* that, being usually not less than 35, they have been engaged in Metal Finishing for at least 15 yrs, of which a large part has been spent in an important position of responsibility *or* that, being 30 or over, and having been engaged in metal finishing for at least 10 yrs, they have been Licentiates for a min of 5 yrs.

Licentiate (LIMF): Must have adequate practical experience in Metal Finishing and either has possession of the Advanced Technicians Diploma in Metal Finishing together with an approved industrial project, or have passed an exempting exam (such as an approved HND or HNC in Chemistry, Metallurgy or Engineering subjects, together with a pass in an approved supplementary course in a Metal Finishing Technology together with a suitable project).

EXAMINATIONS:

An examination for the Institute Foundation Certificate is held for candidates completing an introductory course.

Technician's Certificate in Metal Finishing consists of two modules – General Principles, a broad introduction to finishing processes, and Plating Practice. No academic qualifications are required.

Advanced Technician's Certificate in Metal Finishing follows on from the Technician's Certificate and consists of modules in Electrochemistry, Materials Science, Surface Coating, and Process Management.

Advanced Technician's Diploma in Metal Finishing is awarded for those who complete a suitable project post the Advanced Certificate level.

Technical Courses

The IMF provides Training routes for the Surface Engineering and Coatings industry, to Foundation, Ordinary and Advanced Certificate, Diploma and Licientiateship level of the Institute's qualifications. Taught courses for Foundation and Ordinary certificates are offered through the IMF's Midland and London Branches as well as by a number of Independent centres. Alternatively, Distance Learning routes, based on the Open Tech System, are offered for Ordinary and Advanced Certificates as well as the Diploma and Licientiate levels. At present, 4 modules cover a range from General Principles(MFI) to Process Management(MF4) covering Plating Practice(MF2), Electrochemistry(MF3a), Materials Science(MF3b) and Surface Coating(MF3c); modules on Paint and Powder Coating should be available towards the end of 1998.

CPD

Through Branch and Group Meetings, Conferences, Special courses and Symposiums the IMF offers opportunity for continuous professional development for anyone working in the Surface Engineering and Coatings field. Procedures are in hand for linking the CPD portfolio for part recognition for the Institute's formal qualifications. Information on all these courses can be obtained from the above address.

University Qualifications

The following universities offer qualifications in Metallurgy and related subjects. Full details may be found in Part 4, under the entry for the appropriate university.

FIRST DEGREES AWARDED BY UNIVERSITIES

Birmingham; Bucks. Coll.; Central England; De Montfort, Leicester; Leeds; Liverpool; London Guildhall; Manchester; Oxford; Sheffield Hallam; Surrey; UMIST

HIGHER DEGREES AWARDED BY UNIVERSITIES

Central England; Kent (Kent Institute of Art & Design); Leeds; London Guildhall; Manchester; Royal College of Art; Sheffield; UMIST

DIPLOMAS AWARDED BY UNIVERSITIES
Bradford (Bradford & Ilkley Community College); Central England

CERTIFICATES AWARDED BY UNIVERSITIES
Central England

National Certificates and Diplomas

BTEC National Certificates/Diplomas: Metals Technology
BTEC Higher National Certificates/Diplomas: Metals Technology

NVQs

Level 1: High Pressure Aluminium Die Casting; Stock, Process and Supply Steel and Metal Products
Level 2: Cold Working of Metals; Finishing Metal Products; Hot Rolling; Iron Making; Metal Forging; Metal Industry Laboratory Services; Steel Casting; Steel Making; Steel Refining; Stock, Process and Supply Steel and Metal Products
Level 3: Cold Working of Metals; Finishing Metal Products; Hot Rolling; Iron Making; Metal Forging; Metal Industry Laboratory Services; Steel Casting; Steel Industry Operations; Steel Making; Steel Refining; Stock, Process and Supply Steel and Metal Products

City & Guilds

0670 Iron and Steel Production Technology; 0671 Iron and Steel Production Technology

Useful Addresses

Steel Industry National Training Organisation, 5/6 Meadowcourt, Amos Road, Sheffield S9 1BX Tel: 0114 244 6833 Fax: 0114 256 2855

METEOROLOGY AND CLIMATOLOGY

METEOROLOGICAL OFFICE COLLEGE

Shinfield Park, Reading, Berkshire RG2 9AU Tel: 01344 855406 Fax: 01344 855410
e-mail: met-training@meto.gov.uk
The Meteorological Office College is part of the Met. Office. It provides meteorological and technical training for its own staff. For meteorology training a number of places are usually available on each course for those outside the organisation on a fee paying basis.
Forecaster Foundation Training Programme: 26 wks over 15 mths, comprising the Meteorological Observer Training & Analysis, Initial and Advanced Forecasting courses. Entry: Mathematics or Physics degree. Certification: the Met Office certificate of forecasting competence. WMO recognition as class II specialists in Dynamic, Physical and Synoptic Meteorology.
Forecaster Professional Development Programme: 4 wks comprising the Numerical Weather Prediction Appreciation workshop, Satellite Imagery Interpretation, Summer & Winter Mesoscale Meteorology workshops, all 1 wk. Entry: Completed Forecaster Foundation Training Programme or similar. Certification: The Met. Office awards certificates of attendance.
Meteorology for Research Programme: 15 wks comprising parts 1& 2 of the Meteorology for Graduates course. Entry: Good degree in Mathematical or Physical subject. Certification: The Met Office awards s certificate of completion. WMO recognition as Class I specialists in Dynamics, Physical & Synoptic Meteorology.

University Qualifications

The following universities offer qualifications in Meteorology and Climatology and related subjects. Full details may be found in Part 4, under the entry for the appropriate university.

FIRST DEGREES AWARDED BY UNIVERSITIES
East Anglia; Edinburgh; Liverpool; Reading

HIGHER DEGREES AWARDED BY UNIVERSITIES
Birmingham; East Anglia; London (University College (UCL)); Plymouth; Reading; Sheffield

DIPLOMAS AWARDED BY UNIVERSITIES
Nottingham Trent (Southampton Institute); Reading

MICROSCOPY

Membership of Professional Institutions and Associations

THE ROYAL MICROSCOPICAL SOCIETY
37-38 St Clements, Oxford OX4 1AJ Tel: 01865 248768 Fax: 01865 791237
MEMBERSHIP:
Fellow: Any person over 21 who has a genuine interest in Microscopy.
Corporate Member: This category of membership is specially intended to enable scientists from overseas and members of colleges and schools to attend the Society's meetings and courses. It is possible for academic, research and manufacturing organisations, and schools with well-developed science departments to join the Society so that their staff and pupils may attend meetings at reduced rates and receive the Society's publications.
Junior Member: Any person whose work or study involves the use of the microscope, who is between 16 and 25½.
Diploma (DipRMS): This Diploma is awarded to Fellows for work at postgraduate level in the field of Microscopy. Candidates must have a relevant degree and/or practical experience in Microscopy, have attended courses organised by the Society and have submitted a thesis or other examinable evidence of proficiency in microscopy, eg published work, or patents. They may select as fields of work, aspects of Light Microscopy or Electron Microscopy or other forms of Microscopy or any combination of these. If the thesis is accepted, candidates must take an oral exam. Special provision may be made for overseas candidates.
Qualification in the Technology of Microscopy (TechRMS): This is primarily for those engaged in practical microscopy and designed to encourage the study of fundamentals and the instruments and techniques in current use. Candidates are advised to attend courses organised by the society, must sit an authorised examination and then submit a short work project. If a credit is obtained, the project is examined by RMS examiners and if successful, candidates must take an oral examination which covers both the work project and the syllabus. The syllabus has a compulsory section on fundamentals of microscopy, light and electron microscopes and image recording, together with sections on either biological microscopy or the microscopy of materials.

MUSEUM AND RELATED WORK

Membership of Professional Institutions and Associations

THE MUSEUMS ASSOCIATION
42 Clerkenwell Close, London EC1R 0PA Tel: 020 7608 2933 Fax: 020 7250 1929
e-mail: info@museumsassociation.org Website: museumsassociation.org
MEMBERSHIP:
Honorary Fellow: There is a limited number of Honorary Fellows, nominated by the Council and elected by the Association.

Fellowship of the Museums Association (FMA): Open to individual Members of the Association who have held the Associateship of the Museums Association (AMA) for at least 5 yrs, or are able to demonstrate an equivalent level of attainment. Fellowship conditions are: demonstrating a high level of professional experience, development and contribution in any area of museum work; undertaking at least 2 yrs' Continuing Professional Development (CPD); and attendance at a Fellowship appraisal.

Associateship of the Museums Association (AMA): Replaced **Museums Diploma** in 1996. Associate Membership is open to all those who work for or in museums. Routes include the registration of HE qualifications/NVQs/SVQs; set periods of experience; 10 days' Continuing Professional Development (CPD) over 2 yrs; and a structured professional review. Further details and an introductory leaflet are available from the Professional Development Manager at the Museums Association.

University Qualifications

The following universities offer qualifications in Museum and Related Work and related subjects. Full details may be found in Part 4, under the entry for the appropriate university.

FIRST DEGREES AWARDED BY UNIVERSITIES
Anglia; Buckingham; Central Lancashire; Cheltenham & Gloucester; De Montfort, Leicester; East Anglia (Otley College); Essex (Writtle College); Greenwich; Huddersfield; Hull (Bishop Grosseteste College); Kent; Leeds; Lincolnshire; Lincolnshire (Bishop Burton College); Liverpool (Chester College of H.E.); London Guildhall; London Institute (Camberwell College of Arts); Luton; Oxford Brookes; Plymouth; Southampton (King Alfred's College); Surrey (St Mary's, Strawberry Hill); Teesside; Wales (University of Wales, Bangor); Worcester

HIGHER DEGREES AWARDED BY UNIVERSITIES
Birmingham; Bournemouth; Bristol; Bucks. Coll.; City; Durham; East Anglia (Otley College); Essex; Greenwich; Leicester; London (Courtauld Institute of Art); London (Goldsmiths College); London (Institute of Education); London (University College (UCL)); London Institute (Camberwell College of Arts); Newcastle; North London; Northumbria; Nottingham Trent; Oxford; Plymouth; Portsmouth; Royal College of Art; Salford; Sheffield; Sheffield Hallam; Southampton (Winchester School of Art); St Andrews; Wales (Cardiff University); Wales (University of Wales, Bangor)

DIPLOMAS AWARDED BY UNIVERSITIES
Birmingham; De Montfort, Leicester; East Anglia (Otley College); East Anglia (Suffolk College); Leicester; London (Courtauld Institute of Art); Luton; Manchester; Newcastle; Nottingham Trent; Oxford; Oxford Brookes; Plymouth; Salford; St Andrews

CERTIFICATES AWARDED BY UNIVERSITIES
Bournemouth; Essex; Lincolnshire (Bishop Burton College)

NVQs
Level 2: Heritage Care & Visitor Services
Level 3: Museums, Galleries & Heritage (Collection Care & Visitor Services)
Level 4: Museums, Galleries & Heritage (Collection Management & Interpretation); Museums, Galleries & Heritage (Conservation)
Level 5: Museums, Galleries & Heritage (Collection Management & Interpretation); Museums, Galleries & Heritage (Conservation)

SVQs
Level 3: Museums, Galleries & Heritage: Collection Care & Visitor Services
Level 4: Museums, Galleries & Heritage: Collection Management or Conservation
Level 5: Museums, Galleries & Heritage: Conservation

Useful Addresses

Cultural Heritage National Training Organisation, First Floor, Glyde House, Glydegate, Bradford BD5 0UP Tel: 01274 391092 Fax: 01274 394890

MUSIC

Musical Education and Training

Most children and young people before the age of entry to further and higher education take graded written and practical exams in musicianship, singing and instruments. These are designed to mark the progress of learners and the certificates awarded are not strictly speaking qualifications, although Grades VII and VIII are sometimes used to indicate the minimum standard required of entrants by colleges training professional musicians. Grade exams for those learning various instruments are conducted by the Associated Board of the Royal Schools of Music, Trinity College of Music, Guildhall School of Music & Drama and the London College of Music. Further music courses may be taken at Birmingham School of Music; Royal Northern College of Music; The Royal Scottish Academy of Music and Drama. The Royal College of Organists also awards diplomas.

PERFORMERS:
Music colleges offer courses for intending performers. Here the emphasis is on practical work, rehearsal and performance. They also provide courses which, while still demanding a high standard in practical work, give more time for an all-round training in general musicianship.

TEACHERS:
Awards made by the various colleges of music are no longer acceptable by the DES as offering qualified status. Graduates and other students must also take a teaching diploma. In Scotland the BA (Music Education) (formerly DipMusEd) awarded by the Royal Scottish Academy of Music and Drama carries graduate status for salary purposes but intending school-teachers must take a 1-yr course of professional training. Students succeeding in the 3-yr diploma course in Music at Aberdeen or Dundee Colleges of Education or St Andrew's College of Education, Glasgow, are eligible for a Teacher's Certificate.

Qualifications Awarded by Colleges of Music

BIRMINGHAM CONSERVATOIRE
(Faculty of Music, University of Central England)

Paradise Place, Birmingham B3 3HG Tel: 0121 331 5901/2 Fax: 0121 331 5906
e-mail: conservatoire@uce.ac.uk

EXAMINATIONS:
BMus: (1 yr Cert HE; 2 yrs Dip HE; 3 yrs BMus; 4 yrs BMus (Hons)). Western classical music forms the focus of this course, on which most instruments, voice, or composition may constitute the principal study. There is a very wide range of additional and optional studies, including conducting, chamber music, community music, accompaniment, etc. Students participate in a full range of instrumental or vocal ensembles, which include 2 symphony orchestras, several bands, opera groups and choirs.
BMus (R ga Sangeet): (1 yr Cert HE; 2 yrs Dip HE; 3 yrs BMus; 4 yrs BMus (Hons)). This course covers both practical and theoretical aspects of the rich musical tradition of Northern India, Pakistan and Bangladesh. Students may specialise in sitar, voice or tabla. The course has been developed jointly with the University of Delhi.
BMus (Jazz): (1 yr Cert HE; 2 yrs Dip HE; 3 yrs BMus; 4 yrs BMus (Hons)) This course is designed to offer a broadly-based education for musicians who wish to pursue the study of jazz. Principal study tuition is available in a variety of instruments and voice. There is a wide range of classes in improvisation and ensemble playing. For all of these courses a very high standard in principal

study is required at entry. Minimum formal requirements are 5 different subjects: 3 or 4 at GCSE (Grade C) and 1 or 2 at A Level.

BEd Music (Secondary): A 2 yr course for mature students with the equiv of 1 yr in higher education (eg professional experience). Details from the Faculty of Education, Westbourne Road, Edgbaston, Birmingham B15 3TN Tel: 0121 331 6141.

GUILDHALL SCHOOL OF MUSIC & DRAMA

Silk Street, Barbican, London EC2Y 8DT Tel: 020 7628 2571 Fax: 020 7256 9438
Website: www.gsmd.ac.uk

FULL-TIME MUSIC COURSES:

BMus Course: 4 yrs with an exit point after 3 yrs (DipGSM).

Teaching Qualifications: The BMus is accepted by the DFE for the status of qualified teacher for the Graduate addition to salary including Good Honours' for those obtaining either a first or second class pass in the final exam, provided the holder also gains a Certificate in Education by completing a course of professional teacher-training at a College of Higher Education or a university department of education.

Postgraduate and Advanced Music Courses: These are designed for singers and instrumentalists who have reached a high standard of performance and involve a minimum of 1yr FT study. Candidates will normally be expected to have obtained (or be about to obtain) a recognised diploma or degree in music as a result of completing at least 3 yrs in a music college or university music department.

The following degrees and higher diplomas are offered:

1. **Mmus Degree in Music Performance:** Subject to validation.
2. **MMus in Composition:** Validated by City University.
3. **Postgraduate Diploma in Music Performance**
4. **Diploma in Music Therapy (DipMth):** (GSMD – York).
5. **Concert Recital Diploma:** Equivalent to European Premier Prix and awarded on the basis of a public recital examination.
6. **Certificate of Advanced Study:** Awarded on satisfactory completion of postgraduate or advanced course where no other qualification is involved.

Diploma in Continuing Professional Development (Guildhall School of Music & Drama): A modular programme aimed at performance, composers, teachers and arts co-ordinators who already have some professional experience in creative approaches to performance and communication.

MEMBERSHIP:

2 Honorary Diplomas are awarded for service to music or drama.

Fellowship (FGSM): To professors, examiners and past students (the title 'Fellow Emeritus' may also be conferred in exceptional circumstances).

Honorary Membership (HonGSM): For services to music or drama.

EXAMINATIONS SERVICE:

The Guildhall School, through its Department of Initial Studies, also offers a range of graded examinations, recital certificates and licentiate diplomas for candidates throughout the UK and abroad. These examinations are available for most musical instruments and a broad range of speech, communication and drama subjects, including group and classroom based learning. Examinations enquiries: Tel: 020 7382 7167 Fax: 020 7382 7212 e-mail: exams@gsmd.ac.uk

LONDON COLLEGE OF MUSIC AND MEDIA

Thames Valley University, St Mary's Road, Ealing, London W5 5RF Tel: 020 8231 2364
Fax: 020 8231 2433 e-mail: lcm.exams@tvu.ac.uk Website: www.elgar.tvu.ac.uk/lcmexams

INTERNAL DEGREES & DIPLOMAS:

BMus Performance/Composition (3 yrs)
DipHe in Popular Music Performance (2yrs)
Foundation in Popular Music Performance (1yr)DipHe in Music Technology (2yrs)
PG/Dip/ MMus Performance (1yr FT, 2yrs PT)
MMus in Composing Concert Music (1yr)

MMus in Composing for Film and Television (1yr)
MMus in Composing for the Theatre (1yr)
MMus in Composing for New Media (1yr)
Media Arts Major (2yrs DipHE, 3yrs Degree)
Advertising Minor (duration depends on major) & Major
Digital Arts Major and Minor (3yrs)
Media Studies Minor (duration depends on Major)
Multimedia Computing Major and Minor (3yrs)
Music Minor (duration depends on Major)
Photography Minor (duration depends on Major)
Radio Broadcasting Minor (duration depends on Major)
Sound and Music Recording Minor (duration depends on Major)
Journalism Minor (duration depends on Major) & Major
Video Production Minor (duration depends on Major)
MA/PGDip in Film and the Moving Image (1yr FT, 2yrs PT)
MA/PGDIP in Radio Broadcasting (2yrs PT)
BSc in Multimedia Computing Major and Minor (2yrs HND, 3yrs Degree)
BA in Digital Arts Major and Minor (2yrs DipHE, 3yrs Degree)
MA in Multimedia Computing, subject to variation, (duration not yet decided)
MA in Computer Arts
MA in Multimedia Computing
BSc Interactive Software Design
Digital Animation (minor)
BA Design for Interactive Media

INTERNAL AND EXTERNAL AWARDS:
Performers' Diploma of Associate in either a Musical Subject or Speech and Drama Subject (ALCM): This exam is both theoretical and practical.
Associate in Music – Theoretical Diploma (AMusLCM).
Performers' Diploma of Licentiate in either a Musical Subject or Speech and Drama Subject (LLCM): Candidates must hold the Associate Diploma.
Teachers' Diploma in either a Musical Subject or Speech and Drama Subject (LLCM(TD)): Candidates must be at least 18 and must already hold the Associate Diploma.
Licentiate in Music – Theoretical Diploma (LMusLCM): Candidates must hold the AMusLCM.
Diploma of Fellowship (FLCM): This may be taken as a Performer in music or as a Composer or by Thesis. Licentiates of the College (LLCM or LLCM(TD)) may enter for the Fellowship Diploma in the same subject. It may also be taken for performance in Speech and Drama.
BMus
BA(Humanities)

GRADE EXAMINATIONS are offered by:
London College of Music introductory exams in Pianoforte, Violin, Cello, Recorder, Guitar, Electronic Organ and Keyboard, Speech and Drama and Oral Communication. Grades I-VIII: Practical and theoretical in all instrumental and vocal subjects; Speech and Drama; Oral Communications; Verse Speaking; Reading; Acting; Music Theatre; Gospel Music. Certificates are awarded as Pass, Merit and Honours. Examinations in Ensemble Playing: 4 divisions-Preliminary; Intermediate; Advanced and Recital. Certificates are awarded as Pass, Merit and Honours.

ROYAL ACADEMY OF MUSIC

Marylebone Road, London NW1 5HT Tel: 020 7873 7373 e-mail: registry@ram.ac.uk
Website: www.ram.ac.uk

EXAMINATIONS:
Master of Music: Taken after a 2 yr course in musical performance or composition with complementary academic and supporting studies. Students must already hold an honours degree, usually in music or composition. Degrees are awarded by the University of London.
Bachelor of Music: Taken after a 4 yr course in musical performance or composition with complementary academic and supporting studies. Degrees are awarded by the University of London.

Postgraduate Performance: Taken after a 2 yr course in musical performance. Students will already perform to a high standard and intend to follow a performance career.

MPhil Research Programme: A 2 yr award in Performance or Composition, offered under the regulations of the University of London.

PhD Research Programme: A 3 yr award in Performance or Composition, offered under the regulations of the University of London. Concentrates primarily on academic work but also requires the highest possible practical standards.

ROYAL COLLEGE OF MUSIC

Prince Consort Road, South Kensington, London SW7 2BS Tel: 020 7589 3643 Fax: 020 7589 7740
Website: www.rcm.ac.uk

The College provides postgraduate courses leading to the degree of **MMus(RCM) in Performance Studies**, in **Conducting Studies in Chamber Music**, in **Composition** and in **Composition for Screen**. The College also awards a **PGDip(RCM)** to students undertaking postgraduate pathways for Solo & Ensemble Recitalists, Orchestral Musicians, Early Music Specialists, Opera Singers, Concert Singers, Composers, Conductors and others. In addition, the College awards a **DMus Research Degree** examined by thesis and performance or composition.

BMus(Hons): Obtained at the conclusion of a 4 yr FT course.

THE ROYAL COLLEGE OF ORGANISTS

7 St Andrew Street, Holborn, London EC4A 3LQ Tel: 020 7936 3606 Fax: 020 7353 8244
e-mail: exams@rco.org.uk. Website: www.rco.org.uk

MEMBERSHIP:
Open to all persons interested in the organ, choir training and related areas. Full details of application available from the Registrar of the College.

Fellowship of the Royal College of Organists (FRCO): Must be members of the College, who hold the Diploma of Associateship. The Fellowship is obtained by exam taken in 2 sections, Written Papers and Organ Playing. There are no specific educational requirements for admission to the exam.

Associateship of the Royal College of Organists (ARCO): Must be members of the College. The Associateship is obtained by exam taken in 2 sections, Written Papers and Organ Playing. There are no specific educational requirements for admission to the exam.

EXAMINATIONS:
Choir-Training Diploma of the Royal College of Organists (CHD): This exam is open to subscribing members of the College. It consists of an exam taken in 2 sections, Written Paper and Practical.

Organ Teaching Diploma of the Royal College of Organists (DipTCR): This exam is open to Fellows and Associates of the College who are subscribing members. It consists of an exam in 2 sections, Written Paper and Practical.

Preliminary Certificate: This exam is open to full individual or student members of the College. It consists of an exam taken in 2 sections, Written Paper and Organ Playing.

ROYAL NORTHERN COLLEGE OF MUSIC

124 Oxford Road, Manchester M13 9RD Tel: 0161 273 6283 Fax: 0161 273 7611

MEMBERSHIP:
Companionship (CRNCM): An honorary award to mark service of exceptional distinction to the College.

Fellowship (FRNCM): An honorary award conferred upon distinguished musicians.

Honorary Membership (Hon RNCM): An honorary award conferred on non-musicians who have given distinguished service to the College or in other areas of music.

POSTGRADUATE AWARDS: (Both in affiliation with the University of Manchester)
Master of Music in Performance or in Composition (MusM(Perf)): 2 yrs.

Diploma in Advanced Studies in Performance and **Diploma in Advanced Studies in Composition:** 1 or 2 yrs, but in the case of singers, up to 3 yrs.

GRADUATE AWARDS:

Bachelor of Music (Hons) (BMus (Hons)/Grad RNCM): 4 yrs. Final classification weighted 50% practical, 50% supporting academic work.

Bachelor of Arts (Music) (BA (Music)/Grad RNCM): 4 yrs. Course content similar to B(Mus) (above), but with less extensive academic component. Holders of either degree are eligible to apply for postgraduate certificate in education courses or higher degree study. Circulate of the Royal Northern College of Music: 4 yrs joint course in acquisition with the University of Manchester, Department of Music.

DIPLOMA AWARD:

Diploma in Professional Performance (PPRNCM): 4 yr course known as the Professional Performance Course' for students of exceptional practical accomplishment. For advanced students, entry direct to the third yr of the course is sometimes possible. The award is also available for established ensembles.

THE ROYAL SCHOOLS OF MUSIC – JOINT AWARDS

e-mail: abrsm@abrsm.ac.uk Website: www.abrsm.ac.uk

The Royal Academy of Music, the Royal College of Music, the Royal Northern College of Music and the Royal Scottish Academy of Music and Drama incorporate under the title of the **Associated Board of the Royal Schools of Music**. This examining board has its offices at 14 Bedford Square, London WC1B 3JG and awards the diploma of **Licentiate of the Royal Schools of Music (LRSM)** in composition, music in the school curriculum, teaching, performance, direction and piano accompaniment. A professional development course is available for instrumental and singing teachers. The CT ABRSM is a one-yr part time course leading to the award of the Certificate of Teaching ABRSM. The Associated Board also offers a series of pre diploma exams at all levels starting with a preparatory test. These are available worldwide.

THE ROYAL SCOTTISH ACADEMY OF MUSIC AND DRAMA

100 Renfrew Street, Glasgow G2 3DB Tel: 0141 332 4101 Fax: 0141 332 8901
e-mail: registry@rsamd.ac.uk Website: www.rsamd.ac.uk

QUALIFICATIONS:

BMus (Performance): 4 yr course for especially gifted potential performers. Standards for entrance: Musical, approximately Grade 8 (Final) of the Associated Board of the Royal Schools of Music in the principal study; Educational, passes in 3 subjects at SCE Higher Grade or passes in 2 subjects at GCE Advanced Level or recognised equivalents.

BA (Musical Studies): 3 yr FT course with extension, by selection, to a 4th Hons yr. The musical and educational standards for entrance are as for the BMus (Performance). Admission is by competitive audition.

BEd (Music): 4 yr FT course in collaboration with St Andrew's College of Education. The course is designed primarily for students wishing to become class teachers of music in schools, and its successful completion leads to the award of a degree along with a Teaching Qualification (Secondary Education).Standards for entrance: Musical, normally equivalent to Grade 7 (ABRSM) in the Principal Study; Educational, passes in 3 subjects at SCE Higher Grade and in 2 other subjects at Standard Grade (Grades 1-3) or passes at GCE A Level (A-D) in at least 2 subjects and in 3 other subjects at GCSE Level (A-C). English at SCE Higher Grade or English Language and English Literature at GCE O Level is necessary. Admission is by competitive audition. Further details of this course are available from the Academic Registrar.

BA (Scottish Music): 3 yr FT course. Standards for entrance: Musical, a strong indication of performing is sought at the entrance audition for this course; Educational, as for the BMus (Performance) and BA (Musical Studies). Admission is by competitive audition.

MMus (Performance or Composition or Conducting): 1yr FT or 2 yrs PT. Entry is open to graduates or diplomates of universities, polytechnics or colleges who have already undertaken extensive study in the area of specialisation.

MMus (Opera or Advanced Opera): 1 yr FT. Entry to MMus (Opera) is open to graduates or diplomates of universities, polytechnics or colleges who have already undertaken extensive study in the area of specialisation. Entry to MMus (Advanced Opera) is only available to those who have completed the MMus (Opera) course or pursued equivalent operatic study at postgraduate level.

Postgraduate Diploma in Music: 1 yr FT course in Performance/Opera/Composition/Conducting/Teaching. Teaching course also available PT over 2.5 yrs. Entry open to graduates of conservatoires or music colleges.

TRINITY COLLEGE OF MUSIC

Mandeville Place, London W1M 6AQ Tel: 020 7935 5773 Fax: 020 7224 6278
e-mail: info@tcm.ac.uk Website: www.tcm.ac.uk

INTERNAL COURSES:

BMus (Hons) Degree: 4 yrs FT. The BMus (Hons) course is a performance-centred course, which builds the student's all-round skills and confidence in addition to technique. Through a series of projects and core and elective modules, students cover every aspect of being a professional musician: exercising imagination; strengthening practice, rehearsal and performance skills; selecting repertoire concert and project planning; recording; dealing with finances and effective promotion.

Core modules develop and expand the instrumental, vocal, compositional or conducting skills of the student. Performance projects involve students in using these skills in real-life situations. Core modules include: Principal Study (including weekly one-to-one tuition); Large Group and Small Group Performance (including Composition Performance); Applied Performance Projects; Departmental Studies; Contextual Studies; and Musicianship.

Elective modules give students the opportunity to specialise in areas beyond their Principal Study. A selection of elective modules is offered in the third and fourth yrs. The options variously include: Alexander Technique; Analysis; Applied Music and Video Technology; Arrangement and Musical Direction; Choral Conducting; Dalcroze Eurythmics; Improvisation; Instrumental Conducting; Kod ly Musicianship; Languages; Music Business Management (final yr only); Music Therapy (final yr only); Musical Techniques; Performance Practice and Historical Perspectives; Additional Instrumental or Vocal Study (subject to approval by the Head of Department).

BA (Hons) Performance and Teaching Studies (available to non-EU students only): This course offers English language support alongside the programme structure at no extra cost to the student. The course integrates all the areas of study (performance, performance-teaching skills and theoretical elements) and is designed for aspiring instrumentalists, vocalists and teachers of music performance. Students complete the first yr of their course at Chichester College of Arts, Science and Technology, in the College's purpose-designed music block. There they benefit from the support offered by Chichester College's International Department and the in-house intensive English language tuition offered within it. Principal Study lessons are at the heart of the course. Additional performance-centred modules develop and expand the instrumental or vocal skills of the student and these are integrated with a full range of supporting academic studies. A wide choice of elective modules allows specialisation in areas beyond the core modules.

Core modules include Principal Study (including weekly one-to-one tuition); Rehearsal Skills and Chamber Music; Performance Practice and Historical Studies; Applied Theoretical Studies; Pedagogy and Music and Information Technologies. A selection of optional credit-bearing **elective modules** is offered in yrs 2 and 3 of the course, from the following: Alexander Technique; Applied Music Technology; Arrangement and Musical Direction; Choral Conducting; Dalcroze Eurythmics; Improvisation; Instrumental Conducting; Kod ly Musicianship; Music Business Management; Music Therapy; Personal Project and Languages (French, German, Italian, Spanish or Japanese). In addition, English language coaching is available throughout the course if required.

MMus Degree in Performance Studies: 1yr FT. This course emphasises individual attainment in performance, and offers an imaginative, complementary Academic Studies programme as an essential element of an integrated approach to advanced performance training. The Performance component for 2000/2001 offers Principal Study options in Solo Performance; Chamber Music; Conducting; Organ and Church Music Studies; or Piano Accompaniment. Special features of the MMus include a Mentor Scheme and Approved Professional Studies. The Academic component is designed to support the performer in developing familiarity with a representative selection of performance practice sources and texts, practical research techniques and a working knowledge of the principles of preparing a performance edition from source material.

MA (Music Education): 1yr FT/2-3 yrs PT. This degree has been designed to facilitate PT study by those who wish to continue their work without a career break. It provides for the continuing development of the professional performer, the teacher or the composer who wishes to continue their professional career while undertaking studies directly related to their own work situation. It is also available as a 1 yr, FT course to new graduates who wish to acquire the specialist skills needed in education or community based music projects.

Fellowship Diploma in Music (FTCL): A postgraduate diploma in performance for all instruments and voice, or in composition. Candidates must already hold the LTCL Diploma in the same subject.

Licentiate Diploma in Performance or Instrumental/Vocal Teaching (LTCL): A practical diploma for which candidates must already hold the AMusTCL written diploma (and for teachers ATCL in the same subject as well).

Licentiate Diploma in Music Theory, Composition and Literacy (LMusTCL): Written diploma – one 3 hr paper.

Associate Diploma in Performance (ATCL): All instruments and voice. ATCL(Recital) option which includes performances only.

Associate Diploma in Music Theory and Analysis (AMusTCL): Written diploma – one 3 hr paper.

Individualised Programmes of Study: These can be arranged for students from home and overseas. They will receive 1 1/2 hrs of individual tuition a wk. In addition they may attend such classes as are suited to their course of study.

Postgraduate Certificate, Diploma and Advanced Diploma: 1yr FT/2-3 yrs PT. These courses are designed for graduates of strong performance ability to develop their musical technique and informed performance. Students receive 1 1/2 hrs of individualised tuition a wk, watching and performance opportunities, solo and ensemble.

WELSH COLLEGE OF MUSIC AND DRAMA

Castle Grounds, Cathays Park, Cardiff CF10 3ER Tel: 029 2034 2854 Fax: 029 2039 1304
 e-mail: Music@wcmd.ac.uk Website: www.wcmd.ac.uk

BMus (Hons): Throughout all 4 yrs a minimum of 50% is devoted to practical performance through the student's Principal Study and the Professional Studies module which encompasses chamber music, larger ensembles and bands, orchestras, choral and operatic work in addition to solo performance. The normal entrance criterion is two grade Cs at A level, however an exceptional candidate with a high level of practical performance may be accepted with lower grades or with alternative qualifications.

MMus: It may be taken as a 1 yr FT course or a 2 yr PT course. Intended for singers and instrumentalists who have already reached a high standard in performance and wish to develop their creative, critical and analytical skills. Grants are discretionary. Designated for mandatory grant aid.

Advanced Diploma in Music: A course of intensive study in Performance, Instrumental or Vocal Teaching, Early Music, Jazz, Composition, Conducting, Music Technology or Repetiteur Training. May be taken as a 1 yr FT course or as a 2 yr PT course. Grants are discretionary.

HND Performing Arts (Popular Music): A 2 yr course at pass degree level which aims to provide technical and vocational skill training for all aspects of the commercial and popular music industries. Designated for mandatory grant aid. Course details: Tel: 01639 634271.

Postgraduate Diploma in Music Therapy: A 1 yr FT postgraduate training course in music therapy leading. Successful candidates gain a postgraduate diploma and are qualified to seek employment as music therapists.

Grade Examinations

THE ASSOCIATED BOARD OF THE ROYAL SCHOOLS OF MUSIC

(Incorporating the Royal Academy of Music; Royal College of Music; Royal Northern College of Music; and the Royal Scottish Academy of Music and Drama)

24 Portland Place, London WC1B 3JG Tel: 020 7636 5400 Fax: 020 7637 0234
 e-mail: abrsm@abrsm.ac.uk Website: www@abrsm.ac.uk

The Associated Board is an international examining body which offers a system of graded music examinations in over 80 countries around the world. The Associated Board was established in 1889 to provide schools, private teachers of music and the general public with a scheme of music examinations of recognised authority. The Board offers a scheme of examinations suitable for candidates at different stages of ability in keyboard, stringed, woodwind, brass and percussion instruments, jazz piano, jazz ensembles, singing, practical musicianship, instrumental ensembles, choral singing and theory. The Board's practical examinations start with a Preparatory Test followed by the numbered grades. The Grades commence at Grade 1 and are numbered progressively in order of difficulty to Grade 8 which leads on to diploma examinations. There are 3 levels of diploma: DipABRSM, LRSM and FRSM. At each level there are 3 subject lines: Performing, Teaching or Directing. The

CT ABRSM Professional Development Course for instrumental and singing teachers is a PT course running at Regional Centres. It is intended for both new and established teachers, and while no formal qualifications are required for entrance, students should have at least 1 yr's teaching experience. Students who successfully complete the course are awarded the Certificate of Teaching, and are entitled to use the letters CT ABRSM after their names.

Membership of Professional Institutions and Associations

THE INCORPORATED SOCIETY OF MUSICIANS

10 Stratford Place, London W1N 9AE Tel: 020 7629 4413 Fax: 020 7408 1538
e-mail: membership@ism.org Website: www.ism.org
Chief Executive: Neil Hoyle

MEMBERSHIP:

Full Members: Professional musicians, normally holding recognised qualifications or equivalent skills, who are elected to the Society. They receive a fully comprehensive package of services, and are entitled to stand for office and vote. There are about 4,500 Full Members.

Associate Members: Usually amateurs and music lovers, though professionals can apply for this category if they wish. They receive a limited package of benefits and rights. There are about 300 Associate Members.

Student Members: Must be engaged in study for a recognised professional musical qualification. They receive a limited package of benefits and rights, geared to young musicians' needs. There are about 120 Student Members.

Corporate Members: Businesses, organisations, colleges and schools who wish to support the Society and its work. They are entitled to benefits such as major discounts on advertising, and have a special representative on the Society's Council. There are about 150 Corporate Members.

EXAMINATIONS:

The ISM is a professional association. It does not conduct exams, though it publishes registers of specialists among its members – performers and composers, musicians in education and private teachers – who have, in the Society's view, attained certain minimum levels of professional merit.

University Qualifications

The following universities offer qualifications in Music and related subjects. Full details may be found in Part 4, under the entry for the appropriate university.

FIRST DEGREES AWARDED BY UNIVERSITIES

Anglia; Anglia (Colchester Institute); Barnsley; Bath Spa; Belfast; Birmingham; Brighton; Bristol; Brunel; Bucks. Coll.; Cambridge; Central England; Central Lancashire; City; Coventry; De Montfort, Leicester; Derby; Durham; East Anglia; Edinburgh; Exeter; Exeter (Truro College); Glasgow; Glasgow Caledonian; Hertfordshire; Huddersfield; Hull; Keele; Kent (Canterbury Christ Church University College); Kingston; Lancaster; Leeds; Leeds (Bretton Hall); Leeds (Leeds College of Music); Leeds (The College of Ripon & York St John); Leeds Metropolitan; Liverpool; Liverpool (Liverpool Hope University College); London (Goldsmiths College); London (Imperial College of Science, Technology & Medicine); London (King's College London); London (Royal Holloway); London (School of Oriental & African Studies); London Guildhall; Manchester; Manchester Metropolitan.; Middlesex; Napier; Newcastle; Northampton; Nottingham; OU (Northern College of Education); Oxford; Oxford Brookes; Plymouth; Plymouth (Dartington College of Arts); Reading; Royal Scottish AMD; Salford; Sheffield; South Bank; Southampton; Southampton (Chichester Institute of Higher Education); St Martin; Staffordshire; Strathclyde; Sunderland; Surrey; Surrey (University of Surrey Roehampton); Sussex; Thames Valley; Ulster;

Wales (Cardiff University); Wales (Swansea Institute of Higher Education); Wales (University of Wales Institute, Cardiff); Wales (University of Wales, Bangor); Westminster; Wolverhampton; York

HIGHER DEGREES AWARDED BY UNIVERSITIES

Aberdeen; Anglia; Anglia (Colchester Institute); Bath Spa; Belfast; Birmingham; Bristol; Bucks. Coll.; Cambridge; Central England; City; City (Guildhall School of Music & Drama); City (The Centre for Nordoff-Robbins Music Therapy); Durham; East Anglia; Edinburgh; Exeter; Glasgow; Hertfordshire; Huddersfield; Hull; Keele; Kingston; Lancaster; Leeds; Leeds (Leeds College of Music); Liverpool; Liverpool (Liverpool Hope University College); London (Goldsmiths College); London (Institute of Education); London (King's College London); London (Royal Holloway); London (School of Oriental & African Studies); Manchester; Middlesex; Newcastle; Nottingham; Oxford; Plymouth (Dartington College of Arts); Reading; Royal Scottish AMD; Salford; Sheffield; Southampton; Southampton (Chichester Institute of Higher Education); St Martin; Surrey; Surrey (University of Surrey Roehampton); Sussex; Ulster; Wales (Cardiff University); Wales (University of Wales, Bangor); York

DIPLOMAS AWARDED BY UNIVERSITIES

Anglia; Bath Spa; Blackburn; Brighton; Bristol; Bucks. Coll.; Central England; City; Doncaster; Durham (New College Durham); Edinburgh; Hertfordshire; Hull; Leeds; Leeds (Leeds College of Music); Lincolnshire (Hull College); Manchester; Newcastle; Reading; Royal Scottish AMD; Salford; Teesside; Thames Valley; Ulster

CERTIFICATES AWARDED BY UNIVERSITIES

Anglia; Bath Spa; Brighton; Huddersfield; Leeds (Leeds College of Music); Leeds Metropolitan; Leicester; London (Goldsmiths College); London (King's College London); Middlesex; North London; Oxford (Westminster College, Oxford); Salford; Sunderland; Sussex; Ulster; Wales (University of Wales Institute, Cardiff); Wales (University of Wales, Bangor)

National Certificates and Diplomas

BTEC National Certificates/Diplomas: Music Technology; Popular Music
BTEC Higher National Certificates/Diplomas: Music Technology

NVQs

Level 4: Music Performance

Other Awards

The Archbishop of Canterbury's Diploma in Church Music (ADCM): Open to members of any Church which is a member of the World Council of Churches and to members of the Roman Catholic Church. Only those who have already obtained the Fellowship Diploma and the Choir-Training Diploma of the Royal College of Organists are eligible to enter for the exam. The exam takes the form of written papers and is administered by the Royal School of Church Music, Cleveland Lodge, Westhumble, Dorking, Surrey, RH5 6BW Tel 01306 877676 Fax 01306 887260.

'Canterbury' or 'Lambeth' degrees: By tradition and by virtue of his former office of Papal Legate, the Archbishop of Canterbury has the power to grant degrees, including a doctorate of music **(DMusCantuar).** This degree may from time to time be conferred on musicians of merit, including cathedral organists.

Fellow of the Royal School of Church Music (FRSCM): For distinguished services to Church Music.

Associate of the Royal School of Church Music (ARSCM): For those who have distinguished themselves in their chosen field of Church Music.

OPERATIC TRAINING:

The National Opera Studio, Morley College, 61 Westminster Bridge Road, LondonSE1 7HT Tel 0171-928 6833/261 9267 Fax 0171-928 1810.The Studio caters for advanced postgraduate trainees on the brink of the profession and for the needs of young professional singers under engagement, or likely to obtain engagement, with an Opera Company. It does not set any exams or award any qualifications, but was set up by the Arts Council as a purely professional training body. Levels of membership: 12 Singers and 3 Repetiteurs per yr.

MUSICAL INSTRUMENT TECHNOLOGY

Membership of Professional Institutions and Associations

THE INCORPORATED SOCIETY OF ORGAN BUILDERS

Secretary, D M van Heck,, Freepost,, Liverpool L3 3AB

MEMBERSHIP:

Fellow (FISOB): A person shall only be admitted as a Fellow if he or she holds a position of authority in the craft of organ building and has been an Associate Member for not less than 5 yrs; or has had recognised training in the craft of organ building and 15 yrs' practical experience (excluding the period of recognised training), and has both passed such exam or exams (if any) as the Council may require.

Ordinary Member (MISOB): A person shall only be admitted as an Ordinary Member if he or she has had recognised training in the craft of Organ Building and has had 5 yrs' experience (excluding a period of recognised training) in the craft; and is sponsored by 2 Members of the Society (other than Students), and holds a recognised Certificate of Competence in the craft of Organ Building or has passed such exam or exams as the Council may determine.

Associate Member (AISOB): A person shall only be admitted as an Associate Member if he or she has been an Ordinary Member of the Society for not less than 5 yrs; or has had recognised training in the craft and 10 yrs' practical experience in such craft (excluding a period of recognised training); and has both passed such exam or exams (if any) as the Council may determine.

Student Member: A person shall only be admitted as a Student Member if he or she is undergoing recognised training in the craft of Organ Building; or has entered upon but not completed 5 yrs' practical experience (excluding a period of recognised training) in such craft; and is sponsored by a Fellow, Counsellor, Associate or Ordinary Member of the Society.

Counsellor (CISOB): A person shall only be admitted as a Counsellor if (though failing to qualify as a Student, Ordinary Member, Associate Member or Fellow of the Society) he or she holds and has held a position of responsibility in the craft of organ building for more than 10 yrs and is both sponsored by 2 Members, and is accepted by the Council.

PIANOFORTE TUNERS' ASSOCIATION

10 Reculver Road, Herne Bay, Kent CT6 6LD Tel: 01227 368808 Fax: 01227 368808
Website: www.pianotuner.org.uk.

MEMBERSHIP:

Membership: A candidate must: (a) *either* (i) have trained as a Pianoforte Tuner Technician or Maker in a reputable factory or workshop for not less than 3 yrs, or have completed an approved course in Pianoforte Tuning or Technical studies at a recognised college and have gained the proficiency certificate, and have subsequently earned his or her living as a Pianoforte Tuner, Technician or Maker for a period (at least 2 yrs), which combined with the training period, is at least 5 yrs *or* (ii) have earned his or her living as a Pianoforte Tuner, Technician or Maker for at least 7 yrs; and (b) at the time of application, currently be engaged FT in the piano industry; and (c) *either* (i) pass a test of tuning and elementary repairs plus an oral test of knowledge of tuning, construction and repair of pianos, *or* if applying for Technician Membership (ii) pass an assessment of practical ability in a specialist field of piano technology.

Associateship: May be granted by the Executive Council to any applicant who must: (a) *either* (i) have trained as a Pianoforte Tuner, Technician or Factory Operative in a reputable factory for not less than 3 yrs or have gained an approved course from a recognised College *or* (ii) be a member of another tuners' association and satisfy the Executive Council that his tuning proficiency can be shown to be of a satisfactory standard or have earned a living as a Pianoforte Tuner for at least 7yrs; and (b) at the time of application, currently be engaged in the piano industry.

Student: Receiving instruction in a training establishment or workshops acceptable to the PTA, or who has received instruction as above and gained the necessary proficiency certificate may be registered as PTA Students and may attend all PTA General Meetings on a non-voting basis. They may not publicly advertise their Registration and may not use the PTA name or emblem.

Patrons: Any person may become a Patron of the PTA upon payment of an annual subscription.

He or she will be invited to all General Meetings on a non-voting basis, but may not publicly advertise their PTA connection or use the PTA name or emblem for the purpose of business.

University Qualifications

The following universities offer qualifications in Musical Instrument Technology and related subjects. Full details may be found in Part 4, under the entry for the appropriate university.

FIRST DEGREES AWARDED BY UNIVERSITIES
Anglia; York

National Certificates and Diplomas

BTEC National Certificates/Diplomas: Musical Instrument Technology
BTEC Higher National Certificates/Diplomas: Musical Instrument Technology
Scotland
SQA HNC: Musical Instrument Technology; Music Technology
SQA HND: Stringed Keyboard Instrument Technology; Repair and Restoration; Stringed Instrument Technology: Repair and Construction; Wind Instrument Technology: Repair and Construction

City & Guilds

5630 Stringed Keyboard Instrument Manufacture

Other Qualifications

National Diploma for Visually Impaired Pianoforte Tuners: Awarded by the Association for the Education and Welfare of the Visually Handicapped: normally taken after a training course at the Royal National College for the Blind, although candidates may be allowed to enter if they have taken a comparable course of training. The exam consists of 3 sections:
Section 1: The candidate is required to show their ability in the following: chipping up; tuning a piano at the existing pitch; raising or lowering the pitch.
Section 2: A practical test of repairs, diagnosis and correction of faults.
Section 3: A viva voce exam on the technical, professional and commercial aspects of the piano trade. For more information contact: Hon Secretary, 8 Baldock Street, Ware, Hertfordshire SG12 9DZ Tel & Fax 01920 469485.

NAVAL ARCHITECTURE

Membership of Professional Institutions and Associations

THE ROYAL INSTITUTION OF NAVAL ARCHITECTS

10 Upper Belgrave Street, London SW1X 8BQ Tel: 020 7235 4622 Fax: 020 7259 5912
e-mail: membership@rina.org.uk
MEMBERSHIP:
Membership of The Royal Institution of Naval Architects is international, reflecting the global nature of naval architecture and the maritime industry, and provides access to the wide range of benefits and services which RINA is able to offer. There are 7 grades of RINA membership to suit all those involved or interested in naval architecture and maritime technology, whether in a technical capacity or in non-technical occupations. The grades of membership reflect the levels of education, training, experience and professional responsibility achieved.
Fellow (FRINA): Persons who have held a position of superior professional responsibility in the fields of naval architecture or maritime engineering.
Member (MRINA): Persons who are primarily concerned with the progress of maritime technology through innovation, creativity and change, the development and use of new

technologies, the promotion and use of advanced design and production methods, and the pioneering of new engineering services and management techniques in the field of naval architecture and maritime technology.

Associate Member: Persons who are primarily concerned with the management of existing technology at peak efficiency, in the fields of naval architecture and maritime technology, with managerial responsibility as leaders of teams or with individual responsibility at a high level.

Associate: Persons who are primarily concerned with the application of proven engineering techniques to the solution of practical problems in the fields of naval architecture and maritime technology.

Graduate Member: Persons who have gained the academic qualification and are undertaking the training required for the grade of Member, Associate Member or Associate.

Student Member: Persons who have achieved or are studying to achieve the academic qualification required for Graduate Member.

Companion: Persons who are interested or involved in naval architecture and maritime engineering, but whose professional qualifications and experience were gained in other fields. Further information on the requirements for membership and advice on application may be obtained from the Membership Department at the above address.

University Qualifications

The following universities offer qualifications in Naval Architecture and related subjects. Full details may be found in Part 4, under the entry for the appropriate university.

FIRST DEGREES AWARDED BY UNIVERSITIES

Glasgow; London (University College (UCL)); Newcastle; Nottingham Trent (Southampton Institute); Southampton; Strathclyde

HIGHER DEGREES AWARDED BY UNIVERSITIES

London (University College (UCL))

DIPLOMAS AWARDED BY UNIVERSITIES

Glamorgan; Glasgow; London (University College (UCL))

City & Guilds

2410 Shipbuilding Craft Studies; 2420 Shipbuilding; 2450 Yacht and Boatbuilding and Ship Joinery Craft Studies

NAVIGATION, SEAMANSHIP AND MARINE QUALIFICATIONS

FISHING VESSEL CERTIFICATION – ENGINEER OFFICER

The **Fishing Vessels (Certification of Deck Officers and Engineer Officers) Regulations 1984** require sea-going vessels with propulsive power of 750 kW or more to carry at least two qualified Engineer Officers, the Chief Engineer to hold a **(Fishing Vessel) Class 1 Certificate** and the Second Engineer to hold at least a **(Fishing Vessel) Class 2 Certificate** regardless of the vessel's length, tonnage and area of operation.

Engineer Officer (Fishing Vessel) Class 2: To qualify for the issue of a Certificate of Competency as Engineer Officer (Fishing Vessel) Class 2, a candidate must be not less than 19, have completed a period of sea-service in an engineering capacity on fishing vessels of not less than 100 kW propulsive power (ranging from 6 mths for those with a full engineering apprenticeship to 30 mths for those with no formal engineering training) and then passed the required test and examination.

Engineer Officer (Fishing Vessel) Class 1: To qualify for the issue of a Certificate of Competency as Engineer Officer (Fishing Vessel) Class 1 a candidate must have performed at least 21 mths watch-keeping sea-service as an Engineer Officer on a vessel with propulsive power of 750 kW or more and passed the required test and examination.

The Fishing Vessels Officers Regulations are due to be revised soon to take on board the recently developed system of Vocational Qualification.

FISHING VESSEL CERTIFICATION – DECK

The **Fishing Vessels (Certification of Deck Officers and Engineer Officers) Regulations 1984** require sea-going fishing vessels of 16.5m or more in length to have certificated officers, the number and type of certificates being dependent on the size and power of the vessel and the area of operation, whether within the limited area or in unlimited area. The provision for issue of the Certificate of Service based on experience alone no longer exists.

Deck Officer (Fishing Vessel) Class 3: This is a voluntary qualification in the sense that one can also take the Class 2 examination without having obtained Class 3. A candidate for the Class 3 certificate must be not less than 19, have served 2 yrs on board fishing vessels with at least 18 mths in a deck capacity and then have passed the required test and examination.

Deck Officer (Fishing Vessel) Class 2: A candidate must be not less than 20, have served at least 3 yrs at sea in an acceptable deck capacity, 2 yrs of which on board a fishing vessel not less than 12m long and then have passed the required test and examination.

Deck Officer (Fishing Vessel) Class 1: A candidate must be not less than 21 yrs of age; have served as a watch-keeping deck officer in fishing vessels not less than 12m long whilst holding a Deck Officer Certificate of Competency (Fishing Vessel) Class 2 for either 12 mths in fishing vessels operating in unlimited waters or 6 mths in fishing vessels operating in unlimited waters plus 12 mths in fishing vessels operating in limited waters or at least 2 yrs in fishing vessels operating within limited waters and then have passed the required test and examination. The Fishing Vessels Officers Regulations are due to be revised soon to meet the requirements of the recently adopted International Convention on Standards of Training, Certification and Watch-keeping for Fishing Vessel Personnel, 1995, and to take on board the recently developed system of Vocational Qualifications.

Membership of Professional Institutions and Associations

THE NAUTICAL INSTITUTE

202 Lambeth Road, London SE1 7LQ Tel: 020 7928 1351 Fax: 020 7401 2817
e-mail: sec@nautinst.org Website: www.nautinst.org

MEMBERSHIP:
Fellows (FNI): Must have held positions of superior professional responsibility, been a member for 5 yrs and made a significant contribution to the advancement of Nautical Science and the nautical profession.

Members (MNI): Must hold: (a) a British Foreign-Going Master's Certificate of Competency or a similar qualification recognised by Council; (b) the appropriate ship command exam in the seaman specialisation of the Royal Navy; (c) a First Class Licence issued by a recognised Pilotage Authority and 3 yrs' experience as a 1st class pilot.

Associate Members (AMNI): Must hold: (a) British Class III Certificate of Competency or its equivalent; (b) a Royal Naval Bridge Watchkeeping Certificate with an Ocean Navigation Certificate or a similar qualification approved by Council.

Associates: Must hold a Class V Certificate of Competency and be at least 19.

Companions: Any person such as a naval architect, marine engineer or yachtsman, not being a qualified member of the Nautical Profession, satisfies Council that his or her association with the Institute will promote the general advancement or application of Nautical Science.

Students: Must be at least 16, be undergoing a course of training approved by the Council and intend to become Associate Members of the Institute.

EXAMINATIONS:
The Harbour Masters Certificate
The Nautical Surveyors Certificate
The Dynamic Positioning Operators Certificate
The Command Diploma

Pilotage Certificate
Management Diploma
Square Rig Sailing Ship Certificate

THE ROYAL INSTITUTE OF NAVIGATION

1 Kensington Gore, London SW7 2AT Tel: 020 7591 3130 Fax: 020 7591 3131
e-mail: info@rin.org.uk Website: www.rin.org.uk

MEMBERSHIP:

Honorary Members (HonMRIN): Distinguished persons on whom the Institute wishes to confer an honorary distinction.

Fellows (FRIN): Must have been Members for at least 3 yrs, holding certain qualifications, which include having made a contribution of value to Navigation.

Members (MRIN): Must be not less than 21 and must satisfy the Institute of their interest in Navigation.

Student Members: Must be under 25 and be studying at a recognised school or university with a view to making Navigation or an allied interest their career.

Corporate Members: Companies, schools, universities, government departments and similar organisations at home and abroad who are directly or indirectly interested in the science of Navigation.

Associates: Those wishing to join a special interest group and who feel that full membership is inappropriate.

Junior Associates: Those 18 or under with an interest in navigation.

University Qualifications

The following universities offer qualifications in Navigation, Seamanship and Marine Qualifications and related subjects. Full details may be found in Part 4, under the entry for the appropriate university.

FIRST DEGREES AWARDED BY UNIVERSITIES

Liverpool John Moores; Nottingham Trent (Southampton Institute); Plymouth

HIGHER DEGREES AWARDED BY UNIVERSITIES

Bournemouth; City; Exeter; Hull; Liverpool John Moores; Nottingham; Plymouth; Portsmouth; St Andrews; Wales (Cardiff University)

DIPLOMAS AWARDED BY UNIVERSITIES

Hull; Plymouth; St Andrews

CERTIFICATES AWARDED BY UNIVERSITIES

Warwick

National Certificates and Diplomas

BTEC National Certificates/Diplomas: Maritime Technology; Nautical Science
BTEC Higher National Certificates/Diplomas: Marine Operations; Maritime Technology; Nautical Science

SVQs

Level 2: Merchant Vessel Operations
Level 3: Merchant Vessel Engineering; Merchant Vessel Operations
Level 4: Merchant Vessel Engineering; Merchant Vessel Operations

Education and Training for the Merchant Navy

There are 3 principal types of qualified officer in the Merchant Navy – Navigating (or Deck) Officers, Engineer Officers and Radio Officers. The training schemes are being amended to include N/SVQs, and the Merchant Navy Training Board is the industry lead body for this. For further information contact Mr R Matthews, Director, The Merchant Navy Training Board, Carthusian Court, 12 Carthusian Street, London EC1M 6EB.

Deck Department

Deck Officer Class 5: This is a Navigational Watch-keeping certificate for near-coastal voyages (Limited European Trading Area). Candidate must not be less than 19 and must have served at sea on ordinary trading vessels in the deck department for 42 mths. At least 6 mths of the last 12 mths must have been spent on navigational watch-keeping duties on the Bridge under supervision of a certificated officer. Three wks' remission of sea-service for attendance at an ENS course and 3 mths for completion of an approved preparatory course will be given.

Deck Officer Class 4: This is an unrestricted Navigational Watch-keeping certificate. The sea-service and other qualifying requirements are same as for Deck Officer Class 5 except that those following an approved cadet training programme will require 20-30 mths' sea-service. Holders of Deck Officer Class 5 certificates may also take the Class 4 exam in which case he/she will be exempted from the Coastal Navigation paper in the written exam.

Deck Officer Class 3: There is no qualifying sea-service requirement for the Class 3 Bridging exam which comprises written exams in Applied Science, Mathematics (Pure and Applied) and Principles of Navigation. Candidates may take this exam at the same time as, or even before, completing Class 4, but a certificate of competency as Deck Officer Class 3 will not be issued before the candidate has qualified for the issue of a Class 4 certificate. Persons having passed GCE A level (or equiv) in Physics and Mathematics (A to E grade) may be exempted from these 2 subjects, and persons holding National Diploma in Nautical Science which includes all three Bridging subjects may be exempted from Class 3 exam.

Deck Officer Class 2: This is the unrestricted Chief Officer's certificate. A candidate must be not less than 21, must have qualified for the issue of Class 3 certificate and have served for not less than 12 mths at sea as Bridge Watch-keeping Officer in ordinary trading vessels while holding a certificate of competency not less than Class 4. At least 6 mths of this period must have been served in vessels trading between places: at least one of these places should be situated beyond the limits of the Limited European Area and the most distant ports visited should be at least 500 miles apart. Candidates who are unable to meet this requirement will be admitted to the exams but any resulting certificate will be endorsed to limit its use.

Deck Officer Class 1 Master Mariner (NVQ LEVEL 5): This is the unrestricted Master's certificate. A candidate must be not less than 23 and must have 42 mths' watch-keeping service of which at least 18 mths must have been while holding a Class 2 certificate. At least 18 mths of this total period of 3½ yrs must be served in vessels trading between places at least one of which is situated beyond the limits of the Limited European Area and where the most distant ports visited are at least 500 miles apart. Candidates who are unable to meet this requirement will be admitted to the exams but any resulting certificate will be endorsed to limit its use to within the Limited European Area only.

Extra Master: The exam for an Extra Master's certificate is voluntary and intended for officers who wish to prove their superior qualifications and have a certificate of the highest grade granted by the UK Administration. Details are given in Merchant Shipping Notice No M1126 obtainable free of charge from Marine Offices.

Command Endorsements: There are 2 levels of command endorsement exam. A candidate for any command endorsement must be not less than 23 yrs old and must have served 3 yrs at sea as a watch-keeping deck officer while holding a certificate of competency. Limited European Command Endorsement (CLE) is more suitable for tugs, dredgers, standby vessels, seismic and oceanographic survey vessels and other merchant ships of less than 1600 GT operating within the Limited European Area. A candidate must hold at least a Deck Officer Class 5 certificate. Extended European Command Endorsement (CEE) is suitable for those who intend to command vessels under 5000 GT operating within the Extended European Area. A candidate must hold a certificate of competency as Deck Officer of at least Class 4. Holders of a Deck Officer Class 2 certificate (obtained after December 1987) are exempted from the written part of the exam.

Dangerous Cargo Endorsements: Required for service on tankers in the capacity of Master or Chief Officer (also required for Chief and Second Engrs Officer). There are 3 types of DCE, ie Petroleum, Chemical and Gas, for respective types of tankers. An endorsement can be obtained by attending an appropriate shore-based Tanker Safety Course and then completing the required sea-service as below: a) 6 mths' service on a relevant type of tanker *or* b) 14 days' training followed by 3 mths' service *or* c 28 days' approved intensive shipboard training. Details, including a list of training centres, are given in M1549.

Restrictive Endorsements: Endorsements on certificates of competency (eg Voyages within Limited European Area only, Tug Service only, Standby vessels only, Dredgers only) are made where a candidate does not have the required trading ship or trading area experience. Such restrictions apply for service in a capacity higher than basic watch-keeping officer. An officer can acquire the required experience by serving as a watch-keeping officer on a trading ship or in the extended or unlimited trading areas so that the endorsement can be withdrawn.

Ancillary Courses: A candidate for a Deck Officer Certificate of Competency will also have to produce the following certificates before a certificate of competency can be issued: 1. Medical Fitness; 2. Eye-sight; 3. First Aid at Sea (valid for 5 yrs); 4. Efficient Deck Hand (EDH); 5. Certificate of Proficiency in Survival Craft (CPSC); 6. 4-day Fire-fighting course; 7 Global Maritime Distress & Safety System (GMDSS) Operator Licence; 8. Electronic Navigational System (ENS).Candidates for Class 2 and Command Endorsements have to undertake the following additional courses: Navigational Control Course (NCC) and Ship Captain's Medical Training (SCMT).

Ratings (Deck): Initial training comprises: 1-day Basic Sea Survival, 2-day Fire-fighting and Basic First Aid courses, which are available at the National Sea Training College, Gravesend, after which one can join a merchant ship as a Trainee Seaman. On completion of 2 mths' sea-service the trainee can be promoted/employed as Category 3 Seaman. On completion of 12 mths' service as a Deck Rating or 18 mths' service as General Purpose Rating (GP) and having obtained a Steering certificate, a Bridge Watch-rating certificate and an EDH certificate, the seaman can be employed as an Efficient Deck Hand or Category 2 Seaman. On completion of a further 24 mths' sea-service as a Deck or GP Rating and having obtained CPSC, the seaman can be employed as an AB or Category 1 Seaman. Details are given in M780, M1096 and M1501.

Ship's Cook's Certificate: Details are given in M1482.

List of Colleges: There are a number of colleges which provide preparatory courses leading to Deck Officers exams. The UK-MSA approved Cadet Training Scheme leads to Part I of HND (BTEC/SCOTVEC), covering the written syllabi of Class 4 & 3, and thereby providing exemption from the written subjects except for pure professional safety subjects conducted by SCOTVEC on behalf of the Marine Safety Agency (MSA). The written syllabus of Class 2 forms Part II of HND (BTEC/SCOTVEC) and entitles the successful candidates to Higher National Diploma; and the candidates then have to take only 2 more SCOTVEC papers as part of the written exam for Class 2 certificate (the other parts being Oral and Signal). Others who do not follow the full HND course but successfully complete a course of study equating to Deck Officers written syllabus are awarded Certificate of Achievement (BTEC/SCOTVEC) as evaluation of the written part of the syllabus (except for the MSA/SCOTVEC papers). Candidates with UK A levels or OND with Physics and Mathematics are exempted from these papers in Class 3 Bridging exam. Blackpool & the Fylde College, Fleetwood Nautical Campus, Broadwater, Fleetwood, Lancashire, FY7 8JZ Tel 01253 52352. Glasgow College of Nautical Studies, 21 Thistle Street, Glasgow, G5 9XB Tel 0141-429 3201. Liverpool John Moores University, School of Engineering & Technology Management, Byrom Street, Liverpool L3 3AF Tel 0151-231 2121. Lowestoft College of Further Education, Department of Maritime Studies, St Peters Street, Lowestoft, Suffolk NR32 2NB Tel 01502 583521. North Atlantic Fisheries College, Port Arthur, Scalloway, Shetland ZE1 OUN Tel 0159 588328. Southampton Institute of Higher Education, Warsash Campus, Newtown Road, Warsash, Southampton SO3 9ZL Tel 01489 576161. South Tyneside College, Faculty of Nautical Science, St George's Avenue, South Shields, Tyne & Wear NE34 6ET Tel 0191 4560403. The National Sea Training College, Denton, Gravesend, Kent DA12 2HR Tel 01474 363656.

Fishing Vessels: Initial training of a sea-going Fisherman (Deck Department), known as the Fishermen's Safety Training, comprises Basic Sea Survival, Basic First Aid and Basic Fire-fighting. Details are given in M1367.

Deck Officer (Fishing Vessel) Class 3: A candidate must be not less than 19 yrs of age, and have served 2 yrs on fishing vessels of which at least 18 mths has been in a deck capacity.

Deck Officer (Fishing Vessel) Class 2: A candidate must be not less than 20 yrs of age and have served at least 3 yrs at sea in an acceptable deck capacity of which a minimum of 2 yrs has been served on fishing vessels of not less than 12m in length. The holder of a Class 2 (FV) certificate will be eligible to be second in command of any fishing vessel and in charge of fishing vessels up to 24m in length operating within the Limited Area.

Deck Officer (Fishing Vessel) Class 1: A candidate must be not less than 21 yrs of age and have served as a deck watch-keeping officer in fishing vessels of not less than 12m in length whilst holding a deck officer certificate of competency (Fishing Vessel) Class 2 for either 12 mths in the Unlimited Area, or 6 mths in the Unlimited Area with a further 12 mths in the Limited Area, or 24 mths in the Limited Area (at the discretion of the Chief Examiner). The holder is eligible to command any fishing vessel in the Unlimited Area an also Standby and Survey vessels.

Training Centres: Details of training centres can be obtained from the Sea Fish Industry Training Authority, St Andrews's Dock, Hull HU3 4QE Tel 01482 27837.

Boatmasters' Licences: A Boatmaster's Licence is a requirement for a person in charge of a local passenger vessel (carrying more than 12 passengers). There are 3 grades of licence. The requirement for the Master of a local passenger vessel to hold a certain grade of licence depends on the area of operation and number of passengers carried. Details are given in M1525.

Yachts & Other Pleasure Craft: There are 2 types of Yachtmaster's certificate ie Off-shore and Ocean. These non-statutory certificates are issued by the Royal Yachting Association and are intended for those sailing in private pleasure craft of up to 80 GT. However, these qualifications can also be used by Skippers of pleasure craft of up to 24m in length when used commercially, provided the craft complies with the relevant Code of Practice. Such craft must not carry cargo or more than 12 passengers. Details can be obtained from the Royal Yachting Association, RYA House, Romsey Road, Eastleigh, Hants SO5 4YA Tel 01703-629962.

Vocational Qualifications (N/SVQ): Persons aspiring for Certificates of Competency both in the Merchant Navy as well as the Fishing industry can now also follow the N/SVQ route. Approved Training Centres will act as Assessment Centres and Oral examination will still be conducted by the MSA surveyors at MSA Marine Offices.

Radio-Communication: The **GMDSS (Global Maritime Distress & Safety system) Operator's Certificate** is issued by the Radio-communication Authority under the Department of Trade and Industry. The **Radio Maintenance Certificate** is issued by the Association of Marine Radio and Electronic Colleges under the authority of the Marine Safety Agency of the Department of Transport. Further information about both certificates can be obtained from the AMREC secretariat at the Wray Castle College, PO Box 4, Ambleside, Cumbria LA22 OJB Tel 015394 32320.

Deck Officer

The main entry is as a cadet aged 16-19 under scheme (a) or (b): however, (c) offers entry to those who wish to take a degree course immediately after leaving school or who may have embarked on such a course before deciding to seek a career at sea, while (d) and (e) provide scope for those who, while not having quite the academic qualifications normally required, are considered to be in all other respects suitable and of good potential.

(a) BTEC and SQA Diplomas: Entry qualifications are 4 passes at GCE O level or SCE O grade (grade C or above) or equivalent, including mathematics, a science subject (preferably physics) and 2 other academic subjects, 1 of which must test command of the English language. The scheme usually takes the following pattern: Phase 1: Induction– a short familiarisation and safety course; Phase 2: Initial sea phase: sea service of about 9 mths. A planned study course provides continuity of academic work and an introduction to vocational studies. During this time the cadet begins his practical training; Phase 3: A residential training course held in a Nautical College; Phase 4: Sea service of approximately 12 mths; correspondence course and practical training; Phase 5: a residential college course leading to the BTEC or SQA Diploma and Class 4 Certificate exams. Candidates who have passed both for the Diploma and for Class 4 will qualify without further exam for Class 3. (The Scheme can be extended to Higher Diploma level, studies for which are continued at sea and completed when the candidate takes his Class 2 Certificate.)

(b) A level entrant scheme: Entry requirements are at least 5 GCE passes at Grade C or above, or equivalents; 1 subject must be English or a subject testing the use of English. 2 subjects must be at A level, 1 of which must be mathematics or physics; where only 1 A level is held it must be mathematics or physics but 2 subjects must have been studied to A level. The scheme is broadly similar in pattern to BTEC but with shorter college phases and leading directly to the Class 3 exam. Candidates may be exempt from certain subjects in that exam, depending on A level passes.

(c) Graduate Entry Scheme: A postgraduate scheme for prospective officers who have a suitable degree, run by the Liverpool Polytechnic in conjunction with certain shipping companies, and offering those who wish to do so the opportunity to complete a degree course before going to sea. As with the A level scheme, the period of college training is reduced and the scheme leads directly to the Class 3 Certificate.

(d) Short Sea Trade Cadetship: A sponsored Cadetship offered by certain companies operating in the Limited and Extended Trading Areas (roughly UK, Scandinavia, the Baltic, the Mediterranean and NW Europe). It follows a sandwich pattern similar to that of BTEC and leads to the Class 4 exam. Successful candidates can then go to the Class 3 and the Higher Certificates, either in the limited or Deep Sea trades. Candidates must have reached O level in appropriate subjects and have passed in mathematics, English or a subject testing the use of English, and, preferably, in physics.

(e) Class 5 Scheme for Ratings: A sponsored training scheme following a sandwich pattern on the lines of that of BTEC and leading to the Class 5 exam. Trainees serve at sea as ratings but if they are successful they become qualified as junior officers in ships on the limited trades and may go on to Class 4 and 3 and then on to Higher Certificates in limited or Deep Sea trades. Training commences at the National Sea Training Coll, Gravesend, and entry requirements are at least 3 CSE passes (grade 3 or above) in mathematics, a suitable science subject (preferably physics) and a subject testing English; or a pass in an industry-approved entry test.

Engineer Officers : Certificates of Competency

British ships must carry certain engineer officers holding **Certificates of Competency** awarded or recognised by the DTp. Certificates of Competency are granted as follows:

Steam Certificates qualify the holders to serve as engineers in a statutory capacity in steamships.
Motor Certificates qualify the holders to serve as engineers in a statutory capacity in motor ships propelled by internal combustion reciprocating engines.
Combined Steam and Motor Certificates qualify the holders to serve as engineers in a statutory capacity in both steam and motor ships.
Service Endorsements to Certificates of Competency enable the officer to sail in the capacity of Chief Engineer on restricted vessels. There is also an **Extra First Class Certificate** which is awarded after exam and is intended for officers who wish to possess certificates of the highest grade granted by the DTp. This Certificate is a necessary qualification for some governmental and professional appointments. To qualify for the issue of a **Class 1, Class 2, Class 3 or Class 4** Certificate of Competency in the UK each candidate must: satisfy the initial training requirements set out below, have completed the qualifying sea service set out below, hold an approved and valid medical fitness certificate for sea service; pass the examination.
INITIAL TRAINING:
Workshop service or other industrial training completed before the age of 16 will not be accepted. Each candidate must have received one of the forms of training specified in 1, 2 and 3 as follows:
1. Engineer Cadet: Each such candidate must have satisfactorily completed 1 of the courses of engineer cadet training approved by the Department. Details of engineer cadet training schemes and the list of shipping companies participating in them can be obtained from the Merchant Navy Training Board (MNTB), 2/5 Minories, London EC3N 1BJ.
2. Engineering Craftsman: Each such candidate must have satisfactorily completed at least 3 yrs training in engineering craft practice to the satisfaction of the Department, or have completed the Engineering Industry Training Board (EITB) modular system of training for engineering craftsmen.
3. Engineer Graduate: Each such candidate must have satisfactorily completed a FT course of study to at least the standard of the HND in Engineering for a period of not less than 3 yrs at a polytechnic or university, together with 12 mths' engineering training to the satisfaction of the Department.
Engine room Rating to Engineer Officer Scheme: Each such rating satisfactorily completing a course of training approved by the Department may proceed to sea as an uncertificated engineer officer and perform the sea service set out below. Alternatively, qualifying sea service as an engine room rating, whilst in possession of the MNTB Motorman Certificate, and as nominated assistant to the engineer officer in charge of the watch will be considered provided it has been performed on completion of the course. Details of approved schemes can be obtained from the MNTB at the address given above.
Royal Navy Personnel: Engineer Officers who have specialised in marine engineering, marine engineering artificers and mechanicians, on active service or retired, may be examined for Certificates of Competency under the same conditions that apply to Merchant Navy personnel.
Engineer Officers – Certificates of Competency: To qualify for the issue of an initial certificate of

competency each candidate must have attended a 4-day fire fighting course and a first aid at sea course.

To qualify for the issue of a **Class 4 Certificate of Competency,** each candidate must have completed a period of qualifying sea service in ships of not less than 350 kilowatt registered power as follows:

1. Motor Certificate: 6 mths, of which at least 4 mths must have been spent in watch-keeping on the main propelling machinery of motor ships.

2. Steam Certificate: 6 mths, of which at least 4 mths must have been spent in watch-keeping on the boilers and main propelling machinery of steam ships.

3. Combined Certificate: 8 mths, of which at least 4 mths must have been spent in watch-keeping on the main propelling machinery of motor ships and at least 4 mths must have been spent in watch- keeping on the boilers and main propelling machinery of steam ships.

4. Service Endorsement: 6 mths, whilst in possession of a Class 4 Certificate of Competency. This service must be performed in motor ships for a Service Endorsement to a motor certificate and in steam ships for a Service Endorsement to a steam certificate.

To qualify for the issue of a **Class 3 Certificate of Competency,** each candidate must have completed a period of qualifying sea service in ships of not less than 350 kilowatt registered power as follows:

Class 3 Certificate: 12 mths, of which at least 8 mths must have been spent in watch-keeping on the main propelling machinery of motor ships. The remaining period may have been spent in watchkeeping on the main propelling or auxiliary machinery of motor or steam ships, or on day work.

Service Endorsement: 12 mths, whilst in possession of a Class 3 Certificate of Competency. This service must be performed in motor ships.

To qualify for the issue of a **Class 2 Certificate of Competency,** each candidate must have completed a period of qualifying sea service in ships of not less than 750 kilowatt registered power as follows:

1. Motor Certificate: 18 mths, of which at least 9 mths must have been spent in watch-keeping on the main propelling machinery of motor ships. The remaining period may have been spent in watch-keeping on the main propelling or auxiliary machinery of motor or steam ships, or on day work.

2. Steam Certificate: 18 mths, of which at least 9 mths must have been spent in watch-keeping on the boilers and main propelling machinery of steam ships. The remaining period may have been spent in watch-keeping on the main propelling or auxiliary machinery of motor or steam ships, or on day work.

3. Combined Certificate: 18 mths, of which at least 9 mths must have been spent in watch-keeping on the main propelling machinery of motor ships and at least 9 mths must have been spent in watch-keeping on the boilers and main propelling machinery of steam ships.

Service Endorsement: 12 mths, whilst in possession of a Class 2 Certificate of Competency, provided that this period together with the period of qualifying sea service actually performed before obtaining a Class 2 Certificate of Competency, exclusive of remission, amounts to not less than 36 mths. This additional service of not less than 12 mths must be performed on motor ships for a Service Endorsement to a motor certificate and in steam ships for a Service Endorsement to a steam certificate. Where a candidate is in possession of a Class 2 Combined Certificate of Competency, this additional service of not less than 12 mths may be performed in either motor ships or steam ships.

To qualify for the issue of a **Class 1 Certificate of Competency,** each candidate must have completed a period of qualifying sea service in ships of not less than 1,500 kilowatt registered power as follows:

1. Motor Certificate: 18 mths, of which at least 9 mths must have been spent in charge of a watch on motor ships of not less than 3,000 kilowatt registered power whilst holding a Class 2 Certificate of Competency, or as Chief Engineer Officer in motor ships whilst holding a Class 2 Motor Certificate of Competency with Service Endorsement.

2. Steam Certificate: 18 mths, of which at least 9 mths must have been spent in charge of a watch in steam ships of not less than 3,000 kilowatt registered power whilst holding a Class 2 Certificate of Competency, or as Chief Engineer Officer in steam ships whilst holding a Class 2 Steam Certificate of Competency with Service Endorsement. *Note.* Service on vessels of less than 3,000 kilowatt registered power may be considered at a reduced rate at the discretion of the Department.

Marine Engine Operator Licences Marine engine operator licences are issued for personnel serving as Chief Engineer on vessels having a registered power of less than 750 kilowatt and as Second Engineer on vessels having a registered power of less than 1,500 kilowatt when they are operating in specified areas.

Entry Requirements – Marine Engine Operator examination: Sea service or other industrial training completed before the age of 16 will not be accepted. 24 mths sea service in ships of not less than 200 kilowatt registered power or 2 yrs shore employment with an engineering background acceptable to the Department; and 10/12 wks basic engineering skills course which may be based on the MNTB syllabus for prospective Petty officer (Motorman) or similar DTp approved course, this requirement may be waived in certain cases where the shore employment is of suitable quality; and 6 mths qualifying sea service as a trainee marine engine operator in ships of not less than 200 kilowatt registered power before exam for the marine engine operator licence. Sea service and training may be performed in a dual purpose capacity provided such service is accurately described by appropriate entries in the crew agreement such as 'deck officer/trainee engine operator', and provided such service is covered by sea service testimonials which should state the type of main propelling machinery and the nature of the duties performed. The Department will be prepared to approve structured training programmes which provide sea service, basic engineering skills training and qualifying sea service as a trainee engine operator within a 24-mth period.

Entry Requirements – Senior Marine Engine Operator examination: 6 mths qualifying sea service as marine engine operator in ships of not less than 200 kilowatt registered power, whilst holding the marine engine operator licence.

Merchant Navy Certificates of Competency

Marine Safety Agency (an Executive Agency of the Department of Transport), Spring Place, 105 Commercial Road, Southampton SO15 1EG Tel 01703-329242 Fax 01703-329252

Senior Certification

After obtaining their Class 3 Certificate officers return to sea but must continue their studies in order to obtain higher qualifications. After some 18 mths' sea service they can sit for Class 2 (the qualification for a Chief Officer) and after a further 2 yrs at sea they may qualify as Master Mariner by passing the Class 1 exam. They can also study for a nautical degree, for the Extra Master Certificate, or in other aspects of shipping or general transport operations and management.

Useful Addresses

Merchant Navy Training Board, Carthusian Court, 12 Carthusian Street, London EC1M 6EZ
Tel: 020 7417 8400 Fax: 020 7276 2080
Ship Safe Training Group Ltd, 2nd Floor, 135 High Street, Rochester, Kent ME1 1EW
Tel: 01634 405252 Fax: 01634 405242
Maritime and Coastguard Agency, Bay 2/11, Spring Place, 105 Commercial Rd, Southampton, SO15 1EG Tel: 01703 329242 Fax: 01703 329252

NON-DESTRUCTIVE TESTING

Membership of Professional Institutions and Associations

THE BRITISH INSTITUTE OF NON-DESTRUCTIVE TESTING

1 Spencer Parade, Northampton NN1 5AA Tel: 01604 630124 Fax: 01604 231489
e-mail: info@bindt.org Website: www.bindt.org

MEMBERSHIP:
Honorary Fellow (HonFInstNDT): Distinguished persons intimately concerned with non-destructive testing or a science allied to it whom the Institute especially wishes to honour.

Honorary Member (HonMInstNDT): Any person whom the Institute wishes to honour is eligible for Honorary Membership.

Fellow (FInstNDT): Members of not less than 5 yrs' standing who have reached the age of 35 may be elected to Fellowship. The academic qualifications for Fellow are at degree level.

Member (MInstNDT): Persons who have reached 23 who have 5 yrs' non-destructive testing experience and hold a position of responsibility may be elected to Membership. The academic qualifications for Membership are at HNC level or NDT Certification at Level 3.

Graduate Members (GradInstNDT): Persons who have reached 21, who have 3 yrs' experience in non-destructive testing and a high degree of competence in any specific NDT method may be elected to Graduate Membership. The academic qualifications for Graduate Membership are at ONC level or NDT Certification at Level 2.

Practitioner Members (PInstNDT): Persons who have Level 1 Certification in NDT or academic qualifications at City & Guilds Part 2 Craft Level or equivalent, plus 3 yrs combined approved training and experience in NDT.

Corporate Members: Are eligible for registration as Chartered Engineer, Incorporated Engineer or Engineering Technician as appropriate to educational qualifications, NDT training, experience and age. Chartered Engineers and Incorporated Engineers can be registered in Europe with FEANI.

Student Members: Students of science, engineering, metallurgy or allied subjects and/or trainees or assistants engaged in the practice of non-destructive testing may be granted Student Membership. They receive a free Log-Book. The Institute also has **Subscribers, Licentiates, Companions** and **Associates** (firms and other organisations).

QUALIFICATIONS:
Personnel Certification in Non-Destructive Testing Ltd: PCN is an accredited independent certification body, complying with the criteria of European standard EN 45013. PCN is part of the Certification Services Division of the British Institute of Non-Destructive Testing.

NURSERY NURSING

COUNCIL FOR AWARDS IN CHILDREN'S CARE AND EDUCATION
(Incorporating CEYA and NNEB)

8 Chequer Street, St Albans, Hertfordshire AL1 3XZ Tel: 01727 847636 Fax: 01727 867609
Website: www.cache.org.uk
The Council enables professional workers in children's care and education to gain access to training and assessment so that they provide the highest quality service to children and families. The Council also acts as a focus for national standards in children's care and education.

QUALIFICATIONS:
For those who require a course of training before beginning work with children there are the **CACHE Certificate in Child Care and Education** and the **CACHE Diploma in Nursery Nursing (NNEB).** These are both college-based courses. Candidates are assessed through a series of assignments and a large percentage of time is spent in practical training in the workplace. Each course is designed to provide the level of underpinning knowledge and understanding needed for NVQs in Early Yrs Care and Education. The **Advanced Diploma in Child Care and Education (ADCE)** can also provide a bridge between further and higher education and professional development for those already working in this sector. CACHE has also developed Professional Development Awards in its short course programme. For those already working with children, the Council offers **NVQs in Early Yrs Care and Education** and **NVQs in Playwork.** Candidates are assessed to National Occupational Standards by qualified assessors. Registration is via approved NVQ Assessment Centres. Please write to the above address for general information leaflets and a full list of NVQ Assessment Centres and Study Centres.

We now also offer The Key Skills Units and the CACHE Specialist Teacher Assistant (STA) Award and have developed a new award with the NCMA, Developing Childminding Practice which will become the foundation of a national training scheme for childminders. Courses and awards are constantly being developed – contact CACHE for an up-to-date list.

THE SOCIETY OF NURSERY NURSING

40 Archdale Road, East Dulwich, London SE22 9HJ Tel: 020 8693 0555 Fax: 020 8693 0555 e-mail: snn@totalise.co.uk

MEMBERSHIP:

Fellow (FSNN): Must have: (a) reached the age of 30, and have passed the Certificate and the Diploma professional exam, or have been exempted from them; (b) been employed for at least 2 yrs in a nursery establishment; (c) produced a satisfactory letter from employers as well as 2 testimonials as to character and suitability; and (d) passed an assessment interview.

Associate (ASNN): Must have: (a) reached the age of 25, and have passed the Certificate and the Diploma professional exam, or have been exempted from them; (b) been employed for at least 2 yrs in a nursery or similar establishment; (c) produced a satisfactory letter from their employers as well as producing 2 testimonials as to character and suitability.

Graduates (GSNN): Must have passed the Certificate and the Diploma professional exam or have been exempted from them, as a result of passing other equivalent exams, but unable to fulfil the other conditions of Associate Membership. Holders of other nursery nursing qualifications, eg NNEB, BTEC, City & Guilds may apply for membership but must fulfil the other conditions as well.

EXAMINATIONS:

The Certificate exams are equivalent to NVQ Levels 1 & 2. The Diploma exams are equivalent to NVQs Level 3 & 4.The subjects for both the Certificate and the Diploma examinations are the same but the Diploma exam is of a higher level. To pass both Certificate and the Diploma exams, candidates must pass the theory and practical work placement assessment achieving 65%, pass a case study paper achieving 65%, pass the complementary studies paper achieving 65%, as well as passing the interview.

Subjects: The exam subjects are: (1) Child Development and Early Childhood; (2) Childcare and Health; (3) First Aid and Safety; (4) Social and Environmental Studies; (5) Subjects Affecting Special Needs; (6) Management Information Systems and Data Processing; (7) Legal Aspects of Nursery Nursing; (8) Psychological Aspects of Child Development; (9) Work Placement – Practical Experience and Training; (10) A Case Study on any subject chosen from the above.

Complementary Studies: Any 2 of the following: (1) Art and Craft; (2) Music and Drama; (3) Needlework; (4) Home Economics; (5) Literature; (6) Physical Education; (7) Woodwork; (8) A Foreign Language.

University Qualifications

The following universities offer qualifications in Nursery Nursing and related subjects. Full details may be found in Part 4, under the entry for the appropriate university.

FIRST DEGREES AWARDED BY UNIVERSITIES

Birmingham (Birmingham College of Food, Tourism and Creative Studies); Brighton; Derby

HIGHER DEGREES AWARDED BY UNIVERSITIES

Leeds Metropolitan

DIPLOMAS AWARDED BY UNIVERSITIES

Belfast

CERTIFICATES AWARDED BY UNIVERSITIES

Belfast; Glasgow

National Certificates and Diplomas

BTEC National Certificates/Diplomas: Child Care; Childhood Studies (Nursery Nursing)

Scotland

SQA HNC: Working with Children In Their Early Yrs

NVQs

Level 2: Early Yrs Care & Education

Level 3: Caring for Children & young People; Early Yrs Care & Education

SVQs

Level 2: Care; Early Yrs Care and Education
Level 3: Care; Early Yrs and Care and Education
Level 4: Care

Other Vocational Awarding Bodies

ABC: Playwork with Children over 5

NURSING, MIDWIFERY AND HEALTH VISITING

Nursing, Midwifery and Health Visiting education and preparation in the UK are the responsibility of:

The English National Board for Nursing, Midwifery and Health Visiting: Victory House, 170 Tottenham Court Road, London W1P 0HA Tel 0171-388 3131 Fax 0171-383 4031 Website: www.enb.org.uk

The National Board for Nursing, Midwifery and Health Visiting for Scotland: 22 Queen Street, Edinburgh EH2 1NT Tel: 0131-226 7371 Fax: 0131 225 9970

The National Board for Nursing, Midwifery and Health Visiting for Northern Ireland: Centre House, 79 Chichester Street, Belfast BT1 4JE Tel: 01232 238152 Fax: 01232 333298

The Welsh National Board for Nursing, Midwifery and Health Visiting:2nd Floor, Golate House, 101 St Mary's Street, Cardiff CF1 1DX Tel: 01222 261400 Fax: 01222 261499

Candidates must undertake an educational programme at an institution approved by the relevant Board, and be successful in the continuous assessment scheme in order to have their names entered on the Professional Register of the:

UK Central Council for Nursing, Midwifery and Health Visiting (UKCC): 23 Portland Place, London W1N 4JT. Tel: 0171-637 718, www.ukcc.org.uk

The parts of the Professional Register of the UKCC are as follows:

Part	Designation	Abbreviation
1	First level nurses trained in general training	RGN**
2	Second level nurses trained in general nursing (England and Wales)	EN(G)**
3	First level nurses trained in the nursing of persons suffering from mental illness	RMN**
4	Second level nurses trained in the nursing of persons suffering from mental illness (England and Wales)	EN(M)**
5	First level nurses trained in the nursing of persons with learning disabilities	RNMH**
6	Second level nurses trained in the nursing of persons with learning disabilities (England and Wales)	EN(MH)**
7	Second level nurses (Scotland and Northern Ireland)	EN**
8	Nurses trained in the nursing of sick children	RSCN**
9	Nurses trained in the nursing of persons suffering from fever	RFN
10	Midwives	RM
11	Health Visitors	RHV
12	First level nurses trained in adult nursing	RN
13	First level nurses trained in mental health nursing	RN
14	First level nurses trained in learning disabilities nursing	RN
15	First level nurses trained in children's nursing	RN

** May use abbreviation RN (optional)

Nurse Education

Parts 12–15

Pre-registration Diplomas in Higher Education programmes of education are designed to give the student a carefully integrated combination of academic study and practical nursing experience within hospitals and in the community. The courses are of 3 yrs duration, commencing with an 18 mth Common Foundation Programme. Students then progress to a specialist branch for a further 18 mths. The specialist branches are: adult nursing, mental health nursing, learning disability nursing, children's nursing. The minimum educational entry requirements are 5 subjects at GCSE grade C or above or UKCC approved equivalent, a pass in an educational test approved by the UKCC or a vocational qualification approved by the UKCC. Successful completion of the course leads to a professional qualification as a Registered Nurse on Part 12, 13, 14 or 15 of the UKCC Professional Register and a diploma in higher education. Degree courses combined with a Registered Nurse qualification are also available. The programmes combine nurse education with a variety of degrees in nursing, for example, BA (Hons), BN (Hons) or BSc (Hons) in Nursing Studies.

Parts 1, 3, 5 & 8
Nurse education programmes leading to entry on Parts 1, 3, 5 and 8 of the Professional Register are being replaced by the pre-registration diploma and degree programmes of education.

Shortened Programmes
Shortened programmes of nurse preparation are available to those already holding a nursing or midwifery qualification on another part of the Professional Register and to graduates with a health-related degree.

Parts 2, 4, 6 and 7 of the Professional Register
Courses leading to Parts 2, 4 and 6 have been discontinued. Students continue to be admitted to courses leading to Part 7 of the Register in Scotland and preparation takes 18 mths. The min educational entry requirement is that the entrant must provide evidence of having attained a min required standard of general education extending over a period of at least 10 yrs. The min age of entry is 17½.

Second to First Level Nursing Programmes of Education
Second to first level nursing programmes from Parts 2, 4, 6 or 7 to 1, 3, 5, 8, 12, 13, 14 or 15 are provided in a number of educational institutions.

Midwifery

There are 2 types of educational programme leading to a qualification as a midwife and a diploma in higher education or degree: Pre-registration midwifery programmes of 3 or 4 yrs' duration. Post-registration midwifery programmes (shortened) of not less than 78 wks for those already registered on Part 1 or Part 12 of the Professional Register. For the pre-registered programme there is an educational entry requirement of either 5 subjects at GCSE grades A, B or C, including English and a science subject, or a vocational qualification approved by the UKCC, or a pass in the UKCC Educational Test or other UKCC-approved qualification. The min age of entry to midwifery training is 17½.

Health Visiting

Part II of the Professional Register All entrants to traditional health visitor education programmes must be on Parts 1 or 12 of the Register. Entrants to specialist practitioner programmes in public health nursing (health visiting) must be entered on Parts 1, 2, 3, 4, 5, 6, 7, 8, 12, 13, 14, or 15 of the Register.

CONTINUING EDUCATION AND PROFESSIONAL DEVELOPMENT
The English National Board (ENB) has developed and introduced a framework and Higher Award for Continuing Professional Education. The framework provides a flexible and coherent system for continuing education, allowing the practitioners to plan their professional development based on 10 key characteristics which describe the skill and expertise of practitioners working closely with patients and clients. Practitioners who aim for the Higher Award gain both a professional and academic qualification at First or Higher degree levels. The United Kingdom Central Council for Nursing, Midwifery and Health Visiting has agreed a model for education and practice beyond registration with explicit standards for programmes leading to the qualification of specialist preparation. The term "specialist practitioner" refers to both the specialist practitioner based in an institution and the specialist community practitioner. There are increasing numbers of nursing, midwifery and health related First and Higher degree programmes available. Further details can be obtained from the National Boards, please see addresses under the entry for Nurse Education.

Further information on Nursing and Midwifery Education can be obtained from:
England
Careers Section, English National Board for Nursing, Midwifery and Health Visiting, PO Box 2EN, London W1A 2EN Tel: 020 7391 6200 *or* 6205 Fax: 020 7391 6207 E-mail: enb.careers@easynet.co.uk
Scotland
CATCH, PO Box 21, Edinburgh EH2 1NT.
Wales
Careers Officer, Welsh National Board for Nursing, Midwifery and Health Visiting, 2nd Floor, Golate House, 101 St Mary's Street, Cardiff CF1 1DX Tel: 029 2026 1400 Fax: 029 2026 1499
Northern Ireland
Recruitment Officer, National Board for Nursing, Midwifery and Health Visiting for Northern Ireland, Centre House, 79 Chichester Street, Belfast BT1 4JE Tel 028 9023 8152 Fax 028 9033 3298

THE ROYAL COLLEGE OF NURSING

20 Cavendish Square, London W1M 0AB Tel: 020 7409 3333 Website: www.rcn.org.uk
The Royal College of Nursing (RCN), with a membership of over 320,000, is the voice of nursing in the UK, for qualified nurses as well as those in training. Its primary aim is the promotion of the art and science of nursing. As a professional organisation, it promotes the development of the profession of nursing and seeks to raise the standard of the practice to the consumers of health care. It has a Department of Nursing Policy and Practice which is responsible for responding to members' professional opinion. As a professional union, it represents the interests of nurses, both individually and collectively, working for improvements in terms and conditions of service and protecting the interests of its members.

Post-Registration Qualifications

DEGREE, DIPLOMA AND CERTIFICATE COURSES RUN BY THE RCN INSTITUTE OF ADVANCED NURSING EDUCATION

20 Cavendish Square, London W1M 0AB Tel: 020 7355 1396 Fax: 020 7495 3361
The RCN Institute of Advanced Nursing Education is an Institution of Higher Education and is accredited by the University of Manchester. The Institute offers the widest range of courses for health care professionals in the UK. Our undergraduate modular scheme has over 1,300 students currently taking over 25 different courses with a choice of 90 modules. Our programme meets the needs of students from a variety of cultural backgrounds. During the past 4 yrs, students from 35 nations have benefited from our courses, most of them sponsored by their governments. We have also assisted in the setting up of courses in developing countries.

The Undergraduate Modular Scheme
Courses are offered at degree, diploma and certificate level within a comprehensive modular scheme, designed to give maximum flexibility and individually tailored courses. Modules in the Institute's programme are validated by the University of Manchester and the Royal College of Nursing and can be credited towards a degree of that University. They may also count towards an RCN certificate or diploma.

Undergraduate courses
Unless specifically stated otherwise, a course may be taken on FT/PT basis. Students registered for FT degree courses are eligible for a mandatory grant through their local education authority, subject to the current conditions. Courses are divided into 5 programme areas according to the dominant subject area of the course.

EDUCATION AND HEALTH STUDIES:
Diploma in Health Studies: This course provides participants with the opportunity to: i) develop an increased understanding of health-related concepts and other relevant disciplines; ii) consider the application of this understanding to their area of professional practice; iii) develop a more critical, reflective approach to practice.
BSc (Hons) in Child Health: This course has been designed to enable participants to advance the nursing care of children; enrich and extend their knowledge of child health; promote a more research-minded approach to child health and the care of sick children; develop their educational role in the interest of family and enhance their ability to manage and effect change.

BSc (Hons) in Health Studies: This course aims to enable health care specialists to acquire a broad knowledge base in Health Studies.

MANAGEMENT STUDIES PROGRAMME:

Certificate in Health Services Management: 1 yr PT. Aims to enhance personal managerial and communication skills and develop knowledge of healthcare and the principles of resource management.

Diploma in Health Services Management: Designed to enable health care professionals to cope with changing and uncertain environments and to prepare them to become better managers. Aims to increase students' self-awareness; to develop their knowledge and understanding of the use of the behavioural sciences in the workplace; to provide a knowledge-base of management and organisational theory and to manage change more effectively.

BSc (Hons) in Health Services Management: Seeks to give students a thorough knowledge-base for carrying through effective management decisions and to enable students to reach a high sense of personal, interpersonal and group process skills.

MIDWIFERY STUDIES PROGRAMME:

Diploma in Professional Studies (Midwifery): Aims to promote excellence in midwifery practice through the advanced study of midwifery and related disciplines and to facilitate the professional and personal development of registered midwives.

BSc (Hons) in Midwifery Studies: Aims to further promote excellence in midwifery practice through the encouragement of innovative and research-based practice, the generation of midwifery theory, and to further the growth of midwifery as a profession with a unique body of knowledge.

NURSING STUDIES PROGRAMME:

Certificate in Counselling Skills: 1 yr PT. Aims to develop the counselling role of the health care professional whether in health care practice, education or management. The main aims are to enable students to increase their awareness of the importance of effective communication, to develop the necessary skills and attitudes to enhance the individual's communication in all settings; to acquire appropriate strategies for encouraging communication skills in colleagues, learners and patients/clients.

Diploma in Infection Control Nursing: 2 yrs PT. Trains students to practice safely and effectively as infection control nurses. There is increased emphasis on nursing theory and interpersonal skills, as well as imparting specialist knowledge and skills in infection control.

Diploma in Nursing Studies: Aims to promote excellence in nursing practice through the advanced study of nursing and related disciplines, and through encouragement of innovative and research-based practice.

BSc Hons in Nursing Studies: Equally relevant for those in nursing education as for those in nursing practice. The essential theme is the study of nursing and the application of knowledge from related disciplines.

PRIMARY HEALTH PROGRAMME:

BSc (Hons) in Health Studies (Nurse Practitioners/Occupational Health): 2 yrs PT, 3 yrs PT. These courses aim to prepare participants for changing professional roles in a range of community settings; to enhance and extend their knowledge, skills and experience in community-based nursing; to promote their clinical decision-making skills in order to meet clients' health related needs; to foster a more research-minded approach to professional practice; to broaden and deepen the participants' knowledge and understanding of concepts of health and their relevance for practice; to facilitate the personal and professional development of each participant.

THE POSTGRADUATE PROGRAMME

Masters' degrees and 2 Postgraduate Diplomas are on offer together with a research IDHd programme.

Postgraduate Diploma in Education: 1 yr FT/2 yrs PT. Designed to prepare suitably experienced first level graduate midwives and nurses for a teaching role, extending their professional knowledge, skills and managerial capabilities.

MSc in Child Health: FT/PT. The course will meet the needs of registered children's nurses and health visitors.

MSc in Community Nursing: FT/PT. The course aims to prepare students for advanced clinical practice in community settings since they will be expected to be nurse consultants, teachers and to influence policy. Advanced clinical assessment skills will be offered as well as the opportunity to study wider health issues.

MSc in Health Studies: FT/PT. The course aims to prepare students for advanced practice in a variety of health care settings. Participants will consider critically their own personal and professional development needs; develop an in-depth knowledge-base of health and related studies to underpin nursing practice, as well as further skills of analysis and problem solving.

Postgraduate Diploma in Health Services Management: FT/PT. Aims to facilitate the development of managers at senior level in health service organisations. The main aims of the course are to enable students to develop their knowledge and skills: the management of effective and efficient utilisation of human, financial, material and information resources within a health care organisation; the development of strategies to cope with manned and imposed change and the development of a philosophy of management.

MSc in Health Services Management: FT/PT. Enables students to enhance their academic and professional credibility through an in-depth study of management and related studies. Students will further develop their expert knowledge and skills in management, research, change agency and consultancy.

MSc in Midwifery: FT/PT. Aims to evaluate maternity care provision critically; to apply existing research and initiate, collate and disseminate new research work; to identify areas where change is required; to enable advocacy for individuals, families and communities in maintaining and improving standards of care; and to develop support and resource skills to empower others in the provision of maternity care.

MSc in Nursing: FT/PT. Aims to develop students' critical insight into the ways in which expert knowledge is generated and valued, and to provide the support and resources necessary for students to conduct an in-depth research study in nursing.

POSTGRADUATE DEGREE OF THE UNIVERSITY OF EDINBURGH

Department of Nursing Studies, George Square, Edinburgh EH8 9LL Tel: 0131 650 3890 Fax: 0131 650 3891 e-mail: nursing@ed.ac.uk Website: www.ed.ac.uk/~nursing

Diploma/MSc in Nursing (Health Studies) (1 yr FT or 2/3 yrs PT) is a flexible programme offered to allow experienced, able nurses and other health care professionals to extend their knowledge of therapeutic care in nursing and related disciplines. Students take 2 core units: Issues & Trends in Nursing & Health Care; Research Methods and Elementary Statistical Theory. They then choose 4 further units from a range of options covering clinical and management studies. Assessment is mainly by course work. Other course requirements: an Application Unit and a dissertation.

MSc/Diploma in Nursing (Education) (1 yr FT or 2/3 yrs PT) is designed mainly for graduates who possess nursing and teaching qualifications. The course consists of two core units: Issues & Trends in Nursing & Health Research Methods & Elementary Statistical Theory. One optional unit is taken from the programme offered in the Department of Nursing Studies, and three from the Department of Education & Society.

Diploma/MSc in Nursing (Cancer Nursing) (1 yr or 2/3 yrs PT) is designed for nurses with experience in cancer nursing (in any setting), to extend their knowledge of the scientific basis of cancer nursing and the concepts which underpin the delivery of care to individuals with cancer and their families. Students take four course units: Science & Treatment of Cancer, Nursing Management in Cancer Care, Coping with Cancer as a Chronic Illness and Research Methods & Elementary Statistical Theory, along with two half-units and the unit from the MSc in Nursing & Health Studies. Students undertake a dissertation if course work is of a suitable standard, on the basis of which the MSc may be awarded.

Diploma/MSC in Nursing (Child Health) (1yr FT or 2/3 yrs PT) provides a unique opportunity for personal and professional development to experienced paediatric nurses and health visitors, or other health care professionals with a specialist interest in child health. Students take four core units: Chronic Illness and Disability in Childhood; Ethical, Legal and Social Issues in Child Health; Family Nursing; Research Methods and Elementary Statistical Theory. Two optional units are chosen from the programme offered from the MSc in Nursing & Health Studies. Students also undertake a Dissertation if coursework is of a suitable standard, on the basis of which the MSc may be awarded.

THE ROYAL COLLEGE OF MIDWIVES
15 Mansfield Street, London W1M 0BE Tel: 020 7312 3535 Fax: 020 7312 3536
The Royal College of Midwives is the largest midwifery organisation in the world and exists to promote and advance the art and science of midwifery and to increase the efficiency of midwives. There are 230 branches throughout the UK and a national headquarters in each country. Over 90 per cent of practising UK midwives are members of the RCM which provides leadership and support in all professional, educational and employment matters affecting midwives and midwifery. In addition to its world-wide network of midwifery clinicians, teachers and researchers, the RCM is closely linked with the 5 UK statutory bodies, central government and the other medical royal colleges. It is an active member of the International Confederation of Midwives and proud to be the only WHO Collaborating Centre for Midwifery. The organisation provides consultancy and advice, organises and facilitates continuing professional development programmes and is active in midwifery research. The RCM promotes the development and exchange of midwifery knowledge and pursues activities to improve maternity care and the health of women and families nationally and internationally.
The General Secretary is Karlene Davis.

University Qualifications

The following universities offer qualifications in Nursing, Midwifery and Health Visiting and related subjects. Full details may be found in Part 4, under the entry for the appropriate university.

FIRST DEGREES AWARDED BY UNIVERSITIES
Abertay, Dundee; Anglia; Anglia (City College, Norwich); Birmingham; Bournemouth; Bradford; Brighton; Bristol; Brunel; Bucks. Coll.; Central England; Central Lancashire; City; Coventry; De Montfort, Leicester; Derby; East Anglia; East Anglia (Suffolk College); Edinburgh; Glamorgan; Glasgow; Glasgow Caledonian; Greenwich; Hertfordshire; Huddersfield; Hull; Keele; Kent (Canterbury Christ Church University College); Kingston; Leeds; Leeds Metropolitan; Liverpool; Liverpool (Chester College of H.E.); Liverpool John Moores; London (King's College London); Luton; Manchester; Manchester Metropolitan.; Middlesex; Napier; Northampton; Northumbria; Nottingham; Oxford Brookes; Paisley; Plymouth; Queen Margaret; Reading; Robert Gordon; Salford; Sheffield; Sheffield Hallam; South Bank; South Bank (Farnborough College of Technology); Southampton; St Martin; Sunderland; Surrey; Teesside; Thames Valley; Ulster; Wales (College of Medicine); Wales (North East Wales Institute); Wales (University of Wales, Bangor); Wales (University of Wales, Swansea); Wolverhampton; Worcester; York

HIGHER DEGREES AWARDED BY UNIVERSITIES
Aberdeen; Belfast; Birmingham; Bournemouth; Bradford; Brighton; Bucks. Coll.; Cambridge; Central England; City; Coventry; De Montfort, Leicester; Derby; Dundee; Edinburgh; Essex; Glamorgan; Glasgow; Hull; Keele; Leeds; Leeds Metropolitan; Liverpool; Liverpool (Chester College of H.E.); Liverpool John Moores; London (Imperial College of Science, Technology & Medicine); London (King's College London); Manchester; Middlesex; Napier; Newcastle; Nottingham; Portsmouth; Reading; Salford; Sheffield; Sheffield Hallam; South Bank; Southampton; St Martin; Stirling; Sunderland; Surrey; Thames Valley; Ulster; Wales (College of Medicine); Wales (North East Wales Institute); Wales (University of Wales, Bangor); Wales (University of Wales, Swansea); Wolverhampton

DIPLOMAS AWARDED BY UNIVERSITIES
Aberdeen; Anglia; Bournemouth; Bradford; Brighton; Bristol; Bucks. Coll.; Central England; Central Lancashire; City; Coventry; De Montfort, Leicester; Derby; Dundee; Durham (Darlington College of Technology); East Anglia; East Anglia (Suffolk College); Edinburgh; Glamorgan; Glasgow; Hull; Kent (Canterbury Christ Church University College); Leeds; London (King's College London); Middlesex; Napier; Northampton; Paisley; Reading; Salford; South Bank; Southampton (Chichester Institute of Higher Education); St Martin; Stirling; Stockport; Sunderland; Ulster; Wales (College of Medicine); Wales (North East Wales Institute); Wolverhampton; Worcester

CERTIFICATES AWARDED BY UNIVERSITIES
Aberdeen; Bradford (Bradford & Ilkley Community College); Brighton; Bristol; Central England; Central Lancashire; Hertfordshire; Middlesex; Salford; Ulster; Wales (College of Medicine); Warwick

OTHER COURSES AWARDED BY UNIVERSITIES
Anglia; Northampton

PROFESSIONAL COURSES AWARDED BY UNIVERSITIES
Luton

PROFESSIONAL QUALIFICATIONS AWARDED BY UNIVERSITIES
Glamorgan

Other Vocational Awarding Bodies

ABC: Home Nursing

OCCUPATIONAL THERAPY

Membership of Professional Institutions and Associations

THE COLLEGE OF OCCUPATIONAL THERAPISTS
106-114 Borough High Street, Southwark, London SE1 1LB Tel: 020 7357 6480 Fax: 020 7450 2299
Website: www.cot.co.uk
A BSc degree in Occupational Therapy (normally with Hons) is awarded to students who have
successfully completed a prescribed course of education. FT or PT courses leading to the degree
qualification are 3/4 yrs long: 2 yr accelerated courses are available for graduates with a relevant
degree; 4 yr PT courses are available to people with experience of working in occupational
therapy. Some of the following subjects are studied during the course: the principles and practice
of occupational therapy; biological, behavioural and medical sciences; communication and
management; therapeutic use of activity. Additionally, students must usually have completed at
least 1000 hrs of fieldwork placement before qualifying. The minimum entry qualifications are:
students must have reached the age of 18 (17½ in Scotland) and have obtained 5 GCE/GCSE
subjects of which 2 must be at A Level or 6 SCE subjects of which 3 must be at H grade or an
equivalent as recognised by Higher Education eg BTEC National Diploma or a validated Access
Course. Mature candidates are welcome to apply, but are expected to show evidence of and
attainment in a course of recent academic study to A Level standard (or its equivalent). Contact
individual schools for their specific entry requirements.The British Association of Occupational
Therapists has around 22,000 members.

University Qualifications

*The following universities offer qualifications in Occupational Therapy and related subjects. Full details
may be found in Part 4, under the entry for the appropriate university.*

FIRST DEGREES AWARDED BY UNIVERSITIES
Anglia (Colchester Institute); Brighton; Brunel; Coventry; Derby; East Anglia; Exeter (St Loye's
School of Health Studies); Glasgow Caledonian; Kent (Canterbury Christ Church University
College); Leeds (The College of Ripon & York St John); Liverpool; Northampton; Northumbria;
Oxford Brookes; Queen Margaret; Robert Gordon; Salford; Sheffield Hallam; Southampton; St
Martin; Teesside; Ulster; Wales (College of Medicine)

HIGHER DEGREES AWARDED BY UNIVERSITIES
Aberdeen; Birmingham; Brighton; Brunel; Coventry; East London; Exeter (St Loye's School of
Health Studies); Hertfordshire; Nottingham; Sheffield Hallam; St Martin; Surrey; Wales (College
of Medicine); York

DIPLOMAS AWARDED BY UNIVERSITIES
Brighton; Bristol; Hertfordshire; London (Queen Mary & Westfield College (incorporating St
Bartholomew's and the Royal London School of Medicine & Dentistry)); Manchester

CERTIFICATES AWARDED BY UNIVERSITIES
Aberdeen

OPHTHALMIC OPTICS

Advanced Professional Qualifications

Fellowship of The College of Optometrists (FCOptom): The College offers a higher (Fellowship) diploma, mainly in clinical subjects, for Members and holders of approved qualifications.

Diploma in Contact Lens Practice (DCLP): May be taken by diplomates of the College and by holders of any recognised qualification in Optometry.

Diploma in Orthoptics (DOrth): May be taken by diplomates of the College and by holders of any recognised qualification in Optometry.

The following are no longer examining bodies:

The British Optical Association (FBOA), The Worshipful Company of Spectacle Makers (FSMC), The Scottish Association of Opticians (FSAO).

Professional Qualifications

To secure registration by the **General Optical Council** (41 Harley Street, London W1N 2DJ E-mail: GOC@optical.org Website: www.optical.org) and to practise as an optometrist in the UK it is necessary to pass the qualifying exam of **The College of Optometrists** (42 Craven Street, London WC2N 5NG) and to satisfy the conditions with regard to training and clinical experience required by the College and General Optical Council.

Approved training courses are offered at 8 universities, leading to a BSc degree in Optometry or Vision Sciences. Upon graduating the student passes or gains exemption from the Part I professional qualifying exam and is then eligible to commence a pre-registration yr of graduate clinical training, towards the end of which period he/she sits for the professional qualifying exam of the College. Upon satisfactory completion the student is eligible for registration by the General Optical Council. This enables them to apply for Membership of the College (MCOptom).

University Qualifications

The following universities offer qualifications in Ophthalmic Optics and related subjects. Full details may be found in Part 4, under the entry for the appropriate university.

FIRST DEGREES AWARDED BY UNIVERSITIES

Anglia; Aston; Bradford; City; Glasgow Caledonian; Heriot-Watt; Southampton; Ulster; UMIST; Wales (Cardiff University)

HIGHER DEGREES AWARDED BY UNIVERSITIES

Bradford; Bristol; City; Glasgow; Heriot-Watt; London (Imperial College of Science, Technology & Medicine); London (University College (UCL)); Manchester; Reading; Salford; UMIST

DIPLOMAS AWARDED BY UNIVERSITIES

Bristol; London (University College (UCL)); Manchester; Reading; Salford

CERTIFICATES AWARDED BY UNIVERSITIES

Anglia; Bristol; London (University College (UCL))

OPTICIANS (DISPENSING)

Membership of Professional Institutions and Associations

THE ASSOCIATION OF BRITISH DISPENSING OPTICIANS

6 Hurlingham Business Park, Sulivan Road, London SW6 3DU Tel: 020 7736 0088
Fax: 020 7731 5531 e-mail: general@abdo.org.uk Website: www.abdo.org.uk

MEMBERSHIP:
Fellowship (FBDO): This can be taken after: (i) a 2-yr FT course, with 1 yr of approved practical experience following the Final exam; (ii) 3 yrs' practical experience in employment supplemented by PT classes at a technical college or by a correspondence course; (iii) a 3 yr FT BScHons in Optical Management offered at Anglia Polytechnic University or a BSc in Opthalmic Dispensing with Management at Bradford & Lilay Community College. Entry requirements are 5 GCSEs Grades A-C including Maths or Science and English, plus 2 A Levels for those considering a degree.

The Fellowship Exam: Minimum entry requirements for all systems of Training are: 5 GCSE passes, Maths (Grade A or B), English, another science-based subject and 2 further (optional) subjects (ie A, B or C grade passes) which include English, Maths or Physics. Candidates must be at least 17 at the date of the preliminary exam. The exam is in 2 parts – Part One and Final Dispensing. Both have practical and theoretical sections and the subjects include Light, Prisms and Lenses; Ocular Anatomy and Physiology; General and Visual Optical Principles; Practical Work on Lenses and Frames including Fitting.

OTHER AWARDS:
Diploma of Honours Fellowship (FBDO(Hons)): Granted to students who pass the Final Dispensing and also an exam in 1 of: Contact Lens Practice; Geometric Optics of Ophthalmic Lenses; or Low Visual Acuity. Those who obtain the Fellowship Diploma and the Diploma in Contact Lens Practice are entitled to style themselves FBDO(Hons)CL.

Diploma in Contact Lens Practice (CL(ABDO)): Can be taken by members who have not passed the Fellowship exam. Candidates must normally hold the qualifying diploma of a recognised optical body. The exam is theoretical and practical; it covers Anatomy; Pathology of the Eye and the Adnexa; Physiology; Optics; Indications for use of Contact Lenses and Clinical Procedure. The practical exam is taken in 2 parts. The second part requires submission of case histories of a prescribed number of patients and deals with advanced aftercare.

Diploma in Geometric Optics of Ophthalmic Lenses: Open only to those who have passed the Final Theoretical Dispensing exam. If the student has passed the Full Dispensing exam the addition of this Diploma qualifies him/her for Honours Fellowship. The exam covers advanced general optical principles and the study of various types of complex lenses.

Diploma in Low Visual Acuity: Open only to qualified opticians who wish to enhance their knowledge of the dispensing of low vision aids.

University Qualifications

The following universities offer qualifications in Opticians (Dispensing) and related subjects. Full details may be found in Part 4, under the entry for the appropriate university.

FIRST DEGREES AWARDED BY UNIVERSITIES
Anglia; Bradford (Bradford & Ilkley Community College); Glasgow Caledonian

DIPLOMAS AWARDED BY UNIVERSITIES
Bradford (Bradford & Ilkley Community College)

SVQs
Level 2: Optical Support Services

ORTHOPTICS

Membership of Professional Institutions and Associations

BRITISH ORTHOPTIC SOCIETY
Tavistock House North, Tavistock Square, London WC1H 9HX Tel: 020 7387 7992
Fax: 020 7383 2584 e-mail: bos@orthoptics.org.uk

MEMBERSHIP:
Members are qualified orthoptists who hold the Diploma of the British Orthoptic Society (DBO) or a degree in orthoptics. Student Members are those working to qualify as orthoptists.

EXAMINATIONS:
Degrees in orthoptics are offered by Liverpool University and Sheffield University. Entry requirements are normally 3 A Levels or Scottish Highers. Preference is given to candidates with a Science subject. The courses incorporate both theory and clinical teaching and include in depth study of orthoptics, optics, anatomy and physiology. Other areas such as applied sciences, statistics and research methodology are also covered. Post-registration degrees are available to orthoptists who hold the DBO. These are offered by the University of Sheffield.

University Qualifications

The following universities offer qualifications in Orthoptics and related subjects. Full details may be found in Part 4, under the entry for the appropriate university.

FIRST DEGREES AWARDED BY UNIVERSITIES
Glasgow Caledonian; Liverpool;

PACKAGING

Membership of Professional Institutions and Associations

THE INSTITUTE OF PACKAGING
Sysonby Lodge, Nottingham Road, Melton Mowbray, Leicestershire LE13 0NU Tel: 01664 500055 Fax: 01664 564164 e-mail: info@iop.co.uk Website: www.iop.co.uk
The Institute of Packaging is the awarding body for packaging qualifications.

MEMBERSHIP:
Fellows (FInstPkg): Are usually over 35 yrs of age; have been a Member for 5 yrs; have held a responsible executive, administrative or similar position in the profession of packaging for at least 10 yrs; can produce evidence of their contribution to the art and / or science of packaging; and have 3 referees (all of whom must be Members and at least 1 of whom must be a Fellow) sponsoring their application. The Council may confer the grade of Fellow upon any Member of the Institute in recognition of outstanding service to the Institute where the Certificate of Merit is deemed inappropriate, or any person of eminence in the practice of packaging technology, management, administration or related disciplines.
Diploma Members (MInstPkg(Dip)): Must have passed all parts of the Institute's membership qualifying exam (see below).
Members (MInstPkg): Must have held, and continue to hold, a responsible position in packaging for a period of 5 yrs, and have provided evidence satisfactory to the Council that either their knowledge of packaging in general or their profound knowledge of a specific area of packaging is compatible with the status of Membership as attained by passing the qualifying exam.
Associates (AInstPkg): Must work (or be seeking work) in packaging or a related industry and whilst not currently qualified for Member status are considered capable of furthering the objectives of the Institute, or are studying for the Diploma.
Student Member: A junior grade of membership for those studying for the IOP Diploma exam and for FT college or university students.

EXAMINATIONS:
The Diploma in Packaging Technology: Awarded to those who successfully pass all 3 parts of the exam. These are:
Part 1: Successfully complete a series of continuous assessment objective tests on the fundamentals of packaging as part of the chosen study method and gain a credit exemption, or sit a written paper (Paper 1).
Part 2: Successfully complete 2 more written papers – Paper 2: Packaging materials forms and components; and Paper 3: Packaging design, development and production.

Part 3: Complete a 10,000 word dissertation within 6 mths of successfully passing Part 2. The Diploma is equiv to an HND/NVQ Level 4, is university CATS accredited and is accepted by Brunel and Loughborough Universities for entrance to the MSc in Packaging Technology.
Training: Short technical courses at the Packaging School in Melton Mowbray; intensive pre-exam courses at other venues; IOP supported PT courses for the diploma at various venues and a comprehensive open learning course and DL provision for those unable to attend scheduled courses.

University Qualifications

The following universities offer qualifications in Packaging and related subjects. Full details may be found in Part 4, under the entry for the appropriate university.

FIRST DEGREES AWARDED BY UNIVERSITIES
London Institute (London College of Printing); Sheffield Hallam; Surrey Institute; Wales (Swansea Institute of Higher Education)

HIGHER DEGREES AWARDED BY UNIVERSITIES
Surrey Institute

DIPLOMAS AWARDED BY UNIVERSITIES
Hertfordshire (West Herts College)

National Certificates and Diplomas

BTEC National Certificates/Diplomas: Design (Packaging)
BTEC Higher National Certificates/Diplomas: Design (Packaging)

NVQs

Level 1: Packaging Operations (Pharmaceutical)
Level 2: Packaging Operations (Pharmaceutical)

Useful Addresses

Corrugated Packaging Association, 2 Saxon Court, Freeschool Street, Northampton NN1 1ST Tel: 01604 621002 Fax: 01604 620636

PATENT AGENCY

THE CHARTERED INSTITUTE OF PATENT AGENTS

Staple Inn Buildings, High Holborn, London WC1V 7PZ Tel: 020 7405 9450 Fax: 020 7430 0471
e-mail: mail@cipa.org.uk Website: www.cipa.org.uk

MEMBERSHIP:
Fellows (CPA): Are Chartered Patent Agents who have passed the Institute's exams or their equivalent and have had their names entered on the Register of Patent Agents.
Associates: Are either technical assistants who have passed the Institute's foundation level exam; or those whose connection with the law, the arts or science is considered by the Council to enable them to advance the objects of the Institute.
Foreign and British Overseas Members: Are those qualified patent agents practising abroad.
Studentship: Open to pupils and technical assistants (ie those who, having obtained the preliminary requirements for the Institute's exams, work under a Registered patent agent while studying for the exams).

EXAMINATIONS:
The Exam System was revised from 1st June 1991 to take account of the introduction of a Register of Trade Mark Attorneys to complement the existing Register of Patent Agents. A Joint Exam

Board has been set up with the Institute of Trade Mark Agents to administer a modular exam leading to qualification for entry on both registers. Entrants to the profession should have obtained: (a) GCSE with grades A, B or C in at least 5 subjects, including English; and GCE A Level in at least 2 subjects, one of which must be a science or engineering subject; or (b) a degree; or (c) passes at any other exams which the Joint Examinations Board accepts are equivalent to those above. In practice, a degree in science or technology is required for entry to the profession as a trainee patent agent, or in any subject for those training as Trade Mark Agents. To qualify for entry in the Register of Patent Agents, candidates must pass the Patents Foundation Paper, the Common Foundation Module and the Patents Advanced Module, and must have completed a period of 2 yrs FT practice under the supervision of a registered patent agent, or solicitor, or 4 yrs FT practice if not under such supervision. Candidates who pass the Trade Marks Foundation Module, the Common Foundation Module and the Trade Marks Advanced Module are eligible for entry on the Register of Trade Mark Agents after they have completed a similar period of training. Agents whose names have been entered in one register will qualify for the other register by passing the relevant Advanced Module. Exemption from all Foundation Papers is granted to those awarded the Certificate in IP Law after successful completion of a 3 mth FT course at either Manchester University or Queen Mary & Westfield College, University of London.

THE EUROPEAN QUALIFYING EXAMINATION:
Patent Agents will normally be expected to qualify to practise before the European Patent Office, for which they must pass the European Qualifying Exam and be entered on the list of professional representatives before the European Patent Office. Candidates for this exam must: (a) possess a scientific or technical degree or equivalent; and (b) have had at least 3 yrs' training with a professional representative entered on the European List.

PATENT EXAMINERS:
The Patent Examiner is a civil servant working for the Department of Industry and concerned with scrutinising all applications for patents. (There are no specific exams for Patent Examiners who are normally graduates or diploma holders in Science or Engineering.)

University Qualifications

The following universities offer qualifications in Patent Agency and related subjects. Full details may be found in Part 4, under the entry for the appropriate university.

FIRST DEGREES AWARDED BY UNIVERSITIES
Manchester

PENSION MANAGEMENT

Membership of Professional Institutions and Associations

THE PENSIONS MANAGEMENT INSTITUTE
PMI House, 4-10 Artillery Lane, London E1 7LS Tel: 020 7247 1452 Fax: 020 7375 0603
e-mail: education@pensions-pmi.org.uk Website: www.pensions-pmi.org.uk

MEMBERSHIP:
Fellow (FPMI): Applicants must already be an Associate and have at least 8 yrs' relevant practical experience and fulfil CPD requirements.
Associate (APMI): Applicants will have successfully completed the Institute's exams and have had a period of not less than 3 yrs' relevant practical experience.
Student: Applicants must be at least 18 and possess either: (a) at least 2 GCE A Levels and 3 GCSEs, the latter to include English Language and Mathematics; or (b) an ONC in Business Studies; or (c) a BTEC NC; or (d) any other public exam or experience which in the opinion of the Council is equivalent. Possession of the Qualification in Pensions Administration (QPA) is an entry for studentship for the Pensions Management Institute, but does not entitle the holder to be exempt from any of the Institute's exams.

The Institute's exams cover the whole range of knowledge and experience required in relation to the operation, management and administration of pension funds, schemes and arrangements of all kinds. The exams comprise 9 papers, covering: (1) Introduction to Pension Schemes and Social Security; (2) Law; (3) Taxation; (4) Scheme Design; (5) Scheme Constitution and Documentation; (6) Scheme Administration and Financing; (7) Investment of Assets; (8) Remuneration and Other Benefits; (9) Communication and Management. The Pensions Management Institute is also the awarding body for 2 qualifications, each of which is a NVQ and a SVQ. One, the **Qualification in Pensions Administration (QPA)**, is at Level 4, the other, the **Qualification in Public Sector Pensions Administration**, is at Level 3. Both are standards based qualifications where the industry itself has defined the tasks of a pensions administrator and identified the criteria that must be satisfied if tasks are to be performed to standard. There are no entry requirements for either qualification. The Level 4 N/SVQ is for all pensions administrators, regardless of sector. It comprises 9 units, assessed by case study examinations and by work based assessments. The Level 3 N/SVQ is for all administrators of public sector schemes. It comprises 10 units, all of which are assessed in the workplace. The Institute also offers a **Certificate of Essential Pensions Knowledge** for trustees of occupational pensions schemes. A specialist **Diploma in International Employee Benefits** was introduced in 1996.

NVQs

Level 4: Pensions Administration

SVQs

Level 4: Pensions Administration

PERSONNEL MANAGEMENT

Membership of Professional Institutions and Associations

CHARTERED INSTITUTE OF PERSONNEL AND DEVELOPMENT

CIPD House, 35 Camp Road, London SW19 4UX Tel: 020 8971 9000 Fax: 020 8263 3333
e-mail: cipd@cipd.co.uk Website: www.cipd.co.uk

CORPORATE MEMBERS:
Fellow (FCIPD): An applicant for Fellowship must be a Member of the Institute, have worked in personnel and development or one of its specialisms at a professional level for at least 10 yrs and have undertaken appropriate continuing professional development.
Member (MCIPD): An applicant for Corporate Membership must be a Graduate of the Institute, have performed executive and/or advisory duties in personnel and development or one of its specialisms for at least 3 yrs, and have undertaken appropriate continuing professional development.

NON-CORPORATE MEMBERS:
Graduate (Graduate CIPD): Obtained by meeting the Institute's professional standards in 3 fields – core management, core personnel and development, and a range of generalist or specialist electives.
Licentiate (Licentiate CIPD)): Obtained by meeting the Institute's professional standards in any one or two of the above fields, or by gaining an N/SVQ at Level 4 in Management, Personnel or Training & Development.
Associate (Associate CIPD): Obtained by gaining 1 of the Institute's certificate level qualifications, either in Personnel Practice or in Training Practice, an N/SVQ at Level 3 in Training & Development, Level 3 Personnel Support, Level 3 Recruitment Consultancy or any 1 of a small number of other approved qualifications.
Affiliateship: Affiliateship is available to those working in personnel development or one of its

specialisms, those engaged in executive, advisory, teaching or research duties, or those in a profession or occupation where knowledge of the principles of personnel and development is desirable. Affiliateship offers the Institute's services, but does not confer any professional qualification or status. Discounted sub-grades are available for those engaged on a study or assessment programme leading to an CIPD qualification and/or membership.

PROFESSIONAL QUALIFICATION SCHEME:
This incorporates 3 elements – core management, core personnel & development and a range of elective modules, of which 4 must be chosen. The Institute also offers a **Certificate in Personnel Practice** and a **Certificate in Training Practice**, which are lower level skills-based qualifications. The Institute is approved as an awarding body for NVQs in Management (Levels 3, 4 & 5) Training & Development (Levels 4 & 5), Personnel (Level 3, 4, & 5), and Recruitment Consultancy (Level 3).For further information on qualifications and assessments please contact the Membership Development or Professional Education departments at CIPD House.

University Qualifications

The following universities offer qualifications in Personnel Management and related subjects. Full details may be found in Part 4, under the entry for the appropriate university.

FIRST DEGREES AWARDED BY UNIVERSITIES

Abertay, Dundee; Anglia (City College, Norwich); Anglia (Colchester Institute); Aston; Bath; Bradford; Bradford (Bradford & Ilkley Community College); Bucks. Coll.; Central England; Central Lancashire; Cheltenham & Gloucester; Coventry; De Montfort, Leicester; Derby; Doncaster; Doncaster (Dearne Valley Business School); East Anglia (Suffolk College); East London; Glamorgan; Greenwich; Keele; Lancaster; Leeds; Lincolnshire; London (London School of Economics & Political Science); Luton; Manchester (Warrington Collegiate Institute, Faculty of H.E,); Middlesex; Napier; North London; Northampton; Northumbria; Nottingham Trent (Southampton Institute); Paisley; Plymouth; South Bank; Staffordshire; Stirling; Strathclyde; Sunderland; Surrey (University of Surrey Roehampton); Teesside; Thames Valley; UMIST; Wales (North East Wales Institute); Wales (Swansea Institute of Higher Education); Wolverhampton

HIGHER DEGREES AWARDED BY UNIVERSITIES

Aberdeen; Abertay, Dundee; Anglia; Anglia (City College, Norwich); Aston; Bournemouth; Bradford; Bristol; Brunel; Bucks. Coll.; Central England; Central Lancashire; Cheltenham & Gloucester; City; Coventry; De Montfort, Leicester; Derby; East Anglia; East London; Exeter; Glamorgan; Greenwich; Heriot-Watt; Heriot-Watt (Edinburgh College of Art); Heriot-Watt (Scottish Borders Campus); Hertfordshire; Keele; Kingston; Lancaster; Leeds; Leeds Metropolitan; Lincolnshire; Liverpool; London (Institute of Education); London (London School of Economics & Political Science); London Guildhall; Luton; Manchester; Manchester Metropolitan.; Middlesex; Napier; Newcastle; North London; Northampton; Nottingham Trent; Nottingham Trent (Southampton Institute); Portsmouth; Salford; Sheffield Hallam; South Bank; Stirling; Strathclyde; Sunderland; Surrey; Surrey (University of Surrey Roehampton); Teesside; Thames Valley; Ulster; UMIST; Wales (Cardiff University); Wales (Swansea Institute of Higher Education); Wales (University of Wales College, Newport); Warwick; Westminster; Wolverhampton

DIPLOMAS AWARDED BY UNIVERSITIES

Anglia (City College, Norwich); Aston; Birmingham (Birmingham College of Food, Tourism and Creative Studies); Blackburn; Bournemouth; Bradford; Bradford (Bradford & Ilkley Community College); Brighton; Bucks. Coll.; Central England; Cheltenham & Gloucester; Coventry; De Montfort, Leicester; Doncaster; Doncaster (Dearne Valley Business School); Durham; Durham (New College Durham); Glamorgan; Glasgow Caledonian; Hertfordshire; Lancaster; Leeds Metropolitan; Lincolnshire; Manchester Metropolitan.; Middlesex; Napier; North London; Northampton; Nottingham Trent; Oxford Brookes; Plymouth; Salford; South Bank; Stirling; Strathclyde; Teesside; Thames Valley; Ulster; Wales (Swansea Institute of Higher Education); Warwick; Wolverhampton

CERTIFICATES AWARDED BY UNIVERSITIES

Bradford (Bradford & Ilkley Community College); Central England; Cheltenham & Gloucester;

Coventry; De Montfort, Leicester; Durham; East London; Glamorgan; Lincolnshire; Lincolnshire (Hull College); London Guildhall; North London; Nottingham Trent (Southampton Institute); South Bank; Wolverhampton

OTHER COURSES AWARDED BY UNIVERSITIES
Northampton

POSTGRADUATE DIPLOMAS AWARDED BY UNIVERSITIES
Heriot-Watt

NVQs
Level 3: Recuritment Consultancy
Level 3: Supporting Workplace Organisation and Representation

SVQs
Level 3: Personnel Support; Training and Development
Level 4: Personnel Management; Training and Development
Level 5: Personnel Strategy; Training and Development

Higher National Diplomas
Personnel Administration/Personnel Management may be taken as optional subjects in programmes for the **BTEC HND** in Business and Finance.

Useful Addresses
Employment National Training Organisation, Room 32, 4th Floor, Kimberley House, 47 Vaughan Way, Leicester LE1 4SG Tel: 0116 251 7979 Fax: 0116 251 1464

PHARMACY

Membership of Professional Institutions and Associations

THE COLLEGE OF PHARMACY PRACTICE
Sir Williams Lyons Road, Barclays Venture Centre, University of Warwick Science Park, Coventry CV4 7EZ Tel: 024 7669 2400 Fax: 024 7669 3069
e-mail: cpp@collpharm.org.uk Website: www.collpharm.org.uk
The College was founded in 1981 to promote and maintain a high standard of pharmacy practice. Membership is open to UK registered pharmacists in all branches of the profession. Members are either
Founder Members (MCPP) or **Practitioner Members (MCPP)** who have passed the College Membership Exam or completed the Membership by Practice Scheme. This latter route uses a Continuing Professional Development Portfolio, formal submission and interview.
Associates (ACPP) are not full members of the College but are usually preparing for Membership. All Members and Associates are expected to fulfil 30 hrs of continuing education per yr. A Professional Development Programme was launched in April 1997 to provide an infrastructure for College Members to plan and progress their own professional development. Members can work towards the **Advanced Award** and ultimately **Fellowship (FCPP)** – the highest award of the College which recognises the highest levels of professional practice including a significant contribution to professional development.

THE PHARMACEUTICAL SOCIETY OF NORTHERN IRELAND
73 University Street, Belfast BT7 1HL Tel: 028 9032 6927 Fax: 028 9043 9919
e-mail: chief.exec@psni.org.uk

MEMBERSHIP:
Member (MPS): One whose name is included in the Register of Pharmaceutical Chemists for Northern Ireland.
Student: One who has satisfied the regulations for admission to: (1) a first degree course in pharmaceutics of a university or institution of similar academic status in Northern Ireland; or (2) a university or other institution in GB awarding a degree recognised by the Royal Pharmaceutical Society of GB, and being so registered. Candidates wishing to become registered as Pharmaceutical Chemists must hold a degree of a UK university obtained under conditions approved by the Council of the Society. A graduate must undergo a 1 yr period of practical training under the supervision of a registered pharmaceutical chemist and pass the registration exam set by the Society.

THE ROYAL PHARMACEUTICAL SOCIETY OF GREAT BRITAIN

1 Lambeth High Street, London SE1 7JN Tel: 020 7735 9141 Fax: 020 7735 7629
e-mail: enquiries@rpsgb.org.uk Website: www.rpsgb.org.uk

36 York Place, Edinburgh EH1 3HU Tel: 0131 556 4386 e-mail: 101561.2226@compuserve.com

MEMBERSHIP:
Fellows (FRPharmS): Elected for distinguished service within the profession.
Member (MRPharmS): Membership of the Society is available only to those who have a degree in pharmacy, have satisfactorily completed a 1 yr period of pre-registration training in a pharmacy and passed the Royal Pharmaceutical Society's registration exam. Both the pharmacy and the tutor appointed to supervise the graduate must be approved by the Royal Pharmaceutical Society. Candidates may then apply to the Royal Pharmaceutical Society for admission to the Register of Pharmaceutical Chemists.

University Qualifications

The following universities offer qualifications in Pharmacy and related subjects. Full details may be found in Part 4, under the entry for the appropriate university.

FIRST DEGREES AWARDED BY UNIVERSITIES

Aberdeen; Aston; Bath; Birmingham; Bradford; Brighton; Bristol; Central Lancashire; Coventry; De Montfort, Leicester; Dundee; East London; Edinburgh; Glasgow; Greenwich; Hertfordshire; Leeds; Liverpool; Liverpool John Moores; London (King's College London); London (University College (UCL)); Luton; Manchester; Newcastle; Nottingham; Nottingham Trent; OU (NESCOT); Portsmouth; Robert Gordon; Sheffield; Southampton; St Andrews; Strathclyde; Sunderland; Wales (Cardiff University); Wolverhampton

HIGHER DEGREES AWARDED BY UNIVERSITIES

Aberdeen; Aston; Bath; Belfast; Birmingham; Bradford; Brighton; Bristol; City; Coventry; De Montfort, Leicester; Derby; East London; Glasgow; Heriot-Watt; Hertfordshire; Hull; Keele; Kingston; Leeds; Liverpool; Liverpool John Moores; London (King's College London); London (Queen Mary & Westfield College (incorporating St Bartholomew's and the Royal London School of Medicine & Dentistry)); London (The School of Pharmacy); London (University College (UCL)); Manchester; Nottingham; OU (NESCOT); Portsmouth; Southampton; Strathclyde; Sunderland; Surrey; Wales (Cardiff University)

DIPLOMAS AWARDED BY UNIVERSITIES

Aberdeen; Aston; Bradford; East London; Greenwich; Hertfordshire; Leeds; London (King's College London); London (Queen Mary & Westfield College (incorporating St Bartholomew's and the Royal London School of Medicine & Dentistry)); London (The School of Pharmacy); Manchester; Strathclyde; Sunderland; Wales (Cardiff University)

CERTIFICATES AWARDED BY UNIVERSITIES

Aston; Leeds; Sunderland

National Certificates and Diplomas

BTEC Higher National Certificates/Diplomas: Science (Industrial Pharmaceutical); Science (Pharmaceutical)

BTEC Higher National Certificates/Diplomas: Science (Industrial Pharmaceutical); Science (Pharmaceutical)

NVQs

Level 3: Pharmacy Services

SVQs

Level 3: Pharmacy Services

Other Qualifications

The College of Pharmacy Practice: Members of the College (MCPP) consist of the original Founder Members and those who have passed the Membership Exam. The aim of the Exam is to assess the knowledge and skills needed to exercise a high standard of pharmacy practice. It is open to Associates of the College who have been in practice for a minimum of 3 yrs and consist of 5 Assessments as follows: Supply and Dispensing of Medicines; Specialist Knowledge; Response to Practice-Related Problems; Practice Workbook and Oral; Structured Practical Assessment. Recognition of other postgraduate qualifications and published work may be used to claim exemption from some of the Assessments.

Useful Addresses

Association of the British Pharmaceutical Industry 12 Whitehall, London SW1A 2DY
Tel: 020 7930 3477 Fax: 020 7747 1411

PHOTOGRAPHY

Membership of Professional Institutions and Associations

BRITISH INSTITUTE OF PROFESSIONAL PHOTOGRAPHY

Fox Talbot House, 2 Amwell End, Ware, Hertfordshire SG12 9HN Tel: 01920 464011
Fax: 01920 487056 e-mail: bipp@compuserve.com Website: www.bipp.com

MEMBERSHIP:

Honorary Fellows (HonFBIPP): Elected from among distinguished professional photographers.

Fellow (FBIPP): This is awarded for distinguished ability in professional photography. A Fellow may describe himself as an 'Incorporated Photographer' or 'Incorporated Photographic Technician'.

Associates (ABIPP): Must either have passed approved exams in photography with appropriate period of experience, or submit a thesis on an approved photographic subject or examples of work. Associates may describe themselves as 'Incorporated Photographers' or 'Incorporated Photographic Technicians'.

Licentiates (LBIPP): Must be at least 18 and must have passed approved exams in photography or can submit evidence of their photographic or technical ability. Licentiates may describe themselves as 'Incorporated Photographers' or 'Incorporated Photographic Technicians'.

Graduate: One who has successfully completed a recognised course in photography, is engaged in professional photography but is not yet qualified, either by age, or experience, to take up corporate membership.

Student: Available for those pursuing a course in photography at an educational establishment.

Affiliate: Open to persons who have a professional interest in photography, and because of age or other limitations have not yet, or may be unable, to qualify for corporate membership.

Licentiateship may be awarded to candidates who have successfully completed a course, recognised by the BIPP, leading to a degree, HND or HNC. Following 2 yrs' relevant experience at the appropriate level, such candidates may apply for Associateship. Candidates with a degree, HND or HNC in any subject from an educational establishment in the UK, and who have been employed at the appropriate level in professional photography, imaging or photo technology for a minimum of 2 yrs, may apply for the Licentiateship. Applications for Associateship may be made immediately by candidates who have successfully completed the **BIPP Professional Qualifying Exam**.

MASTER PHOTOGRAPHERS ASSOCIATION

Hallmark House, 1 Chancery Lane, Darlington, Co Durham DL1 5QP Tel: 01325 356555 Fax: 01325 357813 e-mail: generalenquiries@mpauk.com

The Master Photographers Association is now the UK's only fully qualified organisation for practising FT professional photographers. There is a comprehensive range of free benefits including business building promotions, pricing guidance, legal support, business and promotional stationery, friendly and informative regional meetings and trade magazine offered by the Association. Members may apply for qualification through submission of prints on 3 levels:

Licentiate (LMPA) is to show evidence of competence and ability to create merchantable-quality photography,

Associate (AMPA) is given in recognition of excellence in technique and/or creative interpretation, and

Fellowship (FMPA) is the highest award given in recognition of absolute excellence. The Qualifications Panel meets 4 times a yr in respect of Licentiate submissions and twice a yr for Associate and Fellowship submissions. There is also a separate Video category for this specialised field.

THE ROYAL PHOTOGRAPHIC SOCIETY

The Octagon, Milsom Street, Bath BA1 1DN Tel: 01225 462841 Fax: 01225 448688 e-mail: rps@rps.org Website: www.rps.org

MEMBERSHIP:

Honorary Fellow (HonFRPS): Elected by the Council. Are distinguished persons who, from their position or attainments, are intimately connected with the science or art of photography, its practice and applications.

Honorary Member: One who has rendered distinguished service to the Society or to photography. **Fellow (FRPS):** Associates may apply for Fellowship by submitting photographic work. Fellowship is granted in various categories and a candidate may be admitted in 1 or more categories. Outstanding ability and individuality or originality are required of applicants for this award. The categories are: Applied; Film and Video; Nature; Portraiture, Theatrical & Wedding; Research & Development; Printing; Science; Slide-Sound Sequences; Visual Art; Contemporary; Documentary, Visual Journalism and Travel. There is also a direct application route to the Fellowship for those with a photographic reputation at the highest level, based on CV/referees and photographic achievements such as exhibitions, publications, awards etc.

Associate (ARPS): Licentiates, Members and Non-Members may apply for Associateship by submitting photographic work in 1 or more of the categories listed under Fellowship above. Associateship may be granted in more than 1 category. The award is granted in recognition of photography of good technical standard and aspects such as choice and treatment of subject and presentation are taken into account. Certain courses are also recognised, eg degree.

Licentiate (LRPS): The Licentiateship may be granted to any Member or Non-Member who satisfies the Council of their competence and ability in still photography, film and video or slide-sound sequences; or upon evidence of passing a recognised course in photography. Reciprocal arrangements also exist with other organisations, eg MPA for both LRPS & ARPS.

Ordinary Member: Membership is open to anyone interested in photography, amateur or professional.

QUALIFICATIONS:

The RPS Imaging Scientist Qualifications provide a structure leading to professional qualifications for engineers, scientists and technologists whose professional activities are concerned with quantitative or mechanistic aspects of imaging systems or their application. Successful candidates automatically qualify for the appropriate level of Society Distinction.

Qualified Imaging Scientist (QIS): For those with academic qualifications below degree level (LRPS).
Graduate Imaging Scientist (GIS): For those with a first degree (ARPS).
Accredited Imaging Scientist (AIS): For those with postgraduate experience as Imaging Scientists (ARPS).
Accredited Senior Imaging Scientist (ASIS): The senior professional qualification for established scientists (FRPS).

University Qualifications
The following universities offer qualifications in Photography and related subjects. Full details may be found in Part 4, under the entry for the appropriate university.

FIRST DEGREES AWARDED BY UNIVERSITIES
Bradford (Bradford & Ilkley Community College); Brighton; Central England; Central Lancashire; Cheltenham & Gloucester; De Montfort, Leicester; Derby; Glasgow (Glasgow School of Art); Kent (Kent Institute of Art & Design); Lancaster (Blackpool and The Fylde College); London Institute (Camberwell College of Arts); London Institute (London College of Fashion); London Institute (London College of Printing); Manchester Metropolitan.; Napier; Northumbria; Nottingham Trent; Nottingham Trent (Southampton Institute); OU (NESCOT); Plymouth; Portsmouth; Surrey Institute; Teesside; Thames Valley; Wales (University of Wales College, Newport); Westminster; Wolverhampton

HIGHER DEGREES AWARDED BY UNIVERSITIES
Central England; De Montfort, Leicester; Derby; Glasgow; Kent (Kent Institute of Art & Design); London (Goldsmiths College); London Institute (Central Saint Martins College of Art & Design); Royal College of Art; Sunderland; Surrey Institute; Wales (University of Wales College, Newport); Westminster

DIPLOMAS AWARDED BY UNIVERSITIES
Bradford (Bradford & Ilkley Community College); De Montfort, Leicester; Exeter (Truro College); Glamorgan; Glasgow; Greenwich; Kent (Kent Institute of Art & Design); Leeds (Leeds College of Art & Design); Lincolnshire (Grimsby College); London Institute (London College of Fashion); Thames Valley; Wales (Swansea Institute of Higher Education); Wolverhampton

CERTIFICATES AWARDED BY UNIVERSITIES
Leeds Metropolitan; Lincolnshire (Hull College); London (University College (UCL))

National Certificates and Diplomas
BTEC National Certificates/Diplomas: Design (Photography); Medical Photography; Photographic Technology
BTEC Higher National Qualifications are offered in: Design (Photographic Laboratory Practice); Design (Photography); Medical Photography; Photographic Technology
Scotland
SQA HNC: Photojournalism; Photography
SQA HND: Photography; Photography with Audio-Visual Production
SQA Advanced Diploma: Illustrative Photography.

NVQs
Level 2: Operating Photofinishing Systems; Photography
Level 3: Photographic Processing; Photography
Level 4: Photography

SVQs
Level 2: Photography

Level 3: Photography; Photographic Processing; Printing Photographic Material
Level 4: Newspaper Journalism: Press Photography; Photography

City & Guilds

9231 Photography

Qualification in Photography

(See also Journalism)

National Certificate in Photojournalism of the National Council for the Training of Journalists:
Awarded towards the end of up to 2 yrs' provincial newspaper training/experience and course attendance for trainee press photographers; training is on the job and by FT or PT courses. Course subjects include General Photographic Theory, Law Affecting Press Photography, Caption-writing (with exams) and Practical Press Photography. Direct entry recruits to provincial newspapers need 5 GCE O level passes or GCSEs or the equivalent, including English Language, with certain exceptions in England and Wales, or 3 O levels including English, in Scotland.
For the FT 1-yr course in press photography, to be followed by 18 mths' on-the-job training and experience, the entry requirements are 1 GCE A level/SCE H grade and 4 GCE/SCE O levels, including English Language.

PHYSICS

Membership of Professional Institutions and Associations

THE INSTITUTE OF PHYSICS

76 Portland Place, London W1N 3DH Tel: 020 7470 4800 Fax: 020 7470 4848
e-mail: physics@iop.org Website: www.iop.org

MEMBERSHIP:
Chartered Physicist (CPhys): A designation which may be used by Fellows and Members of the Institute.
Fellowship (FInstP): Age at least 30. Requirements: candidates must have completed at least 7 yrs' responsible work in physics or its applications, or at least 10 yrs' experience in responsible work demanding a knowledge of physics, and have made an outstanding contribution in physics or in a related field.
Membership (MInstP): Requirements: a min age of 25, a physics degree or degree qualification in an acceptable related discipline and evidence of appropriate post-graduation experience. Experience demanded varies according to the candidate's academic qualification, the minimum period being 4 yrs in the case of a physics graduate who has attained a first or second class honours classification. The period of required experience must include at least 1 yr in paid FT employment applying a knowledge of physics. For those over 30, appropriate experience can sometimes be accepted in lieu of academic qualifications.
Graduate Membership (GradInstP): Requirements: a min age of 20 and an academic qualification acceptable for MInstP.
Associate: Requirements: a min age of 20 and an HND in Applied Physics or acceptable equiv qualification. For those over 30 appropriate experience can sometimes be accepted in lieu of academic qualifications.
Studentship: Requirements: a min age of 16. Open to those following an appropriate course of study in Physics or a related discipline.

EXAMINATION:
The Institute's Graduateship exam, which is generally accepted as being fully equivalent to a UK Honours degree in physics, was last held in 1984.Substantive changes to the qualifications listed above are being proposed in 2000. Please contact the Institute's Admissions Manager for up-to-date information.

University Qualifications

The following universities offer qualifications in Physics and related subjects. Full details may be found in Part 4, under the entry for the appropriate university.

FIRST DEGREES AWARDED BY UNIVERSITIES
Aberdeen; Bath; Belfast; Birmingham; Brighton; Bristol; Central Lancashire; City; Dundee; Durham; East Anglia; Edinburgh; Exeter; Glasgow; Glasgow Caledonian; Heriot-Watt; Hertfordshire; Hull; Keele; Kent; Lancaster; Leeds; Leicester; Lincolnshire (Hull College); Liverpool; Liverpool John Moores; London (Imperial College of Science, Technology & Medicine); London (King's College London); London (Queen Mary & Westfield College (incorporating St Bartholomew's and the Royal London School of Medicine & Dentistry)); London (Royal Holloway); London (University College (UCL)); Loughborough; Manchester; Newcastle; Northumbria; Nottingham; Nottingham Trent; Oxford; Paisley; Reading; Robert Gordon; Salford; Sheffield; Sheffield Hallam; Southampton; St Andrews; Staffordshire; Strathclyde; Surrey; Sussex; UMIST; Wales (Cardiff University); Wales (University of Wales, Aberystwyth); Wales (University of Wales, Swansea); Warwick; York

HIGHER DEGREES AWARDED BY UNIVERSITIES
Aberdeen; Belfast; Birmingham; Bristol; Cambridge; Central Lancashire; Dundee; Durham; East Anglia; Edinburgh; Essex; Exeter; Glasgow; Heriot-Watt; Hertfordshire; Hull; Keele; Kent; Lancaster; Leeds; Leicester; Liverpool; Liverpool John Moores; London (Imperial College of Science, Technology & Medicine); London (King's College London); London (Queen Mary & Westfield College (incorporating St Bartholomew's and the Royal London School of Medicine & Dentistry)); London (Royal Holloway); London (University College (UCL)); Loughborough; Manchester; Newcastle; Paisley; Portsmouth; Reading; Salford; Sheffield; Sheffield Hallam; St Andrews; Surrey; Sussex; UMIST; Wales (North East Wales Institute); Wales (University of Wales, Aberystwyth); Wales (University of Wales, Swansea); York

DIPLOMAS AWARDED BY UNIVERSITIES
Aberdeen; Edinburgh; Hertfordshire; Kent; Lancaster; Leeds; London (King's College London); London (Queen Mary & Westfield College (incorporating St Bartholomew's and the Royal London School of Medicine & Dentistry)); London (University College (UCL)); Manchester; Salford; Staffordshire

CERTIFICATES AWARDED BY UNIVERSITIES
Brunel; London (Goldsmiths College); Southampton; Staffordshire; Wales (University of Wales, Bangor)

National Certificates and Diplomas
BTEC Higher National Certificates/Diplomas: Science (Physics)

PHYSIOTHERAPY

Membership of Professional Institutions and Associations

THE SMAE INSTITUTE
(Incorporating the Open College of Chiropody & Podiatry)

The New Hall, Bath Road, Maidenhead, Berkshire SL6 4LA Tel: 01628 621100/ 632440/ 632449 Fax: 01628 674483

MEMBERSHIP:
Member (MSF)(MABPhys): Available to Graduates of the Institute.

EXAMINATIONS:
The Institute, founded in 1919, provides research and training in osteopathy. Basic training

includes Remedial Massage, Medical Electricity and Manipulative Procedures. Postgraduate studies cover Sports Injuries and include Biomechanics and Orthotics. Candidates for the courses and exams need a minimum of 5 GCE/GCSEs and should be able to devote at least 4 hrs a day during the initial training period. Study is by distance learning, supporting lectures and video training together with regular practical sessions with patients. Before progressing to full practical training, students must sit a series of exams covering the 3 basic disciplines; these exams are marked externally by registered medical consultants. Diplomas are available in Sports Therapy, and Orthotics and Biomechanics.

THE CHARTERED SOCIETY OF PHYSIOTHERAPY

14 Bedford Row, London WC1R 4ED Tel: 020 7306 6666 Fax: 020 7306 6611
e-mail: education@csphysio.org.uk Website: www.csp.org.uk

MEMBERSHIP:
Fellows (FCSP): Members who make an exceptional contribution to the advancement of the profession.
Members (MCSP): Must have successfully completed an approved 3 yr or 4 yr hons degree leading to eligibility for membership of the Chartered Society of Physiotherapy and for state registration by the Physiotherapists Board at the Council for Professions Supplementary to Medicine.

TRAINING REQUIREMENTS:
Candidates for entry to training must have GCSE or SCE O Level passes in a *minimum* of 5 subjects including English and 2 sciences, and at least 3 passes at A Level grade C or above, or 4 at H grade, 1 of which should be a Biological Science. Equivalent qualifications such as BTEC, Science or Health Studies GNVQ Level 3 may be acceptable.
There are 30 institutions offering programmes leading to state registration/membership and the Chartered Society of Physiotherapy.

University Qualifications

The following universities offer qualifications in Physiotherapy and related subjects. Full details may be found in Part 4, under the entry for the appropriate university.

FIRST DEGREES AWARDED BY UNIVERSITIES
Brighton; Brunel; Coventry; Hertfordshire; Keele; Kingston; Leeds (The College of Ripon & York St John); Leeds Metropolitan; London (King's College London); Luton; Oxford Brookes; Salford; Wales (College of Medicine)

HIGHER DEGREES AWARDED BY UNIVERSITIES
Brighton; Coventry; Glasgow Caledonian; Hertfordshire; Leeds Metropolitan; Sheffield Hallam; Surrey (University of Surrey Roehampton); Ulster

DIPLOMAS AWARDED BY UNIVERSITIES
Birmingham; Hertfordshire

CERTIFICATES AWARDED BY UNIVERSITIES
Manchester Metropolitan

PLASTICS AND RUBBER
(including Polymer Science and Engineering)

Membership of Professional Institutions and Associations

SCHOOL OF POLYMER TECHNOLOGY
The University of North London, 166-220 Holloway Road, London N7 8DB Tel: 020 7753 5128 Fax: 020 7753 5081 Website: www.unl.ac.uk

QUALIFICATIONS:

National Certificate (Polymer Technology): Obtained on successful conclusion of a 1 yr FT or 2 yr PT course. The course is also available through distance learning. Candidates must hold GCE O Level or GCSE passes (Grades A, B or C) in English, Mathematics and a Science subject and 1 other, or an equivalent qualification.

BSc(Hons) Polymers &/with a number of subjects including computing, chemistry and business: Awarded after a 3 yr FT or 4 yr S course. Entry requirement for BSc courses is 5 GCSE passes, including Mathematics, and 2 A Level passes, including a physical science or engineering subject; or a BTEC NC/ND with merit grades in 3 appropriate Level III units.

BEng (Hons) Polymer Engineering: Awarded after a 3 yr FT or 4 yr S course. PT mode available. Direct entry into Part 2 possible for FT or PT mode with entry requirement of HNC/D in relevant subject.

MSc Polymer Science and Engineering: Awarded after 1 yr FT or 2 yr PT course to holders of a Science honours degree, or equivalent. February and September start.

MSc Manufacture and Design for Polymer Products: Awarded after 3 yrs PT course. Open to holders of science or engineering degrees and those with relevant industrial experience. The course is in collaboration with the Open University and is studied by a combination of short courses and distance learning. The course is part of the EPSRC IGDS programme.

MSc Polymers, Polymer Manufacture & Product Manufacture: 1 yr course open to holders of Science Hons degrees. It is a European course based here, and in France and Spain

MPhil and PhD: Awarded to suitably qualified graduates after a 2 or 3 yr FT period of research and postgraduate study.

Higher National Diploma/Certificate in Polymer Technology: 2yr FT/PT courses. Entry is 1 A Level pass or BTEC National Certificate.

NVQ Awards: The School is an approved centre and able to assess candidates and prepare candidates for assessment.

University Qualifications

The following universities offer qualifications in Plastics and Rubber and related subjects. Full details may be found in Part 4, under the entry for the appropriate university.

FIRST DEGREES AWARDED BY UNIVERSITIES
Coventry; Leeds; Manchester; Manchester Metropolitan.; Napier; North London; Sheffield; UMIST; Wolverhampton

HIGHER DEGREES AWARDED BY UNIVERSITIES
Belfast; Central England; Coventry; Lancaster; Leeds; Loughborough; Manchester; Manchester Metropolitan.; North London; UMIST

DIPLOMAS AWARDED BY UNIVERSITIES
Lancaster; Loughborough; Napier; North London

CERTIFICATES AWARDED BY UNIVERSITIES
Napier; North London

OTHER COURSES AWARDED BY UNIVERSITIES
North London

National Certificates and Diplomas

BTEC National Certificates/Diplomas: Science (Polymer Technology)
BTEC Higher National Certificates/Diplomas: Science (Polymer Technology)
Scotland
SQA HNC: Toolmaking (Polymer Moulds)
SQA Advanced Diploma in Plastics Moulding Technology.

NVQs

Level 1: Plastic Processing Operations; Processing Rubber (General Rubber Goods); Processing Rubber (Retreading Tyres); Processing Rubber (Tyre Manufacture)

Level 2: Fibre Reinforced Plastic Lamination; Plastics Processing Operations; Processing Rubber (General Rubber Goods); Processing Rubber (Retreading Tyres); Processing Rubber (Tyre Manufacture)
Level 3: Polymer Processing – Product Development; Polymer Processing Technology

SVQs
Level 1: Plastics Processing Operations; Processing Rubber; General Rubber Goods; Processing Rubber: Retreading Tyres or Tyre Manufacture
Level 2: Plastics Processing Operations; Processing Rubber: General Rubber Goods or Retreading Tyres or Tyre Manufacture
Level 3: Polymer Processing Product Development; Polymer Processing Technology

Useful Addresses
British Polymer Training Association, Coppice House, Halesfield 7, Telford, Shropshire TF7 4NA
Tel: 01952 587020 Fax: 01952 582065

PLUMBING

Membership of Professional Institutions and Associations

THE INSTITUTE OF PLUMBING

64 Station Lane, Hornchurch, Essex RM12 6NB Tel: 01708 472791 Fax: 01708 448987
e-mail: info@plumbers.org.uk Website: www.plumbers.org.uk/www.registeredplumber.com
MEMBERSHIP:
Fellow (FIOP): Aged over 25 working, for example, as a director manager or senior engineer in a consulting, manufacturing or installation company with qualifications or experience equivalent to NVQ Level 4 or 5. Suitably qualified applicants can be registered as Incorporated Engineers with the Engineering Council.
Member (MIP): Aged over 23, perhaps working as an established self-employed practitioner, partner, foreman, supervisor or technician with qualifications or experience equivalent to NVQ Level 3. Suitably qualified applicants can be registered as Engineering Technicians with the Engineering Council.
Associate (AIP): Aged over 20 working, for example, as a self-employed operative with qualifications or experience equivalent to NVQ Level 2.
Registered Plumber (RP): Description granted to applicants aged over 20 yrs who have suitable on-site experience.
Companion (CompIP): Open to anyone who is connected with the plumbing industry and supports the work of the Institute.
Trainee: Applicants will be studying for a qualification which will lead to a level of competence in one or more aspects of plumbing.
Industrial Associate: This category is for material and product manufacturers, plumbers' merchants, professional and other organisations who support the objectives of the Institute.

NVQs
Level 2: Mechanical Engineering Services (Plumbing); Plumbing
Level 3: Mechanical Engineering Services (Plumbing); Plumbing

SVQs
Level 2: Mechanical Engineering Services: Plumbing
Level 3: Mechanical Engineering Services: Plumbing

City & Guilds
2480 Marine Plumbing and Coppersmith's Work

Useful Addresses
Association of Plumbing and Heating Contractors, 14 Ensign House, Ensign Business Centre, Westwood Way, Coventry CV4 8JA Tel: 01203 470626 Fax: 01203 470942

British Plumbing Employers Council (Training) Ltd, 2 Walker Street, Edinburgh EH3 7LB Tel: 0131 225 2255 Faax: 0131 226 7638

POPULATION REGISTRATION

Membership of Professional Institutions and Associations

THE INSTITUTE OF POPULATION REGISTRATION
The Register Office, Goldings, London Road, Basingstoke, Hants RG21 4AN Tel: 01256 350745

The Institute consists of people engaged in the Births, Marriages and Deaths Registration Service and in work associated with the production of Vital, Health and Social Statistics, including the Census of Population.

Fellowship (FIR) is awarded to Members in recognition of outstanding service to the Institute.

Members (MIR) must have been Licentiates for at least 5 yrs and have produced a thesis on any registration related topic which, in the opinion of the Management Committee, reaches the necessary standard of knowledge, research and professional competence.

Licentiates (LIR) must at the time of their application be actively engaged in the profession. The Management Committee is currently considering how the Licentiate status will be awarded in the future.

Associates are those who are employed in the profession or associate professions.

The Institute also elects as **Honorary Members** such people as in their opinion merit the honour.

THE INSTITUTE'S EXAMINATIONS:

The Institute recognises the Registrar General for England and Wales as the sole arbiter of registrars' qualifications and standards (in England and Wales) and has therefore suspended its examining role.

University Qualifications

The following universities offer qualifications in Population Registration and related subjects. Full details may be found in Part 4, under the entry for the appropriate university.

FIRST DEGREES AWARDED BY UNIVERSITIES
London (London School of Economics & Political Science); Southampton

HIGHER DEGREES AWARDED BY UNIVERSITIES
Dundee; Exeter; Liverpool; London (London School of Economics & Political Science)

PRINTING
(including Paper Science)

Membership of Professional Institutions and Associations:

BRITISH PRINTING INDUSTRIES FEDERATION
11 Bedford Row, London WC1R 4DX Tel: 020 7915 8300 Fax: 020 7405 7784

EXAMINATIONS:
The Federation conducts annual exams in: Estimating, Introduction to Printing Technology, Print Sales & Print Order Processing. Candidates must be at least 18 yrs of age. Open Learning courses run by the Federation provide instruction in Introduction to Printing Technology, Print Order Processing, and Estimating. Courses are offered by printing departments of various colleges of further education throughout the UK in all these subjects.

NVQs: Levels 1, 2 & 3. In Print Production and Print Administration. Modern apprenticeships for 16 and 17 yr olds are available and there are schemes for both Production and Print Administration to NVQ Levels 2 & 3. New NVQs will be available in 1997 in Desk Top Publishing, Digital Printing, Print Finishing and Hand Binding.

LONDON COLLEGE OF PRINTING

Elephant and Castle, London SE1 6SB Tel: 020 7514 6569 e-mail: info@lcp.linst.ac.uk Website: www.lcp.linst.ac.uk

School of Media at Herbal House, Back Hill, London EC1R 5EN.The College is a specialist college for Further and Higher Education and is a constituent college of The London Institute. It is the only college of its kind in the country and offers a wide range of courses in its specialist areas, from foundation to postgraduate and postexperience qualifications. FT courses include: Advertising, Bookbinding, Business Management, Display Design, Film & Video, Graphic Design, Interior Design, Journalism, Marketing, Retail Studies, Media, Photography, Photojournalism, Printing Planning and Production, Printing Management, Publishing, Radio Journalism, Retail Design, Screenprinting, Textile Design, Travel and Tourism. PT courses: For those already in employment, the College offers a wide variety of courses – day release, evenings or block in many of the areas listed above. Short courses: The College's Professional Development Unit mounts a large number of tailor-made courses to meet individual training needs. It also specialises in seminars, conferences and a range of short courses in the College's specialist areas.

THE INSTITUTE OF PRINTING

The Mews, Hill House, Clanricarde Road, Tunbridge Wells, Kent TN1 1PJ
Tel: 01892 538118/518028 Fax: 01892 518028
e-mail: iop@globalprint.com Website: www.globalprint.com/uk/iop

MEMBERSHIP:
Honorary Fellows: Elected in recognition of outstanding services to printing or to the Institute.
Fellows (FIOP): Must have the qualifications necessary to become a Corporate Member. They must have been engaged for a sufficient period in an important position of responsibility in or connected with industry and have made a distinctive contribution to the science, art and/or professional management of printing.
Members (MIOP): Must have been engaged for at least 3 yrs in a relevant position of responsibility since becoming a Graduate Member; or have been engaged for at least 5 yrs in a relevant position of substantial responsibility or have been engaged in a position of relevant responsibility for at least 3 yrs and have attained a relevant degree or equivalent academic or vocational qualification or have contributed an original paper to an appropriate publication, relevant to the industry.
Graduates (GradIOP): Must have successfully completed a degree level course approved by the Institute.
Students: Must be following, or intending to follow, an approved course of further education acceptable to the Council.
Associates: Must have suitable experience in or connected with printing.

University Qualifications

The following universities offer qualifications in Printing and related subjects. Full details may be found in Part 4, under the entry for the appropriate university.

FIRST DEGREES AWARDED BY UNIVERSITIES

Anglia; Dundee; Glasgow (Glasgow School of Art); Heriot-Watt (Edinburgh College of Art); London Institute (London College of Printing); UMIST; Wolverhampton

HIGHER DEGREES AWARDED BY UNIVERSITIES
Bradford (Bradford & Ilkley Community College); Bristol; Heriot-Watt; London Institute (Camberwell College of Arts); Northampton; Royal College of Art; UMIST; Wales (University of Wales, Swansea)

DIPLOMAS AWARDED BY UNIVERSITIES
Brighton; Hertfordshire (West Herts College); London Institute (London College of Printing)

POSTGRADUATE DIPLOMAS AWARDED BY UNIVERSITIES
Heriot-Watt

National Certificates and Diplomas

BTEC National Certificates/Diplomas: Printing
BTEC Higher National Certificates/Diplomas: Print Production (Technology and Management); Printing
Scotland
SQA HNC: 3-Dimensional Design; 3-Dimensional Design & Furniture Design; 3-dimensional Design (industrial Design); 3-Dimensional Design (Jewellery); 3-Dimensional Design (Pottery & Ceramics); Electronic Publishing; Exhibition Design; Graphic Design; Graphic Reproduction; Graphic Design & Illustration; Illustration & Media Design; Illustration; In-House Publishing; Print Management with Production; Print Production & Quality Control; Print Sales & Marketing; Spatial Design (Display Design); Spatial Design (Interior Design); Spatial Design (Interior Planning).
SQA HND: 3-Dimensional & Furniture Design; 3-Dimensional Design (Industrial Design); 3-Dimensional Design (Jewellery); 3-Dimensional Design (Pottery & Ceramics); Exhibition Design; Graphic Design; Graphics and Illustration; Illustration; Illustration & Media Design; Information & Media Technology; Spatial Design (Interior Design); Practical Journalism; Print Management with Production; Publication Production; Editing and Design.
SVQ Advanced Diploma: Medical Illustration; Spatial Design.

NVQs

Level 2: Machine Printing; Mechanised Binding; Non-impact Printing; Periodical Production: Advertisement Production; Print Commercial; Print Finishing
Level 3: Machine Printing; Mechanised Binding; Periodical Production: Advertisement Production; Print Commercial; Print Finishing
Level 4: Periodical Production: Advertisement Production

SVQs

Level 2: Machine Printing; Mechanised Binding; Print Commercial; Print Finishing; Non Impact Printing; Origination
Level 3: Machine Printing; Mechanised Binding; Print Commercial; Print Finishing; Printing Photographic Material; Origination

City & Guilds

5260 Printing and Graphic Communications

Useful Addresses

British Printing Industries Federation, 11 Bedford Row, London WC1R 4DX Tel: 020 7915 8300 Fax: 020 7405 7784
Paper Education and Training Council, Papermakers House, Rivenhall Road, Westlea, Swindon SN5 7BD Tel: 01793 889600 Fax: 01793 886363

PRISON SERVICE

HM PRISON SERVICE, ENGLAND AND WALES

HM Prison Service, Room 329, Cleland House, Page Street, London SW1P 4LN Tel: 020 7217 6437
Website: www.hmprisonservice.gov.uk
The Prison Service recruits honours graduates from any discipline to join its accelerated promotion scheme for potential senior managers. Whilst members of the scheme start as Prison Officers, it is expected that after 1 yr they will be junior managers (Principal Officers) and that in less than 5 yrs they will have reached prison Governor 4; the grade of most Deputy Governors. Members of the scheme will have demonstrated that they have at least the potential to become Governors of large prisons, and preferably to progress to the highest levels of prison service management. 'Her Majesty's Prison Service serves the public by keeping in custody those committed by the courts. Our duty is to look after them with humanity and help them to lead law-abiding and useful lives in custody and after release.'

SCOTTISH PRISON SERVICE

Calton House, 5 Redheughs Rigg, Edinburgh EH12 9HW Website: www.sps.gov.uk/
The Scottish Prison Service is an Executive Agency with its Chief Executive reporting to the Scottish Parliament. With nearly 4,600 staff, it runs 19 establishments ranging from Young Offenders Institutions through Open Prisons to High Security Units. At present, entry to the Service is at Discipline Officer level although there is a fast track scheme to allow Officers to proceed quickly through the uniformed grades to Governor level. Entry requirements at Officer level is 5 O Level grades including English and Maths, or 3 yrs' supervisory experiences. Candidates must pass a psychometric test and a physical training assessment prior to interview.(For Probation Work see Social Work.)

University Qualifications

The following universities offer qualifications in Prison Service and related subjects. Full details may be found in Part 4, under the entry for the appropriate university.

HIGHER DEGREES AWARDED BY UNIVERSITIES

Cambridge; Greenwich

DIPLOMAS AWARDED BY UNIVERSITIES

Birmingham

RESEARCH DEGREES AWARDED BY UNIVERSITIES

Exeter

OCR

OCR offer the following awards:
Custodial Care Levels 2 & 3

Useful Addresses

Prison Service College, Aberford Road, Wakefield, West Yorkshire WF1 4DE Tel: 01924 434100

PROFESSIONAL INVESTIGATION

THE INSTITUTE OF PROFESSIONAL INVESTIGATORS

Secretary General: J.D. Cole, Suite 353, Glenfield Park Business Centre, Blakewater Road, Blackburn, Lancashire BB1 5QH Tel: 01254 680072 Fax: 01254 59276 e-mail: admin@ipi.org.uk
Website: www.ipi.org.uk
The Institute of Professional Investigators was founded in 1976 as a professional body, catering

primarily for the work and educational needs of professional investigators of all types and all specialisations. Actual voting Membership is in the category of **Member (MIPI)** and **Fellow (FIPI)**, with the faculties of **Affiliateship** being offered to those who are otherwise suitable for Membership, but who lack recognised vocational or academic qualifications which they are required to obtain within 3 yrs, and **Associateship** being offered to those with long experience in investigation but without formal qualifications. Advancement to Fellow is by submission and acceptance of a thesis/dissertation. The Institute has adopted a completely new and updated approach for the acceptance of entry qualifications. Appropriate recognised specialist vocational qualifications of a suitable standard are now acceptable as qualification for entry. The Institute also operates update and refresher training and educational facilities to NVQ standards, including an assessment process, success in which is acceptable as a qualification for entry. Direct entry is also available for those with appropriate academic qualification and investigatory experience.

University Qualifications

The following universities offer qualifications in Professional Investigation and related subjects. Full details may be found in Part 4, under the entry for the appropriate university.

DIPLOMAS AWARDED BY UNIVERSITIES
Loughborough

CERTIFICATES AWARDED BY UNIVERSITIES
Loughborough

NVQs

Level 3: Investigation; Investigation Scenes of Incidents
Level 4: Investigation

PSYCHOANALYSIS

THE BRITISH PSYCHO-ANALYTICAL SOCIETY
Byron House, 112a-114 Shirland Road, London W9 2EQ Website: www.psychoanalysis.org.uk

MEMBERSHIP:
The Society has **Members** and **Associate Members,** who are elected after a qualifying training and who may describe themselves as 'psychoanalysts'. The overall membership is approximately 450. The Society is affiliated to the International Psychoanalytical Association and its training organisation is the only one recognised by the Association as authorised to train psychoanalysts in the UK.

TRAINING:
Applicants for training are eligible for consideration if they are: (a) medically qualified or undergoing medical training; (b) not medically qualified with a university degree or its equivalent, who have either had clinical experience or have carried responsibilities deemed adequate in the course of their professional work. The most appropriate disciplines would include social work, anthropology, psychology and sociology. The length of training varies, but the minimum is 4 yrs' PT study. The training consists of: (1) a personal psychoanalysis; (2) a 3 yr course of lectures and seminars requiring attendance on 3 evenings a wk during term time; (3) psychoanalysis of patients under supervision. Qualification occurs when a candidate has reached a satisfactory standard – determined through continuous course assessment. A training in the psychoanalysis of children may be undertaken by qualified analysts or advanced students.

University Qualifications

The following universities offer qualifications in Psychoanalysis and related subjects. Full details may be found in Part 4, under the entry for the appropriate university.

HIGHER DEGREES AWARDED BY UNIVERSITIES
Belfast; Brunel; East London; Essex; Leeds; Leeds Metropolitan; London (Goldsmiths College); London (University College (UCL)); London Guildhall; Middlesex; Sheffield; York

DIPLOMAS AWARDED BY UNIVERSITIES
Dundee; East London; Leeds; Leeds Metropolitan; Oxford

CERTIFICATES AWARDED BY UNIVERSITIES
Belfast

PSYCHOLOGY

Membership of Professional Institutions and Associations

BRITISH PSYCHOLOGICAL SOCIETY

St Andrews House, 48 Princess Road East, Leicester LE1 7DR Tel: 0116 254 9568 Fax: 0116 247 0787 e-mail: mail@bps.org.uk Website: www.bps.org.uk

(Incorporated by Royal Charter in 1965)

MEMBERSHIP:

Chartered Psychologist (CPsychol): Status is granted to Members of The British Psychological Society who have been entered in the Register of Chartered Psychologists maintained by the Society under the terms of its Royal Charter of Incorporation. Entry in the Register is granted to Members who are judged to have reached a standard sufficient for professional practice in psychology without supervision following at least 6 yrs' undergraduate education and postgraduate training in psychology.

Fellowship (FBPsS): Awarded to Members of the Society in recognition of higher psychological qualifications and of an outstanding contribution to the advancement or dissemination of psychological knowledge or practice over at least 10 yrs.

Associateship Fellowship (AFBPsS): Awarded to Graduate Members of the Society who have either met the postgraduate requirement for registration as Chartered Psychologists and successfully completed a further period of study or practice of psychology for at least 2 yrs, or have engaged in the application, discovery, development or dissemination of psychological knowledge or practice for at least 7 yrs.

Graduate Membership: Awarded to people who hold an approved university honours degree in Psychology or a recognised equivalent, or an approved postgraduate qualification in Psychology.

Foreign Affiliates: Members of foreign psychological societies, mainly those which are affiliated to the International Union of Psychological Sciences, may be elected Foreign Affiliates.

Affiliates: Need have no technical qualifications in Psychology; they are those who are interested in the Society's work but who are not qualified to be elected as Graduate Members.

Student Subscribers: Are honours degree students of Psychology in universities or other institutions or may be, in certain circumstances, postgraduate students studying for a higher degree in Psychology.

EXAMINATIONS:

Qualifying Examination of the Society: Candidates must hold a degree from a recognised university or polytechnic or other institution. The exam comprises 1 written paper in each of the following: (1) Biological Foundations and Cognitive Processes; (2) Individual Differences, Social and Developmental Psychology; (3) Research Design and Quantitative Methods in Psychology; (4) General Paper; (5) Advanced Option Paper and a practical component. A pass in the Qualifying Examination confers on the candidate eligibility for Graduate Membership of the Society and the Graduate Basis for Registration as a Chartered Psychologist.

Doctorate in Clinical Psychology: Candidates must have the Graduate Basis for Registration and will normally be allowed to enrol if they have been accepted as a trainee clinical psychologist on a society accredited training course in clinical psychology. British NHS trainee clinical psychologists are normally required to have completed a 3 yr training course in clinical psychology, 1 such course now leads to the Doctorate in Clinical Psychology. The exam comprises 5 extended essays, 5 reports of clinical activity, 5 evaluations of clinical competence, 2 small-scale research projects, a research dissertation and an oral exam. The Doctorate is validated by the Open University. All enquiries should be directed to the British Psychological Society.

Diploma in the Applied Psychology of Teaching: Candidates become eligible for registration as Chartered Psychologists as Teachers and Lecturers in Psychology. Before enrolment they must have the Graduate Basis for Registration and are normally required to have had 4 yrs' teaching experience under the guidance of a Chartered Psychologist who is Teacher of Psychology. The Exam comprises: (1) 4 unseen written papers; (2) Applied Teaching Assessment comprising – 4 case studies demonstrating the application of the theoretical material covered in Section A; 6 examples of the candidate's actual work on course structure and evaluation, eg samples of work assessed by the candidate; evidence of competence as a teacher from approved observers' reports on 4 occasions; a video recording of an actual teaching session; (3) a dissertation; (4) an oral examination at the discretion of the examiners. Candidates will normally be required to follow a 2 yr FT or equivalent PT path leading to the diploma.

Diploma in Counselling Psychology: Candidates must have the Graduate Basis for Registration. They are normally required to follow a 3 yr FT or equivalent PT path leading to the Diploma involving supervised counselling psychology practice. The exam is based on submitted reports of counselling work, unseen written exam papers, essays, reports of research projects and an oral exam.

Postgraduate Certificate in Occupational Psychology: Candidates, who must hold the Graduate Basis for Registration, may enter for this examination consisting of 4 written papers taken over 2 days. The Certificate part-fulfils the requirements for registration with the Society as a Chartered Occupational Psychologist.

Diploma in Educational Psychology: Candidates must have the Graduate Basis for Registration, and will normally be allowed to enrol only if they have been accepted for employment as trainee educational psychologists in a psychological service. They are normally required to follow a 3 yr training of continuous supervised practical experience and study. The exam comprises 3 unseen written papers, assessment of practical and research competence through submission of professional work portfolios, a small-scale research project, research dissertation, supervisors' reports and an oral exam.

University Qualifications

The following universities offer qualifications in Psychology and related subjects. Full details may be found in Part 4, under the entry for the appropriate university.

FIRST DEGREES AWARDED BY UNIVERSITIES

Aberdeen; Abertay, Dundee; Anglia; Anglia (City College, Norwich); Aston; Bath; Bath Spa; Belfast; Birmingham; Bournemouth; Bradford; Bradford (Bradford & Ilkley Community College); Bristol; Brunel; Buckingham; Bucks. Coll.; Central England; Central Lancashire; Cheltenham & Gloucester; City; Coventry; De Montfort, Leicester; Derby; Dundee; Durham; East Anglia; East Anglia (Suffolk College); East London; Edinburgh; Essex; Exeter; Glamorgan; Glasgow; Glasgow Caledonian; Greenwich; Heriot-Watt; Hertfordshire; Huddersfield; Hull; Keele; Kent; Kent (Canterbury Christ Church University College); Kingston; Lancaster; Lancaster (Edge Hill College of Higher Education); Leeds; Leeds (Leeds, Trinity & All Saints); Leeds (The College of Ripon & York St John); Leeds Metropolitan; Leicester; Lincolnshire (Lincoln University Campus); Liverpool; Liverpool (Chester College of H.E.); Liverpool (Liverpool Hope University College); Liverpool John Moores; London (Birkbeck, University of London); London (Goldsmiths College); London (London School of Economics & Political Science); London (Royal Holloway); London (University College (UCL)); London Guildhall; Loughborough; Luton; Manchester; Manchester Metropolitan.; Middlesex; Napier; Newcastle; North London; Northampton; Northumbria; Nottingham; Nottingham Trent; Nottingham Trent (Southampton Institute); Oxford; Oxford Brookes; Paisley; Plymouth; Portsmouth; Queen Margaret; Reading; Salford (Halton College); Sheffield; Sheffield Hallam; South Bank; Southampton; Southampton (King Alfred's College); Southampton (University of Southampton New College); St Andrews; St Martin; Staffordshire; Stirling; Strathclyde; Sunderland; Surrey; Surrey (University of Surrey Roehampton); Sussex;

Teesside; Thames Valley; Ulster; Wales (Cardiff University); Wales (North East Wales Institute); Wales (University of Wales Institute, Cardiff); Wales (University of Wales, Bangor); Wales (University of Wales, Swansea); Warwick; Westminster; Wolverhampton; Worcester; York

HIGHER DEGREES AWARDED BY UNIVERSITIES

Aberdeen; Aston; Bath; Belfast; Birmingham; Bristol; Brunel; Bucks. Coll.; Cambridge; Central Lancashire; Cheltenham & Gloucester; City; Coventry; Cranfield; Dundee; East London; Edinburgh; Essex; Exeter; Glamorgan; Glasgow; Heriot-Watt; Hertfordshire; Hull; Keele; Kent; Lancaster; Leeds; Leicester; Liverpool; Liverpool (Chester College of H.E.); Liverpool (Liverpool Hope University College); Liverpool John Moores; London (Birkbeck, University of London); London (Goldsmiths College); London (Heythrop College); London (Institute of Education); London (King's College London); London (London School of Economics & Political Science); London (University College (UCL)); London Guildhall; Luton; Manchester; Middlesex; Newcastle; Northampton; Nottingham; Plymouth; Portsmouth; Reading; Sheffield; Southampton; St Andrews; Staffordshire; Stirling; Strathclyde; Surrey; Surrey (University of Surrey Roehampton); Sussex; Teesside; Ulster; UMIST; Wales (Cardiff University); Warwick; Westminster; Wolverhampton; York

DIPLOMAS AWARDED BY UNIVERSITIES

Bath Spa; Birmingham; Bristol; City; Durham; East Anglia; Edinburgh; Exeter; Exeter (Truro College); Glamorgan; Hertfordshire; Hull; Leeds; Leicester; Liverpool; Liverpool (Chester College of H.E.); London (Birkbeck, University of London); London (Goldsmiths College); London (Institute of Education); London (King's College London); London (Royal Holloway); London Guildhall; Nottingham; Oxford; Plymouth; Reading; Staffordshire; Sunderland; Sussex; Thames Valley; Ulster; Wales (Cardiff University); Wales (College of Medicine); Wales (North East Wales Institute); Westminster

CERTIFICATES AWARDED BY UNIVERSITIES

Central Lancashire; City; Exeter; Glamorgan; Leicester; London (Birkbeck, University of London); London (Goldsmiths College); London Guildhall; Staffordshire; Surrey (University of Surrey Roehampton)

POSTGRADUATE DIPLOMAS AWARDED BY UNIVERSITIES

Central Lancashire

PROFESSIONAL QUALIFICATIONS AWARDED BY UNIVERSITIES

East London

PSYCHOTHERAPY

ASSOCIATION OF CHILD PSYCHOTHERAPISTS

120 West Heath Road, London NW3 7TU Tel: 020 8458 1609 Fax: 020 8458 1482
e-mail: acp@dial.pipex.com
Members can be admitted to the Association after completing postgraduate training recognised by the ACP. The minimum requirements for entry into the training presently available are a degree and experience of working with young children. Details of training and the work of Child Psychotherapists in the NHS and private practice can be obtained from the Association at the above address.

BRITISH ASSOCIATION OF PSYCHOTHERAPISTS (BAP)

37 Mapesbury Road, London NW2 4HJ Tel: 020 8452 9823 Fax: 020 8452 5182
e-mail: mail@bap-psychotherapy.org Website: www.bap-psychotherapy.org
The BAP has, for over 35 yrs, trained and qualified Psychotherapists according to the highest professional standards. The BAP runs separate parallel training courses in Psychoanalytic

Psychotherapy and Jungian Analytic Psychotherapy for Adults. The Jungian Section was approved for Membership by the International Association for Analytical Psychology (IAAP) in 1986. These trainings last a *minimum* of 4 yrs from the commencement of theoretical training. The student should be in therapy with an approved therapist at least 3 times a wk throughout the training and until qualification. A Training in Child and Adolescent Psychotherapy was begun in 1982 and recognised by the Association of Child Psychotherapists (ACP) in 1986; students can therefore expect to become eligible, upon qualification, for employment under the NHS. The training lasts a *minimum* of 4 yrs. In addition, the BAP offers a Training in Adult Psychotherapy for Child Psychotherapists already registered with the ACP. This training lasts a *minimum* of 2 yrs. Upon qualification, members of the BAP are eligible for registration nationally with the British Confederation of Psychotherapists and/or the IAAP or ACP. In addition to its main professional courses, the Psychoanalytic, Jungian and Child Sections of the BAP offer shorter external courses of particular interest to workers in the helping professions, who wish to extend their understanding of a psychodynamic way of working in their day to day work. Since 1997, the BAP, in association with the Department of Psychology at Birbeck College, has offered a Diploma/MSc course in the Psychodynamics of Human Development. This PT course will enable students to develop an understanding of psychoanalytic or Jungian approaches to the study of human development, and to consider the contribution of recent research in child development. External courses offered in 2000/2001 include: From Infancy to Adulthood: Observing, Thinking, Experiencing; Infant Observation Seminars – a Jungian Approach; Jungian Thought in the Modern World; Trauma and Abuse Seminars; Collaborative Workshops on the Psychodynamics of Education. Full details of all these courses can be obtained from the Secretary at the above address or from the BAP website. Alongside its education programmes, the BAP also offers a Supervision Service and a Consultation Service for the media, and a prompt assessment and referral system for children, adolescents and adults requiring psychotherapy.

NATIONAL COLLEGE OF HYPNOSIS AND PSYCHOTHERAPY

12 Cross Street, Nelson, Lancashire BB9 7EN Tel: 01282 699378 Fax: 01282 698633
e-mail: hypnosis_nchp@compuserve.com Website: www.nchp.clarets.co.uk
Nationwide training in Hypnotherapy and Psychotherapy for suitable, well-motivated people seeking a new career. We also train people already engaged in complementary health practice, doctors, nurses and other professionals. Comprehensive courses are held on a PT basis at weekends in established teaching centres in London, Glasgow, Liverpool and N. Ireland. Courses are externally accredited by the British Accreditation Council for Independent Further and Higher Education. Successful completion of the 3 stage training leads to the awards of the College:
Certificate in Hypnotherapy and Psychotherapy at the end of Stage 2, based on internally and externally assessed coursework, and exam, and
Diploma in Hypnotherapy and Psychotherapy at the end of the Stage 3, after completion of a minimum 5000 word dissertation which is marked by assessors independent of the College, and a practical exam. Training to Diploma level takes approximately 2 yrs PT. Continuing Professional Development courses and seminars for students and practising therapists are held in various locations. The National College is the main training faculty for the National Register of Hypnotherapists and Psychotherapists (NRHP). Both National College and National Register are members of the British Association for Counselling, the United Kingdom Council for Psychotherapy (UKCP) and the European Association for Hypno Psychotherapy. Suitably qualified graduates can be recommended for UKCP registration by the NRHP.

NATIONAL COUNCIL OF PSYCHOTHERAPISTS

Secretary, Nationwide Referrals and General Enquiries, PO Box 6072, Nottingham NG6 9BW
Tel: 0115 9131 382 Fax: 0115 9131 382
e-mail: ncphq@talk21.com Website: www.natcouncilofpsychotherapists.org
MEMBERSHIP:
Licentiate Member (LNCP): Licentiate Membership is determined by consideration of the applicant's professional training, competence and development as outlined below and all areas are considered to be compulsory. Also implicit is the requirement that applicants will possess those personal qualities which make them suitable for the profession of psychotherapy.

Training Requirements: (a) The applicant must have successfully undertaken a relevant training programme of no less than 1 yr FT or 2 yrs' PT duration (ie combined theoretical and practical training in at least 1 established psychotherapeutic approach) or its equivalent, of not less than 900 hrs overall, consisting of a min 180 hrs of face-to-face tuition; reading assignments: preparation of reports/theses; opportunities for group interaction; personal supervision and personal therapy of the type relevant to the course; *or* (b) where the applicant has less formal training in psychotherapy than the above but can provide evidence of sufficient training and clinical experience in terms of time and commitment which would equate with an acceptable qualification. The burden of proof, here, lies squarely with the applicant.

Competence: (a) The applicant must submit 2 case studies (min 1500 words each) plus a short autobiography, all to be typed doubled-spaced. Also required is *either* a personal interview or a letter of recommendation from a Full Member of the National Council (ie MNCP/FNCP); *or* (b) the applicant may sit a 3 hr written exam on psychology and psychotherapy and will need to achieve the required pass mark. (*Note:* Details available from the Secretary.) This to be followed by an oral board. An autobiography is also required.

Development: The applicant must furnish all necessary details and sign the Commitment to Personal and Professional Development (inherent within the application form).

Full Member (MNCP): The applicant must have been a Licentiate Member, under supervision, for a min of 1 yr; submit a written essay (min 3000 words) on a relevant topic which successfully demonstrates his/her belief and practice and which offers evidence of at least 1 major theoretical approach; submit 1 'in depth' case history (min 3000 words) which demonstrates their ability to integrate their preferred methodology with 1 particular client throughout a typical full length course of therapy; provide full contact details of 2 professional referees.

Fellow (FNCP): Cannot be applied for. Awarded to Full Members for exceptional service to the field of psychotherapy generally and the National Council in particular.

THE NATIONAL REGISTER OF HYPNOTHERAPISTS AND PSYCHOTHERAPISTS

12 Cross Street, Nelson, Lancashire BB9 7EN Tel: 01282 716839 Fax: 01282 698633
e-mail: nrhp@btconnect.com Website: www.nrhp.co.uk

A professional association of qualified therapists who have trained with the National College of Hypnosis and Psychotherapy and equivalent trainings. There are 4 grades of membership relating to the successful completion of National College courses:

Affiliate (NRHP (Affil)), upon completion of the Stage 1 Foundation Course; **Associate (NRHP (Assoc)),** for holders of the College Certificate; **Full Membership (MNRHP),** for holders of the College Diploma in Hypnotherapy and Psychotherapy; and **Full Membership (equivalent) (MNRHP(Eqv)),** for UKCP Registered Hypno-Psychotherapists who have trained with UKCP organisations other than the NCHP. The National Register provides a referral service for members of the public seeking a qualified therapist, and publishes a Directory of Practitioners and a members newsletter. It also offers Continuing Professional Development, has a system of therapist supervision and organises an annual Summer Conference for members. All members are required to adhere to a Code of Ethics and carry appropriate insurance. In common with the National College, the National Register is a member of the British Association for Counselling, the United Kingdom Council for Psychotherapy (UKCP) and the European Association for Hypno Psychotherapy. Suitably qualified members can be recommended for UKCP registration.

THE NATIONAL SCHOOL OF HYPNOSIS AND PSYCHOTHERAPY

Registrar, N-SHAP, 28 Finsbury Park Road, London N4 2JX Tel: 020 7359 6991
Website: www.users.globalnet.co.uk/~enneauk/

N-SHAP was founded in 1980 in response to demands for training beyond standardised command and relaxation techniques. Approaches incorporate some of the latest findings of brain/mind research. Free 22-page guide to training and registration despatched on application.

MEMBERSHIP:

Affiliate Membership: On commencement of Part II, trainees may apply for Affiliate Membership of Central Register of Advanced Hypnotherapists (CRAH) provided they are undergoing approved clinical supervision.

Associate Membership: Granted to diploma holders who have been in practice with satisfactory supervisor reports for several mths.

Full Membership: May be applied for after completion of Part III of the course and a minimum of 2 yrs' supervision. N-SHAP graduates may also apply to British Register of Complementary Practitioners, administered by Institute for Complementary Medicine. Those wishing to apply for registration with UK Council for Psychotherapy will generally be required to complete N-SHAP Part IV and undertake 4 essay assignments unless accredited with prior learning.

EXAMINATIONS:

Dip THP (N-SHAP): Qualification depends on satisfactory class attendance (10 weekends) and execution of class assignments, teachers' reports and 1 day formal Diploma exams – practical and written.

Dip AdvHYP (N-SHAP): Awarded to graduates after further training with mini-dissertation requirement, provided such graduates have been in practice under supervision for a required period.

N-SHAP is currently working towards university accreditation at Master's level.

THE PSYCHOTHERAPY CENTRE

67 Upper Berkeley Street, London W1H 7DH Tel: 020 7723 6173
e-mail: principal@the.psychotherapy.centre.fsnet.co.uk
Website: www.the-psychotherapy-centre-freeserve.co.uk

TRAINING COURSES:
The course is concerned with helping people who have relationship, emotional or psychogenic problems, enabling them to free themselves of these problems and function healthily and effectively. It is based on understanding relevant psychological, social and physiological factors. The training is competence-orientated and mainly experiential. Prospective trainees, to gain insight and ensure that they are reasonably free of neuroses which could adversely affect their treatment of patients, first of all have extensive therapy with a practitioner designated for this purpose by The Psychotherapy Centre. The therapy, evolved in the light of 4 decades of experience and long-term follow-ups of results, is holistic, non-interpretative, non-suppressive, and free of indoctrination, theory, religion or drugs. It is followed by lectures and practical work, including giving therapy under supervision and giving talks. The course, including therapy, normally takes 4 yrs FT or PT.

ADMISSION REQUIREMENTS:
Applicants must have exceptional integrity and intelligence and a university degree.

EXAMINATION:
A **Diploma in Psychotherapy** may be obtained by passing written, multiple-choice and practical exams at the end of the course, in conjunction with cumulative assessment during the course.

University Qualifications

The following universities offer qualifications in Psychotherapy and related subjects. Full details may be found in Part 4, under the entry for the appropriate university.

FIRST DEGREES AWARDED BY UNIVERSITIES
Central England; Coventry

HIGHER DEGREES AWARDED BY UNIVERSITIES
Central England; City; City (School of Psychotherapy & Counselling at Regent's College); De Montfort, Leicester; Essex; Kent; Leeds; Leeds Metropolitan; London (Birkbeck, University of London); London (Goldsmiths College); London (King's College London); London (University College (UCL)); Portsmouth; Sheffield Hallam

DIPLOMAS AWARDED BY UNIVERSITIES
Belfast; Bournemouth; Brighton; Central England; Kent; London (Goldsmiths College); London (King's College London); London (University College (UCL)); Sheffield; Surrey (University of Surrey Roehampton); Sussex

CERTIFICATES AWARDED BY UNIVERSITIES
Leeds Metropolitan; Surrey (University of Surrey Roehampton)

POSTGRADUATE CERTIFICATES AWARDED BY UNIVERSITIES
Warwick

NVQs

Level 2: Service Support (Advice, Guidance, Counselling and Psychotherapy)

SVQs

Level 2: Services Support: Advice, Guidance, Counselling and Psychotherapy

PUBLIC ADMINISTRATION AND LOCAL GOVERNMENT

Membership of Professional Institutions and Associations

THE INSTITUTE OF PUBLIC SERVICE MANAGEMENT

9 Parkland Drive, Rossington, Doncaster DN11 0XN Tel: 01302 286 0762
e-mail: ipsm@cyberphile.co.uk
The Institute of Public Sector Management, established in 1983, provides a broad-based professional institute for managers employed in the public sector in general, but primarily in local government. There are many managers working in the public and charity sectors who can benefit from joining a professional body of like-minded officers who are interested in the promotion of best management practice. IPSM aims to promote and advance efficient management and administration, develop the usefulness of the service provided by its members, and encourage the training and education of staff. Members are entitled to use the designatory letters IPSM and attend national and local conferences and seminars organised by IPSM. They also have the opportunity to participate in the running of the institute through the Council. The Institute provides members with a help-desk facility and is able to draw on a considerable bank of expertise across a wide range of disciplines, as well as providing a networking facility. Full members must have an administrative qualification of at least BTEC Higher National Award standard. They must have been employed in the public or charity sector for at least 12 mths prior to their application. Senior managers in the public and charity sectors are also eligible. Student membership is open to persons studying for qualifications recognised for full membership.

University Qualifications

The following universities offer qualifications in Public Administration and Local Government and related subjects. Full details may be found in Part 4, under the entry for the appropriate university.

FIRST DEGREES AWARDED BY UNIVERSITIES

Anglia; Aston; Bath; Belfast; Birmingham; Bradford (Bradford & Ilkley Community College); Brighton; Bristol; Brunel; Bucks. Coll.; Central England; Central Lancashire; Cheltenham & Gloucester; Coventry; De Montfort, Leicester; Durham; East Anglia (Suffolk College); Edinburgh; Essex; Glamorgan; Glasgow Caledonian; Hertfordshire; Hull; Keele; Kent; Leeds; Leeds Metropolitan; Lincolnshire (Lincoln University Campus); Liverpool John Moores; London (Goldsmiths College); London (London School of Economics & Political Science); London (Royal Holloway); London Guildhall; Loughborough; Luton; Manchester; Manchester Metropolitan.; Middlesex; Newcastle; North London; Nottingham; Paisley; Plymouth; Portsmouth; Queen Margaret; Salford; Sheffield; Sheffield Hallam; South Bank; Southampton; Stirling; Surrey (University of Surrey Roehampton); Sussex; Teesside; Ulster; Wales (Cardiff University); Wales (University of Wales, Bangor); Wales (University of Wales, Swansea); Warwick; Wolverhampton; York

HIGHER DEGREES AWARDED BY UNIVERSITIES

Abertay, Dundee; Anglia; Aston; Bath; Birmingham; Brighton; Bristol; Brunel; Cheltenham & Gloucester; Coventry; East Anglia; Edinburgh; Essex; Glamorgan; Glasgow; Greenwich; Hertfordshire; Hull; Kent; Leeds; Leeds Metropolitan; Leicester; Liverpool; Liverpool John Moores; London (Birkbeck, University of London); London (Goldsmiths College); London (London School of Economics & Political Science); London (Queen Mary & Westfield College (incorporating St Bartholomew's and the Royal London School of Medicine & Dentistry)); London (Royal Holloway); London (University College (UCL)); Luton; Manchester; Middlesex; Napier; Newcastle; North London; Northampton; Nottingham; Oxford; Plymouth; Portsmouth; Sheffield; Sheffield Hallam; South Bank; Stirling; Sunderland; Sussex; Ulster; Wales (University of Wales, Bangor); Warwick; Westminster; York

DIPLOMAS AWARDED BY UNIVERSITIES

Aston; Birmingham; Blackburn; Bradford (Bradford & Ilkley Community College); Bristol; De Montfort, Leicester; Edinburgh; Glasgow; Hertfordshire; Hull; Kent; Leeds; Luton; Manchester; Napier; Newcastle; Strathclyde; Teesside; Ulster

CERTIFICATES AWARDED BY UNIVERSITIES

Brighton; Leeds Metropolitan

OTHER COURSES AWARDED BY UNIVERSITIES

Leeds Metropolitan

National Certificates and Diplomas

BTEC National Certificates/Diplomas: Public Services
Scotland
SQA HNC: Police Studies; Public Administration

Local Government

The Improvement and Development Agency, Layden House, 76-86 Turnmill Street, London EC1M 5LG Tel 020 7296 6600 Fax 020 7296 6666. The Agency brings together a range of services in support of management and people-related matters. Its fundamental role is to help local authorities to be more effective in their work, particularly in the way in which services are delivered, and the way in which they provide democratic leadership in their communities during a time of great change.
EXAMINATIONS AND QUALIFICATIONS:
The Diploma in Careers Guidance and the Diploma in Trading Standards: The Improvement and Development Agency, through its Careers Guidance Training Council and Diploma in Trading Standards Council, respectively awards the Diploma in Careers Guidance and the Diploma in Trading Standards.
N/SVQs in Guidance: In partnership with the Institute of Careers Guidance and SQA, the Agency awards these qualifications.
NVQs in Management; Training & Development; Customer Service: The Agency has now been approved to offer these qualifications For further information relating to these see under 'Employment and Careers Services' and 'Diploma in Trading Standards'.
Diploma in the Management of Care Services: The Agency awards this qualification, which is open to all managers in the care sector. The qualification is gained by achieving competence against set standards and having that competence assessed and verified.
NVQs for the Emergency Fire Services: Acting in the name of the Fire Services Awarding Body, the Agency awards these new qualifications.
SVQ for the Emergency Fire Services: Acting in the name of the Fire Service Awarding Body, the Agency awards these new qualifications jointly with SQA.

PUBLISHING

LONDON SCHOOL OF PUBLISHING

David Game House, 69 Notting Hill Gate, London W11 3JS Tel: 020 7221 3399
e-mail: lsp@easynet.co.uk
Provides training to those already in publishing or for those who wish to enter publishing as a career. All courses are for graduates. Present courses on offer are: Editorial, Magazine Editorial, Picture Research, Book Commissioning, Sales and Marketing for Publishing, Quark XPress and Publishing: An Introduction. All courses are run in the evening between 6.30 – 8.30 pm on one evening a wk for 10 wks. A **Certificate** is issued (which is approved by the National Union of Journalists) at the end of each course that is recognised by our Advisory Board of publishing professionals. Most courses are concluded by a 2 hr written exam, after successful completion of which a certificate will be issued.

SOCIETY OF TYPOGRAPHIC DESIGNERS

Chapelfield Cottage, Randwick, Stroud, Gloucestershire GL6 6HS Tel: 01453 759311
Fax: 01453 767466
This is a professional society open to typographers and graphic designers who submit to the membership committee evidence of their skills in their chosen category of membership, and agree to accept the aims and principles of the Society. Further information can be obtained from the Secretary.

University Qualifications

The following universities offer qualifications in Publishing and related subjects. Full details may be found in Part 4, under the entry for the appropriate university.

FIRST DEGREES AWARDED BY UNIVERSITIES

London Institute (London College of Printing); Loughborough; Middlesex; Napier; Oxford Brookes; Robert Gordon

HIGHER DEGREES AWARDED BY UNIVERSITIES

City; Leeds; London (University College (UCL)); Manchester; Napier; Plymouth; Stirling

DIPLOMAS AWARDED BY UNIVERSITIES

City; Hertfordshire (West Herts College); London Institute (London College of Printing); Napier; Oxford Brookes; Plymouth; Stirling

National Certificates and Diplomas

BTEC National Certificates/Diplomas: Design (Bookbinding)
BTEC Higher National Certificates/Diplomas: Design (Bookbinding)

NVQs

Level 2: Publishing
Level 3: Publishing

Other Vocational Awarding Bodies

ABC: Desk Top Publishing

Useful Addresses

Publishing Training Centre, 45 East Hill, Wandsworth, London, SW18 2QZ Tel: 020 8874 2718 Fax: 020 8870 8985
Institute of Publishing, Essex Lodge, Barnes High Street, London SW13 0LW Tel/Fax: 020 8392 2927

PURCHASING AND SUPPLY

Membership of Professional Institutions and Associations

THE CHARTERED INSTITUTE OF PURCHASING AND SUPPLY

Easton House, Easton on the Hill, Stamford, Lincolnshire
PE9 3NZ
Tel: 01780 756777
Fax: 01780 751610
 e-mail: info@cips.org
Website: www.cips.org.

MEMBERSHIP:
Fellow (FCIPS): Fellowship is awarded by assessment and is defined thus: a **Corporate Member (MCIPS)** who, in the opinion of the Council of the Institute: (i) has demonstrated outstanding competence and achievement in purchasing and supply, a high level of professional knowledge and experience, and responsibility at a senior management level in an enterprise of significant size; *or* (ii) has made or is making a significant contribution towards the advancement of the purchasing and supply profession.
Corporate Member (MCIPS): A person who has either completed the Institute's 2 stage professional exams or has satisfied the Institute's criteria for assessment by alternative routes, which may include a requirement for a written submission, a project and evidence or CPD, and who has been engaged wholly or mainly in a position of responsibility in purchasing and supply for 3 yrs or more.
Student or Associate: A person who either wishes to study for one of the CIPS qualifications, or is pursuing the professional competence route to Corporate Membership.
Affiliate: Those who have an interest in purchasing and supply chain management but do not wish to commit themselves to one of the assessment processes may join as an Affiliate.

EXAMINATIONS:
Graduate Diploma in Purchasing and Supply: Minimum entry qualifications are 5 GCE or GCSE passes, of which at least 2 must be at A Level. The exams consist of a Foundation Stage and a Professional Stage. Many students pursue a BTEC Higher Award or a SCOTVEC equivalent to obtain substantial exemptions from the Institute's Foundation exams. Similarly those holding recognised degrees, diplomas or other professional qualifications will be considered under the exemptions policy. Many colleges offer PT and FT study facilities and there are also correspondence courses. NVQ/SVQs in Procurement also provide a route to CIPS membership.
Certificate in Purchasing and Supply: Open access. Suitable for newcomers to purchasing and supply. Leads to the
Advanced Certificate in Purchasing and Supply for those who want to develop their understanding of operational issues.

University Qualifications

The following universities offer qualifications in Purchasing and Supply and related subjects. Full details may be found in Part 4, under the entry for the appropriate university.

FIRST DEGREES AWARDED BY UNIVERSITIES
Glamorgan; Manchester Metropolitan.; Northumbria

HIGHER DEGREES AWARDED BY UNIVERSITIES
Salford; Staffordshire

DIPLOMAS AWARDED BY UNIVERSITIES
Napier; Salford

PROFESSIONAL QUALIFICATIONS AWARDED BY UNIVERSITIES
Glamorgan

NVQs

Level 2: Procurement
Level 3: Procurement
Level 4: Procurement

QUALITY ASSURANCE

Membership of Professional Institutions and Associations

THE INSTITUTE OF QUALITY ASSURANCE

12 Grosvenor Crescent, London SW1X 7EE Tel: 020 7245 6722 Fax: 020 7245 6788

e-mail: reception@iqa.org Website: www.iqa.org

CORPORATE MEMBERS:
Honorary Fellows (HonFIQA): Are limited in number and have rendered, or are in a position to render, conspicuous service to the Institute.
Fellows (FIQA): Must be at least 35, of degree level qualification in a subject acceptable to the Institute's Council and must hold qualifications deemed equivalent to the Institute's QA Management Exams. They must normally have been a Member for at least 5 yrs and must have held a senior professional or managerial position with QA responsibilities for at least 5 yrs.
Members (MIQA): Must be at least 26 and must normally possess the academic qualifications shown above for Fellow. They must also have a minimum of 5 yrs' experience in QA (of which at least 2 yrs have been devoted to practical training) and a minimum of 2 yrs in a responsible QA appointment.

NON-CORPORATE MEMBERS:
Associate Members (AMIQA): Must be at least 26. They must have satisfactorily completed studies to a level equivalent to the full Institute's membership exams (ie HNC/HND and passed the Institute's 2 mandatory QA papers) and fulfil the experience requirements shown above for Member.
Licentiates (Lic IQA): Must be at least 21 and hold a degree level qualification in a subject acceptable to the Institute's Council and to be currently involved in QA. Alternatively they must have satisfactorily completed studies to the level of the Institute's membership exam and have 2 yrs' experience in QA.
Students: Must be at least 17 and be pursuing a course of study leading to a qualification or grade of membership in IQA.
Affiliate: Open to those who have an interest in QA but are not eligible for any other grade of membership.

EXAMINATIONS:
The Institute's exams consist of 2 compulsory papers (the A11 Introduction to Quality Assurance and the A12 Principles & Techniques of Quality Management), 2 optional papers, IQA Diploma for Associate Member, followed by the IQA Advanced Diploma for Member. Existing qualifications may give exemption to some of the above examinations. Please contact the Education Department for clarification. Other exams may give exemption from parts of the IQA exams. Please contact the Institute for further information on these and the IQA's examinations.

University Qualifications

The following universities offer qualifications in Quality Assurance and related subjects. Full details may be found in Part 4, under the entry for the appropriate university.

FIRST DEGREES AWARDED BY UNIVERSITIES
Central Lancashire; Huddersfield; Lancaster (Blackpool and The Fylde College); Leeds Metropolitan; Paisley; Salford; Staffordshire; Wales (University of Wales, Bangor)

HIGHER DEGREES AWARDED BY UNIVERSITIES
Birmingham; Bristol; Cranfield; Glamorgan; Greenwich; Hertfordshire; Leeds; Leeds

Metropolitan; Lincolnshire; London (King's College London); Napier; Newcastle; Nottingham Trent; Paisley; Portsmouth; Salford; South Bank; Stirling; Warwick; Wolverhampton

DIPLOMAS AWARDED BY UNIVERSITIES
Birmingham; Leeds; Napier; Newcastle; Paisley; Salford; Stirling

CERTIFICATES AWARDED BY UNIVERSITIES
Leeds; Newcastle; Sunderland

OTHER COURSES AWARDED BY UNIVERSITIES
Northampton

National Certificates and Diplomas

Scotland
SQA HNC: Quality Assurance
SQA HND: Quality Management
Certificate in Quality Assurance

NVQs
Level 4: Quality Management

City & Guilds
7430 Quality Assurance

RADIOGRAPHY
(See note on State Registration)

Membership of Professional Institutions and Associations

THE SOCIETY AND THE COLLEGE OF RADIOGRAPHERS

THE SOCIETY OF RADIOGRAPHERS

207 Providence Square, Mill Street, London SE1 2EW
Tel: 020 7740 7200 Fax: 020 7740 7204
e-mail: info@sor.org
Website: www.sor.org

Radiography comprises 2 disciplines: Diagnostic Radiography and Therapeutic Radiography. Diagnostic Radiographers are responsible for producing high quality image on film and other recording materials which help to diagnose disease and the extent of injuries. Therapeutic Radiographers help to treat patients, many of whom have cancer, using ionising radiation and sometimes drugs. Membership is open to holders of a UK degree in either diagnostic or therapeutic radiography; the College's diploma (DCR); or an overseas qualification recognised as equiv by the College. The profession is now an all-graduate entry profession and the College's own diploma (DCR) has been withdrawn as a route to qualification with effect from April 1995.At least 50% of the curriculum is a clinical education programme within hospital departments though the academic and clinical components are fully integrated. The entry requirements for all courses are the University general requirements (eg 2 A Levels and 3 GCSE Grade C and various combinations of these including AS Levels). BTEC HNC, and GNVQ are acceptable as is entry through an Access Course. The majority of College specialist qualifications are being phased out in favour of post/graduate MSc courses.

University Qualifications

The following universities offer qualifications in Radiography and related subjects. Full details may be found in Part 4, under the entry for the appropriate university.

FIRST DEGREES AWARDED BY UNIVERSITIES

Bristol; Central England; City; Cranfield; East Anglia (Suffolk College); Hertfordshire; Kent (Canterbury Christ Church University College); Kingston; Portsmouth; Salford; Teesside; Ulster; Wales (University of Wales, Bangor)

HIGHER DEGREES AWARDED BY UNIVERSITIES

Central England; Kingston; Portsmouth; Salford; Wales (University of Wales, Bangor)

DIPLOMAS AWARDED BY UNIVERSITIES

Bradford; Central England; Liverpool

CERTIFICATES AWARDED BY UNIVERSITIES

Central England; City; Hertfordshire; Wales (University of Wales, Bangor)

RETAIL

MEMBERSHIP OF PROFESSIONAL INSTITUTIONS AND ASSOCIATIONS

THE BOOKSELLERS ASSOCIATION OF GREAT BRITAIN AND IRELAND

272 Vauxhall Bridge Road, London SW1V 1BA Tel: 020 7834 5477
Membership is by subscription.
Diploma in Professional Bookselling: Launched in April 1996, this is designed for booksellers seeking a recognised qualification. It is a self-study programme of 15 modules covering all aspects of bookselling and is generally assessed by tutors accredited by the Booksellers' Association.

BOSS (REPRESENTING THE UK STATIONERY AND OFFICE PRODUCT INDUSTRY)

6 Wimpole Street, London W1M 8AS Tel: 020 7637 7692
The Federation conducts exams in product knowledge to Diploma standards.
A minimum of 8 subject passes is required.
Diploma: For candidates who have been in the stationery and office machines trade for not less than 6 months.

THE BRITISH ANTIQUE DEALERS' ASSOCIATION

20 Rutland Gate, London SW7 1BD Tel: 020 7589 4128 Fax: 020 7581 9083 e-mail: enquiry@bada.demon.co.uk Website: www.bada.org
A member may be described as a 'Member of the British Antique Dealers' Association' or as a 'Member of the BADA'. (The use of designatory letters such as MBADA after the name is not permitted). Applicants must be sponsored by at least 2 members and their eligibility is determined by reference to evidence that they are established in business in the Antique Trade and carry a stock of antiques; that they have carried on their business in the Antique Trade for not less than 3 yrs immediately before their application, unless the Council of the Association decides in a particular case on a shorter period; that they are persons of integrity or, in the case of corporations, that they are under the control of such a person; that they have or command the degree of knowledge required to enable them to buy and when selling to describe the antique goods in which they deal.

THE CO-OPERATIVE COLLEGE

Stanford Hall, Loughborough, Leicestershire LE12 5QR Tel: 01509 857218 Fax: 01509 857263
e-mail: library@co-op.ac.uk

Certificate in Policy Studies: A continuously assessed and examined 23 week residential course for mature students. It provides social sciences and business pathways and leads to an HE Access certificate. Students accepted qualify for FEFC scholarships.

Diploma in Management Studies (IM), Certificate in Management Studies and Certificate in Supervisory Management are all PT and DL, with residential workshops.

NVQ/SVQ: A range of management, retail, customer service, training & development, human resource development and administration programmes, primarily at Levels 2, 3 & 4, to help meet the needs of the co-operative and mutual sectors.

A wide range of short courses particularly related to the co-operative and social economy secotrs are also offered including **Director and Member Training for Co-operatives. A Pension Fund Trustee Development Programme** has also been introduced. **Credit Union Training** is also undertaken here at the Co-operative College.

THE GUILD OF ARCHITECTURAL IRONMONGERS

8 Stepney Green, London E1 3JU Tel: 020 7790 3431 Fax: 020 7790 8517
e-mail: ironmongers@compuserve.com Website: www.gai.org.uk

MEMBERSHIP:

Full Membership: is open to bona fide Architectural Ironmongers and Builders Merchants with an interest in ironmongery, who hold adequate stocks in relation to turnover of architectural ironmongery and are equipped to provide the technical expertise, delivery and other facilities for meeting the requirements of the districts served, and who comply with the rules. Full membership is also open to certain manufacturers who meet the membership criteria.

Subsidiary Membership: is only available to subsidiaries of Full Members.

Branch Membership: is only available to branches of Full Members.

Associate Membership: is available to manufacturers of any type of architectural ironmongery (or such other products as the Executive Committee may decide to be suitable) who carry on a business in a manner compatible with the interests and standing of Architectural Ironmongers.

Overseas Membership: Membership of the Guild is available to an overseas applicant who complies with the rules and who carries on business in a manner compatible with the interest of Architectural Ironmongers.

Institute Section: Open to individuals actively engaged in the business of architectural ironmongery who has: *either* gained the GAI Diploma; *or* had such practical training and a minimum of 10 yrs experience.

Membership categories are Fellow, Member and Student. The Institute section has its own National and Regional Committees and holds meetings throughout the country for the membership.

EXAMINATIONS:

The Guild provides a 4 yr course of training. Students are not permitted to take the second year course until they have passed the first year exam, or take the third year courses until they have passed the second year exam. On successful completion of the fourth year exam, students will be awarded a GAI Diploma (DipGAI).

A Certificate is awarded on successful completion of the third year exam.

INSTITUTE OF BUILDERS' MERCHANTS

Parnall House, 5 Parnall Road, Harlow, Essex, CM18 7PP Tel: 01279 419650 Fax: 01279 419650

To improve through lectures, classes and courses of instruction the technical and general knowledge of persons engaged in or about to engage in the trade of a builders' merchants; to award diplomas, certificates and other distinctions; to encourage and undertake research and invention.

MEMBERSHIP:

Fellow (FIBM): Entry is for those who have rendered outstanding service to the local branch or Institute and may be invited by the Governers to become a Fellow.

Member (MIBM): Applicants must have attained NVQ Level 4 at least, but other professional qualifications will be considered by the Membership Committee.

Associate (AinstBM): Applicants should have attained NVQ Level 3 at least, or have 3 yrs' work experience within the industry.

Corporate (CIBM): Applicants must hold a position in a profession or industry that is allied to or serves the builders' merchant trade.

Student Grade: This grade is open to anyone involved in Level 2 NVQs modern apprenticeships.

INSTITUTE OF GROCERY DISTRIBUTION

Letchmore Heath, Watford, Hertfordshire WD2 8DQ Tel: 01923 851930 Fax: 01923 852531
e-mail: training@igd.org.uk
Individual Members (MIGD): open to persons who have achieved success in the Post Graduate Certificate in Food & Grocery Industry Management.

EDUCATION COURSES:
Foundation Certificate in Management: (accredited by Manchester Metropolitan University) An introduction to the food and grocery sector for junior and aspiring managers, consisting of 5 workshops, spread over a year.
Post Graduate Certificate in Food & Grocery Industry Management: (validated by the University of Edinburgh and carrying 60 CATS points) A postgraduate programme tailored for aspiring middle managers in the industry. The course consists of 4 core units, plus 2 option units spread over a year.

THE INSTITUTE OF MASTERS OF WINE

Five King's House, Queen Street Place, London EC4R 1QS Tel: 020 7236 4427 Fax: 020 7213 0499
e-mail: institute-of-masters-of-wine@compuserve.com
Examination for Membership:
The exam for membership is not intended for novices or new entrants to the wind industry and can be passed only by those who are able to demonstrate considerable experience and a deep understanding of all aspects of wine industry affairs. In addition to a searching written exam, candidates must pass a 3-part practical exam in the knowledge, appreciation and comparison of different types of wine. There are provisions for half-passes to be completed within 2 yrs; if a candidate fails to pass 1 written paper s/he may sit that paper again the following year.
If resident in the UK they shall have usually passed the Diploma exams of the Wine and Spirit Education Trust.

THE MEAT TRAINING COUNCIL

PO Box 141, Winterhill House, Snowdon Drive, Milton Keynes MK6 1YY Tel: 01908 231062
Fax: 01908 231063 e-mail: info@meattraining.org.uk Web-site: www.meattraining.org.uk
The Meat Training Council is the lead body, National Training Organisation (NTO) and awarding body for NVQ Levels 1, 2, 3 & 4 in Meat. SVQs are awarded with SQA. Professional membership is administered by the Worshipful Company of Butchers via its Guild of Freemen.
Meat Intermediate Technical Certificate: This replaced the existing Associateship examination course from September 1999 onwards. It is a progression award/related vocational qualification designed to cover the underpinning knowledge and understanding content of the Council's S/NVQ Level 3 Meat Processing (Technical Operations). The award is based on five mandatory modules and two optional modules. The optional modules are designed to fit six industry sectors: abattoir, wholesale/catering, poultry, manufacturing, retail/supermarkets and enforcement. Awarded by the Council.
Graduate Membership Exam: Designed to enable those in the meat industry to gain a senior qualification as a result of an intensive course of study. It gives an understanding of modern principles and techniques used by management with specific relevance to all sectors of the meat industry; to encourage a positive attitude towards management; to help people apply konwledge, skills and understanding gained from a study associated with a business environment and to develop skills in communicating. This course comprises compulsory core and optional specialist modules. Awarded by the Council.
Level 1: entry level qualification; Level 2: four qualifications; Level 3: Meat Processing (Technical Operations). Level 4: Meat Processing Management (Technical and Production). Designed for operational and technical skills, and all awarded by the Council.

MEMBERSHIP
Successful candidates are automatically eligible to join the Worshipful Company of Butchers Guild of Freemen.

Affiliate Grade (AFFInstM): Achievement of the NVQ Level 2 qualification.
Associate Grade (AinstM): Success in the Meat Intermediate Technical Certificate or achievement of NVQ Level 3.
Graduate Members (GMInstM): Success in the Membership exam or achievement of NVQ Level 4.

THE SOCIETY OF SHOE FITTERS

Secretary: Mrs Laura West, The Anchorage, 28 Admirals Walk, Hingham, Norfolk NR9 4JL Tel: 01953 851171 Fax: 01953 851171

The Society is a professional institute engaged in the training of shoe fitters and assisting the public in obtaining fitting services. Entrance is by exam or specialised training course. Successful candidates become **Members (MSSF)** of the Society of Shoe Fitters or **Fellows (FSSF).**

NATIONAL CERTIFICATES AND DIPLOMAS
BTEC Higher National Certificates/Diplomas:
Retail Management
Scotland
SQA HNC: Retail Display; Retail Marketing; Retail Management

NVQS/SVQS
Level 2: Distribution & Warehousing Operations; Distributive Operations; Retail Operations; Retail Sales Delivery

GNVQS
3735 Retail and Distributive Services

SCIENCE (GENERAL)

University Qualifications

The following universities offer qualifications in Science (General) and related subjects. Full details may be found in Part 4, under the entry for the appropriate university.

FIRST DEGREES AWARDED BY UNIVERSITIES
Aberdeen; Anglia; Anglia (City College, Norwich); Bath; Birmingham; Bournemouth; Bristol; Brunel; Cambridge; Central Lancashire; Coventry; Coventry (Newman College of Higher Education); Cranfield; De Montfort, Leicester; Derby; Dundee; Durham; East Anglia (Lowestoft College); East London; Essex (Writtle College); Exeter (The College of St Mark & St John); Glamorgan; Glasgow Caledonian; Greenwich; Heriot-Watt; Hertfordshire; Hertfordshire (West Herts College); Huddersfield; Hull; Kent; Kent (Canterbury Christ Church University College); Kingston; Lancaster; Lancaster (Edge Hill College of Higher Education); Leeds; Leeds (Leeds, Trinity & All Saints); Leicester; Lincolnshire (Lincoln University Campus); Liverpool; Liverpool (Chester College of H.E.); Liverpool (Liverpool Hope University College); Liverpool John Moores; London (Birkbeck, University of London); London (Imperial College of Science, Technology & Medicine); London (King's College London); London (Queen Mary & Westfield College (incorporating St Bartholomew's and the Royal London School of Medicine & Dentistry)); London (Royal Holloway); London (University College (UCL)); Manchester; Manchester Metropolitan.; Napier; Newcastle; North London; Northampton; Northumbria; Nottingham Trent; OU (NESCOT); Oxford Brookes; Paisley; Plymouth; Reading; Robert Gordon; Salford; Sheffield Hallam; South Bank; Southampton (Chichester Institute of Higher Education); Southampton (King Alfred's College); St Martin; Stirling; Strathclyde; Sunderland (City of Sunderland College); Surrey (University of Surrey Roehampton); Sussex; Ulster; Wales (Cardiff University); Wales (University of Wales Institute, Cardiff); Wales (University of Wales, Bangor); Wolverhampton

HIGHER DEGREES AWARDED BY UNIVERSITIES
Belfast; Bristol; Cranfield; De Montfort, Leicester; East London; Edinburgh; Glamorgan; Glasgow; Glasgow Caledonian; Greenwich; Kent; Lancaster; Leeds; Leicester; Liverpool; London (Birkbeck,

University of London); London (Imperial College of Science, Technology & Medicine); London (King's College London); London (University College (UCL)); Loughborough; Luton; Manchester; Newcastle; Northumbria; OU (NESCOT); Reading; Sheffield Hallam; St Martin; Strathclyde; Surrey (St Mary's, Strawberry Hill); Surrey (University of Surrey Roehampton); Sussex; Ulster

DIPLOMAS AWARDED BY UNIVERSITIES
Bradford (Bradford & Ilkley Community College); Bristol; Central Lancashire; Coventry; De Montfort, Leicester; Edinburgh; Glamorgan; Kent; Lancaster; Leeds; Liverpool (Liverpool Hope University College); London (Birkbeck, University of London); Loughborough; Manchester; Newcastle; Paisley; Strathclyde; Surrey (St Mary's, Strawberry Hill); Ulster; Wales (University of Wales, Bangor)

CERTIFICATES AWARDED BY UNIVERSITIES
Anglia; Anglia (City College, Norwich); Bristol; Brunel; Central Lancashire; Durham; Exeter (The College of St Mark & St John); Huddersfield; Keele; Liverpool John Moores; London (Birkbeck, University of London); London (Goldsmiths College); Loughborough; Newcastle; Nottingham; Oxford (Westminster College, Oxford); Sheffield Hallam; St Martin; Sunderland; Sussex; Wales (University of Wales Institute, Cardiff); Wales (University of Wales, Bangor)

OTHER COURSES AWARDED BY UNIVERSITIES
Bournemouth; Essex (Writtle College); Huddersfield; Wales (University of Wales Institute, Cardiff)

National Certificates and Diplomas
BTEC National Certificates/Diplomas: Science
BTEC Higher National Certificates/Diplomas: Science

GNVQs
3729 Science

SECRETARIAL AND OFFICE WORK
(See also Office Technology)

Many private and local authority colleges award their own Certificates and Diplomas to students who successfully complete their courses. Such courses may cover simply the office skills or may include 1 or more modern languages, commercial background, liberal studies or other subjects. Many of these colleges also prepare their students for the external exams of nationally recognised bodies.

INSTITUTE OF QUALIFIED PRIVATE SECRETARIES
First Floor, 6 Bridge Avenue, Maidenhead, Berks SL6 1RR Tel: 01628-625007 Fax: 01628-624990 e-mail: office@iqps.org Website: www.iqps.org
AIMS:
The objects of the Institute are to facilitate and encourage the training and continuing professional development of secretaries and to enable them to make a maximum contribution in their field of activity.
MEMBERSHIP:
Membership is open to secretaries, PAs, administrators and lecturers in Business Studies.

University Qualifications
The following universities offer qualifications in Secretarial and Office Work and related subjects. Full details may be found in Part 4, under the entry for the appropriate university.

FIRST DEGREES AWARDED BY UNIVERSITIES
Lincolnshire; Plymouth

HIGHER DEGREES AWARDED BY UNIVERSITIES
De Montfort, Leicester

DIPLOMAS AWARDED BY UNIVERSITIES
Anglia (City College, Norwich); Brunel; De Montfort, Leicester; Durham (New College Durham); Napier

CERTIFICATES AWARDED BY UNIVERSITIES
Bradford (Bradford & Ilkley Community College); Brunel; Napier

National Certificates and Diplomas

Scotland
SQA HNC: Administration Management
SQA HND: Administration Management

NVQs

Level 1: Administration
Level 2: Administration
Level 3: Administration
Level 4: Administration

SVQs

Levels 1: Administration
Levels 2: Administration
Levels 3: Administration
Levels 4: Administration

OCR

OCR offer **RSA Text Processing Modular Awards** and various other awards in text processing and business and administration. Contact OCR for further details.

LONDON CHAMBER OF COMMERCE AND INDUSTRY EXAMINATIONS BOARD (LCCIEB)

QUALIFICATIONS:
Diploma in Secretarial Administration (DSA); Private Secretary's Diploma (PSD); Executive Secretary's Diploma (ESD); Diploma in Administration; Diploma in Business Administration.
Single Subject Skills Exams: Text Production; Shorthand; Audio Transcription; Practical Word Processing; Word Processing; Information Processing; Practical Computing.

EUROQUALIFICATIONS:
A suite of new awards for bilingual secretaries/administrators (shown below) were introduced in 1992. These are available in English (for non-native English speakers), French, German and Spanish.
Diploma in European Business Administration; European Executive Assistant Certificate.
Holders of all secretarial diplomas are eligible for various levels of membership of the Institute of Qualified Private Secretaries, 21 Whitelodges Ladies, Cookham, Maidenhead SL6 9LZ.

PITMAN QUALIFICATIONS

Shorthand Speed; Typewriting; Typewriting Speed Test; Audio-Transcription; Office Procedures; Administration and Secretarial Procedures; Business Studies; Text Production Skills; Word Processing Techniques; Keyboarding; Practical Word Processing; Practical Data Processing; Practical Spreadsheet Processing; Book-keeping & Accounts; Accounting; Computerised Accounts; Cost & Management Accounting; Commercial Numeracy; English for Business Communications; English for Office Skills; English for Speakers of Other Languages (ESOL);

ESOL for Young Learners; Spoken ESOL; Text Production Skills (French); Text Production Skills (German); Text Production Skills (Spanish); Desktop Publishing

Other Vocational Awarding Bodies

ABC: Keyboarding

SECURITY

Membership of Professional Institutions and Associations

INTERNATIONAL INSTITUTE OF SECURITY

Company Secretary, Suite 8, The Business Centre, 57 Torquay Road, Paignton, Devon TQ3 3DT
Tel: 01803 663275 Fax: 01803 663251 e-mail: iisec@btinternet.com
The Institute is a professional examining body specialising in subjects relating to security measures against loss through theft, fraud, fire, other damage and waste.

MEMBERSHIP:
Fellow (FIISec): Fellowship is awarded on the basis of a thesis on a subject approved by the Governors and undertaken after a soecified period of Membership of 2 yrs. Honorary Fellowship is also available to people of outstanding eminence within the security profession, at the invitation of the Board.
Member (MIISec): Certificate in Security Management Level II: Jointly accredited by the City & Guilds of London Institute (Scheme 7252). Membership is available after successfully completing the Level II exam and subsequently registering with the Institute.
Graduate (GradIISec): Certificate in Security Management Level I: Jointly accredited by the City & Guilds of London Institute (Scheme 7251). Graduateship is available after successfully completing the Level I exam and subsequently registering with the Institute.

EXAMINATIONS:
Membership: Candidates must show that they have a comprehensive knowledge and experience of commercial or industrial security and the duties and responsibilities of a Chief or Senior Security Officer. Questions are based on the law as it concerns security practices, including its relation to fire, techniques and aids to security and the management/administration of a security department.
Graduateship: Questions are set on a general security duties including crime and fire prevention, security of premises and property, emergency situations, safety and English law. Additional modules are available to both Graduates and Members in Retail Security.

University Qualifications

The following universities offer qualifications in Security and related subjects. Full details may be found in Part 4, under the entry for the appropriate university.

FIRST DEGREES AWARDED BY UNIVERSITIES

Glamorgan; London (Royal Holloway)

HIGHER DEGREES AWARDED BY UNIVERSITIES

Bradford; Cranfield; Glamorgan; Hull; Keele; Lancaster; Leicester; Liverpool (Chester College of H.E.); London (Royal Holloway); London (University College (UCL)); Loughborough; Manchester; Reading; St Andrews

DIPLOMAS AWARDED BY UNIVERSITIES

Bradford; Hull; Lancaster; Leicester; Liverpool (Chester College of H.E.); London (Royal Holloway); Loughborough; St Andrews

CERTIFICATES AWARDED BY UNIVERSITIES
Liverpool (Chester College of H.E.); Loughborough

NVQs

Level 2: Fire, Security and Emergency Alarm Systems; Locksmithing; Retail and Leisure Security; Security, Safety and Loss Prevention
Level 3: Security Systems Technical Services

SVQs

Level 2: Security Guarding; Specifying Security/Emergency Systems; Transporting Property Under Guard; Maintaining Security & Emergency Systems
Level 3: Security Systems: Technical Services

Useful Addresses

NACOS (National Approval Council for Security Systems), Queensgate House, 14 Cookham Road, Maidenhead, Berks SL6 8AJ Tel: 01628 637512 Fax: 01628 773367
SITO Ltd (formerly Security Industry Training Organisation Ltd), Security House, Barbourne Road, Worcester WR1 1RS Tel: 01905 20004 Fax: 01905 724949

SHIPBROKING

INSTITUTE OF CHARTERED SHIPBROKERS

3 St Helen's Place, London EC3A 6EJ Tel: 020 7628 5559 Fax: 020 7628 5445
e-mail: icslon@dial.pipex.com Web-site: www.ics.org.uk
Fellows (FICS) must be at least 25, be a principal or director or hold a responsible position in Shipbroking and have passed the Qualifying Examinations.
Members (MICS) must be at least 21 and have, normally, 4 yrs' experience in Shipbroking and have passed the Qualifying Examinations.
Honorary Members are persons elected for outstanding services to the profession.
Retired Members are those with less than 25 yrs' membership who, having retired from business life, pay a reduced subscription until they qualify for Life Membership.
Life Members are Retired Members with 25 or more yrs' membership.

EXAMINATIONS
Qualifying Examination Structure:
Group 1 (All subjects require) Introduction to Shipping; Law of Carriage of Goods by Sea; Economics of Sea Transport & International Trade; Shipping Practice
Candidates may select the following options in respect of Groups 2 and 3:
Option *A*: Two subjects from Group 2 and one from Group 3
Option *B*: Three subjects from Group 2 and none from Group 3
Option *C*: One subject from Group 2 and two from Group 3. If this option is chosen only one Group 3 is exemptible, the other **MUST** be taken with this Institute.
Group 2: Dry Cargo Chartering; Ship Management; Ship Sale and Purchase; Tanker Chartering; Liner Trades; Port Agency
Group 3: Shipping Law; Marine Insurance; Financial and Management Accounting; International Through Transport
Exemptions: candidates with relevant professional or educational qualifications validated by the Institute will be able to apply for exemptions, on a subject for subject basis, from all subjects except Shipping Practice in Group 1 and the specialist subjects comprising Group 2.
Foundation Diploma in Shipping: Exam Structure: Comprises 2 subjects: Introduction to Shipping and one of the following specialist subjects: Dry Cargo Chartering; Ship Management; Tanker Chartering; Ship Sale & Purchase; Liner Trades; Port Agency. Candidates must sit and pass both subjects during the same exam session in order to be awarded this Diploma.

SOCIAL WORK
(See also Probation Work)

England and Wales

Probation Officers deal with people who are placed by the courts under their supervision. They are also responsible for the after-care of persons released from prison service establishments who are 17 and over, for the supervision of prisoners released on parole under the provisions of the Criminal Justice Act 1967 (as amended by the 1972 Act), and, under the provisions of the Powers of Criminal Courts Act, 1973, for the administration of the community service by offenders scheme as an alternative to imprisonment. They also undertake a wide range of duties for the courts in connection with divorce, separation proceedings, adoption and other non-criminal matters where their social work can be applied. Further information about the probation service as a career, current salaries and the arrangements for training and sponsorship, may be obtained from the Home Office, Probation Division, Room 442, 50 Queen Anne's Gate, London SW1H 9AT, or the CCETSW Information Offices in England and Wales.

Membership of Professional Institutions and Associations

THE BRITISH ASSOCIATION OF SOCIAL WORKERS
16 Kent Street, Birmingham B5 6RD Tel: 0121 622 3911 Fax: 0121 622 4860
With its continuing mission to campaign for and defend the values, principles and ethics of social work, BASW confronts the many challenges and opportunities facing social workers and the profession both at a national and international level. BASW members receive all the benefits of a first class Advice and Representation Service, personal professional indemnity insurance, our magazine-*Professional Social Work*, the *Code of Ethics for Social Work*, as well as access to Parliament, the press, and over 75 professional and public bodies. BASW is probably Britain's largest social work publishing house, with numerous books and journals in print, including the prestigious *British Journal of Social Work*.

University Qualifications

The following universities offer qualifications in Social Work and related subjects. Full details may be found in Part 4, under the entry for the appropriate university.

FIRST DEGREES AWARDED BY UNIVERSITIES
Anglia; Anglia (Colchester Institute); Bath; Bradford; Brighton; Bristol; Brunel; Bucks. Coll.; Central England; Central Lancashire; Coventry; Derby; East Anglia; East London; Edinburgh; Glasgow; Glasgow Caledonian; Greenwich; Hertfordshire; Huddersfield; Hull; Lancaster; Lancaster (Edge Hill College of Higher Education); Leeds Metropolitan; Lincolnshire; Manchester Metropolitan.; Middlesex; North London; Northampton; Northumbria; Nottingham Trent; OU (Northern College of Education); Paisley; Portsmouth; Robert Gordon; Salford; Sheffield Hallam; South Bank; Southampton; Southampton (Chichester Institute of Higher Education); Southampton (King Alfred's College); Stirling; Strathclyde; Sunderland; Surrey (University of Surrey Roehampton); Sussex; Teesside; Ulster; Wales (Cardiff University); Wales (University of Wales Institute, Cardiff)

HIGHER DEGREES AWARDED BY UNIVERSITIES
Anglia; Belfast; Birmingham; Bournemouth; Bradford; Bradford (Bradford & Ilkley Community College); Brighton; Bristol; Central England; Central Lancashire; Cheltenham & Gloucester; Coventry; De Montfort, Leicester; Dundee; Durham; East Anglia; East London; Edinburgh; Exeter; Glasgow; Glasgow Caledonian; Hertfordshire; Huddersfield; Hull; Keele; Kent; Kingston; Leeds Metropolitan; Leicester; Lincolnshire; Liverpool; Liverpool (Liverpool Hope University College); Liverpool John Moores; London (Goldsmiths College); London (King's College London); London (Royal Holloway); Manchester; Manchester Metropolitan.; Middlesex; North London; Nottingham; Paisley; Plymouth; Reading; Salford; Sheffield Hallam; South Bank; Southampton; Southampton (Chichester Institute of Higher Education); Stirling; Strathclyde; Surrey (University of Surrey Roehampton); Sussex; Ulster; Wales (Cardiff University); Wales (University of Wales, Bangor); Wales (University of Wales, Swansea); Westminster; York

DIPLOMAS AWARDED BY UNIVERSITIES

Anglia; Anglia (City College, Norwich); Anglia (Colchester Institute); Birmingham; Bournemouth; Bradford (Bradford & Ilkley Community College); Brighton; Bristol; Bucks. Coll.; Central England; Central Lancashire; Cheltenham & Gloucester; De Montfort, Leicester; Dundee; Durham; Durham (New College Durham); East Anglia (Suffolk College); East London; Edinburgh; Exeter; Glasgow; Hertfordshire; Hull; Kent (Canterbury Christ Church University College); Lancaster; Leeds (Bretton Hall); Leeds Metropolitan; Liverpool; Liverpool (Liverpool Hope University College); London (Goldsmiths College); Luton; Manchester; Manchester (Warrington Collegiate Institute, Faculty of H.E,); Northampton; Northumbria; Paisley; Reading; Salford; South Bank; Southampton (Chichester Institute of Higher Education); Staffordshire; Stirling; Teesside; Ulster; Wales (University of Wales Institute, Cardiff); Warwick; Wolverhampton; Worcester

COLLEGE DIPLOMA AWARDED BY UNIVERSITIES

Salford

CERTIFICATES AWARDED BY UNIVERSITIES

Anglia (City College, Norwich); Brighton; Bristol; Central England; Cheltenham & Gloucester; Dundee; Leicester; Liverpool John Moores; Manchester; Manchester (Warrington Collegiate Institute, Faculty of H.E,); Northampton; Nottingham; Paisley; Sunderland

OTHER COURSES AWARDED BY UNIVERSITIES

Central Lancashire

POSTGRADUATE DIPLOMAS AWARDED BY UNIVERSITIES

Central Lancashire

PROFESSIONAL COURSES AWARDED BY UNIVERSITIES

Leeds Metropolitan; Luton; Manchester Metropolitan

RESEARCH DEGREES AWARDED BY UNIVERSITIES

Exeter

National Certificates and Diplomas

BTEC National Certificates/Diplomas: Caring Services (Social Care)
BTEC Higher National Certificates/Diplomas: Caring Services (Care Management); Caring Services (Counselling); Caring Services (Guidance); Caring Services (Managing Care); Caring Services (Practice Management); Caring Services (Social Care)
Scotland
SQA HNC: Counselling; Social Sciences; Social Sciences with Management; Social Sciences with Information Technology
SQA HND: Social Sciences; Social Sciences with Management; Social Sciences with Information Technology

NVQs

Level 2: Care; Community Work; Custodial Care
Level 3: Advice; Care; Community Work; Custodial Care; Guidance
Level 4: Advice; Care; Community Work; Guidance

SVQs

Level 2: Care; Community Work
Level 3: Care; Advice; Community Work; Guidance; Group and Foster Care Counselling
Level 4: Care; Advice; Community Work; Guidance

City & Guilds

3560 Practical Caring Skills

Other Qualifications

NEIGHBOURHOOD WORK:
People who wish to take up some form of Neighbourhood Work take a degree or diploma in Sociology, Social Studies or Social Administration, preferably one which includes study of Community Organisation. Neighbourhood Work also includes work as a Warden in a residential settlement and work as a Community Centre Warden. The following centres run a 2-yr course providing recognised qualifications for youth and community workers: Westhill Coll of Education; Bulmershe CHE; Crewe and Alsager CHE; Derbyshire CHE; Bradford & Ilkley Community Coll; Leicester University; (in association with NE London University); Manchester Metropolitan University; Matlock CHE; NE Wales IHE; Sunderland University.

Social Work Training

The Central Council for Education and Training in Social Work (CCETSW), Derbyshire House, St Chad's Street, London WC1H 8AD Tel 020 7278 2455, www.ccetsw.org.uk, has statutory responsibility for promoting and recognising courses of training in all fields of social work and for approving the training of social workers for approval under mental health legislation. The professional qualification for social work awarded by CCETSW is the Diploma in Social Work (DipSW). This forms part of a continuum of education, training and qualifications currently being promoted by CCETSW for all social care and social work staff in the personal social services. This includes a new framework for Post-qualifying education and training for social care and social work personnel in all service sectors.

THE DIPLOMA IN SOCIAL WORK (DIPSW)

This award is the professional qualification for all social workers in the UK, and is attainable by a number of different routes. DipSW programmes comprise at least 2 yrs' study and supervised practice, including a final assessed placement of a minimum of 80 days. Applicants to DipSW programmes must be suitable to become a social worker, at least 22 yrs of age when they receive the award, and without a criminal record. Most programmes require applicants to have had social work-related experience. Those under the age of 21 should have *either* 2 A level passes of grade E or above and 3 GCSE passes of grade C or above; *or* 5 passes for the Scottish Certificate in Education (including 3 at higher level) *or* any other educational, professional or vocational qualifications deemed to be equivalent. For further information on the DipSW and on other routes for entry, consult the CCETSW handbook *How to Qualify for Social Work.*

POST-QUALIFYING STUDIES

The post-qualifying framework was developed to allow social workers and probation officers to gain formal recognition for their continuing professional development and to provide a means for relating common minimum standards across the wide variety of social work education and training. The following awards are open to all staff of the personal social services who hold a professional social work qualification such as the DipSW, CQSW, CSS or recognised equivalent.

The Post-Qualifying Award in Social Work (PQSW) is designed to recognise the developing skills of social workers and has three, developmental, components – concerned initially with the consolidation of learning at qualification level; secondly with work of increasing complexity and finally with the candidate taking some responsibility for the learning and practice of others. This level of professional competence should be achievable by all qualified and experienced social workers who have been offered proper induction, support and training opportunities.

The Advanced Award in Social Work (AASW) is designed to recognise the higher level skills of social workers involved in policy-making, teaching, management, research and innovative practice. Work towards the AASW can be pursued via four 'pathways' – practice, management, research and education, and training. Although a candidate will 'major' in one of the areas, competence at this level will necessarily involve reference to the other three pathways. To register for a PQSW or an AASW, candidates need to register with the CCETSW-approved post-qualifying education and training consortium which covers the area in which they work, or if they are not currently in employment, the area in which they live. The consortium will have systems for providing support and guidance, including the appointment of supervisors and mentors. They will also be responsible for assessment. For further details, contact the CCETSW.

SOCIOLOGY

Membership of Professional Institutions and Associations

THE INTERNATIONAL INSTITUTE OF SOCIAL ECONOMICS

Enholmes Hall, Patrington, Hull, East Yorkshire HU12 0PR Tel: 01964 630033 Fax: 01964 631716
e-mail: hr24@dial.pipex.com

CORPORATE MEMBERSHIP:

Fellow (FIISE): Fellowship may be granted to persons already qualified as Members (see below) who have had at least another 10 yrs' approved experience; or who, being so qualified, have had at least 5 yrs' approved experience; or who have rendered outstanding service to the profession.

Member (MIISE): Membership may be granted to persons already qualified as Associate Members who have had at least 5 yrs' approved experience; or persons having a postgraduate degree or equivalent qualification in a course containing an approved balance of Social Economic subjects.

Associate Member (AMIISE): Associate Membership may be granted to persons whose first degree or equivalent qualification was obtained in a course containing an approved balance of Social Economic subjects; or who have at least a recognised first degree or an equivalent qualification, and an approved postgraduate degree or diploma in Social Economic subjects; or are considered to have suitable practical experience and alternative educational or other appropriate qualifications. Submission of an approved dissertation, research paper or published work will normally be required.

NON-CORPORATE MEMBERSHIP:

Affiliate Membership: Open to students on an approved course of study who would, on its satisfactory completion, be acceptable as Associate Members, or persons not otherwise qualified as Associate Members, Members or Fellows, but whose activities, experience, or academic work provide significant contributions to the advancement of Social Economics, and who are elected by a majority of the Council.

Organisation Membership: May be granted to organisations either pursuing Social Economic objectives or wishing to see such objectives forwarded.

University Qualifications

The following universities offer qualifications in Sociology and related subjects. Full details may be found in Part 4, under the entry for the appropriate university.

FIRST DEGREES AWARDED BY UNIVERSITIES

Abertay, Dundee; Anglia; Anglia (City College, Norwich); Anglia (Colchester Institute); Aston; Barnsley; Bath; Bath Spa; Belfast; Birmingham; Bradford; Bradford (Bradford & Ilkley Community College); Brighton; Bristol; Brunel; Bucks. Coll.; Central England; Central Lancashire; Cheltenham & Gloucester; City; Coventry; De Montfort, Leicester; De Montfort, Leicester (De Montfort University Bedford); Derby; Doncaster; Durham; East Anglia; East London; Edinburgh; Essex; Exeter; Exeter (The College of St Mark & St John); Glamorgan; Glasgow Caledonian; Greenwich; Hertfordshire; Huddersfield; Hull; Keele; Kent; Kent (Canterbury Christ Church University College); Kingston; Lancaster; Lancaster (Edge Hill College of Higher Education); Leeds; Leeds (Bretton Hall); Leeds (Leeds, Trinity & All Saints); Leeds (The College of Ripon & York St John); Leeds Metropolitan; Leicester; Lincolnshire (Grimsby College); Liverpool; Liverpool (Chester College of H.E.); Liverpool (Liverpool Hope University College); Liverpool John Moores; London (Birkbeck, University of London); London (Goldsmiths College); London (London School of Economics & Political Science); London (Royal Holloway); London Guildhall; Loughborough; Luton; Manchester; Manchester Metropolitan.; Middlesex; Napier; Newcastle; North London; Northampton; Northumbria; Nottingham; Nottingham Trent; Nottingham Trent (Southampton Institute); Oxford Brookes; Paisley; Plymouth; Portsmouth; Queen Margaret; Reading; Salford; Sheffield; Sheffield Hallam; South Bank; Southampton; Southampton (Chichester Institute of Higher Education); St Martin; Staffordshire; Stirling; Strathclyde; Sunderland; Surrey; Surrey (St Mary's, Strawberry Hill); Surrey (University of Surrey Roehampton); Sussex; Teesside; Ulster;

Wales (Cardiff University); Wales (North East Wales Institute); Wales (Swansea Institute of Higher Education); Wales (University of Wales College, Newport); Wales (University of Wales, Bangor); Wales (University of Wales, Swansea); Warwick; Westminster; Wolverhampton; Worcester; York

HIGHER DEGREES AWARDED BY UNIVERSITIES
Aberdeen; Anglia; Bath; Birmingham; Birmingham (The University of Birmingham, Westhill); Bradford; Brighton; Bristol; Cambridge; Cheltenham & Gloucester; Coventry (Newman College of Higher Education); De Montfort, Leicester (De Montfort University Bedford); Dundee; Durham; East London; Edinburgh; Essex; Exeter; Glamorgan; Glasgow; Greenwich; Hertfordshire; Huddersfield; Hull; Kent; Lancaster; Lancaster (Edge Hill College of Higher Education); Leeds; Leeds Metropolitan; Leicester; Lincolnshire; Liverpool; Liverpool John Moores; London (Goldsmiths College); London (Institute of Education); London (King's College London); London (London School of Economics & Political Science); London (Queen Mary & Westfield College (incorporating St Bartholomew's and the Royal London School of Medicine & Dentistry)); London (Royal Holloway); London (University College (UCL)); Luton; Manchester; Manchester Metropolitan.; Middlesex; Napier; Newcastle; North London; Northumbria; Nottingham; Nottingham Trent; Oxford; Plymouth; Reading; Salford; South Bank; Southampton; Staffordshire; Strathclyde; Surrey; Surrey (University of Surrey Roehampton); Wales (University of Wales, Bangor); Wales (University of Wales, Swansea); Warwick; Westminster; York

DIPLOMAS AWARDED BY UNIVERSITIES
Aston; Bath Spa; Birmingham; Blackburn; Bradford; Bristol; Cheltenham & Gloucester; Durham; East London; Edinburgh; Glasgow; Greenwich; Hertfordshire; Hull; Kent; Leeds; Leicester; London (London School of Economics & Political Science); London (Royal Holloway); Luton; Manchester; Napier; Newcastle; North London; Plymouth; Reading; Salford; Staffordshire; Strathclyde; Teesside; Warwick

CERTIFICATES AWARDED BY UNIVERSITIES
Bristol; Cheltenham & Gloucester; Durham; Essex; Kent; London (Goldsmiths College); Sheffield Hallam; Staffordshire; Surrey (University of Surrey Roehampton); Wales (University of Wales, Bangor)

SPEECH AND LANGUAGE THERAPY

Membership of Professional Institutions and Associations

ROYAL COLLEGE OF SPEECH AND LANGUAGE THERAPISTS

2 White Hart Yard, London SE1 1NX Tel: 020 7378 1200 Fax: 020 7378 7254
e-mail: academic@rcslt.org Website: www.rcslt.org
An undergraduate degree or postgraduate qualification from an accredited course is necessary to qualify as a speech and language therapist. RCSLT issues to graduates the certificate which confers eligibility to practise in the National Health Service.

EXAMINATIONS:
3 and 4 yr degree courses are offered at 15 Universities and Higher Education Institutions. Applications are made through UCAS. NHS Bursaries are available and there is no student contribution to fees. Pre-entry requirements vary from one education establishment to another. If you are seriously interested in following a speech and language therapy career it is advisable to check at an early stage with the various establishments that your choice of A Level subjects (or alternative exams) will be appropriate. Special arrangements may be negotiable for mature students. There are 5 postgraduate courses (in London, Reading, Sheffield and Newcastle) for graduates from other disciplines who wish to gain a speech and language therapy qualification. Accredited courses are run at the following institutions:3 and 4 yr Undergraduate Courses: Leeds Metropolitan University; De Montfort University; Manchester Metropolitan University; University of Strathclyde (Jordanhill Campus); Queen Margaret University College (Edinburgh);

University of Central England in Birmingham; City University; Manchester University; Newcastle University; Reading University; Sheffield University; University of Wales Institute, Cardiff; University College, London; University of Ulster; College of St Mark & St John (Plymouth).2 yr Postgraduate Courses: City University; University College London; Newcastle University; Reading University; Sheffield University.

University Qualifications

The following universities offer qualifications in Speech and Language Therapy and related subjects. Full details may be found in Part 4, under the entry for the appropriate university.

FIRST DEGREES AWARDED BY UNIVERSITIES
Central England; City; De Montfort, Leicester; Exeter (The College of St Mark & St John); London (University College (UCL)); Manchester; Manchester Metropolitan.; Newcastle; Sheffield; Strathclyde; Ulster

HIGHER DEGREES AWARDED BY UNIVERSITIES
City; De Montfort, Leicester; Edinburgh; Essex; Leeds Metropolitan; London (Institute of Education); London (University College (UCL)); Manchester; Reading; Sheffield

DIPLOMAS AWARDED BY UNIVERSITIES
City; Edinburgh; London (University College (UCL))

CERTIFICATES AWARDED BY UNIVERSITIES
Newcastle

SPORTS SCIENCE
(See also Physiotherapy)

Membership of Professional Institutions and Associations

INTERNATIONAL INSTITUTE OF SPORTS THERAPY
(See International Institute of Health & Holistic Therapies, listed under Vocational Training Charitable Trust in the Beauty Therapy and Beauty Culture Section)

University Qualifications

The following universities offer qualifications in Sports Science and related subjects. Full details may be found in Part 4, under the entry for the appropriate university.

FIRST DEGREES AWARDED BY UNIVERSITIES
Aberdeen; Abertay, Dundee; Barnsley; Bath; Birmingham; Bradford; Brighton; Brunel; Bucks. Coll.; Central Lancashire; Cheltenham & Gloucester; Coventry; De Montfort, Leicester; De Montfort, Leicester (De Montfort University Bedford); Durham; East Anglia (Suffolk College); Essex; Essex (Writtle College); Exeter; Exeter (The College of St Mark & St John); Glamorgan; Glasgow; Greenwich; Heriot-Watt; Hertfordshire; Huddersfield; Hull; Kent (Canterbury Christ Church University College); Kingston; Lancaster (Edge Hill College of Higher Education); Leeds; Leeds (Leeds, Trinity & All Saints); Leeds (The College of Ripon & York St John); Leeds Metropolitan; Liverpool (Chester College of H.E.); Liverpool (Liverpool Hope University College); Liverpool John Moores; Loughborough; Luton; Manchester (Warrington Collegiate Institute, Faculty of H.E,); Manchester Metropolitan.; North London; Northampton; Northumbria; Nottingham Trent; Nottingham Trent (Southampton Institute); Oxford Brookes; Plymouth; Portsmouth; Salford; Sheffield Hallam; South Bank; Southampton (Chichester Institute of Higher Education); Southampton (King Alfred's College); Southampton (University of Southampton New College); St Martin; Staffordshire; Stirling; Strathclyde; Sunderland; Surrey (St Mary's, Strawberry Hill); Surrey (University of Surrey Roehampton); Teesside; Ulster; Wales (North East

Wales Institute); Wales (Swansea Institute of Higher Education); Wales (University of Wales College, Newport); Wales (University of Wales Institute, Cardiff); Wales (University of Wales, Bangor); Wales (University of Wales, Swansea); Wolverhampton; Worcester

HIGHER DEGREES AWARDED BY UNIVERSITIES
Birmingham; Bristol; Brunel; Cheltenham & Gloucester; City; De Montfort, Leicester; De Montfort, Leicester (De Montfort University Bedford); Essex; Exeter (The College of St Mark & St John); Glasgow; Hertfordshire; Leeds Metropolitan; Liverpool; Liverpool (Chester College of H.E.); Liverpool (Liverpool Hope University College); Liverpool John Moores; London (Birkbeck, University of London); London (Queen Mary & Westfield College (incorporating St Bartholomew's and the Royal London School of Medicine & Dentistry)); Loughborough; Luton; Manchester; Manchester Metropolitan.; Nottingham; Salford; Southampton (Chichester Institute of Higher Education); St Andrews; Staffordshire; Surrey (University of Surrey Roehampton); Ulster; Wales (College of Medicine); Wales (University of Wales Institute, Cardiff); Wales (University of Wales, Bangor)

DIPLOMAS AWARDED BY UNIVERSITIES
Blackburn; Brighton; Bucks. Coll.; Central Lancashire; City; Coventry; De Montfort, Leicester (De Montfort University Bedford); Doncaster; Durham (New College Durham); Exeter; Exeter (Truro College); Glamorgan; Greenwich; Hertfordshire; Leicester; Lincolnshire (Bishop Burton College); Lincolnshire (Grimsby College); Lincolnshire (Yorkshire Coast College); Liverpool (Chester College of H.E.); London (Queen Mary & Westfield College (incorporating St Bartholomew's and the Royal London School of Medicine & Dentistry)); Luton; North London; Salford; Southampton (King Alfred's College); Teesside; Ulster; Worcester

CERTIFICATES AWARDED BY UNIVERSITIES
Brighton; Bristol; Brunel; Exeter (The College of St Mark & St John); Leeds Metropolitan; Liverpool (Chester College of H.E.); Liverpool John Moores; Southampton; Southampton (Chichester Institute of Higher Education); Wales (University of Wales Institute, Cardiff)

PROFESSIONAL COURSES AWARDED BY UNIVERSITIES
Luton

National Certificates and Diplomas
BTEC National Certificates/Diplomas: Science (Sports Studies)
BTEC Higher National Certificates/Diplomas: Science (Sports Studies)

STATISTICS
(See also Mathematics)

Membership of Professional Institutions and Associations
THE ROYAL STATISTICAL SOCIETY
12 Errol Street, London EC1Y 8LX Tel: 020 7638 8998 Fax: 020 7256 7598

e-mail: rss@rss.org.uk Website: www.rss.org.uk

MEMBERSHIP:
Fellow: Fellowship is by election, but is open to anyone with a genuine interest in statistics.
Chartered Statistician (CStat): Professional grade awarded to those with a good honours degree (or equivalent) in statistics, together with at least 5 yrs' responsible professional experience as a statistician.
Graduate Statistician (GradStat): Professional grade awarded to those with a good honours degree (or equivalent) in statistics, but without the necessary professional experience to qualify as CStat.
Affiliate: Corporate bodies and institutions may be admitted to affiliation with the Society.

EXAMINATIONS:
The Society merged with the Institute of Statisticians in 1993 and is continuing to operate the exams originally run under the name of the IOS. The aim of these exams is to provide a route into the statistical profession for those in countries where few, if any, university courses are available, and for those in the UK who cannot pursue an undergraduate degree course, or who wish to convert from another discipline after some yrs' work.

The exams are held in May and there are 3 levels:

Ordinary Certificate (2 papers), **Higher Certificate** (3 papers: Statistical Theory; Statistical Methods; Statistical Applications and Practice), and **Graduate Diploma** (4 compulsory papers: Applied Statistics I and II; Statistical Theory and Methods I and II; and an option paper with questions on economic statistics, econometrics, medical statistics, biometry, industrial statistics and operational research.

University Qualifications

The following universities offer qualifications in Statistics and related subjects. Full details may be found in Part 4, under the entry for the appropriate university.

FIRST DEGREES AWARDED BY UNIVERSITIES

Aberdeen; Anglia; Bath; Belfast; Birmingham; Brighton; Bristol; Brunel; Central Lancashire; City; Coventry; Derby; Dundee; East Anglia; Edinburgh; Essex; Exeter; Glamorgan; Glasgow; Glasgow Caledonian; Greenwich; Heriot-Watt; Hertfordshire; Huddersfield; Hull; Keele; Kent; Kent (Canterbury Christ Church University College); Kingston; Lancaster; Leeds; Liverpool; Liverpool (Chester College of H.E.); Liverpool John Moores; London (Birkbeck, University of London); London (Goldsmiths College); London (Imperial College of Science, Technology & Medicine); London (London School of Economics & Political Science); London (Queen Mary & Westfield College (incorporating St Bartholomew's and the Royal London School of Medicine & Dentistry)); London (Royal Holloway); London (University College (UCL)); Luton; Manchester; Middlesex; Napier; Newcastle; North London; Nottingham; Oxford Brookes; Plymouth; Portsmouth; Reading; Sheffield; Sheffield Hallam; Southampton; St Andrews; Staffordshire; Strathclyde; Surrey; Sussex; Ulster; UMIST; Wales (University of Wales, Aberystwyth); Wales (University of Wales, Swansea); Warwick; York

HIGHER DEGREES AWARDED BY UNIVERSITIES

Aberdeen; Birmingham; Bristol; Brunel; Cambridge; Central Lancashire; City; Essex; Exeter; Glasgow; Greenwich; Kent; Lancaster; Leicester; Liverpool John Moores; London (Birkbeck, University of London); London (Goldsmiths College); London (London School of Economics & Political Science); London (Queen Mary & Westfield College (incorporating St Bartholomew's and the Royal London School of Medicine & Dentistry)); London (Royal Holloway); London (University College (UCL)); Manchester; Napier; Oxford; Plymouth; Reading; Salford; Sheffield Hallam; Southampton; St Andrews; UMIST; Warwick; York

DIPLOMAS AWARDED BY UNIVERSITIES

Central Lancashire; City; Exeter; Glasgow; Hull; Lancaster; Leicester; London (Birkbeck, University of London); London (London School of Economics & Political Science); London (University College (UCL)); Manchester; Middlesex; Napier; Nottingham; Oxford; St Andrews; Staffordshire

CERTIFICATES AWARDED BY UNIVERSITIES

London (Birkbeck, University of London); Staffordshire

Higher National Diplomas

Courses for the HND in Mathematics, Statistics and Computing are listed under 'Computing and Information Technology'.

STOCKBROKING AND SECURITIES

INSTITUTE OF INVESTMENT MANAGEMENT AND RESEARCH

21 Ironmonger Lane, London EC2V 8EY Tel: 020 7796 3000 Fax: 020 7796 3333
e-mail: contact@iimr.org.uk Website: www.iimr.org.uk

MEMBERSHIP:

Fellows (FIIMR): Members eligible for election are those who have been Associate Members for not less than 10 consecutive yrs, have submitted an original work contributing to the activities of the investment community or have made a significant contribution to the work of the Institute.

Associates (AIIMR): Student Members who have passed the Associate Exam and have been professionally engaged in investment analysis or portfolio management, or an equivalent activity for at least 2 yrs.

Accredited Members: Student Members who have passed the Associate Exam, but not yet obtained the relevant professional experience.

Student Members: Persons must be 18 and have reached an academic standard at least equivalent to Grade C GCE in 5 subjects at O Level or GCSE which includes (i) English or English Language and (ii) Mathematics or Commercial Mathematics and to have passed the Investment Management Certificate. Student Membership is open for 3 yrs, during which a Student must pass the Associate Exam though this period may be extended if he can show good reason for being unable to complete the exam within that period.

EXAMINATIONS:

Associate Exam: 2 parts – Part 1: Consisting of Securities and Investment; Economic and Applied Statistical Analysis; and Interpretation of Accounts and Corporate Finance; and Part 2: Consisting of Portfolio Management; Investment Regulation and Practice; and a Case Study.

Investment Management Certificate: 3 hr multiple choice paper covering regulation, markets, statistics, accounting, economics and portfolio management. This is a basic competence test designed for investment managers regulated by IMRO and PIA.

THE SECURITIES INSTITUTE

Centurion House, 24 Monument Street, London EC3R 8AQ Tel: 020 7645 0600 Fax: 020 7645 0601
Website: www.securities-institute.org.uk

The Institute is the largest professional body for practitioners in stockbroking, derivatives markets, investment management, corporate finance and related activities. The Institute presently has over 17,000 Full, Associate, Affiliate and Student Members. Securities Institute (Services) Ltd, a subsidiary company, runs updating courses, professional seminars and other training courses for practitioners.

EXAMINATIONS:

Securities Institute Diploma: Professional level exam designed for those with 2-3 yrs' experience . 3 passes from the following 10 subjects – Regulation and Compliance; Interpretation of Financial Statements; Bond and Fixed Interest Markets; Private Client Investment Advice and Management; Investment Analysis; Fund Management; Financial Derivatives; Corporate Finance; Operations Management; International Operations Management – achieves the SIE Diploma, leading to full membership of the Securities Institute.

Investment Administration Qualification: A benchmark qualification for individuals who are employed in the operations/settlement/administrative needs for a financial institution. A pass in 3 modules achieves the Qualification. Modules include: Introduction to Securities and Investment, Regulatory Environment, Treasury Operations, Global Custody, CREST Settlement, Derivatives Operations, OEICs Administration, UTA Administration, ISA Administration, Portfolio Performance Measurement, International Settlement.

International Capital Markets Qualification (ICMQ): ICMQ and the IIAC are qualifications aimed at employees working overseas in 'emerging markets' in places such as the Far East, Africa and Eastern Europe. The ICMQ is made up of 3 modules and is set at an introductory level. The IIAC Certificate follows the ICMA and is made up of 4 modules. All of the examinations are made up of multiple choice questions with the exception of Financial Advice.

Investment Administration Qualification (IAQ): This range of workbook-based modules includes the Introduction to Securities and Investment – the ideal introduction to financial services (linked to 1 hr multiple choice exam). Other subjects are Crest Settlement, Derivatives Operations, International Settlement, IMRO Regulatory Environment, SFA Regulatory Environment, Unit Trust Administration, ISA Administration, OEIC Administration, PEP Administration, Treasury Operations, Portfolio Performance Measurement, and Global Custody. 3 subject passes achieves the Merit Award.

Investment Advice Certificate (IAC): The IAC is the benchmark exam for specialists engaged in the investment of private clients' capital. The exam comprises 3 papers – Introduction to Financial Services, Investments and Products, and Financial Advice. Individuals take 1, 2, or all 3 papers depending on the nature of their work and the relevant regulatory requirements.

SFA Registered Persons Exams: The Securities Institute administers the Securities and Futures Authority exams: Securities Representative, Securities and Financial Derivatives Representative, Futures and Options Representative and Corporate Finance Representative. SFA is the self-regulating organisation responsible for authorising investment business dealing in securities, futures and options. Employees of such firms must register as Representatives before advising clients on investments or as Traders before committing their firm in market dealings.

Note: UK regulatory requirements may change during 2001 due to the implementation of the Financial Services and Markets Act.

University Qualifications

The following universities offer qualifications in Stockbroking and Securities and related subjects. Full details may be found in Part 4, under the entry for the appropriate university.

FIRST DEGREES AWARDED BY UNIVERSITIES
Glamorgan

HIGHER DEGREES AWARDED BY UNIVERSITIES
City; Glasgow Caledonian; London Guildhall; Reading; York

PROFESSIONAL COURSES AWARDED BY UNIVERSITIES
Leeds Metropolitan

SURGICAL, DENTAL AND CARDIOLOGICAL TECHNICIANS
(See also Dental Ancillary Staff)

Membership of Professional Institutions and Associations

THE BRITISH INSTITUTE OF DENTAL AND SURGICAL TECHNOLOGISTS

PO Box 196, Bingley BD16 1XX Tel: 01274 589568 e-mail: bidst@btinternet.com

ALL SECTIONS:
Life Members: Those who have been Fellows or Licentiates of the Institute for a continuous period not less than 15 yrs and whose subscriptions have been paid up to date throughout the period of Membership and who have reached retirement age and receive no income, and who are recommended by the section committee.

SURGICAL SECTION:
Fellows (FBIDST): Fellowship will be awarded by Council only after 4 yrs in continuous membership at Licentiate grade to those who hold a relevant BTEC Higher Certificate, or CGLI Advanced Certificate, on either the reading of a paper at a recognised scientific meeting, or the publication of a paper in an approved Scientific Journal. This award to be subject to recommendation or ratification by the Surgical Section Committee.

Licentiates (LBIDST): (a) Applicants who have passed the final exam in courses of education prescribed by the Council and are not less than 24; (b) those of not less than 25 who have been practising as surgical technologists for not less than 10 yrs.

Associates: Applicants who have experience or are undertaking a course of education but who in the opinion of the Council are not yet qualified for Licentiate.

DENTAL SECTION:

Fellows (FBIDST): Fellowship will be awarded by Council only after 5 yrs in continuous membership at Licentiate grade to those who hold a relevant BTEC Higher Certificate, or CGLI Advanced Certificate, on either the reading of a paper at a recognised scientific meeting, or the publication of a paper in an approved Scientific Journal. This award to be subject to recommendation or ratification by the Central Dental Council.

Licentiates (LBIDST): (a) Those who have successfully completed the full TEC, BTEC programme or SCOTEC diploma programme; or (b) those who hold the Final Certificate of the C&G; or (c) those who hold the First Class Certificate of HM Forces; or (d) those who have passed another exam recognised by the Institute for this grade of membership.

Associates: Those who have successfully completed 8 units of the TEC, BTEC, or SCOTEC Certificate or Diploma programme, or who hold the CGLI Intermediate Certificate.

University Qualifications

The following universities offer qualifications in Surgical, Dental and Cardiological Technicians and related subjects. Full details may be found in Part 4, under the entry for the appropriate university.

FIRST DEGREES AWARDED BY UNIVERSITIES
Manchester Metropolitan.; Strathclyde; Wales (University of Wales Institute, Cardiff)

HIGHER DEGREES AWARDED BY UNIVERSITIES
Bristol; Dundee; Glasgow; London (Queen Mary & Westfield College (incorporating St Bartholomew's and the Royal London School of Medicine & Dentistry)); Strathclyde

DIPLOMAS AWARDED BY UNIVERSITIES
Dundee; Strathclyde; Wales (University of Wales Institute, Cardiff)

SURVEYING

University Qualifications

The following universities offer qualifications in Surveying and related subjects. Full details may be found in Part 4, under the entry for the appropriate university.

FIRST DEGREES AWARDED BY UNIVERSITIES
Abertay, Dundee; Anglia; Brighton; Bristol; Central England; Central Lancashire; City; Coventry; De Montfort, Leicester; East London; Exeter; Glamorgan; Glasgow Caledonian; Greenwich; Heriot-Watt; Kingston; Leeds Metropolitan; Liverpool John Moores; Luton; Napier; Newcastle; Northumbria; Nottingham Trent; Nottingham Trent (Southampton Institute); Plymouth; Portsmouth; Reading; Robert Gordon; Salford; Sheffield Hallam; South Bank; Staffordshire; Ulster; UMIST; Westminster; Wolverhampton

HIGHER DEGREES AWARDED BY UNIVERSITIES
Aberdeen; City; Glasgow; Kingston; London (University College (UCL)); Nottingham

DIPLOMAS AWARDED BY UNIVERSITIES
Abertay, Dundee; Glamorgan; London (University College (UCL)); Luton; Northampton; Northumbria

PROFESSIONAL QUALIFICATIONS AWARDED BY UNIVERSITIES
East London

National Certificates and Diplomas

BTEC National Certificates/Diplomas: Mine Surveying; Surveying; Surveying (Cartography); Surveying (Engineering)
BTEC Higher National Certificates/Diplomas: Mine Surveying; Minerals Surveying; Surveying; Surveying (Air Survey); Surveying (Cartography); Surveying (Engineering)
Scotland
SQA HNC: Built Environment; Construction Management; Construction Practice; Quantity Surveying
SQA HND: Construction Surveying; Quantity Surveying; Built Environment (Quantity Surveying)
SQA Advanced Certificate: Construction Practice
SQA Advanced Diploma: Construction Surveying

NVQs

Level 3: Fenestration Surveying
Level 2: Surveying Support

City & Guilds

6270 Quantity Surveying

SWIMMING INSTRUCTION

Membership of Professional Institutions and Associations

HALLIWICK ASSOCIATION OF SWIMMING THERAPY

c/o ADKC Centre, Whitstable House, Silchester Road, London W10 6SB Tel: 020 8968 7609
Fax: 020 8968 7609 e-mail: obk@obk.co.uk Website: www.co.uk/halliwick/index.html
A voluntary Association which aims to teach swimming and safety in water, and to encourage confidence regardless of the severity of the Disability. It exists to provide opportunities for recreational swimming to disabled people of all types and ages. The Association works through regional associations to which local clubs can affiliate, and provides **instructor training**. The Association organises regional and national galas. It also publishes books and has issued 3 videos. **Proficiency tests** held by the Association are aligned to the Halliwick Method. A high standard of teaching and exams is maintained. Courses for volunteers and professions are already arranged in many parts of the country. Applications for others will be considered.

THE SWIMMING TEACHERS' ASSOCIATION

Anchor House, Birch Street, Walsall, West Midlands WS2 8HZ
Tel: 01922 645097
Fax: 01922 720628
e-mail: sta@sta.co.uk
Website: www.sta.co.uk

GRADES OF MEMBERSHIP:
Fellow Members, Diploma Members, Qualified Members and Associate Members are all entitled to vote.
Student Members and Honorary Associate Members are not entitled to vote.
EXAMINATIONS:
Student Teachers' Certificate: This examination course is designed to provide preliminary

training in swimming teaching for young people aged 14-18.

Basic Teachers' Certificate: This examination course is the introduction to swimming teacher training and the pre-requisite for the Swimming Teachers' Certificate Examination.

Swimming Teachers' Certificate: This examination qualifies candidates to teach swimming.

Teachers' Certificate for Teaching Swimming: This 2 part examination course is designed specifically to train qualified school teachers to teach swimming to Key Stage 2 – TCTS(P) or Key Stages 3 and 4 TCTS(S).

The National Aquatic Rescue Standards for Pool Lifeguards: A course to provide qualified lifeguards. The award is valid for 24 mths and carries a water test depth endorsement.

The National Aquatic Rescue Standards for Swimming Teachers and Poolside Helpers: A course to provide qualified poolside helpers. The award is valid for 24 mths and carries a water test depth endorsement.

The National Aquatic Rescue Standards for Pool Attendants: A course to provide qualified poolside helpers. The award is valid for 24 mths and carries a water test depth endorsement.

The National Aquatic Rescue Standards – Emergency Responders: A course to train those experienced in primary life support to act as emergency responders. This includes use of oxygen and automated defibrillation equipment.

The National Aquatic Rescue Standard – Spinal Module: A course to train those who hold practical lifeguarding skills in the knowledge and treatment required for suspected spinal injuries.

Parent and Child Module: A module for qualified swimming teachers that covers the special aspects of teaching babies and very young children.

Aquacise: A course for swimming teachers who wish to teach therapeutic water exercises, with particular emphasis on antenatal exercises, on remedial exercises following illness or operations and general water fitness exercises.

Disabilities Awareness Certificate: A course to train qualified helpers and qualified swimming teachers in the correct treatment and handling of those with more severe disabilities.

First Aid at Work: A range of First Aid courses including First Aid at Work and Appointed Persons Certificate, both of which comply with HSE requirements. An extension module to First Aid at Work covers support in pregnancy, childbirth, febrile convulsions and use of specialised first aid equipment.

Tutors: The STA also runs courses to train tutors for the above examinations; within the regions seminars are regularly held on topics of interest to swimming teachers.

TAXATION

Membership of Professional Institutions and Associations

THE ASSOCIATION OF TAXATION TECHNICIANS

ASSOCIATION OF TAXATION TECHNICIANS

12 Upper Belgrave Street, London SW1X 8BB
Tel: 020 7235 2544
Fax: 020 7235 4571
e-mail: info@att.co.uk
Website: www.tax.org.uk

MEMBERSHIP:

Member (ATT): Membership is restricted to those who have passed either the Association's exam *and* who have a minimum of 2 yrs' acceptable current practical experience in UK taxation *or* to those who are Fellows or Associates of The Chartered Institute of Taxation.

EXAMINATIONS:

Candidates must meet the minimum educational requirements of 4 GCSEs (not craft subjects) at Grade C or above including English Language and Mathematics or certain professional experience. Further details may be obtained from the Association. Candidates must have registered with the Association for at least 7 mths before they may attempt the exams. The exam covers Personal Taxation in the first paper and Taxation of Businesses in the second paper. In addition there are 2 papers on the Principles of Law and the Principles of Accounting. Exemptions for the 2 papers will be granted to those who have successfully studied at A Level or above.

Distinctions: Distinctions are awarded to candidates in the exam who achieve an exceptionally high standard. Such certificates are additional to various prize awards.

THE CHARTERED INSTITUTE OF TAXATION

THE CHARTERED INSTITUTE OF TAXATION

12 Upper Belgrave Street, London SW1X 8BB
Tel: 020 7235 9381
Fax: 020 7235 2562
e-mail: post@ciot.org.uk
Website: www.tax.org.uk.

MEMBERSHIP:

Fellow (FTII): Fellowship is restricted to those who have submitted an acceptable thesis and who can produce satisfactory evidence of specialisation in taxation for at least 3 yrs prior to the date of their application. Theses may only be submitted by those who are already associates.

Associates (ATII): Applicants must have passed the Associateship exam and have demonstrated 3 yrs' professional experience in UK taxation.

Subscribers: The Institute has a class of subscribers for certain limited technical information but they are not members of the Institute.

EXAMINATIONS:

Candidates must have been registered as a student with the Institute for 6 mths and hold a Certificate of Eligibility. To obtain a Certificate of Eligibility a student must have passed the exam of The Association of Taxation Technicians or the qualifying exam for one of certain professional bodies. Further details may be obtained from the Education Department.

Associateship Exam: Covers practice ethics and administration, general taxation, interaction of taxes and 1 further paper from a choice of 4 options: general practice including owner managed companies; taxation of individuals, trusts and estates; taxation of companies, their shareholders and employees; and indirect taxation.

University Qualifications

The following universities offer qualifications in Taxation and related subjects. Full details may be found in Part 4, under the entry for the appropriate university.

FIRST DEGREES AWARDED BY UNIVERSITIES
Abertay, Dundee; Bournemouth; London Guildhall

HIGHER DEGREES AWARDED BY UNIVERSITIES
Bournemouth; Dundee

PROFESSIONAL COURSES AWARDED BY UNIVERSITIES
London Guildhall; Manchester Metropolitan

TAXI DRIVERS (LONDON)

Cab drivers and cab proprietors in the Metropolitan Police District and City of London are licensed by an Assistant Commissioner of the Metropolitan Police, through the **Public Carriage Office** at 15 Penton Street, Islington N1 9PU.

A cab driver's licence is valid for 3 yrs and a cab proprietor's licence for 1yr. Applicants are required to satisfy the Licensing Authority that they are in all material respects fit to hold a licence. Before a cab driver's licence is issued an applicant must pass a 'Knowledge of London' exam, which consists of a written test and successive oral exams conducted at intervals before examiners at the Public Carriage Office and continuing until such time as an applicant attains a degree of knowledge that enables him or her to undertake hirings by a reasonably direct route. The Public Carriage Office is concerned only with the exam of candidates and not with their tuition. A full cab driver's licence, known as an 'All London' licence, enables a cab driver to ply for hire over the whole of the Metropolitan Police District and City of London. The holder of such a licence must have a thorough knowledge of the Central London area, know the precise location of important public buildings, hotels, theatres etc, and also have a good working knowledge of the remainder of the district in which he or she is licensed to ply for hire. Licences are also issued to drivers to ply for hire in 21 suburban sectors of London only. Suburban drivers must have an intimate knowledge of the sector as well as some idea of the Central London area.

All cab drivers must pass a driving test on a cab before being licensed. Licences are not issued to persons under 21.

TEACHING/EDUCATION

OCR Teacher/Trainer Qualifications

OCR offer various teacher/trainer awards in Counselling, Learning Disabilities, Teaching foreign languages to adults, Information Technology, Administration, Numeracy & Exercise to music. Contact OCR for more details.

Initial Qualifications in England and Wales

RECOGNITION:
To obtain a teaching appointment in maintained schools in England and Wales, it is necessary to be a

qualified teacher. In order to be qualified, teachers must have satisfactorily completed an approved course of initial training or be exceptionally recognised as a qualified teacher under the Education (Teachers) Regulations 1989.

OTHER APPROVED COURSES OF TRAINING:
Courses of initial training at institutions providing teacher training: a course of training leading to registration as a primary or secondary school teacher in Scotland. A course of training in Northern Ireland, approved by the Ministry of Education for Northern Ireland, leading to recognition as a school teacher.

APPROVED COURSES OF TRAINING IN ENGLAND AND WALES:
Initial teacher training courses in England and Wales are provided by Colleges and University Departments of Education. The main courses available are Bachelor of Education (BEd) degrees for non-graduates and Post-graduate Certificates of Education (PGCEs) for graduates. BEd degrees usually last 4 yrs for an honours degree although there are some 2 yr BEd degrees in the secondary shortage subjects for holders of certain specialist qualifications. PGCEs generally last 1 yr but there are some 2 yr conversion PGCEs in the shortage subjects for those whose degrees are in other subjects but did, nonetheless contain about 1 yr of relevant subject study at a higher educational level. There are also some 2 yr Articled Teachers Scheme PGCEs which are largely school based and for which students are paid a bursary by the LEA in which they are studying. In addition to these there are some 4 yr courses that combine professional training and study for a degree.Details of courses and institutions are given in the *NATFHE Handbook of Initial Teacher Training*. This is published by the National Association of Teachers in Further and Higher Education and is available from Linneys ESL, 121 Newgate Lane, Mansfield, Nottinghamshire NG18 2PA.

QUALIFICATIONS FOR ADMISSION TO TRAINING:
Students entering 4 yr BEd (Hons) courses will normally be expected to have 3 GCSE/O levels, grade C or above, and 2 GCE A levels (or equivalent qualifications) while entrants to PGCE courses require a UK degree or a recognised equivalent. All entrants to courses of initial teacher training, whether undergraduate or postgraduate, will be expected to provide evidence of a level of competence in English language and mathematics equivalent to at least GCSE/O level grade C standard. Applications for undergraduate courses are made through UCAS, Fulton House, Jessop

Avenue, Cheltenham, Glos, GL50 3SH, and postgraduate applications through the Graduate Teacher Training Registry, PO Box 239, Cheltenham, Glos, GL50 3SL.

DIPLOMA OF HIGHER EDUCATION:
Many colleges of education and colleges or institutes of higher education now offer a range of courses in addition to teacher-training, leading to awards such as BA, BSc and DipHE. The latter is awarded after a 2-yr course equivalent in standard to the first 2 yrs of a degree, and the normal entry qualifications for the course are the same as for a degree course, *viz*, 5 GCE or GCSE passes including 2 at A level. In addition to being a terminal qualification, the DipHE provides a foundation for further study, leading to a degree or professional qualification.

FURTHER EDUCATION TEACHER TRAINING CENTRES:
1-yr FT courses of professional training for students with technical qualifications who wish to teach in further education institutions are offered at: Bolton IHE; University of Greenwhich, London SW15; Huddersfield University; Wolverhampton University; University College Cardiff, Department of Education. These colleges also offer PT courses for serving teachers in colleges of further education who are seconded by their education authorities. PT courses are also run at: University of the West of England at Bristol; Bulmershe CHE; Derby University; Dorset IHE; Essex IHE; Hertfordshire University; De Montfort University, Leicester; Lincoln CT; Middlesex University; Nene Coll, Northampton; New Coll, Durham; NE Wales IHE; Oxford Brookes University; Plymouth University; Portsmouth University; Nottingham Trent University

TEACHERS OF HANDICAPPED CHILDREN:
There are no longer any initial teacher training courses specifically for children with special needs. These have been phased out and replaced with in-service courses for already qualified teachers.
In-Service Training Courses: Teachers of handicapped pupils may be seconded to attend 1-yr courses which are held in University Departments of Education, polytechnics and other colleges of higher education throughout the country. A number of these courses offered on a PT basis are also available. 1-term courses primarily designed for remedial teachers in ordinary schools, can also be taken.

Initial Qualifications in Northern Ireland

RECOGNITION:
To be recognised as a teacher in Northern Ireland candidates must have qualifications acceptable to the Department of Education for Northern Ireland.
Primary School Teachers: To become eligible for recognition as a qualified teacher in a primary school a candidate must have successfully completed a course of professional teacher training, normally of 4 yrs' duration, approved by the Department. Untrained graduates are only qualified for recognition in Institutes of FE.
Secondary School Teachers: To become eligible for recognition in a secondary school candidates must have a degree, diploma or certificate approved by the Department or have successfully completed a course of professional teacher training, normally of 4 yrs' duration, approved by the Department. A university degree or qualification accepted as equivalent, which was acquired after 31 December 1973, is not accepted for recognition purposes unless accompanied by approved professional training.
Special School Teachers: To become eligible for recognition in special schools candidates must normally have qualifications which would entitle them to recognition in primary or secondary schools. Teachers of blind or deaf or partially hearing pupils must have a special diploma or certificate regarded as appropriate by the Department.
Institutions of Further Education: The qualifications normally required for recognition as a qualified teacher are successful completion of a degree, diploma, certificate or FT course of teacher training approved by the Department or such other qualifications together with suitable experience that the Department recognises. The completion of a course of teacher training is not a mandatory requirement for recognition.
Approved Qualifications: The qualifications required as a condition of recognition are almost identical with those recognised by the DfEE in England and Wales for the normal route to Qualified Teacher Status. Full details may be obtained from the Department of Education, Waterside House, 75 Duke Street, Londonderry BT47 1FP. The qualifications fall into 2 broad groups, university degrees and/or certificates of education obtained in the UK and specialist

qualifications in Art, Commercial Subjects, Crafts, Domestic Science, Music, Physical Education, Speech Training and Woodwork.

PROBATION:
A teacher who is recognised as a qualified teacher is placed on probation for an initial period of 3 or 6 terms during which recognition is provisional. The period of 3 terms applies to teachers who have successfully completed an approved course of teacher training and the period of 6 terms to teachers who have not taken such a course.

INITIAL TRAINING OF TEACHERS:
1. FT courses of initial training are provided by the 2 colleges of education and the 2 universities. PT courses are provided by the Open University. Training is phase related, ie the professional studies and school experience elements of the courses on offer are orientated towards teaching in either primary or secondary schools.2. The 2 colleges of education are: Stranmillis, a non-denominational, co-educational college managed by a governing body on behalf of the Department of Education for Northern Ireland, and St Mary's, a co-educational college under Roman Catholic management. The colleges offer primary orientated 4-yr courses leading to the award of a BEd (Hons) degree of Queen's University or 1-yr Postgraduate Certificate in Education courses and, in addition, secondary orientated BEd courses in Craft, Design and Technology, Business Studies and Religious Studies.3. The Queen's University of Belfast offers a secondary orientated 1-yr Graduate Certificate in Education course. The University of Ulster provides courses of initial teacher training on 2 of its campuses, at Coleraine and Jordanstown. One yr Postgraduate Certificate in Education courses in some non-practical subjects are offered at Coleraine. At Jordanstown, secondary orientated 1 yr Postgraduate Certificate in Education courses are available for intending teachers of Art, Music, Home Economics, Physical Education and Technology.

REQUIREMENTS FOR ADMISSION TO TRAINING:
Department of Education Regulations require that a student will not be admitted to the college or university unless the authorities are satisfied as to his/her good character and health, physical capacity for teaching and suitability for the teaching profession in other respects. Initial teacher training institutions must satisfy themselves that entrants to courses have the personal and intellectual qualities suitable for teaching and show evidence of professional potential. Entrants to undergraduate courses are normally expected to have at least 2 A levels and 3 GCSE grade C passes (or equivalent qualifications). Mature applicants for undergraduate courses who lack these qualifications may be admitted as special entrants if they have suitable personal qualities and appropriate experience of adult and working life. Entrants to postgraduate courses should have a recognised UK degree or an equivalent qualification. In the case of equivalent qualifications, it is a matter for an admitting institution to decide on an applicant's acceptability. All entrants to courses of initial teacher training must be able to demonstrate a level of competence in English Language and mathematics equivalent to at least GCSE grade C standard. It is emphasised that the above are minimum entry requirements but that many institutions expect prospective students to hold more than the minimum qualifications.

Initial Qualifications in Scotland

RECOGNITION AS A TEACHER:
In Scotland only teachers who are registered with the General Teaching Council (GTC) for Scotland, (Clerwood House, Clermiston Road, Edinburgh EH12 6UT Tel: 0131 314 6000 Website: www.gtcs.org.uk) may be appointed to posts in education authority schools. Automatic entitlement to registration is secured by successful completion of a course of initial teacher education at a Scottish teacher education institution leading to the award of a Teaching Qualification. Provision exists, however, for the exceptional admission to the Register of teachers from outside Scotland whose qualifications are considered by the Council to be broadly equivalent to those required of Scottish teachers. The Council welcomes applications from qualified teachers outside Scotland. There is an annual fee for registration. Teachers wishing to take up permanent posts in further education establishments do not need to be registered or hold a Teaching Qualification but they must hold the qualifications necessary for entry to a course leading to the award of a Teaching Qualification (Further Education) and have relevant industrial or commercial experience. The following Teaching Qualifications are issued by the teacher education institutions:

Teaching Qualification (Primary Education): A certificate of competency to teach in primary schools and departments.

Teaching Qualification (Secondary Education): A certificate of competency to teach a specified subject or group of subjects in secondary schools or departments.

Teaching Qualification (Further Education): A certificate of competency to teach a specified subject or group of subjects in further education centres.

Special Qualifications. Registered teachers may undertake a supplementary course leading to the award of a Special Qualification in order to specialise in 1 of the following areas: as a nursery teacher; an infant teacher; a teacher of 1 or more categories of pupils requiring special education; a learning support teacher in primary or secondary schools or departments, or a teacher in the upper primary school.

PROBATION:
After successfully completing an approved course of study teachers are awarded a Teaching Qualification by their teacher education institution and, on applying to the GTC, a provisional registration certificate. The Certificate confers the status of qualified teacher during a period of 2 yrs' approved probationary service in Scottish schools. On successfully completing their probation teachers receive from the Council the appropriate Certificate of Full Registration, which is their mark of final recognition as qualified teachers.

TEACHER EDUCATION:
The responsibility for teacher education in Scotland is entrusted to 6 teacher education institutions.

Institution	Type of course
University of Paisley	Primary Education
Faculty of Education, Ayr Campus, Ayr KA8 0SR	Secondary Education
University of Strathclyde	Primary Education
Faculty of Education	Secondary Education
Jordanhill Campus, Southbrae Drive, Glasgow G13 1PP	Further Education
Northern College	Primary Education
Aberdeen Campus, Hilton Place	Secondary Education
Aberdeen AB24 4FA	
Dundee Campus, Gardyne Road, Broughty Ferry,	
Dundee DD5 1NY	Primary Education
Moray House Institute of Education,	
the University of Edinburgh	
(Incorporating the Scottish Centre for Physical Education,	
Movement and Leisure Studies)	
Holyrood Campus, Holyrood Road	Primary Education
Edinburgh EH8 8AQ	Secondary Education
Cramond Campus Cramond Road North,	
Edinburgh EH4 6JD	Physical Education
The University of Edinburgh Faculty of Education	Primary Education
St Andrew's Campus, Duntocher Road, Bearsden,	
Glasgow G61 4QA	Secondary Education
University of Stirling,	Secondary Education and Further
Dept of Education, Stirling FK9 4LA	Education

ENTRY REQUIREMENTS:
Primary Education: There are 2 methods of obtaining this qualification: (a) a degree of a UK university (including the Open University) followed by a 1-session (October to June) course at a teacher education institution; (b) a 4-yr course at a teacher education institution leading to the award of the Degree of Bachelor of Education in which academic studies and professional training proceed concurrently. Entrance qualifications for this degree will be similar to those of normal university entrance.All candidates are required to have a pass in English at Higher grade and Mathematics at either grade of the Scottish Certificate of Education (or equivalent). From session 2000-2001, Mathematics will have to be offered at a minimum of standard grade credit (ie grades 1 or 2).

Secondary Education: There are 2 methods of obtaining this qualification: (a) a degree which, as a general rule, contains passes in 2 graduating courses in the subject or subjects to be taught (3 from the yr 2000) and followed by 1 session postgraduate Certificate in Education course. (An SCE Higher grade pass in English is also required) (b) concurrent BEd degree or BA/BSc plus Diploma in Education offered at certain teacher education institutions. Entrance requirements are similar to those required for normal university entrance and include an SCE Higher grade pass in English (or equivalent) and specific requirements as necessary for particular qualifications. Candidates are advised to communicate direct with the Admissions Office of the Scottish institution of their choice as not all secondary subjects are offered at each establishment.

Further Education: Teacher education is open mainly to candidates with acceptable technical or commercial qualifications who have been employed in industry or commerce, who hold a recognised appointment in further education and who are seconded to the course on full salary by their employing college. The minimum technical qualification is generally an HNC or a Full Technological Certificate of the CGLI. Advice on qualifications which are acceptable as pre-entry requirements may be obtained from the institution concerned.

Notes: 1. Full details of entry requirements may be found in the *Memorandum on Entry Requirements to Courses of Teacher Education in Scotland*, Scottish Office Education and Industry Department – published annually by HMSO. 2. For details of Scottish Certificate of Education (SCE) equivalences consult the appropriate Scottish teacher education institution.

Membership of Professional Institutions and Associations

THE COLLEGE OF TEACHERS

Coppice Row, Theydon Bois, Epping, Essex CM16 7DN Tel: 01992 812727 Fax: 01992 814690
e-mail: collegeofteachers@mailbox.ulcc.ac.uk

HONORARY AWARDS:

Charter Fellow (HonFCP): Chosen each yr from among today's most distinguished practitioners of education.

INDIVIDUAL MEMBERSHIP:

Ordinary Fellow (FCollP): The senior Class of Membership, reserved for those who have made an outstanding contribution to education. Minimum requirements for application: evidence of an outstanding contribution to education through high academic qualifications or a significant contribution to educational literature; tenure of a position of considerable responsibility in education (or 10 yrs in work demanding a knowledge of education). Holders of the Fellowship (FCP) qualification are normally eligible for election to this class of Membership. This grade is no longer available to new members.

Member (MCollP): The Class of Membership applicable to a practising educationist. Minimum requirements for application: a professional qualification and experience in teaching or the education service. Holders of the Associate (ACP), Licentiate (LCP) and DipASE qualifications are normally eligible for election to this class of Membership. New members will be MCT and cannot upgrade to FCollP.

Student: A transitional category to which persons wishing to be associated with the College, but who are not eligible for election as Ordinary Fellows or as Members, may be elected. Candidates for College awards are automatically elected to this category, unless they are already full members.

All members receive a newsletter and the College's journal *Education Today*

ACADEMIC QUALIFICATIONS:

Under the terms of a supplemental Royal Charter which came into effect on the 15th May 1998: the former 'College of Preceptors' became the 'College of Teachers'. The qualifications offered by the College will continue to be at the same levels as before. The College of Teachers is legally the same body as the former College of Preceptors, and so the only effective change is one of name. For the information of candidates, students, members, holders of qualifications, and others interested, the validity and standing of qualifications will not be affected. Do please contact the new College if you have any problems arising from this change of name, or anyone with whom you deal requires further information. The College will be pleased to provide any further assistance needed.

Fellow (FC.T): An award at masters' level conferred on the basis of a research thesis of about 50,000 words or for published work, professional papers or professional record. Candidates normally need to be graduates (or holders of the LC.T) and experienced qualified teachers. For the FC.T by professional record, teachers will have to have responsibility for a major area, and the staff development within it.

Licentiate (LC.T): The College's qualification at degree level. Now only awarded tp TESOL (Teaching English to Speakers of Other Languages) students.

Associate (AC.T): The College's basic qualification for teachers. There is a Foundation Scheme (Mode A) in which the AC.T is awarded by exam, a range of schemes (Mode B) in which the AC.T is awarded by thesis and AC.Ts can also be awarded for approved courses conducted by institutions accredited by the College (Mode C). The College accredits 2 distance learning institutions to offer an AC.T in the Theory & Methodology of Teaching English to Speakers of Other Languages (TESOL). The AC.T recognises significant work above the basic qualification level for teachers. Candidates normally need to be qualified teachers with at least 1 yr's experience. In 1990 Council approved the award of AC.Ts with subsidiary designation (eg AC.T (Special Needs)) to candidates who are not necessarily teachers, but who qualify at AC.T level in fields related to education. An AC.T with subsidiary designation does not, on its own, allow candidates to register for the higher qualifications of the College.

Certificate of Educational Studies (COES): A first level qualification instituted by Council in 1990 specifically for people like School Governors who are not professionals but who play a significant role in education.

The College awards **Diplomas (DipCP)** and **Advanced Certificates (A.Cert)** to successful candidates from accredited courses. The current ones are all in the field of TEFL (Teaching English as a Foreign Language).

THE EDUCATIONAL INSTITUTE OF SCOTLAND

46 Moray Place, Edinburgh EH3 6BH Tel: 0131 225 6244 Fax: 0131 220 3151
e-mail: tdugmore@eis.org.uk Website: www.eis.org.uk

MEMBERSHIP:

Fellow of the EIS (FEIS): On the nomination of the Board of Examiners of the EIS, the Grade of Fellow may be conferred on:

1. Members of the EIS who have attained eminence as teachers or lecturers, who have rendered valuable service to the Institute and who have been recommended as being worthy of the honour of the Grade of Fellow by the local association or self governing association to which they belong.
2. Members of the EIS of not less than 5 yrs' standing who present a thesis, not previously presented for any degree or diploma, which, in the judgement of the Board of Examiners, constitutes an original contribution to learning in relation to education. A thesis under this section shall be sent to the General Secretary not later than 1 October in each yr.
3. Persons who have rendered signal service to education in Scotland or elsewhere. It shall be competent for local associations and self governing associations to transmit to the General Secretary of the Institute on or before the last day of February in each yr the names of persons who have rendered signal service to education and whom they wish to recommend as being worthy of the honour of the Grade of Fellow together with a statement of the nature and extent of their service to education.

Honorary Fellows (Hons FEIS): On the nomination of the Board of Examiners of the EIS, the Grade of Honorary Fellow may be conferred on persons who have rendered signal service to education in Scotland or elsewhere.

Personal applications for the grade of Fellow or Honorary Fellow are not accepted except in the case of those presenting a thesis.

THE SOCIETY OF TEACHERS IN BUSINESS EDUCATION

88 Springfield Road, Millhouses, Sheffield S7 2GF Tel: 0114 236 3659 Fax: 0114 235 2671
e-mail: gensec@stbe.demon.co.uk

MEMBERSHIP:

Fellow (FSBT): Shall be not less than 25 and shall be a Member or qualified to be a Member and shall have been engaged in teaching a business subject for a consecutive period of not less than 3 yrs.

Member (MSBT): Shall be not less than 21 and shall hold (i) a teacher's certificate recognised by the Department for Education in respect of a business subject or group of business subjects, or (ii) a teacher's certificate or diploma awarded by those examining bodies determined by the Society as being of a relevant standard, or (iii) a degree of a university recognised by the Council provided evidence is produced of a knowledge of, and experience in, teaching 1 or more business subjects, or (iv) a certificate or diploma awarded by exam, by an appropriate professional body or other body as may from time to time be determined by the Council, provided that such a person can produce evidence of teaching 1 or more business subjects.

Registered Student: A person studying for an exam leading to the award of an appropriate teacher's certificate or diploma and who intends to seek membership upon successful completion of this may be placed on the Society's List of Registered Students.

THE SOCIETY OF TEACHERS OF THE ALEXANDER TECHNIQUE

129 Camden Mews, London NW1 9AH Tel: 020 7284 3338 Fax: 020 7482 5435
e-mail: info@stat.org.uk Website: www.stat.org.uk

The Alexander Technique is a system of psycho-physical re-education. It teaches us a way of regaining our natural human birthright of upright, poised awareness in all activity. Restoration of natural poise brings relief from a range of conditions where excess muscular tension is a contributory factor. There is also an improvement in general wellbeing, both mental and physical.

TRAINING:

A 3yr FT training course is offered at a number (15) of Training Schools recognised and approved by the Society of Teachers of the Alexander Technique (STAT). Qualification is by continuous assessment leading to Professional Competence Certification by the Head of Training School and Full Membership of STAT, which is the professional body. Full Membership is restricted to those who have completed a 3 yr FT course. Application should be made to the Head of the Training Course chosen and admission is solely at the discretion of the Head of the Training Course. A complete list of Training Courses currently recognised by STAT can be obtained by writing to the Administrator enclosing an A5 SAE. Some LEAs and charitable bodies make discretionary awards, but students must be prepared to make their own financial arrangements.

University Qualifications

The following universities offer qualifications in Teaching/Education and related subjects. Full details may be found in Part 4, under the entry for the appropriate university.

FIRST DEGREES AWARDED BY UNIVERSITIES

Anglia; Anglia (City College, Norwich); Bath; Bath Spa; Bradford; Bradford (Bradford & Ilkley Community College); Brighton; Bristol; Brunel; Cambridge; Central England; Central Lancashire; Cheltenham & Gloucester; Coventry (Newman College of Higher Education); De Montfort, Leicester; De Montfort, Leicester (De Montfort University Bedford); Derby; Durham; East Anglia; East Anglia (Suffolk College); East London; Essex; Exeter (The College of St Mark & St John); Glasgow; Greenwich; Heriot-Watt; Hertfordshire; Huddersfield; Hull; Keele; Kent (Canterbury Christ Church University College); Kingston; Lancaster; Lancaster (Edge Hill College of Higher Education); Leeds; Leeds (Bretton Hall); Leeds (Leeds, Trinity & All Saints); Leeds Metropolitan; Liverpool; Liverpool (Chester College of H.E.); Liverpool (Liverpool Hope University College); Liverpool John Moores; London (Goldsmiths College); London (King's College London); Loughborough; Luton; Manchester; Manchester (Warrington Collegiate Institute, Faculty of H.E,); Manchester Metropolitan.; Middlesex; Newcastle; North London; Northampton; Northumbria; Nottingham Trent; OU (Northern College of Education); OU (The Central School of Speech & Drama); Oxford (Westminster College, Oxford); Oxford Brookes; Paisley; Plymouth; Sheffield Hallam; Southampton; Southampton (Chichester Institute of Higher Education); Southampton (King Alfred's College); St Martin; Stirling; Stockport; Strathclyde; Sunderland; Sunderland (City of Sunderland College); Surrey (St Mary's, Strawberry Hill); Surrey (University of Surrey Roehampton); Wales (Cardiff University); Wales (North East Wales Institute); Wales (Swansea Institute of Higher Education); Wales (University of Wales College, Newport); Wales (University of Wales Institute, Cardiff); Wales (University of Wales, Aberystwyth); Wales (University of Wales, Bangor); Wales (University of Wales, Swansea); Wolverhampton; Worcester; York

HIGHER DEGREES AWARDED BY UNIVERSITIES

Aberdeen; Anglia; Anglia (City College, Norwich); Aston; Bath; Bath Spa; Belfast; Birmingham; Birmingham (The University of Birmingham, Westhill); Bradford; Bradford (Bradford & Ilkley Community College); Brighton; Bristol; Brunel; Buckingham; Cambridge; Central England; Central Lancashire; Cheltenham & Gloucester; City; De Montfort, Leicester; De Montfort, Leicester (De Montfort University Bedford); Derby; Dundee; Durham; East Anglia; East Anglia (Otley College); East London; Edinburgh; Essex; Exeter; Exeter (The College of St Mark & St John); Glamorgan; Glasgow; Greenwich; Heriot-Watt; Hertfordshire; Huddersfield; Hull; Keele; Kent; Kingston; Lancaster; Lancaster (Edge Hill College of Higher Education); Leeds; Leeds (Bretton Hall); Leeds (Leeds, Trinity & All Saints); Leeds (The College of Ripon & York St John); Leeds Metropolitan; Leicester; Liverpool; Liverpool (Chester College of H.E.); Liverpool (Liverpool Hope University College); Liverpool John Moores; London (Birkbeck, University of London); London (Goldsmiths College); London (Institute of Education); London (Jews' College); London (King's College London); London (University College (UCL)); Loughborough; Luton; Manchester; Manchester Metropolitan.; Middlesex; Napier; Newcastle; North London; Northampton; Nottingham; Nottingham Trent; OU (Northern College of Education); OU (The Central School of Speech & Drama); Oxford (Westminster College, Oxford); Oxford Brookes; Paisley; Plymouth; Portsmouth; Reading; Sheffield; Sheffield Hallam; South Bank; Southampton; Southampton (Chichester Institute of Higher Education); Southampton (King Alfred's College); St Martin; Staffordshire; Stirling; Strathclyde; Sunderland; Surrey; Surrey (St Mary's, Strawberry Hill); Surrey (University of Surrey Roehampton); Sussex; Ulster; Wales (Cardiff University); Wales (College of Medicine); Wales (University of Wales College, Newport); Wales (University of Wales Institute, Cardiff); Wales (University of Wales, Aberystwyth); Wales (University of Wales, Swansea); Warwick; Westminster; Wolverhampton; Worcester; York

DIPLOMAS AWARDED BY UNIVERSITIES

Aberdeen; Anglia; Anglia (City College, Norwich); Aston; Barnsley; Bath Spa; Belfast; Birmingham; Birmingham (Birmingham College of Food, Tourism and Creative Studies); Bradford; Bradford (Bradford & Ilkley Community College); Brighton; Bristol; Brunel; Central England; Cheltenham & Gloucester; City; City (Laban Centre London); De Montfort, Leicester (De Montfort University Bedford); Derby; Doncaster; Dundee; Durham; East Anglia (Suffolk College); East London; Edinburgh; Essex; Exeter; Exeter (The College of St Mark & St John); Exeter (Truro College); Glamorgan; Glasgow; Hertfordshire; Hull; Hull (Bishop Grosseteste College); Kingston; Lancaster; Lancaster (Edge Hill College of Higher Education); Leeds; Leeds (Bretton Hall); Leeds (Leeds, Trinity & All Saints); Leicester; Lincolnshire (East Yorkshire College); Liverpool; Liverpool (Chester College of H.E.); Liverpool (Liverpool Hope University College); Liverpool John Moores; London (Goldsmiths College); London (Institute of Education); London (King's College London); London (University College (UCL)); Loughborough; Manchester; Manchester Metropolitan.; Napier; Newcastle; Northampton; Nottingham; Nottingham Trent; OU (Northern College of Education); Oxford; Oxford Brookes; Paisley; Plymouth; Reading; South Bank; Southampton (Chichester Institute of Higher Education); Southampton (King Alfred's College); Stirling; Strathclyde; Surrey (St Mary's, Strawberry Hill); Surrey (University of Surrey Roehampton); Sussex; Ulster; Wales (College of Medicine); Wales (North East Wales Institute); Warwick; Wolverhampton; Worcester; York

CERTIFICATES AWARDED BY UNIVERSITIES

Aberdeen; Anglia; Anglia (City College, Norwich); Aston; Bath Spa; Belfast; Birmingham (The University of Birmingham, Westhill); Bradford (Bradford & Ilkley Community College); Brighton; Bristol; Brunel; Cambridge; Central England; Central Lancashire; Cheltenham & Gloucester; De Montfort, Leicester; De Montfort, Leicester (De Montfort University Bedford); Derby; Dundee; Durham; East London; Edinburgh; Essex; Exeter; Exeter (The College of St Mark & St John); Glamorgan; Glasgow; Greenwich; Hertfordshire; Huddersfield; Hull; Hull (Bishop Grosseteste College); Keele; Kingston; Lancaster; Lancaster (Edge Hill College of Higher Education); Leeds; Leeds (Leeds, Trinity & All Saints); Leeds (The College of Ripon & York St John); Leeds Metropolitan; Leicester; Liverpool; Liverpool (Chester College of H.E.); Liverpool John Moores; London (Goldsmiths College); London (Institute of Education); London (King's College London); Loughborough; Manchester; Manchester Metropolitan.; Middlesex; Newcastle; North London;

Northampton; Northumbria; Nottingham; Nottingham Trent; OU (Northern College of Education); Oxford; Oxford (Westminster College, Oxford); Oxford Brookes; Paisley; Reading; Sheffield Hallam; South Bank; Southampton; Southampton (Chichester Institute of Higher Education); Southampton (King Alfred's College); St Martin; Stirling; Sunderland; Surrey (St Mary's, Strawberry Hill); Surrey (University of Surrey Roehampton); Sussex; Ulster; Wales (Cardiff University); Wales (College of Medicine); Wales (University of Wales College, Newport); Wales (University of Wales Institute, Cardiff); Wales (University of Wales, Bangor); Warwick; Westminster; Wolverhampton; Worcester; York

OTHER COURSES AWARDED BY UNIVERSITIES
Leeds Metropolitan; Manchester Metropolitan.; Northampton; Sunderland (City of Sunderland College); Wales (University of Wales Institute, Cardiff)

POSTGRADUATE CERTIFICATES AWARDED BY UNIVERSITIES
Coventry (Newman College of Higher Education); Wales (University of Wales, Aberystwyth); Warwick

POSTGRADUATE DIPLOMAS AWARDED BY UNIVERSITIES
Central Lancashire

PROFESSIONAL COURSES AWARDED BY UNIVERSITIES
Leeds Metropolitan; London Guildhall; Luton

National Certificates and Diplomas
BTEC National Certificates/Diplomas: Learning Resources Technology
BTEC Higher National Certificates/Diplomas: Learning Resources Technology

NVQs
Level 3: Outdoor Education, Development Training, Recreation
Level 3 and 4: School Administration

City & Guilds
7307 Further and Adult Education Teachers' Certificate; 7321 Learning Support; 7401 Continuing Professional Development; 9281 Teaching Basic Communication Skills

Post-Credential Diplomas
There are numerous supplementary and refresher courses for serving teachers with appropriate experience, some of which lead to the award of Institute of Education supplementary certificates. Diplomas are usually awarded only after special courses of advanced study
.Further information can be obtained directly from Local Education Authorities.

Montessori International Diploma

The Maria Montessori Training Organisation, 26 Lyndhurst Gardens, London NW3 5NW
 Tel: 020 7435 3646 Fax: 020 7431 8096 Website www.montessori-ami.org
The Maria Montessori Training Organisation is the International Training Centre in Britain of the Association Montessori Internationale (AMI). The courses provide underpinning knowledge for NVQ levels 2 and 3. The Montessori International Diploma Course can be studied on a 1 yr FT/18 mths to 2 yrs PT basis.

EXAMINATIONS:
Examinations consist of 5 separate elements: 1. **Theory:** One Paper – 3 hrs; 2. **Method:** One Paper – 3 hrs; 3. **Practical:** Oral Examination – in the presence of an AMI appointed external examiner; 4. **Presentation Files:** prepared during the course; 5. **School Visits** – practice and observation. Attendance at lectures, practical sessions and the other mandatory activities – as well as the student's standard of work and general attitude throughout the course, will also be considered in the final assessment for a Diploma.

Other Awards

ASSOCIATION FOR THE EDUCATION AND WELFARE OF THE VISUALLY HANDICAPPED
Hon Secretary: Mrs J M Stone, School of Education, University of Birmingham, PO Box 363, Birmingham B15 2TT Tel: 0121 414 4799/4847Teachers in schools for the visually handicapped in England and Wales must have taken 1 of the following courses conducted by Birmingham University:

BPhilEd: 1 yr FT course, and 6 mths PT.

Diploma in the Education of the Visually Handicapped: 1 yr FT course. Since 1981, this Diploma may also be taken as a 2 yr PT course.

The School Teachers Diploma of the College of Teachers of the Blind exam conducted by the AEWVH has been phased out; all candidates are now referred to Birmingham University.

Other Vocational Awarding Bodies

ABC: Teachers' Certificate (Post-16)

TECHNICAL COMMUNICATIONS

Membership of Professional Institutions and Associations

THE BRITISH ASSOCIATION OF COMMUNICATORS IN BUSINESS

42 Borough High Street, London SE1 1XW Tel: 020 7378 7139 Fax: 020 7378 7140
e-mail: enquiries@bacb.org Website: www.bacb.org.uk

GRADES OF MEMBERSHIP:

Fellow (FCB): Fellows are elected by the Council and must be of the highest standing in the field of internal corporate communication.

Member: (a) (MCB Dip) An Associate who has completed at least 2 yrs in internal corporate communication and who has passed the Certificate and Diploma Exams. **(b) (MCB)** One who has been engaged in internal corporate communications for at least 10 yrs and has demonstrated his or her professional ability and competence to the satisfaction of the Membership Committee. Experience must include having had management responsibilities.

Associate Member: A person who is engaged in corporate communication.

Student: Must be enrolled in a formal course of relevant further education and/or be studying on-the-job training or otherwise for a relevant exam.

THE INSTITUTE OF SCIENTIFIC AND TECHNICAL COMMUNICATORS

Blackhorse Road, Letchworth, Herts SG6 IYY Tel: 01462 486825
e-mail: istc@istc.org.uk Website: www.istc.org.uk

CORPORATE MEMBERSHIP:

Fellow (FISTC): Must have been a Member for at least 2 yrs, have passed an appropriate exam and have exercised supervisory responsibility in the field of scientific and technical communication for at least 4 yrs; or have exercised such responsibility for at least 3 yrs and have either suitable comprehensive knowledge or relevant special knowledge; or have appropriate professional education and experience and have submitted a thesis of an acceptable standard on a suitable subject. In their evaluation the Institute is assisted by a panel of adjudicators. At their discretion a thesis may consist of or embody any work produced by the candidate during the 10 yr period immediately prior to his application. A written thesis must be at least 6000 words in length but not more than 12,000 words in length, and must be submitted within 1_yr from the date of approval of the subject matter by the Council.

Member (MISTC): Must possess an acceptable qualification or have had equivalent experience in a branch of science or technology in which they are engaged as communicators and have passed relevant exams and have had at least 5 yrs' suitable experience (of which at least 2 must have been in a responsible position in suitable practice); or have had at least 5 yrs' experience as above (3 in a responsible position) and have either relevant comprehensive knowledge or relevant specialist knowledge.

NON-CORPORATE MEMBERSHIP:
Associate Members: Those persons who wish to be associated with the Institute to further their knowledge of scientific and technical communication.
Student Members: Must either have enrolled in a formal course of relevant further education or be employed in the field of Technical Communication and be studying, by on-the-job training or otherwise, for a relevant exam.

University Qualifications

The following universities offer qualifications in Technical Communications and related subjects. Full details may be found in Part 4, under the entry for the appropriate university.

FIRST DEGREES AWARDED BY UNIVERSITIES
Abertay, Dundee; Aston; Birmingham; Coventry; Essex; North London; Reading

HIGHER DEGREES AWARDED BY UNIVERSITIES
Napier; Newcastle; Surrey

DIPLOMAS AWARDED BY UNIVERSITIES
Reading

NVQs

Level 2: Providing a Telecommunications Service; Providing External Telecommunications Equipment
Level 3: Providing a Telecommunications Service

City & Guilds

5360 Communication of Technical Information

TEXTILES

Membership of Professional Institutions and Associations

THE TEXTILE INSTITUTE

4th Floor, St James's Buildings, Oxford Street, Manchester M1 6FQ Tel: 0161 237 1188
Fax: 0161 236 1991 e-mail: tiihq@textileinst.org.uk Website: www.texi.org
The Textile Institute covers all disciplines – from technology and production to design, development or marketing – relating to fibres and fabrics, clothing and footwear, interior and technical textiles.

MEMBERSHIP:
Fellows (CText FTI): Are Chartered Members of The Textile Institute. Candidates must be able to demonstrate that they have attained a standard of professional competence at least equal to that required for the Associateship, and that they have made a major personal creative contribution to: (a) industrial or commercial operation or organisation in the textile industry in ways that have a specific textile connotation; or (b) the advancement of knowledge through research, normally shown by publication; or (c) the advancement of technology in practice, as shown by developments in machinery, processes, or products; or (d) textile design; or (e) textile education, training, or communication.
Associates (CText ATI): Are Chartered Members of The Textile Institute who must have at least 2 yrs' approved experience in the textile industries. Candidates must also (a) have passed the prescribed exams of The Textile Institute; or (b) hold a TI-accredited degree or other approved in

a textile-related subject; or (c) hold an appropriate degree or equivalent qualification in a relevant discipline and be able to show evidence of a broad general knowledge of textiles in related areas and have at least 5 yrs relevant professional experience after graduation; or (d) be able to show evidence of practice in the textile industries or other relevant occupation that demonstrates a development of professional skill to a level comparable to an appropriate degree and its application over a period of at least 10 yrs and have a broad general knowledge of related textiles. **Licentiates (LTI):** Must have at least 2 yrs' relevant experience. Applicants must also (a) have passed the prescribed Textile Institute exams; or (b) hold a TI-accredited degree or diploma in a textile-related subject; or (c) hold an appropriate degree or diploma in a relevant discipline and be able to show evidence of a specialised knowledge of one aspect of textiles or a broad general knowledge of textiles; or (d) be able to show evidence of practice in the textile industries or a related occupation that demonstrates the development of professional skill in a special area over a period of at least 10 yrs.

Personal Membership: Open to anyone interested in the textile industries and in promoting the objects of the industries, of any nationality, anywhere in the world (the Textile Institute has members in 100 countries). Applicants for any of the professional qualifications must be personal members of the Institute and must remain in membership in order to retain use of their qualifications.

Company Patron Membership: Open to any company or organisation enabling them to demonstrate their interest in, and commitment to, the textile industries.

TRAINING:
A complete list of all degrees and other qualifications that are approved as satisfying the academic requirements for the award of ATI or LTI is available from the Institute.

University Qualifications

The following universities offer qualifications in Textiles and related subjects. Full details may be found in Part 4, under the entry for the appropriate university.

FIRST DEGREES AWARDED BY UNIVERSITIES
Bradford (Bradford & Ilkley Community College); Bucks. Coll.; Central England; De Montfort, Leicester; Derby; Dundee; East London; Glamorgan; Glasgow (Glasgow School of Art); Heriot-Watt (Edinburgh College of Art); Heriot-Watt (Scottish Borders Campus); Huddersfield; Leeds; Leeds (Bretton Hall); Leeds (Leeds College of Art & Design); Liverpool John Moores; London (Goldsmiths College); London Guildhall; London Institute (Central Saint Martins College of Art & Design); London Institute (Chelsea College of Art & Design); Loughborough; Manchester Metropolitan.; Middlesex; Nottingham Trent; Plymouth (Falmouth College of Arts); Southampton; Southampton (Winchester School of Art); Surrey Institute; Ulster; UMIST

HIGHER DEGREES AWARDED BY UNIVERSITIES
Brighton; Central England; Derby; Heriot-Watt; Heriot-Watt (Scottish Borders Campus); Huddersfield; Leeds; London (Goldsmiths College); London Institute (Central Saint Martins College of Art & Design); London Institute (Chelsea College of Art & Design); Manchester Metropolitan.; Nottingham Trent; Royal College of Art; Southampton; Southampton (Winchester School of Art); Surrey Institute; Ulster; UMIST

DIPLOMAS AWARDED BY UNIVERSITIES
Bath Spa; Blackburn; Bournemouth; Bucks. Coll.; Central England; De Montfort, Leicester; Glamorgan; Huddersfield; Leeds; London (Goldsmiths College); London Institute (Central Saint Martins College of Art & Design); Manchester Metropolitan.; Nottingham Trent; Ulster

CERTIFICATES AWARDED BY UNIVERSITIES
Bournemouth; Bradford (Bradford & Ilkley Community College); Central England; De Montfort, Leicester; Lincolnshire (Bishop Burton College); Lincolnshire (Hull College); London (Goldsmiths College)

POSTGRADUATE DIPLOMAS AWARDED BY UNIVERSITIES
Heriot-Watt

National Certificates and Diplomas

BTEC National Certificates/Diplomas: Design (Textiles); Design (Embroidery); Science (Leather Technology); Science (Textile Coloration); Textiles; Textiles (Care); Textiles (Laundry Technology)
BTEC Higher National Certificates/Diplomas: Design (Textiles); Management of Textile Aftercare; Science (Leather Technology); Science (Textile Coloration); Textiles; Textiles (Care)
Scotland
SQA HNC: Stitched Textile and Fashion Design; Textiles; Textile Technology; Textile Art
SQA HND: Textile Technology; Stitched Textiles with Fashion Design; Textile Art

NVQs

Level 1: Manufacturing Textiles
Level 2: Surface Pattern Textile Design

SVQs

Level 1: Manufacturing Sewn Products; Manufacturing Textiles
Level 2: Manufacturing Sewn Products; Design: Constructed Textile Design; Design: Surface Pattern Textile Design; Manufacturing Textiles
Level 3: Handcraft Tailoring; Textiles Coloration; Manufacturing Textiles

City & Guilds

4140 Textile Techniques; 7815 Basic Sewing Skills

Other Vocational Awarding Bodies

ABC: Sewing and Textiles

Useful Addresses

CAPITB Trust, 80 Richardshaw Lane, Pudsey, Leeds LS28 6BN Tel: 0113 2393355 Fax: 0113 239 4118
Confederation of British Wool Textiles, Merrydale House, Roydsdale Way, Bradford BD4 6SB Tel: 01274 652207 Fax: 01274 682293
National Textile Training Group (NTTG), Jarodale House, 7 Gregory Boulevard, Nottingham NG7 6LD Tel: 0115 953 1866 Fax: 0115 962 5450
Scottish Textiles Network, 22a Palmerston Place, Edinburgh EH12 5AL Tel/Fax: 0131 623 6677
SPA (Screen Printing Association) UK Ltd, Association House, 7A West Street, Reigate, Surrey RH2 9BL Tel: 01737 240792 Fax: 01737 240770

TIMBER TECHNOLOGY

Membership of Professional Institutions and Associations

INSTITUTE OF WOOD SCIENCE

Stocking Lane, Hughenden Valley, High Wycombe, Buckinghamshire HP14 4NU
Tel: 01494 565374 Fax: 01494 565395
e-mail: iwscience@aol.com Website: www.iwsc.org.uk
The Institute of Wood Science is the examining body for the UK timber trade, giving qualifications at Certificate (Intermediate) and Associate levels.
The syllabus of the Institute of Wood Science Course is a comprehensive one, covering all aspects of wood technology, including utilisation. Both levels are based on a workbook concept and are designed to provide information leading to self-seeking study for completion. Several practical exercises are included to complement the theory.
For the **Certificate level** there are 5 modules and each module requires 60 hrs study, ie 30 hrs

guided study and 30 hrs DL. The **Associate level** has a core module concerned with wood as a material and its handling and processing, and a project study with 1 additional module to complete the course requirement. There is no fixed time for completion of the course but it is expected to take no less than 1 yr.

Successful students are awarded a nationally recognised professional qualification and membership of the IWSc. Those successful at Certificate level may use the letters **CMIWSc** and those at Associate level **AIWSc**.

University Qualifications

The following universities offer qualifications in Timber Technology and related subjects. Full details may be found in Part 4, under the entry for the appropriate university.

HIGHER DEGREES AWARDED BY UNIVERSITIES
Bournemouth

National Certificates and Diplomas

BTEC National Certificates/Diplomas: Timber Trade and Technology

NVQs

Level 2: Sawmilling; Wood Preserving – Industrial Pre-Treatment (Construction); Woodmachining; Woodturning
Level 3: Woodmachining; Woodturning

SVQs

Level 1: Wood Occupations (Construction)
Level 2: Woodmachining; Wood Occupations (Construction)
Level 3: Woodmachining; Wood Occupations (Construction)

Useful Addresses

Timber Trades Training Association, Suite 4, Cornwall House, Station Approach, Princes Risborough, Buckinghamshire HP27 9DN Tel: 01844 342064 Fax: 01844 342069

TOWN AND COUNTRY PLANNING

THE ROYAL TOWN PLANNING INSTITUTE

26 Portland Place, London W1N 4BE Tel: 020 7636 9107 Fax: 020 7323 1582
e-mail: online@rtpi.org.uk Website: www.rtpi.org.uk

CORPORATE MEMBERS:
Fellow (FRTPI): Members over 30 in senior positions and with the requisite practical experience/contribution to the profession may apply after at least 5 yrs' membership.
Member (MRTPI): Candidates must have successfully completed an accredited course and have at least 2 yrs' satisfactory town planning experience. A special entry arrangement exists for those with a graduate level qualification (with acceptable Planning content) plus 10 yrs' relevant town planning experience.
Note: Special arrangements are available to members of the Royal Australian and New Zealand Planning Institutes and for suitably qualified planners who come within the terms of the EC General Directive on Higher Education Diplomas.
Legal Member (LMRTPI): Formerly open to qualified legal practitioners of at least 30 who had passed the Legal Membership exam and had appropriate experience. This class is now closed.

NON-CORPORATE MEMBERS:
Legal Associate: This non-corporate class, without the right to the use of designatory letters, has replaced the former Legal Membership class. It is open to qualified legal practitioners who have

passed the joint RTPI/Law Society exam and have obtained appropriate experience.

International Associate: This non-corporate class, without the right to use designatory letters, is open to those in membership of a professional institute constituted outside the UK whose objects are similar to those of the RTPI. Applicants must not be ordinarily resident in the UK or the Republic of Ireland and must not be eligible for Corporate Membership of the RTPI.

Technical Member (TechRTPI): This non-corporate class is open to planning support staff with the equivalent of an HNC in Planning plus 2 yrs' experience in planning support. N/SVQs are available for this class of membership.

Student Member: Candidates must either be or have been in suitable employment or be or have been engaged in suitable studies with a view to entering the profession, and satisfy the minimum academic requirements. Applicants must not be eligible for Corporate Membership of the RTPI.

HONORARY MEMBERSHIP:
The Institute may elect **Honorary Members** and **Honorary Corresponding Members**.

METHODS OF ENTRY TO THE PROFESSION:
Methods of entry to the profession are by taking a degree or diploma accredited by the Institute as satisfying the academic requirements for membership. In addition, candidates must have 2 yrs' relevant practical experience in town planning.

University Qualifications

The following universities offer qualifications in Town and Country Planning and related subjects. Full details may be found in Part 4, under the entry for the appropriate university.

FIRST DEGREES AWARDED BY UNIVERSITIES
Bristol; Central England; Coventry; De Montfort, Leicester; Doncaster; Dundee; Durham; Leeds Metropolitan; Liverpool John Moores; London (University College (UCL)); Manchester; Newcastle; Nottingham Trent; Oxford Brookes; Reading; Salford; Sheffield Hallam; Wales (Cardiff University); Westminster

HIGHER DEGREES AWARDED BY UNIVERSITIES
Belfast; Bristol; Central England; Coventry; Dundee; East London; Glasgow; Heriot-Watt; Heriot-Watt (Edinburgh College of Art); Hull; Kent; Leeds Metropolitan; Leicester; Liverpool; Liverpool John Moores; London (London School of Economics & Political Science); London (University College (UCL)); Loughborough; Manchester; Newcastle; Oxford Brookes; Reading; Sheffield Hallam; South Bank; Strathclyde; Wales (Cardiff University); Westminster

DIPLOMAS AWARDED BY UNIVERSITIES
Bristol; Central England; Heriot-Watt (Edinburgh College of Art); Liverpool; London (University College (UCL)); Manchester; Newcastle; Oxford Brookes; Reading; Sheffield; South Bank; Strathclyde; Wales (Cardiff University); Westminster

POSTGRADUATE DIPLOMAS AWARDED BY UNIVERSITIES
Heriot-Watt

PROFESSIONAL COURSES AWARDED BY UNIVERSITIES
Leeds Metropolitan

National Certificates and Diplomas

BTEC National Certificates/Diplomas: Land Administration (Planning)
BTEC Higher National Certificates/Diplomas: Land Administration (Planning)
Scotland
SQA HNC: Built Environment; Built Environment (General); Built Environment (Building Control); Built Environment (Building Inspection and Supervision); Community and Local Economic Development; Community Arts.
SQA HND: Built Environment; Built Environment (General); Built Environment (Building Control); Built Environment (Building Inspection and Supervision); Built Environment Studies; Community and Local Economic Development; Community Arts.

TRADING STANDARDS

Membership of Professional Institutions and Associations

IMPROVEMENT AND DEVELOPMENT AGENCY

Layden House, 76/86 Turnmill Street, London EC1M 5LG Tel: 020 7296 6600 Fax: 020 7296 6666
Website: www.idea.gov.uk

The IDA through its Assessment Committee is responsible for the award of the **Diploma in the Management of Care Services** incorporating a certificated S/NVQ in Management at Level 4 and unit certification for the ENTO Units undertaken (D32 and D33 or D34). This qualification is awarded after achieving registered competence against set national standards, and is available to all managers in the care sector. Programmes are available throughout Britain and are negotiated locally with employers participants and approved centres. Programmes consist of the assessment of competence, collation of evidence and underpinning knowledge and understanding in managing the care services centre.

The Agency, through its Diploma in Trading Standards Council, conducts the assessment procedure, and awards the **Diploma in Trading Standards**. Exemptions from Papers I-IX are available to graduates, with a 2:2 or above, from specific courses at Manchester Metropolitan, Glasgow Caledonian and Teeside Universities, and at the University of Wales Institute, Cardiff. Possession of the Diploma in Trading Standards satisfies the statutory requirements formerly met by successful completion of the DTI Certificate in Weights and Measure examinations.

THE INSTITUTE OF TRADING STANDARDS ADMINISTRATION

3/5 Hadleigh Business Centre, 351 London Road, Hadleigh, Essex SS7 2BT Tel: 01702 559922
Fax: 01702 551161 e-mail: institute@itsa.org.uk Website: www.tradingstandards.gov.uk

MEMBERSHIP:

Fellow (FITSA): Fellowship may be granted to any member of at least 10 yrs' standing who has made an original contribution to knowledge or has rendered distinguished service to the Institute.

Life Members: Are elected by Council in recognition of exceptional services to the Institute.

Member (MITSA): Candidates should have gained either a Diploma in Trading Standards or a Diploma in Consumer Affairs, and should hold a suitable appointment.

Associate Member (AITSA): A person employed in an occupation acceptable to the Management Board and who holds Part 1 of the Diploma in Trading Standards, or Part 1 of the Diploma in Consumer Affairs. A person who does not hold the appropriate qualification but whose length of service in their qualifying appointment is acceptable may also be admitted as an Associate.

Retired Members or Retired Associates: May continue to use the designatory letters awarded.

Student Member: A person who is registered as a student for the Diploma in Trading Standards, or the Diploma in Consumer Affairs.

Affiliate Member: A person who is not eligible for any other class of membership but who is desirous of promoting the interests and objectives of the Institute.

International Membership: Those persons resident outside the UK who share the aims and objectives of the Institute and who hold engagements acceptable to the Institute.

University Qualifications

The following universities offer qualifications in Trading Standards and related subjects. Full details may be found in Part 4, under the entry for the appropriate university.

FIRST DEGREES AWARDED BY UNIVERSITIES

Glasgow Caledonian; Liverpool John Moores; Manchester Metropolitan.; North London; Queen Margaret; Ulster

TRAINING

Membership of Professional Institutions and Associations

THE INSTITUTE OF PERSONNEL AND DEVELOPMENT
The Institute of Personnel and Development (IPD), IPD House, 35 Camp Road, Wimbledon, London SW19 4UX Tel: 020 8971 9000 Fax: 020 8263 3333

University Qualifications

The following universities offer qualifications in Training and related subjects. Full details may be found in Part 4, under the entry for the appropriate university.

FIRST DEGREES AWARDED BY UNIVERSITIES
Salford; Sunderland; Wales (Cardiff University)

HIGHER DEGREES AWARDED BY UNIVERSITIES
Bristol; Leeds Metropolitan; Leicester; London (Institute of Education); Reading; Sunderland; Wales (University of Wales College, Newport)

DIPLOMAS AWARDED BY UNIVERSITIES
Bristol; City; Durham; Durham (New College Durham); London (Goldsmiths College); Manchester; Reading; Westminster

CERTIFICATES AWARDED BY UNIVERSITIES
Bradford (Bradford & Ilkley Community College); Durham; Wales (University of Wales College, Newport)

OTHER COURSES AWARDED BY UNIVERSITIES
Leeds Metropolitan

PROFESSIONAL COURSES AWARDED BY UNIVERSITIES
Luton

National Certificates and Diplomas

Scotland
SQA HNC: Training & Development

NVQs

Level 3: Training & Development
Level 4: Training & Development (Human Resource Development); Training & Development (Learning Development)
Level 5: Training and Development Strategy

SVQs

Level 3: Training & Development
Level 4: Training & Development (Human Resource Development); Training & Development (Learning Development)
Level 5: Training and Development Strategy

Useful Addresses

Employment NTO, Kimberley House, 47 Vaughan Way, Leicester LE1 4SG Tel 0116 251 7979 Fax: 0116 251 1464

TRANSPORT

Membership of Professional Institutions and Associations

THE INSTITUTE OF TRAFFIC ACCIDENT INVESTIGATORS

Gen Secretary: David W. Hutson, 22 Valley Drive, West Park, Hartlepool TS26 0AE
Tel: 01429 427087 Fax: 01429 864489 e-mail: gensec@itai.org Website: www.itai.org
A registered charity whose aims are to provide a means for communication, education, representation and regulation in the field of traffic accident investigation, thereby seeking to promote a professional approach to the subject.

ENTRY REQUIREMENTS:
Affiliate Membership: Open to any person with an interest in the subject of accident investigation.
Member (MITAI): Affiliates of at least 2 yrs standing may apply for transfer to Member grade. Applicants must provide proof of their qualifications, personal involvement and experience in a specialist field that relates directly to accident investigation. Applicants are required to supply a portfolio containing clear evidence of their Continued Professional Development (CPD's) completed for the previous 2 yrs, currently a minimum of 18 hrs of study time per yr. Applicants will require 2 Sponsors, each of whom should be Members of the Institute. 2 full files relating to 'Accident Investigation' must be submitted for assessment, at least 1 of the submissions must have been completed within the previous 2 yrs and the other must not be more than 5 yrs old. All applicants are required to produce a 2500 word report, the basis of which will be to expand on their submitted work files.

INSTITUTE OF TRANSPORT ADMINISTRATION (IOTA)

The Mill House, 12 Nightingale Road, Horsham RH12 2NW Tel: 01403 242412
e-mail: director.iota@btclick.com Website: www.iota.org.uk

QUALIFICATION FOR MEMBERSHIP:
Fellow (FInstTA): Granted to persons of special distinction and eminence from within the Institute and at the discretion of the National Council, to persons outside the Institute who have made an outstanding contribution to transport.
Member (MInstTA): Granted to persons who have been Associate Members for at least 2 yrs and have given proof of their ability to hold positions of high administrative responsibility within the transport industry. Persons holding high executive appointments, possessing extensive experience in industry, commerce and transport may also be granted the grade of Member by the Council.
Associate Member (AMInstTA): Associate Membership may be granted to persons who possess a minimum of 2 yrs' transport experience at an adequate level. Persons of approved managerial status within the transport industry may be granted Associate Membership by the Council.
Associates (AInstTA): Applicants who, while not necessarily employed directly in transport administration, fill ancillary appointments within the transport industry.
Student: Open to men and women aged 16 and over who intend to make their careers in the transport industry.

THE INSTITUTE OF LOGISTICS AND TRANSPORT

The Institute of Logistics and Transport, Logistics and Transport Centre, Earlstrees Court, Earlstrees Road, Corby, Northants NN17 4XQ Tel: 01536 740100 Fax: 01536 740101
Website: www.iolt.org.uk

MEMBERSHIP GRADES:
Fellows (FCIT, FILT): Fellowship of the Institute is open to those Chartered Members who have at least 7 yrs' experience in a position or positions of high responsibility in the management of logistics or transport. Fellowship is also granted to people who have attained a position of eminence in logistics or transport.
Chartered Member (MCIT, MILT): Candidates for election or transfer to the grade of Chartered Member should hold the Institute's Advanced Diploma or an exempting qualification (usually an

approved degree) and have at least 5 yrs' relevant experience in logistics or transport, including at least 2 at a senior level. A postgraduate programme is available to candidates whose qualifications meet only part of the requirements for exemption from the Advanced Diploma. The Professional Route enables experienced logistics or transport professionals, who do not fully meet the academic requirements for Chartered Membership, to demonstrate that they broadly satisfy the Institute's criteria. Alternatives include writing a professional essay, delivering a professional paper, submitting previously published works and/or undergoing a professional interview. Candidates are required to provide evidence of their experience through a CV and an application form.

Member (MILT): Candidates for election or transfer to the grade of Member should hold an approved qualification at level 3 or 4* in logistics or transport and have management responsibility which involves planning, making decisions, directing and accountability for the use and performance of resources. Candidates with a level 3 qualification should have at least 3 yrs' relevant work experience; candidates with a level 4 qualification should have at least one yr's relevant work experience. Candidates are required to provide evidence that they meet the above criteria, either by a CV or though the application form. Candidates without an appropriate qualification but with management responsibility over an extended period (at least 5 yrs) may submit a portfolio of evidence for consideration under the Accreditation of Prior Experience (APA) process.

Affiliate: Affiliate Membership is open to those who are interested in logistics or transport and who support the aims of the Institute but who may not, for a variety of reasons, qualify for Membership. This grade includes those studying for educational qualifications in logistics or transport.

*Level 3 qualifications include relevant N/SVQs at level 3 and the ILT Certificate qualification. Level 4 qualifications include relevant N/SVQs at level 4, relevant HNC/HNDs and the ILT Diploma

TRANSPORT

QUALIFICATIONS:

The Introduction to Transport: This single unit course is especially suited to anyone who has considered entering the transport industry from school, or for those people working in transport organisations in a non-operational role and who wish to know more about the industry they are supporting.

ILT Certificate in Transport: A modular examination-based programme for first line managers and supervisors providing core and optional units such as Management, Passenger Transport and Freight Transport. It is also possible to gain exemption from the national and international CPC if the appropriate options are taken.

ILT Diploma in Transport: The Diploma is set at the operational level of transport management and provides the general transport-related knowledge required by a manager at this level. Starting with the economic, financial and human resource management aspects of transport operational management, students can then choose to specialise in either the multi-modal movement of goods or of people. All Certificate and Diploma level qualifications provide the necessary educational qualification for membership of the Institute (MILT) when considered with relevant experience.

The Advanced Diploma in Transport: The Advanced Diploma follows on from the Diploma in Transport and takes the level of study up to that of strategic management. Two core units deal with the development of transport policy at the local national and international levels and with the strategic managerial aspects of economics, finance and human resources that were covered at the optional level in the Diploma. Students may then chose to study either Transport Planning or Transport and Society, or any other relevant unit. The Advanced Diploma is at the level of honours degree and provides the educational qualification for Chartered Membership (MCIT).

MSc in Logistics or Passenger Transport Management: The MSc in Logistics or Passenger Transport Management are masters degrees offered by ILT and validated by Aston University. The qualifications are offered entirely by distance learning with materials and support provided by the Institute of Logistics and Transport. This unique 3-yr programme for professionals addresses strategic issues in Passenger Transport Management and Logistics.

NB: Refer to the section on Distribution for further ILT qualifications.

University Qualifications

The following universities offer qualifications in Transport and related subjects. Full details may be found in Part 4, under the entry for the appropriate university.

FIRST DEGREES AWARDED BY UNIVERSITIES
Aston; Bradford; Bristol; Bucks. Coll.; Coventry; Huddersfield; Leeds; Liverpool John Moores; London Guildhall; Loughborough; Napier; Oxford Brookes; Salford; Staffordshire; Ulster; Wales (Swansea Institute of Higher Education)

HIGHER DEGREES AWARDED BY UNIVERSITIES
Aston; City; Coventry; Cranfield; Leeds; London (Imperial College of Science, Technology & Medicine); London (University College (UCL)); London Guildhall; Newcastle; North London; Nottingham Trent (Southampton Institute); Plymouth; Salford; Sheffield Hallam; Wales (Cardiff University); Wales (Swansea Institute of Higher Education); Westminster; York

DIPLOMAS AWARDED BY UNIVERSITIES
Leeds; Newcastle; Salford; Wales (Swansea Institute of Higher Education)

CERTIFICATES AWARDED BY UNIVERSITIES
Salford

National Certificates and Diplomas

BTEC National Certificates/Diplomas: Motor Vehicle Studies (Parts); Shipping and Transport Studies

NVQs

Level 1: Maintaining Automotive Vehicles; Vehicle Maintenance – Service Replacement; Vehicle Parts Distribution & Supply; Vehicle Valeting
Level 2: Lift Truck Operations; Maintaining Automotive Vehicles; Organising Road Transport Operations; Rail Transport (Signal Operations); Rail Transport – Driving; Rail Transport – Shunting; Vehicle Maintenance Service Replacement; Vehicle Body Fitting; Vehicle Mechanical & Electronic Systems – Unit Replacement; Vehicle Parts Distribution & Supply
Level 3: Maintaining Automotive Vehicles (Body Structures & Claddings); Maintaining Automotive Vehicles (Electrical/ Electronic); Maintaining Automotive Vehicles (Mechanical); Motorcycle Mechanical and Electronic Systems – Maintenance & Repair; Vehicle Body Repair; Vehicle Mechanical & Electronic Systems – Maintenance & Repair (Heavy Vehicles); Vehicle Mechanical & Electronic Systems – Maintenance Repair (Light Vehicles); Vehicle Parts Distribution and Supply; Vehicle Refinishing
Level 4: Co-ordinating Automotive Maintenance
Level 5: Directing Automotive Maintenance

SVQs

Level 1: Assisting in Road Haulage and Distribution Operations
Level 2: Bus & Coach Driving & Customer Care; Lift Truck Operations; Organising Road Transport Operations; Rail Transport (Driving); Rail Transport (Passenger Services); Rail Transport (Shunting); Rail Transport (Signal Operations); Transporting Goods by Road
Level 3: Driving Instruction: Passenger Carrying Vehicles
Level 4: Piloting Transport Aircraft

OCR

Exams are offered for:
Certificates of Professional Competence required by regulations for those in the occupations of Road Passenger Transport Operator and Road Haulage Operator.

TRAVEL AND TOURISM

Membership of Professional Institutions and Associations

CONFEDERATION OF TOURISM, HOTEL AND CATERING MANAGEMENT

118-120 Great Titchfield Street, London W1P 7AJ Tel: 020 7612 0170 Fax: 020 7612 0170
e-mail: info@cthcm.com Website: www.cthcm.com

The Confederation of Tourism Hotel and Catering Management was established in 1982 to provide recognised standards of management training appropriate to the needs of the hotel and travel industries, via its syllabi, examinations and awards. Those studying for the examinations of the Confederation are offered a structured learning process, encompassing both the theoretical and practical aspects of the industry, together with a clearly defined path of development through progressive grades of membership. The Confederation offers four externally examined Diploma training programmes, each of which will normally take an academic yr to complete, and four grades of membership each indicating a level of personal development.

TRAINING PROGRAMMES:

Diploma in Hotel Management: Aims to provide students with a broad understanding of the operational aspects of the international hotel industry, and a knowledge of the underlying principles involved.

Syllabus content: Food and beverage operations, food science, hygiene and nutrition, front office operations, facilities and accommodation operations, hospitality costing and control, supervisory management, marketing, tourism, computing, business communication.

Advanced Diploma in Hotel Management: Aims to provide an understanding of the managerial, decision making and leadership aspects of the international hotel industry and to develop independent research and study skills which will be required when working at senior managerial level in the industry.

Syllabus content: Food and beverage management, food and beverage production, facilities and accommodation management, management accounting, human resource management, management research report.

Diploma in Travel Agency Management: Aims to provide students with a broad understanding of the operational aspects of travel agency management and airline ticketing, along with an understanding of the tourism industry.

Syllabus content: Travel geography, the tourism industry, travel agency operations, fares and ticketing levels one and two, computer reservations systems, travel agency law, business computing, sales and marketing, finance for the travel industry.

Advanced Diploma in Tour Operation and Management: Aims to provide an understanding of the managerial, decision making and leadership aspects of the international tour operation industry and to develop the independent research skills which will be required when working as a senior manager in the industry.

Syllabus content: Tour operations, tour management, resort representation, advanced fares calculation, advanced computer reservation systems, brochure and website design.

ADMISSIONS REQUIREMENTS:

The selection of students for admission to the courses at Diploma level is at the discretion of individual educational establishments. No specific educational qualifications are required, although it is desirable for applicants to have completed formal secondary education.

For selection on to a course at Advanced Diploma level the applicant must have been successful in, or exempted from, the Diploma level course. Exemptions are granted at the discretion of the Confederation on the basis of previous education and experience.

Examination results and certificates

Each candidate will receive a record of performance in one of four grades for each component of the examination. The grades are Distinction, Credit, Pass and Referral. Qualifications are awarded to those candidates who achieve at least a pass grade in all components of their course.

GRADES OF MEMBERSHIP:

Student Member: This classification is for those who have enrolled on a CTHCM course at a registered CTHCM centre.

Associate Member (AMCTHCM): Awarded to those who have passed or been exempted from the Diploma level examination. Holders of equivalent qualifications acceptable to the Confederation may also be granted associate membership.

Member (MCTHCM): Awarded to those who have passed or been exempted from the Advanced Diploma level examinations, and hold at least 2 yrs' experience in the industry. Holders of equivalent qualifications acceptable to the Confederation may also be granted membership, as may those who have at least 10 yrs relevant experience.

Fellow (FCTHCM): Awarded at the discretion of the Confederation to those who have achieved positions of significant responsibility in the industry, or who have made notable contributions to the work of the Confederation.

ENGLISH HERITAGE

23 Savile Row, London W1X 1AB Tel: 020 7973 3000 Fax: 020 7973 3883
Contact English Heritage for information on qualifications.

INSTITUTE OF TRAVEL AND TOURISM

113 Victoria Street, St Albans, Hertfordshire AL1 3TJ Tel: 01727 854395 Fax: 01727 847415
e-mail: itt@dial.pipex.com

MEMBERSHIP:

Fellows (FInstTT): Must pass the Institute's professional paper at Fellowship level or have been a Full Member for 10 yrs or 5yrs by substantial contribution to the institution or industry.

Full Members (MInstTT): Must pass the Institute's professional paper or 5 yrs' experience in the Travel & Tourism industry at management level or hold a recognised qualification exempting them from it.Details of the Institute's exemptions may be obtained from the Membership department. A list of FT courses recognised for exemption is also available.

Associate Members (AInstTT): Must hold an accredited certificate from an Institute approved college or COTAC II or other recognised qualifications or 5 yrs' experience in the Travel & Tourism Industry.

Affiliate Members (Non-Corporate): Must hold Level I C&G Travel and Tourism qualifications, eg COTAC I, COTICC I or Airline I Qualification or Level 2 NVQ in Travel Services or Intermediate GNVQ in Leisure & Tourism.

Student Members (Non-Corporate): Must be studying at an Institute approved college.

INTERNATIONAL INSTITUTE OF HOSPITALITY TOURISM & MANAGEMENT (IIHTM)

Secretary General: Mr R. A. Wright BA (Hons). DMS., MA., MEd.,

Registered Office: 43 Gower Street, London WC1E 6HH Tel: 020 7274 2166 Fax: 020 7274 1226
e-mail: Intloffice@clc-london.ac.uk

The Institute aims to provide a service to all categories of personnel in the Hotel, Catering, Tourism and Food Industries throughout the world. It offers recognised examinations and qualifications in all of these sectors. It maintains high academic standards through its Council, appointed from senior members of industry and education. Standards are also supported by consultation with industry and other examining bodies in the relevant fields. The Institute's courses are offered world-wide on the basis of equal opportunity for all.

The Institute has two areas of work

Membership – offering suitably qualified and experienced personnel the opportunity to obtain recognition for their qualification and experience via corporate membership of the Institute.

Educational qualifications – the Institute offers a variety of educational courses and examinations to be studied at recognised centres throughout the world. These are at different levels: successful completion can lead to awards ranging from **student members to fellowship award of the Institute.**

MEMBERSHIP:

Fellowship (FIIHTM): Awarded to distinguished members of the industry in recognition of their work and contribution to the various industries covered by the Institute.

Membership (MIIHTM): Awarded by the Institute to holders of the Institute's Higher Diploma and who have 2 yrs' experience in the industry. Holders of equivalent qualifications acceptable to the Institute may also be granted Membership. Candidates who have at least 10 yrs' experience in the industry in a relevant craft, supervisory or management position may also be granted Membership.

Associate Membership (AMIIHTM): Associate Membership will be awarded to holders of the Institute's Advanced Diploma. Holders of equivalent qualifications may also be granted Associate Membership.

Student Membership: Students who have completed secondary education and are enrolled on an Institute's Certificate level course at a recognised and registered centre must register as Student Members. On successful completion of their course they will be eligible to proceed to the appropriate category of membership.

EXAMINATIONS:

The Institute will provide course structures, syllabus, schemes of work and subject modules in a variety of areas. These are continuously updated, amended and additions made. Please contact the Institute for up-to-date material in any area that you are interested in. Please note that full course materials will only be sent to recognised centres whose registration is up to date.

The Institute will set and hold examinations at **Certificate**, **Diploma**, **Advanced Diploma** and **Higher Diploma** level at recognised centres throughout the world. These will be at times and intervals to suit the academic yr in each country. The examinations will be externally set, marked and moderated covering all subjects at the various levels. The Institute will also accredit and issue Certificates for approved single subject examinations. This process is in addition to the accreditation of full-time courses.

Current programmes of study are as follows:

1. **Certificate in Hotel, Restaurant and Tourism Management**
2. **Diploma in Hotel, Restaurant and Tourism Management**
3. **Advanced Diploma in Hotel, Restaurant and Tourism Management**
4. **Higher Diploma in Hotel, Restaurant and Tourism Management**
5. **Certificate in Travel & Tourism Management**
6. **Diploma in Travel & Tourism Management**
7. **Advanced Diploma in Travel & Tourism Management**

Syllabi, course structure, sample examination papers and course guidelines are available from the Institute.

THE TOURISM MANAGEMENT INSTITUTE

c/o Hon Secretary: Stephen Watson MTMI, University College, Scarborough YO11 3AZ Tel: 01723 362392 Fax: 01723 370815 e-mail: stephenw@ucscarb.ac.uk Website: www.tmi.org.uk

The Tourism Management Institute is the professional institute for tourism destination management in the UK. Its mission is to advance tourism destination management for the economic, social and environmental benefit of recipient host communities. Corporate membership of the Institute (Fellows, Members and Associates) is open to qualified professionals in tourism management whereas non-corporate membership is for Students and Affiliates (commercial and educational bodies) whose activities are relevant and supportive to practitioners and the function of tourism management.

University Qualifications

The following universities offer qualifications in Travel and Tourism and related subjects. Full details may be found in Part 4, under the entry for the appropriate university.

FIRST DEGREES AWARDED BY UNIVERSITIES

Abertay, Dundee; Anglia; Anglia (City College, Norwich); Anglia (Colchester Institute); Barnsley; Bath Spa; Birmingham (Birmingham College of Food, Tourism and Creative Studies); Bournemouth; Brighton; Bristol; Buckingham; Bucks. Coll.; Central Lancashire; Cheltenham & Gloucester; Coventry; Derby; East Anglia (Suffolk College); Essex (Writtle College); Exeter (The College of St Mark & St John); Glamorgan; Glasgow Caledonian; Greenwich; Hertfordshire; Huddersfield; Hull; Kent (Canterbury Christ Church University College); Lancaster (Blackpool and The Fylde College); Leeds (The College of Ripon & York St John); Leeds Metropolitan; Lincolnshire (Grimsby College); Lincolnshire (Lincoln University Campus); Liverpool (Chester College of H.E.); Liverpool John Moores; London (Wye College); Luton; Manchester

Metropolitan.; Napier; North London; Northumbria; Nottingham Trent (Southampton Institute); Oxford Brookes; Paisley; Plymouth; Portsmouth; Queen Margaret; Robert Gordon; Salford; Sheffield Hallam; South Bank; Southampton (King Alfred's College); Staffordshire; Stirling; Strathclyde; Sunderland; Teesside; Thames Valley; Wales (Swansea Institute of Higher Education); Wales (University of Wales Institute, Cardiff); Wales (University of Wales, Aberystwyth); Wales (University of Wales, Bangor); Westminster; Wolverhampton

HIGHER DEGREES AWARDED BY UNIVERSITIES
Anglia; Birmingham (Birmingham College of Food, Tourism and Creative Studies); Bournemouth; Brighton; Buckingham; Bucks. Coll.; Central Lancashire; Derby; Exeter (The College of St Mark & St John); Glasgow; Glasgow Caledonian; Greenwich; Hull; Kent; Lancaster; Luton; Manchester Metropolitan.; Middlesex; Napier; North London; Northumbria; Oxford Brookes; Plymouth; Portsmouth; Sheffield Hallam; Staffordshire; Strathclyde; Surrey; Thames Valley; Ulster; Wales (University of Wales Institute, Cardiff); Westminster

DIPLOMAS AWARDED BY UNIVERSITIES
Anglia; Anglia (City College, Norwich); Barnsley; Birmingham (Birmingham College of Food, Tourism and Creative Studies); Blackburn; Bournemouth; Bradford (Bradford & Ilkley Community College); Brighton; Bucks. Coll.; Central Lancashire; Durham (New College Durham); Glasgow; Greenwich; Lincolnshire (Grimsby College); Lincolnshire (Hull College); Lincolnshire (Yorkshire Coast College); Luton; Manchester Metropolitan.; Northumbria; Plymouth; Portsmouth; Salford; Southampton (King Alfred's College); Strathclyde; Ulster; Wales (Swansea Institute of Higher Education); Worcester

CERTIFICATES AWARDED BY UNIVERSITIES
Anglia (City College, Norwich); Bournemouth; Brighton; Leeds Metropolitan; Liverpool John Moores; Newcastle; North London

POSTGRADUATE DIPLOMAS AWARDED BY UNIVERSITIES
Birmingham (Birmingham College of Food, Tourism and Creative Studies); Thames Valley

PROFESSIONAL COURSES AWARDED BY UNIVERSITIES
Manchester Metropolitan

National Certificates and Diplomas
BTEC National Certificates/Diplomas: Travel and Tourism
BTEC Higher National Certificates/Diplomas: Tourism Management; Transport Studies; Travel and Tourism; Travel and Tourism Management
Scotland
SQA HNC: Tourism; Travel; Travel and Tourism
SQA HND: Tourism; Travel with Tourism

NVQs
Level 2: Handling Air Passengers; Maintaining & Operating Caravan Parks; Port Passenger Operations; Providing Air Passenger Ticketing Services; Rail Transport – Passenger Services; Tourist Information; Transporting Passengers by Road – Passenger Support Services; Transporting Passengers by Road – Short Itineraries; Travel Services; Travel Services (Commentaries and Interpretation for Tourism); Travel Services (Tour Operations)
Level 3: Handling Air Passengers; Providing Air Passenger Ticketing Services; Tourist Information; Transporting Passengers by Road – Long Itineraries; Travel Services; Travel Services (Commentaries and Interpretation for Tourism); Travel Services (Supervising); Travel Services (Tour Operations)
Level 4: Travel Services (Environmental and Heritage Interpretation); Travel Services (Guiding and Tour Managing); Travel Services (Leisure and Business Travel); Travel Services (Tour Operations)

SVQs

Level 2: Tourist Information; Travel Services; Travel Services (Tour Operations); Travel Services: Commentaries and Interpretation for Tourism
Level 3: Tourist Information; Travel Services; Travel Services (Tour Operations); Travel Services: Commentaries and Interpretation for Tourism

GNVQs

3725 Leisure and Tourism

OCR

OCR offer the following awards:
Tourist Information Levels 2 & 3
Travel Services (Leisure & Business) Levels 2, 3 & 4
Travel Services (Commentaries & Interpretation for Tourism) Levels 2 & 3
Travel Services (Tour Operations) Levels 2, 3 & 4
Travel Services (Supervising) Level 3
Travel Services (Environmental & Heritage Interpretation) Level 4
Travel Services (Guiding & Tour Managing) Level 4

City & Guilds

4838 Business Travel

Useful Addresses

Travel Training Company, The Cornerstone, The Broadway, Woking, Surrey GU21 5AR Tel: 01483 727321 Fax: 01483 756698
Caravan Industry Training Organisation, 74-76 Victoria Road, Aldershot, Hampshire GU11 1SS Tel: 01252 344170 Fax: 01252 322596

VETERINARY SCIENCE

Membership of Professional Institutions and Associations

THE ROYAL COLLEGE OF VETERINARY SURGEONS

Belgravia House, 62-64 Horseferry Road, London SW1P 2AF Tel: 020 7222 2001
Fax: 020 7222 2004 e-mail: admin@rcvs.org.uk Website: www.rcvs.org.uk

MEMBERSHIP:
Total Membership (all registers): 19,250
Member (MRCVS): To practise as a veterinary surgeon in Great Britain it is necessary to be registered with the Royal College of Veterinary Surgeons. Registration (other than temporary registration) carries with it membership of the Royal College. To qualify for membership the applicant must hold a veterinary degree granted by a British University or hold a veterinary qualification awarded by one of the Member States of the EU (and be a citizen of one of those Member States), or hold another overseas veterinary qualification which is currently recognised by the College for registration without further examination. All other veterinarians must pass the College's statutory examination for membership before being entitled to registration. The veterinary degree course lasts 5/6 yrs.
Fellow (FRCVS): The Diploma of Fellowship may be acquired, by members of the Royal College, not less than 5 yrs after graduation by thesis or, not less than 20 yrs after graduation by meritorious contributions to learning.
Supplementary Veterinary Register: There is also a Supplementary Veterinary Register of veterinary practitioners who have no academic qualification but are qualified to practise by

experience. Under the Veterinary Surgeons Act (1966) no further entries may be made in this Register. Members of the Royal College of Veterinary Surgeons (or holders of qualifications which would enable them to be registered by that College) are qualified to take up membership of The British Veterinary Association, 7 Mansfield Street, London W1M 0AT.

QUALIFICATIONS:

Certificates and Diplomas: The Royal College also has power to award postgraduate Certificates and Diplomas in a number of subjects, including cattle, sheep and fish health and production, pig medicine, poultry medicine and production, laboratory animal science, aspects of equine studies and small animal medicine and surgery, veterinary anaesthesia, ophthalmology, dermatology, cardiology, reproduction, public health and radiology, animal welfare science, ethics and law, state veterinary medicine, zoological medicine, by examination.

Certificate in Veterinary Nursing: The RCVS Certificate in Veterinary Nursing and S/NVQ Levels 2 and 3 may be awarded following 2 yrs' training in approved veterinary practices. Training is assessed in the workplace and also by examinations.

Diploma in Advanced Veterinary Nursing (Surgical or Medical): May be awarded following a further 2 yrs study and training in veterinary practices and success in the relevant examination. Only qualified veterinary nurses may be included on the List of Veterinary Nurses held by the Royal College of Veterinary Surgeons and thereby have the legal authority to undertake certain additional procedures allowed by the 1991 Amendment to Schedule III of the Veterinary Surgeons Act 1966.

University Qualifications

The following universities offer qualifications in Veterinary Science and related subjects. Full details may be found in Part 4, under the entry for the appropriate university.

FIRST DEGREES AWARDED BY UNIVERSITIES

Aberdeen; Adams; Anglia; Belfast; Bristol; Cambridge; De Montfort, Leicester; East Anglia (Otley College); East Anglia (Suffolk College); East London; Edinburgh; Essex (Writtle College); Glasgow; Lancaster; Leeds; Lincolnshire (Bishop Burton College); Liverpool; London (Imperial College of Science, Technology & Medicine); London (Royal Veterinary College); London (Wye College); Luton; Middlesex; Newcastle; Nottingham; Nottingham Trent; OU (NESCOT); Plymouth; Reading; Wales (University of Wales, Aberystwyth)

HIGHER DEGREES AWARDED BY UNIVERSITIES

Aberdeen; Cambridge; Edinburgh; Essex (Writtle College); Glasgow; Keele; Liverpool; London (Royal Veterinary College); Stirling; Wales (University of Wales, Aberystwyth)

DIPLOMAS AWARDED BY UNIVERSITIES

Aberdeen; Central Lancashire; De Montfort, Leicester; East Anglia (Otley College); East Anglia (Suffolk College); Edinburgh; Glamorgan; Greenwich; Lincolnshire (Bishop Burton College); Liverpool; Reading; Salford; Stirling; Worcester

National Certificates and Diplomas

BTEC National Certificates/Diplomas: Animal Care; Science (Animal Technology)
BTEC Higher National Certificates/Diplomas: Animal Care; Science (Animal Science); Science (Animal Technology)

NVQs

Level 1: Animal Care
Level 2: Caring for Animals
Level 3: Animal Training; Animal Welfare and Management; Pet Care and Supply; Veterinary Nursing

SVQs

Level 1: Animal Care
Level 2: Caring for Animals; Veterinary Nursing
Level 3: Animal Training; Animal Welfare & Management; Pet Care & Supply; Veterinary Nursing

Regional Examining Bodies
CENTRAL
Animal Care (Small Animals) Phase 1 & Phase 2 (180 hrs each)

Useful Addresses
Royal College of Veterinary Surgeons, Belgravia House, 62–64 Horseferry Road, London SW1P 2AF Tel: 020 7222 2001 Fax: 020 7222 2004
Animal Care ITO Ltd Second Floor, Burgess Building, The Green, Stafford ST17 4BL Tel : 01785 227399 Fax: 01785 229015

WASTES MANAGEMENT

Membership of Professional Institutions and Associations

THE INSTITUTE OF WASTES MANAGEMENT

9 Saxon Court, St Peter's Gardens, Northampton NN1 1SX Tel: 01604 620426 Fax: 01604 621339 Website: www.iwm.co.uk

CORPORATE MEMBERSHIP:
Fellow (FIWM): Conferred on a Member of at least 7 yrs' standing who has shown evidence of distinguished professional attainment in the sphere of wastes management.
Member (MIWM): Open to those who possess an appropriate degree, or other recognised qualification, have 4 yrs' relevant experience and undergone a period of post-qualification vocational training.
Licentiate (LIWM): Open to those who possess an appropriate degree, have at least 1 yr's relevant experience and undergone a period of post-qualification vocational training.
NON-CORPORATE MEMBERSHIP:
Graduate Member (GradMIWM): Open to those with an appropriate degree and who are concerned with the management of wastes.
Associate Member (AssocMIWM): Minimum age 23 yrs possessing 2 A Levels or an HNC qualification, and with 5 yrs' experience in the wastes management industry.
Technician Member (TechMIWM): Minimum age 21 yrs and qualified to National Certificate level, and with 3 yrs' experience in the wastes management industry.
Affiliate Member: A person who is involved with wastes management, but is not eligible for any other grade of membership.
Student Member: Minimum age 16, a person undertaking a course of study and exams, both FT and PT, relevant to the wastes management industry.
Affiliated Organisation: Available to any company or organisation which is involved with the wastes management industry and which supports the aims and objectives of the Institute.
EXAMINATIONS:
Courses leading to qualifications in Wastes Management, accredited by the Institute, are available at HNC, first degree, PgD and MSc levels, at a number of Colleges and Universities in the UK. It is possible to study for a number of these on a PT or distance-learning basis. Up-to-date details of these, and information concerning the availability of such courses, should be obtained from the Education & Training Department at the Institute's offices.

University Qualifications
The following universities offer qualifications in Wastes Management and related subjects. Full details may be found in Part 4, under the entry for the appropriate university.

FIRST DEGREES AWARDED BY UNIVERSITIES
Lancaster; Northampton; Staffordshire

HIGHER DEGREES AWARDED BY UNIVERSITIES
Central Lancashire; Glamorgan; Glasgow Caledonian; Leeds; Loughborough; Luton; Paisley; Sunderland

DIPLOMAS AWARDED BY UNIVERSITIES
Loughborough; Paisley

CERTIFICATES AWARDED BY UNIVERSITIES
Lincolnshire (Bishop Burton College); Wales (University of Wales Institute, Cardiff)

NVQs
Level 2: Removal of Hazardous Waste (Asbestos); Water Industry Operations (Sewerage Maintenance)
Level 3: Landfill Operations – Inert Waste; Removal of Hazardous Waste (Asbestos); Transfer Operations – Inert Waste; Treatment Operations – Inert Waste
Level 4: Managing Incinerator Operations – Special Waste; Managing Landfill Operations – Biodegradable Waste; Managing Landfill Operations – Special Waste; Managing Transfer Operations – Biodegradable Waste; Managing Transfer Operations – Clinical or Special Waste; Managing Treatment Operations – Biodegradable Waste; Managing Treatment Operations – Clinical or Special Waste

SVQs
Level 1: Waste Management Operations
Level 2: Operating Process Plant: waste water or water or sludge; Waste Management Operations
Level 3: Managing Civic Amenity Site Operations; Managing Landfill Operations; Managing Treatment Operations; Managing Treatment Operations (special waste); Regulating Waste Management; Waste Management Supervision
Level 4: Managing Incineration Operations (special waste); Managing Landfill Operations (biodegradable waste; special waste); Managing Transfer Operations (special waste); Regulating Waste Management

WATCH AND CLOCK MAKING AND REPAIRING

Membership of Professional Institutions and Associations

BRITISH HOROLOGICAL INSTITUTE LTD
Upton Hall, Upton, Newark, Nottinghamshire NG23 5TE Tel: 01636 813795/6 Fax: 01636 812258 e-mail: clocks@bhi.co.uk Website: www.bhi.co.uk
MEMBERSHIP:
Fellowship (FBHI): May be conferred upon satisfaction of the following 3 requirements: either gaining a Pass with Merit in the Institute's Final Grade Exam in Technical Horology (or recognised equivalent) or passing a special 3 hr exam in Technical Horology, completing a 5000 word dissertation or practical piece, viva voce. Candidates must be over 32 yrs of age, able to provide details of 3 referees (of whom at least 2 should preferably be Fellows of the Institute) and have completed 5 yrs FT professional experience in horology after training.
Membership (MBHI): May be conferred (1) upon any Graduate Member professionally engaged in horology who has gained a Pass Certificate in the Institute's Final Grade Exam in Technical Horology (or has passed such other exam as Council may consider appropriate) and who has had, in addition, at least 5 yrs FT professional experience in the horological industry; (2) upon any professionally engaged Horologist not necessarily qualified by exam in horology who has served at least 10 yrs at the bench on clock or watch work and whose application is supported by his local

branch or, in the absence of a local branch, by 2 written recommendations of Fellows of the Institute; (3) after 5 yrs' experience and after passing specific practical tests. Details available on enquiry.

Graduate Membership (GradBHI): May be conferred (1) upon any person who has gained a Pass Certificate in the Institute's Final Grade Exam in Technical Horology (or has passed such other exam as Council may consider appropriate); (2) upon any person who gained a Pass Certificate in the Institute's Final Exam in Technical Horology and who has also received a recognised College Diploma based on a BHI-approved syllabus.

Associateship: May be granted to any person having an interest in horology, on payment of the appropriate annual subscription.

Student Membership: May be granted to any bona fide student of horology who is serving a term of apprenticeship, or is undergoing an approved course of training in horology.

EXAMINATIONS:

Exams in Technical Horology: The stages (Preliminary, Intermediate and Final) may be taken during a 5 yr term of apprenticeship or as a mature student. FT and PT courses are available at some technical colleges and the Institute runs its own correspondence course. In each Grade successful students are awarded either a Pass with Merit or Pass Certificate for obtaining 66% or 40% marks respectively. The exams cover Horological Theory, Technical Drawing and Practical Work.

THE BRITISH HOROLOGICAL INSTITUTE

Upton Hall, Upton, Newark, Nottinghamshire NG23 5TE Tel: 01636 813795/6 Fax: 01636 812258 e-mail: clocks@bhi.co.uk Website: www.bhi.co.uk

MEMBERSHIP:

Fellowship (FBHI): May be conferred upon satisfaction of the following three requirements: either gaining a Pass with Merit in the Institute's Final Grade Exam in Technical Horology (or recognised equivalent) or passing a special 3 hr exam in technical horology; completing a 5000 word dissertation or practical piece; viva voce. Candidates must be over 32 yrs of age, be able to provide details of 3 referees (of whom at least two should preferably be Fellows of the Institute) and have completed 5 yrs' full-time professional experience in horology after training.

Membership (MBHI): May be conferred (1) upon any Graduate Member professionally engaged in horology who has gained a 'pass' certificate in the Institute's final grade exams in technical horology (or has passed such other exam as Council may consider as appropriate) and who has had in addition, at least 5 yrs' FT professional experience in the horological industry; (2) upon any professionally engaged Horologist not necessarily qualified by exam in horology who has served at least 10 yrs at the bench on clock or watch work and whose application is supported by his local branch or, in the absence of a local branch, by 2 written recommendations of Fellows of the Institute; (3) after 5 yrs' experience and after passing specific practical tests. Details available on enquiry.

Graduate Membership (GradBHI): May be conferred (1) upon any person who has gained a 'pass' certificate in the Institute's final grade exam in technical horology (or who has passed such other exams as the BHI Council may consider as appropriate); (2) upon any person who gained a 'pass' certificate in the Institute's final exams in technical horology and who has also received a recognised College Diploma based on a BHI-approved syllabus.

Associateship: May be granted to any person having an interest in horology, on payment of the appropriate annual subscription.

Student Membership: May be granted to any bona fide student of horology who is serving a term of apprenticeship, or is undergoing an approved course of training in horology.

University Qualifications

The following universities offer qualifications in Watch and Clock Making and Repairing and related subjects. Full details may be found in Part 4, under the entry for the appropriate university.

DIPLOMAS AWARDED BY UNIVERSITIES
Central England

WELDING

Membership of Professional Institutions and Associations

THE WELDING INSTITUTE

Granta Park, Great Abington, Cambridge CB1 6AL Tel: 01223 891162 Fax: 01223 894219
e-mail: twi@twi.co.uk Website: www.twi.co.uk

PROFESSIONAL MEMBERSHIP:

Honorary Fellow (HonFWeldI): Honorary Fellowship is conferred in respect of outstanding contributions to the theory or practice of welding or of 1 of the allied processes, or in recognition for other special causes.

Fellow (FWeldI): Applicants must be over 35, hold an Engineering Council accredited degree (or be CEng), and have held an important relevant position of technical or scientific responsibility for not less than 10 yrs, or have made such noteworthy contribution to the technology of welding or 1 of the allied processes either in practice or in theory that their election will advance the interests of the Institute.

Senior Member (SenMWeldI): Applicants must be over 30, hold an Engineering Council accredited degree (or be CEng), have demonstrated a specified level of knowledge of welding technology (various options available) and have undergone at least 2 yrs' training in engineering or in another appropriate field and, in addition, have had at least 2 yrs' responsible experience related to welding and joining technology.

Member (MWeldI): Applicants must be over 25, hold an Engineering Council accredited degree (or be CEng), have undergone at least 2 yrs' training in engineering or in another appropriate field and, in addition, have had at least 2 yrs' responsible experience related to welding and joining technology.

Incorporated Member (IncMWeldI): Applicants must be over 25, hold an approved SQA or Edexel HNC in Fabrication and Welding Engineering or another approved qualification and have had at least 2 yrs' training and 3 yrs' experience at the appropriate level with responsibilities for welding or one of the allied processes.

Technician (TechWeldI): Applicants must be over 21, hold an approved SQA/BTEC Certificate in Fabrication and Welding Engineering or another approved qualification and have had at least 2 yrs' training and 1 yr's experience at the appropriate level with responsibilities for welding or some other field of science or technology or one of the allied processes.

Graduate (GradWeldI): Applicants must hold an accredited first degree in engineering or materials, or an accredited BTEC or SQA National or Higher National Award or equivalent.

Senior Associate (SenAWeldI): Must be over 30 and have been involved with welding or allied activities for at least 10 yrs, and have held a post of responsibility for at least 5 of these.

REGISTRATION:

Corporate Membership: May qualify for registration as Ceng. Incorporated Members are normally eligible for registration as IEng and Technicians as EngTech.

VOCATIONAL QUALIFICATIONS:

The Welding Institute is accredited by the UK Department of Trade and Industry to confer vocational qualifications under the Certification Scheme for Welding and Inspection Personnel. Categories of certification include Welding Engineers, Welding Technicians, Welding Inspectors, Welding Supervisors, Welding Technical Representatives, Welding Instructors, Underwater Inspectors and Non-Destructive Testing Personnel.

National Certificates and Diplomas

Scotland
SQA HNC: Fabrication and Welding Engineering; Fabrication and Welding Technology
SQA HND: Fabrication and Welding Engineering

NVQs

Level 1: Joining Materials by Welding
Level 3: Joining Materials by Welding

SVQs

Level 1: Joining Materials by Welding
Level 2: Joining Materials by Welding
Level 3: Joining Materials by Welding

City & Guilds

2190 Welding and Fabrication Inspection and Quality Control; 2290 Welding and Fabrication Competences; 5990 Construction Services Welding

Other Vocational Awarding Bodies

ABC: Welding and Fabrication Practice

WELFARE

(See also Social Work)

Membership of Professional Institutions and Associations

THE COMMUNITY AND YOUTH WORK ASSOCIATION – YDA

General Secretary: C Shaw, 122 Rochdale Road, Oldham OL1 1NT Tel: 01457 834943 Fax: 01522 524305

MEMBERSHIP:
Fellowship (FCYW): Strictly limited to founder members, honorary representatives of long standing and others whose work for the association and youth work merits this award.
Membership (MCYW): Awarded to suitable applicants who are usually already associates and have a number of yrs of experience in their field and to JNC qualified workers after 3 yrs.
Associateship (ACYW): Available to those who have completed the Association's basic course or that of another acceptable agency or a local authority, and have suitable experience.
Affiliateship: Available for organisations and individuals who wish to receive publications, attend meetings and support the work of the Association or who are youth workers who do not wish to apply for another grade.
Students: Students preparing for full membership are registered as Affiliates. The basic course covers an introduction to Youth and Community Studies, Current Issues in Community and Youth Work, and First Aid and Social and Economic Studies. Persons with an appropriate professional qualification may be exempted from these requirements.

EXAMINATION:
Diploma of Community Youth & Social Welfare: Operated jointly with the New Institute of Social Welfare (ISW) and replacing the Diploma in Youth Development and the ISW Dip. Assessment for entry takes into account DipSW/CQSW (CCETSW), CertYCW/DipHE (JNC for Youth Workers & Community Centre Wardens) and relevant NVQ/SVQ or RAMP accredited schemes (12 mths).
Certificate in Youth and Community Work (CertYCW): The Association is currently liaising with Cert/DipHE awarders regarding the sponsorship of courses. (This does not indicate association recognition of all DipHE), (2 yrs).
Overseas Diploma: The Association welcomes international membership and operates a scheme for special assessment for overseas associates, (2 yrs).
College Diploma Endorsement Scheme: A scheme whereby college awards are endorsed for membership, it is open on a block basis to colleges approved by the association guaranteeing levels of membership or offering a joint award.
Diploma in Management Studies (Youth Services): This postgraduate award is offered by flexi-study (12 mths).

INSTITUTE OF SOCIAL WELFARE

Rear Vicarage,, Stockport Road, Mossley, Lancs OL5 0QY Tel: 01457 834943 Fax: 0161-624 1907
Following the dissolution of the Institute of Social Welfare in 1990, the new Institute of Social Welfare was formed. The Broad Church Social Welfare policy of the former institute was adopted. The Institute has introduced a diploma scheme as a route to post qualification study. The ISW is a body of people drawn from different professions whose aim is the improvement of social and community services. It admits to membership workers in social services departments, hospitals, education welfare, race relations, prison service, probation, youth service, day care, residential and nursery services from state, voluntary and independent agencies. The Institute recognises the professional and the non-professional as essential colleagues in the network of care.

MEMBERSHIP:
Fellowship (FISW): Members whom the Council consider have rendered distinctive service to social welfare, and all holders of the Institutes Diploma in Social Welfare.
Member (MISW): Persons engaged in the social services or as FT or PT officers of approved bodies or holders of professional qualifications approved by the council of the Institute but not holding the Institute's own Diploma.
Affiliate: Any person or organisation wishing to further the aims of the Institute.
Overseas Associate: The Institute maintains a register of overseas qualified members by direct admission.
Diploma in Community Youth & Social Welfare: An opportunity for post-qualification/experience study by established professionals via an approved centre and a route to Fellowship (awarded with the YDA q.v.).

INSTITUTE OF WELFARE OFFICERS

3rd Floor, Newland House, 137-139 Hagley Road, Edgbaston, Birmingham B16 8UA
Tel: 0121 454 8883 Fax: 0121 454 7873
e-mail: info@instituteofwelfare.co.uk Website: www.instituteofwelfare.co.uk

CORPORATE MEMBERS:
Companion: Wholly within the gift of the Institute, and is the highest professional grade.
Fellow: Must have been a member for at least 5 yrs, and must be holder of the Diploma in Welfare or its equiv (ie must have been a practising Welfare Officer for at least 7 yrs).
Member: Must have been in post for at least 2 yrs as a practising Welfare Officer and hold the Diploma in Welfare Studies or equiv.
Associate Member: Holder of the Certificate or Diploma in Welfare Studies but less than 2 yrs' experience of Welfare practice.

NON-CORPORATE MEMBERS:
Student: Undertaking the Institute's Foundation Certificate or Diploma in Welfare Studies course.
EXAMINATIONS:
The Institute has now published syllabus and exam regulations which can be obtained from the address above.

University Qualifications

The following universities offer qualifications in Welfare and related subjects. Full details may be found in Part 4, under the entry for the appropriate university.

FIRST DEGREES AWARDED BY UNIVERSITIES

Anglia; Bradford (Bradford & Ilkley Community College); Brunel; Bucks. Coll.; Central Lancashire; Coventry; De Montfort, Leicester; Derby; Durham; Exeter (The College of St Mark & St John); Kent; Kingston; Lancaster (Edge Hill College of Higher Education); Leeds; Leeds (Bretton Hall); Leeds Metropolitan; Liverpool (Chester College of H.E.); Liverpool John Moores; Manchester Metropolitan.; Northampton; Paisley; Plymouth; Reading; Southampton (Chichester Institute of Higher Education); Sunderland; Teesside; Wales (University of Wales College, Newport); Wolverhampton; Worcester

HIGHER DEGREES AWARDED BY UNIVERSITIES

Bradford; Brighton; Bristol; Brunel; Central Lancashire; Cheltenham & Gloucester; Dundee; East Anglia; East London; Edinburgh; Hertfordshire; Keele; Kent; Leeds Metropolitan; Leicester;

Liverpool (Liverpool Hope University College); London (Goldsmiths College); London (Imperial College of Science, Technology & Medicine); London (King's College London); London (London School of Economics & Political Science); London (University College (UCL)); Manchester; Manchester Metropolitan.; Middlesex; Nottingham; Sussex; Wales (College of Medicine); Wales (University of Wales, Swansea)

DIPLOMAS AWARDED BY UNIVERSITIES
Bradford (Bradford & Ilkley Community College); Brighton; Central Lancashire; De Montfort, Leicester; Derby; Dundee; Durham; East London; Exeter (The College of St Mark & St John); Exeter (Truro College); Hertfordshire; Leeds Metropolitan; Leicester; Lincolnshire (Grimsby College); Lincolnshire (Hull College); Liverpool (Chester College of H.E.); London (Goldsmiths College); London (King's College London); Manchester; Salford; Southampton (Chichester Institute of Higher Education); St Martin; Wales (College of Medicine); Wales (North East Wales Institute)

CERTIFICATES AWARDED BY UNIVERSITIES
Central Lancashire; Dundee; Durham; East London; Leeds; Liverpool (Chester College of H.E.); London (Birkbeck, University of London); Nottingham; OU (Northern College of Education); St Martin

OTHER COURSES AWARDED BY UNIVERSITIES
Leeds Metropolitan

PROFESSIONAL COURSES AWARDED BY UNIVERSITIES
Luton

National Certificates and Diplomas
BTEC National Certificates/Diplomas: Caring Services (Nursery Nursing); Caring Services (Social Care)
BTEC Higher National Certificates/Diplomas: Caring Services (Care Management); Caring Services (Counselling); Caring Services (Guidance); Caring Services (Managing Care); Caring Services (Practical Management); Caring Services (Social Care)

NVQs
Level 2: Care
Level 3: Care
Level 4: Care

SVQs
Level 2: Early Yrs Care and Education
Level 3: Early Yrs Care and Education

GNVQs
3724 Health and Social Care

OCR
OCR offer the following awards:
Advice, Guidance, Counselling & Psychotherapy Service Support Level 2
Advice Levels 3 & 4 in
General Advice; Money Advice; Welfare Rights; Housing Advice & Business Advice.
Guidance Levels 3 & 4.

City & Guilds
9249 Youth Worker Awards

Other Vocational Awarding Bodies
ABC: Caring for People; Caring Skills; Community and Health Care; Youth and Community Workers' Certificate

Part 6

Bodies Accrediting Independent Institutions

The British Accreditation Council for Independent Further and Higher Education (BAC)

The BAC was established in 1984 and exists 'to define, monitor and improve standards in independent further and higher education institutions'. It accredits independent institutions which meet its required criteria. Its sponsors include the chief bodies responsible for the maintenance of academic standards in Britain: universities, colleges, national validating bodies, and public and professional examining boards, and also those, such as the British Council, with a particular concern for overseas students.

The process of accreditation involves an initial application; the determination of eligibility for accreditation, including a preliminary visit by an inspector; and a full institutional inspection followed by a decision on accreditation by the Accreditation and Recognition Committee of the BAC. Accreditation is conditional upon re-inspection within five years. During this period, each accredited institution is required to furnish an annual report on its activities in a manner prescribed by the BAC and is visited by a BAC reporting inspector. The BAC reserves the right, however, to review the accreditation of an institution at any time if reasonable grounds exist.

Institutions seeking BAC accreditation must satisfy the BAC under *all* the following heads:

  (i)   Premises and Health & Safety;
 (ii)   Administration and staffing;
(iii)   Quality management, including the effectiveness of the monitoring of experiences of students in joining and pursuing the programmes provided;
 (iv)   Welfare arrangements, including career advice and counselling where appropriate; and
  (v)   Teaching and learning, involving an assessment of the professional competence of academic staff.

In addition, the BAC enquires into the legal and financial viability of institutions. Discussions have also been held with Home Office representatives to ensure that the criteria used by the BAC are consistent with those required by the Home Office of bona fide institutions enrolling overseas students.

The BAC has worked closely with two other accrediting bodies to try and present a clearer picture of accreditation in the independent sector. These bodies are the British Council's English Language Recognition Scheme for English Language Schools and the Open and Distance Learning Quality Council. Accreditation by these three accrediting bodies has been welcomed by the Secretary of State for Education as the only public guarantee of standards in institutions in the independent sector of further and higher education.

Further details of the work of the BAC and a current list of accredited institutions may be obtained from Robin Laidlaw, Chief Executive, BAC, Westminster Central Hall, Storey's Gate, London SW1H 9NH Tel 020 7233 3468 Fax 020 7233 3470 e-mail: info@the-bac.org website: www.the-bac.org

The British Council

The British Council runs the English in Britain accreditation scheme for the inspection and accreditation organisations which provide courses in English as a Foreign Language (EFL) in Britain.

The scheme is managed jointly by the British Council, ARELS (the Association of Recognised English Language Services) and BASELT (the British Association in State English Language Teaching). One of its aims is to effectively promote accredited UK ELT through the British Council's network of overseas of fices.

Under the terms of the scheme, institutions are inspected rigorously every three years in the areas of management and administration, premises, resources, professional qualifications, academic management teaching and welfare. The scheme also includes a system of random spot checking. The management and policy of the scheme is conducted by an independent board while a separate independent committee reviews inspectors' reports.

Some 80 per cent of recognised schools are also members of ARELS which insists on British Council recognition as a criterion for their membership. In addition, all ARELS members, of which there are 220, are required to abide by the Association's Code of Practice and Regulations. Established in 1960, ARELS exists to raise the high standards of its members even further through conferences, training courses and publications. The association also represents the interests of members and students to government bodies and promotes the teaching of English in Britain at homes and overseas.

All accredited state sector colleges and universities are BASELT members. The Council works closely with both associations in the development of the scheme.

Further information on the English in Britain: Accreditation scheme may be obtained from the Accreditation Unit, The British Council, Bridgewater House, 58 Whitworth Street, Manchester M1 6BB Tel 0161 957 7098 Fax 0161 951 7074. Further information on ARELS may be obtained from ARELS, 2 Pontypool Place, Valentine Place, London SEX 8QF, Tel 020 7242 3136 Fax 020 7928 9378.

The Open and Distance Learning Quality Council

ODL QC was established in 1969 as the Council for the Accreditation of Correspondence Colleges, a joint initiative of the then Labour government and representatives of the sector. It is the principal accrediting body for a wide variety of providers of open and distance learning in the UK, from commercial colleges to professional and public sector institutions. Now independent, it nevertheless continues to have the informal support of government.

ODL QC promotes quality by:

- establishing standards of education & training in open and distance learning;
- recognising good quality provision, wherever it occurs;
- supporting and protecting the interests of learners;
- encouraging the improvement of existing methods and the development of new ones;
- linking open and distance learning with other forms of education & training; and
- promoting wider recognition of the value of open & distance learning

Accreditation includes a rigorous assessment of an educational provision, including materials, tutorial support, publicity, contractual arrangements with learners and general administrative procedures, each of which is measured against the Council's published benchmark standards. If accredited, the provider is monitored on a regular basis and reassessed at least once every three years.

The Council promotes those colleges which it accredits and which are, by definition, quality providers of ODL, and acts as honest broker in matching accredited colleges to potential markets. A list of courses offered by accredited providers is circulated widely, both in this country and abroad, and is also included on the Council's website, www.odlqc.org.uk/odlqc

The Council also seeks to protect the interests of learners by promoting the importance of accreditation, and by offering advice and support directly to learners. At the same time, knowledge of good practice is disseminated more widely, and quality encouraged wherever open and distance learning occurs.

The Council consists of members nominated by professional and public bodies involved in education, as well as representatives of accredited providers, and has strong links with other bodies in the sector, both in the UK and abroad.

All enquiries should be addressed to the Chief Executive, ODL QC, 16 Park Crescent, London W1B 1AH, Tel 020 612 7090, email odlqc@dial.pipex.com

The Conference for Independent Further Education (CIFE)

CIFE was founded in 1973 to promote strict adherence by independent sixth form and tutorial colleges to the highest standards of academic and professional integrity. All member colleges must be accredited by the British Accreditation Council for Independent Further and Higher Education

(BAC), or optionally or as well as the Independent Schools Joint Council (ISJC) if they are registered by the Department for Education and Employment (DfEE) as schools. Candidate membership is available for up to 3 yrs for colleges seeking BAC of ISJC accreditation within that period for colleges which otherwise satisfy CIFE's own exacting membership criteria. All colleges must also abide by stringent codes of conduct and practice, the character and presentation of their published exam results are subject to regulation and the accuracy of the information must be validated by BAC as academic auditor to CIFE. Full Members are subject to reinspection by their accrediting bodies. There are 33 colleges in full or candidate membership of CIFE at present, spread throughout England but with concentrations in London, Oxford and Cambridge.

CIFE colleges offer a wide range of GCSE A and A/S level courses. In addition some CIFE colleges offer English language tuition for students from overseas and degree-level tuition. A number of the colleges offer summer holiday academic courses, and most of them also provide A level and CCSE revision courses during the Christmas and/or Easter holidays. Further information on CIFE may be obtained from the Secretary, Dr Elizabeth Cottrell, Flat 2, 295 Ladbroke Grove, London W10 6HE.

Part 7

Study Associations and the 'Learned Societies'

The study associations consist of persons who wish to increase their knowledge of a particular subject or range of subjects; they may be professionals or amateurs. Some associations consist almost entirely of specialists (eg the Royal Statistical Society); others (eg the Royal Geographical Society and the Zoological Society of London) have a more general membership. The learned societies usually have one grade of membership, fellows or members. Some also admit group members (such as schools or libraries) called corporate members, and junior associate, corresponding and overseas members, who pay lower subscriptions. Some also elect honorary fellows or members. The members of some societies may use designatory letters, but this does not mean that the holder is 'qualified' in the same sense as a doctor or a chartered accountant.

Membership of some learned societies is by election and is commonly accepted as distinguishing the candidate by admission to an exclusive group. Candidates may be selected in respect of pre-eminence in their subject or in the public service. The chief associations of this type are the Royal Society (founded 1660 and granted Royal Charters in 1662 and 1663), the Royal Academy of Arts (founded 1768) and the British Academy (founded 1901).

The Royal Society was established to improve 'natural knowledge' and is mainly concerned with science, in pure and applied science and technology. Election to Fellowship (FRS) is regarded as one of the highest distinctions. The Society elects Royal Fellows, Fellows and Foreign Members.

The Royal Academy was established to cultivate and improve the arts of painting, sculpture and architecture. There are two main grades of membership, Academicians (RA), including Senior Academicians, and Associates (ARA); there are also a small number of Honorary Academicians.

The British Academy was established to promote historical, philological and philosophical studies. The Academy has Fellows (FBA), Corresponding Fellows and a small number of Honorary Fellows.

A list of Learned Societies and Study Associations can be found below.

Occupational Associations

The occupational associations do not qualify practitioners but organise them. Some co-ordinate the activities of specialists (eg the Society of Medical Officers of Health) and others promote the individual and collective interests of professionals working in a wider area. Both also seek to safeguard the public interest and to offer an educational service to their members. The latter type of association is especially numerous among teachers, who have over 20 associations (eg the National Union of Teachers, the Educational Institute of Scotland, the National Association of Schoolmasters/Union of Women Teachers and the National Association of Head Teachers), and is represented in the medical profession by the British Medical Association. Both types of association usually have only one grade of membership.

List of Study Associations and Learned Societies*

(* This list largely excludes qualifying bodies covered in Part 5)

DATE OF FOUNDATION	TITLE
Agriculture and related subjects	
1926	Agricultural Economics Society
] 952	British Agricultural History Society
1945	British Grassland Society
1944	British Society of Animal Production
1947	British Society of Soil Science
1921	Commonwealth Forestry Association
1947	Fertiliser Society

DATE OF FOUNDATION	TITLE
1927	Herb Society of Great Britain
1925	Institute of Foresters
1938	Institution of Agricultural Engineers
1839	Royal Agricultural Society of England
1882	Royal Forestry Society of England,, Wales and N Ireland
1784	Royal Highland and Agricultural Society of Scotland
1804	Royal Horticultural Society
1854	Royal Scottish Forestry Society
1904	Royal Welsh Agricultural Society
1931	Society for Applied Bacteriology
1943	Society of Dairy Technology
1945	The Soil Association

Anthropology and related subjects

1951	British Sociological Association
1907	Eugenics Society
1931	Institute for the Study and Treatment of Delinquency
1921	National Institute of Industrial Psychology
1843	Royal Anthropological Institute of Great Britain and Ireland
1823	Royal Asiatic Society of Great Britain and Ireland
1901	Royal Society for Asian Affairs

Archaeology

1924	Ancient Monuments Society
1843	British Archaeological Association
1846	Cambrian Archaeological Association
1944	Council for British Archaeology
1908	Prehistorical Society
1843	Royal Archaeological Institute

Art

1936	Faculty of Royal Designers for Industry
1950	International Institute for Conservation of Historic and Artistic Works
1888	National Society for Art Education
1899	Pastel Society
1768	Royal Academy of Arts
1814	Royal Birmingham Society of Artists
1831	Royal Institute of Painters in Watercolours
1883	Royal Institute of Oil-Painters
1826	Royal Scottish Academy of Painting,, Sculpture and Architecture
	Royal Society of British Artists
1904	Royal Society of British Sculptors
1904	Royal Society of Marine Artists
1895	Royal Society of Miniature Painters,, Sculptors and Gravers
1884	Royal Society of Painter-Etchers and Engravers
1804	Royal Society of Painters in Watercolours
1891	Royal Society of Portrait Painters
	Senefelder Group of Lithographers
1919	Society of Graphic Artists
1952	Society of Portrait Sculptors
	Society of Wildlife Artists
	Society of Women Artists
1952	United Society of Artists

Biology and related subjects

1904	Association of Applied Biologists

DATE OF FOUNDATION	TITLE
1960	Biological Engineering Society
1836	The Botanical Society of the British Isles
1836	The Botanical Society of Edinburgh
1896	British Bryological Society
1913	The British Ecological Society
1896	The British Mycological Society
1858	The British Ornithologists' Union
1959	British Society for Cell Biology
1933	The British Trust for Ornithology
1929	Freshwater Biological A
	Human Biology
1937	The Systematics Association
1826	The Zoological Society of London

Chemistry
1841	The Chemical Society
1911	The Biochemical Society
1913	The Institute of Petroleum
1918	Oil and Colour Chemists' Association
1881	Society of the Chemical Industry
1897	Society of Leather Technologists and Chemists

Economics, Philosophy and related subjects
1927	Economics History Society
1956	Institute of Economic Affairs
1915	Philosophical Society of England
1920	Royal Institute of International Affairs
1834	Royal Statistical Society
1954	Scottish Economic Society

Engineering
1847	The Architectural Association
1966	Concrete Society
1946	Faculty of Building
1976	Fellowship of Engineering
1881	Institute of British Carriage and Automobile Manufacturers
1978	Institute of Concrete Technology
1899	Institute of Refrigeration
1959	Institution of Nuclear Engineers
1920	Newcomen Society for the Study of the History of Engineering and Technology
1916	Royal Incorporation of Architects in Scotland
1860	Royal Institution of Naval Architects,
1927	Royal Television Society
1854	Society of Engineers
1958	Society of Environmental Engineers

Geography, Geology and related subjects
1949	British Geotechnical Society
1940	British Society of Rheology
1931	Gemmological Association of Great Britain
1893	Geographical Association
1807	Geological Society
1858	Geologists Association
1846	Hakluyt Society

DATE OF FOUNDATION	TITLE
1933	Institute of British Geographers
1876	Mineralogical Society of Great Britain and Ireland
1847	Palaeontographical Society
1957	Paleontological Association
1830	Royal Geographical Society
1884	Royal Scottish Geographical Society

History and related subjects

1902	British Academy for the Promotion of Historical
1903	British Numismatic Society
1888	British Record Society
1932	British Record Association
1964	Furniture History Society
1869	Harleian Society
1906	The Historical Association
1868	Royal Historical Society
1836	Royal Numismatic Society
1717	Society of Antiquaries of London
1780	Society of Antiquaries of Scotland
1956	Society of Architectural Historians in Great Britain
1947	Society of Archivists
1911	Society of Genealogists
1953	Scottish Genealogy Society
1886	Scottish History Society
1897	Scottish Record Society

Law

1958	British Institute of International and Comparative Law
1887	The Selden Society

Literature and Arts

1892	Bibliographical Society
1960	British Society of Aesthetics
1933	British Film Institute
1904	Classical Association
1915	Design and Industries Association
1906	English Association
1842	Philological Society
1909	Poetry Society
1874	Royal Musical Association
1884	Society of Authors
1823	Royal Society of Literature of the United Kingdom

Mathematics and Physics

1924	Astronomical Society of Edinburgh
1890	The British Astronomical Association
1966	British Biophysical Society,
1927	The British Institute of Radiology
1933	The British Interplanetary Society
1930	The Institution of Electronics
1871	The Mathematical Association
1820	The Royal Astronomical Society
1850	The Royal Meteorological Society

Medicine

DATE OF FOUNDATION	TITLE
1887	The Anatomical Society of GB and Ireland
1932	Association of Anaesthetists of GB and Ireland
1933	Association of British Neurologists
1957	Association for Child Psychology and Psychiatry
1953	The Association of Clinical Bio-chemists
1927	The Association of Clinical Pathologists
1972	Association of Psychiatrists in Training
1920	Association of Surgeons of GB and Ireland
1957	The Association for the Study of Medical Education
1959	The British Academy for Forensic Sciences
1977	British Association of Clinical Anatomists
1950	British Association of Forensic Medicine
1963	British Association of Manipulative Medicine
1962	British Association of Oral Surgeons
1965	British Association of Orthodontists
1943	British Association of Otolaryngologists
1954	British Association of Paediatric Surgeons
	British Association of Plastic Surgeons
	British Association of Rheumatology and Rehabilitation
1964	British Association of Social Psychiatry
1973	British Association of Surgical Oncology
1945	British Association of Urological Surgeons
1934	The British Diabetic Association
1948	The British Geriatric Society
1832	British Medical Association
1950	The British Neuropathological Society
1953	The British Occupational Hygiene Society
1918	The British Orthopaedic Association
1928	The British Paediatric Association
1931	The British Pharmaceutical Society
1913	The British Psycho-Analytical Society
1948	British Society for Allergy and Clinical Immunology
1962	British Society for Clinical Cytology
1937	The British Society of Gastro-enterology
1960	British Society for Haematology
1947	The British Society for Research on Ageing
1965	Chiropractic Advancement Association
1947	Ergonomics Society
1950	The Faculty of Homeopathy
1959	The Forensic Science Society
1813	Harveian Society of London
1936	The Heberden Society
1819	The Hunterian Society
1969	Institute of Occupational Medicine
1964	Institute of Pharmacy Management International
1773	The Medical Society of London
1922	The Medical Society for the Study of Venereal Diseases
1901	The Medico-Legal Society
1941	The Nutrition Society
1880	The Ophthalmological Society of the UK
1925	Osteopathic Association of Great Britain
]906	Pathological Society of Great Britain and Ireland
1734	Royal Medical Society
1875	The Royal Sanitary Association of Scotland
1805	The Royal Society of Medicine

DATE OF FOUNDATION	TITLE
1907	The Royal Society of Tropical Medicine and Hygiene
1926	The Society of British Neurological Surgeons
1946	The Society of Endocrinology
1884	The Society for the Study of Addiction (to Alcohol and Other Drugs)
]950	Society for the Study of Fertility
1933	The Society of Thoracic and Cardiovascular Surgeons of Great Britain and Ireland
1945	The Thoracic Society

Science – General

1924	ASLIB
1831	The British Association for the Advancement of Science
1901	The British Psychological Society
1956	The British Society for the History of Science
1960	The British Society for the Philosophy of Science
1925	The Royal Institute of Philosophy
1799	The Royal Institution of Great Britain
1660	The Royal Society
1754	The Royal Society of Arts
1783	The Royal Society of Edinburgh

Town and Country Planning

1899	Town and Country Planning Association

General Index

NOTE: In addition to the abbreviations listed at the beginning of the book, the following are used throughout the index; FE - Further Education; HE - Higher Education. Universities are listed under locations eg: Aberdeen, University of.

Index of Advertisers

Visit Kogan Page on-line

Comprehensive information on
Kogan Page titles

Features include

- complete catalogue listings,
  including book reviews and
  descriptions

- special monthly promotions

- information on NEW titles and
  BESTSELLING titles

- a secure shopping basket facility
  for on-line ordering

PLUS everything you need to know
about KOGAN PAGE

http://www.kogan-page.co.uk